COMMERCIAL LAW
for
BUSINESS AND ACCOUNTING STUDENTS

A COMPLETE BUSINESS LAW TEXT AND CPA LAW REVIEW

By

DR. WILLIAM T. SCHANTZ

B.S., J.D., L.L.M. (Taxation)
Professor of Law, Portland State University
Attorney at Law
Member of Oregon Bar

Assisted By

DR. JANICE E. JACKSON

B.A., J.D.
Assistant Professor of Law, Portland State University
Attorney at Law
Member of Oregon Bar

ST. PAUL, MINN.
WEST PUBLISHING CO.
1980

This book contains quotations from prior Uniform CPA Examinations and Unofficial Answers published by and copyrighted © in 1966, 1967, 1968, 1971, 1973, 1974, 1975, 1976, 1977, and 1978 by the American Institute of Certified Public Accountants, Inc. Such passages have been reprinted with the permission of the AICPA.

Library of Congress Cataloging in Publication Data

Schantz, William T
    Commercial law for business and accounting students.
    Includes index.
    1. Commercial law—United States. I. Title.

KF889.S24   346'.73'07   79–18028

ISBN 0-8299-2061-7

Schantz–Comm.Law Bus. & Acct.Stud. MTB

3rd Reprint—1982

DEDICATION

For my friends Jim Manning and Dee Taylor

William T. Schantz

*

PREFACE

Our teaching of the subject of commercial (business) law has provided us the basis for identifying four distinct groups of students taking business law courses:

(1) The "business major" who needs the knowledge of business law as one of several important tools to be used in making future business decisions;

(2) The "accounting major" who needs this same knowledge so as to be able to understand the commercial operations of his or her future clients (and also to pass the "business law" part of the Uniform CPA Examination);

(3) The "pre-law major" who seeks a broad exposure to all aspects of law as it relates to the business world (and who also uses business law to test his or her aptitude for an advanced study of law); and

(4) The "other major" who, whether concentrating in history, art, engineering, literature, pre-med, music, education, or journalism, faces a lifetime of purchasing property, making contracts, writing checks, buying insurance, borrowing money, signing mortgages, writing wills, and so forth. Knowledge of commercial law is simply essential to living in a complex world.

The study of business law should be the same for all students. The objective must be to provide a complete, up-to-date coverage that is not only interesting to read and easy to understand, but which also results in knowledge that will be retained and used in the future. This text was written to accomplish this objective.

Complete coverage. This text completely covers all business law subject matters including several not covered by other texts such as banking, registration of securities, labor law, suretyship, professional responsibility, and business torts. Each of the 16 business law concepts tested on the law part of the Uniform CPA Examination is exhaustively treated.

Additionally, and perhaps more importantly, this text puts the subject matter into its logical order. The effective study of law requires building from concept to concept. The ordering of the material is very important. For example, understanding the "risk of loss" provisions of Article 2 of the Uniform Commercial Code dealing with sales of goods requires some understanding of insurance, negotiable instruments, bailments, carriers, warehousemen, and documents of title. It has never made sense to us to treat sales of goods before negotiable commercial paper or insurance. For this reason, the middle chapters of this text build from Chapter 11 (insurance) to Chapters 12 through 15 (negotiable instruments and banking) to Chapter 16 (bailments, carriers, warehousemen, and documents of title) to Chapters 17 through 19 (sales, including risk of loss provisions). When the student

v

PREFACE

reaches Chapter 17 and is exposed to the "special property and insurable interest" of the buyer, the student knows what is meant by "insurable interest" by reason of having previously studied insurance. And the student fully understands the use of negotiable drafts and negotiable documents of title to facilitate the sales transaction because of his or her previous study of these instruments. In the same manner, most contracts deal with elements of real or personal property. The law of sales always involves contracts dealing with goods (personal property). Other contracts control the purchase and sale of homes and govern thousands of other real property transactions daily. Since most contracts involve property, and because property is the underlying element of commercial law, this text thoroughly explains the law of property as a background to a complete study of the law of contracts. Throughout the book, whenever relevant, previously covered law is related to new material so that a complete relationship of concepts is presented.

Complete coverage also means the ability to cover all the material in a reasonable timeframe. The subject matter of business law is so extensive and far-reaching that it is tempting to provide more material than can be used. This text has 30 chapters designed to be covered in 30 weeks, i. e., one chapter a week. We have planned the text so that the subject matter will divide for a three term or two semester course by teaching ten chapters in each of three terms or fifteen chapters in each of two semesters. In the three term course, property and contracts are taught the first term; insurance, commercial paper, banking, bailments, sales, and the employer-employee relationship the second term; and agency, methods of doing business, securities, antitrust, bankruptcy, secured transactions, professional responsibility, trust and estates the third term. Using two semesters, the first semester covers property, contracts, insurance, commercial paper, and banking; and the second semester covers the other fifteen chapters.

Since each area of law within the text is also complete in itself, the text will easily adjust to a one term course on a ten week timeframe in a variety of ways. For example, a one term course could cover contracts (with weeks 1–4 spent on Chapters 7–10), insurance (week 5 on Chapter 11), the employer-employee relationship (week 6 on Chapter 20), methods of doing business as a partnership or corporation (weeks 7 and 8 on Chapters 22 and 23), bankruptcy (week 9 on Chapter 26), and wills and estates (week 10 on Chapter 30).

For the CPA candidate, all subject matters tested on the law part of the Uniform CPA Exam are covered, including registration of securities, suretyship, and professional responsibility. The problem selection was based on a detailed study of all Uniform CPA Exams given over the last 15 years; every effort was made to treat all business law concepts tested on the Uniform Exam.

We believe our coverage of commercial law is the most complete coverage ever presented. At the same time, the material may be fully covered within the appropriate timeframes of business law courses.

PREFACE

Up-to-date coverage. This text reports the most recent statutes, cases, and interpretations of the law. For example, in our study of contracts, we have included the most recent tentative drafts of the Restatement Second of the Law of Contracts. Statutes include, among many others:

The 1979 Bankruptcy Act;

The 1978 Age Discrimination in Employment Act;

The 1977 Amendments to the Fair Labor Standards Act;

The 1977 Foreign Corrupt Practice Act;

The 1978 Amendments to the Securities Exchange Act;

The 1975 Magnuson-Moss Warranty Federal Trade Commission Improvement Act;

The 1976 Tax Reform Act;

The 1978 Fair Debt Collection Practices Act; and

The 1978 Right to Financial Privacy Act.

On June 25, 1979, the American Institute of Certified Public Accountants announced that beginning with the November 1979 examination, candidates will be expected to deal with the following additional subjects: "The new Federal Bankruptcy Act effective in 1979" (covered completely in Chapter 26); "The 1972 amendments to the Uniform Commercial Code" (covered completely throughout the text); "The Foreign Corrupt Practices Act of 1977" (covered completely in Chapter 24); and "Product liability of sellers of goods under the Uniform Commercial Code as amended in 1972 and under common law" (covered completely in Chapter 19).

Our cases have been chosen to reflect the most important and most recent interpretations of the law. For example, Chapter 20 dealing with the employer-employee relationship includes both the *Allan Bakke* and *Brian Weber* "reverse discrimination" cases.

Interesting to read coverage. Commercial law is a fascinating subject because it deals with the rights and responsibilities of individuals in the marketplace. We believe the subject is made all the more interesting because of some special features within the text. We selected our cases very carefully, choosing them not only because of the important rules of law they illustrate, but also because of their intriguing facts. For example, in Chapter 1, the case of *Katko v. Briney* is the famous "spring-gun" case; the case of *Lieber v. Mohawk Arms* deals with the question of who is entitled to Adolph Hitler's uniform. In Chapter 8, the case of *Columbia University v. Jacobsen* resolves the question of whether Columbia falsely represented that it would teach the defendant wisdom, truth, and beauty. Chapter 9's *Marvin v. Marvin* (popularly known as the "palimony" case) concerns the legality of an agreement of unmarried parties to live together and share earnings. Chapter 11's *Liberty National v. Weldon* presents the case of an aunt who killed her two and one-half year old niece to collect life insurance. And in Chapter 25, the National Labor Relations Board must decide whether it is an unfair labor practice for telephone company employees to wear sweat-

PREFACE

shirts to work bearing the slogan, "Ma Bell is a Cheap Mother." We believe the cases in every chapter are uniquely interesting.

Our examples are designed to create and maintain interest, with some examples carrying through entire chapters. For example, in Chapters 22 and 23, the same hypothetical small business (a sporting goods operation) is used to illustrate the sole proprietorship, partnership, and corporate forms of doing business. The student can picture himself or herself in similar future circumstances and see why he or she might select one form of business organization over another.

Finally, our book of supplementary materials that accompanies the text provides one or two exercises for the student to complete as he or she reads the chapter material. Having our students do these exercises as they read the material has substantially increased their interest and their knowledge.

Easy to read coverage. Our efforts in preparing this text were devoted not only to providing a complete and interesting coverage of commercial law but also to providing a book that is as readable as possible. We very purposefully started each chapter section with a question. We urge the student to read each question carefully, then, after reading the section that follows, to try to answer the question in his or her own words. If the student cannot answer the question, he or she should reread the material in the section until he or she can do so. In every case, we have provided complete explanations and where the subject matter is particularly difficult have used special illustrations to aid in the explanations. There are, for example, special illustrations dealing with land description in deeds (Chapter 6); consideration in unilateral and bilateral contracts (Chapter 9); negotiability requirements for checks, notes, and drafts (Chapter 13); buyer's and seller's remedies (Chapter 18); and the results of using the corporate form of business organization versus the partnership and sole proprietorship methods (Chapters 22 and 23). Each illustration provides the student with a unique tool enabling him or her to grasp the most intricate of business law subject matters.

All relevant statutory sections (including the Uniform Commercial Code and the Official Comment to the Code) are included within the text itself rather than in appendices. As a result, the student is able to read the relevant statutory section as he or she reads the text material. Included among these statutes are relevant sections of the Uniform Commercial Code, the Fair Labor Standards Act, the Uniform Partnership Act, the Uniform Limited Partnership Act, the federal and state securities laws, and many others. In the supplement that accompanies the text, the Uniform Commercial Code is reproduced in its entirety for use as a side-by-side reference with the text.

Retention of knowledge. The text and supplementary materials book include several special items designed to help the student learn and to retain the law for future use. The text of each chapter is followed by two or three cases and ten problems which thoroughly test the student's grasp of the chapter material. In 29 of the 30 chapters (all but Chapter 1), some of the problems are taken from actual law sections of Uniform CPA Examina-

PREFACE

tions given over the last several years. The CPA questions have been categorized according to chapter subject matter and are excellent problems for any business law student whether or not the student intends to take the Uniform CPA Exam. In the supplementary materials book, there is provided an extensive outline of each chapter of the text which the student may use for study and review. The supplement also provides additional cases which may be used within the classroom or as homework materials. Each case is preceded by a number of probing questions designed to test the student's understanding of the case and to help him or her pinpoint the important legal issues involved. The supplement also includes extra CPA problems taken from the law part of past Uniform CPA Exams. We are confident that the cases, problems, exercises, and outlines provide the student with what he or she needs to learn and retain a knowledge of commercial law.

The textbook also contains a special appendix entitled "The American Legal Environment in a Nutshell". This appendix completely describes the American legal system in a nutshell. It summarizes definitions and sources of law in the United States; the dual court system; the check and balance system; stare decisis; procedures for civil, criminal, administrative, equity, juvenile, and domestic relations cases; as well as the substantive law of torts, crimes, taxation, environmental law, consumer protection, and domestic relations. The "Nutshell" is approximately 50 pages in length. It presents a very complete picture of the American legal system to the beginning law student who has not yet taken a course in basic American Law or the Court System. And for the student who has taken such a course, it provides an excellent summary and review. The appendix also contains a complete glossary of legal terms.

Footnotes to the text, which have been kept to a minimum, are numbered consecutively, beginning anew with each chapter. Footnotes to the cases are from the actual court opinions; their numbers are unchanged.

We believe we have accomplished our goal of providing a complete, up-to-date coverage of the subject matter of business law—a coverage that is both interesting to study and easy to understand. We think that professors and students alike will enjoy using the text. We hope that we have contributed something to students that will be of substantial value to them now as they are learning, and also of great practical benefit to them later as they live their lives in a commercial world.

WTS
JEJ

Portland, Oregon
November, 1979

*

ACKNOWLEDGMENTS

Much more appreciation goes to all the people who helped with *Commercial Law for Business and Accounting Students: A Complete Business Law Text and CPA Law Review*.

Mrs. Gina Green, who, as secretary to the Finance-Law Department at Portland State University until a few months ago, devoted many hours to finishing the final manuscript including preparing the many illustrations for camera copy. We have truly missed Gina since she, Bud, and their family returned to Missouri. We extend them our best wishes always.

Miss Cynthia Rein, who assisted Gina, proofread the manuscript, sorted, copied, and did many other miscellaneous activities. Cindy, our work-study student, is a music major, sings beautifully, and will find great success in the future.

Miss Mary Mertens, who digested *The American Legal Environment: Individuals, Their Business, and Their Government* to produce our special appendix entitled "The American Legal Environment in a Nutshell". Mary was a fine editor of our college newspaper and is now an excellent law student at Notre Dame.

Mr. John Urness, who prepared the outlines of all thirty chapters for the book of supplementary materials that accompanies this text and also did the glossary. John was an exceptional student in both the undergraduate and MBA programs at Portland State University and one of the finest ever of football players. He was named to the academic All American team, led the Portland State Vikings on the football field, and served as graduate assistant to the Finance-Law Department. He will be an outstanding law student at the University of Oregon and a fine attorney.

Mr. Thomas Howe, who worked long and hard to create a splendid index for this text. Tom also has been an excellent student in our business school. He can look forward to achieving additional excellence at Lewis and Clark Law School and to a fine career as an attorney.

Finally, to a good friend Ray Hughey. Ray did not work on this book as such, but by taking Bill Schantz away from it on some several days in pursuit of the wiley steelhead and salmon, he contributed much to the author's peace of mind. And we even caught a few that got by the trollers and the Indians.[1]

---

[1] On July 2, 1979 the Supreme Court of the United States, in the case of State of Washington v. Puget Sound Gillnetters Association, 99 S.Ct. 3055 (1979), ruled that treaties entered into one hundred and twenty-five years earlier between the United States and Indian tribes of the Pacific Northwest (Treaty of Medicine Creek, Treaty of Neah Bay, Treaty with the Yakamas etc.) provide that the Indians are entitled to up to 50% of anadromous fish (salmon and steelhead) returning from the ocean to fresh water places of their origin to spawn. This settled a controversial issue between some 6,600 commercial trollers and 800 Indians who make their livelihood by commercial fishing. The Indians are very good fishermen; so are the trollers. Nearly a half million other individuals are licensed to engage in sport fishing in the Pacific Northwest and compete for what is left.

SUMMARY OF CONTENTS

SUMMARY OF CONTENTS

TABLE OF CONTENTS

TABLE OF CONTENTS

TABLE OF CONTENTS

TABLE OF CONTENTS

TABLE OF CONTENTS

TABLE OF CONTENTS

TABLE OF CONTENTS

TABLE OF CONTENTS

TABLE OF CONTENTS

CHAPTER 10. OTHER FACTORS AFFECTING THE RIGHTS OF CONTRACTING PARTIES: CONDITIONS, THE STATUTE OF FRAUDS, INTERPRETATION OF CONTRACTS, THE PAROL EVIDENCE RULE, DISCHARGE, BREACH OF CONTRACT AND DAMAGES
—Continued

TABLE OF CONTENTS

TABLE OF CONTENTS

TABLE OF CONTENTS

XXIX

TABLE OF CONTENTS

TABLE OF CONTENTS

TABLE OF CONTENTS

TABLE OF CONTENTS

TABLE OF CONTENTS

TABLE OF CONTENTS

TABLE OF CONTENTS

TABLE OF CONTENTS

TABLE OF CONTENTS

TABLE OF CONTENTS

TABLE OF CONTENTS

TABLE OF CONTENTS

CHAPTER 30. TRANSFERRING PROPERTY AT DEATH: WILLS—Continued

*

TABLE OF CASES

The principal cases are in italic type. Cases cited or discussed are in roman type. References are to Pages.

TABLE OF CASES

TABLE OF CASES

*

NOTE TO STUDENTS

SPECIAL APPENDIX A COMPLETELY DESCRIBES THE AMERICAN LEGAL SYSTEM IN A NUTSHELL. The appendix summarizes definitions and sources of law in the United States; the dual court system; the check and balance system; stare decisis; procedures for civil, criminal, administrative, equity, juvenile, and domestic relations cases; as well as the substantive law of torts, crimes, taxation, environmental law, consumer protection, and domestic relations. If you have not taken a course in Basic American Government or the Court System, you will find that this summary presents a very complete picture of the American legal system. If you have taken such a course, Appendix A will provide you with an excellent summary and review.

THE TEN PROBLEMS AT THE END OF EACH CHAPTER INCLUDE PROBLEMS TAKEN FROM LAW SECTIONS OF PAST UNIFORM CPA EXAMS. The problems, including the CPA problems, are excellent for any student whether or not the student intends to take the Uniform CPA Exam.

APPENDIX B PROVIDES A COMPLETE GLOSSARY OF LEGAL TERMS.

A SUPPLEMENTARY MATERIALS BOOK, CONTAINING THREE HELPFUL STUDY AIDS, IS AVAILABLE FOR USE WITH THIS TEXT. The supplement includes:

(1) ONE OR TWO EXERCISES FOR EACH CHAPTER TO BE COMPLETED AS STUDENTS FIRST READ THE CHAPTER. The exercises are invaluable in helping students learn and retain the subject matter of business law.

(2) STUDY AND REVIEW OUTLINES FOR EACH CHAPTER IN THE TEXT.

NOTE TO STUDENTS

(3) THE COMPLETE TEXT OF THE UNIFORM COMMER-
CIAL CODE, THE UNIFORM PARTNERSHIP ACT, THE UNI-
FORM LIMITED PARTNERSHIP ACT, AND THE MODEL BUSI-
NESS CORPORATION ACT, FOR USE AS A SIDE–BY–SIDE REF-
ERENCE WITH THE TEXT.

The supplement also contains additional court cases with follow-up questions designed to pinpoint the important legal issues presented. And, finally,
it provides extra CPA problems taken from the law part of past Uniform
CPA Exams.

COMMERCIAL LAW

FOR

BUSINESS AND ACCOUNTING

STUDENTS

Chapter 1

BUSINESS LAW AND OWNING PROPERTY

What is the need for commercial law?

**"Anything worth having is
worth cheating for."**

W. C. Fields

W. C. Fields was a very funny man. Unfortunately, some of what he said in jest and great levity accurately describes the less-than-ideal yet often-found traits and characteristics of many people. The instinct to acquire, to own, and to keep property is one of the strongest forces inherent in the human animal.

Robert Ardrey in his book *The Territorial Imperative*[1] writes about such instincts.

He says:

We acknowledge a few such almighty forces, but very few; the will to survive, the sexual impulse, the tie perhaps between mother and infant * * *. And it may come to us as the strangest of thoughts that the bond between a man and the soil he walks on should be * * * [the most] powerful * * *. [It is a] force shaping our lives in countless unex-

pected ways * * *. There is the need for security * * *. The predator fights for a net gain in security, whether in loot [or] land * * *. The defender, on the other hand, fights to conserve security * * *. Several hundred million years of biological evolution have altered not at all the psychological tie between proprietor and property.

Thus it is that the great issues and conflicts of today's world can be explained in terms of property. We have territorial disputes between Israelis and Palestinians. We ask ourselves, who controls the Suez Canal? Or the Panama Canal? How much should the world pay for Arab oil? To what extent should Arab investment be permitted in the United States? Should our country ship millions of bushels of grain to Russia? To India? Will the extension of our territorial waters (fishing rights) out to 200 miles serve to eliminate a source of food vital to the Japanese people? Does nuclear energy development provide jobs (prop-

1. Robert Ardrey, *The Territorial Imperative*, Kingsport Press, 1966, pages 6, 336–337.

1

erty) and power (property), or destroy the environment (property)? And what of the 20 year Vietnam war fought over control of the territory (property) of South Vietnam? Certainly, the media talks of the "haves" and "have-nots" in explaining our great social issues: the "Third World" has emerged to demand its share, and, each year, United States property owners and wage earners pay hundreds of millions of dollars in property and income taxes to federal and state governments, which, in turn, spread the tax revenues (property) around in human resource programs and finance the purchase of important defense properties.

But it is not with these great issues of the day that our text is concerned (although business or commercial law certainly has a constant and major impact on these issues). Rather, our text will deal with the many commercial law rules governing the millions of daily transactions that make up the world of business and finance—rules that are absolutely necessary to the daily intercourse of business. Even Ayn Rand, an author well known for her controversial position that government should be limited in function to the protection of rights, agrees with the need for commercial law rules, in her book *The Virtue of Selfishness.*[2]

She says:

In a free society, men are not forced to deal with one another. They do so only by voluntary agreement and, when a time element is involved, by *contract.* If a contract is broken by the arbitrary decision of one man, it may cause a disastrous financial injury to the other * * *. The protection and enforcement of contracts through courts of civil law is the most crucial need of a peaceful society; without such protection, no civilization could be developed or maintained.

Man cannot survive, as animals do, by acting on the range of the moment. Man has to project his goals and his actions and plan his life long-range. * * * No man may obtain any values from others without the owners' consent and * * * a man's rights may not be left at the mercy of the unilateral decision, the arbitrary choice, the irrationality, *the whim* of another man.

Such, in essence, is the proper purpose of a government: to make social existence possible to men, by protecting the benefits and combating the evils which men can cause to one another. [Emphasis added.]

———

As stated forcefully in the quotation, there is a need for commercial law for three reasons:

(1) People must be able to plan and project, i. e., be able to predict to some considerable degree the results of their work and other transactions. Commercial rules (laws) that people can learn in advance and rely upon in their dealings with others are essential before business can operate, people can invest, and consumers can buy.

(2) People must not be allowed to take advantage of others in their quest for property, wealth, and power, i. e., W. C. Fields' quip must not become the modus operandi. Commercial law rules that operate to prevent cheating are required.

(3) Finally, people must feel secure in their commercial transactions and other contracts. It is only where individuals know that their agreements will be binding and enforceable in the courts that they will feel free to contract to buy a house, work for another, borrow money from a bank, sell goods to a customer, in-

2. Ayn Rand, *The Virtue of Selfishness,*
The New American Library, 1964, pages
110–112.

crease inventory, purchase common stock, or protect an insurable interest.

How important are concepts of property to commercial (business) law?

Survival is a basic instinct of the human race. From time immemorial, every individual has needed certain minimal amounts of property, including such bare essentials as food, clothing, and shelter, in order to survive. And with the rise of modern civilization, people are demanding much more than the simple necessities of life. To meet the demand, business makes available hundreds of thousands of products imaginatively conceived in the minds of human beings. People spend their lives working hard to manufacture and sell such products, and to provide related services, while at the same time producing personal incomes that they themselves can use to acquire property and enjoy life.

Commercial law is inextricably tied to these "survival" activities and to the concept of private ownership of property. The law provides enforceable rules defining "property", placing limitations on its ownership, specifying ways of acquiring and transferring it, and setting down various methods for doing business in goods, services, and other property. These rules of commercial law enable our economic system to provide a maximum return in goods and services to the American people because they recognize the institution of private property, which rewards individual initiative and energy and therefore makes for greater economic activity.

The concept of property is thus the underlying element of all commercial law. For that is what commercial law is about, whether one is concerned with banking, buying, selling, financing, transporting, insuring, incorporating, entrusting, probating, or bankrupting.

What are the sources of commercial law?

There are three sources of law in the United States: (1) written law; (2)

common law; and (3) administrative law.

Written law, as the term is used here, is narrowly defined to include federal and state constitutions, treaties made by the president with foreign nations, and statutes written and passed by the federal Congress, the state legislatures, or by local governmental units such as city or county commissions. To put it simply, "written" law is law found in one of three formal documents—a constitution, treaty, or statute. Written law is important to the study of commercial law because all three kinds of written documents may be used to create commercial law, to expand it, or to restrict its scope of operation. For example, the U. S. Constitution contains numerous provisions regarding "commerce", "property", and "contracts"; treaties and executive agreements with other governments have an unparalleled influence on international trade and business; and statutes like the Uniform Commercial Code control many aspects of commercial transactions.

Still, there are many situations that are not regulated by a constitution, treaty, or statute. This is where the *common law* comes into play: if there is no written law to guide a judge in making a decision or settling a dispute, the judge must decide the case by looking to unwritten, judgemade rules (common law rules) applied to similar cases in the past. This is how common law developed and continues to develop. And, while common law rules can be superseded or modified by statute, the common law, as one of the three sources of law in our country, still has a vital and major impact on commercial law.

To understand how the general law of business came into being, it is necessary to travel back in time hundreds of years to a Europe in which business law was designated as "mercantile law" or "the law merchant". Before the first common law courts existed in England, a system of so-called "mercantile courts" had evolved to settle the disputes of the merchants and traders of the time. Frequently, the mercantile judges were appointed at fairs where the merchants came to sell their goods. When disputes arose, the merchant courts would promptly settle the issues so that the traveling merchants would not be detained. The courts' decisions were based on a system of rules, customs, and usages generally accepted by the merchants and traders themselves. The courts enforced their decisions by ostracizing any merchant who refused to accept them. It was necessary for the "law merchant" to operate this way: even after the early common law courts came into existence, they would not help the merchants resolve their disputes or enforce their mercantile decisions. It was not until the 18th Century that the common law courts discarded the notion that it was beneath their dignity to enter into commercial law matters, and took the law merchant completely into the common law system. By accepting the "law merchant", the common law courts gave the force of law to the custom and usage of merchants. The resulting business or commercial law, which has its roots completely in the customs and usages of the medieval merchants, has now been carried one step further by the partial codification of the common law into statutory form.

Specifically, all the state legislatures[3] in the United States have adopted, with but minor variation, a written statute called the Uniform Commercial Code. The widespread adoption of the Code (in all states but Louisiana) has led to the almost uniform regulation of certain business transactions in our country.

The Code itself is an extremely detailed instrument. It contains more than 400 sections covering many areas of commercial law, with greatest emphasis on the law of sales and the use of checks and promissory notes. The purposes of the UCC are stated in Section 1–102.

The UCC provides:

(1) This Act shall be liberally construed and applied to promote its underlying purposes and policies.

(2) Underlying purposes and policies of this Act are:

   (a) To simplify, clarify and modernize the law governing commercial transactions;

   (b) To permit the continued expansion of commercial practices through custom, usage and agreement of the parties;

   (c) To make uniform the law among the various jurisdictions.

———

Many aspects of commercial law, however, remain unchanged by the Uniform Commercial Code and are still controlled by common law rules. For example, the bulk of property law and contract law is based on common law and applies irrespective of the Uniform Commercial Code. Thus, both the UCC and the common law will be very important to our study of business or commercial law.

Administrative law, the third source of law in our country, will also be important to our commercial law study. Administrative law is law resulting from the work of an administrative agency. An administrative agency is a governmental authority other than a court or legislature that functions like a court or legislature in that it decides cases and/or makes rules that directly affect people and business.

Administrative agencies have been created by Congress for two reasons. First, the regulation of certain fields requires a nonlegal expertise. It is simply impossible for presidents, governors, senators,

3. However, Louisiana has adopted only two of the nine Articles of the Code.

congressmen, or judges to know enough about technical fields and industries to make good, workable regulations governing their operation. Radio, TV, transportation, atomic energy, air and water pollution, aeronautics, and space exploration are all areas where nonlegal experts must do the rulemaking if we are to have rules that make sense. Second, administrative agencies are needed to answer the mechanical questions that would otherwise overwhelm the courts in volume alone. For example, agencies such as the Social Security Administration and the Veterans Administration can easily decide who qualifies for benefits, how long the benefits should continue, and what kinds of benefits are called for, without any assistance from the courts. And it makes good sense to allow the courts to devote their time to more controversial matters.

Administrative law is important to commercial law because the rules and decisions of administrative agencies, particularly those of the Interstate Commerce Commission, the Federal Trade Commission, the Securities and Exchange Commission, and the Environmental Quality Commission, have a profound and lasting impact on the law of business.

In conclusion, all three sources of law —written, common, and administrative —are important to a study of commercial law. And while our text will emphasize the written law of the Uniform Commercial Code, we will also explore all applicable common law as well as rules and decisions of administrative agencies.

What is property?

"Property", as the term is used in this text, is first of all a legal concept. And while a "concept" is but a general thought or idea conceived in some detail, a legal concept is something more—it is a specifically defined division or part of the whole law (i. e., a division or part of the law that has been authoritatively defined by the legislative, executive, or ju-

dicial branches of government). There are a great many legal concepts within our system of law. It is the division of law into concepts that enables lawyers (men and women trained in the study of legal concepts) to categorize problems and resolve disputes. A lawyer can take any particular fact situation and place it within a specific category or subject matter area of the law; certain rules unique to the category or area will then apply. For example, say you tell your lawyer that a speeding motorist failed to stop at a stop sign and ran into your automobile, causing you extensive property damage. Your lawyer will recognize that negligence, a legal concept of tort law, is involved and will apply the rules of negligence to your problem. Your lawyer is familiar with these rules and principles from his or her legal study, and he or she knows where to look for any changes in the law.

Or say someone robs and beats you, and you wind up in the hospital. Your lawyer will apply the rules and principles of another legal concept—intentional tort —to help you recover damages for your personal loss and injury. Law enforcement officials will utilize, not tort, but the legal concept of crime to arrest your assailant.

If you buy a new TV-stereo that does not work, the legal concept of sales will apply. And if you need a divorce, domestic relations law (a legal concept dealing with divorce, alimony, and child support) will provide the answers.

So it is with every fact situation, including those in a commercial law or business law setting. Each must be placed within a specific legal concept authoritatively defined in one or more of the three sources of law—written, common, or administrative. This text will cover all the legal concepts dealing with commercial or business law, including the seventeen legal concepts that are covered in the business law section of the CPA exam. We will begin our study with the concept of property, breaking it into its two main parts—real property and personal property. We will then proceed to cover the rules and principles of the legal concepts of contract, insurance, assignment, negotiable instruments, bailments, carriers, documents of title, sales, employer-employee, agency, partnership, corporation, securities regulations, antitrust and labor law, bankruptcy, secured transactions, suretyship, professional responsibility, trust, wills, and estates. Each of these legal concepts is an authoritatively defined category of law into which fact situations can be placed with the result that certain rules and principles will apply.

It should be pointed out that no matter what individual legal concept or category is involved, the primary concept of our law—that is, the fundamental or basic element of our entire legal system—always remains the same. And that is the notion of legal rights and duties. Whether we are discussing contracts, sales, agency law, bailments, corporations, property law, or any other of the many hundreds of specific legal concepts contained within our legal system, it always comes down to a basic discussion of legal rights and duties. A legal "right" is a legal capacity to act or to demand action or forbearance on the part of another. A legal "duty" is a legal obligation to act or to refrain from acting. Whenever there is a legal right in one person or group, there is always a correlative duty in some other person or group. As the protection and guarantee of individual rights is the single most important objective of our legal system, it comes as no surprise that the whole of our law is a system of control designed to create, recognize, and enforce legal rights and duties.

This chapter section asks the question, "What is property?" Knowledge of the primary concept of our law (i. e., the notion of legal rights and duties) is essen-

tial to understanding the answer to this question, an answer best found in thorough consideration of:

(1) The long established common law distinction between property rights and personal rights (i. e., transferability versus nontransferability);

(2) Other traditional common law characteristics of property;

(3) The meaning of the term "property" as used in the 14th Amendment of the U.S. Constitution, which states that "life, liberty or *property*" (emphasis added) may not be taken away without "due process of law"; and

(4) Legislative expansion of the concept of property in statutes enlarging the scope of traditional property interests, or creating new property interests.

(1) *The common law distinction between property rights and personal rights.* In keeping with the primary concept of our law, the common law has traditionally recognized two types of individual rights —personal rights and property rights. The difference between the two is found in their transferability. If a right can be disposed of or transferred by gift, sale, or assignment, it is a property right. If a right cannot be disposed of, but can be exercised only by the person possessing it (i. e., the owner cannot give it away or sell it to another), it is a personal right. Personal, nontransferable rights include such Bill of Rights protections as freedoms of religion, speech, press, and assembly. Civil rights are nontransferable; and so are rights to vote, to marry, and to make a will.

Property or transferable rights, on the other hand, include real property rights and personal property rights (not to be confused with personal rights as defined above). The term "real" refers to the earth; accordingly, real property rights are rights with respect to real estate (land and things permanently attached to land such as buildings and their fixtures). All other property rights are personal property rights—transferable rights that are unconnected to real estate. The legal concepts of real and personal property will be treated in detail in the chapters that immediately follow.

(2) *Other traditional common law characteristics of property.* The word "property" is derived from the Latin word "proprius" meaning "belonging to one" or "one's own". Way back in the 1700's, Professor Blackstone wrote in his *Commentaries* as follows

He wrote:

There is nothing which so generally strikes the imagination, and engages the affections of mankind, as the right of property; or that sole and despotic dominion which one man claims and exercises over the external things, of the world, in total exclusion of the right of any other individual in the universe.[4]

———

Corpus Juris Secundum, a legal "encyclopedia" of the law, modernly describes the common law concept of property in the following language.

It says:

Property is considered to be the highest right which a man can have to anything, real or personal, being a complex bundle of rights, duties, powers, and immunities, comprising a vast variety of rights, with certain rights such as the right of use, the right of enjoyment and the right of disposal considered to be the constituent elements or essential attributes of property. It is generally recognized that property includes the right of *acquisi-*

tion, the right of *dominion*, the right of *possession*, the right of *use and enjoyment*, the right of *exclusion*, and the right of *disposition*. There are frequent statements to the effect that these rights may be exercised to the exclusion of all others, freely, and without restriction, and without control or diminution save only by the laws of the land, and that anything which destroys one or more of the elements of property to that extent destroys the property itself, although title and possession remain undisturbed.[5] (Emphasis added.)

———

And, in Citizens State Bank of Barstow, Texas v. Vidal, 114 F.2d 380 (10th Cir. 1940), the court states that the "essential ingredients" of property are that it be subject to ownership, transfer, and exclusive possession and enjoyment, and that it exist in such form that it may be brought within a court's dominion and control through some legally recognized process.

(3) *The meaning of the term "property" as used in the 14th Amendment of the U.S. Constitution, which states that "life, liberty or property" may not be taken away without "due process of law."* Common law definitions of property evolved over a very long period of time, with judges creating and following legal precedents without the benefit of written law (constitutions, treaties, or statutes) as a guide.

However, the U.S. Constitution also makes reference to the concept of "property"; and its use of that term in the 14th Amendment (passed in 1868) carries the meaning of "property" several steps beyond its common law definition. The 14th Amendment states in part: "[N]or shall any state deprive any per-

———

4. 2 *Blackstone's Commentaries* 2, 15.

5. 73 *Corpus Juris Secundum*, 142–144.

son of life, liberty, or property without due process of law." In interpreting this provision, the United States Supreme Court has defined "property" to include some interests that are nontransferable —interests that clearly do not fit within traditional common law definitions of the term "property". Most of the "new property" interests protected by the Amendment are interests given by government to businesses and individuals. In modern years, government has become a major source of wealth, distributing benefits of all kinds, including food stamps, money, other welfare benefits, services, contracts, licenses, and franchises. More specifically, government grants:

(a) *Occupational licenses.* Licenses required before an individual may practice law, medicine, or engage in a number of occupations requiring little formal education;

(b) *Franchises.* Exclusive rights to operate a TV station, bus line, air carrier, liquor store, national park concession, etc.;

(c) *Direct income benefits.* Benefits including social security, unemployment compensation, aid to dependent children, veteran's benefits, and workmen's compensation;

(d) *Contracts.* Billions of dollars paid to businesses (many of which do all or nearly all their business with the government) in the form of government contracts and research grants;

(e) *Subsidies.* Billions of dollars used to subsidize or support agriculture and other industries.

Many of these government-granted interests have been deemed "property" interests within the meaning of the 14th Amendment (therefore requiring due process of law before they may be denied or taken away) even though they are not "transferable" interests as defined at common law. For example, almost all Americans who work pay social security taxes and are eligible for social security benefits. Yet, while the right to such benefits is generally considered nontransferable, the right to receive benefits has been held to constitute "property" for purposes of the 14th Amendment. Nor may occupational or professional licenses be denied or taken away without providing the adversely affected party with adequate notice and hearing—with an opportunity to be heard. Similarly, some "minimum" notice and hearing is required before an individual may be deprived of his or her livelihood, whether he or she is a licensed doctor, lawyer, taxi driver, or real estate broker. And in New York, the courts have held that a driver's license is "of tremendous value to an individual and may not be taken away except by due process." Wignall v. Fletcher, 303 N.Y. 435, 441, 103 N.E.2d 728, 731 (1952).

As to welfare benefits, the U.S. Supreme Court made clear in its 1970 decision in Goldberg v. Kelly, 397 U.S. 254, 90 S.Ct. 1011, 25 L.Ed.2d 287, that due process is required before welfare benefits may be discontinued or suspended. The court suggested that once eligibility has been determined, statutory welfare *entitlements* (an entitlement is simply a benefit available to individuals who meet certain criteria or conditions) are to be treated on an equal footing with more traditional forms of property. The following quote is found in a footnote to the *Goldberg* opinion.

It says:

It may be realistic today to regard welfare entitlements as more like "property" than a "gratuity." Much of the existing wealth in this country takes the form of rights that do not fall within traditional common-law concepts of property. It has been aptly noted that "society today is built around entitlement. The automobile dealer has his franchise, the doctor and lawyer their professional licenses, the worker his union membership, contract, and pension rights, the executive his contract and stock options; all are devices to aid security and independence. Many of the most important of these entitlements now flow from government; subsidies to farmers and businessmen, routes for airlines and channels for television stations, long term contracts for defense, space, and education; social security pensions for individuals. Such sources of security, whether private or public, are no longer regarded as luxuries or gratuities; to the recipients they are essentials, fully deserved, and in no sense a form of charity." [6]

And, in 1975, in Goss v. Lopez, 419 U.S. 565, 95 S.Ct. 729, 42 L.Ed.2d 725, the U.S. Supreme Court held that high school students who had been temporarily suspended from their high schools without a hearing either prior to suspension or within a reasonable time thereafter, had been denied due process of law contrary to the 14th Amendment.

The Court stated:

Among other things, the state is constrained to recognize a student's legitimate entitlement to a public education as a property interest which is protected by the Due Process Clause and which may not be taken away for misconduct without adherence to the minimum procedures required by that clause.

In summation, it can only be concluded that the term "property", as used in the 14th Amendment, includes interests neither included in nor contemplated by the traditional common law definition of that term. Still, the 14th Amendment applies only where there is action by the state to deny or take away a property interest without due process of law. If the state is not involved, there is no constitutional protection. There is, for instance, no common law property right in private employment. However, at least one Law Review has urged the development of such a right to prevent arbitrary dismissal of employees.[7] Such a right would not prevent an employer from discharging employees for cause, but it would prevent dismissal for arbitrary or non-job-related reasons. The courts have yet to accept such a new common law property right, relying instead on the legal concept of contract to govern the employer-employee relationship.

(4) *Legislative expansion of the concept of property in statutes enlarging the scope of traditional property interests, or creating new property interests.* The common law crime of larceny required the trespassory taking and carrying away of the *personal property* of another with intent to steal the property. Modern criminal codes have generally eliminated use of the term "larceny", and classify such acts under "theft". At the same time, the modern codes have expanded the definition of "theft" to include the stealing of services as well as the stealing of personal property. For example, the State of Oregon's modern Criminal Code provides as follows.

---

6. 397 U.S. at 262, Footnote 8, quoting Reich, *Individual Rights and Social Welfare: The Emerging Legal Issues*, 74 Yale L.J. 1245, 1255 (1965).

7. Levine, Philip J., *Towards a Property Right in Employment*, 22 Buffalo Law Review, page 1,081, 1972–73. And it should be pointed out that, in recent years, the U.S. Supreme Court has appeared to recognize a property right or "entitlement" in *government* jobs (as opposed to private jobs).

It says:

Or.Rev.Stat. § 164.125 (1973). *Theft of services.* (1) A person commits the crime of theft of services if:

(a) With intent to avoid payment therefor, he obtains services that are available only for compensation, by force, threat, deception or other means to avoid payment for the services. (Emphasis added.)

———

This classification of "theft" falls under the broader statutory heading of "offenses" against "property", indicating that, at least within the criminal law concept, one may have a property right in his or her labor.

In the commercial or business law area, you will recall that the Uniform Commercial Code governs a wide variety of commercial transactions in all our states. The UCC creates a new "property" right in one "sales" law situation. Generally, in a contract (a legally binding agreement) for the sale of goods, the seller's first job after formation of the contract is to manufacture or select the goods that are to be shipped or otherwise delivered to the buyer. At some point in time, the seller will identify the exact goods to be shipped, delivered, or held for the purchaser. This activity is called "identification" of the goods to the contract. UCC Section 2–501. Identification of the goods creates a special property interest in the buyer which gives the buyer important property rights, including the right to insure the goods, the right to obtain the goods if the seller becomes insolvent, the right to inspect the goods, and the right to recover damages from anyone who injures the identified goods. This special property right will be discussed in detail in Chapter 17 of the text, dealing with the law of sales as governed by the Uniform Commercial Code.

How does the law protect an individual against damage or threat of damage to property?

Any unreasonable interference with another's personal or property interests is called a legal "tort". Put simply, a "tort" is socially unreasonable conduct—conduct society will not tolerate—that adversely affects another's interests, causing personal loss or property loss. The legal concept of tort law is designed to measure the amount of loss sustained and to equitably "adjust" the loss by providing compensation for the tort victim.

Thus, the law of torts allows a person to recover money damages for sustaining what are termed "intentional" torts (in tort law, a person is said to intend the reasonable, natural, or probable consequences of his or her acts—a malicious or harmful intent is not required). Intentional torts include "battery" (an unpermitted, offensive, or unprivileged touching of one's person, e. g., socking someone in the nose); "assault" (the state of being placed in apprehension or fear of an imminent battery, e. g., shaking a fist angrily at someone); "false imprisonment" (confinement without legal justification, e. g., locking someone in the closet); "infliction of mental distress" (creation of emotional disturbance by outrageous actions, e. g., falsely notifying someone by telegram that a loved one has been killed); "defamation of character" (holding one up to public ridicule or scorn, e. g., falsely and publicly calling someone a rapist); and "invasion of privacy" (unjustified interference with someone's private life, e. g., spying, wiretapping, or exposing intimate details about a person's private life).

In addition to the intentional torts (and there are many, many more) is the tort of negligence which requires no intent on the part of the tortfeasor (person committing the tort), but simply carelessness. Negligence is perhaps best defined as unintentional conduct that falls below the standard established by law for the protection of others against unreasonably great risk of harm to either person or property. To constitute negligence, the risk must be foreseeable at the time the conduct occurs, and, in light of that risk, the defendant's actions must be unreasonable. For example, many negligence cases arise out of automobile accidents in which one party's careless driving has resulted in personal injury or property loss to another party. However, where an accident is unforeseen and unavoidable (e. g., where a child unexpectedly darts out in front of an automobile, and the driver has no time or opportunity to miss hitting the child), there is no negligence and no liability.

How do courts determine whether any particular conduct is negligent? Most apply what is called the "reasonable prudent person" test and define negligence as the failure to do what a reasonable, prudent person would do under the same or similar circumstances. In an emergency situation, for example, it might be "reasonable" to react with panic or confusion. In addition, the plaintiff (the party who brings the lawsuit) must establish four elements to prove negligence:

(1) The plaintiff must show that the defendant had a *duty* to act according to a certain standard of conduct. This duty varies with the situation and circumstances. While a doctor has a high duty of care to a patient, a landowner has very little duty to a trespassing adult. In later chapters, we will consider the duties of various kinds of bailees, common carriers, and warehousemen.

(2) Once duty is established, the plaintiff must prove that the defendant *breached* the duty—that he or she failed to conform to the required standard of conduct.

(3) The plaintiff must also prove that the defendant's breach of duty *caused* the injury. The defendant's conduct causes the injury only where it is a material element or substantial factor in bringing the injury about.

(4) Finally, the plaintiff must prove that he or she suffered *actual loss* or *damage*.

Negligence is a very important tort concept that will come up often in our study of commercial law, particularly in the areas of property, insurance, banking, bailments, and agency.

Are there any intentional torts and defenses to intentional torts that provide protection for property interests?

There are several intentional torts and defenses to such torts that provide invaluable protection for real property and personal property interests. They are best summarized under the following headings: (1) Intentional torts relating to real property; (2) Intentional torts relating to personal property; and (3) Defenses regarding property.

(1) *Intentional torts relating to real property.*

Trespass to land. Any physical entry upon the surface of land is a trespass, including walking on the land, digging under it, flooding it, breaking into a building on the land, or causing others to trespass on the property.

Nuisance. The tort of nuisance is the use of one's own land in such manner as to unreasonably interfere with another's use and enjoyment of his or her land. Possession of a property right in real estate carries with it a right to quiet enjoyment of the property. Any unreasonable interference with the owner's comfort or convenience constitutes a private nuisance, including excessive noise, vibration, pollution, smoke, heat, odor, or fire hazard.

Many times, a nuisance is also a trespass (e. g., where one property owner diverts stagnant water from his or her property, and it floods a neighbor's land).

(2) *Intentional torts relating to personal property.*

Conversion. A person who seriously interferes with another's personal property (goods, things, documents, stock certificates) may be forced by a court of law to purchase the property from its lawful owner at its fair market value. Such a serious interference is called a conversion, and always results in a forced sale of the goods to the interfering party. The interfering party, however, must intend to convert the property (again, a hostile intent is not required, but simply an intent to exercise control over the property inconsistent with the owner's rights). Thus, if a party intentionally steals another's property, destroys it, or seriously damages it, he or she will be liable for the tort of conversion. But if the damage results from the party's carelessness, then the tort action must be based on negligence, not conversion.

Suppose the property owner wants the "converted" item returned? If someone intentionally carries off your TV set and you sue the party for conversion, you will receive the TV set's fair market value in cash, but the converter will be allowed to keep your former property. If you prefer to keep the TV rather than "sell" it to the converter, you should forego a conversion action and ask the court for a decree requiring the interfering party to return the item to you. A request to the court for the return of specific goods is called a suit to "replevin" the goods.

Trespass to chattels. Intentional interference with personal property not serious enough to justify a forced sale of the property in a conversion action is called a trespass to chattels. Trespass to chattels is often called "the little brother of conversion" because it provides recovery for

intentional damage insufficient to be classified as a conversion. For example, someone who merely scratches the wood cabinet on your TV set has not caused sufficient damage to justify a forced sale; but the wrongdoer has "trespassed to the chattel" and must pay for the damage inflicted.

(3) *Defenses regarding property.* Sometimes, an individual is privileged to do an act that would otherwise be tortious. Thus, the law of torts recognizes that a person who is in great danger of physical harm may use reasonable force in self-defense without incurring liability for battery or assault. Self-defense is permissible whenever force is reasonably necessary to prevent harmful contact or confinement. However, force cannot be used once the danger has passed, and only the amount of force necessary to prevent harm is privileged.

Along the same line, there are two important tort defenses that relate specifically to property:

(a) *Defense of property.* An individual is entitled to use reasonable force to protect his or her property. However, the law values human life (even that of a thief) more highly than it values property, and force likely to cause death or great bodily injury may never be used to protect property interests alone. Nor may such force be exerted indirectly in the form of spring guns or vicious watch dogs maintained on the premises to protect property. These kinds of protection fall outside the scope of the defense privilege. (Some jurisdictions prohibit the use of dangerous mechanical devices or dogs to discourage trespassing and petty theft, but permit their use to protect against serious crimes such as burglaries.)

(b) *Recapture of chattels.* A person whose property has been wrongfully taken is justified in using reasonable force to retake the property if he or she does so immediately. However, the use of force is privileged only so long as the property owner is in "fresh pursuit" of his or her property. If the pursuit stops for any length of time, the property owner must turn the chase over to law enforcement personnel. Thus, where a person in fresh pursuit of wrongfully taken proper- ty breaks down a door, enters a building, and holds the thief captive until the law arrives, the defense of "recapture of chattels" may be successfully asserted to charges of trespass, battery, and false imprisonment.

CASES

CASE 1—*A driver's license is an "entitlement" protected by the 14th Amendment.*

BELL v. BURSON

Supreme Court of the United States, 1971.
402 U.S. 535, 91 S.Ct. 1586, 29 L.Ed.2d 90.

Mr. Justice BRENNAN delivered the opinion of the Court.

Georgia's Motor Vehicle Safety Responsibility Act provides that the motor vehicle registration and driver's license of an uninsured motorist involved in an accident shall be suspended unless he posts security to cover the amount of damages claimed by aggrieved parties in reports of the accident. The administrative hearing conducted prior to the suspension excludes consideration of the motorist's fault or liability for the accident. The Georgia Court of Appeals rejected peititioner's contention that the State's statutory scheme, in failing before suspending the licenses to afford him a hearing on the question of his fault or liability, denied him due process in violation of the Fourteenth Amendment: the court held that " 'Fault' or 'innocence' are completely irrelevant factors."

Petitioner is a clergyman whose ministry requires him to travel by car to cover three rural Georgia communities. On Sunday afternoon, November 24, 1968, petitioner was involved in an accident when five-year-old Sherry Capes rode her bicycle into the side of his automobile. The child's parents filed an accident report with the Director of the Georgia Department of Public Safety indicating that their daughter had suffered substantial injuries for which they claimed damages of $5,000. Petitioner was thereafter informed by the Director that unless he was covered by a liability insurance policy in effect at the time of the accident he must file a bond or cash security deposit of $5,000 or present a notarized release from liability, plus proof of future financial responsibility, or suffer the suspension of his driver's license and vehicle registration. Petitioner requested an administrative hearing before the Director asserting that he was not liable as the accident was unavoidable, and stating also that he would be severely handicapped in the performance of his ministerial duties by a suspension of his licenses. A hearing was scheduled but the Director informed petitioner that "[t]he only evidence that the Department can accept and consider is: (a) was the petitioner or his vehicle involved in the accident; (b) has petitioner complied with the provisions of the Law as provided; or (c) does petitioner come within any of the exceptions of the Law." At the administrative hearing the Director rejected petitioner's proffer of evidence on liability, ascertained that petitioner was not within any of the statutory exceptions, and gave petitioner 30 days to comply with the security requirements or suffer suspension. * * *

If the statute barred the issuance of licenses to all motorists who did not carry liability insurance or who did not post security, the statute would not, under our cases, violate the Fourteenth Amendment. It does not follow, however, that the amendment also permits the Georgia statutory scheme where not all motorists, but rather only motorists involved in accidents, are required to post security under penalty of loss of the licenses. Once licenses are issued, as in petitioner's case, their continued possession may become essential in the pursuit of a livelihood. Suspension of issued licenses thus involves state action that adjudicates important interests of the licensees. In such cases the licenses are not to be taken away without that procedural due process required by the Fourteenth Amendment. This is but an application of the general proposition that relevant constitutional restraints limit state power to terminate an entitlement whether the entitlement is denominated a "right" or a "privilege." Sherbert v. Verner, 374 U.S. 398 (1963) (disqualification for unemployment compensation); Slochower v. Board of Higher Education, 350 U.S. 551 (1956) (discharge from public employment); Speiser v. Randall, 357 U.S. 513 (1958) (denial of a tax exemption); Goldberg v. Kelly [397 U.S. 254 (1970)] (withdrawal of welfare benefits).

We turn then to the nature of the procedual due process which must be afforded the licensee on the question of his fault of liability for the accident.

The hearing required by the Due Process Clause must be "meaningful," and "appropriate to the nature of the case." It is a proposition which hardly seems to need explication that a hearing which excludes consideration of an element essential to the decision whether licenses of the nature here involved shall be suspended does not meet this standard.

* * * [I]t is fundamental that except in emergency situations (and this is not one) due process requires that when a State seeks to terminate an interest such as that here involved, it must afford "notice and opportunity for hearing appropriate to the nature of the case" *before* the termination becomes effective.

We hold, then, that under Georgia's present statutory scheme, before the State may deprive petitioner of his driver's license and vehicle registration it must provide a forum for the determination of the question whether there is a reasonable possibility of a judgment being rendered against him as a result of the accident. * * *

Reversed and remanded.

CASE 2—*Spring guns and other man-killing devices are not justifiable against a petty thief.*

KATKO v. BRINEY

Supreme Court of Iowa, 1971.
183 N.W.2d 657.

MOORE, Chief Justice.

The primary issue presented here is whether an owner may protect personal property in an unoccupied boarded-up farm house against trespassers and thieves by a spring gun capable of inflicting death or serious injury.

We are not here concerned with a man's right to protect his home and members of his family.   Defendants' home was several miles from the scene of the incident to which we refer infra.

Plaintiff's action is for damages resulting from serious injury caused by a shot from a 20-gauge spring shotgun set by defendants in a bedroom of an old farm house which had been uninhabited for several years.   Plaintiff and his companion, Marvin McDonough, had broken and entered the house to find and steal old bottles and dated fruit jars which they considered antiques.

At defendants' request plaintiff's action was tried to a jury consisting of residents of the community where defendants' property was located.   The jury returned a verdict for plaintiff and against defendants for $20,000 actual and $10,000 punitive damages.

* * *

Most of the facts are not disputed.   In 1957 defendant Bertha L. Briney inherited her parents' farm land in Mahaska and Monroe Counties.   Included was an 80-acre tract in southwest Mahaska County where her grandparents and parents had lived.   No one occupied the house thereafter.   Her husband, Edward, attempted to care for the land.   He kept no farm machinery thereon.   The outbuildings became dilapidated.

For about 10 years, 1957 to 1967, there occurred a series of trespassing and housebreaking events with loss of some household items, the breaking of windows and "messing up of the property in general".   The latest occurred June 8, 1967, prior to the event on July 16, 1967 herein involved.

Defendants through the years boarded up the windows and doors in an attempt to stop the intrusions.   They had posted "no trespass" signs on the land several years before 1967.   The nearest one was 35 feet from the house.   On June 11, 1967 defendants set "a shotgun trap" in the north bedroom.   After Mr. Briney cleaned and oiled his 20-gauge shotgun, the power of which he was well aware, defendants took it to the old house where they secured it to an iron bed with the barrel pointed at the bedroom door.   It was rigged with wire from the doorknob to the gun's trigger so it would fire when the door was opened.   Briney first pointed the gun so an intruder would be hit in the stomach but at Mrs. Briney's suggestion it was lowered to hit the legs.   He admitted he did so "because I was mad and tired of being tormented" but "he did not intend to injure anyone".   * * *

Plaintiff lived with his wife and worked regularly as a gasoline station attendant in Eddyville, seven miles from the old house.   He had observed it for several years while hunting in the area and considered it as being abandoned.   He knew it had long been uninhabited.   In 1967 the area around the house was covered with high weeds.   Prior to July 16, 1967 plaintiff and McDonough had been to the premises and found several old bottles and fruit jars which they took and added to their collection of antiques.   On the latter date about 9:30 p. m. they made a second trip to the Briney property.   They entered the old house by removing a board from a porch window which was without glass.   While McDonough was looking around the kitchen area plaintiff went to another part of the house.   As he started to open the north bedroom door the shotgun went off striking him in the right leg above the ankle bone.   Much of his leg, including part of the tibia, was blown away.   Only by McDonough's assistance was plaintiff able to get out of the house and after crawling some distance was put in his vehicle and rushed to a doctor and then to a hospital.   He remained in the hospital 40 days.

Plaintiff's doctor testified he seriously considered amputation but eventually the healing process was successful. Some weeks after his release from the hospital plaintiff returned to work on crutches. He was required to keep the injured leg in a cast for approximately a year and wear a special brace for another year. He continued to suffer pain during this period.

There was undenied medical testimony plaintiff had a permanent deformity, a loss of tissue, and a shortening of the leg.

* * *

Plaintiff testified he knew he had no right to break and enter the house with intent to steal bottles and fruit jars therefrom. He further testified he had entered a plea of guilty to larceny in the nighttime of property of less than $20 value from a private building. He stated he had been fined $50 and costs and paroled during good behavior from a 60-day jail sentence. Other than minor traffic charges this was plaintiff's first brush with the law. * * *

The main thrust of defendants' defense in the trial court and on this appeal is that "the law permits use of a spring gun in a dwelling or warehouse for the purpose of preventing the unlawful entry of a burglar or thief".
* * *

In the statement of issues the trial court stated plaintiff and his companion committed a felony when they broke and entered defendants' house. * * * [T]he court referred to the early case history of the use of spring guns and stated under the law their use was prohibited except to prevent the commission of felonies of violence and where human life is in danger.
* * *

* * * ["O]ne may use reasonable force in the protection of his property, but such right is subject to the qualification that one may not use such means of force as will take human life or inflict great bodily injury. Such is the rule even though the injured party is a trespasser and is in violation of the law himself."

* * * "An owner of premises is prohibited from willfully or intentionally injuring a trespasser by means of force that either takes life or inflicts great bodily injury; and therefore a person owning a premise is prohibited from setting out 'spring guns' and like dangerous devices which will likely take life or inflict great bodily injury, for the purpose of harming trespassers. The fact that the trespasser may be acting in violation of the law does not change the rule. The only time when such conduct of setting a 'spring gun' or a like dangerous device is justified would be when the trespasser was committing a felony of violence or a felony punishable by death, or where the trespasser was endangering human life by his act."

* * *

The overwhelming weight of authority, both textbook and case law, supports the trial court's statement of the applicable principles of law.

Prosser on Torts, Third Edition, pages 116–118, states:

" * * * the law has always placed a higher value upon human safety than upon mere rights in property, it is the accepted rule that there is no privilege to use any force calculated to cause death or serious bodily injury to repel the threat to land or chattels, unless there is also such a threat to the defendant's personal safety as to justify a self-defense. * * * spring guns and other man-killing devices are not justifiable against a mere trespasser, or even a petty thief. They are privileged only against those upon whom the landowner, if he were present in person would be free to inflict injury of the same kind."

* * *

In Volume 2, Harper and James, The Law of Torts, section 27.3, pages 1440, 1441, this is found: "The possessor of land may not arrange his premises intentionally so as to cause death or serious bodily harm to a trespasser. The possessor may of course take some steps to repel a trespass. If he is present he may use force to do so, but only that amount which is reasonably necessary to effect the repulse. Moreover if the trespass threatens harm to property only—even a theft of property—the possessor would not be privileged to use deadly force, he may not arrange his premises so that such force will be inflicted by mechanical means. If he does, he will be liable even to a thief who is injured by such device."

* * *

In Hooker v. Miller, 37 Iowa 613, we held defendant vineyard owner liable for damages resulting from a spring gun shot although plaintiff was a trespasser and there to steal grapes. At pages 614, 615, this statement is made: "This court has held that a mere trespass against property other than a dwelling is not a sufficient justification to authorize the use of a deadly weapon by the owner in its defense; and that if death results in such a case it will be murder, though the killing be actually necessary to prevent the trespass. The State v. Vance, 17 Lowa 138." At page 617 this court said: "[T]respassers and other inconsiderable violators of the law are not to be visited by barbarous punishments or prevented by inhuman inflictions of bodily injuries."

* * *

In addition to civil liability many jurisdictions hold a land owner criminally liable for serious injuries or homicide caused by spring guns or other set devices. See State v. Childers, 133 Ohio 508, 14 N.E.2d 767 (melon thief shot by spring gun); Pierce v. Commonwealth, 135 Va. 635, 115 S.E. 686 (policeman killed by spring gun when he opened unlocked front door of defendant's shoe repair shop); State v. Marfaudille, 48 Wash. 117, 92 P. 939 (murder conviction for death from spring gun set in a trunk); State v. Beckham, 306 Mo. 566, 267 S.W. 817 (boy killed by spring gun attached to window of defendant's chili stand); State v. Green, 118 S.C. 279, 110 S.E. 145, 19 A.L.R. 1431 (intruder shot by spring gun when he broke and entered vacant house. Manslaughter conviction of owner-affirmed); State v. Barr, 11 Wash. 481, 39 P. 1080 (murder conviction affirmed for death of an intruder into a boarded up cabin in which owner had set a spring gun).

* * *

The jury's findings of fact including a finding defendants acted with malice and with wanton and reckless disregard, as required for an allowance of punitive or exemplary damages, are supported by substantial evidence.

* * *

* * *

Study and careful consideration of defendants' contentions on appeal reveal no reversible error.

Affirmed.

CASE 3—*Who gets Adolph Hitler's uniform and cap?*

LIEBER v. MOHAWK ARMS, INC.

Supreme Court, Oneida County, 1970.
64 Misc.2d 206.

J. Robert LYNCH, Justice:

* * * The facts are undisputed.

In 1945 the plaintiff, then in the United States Army, was among the first soldiers to occupy Munich, Germany. There he and some companions entered Adolph Hitler's apartment and removed various items of his personal belongings. The plaintiff brought his share home to Louisiana. It included Hitler's uniform jacket and cap and some of his decorations and personal jewelry.

The plaintiff's possession of these articles was publicly known. Louisiana newspapers published stories and pictures about the plaintiff's collection and he was the subject of a feature story in the Louisiana State University Alumni News of October, 1945. There is some indication that the articles were occasionally displayed to the public.

In 1968 the collection was stolen by the plaintiff's chauffeur who sold it to a New York dealer in historical Americana. The dealer sold it to the defendant who purchased in good faith. Through collectors' circles the plaintiff soon discovered the whereabouts of his stolen property, made a demand for its return that was refused, and commenced this action seeking the return.

The defendant resists and asks * * * judgment on the ground that the plaintiff cannot succeed in the suit since he "never obtained good and legal title to this collection", that "the collection properly belongs to the occupational military authority and/or the Bavarian Government".

This defense, title in a third party, was at one time effective. But it did not survive the enactment of the Civil Practice Law and Rules, section 7101 of which provides for the recovery of a chattel by one who has the superior right to possession. In proposing the elimination of this defense the draughtsmen of the CPLR sought to prevent the very thing being attempted by the defendant here. "The present law thus allows a defendant who has a lesser right to possession than the plaintiff to keep the property and withstand a replevy by asserting the superior right of a third person, even though there is no assurance that he will turn over the property to the third person. There is no good reason to perpetuate this situation, for if the holder of a chattel is genuinely concerned about the rights of the true owner, he may employ the modern procedural device of interpleader to protect them, or may merely notify the person who claims to be the true owner and the latter may intervene."

[W]e find that the plaintiff must recover possession of the chattels. The defendant, despite its good faith, has no title since its possession is derived from a thief (Uniform Commercial Code, § 2–403; Bassett v. Spofford, 45 N.Y. 387). The plaintiff's possession prior to the theft and since 1945 is unquestioned. * * *

* * *

[J]udgment is granted to the plaintiff.

PROBLEMS

1. Sally Carpenter is incensed when her welfare benefits are cut off without notice of any kind. Sally demands a hearing on the matter but Harvey Price, the welfare officer, refuses to schedule one. Sally marches down to the welfare office and accosts Harvey. When he refuses to reopen her case, Sally kicks him in the shin and pushes his typewriter on the floor, seriously damaging it. Is Sally entitled to a hearing regarding denial of her welfare benefits? *yes - 14th Amendment* If so, on what basis? Does Harvey have any legal recourse against Sally for the kick *intentional tort battery* on the shin and the damage to his typewriter? *conversion* Explain.

2. Sally's welfare benefits are reinstated. Sally is in need of some extra *Not transferrable Prop.* cash so she sells her right to the benefits to Mark Harris for $250. Sally also sells Mark her portable TV for $50 and her old Chevy for $175. Mark attempts to collect Sally's benefits from the welfare department, but the department refuses to pay them to Mark. When Mark leaves the department, he see Fred Willard driving away in the Chevy. Mark immediately gives chase on foot. He catches up to the car at the corner stoplight, pulls Fred from the auto, and punches him in the nose when Fred puts up a fight. Answer the following:

   (a) Does Mark have a right to collect Sally's welfare benefits? Explain. *No - not transferrable*

   (b) Does Mark have a right to possession and use of the portable TV and the old Chevy? Explain. *yes - personal prop.*

   (c) Does Fred Willard have any legal recourse against Mark for the punch in the nose? Explain. *no - "fresh pursuit" recapture chattel battery but*

3. Answer the following "True" or "False" and give reasons for your answers:

   F (a) The primary concept of our law is the protection of commercial interests under the Uniform Commercial Code. *Rights & Duties*

   F (b) Government contracts and subsidies fall within traditional common law definitions of property.

   T (c) Personal rights may not be transferred.

   F (d) A person whose personal property has been wrongfully taken may obtain return of the property by suing for conversion.

   T (e) Property is the underlying concept of all commercial law.

4. Why is commercial law necessary? *plan & project*

5. Name and define the three sources of law. *written, common, Admin*

6. Jean Campbell and Rhonda Martin are suspended from high school without notice or hearing of any kind. Having nothing else to do, Jean and Rhonda climb over a fence onto Mike Carter's private property and trample Mike's prize flower bed. An angry Mike appears, waving a loaded pistol at the girls.

   (a) What are Jean's and Rhonda's rights with regard to the suspension from high school? *Hearing & notice - 14th*

   (b) Does Mike have any legal recourse against the girls for their having trampled his flower bed? Explain. Does it matter that the girls did not "intend" to trample the flowers? Explain.
   Trespass - tort

(c) Does Mike have a right to use the gun to protect his property? Explain. *Reasonable force*

7. Daydreaming about steelhead fishing, Carl Stryker carelessly drives his van into Molly Hanson's new sportscar. Does Molly have any legal recourse against Carl? Explain. *neg* Assuming Molly has legal recourse, what test will the court apply? *Reasonably prud person* Is Molly likely to recover? Explain.

1 Duty 2 Breach ← causation 3 ✓ Damages

8. Molly is driving home in what is left of her sportscar. Suddenly, a young boy darts out in front of her car, and Molly is unable to avoid hitting the child. Can the child recover from Molly for his injuries? *no* If so, on what basis? If not, why not? *unavoidable accident*

9. Sara Travers has had a bad day. First, she found young Billy Tucker scraping paint off the side of her car. Then, while Sara was shopping, the store detective detained her in a locked room for 20 minutes, mistakenly thinking that she had stolen something. Now Sara's home, but her neighbors are playing such loud music and making so much noise that Sara can't sleep. What are Sara's legal rights, if any, against Billy Tucker, the store detective, and the noisy neighbors?

Tucker Trespass to chattels Dect False imprisonment noisy neighbors nuisance

10. Ray Hewitt becomes upset when the coffee shop waitress charges him 20¢ extra for a single coffee refill. Ray shakes his fist menacingly at the waitress then leaves the coffee shop, but not before taking a set of beer mugs belonging to the shop owner, Jim Walker. All day long Jim broods about the theft; that evening, he takes action. He goes to Ray's home, and when Ray opens the door Jim clubs him on the head and retakes the beer mugs. Jim then returns to the coffee shop, pleased that he has taken care of the problem himself.

(a) What legal recourse, if any, does the waitress have against Ray Hewitt? *Assault ← if fear of battery*

(b) What legal recourse, if any, does Ray Hewitt have against Jim Walker? *Battery, trespass   conversion*

(c) What defense is Jim likely to offer for his action in clubbing Ray? Is the defense a good one? Explain.
Recapture of chattels

*Defenses for negligence
unavoidable
last clear chance
comparative negligence*

Chapter 2

MESHING REAL AND PERSONAL PROPERTY: MINERALS, TREES, CROPS, FIXTURES, AND RENTALS

How do you distinguish between real property and personal property?

We saw in Chapter 1 that, whereas personal rights are nontransferable, property rights may be freely transferred by gift, sale, or assignment. Property or transferable rights may be further divided into two mutually exclusive categories—*real property* rights and *personal property* rights. It is easy to understand the difference between these two kinds of property rights if you begin by making the term "real property" synonymous with the word "land". Start out by visualizing a great expanse of barren land. This is "real" property as the term is used in law. Realize that real property—or land —includes not only the crust of the earth, but also the area below the surface of the land, as well as the airspace above.

Now, imagine moving across this great expanse of barren land until you reach an area covered by a forest of trees. The trees and any other natural vegetation found on the land are a part of the land and are considered real property. However, as will be explained shortly, the trees become personal property when they are cut or severed from the land. Imagine still further, if you will, the appearance of a farmhouse with its barn, fences, crops, and animals. The house, barn, and fences are almost certain to be a part of the land, although there is a slim chance that they will qualify as personal property, and not land, under the law of "fixtures" (a legal concept explained later in the chapter). As for the crops growing in the fields, they clearly start out as part of the land (as real property), but by virtue of a Uniform Commercial Code rule, may become personal property even before they are cut or harvested.

And what about the cattle grazing in the pasture? There is no question but what the cattle are classified under the law as personal property. Yet cattle, as a distinct item of personal property, are unique in many respects. Historic records show that long ago, people were more interested in owning cattle than in owning land. Men and women lived as nomads, driving their cattle north during the summer months and south during the winter. As nomads, people had little use for land ownership, but ownership of cattle was vital to their livelihood. For this reason, the first property laws to come into being (crude though they were) were those dealing with the ownership, transfer, and sale of cattle, and the disposition of cattle upon the owner's death. The word "chattel," which comes initially from the word cattle, is a legal term still important to understanding the modern law of property. *Black's Law Dictionary* defines "chattel" in this way.

It says:

An article of personal property; any species of property not amounting to a freehold or fee in land. * * * A thing personal and movable. * * * Things which in law are deemed personal property, they are divisible into chattels real and chattels personal.[1]

1. Henry Campbell Black, *Black's Law Dictionary*, Revised Fourth Edition, West Publishing Co., 1968, p. 299.

"Personal chattels" are defined as "movable things".[2] "Real chattels" are "such as concern, or savor of, the realty, such as leasehold estates * * * [a]n interest in real estate less than freehold."[3] And a "chattel mortgage" is "a mortgage on chattels * * * [a] transfer of some legal or equitable right in personal property or creation of a lien thereon as security for payment of money or performance of some act."[4] (This chapter deals with the law regarding chattels real, i. e., the rental of real estate and the landlord-tenant relationship. Chapter 27 deals with "secured transactions", including the law on chattel mortgages.)

One final scene might be added to our imaginative trip across the land. Picture for a moment a coal mine, a gold mine, or an oil field. While minerals in their natural state are unquestionably a part of the land, the mineral rights (real property rights) in land may be sold or retained separately from the other real property rights in the land. At some point in time, as the minerals are removed from the earth, they become chattels (personal property).

In distinguishing between real property and personal property, our starting point has been the earth itself. Subtracting from the earth (e. g., in the case of minerals, oil, natural gas, trees, and crops), it is possible to change real property into personal property. Adding to the earth (e. g., in the case of lumber, gravel, cement, pipes, furnaces, doors, hanging lamps, and TV antennas), personal property may be converted into real property. The emphasis is on removal or attachment.

One additional and important factor in distinguishing between real and personal property is the *time* involved. Unless an individual's interest in land can last forever, or at least for the duration of the

individual's lifetime, the interest is classified as personal property, not real property. This rule that any interest in land of potentially infinite or lifetime duration is real property, and any other interest is personal property stems from early English common law; the rule was later adopted into the United States legal system. Thus, at early English common law, a landowner who was wrongfully deprived of possession of his or her land could bring a legal action to regain possession only if he or she owned what was termed a "freehold estate" (i. e., an interest in land of potentially infinite or lifetime duration). An interest of potentially infinite duration was and is referred to legally as a "fee" interest. An interest of lifetime duration was and is referred to legally as a "life estate". The owner of a fee interest or life estate could bring a case in court called a "real action" to recover possession of the property. The owner of less than a freehold estate (e. g., the owner of a "leasehold" interest, i. e., an interest in land for a limited period—months, years, etc.) could bring only what was termed a "personal action" to recover money damages, not the property itself.

And that is where the terms "real property" and "real estate" have come from—from law defining real property as land interests of potentially infinite (fee interest) or lifetime (life estate) duration. All other property is personal property. For this reason, an interest in land that is limited to a term for years (a typical lease or rental agreement) is not real property but is called a "chattel real". It is a chattel interest in real property. This is not to say that, modernly, a person who is wrongfully deprived of possession of land that he or she has leased for a period of years cannot regain possession of the land in the courts—but only that historically he or

2. Ibid.
3. Ibid.

4. Id. at p. 300.

she could not do so through a real action. However, it is still correct to classify interests in land that are less than fee or life estate interests as personal property. In later sections of this chapter, we will explore the law of "chattel real"—that is, the law of landlord-tenant.

In conclusion, the following two factors must always be considered in distinguishing between real and personal property:

(1) *The physical characteristics of and the relationship to the land of property either subtracted from or added to real property.* Minerals, trees, crops, improvements to the earth, and the like are sometimes real property and sometimes personal property, depending upon their classification under a variety of legal rules and principles to be explored in the chapter material immediately following.

(2) *The length of time the interest in land can last.* If the interest can last forever or for life, it is real property. If it can last only for a shorter period of time, it is a chattel real and personal property.

When do minerals, trees, crops, and the like change from real property to personal property?

Article 2 of the Uniform Commercial Code, entitled "Sales", states at Section 2–102 that "unless the context otherwise requires, this Article (Sales) applies to transactions in goods. * * * " *Black's Law Dictionary* defines the term "goods" as follows.

It says:

The term "goods" is not so wide as "chattels," for it applies to inanimate objects, and does not include animals or chattels real, as a lease for years of house or land, which "chattels" does include.[5]

Moving on to "goods and chattels," *Black's* states:

This phrase is a general denomination of personal property, as distinguished from real property; the term "chattels" having the effect of extending its scope to any objects of that nature which would not properly be included by the term "goods" alone, e. g., living animals, emblements, and fruits, and terms under leases for years.[6]

The Uniform Commercial Code definition of "goods" encompasses both "goods" and "goods and chattels" as defined in *Black's Law Dictionary*, excluding only rental terms for years (i. e., chattels real).

The UCC provides:

Section 2–105. Definitions: * * *
(1) "Goods" means all things (including specially manufactured goods) which are movable at the time of identification to the contract for sale. * * * "Goods" also includes the unborn young of animals and growing crops and other identified things attached to realty as described in the section on goods to be severed from realty (Section 2–107).

As a result of the UCC definition "goods", which are always and without exception classified as personal property, include animals and their unborn young, growing crops, timber, and other things to be severed from land or realty.

The timing of when crops, timber, minerals, structures, and the like change from real estate to personal property is controlled by Section 2–107 of the Uniform Commercial Code as follows.

The UCC provides:
(1) A contract for the sale of minerals or the like (including oil or gas) or a structure or its materials

5. Henry Campbell Black, Ibid, p. 823.   6. Ibid.

to be removed from realty is a contract for the sale of goods within this Article if they are to be *severed by the seller.*

* * *

(2) A contract for the sale apart from the land of growing crops or other things attached to realty and capable of severance without material harm thereto but not described in subsection (1) or of timber to be cut is a contract for the sale of goods within this Article *whether the subject matter is to be severed by the buyer or by the seller* even though it forms part of the realty at the time of contracting, and the parties can by identification effect a present sale before severance. (Emphasis added.)

The quoted provisions deal with four categories of things: minerals, structures, crops, and timber. The provisions determine whether these items will be considered real property or personal property at the time an agreement to sell them is made. However, to obtain the complete picture for our study, it is necessary to inquire whether these items are real property or personal property prior to the making of any agreement to sell them. The following conclusions apply:

Minerals. Because land, at common law, extends to the center of the earth, any surface or subsurface minerals are a part of the land (i. e., real property). The landowner may sell or retain the minerals independently of the rest of the land.

Structures. Structures on land are usually, but not always, a part of the land and real property. The classification of a particular structure as either real or personal property is controlled by the law of "fixtures" (as discussed in a later section of this chapter). For now, it is enough

to realize that if a structure is placed on land with the intention that it remain personal property and not become part of the land, then the structure will continue to be personal property. Generally, such intent is not present, and the structure becomes a part of the real estate.

Crops. Annual crops that are produced by labor (as opposed to growing naturally) are called "fructus industriales" and are considered personal property under the common law. Annual crops include corn, wheat, potatoes, barley, etc.

Timber. All trees, bushes, grasses, and the like which do not require annual cultivation are considered part of the land (i. e., real property) and are called "fructus naturales".

Now let's "mesh" the common law rules designating these items as real or personal property with the Uniform Commercial Code rules on removal of these items from the land. The following legal conclusions can be made:

(1) *Minerals.* Minerals always start out as real property; however, they become personal property at the time a sales agreement is entered into if the minerals are to be severed from the land *by the seller.* Where severance is left to the buyer, the minerals remain real property and do not change into personal property until the buyer actually removes them from the earth. Similarly, where no sales agreement is involved, and the owner of the real property mines or removes the minerals for his or her own use, the act of removal or mining serves to convert the real property into personal property.

(2) *Structures.* As previously stated, a structure may or may not be real property prior to an agreement for sale depending on the original intention of the party who placed the structure on the land (in most cases, the party's intention is that the structure become a part of the real estate). Like minerals, a real prop-

erty structure becomes personal property at the time a sales agreement is entered into if the structure is to be removed by the seller. If the buyer is to remove the structure, it is real property until its removal.

(3) *Crops.* With respect to a contract of sale, annual crops ("fructus industriales") are generally considered personal property without regard to their severance from the land. However, there are exceptions where annual crops will be treated as part of the land they grow on. First, where a deceased person's will states that land is to go to a certain party, it is usually held that the specified party is entitled to any crops growing on the land at the time of the owner's death (this being the probable intent of the decedent). Second, where a person mortgages his or her land, it is the general rule that any crops growing on the land are included within the scope of the mortgage (unless expressly excepted in writing) and will be sold along with the land if foreclosure is necessary. Third, it is a common law rule that a transfer of land ordinarily carries with it all crops growing on the land, except where the crops are reserved by agreement of the parties. However, if the crops have already been harvested (severed from the land) prior to the transfer, they will not pass with the conveyance, but will belong to the former owner. In a few states, crops that have ripened and are ready for harvest will not pass with the land on the theory that ripened crops no longer need the soil and have been "constructively severed" from the land.

(4) *Timber.* Like crops, timber ("fructus naturales") is considered personal property at the time a sales agreement is made without regard to who is to sever the timber from the land. However, this was not always the case. Under original Section 2–107 of the UCC, timber was treated like minerals rather than crops. But several timber-growing

states changed the Code provision because of the financing advantages of treating timber like "goods"; and, in 1972, the UCC itself was amended to reflect this change.

(5) *Other property.* As to property other than minerals, structures, crops, and timber that is attached to realty (e. g., fences, electrical appliances, irrigation equipment, or anything else constituting less than a structure), the property will initially start out as real or personal property depending upon the intent of the attaching party. Property that starts out as real property will become personal property at the time a sales agreement is entered into if the property can be removed from the land without doing material harm to the realty. If material harm would result, the item will become personal property only upon its actual removal from the land.

Are there any special rules regarding oil?

Oil producing states have taken one of two legal positions on oil ownership. Some states, including Arkansas, Kansas, Mississippi, Ohio, Pennsylvania, and Texas maintain that oil, like coal and other minerals, can be the subject of ownership and transfer even before it is pumped to the surface. In these so-called "ownership" states, a transfer of oil rights is treated by the courts as a transfer of land, creating two vertical layers of ownership in the real property.

Other states, including California and Oklahoma, insist that oil cannot be the subject of ownership until it is pumped to the surface of land and taken possession of. Courts in these "nonownership" states reason that, although oil is initially trapped in rocks, it moves underground once drilled from one location to another in search of a low pressure area. Because the oil moves, the courts hold that it cannot be "owned" until it is brought to the surface of the land, at which point it becomes personal property.

What this means in practical terms is that, in ownership states, oil is the subject of ownership as part of the real property under the surface of the land. As real property, the oil can be transferred by deed like any other real property interest. (However, even with a deed, it is customary for the landowner to receive a fixed percentage of the oil produced in return for transfer of the oil rights.) In nonownership states, oil is not the subject of ownership until it is brought to the surface as personal property. In such states, the landowner cannot transfer ownership of oil rights by deed, but can only grant a privilege to an oil company to drill on the land under what is termed an "oil lease". The oil company pays rent, called an oil royalty, to the landowner for the right to take the oil from the land. The rent or royalty is usually computed as a percentage share of all oil produced, such as a 10% interest.

Courts in all states, ownership and nonownership alike, agree that once an oil well is drilled on a person's land, that person will own all oil and gas produced from the well even though some of the oil or gas has moved underground from a neighbor's adjoining land. To guard against application of this "rule of capture", adjacent landowners are advised to drill "offset wells" to trap their own oil and gas and prevent them from seeping away.

What is the law on "fixtures?"

A fixture is an article, once personal property, that has become so closely connected to real property as to lose its status as a chattel and become a part of the land. The first and most important test in determining whether a particular item of personal property has become a fixture is the annexor's intent in having added the chattel to the realty. Did the annexor (person adding the property) intend to make a permanent improvement to the land? If he or she did, that intent will be controlling, and the chattel added to the property will be a legal fixture. It is not the annexor's secret or undisclosed intent that is considered, but rather the annexor's apparent intent as evidenced by his or her conduct and statements at the time of the annexation.

The only time the annexor's intent to make a permanent improvement will be disregarded is where the annexation is wrongful because the annexor does not own the chattel he or she adds to the real property. It is simply not fair to deprive the chattel owner of his or her personal property just because the annexor intended to permanently and wrongfully add the property to his or her (or another's) land. An exception to this rule arises where the chattel loses its identity by the incorporation. For example, where a single stolen brick is built into a wall containing many hundreds of bricks, it would obviously be impossible to identify and recover the specific stolen property. The stolen brick, in this case, becomes the property of the landowner (under the laws of "accession" to be studied in Chapter 3), and the chattel owner's remedy is an action against the wrongdoer for the tort of conversion.

Wrongful annexations aside, if the annexor's intent were discoverable in every situation, it would be an easy matter to determine whether a particular item of personal property had become a legal fixture when attached to the land. The annexor's intent, however, is not always readily apparent, and the courts must frequently look to other tests (tests that are said to indirectly prove intent) to make this determination.

The second test used by the courts to determine whether or not a chattel is a legal fixture is the manner in which the article is affixed to the real estate. If the article is so permanently attached to the land or a building on the land that it cannot be removed without causing substantial injury to the real property, it will be a fixture unless a contrary intent on the part of the annexor can be shown. At early common law, the manner of affixation was the only fixture test used, and an article simply could not be a fixture unless it was physically attached to the realty by means of bolts or screws or the like. This is no longer true, and chattels are modernly held to be fixtures though they are not physically attached to the land in any way so long as the annexor clearly intended the chattel to become a permanent part of the realty.

The third test of a legal fixture is the adaptability of the chattel to the real estate, particularly to the land's business use or other specifically intended purpose. Thus, an item installed in a building to carry out the purpose for which the building was constructed (e. g., a screen in a movie theatre) will usually be considered a fixture.

In summary, there are three tests for a legal fixture:

(1) *The annexor's objective intent.* This test is controlling, and if intent can be readily determined, there is no need to go on to tests 2 and 3, which are primarily used as indirect evidence of intent.

(2) *The manner of affixation.* If the item is so permanently connected to the land that its removal will substantially damage the real property, the item will be a fixture (unless the annexor's intent is to the contrary).

(3) *The adaptability of the chattel to the real estate.* If the article is appropriate and necessary to the usual and normal use of the real property, it will most likely be a fixture (again, unless the annexor's intent is to the contrary).

With regard to whether a chattel has become a fixture, does it make any difference who affixed the item to the real estate?

Yes. In a number of situations, it is not necessary to resort to the three fixture tests enumerated above because the relationship between the annexor and landowner will govern whether or not the chattel has become a fixture. Four important relationships to consider are: (1) tenant-landlord; (2) licensee-landowner; (3) trespasser-landowner; and (4) life estate interest holder-remainderman (the remainderman is the party entitled to possession of the property upon the death of the life estate holder or life "tenant").

(1) *Tenant-landlord.* Under the old common law, if a tenant (a renter of land, buildings, or apartments) installed chattels in a permanent manner on leased property, the chattels became fixtures belonging to the landlord. After a time, the courts developed an exception for articles termed "trade fixtures" that were installed by the tenant for the purpose of his or her trade or business. This exception for business-related chattels installed by a "commercial" tenant was developed to protect businesspeople from losing valuable tools of their trade. The exception was broadly defined to include any chattels used primarily for a trade or business, including agriculture and mining. "Trade fixtures", as that term was used at common law, were not legal fixtures because they remained personal property even when attached to the land, and were removable by the tenant upon expiration of the lease. However, the tenant was required to reimburse the landlord for any damage caused by removal of the trade fixtures; and if the trade fixtures could not be removed without causing irreparable injury to the real property, the "fixtures" could not be removed at all.

Needless to say, landlord-tenant law has come a long way since early common law in extending protection to tenants; and it is now the law that a tenant may remove any chattels he or she installs on leased premises regardless of whether the chattels are used in a trade or business. The tenant's only obligation is to repair or pay for any damage to the realty caused by removal of the chattels. As at common law, where removal would result in irreparable damage to the real property, removal cannot be made. Generally, the tenant has a right to remove his or her personal property within a reasonable time after expiration of the lease (although a few courts have ruled that removal must be before the term ends). If the tenant fails to remove the property within a reasonable time, the tenant is said to have abandoned his or her ownership rights, and the landlord becomes the new owner. Of course, the landlord is always free to reject ownership of abandoned chattels, and can force the tenant to remove the property from the premises or face liability in court for trespass.

(2) *Licensee-landowner.* A licensee is a person who has a right to go upon land only for a particular purpose. *Black's Law Dictionary* defines "licensee" in this way.

It says:

Person privileged to enter or remain on land by virtue of possessor's consent, whether given by invitation or permission. * * * Person using premises through owner's sufferance only, without any enticement, allurement, or inducement and for his own personal benefit, convenience, and pleasure. * * * Person who has mere permission to use land, dominion over it remaining in owner, and no interest in nor exclusive possession of it being given to occupant.[7]

An example of a licensee is an individual who attends a free concert at a thea-

tre, or who obtains permission to place a sign on another's property. Modernly, if a licensee attaches chattels to the land he or she has permission to use, the licensee can remove the chattels subject only to a duty to repair any damage caused. The rules for licensees are thus the same as the rules for tenants.

(3) *Trespasser-landowner.* Ordinarily, a trespasser who takes possession of another's real property and improves the land by attaching chattels will lose the chattels to the landowner regardless of the trespasser's good faith in making the annexation. However, some courts have allowed innocent trespassers who make improvements to recover from the landowner the amount by which the improvements increase the value of the land. And a few states have passed statutes authorizing innocent trespassers to remove any chattels they mistakenly attach to land (subject, of course, to a duty to pay for any damage caused by the removal).

(4) *Life estate interest holder-remainderman.* As will be explained in detail in Chapter 4, land may be divided in such a way that one person possesses a life estate in the land (a possessory interest for the period of the individual's lifetime), and another a remainder interest (complete possession and ownership of the land upon the death of the life tenant). Who owns chattels attached to the land by the life tenant prior to his or her death? The rule has long been that the life tenant does. In attaching the chattels the life tenant presumably intends to benefit only himself or herself, and not the remainderman. The life tenant may thus remove any chattels he or she affixes to the land, and after the life tenant's death, his or her heirs may do so. Of course, the chattels must be removed within a reasonable time after the life tenant's death, and any damage to the

7. Henry Campbell Black, *Black's Law Dictionary*, Revised Fourth Edition, West Publishing Co., 1968, p. 1,070.

realty must be repaired or paid for (again, where removal would cause irreparable damage to the real property, the chattels become legal fixtures).

Finally, where the life tenant goes beyond merely attaching chattels and actually builds a house, barn, garage, or other building, the courts presume an intent to permanently benefit the land, and deem the new addition an unremovable fixture.

What difference does it make whether something is classified as real property or personal property?

There are seven very practical reasons why it is important to determine whether an article is real property or personal property.

(1) *Sales and other transfers of real estate.* Because fixtures are real, not personal property, they are included in any sale or other transfer of the realty. Thus, the classification of property as either chattel or fixture is crucial to determining whether or not the sale or transfer includes the built-in appliances, the air-conditioning system, the built-in stereo set, the TV antenna, the storm windows, the rugs, the hanging lamps, etc.

(2) *Eminent domain condemnation proceedings.* The 5th Amendment of the United States Constitution states that property shall not be taken for public use without just compensation. Thus, in eminent domain or condemnation proceedings by the government, the government must reimburse the landlord for the reasonable value of his or her real property. Whether the government must pay the landlord the reasonable value of chattels affixed to the land, or whether the landlord must remove the chattels as personal property, depends upon the classification of the chattels as personal property or fixtures.

(3) *Creditors' rights.* A buyer purchasing chattels on credit may give a security interest to the seller of the chattel (call-

ed a "chattel mortgage" in the past, a security interest gives the security interest holder the right to repossess the chattel if the buyer gets behind in payments). If the chattel is later attached to realty so as to become a fixture, the rights of the security interest holder may be placed in jeopardy (assuming proper filings have not been made to protect the security interest —see ch. 27, "Secured Transactions"). If the chattel is not a fixture, the seller's security interest is paramount.

The same kind of problem may result where a mortgage is placed on the real property, making the real estate subject to sale if the mortgage debt is not repaid. Whether chattels subsequently attached to the real estate are subject to sale in the event of a mortgage default will again depend on whether or not the chattels are classified as personal property or fixtures.

(4) *Taxation.* Most states levy taxes on both real estate and personal property (although the personal property tax often applies only to business). The applicable tax rates will vary depending upon the classification of the property as either real property or personal property.

(5) *Distribution of property at death.* Frequently, a decedent (dead person) will leave a will providing for distribution of his or her real property to one beneficiary, and his or her personal property to another. The classification of the decedent's property interests as either real or personal property will thus substantially affect the survivors' interests.

(6) *Requirements for transfer of property.* While certain formalities are required to transfer real estate, including the execution and delivery of a written document called a deed (See Ch. 4), personal property may be transferred without any formality whatsoever (e. g., it is possible to sell a TV set by merely delivering it to the buyer in exchange for cash).

In addition, the rule that an oral contract or agreement to buy or sell an interest in real property will not be enforceable in court unless it is evidenced by a written memorandum containing the essential terms of the agreement does not apply to contracts to buy or sell personal property unless the value of the personal property equals or exceeds $500.00 (See Ch. 10 regarding the Statute of Frauds).

(7) *Determination of applicable law.* Real property is generally governed by the law of the location of the real estate without regard to where the real property owner resides. In contrast, personal property is controlled by the law of the owner's domicile (or residence) no matter where the personal property is located. Thus, if a person living in Oregon and owning property in Florida dies without a will, the laws of Florida will govern the distribution of any real estate located in Florida, while the laws of Oregon will govern the distribution of any personal property located there.

How is a landlord-tenant relationship created?

A landlord-tenant relationship arises only from what is termed a "lease". A "lease" is a binding agreement by a real property owner, called a landlord, to rent real property to a second party, called a tenant, coupled with a conveyance or transfer to the tenant of the right to exclusive possession of the property. A lease is thus both a contract (binding agreement) and a conveyance (transfer), and it is the only method by which the landlord-tenant relationship may be created. Other legal concepts may involve the right to *use* real property, but they are not lease agreements because they do not result in the transfer of the right to exclusive possession. For example, a person who rents a hotel or motel room is not a tenant, but is a licensee (the holder of a license). The brief period of use of the room, together with the high degree of control reserved by the hotel or motel management, indicates that a mere

privilege to use the premises was intended rather than a transfer of the right to exclusive possession. Similarly, a lodger's contract for room and board is not a lease, but a mere license to use the room. And an employee who lives on his or her employer's premises as a condition of employment is a licensee, and not a tenant.

In close cases where the intent of the parties is not clear, the courts will look at the following factors to determine whether a particular relationship is a lease or a license:

(1) What the parties themselves call the agreement;

(2) Whether the agreement calls for the payment of rent (indicates a lease);

(3) Whether the agreement gives possession for a term (a definite period) or for an unlimited time (the former suggests a lease, the latter a license);

(4) The specificity with which the real property is described (the more specific the description, the more likely a lease);

(5) The limitations, if any, on the use of the real property (excessive limitation indicates a license).

The determination of whether the relationship is a lease or license is important because a tenant possesses legal rights far superior to those of a licensee. Not only is the tenant entitled to exclusive possession of the property (as opposed to mere use), but he or she has a right to notice prior to eviction unless the lease specifies a definite ending date. The licensee, on the other hand, has no right to notice. And, whereas the tenant can justifiably use reasonable force (called "self-help") to remove trespassers from the leased premises, the licensee must look to the licensor for their removal. Finally, a lease agreement is not affected by the landlord's conveyance (transfer) of the land to a third party, but a conveyance does serve to terminate a license.

What are the requirements for a lease?

Because a lease is a contract as well as a conveyance, all the requirements of a valid contract must be present, including (1) mutual assent, (2) consideration, (3) capacity of parties, and (4) legality of subject matter (these elements are discussed in detail in Chapters 7–10, Contract Law). Under the terms of the contract, the tenant agrees to pay rent, and both landlord and tenant make other promises relating to the real estate in question. The legal interest transferred to the tenant is called a "leasehold estate" and may take any one of several tenancy forms (as discussed in the following section).

As for formalities, while many lease agreements are put into writing as a matter of course, only lease agreements for periods greater than one year (in a few states, three years) have to be written in order to be enforceable (See Ch. 10). The written lease should in every case identify the landlord as "lessor" and the tenant as "lessee"; and both parties should be of age and of sound mind.

As a general rule, the written lease must describe the real property involved (i. e., the leased premises) with certainty. While the lease does not have to specify a due date for rent (in which case the rent will be due at the end of the rental period), most written leases expressly make rent payable in advance on the first day of each month. In all cases, the lessor must sign the instrument in order to effectuate the transfer. While it is customary for the lessee to sign as well, his or her signature is not technically required: the lessee accepts the lease by taking possession of the leased premises.

In many states, the lease must also be witnessed or acknowledged (notarized), particularly where the lease is for a substantial period of time. And in a number of states, a lease for more than one year (in a few states, three years), must be recorded in the county land records in order to put third parties (who might purchase or otherwise make claim to the real property) on notice of the tenant's rights. States requiring recordation include California, Florida, Georgia, Hawaii, Idaho, Indiana, Minnesota, Mississippi, Montana, New Mexico, North Carolina, Ohio, Oklahoma, Rhode Island, Tennessee, Wisconsin, and Wyoming. In other states (and for shorter term leases in all states), the tenant's possession puts the whole world on constructive notice of the tenant's rights.

Finally, it is important to remember that no writing at all is required for a lease that can last for a period of time less than one year. The lease may be entirely verbal and it will still accomplish both a contract and a conveyance.

What kinds of leasehold estates can be created by a lease relationship?

Any one of the following four tenancies or leasehold estates can be created by a lease relationship:

(1) A tenancy for years;

(2) A tenancy from period to period;

(3) A tenancy at will; and

(4) A tenancy at sufferance.

Tenancy for years. A tenancy or estate for years is a tenancy that has a fixed or definite beginning and end at the time of creation of the tenancy. Thus, a tenancy created to last a specific number of days, weeks, months, or years is an estate for years (e. g., a tenancy for "six months"), as is a tenancy created to last a period of time computable by reference to a calendar (e. g., a tenancy "from May 1st until next Independence Day"). All that is required is that the tenancy have a specific beginning and a specific ending determined at the time the lease is entered into.

Unless the lease states otherwise, the tenancy for years begins at the earliest moment of the first day of the tenancy and terminates on the last day at midnight. *Because both parties know from the outset exactly when the tenancy will end, the tenancy terminates automatically without either party giving notice.*

How long can an estate for years last? At common law, there was no restriction placed on the length of a tenancy for years (estates for a 100 or even a 1,000 years were not unheard of). Modernly, many states do restrict the duration of estates for years, as does California, where leaseholds on farm property may last no longer than 51 years, and on urban property no longer than 99 years.

Tenancy from period to period. A tenancy from period to period is an estate that continues from year to year, or from month to month, or for other successive fractions of a year until terminated by proper notice from either party. The beginning date of the tenancy as well as the period of the estate (i. e., yearly, monthly, weekly) are always certain—it is only the ending date that is unknown. Although the tenancy continues from one period to the next, the terms and conditions of the tenancy remain the same for each period unless a new agreement is entered into.

Proper notice must always be given to terminate a periodic tenancy. Under the common law, this was notice given one "period" in advance for a month to month or week to week tenancy (i. e., one month's notice, or one week's notice), and six months in advance for a tenancy from year to year. In every case, the notice had to fix the end of the period as the date for termination.

Modern statutes generally do away with the latter requirement, at least in the case of the month to month tenancy. There, written notice given 30 days in advance of the desired termination date is usually sufficient to terminate the tenancy; and the 30 day notice period can begin and end at any time. For a year to year tenancy, while some statutes again require only a 30 day notice given at anytime, other statutes insist upon a 60 day written notice prior to the end of the term.

The death of either the landlord or tenant will not affect a tenancy for years or tenancy from period to period. The rights of the parties will continue on in their respective heirs or beneficiaries.

Tenancy at will. A tenancy at will is an estate that is terminable at the will of either landlord or tenant. Although such a tenancy holds little potential for longevity, it does give the tenant exclusive possession of the property for the duration of the tenancy as well as the right to maintain an action of trespass against any person who wrongfully comes onto the property.

To be "terminable at will" means that the tenancy will come to an end when either party, landlord or tenant, indicates his or her intention that the estate cease to exist. The landlord normally manifests such intent by giving notice to the tenant; the tenant usually implies such intent by simply abandoning the property. Statutes in most states now require landlords, but not tenants, to give a 30 day written notice to terminate an estate at will. Even where the landlord sells the property, or where he or she dies leaving the property to another in a will or allowing it to pass according to the state laws of intestacy (laws controlling the distribution of property when there is no will), the notice must still be given or the tenancy will not come to an end.

The tenant, on the other hand, need give no formal notice to terminate the tenancy. And if the tenant dies or attempts to transfer his or her interest to another, the tenancy will automatically end. This is because the estate at will is considered a personal relationship between landlord and tenant—the tenant does not have a right to substitute another in his or her place.

Tenancy at sufferance. A tenancy at sufferance is the "estate" that results when a tenant in lawful possession of property under one of the other three leasehold estates remains in possession of the leased real property after expiration of the term of the lease without the consent of the landlord. At the time the tenancy is created, the landlord has the option either to treat the holdover tenant as a trespasser or to continue treating him or her as a tenant. If the landlord chooses the first alternative, he or she may use reasonable force to re-enter the premises and evict the holdover tenant (a landlord never has to give notice to a tenant at sufferance). Or the landlord may institute legal eviction proceedings in court. In any event, the trespassing tenant will be liable to the landlord in money damages, generally in an amount measured by the reasonable rental value of the premises during the period of unauthorized occupancy.

Of course, the landlord may choose to treat the holdover tenant, not as a trespasser, but as a tenant from period to period (if the landlord takes no steps to evict the holdover tenant within a reasonable period of time, the courts will imply that the landlord has so elected). The "period" of the new tenancy will depend in large part on the period of the old. Thus, if the tenant originally had a lease for at least a year—whether as an estate for years or as an estate from year to year —the landlord can hold the tenant for another year's period (although, even here, if the rent was paid on a monthly basis, most jurisdictions would only hold the tenant to an additional month to month tenancy). Some recent holdings indicate that a landlord cannot bind a holdover tenant to a full new term if the tenant's reason for not vacating the premises was legally excusable (e. g., illness).

Can a landlord legally refuse to rent to someone?

The federal Fair Housing Act of 1968 prohibits a landlord from refusing to sell or rent to an individual on the basis of race, color, religion, or national origin. Most states also have statutes prohibiting discrimination on these grounds in the rental or sale of real property, and many states additionally outlaw discrimination on grounds of sex, age, handicap, or having children.

Along the same line, the Civil Rights Act of 1866 states: "All citizens of the United States shall have the same right, in every state and Territory, as is enjoyed by the white citizens thereof to inherit, purchase, lease, sell, hold, and convey real and personal property." In the 1968 case of Jones v. Mayer Co., 392 U. S. 409, 88 S.Ct. 2186, 20 L.Ed.2d 1189, the U.S. Supreme Court held that this Act of Congress bars all racial discrimination, private as well as public, in the sale or rental of property. An individual who has been discriminated against may complain to the Department of Housing and Urban Development which will investigate the complaint and try to eliminate the complained of conduct. The injured party may also go to federal court and obtain an injunction (a court order) requiring the other party to stop discriminating. Or the injured party may simply petition the court for money damages from the wrongdoer in an amount to cover the actual loss suffered plus up to $1,000 in "punitive" damages ("punitive" damages are "penalty" damages that vary in amount according to the outrageousness of the wrongdoer's conduct). If the injured party cannot afford to hire an attorney, the court will appoint a lawyer to assist the party with his or her discrimination case.

What are the rights and duties of landlords and tenants?

The lease relationship creates certain rights and duties in both the landlord and tenant. A landlord, to begin with, has a duty to transfer possession to the tenant at the beginning of the tenancy. The landlord's duty is to deliver actual possession of the property, and if the previous tenant has not vacated the premises when the new tenant's lease begins, the new tenant can rescind (i. e., terminate) the lease or recover money damages.

The landlord also has a duty to provide the tenant with quiet, uninterrupted possession and enjoyment of the real property during the period of the lease agreement. This is called the landlord's "covenant" or promise of quiet enjoyment. If during the term of the lease, the landlord wrongfully evicts the tenant (or allows another to do so) from all or any portion of the real estate, the tenant is completely excused from paying rent until possession of the property is restored. Where, on the other hand, the tenant is evicted from only a part of the leased premises, not by the landlord, but by a third party who holds an interest in the land superior to the tenant's interest (e. g., a mortgage holder, called a "mortgagee", of the property who recorded his or her interest in the land in the county land records office before the tenant's leasehold agreement came into being), the tenant will not be completely excused from paying rent, but will be responsible for rent on whatever portion of the property remains in his or her possession. A third party's interest is not superior, however, where it is subsequent in time to creation of the leasehold, or prior in time but unrecorded (the tenant, in this case, would have no reason to know of the interest). Thus, where a mortgagee whose interest in the land is "inferior" to the tenant's is forced to foreclose (i. e., take over ownership of the property because the owner has failed to make his or her mortgage payments), the mortgagee simply becomes the new landlord with the same rights and duties as the old owner.

And it is not always necessary for the landlord to come onto the property and physically oust the tenant from the leased premises before the landlord will be liable for a wrongful eviction. If the landlord so seriously interferes with the tenant's use and enjoyment of the real estate that the tenant is forced to leave the property, the landlord is said to have made a "constructive eviction", which, like a regular eviction, relieves the tenant of any further obligation to pay rent. In any event, it must be "reasonable" for the tenant to leave the premises in view of the landlord's conduct; and the tenant can never claim constructive eviction unless he or she actually leaves the premises. The tenant cannot remain in possession and simply refuse to pay rent. Examples of constructive eviction by the landlord include turning off heat, electricity, or water; making excessive noise; permitting the building to become infested with rats; and failing to provide air conditioning in windowless buildings.

In addition to the landlord's covenant of quiet enjoyment is the landlord's "implied" covenant of habitability of the premises. Landlord-tenant law implies a promise on the part of the landlord that the premises are, at least initially, in a habitable (i. e., liveable) condition. The law recognizes that the tenant typically has little or no opportunity to inspect the premises and determine whether there are any defects in plumbing, heating, etc. before he or she takes possession of the property. "Habitability" is generally defined as meaning compliance with the local housing code. A housing code is a city, county, or state statute that establishes certain minimum standards to be met by dwellings intended for human occupancy, including specifics as to space requirements and essential facilities, e. g., bathroom, kitchen, utilities. (In 1954, a federal urban renewal law was passed providing for disbursement of federal urban renewal funds to local governmental units possessed of a local housing code. Because of this, local housing codes have been adopted nearly everywhere.) A landlord who fails to provide premises that comply with the local housing code has breached the implied covenant of habitability. The tenant, in this case, can either vacate the premises and recover any prepaid rent or remain in possession and recover money damages for the breach.

Assuming the landlord does provide the tenant with initially habitable premises, who is responsible for maintaining the premises in good condition? At common law, the landlord had no continuing duty to repair the premises, and if the leasehold property became untenantable in time, it was up to the tenant to remedy the situation. Certainly, it was not unfair to hold the tenant responsible for causing damage (termed "waste") to the property in excess of the ordinary wear and tear to be expected from everyday living. But it soon became apparent that structural and other repair work necessitated, for the most part, by the mere passage of time, was best left to the landlord —the owner of the property and the person in the best financial position to make the repair. Accordingly, while modern landlord-tenant law still holds the tenant accountable for "affirmative" and "permissive" waste of the property ("affirmative" waste is a voluntary act on the part of the tenant that damages the premises or substantially changes the premises, such as breaking down a door; while "permissive" waste is a negligent failure to act on the part of the tenant which results in damage or decay to the property, such as carelessly leaving a window open during a rainstorm, thereby ruining the wallpaper of the leased premises), the

law has broken with common law tradition to impose an affirmative duty of repair upon the landlord, generally extending the landlord's covenant of habitability throughout the period of the lease. Thus, it is up to the landlord to maintain the premises in a "tenantable" condition that complies with the local housing code. Several states have additionally defined by statute "essential services" that the landlord must provide, including proper facilities for lighting, heating, water, etc.

Assuming the landlord fails to maintain the premises, can the tenant withhold payment of rent? Under the common law, the answer is no. At common law, the rights and duties of the landlord and tenant are said to be "independent" of each other: if the landlord or the tenant breaches a covenant (promise), the other party may not, in turn, breach a covenant, but can only seek relief in court.[8] However, to some extent, the rule of independent covenants has been changed by modern landlord-tenant statutes. For example, in many states, if the landlord fails to make needed repairs, the tenant has a legal right to withhold payment of the rent, placing it into a fund unavailable to the landlord until the repairs are made; use all or part of the rent to make the repairs, paying to the landlord only what is left; or petition the court to place the building in "receivership" and appoint a "receiver" to collect the rent and make the necessary repairs. To give force to these tenant's remedies, recent statutes and court holdings in many states prohibit a landlord from retaliating against a tenant who uses the remedies by giving the tenant notice of eviction. Prohibitions against retaliatory eviction are particularly important to the month to month tenant who, in the normal case, may be given 30 days written notice at anytime for any reason.

8. An exception arises in the case of a breach of the covenant of quiet enjoyment (wrongful eviction).

Despite the landlord's responsibility for maintaining the leased premises in a habitable condition, the landlord is generally not liable for injury that occurs on the property to the tenant or the tenant's guests. One exception to this rule arises where the injury occurs as a result of a concealed dangerous condition (e. g., a rotting floor) that the landlord knew about at the beginning of the tenancy and failed to disclose to the tenant. Of course, if the tenant knew about the condition and accepted the premises anyway, the landlord would not be responsible for injury resulting from the condition unless the tenant was in such a bad bargaining position as to make the leasehold agreement "unconscionable." (Simply put, an "unconscionable" contract is one containing provisions that are extremely unfair to one of the parties to the contract who had very little bargaining power in entering into the agreement, e. g., an individual with little money and no home who agrees to anything in order to obtain a month to month tenancy—unconscionable contracts are dealt with in detail in Ch. 8.)

A second exception to the "no liability" rule comes into play where the landlord leases premises to a tenant who informs the landlord of his or her intention to use the premises for a public purpose, such as a business, and a member of the general public is injured on the leased premises as the result of a defective condition that the landlord warned the tenant about at the time of creation of the leasehold agreement. If the landlord knew or had reason to know that the tenant was unlikely to remedy or repair the defect prior to opening up the property to the public, the landlord will be liable to the injured party.

A landlord is also liable for injury to a tenant or tenant's guest resulting from the defective condition of "common areas" adjacent to the leased premises that remain under the landlord's control (e. g., elevators, stairways, or hallways in an apartment building).

A very few courts (and it does not appear to be the trend) have altogether rejected that "no liability" rule and hold that the landlord's implied warranty of habitability establishes a tort duty on the part of the landlord not only to deliver the real property in a safe condition, but to maintain it that way throughout the period of the lease agreement. Under this interpretation, any tenant or guest injured on the property as the result of a defective condition could rightfully sue the landlord for money damages.

Let us move now from landlord obligations and duties to the tenant's duty to pay rent. Every tenant shares this duty even where no express promise to pay rent can be found (in which case, the duty is to pay a "reasonable rental value"). Occasionally, premises rented for commercial or business use by the tenant will utilize what is termed a "percentage lease" in which the tenant pays not only a minimum monthly rent, but, also at the end of the business year, a percentage of the tenant's gross receipts. Because the rent (which varies) is necessarily dependent on the success of the tenant's business, it is generally said that the tenant has a duty to use reasonable diligence to produce as many receipts as possible.

What are the landlord's rights if the tenant fails to pay his or her rent? At common law, the landlord had an unlimited right called the right of "distress" to enter the leased property and seize the tenant's chattels, holding them until the rent was paid (and, if necessary, selling them to collect the unpaid rent). Modernly, the right of "distress" has been strictly limited by statute in most states, and some states have altogether abolished it. States that still permit "distress" generally require prior notice to the tenant coupled with an opportunity to protest the action in advance in a hearing before a judge. Generally, the seizure will be denied unless the court determines that the tenant is likely to remove or destroy the property. And, even where "distress" is ordered by the court, that portion of the tenant's property necessary for day-to-day living will usually be exempt from seizure.

States that have abolished distress generally permit the landlord to remove the tenant's property from the leased premises only where the tenancy agreement has come to an end and it is necessary to clear out the dwelling unit in order to rent to a new tenant. The landlord, in this case, has a duty to store any chattels he or she removes from the premises and to give the tenant ample time and opportunity to claim them. If the tenant fails to claim the property in a reasonable time, and the goods must ultimately be sold, the landlord is entitled to reasonable storage costs only—he or she cannot apply the proceeds of the sale against the tenant's unpaid rent. And any surplus proceeds after deduction for storage must be returned to the tenant. The landlord's sole remedy with regard to the unpaid rent is to sue the tenant in court for breach of the rental agreement.

The right of "distress" aside, can the landlord legally use force to retake possession of the leased premises from a tenant who is behind in his or her rent? In a majority of states, the answer is no, and a tenant ousted by force may generally sue to recover money damages and/or possession of the premises. Nearly every state, however, has enacted a summary (brief and informal) statutory procedure by which a landlord can legally evict a tenant in default on his or her rent. Called an *"unlawful detainer proceeding"*, this statutory procedure requires the landlord to give notice to the tenant that he or she must pay all rent due within a short period of time (typically 3–10 days) or else the tenant must vacate the premises. If the tenant fails to pay the rent within the specified time and refuses

to move, the landlord files suit in court asking for an order directing the tenant to give up possession of the property. The tenant then has up to five days time in which to file an "answer" to the landlord, raising any applicable defenses to payment (such as use of the rent to make needed repairs, withholding the rent until repairs are made, or retaliatory eviction by the landlord). If the tenant fails to file an answer, he or she will lose the case by default. And, even if the tenant does file an answer, any defenses raised must be proved in the courtroom hearing, or the tenant will lose there as well. Where the tenant loses by either default or decision, the landlord will receive a "writ of possession" from the court ordering the sheriff to direct the tenant to move, and, if the tenant fails to move, to physically oust him or her from the property.

What are the landlord's rights in the event the tenant leaves the leased premises prior to the end of the term?

Sometimes, a tenant finds it necessary to leave the leased premises prior to the end of the term (e. g., where the tenant finds employment in another city or has to move for personal or family reasons). A *surrender* occurs where the tenant voluntarily gives up possession of the premises, and the landlord accepts possession with *intent* that the lease be terminated. The tenant, in this case, is excused from any further obligation under the lease agreement.

However, many times, the landlord refuses to accept possession and terminate the agreement, and the tenant simply *abandons* the premises. Generally speaking, the landlord has two options in this situation. First, he or she may let the premises sit idle and sue the tenant for the rent as it falls due (the majority rule is that the landlord is not obligated to re-let the premises). *Or* the landlord may retake possession of the premises, relet them, and hold the original tenant for the difference between the old rental and the new rental. Under the majority rule, the landlord's retaking of possession does not effect a surrender so long as the landlord notifies the tenant of his or her intention to relet the premises and to hold the tenant responsible for any deficit in rent. A minority of jurisdictions give the landlord a third option and allow him or her to sue at once for all rent due under the entire period of the lease (set off by the reasonable rental value of the premises for that period).

These common law remedies have been codified by statute in a number of states.

What are the newest trends in land-lord-tenant law?

The Uniform Residential Landlord-Tenant Act (URLTA), a modern statutory breakthrough for tenants, has been adopted with but minor variation in some thirteen states (including Alaska, Arizona, Delaware, Florida, Hawaii, Kansas, Kentucky, Nebraska, New Mexico, Ohio, Oregon, Virginia, and Washington), and several other state legislatures are likely to pass the Act in the near future. The URLTA includes the following important provisions:

(1) An express warranty of habitability requiring the landlord to "comply with the requirements of applicable housing codes materially affecting health and safety." This means that the landlord must maintain the premises in a safe and habitable condition and provide essential services, including water, heat, electricity, etc.

(2) A provision permitting the tenant to make minor repairs and deduct their cost from the next rental payment (generally up to $100 or $\frac{1}{2}$ the monthly rent payment, whichever is greater). There is some variation from state to state with respect to the kinds of repairs that can be made, with some states limiting repairs to

utilities and essential services. Another common limitation is that repairs can be made only once every 12 month period.

(3) A provision prohibiting the landlord from taking retaliatory action against a tenant who attempts to organize other tenants, joins a tenants' union, or reports a housing code violation by the landlord. Retaliatory intent is presumed where landlord action (including raising rent, decreasing services, or evicting the tenant) follows the tenant activity within a certain period of time (usually six months). Up to that time, the burden is on the landlord to disprove retaliatory motives; after that time, the legal burden shifts and it is up to the tenant to prove retaliatory intent.

(4) A provision abolishing the landlord's "distress" (seizing the tenant's personal property) and "distraint" (locking the tenant behind in rent out of the real property). Where the landlord acts in disregard of the statute to seize the tenant's property or to lock the tenant out of the premises, the tenant may generally recover money damages in an amount three times his or her monthly rent, or treble damages (i. e., three times the actual loss suffered) plus attorneys' fees. (But, remember, the landlord does have a legal right to "store" the goods of a tenant who has abandoned the leasehold premises.)

(5) A provision limiting security deposits collected by the landlord to an amount no greater than one month's rent. Any deductions from the deposit must be fairly made and itemized in writing; all unclaimed amounts must be returned to the tenant within 14 days of termination of the tenancy. If the landlord fails to comply with the URLTA provisions, the tenant may recover twice the amount of his or her rent in money damages.

(6) A provision prohibiting the landlord from turning off the utility services of a tenant in default on rent payments.

In addition to the URLTA, there are certain other provisions appearing in some state landlord-tenant statutes that change the traditional common law lease relationship mostly for the benefit of the tenant who is considered to be in an inferior bargaining position. For example, as mentioned earlier in the chapter, several states have authorized the appointment of a receiver to collect tenant rents from buildings that have become badly dilapidated. The receiver uses the rents to make needed repairs, then returns the building, along with any remaining rent, to the landlord. States having enacted receivership laws include Connecticut, Delaware, Illinois, Indiana, Massachusetts, Michigan, Minnesota, Missouri, New Jersey, New York, Ohio, Rhode Island, and Wisconsin. The only problem these states have encountered is that the amount of rent collected is often inadequate to accomplish the needed repairs.

Other jurisdictions permit a tenant to sue in court for what is called "retroactive rent abatement" and recover rent paid to a landlord who has failed to maintain the premises in a habitable condition. The theory behind the action is that the rent could have been withheld originally, but was not withheld because of the tenant's oversight or ignorance of the law. This course of action has been effective in encouraging landlords to maintain their real property in good condition and prevent the property from deteriorating.

Still other jurisdictions permit the tenant to obtain an injunction (court order) requiring the landlord to specifically perform his or her duties of "habitability" (i. e., forcing the landlord to actually make the needed repairs).

A new law that has been adopted in a very few states requires a landlord to make a security deposit (landlords have long required tenants to make such deposits) out of which emergency repair funds can be taken if the landlord fails to maintain the premises in a habitable condition. The typical law requires the landlord to deposit with a government agency a specific sum of money per rental unit to ensure compliance by the landlord with his or her rental obligations. The funds can be used only in emergency situations that pose a threat to the tenant's health or safety, and the tenant must give the landlord adequate notice and opportunity to make the repairs before dipping into the security deposit fund.

Another new and more informal procedure is a joint effort by the tenant and mortgagee of the leased property to pressure the landlord-owner into making needed repairs. This procedure will work only where the mortgagee is interested in getting the building into better condition, not in foreclosing the mortgage (in many cases, the mortgagee does not want to foreclose and end up owning a building that may be unmarketable because of existing leasehold interests). Joint negotiation with the landlord-owner may result in the mortgagee's temporary suspension of mortgage payments on condition that the landlord use the mortgage payment money to restore the leasehold premises to a good and "habitable" condition.

In an effort to take the burden off the tenant, local housing authorities in some states have established a "certificate of habitability" program under which landowners desirous of leasing their property must submit to advance inspection for habitability and periodic inspection thereafter for continued maintenance of the property. Only landowners with current certificates of habitability can legally lease their property.

And, finally, special landlord-tenant courts have been created in some states to deal exclusively with disputes arising out of landlord-tenant relationships. The result is a quick resolution of controversies as well as a substantial reduction in cost to the parties.

CASES

CASE 1—*Did the "Fathers" own the coolers?*

PREMONSTRATENSIAN FATHERS v. BADGER MUTUAL INS. CO.

Supreme Court of Wisconsin, 1970.
46 Wis.2d 362, 175 N.W.2d 237.

This is an action to recover upon a fire insurance policy, the coverage clause of which provides:

"When the insurance under this policy covers a building, such insurance shall cover on the building, * * * all permanent fixtures. * * *"

The Premonstratensian Fathers, called Fathers, are the owners of a one-story building, insured by the property insurance policy in question, which is used as a supermarket. The building was originally constructed in 1958 by the Jacobs Realty Corporation. * * * Following the construction of the supermarket, the business has been continually run as a retail grocery business, offering a wide variety of canned goods, frozen goods, produce and meats.

* * * On March 7, 1960, Jacobs * * * deeded * * * the land and the improvements to the Fathers. On March 7, 1960, the Fathers leased the premises back to the Jacobs Brothers Stores, Inc. for a term of twenty years. The lease further provided that the lessee was to provide fire insurance on the building and the fixtures in the name of the lessor. Following this lease, the premises were operated in exactly the same manner as it had been since the initial construction. The lessee then provided the insurance which is the subject of the instant lawsuit.

On June 1, 1964, the building and improvements were severely damaged by a major fire. Following the fire, the building was replaced with a new building, and the interior of the building is substantially the same as that prior to the fire and is still run as a supermarket. The defendant-insurers paid to the plaintiff the sum of $83,000 for the loss suffered to the building, but have refused to pay a claim in the amount of $23,551.02 for the destruction of five Hussman walk-in coolers which were situated in the building. The grounds upon which the insurers have refused to pay the claim of the Fathers, and upon which they relied in both the trial court and in this court are: (1) The coolers are not the property of the Fathers, and (2) even if the coolers are the property of the Fathers, they are not insured property. There is no issue as to the amount of the damages, or whether the policy was in full force and effect on the date of the fire. The trial court concluded that the coolers are insured property and granted judgment for the plaintiff.

The coolers which are the subject of this dispute are walk-in type coolers. There are five of these: two meat coolers, a deep-freeze, a produce cooler, and a dairy cooler. A further description of the coolers is set forth in the opinion.

Connor T. HANSEN, Justice.

Although the insurers have divided their argument into two sections, the basis of the entire appeal is a consideration of the legal status of the coolers. If the coolers are determined to be common-law fixtures, and were such at the time of the construction of the building and the installation of the coolers, then they would have passed to the Fathers under the warranty deed of March 7, 1960, and they would be insured under the terms of the policy. The issue then is whether these coolers constitute fixtures.

The rule which has developed in Wisconsin as to what constitutes a fixture is not really a comprehensive definition, but rather a statement of the factors which are to be applied to the fact and circumstances of a particular case to determine whether or not the property in question does constitute a fixture:

> " * * * Whether articles of personal property are fixtures, i. e., real estate, is determined in this state, if not generally, by the following rules or tests: (1) Actual physical annexation to the real estate; (2) application or adaptation to the use or purpose to which the realty is devoted; and (3) an intention on the part of the person making the annexation to make a permanent accession to the freehold."

It is the application of these tests to the facts of a particular case which will lead to a determination of whether or not an article, otherwise considered personal property, constitutes a common-law fixture, and hence takes on the nature of real property. * * *

ANNEXATION.

Annexation refers to:

> " * * * the act of attaching or affixing personal property to real property and, as a general proposition, an object will not acquire the status of a fixture unless it is in some manner or means, albeit slight, attached or affixed, either actually or constructively, to the realty."

It has been held in Wisconsin that physical annexation, although a factor to be considered in the determination, is of relative unimportance:

> " * * * it has often been said by this court that the matter of physical annexation of the article * * * is relatively unimportant. * * *."

The trial court ably pointed out the physical facts which led to its conclusion that there is indeed annexation in this case. The more important of these are as follows: (1) The exterior walls of the cooler, in four instances, constituted the interior wall of another room. (2) In the two meat coolers, a meat hanging and tracking system was built into the coolers. These tracks were used to move large cuts of meats from the cooler area into the meat preparation areas, and were suspended from the steel girders of the building structure by means of large steel bolts. These bolts penetrated through the roof of the cooler supporting wooden beams, which, in turn, supported the tracking system. The tracking in the coolers was a part of a system of tracking throughout the rear portion of the supermarket. (3) The coolers were attached to hardwood plank which was, in turn, attached to the concrete floor of the supermarket. The attachment of the plank to the floor was accomplished through the use of a ramsetting gun. The planks were laid on the floor, and the bolts were driven through them into the concrete floor, where they then exploded, firmly fixing the coolers into place. * * *

These factors adequately support the conclusion that the coolers were indeed physically annexed to the premises. * * *

ADAPTATION.

Adaptation refers to the relationship between the chattel and the use which is made of the realty to which the chattel is annexed. The use of the realty was that of a retail grocery, commonly known as a supermarket. This was the intent of the parties at the time of the construction of the building, and the intent of the parties throughout the entire history of the business. The fact of operation has borne out this intent. In a business which carries fresh foods, frozen foods, produce, meats and butter, coolers used for storage and handling of these perishables are patently related to the use of the building. In fact, it would be hard to picture any equipment more closely related to the operation of a supermarket, where large quantities of perishables must, of necessity, be purchased for storage and processing.
* * *

INTENT.

This court has repeatedly held that intent is the primary determinant of whether a certain piece of property has become a fixture. The relevant intent is that of the party making the annexation. * * *

In its decision, the trial court found, as a reasonable and legitimate inference from all the facts and circumstances surrounding the placement of the coolers onto the realty, that there was an intention that the coolers became a permanent accession to the realty; that when Jacobs Realty Corporation conveyed the land together with all buildings and improvements thereon * * *, the intention still prevailed that the coolers were a permanent accession to the realty * * *.

* * * As this court has stated:

"* * * Although it is true that, in applying that doctrine, the question of whether such machines constitute fixtures is largely one of intent, that intent may be considered established conclusively by the fact that the machines in question were clearly adapted to, *and were in fact put by the owner of the realty and the machines to, the use to which he devoted the realty and the installed machines as an entirety.* * * *" (Emphasis added.) * * * Judgment affirmed.

CASE 2—*"Operation Equality"*—*"all citizens have the same right to inherit, purchase, lease, sell, hold and convey real and personal property."*

BUSH v. KAIM

United States District Court, N.D.Ohio, E.D.1969.

297 F.Supp. 151.

LAMBROS, District Judge:

This is a civil action arising under the Civil Rights Act of 1866, Title 42, U.S.C.A. § 1982. * * *

The plaintiffs, Reginald Bush, Jr., and Rita Mae Bush, are husband and wife; they are negroes; they have a four-month old daughter, Adrienne Bush.

Mr. Bush has recently been employed by the Mead-Johnson Laboratories as a medical sales representative. In connection with this employment, he was required to relocate in or near Cleveland, Ohio.

In order to secure suitable housing for himself and his family, he came to Cleveland on or about October 21, 1968. * * *

* * * In the Cleveland Plain Dealer edition of Saturday, November 9, 1968, Mr. Bush noticed the following advertisement: "Eastlake ranch, 2-bedrm, carpeted living rm, attached garage; spotless, $150. Reference 261–2820."

* * *

The defendants, Frank A. Kaim and Carolyn Kaim, are the owners of the property which was advertised as indicated above in the Cleveland Plain Dealer. This property is a single-family house located at 813 Stevens Blvd. in Eastlake, Ohio. This is the only rental property owned by these defendants. Mr. Kaim is a real estate agent and is experienced in the rental and sale of real property.

Mr. Bush called the number indicated in the advertisement at about 6:00 p. m. on the evening of Saturday, November 9th. He spoke with Carolyn Kaim. He asked to come out and view the property. Arrangements were made for him to come out that evening. Mrs. Kaim gave him directions to reach the property.

Bush arrived at about 8:30 that evening. Mr. Kaim met him at the door and showed him through the house. During the course of this tour and after they had been through a few rooms, Mr. Kaim told Bush that he had been showing the house to a number of other people and had received part of a rental deposit from a man to whom he had shown the house that day. Kaim also stated that he had not yet had time to tell his wife about this deposit, but that he was fairly certain the people who gave him the deposit would rent the house. Bush asked Kaim to call him the next day and let him know if the house had been taken. Although Mr. Kaim agreed to call the plaintiff, he never did so.

During the course of the meeting between Kaim and Bush, Kaim asked Mr. Bush whom he worked for, and Bush told him. Mr. Kaim did not ask the size of Mr. Bush's family; he did not ask him his age; he did not ask for credit references; and he did not request Mr. Bush to fill out a rental application.

Mr. Bush became suspicious as a result of his meeting with Mr. Kaim. He called a Mrs. Talbot, who works for Operation Equality and told her what had occurred. He asked her to verify whether the house was in fact rented. She referred him to Mrs. Catherine Worley, a part-time employee of Operation Equality. Arrangements were made whereby Bush and Mrs. Worley would go out to the house on Monday to see if Bush could rent it. If they were unsuccessful, another Operation Equality volunteer would then appear at the house and attempt to rent it.

* * *

Mrs. Worley called Mrs. Joan M. Maguire, another Operation Equality volunteer. * * *

She had previously, in a phone conversation, instructed Mrs. Maguire to make an appointment to rent the house the following day. Mrs. Worley, Mrs. Maguire, and Mrs. Maguire's husband are white.

On Monday morning, Mrs. Worley called Mrs. Kaim sometime between 11:00 and 12:00 a. m. Mrs. Worley asked if the house was still available for rent. Mrs. Kaim said it was. She made an appointment to come out and view the house.

Mrs. Maguire also called up and asked if the house was for rent. The woman who answered the phone stated that it was. She then made an appointment to come out and view the house.

Mrs. Worley and Mr. Bush drove out to the house on Monday afternoon. They arrived at about 1:30. Mrs. Roland, who was at that time a tenant in the house, opened the door and allowed them to enter. Soon after, Mrs. Kaim arrived.

* * *

Mr. Bush introduced himself and Mrs. Worley. He stated that he had come to rent the house. * * *

* * * Mrs. Kaim declined to rent the property to Mr. Bush at that time. Mrs. Worley and Mr. Bush, unsuccessful in their attempt to rent the house, then left. They drove to the corner of the block, parked the car, and waited.

A few minutes later, Mrs. Maguire drove around the corner and proceeded to the Kaim house. She waved to Mrs. Worley and Mr. Bush as she drove by.

Mrs. Maguire was in the house for ten to fifteen minutes. Mrs. Kaim showed Mrs. Maguire around the house. * * *

* * *

Mrs. Maguire asked if the house had been rented, and Mrs. Kaim replied that it had not. Mrs. Kaim asked Mrs. Maguire if she wanted to rent the house. Mrs. Maguire said yes. Mrs. Maguire asked Mrs. Kaim if she would accept $50.00 as deposit, and Mrs. Kaim said yes. Mrs. Maguire gave Mrs. Kaim her personal check for $50.00 which Mrs. Kaim accepted.

* * *

The Court has studied the significant portions of the testimony of all the witnesses. The Court has concluded that the Kaims declined to rent to Mr. Bush solely for the reason that he was a negro and for no other reason.

* * *

* * *

This action arises under the provisions of Title 42 U.S.C.A. § 1982, the so-called Civil Rights Act of 1866.

That Act provides:

"All citizens of the United States shall have the same right, in every State and Territory, as is enjoyed by white citizens thereof to inherit, purchase, lease, sell, hold, and convey real and personal property."

Plaintiffs' allege that they have been denied the "same right" to lease property guaranteed them by Section 1982 solely on the basis of their race.

* * *

The landmark case interpreting Section 1982 is Jones v. Alfred H. Mayer Co., 392 U.S. 409, 88 S.Ct. 2186, 20 L.Ed.2d 1189 (1968). * * *

The precise issue before the Supreme Court in Jones v. Mayer was whether Section 1982 barred *all* racial discrimination, or merely discrimination which was the product of state action. The Court stated: "We hold that Section 1982 bars *all* racial discrimination, private as well as public, in the sale or rental of property, and that the statute, thus construed, is a valid exercise of the power of Congress to enforce the Thirteenth Amendment."

The issue of whether Section 1982 bars private discriminations in the sale or rental of houses can no longer be debated. This issue is conclusively settled by Jones v. Mayer.

* * *

The Court also set forth the standard to be utilized in determining whether an individual had been deprived of rights guaranteed him under Section 1982: "So long as a Negro citizen who wants to buy or rent a home can be turned away simply because he is not white, he cannot be said to enjoy 'the *same* right * * * as is enjoyed by white citizens * * * to * * * purchase [and] lease * * * real and personal property.' 42 U.S.C., § 1982." (Emphasis is Court's.) As the Court went on to state, Section 1982 "must encompass every racially motivated refusal to sell or rent." * * *

* * *

In sustaining his burden for proving that there has been a prohibited discrimination under the Act, the plaintiff must show each of the following elements: (1) that the owner (or responsible party) placed the property on the open market for sale or rental, (2) that the plaintiff was willing to rent or purchase the property on the terms specified by the owner, (3) the plaintiff communicated this willingness to the owner at a time when the property was available for sale or rent, (4) that the owner refused to rent or sell the property to the plaintiff on the terms which the owner indicated would otherwise be satisfactory, and (5) that there is no apparent reason for the refusal of the defendant to rent the property to the plaintiff other than the plaintiff's race.

The defendant may then come forward and rebut the evidence establishing any of these elements, or he may show that there were reasons other than the plaintiff's race underlying his refusal to rent to the plaintiff.

Section 1982 does not prohibit an owner from considering factors *other than* race in determining whether to sell or rent his property to a negro, or to any other person for that matter. An owner can refuse to rent or sell to anyone, negro or white, for any reason he chooses so long as the motivating reason for this decision is not the individuals race or color."

The statute guarantees to negroes only the "same right" as is enjoyed by white citizens. It does not purport to grant to negroes rights which exceed those of white or other citizens. It provides merely that an owner may not refuse to rent to a negro solely on the basis of his race. Thus, an owner may refuse to rent to a negro for any reason he would refuse to rent to a white man. The statute merely prohibits him from refusing the negro solely because he is a negro.

* * * Such factors, which an owner might consider, include the credit standing of the applicant, his assets, his financial stability, his reputation in the community, his age, the size of his family, the ages of his children, his past experience as a lessee or tenant, the length of time he plans to occupy the premises, and whether he is or is not a transient.

* * *

* * * The Court may consider a number of things in determining whether the owner actually utilized relevant non-racial elements in deciding whether to rent to the plaintiff as opposed to another individual: (1) Did the owner request information relevant to these subjects from the plaintiff, (2) did the owner request such information from other applicants, (3) did he secure such information from other sources, (4) did he request this information from the plaintiff and/or from the other applicants during the period in which he was selecting a tenant, (5) did the owner make any attempt to follow up on this information or to check its accuracy, (6) did he perform this follow-up or checking process during the time in which he was deciding to whom to rent, (7) were there other applicants with better or more desirable ratings in these areas than the plaintiff.

The above are some of the elements which the Court may consider in determining whether the defendant's decision not to rent to the plaintiff was racially motivated or not. There may, of course, be other factors, and the above is not an exclusive list.

In the present case, certain differences other than race did exist between the Bushes and the Maguires. Nevertheless, although these differences did exist, the evidence establishes that the defendants did not consider them in refusing the plaintiffs. Rather, they based their decision not to rent to the plaintiffs solely upon considerations of race.

* * *

The Court seeks to restore to the plaintiffs that of which they have been deprived. The defendants held their property out for rental under certain terms and conditions. * * * The defendants, in refusing to rent to the plaintiffs, have deprived them of the right to enter into a lease for these premises under these terms and conditions. It was a rental of the property under these terms that the Kaims held forth to the white applicants; and it is a rental of the property under these terms that they have deprived the plaintiffs.

I

* * *

It is ordered that the defendants permit the plaintiffs to occupy the above-mentioned premises. * * *

PROBLEMS

1. Patti Schroeder signs a written lease, agreeing to rent an apartment from "The Keyes Company" for a two year period, the rent to be paid in monthly installments of $250. Patti is happy with the rented premises until one spring day when she forgets to close her glass sliding doors and an unexpected shower damages the apartment wall and floor. Patti insists that The Keyes Company has a duty to keep the premises in repair, but the Company refuses to repair the water damage. A week later, and twelve months before the lease expires, Patti leaves the rented premises and moves in with her sister Cindy. Upon discovering that Patti has left, The Keyes Company retakes possession of the apartment. In a back closet, the Company finds a color TV, some clothing, and other personal items forgotten by Patti; the Company sells the property and applies the proceeds towards Patti's unpaid rent. A few days later, and without informing Patti, the Company relets the premises for $200 a month. Twelve months later, the Company sues Patti for $750 (the $600 difference between the old rent and the new rent for the 12 month period plus $150 for the water damage to the apartment). Patti seeks your advice.

    (a) What type of tenancy did Patti enter into? *Tenancy for years*

    (b) As between The Keyes Company and Patti, who is responsible for the water damage to the apartment? Explain. *Patti permissive waste of property*

    (c) Did The Keyes Company have a right to relet the premises when Patti moved in with her sister? Explain. *yes abandonment*

    (d) Did the Company have a right to sell Patti's property? Explain. *notice, hearing   no, only to store*

    (e) Is Patti responsible for the $600 rent deficit? Explain. *no tenant must be notified - surrender*

2. Ted Spencer rents an apartment from The Keyes Company on a monthly basis. The rent is $225 a month, and Ted is required to pay a one-time, refundable security deposit of $450. The apartment is inhabitable when Ted takes possession of the premises, but, a few months later, the heating system malfunctions, and the apartment is too cold for comfort. Ted complains to The Keyes Company, but the Company refuses to repair the heating. Ted reports the problem to the local housing authority (thinking that it may be a housing code violation), and he joins the neighborhood tenant's union to learn more about his rights as a tenant. Angry that Ted has contacted the housing authority and joined the tenant's union, The Keyes Company gives Ted 30 days notice of termination of the tenancy. When Ted pays no heed to the notice, the Company physically ousts him from the premises and locks him out. What is more, the Company refuses to refund Ted's security deposit. Assuming the Uniform Residential Landlord Tenant Act applies, answer the following:

    (a) What type of tenancy agreement did Ted enter into? *period to period*

    (b) Did The Keyes Company have a duty to repair the heating system? Explain. If your answer is yes, how could Ted have enforced this duty? *yes, affirmative duty to repair   URLTA   put money in holding*

    (c) What legal rights, if any, does Ted have against the Company for the physical ouster, the lockout, and the refusal to refund the security deposit? *Damages   no retaliatory action within 6 mos.   no greater than 1 mo. rent   - itemized deductions   abolished   treble damages + fees   - 14 days   may recover double damages*

(d) Assuming Ted would like to return to the apartment, does he have a legal right to repossession of the premises? Explain. *yes - retaliation prohibited*

3. How would your answers to # 2 above differ if the URLTA were not in effect?

4. Answer the following "True" or "False" and give reasons for your answers.

   F (a) A lease is a freehold estate.

   T (b) In a contract for the sale of minerals, the minerals become personal property at the time the contract is entered into if the minerals are to be severed by the <u>seller</u>.

   T (c) Like annual crops, timber is considered personal property at the time a sales agreement is made without regard to who is to sever the timber from the land.

   F (d) A trespasser who places a fixture on land will ordinarily be allowed to remove the fixture.

   F (e) The majority rule is that a landlord has a duty to make the premises safe for the tenant and his or her guests. *except ① concealed danger ② use of public purpose*

5. Answer the following:

   (a) The Keyes Company refuses to rent to Jeff Temple solely on the basis of his race. What legal recourse, if any, does Jim have against the Company? *Damages, restore inequity*

   (b) Though Joanne Hastings has been given 30 days notice of termination of her month to month tenancy, Joanne refuses to leave the premises at the end of the 30 days. What legal rights, if any, does her landlord have in this situation? *Tenant of Sufferance - Trespasser - evicted Holdover tenant*

   (c) After renting a house from Dan Patton, Gail Roper is evicted from the premises by a mortgagee who recorded his mortgage before Gail entered into the lease agreement. What are Gail's rights, if any, against Dan Patton? Against the mortgagee? Would your answer differ if the mortgagee had recorded his interest after Gail entered into the lease agreement? Explain. *① breach of quiet enjoyment ② none against mortgagee ③ same rights as against Dan*

6. Vance obtained a 25 year leasehold interest in an office building from the owner, Stanfield.

   (a) Vance's interest is non-assignable.

   (b) The conveyance of the ownership of the building by Stanfield to Wax will terminate Vance's leasehold interest.

   (c) Stanfield's death will not terminate Vance's leasehold interest.

   (d) Vance's death will terminate the leasehold interest.

   [# 41, November, 1976 CPA Exam]

7. Donaldson, Inc. loaned Watson Enterprises $50,000 secured by a real estate mortgage which included the land, buildings, and "all other property which is added to the real property or which is considered as real property as a matter of law." Star Company also loaned Watson $25,000 and obtained a security interest in all of Watson's "inventory, accounts receivable, fixtures, and other tangible personal property." There is insufficient property to satisfy the two creditors. Consequently, Donaldson is attempting to include all property possible under the terms and scope of its real estate mortgage. If Donaldson is suc-

cessful in this regard, then Star will receive a lesser amount in satisfaction of its claim. What is the probable outcome of Donaldson's action?

(a) Donaldson will not prevail if the property in question is detachable trade fixtures.

(b) Donaldson will prevail if Star failed to file a financing statement.

(c) Donaldson will prevail if it was the first lender and duly filed its real property mortgage.

(d) The problem will be decided by taking all of Watson's property (real and personal) and dividing it in proportion to the respective debts.

[# 29, May, 1978 CPA Exam]

8. You are the accountant for the Ajax Washing Machine Company. The Company installs and operates coin metered washing machines in the basements of apartment houses for the use and convenience of the tenants in the building. While auditing the records of Ajax, you found the following:

Ajax recently entered into an agreement with the owner of a building under which the building owner granted Ajax permission to install and maintain a coin metered washing machine for a period of three years from the date of installation. Ajax retains ownership of the machine and is to keep all proceeds derived from its use, paying the owner a fixed monthly amount for the privilege of having the machine in the building. The agreement further provides that the building owner will furnish Ajax space which the owner chooses and the power required for the operation of the machine. In addition, the owner agrees that he will allow Ajax to enter the building to service the machine.

Recently the building owner sold his property to a new owner who has disconnected the machine and who refuses to comply with the agreement which, he alleges, is not binding on him.

Required: (a) List and describe the essential elements required for a lease. *Mutual assent, consideration, Capacity, legality*

(b) List and describe the essential elements required for a license. *Priviledge to use premises*

(c) Did the agreement between the parties create a lease or a license? Explain.

(d) Must the new owner of the building honor the agreement entered into between the former owner and Ajax? Explain. *no license is revocable*

(e) If the agreement had been called a "Lease" and if Ajax had been referred to as the "Tenant" and the former owner as the "Landlord", would your answer to "d" change? Explain. *no*

[# 6 , May, 1967 CPA Exam]

9. Ambrose agreed to pay a specified rental to Lord under a lease agreement calling for rental of one of two identical side-by-side theaters owned by Lord (Theater "A" and Theater "B"). It was later agreed that Theater "A" would be used for the run of the play but not to exceed nine months in return for a fixed weekly fee plus a percentage of gross receipts. Under these circumstances

(a) The lease if oral would be void.

(b) The lease, even if written, would be illusory since *no* set lease term is provided.

(c) If the interior of Theater "A" was burned out by fire, Lord would probably be excused from performance even though Theater "B" was available and Ambrose was willing to accept the substitution.

(d) The lease if oral would be valid and not voidable.

[# 36, May, 1974 CPA Exam]

10. Under certain circumstances personal property may be converted into and become a part of real property. Which of the following is *least* relevant in ascertaining whether this has occurred?

(a) The mode and degree of annexation.

(b) The use and purpose the property serves in relation to the real property.

(c) The legal formalities which the parties satisfied in relation to the property in question, such as a signed, sealed, and witnessed document.

(d) The actual intent of the parties.

[# 38, May, 1977 CPA Exam]

Chapter 3

ACQUIRING OWNERSHIP OF PERSONAL PROPERTY BY OTHER THAN PURCHASE: WILD THINGS, ABANDONED PROPERTY, FINDERS' RIGHTS, ACCESSION, CONFUSION, GIFTS, PATENTS, COPYRIGHTS

What are the two types of personal property?

In our broad overview of property rights in Ch. 2, we saw that there are two types of property (i. e., transferable) rights—real property rights (land and its fixtures) and personal property rights. Personal property rights, the subject matter of this chapter, may be further classified into "tangibles", called *choses in possession*, and "intangibles", called *choses in action*. A tangible personal property right refers to something with material substance—something you can touch. This book, for example, is a tangible or chose in possession. And so is a table, a lamp, a telephone, a TV set, an automobile, an airplane, and an ocean liner. An intangible, on the other hand, has no material substance. It is called a chose in "action" because, in the event of a dispute, it is necessary to bring a legal action in court to effectuate the right. Since a chose in action has no material substance, it would be impossible to enforce the right in any other way (e. g., by taking possession of the property). Intangible personal property rights include patents, copyrights, common stock rights, bonds, accounts receivable, business goodwill, and any other transferable contract right.

While ownership of an intangible is sometimes evidenced by a written document of one kind or another, the paper containing the writing should not be confused with the property itself. For example, the owner of a patent right (patent rights are considered in a later section of this chapter) will possess a certificate of patent ownership; the purchaser of 100 shares of IBM corporate stock will hold a stock certificate evidencing his or her shareholder status; and a borrower of money will frequently sign a promissory note (See Chapters 12–15 on negotiable instruments), containing the debtor's promise to repay the lender in full. Each of these writings is but evidence of an intangible personal property right. If the paper is lost or destroyed, ownership of the right continues (although, without the writing, it may be more difficult to prove the existence of the right).

What is the most common way to acquire ownership of personal property?

Ownership of personal property is most commonly acquired by purchase. The purchase and sale of goods is governed by the law of contracts and sales. The purchase and sale of corporate stock is strictly regulated by the federal Securities and Exchange Commission (which administers the federal securities laws) and state "Blue Sky" laws; and drafts, notes, and checks (other intangibles) are controlled by the law of negotiable instruments.

The purchase and sale of personal property is explored in detail in later chapters of the text. This chapter is concerned with the acquisition of personal property by means other than purchase. And there are several other ways of acquiring ownership of such property. For example, a person may acquire ownership

51

of abandoned property or wild things (e. g., fish, birds, and other wild animals that belong to no one) simply by taking the property into legal possession. The finder of lost property may ultimately acquire title if the true owner cannot be located. And a person may obtain ownership of personal property by means of accession, confusion, gift, patent, or copyright law. In each of these situations an individual acquires ownership of personal property by means other than purchase.

Ownership of property (real or personal) is generally referred to as "title". And it is important to realize that title is not a written paper. It is a legal concept indicating ownership—that is, a legally protected interest in property good as against the whole world. Ownership or title may be evidenced by a written "document of title" or "title certificate" (and usually is in the case of large items like cars, boats, and airplanes), but these papers are merely evidence of ownership and are not required. The owner of a book, a table, a lamp, or a TV set may possess nothing in writing to indicate ownership, but he or she will possess title (a legally protected interest in the property) nonetheless.

Title or ownership is important because it confers upon the owner of the property the exclusive right to use, possess, and dispose of the property. Disposition encompasses lifetime transfers as well as distribution to heirs and beneficiaries upon the owner's death.

But, as pointed out in Ch. 1, title is not the only legally recognized property interest; and a party without title may still have important rights and obligations with respect to the property at issue. For example, the Uniform Commercial Code creates in the purchaser of goods a "special property interest" once the goods have been identified to the contract of sale. In addition, the purchaser may bear the risk of loss or destruction of the

goods even before title (i. e., ownership) has been transferred to him or her. And the seller may retain a security interest in the goods even after title has passed to the purchaser. Apart from the sales situation, a person may acquire rightful possession of property belonging to another (called a bailment) and possess superior rights to all but the true owner (the party with title). What each of these situations has in common is that a person without title or ownership of property nevertheless possesses valuable rights in the chattel. Each of these areas is treated in detail in later chapters of the text.

Like title or ownership, "possession" is a legal term with a special meaning. To legally possess personal property, a person must: (1) intend to exercise control over the chattel; and (2) physically control the chattel to an appreciable extent (i. e., exercise a sufficient amount of physical control over the property). Both factors are essential to establishing legal possession. For example, a person who is unaware of the existence of a chattel within his or her physical control (e. g., a valuable ring in the pocket of an old coat) does not intend to possess the property and is not in legal possession of the chattel (the result would be contrary if the individual consciously intended to possess the contents of the coat's pocket, whatever they might be). And a person who picks up an article from the street or from a store counter (e. g., a necktie or a book), examines it, and ultimately discards it has custody only and not legal possession because there is neither intent to exercise control over the item, nor sufficient physical control of the property. The same is true of an individual who tries on clothing to determine whether or not to buy.

Proof of possession—legal possession —is extremely important in cases involving the acquisition of title to wild things, abandoned property, and other property found on public and private premises.

How does a person become the owner of (i. e., obtain title to) "wild things"?

Title, you will recall, means ownership. And ownership of property confers upon the owner the right to exclude all others from use or enjoyment of the property. The owner, in turn, becomes subject to the many duties of property ownership, including the duty to pay any taxes levied on the property, and the duty to use the property safely so as not to cause injury to others.

In the vast majority of cases, possession alone will not establish ownership of property. But where wild animals (*ferae naturae*) as opposed to domestic animals (*domitae naturae*) are concerned, legal possession of the animals (including fish found in rivers, lakes, and oceans) will generally be sufficient to vest all title and ownership rights in the possessing party. Until wild things are taken into possession, they belong to no one. Once reduced to possession, it is essential that the law protect the possessor's exclusive use and enjoyment of the property by recognizing the possessor as the party with legal title.

But remember, legal possession demands sufficient physical control of the property coupled with an intent to control or possess it. This is not to say that actual physical control of a wild animal is always necessary to obtain title. While merely chasing a wild animal with intent to possess it will never constitute legal possession no matter how close the pursuit may be, a hunter who is in fresh pursuit of a wild animal that he or she has mortally wounded is the legal owner of the animal despite the intervention of an outsider who completes the kill and captures the wild thing. The hunter's actual physical possession of the animal is close to inevitable, and there exists "sufficient physical control" to establish legal possession and ownership. Similarly, a party who confines a wild animal in an en-closed place under the party's private control and takes reasonable precautions to prevent the animal from escaping has exercised sufficient physical control (coupled with intent to control) to establish legal possession and ownership.

Suppose a wild animal that is reduced to possession escapes from its owner. Unless the animal has been tamed or domesticated to the point that it will eventually return to its place of captivity, the animal reverts to its wild state and again belongs to no one. Thus, wild pigeons trained as homing pigeons remain the property of their owner though they fly freely far from the owner's land, while a red fox that escapes from its cage with no intention of returning reverts to nature and is wild once more. A single exception to the general rule arises where a formerly wild animal, not native to its place of captivity (e. g., an elephant housed in a private zoo in Anaheim, California), escapes from its owner-captor. Though the animal has no intention of returning to its place of captivity, the owner retains title and has superior rights to anyone who subsequently captures the animal.

Finally, it must be mentioned that a landowner has a common law right to any wild animals (including birds or fish) that are taken from his or her land by trespassers. Many landowners post "no hunting" and "no fishing" signs to help enforce this right.

Of course, all these rules are subject to statutory restrictions dealing with the licensing of hunters and fisherpeople, and regulating seasons, bag limits, and fish and game conservation.

Does a person become the owner of abandoned personal property simply by taking possession of it?

A person who intentionally relinquishes ownership and possession of a chattel without placing title in someone else is said to "abandon" the personal property.[1] The common law rule is that abandoned property belongs to no one, and the first person to take the property into legal possession (i. e., the first person to exercise sufficient physical control over the property with intent to acquire ownership) obtains legal title.

The common law rule has been changed by statute in some states, the statutes declaring that all abandoned property belongs to the state. Any person who finds abandoned property must report the discovery to the appropriate state agency. If it chooses, the agency may disclaim the state's interest in the abandoned property and award the property to the finder.

Acquiring title to personal property by taking possession of wild things or abandoned property is known in the law as acquiring title by *"occupation"*.

What is the law generally regarding finders of personal property?

Closely related to the subject of abandoned property is the law regarding finders of personal property. A person who finds *lost* personal property does not acquire title by the mere act of finding the property, or by the act of taking the property into legal possession (as is sufficient with abandoned property). However, in several instances, the finder will ultimately acquire ownership of the chattel if the true owner cannot be found. And prior to that time, he or she will possess a "finder's rights", meaning that he or she will be entitled to possession of the property against everyone in the whole world except the true owner. Where the finder possesses such rights, he or she can bring an action for conversion or trespass to the chattel against any third person who interferes with his or her possession of the property. And if a third party success-

fully deprives the finder of possession, the finder can bring a suit in "replevin" and recover the chattel.

But on many occasions, it is not the finder who will possess superior rights to the chattel and ultimately acquire title—rather, it is the owner of the "locus in quo" (i. e., the owner of the "place in which" the chattel was found). And, in a few cases, the state will acquire title—not the finder, and not the owner of the locus in quo.

As between the finder, the owner of the locus in quo, and the state, the question of who will ultimately obtain title to a particular chattel depends upon a consideration of the following:

(1) The classification of the property as either:

(a) Abandoned property;

(b) Lost property;

(c) "Treasure Trove";

(d) Property other than treasure trove that is embedded in the earth; or

(e) Misplaced property.

(2) Whether the property was found in a public or private place.

(3) Whether the finder is a trespasser on the real property (as opposed to a person rightfully present on the land), or an employee of the landowner on whose property the chattel was found.

(4) Whether there are any statutory procedures for acquiring title to the property.

(1) *The classification of the property.*

If the found property is *abandoned property* (ownership and possession of which the true owner intentionally and permanently relinquished), the finder will ordinarily acquire title to the property merely by taking it into legal possession.

---

1. It should be pointed out that real property cannot be abandoned.

Lost property differs from abandoned property in two ways. First, while abandoned property is intentionally and permanently given up by its owner, lost property is unintentionally and accidentally lost or left behind by its owner through carelessness, inadvertence, or neglect. The owner of lost property has no intention of relinquishing title or possession of the property—the owner simply has no idea where the property is. Second, whereas abandoned property belongs to the first person to take it into legal possession, lost property does not belong to the finder or person first to possess it: it continues to belong to the true owner. However, as stated previously, the finder of the lost property may be entitled to possession of the chattel against all but the true owner, and if the true owner cannot be located, the finder may ultimately acquire title (again, depending upon where the item is found, who finds it, and what applicable "finders' statutes" say).

In some cases, it is difficult to determine whether property is abandoned or lost. In making the determination, the courts will generally inquire into the location where the chattel was found (e. g., property found in a public dump is probably abandoned, while property found in a public restaurant appears to be lost) and the value of the item (the more valuable the property, the more likely it is lost and not abandoned).

Treasure trove, to be distinguished from both abandoned and lost property, is defined as coin or bullion (and modernly paper money) found buried in the ground. Treasure trove is not abandoned property because the owner who buried it had no intention of relinquishing his or her rights in the money or gold. And it is not lost property because there was nothing accidental about its burial in the soil—the owner intentionally hid the treasure in the ground, fully expecting to return for it at a later date, but, for some unexplained reason, failing to return.

Treasure trove rules are of ancient origin, dating back to the time of the Roman conquerors who hid treasure in England prior to being forced out of the British Isles. Originally, it was held that treasure trove belonged to the king or sovereign. Later, because the sovereign wanted to encourage the discovery of buried treasure, the finder was given a right to share in the treasure trove. Modernly, unless a state, by statute, claims title to all or part of any treasure trove discovered within its boundaries (and several states do), the finder will obtain title and become the owner of the property. This is a fair result because the true owner is hardly likely to appear and make claim to the treasure.

Objects other than treasure trove found embedded in the soil are given, not to the finder of the property, but to the owner of the land, called the owner of the locus in quo. The property is given to the landowner rather than the finder because the property is considered to be a part of the soil itself. For example, in Allred v. Biegel, 20 Mo.App. 818, 219 S.W.2d 665 (1949), an ancient Indian canoe found embedded in the soil was awarded to the landowner, not the finder.

And it makes no difference whether the article was originally lost, abandoned, or mislaid ("mislaid" property will be defined shortly): if it is embedded in the soil, and the true owner cannot be found, the owner of the locus in quo will acquire title. Of course, the deeper the property is embedded in the soil, the more sense it makes to classify the article as "part of the land". Even so, there have been cases awarding title to the landowner to objects found but a few inches below the surface of the soil.

The final classification of property important to our study of finders' rights is *mislaid* or *misplaced property*. Mislaid property is property that the owner has voluntarily and intentionally put down in a particular location, only to subsequently forget where he or she has placed the property. The property is not abandoned because the owner intends to reclaim it; and it is not lost because the owner intentionally set it down. When mislaid property is found, the general rule is that the owner of the "locus in quo" possesses superior rights to the finder. The theory behind the rule is that, once the true owner remembers where he or she mislaid the chattel, the true owner will return to that place in search of the mislaid property. If the owner of the "locus in quo" has possession of the property, the true owner will have little difficulty in locating his or her chattel. And if the true owner never returns to claim the property, the owner of the "locus in quo" (rather than the finder) is entitled to ownership for having cared for the property in anticipation of the true owner's return.

In cases where it is difficult to determine whether goods are lost or misplaced, the courts will carefully scrutinize the physical placement of the goods at the time of their discovery. For example, goods found on a table, in a drawer, under a mattress, or in a forgotten vault or other secret place indicate intentional placement by the owner and are more likely mislaid than lost. Goods found on the floor or on the ground, on the other hand, suggest an accidental separation from their owner and are probably lost rather than mislaid.

(2) *Whether the property was found in a public or private place.*

In all but a few states, lost property found on public or semi-public property goes to the finder rather than the owner of the locus in quo.

The finder of the lost chattel has superior rights to all but the true owner (including the owner of the locus in quo)

and will ultimately obtain title if the true owner cannot be located. For example, an umbrella or other item of personal property lost and found in a restaurant or theater, or on a bus or train will belong to the finder unless the true owner can be located to claim it. Oftentimes, and particularly where the item is left on a public conveyance, such as a bus or train, the property will be classified as mislaid rather than lost (if at all logically possible) in order to give the true owner every opportunity to return and collect his or her property from the owner of the locus in quo.

Where lost property is found not on public but on private property, the old common law view, and the traditional view in a majority of states, is that the owner of the locus in quo and not the finder is entitled to possession of the chattel and ultimately title if the true owner cannot be found. Again, the theory behind the rule is that the true owner is likely to look for the chattel at the site of the loss—giving possession to the owner of the locus in quo, rather than the finder (who may never return to the discovery site) assists the true owner in relocating his or her property.

However, a sizeable minority of states (and it appears to be the trend) have rejected the traditional rule preferring the owner of the locus in quo over the finder. The minority holds that the finder of lost property has superior rights to possession (and ultimately title) even where the property is found on private premises. These states claim that the traditional rule discourages finders from reporting their discoveries since the owner of the locus in quo will always be allowed to deprive the finder of possession. And since the finder would presumably attempt to locate the true owner if permitted to keep possession (several statutes require public notice of the find), it really makes little practical difference from the true owner's standpoint who holds onto the property until he or she can reclaim it.

(3) *Whether the finder is a trespasser on the real property (as opposed to a person rightfully present on the land), or an employee of the owner of the locus in quo.*

As a means of discouraging trespassing, it is generally held that a trespasser on real property has no rights, and this holds true for a trespassing finder. Thus, a finder who is wrongfully present on the land at the time of making the discovery acquires no legal rights to possession or ownership of the property whether the chattel is abandoned, lost, mislaid, treasure trove, or property other than treasure trove embedded in the ground. The owner of the locus in quo and, in some cases, the state, will always have a superior claim.

Where the finder is rightfully present on the land (as is the case with a social guest of the landlord, a business visitor, and any other person present on the property with the landowner's permission), the finder generally acquires rights to possession and title as outlined above. However, an exception arises where the finder also happens to be an employee of the landowner who finds the property during the course of employment and who either (1) has a duty to turn over to the employer any personal property found on the land; or (2) knows or should know as a reasonable person that the landowner intends to exercise control with respect to everything found on the real property. If these conditions are satisfied, the employer-landowner will always be entitled to possession of the chattel (and ultimately title if the true owner cannot be located) even in situations that would ordinarily place superior rights in the finder of the property (e. g., lost property on semi-public land). Of course, where the property is mislaid, rather than lost, the owner of the locus in quo will be entitled to possession over the finder in any case.

When does an employee have a duty to turn over to the employer-landowner any personal property found on the premises? An easy example is a hotel maid who discovers a watch while cleaning a rented hotel room. Another is a country club janitor who finds a club member's ring while cleaning out the swimming pool. In each case, the employee has a duty to turn the property over to the employer—the owner of the locus in quo—because the true owner is likely to look to the employer for return of the missing article.

When does an employer-landowner intend to exercise control over everything found on the premises? Generally, the existence of a contract duty on the part of the employer to care for property brought onto his or her business premises indicates such intent. For example, an employee of an owner-operator of a safe-deposit vault has good reason to know that his or her employer intends to exercise control over any property found on the premises. The employer has a contract duty to care for customers' property brought into the vault area, and customers who lose property will look to the employer for the property's return. Because of this, the employer (the owner of the locus in quo), and not the employee who discovers the property, has superior rights to possession and ultimately title. Another example is an owner-operator of a large deep freeze area containing many individual frozen food lockers. Again, the employer has a contract duty to care for customers' property brought onto the business premises; and if an employee finds a "lost" package of frozen meat on the floor of the deep freeze area, the employer is entitled to possession of the meat and ultimately title if the true owner cannot be found.

(4) Whether there are any statutory procedures for acquiring title to the property.

Statutes in many states require a finder of lost property (not including abandoned, mislaid, or treasure trove property) to report the discovery to the appropriate state official (usually the county clerk) within 10 to 15 days after making the discovery. The finder must also advertise the find by posting notices and/or placing ads in the county newspaper. If the true owner does not turn up to claim the property within six months to one year's time, the finder will acquire title to the lost property. However, some states require the finder to pay the county treasurer one-half the value of the lost money or chattels. If the owner does show up to claim the property, the owner must pay any costs and charges incurred by the finder in caring for the property, as well as reasonable compensation for the finder's time and effort.

A finder who fails to follow the statutory procedure and simply keeps the lost property is generally liable, upon discovery, for twice the amount of the chattel's value (usually, the finder is required to reimburse the owner for the full value of the chattel and to pay a "penalty" of one-half the chattel's value to the owner, and one-half to the county).

Are there any other rules regarding finders of personal property?

By now, it is readily apparent that the law of finders' rights is an extremely complex legal concept with many interrelated rules and principles. By committing these various rules and principles to memory, it is possible to master this often confusing concept and to balance the competing interests of chattel owner, finder, owner of the locus in quo, and state.

In conclusion, and before we move on to other methods of acquiring ownership of personal property, it is necessary to point out a few additional rules pertaining to finders of *lost* personal property.

(1) A person who finds lost property has no legal obligation to take charge of the property. However, if the finder does take charge of the chattel, he or she has a duty to use reasonable care to preserve the chattel and to make reasonable efforts to locate the true owner. The finder holds the property as a *bailee* for the true owner. A *bailment* may be defined as the rightful possession of another's personal property. As will be explained in detail in Ch. 16, a bailment which is not based on a contract (as in the finder situation) is called a "gratuitous" bailment. If the finder (the gratuitous bailee) fails to search for the true owner, or fails to restore the chattel to the owner once the owner is located, the finder will be liable for conversion of the property.

(2) A finder of lost property is not entitled to compensation for his or her services absent a statute providing for compensation or an offer of reward extended by the chattel owner. However, the finder is entitled to reimbursement from the owner for actual expenses incurred in protecting and preserving the property and in advertising to locate the owner. But the right of reimbursement does not confer a "possessory lien" upon the finder. If the owner refuses to reimburse the finder, the finder's sole remedy is to bring a legal action in court against the owner to recover money damages—the finder cannot retain possession of the property until the owner agrees to reimburse him or her; nor can the finder sell the owner's property and collect reimbursement from the sales proceeds.[2]

2. A "lien" is simply a claim or charge against real or personal property that secures the payment of a debt or other promised performance. The real estate mortgage or lien on real estate is the legal tool that enables millions of Americans to

(3) A person cannot claim possession of or title to property that is not really lost, or claim finders' fees or reimbursement rights in such a case. For example, in People v. Stay, 19 Cal.App.3d 166, 96 Cal.Rptr. 651 (1971), a party claimed to have found shopping carts that were commonly and customarily removed from a grocery store area by shoppers and left on the public street where employees of the store retrieved them. The carts were not "lost" because the store consented to their removal and always knew approximately where they were. The self-proclaimed finder, in this case, was rightfully convicted of larceny.

What is accession?

Literally, *accession* means "something added". As a legal concept, accession refers to a means of acquiring ownership or title to personal property that is "added to" property already in existence—either naturally (as in animal reproduction or crop growth) or by human design, whether intentional or inadvertent, innocent or wrongful. Of course, there is little problem with the title by accession that results in the following situations:

(1) The owner of animals (including birds and fish) gains title to any offspring of the animals.

(2) A person who plants and cultivates crops becomes the owner of the crops he or she harvests.

(3) A person who contracts to have an article of personal property repaired becomes the owner of any materials added to the chattel during the course of the repair.

(4) A person who provides another with all the materials for manufacture of an article obtains title to the finished product.

In each of these situations, the owner of personal property has either intentionally sought the addition of parts or labor to the property, or has been the recipient of a natural growth or reproduction.

The difficult accession cases are those wherein one person unauthorizedly improves or increases in value or otherwise changes personal property belonging to another by adding parts or labor. Because the change or addition is unauthorized, it will always constitute a conversion of the property, or at least a trespass to the chattel (see Ch. 1). Generally, if the change or addition is serious enough to constitute a conversion, the owner may sue the converter and force him or her to pay for the property in return for receiving title to the chattel. If the interference amounts only to a trespass to the chattel, the owner will recover only minimal damages, and title will not pass to the other party.

However, in some cases, a legal action for conversion will be the owner's only remedy because the very act of accession by the "trespassing" party will serve to transfer title from the original owner to the trespasser at the time the parts or labor are added. Where this occurs, the owner will not be able to recover his or her property (as would be possible in an action for trespass to the chattel) but must make do with the recovery of money damages.

own and occupy homes while continuing to pay for them over a 25 to 30 year period. The lienholder (the savings and loan association or other financial institution financing the purchase) does not have a possessory lien because the institution is not in possession of the property against which the lien is charged. And that is what a "possessory lien" is—a claim or charge against property that remains in the lienholder's possession. The possessory lien is not an interest in the property being held, but only a "right of detainer", i. e., a right to hold the property until the owner discharges the indebtedness owing to the lienholder. Possessory liens will be important to our study of commercial law in several areas, particularly with respect to innkeepers, commercial bailments, carriers, warehousemen, and factors.

Not surprisingly, the obvious starting point of any legal analysis of an unauthorized accession is this: did title to the property pass to the "trespasser" by the very act of accession? The answer will often depend on whether the property was taken innocently by mistake, or whether the accession was willful.

Innocent taking by mistake. A person who innocently and mistakenly takes another's property and adds a very great deal of material and/or labor to it will generally acquire title to the property under the rules of accession. In determining whether the innocent wrongdoer has added sufficient parts and/or labor to justify a transfer of title, courts make use of the following two rules:

(1) *Loss of identity rule (also called the doctrine of "specification").* Ordinarily, title will pass to the innocent trespasser if the chattel has lost its original identity and has been converted into a new species (e. g., grapes changed into wine, wheat into flour, or clay into bricks). However, where timber is cut into lumber, firewood, or shingles, there is no change of identity and no transfer of title. The timber has not been so completely altered that it has lost its identity as wood or timber. (It is sometimes said that the test of a "new species" is whether or not the property can be returned to its former crude material state).

(2) *Relative value rule.* Additionally, title will generally pass to the innocent trespasser when there is a great increase in the value of the chattel as a result of the accession. There is no generally accepted formula for measuring a "sufficient increase" in value (although several courts have held that an increase in the property's value by 5 or 6 times will be sufficient). The court simply determines whether it would work a tremendous hardship on the innocent trespasser or otherwise result in a gross injustice to permit the original owner to retain title to the property. For example, in the case

of Wetherbee v. Green, 22 Mich. 311, 7 AR 653 (1871), the defendant, an innocent trespasser, mistakenly believed that he had a license to cut timber growing on land belonging to plaintiff Green ("plaintiff" refers to the party who brings the legal action, "defendant" to the party being sued). After innocently, but wrongfully cutting the trees, the defendant converted the timber into barrel hoops worth 28 times the original value of the timber. The defendant claimed title to the barrel hoops, and the court agreed. The increase in the value of the property was so substantial that it justified the transfer of ownership.

Where title automatically passes to the innocent trespasser, the owner's sole remedy, as previously stated, is to sue the trespasser for conversion. Where title does not pass automatically, the owner may still force the trespasser to purchase the property in exchange for title in a legal action for conversion. In either event, the measure of damages (the amount the original owner can recover from the innocent trespasser or from a third person who has purchased the enhanced property from the innocent trespasser) will be the original value of the property *before* the addition of materials and/or labor. In this way, the innocent trespasser is given credit for his or her labor and/or materials.

Willful wrongdoer. The general rule is that a willful trespasser who deliberately takes another's personal property and adds materials and/or labor to it cannot acquire title by accession even where there is a change in species of the property or a substantial increase in value of the chattel. The innocent party is entitled to return of his or her property along with any additions made by the willful trespasser. This is a good rule because it discourages people from plundering others' property. In the past, the rule has been strictly applied no matter how little the value of the original chattel, or how great the increase in value of the chattel as a result of the materials or labor added.

However, in recent years, the trend has been to recognize an exception where application of the general rule would lead to a ridiculously unjust result. Thus, in most states, where the goods or materials of two different owners are added together or incorporated, title to the resulting product will go to the owner of the "principal thing" or chattel without regard to the parties' fault or wrongfulness. This exception has been placed into statutory form in several states, including California. What is the "principal thing" can be determined by reference to the respective values of each party's goods or materials. Generally, if the materials added by the trespasser increase the value of the innocent party's property by more than 50%, title will pass to the trespasser as owner of the "principal thing" (i. e., owner of the most valuable property). For example, if a willful trespasser steals paint and uses it to paint his or her car, the trespasser will not lose the car, but will acquire title to the paint added to the car. Of course, the owner of the paint will have the right to sue the trespasser for the value of the paint in a legal action for conversion, but the owner cannot demand return of the property itself. To permit him or her to do so would be manifestly unjust even in the case of a willful wrongdoer.

The most recent trend in the law is to recognize yet another exception to the general rule where the willful trespasser adds not primarily materials, but labor to the innocent party's property to produce a chattel of much greater value. For example, a thief who paints a masterpiece upon a stolen canvas or carves a stolen block of wood into a valuable work of art may well obtain title to the finished product through the laws of accession. Again, it would be ridiculous to require

the thief to return the "stolen property" in its altered state.

In cases involving an exception to the general rule, the innocent party has the right to recover money damages from the wrongdoer in a legal action for conversion. And even where the general rule applies, the innocent party has the option of suing for conversion rather than for replevin of the property itself. The innocent party's measure of damages in a conversion action is not the original value of the converted chattel (as is the case where the taking is innocent), but the value of the chattel in its improved condition. Obviously, this results in the imposition of a penalty, and that is what the law intends.

However, if it would be grossly unjust to force the wrongdoer to pay the full value of the improved chattel, the court will make an exception and order payment of a lesser amount (e. g., a thief who carves a stolen block of wood of negligible value into a masterpiece worth $25,000 will not be required to pay the owner of the wood $25,000 for converting the property—$50 would be a more appropriate penalty).

Suppose the trespasser has decreased rather than increased the value of the primary chattel? The owner, in this case, will not be limited to suing for the value of the chattel in its altered state, but can sue for the property's original value.

And whether the taking is unintentional or deliberate, if the original owner of the primary chattel successfully replevins the property, the trespasser cannot sue the owner for the value of any improvements to the chattel, however great or small. Again, the trend in the law is to rule otherwise where application of the general rule would result in substantial injustice to the trespasser.

Before moving on to the acquisition of title to property by means of "confusion", it is necessary to point out the following:

(1) There is no accession and no passage of title or ownership where materials attached to the primary chattel can be removed without causing significant harm to the chattel and without changing the original nature of the property. Accession, in such a case, simply does not apply.

(2) If the personal property added to the primary chattel is subject to a security interest in a third party, accession will not operate to extinguish the third party's interest: the security interest will prevail even over the interest of the original owner. Section 9–314 of the Uniform Commercial Code governs accession with regard to personal property serving as security for a debt and is considered in Ch. 27 dealing with secured transactions.

What is the law as to "confusion" of goods?

In a very few situations, title or ownership of personal property may be acquired by means of *confusion*. Confusion exists where goods owned by different parties are intermingled so that the property of each is no longer separable or distinguishable. Confusion is like accession in that it involves the contribution of distinct parts to a new integral; it is unlike accession in that there is an intermingling only. In accession, the goods of one party are either so changed by the labor of another as to form a new or more valuable chattel, or so physically united to the primary chattel as to become a constituent part of it. In confusion, the goods of each owner retain their original form and characteristics; it is only because of the circumstance of intermingling that each party's goods can no longer be identified, separated, and returned to their proper owners.

Because the law frowns upon the acquisition of title by confusion, it strictly regulates the situations in which it can occur. The following rules and principles are controlling:

(1) There is no confusion so long as each party's property can be identified and returned. Thus, even where several thousand head of branded cattle belonging to different owners are mixed together in one lot, there is no passage of title by confusion—even where one of the owners has wrongfully intermixed the animals so as to gain title to them all. Each owner retains his or her right and title to the cattle, and the only task is the mechanical one of determining which owner owns which cattle by reference to their brands.

(2) Nor is there confusion resulting in a change of ownership where fungible goods are mixed together and the percentage of each party's contribution to the mass is known. "Fungible" goods are goods of the same quality and value, any one unit of which is the same as any other unit, which goods are customarily sold by weight and measure. Examples are grain, oil, or minerals of the same grade. So long as each party knows how much he or she has contributed to the mass, it makes no difference that different goods are in fact returned to each owner—all the goods are identical. For example, if A, B, C, and D each store varying amounts of fungible grain in the same grain elevator (say A puts in ½ the grain; B, ⅓rd; and C and D each ⅙th), and C withdraws portions of the grain placed in the elevator by A, B, or D, it will make no difference to any of the parties so long as C withdraws only a total of ⅙th of the grain—the amount C originally deposited for storage. While the grain is in storage, each party is a concurrent owner as a tenant in common of the grain. This means that each party owns an undivided share of the whole mass limited by the percentage of the total contributed. (Concurrent ownership, in-

cluding tenants in common, is discussed in detail in Ch. 5.)

(3) Nor is there legal confusion where the intermixture of goods results from a natural force or accident, or by act of a third party (whether inadvertent or willful), so that all owners are free from any fault in the intermingling. Each owner, in such a case, stands equal before the law, and, to the extent that his or her contribution can be proved, will recover his or her share of the property. If proportionate ownership cannot be established, each owner will receive an equal share as a tenant in common with the other owners. And if one tenant in common takes possession of all the goods, he or she will not be considered a trespasser as to the other owners so long as he or she makes a proper accounting of the property.

(4) The only time legal confusion exists is where nonfungible goods are indistinguishably intermixed by one of the owners, rendering the goods inseparable. Where the owner intermixes the goods inadvertently without any wrongful intent or willful purpose, no forfeiture will result if it is possible to determine the original values or quantities of the properties intermixed. Where this is impossible, the loss falls on the party who caused the intermixture, and that party loses title to his or her goods.

Where the owner willfully and wrongfully or fraudulently intermixes the goods so as to render them indistinguishable, the wrongdoer forfeits his or her goods entirely. The innocent party or parties acquire complete ownership or title to the goods and have no obligation to

compensate the wrongdoer in any way. For example, in one case, a logger who had borrowed a great deal of money from a sawmill operator had stored his unmarked and unbranded logs in a slough adjacent to the sawmiller's place of business. Fearing that the logger would not repay him, the sawmiller intentionally and wrongfully intermixed his own unbranded and unmarked logs with those of the logger, and subsequently claimed title to them all. The court denied the sawmiller's claim and held that, since the number of logs each party owned could not be exactly (or even close to exactly) determined, the legal concept of confusion applied, and the logger acquired title to all the logs.

What is the law regarding transfer of ownership by gift?

Defined legally, a *gift* is a voluntary transfer of ownership of property without consideration (i. e., without receiving something in return). There are two kinds of gifts, and both are important to our study: (1) inter vivos gifts; and (2) gifts causa mortis.

Inter vivos gifts. To make an effective inter vivos (i. e., lifetime) gift requires three things: (1) proper donative intent on the part of the donor or giftgiver; (2) legal delivery of the gift to the donee or recipient; and (3) proper acceptance of the gift by the donee.[3]

To have the requisite donative intent, the donor must have present mental capacity at the time of making the gift (e. g., he or she may not be incapacitated due to mental illness), and must intend to make an immediate, effective transfer of his or her property interest to the do-

---

3. The CPA Exam lists "five" requirements for a valid, irrevocable inter vivos gift: (1) competent parties; (2) an absence of consideration; (3) the transaction voluntarily and unconditionally entered into by the donor; (4) actual or constructive delivery of the gift to the donee, and (5) requisite intent by the donor to make a gift and pass title to the donee. You will note that all five requirements are encompassed within the "three" text requirements. However, to make the CPA list complete, it is necessary to add to the list text requirement #3—"proper acceptance by the donee".

nee. However, to say that the donor must intend to make a present gift does not mean that he or she must intend to transfer immediate use and enjoyment of the property to the donee. An intent to make an immediate gift of a future interest or future enjoyment of the property is sufficient. An intent merely to transfer property at some future time is not. For example, say that a duck hunter who owns a prize shotgun says to his son, "This shotgun is now yours, but I want to use it until I stop duck hunting." The hunter's statement to his son indicates an intent to make a present gift of the shotgun. However, if the hunter says, "I want you to have this gun when I am through hunting with it," there is no present gift because there is no intent to vest any property right *now* in the son. Sometimes, it is difficult to determine whether the donor's intent is to make a final, present transfer of a future interest or merely to make such a transfer at a future date. In determining whether donative intent exists, the courts look carefully at the donor's words in making the transfer, the kind of property involved, and the relationship of the parties.

Delivery, the second element of a valid inter vivos gift, is accomplished only when the donor in some way gives up dominion and control of the property and transfers it to the donee. The usual method of delivery is physical transfer of the chattel to the donee, but physical delivery is by no means the only method. The delivery requirement may also be satisfied as follows:

(1) Where the nature or location of the property makes physical delivery of possession impossible, delivery can be accomplished by a "symbolic" delivery ceremony. For example, delivery of a grain elevator full of grain might be accomplished by physically delivering a few grains to the donee as a symbol of the entire amount in the elevator.

(2) Where appropriate, the donor can make a "constructive" delivery of the gift property by delivering to the donee the means by which the donee can gain control of the property (e. g., handing over the keys to a car, or the passbook to a savings account).

(3) Or the donor may "deliver" the gift property by transferring physical possession of the chattel to a third person with instructions to deliver the item to the donee. Until the third person actually delivers the chattel, the donor can revoke the instructions and prevent the gift.

(4) A written document, called a deed of gift, containing words of intent to make a present gift is sufficient, without more, to constitute a valid delivery. The delivery requirement is but a safeguard against false claims by people purporting to be donees. Written documentation by the donor serves to authenticate the fact of gift. (Nevertheless, some courts hold that a deed of gift is sufficient only where it can be proved that actual physical delivery of the chattel was impracticable under the circumstances.)

Where a gift of a future interest is made, a written deed of gift is generally required to prove delivery since physical delivery of the chattel is obviously not intended until later. Also, a deed of gift is often used to show delivery or transfer of an intangible personal property right, such as a bank account, promissory note, account receivable, insurance policy, etc. Of course, some of these intangibles can be constructively delivered by the transfer of written documents or other materials evidencing their existence. For example, funds deposited in a savings account may be constructively delivered by transfer of the savings account passbook to the donee. Funds in a checking account, on the other hand, cannot be constructively delivered by drawing a check against the account and delivering the check to the donee. While savings account withdrawals can only be made upon presentation of the passbook (possession of the passbook thus indicates control of the account), a check may be revoked by the depositor at any time by stopping payment. And payment is automatically revoked by the depositor's death or incapacity (possession of the check thus does not indicate control over the checking account funds).

(5) If the donee is already in possession of the chattel at the time the donative intent is expressed, an inter vivos gift will result without any further proof of delivery.

(6) The Uniform Gifts to Minors Act, adopted in many states, provides for delivery of gifts of securities (stocks and bonds) to minors simply by registering the securities in the name of an adult as "custodian" for the minor.

The third and final element required for an inter vivos gift is acceptance by the donee. Obviously, a donee does not have to accept gifts and they cannot be forced upon him or her. However, experience has shown that most donees do accept, and the courts generally presume acceptance unless the donee acts to affirmatively reject the gift. Where the gift is to the donee's benefit, the presumption of acceptance is difficult to overcome. But where acceptance and ownership of the chattel would place a burden upon the donee (e. g., taxes or creditor's claims), the donee may successfully deny the gift for lack of acceptance.

Once all three elements—donative intent, delivery, and acceptance—are present, there is a valid inter vivos gift that serves to irrevocably transfer title or ownership of the gift property to the donee (of course, if the subject of the gift is a future interest only, the donor may retain the present use and enjoyment of the property).

Gifts causa mortis. A gift causa mortis is a conditional gift of personal property made by a person anticipating imminent death. The gift is conditional in that the donee who receives the gift will be entitled to keep the property only if the donor does in fact die as anticipated, the donee survives the donor, and the donor does not revoke the gift before he or she dies.

Like an inter vivos gift, a gift causa mortis requires donative intent, delivery, and acceptance by the donee. To satisfy the intent requirement, the donor must intend to make an immediate present transfer of the property to the donee. If the donor's intent is that the transfer take effect only at the time of his or her death, the attempted gift causa mortis will fail, and the donor's efforts will accomplish nothing. This is because, to be effective, a transfer at death must be provided for in a written will signed by the decedent and at least two witnesses (three in some states) who attest to the decedent's signature in writing.

In many cases, a gift causa mortis operates to effectively transfer personal property out of a donor's will and to a lifetime donee at a time very close to the donor's death, but without the strict formalities required for normal deathtime transfers. By way of example, say that A possesses a valid will leaving his $5,000 diamond ring to his son B. A then suffers a heart attack and is taken to the hospital by his friend C. Believing he is about to die, A says to C, "I am dying; take this ring, it is yours." There is, in this case, a valid gift causa mortis that transfers title and ownership of the ring to C and renders ineffective the will provision leaving the ring to B.

Because a gift causa mortis can transfer property out of a donor's will, it is a disfavored legal concept, and the courts tend to restrict its application. Thus, more evidence is required to prove delivery of a gift causa mortis than is required in the case of an inter vivos gift. Constructive or symbolic deliveries are usually insufficient. For example, it has been held that the mere handing over of a passbook to a savings account or a key to a safe deposit box will not effect a valid gift causa mortis even where accompanied by donative intent and acceptance by the donee. There must generally be an actual physical delivery of the property or a written deed of gift. Some states even require witnesses for a gift causa mortis.

Unlike an inter vivos gift, a gift causa mortis is always revocable by the donor who can revoke it at any time before he or she dies. And the gift is automatically revoked if the donor does not die from the illness or peril that prompted him or her to make the gift. However, the fact that the donor recovers from the particular illness, or escapes from the particular peril, will not affect the rights of a third party who purchased the gift property from the donee in good faith without knowing that the gift was subject to revocation. The donee's sale of the goods to a bona fide purchaser (defined as someone who purchases goods for value without knowledge of any facts suggesting that less than full ownership is being sold) cuts off the donor's ability to revoke the gift; and the donor probably has no further rights or recourse even against the donee.

While the general rule is that the donor must die from the exact illness or peril that prompted the making of the gift, some courts sustain the gift causa mortis even where death results from a totally different cause (e. g., a donor who enters a hospital expecting to die in a cancer operation but suffers a fatal heart attack before the operation can take place). Some courts also require that the peril arise from an outside or external force and so will not sustain a gift causa mortis made in contemplation of suicide.

In conclusion, it is very important to remember that the concept of gift causa mortis applies to personal property only —not to real property. And this rule works both ways. For example, if a donor attempts to make a gift causa mortis out of the contents of a box containing, in addition to items of personal property, a deed to real property, the gift will not be valid as to the deed. And if the same donor executes and delivers the deed to the donee, intending the delivery to be a revocable gift causa mortis, the gift will not be revocable upon the owner's recovery, but will constitute an effective inter vivos gift.

What is the law on patents, copyrights, and trademarks?

Patents, copyrights, and trademarks are intangible personal property rights that can be originally acquired only by compliance with federal statutes. Once acquired, the rights are freely transferable by sale or gift.

Patents. The United States Constitution provides that Congress may pass laws to "promote progress in science and the useful arts." In accord with this power, Congress has created a patent system under which an inventor can receive a patent (i. e., a monopoly or exclusive right) to his or her invention for a limited period of time (17 years). A patent may be granted for "any new and useful art, machine, manufacture, or composition of matter, or any new and useful improvement thereof." A patent cannot be granted for an idea only.

To obtain a patent, the following procedure must be strictly complied with:

(1) The inventor must file a written application for a patent with the Commissioner of Patents in Washington, D.C.;

(2) The application must contain:

(a) A written description of the invention or discovery;

(b) A precise specification of the part, improvement, or change that the inventor claims to be new;

(c) The applicant's affidavit (sworn statement) that he or she believes the invention or discovery to be new and never before known or used; and

(d) A copy of a drawing of the discovery (where a drawing is possible), or sample if the invention is a composition of matter.

If the Patent Office agrees that the article is a new and useful invention or discovery, it will issue a patent giving the patentee an exclusive right to make, use, and sell the invention for 17 years. Anyone who infringes upon the patentee's right will be subject to court ordered injunction and damages.

Copyrights. Common law protection, sometimes called a "common law" copyright, exists for the unpublished work of a poet, composer, or author. So long as the work is not submitted to general circulation, the creator alone has exclusive rights to use and sale of the property, and can obtain an injunction as well as damages against anyone who infringes his or her rights. However, a general publication of the work destroys the common law protection; and, unless the creator obtains a statutory copyright as provided by federal law at the time the work is published, the creator will lose any and all claim to exclusivity. A general publication requires a large distribution or disclosure of the work sufficient to imply abandonment of the common law copyright: a limited publication or distribution will not terminate this right.

The owner or author of literary, dramatic, musical, artistic, and other intellectual works may obtain federal statutory copyright protection for the work at the time of general publication merely by publishing the work with a notice of copyright affixed thereto (the author's name should be followed by the word "copyright", its abbreviation, "copr.", or merely the symbol ©). The owner must affix the copyright notice to each copy published or offered for sale. Also, the owner must pay a small fee to the Copyright Office in Washington, D.C., and provide the Office with two complete copies of the work for the federal Library of Congress.

What the owner receives in return is the exclusive right to use, print, reprint, sell, copy, revise, transform, record, and perform the work publicly. The copyright law formerly provided a 28 year period of protection, subject to renewal for an additional 28 years. The law has now been amended to provide protection for the period of the author's life, plus an additional 50 years (effective Jan. 1, 1978 for works created on or after that date).

The new Statute also provides that even though the copyright owner has exclusive rights to use, sell, copy, etc. the copyrighted material, others are entitled to make "fair use" of the copyrighted work.

Section 107 of the statute states:

Notwithstanding the provisions of Section 106 [providing for exclusive rights], a copyrighted work, including such use by reproduction in copies of phonorecords or by any other means specified by that section, for purposes such as criticism, comment, news reporting, teaching (including multiple copies for classroom use), scholarship, or research, is not an infringement of copyright. In determining whether the use made of a work in any particular case is a fair use the factors to be considered shall include—

(1) the purpose and character of the use, including whether such use is

of a commercial nature or is for nonprofit educational purposes;

(2) the nature of the copyrighted work;

(3) the amount and substantiality of the portion used in relation to the copyrighted work as a whole; and

(4) the effect of the use upon the potential market for or value of the copyrighted work.

————

The new Statute also permits any library to make one copy of a copyrighted work without the copy constituting an infringement of the copyright.

What may be copyrighted?—books, directories, periodicals, newspapers, lectures, sermons, dramatic or musical compositions, maps, works of art, motion pictures, etc. The only requirement is that the item be original. It does not have to be useful or novel or have literary merit or artistic value.

Anyone who infringes the author's statutory copyright is subject to a civil injunction and damages (including the author's lost profits by reason of the infringement). Statutory damages for willful infringement may be as high as $50,000 even though the infringer makes no profit. While an exact reproduction obviously infringes the right, so does extensive paraphrasing and copying.

It is also a federal crime to willfully infringe upon a copyright for profit (1 year in jail, $10,000 fine or both).

Trademarks. The law also provides protection against unauthorized appropriation of a trademark or tradename. According to the federal Lanham Act of 1946, a "trademark" is "any work, name, symbol, or device or any combination thereof adopted and used by a manufacturer or merchant to identify his goods and distinguish them from those manu-

factured or sold by others." Tradenames, on the other hand, do not identify the goods themselves, but, rather, relate to the business or business goodwill.

A person may obtain an exclusive 20 year right to use a trademark or tradename by registering the mark or name with the Patent Office in Washington, D.C. If the right is infringed, the owner may obtain a court ordered injunction in addition to money damages (although damages will be permitted only where the owner's own use of the mark or name is accompanied by a statement that it is "registered in U.S. Patent Office").

Are there any other miscellaneous rules regarding the acquisition of rights in personal property?

Our study of acquiring rights in personal property would not be complete without a discussion of property rights in the following:

Letters. The recipient of a letter acquires by inter vivos gift from the sender all title or ownership rights in the paper, envelope, and stamp. If someone steals the letter or wrongfully destroys it, the owner has a legal right to sue for replevin and recover the letter, or to bring a legal action for money damages for conversion or trespass to chattels.

As to the sender's rights in the letter, you will recall from our previous discussion of common law copyright that it takes a general publication of a writing to destroy the existing common law protection. Delivery of the letter by the sender does not constitute a general publication, and the sender-writer retains all rights to the contents of the writing. Thus, in order to publish the letter or otherwise sell it commercially, the recipient-owner must obtain the sender-writer's consent.

Dead Bodies. Every individual possesses a property right in his or her own body encompassing the right to direct the place and manner of the body's burial. An individual is also free to donate all or any part of his or her body to an organ bank or for use in scientific or related research.

Surviving relatives of a dead person also have property rights in the de-

ceased's body to the extent that they may recover money damages for others' wrongful acts in handling the body (e. g., performing an unauthorized autopsy, mutilating the body, or interfering with the burial).

CASES

CASE 1—*While you are to be commended for your honesty, you do not get to keep the eight one-hundred-dollar bills.*

JACKSON v. STEINBERG

Supreme Court of Oregon, 1948.
186 Or. 129, 200 P.2d 376.

HAY, Justice.

The plaintiff in this case is Mrs. Laura I. Jackson. The defendant is Karl Steinberg, who is engaged in the hotel business in Portland under the assumed business name of Arthur Hotel. Mrs. Jackson was employed by defendant as a chambermaid in his hotel.

The facts of the controversy are not disputed. Plaintiff entered defendant's employ on October 13, 1946. In describing her duties, she testified: "Well, where a guest checks out we are supposed to change the linen and dust and clean up the room, leave clean towels, and arrange the furniture like it should be, and take out anything that doesn't belong in there. Q. What do you do with that you take out? A. If it is of any value we take it to the desk clerk; if it isn't of any value we put in it the garbage." On December 30, 1946, while cleaning one of the guest rooms, she found eight one-hundred-dollar bills, United States currency, concealed under the paper lining of a dresser drawer. The bills were stacked neatly, and her attention was drawn to them only by reason of their bulk having made a slight bulge in the lining. She removed the bills and delivered them immediately to the manager of the hotel, in order that they might be restored to the true owner, if he could be found, and subject to her claims as finder. * * *

The hotel, during the period in question, was much patronized by seamen, some of whom, after being paid off in the Port of Portland, brought considerable sums of money with them into the hotel, usually in bills of large denominations. Defendant made an unsuccessful effort to discover the owner of the bills, by communicating, or attempting to communicate, by mail, with each of the persons who had occupied this particular room from mid-October through December 31, 1946. Plaintiff then demanded of defendant that he return the money to her as finder, but he refused. She then, on July 10, 1947, filed this action in the District Court for Multnomah County, to recover the sum of $800 of defendant as money had and received. * * *

Plaintiff had judgment in the District Court. * * * Defendant appeals from an adverse judgment.

Defendant's theory * * * is that the bills constitute mislaid property, presumed to have been left in the room by a former guest of the hotel, and that, as innkeeper, he is entitled to custody of the bills and bound to hold them as bailee for the true owner. Plaintiff, on the other hand, claims the right to the possession of the bills as treasure trove, as against all persons but the true owner.

Lost property is defined as that with the possession of which the owner has involuntarily parted, through neglect, carelessness, or inadvertence. It is property which the owner has unwittingly suffered to pass out of his possession, and of the whereabouts of which he has no knowledge.

Mislaid property is that which the owner has voluntarily and intentionally laid down in a place where he can again resort to it, and then has forgotten where he laid it.

Abandoned property is that of which the owner has relinquished all right, title, claim, and possession, with the intention of not reclaiming it or resuming its ownership, possession or enjoyment.

"Treasure trove consists essentially of articles of gold and silver, intentionally hidden for safety in the earth or in some secret place, the owner being unknown."

From the manner in which the bills in the instant case were carefully concealed beneath the paper lining of the drawer, it must be presumed that the concealment was effected intentionally and deliberately. The bills, therefore, cannot be regarded as abandoned property.

With regard to plaintiff's contention that the bills constituted treasure trove, it has been held that the law of treasure trove has been merged with that of lost goods generally, at least so far as respects the rights of the finder. * * *

The natural assumption is that the person who concealed the bills in the case at bar was a guest of the hotel. Their considerable value, and the manner of their concealment, indicate that the person who concealed them did so for purposes of security, and with the intention of reclaiming them. They were, therefore, to be classified not as lost, but as misplaced or forgotten property, and the defendant, as occupier of the premises where they were found, had the right and duty to take them into his possession and to hold them as a gratuitous bailee for the true owner.

The decisive feature of the present case is the fact that plaintiff was an employee or servant of the owner or occupant of the premises, and that, in discovering the bills and turning them over to her employer, she was simply performing the duties of her employment. She was allowed to enter the guest room solely in order to do her work as chambermaid, and she was expressly instructed to take to the desk clerk any mislaid or forgotten property which she might discover. It is true that, in the United States, the courts have tended to accede to the claims of servants to the custody of articles found by them during the course of their employment, where the articles are, in a legal sense, lost property. In Hamaker v. Blanchard, 90 Pa. 377, 35 Am.Rep. 664, a servant in a hotel found a roll of bank notes in the public parlor. It was held that, as the money was found on the floor of a room common to all classes of persons, there was no presumption that it was the property of a guest, and that, when the true owner was not found, the plaintiff was entitled to recover it from the innkeeper, to whom she had delivered it. In the case at bar, however, the bills were not lost property.

* * *

In finding for plaintiff herein, the circuit court judge held that his decision should be governed by Danielson v. Roberts, supra, 44 Or. 108, 74 P. 913, 65 L.R.A. 526, 102 Am.St.Rep. 627, and Roberson v. Ellis, 58 Or. 219, 114 P. 100, 102, 35 L.R.A.,N.S., 979. The present case may be distinguished from those cases, however. In the Danielson case, the plaintiffs were employed merely to clean out an old chicken house, in the process of which work they found buried treasure. In the Roberson case, the plaintiff was employed merely to remove from a warehouse certain goods and rubbish, and, while doing so, found some concealed gold coins. The finding of the treasure was, in neither case, within the scope of the employment of the finders. As stated in the Roberson case: "The handling of the property of other people, not connected with the defendant [the owner of the premises], was not in the line of the plaintiff's employment, and would neither impose responsibility nor confer privilege upon the defendant." In the present case, on the contrary, the search for mislaid or forgotten property was expressly within the scope of plaintiff's employment, and the delivery thereof to her employer was a part of her admitted duty.

* * *

Where money is found in an inn on the floor of a room common to the public, there being no circumstances pointing to its loss by a guest, the finder, even if an employee of the innkeeper, is entitled to hold the money as bailee for the true owner. It would seem that, as to articles voluntarily concealed by a guest, the very act of concealment would indicate that such articles have not been placed "in the protection of the house" and so, while the articles remain concealed, the innkeeper ordinarily would not have the responsibility of a bailee therefor. Upon their discovery by the innkeeper or his servant, however, the inkeeper's responsibility and duty as bailee for the owner becomes fixed.

In Flax v. Monticello Realty Co., 185 Va. 474, 39 S.E.2d 308, a hotel chambermaid found a diamond brooch, wrapped in tissue paper, concealed in a crevice in the margin of the mattress of a bed in one of the guest rooms. Thinking that the brooch belonged to the then occupant of the room, the maid placed it upon the bureau. There the guest found it, and laid claim to it as finder. He did, however, deposit it with the hotel manager in order that inquiry might be made to discover the owner. As the owner was not discovered, the guest demanded return of the brooch, and, on being refused, he brought an action in detinue against the hotel proprietor. Held, that an innkeeper is in direct and continued control of his guest rooms, which are to be considered as private rooms; that the brooch was unquestionably to be classified as mislaid and forgotten property; and that the innkeeper occupied the position of bailee for the true owner of the chattel.

The plaintiff in the present case is to be commended for her honesty and fair dealing throughout the transaction. Under our view of the law, however, we have no alternative other than to reverse the judgment of the lower court. It will be reversed accordingly.

CASE 2—*"Mickey Mouse, Mickey Mouse, forever let us hold our banners high * * * M - I - C — K - E - Y — M - O - U - S - E."*

WALT DISNEY PRODUCTIONS v. MATURE PICTURES CORP.

United States District Court, S.D. New York, 1975.
389 F.Supp. 1397.

Kevin Thomas DUFFY, District Judge.

This is an action for a preliminary injunction brought by the plaintiffs as owners of the copyright of Mickey Mouse March and seeking to prevent the use of that music by the defendants in a movie entitled "The Life and Times of the Happy Hooker" and/or "The Life and Times of Xaviera".

The "Mickey Mouse March" was an original song written by Jimmie Dodd and used generally in connection with the Mickey Mouse Club television series. Having at the request of the parties viewed major segments of the taped Mickey Mouse Club, it is clear that these programs were made for an audience comprised mainly of youngsters. The Mickey Mouse March apparently was the theme song for this television series.

In the movie produced and distributed by the defendants, there is a portion where three male actors sing some of the words of the Mickey Mouse March and for a period thereafter of approximately four to five minutes, the Mickey Mouse March is played as background music, while the female protagonist of the film appears to simultaneously gratify the sexual drive of the three other actors while the group of them is located on or near a billiards table. * * * Supposedly, according to the story line of the film, the three male actors were teenagers "whose father had arranged for her (the female protagonist) to be present as a birthday surprise to them."

At the time the cast on the screen is quite bare except that the male actors are wearing "Mouseketeer" hats similar to those worn by the performers in the television productions of the "Mickey Mouse Club".

There can be no doubt that the music played as background in the defendants' film is the copyrighted "Mickey Mouse March". There is no doubt that the plaintiffs, as owners of the copyright, did not give defendants the right to use the song. There is no doubt that the defendants have used the copyrighted material for commercial gain.

The only real question presented is whether the use by defendants of the copyrighted material constitutes "fair use" as a parody.

Defendants claim the music is used to "highlight and emphasize the transition of such teenagers from childhood to manhood * * * in a highly comical setting", and as such is merely a "humorous take-off" on the music.

The exception of "fair use" as described in Rosemont Enterprises, Inc. v. Random House, Inc., 366 F.2d 303, 307 (2d Cir. 1966) lies

"* * * in the constitutional purpose in granting copyright protection in the first instance, to wit, 'To promote the Progress of Science and the Useful Arts.' U.S.Const. art. 1, § 8. To serve that purpose, 'courts in passing upon particular claims of infringement must occasionally subordinate the copyright holder's interest in a maximum financial return to the greater public interest in the development of art, science and industry.' Whether the privilege may justifiably be applied to particular materials turns initially on the nature of the materials, e. g., whether their distribution would serve the public interest in the free dissemination of information and whether their preparation requires some use of prior materials dealing with the same subject matter."

Parody of a copyrighted article is one of the possible situations where the doctrine of fair use will come into play.

The permissible parody of the copyright article is not a complete copy of the original. It can only be permitted "[W]here the parodist does not appropriate a greater amount of the original work than is necessary to 're-call or conjure up' the object of his satire *   *   *."

In the instant case, the use is far from the parody—there is a complete copy of the copyrighted material. The original song lasts for only two minutes, yet defendants used the work over and over again for substantially more time than is required to "conjure up the original". While defendants may have been seeking in their display of bestiality to parody life, they did not parody the Mickey Mouse March but sought only to improperly use the copyrighted material.

The defendants contend that no injunctive relief should be granted because there is no danger of irreparable damage being done through their use of the copyrighted material. In that contention they are totally wrong. Their use of the copyrighted material in the setting provided is such as to immediately compromise the work. Accordingly, a preliminary injunction will issue.

However, this Court recognizes that the issuance of this injunction could be used improperly to publicize either the "Mickey Mouse Club" or the "Life and Times of the Happy Hooker", and an order will enter providing that no such commercialization of this decision will be permitted under the penalty of contempt. Since the need for immediate relief is apparent, this Court will enter its own order simultaneously with the filing of this decision.

PROBLEMS

1. Jay Gerber publishes and copyrights an English literature text entitled, "The World of Thomas Hardy". The text is designed for college level courses, and Jay anticipates handsome royalties. Nellie Franklin, a literature professor at Digby State University, makes 10 copies of the first chapter of the text and distributes them to her students for classroom use. The University Library makes a single copy of the entire text. When student interest in the text grows, the campus bookstore makes 200 copies of the entire text and puts them on sale. What are Jay Gerber's rights, if any, against Nellie Franklin, the University Library, and the campus bookstore?

2. Read and answer the following:

   (a) Henry Dixon is the only passenger on a city bus. He finds an old black umbrella hooked over a seat (the owner intentionally left it there, no longer wanting the umbrella); a valuable ring lying on the floor; and a tote bag containing an expensive camera on the luggage rack above the seats. As between the bus company and Henry Dixon, who is entitled to the umbrella, the ring, and the tote bag? Explain.

(b) Henry works as a janitor at a local night club. While tidying up in the lounge, Henry finds a charm bracelet on the dance floor. As between the nightclub owner and Henry, who is entitled to the bracelet? Explain. *night club – employee*

(c) After work, Henry goes to dinner at his friend Sheila's house. While playing horseshoes in Sheila's backyard, Henry discovers an empty wallet buried under the surface of the soil. As between Sheila and Henry, who is entitled to the wallet? Explain. *Locus in quo – not treasure trove*

(d) On his way home, Henry trespasses over John Murphy's private property. Henry discovers a woman's handbag (containing no identification) under some bushes on the property. As between *P. 57* John and Henry, who is entitled to the handbag? Explain. *locus in quo, trespasser*

3. Jenny Walker works as a salesperson at "Price's Fabric Shop". One day, when Mrs. Price is gone from the shop, Jenny steals eight yards of fine cream colored silk worth $80 and sews it into a wedding dress worth $400. Jenny spends six weeks making the dress; she trims it in lace (of her own) and adds a new nylon zipper (also her own). When Mrs. Price discovers the theft, she sues to replevin the material in its "improved state". Decision? Would your answer differ if Jenny had "innocently" used Mrs. Price's material, believing it to be her own? Explain. *① Accession – Mrs. Price can generally replevin except where "goods" added greatly increases value >50%; damages up to $400 or time greatly increases value* *② sue for value of silk only.*

4. Tom Lovejoy fears that he is going to die when his doctor informs him that he must undergo coronary bypass surgery. Before going into the hospital, Tom conveys his beach lot to his nephew, Frank Lovejoy; Tom delivers the deed to Frank. Tom also gives his watch and ring to his cousin, Karen Kramer. Tom undergoes surgery and recovers completely. He tells Frank that he wants his land back, but Frank refuses. He tells Karen that he wants his watch and ring back, and she refuses.

(a) As between Tom and Frank, who is entitled to the beach lot? Explain. *irrevocable – inter vivos gift* *P. 65*

(b) As between Tom and Karen, who is entitled to the watch and the ring? Explain. *gift causa mortis* *P. 66*

(c) In the event that Karen has sold the watch and ring to a person who took the jewelry for value and in good faith, can Tom replevin the watch and ring? Explain. *no, bfp cuts off rights*

5. Answer the following "True" or "False" and give reasons for your answers:

T (a) The recipient of a letter cannot publish the contents of the letter without the sender's permission. *invasion of privacy*

F (b) The owner of the locus in quo generally prevails over the finder as to treasure trove found on private premises. *true owner won't return*

T (c) The owner of the locus in quo generally prevails over the finder as *P. 50* to lost property found on private premises.

F (d) A person has title to goods only if he or she has a written certificate of title covering the goods. *Title is a concept*

T (e) Legal possession demands more than physical control over property. *intent*

T (f) Legal possession of wild animals is basically synonymous with ownership of the animals.

6. Jake Howard intentionally intermingles his Grade A turkeys with those of Katie Crocker. Katie has no idea which turkeys are hers nor how

many are hers.① How will the law resolve this problem? ②Would your answer differ if Jake had *accidentally* intermingled the turkeys? Explain.②Would it differ if a third party had done the intermingling? Explain.② ①confusion - title passes to Katie ②no forfeiture unless can't distinguish ③no confusion - tenant in common

7. Tazor Corp. owns 25% of the common stock of the 625 Main Street Corporation, and the state where Tazor is incorporated has assessed its personal property tax against the fair value of the stock. The sole asset of 625 Main Street Corp. is an office building. The tax is

   a. Proper because common stock is always personal property.

   b. Improper because a building is real property, and the character of stock as personal or real depends on the dominant character of the assets owned by the corporation.

   c. Improper because stock is a fixture, and fixtures are personal property.

   d. Proper because a building is personal property, and the character of stock as personal or real depends on the dominant character of the assets owned by the corporation.

   [# 38, November 1973 CPA Exam]

8. You were requested by Charles to prepare a net worth statement for him as of December 31, 1967 which will be furnished to his bank. You must determine whether or not a truck having a fair market value of $20,000 should be included in Charles's net worth. Charles was in the trucking business as a sole proprietor during 1967. Filmore, Charles's uncle, looked upon Charles as his favorite nephew and wished to help Charles in business. Filmore decided to present Charles with a new truck which Charles needed but lacked the funds to purchase.

   Filmore invited Charles to lunch and told him about the intent to make a gift of the truck to him. In fact, he told Charles he had hoped to give him the truck right after lunch, but delivery was not to be made to Filmore until the following week. To evidence his intent Filmore wrote the following on a piece of paper:

   "I hereby acknowledge my intent to make a gift of a new truck to my favorite nephew, Charles. Therefore, for good and valuable consideration, consisting of my love and respect for him, I irrevocably promise to deliver said truck to Charles as soon as I receive it.

   Daniel Filmore."

   Filmore had two waiters sign the paper as witnesses and gave it to Charles.

   Filmore later learned that sometime before the luncheon Charles had been complaining to other relatives that "Uncle Filmore is a tightwad and a cheapskate." Consequently, Filmore refused to turn the new truck over to Charles.

   Charles asserts that a valid *inter vivos* gift was made at the luncheon, or, in the alternative, that his uncle was equally bound by the promise he made.

   Required: 1. What are the requirements necessary to establish a valid inter vivos gift? Donative intent Legal delivery proper acceptance

2. Did Filmore make a gift to Charles at the luncheon? Explain. *no — future*

3. Did Filmore make a legally binding contract with Charles for delivery of the truck? Explain. *no; only promise no consideration*

4. Assuming that the truck had actually been delivered to Filmore prior to the luncheon, that he turned the keys over to Charles at the luncheon and that Charles drove the truck back to his own place of business after the luncheon, would Charles be entitled to the truck? Explain. *yes*

[# 8.a., May 1968 CPA Exam]

9. Pierre, owner of Ritz Restaurant, Inc., had in his possession several valuable items which wealthy patrons had lost or left in the restaurant. The total value of these items was in excess of $5,000.

Ritz Restaurant's financial position was poor. Consequently, Pierre decided to pledge the items in question as collateral for a loan. He took the items to Friendly Finance Company and obtained a loan of $3,500 on the property pledged.

Required: As between the original owners of the property and Friendly Finance Company, who is entitled to the property? Explain. *Owners, bailment*

[# 8.b., May 1968 CPA Exam]

10. **Required:** Define the term "fungible goods."

[# 5.b., May 1968 CPA Exam]

goods same qual., value, any one unit is same as another — sold by weight & measure

Chapter 4

THE LAW OF THE LAND: REAL PROPERTY

Why is the study of history so important to understanding real estate law?

It is impossible to understand real property law (real estate law) without treating it from a historical view or perspective because many of the words and principles of this very complicated legal concept date back to feudal England nearly a thousand years ago. Real property words like "fee simple", "life estate", "remainder", and "escheat" originated with the early English kings who sought to control the vast English lands belonging to the reigning monarch since the time of the Norman Conquest in 1066.

At the time of the Norman Conquest, William the Conqueror claimed all the English lands for himself and subsequent rulers. Although William's subjects acquiesced to his claims of ownership, William encountered two major difficulties with respect to managing the land. First, he found it physically impossible to exercise direct control over the property, particularly in face of the primitive transportation and communication systems of the time. Second, he found it difficult to maintain standing armies large enough to protect the land from the constant threat of outside invasion. To solve both problems, William instituted a system of real property ownership and control known as "feudalism" or the "feudal system".

Under feudalism, there was no private ownership of real property—the King owned all the land. However, the King could and did reduce his direct responsibility for management, control, and protection of the property by granting rights

in the land to certain of his favored subjects who were made responsible for caring for the property. Because rights in land (including the right to transfer such rights) could be obtained only at the will of the King, the number and scope of any particular individual's rights in real property became the single most important indicator of that person's status in society. The most favored of the King's subjects received huge grants of land called "estates". The word "estate" comes from the Latin word "status" and correctly so, as the estate a person received fixed his social status in society. The highest and most impressive estate a person could receive from the King was a "fee" estate—an estate of potentially infinite duration. An estate qualified as a "fee" if the grantee or person receiving it could retain the property until death, at which time the property would pass to his or her heirs. Such an estate had the potential of lasting forever.

A person who received land directly from the King was called a "lord", with the King called the "lord paramount". The lord did not obtain rights in the land without acquiring obligations or duties as a condition of using the property and benefiting from it. This conditional service was referred to as "tenure", and there were four kinds: knight service, socage, frankalmoign, and serjeanty. A lord holding land under tenure of *knight service* was required to render military service to the King and to provide a certain number of knights for the King's army. Knight service supplied the King with an army large enough to defend the English lands and to keep order within the country. *Socage* tenure, on the other hand, required either the performance of agricultural services for the King (e. g., cultivating land) or the payment of money rent. Socage tenure forms the basis for our modern real estate taxes on homes, farms, and other real property. Where the grantee or recipient of the property was a Church, *frankalmoign* tenure applied to require the performance of religious services for the King. And, finally, tenure of *serjeanty* ("serjeanty" comes from the Latin "serientia", meaning service) involved the performance of personal services for the King, such as providing the King with beer when he journeyed into the area (County of Berkshire), or holding his head when he crossed the English Channel (County of Kent). Some serjeanty services were purely dignitary in nature (e. g., carrying the King's flag at a coronation); and such dignitary acts, traditionally performed at ceremonies of state and similar functions, are the sole surviving vestiges of serjeanty tenure.

A lord who received rights in land from the King was free, in turn, to grant the rights to others in exchange for his or her own military, agricultural, monetary, religious, or personal service. This process, called *subinfeudation*, was unrestricted, and each holder of rights in land could parcel out a part of the property to obtain service of tenure. However, the land itself was charged with the service created by any prior transfers; and if an individual charged with a prior service failed to perform, the overlord could justifiably proceed against the land and its current occupant to obtain satisfaction.

In addition to the primary duties of tenure (i. e., military, agricultural, monetary, religious, and personal service), the grantee of rights in land from the King or Overlord also became subject to what were termed "incidents" of tenure. These incidents or duties included "aids" (the duty to help pay for the expenses of marriage of the King's or

Overlord's oldest daughter and the knighting of his oldest son); "relief" (the duty of the grantee's heir or relative to pay a specified sum of money to the King or Overlord in order to take the grantee's place with respect to the property); and "escheat" (the duty to return the land to the King or Overlord upon the death of the grantee without heirs). The incident of "relief" is the forerunner of our modern inheritance tax. When a person dies today, his or her estate (now consisting of both real and personal property) is valued and taxed by both federal and state governments at rates running all the way to 70% for extremely large estates. And the incident of "escheat" is still very much a part of our law, as the property of a deceased person will "escheat" or return to the state if the deceased has no will and no spouse, children, brothers, sisters, parents, grandparents, or other relatives to inherit the property. (See Ch. 30).

After the passage of many hundreds of years of feudal tenure, the Crown found that it had no difficulty maintaining a suitable army without the assistance of knight service; and it found that it had no need for massive contributions of agricultural products through tenure of socage. Ultimately, all tenure was reduced to the socage payment of money rent, and the doctrine of tenure, as it developed in 1066, eventually disappeared (although it is interesting to note that even at the time of the colonization of America, William Penn was granted land in what is now Pennsylvania in socage tenure from the King of England who demanded that William pay him two beaver skins each year).

To what extent has the institution of feudalism affected real property law in the United States?

While the institution of feudalism has long since disappeared, the rules, standards, and principles regarding rights in land that grew out of the feudal system continue to have a marked effect on the ownership and use of land in the United States today. Perhaps the most significant outgrowth of feudalism is our legal system's recognition that there can exist many varied interests in one piece of land simultaneously, and that each interest can be held by a different person. One law professor used to illustrate this point by means of analogy to a person with a big bundle of sticks on his or her back. The bundle, in its entirety, represents all the rights possible in a single piece of land, and the holder of the bundle owns all the rights. However, he or she is free to take each stick and give it to a different person: for example, the holder may give one person the right to possess the land for a lifetime (a life estate); another, the interest remaining when the life tenant dies (a remainder); a third, the right to come onto the land periodically for some specific purpose (an easement); a fourth, the right to any crops harvested from the land (a profit); a fifth, the right to dig for coal (mineral rights); a sixth, the right to place a sign on the land (a license); a seventh, the right to rent the land for a year (a lease), etc.

Another remnant of feudalism, and one that is extremely difficult for most students to understand, is the legal concept of a "future interest" in land. A future interest is one that is presently owned, but possession of which is postponed to some future date. Since the owner presently owns the interest, he or she may sell or transfer it, and the interest may be very valuable. The only thing "future" about it is the right to possession: the purchaser or transferee must wait until the specified future time to take actual physical possession. For example, if a man simultaneously transfers land to his wife for her lifetime and, upon her death, to their son and daughter, the son and daughter will immediately own a future interest in the land that will become possessory only

upon the mother's death. Rather than wait until the death of the mother to take possession of the land, the children can immediately sell their interest to another. However, the purchase must also wait until the mother's death to take possession. The value of the future interest will necessarily depend upon when the interest is likely to become possessory. Obviously, the interest will be more valuable if the mother is 90 years old at the time of the sale since the interest will become possessory in a foreseeably short period of time.

Two other important carryovers from feudal times are the possessory fee simple estate (the maximum ownership a person can have in real estate, i. e., the whole bundle of sticks) and the possessory life estate (an estate limited to the life of some person). The creation of a life estate always involves the creation of a future interest that will become possessory at the end of the designated life. And the creation of a fee simple will involve the creation of a future interest if the fee simple is designed to terminate or end upon the happening of a specified event. Fee simples, life estates, and future interests are considered in detail in the sections that follow.

What are the characteristics of the fee simple estate—i. e., the maximum interest one can have in real estate?

As previously stated, real property law has been going through an evolutionary process for nearly a thousand years. Out of the very rigid number of interests in land that developed during the feudal period, two remain important—the fee simple estate and the life estate.

The *fee simple absolute* estate is the maximum or greatest interest that anyone can have in land or real property. Modernly, the fee simple absolute is a possessory estate that has the potential of lasting forever. The owner of the fee simple absolute has five distinct powers with respect to the land. The owner may: (1) use the land as he or she sees fit; (2) abuse or destroy the property; (3) exclusively possess the land; (4) take the fruits (e. g., crops, minerals) of the property; and (5) freely alienate (i. e., transfer) the land. The right to freely alienate property has always been considered a fundamental right of real property in the United States.

To say that the fee simple absolute estate has the potential of lasting forever means that the estate can be passed on indefinitely through generations of the owner's descendants or devisees. If the owner dies "intestate" (without a will) without having previously sold the real property, the state laws of intestacy will determine which relatives or heirs will receive the property (see Ch. 30). The heirs may be lineal heirs (direct up and down relatives, such as children, grandchildren, parents, and grandparents), or collateral heirs (indirect side-by-side relatives, such as brothers and sisters, uncles, aunts, cousins, etc.) A person who dies "testate" (with a will) can leave the property to his or her heirs or to any other designated person. It is only when a person dies without heirs and without a will specifying another person to take the property that the fee simple absolute will come to an end and "escheat" (i. e., pass) to the state. Theoretically, therefore, the fee simple absolute estate can last forever.

However, this was not always the case. In early feudal times, a person who was granted land by the Crown received but a life estate in the property, and upon the grantee's death, the land returned to the grantor King (in cases of subinfeudation, the land returned to the grantor overlord). Ultimately, the law developed to say that the grantee's heirs would be entitled to take possession of the property upon the grantee's death if it was so specified in the original grant. Thus, if the King or Lord granted land with the words "to my friend John Little", John would receive but a life estate, and, upon John's death, the land would return to the grantor. If, on the other hand, the King or Lord granted the land "to my friend John Little and his heirs", John would still receive a life estate, but his heirs would also (at least originally) receive a future interest in the property that would become possessory upon John's death. Still later, the words "and his heirs" were held not to vest any future interest in the heirs of the grantee, but, rather, merely to describe the nature or quantum of the estate passing to the grantee. In short, the words describe a fee simple estate (called an estate of general inheritance) passing to the grantee alone. As owner of the fee, the grantee (in this case, John Little) is free to pass the estate on to his or her heirs at death (in which case the heirs will inherit the property), but he or she is also free to completely dispose of the property during his or her lifetime (in which case, the grantee's heirs will have no claim whatsoever to the property).

It is important to realize that although the words "and his heirs" sound like they are describing actual people, they are, in reality, merely describing a fee simple interest belonging to the grantee alone. They are called *words of limitation* because they limit or define the interest the grantee receives. They create no interest in the grantee's heirs or relatives.

For many years, it was a common law requirement that the words "and his heirs" be used in order to convey a fee simple estate. Thus, a statement that "I give my land to John Little" would convey a mere life estate to John; a statement that "I give my land to John Little and his heirs" would convey a fee simple. The common law rule requiring use of these technical words of limitation or inheritance has been abolished by statute in nearly all our jurisdictions. And modernly, it is possible to convey a fee simple simply by stating that "I transfer my land to John Little" (by using these words, the grantor is held to transfer whatever interest he or she owns—if that interest is a fee simple, that is what the grantee will receive). Where the words "and his heirs" turn up in modern conveyances or transfers of land, they are still considered words of limitation. So if you transfer land to your son, using the language "to my son William and his heirs", your son will receive a fee simple estate, and your grandchildren will receive nothing.

This is not to say that you cannot create a future interest in your grandchildren or in others. You simply cannot do it by using the words of limitation "and his heirs". Words that will effectively create an immediate future interest in relatives or others are called *words of purchase*. Words of purchase indicate *who* will take the interest as opposed to words of limitation which indicate *what* interest is taken. While words of limitation create a fee simple estate, words of purchase give rise to a life estate with accompanying future interests. For example, to say "to my wife, Alice, and then to my son, William" is to give Alice a life estate, and William an immediate interest in the remainder that will become possessory when Alice dies. The words "and then to my son, William" are words of purchase identifying who will take the remainder estate. Similarly, to say "to my son William, and then to his children" is to create an immediate future interest in the children. "Children" is, again, a word of purchase denoting who will take the remainder estate.

What does the grantee receive when the grantor uses language "to John Little *for life,* and then to his heirs"? It was decided in 1581 in the case of Wolfe v. Shelley, 1 Coke Rep. 93b, 76 Eng.Rep. 206 (now popularly referred to as the "Rule in Shelley's Case"), that a specif-

ic grant of a life estate to a grantee, followed by a "remainder" or future interest to the grantee's "heirs" will be effective to convey the full fee simple interest to the grantee, and nothing to the heirs, despite the grantor's stated intent to the contrary. Again, the words "and his heirs" are words of limitation, not vesting any future interest in specific heirs or individuals, but merely describing the interest John receives—in this case, not only a life estate, but the ability to transfer the land during life or upon death.

The purpose of the Rule in Shelley's Case is to promote the free alienability of land by freeing it up for transfer a full generation earlier. But because the effect of the Rule is to disregard the grantor's stated intent, it has been abolished completely or in part in about ⅔rds of our states. Some states, like Oregon, recognize the Rule for lifetime transfers by deed, but abolish it for "testamentary" (deathtime) transfers by will.

Where the Rule in Shelley's Case does apply, it affects only those transfers that specifically grant a life estate interest to the grantee (e. g., "To John Little *for life,* and then to his heirs"). Where the Rule is abolished, John Little, in the example above, receives only a life estate, and his heirs, a future interest.

Are there any limitations on what the owner of a fee simple absolute estate in land can do with the property?

Even the owner of a fee simple absolute estate—the maximum interest possible in land—is substantially restricted in what he or she can do with the property by the following:

(1) *Eminent domain.* Eminent domain refers to the right of government to take private property for public use by means of a "condemnation" proceeding. The Fifth Amendment of the U.S. Constitution provides that property shall not

be taken for public use without payment of just compensation to the property owner. While property may not be taken for a private use, "public use" has been so broadly defined by the courts that it is now synonymous with "public benefit". Under this interpretation of the law, Congress may pass statutes such as the federal Urban Renewal Act which permits condemnation of large urban slum areas as a single entity, rather than proceeding on a structure-by-structure basis. As a result, even relatively new and sound buildings may be taken and condemned in urban renewal projects. Public use, however, is not so broad as to encompass taking property from one private owner and giving it to another for a private purpose, or condemning property in order to create new profit-producing property for the government (e. g., condemning private property in order to build an office building to be rented to raise revenue).

(2) *Police power*. "Police power" refers to government's inherent authority to do whatever is deemed necessary to protect public health, welfare, and morals. Under the police power, government acts to restrict fee simple landowners in the following ways:

Zoning. Governmental authority to pass zoning ordinances restricting the landowner in the uses he or she can make of property arises only after a state has passed an "enabling" act authorizing a town, city, or county to restrict the use of land through zoning. Zoning ordinances or laws must be reasonable or they will not be valid; and they must remain within the proper police power purposes of protecting health, welfare, and morals. The New Jersey statute, for example, states its purposes as: "To lessen congestion in the streets, secure safety from fire, flood, panic, and other dangers; promote health, morals, and the general welfare, provide adequate light and air, prevent the overcrowding of land and buildings;

and to avoid undue concentration of the population." In all cases, the first and foremost purpose of zoning laws is to promote wholesome housing. Landowners may thus be prohibited from constructing apartment houses or buildings for commercial or industrial use in areas of single-family housing. A second purpose of zoning laws is to promote commerce and industry. Within commercial districts, for example, there may be zoned areas for local grocery stores or convenience shopping only, or areas for light industry versus heavy industry. Other zoning laws permit cumulative uses of land within a designated area (e. g., apartment districts in which single family dwellings and multiple housing units may be constructed). And still others control overall structure density by prohibiting the construction of skyscrapers, restricting lot sizes, or permitting the construction of a single house on a particular area (say $\frac{1}{2}$ acre) of land.

Violation of criminal statutes. It is illegal to use property in a manner that violates criminal law (e. g., using the premises for gambling or prostitution or failing to observe statutes and ordinances dealing with noise control, litter, naturally growing things, stagnant water, etc.).

Environmental regulations and statutes. Every landowner must observe the increasingly strict federal and state regulations and statutes prohibiting contamination of the environment with air and water pollution and uncontrolled solid waste disposal.

(3) *Discrimination laws.* A landowner may not use or transfer his or her property so as to discriminate on grounds of race, color, religion, national origin, etc. As pointed out in Ch. 2, American citizens of every race and color have the same right to purchase, lease, sell, hold, and convey both real and personal property.

(4) *Tax laws.* The power to tax real estate is deemed an inherent right of all

state governments. If a real estate owner fails to pay his or her real property taxes, the owner's property may be sold and the taxes collected out of the proceeds.

(5) *Laws protecting owners of adjoining property.* A landowner may not use his or her real property so as to create a nuisance to adjoining landowners. As pointed out in Ch. 1, a nuisance is any unreasonable use of land that prevents another landowner from enjoying his or her property. It may be a nuisance, for example, to burn rubbish in the backyard, play loud music, or keep barking dogs on the property. If so, the nuisance may be enjoined (i. e., stopped) by court order, and the injured landowner may be awarded money damages. In many cases, the nuisance also constitutes a violation of criminal law enacted under the state's police power, and the "guilty" landowner may be subject to fine and/or imprisonment.

(6) *Creditors' rights.* A person who fails to pay his or her lawful debts may be sued in court, and a judgment (court order requiring the debtor to pay) may be rendered aginst the debtor. If the debtor refuses to pay the judgment, his or her property, including any real property held in fee simple absolute, may generally be sold to satisfy the debt. (However, as you will see in Ch. 26, dealing with creditors and bankruptcy, all states exempt or exclude from seizure and sale a portion of the debtor's property, including his or her equity or interest up to a certain amount in a homestead or residence owned in fee simple absolute.)

Are there fee simple estates that are not "absolute"?

A fee simple absolute is the maximum interest one can have in land and is subject only to the restrictions mentioned in the preceding section. A "qualified" fee, on the other hand, is an estate that confers upon its owner all the ordinary rights of a fee simple absolute (i. e.,

rights to use and abuse the land, exclusively possess it, take its fruits, and transfer it by deed or will), but is subject to completely ending or terminating upon the happening of a specified contingency. There are two kinds of qualified fee simple estates: determinable fee simples, and fee simples subject to a condition subsequent.

A *determinable fee simple* may generally be recognized by the grantor's use of the words "so long as" or "until" in the conveyance or transfer to the grantee. For example, say a person conveys a piece of real property as follows: "To John Little and his heirs *so long as* the land is used for farming purposes". The grantee, John, receives a fee simple estate because the interest in real property has the potential of lasting forever. Yet, the fee is qualified because it may come to an end before John Little's death intestate and without heirs by the happening of the specified event—the use of the land for other than farming purposes. If John Little stops using the land for farming purposes or transfers it to another who fails to farm the property, the land will automatically revert (that is, return or go back) to the grantor. Thus, John Little and his transferee do not possess the entire bundle of sticks even while the land is used for farming purposes: one stick, called the *possibility of reverter,* is lacking. The possibility of reverter refers to the grantor's right of automatic return or revesting of his or her property upon the happening of the specified event or contingency. The grantor need take no action to reclaim the property—it automatically returns to his or her estate. In nearly all states, a possibility of reverter is alienable (transferable) by the grantor inter vivos (during life) and transmissible at death by will or intestacy.

Like the determinable fee simple, the *fee simple subject to a condition subsequent* conveys all the ordinary rights of a fee simple absolute to the grantee, but may end or terminate completely upon the happening of a specified condition or event. Unlike the determinable fee, which is generally signaled by use of the words "so long as" and "until", the fee simple subject to a condition subsequent is usually introduced by the words "on condition that", "but if", "on the express condition that", or "provided that". For example, if a grantor deeds land to "John Little and his heirs, *but if* wine, beer, or other intoxicating beverages are ever sold on the premises, then the grantor has the right to re-enter and repossess the land", John Little possesses a fee simple estate in the property subject to a condition subsequent (i. e., the estate is subject to termination upon occurrence of the condition—the sale of intoxicating beverages). Again, in contrast to the determinable fee simple, the fee subject to a condition subsequent does not end automatically upon the happening of the condition, but requires some affirmative action on the part of the original grantor to reclaim the property. The grantor must either come onto the property and repossess it, or obtain a court order terminating the fee estate. If the grantor does nothing, the estate will continue even though the condition has occurred. The grantor's right, in this case, is not a possibility of reverter, but a *right of re-entry for condition broken,* sometimes called a *power of termination.* Under modern law, the right of re-entry is both alienable during life and transferable at death.

Qualified fee simple estates, whether they are determinable fees or fees subject to a condition subsequent, may be created subject to almost any kind of event or condition with one major exception: the grantor may not, by use of a qualified fee simple, restrain or prohibit the grantee from freely alienating (transferring) his or her land. Thus, a grantor may not convey land "to John Little and his heirs, but upon the express condition that John Little shall not be able to dispose of or

alienate this land for a period of five years from the date of this conveyance". Though couched in the language of fee simple subject to a condition subsequent, the provision is nothing more than a *disabling restraint* on alienation and is void. John Little takes a fee simple absolute.

Disabling restraints on alienation are prohibited by law because the right to freely alienate or transfer property is part and parcel of fee simple ownership. As one of the five powers characteristic of the fee simple estate, the right of free alienation was fiercely fought for and not easily won in face of prohibitions on transfer dating back to early feudal England. The victory that took so long in coming cannot now be undermined by grantors who seek to restrict the transfer of property conveyed in fee simple, whether the restriction is for a year, a day, or even a minute.

Suppose the government exercises its power of eminent domain and condemns land subject to either a possibility of reverter or a right of re-entry for condition broken. Because the interest owned is so uncertain, the holder of the right will generally not be entitled to share in the compensation award paid by the government to the owner of the property (although an exception may be made where the condition or terminating event seems substantially certain to occur within a short period of time).

What is a life estate?

The second possessory estate of continued importance is the *life estate,* an estate limited in duration to the lifetime or combined lifetimes of one or more designated individuals. Generally, the measuring life is that of the grantee. For example, a conveyance "to John Little for life" gives John Little a freely transferable interest in the property for as long as he lives; upon his death, the land will revert to the grantor. The grantor who conveys a life estate thus retains a very important "stick", called a "reversion", out of the entire bundle of rights possible in land. The "reversion" is a future interest that will become possessory only upon the death of the measuring life, in this case, John Little. Because the grantor presently holds the future interest, he or she is free to dispose of it during life or at death by will or intestacy. Once the measuring life comes to an end and the future interest becomes possessory, the grantor (or his or her heir or transferee) will receive possession of the land in fee simple absolute.

Where the life estate is measured by the life of someone other than the grantee, the estate is called a life estate "pur autre vie" (a French phrase, meaning "for the life of another"). Say that a grantor conveys land "to John Little for the life of Shirley Short". By the terms of the conveyance, John Little receives a life estate "pur autre vie" (i. e., for the life of Shirley) that will terminate upon the death of Shirley Short, the measuring life. As long as Shirley lives, John Little is free to use the property or transfer the interest; and if John dies before Shirley, the interest will pass on to John's heirs by will or intestacy.

Like a fee simple, a life estate can be made determinable or subject to a condition subsequent. And like a fee simple, it can be freely transferred, leased, or otherwise alienated. The transferee or lessee will, of course, receive a life estate "pur autre vie" unless he or she happens to be the measuring life by the terms of the original conveyance (e. g., where John Little, in the previous example, transfers or sells his interest in the property to Shirley Short, the measuring life of his life estate "pur autre vie"). In that case, the transferee or lessee will own a life estate for his or her own life.

Life estates are very popular estates modernly; they are created not only by deed or other inter vivos transfer but also

by will. One spouse, for example, may write a will leaving a surviving spouse a life estate in property, with a remainder interest (a presently owned future interest that will become possessory upon the death of the surviving spouse) in fee simple to the children.

Life estates may also be created by operation of law, in which event they are referred to as "legal" life estates (as opposed to the "conventional" life estates created by inter vivos transfer or transfer by will). At common law, for example, a surviving spouse automatically received upon the death of his or her spouse a legal life estate in lands owned by the decedent spouse. A surviving wife received a life estate, called "dower", in one-third of each parcel of real estate owned by her husband in fee simple during the marriage. The husband could not defeat the interest by selling or transferring the property prior to his death; under the law, the wife was still entitled to her dower interest in any property conveyed without her consent. A surviving husband, on the other hand, received a life estate, called "curtesy", not in one-third of the deceased wife's real property, but in all the real property owned by the wife during the marriage. The surviving husband was entitled to curtesy only if "issue" (children) capable of inheriting the mother's real property had been born alive to the couple. However, it was not necessary that the issue survive the mother in order for the husband to claim the curtesy interest.

Modernly, common law dower and curtesy have been abolished in nearly all of our states by statutes equalizing the rights of surviving husbands and wives. Generally, the surviving spouse, whether it is the husband or the wife, is entitled to a specific fraction or "forced share" of the deceased spouse's real and personal property. The forced share usually ranges from one-third to one-half of the property (some states utilize a sliding scale fraction that decreases as the deceased spouse's estate increases, thus giving the surviving spouse a smaller fraction of very large estates). The surviving spouse receives, not a life estate in the property, but a complete ownership interest—that is, all the "sticks".

Again, in contrast to the common law, the deceased spouse is free during his or her lifetime to transfer property held in his or her name free and clear of any interest the surviving spouse may have by virtue of the statutory forced share. Of course, if the decedent spouse holds the property in some form of concurrent ownership with the surviving spouse (e. g., as community property, or as joint tenants with the right of survivorship or as tenants in common), the surviving spouse will have a pre-existing interest in the property that cannot be defeated by an unconsented to inter vivos transfer of the decedent spouse. (Concurrent ownership is considered in Ch. 5.)

When does the statutory forced share become important? Obviously, the surviving spouse will have no interest in claiming a statutory forced share where the decedent spouse's will leaves all or a major part of the estate to the surviving spouse. But where the decedent spouse provides by will that the surviving spouse is to receive little or no property, the surviving spouse will be entitled to claim his or her full statutory forced share. Where the decedent spouse leaves no will, the surviving spouse will usually obtain a larger fraction of the estate as state intestacy laws are generally more generous to the surviving spouse than are the statutory forced share provisions for election against the will. (Wills and intestacy laws are considered in detail in Ch. 30.)

What are the rights and duties of a life tenant (the holder of a life estate)?

A life tenant has the following rights and duties:

(1) *The right to use and enjoy the land.* The life tenant is free to use and enjoy the land (including all income produced from the property) in any manner that does not exploit or injure the future interest that will become possessory upon the death of the measuring life. The right to use and enjoy the land includes the right to harvest any crops grown on the property; and, even where a life tenant whose life is also the measuring life dies, thus terminating the life estate, the life tenant's heirs or beneficiaries will have a legal right to come onto the property and harvest any crops or other "fructus industriales" growing at the time of the life tenant's death. However, the right to use and enjoy the land does not include the right to use or exploit natural resources such as timber, minerals, and oil unless the use of the materials is necessary for repair and maintenance of the property. The use of natural resources for repair and maintenance is called *estovers.*

In the rare instance where the life tenant discovers that the land is totally unproductive, and cannot generate income from the property by means of rentals or other use, the courts will generally authorize sale of the property with the proceeds placed in trust for the benefit of the life tenant. For the duration of his or her life, the life tenant will be entitled to the trust income only (not the actual sales proceeds placed in trust). And upon the life tenant's death, the trust will be dissolved, and the proceeds handed over to the future interest holder. (Trusts are considered in detail in Ch. 29.)

(2) *The duty not to commit waste.* The life tenant who exploits or injures the land to the detriment of the future interest holder is said to commit legal *waste.* There are three kinds of waste, and, in each case, the injured future interest holder is entitled to a court order or injunction restraining the life tenant

from further waste of the property. The future interest holder may also be entitled to money damages.

(a) *Affirmative waste* refers to the life tenant's actual destruction of part of the land (e. g., demolishing a building on the property, cutting down trees, exploiting the minerals). Of course, the life tenant will have a legal right to cut down trees and mine minerals if the right is specifically granted by the terms of the original conveyance.

(b) *Permissive waste* occurs where the life tenant allows the land to fall into disrepair, or fails to take reasonable precautions against the harmful effects of nature (e. g., failing to protect the land from erosion). A failure to pay real property taxes which results in the sale of the property by taxing authorities is considered permissive waste; but a failure to provide adequate property insurance, such as fire, earthquake, and wind insurance, is generally not.

(c) *Ameliorating waste* refers to a material change in use of the land, even where the value of the land increases as a result. For example, turning a small dairy farm into a junk yard is ameliorating waste; but so, too, is turning the farm into a private golf course. However, most states now prohibit the future interest holder from suing for ameliorating waste where the change in use of the property is reasonable in light of the surrounding geographical area, and the value of the land after the change is substantially the same or higher.

Thus, it is not ameliorating waste to convert a small dairy farm into a successful commercial office building in a geographical area that has grown increasingly industrial with the passage of time.

(3) *The duty to repair the land.* The life tenant has a duty to use any income or profits from the land to make needed repairs of the property; and, if there are no income or profits, he or she must re-pair to the extent of the land's reasonable rental value. A failure to repair constitutes permissive waste. However, the life tenant is not required to make permanent improvements (such as adding buildings) to the property, although if he or she does so, the improvements become permanent fixtures belonging to the future interest holder at the end of the measuring life. Nor is the life tenant required to insure the property against fire, earthquake, or wind damage.

(4) *The duty to pay all ordinary real estate taxes on the property.* The life tenant has a duty to pay all ordinary real estate taxes on the property, again, to the extent of income or profits from the property or reasonable rental value of the land. Ordinary taxes do not include taxes or assessments for permanent improvements that are likely to outlast the life estate interest and benefit the future interest holder (e. g., a sewer, road, or sidewalk). Assessments for such permanent improvements must be fairly apportioned between the life tenant and the future interest holder on the basis of the life tenant's realistic life expectancy.

(5) *The duty to pay interest on mortgaged property.* If the land is mortgaged, the life tenant has a duty to pay interest on the mortgage to the extent of income and profits or reasonable rental value. The future interest holder must pay the mortgage principal.

(6) *The right to bring legal action for tortious interference with the property.* The life tenant has a right to sue in court for an injunction against any person who tortiously acts to injure the property (e. g., by trespass or nuisance). Additionally, the life tenant may bring a legal action for money damages to compensate him or her for loss to the property. To the extent that the monetary recovery reflects compensation for damage to the future interest, the recovery must be held in trust for the future interest holder.

What kinds of future interests are there?

You will recall from our earlier discussion that a future interest in land is a presently owned interest in property that will not become possessory until a future date or time. Because the interest is presently owned, it may be presently sold or otherwise transferred and it may even create present duties (e. g., the future interest holder's duty to contribute to the cost of permanent improvements assessed by state or local governments). In short, the only thing "future" about a future interest is possession of the property.

We have already described two kinds of future interests: the possibility of reverter retained by the grantor in conveyance of a fee simple determinable, and the right of re-entry for condition broken (also called a power of termination) retained by the grantor in conveyance of a fee simple subject to a condition subsequent. The possibility of reverter automatically revests possession of the fee in the grantor upon occurrence of the specified event or contingency, while the right of re-entry revests possession in the grantor at the time the condition occurs only if the grantor takes some affirmative action to reclaim the property.

Besides the possibility of reverter and the right of re-entry for condition broken, there are four other future interests important to our study: (1) reversions; (2) vested remainders; (3) contingent remainders; and (4) executory interests.

(1) *Reversions.* A reversion is the interest retained by a grantor who conveys away less than he or she owns. A reversion is a future interest because it becomes possessory only after the lesser estate has come to an end. For example, if the owner of a fee simple absolute conveys the property "to John Little for life", the owner has retained a reversion in fee simple that will become possessory (i. e., return to the grantor) only upon John Little's death.

(2) *Vested Remainders.* Like a reversion, a remainder is a future interest that becomes possessory after the expiration or termination of a lesser estate created by the same conveyance. Unlike a reversion, a remainder does not revert to the grantor, but *remains away* from the grantor and passes to another party or parties as specified in the original land grant. For example, if a grantor conveys land "to John Little for life, and then to Shirley Short and her heirs", John Little receives a life estate, Shirley Short receives a remainder in fee simple absolute that will become possessory upon John Little's death, and the grantor retains no reversion interest whatsoever. (Nor do Shirley Short's heirs receive an interest in the land by the terms of the conveyance as the words "and her heirs" are merely words of limitation describing and defining Shirley's remainder interest in fee simple absolute.)

A remainder, by definition, requires three things: first, the interest must be expressly created by the terms of the conveyance; second, the remainder must be preceded (i. e., legally "supported") by a possessory estate that is less than a fee simple (usually a life estate, but sometimes an estate for years as defined in Ch. 2); and, third, the remainder and preceding life estate must be created simultaneously by the same conveyance. Thus, a conveyance "to John Little and his heirs if John Little marries my daughter Shirley Short" does not create a remainder in John Little because there is no prior possessory estate created by the terms of the conveyance to support a remainder (the interest John receives is an "executory" interest to be defined shortly). If, on the other hand, the conveyance is "to John Little for life, and then to John Little's son, Tom, if Tom marries my daughter Shirley Short", Tom's future interest is properly termed a remainder because it is preceded by a possessory estate (John Little's life estate) created by the terms of the same conveyance.

A *vested remainder* is an unconditional remainder granted to an ascertained person or persons (ascertained means known, or alive and in being at the time of the conveyance). Because the grantee is identifiable, and because the remainder is not subject to any condition precedent (i. e., there is no event or contingency other than the termination of the prior possessory estate that must take place before the grantee will have an unconditional right to possession of the property), the remainder will become possessory whenever and however the preceding possessory estate ends. For example, a grant of land "to John Little for life, then to Shirley Short and her heirs" creates a vested remainder in fee simple absolute in Shirley Short because the interest is absolutely certain to become possessory upon the death of John Little: the remainder is to a named person, Shirley Short, and there are no conditions precedent to its becoming possessory other than the termination of John Little's life estate.

Though a vested remainder is unconditional, it may be subject to partial or complete "divestment" (i. e., subject to being reduced or take away). For example, if a grantor conveys land "to John Little for life, then to his children", the conveyance creates a vested remainder interest in fee simple absolute in any of John's children who are living at the time of the conveyance. However, any vested remainder created is subject to partial divestment (or subject to "open" as it is sometimes stated) since any new child born to John Little will have a vested right upon his or her birth to share equally in the property interest, thus ratably reducing every other child's share. The children will ultimately own the property in fee simple absolute as tenants in common (tenancy in common being a form of concurrent ownership).

Now suppose that a grantor conveys land "to John Little for life, then to Shirley Short for life". John Little obviously receives a possessory life estate by the terms of the conveyance, and Shirley Short receives a vested remainder that will become possessory as a life estate upon John Little's death. However, Shirley's vested remainder is subject to complete divestment in the event that Shirley dies before John Little dies: termination of the measuring life of the remainder life estate completely divests Shirley (as well as her lawful intestate heirs or beneficiaries under a will) of any vested remainder interest.

(3) *Contingent Remainders.* In contrast to a vested remainder, a *contingent remainder* is a remainder either granted to one or more unascertained individuals or created subject to a condition precedent (again, a condition or event other than the termination of the prior possessory estate that must take place before the grantee will be entitled to possession of the property). Let's return to the example of a grantor conveying land "to John Little for life, then to his children." If John Little has no children living at the time of the conveyance, the grantees are unascertained and the remainder is contingent—it cannot become possessory, even at the time of John's death, unless children have been born. Up until the birth of John Little's first child, the grantor retains a reversion interest entitling him or her to return of the property in the event that children are never born to John Little.

Similarly, if a grantor conveys land "to John Little for life, then to his son, Tom, if Tom marries Shirley Short", Tom owns a contingent remainder that will not vest until and unless the condition precedent—Tom's marriage to Shirley Short—takes place. If the condition has not occurred by the time of John Little's death, the land will revert to the grantor until such time as Tom and Shirley do get married.

Suppose grantor Robert Small conveys land "to John Little for life and then to the heirs of Robert Small". Under the rules we have studied, it would be logical to conclude that grantor Small intended to create a life estate in John Little and a contingent remainder in his own heirs (the remainder would be contingent because there is a condition precedent—Robert Small's death—that must occur before Small's heirs can be ascertained and identified so as to take the property interest). However, the common law rule, called the *Doctrine of Worthier Title,* held that such a conveyance created, not a remainder in the grantor's heirs, but a reversion in the grantor. The grantor's heirs received nothing by the terms of the conveyance. The Doctrine of Worthier Title reflected the common law viewpoint that it is "worthier" to take land through inheritance than by grant or conveyance. The rationale behind the rule was that it prevented landowners from circumventing payment of inheritance tax on their property by conveying land inter vivos to their heirs by means of a present remainder interest (you will recall that the inheritance tax grew out of the feudal incident of tenure called "relief" which demanded payment of money by any heir desiring to succeed to his or her ancestor's real property). By deeming it "worthier" to take property by inheritance, and by arbitrarily holding that any attempted remainder to the grantor's heirs would always result in a reversion to the grantor and nothing to the heirs, the common law ensured the payment of inheritance tax and promoted the free alienability of land. Applying the rule to the example above, Robert Small and John Little can join together to transfer or sell a complete fee simple interest; if the rule does not apply, the fee simple cannot be sold or transferred until Robert Small dies and his heirs are identified.

While the Doctrine of Worthier Title is still good law in most states today, it is no longer arbitrarily applied, but is considered a rebuttable presumption that can be overcome by the introduction of evidence showing that the grantor really intended to create a contingent remainder in his or her heirs, thus justifying a possible restriction on free alienability of the land. Where the doctrine is found to apply, the grantor retains a reversion interest, and can dispose of the reversion (and ultimately the property itself) without regard to his or her heirs. Of course, in such case, the grantor's reversion is subject to the claims of his or her lawful creditors, but creditors of the grantor's heirs have no rightful claim to the property since the heirs have nothing to reach.

(4) *Executory Interests.* An *executory interest* is any presently owned future interest that does not qualify as a *reversion* (an interest retained by the grantor), a *remainder* (an interest created by express grant in someone other than the grantor and legally supported by a preceding possessory estate created by the same conveyance), a *possibility of reverter* (the interest retained by the grantor of a fee simple determinable), or a *right of re-entry for condition broken* (the interest retained by the grantor of a fee simple subject to a condition subsequent). For example, a conveyance "to Amos Big for life, and then to John Little and his heirs if John Little marries my daughter Shirley Short" creates a contingent remainder in John Little (contingent on John's marriage to Shirley Short) and a life estate in Amos Big to legally support the remainder. But a conveyance "to John Little and his heirs if John Little marries my daughter Shirley Short" does not create a remainder in John Little, vested or contingent, because there is no preceding possessory estate created by the terms of the conveyance. John Little's interest is an executory interest that will *spring* into existence at such time as John marries Shirley Short. As an executory interest, it is not dependent on the existence of a prior possessory estate.

Executory interests may follow any kind of estate, freehold or nonfreehold, including a fee simple. Where the executory interest follows a fee, the fee is said to be a fee simple subject to an executory limitation. For example, without regard to the Rule Against Perpetuities (considered below), a grant of land "to John Little and his heirs so long as the land is used for farming purposes, and if the land is not used for farming purposes, to Shirley Short and her heirs" creates a fee simple interest in John Little that will *shift* over to Shirley Short if and when the land is used for other than farming purposes. The fee subject to executory limitation is similar to a fee simple determinable in that it will automatically come to an end upon occurrence of the stated event; it differs from a determinable fee in that the property will shift over to a third party rather than revert to the grantor.

Executory interests, of which there are several kinds, were not recognized by law until the Sixteenth Century. While, at common law, neither executory interests nor contingent remainders could be transferred inter vivos or at death by will or intestacy, nearly all states modernly permit free transferability of such interests. Valuation of the interests often poses a difficult problem because of the conditional nature of the interests; in most cases, their value is quite small. Finally, the general rule is that executory interests and contingent remainders are subject to the lawful claims of creditors.

What is the rule against perpetuities?

You will recall from our earlier discussion of qualified fees—the fee simple determinable and the fee simple subject to a condition subsequent—that one condition our legal system will not tolerate is a disabling restraint on alienation of land. What this means is that a grantor who transfers property in fee simple cannot restrict the transferee from transferring or conveying the land to others. To permit the grantor to do so would be to undermine one of the chief characteristics of fee simple ownership—the right of free alienability—a right long fought for and not easily achieved in face of the many feudal restrictions on the transfer of land. Accordingly, any attempt by a grantor to restrain alienation is void, and the grantee or transferee is free to transfer the property despite any prohibition on transfer contained in the original conveyance.

Once it was clearly established that landowners could not use qualified fees to restrain the free alienation of land, the landowners began to resort to a variety of legal devices in an effort to tie up the transferred property for long periods of time and keep the property within the same family. Of course, there was no problem keeping the property within the landowner's family for successive generations so long as all family members voluntarily refrained from transferring the property and permitted it to pass by inheritance only to family members. In this way, the property would remain in the family forever, subject only to the rights of government and the claims of creditors. But where the family was uncooperative, or the landowner wanted to restrict an unrelated transferee in his or her ability to further transfer the land, the landowner had to find some means of doing so other than with a qualified fee.

One means employed successfully for many years was the use of successive life estates followed by a final future interest (either a remainder or executory interest). For example, a grantor might convey land "to John Little for life, then to the children of John Little for life, then to the grandchildren of John Little for life, then to the great grandchildren of John Little for life, then to the great great grandchildren of John Little for life, then to the great great great grandchildren of John Little and their heirs."

If the conveyance is given effect, it will not be until John Little's great great great grandchildren are left surviving that the land will finally vest in fee simple as a freely alienable estate. All preceding generations will have but a life estate with no ability to transfer the free simple.

In 1880, in order to prevent landowners from accomplishing with successive life estates and other terms of conveyance what they were already prohibited from doing with qualified fees—that is, restrain the free alienation of land—the courts developed a rule, called the Rule Against Perpetuities, which states as follows: *No interest is good unless it must vest, if at all, not later than 21 years after some life in being at the creation of the interest.* Thus, the Rule Against Perpetuities states that a contingent or conditional interest in land, whether created by inter vivos or deathtime transfer, will be valid only if the interest must vest within "lives in being plus 21 years" (a few states have done away with the concept of measuring lives, substituting by statute a fixed period of time for vesting without regard to lives in being, e. g., 60 years in California). Remember, an interest in land "vests" when it gives an ascertained grantee the unconditional right to possession of the fee simple, life estate, etc. upon the expiration of all prior estates in the land. If there is any possibility, however remote, that an interest will fail to vest within lives in being and 21 years, the interest violates the Rule Against Perpetuities and is void. However, the fact that one interest conveyed in a grant of land is void under the Rule does not mean that all other interests conveyed are void as well: each interest conveyed stands alone and will be upheld if it is not in violation.

How does the Rule Against Perpetuities promote the free alienability of land? By voiding any conditional interest that is not certain to vest within lives in being

and 21 years, the Rule facilitates early transfer of the land without numerous speculative, contingent interests to act as a cloud on title of the property (a "cloud on title" is any outstanding interest that makes the land difficult to value or sell). In the example of successive life estates given above, if John Little has no children at the time of the conveyance, the contingent life estate remainder to John Little's children will still be good because the interest must vest in the children, if at all, within John Little's lifetime and 21 years (all John Little's children will be born or conceived at the time of John's death, John being a measuring life). But if John has no children or grandchildren at the time of the conveyance, the contingent remainder to John Little's grandchildren will not be valid because there is a possibility that the interest will vest in the grandchildren after lives in being plus 21 years (e. g., five years after the conveyance, John Little has a child, then John Little dies, and then twenty-five years later, John Little's child has a son in whom the remainder vests). And the contingent remainders to successive great grandchildren of John Little will not be valid because there is every likelihood that the interests will vest long after the specified time has elapsed. Thus, upon the death of John Little's children, the land will revert to the grantor or his heirs and will be transferable in fee simple absolute: the grantor's attempt to tie up the land for many generations has failed.

As stated, the Rule Against Perpetuities applies only to contingent or conditional interests, i. e., contingent remainders and executory interests. The Rule does not apply to other future interests, including reversions, possibilities of reverter, rights of re-entry for condition broken, and vested remainders. Vested remainders are, by definition, already vested, and reversions and other interests retained by the grantor are considered vested for purposes of the Rule. Again, if there is any possibility that a contingent remainder or executory interest will not vest within 21 years after the death of the last measuring life in being at the time of creation of the interest, the interest will be void from the outset. The law will not wait and see whether such an interest does in fact vest within the specified time. (A small minority of states do "wait and see" whether the interest does in fact vest within the given time, and, if it does, uphold it.)

In determining whether a particular interest will vest within the specified time, time is computed from the effective date of the conveyance (delivery of the deed in the case of an inter vivos transfer and the date of the testator's death in the case of a deathtime transfer).

As to who is the measuring life, generally any number of lives may be stated to be the measuring lives in being so long as there are no serious problems of identification. (A complete stranger may be named as a measuring life if sufficiently identified, but in almost all cases, the measuring life will be a family member or members, or some other person closely associated with the conveyance of land.) Let's take an example. Suppose a person states in a will that "my land shall vest in fee simple in my oldest grandchild 21 years after the death of my last child". At the time the testator (a person who leaves a will) writes the will, he or she may have no children or grandchildren to serve as measuring lives; but, remember, the will is effective only upon the testator's death, and it is at that time that the measuring lives in being will be determined for purposes of the Rule Against Perpetuities. And at the time the testator dies, all his or her children will either be born or in gestation (for purposes of the Rule, "lives in being" include periods of gestation, thus extending the vesting period 21 years and nine months beyond the measuring lives in being in

the case of an unborn child), and all will serve as measuring lives in being. The latest the fee simple will vest and become transferable as a fee will be 21 years (and possibly nine months) from the death of the decedent's last surviving child. Since all the decedent's children are lives in being at the effective date of the will, the Rule Against Perpetuities is not violated.

But an inter vivos or deathtime transfer "to John Little so long as the property is used for farming purposes, and then to Shirley Short and her heirs" does violate the Rule as to Shirley Short. Although it is intended that John Little receive a valid fee subject to an executory limitation, there is simply no way of telling when, if ever, he will stop using the land for farming purposes. Thus, it is possible that Shirley Short's springing executory interest will not vest (become a fee simple that she or her descendants can transfer) within lives in being and 21 years (e. g., if John's heirs stopped farming the property seven generations later, the interest would only then vest in Shirley's estate and go to her heirs—long after the lives in being and 21 years provided for in the Rule Against Perpetuities had passed). Accordingly, Shirley Short's interest in the land is void. John Little has a determinable fee, and the grantor retains a possibility of reverter that will automatically return the property to his or her estate if the land is ever used for other than farming purposes. (Again, a very few states would "wait and see" whether Shirley's interest did in fact vest within the specified time, and, if so, uphold it.)

The application of the Rule Against Perpetuities produces some interesting results. Consider the following example: Linda Gross writes a will leaving land "to John Little for life, remainder to the children of John Little who reach the age of 25 years". If John Little is alive when Linda Gross dies (i. e., when the will takes effect), the contingent remainder interest to his children will not be valid. This is because John Little might have a child many years after the effective date of the will, and then himself die and be dead (along with any other measuring lives) for more than 21 years before his child reaches the age of 25 and qualifies to take the fee. Because this possibility exists, the interest violates the Rule and is void. Upon John Little's death, the land will revert to Linda Gross or her heirs in fee simple absolute. Not so where John Little is dead with surviving children at the time Linda Gross dies. In this case, all the children that John Little will ever have will be lives in being at the effective date of the will, and the interest will vest, if at all, within their lives and 21 years.

Suppose Linda Gross leaves her property as follows: "To John Little for life, remainder to John Little's widow for life, remainder to John Little's children living at the time of her death." Again, the contingent remainder to John Little's children is in violation of the Rule Against Perpetuities because of a possibility known in the law as the *unborn widow's rule*. Assume John Little marries a woman who is born several years after the effective date of the will (thus, John's wife is not a life in being or measuring life). John Little and his wife have children (again, not measuring lives), then John Little dies. Within ten years time, all John Little's children from all previous marriages die, but John's widow lives on for forty more years. She then dies, leaving only children born to her and John Little. Under the terms of Linda Gross' will, these children are entitled to the land in fee simple as tenants in common. However, the Rule Against Perpetuities time period of "lives in being" (John Little and any of his children living at the time of Linda Gross' death) plus 21 years has long since expired. Accordingly, the interest is void

from the outset. Its invalidity, however, does not affect the validity of the life estate granted to John Little, or the life estate granted to his widow who will take her interest immediately upon the death of John Little, one of the measuring lives. When John Little's widow dies, the property will revert to Linda Gross' heirs in fee simple absolute.

Some states, by statute, avoid the impact of the unborn widow's rule by construing the word "widow" to mean "present wife", in which case the interest is not in violation of the Rule Against Perpetuities since the present wife will necessarily be a life in being, and any children born to her and John Little will qualify to take the fee immediately upon her death.

One final example revolves around the so-called *fertile octogenarian rule*—a rule stating that, for purposes of the Rule Against Perpetuities, every person, regardless of age or physical condition, is presumed capable of producing children. Needless to say, this rule produces some very strange results. For example, suppose Linda Gross wills land "to the children of Shirley Short for their lives, then to Shirley Short's grandchildren in fee simple". Even if Shirley Short is 90 years old at the time of Linda Gross' death (the effective date of the will), she is still presumed to be capable of bearing children. Accordingly, it is possible, at least in the realm of legal theory, for Shirley Short to have another child after Linda Gross' death, and for that child to have children who will qualify as Shirley's grandchildren. These grandchildren were not in being at the time of the testator's death and may not even come into existence until well after all measuring lives have passed (Shirley Short, her children and grandchildren living at the time of Linda's death) and 21 years has elapsed. However improbable, it is possible that an interest in land could vest in such a grandchild more than 21 years after all measuring lives have ceased to be. The interest to Shirley's grandchildren is therefore in violation of the Rule Against Perpetuities and is void from the outset.

Because arbitrary application of the fertile octogenarian rule may lead to absurd results, some states have passed statutes making the presumption of continuous fertility a rebuttable presumption that may be disproved by evidence to the contrary.

How did private persons in the United States originally acquire ownership of land?

All privately owned land in the United States once belonged to either the federal government, an individual state government, or to a foreign nation. England first claimed the land comprising our original thirteen colonies, sparingly making grants of land under "socage tenure" to various proprietors and companies, which, in turn, granted portions of their land to other companies and private individuals. With the War For Independence, ownership of the land shifted from England to the individual American states (although much of the private ownership of land that existed prior to the Revolutionary War continued to be recognized). To provide the newly created federal government with a site for its operations, the individual states granted to the federal government the territory known as the District of Columbia. In 1803, the federal government purchased from France the Louisiana Territory, bounded on the east by the Mississippi River, and on the west by a line running approximately along the eastern boundary of Idaho and through the center of Colorado and New Mexico. After the War of 1847, Mexico ceded to the United States the land now comprising California, Nevada, Utah, Arizona, and parts of Colorado and New Mexico. And in 1846, Great Britain ceded to the United States the territory making up our present

Washington, Oregon, and Idaho in exchange for our country's relinquishment of any claim to Canada.

Apart from the limited private ownership of land stemming from colonial "socage tenure", all land in the United States, whether part of the original thirteen colonies, or part of a land grant from a foreign nation, was free from the claims of individual ownership (subject to some exceptions for land privately settled prior to our acquisition of the property). The land was freely alienable by the federal Congress or the state to which it belonged. Thus, over a period of many years, the federal Congress used a variety of methods to dispose of the land it owned—methods designed to aid in the settlement of the country and to promote the Nation's industrial development.

In accordance with presidential proclamation, some land was sold at public sale for a minimum price. When it became apparent that public sale purchasers were dispossessing actual settlers who had been living on the land and improving the property, the sale method was quickly abandoned, and a "pre-emption" system substituted in its place. Under "pre-emption", any individual who settled 160 acres of land, improved the property, and erected a dwelling, was entitled to purchase the land at a minimum price.

However, the "pre-emption" law was repealed in 1891 in favor of a "homestead" law. The homestead law provides that any citizen who does not own 160 acres of land in any state or territory, and who has not previously exercised the homestead right, can make application for a "homestead". If the application is followed by a bona fide occupation and cultivation of the land for five years time, the homesteader is entitled to a certificate of patent for the land without further payment of any kind. As used here, a *patent* is a government-issued document vesting in the patentee complete legal title to land in fee simple absolute and furnishing good and sufficient evidence of the transfer. The federal land patent is signed in the name of the president, sealed with the seal of the general land office, and countersigned (additionally signed to give the document effect) by the land office recorder. Land patents are issued not only by the United States, but also by individual states in granting state-owned lands to private individuals under state laws similar to federal homestead laws. The holder of a federal or state land patent obtains title to the property in fee simple absolute and may freely alienate the land inter vivos or at death by will or intestacy.

In addition to granting land to private individuals under homestead laws, the federal government (which still owns vast areas of land in states all over the Union) grants considerable land to states for educational and townsite purposes. For example, federal law provides that Section 16 of every township granted to a state must be used for the support of schools, including state universities and agricultural colleges (townships, which are discussed in detail in Ch. 6, are divisions of territory in surveys of federally owned public land, each township being six miles square and containing 36 sections). Federal law additionally provides that 500,000 acres of public land to be used for internal improvements shall be granted to each new state as it is admitted to the Union. And individuals desiring to found cities or towns on public land may obtain presidential authorization to locate townsites of not more than 640 acres and to sell lots at a minimum price.

CASES

CASE 1—*"The deed creates only a contingent option."*

ALAMO SCHOOL DIST. v. JONES

District Court of Appeal, First District, Division 1, California, 1960.
182 Cal.App.2d 180, 6 Cal.Rptr. 272.

DUNIWAY, Justice.

On January 2, 1878, Mary A. Jones, as first party, conveyed certain land to H. S. Raven and Jas. Foster as trustees of the Alamo Public School District, as second parties. Respondent (plaintiff below) is the successor in interest of the grantees; appellants (defendants below) are the successors in interest of the grantor. The action was brought for the purpose of obtaining a declaratory judgment as to appellants' rights, if any, under the deed. The pertinent provisions of the deed are as follows: "the said party of the first part, for and in consideration of the sum of Two hundred & fifty Dollars, * * * does by these presents remise, release, and forever quitclaim unto the said parties of the second part and to their successors in office all that certain * * * parcel of land [description follows]. *Subject however to the right of party of first part to purchase said land herein described. Should same ever be abandoned for School purposes, for some consideration herein mentioned.*

"Together with all and singular the tenements, hereditaments and appurtenances thereunto belonging, * * * and the reversion and reversions, remainder and remainders, rents, issues and profits thereof. To Have and to Hold, all and singular, the said premises, together with the appurtenances, unto the said parties of the second part, and to their Successors in office, in trust for the Alamo Public School District   *   *   *   forever." (Italics added.)

It is conceded that the land has been used for school purposes continuously from the time of the conveyance to the present.

The court found that the intention of the grantor was "to grant the property on condition that if the grantees abandoned the property for school purposes, the grantor should have an option to repurchase it for the price stated, and that this right was personal only to the grantor and not reserved expressly or by implication to the heirs and successors of said grantor." It also found that the grantor was dead. It concluded and decreed that appellants have no interest in the property, and that respondent has title in fee simple absolute. No evidence was received, and the appeal presents only the pure question of law as to the nature of the interest, if any, of the grantor and her successors and assigns in the property. We have concluded that the judgment must be affirmed.

*   *   *

The deed does not create a reversion.

Civil Code, section 768, defines a reversion as "the residue of an estate left by operation of law in the grantor or his successors,   *   *   *   commencing in possession on the determination of a particular estate granted *   *   *" The deed before us conveys a fee simple. A reversion can exist only when the estate conveyed is less than a fee simple, i. e., is a "particular estate," the classic example being a reversion arising from the granting of a life estate.

The deed does not create a possibility of reverter.

A possibility of reverter is created when the duration of an estate is limited by a measure of its life additional to that inherent in the estate itself. A fee simple is perpetual. Thus a possibility of reverter is created by the conveyance of a fee simple which is to last "until" a named event, or "during" a period limited by such an event or "as long as," a certain state of facts continues. Any expression conveying the same idea is sufficient. A classic example is "to A in fee simple until St. Paul's falls" or "as long as St Paul's stands." The rule is technical, and is based on the idea that the duration of the estate is limited, so that, when the event upon which it is limited occurs, the estate of the grantee ipso facto terminates, there being thus a "reverter" to the grantor. It is called a "possibility of reverter" because the event upon which the limitation depends may never occur. In the meantime, the grantee has a fee simple estate. We find no words in the deed before us that can be construed to create a possibility of reverter. Nothing in the deed indicates an automatic reversion of the granted estate when the property is "abandoned for school purposes."

The deed does not create a right of entry for condition broken.

The question whether the deed creates such a right is more difficult. A right of entry for breach of condition is clearly recognized in California. In classical theory, it was distinguished from the possibility of reverter by the fact that it was not a limitation upon the estate granted—not a measure of its duration—but a condition upon the occurrence of which the granted estate could be cut off by reentry of the grantor. An example of such a conveyance would be one of a fee simple "upon condition that, if St. Paul's falls, the estate shall terminate." The effect is not to terminate the estate automatically, as a reversion does, but to give the grantor a right of reentry, the estate terminating only if the right is exercised. Our code recognizes such a right. Civil Code, section 707, states: "The time when the enjoyment of property is to begin or end may be * * * made to depend on events. In the latter case, the enjoyment is said to be upon condition." Section 708 says: "Conditions are precedent or subsequent. The former fix the beginning, the latter the ending, of the right." "A right of reentry, or of repossession for breach of condition subsequent, can be transferred." Our courts apply the common law to such a right of reentry—i. e., the estate does not automatically terminate, but does so only if the person having the right exercises it.

We think that if the deed in question had merely been conditioned upon the continued use of the property for school purposes, it would have created a right of reentry for breach of such condition. No particular words need be used, nor need there be any clause of reentry, the right being implied from the imposition of the condition. However, nothing in the present deed says that the estate granted is conditioned upon such use, or that the estate is subject to termination for breach of the condition.

The deed creates only a contingent option.

The language used is the customary language of an option; the grantor is given a contingent right to purchase, and the normal incidents of a right to purchase are two: the payment of the price and a conveyance of the property to the holder of the option. This is quite different from the termination of the estate, by operation of law, upon a reentry * * * Appellants lay great stress upon the words "subject to," contending that these words import a condition. No doubt they may, in a particular case, but we can see no basis for giving them this effect when they are considered in connection with the balance of the language, to which they are merely introductory. We hold that the deed created only a contingent option in the grantor, and not a true future interest, i. e., not a reversion, not a possibility of reverter, and not a right of entry for breach of condition subsequent.

We are assisted in coming to the foregoing conclusion by certain rules of construction. * * * "A fee simple title is presumed to be intended to pass by a grant of real property, unless it appears from the grant that a lesser estate was intended." "A condition involving a forfeiture must be strictly interpreted against the party for whose benefit it is created." * * * The deed purports on its face to grant a fee, and is to be so construed. It does not purport to reserve any present interest in the grantor. And it is to be construed against the contention that it creates a condition involving a forfeiture * * *.

            * * *

No case cited by appellants deals with language in a deed similar to that which appears in the deed before us. It would appear that there is no California case directly in point. Cases in other jurisdictions support our view that this deed created in the grantor only a contingent option to repurchase. In each of the following cases it was so held: Bates v. Bates, 314 Ky. 789, 236 S.W.2d 943 ([grantor] " 'is to have the land at the same price when it ceases to be public property as school house property' "); Gange v. Hayes, 193 Or. 51, 237 P.2d 196, 198 ("if [grantee] * * * should at any time or for any reason, cease operation of its lumbering or planing mill * * * for a period of twenty four consecutive months, [grantor] * * * at its own option to be exercised, can demand and shall receive a Warranty Deed back * * * upon the payment of the original purchase price * * * "); Gearhart v. West Lumber Company, 212 Ga. 25, 90 S.E.

2d 10, 11 (agreement in deed that property "will be used for county school purposes only, and should this provision be violated, the grantor herein shall have the right to purchase the above property for $2,000"); Bond v. Kennedy, 213 Ark. 758, 212 S.W.2d 336, 338 ("in the event either of such conditions is not complied with, the grantor * * * shall have the exclusive option to buy said property for the sum of * * * ($5000.00)"; Corpier v. Thomason, 155 Ark. 509, 244 S.W. 738, 740 (" 'but when ceased to be used for school purposes, that I [grantor] * * * is to have the land at the specified price of $60.' "). The Restatement is in accord (Rest., Property, § 394, Comments b, c; § 394, Comment f).

The contingent option created was personal to the grantor.

Under the rules laid down in Victoria Hospital Ass'n v. All Persons, supra, 169 Cal. 455, 147 P. 124, it would appear that the contingent right of the grantor to repurchase under the deed before us, is nothing more than a contingent right to enforce a personal covenant which is not assignable, and did not pass to appellants as "the heirs at law and successors to" the grantor * * *.

* * * If so construed, it would have to be exercised during her lifetime, and consequently would be valid rather than void under the rule against perpetuities. * * *

* * *

The contingent option, if inheritable, is void under the rule against perpetuities.

If we are in error in our view that the contingent option was personal to the grantor, and if it were transferable and inheritable as appellants contend, then it would be void under the rule against perpetuities. It is now settled that the common law rule against perpetuities, presently embodied in Civil Code, sections 715.1, following, has always been the law in California. We must therefore treat it as having been in effect in 1878. And while there is no California case upon the question, both the Restatement and the cases in other jurisdictions make it clear that a contingent option that may be exercised at a time beyond the period of the rule is void as in violation of the rule.

* * * In Hill v. State Box Co., 114 Cal.App.2d 44, at page 51, 249 P.2d 903, at page 907, there is dictum recognizing that an option which need not be exercised within the period of the rule, and might never come into existence within that period, would be invalid. That is the nature of the option here; so far as its terms are concerned, it could be exercisable for the first time, say, in A.D. 2050, which would certainly be longer than "21 years after some [indeed, any conceivable] life in being at the creation of the interest [in 1878] and any period of gestation." The very fact that, in theory at least, the possibility that the option might be exercised could continue in existence, as a fetter upon the property, for so long a time—possibly for centuries—best illustrates the reason for holding it subject to the rule, and by the rule rendered void.

* * *

Affirmed.

BRAY, P. J., and TOBRINER, J., concur.

CASE 2—*Lives in being plus twenty-one years—the rule against perpetuities.*

NORTH CAROLINA NAT. BANK v. NORRIS

Court of Appeals of North Carolina, 1974.
21 N.C.App. 178, 203 S.E.2d 657.

Action for a declaratory judgment to determine whether certain provisions of the last will of B. F. Montague violated the rule against perpetuities. * * *

B. F. Montague died a resident of Wake County on or about 1 April 1928, leaving a will dated 19 November 1927. At the time of his death, he left surviving a widow, three daughters who were then 38, 40 and 43 years of age, and one grandchild, Thomas A. Norris, Jr., who was then six years of age; there were no children or grandchildren born subsequent to the death of B. F. Montague. Montague's widow, daughters, and only grandchild have successively deceased. Thomas A. Norris, Jr., the grandchild, died 10 January 1973, leaving surviving four children, who are the defendants herein, and a last will naming plaintiff herein as the Executor.

The pertinent provisions in the will of B. F. Montague are the following:

> "FOURTH: I give, devise and bequeath to my three daughters, May M. Allison and Annie M. Hunter and Marjorie M. Norris, all of my estate, below described, during their natural lives and at the death of either of my said daughters, I give, devise and bequeath all of said property to the survivor or survivors alike, and at the death of the last survivor, I give, devise and bequeath all of my estate below described to the child or children of my said daughters for and during the natural life or lives of such child or children (my grandchild or grandchildren) with remainder over to the lawful issue of such grandchild or granchildren forever. In default of such issue from such grandchild or grandchildren, the remainder shall go to Peace Institute of Raleigh, N.C., absolutely and forever. First of all, however, I give, devise and bequeath to my wife, Bettie L. Montague, a life estate in and to all the property below described in this section (Section FOURTH), and at her death, the same shall descend to my said daughters in the manner and form above specified in this section (Section FOURTH)."

There then follows a description of certain tracts of real property in Raleigh, N.C.

If the rule against perpetuities was violated by the foregoing provisions of Montague's will, title to the real property in question would have been vested in his grandchild, Thomas A. Norris, Jr., immediately prior to Norris's death and would now be vested in plaintiff by virtue of Norris's will. If the rule was not violated, title to such property would now be vested in defendants, Montague's great-grandchildren.

The trial court, concluding as a matter of law that the attempted devise of the remainder interest to the testator's great-grandchildren violated the rule against perpetuities, entered judgment that title to the property in question is now vested in plaintiff as Executor under the will of Thomas A. Norris, Jr., subject to the provisions of Norris's will.

From this judgment, the * * * defendant[s] * * * appealed.

PARKER, Judge.

The common-law rule against perpetuities has been long recognized and enforced in this jurisdiction * * *. This rule, which is "not one of construction but a positive mandate of law to be obeyed irrespective of the question of intention," has been stated by our Supreme Court as follows:

> "No devise or grant of a future interest in property is valid unless the title thereto must vest, if at all, not later than twenty-one years, plus the period of gestation, after some life or lives in being at the time of the creation of the interest. If there is a possibility such future interest may not vest within the time prescribed, the gift or grant is void."

The devise which B. F. Montague attempted to make in Item Fourth of his will to his great-grandchildren of the remainder interest after the termination of the successive life estates granted to his widow, his daughters, and his grandchildren, clearly violated the rule. As of the date of the testator's death, which in case of wills is the time at which the validity of the limitation is to be ascertained, the possibility existed, at least insofar as the law views the matter, that one or more children might thereafter be born to one or more of Montague's three surviving daughters. Had this occurred, the life estates which he provided for his grandchildren might well have extended and postponed vesting of the remainder in his great-grandchildren to a date beyond the time prescribed by the rule. It is the possibility, not the actuality, of such an occurrence which renders the grant void. * * * "[I]t should be noted that a remainder to great-grandchildren whose vesting is not limited upon termination of a secondary life estate in a named grandchild, but upon the death of all the creator's grandchildren as a class, is invalid, since other granchildren might be born after the creation of the future interests and postpone the vesting of the remainder beyond the permitted period."

Affirmed.

PROBLEMS

1. Answer the following "True" or "False" and give reasons for your answers:

   (a) Socage tenure forms the basis for our modern real estate taxes on homes, farms, and other real property.

   (b) A future interest is presently owned.

   (c) Carrying the king's flag at a coronation would be an example of frankalmoign tenure.

   (d) The incident of tenure known as "relief" is the forerunner of our modern income tax.

2. Steve Spooner owns three parcels of real property. He conveys the first "to Milly Monroe for life, then to her heirs." He conveys the second parcel "to Bud Seeley for life, then to Steve Spooner's heirs." Finally, he conveys the third parcel "to Helen Hatch."

   (a) What real property interests, if any, are created in Milly Monroe and her heirs under the common law? Under modern statutory law?

(b) What real property interests, if any, are created in Bud Seeley and Steve Spooner's heirs under the common law? Under modern statutory law?

(c) What real property interests, if any, are created in Helen Hatch under the common law? Under modern statutory law?

3. Lola Gordon writes a will leaving her farmhouse "to Rex Stratton and his heirs so long as gambling never takes place on the premises, and if gambling does take place, then to Richard Skinner and his heirs."

(a) What interest, if any, is created in Rex Stratton and his heirs by the terms of the will? *Qual fee simple - determinable*

(b) What interest, if any, is created in Richard Skinner and his heirs by the terms of the will? *Executory interest - but fails on RAP*

(c) In the event that bingo is played on the premises, who specifically will own the property? Explain. *Lola - poss. of reverter*

4. Rex Stratton wants to keep two parcels of real property within his family. He conveys the first "to my son Robert for life, then to Robert's children for life, then to Robert's grandchildren and their heirs." Robert Stratton has no children at the time of the conveyance. The second parcel of real property Rex conveys "to my daughter Sheila and her heirs on express condition that Sheila not transfer the property for a period of ten years."

(a) What interests, if any, are created in Robert, Robert's children, and Robert's grandchildren by the terms of the first conveyance? *life estate contingent remainder violates RAP*

(b) What interests, if any, are created in Sheila and her heirs by the terms of the second conveyance? *Fee Simple Absolute - can't restrict alienation*

(c) In the event that Sheila transfers the property within ten years, who specifically owns the property? Explain. *New owner life estate pur autra vie*

5. Pam McSweeney conveys real property "to Steve Spooner for the life of Sally Cooper, and then to Doug Adams for life." Name and describe all real property interests created by the conveyance. *life estate vested remainder*

6. How did private ownership of real property in the United States come about? *public sale, ... (preemption), homestead*

7. Desiring to provide for her family, Kelly Sanders executes a will leaving her beachfront property "to my son Tim Sanders for life, remainder to Tim's widow for life, remainder to Tim's children living at the time of his widow's death." At the time Kelly executes the will, her son Tim is married to the former Nancy Spencer and they have two children, Keith and Kathy. What interests, if any, are created under the terms of the conveyance? *Tim - life estate, widow - Contingent Remainder children*

8. Before she dies, Kelly Sanders conveys her mountain cabin "to my daughter Gina for life, remainder to my nephew Harold Spencer." Gina moves into the cabin following the conveyance. She finds that there is ample timber on the land for making minor repairs and for use as firewood. A few months later, Tucker Timber Company offers to purchase the standing timber on the property, and Gina agrees to sell. The same day, Gina receives a property tax statement in the mail and a county assessment of $1,500 for the costs of connecting the mountain property to the newly installed county sewer system.

(a) What interests, if any, were created by the conveyance of the cabin? *life estate - Gina   vested Remainder fee simple absolute yes ~ may use nat. res for maintenance*

(b) Did Gina have a right to use the timber for repairs and fire-wood? Explain. Did she have a right to sell the timber to Tuck-er Timber Company? Explain. *no, exploits nat. resources*

yes - to value of rental

(c) Is Gina responsible for paying property taxes on the land? Explain. Is she responsible for the $1,500 assessment? Explain.

partly: improvement

9. *True-False Question.* If X makes a completed unrestricted gift of Blackacre to Y charity, Y charity

F   a. May abandon its title to the property. *cannot abandon real*

F   b. May be required to give up the property to the state if the state exercises its power of eminent domain (for a private purpose).

F   c. May sue X, the former owner of the property, for wasting the property during the time he held it.

F   d. May force X, the former owner of the property, to retake the property if it is found to be unsuitable for Y charity's purposes.

[# 3.L., May 1966 CPA Exam]

10. Abrams owned a fee simple absolute interest in certain real property. Abrams conveyed it to Fox for Fox's lifetime with the remainder interest upon Fox's death to Charles. What are the rights of Fox and Charles in the real property?

a. Charles may *not* sell his interest in the property until the death of Fox.

(b.) Fox has a possessory interest in the land and Charles has a future interest.

c. Charles must outlive Fox in order to obtain any interest in the real property.

d. Any conveyance by either Fox or Charles must be joined in by the other party in order to be valid.

[# 40, May 1977 CPA Exam]

Chapter 5

OWNING PROPERTY WITH OTHER PEOPLE AND INCIDENTAL RIGHTS IN REAL ESTATE: CONCURRENT OWNERSHIP, JOINT TENANCY, TENANCY IN COMMON, COMMUNITY PROPERTY, SUPPORT RIGHTS, WATER RIGHTS, RIGHTS IN AIRSPACE

What term applies to the complete ownership of a single property right by one individual?

A person who owns a real or personal property right by himself or herself, without anyone else sharing in the ownership, is said to own the property in *severalty*. *Black's Law Dictionary* defines "severalty" in these words:

A state of separation. An estate in severalty is one that is held by a person in his own right only, without any other person being joined or connected with him, in point of interest, during his estate therein.[1]

Thus, the interests that you hold in personal property (whether the property is clothing, furniture, a book, a car, a patent right, or common stock) and those you hold in real property (whether the property is held in fee simple absolute, or as a reversion, remainder, or executory interest) are interests in severalty if you are the only person possessing such right or rights. If you are not the only person possessing such rights, but, instead you share your ownership interest with one or more individuals, you do not own the property in severalty, but, rather, *concurrently* (i. e., together) with those others. However, it is important to distinguish concurrent ownership from the situation in which one person owns one or more rights in property, and another person owns entirely different rights in the same property (e. g., with regard to real property, the life tenant and the future interest holder). In this case, each party owns his or her rights in severalty, not concurrently. It is only when two or more people share ownership of the *same* right or rights in property that they are said to own the property concurrently.

What are some practical reasons for owning property concurrently?

Concurrent ownership is often a practical alternative to ownership in severalty for the following reasons:

(1) *Concurrent ownership is a convenient way to invest with others or operate a business with others.* For example, if you and perhaps ten of your friends form an investment club, pooling your resources to buy a diversified portfolio of stocks and bonds and an apartment house consisting of 50 units, how will each member of your club own the property purchased? Certainly, it is possible for each club member to obtain individual rights in the property (i. e., to own the rights in severalty), but this would make little sense. If you bought 100 shares of General Motors stock, 50 shares of IBM,

---

1. Henry Campbell Black, *Black's Law Dictionary*, Revised Fourth Edition, West Publishing Co., 1968, p. 1540.

25 shares of MacDonald Hamburgers, and 75 shares of Texaco, you would have to obtain eleven certificates from each company in order to provide for ownership in severalty for each club member, and each certificate would have to be separately signed and executed in order to make a subsequent sale of the stock. Obviously, it would be much more convenient for you and your friends to own the investments you make together in a concurrent ownership form. The same is true with respect to your 50 unit apartment house and any other real estate you might ultimately purchase. While you could divide the 50 unit apartment house into eleven specifically described 1/11th parts, one part for each club member, there are practical difficulties in doing so (e. g., how do you determine which member gets which portion of the building?). The better solution is for all members to own the apartment house concurrently, each member with an undivided 1/11th interest in the entire property. As you can see, concurrent ownership makes it easier to initially invest in the property, to presently manage it, and to subsequently transfer it to others.

Similar to the investment club situation, you and your friends may desire to operate a business together. Unless you incorporate,[2] you will most likely do business in partnership form. Section 6 of the Uniform Partnership Act defines "partnership" as "an association of two or more persons to carry on as co-owners a business for profit". And it is a rule of partnership law that all partners concurrently own all partnership property acquired for use in operating the business. Again, it makes much more sense for each partner to own an undivided interest in all the partnership property rather than a specifically described portion of each piece of property, real or personal

(e. g., cars, inventory, accounts receivable). This form of concurrent ownership is called *tenancy in partnership* and is described in detail in a later section of this chapter.

(2) *Concurrent ownership enables spouses to share equally in the ownership of property acquired during marriage.* In the typical marriage, both spouses work hard to acquire both real and personal property. Because both parties contribute substantially of their time and effort, it is only fair that the law provide a method of concurrent ownership between husband and wife enabling each spouse to own an undivided one-half interest in all the property acquired. Of course, if the spouses prefer, they can always divide the property equally and hold it in severalty.

(3) *Concurrent ownership may avoid the time and expense of probate.* Some forms of concurrent ownership eliminate the need for probate of the concurrently held property upon the death of one of the co-owners. Probate, as will be explained more fully in Ch. 30, is simply the legal process of transferring a decedent's property (all of his or her property held in severalty and some of his or her property held concurrently with others) to those people lawfully entitled to the property upon the decedent's death (i. e., those people named in the decedent's will or designated as the decedent's intestate heirs if the decedent leaves no will). Probate also serves to protect the interests of creditors of the deceased (nearly all decedents leave some bills, whether they are merely utility bills, doctor bills, or major debts evidenced by mortgages on real estate) and the interests of taxing authorities with respect to death, income, gift, and property taxes owing. In short, the probate process ensures that the right parties end up with the decedent's

---

2. As you will learn in Ch. 23, corporations own property in severalty in the corporate name.

property. It is a desirable process that serves well to protect the decedent's interests and wishes with regard to the final disposition of his or her property.

To illustrate, imagine that your mother dies without a will, leaving you as her only surviving heir. Your mother's savings account in a local bank contains $50,000; and as your mother's debts are paid in full, you are entitled to the full $50,000 free and clear of any creditor's claims. However, you cannot simply appear at the bank and demand your money —the bank has no means of determining whether you are the appropriate person to take it. It is up to the probate court to determine the legitimacy of your claim to your mother's properties (i. e., her estate) and to ultimately order distribution of the money to you.

In contrast to our orderly probate process, the author likes to recall a scene from the movie "Zorba the Greek" in which an old woman lay dying in a small village. The dying woman owned a substantial amount of property in the town, including a hotel with many furnishings. As the old woman approached death, the townspeople systematically removed each of her possessions until all she had left was the bed she lay dying on —even her clothes and other personal belongings had disappeared. Finally, several townspeople gathered around her bed waiting for her to die so as to be first in line for even the bed itself. That is one way of taking care of a decedent's property. Our system of probate is a much better way.

However, our probate system is also time-consuming (in the usual case, 8 to 10 months) and expensive (usually 3–5% of the estate and sometimes more for administration costs, attorneys' fees, appraiser's fees, etc.). For this reason, it is sometimes desirable to avoid probate, and one of the easiest ways to do so is to own property in certain forms of concurrent ownership. This is particularly true for husbands and wives who own their properties together.

What are the five recognized forms of concurrent ownership?

Modernly, there are five recognized forms of concurrent ownership:

(1) Tenancy in common;

(2) Joint tenancy with the right of survivorship;

(3) Tenancy by the entirety;

(4) Community property; and

(5) Tenancy in partnership.

Each of these forms is described in detail in the chapter sections that follow. As you read through the sections, notice the use of the term "tenancy" to describe four of the five methods of owning property concurrently. You will recall that we have previously used the term "tenant" to describe the holder of a life estate (a "life tenant") and to describe lessees of real estate who hold a chattel real (a lease) as periodic tenants, tenants with estates for years, or tenants at will. We now add still another meaning and use of the term "tenant" in describing concurrent ownership forms. Because the term has so many meanings, it is important to carefully distinguish its use in any given situation so that the proper legal application can be made.

What is the difference between a tenancy in common and a joint tenancy with the right of survivorship?

Perhaps the easiest way to distinguish among the five forms of concurrent ownership is to recognize that the law demands specific kinds or elements of "togetherness" for each form of co-ownership. These elements of "togetherness" are known as legal "unities". For example, a tenancy in common requires one "unity" or element of togetherness; a joint tenancy with the right of survivorship requires four "unities"; a tenancy by the entirety requires five, etc.

A *tenancy in common* differs from ownership in severalty in one way—rather than one person owning the interest, two or more people called tenants in common share undivided ownership of the property. This blending of ownership interests so that all interest holders own an undivided share of the whole property is referred to as the *unity of possession*. It is the only unity required for a tenancy in common. Unity of possession demands that each cotenant have equal rights to use, enjoyment, and possession of the property, whether real or personal. With respect to real property, no one tenant has any right to exclusive possession: each tenant has an equal right to use, occupy, and enjoy the premises.

Tenants in common need not own the same fractional share of the property (e. g., if A, B, C, and D own an apartment house or 100 shares of Standard Oil stock as tenants in common, A might own a ½ interest, B a ⅓rd interest, and C and D a ⅙th interest). Nor is it necessary that the tenants in common acquire their interests at the same time or from the same source. And tenants in common are free to transfer their interests at any time without regard to the other tenants' wishes.

As to inheritability, the interest of a tenant in common will pass to the tenant's lawfully designated beneficiaries or heirs upon the tenant's death just as if the property had been held in severalty. Thus, in the A, B, C, D example above, if A dies testate leaving her interest in the apartment house or in the stock to her daughter, Sally, Sally will become a tenant in common with B, C, and D, owning a ½ undivided interest in the property. As to distribution at death, an interest held in tenancy in common must be probated just like any interest held in severalty.

Modernly, any transfer of property to two or more persons is presumed to create a tenancy in common unless some other form of co-ownership is expressly indicated. There is also a presumption that the tenants take in equal shares unless there is evidence that the tenants were intended to share disproportionately.

In contrast to the tenancy in common, a *joint tenancy with the right of survivorship* requires four unities or elements of togetherness:

(1) *Unity of time.* Whereas tenants in common may acquire their interests at different times, each "joint tenant" must acquire his or her interest at the same time.

(2) *Unity of title.* Again in contrast to the tenancy in common, each joint tenant's interest must be created by the same instrument, that is, by the same deed of conveyance, contract of sale, or the like.

(3) *Unity of interest.* The interests must be identical in size and duration. Thus, a transfer of real property to A, B, C, and D as joint tenants with the right of survivorship, each tenant to receive a ¼th interest in fee simple, will create a valid joint tenancy. However, a transfer of the same property, ½ to A, ⅓rd to B, and ⅙th each to C and D as joint tenants with the right of survivorship will not result in a valid joint tenancy, and the survivorship characteristic will not follow. (A few states will uphold the joint tenancy in the case of unequal fractional shares and permit survivorship if that is the clearly expressed intent of the parties. However, no state will recognize a joint tenancy with the right of survivorship in a conveyance "to A and B for life, and, at the same time, to C and D for ten years, all as joint tenants with the right of survivorship". All the parties must have either a life estate, an estate for years, or some other identical interest of the same duration.)

(4) *Unity of possession.* As with the tenancy in common, each cotenant must

have equal rights to use, enjoyment, and possession of the property.

The *right of survivorship* is the single most important characteristic of the joint tenancy. This right means that upon the death of any joint tenant, the deceased tenant's interest passes, not to the tenant's lawfully designated beneficiaries or heirs (as in the case of the tenancy in common), but to the surviving joint tenants. In other words, if A, B, C, and D own an apartment house or a patent right as joint tenants with the right of survivorship, and A dies, B, C, and D will automatically own A's interest. If B then dies, C and D will automatically own B's interest; and, if C dies before D, D will automatically own all the property by himself in severalty. Where the right of survivorship exists, ownership of the property transfers automatically at the moment of death of the fellow cotenant. As a result, the need for probate is eliminated, and use of the joint tenancy with the right of survivorship is the easiest way to avoid probate.

Probate considerations aside, most people who die want their lawfully designated beneficiaries or heirs, and not their surviving cotenants, to receive their property. For example, returning to your investment club situation, you would not want your interest in the club's real estate, stocks, and bonds to go to your fellow club members upon your death—you would want them to go to your spouse and family. For this reason, the law presumes that a person who transfers property to one or more persons intends to create a tenancy in common rather than a joint tenancy with the right of survivorship unless the transferor expressly indicates that the right of survivorship is to accompany the transfer. At common law, express words were not necessary to create a joint tenancy with the right of survivor-

ship: the term "joint tenancy" automatically created the survivorship characteristic, often to the dismay of the transferor who was attempting to create a tenancy in common. To protect transferors, several states technically abolished the common law joint tenancy. However, the practical effect of such laws was simply to establish a presumption in favor of a tenancy in common in the absence of express words creating survivorship. These states include Alabama, Arizona, Florida, Georgia, Kansas, Kentucky, Maine, North Carolina, Ohio, Oregon, Pennsylvania, South Carolina, Tennessee, Texas, Virginia, Washington, and West Virginia. Thus, to modernly ensure creation of a joint tenancy with the right of survivorship, the words "right of survivorship" or "to the survivor" should be used; the words "joint tenancy" or "jointly held" will not be sufficient.[3]

Joint tenancies with the right of survivorship may be created between any two or more related or unrelated natural persons. Because a corporation is an artificial person and not a natural person, it cannot hold property as a joint tenant—being artificial, it could "live" forever, thus ruling out any possibility of "survivorship" for its human cotenants.

And joint tenancies with the right of survivorship may be created for future interests (remainders and executory interests) as well as for interests that are presently possessory. This is true even where the future interest is created in a class or group of people, such as children. Thus, a transfer "to John Little for life, then to his children and their heirs as joint tenants with the right of survivorship" immediately creates in the unborn children of John Little a contingent remainder in fee simple as joint tenants with the right of survivorship. The remainder is contingent upon John Little's having chil-

---

3. However, it should be pointed out that in past CPA exams the term *joint tenant* has been used to mean *joint tenant with the right of survivorship.*

dren; and the remainder is subject to open (i. e., more children may enter the class, thus decreasing each living child's fractional share of the property) until John Little's last child is born. At that time, the remainder will be fully vested in John Little's children as joint tenants with the right of survivorship, and, assuming the children make no inter vivos transfers, the last surviving child will own all the land in severalty in fee simple absolute.

Suppose that one joint tenant makes an inter vivos transfer of his or her interest to an outside party. The transferee, in this case, does not become a joint tenant with the right of survivorship, but a tenant in common with the remaining joint tenants. This is because the transferee does not possess the unities of time and title—the transferee has received his or her interest at a different time and by a different transfer. As a tenant in common, the transferee will own his or her share of the property free and clear of the survivorship rights of the remaining joint tenants (i. e., upon the tenant in common's death, the tenant's property will go, not to the surviving joint tenants, but to the tenant's lawfully designated heirs or beneficiaries).

The joint tenant's transfer to the outside party, however, destroys only the joint tenancy nature of the particular interest transferred: as amongst themselves, the remaining joint tenants' rights are unaffected. Let's take an example. Assume that A, B, C, and D own a 30 acre ranch as joint tenants with the right of survivorship. A transfers his interest to Sally who becomes a tenant in common with B, C, and D. B, C, and D, however, continue to own their interests as joint tenants with each other. If B and C die, D will own ¾th's of the property because of the survivorship characteristic; because there are no other surviving joint tenants, D will become a tenant in common with Sally who owns the other ¼th undivided interest in the property. If D dies, her heirs will receive her ¾th interest as tenants in common with Sally; if Sally dies, her heirs will receive her ¼th interest as tenants in common with D or her heirs.

Suppose that one joint tenant leases jointly held real property to an outside party or even to another joint tenant. Does the lease destroy the unity of possession required for a joint tenancy, thus destroying the joint tenancy itself? The general rule is that the lease does not destroy the unity of possession but merely suspends it during the period of the leasehold—the joint tenancy continues undisturbed.

Suppose that A transfers property he already owns to himself and C as "joint tenants with the right of survivorship". Technically, there is no possibility of satisfying the unities of time and title necessary for a joint tenancy since A originally received his interest in the property from another source and in another transfer. As a result, A and C hold the land as tenants in common, not as joint tenants. However, many people have circumvented this unity problem by first transferring the property to a third party "strawman" who immediately turns around and retransfers the property to the former owner and a third party as tenants in common with the right of survivorship. In the example above, A would transfer the property to B who would then retransfer the property "to A and C as joint tenants with the right of survivorship" (A and C thus sharing unity of time and title from B). Because of this, some modern jurisdictions have simply carved out an exception to the time and title requirement in cases where a property owner transfers property he or she already owns to himself or herself and one or more others as joint tenants with the right of survivorship.

What are the basic rights and duties among tenants in common and joint tenants?

Tenants in common and joint tenants share the same basic rights and duties as follows:

(1) *Use by cotenants.* Each cotenant is entitled to use, possess, and occupy all the property, whether real or personal, subject only to the same rights in his or her cotenants. Thus, the general rule is that a cotenant who takes possession of and uses concurrently held land is under no obligation to pay his or her cotenants for use of the property unless the cotenant has previously agreed to make payment (a few states, such as Washington, hold to the contrary and do require payment). For example, if A occupies and farms real property belonging to A, B, C, and D as tenants in common or as joint tenants with the right of survivorship, A is legally entitled to keep all crop proceeds so long as his use of the property does not interfere with the other tenants' rights to use and occupy the premises (e. g., where B, C, and D have made no objection to A's use of the land, or where they come and go on the property but show no interest in farming). However, no one cotenant may exclude any other cotenant from any part of the property. Such an exclusion is referred to as an *ouster,* and the excluded cotenant may bring suit to regain possession and to recover money damages for the ouster's use of the property. Also, no cotenant is free to commit "waste" by exploiting the property: a cotenant who cuts timber or extracts minerals must account to his or her cotenants and pay them their lawful shares.

(2) *Use by others.* Any income (e. g., rents) resulting from use of the land by parties other than cotenants must be shared equally with all cotenants. And if one cotenant collects money damages in a "trespass" or "nuisance" action (see Ch. 1) against an outside party, the money collected must also be shared with all cotenants.

(3) *Expenses.* All cotenants must share in proportion to their respective interests in the property the cost of expenses necessary to preserve or maintain the property. Thus, a cotenant who pays for repairs or pays taxes owing on the property has a right to recover a proportionate share of the cost from his or her cotenants. This right to recover is called the "right of contribution". It is limited in one respect: where one cotenant is in possession of the property, he or she is obligated to use whatever profits or income are realized from the property to pay for necessary repairs and taxes prior to claiming any contribution from his or her cotenants. The duty of the cotenant in possession is very similar to that of the life tenant as explained in Ch. 4.

(4) *Partition.* At early common law, neither a tenant in common nor a joint tenant had the right to compel his or her cotenants to *partition* the property—that is, to divide the property into severalty interests or to sell the property where division is impossible and divide up the proceeds. Modernly, however, it is recognized that each cotenant has a right to go to court and demand partition. Of course, the result of partition is to destroy the tenancy in common or joint tenancy and to substitute severalty ownership in its place.

What is a tenancy by the entirety?

A tenancy by the entirety is a form of concurrent ownership that can exist only between husband and wife. It requires not only the four legal unities of time, title, interest, and possession (the unities demanded for a joint tenancy with the right of survivorship) but also a fifth unity of *person* (i. e., the marital relationship—for many purposes, the common law treated the husband and wife as one "person").

In most respects, a tenancy by the entirety is similar to a joint tenancy—as with a joint tenancy, the right of survivorship is one of its major characteristics. However, a tenancy by the entirety differs from a joint tenancy in one very important way. Whereas a joint tenancy may be terminated by the voluntary act of any one of the joint tenants (e. g., a joint tenant who makes an inter vivos transfer destroys the joint tenancy with respect to the particular interest transferred), a tenancy by the entirety cannot be terminated by the voluntary and separate act of either husband or wife. Both parties must agree to terminate the tenancy and act together in doing so. Thus, if either husband or wife transfers his or her interest alone, the transfer will be of no effect, and the tenancy by the entirety will continue without interruption. And neither the husband nor the wife may file an individual suit for partition of the property.

However, this is not to say that the tenancy can never be terminated—only that both husband and wife must act together to do so. Additionally, the tenancy is automatically terminated "by operation of law" if the parties obtain a divorce (in which case the former husband and wife automatically become tenants in common with respect to the property); one or both of the parties die; or creditors are entitled to the property (the rights of creditors are discussed in the following section).

While neither husband nor wife acting alone without the other's consent can transfer property held by the entirety, either spouse is free to transfer his or her survivorship interest. For example, say that A and B own a yacht as tenants by the entirety. A cannot transfer her interest to C without B's consent, but she can sell C her right of survivorship. C, of course, must be willing to gamble on A's outliving B, for if A dies before B, B will automatically own the entire yacht, and C will have nothing.

Tenancy by the entirety is no longer recognized in about half our states (in community property states, for instance, the tenancy is inconsistent with the community property system). Where the tenancy is recognized, it generally applies to both real and personal property; where it is not recognized, husbands and wives are still free to own property as joint tenants with the right of survivorship.

As to creation of the tenancy, a transfer to husband and wife in a state that recognizes tenancy by the entirety is presumed to create such a tenancy even though the words "survivor" or "survivorship" are not used. Of course, a tenancy by the entirety will not result if the transferor clearly expresses an intent to the contrary. (Note that this is precisely opposite to the presumption operating *against* creation of a joint tenancy in the absence of express words of survivorship.)

Once a tenancy by the entirety has been created, both spouses modernly have equal control over the property and are entitled to an equal share of the rents and profits.

Suppose that a transferor conveys property "to A and B as tenants by the entirety", but A and B are not lawfully married. In this case A and B will take the property as tenants in common.

Suppose that husband A conveys property he already owns "to husband A and wife B as tenants by the entirety". Here, as in the analogous joint tenancy situation, the unities of time and title are lacking; but, again, the trend in the law is to overlook the missing unities and uphold creation of the tenancy. In any event, there is nothing to prevent the property owner spouse from using a "strawman" to accomplish the same result.

What rights do creditors have against a debtor who owns property as a tenant in common, a joint tenant, or a tenant by the entirety?

Creditors' rights against debtors who own property as tenants in common, joint tenants, or tenants by the entirety differ in the following respects:

(1) *Tenants in common.* A tenant in common's interest in property is like an interest in severalty in that the property will pass, upon the tenant's death, to the tenant's lawful heirs or beneficiaries—not to the surviving cotenants. A creditor of the tenant can thus "reach" the property (i. e., force legal sale of the property pursuant to a court order to pay off the tenant's debt) either at any time while the tenant is living or for the period of probate after the tenant's death. Of course, the maximum interest the creditor can reach is the maximum interest owned by the tenant—an undivided interest in tenancy in common. Sale of the undivided interest will in no way disturb the other tenants in common: the purchaser of the property will merely succeed to the former tenant's interest as a tenant in common with the others.

(2) *Joint tenants with the right of survivorship.* The undivided interest of a joint tenant with the right of survivorship is also subject to the claims of his or her creditors with one major difference: the creditor must "reach" the property before the debtor-joint tenant dies. If the debtor dies first, the creditor will be out of luck, for at the moment of the debtor's death, the debtor's undivided interest passes automatically to the surviving joint tenants or their heirs free and clear of any claims of the deceased tenant's creditors. Where the creditor succeeds in reaching the property prior to the debtor's death, the joint tenancy nature of the debtor's interest in the property will be destroyed, and the purchaser of the interest will become a tenant in common with the remaining joint tenants.

The joint tenants will, of course, remain joint tenants as amongst themselves.

(3) *Tenants by the entirety.* Most jurisdictions that recognize tenancy by the entirety hold that neither tenant's property interest can be "reached" to satisfy the claims of individual creditors of either husband or wife. Only creditors who have a claim against both spouses can force legal sale of the property. This rule is based on the unity of person required for creation of a tenancy by the entirety: because the property is owned by a legal entity or "person" made up of both husband and wife, it would not be fair to allow the individual creditors of only half that "person" to disrupt the tenancy's existence.

A minority of jurisdictions, however, do allow a creditor of either spouse to reach that spouse's interest in the property so long as the creditor does not prejudice the survivorship rights of the non-debtor spouse. What this means is that the creditor can force legal sale of the debtor's interest in the property (and perhaps purchase the interest at the sale himself or herself), but the purchaser will be limited to what the debtor-spouse presently owns—use, enjoyment, and possession of the property coupled with one-half the income and profits. Of course, if the debtor-spouse survives his or her former cotenant spouse, the debtor's creditor will succeed to the entire interest. But if the debtor dies before his or her spouse, the creditor will lose out completely, and the surviving spouse will take the entire interest free and clear of the creditor's claims.

What are the tax implications of holding property as tenants in common versus holding as joint tenants with the right of survivorship or as tenants by the entirety?

Holding property concurrently as joint tenants with the right of survivorship or as tenants by the entirety eliminates the need for probate of the property and thus avoids probate costs. However, there are some tax implications to holding property with the survivorship characteristic that can result in higher death tax costs to the property owner or his or her estate than what costs are saved in bypassing probate. Put simply, "death" taxes are "transfer" taxes imposed by federal and state governments upon the estate of a deceased. Death taxes tax the transfer of the decedent's property to his or her lawful heirs, beneficiaries, or surviving cotenants.

Before 1976, the federal Internal Revenue Code provided that the full value of survivorship property *of any kind* would be included in the estate of the first joint tenant or tenant by the entirety to die *unless* the surviving cotenants could prove that they had contributed to the cost of the property. To the extent that the survivors could prove contribution, a proportionate share of the property's value would be removed from the decedent's estate. Where contribution could not be proved, the full value of the property (the decedent's interest plus the survivors' interests) would be included in the estate for death tax purposes, and the taxes would be higher because the value of the estate would be higher. (If the decedent owned the interest in severalty or concurrently but as a tenant in common, only the value of his or her particular interest would be included, making the death taxes lower.)

The pre-1976 law is still the law except insofar as it relates to property held with the right of survivorship between husband and wife (including joint tenancies and tenancies by the entirety). The Tax Reform Act of 1976 changed the "old" law to provide that where a husband and wife own property with the right of survivorship, only one-half the

value of the property will be included in the estate of the first spouse to die whether or not the surviving spouse contributed to the cost of the property. However, for this new rule to operate, the tenancy must have been subject to gift taxation at the time of its creation. With limited exception,[4] a joint tenancy with the right of survivorship is subject to gift tax at the time of its creation unless the joint tenants contribute equally to the cost of the property. As for a tenancy by the entirety, there is no gift and no gift tax at the time of creation of the tenancy, regardless of the spouses' equality of contribution, unless the husband and wife elect to treat it as a gift at that time. If they choose not to, the new rule under the 1976 Act will not apply, and upon the death of one of the spouses, the surviving spouse will have to prove contribution or the entire interest will be included in the estate of the decedent spouse.

It should also be pointed out that the Tax Reform Act of 1976 combined the federal estate and gift tax law, making the same tax rates applicable to all gift transfers of property, whether made inter vivos or at death. (Formerly, the two were separate taxes, with the gift tax rates 3/4th's of the estate tax rates.) The rates for the combined gift-estate tax range from 18% on the first $10,000 of *taxable transfers* to 70% of taxable transfers above $5 million. However, a donor may give away $3,000 a year to each and every donee without incurring any tax liability (this is called the donor's annual exclusion). And through a complicated system of tax credits, there exists an effective exemption equivalent to $134,000 in 1978, $147,000 in 1979, $161,000 in 1980, and $175,000 in 1981 and thereafter. What this means is that a person who makes combined lifetime

---

4. One exception is the joint bank account with the right of survivorship. Here, no gift is deemed to occur, and there is no

gift taxation, until one party withdraws more than he or she has deposited.

and deathtime transfers of less than these amounts will not have to pay gift or estate tax to the federal government.

Because the exemption figures permit a person to transfer tens of thousands of dollars (up to $175,000 in 1980 and thereafter) together inter vivos and at death without incurring any tax liability, it may be concluded that most people do not have to worry about the tax implications of holding property concurrently with the survivorship characteristic. This is particularly true with regard to a husband and wife (the people most likely to hold property with the right of survivorship) because of the federal marital deduction which excludes from death taxation the first $250,000 in money or other property left to a surviving spouse (the marital deduction is limited to the greater of $250,000 or 50% of the gross estate less deductions for funeral, administration, and other expenses). Because of the federal marital deduction, most husbands and wives find it desirable to hold their property with the survivorship characteristic in order to avoid probate with its attendant costs in time and money.

Does a joint tenant or tenant by the entirety who murders his or her cotenant retain survivorship rights as to the deceased tenant's fractional interest in the concurrently held property?

The majority rule is that if one joint tenant or tenant by the entirety murders his or her cotenant, the surviving killer has no survivorship rights as to the murder victim's fractional interest in the property. Many of the jurisdictions following the majority rule hold that the murderer's act results in the creation of a tenancy in common, with the murder victim's lawful beneficiaries or heirs being tenants in common with the murderer.

Some states go beyond the majority rule to deprive the killer of even his or her own fractional interest in the concurrently held property. Other states permit the killer to keep his or her own interest, but hold that, upon the killer's death, the killer's interest in the property goes to the estate of the murdered cotenant, not to the murderer's beneficiaries or heirs (in effect, treating the situation as though the murder victim had survived the murderer).

In any event, the policy behind the law is to prevent the murderer from profiting from his or her wrongful act.

What is community property?

Community property is a form of concurrent ownership that comes, not from England, but from France and Spain. For this reason, it is recognized only in states with a Spanish heritage, and there are eight: Arizona, California, Idaho, Louisiana, Nevada, New Mexico, Texas, and Washington.

The theory behind community property is that a husband and wife form a "community" (community being the "unity" required for this kind of concurrent ownership). All property, other than separate property, acquired by the spouses during the existence of the community is "community property" belonging to both spouses equally in undivided one-half shares.

Because community property, by definition, excludes *separate property,* it is important to understand "separate property" as that term is used in community property states. Separate property refers to property belonging entirely to one spouse who is free to sell the property, mortgage it, or otherwise use or dispose of it without regard to the wishes of the other spouse. Separate property may be acquired as follows:

(1) *In the absence of "community".* Property acquired by either spouse prior to the marriage is separate property and remains separate throughout the mar-

riage. Also, any property either spouse acquires after dissolution of the marriage is separate, as is any property either acquires while living separate and apart.

(2) *In the presence of "community"*. The following types of property are separate property even when acquired by the husband or wife during marriage:

(a) Property a spouse receives as a gift or inheritance;

(b) Rents, dividends, or other income from separate property (e. g., rent income from an apartment house the wife acquired prior to marriage);

(c) Gains from sales or exchanges of separate property, as well as any property received in exchange for separate property;

(d) Earnings from a "sole trader" business; [5] and

(e) Money damages recovered by a spouse for personal injuries inflicted by the other spouse (damages recovered from anyone else are community property).

(3) *Separate property created by agreement*. The spouses are free to designate what would normally be community property as separate property, and vice versa, by agreement prior to or during marriage.

Other than separate property, all property acquired by the spouses *during marriage* is community property—provided the marriage is a valid one. If the marriage is not valid, the general rule is that community property will not result. An exception exists in the case of a *putative* marriage. A putative marriage (also called a "de facto" marriage) arises where one or both spouses believe in good faith that they are validly married when, in fact, they are not. Typically, the spouses go through a marriage ceremony but one spouse is already married to another. For property acquired by the spouses subsequent to the "marriage" to be considered community property, the spouse claiming putative status must have been unaware of the circumstances rendering the marriage void at the time of entering into the marriage ceremony. If the spouse was unaware of the facts, most courts will hold that all property, other than separate property, acquired during the putative marriage is community property belonging one-half to the innocent spouse. On the other hand, some courts hold that there can be no community property in the absence of a valid marriage, but protect the innocent spouse by distributing the property acquired during the putative marriage as "though it were" community property.

Putative marriage must be distinguished from what the law terms a *meretricious relationship* in which a man and woman merely live together with full knowledge that their relationship is not a legal marriage. Recent court holdings in some community property states, most notably California, have expounded a social policy of protecting "family" relationships as opposed to "marriage" relationships. The courts have held that parties living together as a family unit should be accorded equal rights in property acquired during the relationship regardless of marriage formalities. Thus, in the case of Marriage of Cary, 34 Cal. App.3d 345, 109 Cal.Rptr. 862 (1973), the court held that two parties who had lived together for eight years and had four children, all of whom were given the same "family" name on their birth certificates, should divide equally all property acquired during the relationship

---

5. Most community property states have what are called "sole trader" statutes that permit a spouse who formally alleges the other spouse to be incompetent or im-

provident to go into business for himself or herself. The purpose of such statutes is to insulate the petitioner spouse's earnings from the incompetent spouse's debts.

even though both parties knew from the outset that they were not legally married. Of course, there are decisions to the contrary, and a majority of community property states still hold that community property may arise only from a valid or putative marriage.

What rights does each spouse have with regard to community property? Each has an undivided one-half interest in all community property arising out of the marriage relationship, and each has equal rights in management and control of the property. However, like tenants by the entirety (and unlike joint tenants), both spouses must consent to any transfer of an interest in the property—neither is free to transfer his or her own interest irrespective of the wishes of the other.

How does community property compare with joint tenancy with the right of survivorship insofar as the rights of the "surviving" spouse are concerned? You will recall that in the joint tenancy situation, the joint tenants are not free to dispose of their fractional interests in the property by will: upon the death of each joint tenant, his or her interest passes automatically to the surviving tenant or tenants. In community property states, on the other hand, each spouse is free to will his or her share of the community property as he or she sees fit (a spouse's testamentary transfer of his or her interest does not affect the other spouse's interest in the property). It is only where a decedent spouse fails to dispose of his or her community property by will that the surviving spouse is entitled to *all* the community property—not by right of survivorship, but by virtue of the state intestacy laws. The intestacy laws also give the "surviving" spouse a right to some portion (though usually not all) of the decedent spouse's separate property.

As to creditors' claims, each spouse's separate property is, of course, subject to debts incurred by the owner spouse at any time, whether before or after marriage. However, the separate property of a spouse is never subject to debts incurred by the nonowner spouse. This is not the case with community property which (unlike tenancy by the entirety property) may be reached by creditors of either spouse for debts incurred both before and after marriage. Where the community property is used to satisfy a separate obligation of one spouse, reimbursement from that spouse's separate property may be required.

In the event that the parties obtain a divorce, the community property is usually divided equally between husband and wife regardless of the cause of dissolution. However, the court cannot award one spouse's separate property to the other, although the court may consider the value of the separate assets in determining how much alimony or child support should be paid.

What is a tenancy in partnership?

Earlier in the chapter, we defined a partnership as "an association of two or more persons to carry on as co-owners a business for a profit". A partnership thus requires two things: a community of interest in the business and a sharing of profits.

As to ownership of partnership property, each partner has equal rights to the property in a form of concurrent ownership called *tenancy in partnership*. The legal "unity" required for this form of ownership is the partnership method of doing business. The incidents of ownership are as follows:

(1) Each partner has an equal right to possession of partnership property for partnership purposes (as opposed to private purposes or interests of the individual partners);

(2) All partners must join in any transfer of an interest in partnership property;

(3) Partnership property is subject only to the claims of creditors of the partnership—not to claims of creditors of the individual partners;

(4) Partnership property is not considered community property and is not subject to any property interests of spouses or families;

(5) Partnership property is not part of a deceased partner's estate: upon the death of a partner, the remaining partners automatically receive the decedent's interest in the partnership property until the last surviving partner owns the property in severalty. However, as you will learn in more detail in Ch. 22, the surviving partners must account to the decedent's estate for what is called the partner's "interest in the partnership". This interest has nothing to do with the specific partnership property owned in tenancy in partnership. Rather, it is a partner's share of partnership profits and surplus. It is personal property, and, unlike the partnership assets held in tenancy in partnership, it can be reached by creditors of the individual partner. What is more, the partner may freely transfer his or her "interest in the partnership", although the transferee will not become a partner, but will merely become entitled to receive that partner's share of partnership profits and surplus.

What are incidental rights in real estate?

In addition to major interests in real property (e. g., the "large sticks" of fee simple, life estate, reversion, remainder, and executory interest), there are several lesser interests (i. e., "skinnier sticks") that may be owned with regard to land. They are called *rights of enjoyment incident to land ownership*. The remainder of this chapter is devoted to the three most important incidental rights—water rights, support rights, and rights in airspace.

What kinds of water rights are there?

When water borders land, covers land, or runs under land, it is only natural that surrounding landowners ask the following: Who is entitled to use the water? For what purpose? To what extent? Does anyone "own" the land under the water? The law of water rights was developed to answer these questions and the many others arising from (the frequently heated) controversies over the use and ownership of water. The principles of the law may be summarized as follows:

(1) *Navigable water*. The law of water rights first draws a distinction between navigable and nonnavigable water. Navigable water is water suitable for navigation (i. e., the passage of vessels). Usually, this means that the water must be suitable for *commercial* navigation (e. g., the transportation of goods) whether or not such navigation actually takes place on the water. However, there are some exceptions, and coastal streams along the Western United States are considered navigable even though the streams are suitable only for a guide and one or two sports fisherpersons out after salmon and steelhead. And in some states, particular waters are simply designated navigable by statute.

It is generally recognized that a state holds navigable water in public trust for the benefit of the people in the state. Thus, all members of the public have equal rights with regard to navigation and recreation on the water (e. g., sailing, fishing, swimming). This is true even where the water runs over privately owned land, although in most cases, the riverbeds of navigable waters are owned by the state. The public's right to use the navigable water does not include a right to trespass on privately owned land bordering the waterway—the public's right of use extends to the river or stream only. In the unlikely situation that there is no means of access to the waterway other than across private property, the public may have a limited right of access over the land. However, in no event may the state effectively deprive the landowner of his or her own right of access to the waterway without paying the landowner just compensation.

(2) *Nonnavigable water.* A property owner alongside a nonnavigable river or stream owns the bed of the water to the middle of the river or stream (the same is true with respect to a property owner along the side of a navigable waterway, the bed of which does not belong to the state). Where the middle line of the river or stream serves as the boundary line between two owners (as it often does), the middle line will remain the boundary even though it changes as the result of a *gradual* change in the location of the stream itself. But where the location of the stream changes suddenly and perceptibly, the "old" middle line prior to the change will continue to serve as the boundary—the new middle line will be disregarded. A property owner who gains land as new soil ("alluvion") is gradually deposited from the water onto his or her property, or as water gradually recedes from the land ("dereliction") exposing soil already there, is said to acquire the property by *accretion*. The term accretion applies to the acquisition of new soil by alluvion or dereliction whether or not the landowner owns to the middle of the stream, and regardless of whether the middle line of the stream is changed. But remember, the change must be gradual and imperceptible: floods, storms, and the like that suddenly and perceptibly change the course of rivers and streams will never result in a change of land ownership. Sudden change that does not result in a change of ownership or boundary is termed *avulsion*.

Suppose that an island is formed in a river or stream by the gradual deposit of alluvial matter (soil carried by the sea and gradually washed into position). If formation of the island is gradual, and it accompanies a gradual shifting of the middle line of the river or stream, the island will belong to whoever owns the river or stream bed below it as determined by the new middle line. If the island crosses the new middle line, it will belong to both owners. In the event the formation is not gradual, the boundary will not change, and the island will belong to the owner of the river or stream bed below as determined by the old boundary line. Where the island springs up in the absence of a change in middle line, it makes no difference whether its formation is gradual or sudden—it will belong to the owner of the river bed or stream bed below it.

(3) *Tide waters.* Tide waters are waters in which an ebbing and flowing of water occurs whether in the ocean, a bay, or a river. Generally, all land below the "low-water" mark belongs to the state. With regard to the ocean, all land bordering on the ocean above the ordinary low-water mark, but below the ordinary high-water mark is designated "shore" or "beach" and is held in trust by the state for the benefit of the public.

(4) *Lakes and ponds.* While states vary somewhat as to the ownership of land below lakes and ponds, title to large lakes (including the "Great Lakes") and other large bodies of water belongs in most cases to the states. Only the beds of small lakes and ponds are likely to belong to riparian owners (a riparian owner is a person who owns land next to the water).

(5) *Ice.* Ice formed on nonnavigable and nontidal waters belongs to the riparian owners bordering the water: the ownership of the ice goes to the riparian owner who owns the bed beneath the ice. Where the state owns the bed, as is the case with most navigable waterways, the first member of the public to appropriate the ice acquires ownership.

(6) *Riparian rights.* Riparian landowners who own land bordering streams or lakes enjoy what are called *riparian rights.* Such rights include the right to a stream's natural flow undiminished in quantity, quality, or velocity; the right to a lake's natural level and purity; and the right to use the water for recreation (e. g., swimming, fishing, boating).

To qualify as riparian property (so as to confer riparian rights upon its owner), land must: (1) touch the water of a lake or stream; and (2) fall within the watershed (i. e., within the drainage area of the lake or stream). So long as these two conditions are satisfied, it makes no difference how large the tract of land is, or how much of it is touching on the water.

Suppose that a riparian landowner purchases a tract of land adjoining his or her riparian property, but not itself bordering on the water. Does this new tract of land become riparian property because it is connected to riparian land? There are two legal positions on the "extension" of riparian land. Under the majority rule, called the *unity of title* rule, all land within the watershed that forms a part of a contiguous whole belonging to one person and bordering on the water is riparian land regardless of when ownership of the "part" was acquired. Thus, a riparian owner of a lakeside tract can increase his or her riparian rights by buying up contiguous, though nonlakefront property. The minority rule rejects this position in favor of the *source of title* rule which states that riparian land is the smallest tract of land touching water ever owned by one person (i. e., in that person's history of title to the "riparian" property). Thus, under the minority rule, a riparian owner cannot acquire contiguous property that does not touch water and call it riparian. Nor can he or she transfer a back portion of riparian property that does not touch the water, then later reacquire the property and call it

riparian—once it is cut off from the riparian property, it cannot form part of the smallest riparian tract the owner has ever possessed. As a result, it can never become riparian again, at least not for that particular owner.

How much water is a riparian owner along a river or stream entitled to? The answer depends upon whether the landowner's jurisdiction follows the doctrine of riparian rights or the doctrine of prior appropriation. The *doctrine of riparian rights* is a rule of law stating that a riparian owner is entitled to the flow of the river or stream water in its natural condition to, by, through, and over his or her land, free from unreasonable diminution in quantity and free from unreasonable pollution in quality. However, even among states following the doctrine, there are a variety of factors entering into whether or not a lower riparian owner (i. e., an owner farther down the river or stream) can object to a diversion of water by an upper riparian owner. These factors include:

(a) *Natural flow rule.* Some states apply the "natural flow" rule and hold that the lower riparian owner is entitled to the *natural flow of the water without material diminution in quantity or quality.* This rule may lead to a waste of water resources as even a downstream owner who has more water than he or she needs can legally demand that the upstream owner stop diminishing the natural flow. If the upstream owner refuses to stop, the downstream owner may obtain a legal injunction (court order) requiring him or her to do so.

(b) *Reasonable use rule.* Other states apply the "reasonable use" rule which states that the downstream owner can enjoin (stop or prevent) upper riparian use of the water only if the lower riparian is not receiving enough water for his or her needs. If the lower riparian has no needs, the upstream owner may use all the water.

(c) *Domestic use.* In both natural flow and reasonable use states, the upstream owner is free to take whatever water he or she needs for domestic purposes such as drinking, bathing, irrigating gardens, watering farm animals on a small farm, etc. Such domestic use is permitted even where it substantially and adversely affects the lower riparian landowner.

(d) *Commercial use.* However, the upper riparian cannot take water for commercial purposes (e. g., irrigating a large ranch) unless all lower riparian domestic needs have been satisfied. Of course, where the reasonable use rule is followed, a good deal of water may be available for commercial purposes; under natural flow, there is likely to be little water available for this purpose.

In contrast to the doctrine of riparian rights is the *doctrine of prior appropriation* which states that the first riparian owner to appropriate the water is entitled to use it all. This doctrine is followed by eight extremely arid states, all located in the Western United States. The "first in time, first in right" approach is justified by these states on the basis that there is not enough water for all riparian owners, and that it is better to obtain some beneficial use from what water there is than to lose all benefit by requiring the owners to share the water. Under this theory, it is wholly immaterial whether the prior appropriator uses the water on riparian or nonriparian land, or whether he or she uses it for natural, domestic, or artificial or business purposes. The prior appropriator can even sever the water rights from the land and sell them to a nonriparian for use on nonriparian land. Again, the idea is that it is better to benefit a few farms or mines than to benefit none at all.

(7) *Surface water.* Surface water is water that has no channel (stream bed or other course to follow) but is diffused (spread out) over land. An example would be water resulting from rain, snow, or seepage. Whoever captures surface water owns it and can use the water for any purpose. Thus, Landowner A who lives on a hill above Landowner B is free to stop or diminish the flow of surface water to B's property and to use the water for domestic or commercial purposes; B' has no right to the continued flow of the water.

However, the usual problem with surface water arises, not where a landowner attempts to capture the water, but where the landowner attempts to get rid of the water by changing the natural drainage so that it will flow onto another's property. Whether or not the party who changes the course of the water will be liable to the party on whose land the water flows depends upon which of the following three doctrines is recognized in the landowners' jurisdiction:

(a) *Common enemy doctrine.* This doctrine, followed in about half our states, declares that surface water is a common enemy of all landowners, and that any landowner can do whatever is necessary to change the drainage and get rid of the water. Under this doctrine, a landowner may use any means available to prevent surface water from coming onto his or her land without incurring any liability to neighboring landowners.

(b) *Reasonable interference doctrine.* Gaining support in some states, this doctrine modifies the common enemy doctrine to provide that a landowner may take whatever action is necessary to get rid of surface water only so long as the landowner does not unreasonably interfere with his or her neighbor's land. The landowner will thus be liable for any unnecessary or disproportionate harm to the neighbor's property.

(c) *Natural servitude doctrine.* Close to half our states hold to this position which maintains that lower lands are *ser-*

vient to (i. e., subject to) the natural surface drainage of upper lands. Thus, a lower owner cannot prevent, obstruct, or change the flow of surface water if the result is to injure landowners either above or below his or her land—the landowner's property is servient to the upper land, and the lower owners have a right to the *natural* flow of the surface water. (Some states permit the servient landowner to make *reasonable* changes in the flow of the water, particularly in urban areas where grading of land is necessary for development.)

Of course, in many instances, upper and lower owners do not care whether the flow of the water is changed, and so a landowner will be free to build a dam or use ditches to change the flow of the water. But where upper and lower owners object, or where the result is to damage their property, the dams or ditches will not be permitted.

In conclusion, lower owners are obligated to receive the natural flow of water from above, including the flow of natural flood waters. However, they are not obligated to receive flood waters caused by extraordinary events such as the bursting of a dam on an upper owner's property. The upper owner, in such event, will be liable in money damages for any injury that results to the lower owner's property.

(8) *Percolating water.* Percolating water is water that moves under the ground and through the ground diffusely rather than in a channel. Percolating water is considered a part of the soil and generally belongs to whoever owns the soil through which it moves.

In the Eastern United States, it is generally agreed that the surface owner has an unqualified right to pump as much percolating water from beneath the land as he or she desires. In the Western United States, the surface owner is limited to pumping the amount of water reasona-

bly needed for use on his or her property. In California, for example, adjoining surface owners are considered "joint tenants" as to percolating water beneath their land (because the water moves diffusely, and not through a channel, it does not remain under the same soil for long). As joint tenants, each owner is entitled to pump the amount of water reasonably needed for his or her property.

It might be pointed out that a few Western states apply the prior appropriation doctrine to percolating water and hold that the "first in time is first in right" to all the water. And in many parts of the country, conservation statutes control the extent to which percolating water may be taken from beneath the ground and used.

What kinds of support rights are there?

A landowner is entitled to the support of his or her property in its natural state by adjoining land and may bring legal action against any neighbor who causes his or her land to "sink" as a result of excavation or other activity. There are two kinds of support rights—lateral support and subjacent support.

(1) *Lateral support.* The right to lateral support (i. e., the right to support from adjoining land) is an absolute right of every landowner. For example, if Neighbor A's excavation activity causes Neighbor B's land to sink, slide, or cave in, A will be liable to B whether or not A was negligent.

However, the right of lateral support is for support of the land in its *natural* state—not for support of *structures* on the land (a minority of states extend the right of absolute support to buildings, one kind of structure). Thus if in the example above, Neighbor B's house sinks, B can recover damages for injury to the *land* regardless of A's negligence if he can prove that the land would have sunk even without the structure upon it. But he cannot recover damages for injury to the *house* unless he can prove that A was negligent in how she excavated the property. B's right to recover, then, is not absolute with regard to the structure—he must prove negligence on the part of A. In many jurisdictions, the legal duties imposed upon an excavator are so great that negligence is very easy to find, with the result that excavators are held to an almost absolute duty regarding structures, the same as they are with regard to land.

(2) *Subjacent support.* Subjacent support refers to the landowner's right to support of his or her property from below (i. e., from the land lying under it). If Neighbor A extracts minerals from her property with the result that subjacent support is removed from Neighbor B's property, A will be absolutely liable to B not only for damage resulting to B's *land*, but for damage resulting to any *buildings* on B's land at the time the mining operation began. However, A will not be responsible for damage to buildings constructed after commencement of the mining activity unless A was negligent in how she conducted the operation. A will also be responsible to B for negligently damaging springs or wells or for interfering with underground percolating water.

What kinds of airspace rights are there?

The courts have long recognized that a real property owner may bring a trespass action (see Ch. 1) for an unwarranted intrusion into the airspace above his or her land. How far does a landowner's property right in airspace extend? Long ago, England's Lord Coke stated—"cujus est solum ejus est usque ad coelum" (meaning, literally, the person who owns the soil owns upward into heaven). Obviously, such a broad statement of ownership has little application in today's world of aviation. Modernly, the courts are called upon to balance the property rights of the private landowner against the public's need for aircraft of every size, shape, and description. In striking the balance, the courts have applied the following theories:

(1) *The zone theory.* The "zone theory" divides the airspace above a landowner's property into two strata. The lower, protected zone is limited to the area of the owner's effective possession (i. e., that portion of the land that is essential to complete use and enjoyment of the property whether or not it is actually used). Any intrusion into the lower zone constitutes a trespass; any flight or passage through the upper zone is nonactionable.

(2) *The actual use theory.* Under the "actual use" theory, the landowner's ownership rights extend only to airspace that he or she actually uses in present enjoyment of the property. Interference with such airspace gives rise to a trespass action.

(3) *The nuisance theory.* The "nuisance" theory steers clear of the ownership problems inherent in a trespass action. It focuses, instead, on whether there has been an unreasonable interference with the landowner's use and enjoyment of the land (see Ch. 1 regarding the tort of "nuisance"). Under this theory, the courts have recognized that federal statutes and Civil Aeronautics Board regulations have, in effect, established a public domain and federal highway in the airspace above prescribed minimum altitudes. Above such altitudes, there can be no trespass as the landowner does not "own" the airspace. But whether activity comes from below or above the minimum altitudes, if it unreasonably interferes with the landowner's use and enjoyment of his or her property, it will be actionable on a nuisance theory. In one case, landowners near a public airport complained that aircraft noise deprived them of the substantial use and enjoyment of their property. The court

agreed, stating that the noise amounted to a continuing nuisance. But because of the public need for the airport, the court allowed the aircraft to continue flying over the property. However, it ordered the government which operated the airport to pay just compensation to the land-owners (stating that the government had, for all intents and purposes, "taken" the landowner's property under the power of eminent domain). Thornburg v. Port of Portland, 233 Or. 178, 376 P.2d 100 (1962).

CASES

CASE 1—*The last survivor gets all the money.*

RUSHAK v. RUSHAK

Supreme Court, Appellate Division, Fourth Department, 1967.
281 N.Y.S.2d 940, 28 A.D.2d 807.

On January 14, 1952 Paraska Rushak opened the bank account which is the subject of the present litigation. Subsequently, in December 1959, she converted the account to a joint account, and a signature card was deposited with the bank bearing signatures of Paraska Rushak and her two sons, John and Stephen, stating that the account was jointly owned by the signatories, the survivor being entitled to the balance. The only deposits ever made in the account were made by Mrs. Rushak before the creation of the joint tenancy and the book was kept by her until her death on July 20, 1965. Five days later, on July 25, 1965, her son Stephen also died, leaving John as the surviving joint tenant. The appeal now before us is by John Rushak from a decree determining that the bank account belongs one-half to the estate of Stephen and one-half to John.

There can be no question * * * that in December 1959 Paraska Rushak created a joint tenancy with a right of ownership in the survivor. The fact that there were three, rather than the usual two, joint tenants does not change this result; nor is it affected by the death of one joint tenant. If, during the lifetime of the two surviving tenants, neither disposes of his joint interest, upon the death of the second joint owner the last survivor becomes the sole owner.

It is not important what the intention of either Stephen or John might have been after the death of Paraska as regards the ultimate disposition of the bank account, for they were not then creating a joint tenancy—or any interest—as between themselves. The joint tenancy with the right of survivorship had already been created in 1959 and that tenancy continued up to the death of Stephen, in the absence of any act by either of the brothers to terminate it. The joint ownership of personal property was analogous to a joint estate in lands and until terminated by act of the parties continued subject to the right of sole ownership in the survivor.

Decree unanimously reversed on the law and order granted decreeing that the joint bank account belongs to John Rushak * * *.

CASE 2—*Appellee pumped Horseshoe Lake down to where you could not even fish it.*

HARRIS v. BROOKS

Supreme Court of Arkansas, 1955.
225 Ark. 428, 283 S.W.2d 129.

WARD, Justice.

The issues presented by this appeal relate to the relative rights of riparian landowners to the use of a privately owned nonnavigable lake and the water therein.

Appellant, Theo Mashburn, lessee of riparian landowners conducts a commercial boating and fishing enterprise. In this business he rents cabins, sells fishing bait and equipment, and rents boats to members of the general public who desire to use the lake for fishing and other recreational purposes. He and his lessors filed a complaint in chancery court on July 10, 1954 to enjoin appellees from pumping water from the lake to irrigate a rice crop, alleging that, as of that date, appellees had reduced the water level of the lake to such an extent as to make the lake unsuitable "for fishing, recreation, or other lawful purposes." After a lengthy hearing, the chancellor denied injunctive relief, and this appeal is prosecuted to reverse the chancellor's decision.

Factual Background. Horseshoe Lake, located about 3 miles south of Augusta, is approximately 3 miles long and 300 feet wide, and, as the name implies, resembles a horseshoe in shape. Appellees, John Brooks and John Brooks, Jr., are lessees of Ector Johnson who owns a large tract of land adjacent to the lake, including three-fourths of the lake bed.

For a number of years appellees have intermittently raised rice on Johnson's land and have each year, including 1954, irrigated the rice with water pumped from the lake. They pumped no more water in 1954 than they did in 1951 and 1952, no rice being raised in 1953. Approximately 190 acres were cultivated in rice in 1954.

The rest of the lake bed and the adjoining land is divided into four parts, each part owned by a different person or group of persons. One such part is owned by Ed Harris, Jesse Harris, Alice Lynch and Dora Balkin who are also appellants. In March 1954 Mashburn leased from the above named appellants a relatively small camp site on the bank of the lake and installed the business above mentioned at a cost of approximately $8,000, including boats, cabins, and fishing equipment. Mashburn began operating his business about the first of April, 1954, and fishing and boat rentals were satisfactory from that time until about July 1st or 4th when, he says, the fish quit biting and his income from that source and boat rentals was reduced to practically nothing.

Appellees began pumping water with an 8 inch intake on May 25, 1954 and continued pumping until this suit was filed on July 10, and then until about August 20th. They quit pumping at this time because it was discovered fish life was being endangered. The trial was had September 28, 1954, and the decree was rendered December 29, 1954.

The Testimony. Because of the disposition we hereafter make of this case, it would serve no useful purpose to set out the voluminous testimony in detail or attempt to evaluate all the conflicting portions thereof. The burden of appellants' testimony, given by residents who had observed the lake over a period of years and by those familiar with fish life and sea level calculations, was directed at establishing the *normal* or *medium* water level of the lake. The years 1952, 1953 and 1954 were unusually dry and the water levels in similar lakes in the same general area were unusually low in August and September of 1954. During August 1954 Horseshoe Lake was below "normal", but it is not entirely clear from the testimony that this was true on July 10 when the suit was filed. It also appears that during the stated period the water had receded from the bank where Mashburn's boats were usually docked, making it impossible for him to rent them to the public. There is strong testimony, disputed by appellees, that the *normal* level of the lake is 189.67 feet above sea level and that the water was below this level on July 10. Unquestionably the water was below normal when this suit was tried the latter part of September, 1954.

On the part of appellees it was attempted to show that: they had used the water for irrigation several years dating back to 1931 and Mashburn knew this when he rented the camp site; although they had been pumping regularly since May 25, 1954 the water did not begin to fall in the lake until July 1st or 4th; an agent of the Arkansas Game and Fish Commission examined the lake and the water about July 2nd and found no condition endangering fish life, and similar examinations after suit was filed showed the same condition, and; they stopped pumping about August 20th when they first learned that fish life was being endangered.

* * *

Two Basic Theories. Generally speaking two separate and distinct theories or doctrines regarding the right to use water are recognized. One is commonly called the "Appropriation Doctrine" and the other is the "Riparian Doctrine".

Appropriation Doctrine. Since it is unnecessary to do so we make no attempt to discuss the varied implications of this doctrine. Generally speaking, under this doctrine, some governmental agency, acting under constitutional or legislative authority, apportions water to contesting claimants. It has never been adopted in this state, but has been in about 17 western states. This doctrine is inconsistent with the common law relative to water rights in force in this and many other states. One principal distinction between this doctrine and the riparian doctrine is that under the former the use is not limited to riparian landowners.

Riparian Doctrine. This doctrine, long in force in this and many other states, is based on the old common law which gave to the owners of land bordering on streams the right to use the water therefrom for certain purposes, and this right was considered an incident to the ownership of land. Originally it apparently accorded the landowner the right to have the water maintained at its normal level, subject to use for strictly domestic purposes. Later it became evident that this strict limitation placed on the use of water was unreasonable and unutilitarian. Consequently it was not long before the demand for a greater use of water caused a relaxation of the strict limitations placed on its use and this doctrine came to be divided into (a) the natural flow theory and (b) the reasonable use theory.

(a) *Natural Flow Theory.* Generally speaking again, under the natural flow theory, a riparian owner can take water for domestic purposes only, such as water for the family, live stock, and gardening, and he is entitled to have the water in the stream or lake upon which he borders kept at the normal level. * * *

Reasonable Use Theory. This theory appears to be based on the necessity and desirability of deriving greater benefits from the use of our abundant supply of water. It recognizes that there is no sound reason for maintaining our lakes and streams at a normal level when the water can be beneficially used without causing unreasonable damage to other riparian owners. The progress of civilization, particularly in regard to manufacturing, irrigation, and recreation, has forced the realization that a strict adherence to the uninterrupted flow doctrine placed an unwarranted limitation on the use of water, and consequently the court developed what we now call the reasonable use theory. This theory is of course subject to different interpretations and limitations. In 56 Am.Jur., page 728, it is stated that "The rights of riparian proprietors on both navigable and unnavigable streams are to a great extent mutual, common, or correlative. The use of the stream or water by each proprietor is therefore limited to what is reasonable, having due regard for the rights of others above, below, or on the opposite shore. In general, the special rights of a riparian owner are such as are necessary for the use and enjoyment of his abutting property and the business lawfully conducted thereon, qualified only by the correlative rights of other riparian owners, and by certain rights of the public, and they are to be so exercised as not to injure others in the enjoyment of their rights." It has been stated that each riparian owner has an equal right to make a reasonable use of waters subject to the equal rights of other owners to make the reasonable use. The purpose of the law is to secure to each riparian owner equality in the use of water as near as may be by requiring each to exercise his right reasonably and with due regard to the rights of others similarly situated.

* * * The nucleus of this opinion is, therefore, a definite acceptance of the reasonable use theory. We do not understand that the two theories will necessarily clash in every case, but where there is an inconsistency, and where vested rights may not prevent, it is our conclusion that the reasonable use theory should control.

* * *

The result of our examination of the decisions of this court and other authorities relative to the use by riparian proprietors of water in non-navigable lakes and streams justifies the enunciation of the following general rules and principles:

(a) The right to use water for strictly domestic purposes—such as for household use—is superior to many other uses of water—such as for fishing, recreation and irrigation.

(b) Other than the use mentioned above, all other lawful uses of water are equal. Some of the lawful uses of water recognized by this state are: fishing, swimming, recreation, and irrigation.

(c) When one lawful use of water is destroyed by another lawful use the latter must yield, or it may be enjoined.

(d) When one lawful use of water interferes with or detracts from another lawful use, then a question arises as to whether, under all the facts and circumstances of that particular case, the interfering use shall be declared unreasonable and as such enjoined, or whether a reasonable and equitable adjustment should be made, having due regard to the reasonable rights of each.

* * *

Our Conclusion. After careful consideration, an application of the rules above announced to the complicated fact situation set forth in this record leads us to conclude that the Chancellor should have issued an order enjoining appellees from pumping water out of Horseshoe Lake when the water level reaches 189.67 feet above sea level for as long as the material facts and circumstances are substantially the same as they appear in this record. * * *

[E]ach riparian owner has the right to use the water in the lake for all lawful purposes, so long as his use of the water is not detrimental to the rights of other riparian owners. * * * From the evidence in the record it is plain that when the water of the lake here involved is at normal level the lake is too small in area and content to allow water to be pumped therefrom for irrigating purposes without consequent damage to other riparian owners. * * *

We think the conclusion we have reached is not only logical but practical. Although appellees had quit using water from the lake when this case was tried yet they testified that they intended to use water therefrom in 1955. We might assume that they would want to also use water in subsequent years, so it would seem to be to the best interest of all parties concerned to have a definite level fixed at which pumping for irrigation must cease in order to avoid useless litigation.

* * *

Reversed with direction to the trial court to enter a decree in conformity with this opinion.

PROBLEMS

1. Answer the following "True" or "False" and give reasons for your answers:

    (a) Most people don't have to worry about the gift and estate tax implications of holding property jointly with the right of survivorship or as tenants by the entirety.

    (b) Community property law exists in a majority of states, including California and Arizona.

    (c) A sudden, perceptible change in the course of a nonnavigable river will never result in a change of boundary line between owners.

    (d) A creditor of both spouses can reach property held by the spouses as tenants by the entirety, but a creditor of one spouse cannot reach community property held by the spouses.

    (e) A conveyance of property "¼ to John and ¾'s to Sue, as joint tenants with the right of survivorship" creates a valid joint tenancy.

    (f) A landowner who removes lateral support from an adjoining landowner's property is strictly liable for any damage that results to the adjoining landowner's land and structures.

2. Betty Chase conveys five acres of land, part of which is bordering a stream (and which is within the stream's watershed), "to Paul Stoddard, Gloria Green, and Walter Thompson, each to have an equal, undivided share in the whole of the property." Of the three, only Paul

Stoddard moves onto the land; he cultivates crops (which he sells in the city); takes in a lodger; and makes minor repairs on the property. Paul receives a property tax statement, a copy of which he sends to Gloria and Walter along with a list of repair costs. A few weeks later when Paul diverts water from the stream to irrigate his crops, a downstream owner complains that she doesn't have enough water to run her public resort (which has been in operation for over a year now). To add to Paul's problems, Gloria and Walter tell him that he has no right to live on the land and must leave immediately; that, since he was living there, he is solely responsible for property taxes and repairs; and that they are entitled to a share of all property proceeds and rent money.

(a) What real property interest, if any, was created in Paul, Gloria, and Walter by the terms of the conveyance? *tenancy in common*

(b) Does Paul have a right to divert water from the stream for irrigation purposes? Explain. *Riparian owner no - diminishes use*

(c) Does Paul have a right to live on the land? *yes* To keep all crop and rent proceeds? *Paul keep* Explain. *Rent shared*

(d) Who is responsible for paying property taxes and repair costs? Explain. *Shared, but crop & rent must be applied first*

3. Marsha McKenzie also owns a small tract of land bordering the stream. She purchases an adjoining tract that does not border the stream and there raises a few cows and sheep to provide her with meat, wool, and a steady supply of milk. When Marsha diverts water from the stream to irrigate the adjoining tract for the benefit of the livestock, the downstream owners complain that the flow of the stream has been diminished. Does Marsha have a right to divert the water to the adjoining tract? Explain.

4. Marsha McKenzie marries Greg Brown. After their marriage, Marsha sells her streamfront property and the adjoining tract and places the proceeds in a savings account in her own name; Greg does not join her in the transfer. Over the years, Greg and Marsha acquire a home, expensive furnishings, and a beachhouse. Both Greg and Marsha help pay for these items (however, Marsha works only part-time and does not contribute as much as Greg). After Greg and Marsha have been married 40 years, Greg receives a small inheritance from his father and uses the money to purchase a new car. Not long after, Marsha sells the beachhouse to Bill O'Connell without telling Greg about the sale. Greg dies a few weeks later leaving a will giving "whatever interest in real or personal property I may own to my sister Ruth." Assuming community property law applies, answer the following:

(a) As between Ruth and Marsha, who owns the savings account proceeds? The house and furnishings? The new car? Explain all your answers. *ⓐ marsha sep. prop.* *ⓑ Both tenants in common community* *ⓒ Ruth sep prop*

(b) As between Ruth, Marsha, and Bill O'Connell, who owns the beachhouse? Explain. *Tenants in Common not effective transfer* *Bill has action against marsha*

5. How would your answer to # 4 above differ if Greg and Marsha were not legally married, but were only "living together"?

6. Larry Wilson conveys real property "to Ted Armstrong, Mary Marx, Judy Johnson, and Rick Taylor, equally, in undivided shares with the right of survivorship." Mary is in need of cash so she sells her inter-

[margin handwritten: minority source of title majority unity of title P. 119-20]

est in the land to Marty Michaels. Within ten years time, both Judy and Marty die. Ted then shoots and kills Rick and claims title to all the land.

(a) What interest, if any, was created in Ted, Mary, Judy, and Rick by the terms of the conveyance? Explain. *Joint tenancy w/rt. of survivorship*

(b) What was the effect of Mary selling her interest to Marty Michaels? *Tenant in common*

(c) What was the effect of Judy's death? Of Marty's death? *Ted & Rick get her share*   *Pass to heirs*

(d) Does Ted now have title to all the land? Explain. *No, cannot succeed against Rick*

7. A joint tenancy

(a) Cannot be created by deed.

(b) Will be found to exist by judicial preference if it is unclear as to whether a joint tenancy or tenancy in common was intended by the grantor.

(c) Cannot be created in respect to personal property.

(d) Provides a right of survivorship in the surviving joint tenant.

[# 26, May, 1976 CPA Exam]

8. Olson conveyed real property to his sons, Sampson and David, but the deed was ambiguous as to the type of estate created and the interest each son had in relation to the other. David died intestate (without a will) shortly after Olson. David's widow and children are contending that they have rights in the property. Which of the following would be the widow's and children's best argument to claim valid rights in the real property?

(a) The conveyance by Olson created a life estate in Sampson with a contingent remainder interest in David.

(b) The conveyance by Olson created a joint tenancy with a right of survivorship.

(c) The conveyance by Olson created a tenancy in common.

(d) The widow is entitled to her statutory share.

[# 27, May, 1978 CPA Exam]

9. A joint tenant's interest in real property

(a) Can only be created by deed.

(b) Need not be created at the same time nor pursuant to the same instrument.

(c) Will not pass under the laws of intestate succession.

(d) Cannot be sold or severed during the life of the joint tenancy.

[# 39, May, 1977 CPA Exam]

10. *True or false question.* Brown wished to raise some additional capital for his manufacturing business. Ames, his accountant, suggested that he mortgage his estate, Longacre. Brown then did this receiving a $10,000 loan from Central Bank and giving his mortgage bond in that amount. Brown neglected to advise either Ames or the Bank that he previously had mortgaged Longacre to Collins who failed to record the mortgage. The Bank promptly recorded its mortgage. In anticipation of his son Henry's wedding to Helen Smith, Brown deeded Longacre as

a wedding gift to Henry Brown and Helen Smith. Henry and Helen recorded the deed and were married.

F (a) The deed to Henry and Helen created a tenancy by the entirety.

T (b) If Henry and Helen were married at the time they received the deed, the answer to Item a. would be different.

T (c) Either Henry or Helen may dispose of his or her interest in Longacre without the consent of the other.

T (d) If Henry and Helen were tenants by the entirety in Longacre and Helen dies first, Henry automatically becomes the owner of the entire estate even if Helen's will provides otherwise.

[# 10, May 1971 CPA Exam]

Chapter 6

LIFETIME TRANSFERS OF LAND AND LAND USE PLANNING: DEEDS, ADVERSE POSSESSION, EASEMENTS, PROFITS, COVENANTS, LICENSES, ZONING, AND EMINENT DOMAIN

When and how is real property transferred?

Whether a person owns land in severalty or concurrently with others, there will come a time when that person's interest in land will be transferred into the possession and ownership of another. We have already learned that the Rule Against Perpetuities prohibits a landowner from tying up the ownership of land for countless generations. We know that the free transferability of land is one of the chief characteristics of a fee simple interest in property, and that real estate changes ownership in the United States over and over again. (It is no wonder that thousands of people make a living as real estate salespersons—the potential increase in real property value makes investment in real estate an attractive proposition.)

A landowner may *voluntarily* transfer his or her interest in land during life by gift, sale, or other exchange; or he or she may *involuntarily* part with it inter vivos as the result of adverse possession, creditors' claims, tax sale, or condemnation.

A landowner who does not transfer his or her land during life, either voluntarily or involuntarily, must "voluntarily" part with it at death by will or intestacy (testamentary transfers are "voluntary" in the sense that death is inevitable, and "you can't take it with you"—therefore you transfer it to others).

So you see, every landowner's real property will ultimately be transferred—the only questions are when and how.

Both questions are considered in detail in the following outline.

I. *Voluntary transfers in which the owner desires to pass his or her rights in the real estate to another.*

A. Inter vivos (lifetime) transfers.

1. Kinds of transfers.

   a. *By gift.* As defined in Ch. 3, a gift requires: (1) donative intent on the part of the donor; (2) delivery to the donee; and (3) acceptance by the donee.

   b. *By sale.* A sale is a contract between two parties called the "seller" (or vendor) and the "buyer" (or purchaser) in which the seller transfers ownership of property to the buyer in consideration of the payment or promise of payment of a certain price in money or money's worth.

   c. *By exchange.* An exchange is a reciprocal transfer or "mutual swap" of interests, one "in exchange" for the other. Under our tax laws, many exchanges of property, particularly "like kind" exchanges (i. e., exchanges of the same kind of property, real for real or personal for personal), do not result in the immediate recognition of taxable gain even though a transferor ends up with property worth considerably more than his or her original investment in the exchanged property. For example, if Ernie Entrepreneur buys an apartment house for $100,000, holds it for ten years, then exchanges it for a ranch worth $150,000, Ernie will not immediately recognize any gain for tax purposes. However, to the extent that Ernie also receives money in exchange for the apartment house (e. g., if Ernie receives the ranch plus $5,000), Ernie's gain will be recognized (here, a $5,000 recognized gain). And even where no money is involved, Ernie's full gain will be recognized and taxed upon the ultimate cash sale of the ranch. Thus, the tax advantage of property exchange is merely to postpone the tax—not to eliminate it altogether. Yet postponement itself is extremely valuable for it permits an investor to keep trading (exchanging) properties for properties of higher value without the burden of producing immediate cash for the payment of income taxes.

2. Method of transfer. Whether real estate is transferred by gift, sale, or exchange, a "deed" is used to effectuate the transfer. Students frequently make the mistake of thinking that deeds are contracts —they are not. A deed is simply an instrument required by law to evidence the transfer of real property by gift, contract of sale, or contract of exchange. It is a writing, signed by the grantor, whereby title (ownership) of real property is conveyed (i. e., transferred) from one person to another.

B. Testamentary (deathtime) transfers. (Again, such transfers are voluntary in the sense that death is inevitable for us all. Because you "can't take it with you", you transfer it to others.)

1. Kinds of transfers.

   a. *By will.* A will is a revocable instrument by which a person provides for the disposition of his or her real and personal property upon death.

   b. *By intestacy.* The real and personal property of a person who dies intestate (i. e., without a will) is transferred to the decedent's heirs according to state intestacy statutes specifying who gets what. Generally, these laws give one-half of the decedent's property to his or her surviving spouse, and the other half to the surviving children. Where the decedent has no immediate family, the intestacy laws permit more remote heirs to inherit so long as they are not too far removed. Where the heirs are too remote, or the decedent has no family at all, the decedent's property will "escheat" (i. e., pass) to the state. (Wills and intestate succession are considered in detail in Ch. 30).

2. Method of transfer. One method frequently used in testamentary transfers by will (and in inter vivos gift transfers) is the "trust" arrangement in which real or personal property is transferred (by will, deed, etc.) to a party called a "trustee" who holds and manages the property for the benefit of another. (Trusts are dealt with in Ch. 29.)

II. *Involuntary transfers in which the owner's interest in real or personal property is transferred to another irrespective of the owner's intent or desire.*

A. *Adverse possession.* Adverse possession is a method of acquiring ownership of real property by merely possessing the property in a manner prescribed by statute for a specified period of time (usually 10 or 20 years).

B. *Creditors' rights.* As previously explained, creditors have the ability to "reach" the property of debtors who fail to pay their debts. This means that once a creditor has reduced his or her claim to judgment in a court of law, the creditor can force a sale of the debtor's property to satisfy the judgment. (A judgment is simply a court's decision as to the outcome of a particular claim or controversy.)

C. *Rights of government.* Federal and state governments may deprive an owner of his or her interest in property by means of tax sales and eminent domain.

1. *Tax sales.* Like a creditor, the government may seize and sell the real and personal property of a person who fails to pay his or her taxes.

2. *Eminent domain.* As mentioned briefly in Ch. 2, eminent domain is the power of government to take private property for public use upon the payment of just compensation.

With this broad outline in mind, let's get more specific: deeds, adverse possession, and eminent domain will be considered in this chapter along with both private and governmental land use planning.

What are the requirements of a deed?

A deed is a written instrument expressing a grantor's intent to convey or pass an interest in real property to a grantee. In order to be effective, a deed must be signed by the grantor and it must be delivered by the grantor to the grantee. The requirements of a deed may be summarized as follows:

(1) *In writing.* The transfer of an interest in real property must be evidenced by a writing. Modernly, the appropriate writing is a deed whether the transfer is by gift, sale, or exchange.

(2) *Signed by the grantor.* The written deed must be signed by the grantor —the party making the transfer. If the grantor's signature is forged on the deed, the deed will be of no effect. As for the signature of the grantee, it is not required, nor is it customary.

(3) *Description of the grantee.* The grantee must be sufficiently described in the deed so that it may be ascertained with certainty who is to receive the land. It is not necessary to actually name the grantee so long as he or she may be readily determined from the information given (for example, there is no real problem of identification in a conveyance to "my wife" or to "my children"). However, if the specified grantee is nonexistent or cannot be identified (e. g., in a conveyance merely "to Bill" or "to John"), the deed will be invalid for lack of certainty.

(4) *Words of grant.* The deed must contain words, called words of grant, indicating the grantor's intent to convey an interest in real property to the grantee. No special technical words are required —the word "grant" or the like will do. While many people use the somewhat technical "give, grant, bargain, and sell", this is not a requirement.

The granting clause is important not only because it expresses the grantor's intent to convey, but also because it determines the extent of the estate being transferred. So long as the granting clause clearly states what is being transferred, the granting clause will control even where the rest of the deed is inconsistent. Where the granting clause is unclear, the court will look at the entire instrument to determine the grantor's intent. For example, suppose that a granting clause states "to my son Bill and his heirs and also to Bill and his wife, Anne, and their heirs, jointly with the right of survivorship, forever". The granting clause is inconsistent in that it first appears to create a fee simple interest in Bill alone, but then goes on to suggest a tenancy by the entirety in Bill and Anne in fee simple. The court, in this case, would look to the entire deed instrument to determine which the grantor intended (he or she probably intended a tenancy by the entirety).

Suppose that the deed is silent as to what interest is being transferred. In that case, the law will presume that the grantor intended to convey his or her entire interest in the real property.

(5) *Signature of grantor's spouse.* You will recall from Chapters 3 and 4 that spouses in some states have rights of dower, curtesy, or community property. To release such rights, both spouses must sign any deed of conveyance. In any event, it is always good procedure to have both spouses join in execution of deeds.

(6) *Description of land conveyed.* The test of whether the deed sufficiently describes the land to be transferred is whether the land may be located on the basis of the description with reasonable certainty. Again, as in describing the grantee, all that is required is that the deed provide a means whereby the land may be readily identified. Thus, the description may be by "metes and bounds" (actual measurements and boundaries), by reference to government surveys, by recorded plats (maps or other representations of property subdivided into lots), by streets and numbers, by name of the property, by reference to adjacent property, or by any other nucleus of description.

Land description is considered in detail in a following section.

(7) *Consideration.* Consideration (the giving of money, value, or other benefit to the grantor in exchange for the land) is not required for a valid deed (e.g., a gift transfer of real property by deed requires no consideration). However, consideration will often accompany a transfer by deed because many transfers are the subject matter of contracts of sale or contracts of exchange, and (as you will learn in Ch. 7 dealing with contracts) consideration is required for a valid contract.

Where the grantee does, in fact, purchase the property at its full monetary value, the actual amount that he or she pays for the land does not have to be recited (i. e., stated) on the deed. Often, the purchaser does not want the purchase price publicly known; and, since the purchaser must publicly record the deed in the county land recorder's office in order to protect his or her interest in the property, the best way of keeping the price confidential is to keep it out of the deed. Thus, the language "for value received" or "for $1.00 and other good and valuable consideration" is often found in deeds to show that the grantee was a purchaser—not to show how much he or she paid for the property.

(8) *Acknowledgment.* "Acknowledgment" is required for a valid deed in only a few states, including Arizona and Ohio. "Acknowledgment" refers to a formal declaration made by the grantor in front of a public officer, usually a notary public, that he or she has signed the deed and is transferring the property voluntarily. Upon acknowledgment, the notary public will attach a certificate of acknowledgment to the deed, reciting that the grantor has freely appeared and executed the instrument as his or her voluntary act and deed.

Although very few states require acknowledgment, almost all states provide that an unacknowledged deed cannot be recorded. Thus, a purchaser who fails to obtain an acknowledged deed cannot record the deed and will not be protected against a subsequent purchaser of the same property who obtains and records an acknowledged deed (of course, in this case, the grantor will be in the wrong, and if the original purchaser can catch up with him or her, the purchaser will be able to recover money damages). In any event, the grantee should always insist upon an acknowledged deed, and should never accept one that is unacknowledged.

(9) *Seal.* Historically, the grantor not only had to acknowledge the deed, but had to affix his or her seal thereto as well. Modernly, the requirement of a seal has been dispensed with everywhere.

(10) *Delivery.* The grantor must deliver the deed to the grantee in order to complete the transfer of property. Without delivery the grantor retains title, and the grantee has no ownership interest in the land. What delivery demands is that the grantor signify in some way that the deed is operative. Physical delivery of the deed coupled with the grantor's intent that the delivery be effective to transfer the real property is always sufficient. Whether anything less than this will do depends upon the facts of the particular case. For example, merely handing the deed to the grantee for inspection will never constitute delivery: there is no intent that the physical "delivery" result in transfer of the real property. If the grantor retains physical possession of the deed, there arises a legal presumption against delivery that can only be rebutted by sufficient evidence to the contrary. Where the grantee is in physical possession of the deed, the presumption is in favor of delivery, and, to rebut the presumption, the grantor must introduce sufficient evidence of nondelivery. The fact that a deed has been recorded

also raises a presumption of delivery, as does (at least in some states), the fact that the grantor has acknowledged the deed.

Suppose that the grantor physically delivers the deed to the grantee, but the deed contains a condition that the transfer is not to take effect until the grantor's death. The general rule is that there has been a valid delivery (i. e., a present transfer) of a future interest (a vested remainder in fee simple) to the grantee, with a life estate reserved in the grantor.

Often, the grantor will deliver the deed to a third person with directions to deliver the deed to the grantee only upon the performance of some condition (e. g., the payment of the purchase price). The deed is said to have been placed "in escrow". The third person is called the "escrow agent"; and the instructions defining the conditions that must be met before delivery of the deed are called the "escrow instructions". Placing a deed in escrow protects the purchaser of land against the possible death or disability of the grantor, and it protects the seller by assuring him or her that the purchase price will be paid in full before the deed is physically handed over to the grantee.

(11) *Acceptance.* It is generally agreed that ownership of the property does not pass to the grantee until he or she accepts the deed. However, where the conveyance is beneficial to the grantee (and it usually is), acceptance will be presumed or implied so long as the grantee has knowledge of the deed and fails to indicate his or her rejection of it.

What kinds of deeds are there?

Generally, there are four kinds of deeds used to convey interests in real property: (1) quitclaim deeds; (2) bargain and sale deeds; (3) general warranty deeds; and (4) special warranty deeds.

(1) *Quitclaim deed.* A quitclaim deed is an instrument purporting to convey only what interest, if any, the grantor has in a specified piece of real property. The deed does not purport to transfer the land itself, and the grantor who quitclaims property makes no promise, express or implied, that he or she has good title, or any title or ownership at all. The grantor is merely stating: "If I own any interest, and I may, in fact, own no interest, I am transferring whatever I do own to you." Thus, upon execution of the quitclaim deed, whatever interest the grantor holds in the property will pass to the grantee; if the grantor holds no interest, nothing will be conveyed. In either event, the grantor has made no promise regarding the nature of his or her interest in the land, and will not be responsible or liable if the grantee is later disappointed with the "transfer".

Who is most likely to use a quitclaim deed? Usually, a grantor who believes (but is not certain) that he or she holds an interest in real property that is likely to serve as a defect in title to the property will release his or her "rights" by executing a quitclaim deed. For example, a husband or wife who fails to join his or her spouse in executing a deed to real property might later be asked to release a potential dower or curtesy interest in the land by means of a quitclaim deed.

(2) *Bargain and sale deeds.* A bargain and sale deed is but one step above a quitclaim deed. While a grantor who executes a bargain and sale deed does purport to transfer land to the grantee (and not merely whatever interest, if any, he or she may own in the property), the grantor makes no promise, express or implied, that he or she has good title to the property, or any title at all. Because the grantee pays good value for the land without receiving any assurance (warranty) of title, the grantee is actually in no better position than the grantee of a quitclaim deed.

(3) *General warranty deeds.* A general warranty deed, on the other hand, not only purports to transfer the land itself—it also contains warranties (promises) that the grantor has good title to the property, and that the grantor will protect the grantee from *any and all* claims that should arise from a defect in the grantor's ownership interest. The general warranty deed contains the following specific warranties:

(a) *The covenant of seisin.* The covenant of seisin is the grantor's guaranty that he or she owns the very interest described in the deed; it is the grantor's promise of good title and ownership. If the grantor does not own the interest he or she purports to convey, the grantor breaches this warranty, and the grantee may immediately sue to recover damages.

(b) *The covenant of right to convey.* closely related to the covenant of seisin, this is the grantor's guaranty that he or she has the right to transfer the land.

(c) *The covenant against encumbrances.* The covenant against encumbrances is the grantor's promise that there are no debts outstanding against the property (e. g., mortgages or other liens as will be explained in Ch. 27) and no burdens on the land (e. g., easements and the like as will be defined later in the chapter) other than those described or listed in the warranty deed. If any debts or burdens not disclosed in the deed are later found to exist, the grantor will be liable to the grantee in money damages.

(d) *The covenant for quiet enjoyment.* This covenant is the grantor's promise that the grantee will not be disturbed in his or her possession or enjoyment of the property by some third party's lawful claim of ownership. Thus, if the grantee is rightfully evicted from the premises or otherwise lawfully disturbed in his or her possession of the land by a third party whose title is superior to the grantee's, and whose title existed at the time of the conveyance, the grantor will be liable in damages.

(e) *The covenant for further assurances.* The covenant for further assurances refers to the grantor's promise that where the conveyance is ineffective in perfecting title (ownership) in the grantee, the grantor will execute any additional documents required to perfect title.

With these five warranties, it is no wonder that investors in real property prefer a general warranty deed to quitclaim deeds and deeds of bargain and sale. The grantee who acquires ownership through a general warranty deed is assured of protection from the grantor in the event of future problems regarding title.

(4) *Special warranty deed.* A special warranty deed normally contains all five of the covenants found in the general warranty deed, with one major difference—the covenants found in the special warranty deed apply only to defects in title arising during the grantor's period of ownership of the land, not to defects that may have arisen prior to that time. In other words, the grantor promises only that he or she has not caused any defects in title—not, as in the case of the general warranty deed, that no one else has either. Thus, where title proves defective because of events occurring prior to the grantor's acquisition of title to the property, the grantor will not be liable to the grantee.

Does a grantor have a duty to convey "marketable" title?

A grantor who enters into a binding agreement to sell real property impliedly promises (covenants) that he or she will furnish the buyer with *marketable title* at the time of closing (i. e., at the time the buyer pays the purchase price and the seller delivers the deed to the buyer). Marketable title, often called *merchantable* title, means title reasonably free from

doubt—title that a prudent buyer would accept. The idea behind marketable title is that a buyer should not be required to "purchase a lawsuit". Thus, an outstanding mortgage, lien (claim), or other defect in the property (including outstanding easements, profits, and covenants as will be defined later in the chapter, but generally not including zoning and subdivision restrictions) that is not listed in the contract of sale and is not accepted by the buyer will render the title unmarketable and will enable the buyer to refuse to go through with the purchase.

However, the buyer must insist upon and receive a marketable title prior to paying for the land and accepting delivery of the deed or he or she will be held to have waived the right. This is not to say that the buyer can call off the purchase agreement prior to the closing date because the seller does not have marketable title. There is always a possibility that the seller may obtain marketable title prior to that time, and the law will wait and see whether marketable title exists at the time of closing.

Does a buyer who agrees to accept a quitclaim deed at the time of closing waive his or her right to marketable title? No. Even where the contract of sale provides for delivery by quitclaim deed, the buyer has a right to demand marketable title at the time of closing. The effect of a quitclaim deed is simply to relieve the seller of liability for any unknown defects that become apparent only after closing. To protect himself or herself, the buyer should in any case demand a warranty deed.

The contract of sale may specifically call for a "good record title". This means that the seller must provide marketable title based upon public land records. As you will learn later in the chapter, all states provide for public recordation of deeds and other documents affecting title to real property. The public records show the chain of ownership of the property and list any outstanding interests in the land.

Where "good record title" is demanded, title acquired by adverse possession will not be acceptable. Adverse possession (discussed later in the chapter) is a method of acquiring ownership of real property by merely possessing the property in a manner specified by statute for a designated period of time. Where "good record title" is not demanded, title acquired by adverse possession will qualify as marketable.

Before leaving the area of marketable title, it should be pointed out that the existence of an "encroachment" may also render title unmarketable. An enroachment, as it relates to marketable title, refers to the trespass on land of a physical structure or fixture. An encroachment may exist where: (1) a building or other fixture on the land sold intrudes in part on neighboring land; (2) a building or other fixture on the land sold intrudes upon an adjoining street or alley; or (3) a building or other fixture on adjoining land intrudes upon the land sold. In the case of (1) or (2), title will be unmarketable if the encroachment is likely to result in the institution of suit by either the neighboring landowner or the city for removal of the obstruction. Where the encroachment is *very slight* (e. g., where the landowner's garage extends one-half an inch onto his or her neighbor's property), title will not be rendered unmarketable. It is the policy of the law to permit an obstruction to stand where the trespass is very slight, the cost of removal is great, and the benefit of removal to the landowner is negligible. However, the encroachment of a building one and one-half inches onto neighboring land has been held to render title unmarketable.

So you see, there is no standard yardstick by which to measure the degree of encroachment, and the courts continue to reach their decisions on a case by case basis.

In the case of (3), if the area of land occupied by the encroaching fixture is relatively insignificant, the title will most likely be held marketable, and the buyer will be allowed merely to deduct a portion of the purchase price to reflect the loss in land area.

How is land described on deeds?

We stated previously that every deed must contain a reasonably certain description of the land to be transferred. The test of "reasonable certainty" is whether the location of the land and its boundaries can be determined or fixed with some precision. This test is satisfied by any one of the following methods of land description:

(1) *Metes and bounds.* "Metes" are measures of length in standard measurement units, such as inches, feet, yards, rods, or meters. "Bounds", on the other hand, are both natural and artificial boundaries, such as streams, lakes, trees, and streets. A "metes and bounds" description begins at one starting point on the land and follows the boundaries of the land in "metes and bounds" all the way back to the beginning point. Often, the description will mark the corners of the tract of land by reference to "monuments" (i. e., natural and artificial permanent landmarks on the land, such as fences, stakes, trees, or rivers). For example, a tract of land might be described as follows:

Beginning at a point on the east boundary of North Slavin Road 150 feet north of the north boundary of Westchester Road; running thence east on a line parallel to the north boundary of Montgomery Street 135 feet to the Miller Farmhouse picket fence; thence south in a line parallel to Rock Creek Road 140 feet to the oak tree; thence west in a line parallel to the north boundary of Sumner Street 135 feet to the east boundary of North Slavin Road; thence north along the east boundary of North Slavin Road, 140 feet to beginning.

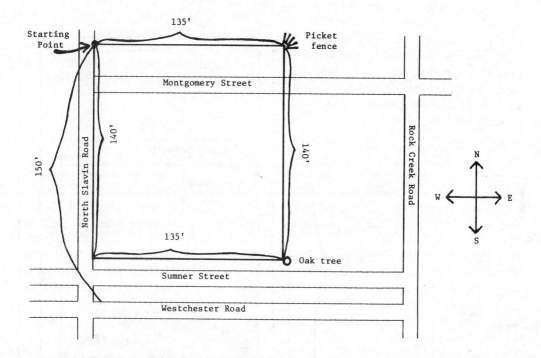

Now let's change the example. Suppose that Grantor A conveys to Grantee B land described as follows.

Beginning at a point on North Slavin Road 150 feet north of the north boundary of Westchester Road; running thence east on a line parallel to the north boundary of Montgomery Street 135 feet to the Bonschi River; thence south along the Bonschi River 145 feet to the old oak tree; thence west in a line parallel to the north boundary of Sumner Street 135 feet to North Slavin Road; thence north along North Slavin Road, 145 feet to beginning.

This land description fails to specify whether the land tract includes or excludes North Slavin Road, and whether it includes or excludes the Bonschi River. The general rule is that the property will be presumed to run to the center of the street or road if the grantor owns that much of the road, and to the center of the river, lake, or stream if the grantor owns that much of the river, lake, or stream bed. This is so whether the land description states that the property "is bounded" by the river, street, road, etc., or whether it merely states that the property runs "to the river, street, road, etc.".

(see following illustration)

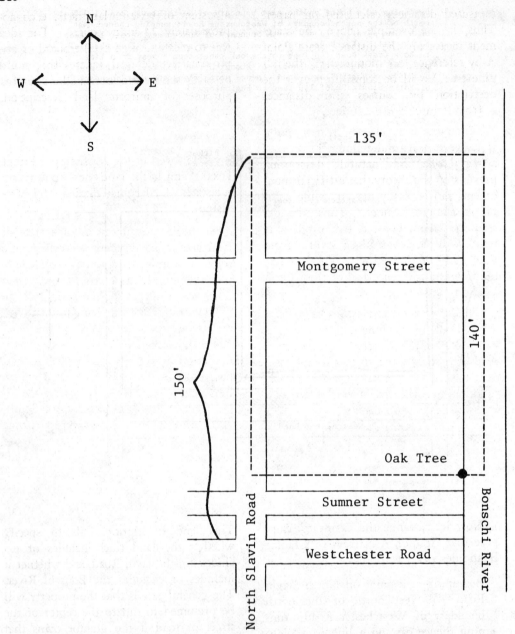

Suppose that the land description contains conflicting statements as to how much property is included within the land tract. For example, if one part of the description states "from Point A to the tall pine tree" (200 feet north of Point A), and another part states "from Point A north 250 feet" (50 feet beyond the tall pine tree), which statement will be controlling? Generally, a description based on monuments (i. e., natural or artificial landmarks) is considered controlling over a description based on "courses and distances" (i. e., a direction and length of line to be run from a starting point). The reasoning behind the rule is that people who buy property are more apt to judge the size of a tract of land by reference to landmarks they have actually seen on the property than by reference to measured distances calculated on paper. Thus, in the example above, the statement measuring the distance from Point A by reference to a monument ("the tall pine tree") will be controlling over the description by courses and distances ("from Point A north 250 feet").

Where the inconsistency in description is between a natural monument and an artificial one, the "natural" description prevails on the theory that artificial monuments can be easily moved, while natural monuments cannot. Thus, the description "from Point A to the tall pine tree" will be controlling over "from Point A to the barbed wire fence" where the tree and the fence fail to coincide in location.

Finally, courses and distances will always prevail over common names, such as the "Manning Lakefront Property". And both courses and distances and common names will prevail over a mere description by quantity, such as "my 850 acres in Mannanuska County".

(2) *Government survey.* In our treaty with England following the War for Independence, the United States acquired that area of land known as the Northwest Territory, an area modernly comprising our states of Illinois, Ohio, Michigan, and Wisconsin. The costs of the Revolutionary War had been unexpectedly high, and in urgent need of revenue to pay off the massive war debt, the United States decided to sell the Northwest Territory to private individuals. The government's decision to sell the territory led to the development of a new method of land description—the government survey. The old method of "metes and bounds" (a method that had served well during the very early history of the United States) simply would not do for a vast wilderness area that was unsettled and uncharted.

The government survey was an effort to divide the unsettled areas of land into a system of rectangular tracts, each approximately 24 miles square. The idea was to create a huge checkerboard of approximately identical squares that could be easily subdivided into smaller units for purposes of uniform land description. The idea was successful, and the government survey system was ultimately utilized in all our lands north of the Ohio River and west of the Mississippi (except Texas), and in the lands now comprising our states of Alabama, Florida, and Mississippi.

To begin the survey in each state or land area, a government surveyor would select a prominent landmark (for example, the mouth of a river), and run a north-south line, called the "principal" or "prime meridian" from that point and to the north-south boundaries of the land. The prime meridian was usually given a numerical or geographical name, such as the "First Prime Meridian" or the "San Bernardino Meridian" (the prime meridian for the government survey of Southern California). Intersecting the prime meridian at a right angle and at another prominent point selected by the surveyor was an east-west line called the "principal" or "prime base line". With the prime base line established, it became an easy task to run east-west lines parallel to the prime base line every 24 miles north and south of the line. These lines were called "standards parallels". However, it was impossible to run north-south lines parallel to the prime meridian every 24 miles east and west of the prime meridian without taking into account the curvature of the earth's surface. Because of the curvature, true north-south lines, no matter how far apart they are originally, will ultimately converge at the north and south poles. Thus, without a periodic correction in the north-south lines to allow for the curvature of the earth's surface, the squares formed by an intersection of the lines with the standard parallels would get smaller and smaller as they approached the north and south poles. The solution in the government survey was to correct the lines every 24 miles, using the standard parallels as correction points. The 24 mile long lines, called "guide meridians", were corrected so as to produce the squarest tracts of land possible.

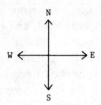

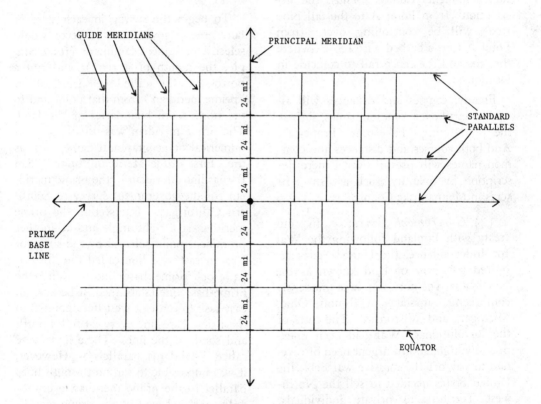

GOVERNMENT SURVEY
DIVISION OF LAND AREA
INTO TRACTS

Once a particular land area had been divided into tracts, each tract was further divided into 16 "townships", each township approximately six miles square in area. The townships, too, were further divided into 36 "sections", each section approximately one square mile in area, and each section containing 640 acres of land. The sections were numbered 1 to 36 always starting with the section in the northeast corner of the township. As needed, the township sections could themselves be divided into quarters and the quarters into quarters, and so on.

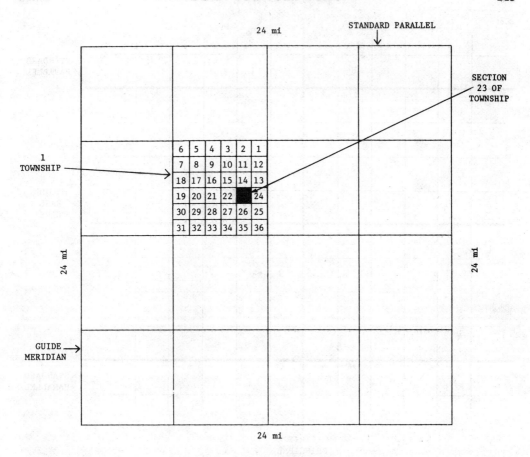

ONE "SQUARE" TRACT IN THE CHECKERBOARD

Each township is identified by its location in the 24 mile tract of land. To facilitate description, each row of townships running north and south is called a "range". The ranges east of the principal meridian are numbered consecutively as they move east, the first row east of the meridian being "Range 1 East"; the ranges west of the principal meridian are numbered consecutively as they move west, the first row west of the meridian being "Range 1 West". Each township is additionally identified by the number of east-west rows of townships intervening between it and the prime base. Again, the east-west rows north of the base line are numbered consecutively as they move north, the first row north of the line being "Township 1 North"; and the east-west rows south of the base line are numbered consecutively as they move south, the first row south of the line being "Township 1 South".

Thus, to properly and completely identify a township for purposes of land description on a deed, both the range and township number must be given. For example, a township in the tenth row south of the prime base line and in the sixth row east of the Second Principal Meridian may be described as "Township 10 South of the Prime Base Line, Range 6 East of the Second Principal Meridian". The legal description may be abbreviated is "T. 10 S., R. 6 E. of the 2nd P.M." If you feel confused at this point, the following illustration should be helpful.

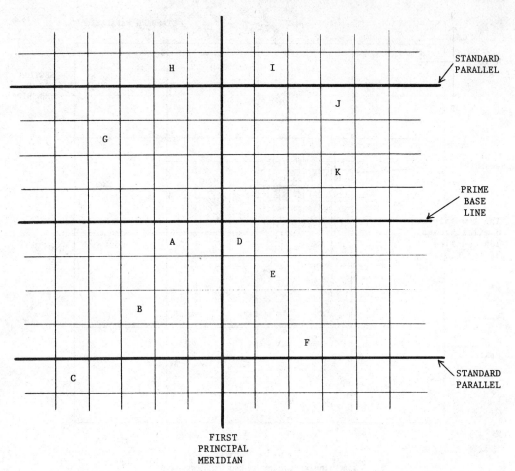

Upon close scrutiny, it can be seen that A is "Township 1 South, Range 2 West"; B is "Township 3 South, Range 3 West"; E is "Township 2 South, Range 2 East"; and J is "Township 4 North, Range 4 East", etc.

Now suppose that a grantor wants to describe land contained in a particular section of a township, or in a particular quarter of a section, or in a particular quarter of a quarter. The following illustration, which is a many times enlarged reproduction of "Square G" from the previous illustration, shows how the northeast quarter of the southwest quarter of section 16 should be described.

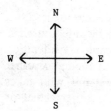

- 6 mi -

6	5	4	3	2	1
7	8	9	10	11	12
18	17	16	15	14	13
19	20	21	22	23	24
30	29	28	27	26	25
31	32	33	34	35	36

The township is
6 miles square,
and contains
36 sections.

Each section is
one mile square and
contains 640 acres.

- 6 mi -

"Square G"

The shaded corner of Section 16 should
be described as follows: "The Northeast
Quarter of the Southwest Quarter of
Section 16, Township 3 North, Range 4
West of the First Principal Meridian".
The description may be abbreviated as:
"NE¼ of SW¼, S.16, T.3N., R.4W. of the
1st P.M."

---

(3) *Plats.* A tract of land ready for residential or other development is often subdivided into building lots. A surveyor subdivides land by first dividing the land into blocks separated by streets, and by then dividing the blocks into lots. The blocks and lots are numbered, and the streets are given names. Often, the subdivided tract is also given a name, such as "Sunset Heights" or "Sylvan Hills". The surveyor then prepares a map of the tract, called a "plat", which is carefully drawn to scale to show the exact dimensions of all blocks and lots, which are identified by number, and all streets, which are identified by name. The "plat" also designates the quarter-section lines of land that has been included in a government survey.

Thus, the legal description of land contained in a platted subdivision may be by block and lot number alone, or by a combination of block and lot number and reference to government survey. For example, where the shaded area in the preceding illustration forms part of a subdivision, the legal description might be as follows: "Lot 8, in Block 3, of Sunset Heights, a subdivision of the Northeast Quarter of the Southwest Quarter of Section 16, Township 3 North, Range 4 West of the First Principal Meridian".

A description by street address alone should never be used to describe land in a deed. Often a street address is not inclusive of the entire property interest intended to be transferred.

Additionally, where a lot is not a perfect square or rectangle, it should never be described as the "west half" or the "south quarter" of a particular piece of property. The result of describing it in this manner will be to transfer either more or less than the portion of property intended. Unless such "irregular" land is platted, it should be described in metes and bounds.

What is the effect of "recording" a deed?

Recording statutes in effect in all our states provide for the recordation of deeds and other documents, such as mortgages, affecting title to real property. To "record" is to officially file a copy of a deed or other instrument with the County Land Recorder's Office. While recording is not essential to making a deed or other instrument valid as between the grantor and grantee, it does serve as "constructive notice" (i. e., inferred or implied notice) to the world at large that there is an outstanding interest in the land. The idea behind recording laws is that the ownership of real property should be determinable from the public record, and that purchasers of land should be able to rely upon these records in entering into real estate transactions— they should not have to worry about secret, unrecorded deeds. Therefore, while a grantee who records will be protected against the claims of all subsequent transferees of the same property, a grantee who fails to record may lose his or her

interest in the land to a subsequent "bona fide" purchaser. A "bona fide" purchaser is one who pays valuable consideration for the land (i. e., gives money or other value for the property) and who takes the land without notice, either actual or constructive, of the grantee's prior claim. Obviously, where the grantee records, there can be no bona fide purchasers for the entire world is on constructive notice of the grantee's interest.

Whether the grantee or a subsequent bona fide purchaser will prevail as to the property will depend in large part upon the kind of recording statute in effect in the particular state. Basically, there are three types: "notice", "race-notice" and "race" statutes.

(1) *Notice statutes.* Under a "notice" statute, a subsequent bona fide purchaser (again, one who pays valuable consideration and takes the property without actual or constructive notice of any prior claims) will always prevail over a prior grantee who has failed to record his or her interest. For example, suppose that A conveys land by deed to B on April 1st. B fails to record, and, on May 1st, A conveys the same land by deed to C. C does not record. In a "notice" jurisdiction, C will prevail so long as he or she is a bona fide purchaser. And it makes no difference as between B and C whether C ever records. Thus, if, in the above example, B records on May 2nd and C has yet to record, C will still prevail. However, C would be wise to record as soon as possible in order to protect himself or herself against subsequent transfers by A to additional bona fide purchasers.

Now let's change the facts. Suppose that, in the example above, C purchases the property from A, knowing that A has already sold the land to B, but that·B has not recorded his or her deed. C, in this case, will not prevail over B because C had *actual* knowledge of the prior transfer at the time of the purchase and cannot qualify as a bona fide purchaser.

One problem that arises in a notice jurisdiction is that it is sometimes difficult to tell who is the prior and who is the subsequent grantee in cases where both parties have failed to record their interests. Often, it boils down to a question of when delivery of each deed occurred; and, since evidence of delivery is often difficult to find, or based entirely on the testimony of the parties concerned, the determination is not an easy one.

(2) *Race-notice statutes.* A subsequent bona fide purchaser is protected under a "race-notice" statute only if he or she records before the prior grantee. Thus, in order to prevail, a subsequent purchaser must not only pay valuable consideration for the property and take the land without actual or constructive notice of the prior transfer, but he or she must also win the "race" to record. Again, if A on April 1st conveys land by deed to B who fails to record, and, on May 1st, A conveys the same land by deed to bona fide purchaser C, C must record before B records or C will not prevail in a "race-notice" jurisdiction.

Unlike a "notice" jurisdiction where priority depends upon the respective delivery dates of the deeds, priority in a "race-notice" jurisdiction depends upon the time of recording.

Of course, if the subsequent transferee has actual knowledge of the prior transfer, winning the "race" to record will be of little consequence. A subsequent transferee with actual knowledge cannot qualify as a bona fide purchaser.

(3) *Race statutes.* In effect in very few states, "race" statutes provide that whoever records first wins—period. It makes no difference whether the subsequent transferee has actual knowledge of the prior transfer so long as he or she wins the "race" to record. Race statutes are thus an exception to the general rule

requiring a bona fide purchaser who takes the land without knowledge of the grantee's prior interest. So, if in a race jurisdiction, A conveys land to B who tells C that she has received a deed from A, and C, acting on this knowledge, persuades A to convey the same land to him, and C records before B, C will prevail.

What are the mechanics of recording?

A grantee "records" a deed by taking it to the County Land Recorder's Office where a copy of the deed is made and filed chronologically in the official records with a special entry included for the date and time of filing. The County Recorder will also index the deed, usually in a "grantor-grantee" index. The deed will be listed twice in the index—first, in the grantor volume, and, second, in the grantee volume. The deed can thus be located by searching either under the grantor's name or under the grantee's. In any case, both volume entries include the names of both parties, a description of the land, and the volume and page number of the records where the copy of the deed may be found. The volumes are alphabetized and periodically re-indexed to make the search easier.

In some cities where land has been platted and broken down into blocks and lots, the County Recorder maintains a "tract index" rather than a "grantor-grantee index". Entries in a tract index are made under block and lot number. Each page of the index deals exclusively with a particular lot of land, and all instruments relating to that particular piece of property are indexed together on the page. Keeping all recorded interests together, rather than separating them as is done in the grantor-grantee index, greatly simplifies any "title" search for outstanding interests in the property.

What kinds of instruments can be recorded?

In addition to acknowledged deeds (you will recall that most states prohibit the recordation of unacknowledged deeds), any instrument affecting an interest in land can and should be recorded, including mortgage agreements and contracts to convey real property in the future. However, deeds containing restrictions on transfer to people of a particular race, color, religion, or national origin cannot be recorded as the Federal Fair Housing Act of 1968 makes it unlawful to print or publish notices, statements, or other documents indicating preference, limitation, or discrimination based on these grounds.

Once a deed or other instrument affecting an interest in land has been properly recorded, the whole world is said to be on constructive notice of the recorded interest.

How is a "title search" made?

A "title search" is a search of public land records for all recorded ownership rights and outstanding interests in a particular piece of real property. Before a buyer will want to commit himself or herself to purchasing a particular parcel of land, he or she will want to conduct a thorough title search, either personally, or through an attorney or title insurance company, to make certain that the seller has good record title. Sometimes, the contract of sale will require the seller to furnish evidence of good record title, and/or to pay for the cost of title insurance.

It is extremely important for the buyer to conduct a title search because, as you will recall, a buyer is held to have constructive notice of any and all recorded interests in the land. If the buyer does not conduct a search, and the seller does not have good title, the buyer will end up paying for the property and receiving nothing in return.

How is a title search made? Where the County Land Recorder maintains a tract index, the search is a simple task.

All recorded interests in the particular piece of property are indexed on one page, and the buyer or his or her representative need look no further (though the buyer or his or her representative will want to go out to the property to make certain that there are no adverse possessors).

However, where a grantor-grantee index is maintained, the search becomes more difficult. In a grantor-grantee index, the recorded interests are not grouped together, but are scattered throughout the two volume index under the alphabetized names of grantor and grantee. In order for a particular recorded interest to serve as constructive notice to the world in general, the recorded interest must be found within the chain of title to the property. The buyer or his or her representative completes a chain of title search by looking first in the grantee index under the seller's name to find out when and from whom the seller acquired title. The buyer or his or her representative then checks for any and all recorded transfers made by the seller after the date on which the seller acquired title. A check is then made in the grantor file for any and all transfers made by the seller's grantor after the date he or she acquired title, and until the date he or she transferred the interest to the seller. The search continues in this manner back and forth between the grantor and grantee volumes until every recorded transfer made by any predecessor in interest after the date he or she acquired title and until the date he or she transferred the interest away has been sought out.

Interests transferred and recorded prior to the date that any particular grantor acquired title or after the date that he or she transferred the interest are "wild" deeds or instruments. They are not within the chain of title, and do not impart constructive notice to a subsequent purchaser. For example, suppose that Seymour Langtry conveys land to Samantha Jones on April 1st. Samantha does not record. On May 1st, Seymour conveys the same land to bona fide purchaser Bill Smith who records immediately. On June 1st, Samantha records. On July 1st, Bill Smith conveys the land to bona fide purchaser Jake Horowitz who also records. As between Samantha Jones and Jake Horowitz, Jake will prevail because Samantha recorded her interest in the land only after Bill Smith recorded his deed. Because Seymour Langtry parted with record ownership and title as of the date of Bill Smith's recording, bona fide purchaser Jake Horowitz would have to look no further in time for transfers made and/or recorded from Langtry. Samantha's deed would thus be a "wild" deed, not in the chain of title, and of no constructive notice to anyone. This is so regardless of the kind of recording statute in effect in the jurisdiction. And it is a good result because it would not be fair to expect purchasers to check for transfers made by a grantor *before* the grantor acquired record title or *after* he or she parted with record title. To require this would be to place an excessive burden upon the title searcher.

Similarly, any other instrument unconnected to the chain of title is a "wild" instrument that does not serve as constructive notice. For example, suppose that Seymour Langtry conveys land to Samantha Jones on April 1st. Samantha does not record, but soon thereafter conveys to Bill Smith who does record. Seymour Langtry then conveys the same land to bona fide purchaser Jake Horowitz who also records. As between Bill Smith and Jake Horowitz, Jake will prevail because the connecting deed from Seymour to Samantha is not recorded, and there is no way that Jake can learn of Bill Smith's claim by an ordinary title search.

Where a deed in the chain of title refers to an instrument outside of the chain, the reference in the deed may be sufficient to impart constructive notice of the unrecorded instrument. The question is whether the title searcher would be likely to run across the reference and whether the reference is sufficiently clear to put the searcher on notice of the claim.

Of course, even where an instrument or claim is not within the chain of title, the purchaser will be on notice of the claim if he or she has actual knowledge of the interest—or enough knowledge that he or she should be expected to inquire further.

What is title insurance?

Title insurance is insurance protection against loss arising from a defect in title or from a lack of good title. Title insurance is generally available in one form or another throughout the United States. Basically, there are two types:

(1) *Lawyer-title policies.* Here, the purchaser of property (or the seller on the purchaser's behalf where the contract of sale so provides) hires an attorney to conduct a title search and to furnish the purchaser with an opinion as to title as well as an abstract of title (an "abstract" is merely a summary of the record title, including all outstanding liens, mortgages, judgments, and similar claims). The abstract is turned over to a title insurance company which issues a policy on the basis of the abstract.

(2) *Title-plant policies.* Some title insurance companies issue policies on the basis of their own title search, rather than an attorney's abstract. Usually, the companies maintain duplicate land records, including a tract index, in the plant's main office.

If the title insurance company is satisfied that good record title exists, the company will issue a policy insuring against loss that may arise from a defect in title. The company may specifically list in the policy any minor defects found on the record for which the company refuses to be liable. Unless the company takes exception to the existing defects of record, the company cannot escape liability. However, the company generally does not insure against the following:

(1) unrecorded liens and easements;

(2) rights of a person in possession on the basis of an unrecorded instrument;

(3) rights that could be ascertained by inspection of the land, by proper survey, or by inquiry of a person in possession;

(4) unrecorded mining claims and water rights;

(5) violation of governmental zoning and use regulations; and

(6) unpaid taxes or assessments.

In some cases, the title insurance company may be willing to sell such extended coverage for a substantial increase in premium.

In any event, the purchaser alone is insured against the covered defects, and the policy does not "run with the land" (i. e., the insurance protection is not transferred with a transfer of the property—any subsequent purchaser must buy his or her own title insurance).

Where a loss occurs, and the title insurance company is liable, the insured landowner's recovery will be the actual market loss he or she suffers, up to the maximum limits of the policy.

What is estoppel by deed?

Occasionally, a grantor will execute a deed of conveyance, purporting to convey real property that he or she does not own. Of course, a grantor who has nothing to convey transfers nothing to a grantee by such a deed of conveyance. However, if the grantor subsequently acquires ownership of the land described in the deed, the grantee will automatically become the owner of the property as a result of *estoppel by deed.*

Estoppel by deed is the rule of law that a person who purports to convey an interest in real property that he or she does not own will later be "estopped" (i. e., stopped) from denying transfer of the interest to the grantee in the event that the grantor subsequently acquires ownership of the land.

Estoppel by deed may conflict with chain of title rules if the grantee who automatically acquires ownership of the land fails to record his or her interest before the grantor conveys to a bona fide purchaser who does record. If the grantee recorded the purported transfer prior to the date on which the grantor actually received ownership of the land, the recorded deed will be a wild instrument outside the chain of title and of no constructive notice to a subsequent bona fide purchaser. The majority rule is that the grantee's rights to the property will be protected only where he or she re-records after the grantor obtains title and before the grantor transfers the land to a subsequent bona fide purchaser.

What is adverse possession?

Adverse possession is a means of acquiring an ownership interest in real property by merely possessing the property in a manner prescribed by statute for a specified period of time. Thus, a person may acquire a life estate or a fee simple absolute interest in land belonging to another if he or she meets the following five conditions:

(1) Actual possession;

(2) Open and notorious possession;

(3) Hostile intent;

(4) Continuous possession throughout; and

(5) Statutory time period.

Actual possession. To begin with, the adverse possessor must actually occupy the property. This does not mean that he or she must in every case live on the property. What is required is that the adverse possessor exercise the kind of use and control over the land that would be expected of the true and lawful owner. Acts appropriate to the property, such as cultivating farmland, and herding cattle on grazing land are sufficient. Some states require less actual use and occupation of the land where the adverse possessor claims the property on the basis of a defective instrument (e. g., a deed forged and delivered to him or her). Where the adverse possessor's claim is not based on a defective instrument, these same states require a "substantial enclosure" of the property, which usually means fencing the property in, cultivating a large portion of it, or improving it substantially.

Open and notorious possession. Possession must be "open and notorious". This means that the possession must be so blatantly obvious that the rightful owner is put on notice that he or she had better take action to defend the property. This does not mean that the rightful owner must actually show up and discover the adverse possessor's presence on the land. All that is required is that the possession be so open and obvious that a reasonable inspection by the lawful owner would not fail to disclose its presence. Thus, a person who secretly cultivates land belonging to another, or who stealthily lives on the property so as not to be discovered, does not possess the land in the open and notorious manner required for adverse possession.

Hostile intent. The possession also requires a "hostile" intent. Hostility, however, does not mean ill feeling—merely an intent to occupy and possess the land in disregard and denial of the true owner's ownership and title. Thus, a statement that "I know this land belongs to someone else, but I am claiming it as my own anyway" is sufficiently hostile. However, a statement that "I do not claim this land as my own even though I occupy it" lacks sufficient hostility.

Similarly, a tenant or licensee who is on the property with the owner's permission can never claim adverse possession.

Where the adverse claimant openly and notoriously possesses the land for the required statutory period, a legal presumption arises that he or she had done so with the required hostile intent. Not so, however, where a boundary dispute arises as to property openly and notoriously, but mistakenly occupied for the statutory period along the boundary line between adjoining property owners. Most courts, in this case, hold that there is no hostile intent where it is reasonable to conclude that the possessor would not have occupied or claimed the land had he or she known that it belonged to a neighbor. Several recent decisions have permitted the disputed boundary to stand on the basis that both property owners accepted the disputed line for the statutory period of time.

The actual possession of a tenant in common or joint tenant is generally not adverse to that of the other cotenants as each cotenant has a right to occupy all the land. However, where one cotenant clearly repudiates the cotenancy, and openly and notoriously claims the entire property for himself or herself, the cotenant is said to possess the land with the required hostile intent.

Continuous possession throughout. The actual, open and notorious, hostile possession must continue for the entire statutory period. Continuous possession, however, does not mean constant possession. Again, what is required is the level of occupancy and use that could be expected of an average owner of the same or similar property. For example, a lakefront summer home that is snowed in during the winter may require occupancy and use only during the summertime.

However, where the adverse claimant at some point abandons the property, intending never to return, the adverse possession will come to an end. If the adverse possessor ever returns to the property, hoping to resume occupancy and use, he or she will have to start all over again for purposes of the statutory period. This is so whether the adverse possessor is gone for two days or two years.

Similarly, an interruption of possession by the true owner will also terminate the continuous use and require the adverse possessor to begin again for purposes of the statutory period. Interruption of use demands that the true owner re-enter the property openly and notoriously for the purpose of regaining possession. It is not sufficient that the true owner post a "no trespassing" sign, or initiate a lawsuit for possession. Of course, if the lawsuit results in a court order declaring that the true owner has the right to possession of the property, this will be a sufficient interruption.

Suppose that A, B, and C hold the same property adversely for successive periods of time that, taken together, equal the statutory period, but, taken separately, do not. Does C, the final adverse claimant, have a lawful claim to the property? The majority rule is that successive adverse possessors cannot "tack" together their periods of possession unless the claimants share a "privity of estate". This means that each successive adverse claimant must succeed to his or her interest by a *voluntary transfer* of possession (either inter vivos or at death) from the preceding possessor. For example, assume that Samantha Jones adversely possesses Seymour Langtry's 40 acre farm for five years, then sells the land in fee simple to Bill Smith who continues to occupy the land and claim it as his own for another three years. Bill Smith then dies, and his daughter, Virginia Smith, claims the property as her father's only intestate heir. Virginia, too, immediately occupies the property and claims it as her own for another twelve years, at the end of which time

she asserts her ownership as an adverse possessor. To satisfy the 20 year statutory holding period in effect in her state, Virginia simply tacks together the twelve, three, and five year holding periods of herself, her father, and Samantha Jones. Under the majority rule, Virginia is now the fee simply absolute owner of the farm. If, on the other hand, Virginia had failed to take immediate possession of the land upon her father's death, she would have been unable to tack the holding periods of her predecessors in possession and would still have eight more years of adverse possession to go.

Because of the requirement of privity of estate, tacking is never allowed where one adverse possessor forces another off the property and begins to hold adversely. Nor is tacking permitted where one adverse possessor abandons the property, and another adverse possessor immediately takes possession—the required privity of estate is not present.

Statutory time period. The adverse possession must continue for the period of time prescribed by statute—20 years in most states, less in others (e. g., 10 years in Oregon). In some states, including California, if the adverse possessor claims the property under "color of title" (i. e., on the basis of a defective instrument, such as a forged deed that the adverse possessor believes to be valid), or enters the property and substantially improves the land or pays all property taxes, the holding period will be cut down to five years. (In some states, the adverse possessor must pay all property taxes on the land whatever the statutory holding period or adverse possession will not result.) In any case, once the statutory period has been satisfied, the statute of limitations will bar any action by the original owner to recover the property.

Suppose that the true owner is disabled and thus unable to interrupt the adverse possessor's continuous use. Does the statutory period continue to run? The general rule is that the statutory period ceases to run, and the statute of limitations is "tolled" or brought to a standstill, where the true owner of the property is unable to assert his or her rights because of a disability such as insanity, imprisonment, or minority. For the period of the true owner's disability, the adverse claimant's possession and use of the land is of no effect.

Once the statutory period of time has run, the original owner's title to the land is completely and automatically extinguished by operation of law, and new title or ownership rights are created in the adverse possessor. Because the adverse possessor has nothing in writing to evidence his or her ownership interest, he or she may wish to file a "quiet title" action in court against the former owner. The purpose of the action is to place *good record title* in the adverse possessor (he or she already has *good legal title*.) Upon proof of all the elements of adverse possession, the court will declare the adverse possessor to be the true and lawful owner of the property, and will issue a judgment making its decision a matter of legal record.

Of course, the adverse possessor need not file a "quiet title" suit—he or she owns good legal title, and the fact that his or her interest does not appear on record is of no consequence. Recording laws simply have no effect upon title acquired by adverse possession, and the adverse possessor is free, regardless of record title, to hold on to the property, or to transfer it by deed, will, or intestacy. For example, suppose that Samantha Jones begins adversely possessing Seymour Langtry's 40 acre farm in 1950. In 1970, the statutory holding period is up, and Samantha acquires title to the property by adverse possession. In 1975, Seymour Langtry, whose name still appears on record as owner of the property, sells and deeds the 40 acre farm to Bill

Smith who immediately records the deed. Who owns the land? Samantha Jones does—Bill Smith owns nothing. At the time Bill received the deed from Seymour, Seymour had nothing to convey: his interest in the farm was extinguished by operation of law in 1970. The fact that Seymour's name appeared as record title holder at the time of the transfer simply has no effect on Samantha's ownership rights. How could Bill Smith (or any other purchaser) have protected himself from this result? Prior to purchasing, he could have gone out to the property and inspected the land for the presence of adverse possessors.

Now let's change the facts a little. Suppose that Seymour Langtry owns, not a fee simple absolute, but a life estate interest in the farm, with the remainder interest in his son, Larry. Again, Samantha Jones begins adversely possessing the land in 1950. In 1970, Seymour's interest in the land is extinguished, and Samantha Jones automatically acquires ownership of Seymour's interest by adverse possession. If, in 1976, Seymour dies, does Samantha have a good defense to Larry Langtry's claims of fee simple ownership? No. By adversely possessing the land from 1950 to 1970, Samantha acquired title to a life estate pur autre vie (for the life of Seymour)—not to a fee simple absolute. This is because an adverse possessor acquires title only to whatever *present possessory interests* are owned by the lawful owner of the property at the time the adverse possession begins. Thus, to obtain title to the fee simple, Samantha must now adversely possess the land for another 20 years (during the period of Larry's fee simple ownership).

Finally, the statutory period for adverse possession does not run against government land. It is therefore impossible to acquire title by adverse possession to land belonging to the United States, the individual states, or any other political subdivision.

What is land use planning and control?

Land use planning refers to the orderly use and development of land so as to obtain the maximum benefit possible from real property. Land use planning is accomplished both by private agreement and by governmental controls. Techniques used privately include licenses, easements, profits, covenants, and general plan restrictions. Public land use controls include zoning, subdivision regulations, and eminent domain. All of these techniques are considered in the following sections.

What is a license?

A license is without doubt the "skinniest stick" in that large bundle of sticks representing all the rights that a person may have with regard to a piece of real property. For a license is not an interest in land, but is a mere privilege, personal to the licensee (the person possessing it), to go onto another's land for a specified purpose. It is oral or written permission to perform acts that would otherwise constitute a trespass.

With limited exception, a license is revocable at the will of the landowner: if the landowner decides to revoke, the license is instantly terminated. For example, a farmer who says to a hunter on Monday, "I give you permission to hunt pheasants on my land all next week", can on Tuesday revoke the permission, and the hunter's license to hunt on the land will be automatically and instantly terminated. If the hunter persists in hunting, he or she will be liable for trespass.

The only two exceptions to revocability are licenses "coupled with an interest" and licenses rendered irrevocable by estoppel. A license "coupled with an interest" is a license tied up to some other legally enforceable interest of the licensee. For example, if Seymour Langtry sells Sa-

mantha Jones three wheelbarrows and a used tractor, and tells Samantha to come onto his land to pick up the property, Samantha will have an irrevocable license for a reasonable period of time to go onto the land for that purpose.

Most courts hold that a license is made irrevocable by estoppel (i. e., the licensor is estopped from revoking it) where the licensee expends a substantial amount of money, time, or effort in reliance upon the license. Thus, if Seymour Langtry gives Samantha Jones permission to come onto his land and put up an expensive billboard for advertising purposes, Seymour will be estopped from revoking the license once Samantha has gone to the expense of installing the sign. Where estoppel is applied, the license will be irrevocable for whatever period of time is required for the licensee to recoup his or her expenses. In the case of Samantha's billboard, this period will be for the natural life of the sign.

Because a license is personal to the licensee, the licensee cannot transfer it either inter vivos or at death. Any attempt to do so will result in termination of the license.

What is an easement?

An easement is a genuine, though nonpossessory, interest in real property that may be owned in severalty or in a form of concurrent ownership. Like a license, an easement is a right to use another's land, but it is much more than a privilege and cannot be revoked by the landowner.

An easement may be classified in the same manner as a possessory estate—for years, for life, or in fee simple. However, an easement can never be classified as a tenancy at will for such a tenancy is by its very nature revocable.

Generally speaking, there are two kinds of easements: *easements appurtenant,* and *easements in gross.* An easement appurtenant is one involving two adjoining parcels of land. One parcel, called the "dominant estate" is in some way benefited by the second parcel, or "servient estate". The servient estate is thus said to be burdened with the easement. For example, suppose that Seymour Langtry owns one acre of land in fee simple absolute. Seymour conveys one-half of the land in fee simple to Samantha Jones, and Seymour also conveys to Samantha an easement giving her the right to cross over Seymour's one-half to get to her property. Samantha's property, the dominant estate, is benefited by the easement of access across Seymour's land; Seymour's property, the servient estate, is burdened with the easement appurtenant. In the event that Samantha conveys her one-half interest or loses it by adverse possession, the easement appurtenant will be transferred along with the dominant estate.

An easement in gross, on the other hand, involves only one parcel of land belonging to someone other than the easement holder, and benefiting the holder personally as opposed to benefiting a servient estate. Thus, an irrevocable right to hunt on another's property or to put up a billboard on the land constitutes an easement in gross (a revocable right to do these things would be merely a license). At common law, an easement in gross was considered personal to the grantee and could not be transferred either inter vivos or at death. Modernly, many states provide for the free transferability of commercial easements in gross, such as a commercial pipeline or utility line, but prohibit the transfer of noncommercial easements unless the deed of conveyance expressly states "to the grantee and his or her heirs or assigns". Still other states permit all easements in gross to be freely transferred, whether they are commercial or noncommercial.

As to the creation of easements, there are three possibilities:

(1) *By express written grant.* Other than implied or prescriptive easements, all easements must be created in writing (any attempt to orally create an easement will result in a mere license). Generally, a testator or grantor will directly grant an easement to a beneficiary or grantee in a will or deed of conveyance. Or a grantor will expressly reserve an easement for himself or herself, while transferring all other rights in the land. For example, Seymour Langtry might convey his one acre of land to Samantha Jones "except that I reserve the right to use the 15 foot strip of land along the western border as a roadway". The effect of such language is to reserve in Seymour an easement of use. If the easement benefits an adjoining parcel of land belonging to Seymour, the easement is appurtenant; if there is no second parcel involved, the easement is in gross.

(2) *By implication.* In the absence of an express easement, an "implied" easement (also called an "easement by necessity") will arise where an easement is strictly necessary to the use or enjoyment of land conveyed or land retained by a grantor. Suppose that Seymour Langtry conveys the back one-half acre of his one acre parcel to Samantha Jones. If the only way Samantha can reach her property from the public road or highway is by crossing the one-half acre retained by Seymour Langtry, the law will imply an easement by necessity permitting her to do so. Because an implied easement, by definition, requires two parcels of land, such an easement is always appurtenant. In the example, Samantha's parcel is the dominant estate and Seymour's the servient.

(3) *By prescription.* Both easements appurtenant and easements in gross may be created by "prescription" (i. e., by adverse use). Acquiring such an easement is similar to acquiring title to a possessory estate in land by means of adverse posses-

sion. Like adverse possession, adverse use or prescription must be open and notorious, continuous and uninterrupted, and hostile as to the true owner. Again, this means that the adverse user must make no attempt to conceal his or her use of the land; that he or she must use the land continuously (although not necessarily constantly) for the entire statutory period; and that he or she must use the land in disregard and denial of the true owner's rights. Thus, if A walks over B's land whenever A happens to be going in that direction for a period of 20 years, A will acquire an easement by prescription. But if A has B's permission to cross over the property, A's use is not adverse to B's ownership rights (A has a license to use the land) and A cannot lay claim to a prescriptive easement.

As to the statutory holding period, if the easement is appurtenant, tacking will be permitted by the dominant estate holders so long as there is privity of estate. If the easement is in gross, tacking will not be permitted because the easement is personal to the holder. The true owner may, of course, interrupt the adverse use and so cause a break in the statutory holding period either by filing suit against the adverse user (compare—merely filing suit will not interrupt adverse possession—a legal judgment is required), or by actually putting a stop to the adverse use. A protest that falls short of halting the adverse use will not be sufficient (for example, posting "no trespass" signs that the user ignores).

How is an easement terminated? To begin with, an easement created by written grant may be released or terminated by written agreement or by deed of conveyance back to the grantor (the deed will be to the grantee in the case of an easement created by reservation in the grantor). An implied easement, on the other hand, terminates when the necessity for the easement ends: mere nonuse by the holder, for no matter how long a pe-

riod, will not terminate the easement unless the holder clearly expresses an intention to abandon the right. And, finally, an easement acquired by prescription, may be lost by prescription in the event of adverse use for the statutory period by the owner of the possessory interest or by any other party.

What is a profit?

A "profit" is very similar to an easement in that it is a genuine interest in real property as opposed to a mere license or privilege. It differs from an easement in that it gives, not an irrevocable right to *use* the land, but an irrevocable right *to take* something away from it, such as minerals, timber, water, oil, or the like. Of course, whenever a profit is granted, an implied easement is also created permitting the profit holder to go onto the property to accomplish the taking.

A profit, like an easement, may be appurtenant or in gross, although a profit in gross, unlike an easement in gross, is always freely transferable because it always has commercial value. A profit may be created by express grant in a deed or will, or it may be created by prescription—it can never be created orally (an oral attempt to create a profit results in a license) or by implication or necessity.

What is a covenant?

A covenant is simply a promise to do something or not to do something. Covenants are frequently contained in deeds of conveyance as a means of restricting the grantee of property in his or her use of the land. For example, a grantee might promise "*not* to use the land for other than residential purposes", "*not* to build other than one-story structures on the land", "*to* maintain a fence", and "*to* rotate crops on the property". As such, the covenants are genuine, nonpossessory interests in land. They belong to the grantor who has a legal right to enforce them.

Like express easements and profits, covenants must be created in writing in order to be valid. Generally, the writing is a deed, which, as you will recall, is signed by the grantor and not by the grantee. However, the grantee is considered bound by any covenants contained in a deed by reason of accepting the deed. Any subsequent purchaser from the grantee is also bound by the covenants so long as the purchaser had either actual or constructive notice (from the recorded deed) of the covenants at the time of purchase. As a result, such covenants are said to "run with the land."

In conclusion, covenants designed to restrict the use of land on the basis of race, creed, color, or sex are in violation of federal and state discrimination laws and cannot be enforced in the courts.

What are "general plan restrictions"?

"General plan restrictions" are restrictions placed upon all lots within a single subdivision as part of a general plan to benefit all lot owners. You will recall from our earlier discussion of plats that a developer who is ready to develop a particular tract of land usually subdivides the land into building lots: the developer has a surveyor divide the land into blocks, and the blocks into lots. A name is then given to the subdivision like "Sunrise Hill" or "Rolling Hill". In order to attract purchasers, the developer may draw up a general plan restricting the use and development of all lots within the subdivision. The idea is to achieve substantial uniformity in land development and make for pleasant living conditions. Thus, the plan may exclude stores or other industrial use, it may prohibit mobile homes, it may limit all buildings to single residences, it may prohibit construction on the front portion of the lots, and it may require approval of all building plans and specifications.

General plan restrictions are closely related to covenants. Where such restrictions are in effect, each lot owner has the right to enforce the restrictions against all other lot owners and future lot purchasers.

Since it would be a cumbersome task to include all lot restrictions in each deed of conveyance, the general practice is to incorporate the restrictions only in the recorded plat or map of the subdivision itself. As every lot purchaser is held to have notice of the recorded plat, all lot purchasers have constructive notice of the general plan restrictions. Where there are so many restrictions that it is impossible to include them all on the recorded plat or map, the restrictions are placed into a separate instrument, called a "declaration of restrictions". The declaration is referred to (i. e., "incorporated by reference") in the plat and recorded simultaneously with it. As an added protection, each individual deed of conveyance makes reference to the fact that the land is sold subject to recorded restrictions.

How is public land use control accomplished?

To this point we have dealt solely with private land use planning as it is achieved through licenses, easements, profits, covenants, and general plan restrictions. Public or governmental land use planning, on the other hand, is primarily accomplished through zoning regulations, subdivision controls, and eminent domain.

(1) *Zoning.* You will recall from our discussion of zoning in Ch. 4 that the power of a town, city, county, or other political subdivision of a state to pass zoning ordinances is dependent upon the passage of a state enabling statute permitting the restriction of landowners in their use of private property. You will also recall that the first and foremost purpose of zoning laws is to promote wholesome housing; a second purpose is to promote commerce and industry.

The power to "zone" property is an important tool in governmental land use planning. To promote wholesome housing, for example, governmental authorities often zone areas exclusively for single-family housing, and areas exclusively for two-family housing—excluded from these areas are apartments and commercial and industrial construction. Commercial areas may be zoned into several categories: C-1 may be limited to "convenience shopping" facilities such as small grocery stores or drugstores; C-2 may permit the construction of a regional shopping center; C-3 may be a downtown commercial district; and C-4 may allow industrial parks or heavy industry.

Within districts, zoning ordinances may regulate overall structure density by prohibiting construction of buildings over a designated height (thus prohibiting construction of skyscrapers in some areas), by restricting lot sizes, by requiring minimum sideyards and backyards between buildings, and by requiring a minimum front yard between residential property and the street.

Because of the need for flexibility in the law, zoning boards are frequently empowered to grant "special exceptions" to zoning ordinances in order to cope with changes in the neighborhood and to provide for beneficial and equitable use of real estate. Thus, it is not unusual to find a small gift shop or beauty shop in a residential neighborhood so long as there is adequate parking and limited advertising. A "variance" (i. e., a nonconforming use) may also be allowed where special hardship is likely to result to a particular landowner if the variance is not granted (for example, a landowner whose lot is peculiarly shaped and thus not suitable for the zoned uses).

(2) *Subdivision controls.* Nearly all local governmental authorities have passed laws requiring subdivision developers to "dedicate" a certain amount of land for streets, parks, schools, and public areas, and to adhere to strict statutory procedures as to the installation of sewers and utility lines and the construction and maintenance of streets and roads (including grading and paving requirements and standards for street lighting).

"Dedication" refers to the voluntary transfer of privately owned land to the government for a public purpose. You will recall from our discussion of real property back in Ch. 4 that most privately owned land originally belonged to the government which transferred it to private individuals by grant, patent, or the like. Dedication is the process of voluntarily transferring privately owned land *back* to the government. Of common law origin, dedication technically requires an "offer" to transfer on the part of the landowner, and an "acceptance" by the public. The landowner's offer may be implied where the landowner acquiesces in a public use of his or her land; acceptance, too, may be inferred from continuous public use of private property. Usually, the practical effect of dedication is to create an easement in the public (via the local governmental unit) to use the land. Sometimes, the dedication will result in a transfer of fee simple ownership to the public. However, anytime the land ceases to be used for the public purpose, it may be reclaimed by the person who dedicated it.

Insofar as subdivision regulations are concerned, filing the plat containing areas marked off for the required purposes constitutes the necessary offer of dedication. However, approval of the plat by the city of other public body does not constitute acceptance of the streets, parks, schools, and other public areas contained therein. The local governmental unit accepts the offered property by passing an ordinance of acceptance, or by actually putting in the streets, schools, parks, and sewers as suggested.

As to how much dedicated property the local governmental unit can require, the courts are in disagreement. They are also in disagreement as to what purposes the property can be put.

In any case, once the dedication is complete, neither the government nor the subdivision developer can use the land for other than the dedicated purposes.

What is eminent domain?

You will recall that "eminent domain" refers to the right of government to take private property for public use upon the payment of just compensation. This power stems from the Fifth and Fourteenth Amendments to the United States Constitution.

With regard to the power, the term "public use" has become synonymous with "public benefit", thus permitting governmental units to condemn whole areas of land, including sound or new buildings for the purpose of urban renewal. Poorly organized vacant land may also be condemned to permit creation of new industrial parks that will benefit the public.

When the government condemns property, it generally acquires a fee simple absolute in the property, and the original landowner retains nothing. Of course, if, in the future, the public use is satisfied, the government may decide to sell or otherwise transfer the property back into private ownership (either to the original owner or another party), thus starting the whole cycle of land ownership all over again. And where the government does not take a fee simple, but rather condemns the land for a limited period of time, the private landowner will retain rights in the property, and will be entitled to its return upon completion of the public use.

In any case, the private landowner will be entitled to "just compensation" for the interest taken—"just compensation" referring to the fair market value of the property.

What duty does a landowner owe a person who comes upon his or her property?

As a final restriction upon land ownership, the law imposes certain duties upon a landowner with regard to people who come upon his or her property. The duty is not the same in every case, but varies with the class of individual who comes upon the land.

(1) *Trespassers.* The landowner's only duty to a trespasser is to warn the trespasser about hidden dangers on the property (e. g., a faulty stairwell) if and when the landowner discovers the trespasser's presence on the land. However, an exception arises in the case of trespassing children under what is called the *attractive nuisance* doctrine. If the landowner maintains a condition on his or her property that poses an unreasonable risk of harm to children, and the owner can anticipate that children are likely to trespass on the land, then the owner will be liable if children do in fact trespass and suffer injury as a result of the condition. A good example of an attractive nuisance is a swimming pool that is inadequately fenced off. Generally, to recover under the attractive nuisance doctrine, a child must be of "tender years" (usually, less than 14 years of age).

(2) *Licensees.* A licensee is a person who has a privilege to enter upon the landowner's property with the consent of the landlord but nothing more (e. g., members of the landowner's family, social guests who come to visit at the invitation of the landowner, door-to-door salesmen, etc.). The landowner's duty to a licensee is the same as his or her duty to a trespasser—that is, to warn the licensee of hidden dangers on the property once the landowner is aware of his or her presence on the land. Again, a higher duty may be imposed with respect to licensee children under the attractive nuisance doctrine.

(3) *Business visitors (also called invitees)*. A business visitor or invitee is a person who comes upon the landowner's property upon the business of the landowner (e. g., a business customer, a restaurant patron, a TV repairer, etc.). The landowner owes a much higher duty to a business visitor than he or she owes to a trespasser or licensee. With regard to a business visitor, the landowner has a duty to make the premises safe—that is to say, to take reasonable precautions to protect the invitee from foreseeable dangers on the property.

CASES

CASE 1—*Upon learning of his terminal cancer he deeded the land to his "daddy", but was there a delivery of the deed?*

HAGEN v. PALMER

Supreme Court of South Dakota, 1973.
210 N.W.2d 164.

DOYLE, Justice.

This is an action to set aside a deed to a quarter section of land for lack of consideration and nondelivery of the deed with the proviso that the plaintiff pay to the defendant any sum due defendant on account of the purchase of said property, less the reasonable value of use of the land during the defendant's possession. The trial court entered judgment for the defendant and plaintiff appeals.

The plaintiff, Ethel C. Hagen, was formerly married to Paul Palmer, deceased, who was the son of Charles Palmer, the defendant in this action. They were married in 1951 and lived with the father until 1953 when they moved to a farming unit consisting of approximately 720 acres owned by the father. The land in dispute is contiguous to the unit owned by the father. On March 19, 1958, Paul Palmer purchased the land in question, one quarter section. He borrowed $600 from the bank and $5000 from his father in order to pay for the land. Paul and his wife Ethel resided on this unit, which included the part rented from the father and the quarter section purchased by Paul, until Paul Palmer died in July 1963. There was no formal lease or rent agreement between Charles Palmer and Paul Palmer. In November 1962, Paul Palmer learned that he had terminal cancer. On January 5, 1963, Paul Palmer and his wife Ethel Palmer executed a warranty deed conveying the quarter section of land in question to Charles Palmer. This warranty deed was drawn in an attorney's office, acknowledged by the attorney, mailed to the Register of Deeds of Hyde County where it was duly recorded and then returned to the attorney. The deed was subsequently mailed to the Paul Palmer residence and placed in their files. The defendant did not see the deed until it was shown to him at the trial. After the death of Paul Palmer, on July 29, 1963, his wife Ethel continued to live on the unit. However, the defendant, Charles Palmer, took possession of the parcel of land in question and leased it, collecting rent from 1964. He also paid the real estate taxes on the land from 1963 to date of trial. Ethel Palmer was the executrix of the estate of Paul Palmer, and the land in question was not included as part of the estate of Paul Palmer.

There are several propositions presented on appeal; however, the question of delivery of the deed is determinative of this lawsuit. The finding of fact and conclusion of law of the trial judge was that a preponderance of the evidence established that the deed executed by Paul and Ethel Palmer on January 5, 1963, was constructively delivered to the grantee, Charles Palmer. The trial court's finding, of course, will not be disturbed on appeal unless clearly erroneous.

The general rule concerning delivery is stated in Powell on Real Property, Vol. 6, ¶ 896, p. 249 at 252, as follows:

> "The finding of delivery rests upon a judicial conclusion that the conduct of the grantor justifies a finding of his intent to treat the deed as an unrecallable instrument giving the grantee what the deed purports to convey him."

SDCL 43–4–9 states:

> "Though a grant be not actually delivered into the possession of the grantee, it is yet to be deemed constructively delivered where the instrument is, by the agreement of the parties at the time of execution, understood to be delivered, and under such circumstances that the grantee is entitled to immediate delivery."

Whether there has been delivery is a question of intent to be found from all the facts surrounding the transaction. "The fact that a deed has been duly executed, acknowledged, and recorded is prima facie evidence of its delivery".

The evidence disclosed affirmative acts by the plaintiff from which the trial court could reasonably find an intent on her part and a knowledge of the intent of Paul Palmer to treat the deed as having been delivered to the grantee. Plaintiff was the executrix of the estate of Paul Palmer and his sole heir, and throughout the proceedings of said estate she made no claim that Paul Palmer had any interest in the land. The plaintiff, together with her husband, Oscar Hagen, leased and paid rent for this land in the year 1965. The defendant was permitted to take possession of the real estate, to lease it from 1964 and to retain all rental therefrom without any objection from the plaintiff. The defendant has also paid all real estate taxes on this property for the years 1963 to date of trial. There was testimony by the defendant that prior to Paul Palmer's death he had two conversations with his son regarding this parcel of land. The first conversation was in the fall of 1962 when Paul told his father, " 'daddy, * * * I am going to give that quarter back to you. * * * I owe it to you.' " The second conversation occurred sometime between January 5, 1963 and July 1963, at which time Paul told his father that he had conveyed the property to him. Plaintiff, herself, testified that she knew that defendant was aware that Paul Palmer had put this parcel of land in the defendant's name and had informed him of this fact. There was testimony of a neighbor who stated that on January 5, 1963, the date of the deed, Paul Palmer had told him that he had transferred the parcel of land in question to his father because he owed money on it and felt he should turn it back to him.

The evidence disclosed that delivery and acceptance of the deed were accomplished by the parties. The plaintiff relies primarily on Cassidy v. Holland, 27 S.D. 287, 130 N.W. 771, in which this court held that:

> "Where a deed is found in the possession of the grantor unexplained, the presumptions in relation to the delivery thereof are exactly opposite to those where the deed comes from the possession of the grantee."

In that case, however, the deed was not recorded and had never been out of the grantor's possession; consequently, the opinion does not apply to the facts in the present case.

* * *

In view of the trial court's express finding of constructive delivery of the deed, supported not only by the testimony of the defendant but by testimony of the plaintiff, and affirmative acts on the part of the plaintiff disclosing an intent that the deed had in fact been delivered, we conclude that judgment for the defendant be affirmed.

CASE 2—*The defendants have established their "hostile, adverse claim of right to pasture and water livestock"—an easement by prescription.*

SCHWENKER v. SAGERS

Supreme Court of Iowa, 1975.
230 N.W.2d 525.

HARRIS, Justice.

This dispute concerns the extent of defendants' right to use a 30 foot wide strip of farmland. The trial court held defendants' rights were limited to ingress and egress to their adjoining land. The trial court issued a writ of injunction restraining defendants from, among other things, using the strip for keeping, feeding and watering livestock. We reverse and remand.

In 1943 defendants purchased a 50 acre tract in Jackson County, Iowa adjacent to land they already owned. To previous owners the 50 acre tract had been "landlocked"; that is, it did not abut a public roadway. Access to the 50 acre tract had been established over the 30 foot strip in question to an east-west public road to the south.

Plaintiff owned the tract from which the 30 foot strip was taken. The strip, which is also used for access purposes by persons other than the parties, amounts to a dirt farm lane. It is enclosed by fences with a gate at the point where it joins the public road. A short distance from the south boundary of defendants' 50 acre tract the strip is crossed by a stream. The stream does not otherwise touch defendants' property. Accordingly through long usage defendants and their predecessors in title utilized the strip for the purpose of watering livestock at the stream.

Although plaintiff disputes it, we believe defendants clearly established their claim they used the entire strip to water and pasture their livestock from the time they acquired the tract in 1943.

The actual use was a considerable enlargement of defendants' recorded rights to the strip, which they originally acquired by quit claim deed. Their immediate grantor acquired the strip by a deed which described an "easement to the use of the * * * [strip] as a roadway jointly with the grantor * * *."

The right of plaintiff, defendants, and others to use the strip as a roadway is not disputed. At issue is defendants' expanded use of the strip for purpose of pasturing and watering livestock. Defendants claim their expanded right by way of prescription.

Until 1964 the question was not of great moment to the parties. In 1964 plaintiff acquired another tract to the north of defendants'. Use of the strip for ingress and egress had been reserved to the owner of that tract and was conveyed to plaintiff. Also in 1964 defendants rented their farm. Plaintiff claims the tenants keep more cattle than defendants did. It is apparent the trend to ever larger farm machinery has aggravated the problems incident to the shared use of the strip.

There are three generally recognized methods of creating an easement: (1) express written grant, (2) prescription and (3) implication. It is not controlling here that there was a more limited written grant as to the same strip in this case. The terms of the written grant are not denied by plaintiff. And defendants do not suggest that the written grant was sufficiently broad to authorize the use to which they were enjoined by the trial court. This is not a claim of easement by implication. Defendants' sole claim of easement in the strip for livestock use was by way of prescription.

"An easement by prescription is created 'by adverse possession, under claim of right or color of title, openly notoriously, continuously, and hostilely asserted against defendants for ten years or more.' [U]se of property does not establish adverse possession. One claiming an easement by prescription must prove by evidence, independent of his use, that an easement was claimed as a matter of right and that the title holder had express notice thereof.

An easement established for a limited use may be expanded by prescription.

Two principles are argued which should be laid aside, not as invalid, but because they are inapplicable.　*　*　*

One principle limits the extent to which a shared easement may generally be used. It is a practical rule, necessary to accommodate the needs of others who share the easement, including the owner of the servient estate.

"The principles governing easement rights are simple and well established. [The easement holder] has the right to use the　*　*　*　strip in the manner and for the purposes it was intended to serve. He cannot use it in a way which imposes additional burdens on the owner of the land through which it runs. [The easement holder's] rights are not exclusive, and [servient owners] may use the easement strip for any purpose not inconsistent with [the] easement.

"Neither　*　*　*　may use the [strip] in violation of the rights of the other.　*　*　*."

The foregoing principle might have aided plaintiff if the recorded easement had not been enlarged by prescription. It does not operate to reduce easement rights but only to define and regulate them. In short, the rule set out　*　*　*　could have been utilized to prevent defendants from acquiring expanded uses. But it is not appropriate to erase or erode rights to such uses after they have been established by prescription.

Another principle governs situations where the use is merely permissive at its inception. Where the use is undertaken by permission of the servient estate owner it is not adverse or under claim of right. Continued use does not, by mere lapse of time, become hostile or adverse. This principle does not prevent prescription from ever running in all cases where the original use was merely permissive. But it is necessary for the user to show the use has become adverse and ceased to be merely permissive. We have held one manner in which a permissive use becomes adverse is by transfer of the servient property.

The trial court noted the servient property in the instant case had been transferred to plaintiff within ten years prior to suit. On this basis it was held defendant had not shown adverse or hostile use for sufficient time to establish a prescriptive right. This was error. The fact less than ten years had run from transfer of the servient estate does not bar establishment of the prescriptive easement for two reasons. Neither the recorded easement nor the expanded easement were permissive in origin. In any event the expanded easement was clearly shown to be hostile and adverse to plaintiff's predecessors in title for a period far in excess of ten years.

IV. Enlargement by prescription of a limited easement is rare. We note and adopt the following:

"The comparatively few cases which a comprehensive search has revealed as involving the point clearly indicate that *where an easement is granted for use in a specified manner or for a specified purpose, an open and continuous use thereof, under a claim of right, for the prescriptive period for purposes or in a manner beyond the scope of the grant, will create an easement of the larger scope by prescription,* although in the majority of such cases the enlarged easement was held in fact not to arise because of a lack of the elements necessary to create it." (Emphasis added).

In the instant case defendants clearly establish their hostile, adverse claim of right to pasture and water livestock. The record shows defendants treated the strip as if they had bought it together with the 50 acre tract in 1943. There was a road gate at the end of the strip. The strip was thereby fenced together with a pasture on the 50 acre tract. Pasture and strip became one common ground where defendants thereafter regularly pastured and watered their cattle.

Defendants were able to show they had received, some 20 years prior to trial, a letter from Hillis Lee, a Maquoketa attorney. Mr. Lee then represented I. M. Bowley, a predecessor owner of the servient estate. Mr. Bowley threatened to put a gate across the strip so as to block access to the stream. At the time Mr. Bowley threatened to do so in order to impel defendants to participate in the upkeep of the north end of the strip. Defendants advised Mr. Lee they had a right to the use of the strip, specifically to the water, and refused to cooperate. The record shows that on the basis of their insistence Mr. Bowley's demands were dropped. They continued to use the strip during approximately 20 years that followed.

The trial court erred in ordering an injunction restraining defendants from using the strip for keeping, feeding and watering livestock.

Judgment of the trial court is reversed and the case is remanded for entry of a judgment in conformity herewith.

PROBLEMS

1. Read and answer the following:

    (a) Although Art Able does not own Redacre, he purports to convey the land to Betty Barker on November 1st. Betty records her deed the same day. On December 1st, Art Able acquires ownership of Redacre. On December 10th, he sells and conveys the land to Connie Carpenter who immediately records her deed. As between Betty Barker and Connie Carpenter, who is entitled to the property? Explain fully. *Connie b+p prevails because Betty did not rerecord deed*

  (b) Abe Arnold conveys Blueacre to Billy Bottoms on January 1st. On February 1st, Abe sells and conveys Blueacre to Cora Castle who has no knowledge of the prior transfer to Billy. On January 2nd *FEB*, Billy records his deed. On January *FEB* 3rd, Cora records her deed. As between Billy and Cora, who prevails under a notice statute? Under a race-notice statute? Under a race statute? Explain your answers fully. *notice – prior grantee must record before 2d conveyance. Race-notice – 1st recorder wins BFP if no recording. RACE STATUTE – 1st recorder wins*

2. Knowing that Andy Amos owns Greenacre, but does not live there, Peter Sammons moves onto the property. He builds a fence around the land, cultivates crops for his own use, and raises some sheep. After a few weeks, Andy Amos posts a "no trespassing" sign on the land, but Peter ignores the sign. Two years pass, then Peter suffers an attack of wanderlust. He "gives" Greenacre to his old friend Zeb Stone who moves onto the property and continues to farm it. 18 years pass. Zeb never records any claim to the land. Then, on March 1st, Andy Amos conveys Greenacre to Beth Biddle. Beth does not record her deed. On April 1st, Andy "gives" Greenacre to Carl Carlson who also fails to record. On May 1st, Andy sells and conveys Greenacre to Darlene Darrow who knows about the prior, unrecorded transfers to Beth Biddle and Carl Carlson. Darlene records her deed the same day. On June 1st, Darlene sells and conveys Greenacre to Ethel Euing who records on June 1st. Assuming the statutory period for adverse possession is 20 years, answer the following: *Beth prevails 1st in time*

  (a) As between Beth Biddle and Carl Carlson (and without regard to Zeb Stone's rights, if any), who is entitled to Greenacre under a notice statute, a race-notice statute, and a race statute? Explain. As between Beth, Carl, and Darlene Darrow? As between Beth, Carl, Darlene, and Ethel Euing? Explain your answers. *notice – Beth / Race-notice – Beth / Race – Darlene* *notice – Ethel (BFP) / Race Notice – Ethel / Race – Ethel*

  (b) Now as between Beth, Carl, Darlene, Ethel, and Zeb Stone, who is entitled to Greenacre? Explain. *Zeb adverse control*

3. Read and answer the following:

  (a) A land description in a deed contains a glaring inconsistency. One part of the description states "from the stake located at the Northeast corner of Miller's fence to the old oak tree" (400 feet east of the stake), while a second part states "from the stake located at the Northeast corner of Miller's fence east 350 feet", and yet a third part states "from the stake located at the Northeast corner of Miller's fence to the Northwest corner of Souder's picket fence" (410 feet east of the stake). Which description controls? Explain. *oak tree*

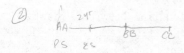

(b) Describe the shaded area of real property in both full and abbreviated form.

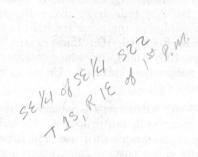

SE¼ of SE¼ of 35, S22
T 1S, R 1E of 1ª P.M.

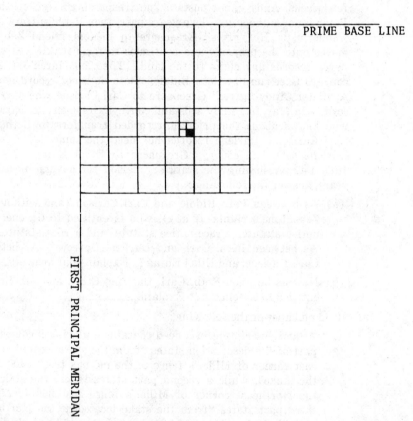

PRIME BASE LINE

FIRST PRINCIPAL MERIDAN

4. Answer the following "True" or "False" and give reasons for your answers:

  T (a) An unacknowledged deed cannot be recorded.

  T (b) Title acquired by adverse possession is "marketable" title.

  F (c) Recording is essential to making a deed valid as between a grantor and grantee.

  T (d) An implied easement is always appurtenant.

  F (e) A license cannot be revoked and may be freely transferred by the licensee.

T (f) An easement appurtenant runs with the land and cannot be revoked.

T (g) Modernly, a commercial easement in gross is freely transferable.

F (h) A profit may be created by express grant or implied by necessity.

F (i) A profit is always freely transferable.

T (j) Dedication refers to the voluntary transfer of publicly owned land to a private landowner.

T (k) Under the government's power of eminent domain, "public use" has become synonymous with "public benefit".

5. In connection with the audit of Fiske & Company, you found it necessary to examine a deed to certain property owned by the client. In this connection, which of the following statements is correct?

   (a) A deed purporting to convey real property, but which omits the day of the month, is invalid.

   (b) A deed which lacks the signature of the grantor is valid.

   (c) A quitclaim deed which purports to transfer to the grantee "whatever title the grantor has" is invalid.

   (d) A deed which purports to convey real property and recites a consideration of $1.00 and other valuable consideration is valid.

   [# 31, May 1978 CPA Exam]

6. Maxwell purchased real property from Plumb and received a warranty deed at the closing. Maxwell neglected to record the deed. In this situation

   (a) A subsequent purchaser from Plumb will obtain a better title to the real property than Maxwell even if the subsequent purchaser is aware of Maxwell's prior purchase.

   (b) Maxwell must record his deed in order to perfect his rights against Plumb.

   (c) Recordation would provide constructive notice of Maxwell's rights to subsequent purchasers of the real property even though they do not have actual notice.

   (d) Maxwell lacks an insurable interest in the property and any fire insurance policy he obtains is void.

   [# 23, May 1976 CPA Exam]

7. Arthur entered into a contract for the sale of real property to Vance for $50,000. Arthur owned the property free and clear of all mortgages. Arthur received $2,500 upon the signing of the contract and agreed to take $22,500 in cash or certified check at the closing and a first mortgage for the balance. In this situation

   (a) The mortgage in question need not be recorded by Arthur to perfect his interest against third parties in that it is a purchase-money security interest.

   (b) Arthur's contract gave Vance an implied covenant that his title would be marketable at the time of closing.

   (c) If the contract is silent on the point, Arthur must deliver a full warranty deed with covenants at the closing.

(d) If Arthur breaches the contract, Vance's only recourse is to sue for damages based upon breach of contract.

[# 27, May 1976 CPA Exam]

8. Hershey, an accountant, performed professional services for Martin for several years without receiving any compensation. Hershey pressed Martin for payment. Martin explained that at the moment he was unable to pay Hershey in cash. However, as payment he offered to deed to Hershey part of his property which he had purchased in an isolated area in another state many years before. Hershey and Martin agreed that Hershey should take a trip to inspect the property before deciding whether or not Hershey would agree to Martin's offer. Expecting that Hershey would accept the property once he saw it, Martin drew and signed a deed for the property and asked Hershey to hold the deed for the property conditionally until his return. Hershey visited the property and found that Ahrens had moved on to the property several years before and that Ahrens considered it his own. Hershey also discovered that Saffer, who bought a strip of adjacent land from Martin, has for a long time regularly crossed the property to visit his land.

Hershey returned home still unsure of whether or not he should accept Martin's proposition. On arrival, however, Hershey learned that Martin had died insolvent and, fearing the loss of his fee, Hershey produced the deed and announced to the executor of the estate that he considered the property his own. Martin's executor questions Hershey's title.

Required: (a) As between Hershey and the executor of Martin's estate, who is entitled to the land? Explain.

(b) Under what theory might Ahrens claim title to the land? What facts would Ahrens have to show to claim title to the land?

(c) Under what theory or theories might Saffer claim the right to cross the land? What facts would Saffer have to prove in order to claim an interest in the land?

[# 5, May 1967 CPA Exam]

9. While vouching additions to the land and buildings accounts during your examination of the financial statements of Dandy Manufacturing, Inc., you learn that Dandy had purchased a factory building from Howard Luff for $247,500. Dandy had engaged the Bigelow Title Insurance Company, Inc., to do the title search and to issue a $247,500 title policy insuring Dandy's fee interest in the real property. Bigelow issued the title policy without exception. Howard Luff gave a typical bargain and sale deed with a covenant against the grantor's acts; or, as it is sometimes referred to, a special warranty deed. It was subsequently discovered that the executor of Luff's father's estate had failed to pay the estate taxes due on the property.

Required: (1) What are Dandy's rights against Luff on the deed? Explain.

(2) What are Dandy's rights against Bigelow Title? Explain.

[# 8(a), May 1973 CPA Exam]

10. Your client, Albert Fall, purchased a prominent industrial park from Josh Barton. At the closing, Barton offered a quitclaim deed. The contract of sale called for a warranty deed with full covenants.

(a) Fall should accept the quitclaim deed since there is no important difference between a quitclaim deed and a warranty deed.

(b) An undisclosed mortgage which was subsequently discovered would violate one of the covenants of a warranty deed.

(c) Fall cannot validly refuse to accept Barton's quitclaim deed.

(d) The only difference between a warranty deed with full covenants and a quitclaim deed is that the grantor of a quitclaim does not warrant against defects post his assumption of title.

[# 8(c), November 1973 CPA Exam]

Chapter 7

THE FIRST REQUIREMENT FOR A CONTRACT: MUTUAL ASSENT

What is a contract?

A contract cannot be seen or touched or be otherwise perceived by the senses. It is a legal concept that exists only in the imagination. You will recall from Ch. 1 that a legal concept is a general thought or idea—a mental formulation on a broad scale and in some detail. The word "concept" comes from the Latin *conceptus*, meaning "thing conceived", and that is what a contract is—"a thing conceived" in the mind as creating legal rights and duties by reason of a bargain or promises between people.

A contract is not a "writing". To be sure, many contracts are evidenced by a writing, but, even where the terms of the contract are written down, the writing itself is not the contract, but merely proof of the contract which will always remain an intangible.

Most contracts are in fact never written down. They are entirely products of the spoken word or of a wordless bargain or exchange. For example, if you purchase a magazine at the supermarket, you enter into a contract whether you orally state to the checker, "I'll take this magazine," or you simply place the magazine on the counter and the checker rings up the sale on the cash register. Similarly, if you place a quarter into a vending machine and receive a candy bar in return, you enter into a contract though nothing is said or put into writing. And the same is true if you place money into a parking meter to pay for an hour's parking (in this case, you enter into a contract with the city, you agreeing to pay a quarter in advance for the city's implied promise to rent you the space for an hour's time).

Whether a transaction is oral, word-less, or written, it constitutes a contract if it is recognized by law as creating legal rights and duties by reason of the bargain or promises (express or implied) of the agreeing parties. A "right" is simply a legal capacity to act or to demand action or forbearance on the part of another; a "duty" is but a legal obligation to act or to refrain from acting.

Thus, "contracts" may be defined as legally recognized promises or bargains made by two or more persons including all rights and duties resulting from the promises or bargains. The law requires four elements for a valid contract: (1) mutual assent, (2) consideration, (3) capacity, and (4) legality. Lacking any one of these four elements, the promises or bargains between parties will not create rights and duties and will not result in a valid contract.

In this chapter and the next, we will consider the first element necessary for a contract—mutual assent (the remaining three elements will be discussed in Ch. 9). However, before moving on to the specifics of mutual assent, a few general questions and answers regarding the law of contracts are in order.

Why do we need the contract concept?

In Ch. 1, we concluded that people need commercial law so as to be able to plan and project secure in the knowledge that their business dealings and agreements with others will be legally binding and enforceable. The basic tool or technique used by commercial law to accomplish this result is the contract. With the exception of illegal acts or promises, a person may use the contract device to commit to or have others commit to almost any present or future undertaking, including the sale of real or personal property, the performance of personal services, or the making of a loan. The law of contracts runs through every facet of modern society, reaching daily into all our lives. Our employment, our recreation, the properties we own, the creditors we owe—all are at some point subject to or governed by the law of contracts.

Through the concept of contracts, the law attempts to ensure that people will receive their reasonable expectations from the promises and bargains they enter into with others. They key word here is "reasonable". Where it is unreasonable to expect a party to carry out a promise exactly or to carry it out at all, the law will not require performance. For example, the law of contracts is unlikely to provide you with a legal remedy where your boyfriend or girlfriend fails to meet you for lunch "as promised", or where a friend who has "promised" to someday give you a valuable painting changes his or her mind. Most reasonable people in your position would not expect such promises to be legally binding or to result in legal remedies for "breach" of contract.

Contract law is complicated precisely because of the underlying notion of the law that not all promises should be legally binding. Obviously, it is very important for a person (particularly a businessperson) to know when the promises he or she makes or receives from others are binding and to what extent they are binding. As a result, many rules of contract law have been developed to determine when a person's promises or bargains will be binding and to what extent the machinery of the legal system will be available to assist the promisee in realizing his or her reasonable expectations if such promises or bargains are not carried out.

Of course, it is just as important to know when your promises or bargains will not be legally binding, and this is the starting point for a study of contracts —to know that promises and bargains

will not be legally binding unless the four elements of mutual assent, consideration, capacity, and legality are present. In other words, you can promise a person anything and the promise will mean nothing legally unless the four elements of a contract are present. While it may be bad manners to miss a luncheon date or a dance, it is not a breach of contract unless a contract was in fact formed (although it is unusual to form a contract regarding such subject matter, it is possible so long as all four elements of a valid contract are present).

So start out with the basic realization that promises in and of themselves usually mean nothing legally unless they form a contract with the required mutual assent, consideration, capacity, and legality. The word "usually" is used because the law will sometimes recognize an exception to the general rule and hold a promise or bargain binding (at least in part) despite the fact that one or more of the four elements of a contract are lacking in order to achieve a fair and equitable result and meet a party's reasonable expectations. In our study of contracts, we will explore the general rule as well as its exceptions.

How does property relate to the concept of contracts?

In the first six chapters of the text, we explored the legal concept of property. Our study of property was a fitting prelude to our study of contract law because contracts often involve the transfer or sale of property or the performance of services in order to make a living and acquire property. This is particularly true in light of the expanding definition of property, as discussed in Ch. 1 (you will recall that property now includes not only transferable rights in real and personal property, but also government entitlements, personal services, special property interests created by statute, and other interests protectible as "property" under the 14th Amendment of the U. S. Constitution).

Thus, contracts seem always to directly or indirectly relate to property. Additionally, most contract rights are themselves property rights as they may be freely transferred to others (such rights are correctly classified as *intangible* personal property rights because they can be neither seen nor physically possessed).

Contract rights are personal rights (rather than property rights) where they involve such close personal relationships or personal services that it would be impossible or unfair to permit their transfer. For example, you may have a binding contract right to the personal services of a surgeon in taking out your appendix: neither you nor the surgeon can transfer that right to another. Or say that you have obtained approval for a loan based upon your good financial position and excellent credit rating—you obviously have no ability to transfer your right to the loan to another (his or her financial position and credit rating may be different).

What are the natural parts of a contract law study?

There is an old saying about the person who became so lost in detail that he or she "could not see the forest because of the trees". As with many other complicated subject matters, the law of contracts is so replete with intricate rules and detail that it is difficult for a student to tie all the rules together so as to gain an understanding of the overall concept. Certainly, it is important to emphasize the specific rules relating to each general principle of contract law, but, at the same time, it is crucial to keep in view the whole of the subject matter of contracts as it is formed by the interaction of its parts.

To begin with, a contract generally requires the presence of four elements— mutual assent, consideration, capacity,

and legality. "Mutual assent" is synonymous with the agreement of the parties and is usually manifested by an offer and an acceptance. As previously stated, the many rules regarding offers, acceptances, and other aspects of mutual assent are presented in this chapter and the next. You will find that even though mutual assent appears to be present, it may not exist because one of the parties has done something to prevent the other from really consenting to the agreement. The "something" may be fraud, duress, undue influence, mistake, or "unconscionable" act. You must understand the specific rules defining such action and determining its effect upon mutual assent if you are to make the proper conclusion as to the existence of mutual assent.

Of course, even if mutual assent exists, there may still be no contract because one of the other three required elements is lacking. Contrary to popular belief, the second requirement of "consideration" does not demand the payment of money, although the payment of money will certainly do. What it does require is that a party either do something or promise to do something that he or she is not already bound to do. The subject of consideration is discussed in detail in Ch. 9.

Assuming that both mutual assent and consideration are present, there will still be no contract unless contractual capacity also exists. A person may be so devoid of reason (i. e., so mentally ill) that he or she will be held not to have entered into a contract despite the apparent existence of mutual assent and consideration. Or a person may be so young that he or she will be given the option of going through with the contract or disaffirming (rejecting) it. A minor (and the age varies from state to state from 18 to 21 years) who chooses to go through with the contract is said to "ratify" the agreement; a minor who disaffirms is said to "rescind" the contract. A contract that may be either ratified or rescinded is called a "voidable" contract.

Finally, if the subject matter of the promises or bargain is illegal, there will be no contract despite the existence of mutual assent, consideration and contractual capacity. Obviously, there is no legally recognized and enforceable contract where two adults (contractual capacity) reach an agreement (mutual assent), one promising to commit murder (consideration) in return for the other's promise to pay him or her a substantial sum of money (consideration). The subject matter —murder—is illegal, and the law will not recognize the agreement as giving rise to legal rights and duties. Of course, there are far more subtle forms of illegality, and they will be dealt with along with contractual capacity in Ch. 9 of the text.

In Ch. 10 you will learn that even a valid contract (valid because of the presence of mutual assent, consideration, capacity, and legality) may be unenforceable because the party seeking to enforce the contract cannot produce the appropriate written evidence required by the Statute of Frauds. The Statute of Frauds does not apply to all contracts: it requires a written memorandum signed by the party against whom enforcement is sought in contracts involving the transfer of an interest in land (and don't forget all the possible real property "interests" or "sticks" as described in the last six chapters); the sale of goods (personal property) for $500 or more; contracts that cannot be performed within one year; contracts in which one person promises to pay the debt of another; contracts in which a person handling the estate of a deceased person promises to pay the decedent's debts out of his or her own funds; and contracts in which a person promises to do something in return for a promise of marriage (however, mutual promises to marry are excluded from the statute).

A valid contract may also be subject to "conditions". In some cases, the contract will not begin to operate unless and until a certain condition occurs—until the condition occurs, neither party has an obligation to perform or carry out the promises made. In other cases, the contract will begin to operate immediately, but each party's obligation to perform will terminate or come to an end upon the occurrence of a specified condition. Sometimes, conditions are implied by law; and, sometimes, each party must perform alternatively as a condition to the continued performance of the other.

Closely related to implied conditions is the subject matter of interpretation of contracts. Generally speaking, there are established rules for interpreting ambiguous contract terms. Also, a rule called the "parol evidence" rule states that when a contract is fully (finally and completely) written by the parties, the written terms of the contract cannot be varied, altered, or changed by the introduction of evidence that occurred prior to or at the time of the writing.

Ultimately, a person who enters into a valid contract will either be "discharged" from further performance under the contract, or he or she will become liable for "breach of contract" for failing to perform as promised. In most cases, contract obligations are discharged by performance of the obligations. Other methods of discharge include objective impossibility (when it is impossible for anyone to perform the contract), novation (the agreed upon substitution of a third party for one of the contracting parties), and, as previously mentioned, the happening of a "condition subsequent" that operates to terminate any further duty of performance under the contract. A party who breaches a contract will be held liable in money damages to the nonbreaching party in an amount calculated to place the nonbreaching party in the same position as he or she would have been in had the contract been carried out. However, the rule of remoteness permits recovery only of damages that are foreseeable; and the rule of mitigation of damages requires the injured party to do all that he or she can to keep the damages to a minimum. The subject matters of conditions, interpretation of contracts, the parol evidence rule, discharge, breach of contract, and damages are all considered in Ch. 10.

Ch. 11 begins with a consideration of third party beneficiary contracts—contracts made by individuals for the benefit of others. The typical example of a third party beneficiary contract is a life insurance contract wherein the insured pays a premium to an insurance company in exchange for the company's promise to pay a specified sum of money upon the insured's death to a third party beneficiary, usually the insured's wife or child. There are many special rules of law dealing with life insurance contracts, and they are presented in detail in Ch. 11 along with the many other aspects of insurance contracts generally.

Another important subject of contract law is "assignment" of contract rights. As noted previously, most contract rights are transferable property rights—"assignment" of the rights is the most common method of transfer. In an assignment, one party assigns (transfers) rights to another who then stands in the same position as his or her assignor (transferor) with regard to the contract. Since the assignee (transferee) is in the same position as the assignor, any defenses that are good against the assignor are also good against the assignee.

On the other hand, a "holder in due course" who takes a special kind of contract called a "negotiable instrument" through a "negotiation" may acquire rights in the contract superior to those of his or her transferor. Negotiable instruments, including checks, drafts, and promissory notes, are designed to serve in commerce as substitutes for money. A "negotiation" is not an assignment; and a "holder in due course" is not an assignee. The fact that a holder in due course may acquire superior rights to those of his or her transferor (as opposed to merely "standing in his or her shoes" as an assignee does) is the chief distinction between assignment of contract rights generally and negotiation of negotiable instruments. It is a result that makes negotiable instruments a very special and important part of our law. For this reason, we take up the study of negotiable instruments directly following assignment of contract rights in Ch. 12.

Once our study of negotiable instruments is complete, we move to the law of banking because banks are the institutions that deal most often with checks, drafts, and promissory notes.

Following banking, we take a look at another kind of negotiable instrument called a "document of title". A document of title is designed not to serve as a substitute for cash but to facilitate the transfer of goods in commercial transport or storage. The subject of commercial transport of goods is controlled by the legal concept of "common carrier" and a special contract known as a "bill of lading". While "common carriers" such as commercial trucks, trains, and cargo jets do not own the property that they transport, they do have rightful possession of it (the rightful possession of another's goods is termed a "bailment" and the many rules governing bailments are considered along with common carriers at this point). A "bill of lading" is a written receipt for goods deposited with a carrier—the bill embodies the contract for carriage (transportation) of the goods, and it acts as documentary evidence of title to the goods. The bill of lading may be a negotiable document of title in which case negotiation of the bill will serve to transfer ownership of the goods to the transferee. And negotiation may create superior rights in the transferee in the same way that negotiation of a negotiable check, draft, or promissory note may create superior rights in a holder in due course.

With regard to stored goods, "warehousemen" are people in the business of commercially storing goods for a price; they are in a bailment relationship with respect to the goods they store. Warehousemen commonly use a written contract called a "warehouse receipt" which, like a bill of lading, may be a negotiable document of title. Again, negotiation of the document will serve to transfer ownership of the goods.

Having in mind a basic understanding of contracts, insurance, negotiable instruments, bailments, common carriers, warehousemen, and documents of title, we move to the law of sales in Chapters 17, 18, and 19. A "sale" is the transfer of ownership of goods to another for a price. The Uniform Commercial Code definition of a "contract" as "the total legal obligation created by a bargain" encompasses sales of goods. Furthermore, the Code contains a great number of special rules governing the law of sales, including provisions as to who bears the risk of loss for goods that are damaged or destroyed after the goods have been sold, but before possession and ownership have been transferred to the buyer; as to what rights are created in the buyer upon identification of the goods to the

sales contract; as to the legal effect of a sale of goods by one who lacks complete ownership (title); and as to the legal remedies of the buyer and seller in the event that the sales contract is breached.

In Ch. 21, we will see that a person can authorize another to contract for him or her. The authorizing party is called the *principal*, the authorized party the *agent*. The principal is bound by his or her agent's contracts just as if he or she had made them personally.

Finally, a study of secured transactions involving both goods and real property is in order. Goods, for example, may be put up as security for the repayment of a loan or for the issuance of credit. Where this occurs, it may be necessary to file a "financing statement" if the security holder's interest in the property is to be protected. A security interest in real property is generally created by a special contract called a "mortgage". Security interests and mortgages (including the many rules governing the creation and protection of such interests) are dealt with in detail in Chapter 27. The closely related subject of "suretyship" is treated in the same chapter (a "surety" is a person who promises to pay for the debt of another).

The following illustration presents a quick look at the "forest" of contract law rules. Keep the specifics in mind, but don't lose sight of the overall picture.

CONTRACTS

*"Don't miss the forest (the overall concept of contracts)
because of the trees (the labyrinthe of rules)."*

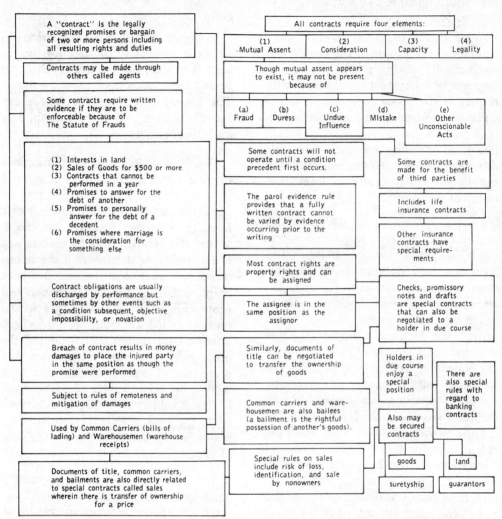

What are the sources of contract law?

The basic law of contracts is common law (i. e., unwritten law resulting from court decisions—see Appendix A). However, there are statutes in every state that affect contracts and control particular contract transactions. By far and away the most important legislation dealing with contracts is the Uniform Commercial Code which has been passed in full by 49 of the 50 states (and in part by Louisiana), as well as the District of Columbia and the Virgin Islands. The Code is divided into ten "Articles", each of which is further divided into "Parts" and "Sections". The "Articles" are entitled:

(1) General Provisions;

(2) Sales;

(3) Commercial Paper;

(4) Bank Deposits and Collections;

(5) Letters of Credit;

(6) Bulk Transfers;

(7) Warehouse Receipts, Bills of Lading and Other Documents of Title;

(8) Investment Securities;

(9) Secured Transactions, Sales of Accounts, Contract Rights and Chattel Paper;

(10) Effective Date and Repealer.

The name "Uniform Commercial Code" may be a misnomer since the Code is really not uniform in all the states. Originally, the Code came out with some "optional" provisions that were adopted by some states and not others. And the Statute has been amended to some extent in nearly every state. Additionally, each state is free to interpret the language of the Code in its courts; and it is not surprising that different states have interpreted some of the same Code provisions in different ways. Be that as it may, the Uniform Commercial Code has resulted in far more uniformity of commercial transactions than existed in pre-Code days. Moreover, the courts look to the Code for guidance in areas not directly covered by the Statute.

It should be noted that the Code applies to the sale of goods but does not apply to the sale of real property, or to the use of real property as security (with the exception of fixtures). Nor does the Code apply to employment or other contracts involving services, to insurance contracts, suretyship transactions, or bankruptcy.

And even where the Code does apply, it may cover only part of the transaction —not all of its aspects. Common law and other statutory law may also come into play. The Code itself states at Section 1–103 that it is to be "supplemented" by the common law.

The UCC provides:

Section 1–103. Supplementary General Principles of Law Applicable

Unless displaced by the particular provisions of this Act, the principles of law, and equity, including the law merchant and the law relative to capacity to contract, principal and agent, estoppel, fraud, misrepresentation, duress, coercion, mistake, bankruptcy, or other validating or invalidating cause shall supplement its provisions.

———

Thus, contract law is a blend of common law and statutory law. Though some of the specifics vary from state to state, the basic rules are largely the same. Our task is to study the basic rules of both the common and the statutory law and to interrelate the rules. It is a formidable task, yet a necessary one if a complete and accurate understanding of contract law is to be achieved.

What is mutual assent?

The first element necessary to formation of a contract is mutual assent. "Mutual assent" is synonymous with "agreement". What it requires is that each party manifest a willingness or agreement to be bound by his or her promise. The requirement of mutual assent is part and parcel of the twofold purpose of the law of contracts: (1) *not* to hold parties to their promises or agreements in the absence of evidence that the parties truly intended or agreed to be bound; and (2) *to* ensure that parties who do make promises and enter into agreements, desiring to be bound, are met with their reasonable expectations. This is an important purpose. Parties should not be bound to unintended promises, promises they were forced to make, or promises that arose out of a mutual mistake about the facts of the situation. On the other hand, parties should be obliged to follow through on intended agreements or promises so that the reasonable expectations of the parties relying upon the promise can be met. The notion that parties should only be bound to their intended agreements and promises is the underlying reason for all the many rules regarding the formation of mutual assent.

The law employs an objective test for determining the presence of mutual assent. Called the *objective theory of contracts,* the rule is that a contracting party may rely upon the apparent intentions of the other party without regard to the party's secret thoughts or subjective, but undisclosed, feelings or reservations. Thus, the test of mutual assent is what a reasonable person in the respective positions of each of the contracting parties would be led to believe by the words and conduct of the other party. So a person who subjectively intends not to enter into an agreement, but who, by words or conduct, leads another to reasonably conclude that the requisite mutual assent is there, will be bound to the agreement despite his or her hidden intent to the contrary. Of course, if the second party has actual knowledge of the first party's true intentions, there will be no mutual assent and no contract. The first party, in this case, does not intend to enter into a contract, and the second party has no reasonable expectations from the promise in light of his or her actual knowledge of the first party's subjective intent.

Now let's look at some examples. If, as a joke, Jeff Jackson offers to sell his $500 golf clubs to Jill Kelley for $25, and Jill, as a reasonable person, believes that the offer is genuine, mutual assent will be found despite Jeff's secret intention not to be bound by the agreement. However, if in light of all the circumstances, Jill should realize as a reasonable person that Jeff would not truly offer to sell the clubs for a mere fraction of their price, no mutual assent will be found,

and Jeff will not be bound to follow through with the agreement. And of course, if Jill knows that Jeff's intent is to play a joke on her, mutual assent will not arise regardless of how reasonable it is to conclude from Jeff's words and conduct that he is serious about entering into an agreement.

The same rules apply to an expression of mutual assent made in anger or great excitement (e. g., a promise to pay $20,000 "to anyone who rescues my mother from the burning house"). For mutual assent to be found in such circumstances, it is necessary that the statement or expression create, in light of all the circumstances, an expectation of legally recognized rights in the mind of a reasonable person.

The objective theory of contracts also takes care of the social obligation situation. Suppose, for example, that Jeff Jackson promises Jill Kelley that he will have lunch with her on Tuesday, or that he will take her to a dance at the college or country club. A reasonable person in Jill's position would realize that Jeff intends only a social obligation and not a binding legal promise with its attendant legal consequences for nonperformance. Understandably and logically, the law will not find the required mutual assent in such a situation.

In conclusion, mutual assent is a showing or manifestation by the parties to one another that they agree to the same bargain at the same time. Where the showing is by oral or written words, the contract is said to be an *express* contract. Where the mutual assent is manifested by conduct alone, the contract is said to be *implied in fact.* Many contracts are partly express and partly implied in fact. For example, if a baseball player who is hit in the mouth with a ball goes into a doctor's office and orally states that she will pay a specified price if the doctor will stitch up her face, an express contract will result. If the baseball player says nothing to the doctor, but merely points to her face, with the result that the doctor performs the necessary medical services, an implied in fact contract will arise for the reasonable value of the medical services. And finally, if the baseball player orally asks the doctor to stitch up her face, but makes no mention of price or payment, a partly express and partly implied in fact contract will arise with the law inferring a promise (a promise implied in fact) on the part of the baseball player to pay a reasonable fee for the doctor's services. Mutual assent is found in each of these examples because a reasonable person in the position of each of the parties would agree that binding promises were intended.

How is mutual assent usually manifested?

Mutual assent is usually manifested by one party making an offer and another party making an acceptance of the offer.

What is an offer?

An offer may be succinctly defined as a definite conditional undertaking. It is a *definite* proposal made by one party (the "offeror") to another party (the "offeree") indicating the offeror's present intent to enter into a contract (i. e., to *undertake* a legally recognized promise or obligation) *conditioned* upon the offeree's completion of the contract by acceptance. The offeree's power to accept is created by the offer itself.

An offer is usually a promise to do or not to do a specific act in the future; it is always conditional in that the undertaking is conditioned upon acceptance by the offeree. As to the terms of the offer, they must always be sufficiently definite that a court can determine the nature and extent of the offeree's reasonable expectations.

Whether or not a particular statement or expression indicates a present intention

to enter into a contract is governed by the objective theory of contracts. If a reasonable person in the position of the offeree would know that the "offer" is intended only as a joke, an opinion, a social obligation, or is made only because the "offeror" is in a state of great excitement or anger, the statement or expression will not constitute an offer.

How are offers distinguished from statements of opinion, preliminary negotiation, statements of intention, or invitations to make an offer?

Rarely does one party's initial communication to another constitute the definite conditional undertaking required for an offer. More often, parties who hope to ultimately enter into a binding contract or agreement begin their discussion with a general conversation about the subject matter involved. They exchange information as needed but do not immediately, and perhaps never, arrive at an offer. This initial bantering back and forth of ideas is called *preliminary negotiation* and its purpose is to acquaint both parties with the details of a possible agreement to come together in the future. Many bargaining transactions, for example, start out with preliminary negotiation over such topics as advertising, marketing, financial history, credit ratings, etc.

At any time either party to a preliminary negotiation makes what can be considered a definite conditional undertaking, an offer arises, creating in the offeree the power to complete mutual assent by making the appropriate acceptance. In determining whether the conversation has moved from preliminary negotiation to an offer, the courts again employ the objective theory of contracts: would a reasonable person in the position of the offeree believe that if he or she accepted the proposal a completed agreement would result without further negotiation of any kind being necessary? Often, the words used by the parties are helpful in making this determination. For example, words such as "Are you interested?" or "Would you pay . . .?" appear to be words of preliminary negotiation, whereas words such as "I'm asking" or "I will pay you the amount of . . ." or "the lowest price I will accept is . . ." or "I offer to sell" look to be words constituting a definite conditional undertaking—that is, an offer.

Apart from preliminary negotiation, one party may merely state an *opinion* without any desire to enter into an agreement. The question of whether particular words constituted an offer or merely an opinion came before the Minnesota courts in the case of Anderson v. Backlund, 159 Minnesota 423, 199 N.W. 90 (1924). In that case, a landowner had rented land to a farmer. One day, the farmer was telling the landowner about his many financial difficulties, and the landowner suggested that it might be a good idea to get more cattle for the pasture. The renter responded, voicing his concern that there would not be enough water for additional cattle because of the unusually dry season then occurring in Minnesota. The landowner quickly replied, "Never mind the water, John, I will see there will be plenty of water because it never failed in Minnesota yet." Shortly thereafter, the renter purchased over 100 more head of cattle, and ultimately suffered a substantial financial loss when the rain did not materialize in Minnesota. The renter sued the landowner in court, claiming that he had bought the extra cattle in reliance upon the owner's promise. The Minnesota court, however, held that no promise had been made—the landowner's statement, the court declared, was merely his opinion as to what the weather would be in the future.

Similarly, a statement of *intention* is not an offer. Suppose that a party says, "I am going to sell my boat for $1,500", and another party immediately responds by saying, "I accept, here is your $1,500". Because the first party's statement is not a definite conditional undertaking, but merely a declaration of intention to sell the boat at a future time, the second party has no power to complete an agreement and his or her purported acceptance does not give rise to mutual assent.

If often happens that a party who desires to enter into a contract will not himself or herself make an offer, but will invite or request others to make offers that he or she can accept or disregard. This is particularly true of merchants (i. e., dealers in goods) who do not want to run the risk of making offers to sell a particular item to a large group of individuals or to the general public: if more than one of the offerees accepts, the offeror may face liability for breach of contract to all but the one offeree who receives the goods. Because such multiple liability is possible, it is very important for merchants to invite offers rather than to make offers to sell their goods.

Thus, it is that merchants or dealers in goods generally send out catalogs, price lists, or circular letters advertising their goods and prices, but not offering to sell them. The advertisements are merely invitations to other merchants or members of the public to make an offer to buy the goods at the prices quoted. It is then up to the dealer to accept the offer or offers made; and, if the dealer does not have any goods in stock at the time the offer is made, he or she simply disregards the offer and mutual assent does not arise.

This is not to say that merchants or dealers cannot make valid offers through their advertisements—merely that it is unusual for them to do so. To help protect merchants, there is a rebuttable presumption in the law that any advertisement placed in a newspaper, handbill, store window, catalog, price list, or circular letter is not an offer to sell, but merely an invitation to another to make an offer to buy. Additionally, the objective theory of contracts works in the merchants' favor as a reasonable person would in most cases conclude that a dealer's advertisement was not intended as a definite conditional undertaking, but merely as an invitation to make an offer.

As a result, if you see an advertisement in your local newspaper that a local supermarket will be selling coffee, sugar, canned goods, and meats at specified prices on Saturday only, you are more than likely being invited, along with other potential customers, to come into the store on Saturday and make an offer to buy the advertised goods at the quoted prices. It is then up to the store to accept your offer at the check-out counter. In the unlikely event that the store has used language in the advertisement that clearly and unmistakeably constitutes a definite conditional undertaking, the store has made an offer that you, as an offeree, have the power to accept.

How definite does a statement have to be in order to constitute an offer?

An offer does not have to contain every possible specific of an agreement in order to satisfy the requirement of definiteness. It need only be "reasonably" definite—that is, sufficiently definite that the court can determine the essential terms of the agreement as intended by the parties so as to meet the reasonable expectations of either party in damages. Suppose, for example, that Bonita Businessperson and Thomas Artistic are graduating from college, Bonita with a degree in business administration, and Thomas with a degree in art. Bonita plans to go into business for herself, while Thomas decides to paint still life for a living. If Bonita offers to pay Thomas a "fair share

of the profits" from her business if Thomas will paint her a "masterpiece", the offer will fail for lack of definiteness. There is no way that a court can determine what a "fair share" of the profits from Bonita's new business might be; nor can the court pass judgment on what would constitute a "masterpiece" from Thomas.

It is generally agreed that the requirement of definiteness is satisfied if the court can determine four essential terms of the agreement: the parties to the contract, the subject matter of the contract, the time for performance by the parties, and the price, if any, involved in the transaction. It is not necessary that all four terms be spelled out expressly or exactly in the offer itself so long as the terms may be readily determined from the entire manifestations of the parties in both the offer and acceptance. In other words, the essential terms must be either expressly stated by the parties or unquestionably implied from their conduct. Suppose, for example, that a party telephones a plumber and requests him or her to come immediately and fix a pipe that has broken and flooded the caller's basement. Although nothing is said as to price, payment of a reasonable fee will be implied in fact from the caller's request for services. Because the price term is not mentioned at all, it is probable that the parties intended the term to be implied at the going rate for plumber's services. However, where the parties make a vague or indefinite reference to price, the offer will fail for lack of definiteness, and no mutual assent or contract will arise. A vague or indefinite reference shows that the parties did have something in mind as to price, and for the court to imply a "reasonable" price in face of the reference would be contrary to the parties' intent. As you can see, there is a considerable difference in result in only vaguely or indefinitely mentioning an essential term and not mentioning it at all.

Similarly, where the implication of "reasonable" terms would be inconsistent with something the parties expressly said, the terms will not be implied by the court. For example, if an offeror specifically states that an essential term is "to be agreed upon" at a later time, and the term is never agreed upon, the court will not imply a reasonable term. To do so would be contrary to the specific intent of the parties. And as the court has no means of determining what the parties did intend, the offer will fail, and mutual assent will not arise. Thus, if in our example above, the caller specifically tells the plumber that they will "agree upon price at a later time", and they later fail to agree, the offer will fail for lack of definiteness and there will be no contract. (Of course, in any case where the plumber actually does the work at the request of the caller, he or she will be able to recover the value of his or her services under the legal theory of "restitution" or "unjust enrichment" without regard to whether a contract exists. As a legal principle separate and apart from contract law, restitution or unjust enrichment provides that a person may not benefit unjustly or inequitably enrich himself or herself at another's expense. Even a person who mistakenly or foolishly confers a benefit upon another is thus entitled to recover the value of the benefit conferred.)

It should be noted that an offer will fail for lack of definiteness because a term is "to be agreed upon" at a future time only where the term is an essential term. An express statement that a minor term is "to be agreed upon" at a future time will not prevent the formation of mutual assent. The court, in this case, will either fill in a "reasonable" term or not require performance of the term at all.

And either an essential term or a minor term may be left open so long as the parties provide some objective standard by which to fill in the term (e. g., an offer to sell "at a price to be decided by appraisers.")

It is also important to realize that the Uniform Commercial Code has liberalized the requirement of definiteness insofar as contracts for the *sale of goods* are concerned. You will recall from Ch. 2 that "goods" are defined in the UCC at Section 2–105:

The UCC provides:

(1) "Goods" means all things (including specially manufactured goods) which are movable at the time of identification to the contract for sale ["identification" is the point in time in which the goods subject to the contract of sale are picked out or set aside] other than money in which the price is to be paid, investment securities and things in action ["things in action" are rights to recover money or other personal property through a court proceeding].

"Goods" also includes the unborn young of animals and growing crops and other identified things attached to realty as described in the section on goods to be severed from realty (Section 2–107).

———

Section 2–107, as you will also recall from Ch. 2, is the Code provision governing the time of transformation of realty into "goods" by reason of its severance from the land.

The UCC provides:

(1) A contract for the sale of minerals or the like (including oil and gas) or a structure or its minerals to be removed from realty is a contract for the sale of goods if they are to be severed by the seller. * * *

(2) A contract for the sale apart from the land of growing crops or other things attached to realty and capable of severance without material harm thereto but not described in subsection (1) or of timber to be cut is a contract for the sale of goods whether the subject matter is to be severed by the buyer or by the seller even though it forms part of the realty at the time of contracting.

Generally speaking, then, the term "goods" includes all movable things; any minerals or structures to be removed from land by the seller; any growing crops or timber to be removed from real property; and any other item to be removed from land so long as it is capable of severance without material harm to the real property.

Under the Uniform Commercial Code, an offer for the sale of "goods" may give rise to mutual assent upon acceptance by the offeree even though the same offer and acceptance would fail for lack of definiteness in the case of a subject matter other than goods (e. g., contracts for personal services such as those of a plumber or lawyer, or sales of insurance or real estate). Section 2–204 of the UCC provides as follows.

The UCC provides:

(1) A contract for [the] sale of goods may be made in any manner sufficient to show agreement, including conduct by both parties which recognizes the existence of such a contract.

(2) An agreement sufficient to constitute a contract for sale may be found even though the moment of its making is undetermined. [This provision particularly applies to situations where there is an exchange of correspondence indicating that the parties intended a binding obligation but failing to disclose the exact time when the contract came into existence.]

(3) Even though one or more terms are left open a contract for sale does not fail for indefiniteness if the parties have intended to make a contract and there is a reasonably certain basis for giving an appropriate remedy.

The specific Code provisions regarding "indefiniteness" in contracts for the sale of goods are summarized below:

Failure to state the price of goods. Oftentimes, businesspeople leave the price term in a sales contract completely open or merely specify a procedure for determining price at some time in the future. And there may be good business reasons for doing so. The seller, on one hand, may believe that the market price is going to rise and so hope to sell at a higher price. The buyer, on the other hand, may believe that the market price is going to fall and so hope to conclude the purchase at a lower price (for a buyer purchasing inventory over a long period of time, the ability to buy at the lower price as the market price falls is crucial to remaining competitive with other dealers).

In recognition of the fact that "open price terms" are frequently necessary and desirable in business transactions, UCC Section 2–305, "Open Price Terms" provides as follows.

The UCC provides:

(1) The parties if they so intend can conclude a contract for sale even though the price is not settled. In such a case the price is a reasonable price at the time for delivery if

(a) nothing is said as to price; or

(b) the price is left to be agreed by the parties and they fail to agree; or

(c) the price is to be fixed in terms of some agreed market or other standard as set or recorded by a third person or agency and it is not so set or recorded.

(2) A price to be fixed by the seller or by the buyer means a price for him to fix in good faith. [Section 2–103 defines "good faith" on the part of a merchant as "honesty in fact and the observance of reasonable commercial standards of fair dealing in the trade".]

(3) When a price left to be fixed otherwise than by agreement of the parties fails to be fixed through fault of one party the other party may at his option treat the contract as cancelled or himself fix a reasonable price.

(4) Where, however, the parties intend not to be bound unless the price be fixed or agreed and it is not fixed or agreed there is no contract. In such a case the buyer must return any goods already received or if unable to do so must pay their reasonable value at the time of delivery and the seller must return any portion of the price paid on account.

———

Thus, with regard to the sale of goods, the Uniform Commercial Code has rejected the rule that an agreement by the parties to agree upon price at a later time makes the transaction fail for lack of definiteness. To ensure that the parties' *intended* agreement is given effect, the law imposes standards of "reasonableness" and "good faith". As stated at U.C.C. Section 1–203.

Every contract or duty within this Act imposes an obligation of good faith in its performance or enforcement.

———

Failure to specify place of delivery. While most commercial sales (i. e., contracts entered into between businesspeople or merchants) expressly provide for the place and method of delivery of the goods, many private sales (i. e., contracts entered into between private persons) altogether omit any mention of delivery place. Where either a commercial or private sale of goods fails to specify the place of delivery, the transaction will not fail for lack of definiteness because of UCC Section 2–308, "Absence of Specified Place for Delivery".

The UCC provides:

Unless otherwise agreed

(a) the place for delivery of goods is the seller's place of business or if he has none, his residence; but

(b) in a contract for sale of identified goods which to the knowledge of the parties at the time of contracting are in some other place, that place is the place for their delivery.

———

Thus, where the place of delivery is not specified in a sale of goods, the place of delivery is the seller's place of business, or, if the seller has no place of business, the seller's residence, unless the goods are known to be elsewhere at the time of contracting.

Failure to specify the time for shipment or delivery of the goods. If the buyer and seller do not agree either expressly or impliedly on the time for delivery of the goods, UCC Section 2–309 provides that the time for delivery shall be a "reasonable" time. What is "reasonable" depends upon many factors, including the nature of the goods (perishable or nonperishable), the nature of the market, the transportation conditions, the purpose for which the goods will be used, and the extent of the seller's knowledge of this purpose.

Failure to specify time of payment for the goods. Where the time for payment is not specified by the parties, payment is due under UCC Section 2–310 at the time and place where the buyer receives the goods. The UCC provides for payment at the time of receipt of the goods in order to facilitate the buyer's right to inspect the goods prior to payment as provided for in UCC Section 2–513. By deferring the buyer's duty to pay until the time and place of his or her receipt of the goods, the buyer can conveniently exercise his or her right of inspection just prior to payment. (Where the parties provide for payment prior to receipt of the goods, the seller must make the goods available for the buyer's inspection prior to payment, although the seller need not give up possession of the goods until payment is received.)

Failure to exactly state the quantity of goods to be sold. Often, a buyer of goods will contract for a seller's entire "output"; or a seller will agree to supply a buyer with all his or her "requirements". Obviously, such contracts are inexact as to the quantity of goods to be sold, but they may be commercially desirable. A buyer, for example, may want to secure a source of supply that enables him or her to easily meet fluctuating market needs—the convenience of dealing with only one seller is an added benefit. A seller, on the other hand, may find that the assurance of a market for his or her goods makes for better planning and scheduling of business operations and helps save storage and marketing costs, thus making for higher profits. It may therefore be to a buyer's benefit to agree to purchase all of a particular seller's output or production of oil, sugar,

lumber, etc.; and it may be to a seller's benefit to contract to provide all of a particular buyer's needs or requirements for tomatoes, green peppers, onions, or color television sets.

Even apart from the UCC, offers to supply "all your requirements" or to sell "the entire output of the factory" are generally considered sufficiently definite as to quantity or nature of the subject matter and will not fail for lack of definiteness. This is because the terms "output" and "requirements" provide objective standards by which the courts can measure the quantities intended by the parties, particularly where there has been a history of business dealings between the parties, or where one or both of the businesses have been established for a considerable period of time.

The language of the Uniform Commercial Code at Section 2–306, "Output, Requirements and Exclusive Dealings" only strengthens this conclusion.

The UCC provides:

(1) A term which measures the quantity by the output of the seller or the requirements of the buyer means such actual output or requirements as may occur in good faith, except that no quantity unreasonably disproportionate to any stated estimate or in the absence of a stated estimate to any normal or otherwise comparable prior output or requirements may be tendered or demanded.

(2) A lawful agreement by either the seller or the buyer for exclusive dealing in the kind of goods concerned imposes unless otherwise agreed an obligation by the seller to use best efforts to supply the goods and by the buyer to use best efforts to promote their sale.

Under Subsection (1), a transaction for "output" or "requirements" is not too indefinite as it is held to mean the "actual good faith" output or requirements of the party.

Subsection (2) deals with "exclusive dealing" contracts wherein a buyer and seller agree that the buyer will have an exclusive right to sell the goods of the seller in a particular area or under a franchise. For example, Randall Retailer may be offered an exclusive right to sell in Walla Walla, Washington the products produced by the "Crispy Potato Chip & Dip" Company. At first glance, the offer appears too indefinite to create in Randall the right to complete an agreement upon acceptance. How much, for instance, is Randall supposed to sell under the terms of the offer? At what price? By imposing upon the seller an obligation to use his or her "best efforts" to supply the goods, and upon the buyer an obligation to use his or her "best efforts" to sell the goods, Section 2–306 of the UCC provides an objective standard by which these factors can be determined and saves the offer and subsequent acceptance from failure for lack of definiteness.

Where particulars of the agreement are left for future determination by one of the parties. Section 2–311 of the UCC provides that an agreement otherwise sufficiently definite to constitute a contract is not rendered invalid by the fact that it leaves particulars of performance to be specified by one of the parties. However, Section 2–311 also provides that "any such specification must be made in good faith and within limits set by commercial reasonableness". "Commercial reasonableness" is not an obscure concept incapable of precise definition, but rather an objective standard measured by the sound business judgment of reasonable persons familiar with the customary practices in the type of transaction involved.

By way of summary and conclusion, the following four principles regarding the requirement of definiteness should be remembered:

(1) Definiteness is required because it is essential that offers (as well as acceptances) be clearly understandable: a court must be able to determine what the parties intended so as to meet their reasonable expectations with money damages or other remedies.

(2) However, the requirement of definiteness does not demand that every detail of the agreement be spelled out with exact precision. Only "reasonable" definiteness is required, and an offer need not even spell out all the *essential* terms so long as the offer makes reference to some objective standard by which to fill in the missing particulars.

(3) Insofar as the sale of goods is concerned, the Uniform Commercial Code has liberalized the definiteness requirement with provisions designed to "fill in the gaps" where essential terms such as price, quantity, or place of delivery are left open.

(4) The trend in the law is to take the UCC approach with regard to all contracts, and not just contracts for the sale of goods. The courts are thus increasingly willing to read in or imply "reasonable" terms to fill in gaps in a contract so long as it is clear that the parties intended to enter into a binding agreement.

Are there any "keys" or guidelines for determining whether particular language constitutes an offer?

As stated previously, the purpose of contract law is twofold: (1) *not* to hold parties to their promises or agreements in the absence of evidence that the parties intended to be bound; and (2) *to* ensure that parties who do make promises and enter into agreements, desiring to be bound, are met with their reasonable expectations. While there is no one rule that tells us whether the particular words used by a person constitute an offer (indicating an intent to be bound), there are several "key" factors or guidelines that may be helpful in making this determination.

To begin with, the primary test is this: Would a reasonable person in the position of the party hearing or reading the words believe that a contract would result upon his or her acceptance of the proposal? In answering this question, the courts look at four things:

(1) *The words used.* If the words of the proposal include "offer" or "promise", it is likely that an offer was intended. The words "I'm asking", or "first come, first served", or "I bid" are also suggestive of an offer. But the words, "Are you interested?", "Would you pay?", or "I'm thinking of selling" do not indicate an intent on the part of the speaker to become immediately bound.

(2) *How definite the words are.* The more definite the words and terms of the proposal, the more likely the proposal is an offer.

(3) *The circumstances in which the words are used.* Words spoken in a state of great excitement or fear rarely indicate true contractual intent even where words such as "offer" or "promise" are used. For example, a statement that "I promise to pay $50,000 to anyone who puts out the fire in my house" is probably not a valid offer. The same is true of a proposal obviously made in jest, or in anger, or as a political promise (e. g., "I promise to eliminate 10% of the bureaucrats in Washington, D.C. if you vote for me.").

(4) *The person to whom the proposal is made.* A statement made to a specific individual or to a small group of individuals is much more likely to constitute an offer than is a statement made to a large group of people or to the general public. This is not to say, however, that offers are never made to large groups or to the general public (an offer of reward, for example, is typically made to the public at large), but merely that they are more often made to small groups or a single individual.

Must the offeree have knowledge of the offer to accept it?

The general rule is that an offeree must know of the existence of an offer before he or she can accept it. This means that the offer must be in some way communicated to the offeree either directly or indirectly (e. g., through a third party) or the offeree will not have the power to accept the offer.

For example, a person who performs an act called for in a public offer of reward generally cannot claim the reward unless he or she performed the act with knowledge of the offer. However, some courts hold that where the person learns of the reward after beginning performance, but before completing it, he or she may claim the reward by completing the called for act with the intention of accepting the offer. For example, suppose that Jeff Jackson finds a billfold and only later learns of a $50.00 reward for "finding and returning" it. In a number of jurisdictions, Jeff will be permitted to collect the reward merely for returning the billfold to its true owner.

It is also held that identical cross-offers sent through the mail do not create mutual assent (offer and acceptance) because neither party has knowledge of the other's offer at the time of the mailing. Thus, where Jeff Jackson sends an offer by mail to Jill Kelley, offering to sell Jill his vacant lot on 4th Street for $6,000, and Jill, in ignorance of this offer, mails an offer to Jeff, offering to buy Jeff's vacant lot on 4th Street for $6,000, there is no mutual assent—no offer and acceptance—and there can be none until one of the parties accepts the other's offer.

However, insofar as the sale of goods is concerned, the rule on identical cross-offers is subject to UCC Section 2–204 which, as you will recall from the previous section, states that "an agreement sufficient to constitute a contract for sale may be found even though the moment of its making is undetermined." Thus, where parties act upon identical cross-offers for the *sale of goods* as though mutual assent is present and a valid contract exists, the courts will find a binding agreement on the basis of Section 2–204.

Who may accept an offer?

The offeror controls not only the terms of the offer, but who can accept the offer. It is a rule of law that only the person or persons to whom the offer is made (i. e., the offeree or offerees) can accept, and this right to accept is nontransferable and nonassignable. Thus, an offeree cannot transfer his or her right to accept to another. Nor can a third party who learns about the offer substitute himself or herself for the offeree even though the offeror is willing to contract with the third party: any contract that results between the offeror and third party will be based on a new offer by the offeror, or on an offer by the third party, in which case the original offeror will become the offeree-acceptor.

Of course, an offer of reward is made to the general public and can be accepted by anyone who knows of the offer. However, once a party has accepted the offer by doing the requested act or acts, the offer cannot then be accepted by another.

In what three ways may an offer request acceptance?

We have defined an offer as a definite conditional undertaking. It is conditional in that the offeror's proposed undertaking or performance will only take place if the offeree responds in the manner requested by the offeror. The offeror will always request acceptance in one of the following three ways:

(1) *A promise for a promise—i. e., a "bilateral" contract.* Put simply, a *bilat-eral contract* is a promise for a promise: the offeror *promises* to do something or to refrain from doing something in exchange for the offeree's *return promise* to do something or not to do something. The offeree accepts the offer by making the requested promise, at which time mutual assent arises and a contract comes into being creating present rights and duties even though both parties are to perform their promises at some time in the future. For example, suppose that Jeff Jackson makes the following offer to Jill Kelley: "I promise to transfer ownership of my Jack Palmer golf clubs together with my golf bag and cart to you on May 1st (three months from today's date) if you promise to mow my lawn once a week for the next three months." Jill responds: "I accept your offer and promise to mow your lawn once a week for the next three months." Here, Jeff's offer (his promise to transfer ownership) is conditioned upon Jill's return promise to mow Jeff's lawn. By making the requested promise, Jill has accepted the offer, and a bilateral contract comes into existence at the moment of acceptance even though both performances (the transfer of ownership and the mowing of the lawn) are to take place in the future.

An offeree thus accepts in a bilateral contract situation by making the requested promise.

(2) *A promise for an act—i. e., a "unilateral" contract.* A *unilateral contract* is a promise for an act: here, the offeror promises to do something or not to do something in exchange for the offeree's performance of a requested act. The offeree accepts the offer by doing the requested act, at which time mutual assent arises and a contract comes into being creating present rights and duties. Suppose, for example, that Jeff Jackson makes the following offer to Jill Kelley: "I promise to transfer ownership of my Jack Palmer golf clubs together with my golf bag and cart to you on May 1st

(three months from today's date) if you mow my lawn once a week for three months." Jeff's offer, in this case, is not conditioned upon Jill's return promise to mow Jeff's lawn, but upon the actual act of mowing the lawn. Jill can accept the offer only by mowing the lawn for three months—not by promising to do so. Since no promise is demanded of Jill Kelley, she never becomes bound to perform. However, once Jill accepts the offer by performing the act, she becomes entitled to the promised performance of Jeff Jackson.

An offeree thus accepts in a unilateral contract situation by doing the requested act.

(3) *An act for a promise—i. e., a "reverse unilateral" contract.* It should be pointed out that nearly all contracts are bilateral or unilateral as described in (1) and (2) above. Occasionally, however, an offeror will offer to perform an act in return for a requested promise from the offeree to do something or not to do something. Because an "act" for a "promise" is exactly the opposite of a unilateral contract, an "act" for a "promise" is called a *reverse unilateral contract.* A good example of a reverse unilateral contract is the payment of money in advance for a promised future performance (e. g., an offer to pay a mortuary $1,000 on the condition that the mortuary promise to take care of your burial expenses upon your death). In a bilateral contract, both the offeror and the offeree are promisors and promisees; in a unilateral contract, the offeror is the promisor and the offeree is the promisee; in a reverse unilateral contract, the offeror is the recipient or promisee of the promise made by the offeree-promisor.

Returning to our previous example, suppose that Jeff Jackson makes the following offer to Jill Kelley: "If you promise to mow my lawn once a week for the next three months, my Jack Pal-mer golf clubs together with my golf bag and cart are now yours." This time, Jeff's offer to perform the act of transferring ownership of the golf clubs, bag, and cart is conditioned upon Jill's making of the requested promise. If Jill responds, "I accept your offer and promise to mow your lawn once a week for the next three months," her acceptance gives rise to mutual assent, at which point Jill becomes the owner of the golf club, bag, and cart, and falls under a contractual duty to carry out her promise.

As you can see, the offeror in a reverse unilateral contract makes no promise, but, instead, performs an act in exchange for the offeree's making of a requested promise.

An offeree thus accepts in a reverse unilateral situation by making the requested promise.

Is an offer revocable?

It is often said that the offeror holds the power of life and death over an offer. What this means is that the offeror may generally revoke the offer at any time up until acceptance by the offeree by effectively communicating the rejection to the offeree.

An offer is revocable even where the offeror expressly promises not to revoke, or expressly promises to hold the offer open for a definite period of time. This is because promises in themselves are not binding: a binding promise requires all the elements necessary for a contract—mutual assent, consideration, legality, and capacity. An offer, by itself, does not even give rise to mutual assent. Thus, if Jeff Jackson offers to sell his golf clubs, bag, and cart to Jill Kelley for $500, Jeff can revoke the offer at any time prior to Jill's acceptance of the offer. Even if Jeff states, "I promise to sell you my golf clubs for $500, and I further promise that you can have 10 days to think this over, during which time I will not revoke the offer," Jeff can still revoke the offer the following day. The offer in and of itself does not give rise to mutual assent, and, as you will learn in a later chapter, there is no consideration for Jeff's promise not to revoke.

Of course, Jeff and Jill can always enter into a *binding* agreement to keep the offer open for ten days. For example, suppose that Jeff states to Jill, "If you will pay me $10.00, I will promise not to sell my golf clubs to anyone else during the next ten day period, during which time you may purchase the clubs for $500." If Jill accepts by paying Jeff the $10.00, mutual assent arises. There is "consideration" or value given in the payment of the $10.00, and, assuming all other elements of a contract are present, a binding agreement comes into being, and Jeff cannot revoke the offer to sell for the full ten day period. During this ten day period, Jill has an "option" to buy the clubs. And that is what a contract the subject matter of which is to keep an offer open is called—an *option contract.* An option contract is much more than a mere offer: it is a binding agreement, and it can be a very valuable asset. For example, the holder of an option to buy an acre of land for $50,000 anytime during the next six months may be able to sell the option for $60,000 in three months time.

The Uniform Commercial Code, Section 2–205, "Firm Offers", creates an important exception to the general rule that an offer is revocable even though it contains an express promise that it will be kept open for a period of time.

The UCC provides:

An offer by a merchant to buy or sell goods in a signed writing which by its terms gives assurance that it will be held open is not revocable, for lack of consideration, during the time stated or if no time is stated for a reasonable time, but in no event may such period of irrevocability exceed three months; but any such term of assurance on a form supplied by the offeree must be separately signed by the offeror.

————

Thus, a written offer to buy or sell goods made and signed by a merchant, and containing an express promise that the offer will be kept open for a period of time, is a "firm offer" and cannot be revoked by the merchant for the time stated or for three months, whichever is less, or, if no time is stated, for a "reasonable" time, again, not to exceed three months. The effect of the UCC provision is that a merchant who promises in a signed writing that he or she will not revoke an offer to buy or sell goods for a period of time may be "estopped" from revoking the offer for up to three months regardless of whether the offeree has given any consideration (value) for the promise not to revoke. The "signing" required is not a formal signature, but merely some authentication of the writing, such as initialing the clause containing the offer not to revoke.

Of course, if the offeree gives consideration for the promise not to revoke, a binding option contract exists rather than a firm offer, and the offer will be irrevocable for the time agreed upon by the parties without regard to the three month maximum applicable to firm offers.

Apart from option contracts and firm offers, the general rule is that an offer is revocable at anytime up until the moment of acceptance. To be effective, the revocation must be communicated to the offeree prior to acceptance. Usually, the offeror directly notifies the offeree that the offer is being revoked. Any words or conduct by the offeror will serve to revoke the offer so long as a reasonable person in the position of the offeree would understand that the words or conduct constitute a revocation (this, again, goes back to the objective theory of contracts). And sometimes the offeree on his or her own acquires reliable information that the offer has been revoked, or that the offeror has entered into a completely inconsistent contract with another party. Such an indirect "communication" will also serve to effectively revoke the offer. Thus, Jeff Jackson's offer to sell his golf clubs to Jill Kelley is effectively revoked when Jill learns from Jeff's mother that Jeff has sold the clubs to Harvey Seymour.

In the case of a reward offer or other offer made to the general public through newspaper, television, or other advertising media, the law does not demand that revocation of the offer be effectively communicated to each of the potential offerees. Because such an offer is made to a number of persons whose specific identities are unknown to the offeror, it would be impossible for the offeror to determine just who had learned of the offer. To place upon him or her the burden of notifying all potential offerees would be unfair in the extreme. Thus, all that is required to revoke an offer made to the general public is publicity of revocation placed in the same advertising medium as the original offer and equal to the original offer in scope and style.

One final problem regarding revocation of offers revolves around revocation of an offer to enter into a unilateral contract (a promise for an act). The general rule that an offeror has the power of life and death over an offer up until the moment of acceptance by the offeree makes perfect sense insofar as a bilateral (a promise for a promise) or reverse unilateral (an act for a promise) contract is concerned. Acceptance in such situations (by the making of the requested promise) takes but a moment of the offeree's time. Nor is there a problem with regard to an offer to enter into a unilateral contract where the requested act can be performed summarily (for example, payment of $50 in one lump sum). But where acceptance in the unilateral con-

tract situation will take a period of time rather than a moment, it would not be fair to permit the offeror to revoke after the offeree has substantially begun to perform, but before he or she has completed performance and accepted the offer. Accordingly, the courts hold that the offeror cannot revoke once the offeree has "substantially" (though not fully) performed, but must allow the offeree to complete the performance and so accept the offer. Let's return to our previous example where Jeff Jackson promises to transfer ownership of his golf clubs to Jill Kelley if Jill mows Jeff's lawn once a week for the next three months. If Jill mows the lawn for four consecutive weeks, intending to accept the offer, Jeff cannot revoke even though Jill has yet to accept the offer by completing the requested act—Jeff must permit Jill to complete her performance since she has already substantially performed.

What possible responses are there to an offer?

Just as the first communication by a party anticipating ultimate mutual assent may be something other than an offer, so may the first response by an offeree be something other than an acceptance. Generally speaking, an offeree may respond to an offer in any one of the following six ways—by:

(1) Rejection, which terminates the offer;

(2) Acceptance, which results in mutual assent;

(3) Something less than an acceptance, which has no legal effect;

(4) A mere inquiry, which also has no legal effect;

(5) Counteroffer, which, again, terminates the offer, but is itself an offer which can be accepted by the original offeror; or by

(6) Something less than a common law acceptance or counteroffer

which nevertheless constitutes a valid acceptance in some circumstances under the Uniform Commercial Code.

Rejection. A rejection is a definite statement by the offeree that he or she does not intend to accept the offer. A rejection serves to terminate the offeree's power of acceptance; it is effective only when it is communicated to the offeror. Thus, where Jeff Jackson offers to sell Jill Kelley his golf clubs, and Jill responds that she is not interested in buying the clubs, Jill's rejection of Jeff's offer terminates her ability to accept, and she cannot later change her mind and claim that she has "accepted" the offer. But where Jill sends a rejection by mail, and before Jeff receives the rejection, Jill telephones Jeff and orally accepts the offer, the acceptance will be valid and the rejection of no effect. The rejection, to be effective, must be communicated— here, Jill had already accepted the offer at the time of communication of the rejection to the offeror, Jeff.

Of course, where a merchant makes a firm offer as defined in U.C.C. Section 2–205, the offeree's rejection of the offer will not terminate his or her power to accept: the firm offer must be kept open for the time stated, up to a maximum of three months.

And where an offer specifically states that it will be left open for acceptance for a certain period of time without regard to rejection, a rejection by the offeree will not terminate his or her capacity to change his or her mind and accept the offer so long as the offeror has not yet revoked the offer.

Acceptance. To accept an offer is to respond in the manner requested by the offeror. An offeree accepts a bilateral contract by making the requested promise; he or she accepts a unilateral contract by performing the requested act. In either case, the result of a valid acceptance is the creation of mutual assent between offeror and offeree—the first element necessary for a contract.

Under the common law, an acceptance is not valid and effective unless it is unequivocal and unqualified. The acceptance must be exact, positive, and unconditional: a response that changes the terms of the offer in any respect is not an acceptance. (The only exception to this rule arises under Section 2–207 of the UCC as will be explained shortly.)

Something less than an acceptance. Sometimes, an offeree's response to an offer indicates an interest in the offer, but is too equivocal or indefinite to qualify as an acceptance. In one case, for example, an offeree responded to an offer by sending a telegram to the offeror stating that the offer "constituted the low bid" and that the offeror "should come on the morning train". The court, in this case, rightfully concluded that the offeree's response was not an acceptance. Though the response indicated an interest in the offer, it simply said nothing more. So where Jeff Jackson offers to sell his Jack Palmer golf clubs together with his bag and cart for $500 to Jill Kelley, and Jill responds, "I am really interested and will work out the details with you in the next few days," there is a valid offer by Jeff, but no acceptance by Jill. Jill's response contains no promise to buy the golf clubs at the stated price—her response is "something less than an acceptance" and has no legal effect whatsoever. Jill can still accept the offer so long as it remains open, and, of course, Jeff can freely revoke the offer at any time prior to her acceptance.

A mere inquiry. A mere inquiry is not an equivocal or indefinite expression of assent to an offer as is "something less than an acceptance"—rather, it is a question, suggestion, or request anticipating a change from the original terms of the offer. However, like "something less than an acceptance", a mere inquiry is not an acceptance and does not give rise to mutual assent; nor does it constitute a rejection of the offer so as to terminate the offeree's power to accept. A mere inquiry simply has no legal effect whatsoever. For example, an offeree often responds to an offer by inquiring whether or not the offeror will perform or sell on terms other than those contained in the offer. Responses such as, "Will you take less?", "Would you be able to deliver immediately rather than next week?", or "Would there be any change in price if I ordered a dozen instead of one?" are all mere inquiry responses. Because a mere inquiry has no legal effect, the offeree is still free after making such an inquiry to accept the original offer so long as he or she does so before the offeror revokes.

Both the mere inquiry and "something less than an acceptance" must be distinguished from what is known as a "grumbling acceptance". A grumbling acceptance is a valid acceptance containing a "grumble" or "simultaneous request". For example, the offeree might respond to an offer by stating,, "I accept your offer, but I sure don't like its terms," or "I accept your offer, but you sure have made a hard bargain," or "I accept your offer, but I wish you would give me a better price," or "I accept your offer, but, if possible, would you ship the goods tomorrow instead of waiting for the 10 days called for in your offer." Though the responses contain a "grumble" or "simultaneous request", all are good acceptances that, unlike the mere inquiry or something less than an acceptance, will give rise to mutual assent.

Thus, if in our golf club example, Jeff Jackson offers to sell the clubs for $500, and Jill Kelley responds, "Would you take $450?", Jill's response is a mere inquiry and has no legal effect. But if Jill responds, "I accept the offer and will pay you $500, but I sure wish you would

have sold the clubs for $450," Jill's response is a good acceptance, although "grumbling", and will give rise to mutual assent between Jeff and Jill.

Counteroffer. If, in response to an offer, an offeree proposes his or her own definite conditional undertaking containing terms different from or at variance with those of the original offer, the offeree has made a "counteroffer". The counteroffer serves to terminate the original offer and reverses the roles of the parties by creating in the original offeror the power to accept the counteroffer and so complete a binding agreement.

For example, if Jeff Jackson offers to sell his golf clubs to Jill Kelley for $500, and Jill responds, "I will give you $350 for the clubs," Jill has made a counteroffer (i. e., a definite conditional undertaking), and it is up to Jeff to decide whether or not to accept the offer. Jill's counteroffer has terminated Jeff's original offer, and Jill can no longer complete an agreement by agreeing to pay $500 for the clubs.

Because a counteroffer is itself an offer, it is easily distinguishable from a mere inquiry and "something less than an acceptance" which have no legal effect whatsoever. A mere inquiry is not an offer but a mere suggestion or request for different terms; and "something less than an acceptance" may indicate the offeree's interest in the original offer, but it offers nothing new. As you continue your study, it is important to keep in mind the distinctions among these three responses to an offer.

Something less than a common law acceptance or counteroffer under the UCC The general rule that an acceptance must be unequivocal, unconditional, and exact or it will constitute something less than an acceptance or a counteroffer is qualified insofar as the sale of goods is concerned by UCC Section 2–207, "Additional Terms in Acceptance or Confirmation".

The UCC provides:

(1) A definite and seasonable expression of acceptance or a written confirmation which is sent within a reasonable time operates as an acceptance even though it states terms additional to or different from those offered or agreed upon, unless acceptance is expressly made conditional on assent to the additional or different terms.

(2) The additional terms are to be construed as proposals for addition to the contract. Between merchants such terms become part of the contract unless:

(a) the offer expressly limits acceptance to the terms of the offer;

(b) they materially alter it; or

(c) notification of objection to them has already been given or is given within a reasonable time after notice of them is received.

(3) Conduct by both parties which recognizes the existence of a contract is sufficient to establish a contract for sale although the writings of the parties do not otherwise establish a contract. In such case the terms of the particular contract consist of those terms on which the writings of the parties agree, together with any supplementary terms incorporated under any other provisions of this Act.

Section 2–207 of the Code was primarily enacted to put an end to the "battle of the forms" between merchant buyers and sellers. The "battle of the forms" refers to the confusion that resulted prior to the Code provision from each party's use of his or her own sales and purchase forms.

For example, a buyer and seller will frequently engage in preliminary negotiation over the telephone. One party will then send a form prepared by his or her attorney to the other party; and the other party will respond by returning his or her own form, carefully drafted to his or her own advantage. Generally, the forms will agree in some respects (e. g., as to price, quality, quantity, and delivery), but differ in others.

Following the common law rules expressed in the preceding pages, the forms taken together will produce something less than an offer and an acceptance— perhaps a counteroffer, something less than an acceptance, a mere inquiry, or a mish-mash of all of these. Generally, the parties will go ahead and perform the agreement and so there will be no problem. But where the deal breaks down, and the parties decide to stress the differences in their forms (each party looking for some means of release from his or her contractual obligations or some way of holding the other party to an agreement that he or she did not intend), the common law rules will be hard pressed for an answer.

To solve this problem with regard to the sale of goods, Section 2–207 of the Code provides that the offeree's injection of different terms will not necessarily constitute a rejection of the original offer nor a counteroffer that serves to terminate the original offer. Unless the original offer expressly limits acceptance to its terms, the additions to the offer will not prevent acceptance by the offeree but will be treated merely as proposals for addition to the contract. And where the transaction is between merchants, the new terms will automatically become part of the contract unless the new terms materially alter the contract or unless the offeror objects to the terms within a reasonable period of time.

For example, suppose that Millicent Manufacturer offers (on her form) "to sell 1,000 pairs of shoes at $10.00 per pair to be ready in 90 days", and Rudy Retailer responds (on his form) by agreeing to buy on Millicent's terms, but adds that the shoes "must be delivered to Martin's store and that a 2% discount is to be allowed if fully paid within 100 days". Millicent does not object to the new terms. Under the common law, Rudy's response does not give rise to mutual assent, but is a counteroffer. However, under the UCC, mutual assent does arise and the additional terms proposed by Rudy automatically become a part of the contract: both parties are merchants, the terms do not materially change Millicent's obligations, and Millicent does not appear to object.

If, in the example above, one or both of the parties are nonmerchants, the additional terms will not prevent acceptance by the offeree; however, the terms will be treated merely as proposals to the contract and will not become a part of the agreement unless the original offeror assents.

Remember, UCC Section 2–207 applies only to the sale of goods—the common law rules apply to all other transactions.

How are offers terminated apart from revocation, rejection, or counteroffer?

You will recall that, with the exception of firm offers and option contracts, an offeror may revoke an offer at any time by effectively communicating the revocation to the offeree. An offeree may also terminate an offer simply by communicating a rejection of the offer to the offeror, or by responding with a counteroffer. Termination of an offer by revocation, rejection, or counteroffer is said to be termination *by act of the parties.*

Termination of an offer may also occur *by operation of law* in the following situations:

(1) *Death or destruction of the subject matter.* An offer ceases to exist by operation of law if a person or thing essential to performance of the contemplated agreement either dies or is destroyed. So if Jeff Jackson offers to sell his Jack Palmer golf clubs for $500 to Jill Kelley, and, before Jill can accept, the golf clubs are destroyed in a fire at Jeff's home, the offer will automatically terminate, and Jill will no longer have any power to accept.

(2) *Death or insanity of the offeror or offeree.* An offer is personal to the offeror and offeree. It follows that if either party dies or becomes insane after the offer is made, but before acceptance, the offer will terminate by operation of law. Thus, if either Jeff Jackson or Jill Kelley dies or becomes insane after Jeff offers to sell his clubs, but before Jill accepts the offer, the offer will automatically terminate by operation of law.

Insanity occurring subsequent to the making of an offer must be distinguished from insanity existing at the time the offer is made. In the latter case, either the offeror or offeree will lack "capacity" to contract ("capacity" being the third element necessary for a contract), and a valid offer and acceptance cannot be made.

Death or insanity occurring subsequent to the making of an offer, but prior to acceptance, must also be distinguished from death or insanity occurring after the offer has been accepted. Assuming that all other elements necessary for a contract are present, the death or insanity will not affect the contract rights and obligations that have already come into being.

(3) *Supervening illegality of the proposed contract.* If the proposal contained in an offer becomes illegal after the offer is made, but prior to acceptance, the offer will terminate by operation of law. For example, where Jeff Jackson offers to sell his collection of handguns for $1,000 to Jill Kelley, and before Jill accepts, a law is passed making it illegal to sell handguns, Jeff's offer to Jill im-

mediately terminates. It should be pointed out that where the law is passed only after Jill accepts Jeff's offer, the subsequent illegality will discharge performance of the parties' remaining contract obligations. (Discharge of contract obligations is discussed in Ch. 10.)

(4) *Lapse of time.* An offer terminates by operation of law upon the expiration of the time stated in the offer, and where no time is specified, at the end of a "reasonable" period of time. What is "reasonable" depends upon such factors as the nature of the subject matter involved, market fluctuations, and local usage and custom. Thus, if Jeff Jackson offers to sell his Jack Palmer golf clubs for $500, the offer to remain open for ten days, the offer will terminate by operation of law at the end of ten days, assuming that Jeff has not earlier revoked the offer. If Jeff fails to specify a time in the offer, the offer will terminate at the end of a reasonable time.

Generally, where an offer states that it will remain open for a certain period of time, such as ten days or 30 days, the time period will begin to run, not from the date the offer was made or dispatched, but from the date it was received by the offeree assuming there has been no delay in receipt. In the case of a delay, the time period will begin to run from the date the offer would have reached the offeree but for the delay.

Can an offer ever be accepted by silence?

Under certain circumstances, silence alone can be the basis for mutual assent. The law of "acceptance by silence" is summarized below.

(1) Generally speaking, silence on the part of the offeree indicates only that the offeree prefers not to waste any of his or her time giving thought to the offeror's proposal. Nothing in the law requires the offeree to consider the offer, and silence by itself without the presence of other factors such as acceptance by silence in previous dealings between the parties, will never constitute acceptance of an offer. Thus, in the vast majority of cases, an offer followed by silence on the part of the offeree does not give rise to mutual assent.

(2) The offeror cannot by the terms of his or her offer force the offeree to either respond to the offer or "accept" by silence. For example, if Jeff Jackson offers to sell his golf clubs to Jill Kelley and states in the offer, "If you don't call me by Friday, you have accepted," or "If you don't mail me a rejection, you have accepted," Jill's silence after receiving the offer is not an acceptance unless she intends her silence to so operate. It is the same as stating, "You accept if you wash your car on Saturday," or "if you go to church on Sunday." An offeror simply cannot "create" an acceptance out of the offeree's silence any more than the offeror can "create" an acceptance out of the performance of some ordinary act that the offeree would be likely to perform regardless of the offer.

(3) The offeror may bind *himself or herself* to accepting the offeree's silence as acceptance by so providing in the offer. For example, where an offer states, "If you want to accept this offer, you can do so by remaining silent," and the offeree remains silent *with intent to accept* the offer, the silence will constitute an acceptance, and both offeror and offeree will be bound to the agreement.

(4) Silence will operate as an acceptance regardless of the offeree's intent where the offeree *unreasonably* fails to speak up and reject the offer. Thus, acceptance will be "deemed" or "implied" where an offeree who has a chance to reject remains silent while an offeror confers upon him or her goods, services, or other benefit under such circumstances that a reasonable person in the offeree's position would understand that the goods or services are being offered with the ex-

pectation of payment. Acceptance is deemed or implied in fact to protect the offering party's reasonable expectations and to prevent unjust enrichment of the offeree.

(5) Silence may also constitute an acceptance in cases where the offeree solicits the offer. The best example is where a company sends out a traveling salesperson to solicit orders, but rather than give the salesperson the power to enter into contracts, the company provides expressly in its forms that "all orders are subject to acceptance by the home office." Because it is only reasonable that the soliciting company notify the party whose order is solicited (i. e., the offeror) within a reasonable period of time if the order cannot be accepted, the law imposes an affirmative duty upon the company to reject the order (the offer) if that is the company's intent. Silent retention of the order for an unreasonable period of time will constitute an acceptance.

The same is true where goods are sent on approval at the request of the recipient-offeree (e. g., where Jill Kelley orders an exercise machine which may be returned to the manufacturer if Jill is not satisfied with the machine after using it for a ten day trial period). If the recipient (the offeree whose approval constitutes acceptance of the goods) retains the goods for an unreasonable amount of time, the retention will be held to constitute an implied acceptance.

(6) In several states, statutes have been passed to protect consumers who do not respond to the receipt of unsolicited merchandise from incurring a contract obligation to pay for the merchandise on a deemed or implied acceptance basis. Such statutes generally provide that where unsolicited merchandise is received as part of a sales offer, the merchandise is considered an unconditional gift that the recipient can use or dispose of as he or she sees fit without incurring obligation of any kind to the offeror-sender.

What is the effective moment of an acceptance (i.e., what is the "deposited acceptance" rule)?

As you know, most communications between an offeror and offeree are legally effective only when they are received by (i. e., communicated to) the recipient party. Thus, an offer is not effective until the offeree has actual knowledge of it; nor is a revocation effective to revoke an offer until the offeree knows of its existence. If the offeree makes a counteroffer, it, too, takes effect only upon its communication to the offeror; and if the offeree rejects the original offer, the rejection will serve to terminate the offer only when the offeror has actual knowledge of it.

The general principle that a communication between offeror and offeree must be received in order to be legally effective has but one exception—the so-called "deposited acceptance" rule. The rule states that, unless the offeror expressly provides to the contrary in his or her offer, the offeree's acceptance of the offer is effective when properly dispatched. Thus, unlike an offer, revocation, counteroffer, and rejection which are effective only when received, an acceptance is effective when sent. At the moment of proper dispatch, the acceptance gives rise to mutual assent between the offeror and offeree even though the offeror has no actual knowledge of the acceptance and will have none until it is received. The reasoning behind the rule is that when the mails or other means of communication are used, one of the parties—either the offeror or offeree—will have no knowledge of the effective time of acceptance. If the acceptance is effective when sent (as the deposited acceptance rule provides), the offeror will not know when mutual assent arises; if the acceptance is effective only when received, the offeree will not know when mutual assent occurs. As between the offeror and offeree, it is the offeror who invites acceptance, and so it is only fair that the offeror should bear the burden of "not knowing" unless he or she expressly provides to the contrary. Also, making acceptance effective at the time of dispatch closes the transaction more quickly and makes for prompt performance of the contract.

The deposited acceptance rule is limited in that the offeror may expressly provide in his or her offer that acceptance will be effective only when received. It is the offeror's offer that creates the power of acceptance, and the offeror is free to limit that power in any manner that he or she desires. (It follows that the offeror is also free to specify the mode of acceptance—e. g., by telephone only, exclusively by telegraph, or by letter alone).

The deposited acceptance rule is also limited in that it requires "proper" dispatch of the acceptance. What is "proper" depends upon what the offeror has authorized. To begin with, if the offeror has expressly specified a "mode of acceptance" in the offer, the express instructions will be controlling. If there are no express instructions, the offeror is said to impliedly authorize the means of communication used in transmitting the offer, and any other means reasonable and customary at the time and place of the transaction (this usually means any other method just as fast and efficient as the means of transmission of the offer). Thus, where parties a considerable distance apart are negotiating by mail, and one party makes an offer by mail, the offeree has the power to accept by mailing a letter of acceptance, properly stamped and addressed, within a reasonable period of time following the offer. If all other elements of a contract are present (consideration, capacity, and legality), the contract will come into being at the time and place of mailing (assuming the offeror has not expressly provided that acceptance is effective only upon receipt).

Similarly, where the offeror telegraphs the offer, the offeree may accept and so

give rise to mutual assent merely by properly directing a telegram of acceptance to the offeror—again, the acceptance is effective upon dispatch of the telegram. A letter of acceptance, on the other hand, would not be a "reasonable" mode of response (a letter is not as fast or efficient as a telegram), and the letter would be effective only upon receipt. (A telegram in response to a letter would obviously be reasonable.)

With regard to the sale of goods, the Uniform Commercial Code continues to recognize the offeror's common law right to specify the mode of acceptance and the effective time of acceptance. Where the offeror does not so specify, the Code at Section 2–206(1)(a) states that an offer may be accepted "in any manner and by any medium reasonable in the circumstances." It is important to note that the Code at Section 1–201(38) modifies the deposited acceptance rule insofar as the sale of goods is concerned. The Section provides that where the offeree uses an improper medium of communication, or where he or she uses a proper means but fails to properly stamp, address, or otherwise direct the acceptance, the effective moment of acceptance will still be the time of dispatch so long as the acceptance is received within the time a properly dispatched acceptance would normally arrive.

The UCC provides:

(38) "Send," in connection with any writing or notice means to deposit in the mail or deliver for transmission by any other usual means of communication with postage or cost of transmission provided for and properly addressed and in the case of an instrument to an address specified thereon or otherwise agreed, or if there be none to any address reasonable under the circumstances. *The receipt of any*

writing or notice within the time at which it would have arrived if properly sent has the effect of a proper sending. (Emphasis supplied.)

One important exception to the deposited acceptance rule arises where an offeree sends both an acceptance and a rejection to the offeror. If the offeree sends the rejection first, the acceptance will be effective only when it is communicated to the offeror. Thus, if the rejection arrives first, the rejection will destroy the original offer, and the acceptance, once received, will operate only as a counteroffer. If, on the other hand, the acceptance arrives first, mutual assent will arise and it will make no difference that the rejection is received a short time thereafter.

However, where the offeree sends the acceptance first, and then the rejection, the acceptance will be effective upon dispatch, and the rejection will be of no effect unless it arrives before the acceptance and the offeree, relying upon it changes his or her position (e. g., by selling the goods to someone else). The offeror, in the latter case, has no way of knowing that mutual assent has already occurred as a result of dispatch of the acceptance. The law will therefore protect the offeror and estop the offeree from asserting the existence of a contract.

What are the rules of mutual assent as to auctions?

The unique rules governing the creation of mutual assent at a public auction are summarized below:

(1) The announcement of advertisement of the auction is not itself an offer. Rather, it is an invitation to the public to come to the auction and make offers through the bidding process. Similarly, when the auctioneer puts the goods up for sale (often called putting the goods "on the block"), he or she is not making an offer to sell the goods, but rather, is inviting the public to make offers to purchase them.

(2) A "bid" on the goods by a member of the public constitutes an offer.

(3) The auctioneer makes an acceptance by dropping the hammer on a particular bid.

(4) Unless the auction is explicitly advertised to be "without reserve", or unless the goods are explicitly put up for sale "without reserve", the auction is presumed to be "with reserve", meaning that the seller is free to reject any and all bids or withdraw the goods from sale at any time prior to acceptance by the auctioneer.

(5) Because a seller who advertises that an auction is to be "without reserve" represents to the public that the goods will be sold to the highest bidder, the seller is estopped from withdrawing the goods from sale once the bidding has begun. A bidder, on the other hand, makes no promise of any kind, and is free to revoke his or her bid at any time up until the moment the hammer falls whether the auction is "with reserve" or "without reserve".

(6) The seller may not personally bid on the goods unless he or she gives public notice of intent to do so prior to or at the time of the auction. This rule is designed to prevent the seller from fraudulently driving up the bid price by secretly bidding against "good faith" bidders. If the seller bids on the goods without giving notice, the sale is fraudulent, and the buyer may either disaffirm the sale or take the goods at the last good faith bid prior to acceptance by the auctioneer.

The above rules are set forth in the Uniform Commercial Code at Section 2–328, "Sale by Auction".

The UCC provides:

(1) In a sale by auction if goods are put up in lots each lot is the subject of a separate sale.

(2) A sale by auction is complete when the auctioneer so announces by the fall of the hammer or in other customary manner. Where a bid is made while the hammer is falling in acceptance of a prior bid the auctioneer may in his discretion reopen the bidding or declare the goods sold under the bid on which the hammer was falling.

(3) Such a sale is with reserve unless the goods are in explicit terms put up without reserve. In an auction with reserve the auctioneer may withdraw the goods at any time until he announces completion of the sale. In an auction without reserve, after the auctioneer calls for bids on an article or lot, that article or lot cannot be withdrawn unless no bid is made within a reasonable time. In either case a bidder may retract this bid until the auctioneer's announcement of completion of the sale, but a bidder's retraction does not revive any previous bid.

(4) If the auctioneer knowingly receives a bid on the seller's behalf or the seller makes or procures such a bid, and notice has not been given that liberty for such bidding is reserved, the buyer may at his option avoid the sale or take the goods at the price of the last good faith bid prior to the completion of the sale. This subsection shall not apply to any bid at a forced sale.

You will note that Subsection (2) provides that if a new bid is made just as the auctioneer is dropping the hammer on another bid, the auctioneer has the option of either closing the sale on the first bid or reopening the bidding. If the auctioneer chooses to reopen the bidding, the bid on which the hammer was falling will be discharged, although the bidder will be free to enter a new bid. The effect of Subsection (2) is to carve out an exception to the general rule that the dropping of the hammer constitutes an acceptance.

Also, Subsection (3) makes clear that, even though an auction "with reserve" is the usual and normal procedure, the point in time that determines whether an auction is "with" or "without reserve" is when the goods are "put up" for sale. To "put up" goods is to describe them to the people present at the auction and to open up bidding on the goods. Until the goods have been "put up" for sale, the goods may be withdrawn from the auction and never presented for sale regardless of whether the auction has been advertised as "with" or "without reserve". Of course, if the seller's "without reserve" advertisement constitutes a firm offer within the meaning of UCC 2–205 (firm offers were discussed in a prior section on revocation of offers), the seller will not be able to withdraw the goods during the time stated in the offer, and, if no time is stated, for a reasonable time.

Finally, it should be noted that Subsection (4), which requires a seller to give public notice of his or her intent to bid at an auction sale, does not apply to "forced" sales. A "forced" sale is a sale of property required by law to satisfy a debt or other obligation (e. g., taxes owing) of the seller. For example, where a property owner fails to pay a judgment rendered against him or her for breach of contract or negligence arising out of an automobile accident, the plaintiff may institute legal procedures resulting in the "forced" sale of the defendant's property.

CASES

CASE 1.—*"High as a Georgia pine"* * * * *mutual assent or "just a bunch of two doggoned drunks bluffing to see who could talk the biggest and say the most"*?

LUCY v. ZEHMER

Supreme Court of Appeals of Virginia, 1954.
196 Va. 493, 84 S.E.2d 516.

BUCHANAN, Justice.

This suit was instituted by W. O. Lucy and J. C. Lucy, complainants, against A. H. Zehmer and Ida S. Zehmer, his wife, defendants, to have specific performance of a contract by which it was alleged the Zehmers had sold to W. O. Lucy a tract of land owned by A. H. Zehmer in Dinwiddie county containing 471.6 acres, more or less, known as the Ferguson farm, for $50,000. * * *

The instrument sought to be enforced was written by A. H. Zehmer on December 20, 1952, in these words: "We hereby agree to sell to W. O. Lucy the Ferguson Farm complete for $50,000.00, title satisfactory to buyer," and signed by the defendants, A. H. Zehmer and Ida S. Zehmer.

The answer of A. H. Zehmer admitted that at the time mentioned W. O. Lucy offered him $50,000 cash for the farm, but that he, Zehmer, considered that the offer was made in jest; that so thinking, and both he and Lucy having had several drinks, he wrote out "the memorandum" quoted above and induced his wife to sign it; that he did not deliver the memorandum to Lucy, but that Lucy picked it up, read it, put it in his pocket, attempted to offer Zehmer $5 to bind the bargain, which Zehmer refused to accept, and realizing for the first time that Lucy was serious, Zehmer assured him that he had no intention of selling the farm and that the whole matter was a joke. Lucy left the premises insisting that he had purchased the farm.

[Judgment was for defendants]

* * *

W. O. Lucy, a lumberman and farmer, thus testified in substance: He had known Zehmer for fifteen or twenty years and had been familiar with the Ferguson farm for ten years. Seven or eight years ago he had offered Zehmer $20,000 for the farm which Zehmer had accepted, but the agreement was verbal and Zehmer backed out. On the night of December 20, 1952, around eight o'clock, he took an employee to McKenney, where Zehmer lived and operated a restaurant, filling station and motor court. While there he decided to see Zehmer and again try to buy the Ferguson farm. He entered the restaurant and talked to Mrs. Zehmer until Zehmer came in. He asked Zehmer if he had sold the Ferguson farm. Zehmer replied that he had not. Lucy said, "I bet you wouldn't take $50,000.00 for that place." Zehmer replied, "Yes, I would too; you wouldn't give fifty." Lucy said he would and told Zehmer to write up an agreement to that effect. Zehmer took a restaurant check and wrote on the back of it, "I do hereby agree to sell to W. O. Lucy the Ferguson Farm for $50,000 complete." Lucy told him he had better change it to "We" because Mrs. Zehmer would have to sign it too. Zehmer then tore up what he had written, wrote the agreement quoted above and asked Mrs. Zehmer, who was at the other end of the counter ten or twelve feet away, to sign it. Mrs. Zehmer said she would for $50,000 and signed it. Zehmer brought it back and gave it to Lucy, who offered him $5 which Zehmer refused, saying, "You don't need to give me any money, you got the agreement there signed by both of us."

The discussion leading to the signing of the agreement, said Lucy, lasted thirty or forty minutes, during which Zehmer seemed to doubt that Lucy could raise $50,000. Lucy suggested the provision for having the title examined and Zehmer made the suggestion that he would sell it "complete, everything there," and stated that all he had on the farm was three heifers.

Lucy took a partly filled bottle of whiskey into the restaurant with him for the purpose of giving Zehmer a drink if he wanted it. Zehmer did, and he and Lucy had one or two drinks together. Lucy said that while he felt the drinks he took he was not intoxicated, and from the way Zehmer handled the transaction he did not think he was either.

December 20 was on Saturday. Next day Lucy telephoned to J. C. Lucy and arranged with the latter to take a half interest in the purchase and pay half of the consideration. On Monday he engaged an attorney to examine the title. The attorney reported favorably on December 31 and on January 2 Lucy wrote Zehmer stating that the title was satisfactory, that he was ready to pay the purchase price in cash and asking when Zehmer would be ready to close the deal. Zehmer replied by letter, mailed on January 13, asserting that he had never agreed or intended to sell.

Mr. and Mrs. Zehmer were called by the complainants as adverse witnesses. Zehmer testified in substance as follows:

He bought this farm more than ten years ago for $11,000. He had had twenty-five offers, more or less, to buy it, including several from Lucy, who had never offered any specific sum of money. He had given them all the same answer, that he was not interested in selling it. On this Saturday night before Christmas it looked like everybody and his brother came by there to have a drink. He took a good many drinks during the afternoon and had a pint of his own. When he entered the restaurant around eight-thirty Lucy was there and he could see that he was "pretty high." He said to Lucy, "Boy, you got some good liquor, drinking, ain't you?" Lucy then offered him a drink. "I was already high as a Georgia pine, and didn't have any more better sense than to pour another great big slug out and gulp it down, and he took one too."

After they had talked a while Lucy asked whether he still had the Ferguson farm. He replied that he had not sold it and Lucy said, "I bet you wouldn't take $50,000.00 for it." Zehmer asked him if he would give $50,000 and Lucy said yes. Zehmer replied, "You haven't got $50,000.00 in cash." Lucy said he did and Zehmer replied that he did not believe it. They argued "pro and con for a long time," mainly about "whether he had $50,000 in cash that he could put up right then and buy that farm."

Finally, said Zehmer, Lucy told him if he didn't believe he had $50,000, "you sign that piece of paper here and say you will take $50,000.00 for the farm." He, Zehmer, "just grabbed the back off of a guest check there" and wrote on the back of it. At that point in his testimony Zehmer asked to see what he had written to "see if I recognize my own handwriting." He examined the paper and exclaimed, "Great balls of fire, I got 'Firgerson' for Ferguson. I have got satisfactory spelled wrong. I don't recognize that writing if I would see it, wouldn't know it was mine."

After Zehmer had, as he described it, "scribbled this thing off," Lucy said, "Get your wife to sign it." Zehmer walked over to where she was and she at first refused to sign but did so after he told her that he "was just needling him [Lucy], and didn't mean a thing in the world, that I was not selling the farm." Zehmer then "took it back over there * * * and I was still looking at the dern thing. I had the drink right there by my hand, and I reached over to get a drink, and he said, 'Let me see it.' He reached and picked it up, and when I looked back again he had it in his pocket and he dropped a five dollar bill over there, and he said, 'Here is five dollars payment on it.' * * * I said, 'Hell no, that is beer and liquor talking. I am not going to sell you the farm. I have told you that too many times before.' "

Mrs. Zehmer testified that when Lucy came into the restaurant he looked as if he had had a drink. When Zehmer came in he took a drink out of a bottle that Lucy handed him. She went back to help the waitress who was getting things ready for next day. Lucy and Zehmer were talking but she did not pay too much attention to what they were saying. She heard Lucy ask Zehmer if he had sold the Ferguson farm, and Zehmer replied that he had not and did not want to sell it. Lucy said, "I bet you wouldn't take $50,000.00 cash for that farm," and Zehmer replied, "You haven't got $50,000 cash." Lucy said, "I can get it." Zehmer said he might form a company and get it, "but you haven't got $50,000.00 cash to pay me to-night." Lucy asked him if he would put it in writing that he would sell him this farm. Zehmer then wrote on the back of a pad, "I agree to sell the Ferguson Place to W. O. Lucy for $50,000.00 cash." Lucy said, "All right, get your wife to sign it." Zehmer came back to where she was standing and said, "You want to put your name to this?" She said "No," but he said in an undertone, "It is nothing but a joke," and she signed it.

She said that only one paper was written and it said: "I hereby agree to sell," but the "I" had been changed to "We". However, she said she read what she signed and was then asked, "When you read 'We hereby agree to sell to W. O. Lucy,' what did you interpret that to mean, that particular phrase?" She said she thought that was a cash sale that night; but she also said that when she read that part about "title satisfactory to buyer" she understood that if the title was good Lucy would pay $50,000 but if the title was bad he would have a right to reject it, and that that was her understanding at the time she signed her name.

     *   *   *

The defendants insist that the evidence was ample to support their contention that the writing sought to be enforced was prepared as a bluff or dare to force Lucy to admit that he did not have $50,000; that the whole matter was a joke; that the writing was not delivered to Lucy and no binding contract was ever made between the parties.

It is an unusual, if not bizarre, defense. When made to the writing admittedly prepared by one of the defendants and signed by both, clear evidence is required to sustain it.

In his testimony Zehmer claimed that he "was high as a Georgia pine," and that the transaction "was just a bunch of two doggoned drunks bluffing to see who could talk the biggest and say the most." That claim is inconsistent with his attempt to testify in great detail as to what was said and what was done. * * * The record is convincing that Zehmer was not intoxicated to the extent of being unable to comprehend the nature and consequences of the instrument he executed, and hence that instrument is not to be invalidated on that ground. It was in fact conceded by defendants' counsel in oral argument that under the evidence Zehmer was not too drunk to make a valid contract.

* * *

The appearance of the contract, the fact that it was under discussion for forty minutes or more before it was signed; Lucy's objection to the first draft because it was written in the singular, and he wanted Mrs. Zehmer to sign it also; the rewriting to meet that objection and the signing by Mrs. Zehmer; the discussion of what was to be included in the sale, the provision for the examination of the title, the completeness of the instrument that was executed, the taking possession of it by Lucy with no request or suggestion by either of the defendants that he give it back, are facts which furnish persuasive evidence that the execution of the contract was a serious business transaction rather than a casual, jesting matter as defendants now contend.

* * *

If it be assumed, contrary to what we think the evidence shows, that Zehmer was jesting about selling his farm to Lucy and that the transaction was intended by him to be a joke, nevertheless the evidence shows that Lucy did not so understand it but considered it to be a serious business transaction and the contract to be binding on the Zehmers as well as on himself. The very next day he arranged with his brother to put up half the money and take a half interest in the land. The day after that he employed an attorney to examine the title. The next night, Tuesday, he was back at Zehmer's place and there Zehmer told him for the first time, Lucy said, that he wasn't going to sell and he told Zehmer, "You know you sold that place fair and square." After receiving the report from his attorney that the title was good he wrote to Zehmer that he was ready to close the deal.

Not only did Lucy actually believe, but the evidence shows he was warranted in believing, that the contract represented a serious business transaction and a good faith sale and purchase of the farm.

In the field of contracts, as generally elsewhere, "We must look to the outward expression of a person as manifesting his intention rather than to his secret and unexpressed intention. 'The law imputes to a person an intention corresponding to the reasonable meaning of his words and acts.'"

At no time prior to the execution of the contract had Zehmer indicated to Lucy by word or act that he was not in earnest about selling the farm. They had argued about it and discussed its terms, as Zehmer admitted, for a long time. Lucy testified that if there was any jesting it was about paying $50,000 that night. The contract and the evidence show that he was not expected to pay the money that night. Zehmer said that after the writing was signed he laid it down on the counter in front of Lucy. Lucy said Zehmer handed it to him. In any event there had been what appeared to be a good faith offer and a good faith acceptance, followed by the execution and apparent delivery of a written contract. Both said that Lucy put the writing in his pocket and then offered Zehmer $5 to seal the bargain. Not until then, even under the defendants' evidence, was anything said or done to indicate that the matter was a joke. Both of the Zehmers testified that when Zehmer asked his wife to sign he whispered that it was a joke so Lucy wouldn't hear and that it was not intended that he should hear.

The mental assent of the parties is not requisite for the formation of a contract. If the words or other acts of one of the parties have but one reasonable meaning, his undisclosed intention is immaterial except when an unreasonable meaning which he attaches to his manifestations is known to the other party. Restatement of the Law of Contracts, Vol. I, § 71, p. 74.

> " * * * The law, therefore, judges of an agreement between two persons exclusively from those expressions of their intentions which are communicated between them. * * *."

An agreement or mutual assent is of course essential to a valid contract but the law imputes to a person an intention corresponding to the reasonable meaning of his words and acts. If his words and acts, judged by a reasonable standard, manifest an intention to agree, it is immaterial what may be the real but unexpressed state of his mind.

So a person cannot set up that he was merely jesting when his conduct and words would warrant a reasonable person in believing that he intended a real agreement.

Whether the writing signed by the defendants and now sought to be enforced by the complainants was the result of a serious offer by Lucy and a serious acceptance by the defendants, or was a serious offer by Lucy and an acceptance in secret jest by the defendants, in either event it constituted a binding contract of sale between the parties.

    * * *

Reversed and remanded.

CASE 2—*Should the existence of an agreement "depend upon the conflicting fine print of commercial forms which cross one another but never meet?" This was "a genuine battle of the forms."*

GAYNOR–STAFFORD INDUSTRIES, INC. v. MAFCO TEXTURED FIBERS

Supreme Court, Appellate Division, First Department, 1976.
52 A.D.2d 481, 384 N.Y.S.2d 788.

BIRNS, Justice:

Both parties to this appeal are merchants in the textile industry.

Beginning in April 1974 they entered into a series of contracts for the purchase by respondent from appellant of substantial quantities of textured polyester yarn. In each instance, respondent placed an oral order with appellant for the yarn. A written order acknowledgment from appellant of the oral order followed and thereafter respondent sent its own form of a written and signed purchase order to appellant. The yarn specified or described was subsequently delivered to respondent.

In October 1974 respondent asked for an extension of time to make payment, and then in November 1974 refused to pay for certain shipments which it asserted did not include "dyeable yarn."

On the face of appellant's order acknowledgments was a statement that "This acknowledges * * * receipt of your order," and the following language appeared:

> "The acceptance of this order is conditional on the assent by the buyer to all of the conditions and terms on the reverse side hereof.

Your assent will be assumed unless you notify us to the contrary immediately upon receipt of this acknowledgment or when you accept delivery, in whole or in part, of the goods described herein."

Respondent's written purchase orders stated at the bottom "Acknowledge promptly if you are unable to ship by date specified." Stamped on the face of each purchase order was the following:

"Unless confirmation is received from the seller, the option to retain or cancel this order remains with the buyer."

One purchase order (# 2706) sent by respondent, had a note on its face reading: "Confirmation of contract # 4375" which appears to indicate that respondent considered appellant's order acknowledgment # 4375 as "the contract" and its own purchase order merely as confirmation of that contract.

On the reverse side of each order acknowledgment was a provision (condition 14) that "all controversies arising out of or relating to this contract * * * shall be settled by arbitration * * * under the Rules of the General Arbitration Council of the Textile Industry * * *."

Respondent contends, as it did below, that it was not aware of the arbitration clause nor bound by its inclusion on the reverse side of the order acknowledgment, and that the form used by appellant which included the arbitration clause should not be deemed superior to the form used by respondent which contained no arbitration clause. Finally, it urges that the arbitration clause was a "material alteration" of the contract, thereby falling within the purview of Uniform Commercial Code section 2–207(2)(b).

Appellant asserts before us, as it did below, that the notation on the face of its order acknowledgments alerted or should have alerted respondent to the said arbitration clause and, moreover, that both appellant and respondent were engaged in textiles and respondent must have been aware arbitration was a trade practice in said business.

Because the sole issue before us is whether there was an agreement to arbitrate, the forms involved and the pertinent section of the Uniform Commercial Code must be examined and considered to determine the answer.

Section 2–207 of the Uniform Commercial Code provides:

"Additional Terms in Acceptance or Confirmation

"(1) A definite and seasonable expression of the acceptance or a written confirmation which is sent within a reasonable time operates as an acceptance even though it states terms additional to or different from those offered or agreed upon * * *.

"(2) The additional terms are to be construed as proposals for addition to the contract. Between merchants such terms become part of the contract unless:

(a) the offer expressly limits acceptance to the terms of the offer;

(b) they materially alter it; or

(c) notification of objection to them has already been given or is given within a reasonable time after notice of them is received."

* * *

Matter of Doughboy Ind. (Pantasote Co.), 17 A.D.2d 216, 233 N.Y.S.2d 488, cited by respondent [does not] justify respondent's position. Although that case was decided a short time before the Code became effective in September 1964, the court examined the official comments of the drafters of the Code under section 2–207 in reaching its decision. The parties in *Doughboy* were not in the textile business and had dealt with each other on only two occasions during a three-month period. There, the face of seller's form brought attention to the terms on the reverse side, which included an arbitration clause and recited that silence or failure to object to the terms would bind the buyer. The buyer remained silent. The buyer's form, however, stated "only signed consent will bind." The court below held that the arbitration clause was not binding in that it was a material alteration and, further, that the seller's arbitration clause and the provision in the buyer's form which stated that only signed consent would bind, were in conflict, thus initiating a genuine "battle of the forms". The court opined that the existence of an agreement to arbitrate should not depend upon the conflicting fine print of commercial forms which cross one another but never meet.

It is undisputed that the parties here were merchants who have had long experience in the textile industry and in fact had dealt with each other for seven months. Hence, Matter of Helen Whiting, Inc. (Trojan Textile Corp.), 307 N.Y. 360, 121 N.E.2d 367, although a pre-Code case, is helpful in disposing of the issue before us. The parties in *Whiting* were in the textile business. An arbitration clause appeared on the reverse side of the seller's form. The buyer claimed not to be bound thereby. The Court of Appeals observed: "From our own experience, we can almost take judicial notice that arbitration clauses are commonly used in the textile industry." Indeed, this Court has cited *Whiting* for the proposition that arbitration is common in the textile industry.

* * * Respondent's claim that the arbitration clause in appellant's form was a "material alteration" of the terms of the contract between the parties is negated by the rule in *Whiting*, supra, that arbitration is common in the textile industry. In these circumstances, the arbitration clause cannot be considered a "material alteration" (Uniform Commercial Code, § 2–207 [2][b]) so as to be binding only where there is affirmative consent. Therefore, respondent's failure to notify appellant within a reasonable time after receipt of the order acknowledgments of its objection to the arbitration clause, gave said clause binding effect (Uniform Commercial Code, § 2–207 [2][c]).

Accordingly, the judgment appealed from should be reversed * * * motion to compel arbitration should be granted.

PROBLEMS

1. On February 1st, Sharon Douglas offers to sell her stereo speakers to Gary Farrell for $450. What is the legal result of each of the following responses by Gary?

    (a) "I will pay you the $450, but I sure wish you would have taken $350." *accept.*

    (b) "I'm sure we can work something out over the next few days." *negotiat*

    (c) "I will give you $350." *counter-offer*

    (d) "Would you accept payment in three monthly installments?" *Inquiry*

    (e) On February 5th, Gary writes Sharon, "I am not interested in your offer." On the morning of February 6th, Gary changes his mind and telegrams Sharon, "I accept your offer." Sharon receives the letter at 2:00 p.m. on February 6th. She receives the telegram at 3:00 p.m. on February 6th. *Rejection*

(f) On February 5th, Gary sends a telegram to Sharon, stating: "I accept your offer." Before she receives the telegram, Sharon telephones Gary and states, "You can forget about the offer—I've decided not to sell my speakers after all." *effective when sent*

2. Sam Ralston promises to pay Jerry Bailey $1,500 if Jerry builds Sam a drift boat for fishing on the Deschutes River. Jerry begins work on the boat, but after he is half finished, Sam calls and states, "I'm withdrawing my offer—you can forget about the boat." What kind of contract, if any, is at issue here? What are the rights and liabilities of the parties? *unilateral — cannot revoke*

3. Read and answer the following:

(a) Judy Banner promises to meet Cliff Winters for lunch at the "Byzantine Bistro". Judy does not show up as promised and Cliff sues Judy for breach of contract. Result? *No mutual assent*

(b) On May 1st, Cliff Winters offers to sell his fine Arabian mare to Liz Gifford. Liz agrees to buy the mare and to take possession of the animal on June 5th. The parties agree to decide upon price at a later time prior to delivery. Assuming the parties do not agree upon price prior to delivery, does the contract fail for lack of definiteness? Explain. *no reasonable price*

(c) On May 1st, Cliff Winters writes to his friend Sharon Douglas and offers to sell Sharon his used motorcycle for $300. On May 2nd, Cliff is fatally injured in an automobile accident. On May 3rd, Sharon posts a letter to Cliff, stating, "I accept your offer. Here is my check for $300." What are Sharon's rights, if any, with regard to the used motorcycle? Explain. Would your answer differ if Sharon had posted her acceptance prior to Cliff's death in the automobile accident? Explain. *(a) offer terminated (b)*

4. Answer the following "True" or "False" and give reasons for your answers:

T (a) A bilateral contract is a promise for a promise.

F (b) A reverse unilateral contract is a promise for an act.

F (c) Advertisements placed in newspapers by department stores, supermarkets, and the like generally constitute offers to sell at the advertised prices.

T (d) Silence on the part of the offeree seldom constitutes an implied acceptance of the offer.

F (e) When an auctioneer puts goods "on the block", he or she is making an offer to sell the goods.

T (f) A seller who advertises that an auction is to be "without reserve" is estopped from withdrawing the goods from sale once the bidding has begun."

5. Normally, the offer initiates the process by which a contract is created. Therefore, the offer is critical insofar as satisfying basic contract law requirements. Which of the following statements is *incorrect*?

(a) The offer may only be expressed in words.

(b) The offer must be communicated to the other party.

(c) The offer must be certain enough to determine the liability of the parties.

(d) The offer must be accepted by the other party.

[# 19, May, 1978 CPA Exam]

6. The distinction between contracts covered by the Uniform Commercial Code and contracts which are *not* covered by the code is

(a) Basically dependent upon whether the subject matter of the contract involves the purchase or sale of goods.

(b) Based upon the dollar amount of the contract.

(c) Dependent upon whether the statute of frauds is involved.

(d) Of relatively little or *no* importance to the CPA since the laws are invariably the same.

[# 35, November, 1976 CPA Exam]

7. A merchant made the following offer: "I offer you 100 cases of No. 3 macaroni at $13.50 per case. This offer is irrevocable for ten days." In which of the following situations would the offer be irrevocable because it is a "firm offer" or option contract under the Uniform Commercial Code?

(a) The offer was made orally and admitted to in court by the seller.

(b) The offer was written and signed by the seller.

(c) The offer was written and signed by the seller, but the second sentence read: "Acceptance must be made within ten days."

(d) Like all previous contracts for macaroni between the offeror and offeree, the offer was made by telephone.

[# 39, May, 1975 CPA Exam]

8. With respect to a contract for the sale of goods, a definite and seasonable expression of acceptance sent within a reasonable time is effective as an acceptance even though it states minor additional terms to those offered, except in which of the following situations?

(a) The acceptance was accompanied by a request that the goods be shipped by truck instead of by rail, if convenient.

(b) The offer impliedly limits acceptance to its terms.

(c) Acceptance is expressly conditional on assent to the additional terms.

(d) The price is in excess of $500.

[# 1, November, 1975 CPA Exam]

9. Sills Corporation of 123 Main Street entered into a contract to sell goods to Baskins of 456 Atlantic Avenue in the same town as Sills. The parties reached an agreement with respect to price and quantity but failed to state the place of delivery.

(a) The place of delivery is the seller's place of business.

(b) The place of delivery is the buyer's place of business.

(c) The contract is unenforceable because of indefiniteness.

(d) The place of delivery is that which is reasonable under the circumstances.

[# 5, November, 1975 CPA Exam]

10. On June 1, 1975, Markum Realty, Inc., offered to sell one acre of land in an industrial park it owned to Johnson Enterprises, Inc. The offer was by mail and, in addition to the other usual terms, stated: "This offer will expire on July 2, 1975, unless acceptance is received by the offeror on or before said date."

Johnson decided to purchase the tract of land and on July 1, telegraphed its acceptance to Markum. The acceptance telegram was delayed due to the negligence of the telegraph company which had admitted that delivery was not made to Markum until July 3. Markum decided not to sell to Johnson because it had received a better offer, but it remained silent and did not notify Johnson of its decision.

When Johnson did not hear from Markum by July 11, its president called the president of Markum and inquired when Johnson might expect to receive the formalized copy of the contract the two companies had entered into. Markum's president responded that there was no contract.

Required: 1. Did a contract result from the above described dealings between Markum and Johnson? Discuss the legal implications of each communication between the parties in your explanation.

2. Assuming a contract did not arise, does Johnson have any legal recourse against the telegraph company? Explain.

[# 4.a., November, 1975 CPA Exam]

Chapter 8

FACTORS THAT PREVENT AGREEMENT EVEN THOUGH THERE APPEARS TO BE MUTUAL ASSENT: MISTAKE, UNDUE INFLUENCE, DURESS, FRAUD, UNCONSCIONABILITY

When is there no mutual assent even though there appears to be a valid offer and acceptance?

We saw in the last chapter that mutual assent is the first of four elements necessary for a valid contract. We learned that mutual assent is usually manifested by one party making an offer and another party making an acceptance of the offer. However, this is not to say that mutual assent arises everytime there looks to be a valid offer and acceptance. Sometimes, there are other factors present that prevent the formation of mutual assent or agreement and warrant the conclusion that a contract was not intended. (Again, this is consistent with the two-fold purpose of contract law: to hold parties only to promises or bargains that they intend to make, and not to hold them to unintended promises or bargains, including promises or bargains induced by force, trickery, mistake, or other inequitable act.)

By way of example, suppose that there exists a written document signed by Sylvia Seller and Archie Buyer wherein Sylvia has promised to sell, and Archie has promised to buy, Sylvia's Lincoln Continental automobile for the cash price of $7,500. From the face of the writing, there appears to be both a valid offer and a valid acceptance—that is, there appears to be mutual assent. Even so, it would not make sense for a court of law to find the existence of mutual assent or agreement between the parties in any one of the following situations:

(1) Sylvia Seller owns two Lincoln Continentals, one a green, four year old model that Sylvia has driven 48,000 miles, and the other a black, two year old model that Sylvia has driven 24,000 miles. Sylvia believes that she has contracted to sell Archie the green car, while Archie believes that he has contracted to purchase the black car. Neither party realizes that the other is thinking of a different "subject matter" at the time the written document is signed. Rather than mutual assent between the parties, there is *mutual mistake*.

(2) Sylvia Seller is 86 years old, in sound mind, but physically infirm. Archie is Sylvia's court appointed guardian whose legal responsibility it is to look after Sylvia's affairs. Archie has carried out his duties to Sylvia's satisfaction for many years, and Sylvia has great faith in Archie's business judgment. As a result, Archie easily persuades Sylvia to enter into a written agreement to sell him her new Lincoln Continental for less than one-half of its fair market value. Though there appears to be mutual assent, Archie has exerted *undue influence* over Sylvia, and there is no agreement between the parties.

(3) Sylvia Seller is a 25 year old married woman who has been having a secret love affair with Archie Buyer. When Sylvia unexpectedly informs Archie that she is terminating the relationship, Archie points a gun at Sylvia and forces her to sign a document stating that she will sell Archie her new Lincoln Continental

for a mere fraction of its fair market value. Archie also threatens to "tell all" to Sylvia's husband, Sylvester, if Sylvia refuses to sign the "agreement". Under *duress*, Sylvia signs but obviously does not intend the agreement. Again, there is no mutual assent despite the apparent offer and acceptance to be found on the face of the written instrument.

(4) For some time, Sylvia Seller has been negotiating to sell a boat to Archie Buyer for the cash price of $7,500. Just as Sylvia and Archie are about to sign the agreement, and while Sylvia is not looking, Archie substitutes in place of the agreement a written document purporting to sell him Sylvia's new Lincoln Continental (valued at $15,000) for the cash price of $7,500. Sylvia signs the document without realizing that the substitution has taken place. Because Sylvia's signature has been *fraudulently* obtained on the document, there is no mutual assent and no valid contract for sale.

(5) In negotiating to sell Archie her Lincoln Continental, Sylvia tells Archie that the automobile is two years old and has 24,000 miles on it, when, in fact, the car is four years old and has been driven 48,000 miles. Relying upon Sylvia's misrepresentation, Archie enters into the agreement. Archie's agreement, in this case, has been *fraudulently induced* and so, again, mutual assent is not present despite the apparent offer and acceptance.

(6) Archie Buyer, who lives next door to Sylvia Seller, uses his life savings of $18,000 to build an addition onto his family residence. After the addition is complete Archie discovers that it extends two feet onto the northeast corner of Sylvia Seller's land. However, the encroachment (as defined in Ch. 6) in no way affects Sylvia's use and enjoyment of her land. In any event, Sylvia agrees to sell the two foot piece of land to Archie for $10,000 payable in five equal installments of $2,000 every two years for the

next ten years. Not only is $10,000 many times the fair market value of the land, but Sylvia additionally insists as part of the contract that Archie agree in writing to purchase her ten year old Lincoln Continental for $7,500. For several months now, Sylvia has been trying unsuccessfully to sell the car at a much lower price. Although offer and acceptance appear to be present, the *unconscionable* (highly inequitable) terms of the agreement negate the possibility of mutual assent, and Archie will not be bound to go through with the agreement.

As the above examples illustrate, the following factors may prevent the creation of mutual assent even though there appears to be a valid offer and acceptance:

(1) Mistake;

(2) Undue influence;

(3) Duress;

(4) Fraud in the execution;

(5) Fraud in the inducement; and

(6) Other unconscionable act.

Each factor is treated in detail in the sections that follow.

What is meant by the term "mistake" as a factor preventing mutual assent?

The American Law Institute (ALI) was created in 1923 with a stated charter purpose to "promote the clarification and simplification of the law and its better adaptation to social needs, to secure the better administration of justice and to carry on scholarly and scientific legal work." The organization's membership is composed of the justices of the U. S. Supreme Court, senior judges of the U. S. Courts of Appeals, the chief judges from the courts of the various states, the presidents and high ranking members of the various national and state bar associations, the deans of many law schools throughout the country, presidents and high ranking members of learned legal societies such as the American Society of Internal Law, and other respected lawyers and law professors.

Upon its creation, the ALI was determined to bring some semblance of order to the ever increasing volume of judicial decisions rendered in the courts on a wide variety of legal concepts, including torts, agency, property, contracts, etc. The Institute felt that it could perform a very valuable service to the law by restating the generally accepted principles of these concepts after thoroughly examining all pertinent cases across the country. The result of the ALI's efforts was the writing and publication of several "Restatements" (orderly, and often multi-volume legal summaries) on various legal topics. The ALI published the *Restatement, Law of Contracts* in 1932. Beginning in 1964, the ALI began tentatively revising the *Restatement of Contracts* so as to bring it up to date with the most recent common law decisions. And in 1973, the Institute published the first seven tentative drafts (covering approximately one-half of the original *Restatement* in revised and edited form) as the *Restatement, Second, Law of Contracts.* The *Restatement, Second* is still tentative and will not be given final approval until all portions of the original *Restatement* have been thoroughly revised. To this end, the ALI periodically issues tentative drafts covering the remaining chapters of the *Restatement*, the most recent publication being the tentative draft on "enforceability of contracts".

From time to time throughout our study of contracts, we will refer to the rules of the original *Restatement* as well as to the revised rules of the tentative *Restatement, Second.* While the rules are but the ALI's opinion as to what the law of contracts is generally and not a definitive treatise on the case law and statutory law of each state and federal jurisdiction, the ALI's opinion is entitled to great re-

spect and carries great weight in the legal community.

Thus we find a starting place for defining "mistake" as a factor preventing mutual assent in the *Restatement, Second,* § 293, Tentative Draft #10: "A mistake is a belief that is not in accord with existing facts." A *mistake* is an erroneous belief relating to the facts as they exist at the time an agreement is made or entered into. The mistake must be as to *facts in existence* or it will not prevent the creation of mutual assent. For example, a person who enters into a contract because of a mistaken prediction as to what will occur in the future makes no mistake as the term is used here. A great many agreements are made with full awareness of a future uncertainty, or with what might be called a "conscious ignorance" of the future. Though aware of the uncertainty, the parties estimate and weigh the possibilities and fix their values accordingly. If future events take an unexpected turn, the parties must still abide by their bargains. For example, suppose that Tom Picker, believing that mild weather will hold until October, agrees with Lois Owner in August that he will pick and harvest all of Lois' tomatoes before the first frost of the year occurs. In September, the weather suddenly changes, and the first frost ruins Lois' tomatoes before Tom has a chance to harvest them. Tom cannot successfully challenge mutual assent on the basis of mistake. Tom's judgment may have been poor, but many enforceable contracts result from bad judgment or bad bargaining. If a party could claim mistake every time his or her bargain turned sour, no one would feel comfortable entering into agreements with others.

Suppose, however, that when Tom agrees to pick and harvest Lois' tomatoes, he believes that he has contracted with regard to Lois' 20 acre field located north of the farm buildings. Lois, on the other hand, thinks that Tom has agreed to pick and harvest her 40 acre field located south of the buildings. Here, in contrast to the prior situation, there is a mistake as to existing facts that prevents the formation of mutual assent. The mistake is properly termed a "latent ambiguity": there is "ambiguity" in that Lois owns two tomato fields and the agreement fails to identify which field is to be picked and harvested; the ambiguity is "latent" in that neither party knows that the other is thinking of a different field. Thus, whereas the offer and acceptance appear to be definite and certain, there is uncertainty arising from extrinsic (outside) facts showing that the parties were thinking of different things at the time of contracting.

The general rule is that there is no mutual assent and no contract in the case of a latent ambiguity if both parties were thinking of different things at the time they entered into the agreement, the interpretations of both parties were reasonable, and neither party knew or had reason to know of the ambiguity or difference in interpretation. The most famous case involving a latent ambiguity is the old English case of Raffles v. Wichelhous, 159 Eng.Rep. 375 (Exch. 1864), in which two parties to a sales contract agreed that a load of cotton should be delivered from Bombay on the ship "Peerless". As it turned out, each party was thinking of a different ship, there being two ships named "Peerless", each scheduled to arrive from Bombay at a different time. Since both parties in the "Peerless" case were thinking of different ships at the time of contracting, and since neither party was aware of the latent ambiguity or uncertainty, there was no mutual assent created despite the apparent offer and acceptance.

Latent ambiguity is thus an area of "mutual mistake"—that is, *both* parties to the contract must be mistaken. And they must be mistaken as to a *material* fact as opposed to a minor or collateral matter. Mutual assent will fail to arise only where the mutual mistake goes to the very heart or basis of the bargain.

Assuming a mutual mistake as to a material fact exists, is the transaction void or voidable? The *Restatement of the Law of Contracts*, Section 294, "When Mistake of Both Parties Makes a Contract Voidable", states:

(1) Where a mistake of both parties at the time a contract was made as to a basic assumption on which the contract was made has a material effect on the agreed exchange of performances, the contract is voidable * * *

A *voidable* contract is one the legal effects of which may be completely avoided by the parties. Usually, where a contract is said to be voidable, at least one of the parties has the option of going through with the agreement or avoiding its legal ramifications entirely. Section 13 of the *Restatement* defines a "voidable contract" as follows.

The Restatement provides:

A voidable contract is one where one or more parties have the power, by a manifestation of election to do so, to avoid the legal relations created by the contract, or by ratification of the contract to extinguish the power of avoidance.

Comment:

    * * *

    b. Grounds of avoidance. Typical instances of voidable contracts are those where one party was an infant, or where the contract was induced by fraud, mistake, or duress, or where breach of warranty or other promise justifies the aggrieved party in putting an end to the contract. Usually the power to avoid is confined to one party to the contract, but where, for instance, both parties are infants, or where both parties enter into a contract under a mutual mistake, the contract may be voidable by either one of the parties. Avoidance is often referred to as "disaffirmance."

*   *   *

e. Power of ratification. The propriety of calling a transaction a voidable contract rests primarily on the traditional view that the transaction is valid and has its usual legal consequences until the power of avoidance is exercised. Where each party has a power of avoidance, there is no legal duty of performance; but the term voidable contract is appropriate if ratification by one of the parties would terminate his power of avoidance and make the contract enforceable against him. Moreover, action may be necessary in order to prevent the contract from producing the ordinary legal consequences of a contract; often such action in order to be effectual must be taken promptly.

As may be concluded from the above definition, a voidable contract generally has these three characteristics:

(1) The contract is valid and remains so unless the power of avoidance is exercised;

(2) A party having power to avoid the contract usually has the correlative power to ratify the contract (i. e., to agree to its terms and provisions);

(3) In the absence of specific words or actions indicating avoidance, the agreement may be held impliedly ratified.

An agreement that is based on a material mutual mistake does not possess the three characteristics stated above. To begin with, the transaction is invalid from the outset as mutual assent never arises. Also, while both parties have the ability to "avoid" the transaction by proving the existence of the mistake, neither party has the power to ratify the agreement (although, once the parties become aware of the mistake, they may certainly agree to enter into the same contract on mutually acceptable and understood terms).

Why, then, does the *Restatement* use the term "voidable" to describe a transaction based on material mutual mistake? It may be to show that there is an absence of mutual assent and to emphasize that neither party has any resulting contract obligations. Also, a mutual mistake usually benefits one of the parties, and generally only the adversely affected party will desire to avoid the agreement: for this reason, the transaction is often said to be "avoidable" to that party.

However, the use of the term "voidable" is confusing. It would be much more accurate simply to say that a transaction based on a material mutual mistake lacks mutual assent and is therefore null and void from the outset. A *void* transaction is one that has absolutely no force and effect and is incapable of legal enforcement. It is technically incorrect to use the term "void" to describe a contract because contracts are, by definition, *legally recognized* promises or bargains made by two or more persons including all resulting rights and duties. While a transaction may be properly termed void, a contract may not be. The better statement is that there is simply no contract at all in the case of a void or nugatory transaction.

Thus, a transaction that is based on a mutual mistake that goes to the very heart of the bargain is *void* from the outset—it is not a *voidable* contract. As neither party has the power to ratify the agreement, the transaction will become valid only if both parties, fully aware of the mistake, agree to enter into a valid contract on those terms. And quite often, the party who is adversely affected by the mistake will want to go through with the contract even on terms including the mistake. In this situation, the adversely affected party is in the position of an offeree who can accept the offer as it was made (mistake included) so long as the offer has not been revoked, withdrawn, or otherwise terminated. Upon acceptance, mutual assent arises, and, assuming that all other required elements are present, a valid contract comes into being.

We have spent a considerable amount of time explaining the difference between "void" and "voidable" for a very important reason. While many of the other factors preventing mutual assent will also result in either a void or voidable transaction, the terms "void" and "voidable" are not confined to this particular legal concept. They will reappear from time to time as we move through other commercial law concepts. The distinction between the two terms is easily confused, so care should be taken to keep their proper meanings in mind.

Does use of an ambiguous term prevent the creation of mutual assent where one party knows what interpretation has been given to the term by the other party?

Sometimes, an ambiguous term having two or more meanings is used, but one party knows exactly which meaning the other party has in mind. In this case, there is no mistake of any kind, and mutual assent arises based upon the innocent party's intent. For example, if, in the "Peerless" case, the two ships were sailing one in October and one in January, and one party knew that the other was thinking of the October sailing, there would be mutual assent based upon the October sailing.

Does mutual assent arise where one party uses words, figures, or symbols that are exact in meaning but that are used by mistake?

Sometimes, a party will make an offer using words, symbols, or figures that are exact in meaning but that are based upon the offeror's mistaken belief as to existing facts. For example, an offeror might submit a bid on a construction job using figures that (unbeknownst to the offeror) are based upon mathematical errors or other erroneous computations.

Such a mistake is referred to in the law as a *unilateral mistake*. It is an error by the offeror in using clear unambiguous words that the offeror would not use if he or she had knowledge of the true facts. The offeror makes the unilateral mistake before he or she makes the offer: at the time of making the offer, the offeror is saying exactly what he or she intends to say, and is conveying exactly the meaning that he or she intends to convey to the offeree. The offeror in the example above might intentionally submit a bid for $15,000, having incorrectly added up a column of figures to arrive at $15,000 rather than the correct total of $25,000. Certainly, the offeror has made a mistake, but it is a unilateral mistake the consequences of which may be entirely different from a mutual mistake.

When a unilateral mistake is made, there are three possible results:

(1) If the offeree knows or has reason to know that the offeror has made a mistake, the result is the same as in the mutual mistake situation—that is, there is no mutual assent and therefore no contract. The offeree "has reason to know" of any mistake that is "palpable" (obvious) under the circumstances. Thus, in Kemper Constr. Co. v. Los Angeles, 37 Cal.2d 696, 235 P.2d 7 (1959), the court held that the offeree had reason to know that the offeror had made a mistake when he submitted a construction

bid some $300,000 less than the next lowest bid. It is often said that the offeree cannot "snap up the offer" knowing that it was made in mistake.

Again, as in the area of mutual mistake, the unilateral mistake must be material; a unilateral mistake as to a relatively minor and unimportant fact will not prevent creation of mutual assent.

(2) If the offeree neither knows nor has reason to know that a mistake has been made, mutual assent will arise based upon the terms proposed by the offeror. This result is in accord with the objective theory of contracts. As you will recall from Ch. 7, the objective theory provides that a contracting party may rely upon the apparent intentions of the other party without regard to the party's secret thoughts or subjective, but undisclosed feelings or reservations. The test applied in determining whether or not mutual assent exists is thus the objective one of what a reasonable person in the position of the offeror or offeree would be led to believe by the words or conduct of the other party. A reasonable person in the position of an offeree who neither knows nor has reason to know that a unilateral mistake has been made would be led to conclude that the offer was made on the terms indicated. It follows that the unilateral mistake will not prevent a finding of mutual assent based upon those terms.

If, upon discovering his or her unilateral mistake, the offeror refuses to go through with the agreement, the offeree may collect money damages for breach of contract (assuming that all other elements of a valid contract are present). Where money damages are not an adequate remedy (e. g., where the property involved is unique), the offeree may obtain a court order requiring the offeror to specifically perform according to the terms of the offer.

(3) Sometimes, though a purely unilateral mistake has been made as described in (2) above, the courts will not require the offeror to go through with the agreement if to do so would result in a tremendous or unconscionable hardship to the party.[1] What is "harsh" or "unfair" is decided by the courts on a case by case basis using the objective standard of whether a reasonable person in view of all the circumstances would conclude that enforcement of the contract would be grossly unfair or inequitable. (In cases of extreme hardship or unfairness, the courts might well conclude that the offeree had reason to know of the mistake, and so find a lack of mutual assent on the basis of (1) above.)

Does mutual assent arise where a mistake is made by an intermediary such as a telegraph company?

Suppose that an offeror uses an intermediary such as a telegraph company or interpreter to send his or her offer, and the intermediary makes a mistake in transmitting the offer to the offeree. Acceptance by the offeree will not give rise to mutual assent if the offeree knows or has reason to know that a mistake has been made. Again, the law will not permit the offeree to "snap up" an offer containing a palpable error.

But where the offeree is unaware of the error and has no reason to know of its existence, the majority rule is that there is mutual assent based upon the terms transmitted to the offeree. The reasoning behind the rule is that, since the offeror chose to use an intermediary, the offeror should bear the risk of any loss resulting from the intermediary's mistake. Supporters of the rule also

1. As will be seen in a later section dealing with "unconscionability", the courts are more and more unwilling to enforce agreements that by their very terms are extremely unfair to one of the parties.

maintain that it is the most practical and convenient result from a business standpoint.

Under the minority view, which may well be the better position, the courts hold that there is no mutual assent and no contract. The minority courts draw an analogy between the mistake in transmission and the mutual mistake situation: in both cases, the parties to the transaction have reached no meeting of the minds, and it cannot be said that they have truly assented to the agreement.

In any event, the intermediary may be liable to the offeror for its negligence in incorrectly transmitting the offer. However, this is seldom a satisfactory remedy since intermediary companies routinely limit their liability by contract with the people who use their services (and the courts routinely uphold such limitations).

Does mutual assent arise where a mistake is caused by a party's failure to read a document before signing it?

Sometimes, an offeree who appears to assent to a written offer by signing it is really mistaken as to the contents of the offer because of a negligent failure to thoroughly read the offer before signing. The general rule is that the offeree is nevertheless legally bound to the terms *as they are written* unless the offeror knows or has reason to know of the offeree's mistake. This, again, is in accord with the objective theory of contracts: by *appearing to accept* the offer by signing the **instrument** (which may be a long and formal document), the offeree has led the offeror (along with any other reasonable person) to conclude that the offeree is either familiar with the terms of the offer and accepts them as is, or that he or she is ignorant of the terms but accepts them anyway without knowing or caring what they are. Despite the offeree's secret or undisclosed intentions, he or she will be held to his or her objective manifesta-

tions and cannot later challenge the existence of mutual assent or the validity of the contract by stating, "I did not know what I signed."

Of course, if the offeror knows or has reason to know of the offeree's mistake, mutual assent will not arise, and the entire transaction will be void. The same is true where the offeror personally brings about the offeree's mistake by fraudulently inducing him or her to sign or accept the instrument without reading it. For example, there is no mutual assent and no contract where an offeror misrepresents the terms of a written offer so as to induce a blind or illiterate offeree to sign or accept the offer. Nor is there mutual assent or a valid contract where an offeror secretly substitutes another document at the last moment, with the result that the offeree signs the instrument without realizing that the substitution has taken place.

Even in the absence of knowledge or fraud on the part of the offeror, mutual assent will not arise if the terms of the purported contract are unconscionable. As with a purely unilateral mistake, an offeree's mistake as to terms resulting from a failure to read the document before signing will not give rise to mutual assent or a valid contract where the effect of enforcing the agreement would be to work a tremendous hardship upon the party. This is particularly true in the case of a so-called *adhesion contract*. An adhesion contract is a "one sided" contract in which the offeror and offeree occupy substantially unequal bargaining positions: the offeree, the party with inferior bargaining power, is forced to "adhere" to the terms dictated by the offeror in order to acquire some essential property or service. For example, suppose that Archie Buyer wants to purchase a new car from Honest Ron Wheeler's New Car Sales Room. Archie may have sufficient bargaining strength to enter into preliminary negotiations with Honest Ron over such matters as car model, color, and option features, but, when it comes down to actually entering into a contract of purchase, Archie will probably be required to sign a standard contract form prepared by the manufacturer. In Ron's words, Archie must either sign the form or forget about buying the car—that is, he must either "take it or leave it". Because Ron occupies a superior bargaining position, and because Archie must "adhere" to the terms dictated by Ron or forget about purchasing the car (which he needs for both work and recreation), the contract is one of "adhesion". If Archie signs the standard contract form without reading its provisions, Archie will not be bound by any terms that prove unfair or unconscionable. The court, in such a case, will either rule that there is no mutual assent and thus no contract, or it will uphold the contract and simply refuse to enforce the unconscionable clauses. The court is considered to have inherent power to refuse to enforce a one sided contract in which one party lacked any meaningful choice.

What is the effect of undue influence on the element of mutual assent?

Black's Law Dictionary defines "undue influence" as "the use, by one in whom a confidence is reposed by another * * * of such confidence * * * for the purpose of taking an unfair advantage over him."[2] The *Restatement, Second, Law of Contracts*, Tentative Draft #11, defines "undue influence" as follows.

The Restatement provides:

Undue influence is unfair persuasion of a party who is under the domination of the person exercising the

persuasion or who, by virtue of the relation between them, is justified in assuming that that person will not act in a manner inconsistent with his welfare.

—————

Thus, for undue influence to exist in a contract situation, one party must be under the domination of another, and the dominating party must use unfair persuasion to overcome the free will or judgment of the other party, causing the party to either make an offer or accept an offer.

For purposes of undue influence, one party is considered "dominated" by another where he or she is justified in assuming that the other will act only in his or her best interests. Thus, a relationship of trust or confidence between the parties, particularly a family or *fiduciary*[3] relationship, will establish the necessary element of domination. Examples of such relationships include parent-child, attorney-client, trustee-beneficiary, and doctor-patient. The idea is that a person with trust and confidence in another is highly vulnerable to the influence of the other. Of course, if it can be shown that one party is dominated by another even in the absence of a relationship of trust and confidence, that will be sufficient for purposes of undue influence.

Assuming that one party dominates another, how much and what kind of influence is undue or improper? Generally speaking, "undue" influence is any persuasion, pressure, or influence short of actual force but stronger than mere advice, that so overpowers the dominated party's free will or judgment that he or

2. Henry Campbell Black, *Black's Law Dictionary*, Revised Fourth Edition, West Publishing Co., 1968, p. 1,698.
3. A "fiduciary" is a person (e. g., a trustee) who has a legal duty to act primarily for the benefit of another (e. g., a trust beneficiary) as to whom he or she stands

in a position of responsibility, trust, and confidence. A fiduciary relationship demands a high degree of good faith on the part of the fiduciary, and a great deal of confidence and trust on the part of the other party.

she cannot act intelligently and voluntarily, but acts, instead, subject to the will of the dominating party in making an offer or accepting an offer. In each case, the degree of persuasion or pressure required will vary depending upon a variety of circumstances including the health and age of the dominated party. The fact that a dominated party is weak, infirm, or aged does not in and of itself establish undue influence. However, it does go toward reducing the amount of persuasion or pressure that will be required for a finding of undue influence. The ultimate issue in every case is whether the dominated party made an offer or accepted an offer, not as a result of his or her own free will, but as a result of the unfair persuasion or pressure of the dominating party. The fact that the resulting bargain is not to the dominated party's benefit strongly suggests undue influence, as does the fact that the dominated party sought no independent advice apart from that of the dominating party.

Where undue influence is found to exist, the dominated party may avoid the contract with one exception: he or she may not avoid where a person other than the dominating party is the other party to the contract and that person has in good faith and without knowledge or reason to know of the undue influence given value in exchange for the agreement or otherwise materially changed his or her position in reliance upon it. In all other cases, if the dominated party chooses to avoid, it is just as if no agreement has been entered into. If he or she elects not to avoid, a valid contract will come into being assuming that all four elements necessary for a valid contract are present.

What is the effect of duress on the element of mutual assent?

Black's Law Dictionary defines "duress" as "any illegal imprisonment, or legal imprisonment used for an illegal purpose, or threats of bodily or other harm, or other means amounting to or tending to coerce the will of another, and actually inducing him to do an act contrary to his free will." [4] Thus, insofar as mutual assent is concerned, duress is any physical or mental coercion that deprives a person of his or her own free will and forces him or her to make an offer or accept an offer. The victim of duress usually knows what he or she is doing, but has no choice or alternative as his or her own free will has been overcome.

In determining whether or not duress exists, the courts use a subjective test. It makes no difference whether an average person in the same situation would yield in face of the threat or force employed so long as the will of the particular individual was overcome. While duress is very similar to undue influence, it differs from undue influence in three ways. First, it generally does not involve a confidential or fiduciary relationship between the parties. Second, the degree of coercion required for duress usually goes far beyond the unfair pressure or persuasion sufficient for a finding of undue influence. And, third, while undue influence makes an agreement voidable, duress makes an agreement sometimes void and sometimes voidable depending upon the kind of duress involved.

(1) *Duress that makes an agreement void.* Duress (mental or physical coercion or force) that reduces its victim to a mere mechanical instrument or automaton who is physically compelled to enter into an agreement against his or her will renders the transaction void (meaningless and of no legal effect). Here, the victim is not merely coerced, but is physically forced to make an offer or accept an offer. Examples include a party who hypnotizes another and directs him or her to

---

4. Henry Campbell Black, *Black's Law Dictionary*, Revised Fourth Edition, West Publishing Co., 1968, p. 594.

sign a contract that he or she does not intend to accept; a party who strongarms a victim, taking his or her hand and physically forcing him or her to sign; a party who furtively drugs or intoxicates another subsequently coaxing or persuading the victim to enter into an undesired agreement. In each case, the victim is reduced to acting mechanically under duress, and, in each case, the transaction is void.

(2) *Duress that makes an agreement voidable.* Where the victim of duress intentionally (as opposed to mechanically) enters into an agreement because of the threat or force employed, the agreement is merely voidable. Here, the duress falls short of reducing the party to an automaton, but anything and everything up to that point is included. Obviously, if one person holds a gun to another's head and threatens to kill the party (or his or her spouse, child, uncle, etc.) unless he or she enters into an agreement, any contract that results is voidable because of the extreme physical duress. But there are far more subtle forms of duress that will make a resulting contract just as voidable. For example, in the case of Thompson Crane & Trucking Co. v. Eyman, 123 Cal.App.2d 904, 267 P.2d 1043 (1954), an accountant refused to give his client some important work papers unless the client agreed to pay a substantially higher fee than was originally agreed upon. The client needed the papers immediately in order to appeal an unfavorable tax assessment and so agreed to the higher price. The court in the *Thompson* case permitted the client to avoid the agreement on the grounds of duress.

Generally speaking, voidable duress requires three things:

(a) *An improper threat.* Not all threats are improper. For example, a threat to take a legitimate civil claim to court against another person is perfectly permissible. The *Restatement, Second,* of the *Law of Contracts,* Tentative Draft #11 defines "improper threat" at Section 318.

The Restatement provides:

(1) A threat is improper if

(a) what is threatened is a crime or a tort, or the threat itself would be a crime or a tort if it resulted in the obtaining of property, or

(b) what is threatened is the instigation of criminal prosecution, or

(c) what is threatened is the commencement of civil process and the threat is made in bad faith, or

(d) the threat is a breach of the duty of good faith and fair dealing under a contract with the recipient.

(2) A threat is improper if the resulting exchange is not on fair terms, and

(a) the threatened act would harm the recipient and would not significantly benefit the party making the threat, or

(b) the effectiveness of the threat in inducing the manifestation of assent is significantly increased by prior unfair dealing by the party making the threat or

(c) what is threatened is otherwise a use of power for a purpose for which it is not designed.

———

(b) *A contract induced by the improper threat.* Again, the test is a subjective one: was the particular person who was subjected to the improper threat induced to enter into an agreement because of the threat? If the party attached importance to the threat in deciding whether or not to enter into the contract, he or she was so induced. And it makes no difference that an average person would have ignored or dismissed the threat. It is not the average person who is most in need of protection—it is the timid, the weak, and the inexperienced.

(c) *No realistic alternative.* Finally, a claim of voidable duress will be sustained only where the victim of the duress had no reasonable alternative (i. e., no "way out") but to submit to the coercion. If, in light of the circumstances, the victim had a reasonable alternative but failed to take it, there will be no finding of duress even though the threat was improper, and even though it induced the victim to enter into the contract. Put simply, then, the presence of a realistic or reasonable alternative rules out the possibility of voidable duress, and so, in a sense, the third and final requirement for voidable duress is the most important of the three.

The examples that follow should be of help to you in understanding the three requirements of voidable duress, particularly the third requirement of no reasonable alternative.

Physical duress. Extreme physical coercion such as pointing a weapon at someone or threatening to kill them is always sufficient to establish voidable duress because there is no reasonable alternative to compliance.

Duress as to property. Generally, there is no voidable duress where a wrongdoer refuses to surrender another's *personal property* or chattels unless and until the property owner agrees to pay the wrongdoer a specified sum of money (or enter into some other kind of agreement). There is no duress because the property owner whose goods have been wrongfully withheld generally has a legal right (a realistic alternative) to go into court and demand their return. If the property owner elects to buy his or her way out of the situation rather than exer-

cise his or her legal remedy, he or she cannot later sue for a "refund" on the basis of duress. Of course, there are situations where the property owner has no choice but to acquiesce to the wrongdoer's demands (e. g., where the property owner needs the goods immediately, or the goods are perishable). In this case, the property owner's payment of money is made under duress, and the transaction is voidable.

The same rules apply where a wrongdoer occupies another's *real property* and refuses to relinquish possession unless and until the landowner pays a specified sum of money or enters into another kind of agreement. Again, there is usually no duress because the landowner has an available legal remedy for the return of his or her property. Of course, if circumstances make it necessary for the landowner to regain possession of the land at once (e. g., to complete a subdivision project or the like), the payment of money or other agreement will be voidable as a product of duress.

Duress by threat of legal action. There is generally no voidable duress where a person threatens to press *criminal* charges against another or to inform authorities of another's criminal activities. Even where the threatening party is acting in bad faith and for private gain, the recipient of the threat has a realistic alternative—he or she can defend against the charge, and, if successful, can bring a tort action against the party who made the threats.

Along the same line, there is usually no voidable duress where a person threatens to institute *civil* proceedings against another unless the other pays a specified sum of money or enters into another agreement. Again, the recipient of the threat can defend against the lawsuit (a realistic alternative), and, if successful, can sue the party who tortiously brought the lawsuit. Of course, if defending against the charge is not a realistic alternative (as where the victim has neither the time nor money needed for a defense), voidable duress will be present, and the victim may set aside any resulting transaction.

Economic duress. Economic duress (also called "business compulsion" or "economic coercion") exists where one party wrongfully jeopardizes another's economic situation and then uses the situation to force the party to enter into an undesired agreement (e. g., refusing to provide needed goods or services until the party enters into an unrelated contract). Where the wrongdoer forces the victim to enter into an agreement with an innocent third party who neither knows nor has reason to know of the duress, the transaction will not be voidable if the third party has in good faith given value for the agreement or otherwise materially changed his or her position in reliance upon it.

And where the victim has any reasonable alternative to succumbing to the wrongdoer's demands (as by purchasing the same or similar goods or services from another supplier), there is no voidable duress whether the agreement is with the wrongdoer personally or with an innocent third party.

What is fraud in the execution?

Fraud in the execution (also called fraud in the factum) makes an agreement null and void—that is, of no legal effect whatsoever. Fraud in the execution occurs in two situations:

(1) *Where a party who intends to enter into a transaction is fooled or tricked into entering into an entirely different transaction.* For example, suppose that Dorothy Devious and Mary Trusting decide to enter into a contract. Dorothy draws up a written agreement and Mary Trusting carefully reads its terms. However, just before Mary signs the instrument, Dorothy surreptitiously (secretly) substitutes a different writing which she induces Mary to sign in the belief that it is the other document. Because of Dorothy's fraud in the execution (the surreptitious substitution of another writing), there is no mutual assent, and the agreement is void.

The same is true where Dorothy orally reads one set of terms to a blind Mary Trusting, then subsequently assists Mary in signing a completely different set of terms. Again, because of Dorothy's fraud in the execution (reading one set of terms while helping Mary sign another), there is no mutual assent, and the agreement is void.

(2) *Where a party who has no intention of entering into any agreement is fooled or tricked into signing an agreement.* For example, suppose that Percy Popstar is asked to sign an "autograph" on what turns out to be a carefully concealed legal document or check. Again, the fraud in the execution (the surreptitious use of the legal document or check) prevents the creation of mutual assent, and the transaction is utterly void and meaningless.

What is fraud in the inducement and what is its effect upon mutual assent?

In all cases, the victim of fraud in the execution has absolutely no intention of entering into the particular agreement that is fraudulently foisted upon him or her. The victim has no knowledge of the character or contents of the writing, and the entire transaction is void.

With regard to fraud in the inducement, on the other hand, the victim of the fraud intends to consent to the particular agreement, but only because a material fact has been misrepresented to him or her by the defrauding party. The agreement induced by the fraud is voidable, not void, and the defrauded party may go through with the agreement or avoid it at his or her option.

Fraud in the inducement such as will serve as a basis for avoiding an agreement requires four things:

(1) A material misrepresentation;

(2) Intent on the part of the party making the misrepresentation that the other party rely upon it;

(3) Justifiable reliance by other party (for example, it would not be justifiable to rely upon a statement one knows to be false); and

(4) Inducement of the agreement by the misrepresentation (i. e., the misrepresentation must prompt the party to enter into the transaction).

Where all four elements of fraud in the inducement are established, the defrauded party may avoid the agreement or pursue a number of alternative legal remedies. The four elements of fraud in the inducement and the legal remedies available to the injured party are discussed in detail in the following sections.

What is material misrepresentation?

Fraud in the inducement generally requires a false representation of a material *fact* as opposed to an *opinion*. The *Restatement, Second, Law of Contracts,* § *310,* Tentative Draft #11, entitled "Assertions of opinion", summarizes the distinctions between assertions of fact and opinion, and contains several helpful illustrations.

The Restatement provides:

(1) An assertion is one of opinion if it expresses only a belief, without certainty, as to the existence of a fact or expresses only a judgment as to quality, value, authenticity, or other similar matters.

Comment: * * * The difference is that between "this is true," and "I think this is true, but I am not sure."

* * * The fact that points of view may be expected to differ on the subject of a statement suggest that the statement is one of opinion. Statements of judgment as to quality, value, authenticity, or similar matters are common examples. For instance, the statement that an automobile is a "good" car relates to a matter on which view may be expected to differ, and the maker of such a statement will normally be understood as expressing only his own judgment and not as making assertions concerning such matters as horsepower or riding qualities.

* * * A seller's statement of the quantity of land or goods is virtually never a statement of opinion, even though he does not suggest that it is based on a survey, weighing or other measurement. The words "more or less" do not change such a statement into one of opinion, and the recipient is justified in believing that the quantity is substantially as stated although the measurement expressed may not be exact. In contrast, a seller's general statement of quality is usually one of opinion. There are, however, instances in which the gradations of quality are so marked that goods are usually sold as of a specified grade and assertion of grade is not one of opinion. A statement of value is, like one of quality, ordinarily a statement of opinion. However, a statement of the price at which something has been offered for sale or sold is not one of opinion.

Illustrations:

1. A, seeking to induce B to make a contract to buy goods, tells B that *he paid* $10,000 for them. A knows that he paid only $8,000 for the goods. The statement is not one of opinion.

2. The facts being otherwise as stated in Illustration 1, A tells B only

that the goods *are worth* $10,000. The statement is one of opinion. [Emphasis added.]

* * * The propensity of sellers and buyers to exaggerate the advantages to the other party of the bargains they promise is well recognized, and to some extent their assertions of opinion must be discounted. * * * [S]ome allowances must be made for seller's puffing and buyer's depreciation.

———

As explained in the *Restatement, Second,* a party may generally not rely upon another's statements as to value or quality—such statements are usually opinions only and not statements of fact. Nor may a party normally rely upon another's statements as to what he or she believes the law to be (though not dealt with in the passage quoted, statements of law are in most cases treated as statements of opinion).

However, there are exceptions, and even opinion-like statements as to value, quality, or law may serve as the basis for fraudulent misrepresentation if it is reasonable for a person to rely upon them. Because the distinction between fact and opinion is so closely related to the subject of justifiable reliance (the third element required for fraud in the inducement), further consideration of the topic is left to the section dealing with reliance.

Not only must the false representation be as to a fact, but the fact must be *material.* Generally, a fact is deemed material if it is likely to induce a reasonable person to assent to the agreement. It is also deemed material regardless of its probable effect upon a reasonable person if it is likely to induce the particular person to whom it is stated to assent because of some special reason or circumstance known to the party making the misrepresentation. A fact is not material if it is

of but peripheral importance to the agreement, or if it makes little or no difference to anyone involved whether the fact is true or false. For example, a landowner's false assertion that his or her property was purchased for $20,000 some 40 years ago when, in fact, the land was purchased for $10,000, makes little or no difference to a prospective purchaser today, and is therefore not a material misrepresentation; however, the landowner's false assertion that he or she paid $20,000 for the land one year ago when, in fact, he or she paid $10,000 is material.

Finally, is it necessary that the party who misrepresents the material fact do so with knowledge of its falsity? At one time, most courts said yes and required actual knowledge on the part of the person making the misrepresentation. But modernly, all courts will find fraud in the inducement where the misrepresentation is made with either of two kinds of *scienter* (knowledge)—*actual* knowledge or *imputed* knowledge. A party has actual knowledge if he or she makes the misrepresentation intentionally or knowingly; a party has imputed or chargeable knowledge if he or she makes the misrepresentation negligently (i. e., because of a careless failure to discover the statement's truth or falsity). A growing number of courts go so far as to provide a legal remedy on a strict liability basis for a completely *innocent* misrepresentation that is made unintentionally and without carelessness of any kind. Thus, whether the misrepresentation is intentional, negligent, or totally innocent, the defrauded party may have a legal remedy; the various remedies available to the defrauded party are considered in a following section.

What intent on the part of the party making the misrepresentation is required in all cases?

In all cases, a party who makes a misrepresentation (whether intentionally, negligently, completely innocently) must *intend* that the other party *rely* upon the misrepresentation in entering into an agreement or fraud in the inducement will not be found. The requirement of intent to induce reliance is thus separate and apart from any scienter requirement; it is either satisfied or not without regard to whether the party making the misrepresentation has actual or chargeable knowledge of the statement's falsity.

Two problems that commonly arise in the area of intent to induce reliance are (1) whether the required intent is present where the party who makes the misrepresentation intends to induce a particular person to rely upon the statement, but, instead, another person hears and relies to his or her detriment; and (2) whether the required intent is present where the party intends to induce a particular agreement, but the person who hears the misrepresentation relies upon it to enter into a completely different agreement.

In the first case, it is generally held that a person other than the particular person intended to be reached or influenced by the party making the misrepresentation cannot claim fraud in the inducement. Of course, the party making the false representation may intend to reach a very large class or number of individuals. For example, say that a manufacturer advertises his or her products in a newspaper, falsely representing one or more material facts about the goods in order to increase sales. The manufacturer may ultimately be liable to a very large group of consumers if the consumers do, in fact, rely upon the misrepresentation in purchasing the goods. Also, anytime the speaker as a reasonable person should anticipate that another is likely to rely upon his or her misrepresentation, the courts will find the required intent to induce reliance on the basis that a speaker intends to reach all who are reasonably foreseeable to rely in light of all the circumstances. This is not to say that a speaker will be liable for fraud in the inducement where a remote investor or casual bystander happens to overhear the conversation and relies upon the speaker's misrepresentation to his or her detriment —here, there is simply no intent, express or reasonably implied, to induce the party's reliance.

In the second case, where a party relies upon the speaker's misrepresentation to enter into a completely different, unintended transaction, there is generally no fraud in the inducement. Again, it cannot be said that there is any intent, express or reasonably implied, to induce the particular agreement that results. For example, suppose that Thomas Manufacturer misrepresents several material facts about his company in order to induce Emily Retailer to enter into an exclusive dealership or franchise agreement with his company. Emily decides not to become an exclusive dealer or franchise operator for Thomas. However, she does rely upon the misrepresentations in purchasing a number of his goods for purposes of resale. In these circumstances, it is unlikely that a claim of fraud in the inducement will be sustained. Thomas Manufacturer made the misrepresentations with the sole intent to induce Emily Retailer to become an exclusive dealer or franchise operator—not to induce her to purchase his goods on any other basis.

What is meant by "justifiable reliance"?

The requirement of *justifiable reliance* means that a party who relies upon another's misrepresentation must have a reasonable basis for doing so or fraud in the inducement will not be found. For example, there is no justifiable reliance where a party relies upon a misrepresentation that is obviously false. However, the falsity of the representation must be apparent from the statement itself or from facts within the knowledge of the person hearing the statement. In this connection, students frequently make the mistake of thinking that there is no justifiable reliance where the person relying upon the misrepresentation could have discovered the falsity of the statement by reasonable investigation. This is not true as there is no duty on the part of the person hearing the misrepresentation to investigate the statement or otherwise check out its truth or falsity. Thus, a party who relies upon another's misrepresentation may have a remedy for fraud in the inducement even though it would have been a simple task to discover that the statement was false.

There is little problem in applying these justifiable reliance rules to misrepresentations of material fact. But suppose that a party misrepresents his or her opinion. Is the party who hears the misrepresentation ever justified in relying upon it? As explained previously in the chapter, a person is ordinarily not entitled to rely upon another's misrepresentations of opinion (e. g., statements as to value or quality, a merchant's "puffing of wares"). However, there are exceptions where reliance upon a misrepresentation of opinion is justified. The *Restatement of Contracts* puts it this way at Section 311, "When Reliance On an Assertion of Opinion Is Not Justified".

The Restatement provides:

To the extent that an assertion is one of opinion only, the recipient is not justified in relying on it unless

(a) the recipient stands in such a relation of trust and confidence to the person whose opinion is asserted that the recipient is reasonable in relying on it, or

(b) the recipient reasonably believes that, as compared with himself, the person whose opinion is asserted has special skill, judgment or objectivity with respect to the subject matter, or

(c) the recipient is for some other special reason particularly susceptible to a misrepresentation of the type involved.

With regard to exception (a), a relationship of trust and confidence means a fiduciary relationship or any other confidential relationship such as a family relationship or relationship arising from membership in the same social, fraternal, or religious organization.

As for exception (b), a party may be justified in relying upon a misrepresentation of opinion if the party has reason to believe that the opinion is made by one with expert knowledge (i. e., special skill or superior knowledge or judgment with respect to the subject matter). For example, it is reasonable to rely upon a jeweler's statement of opinion that a particular jewel is worth $5,000—the jeweler is a gems expert and possesses superior knowledge and judgment with respect to the nature and value of jewels. The same is true of any statement of opinion given by a stock broker, art dealer, or real property appraiser within the area of his or her expertise (because the speaker possesses expert knowledge, his or her opinions within that area of knowledge may be justifiably relied upon). Thus, a party who enters into a contract in reliance upon an expert's misrepresentation of opinion may avoid the contract on the basis of fraud in the inducement. This is so even where the expert is not a party to the agreement with one exception. The exception arises where the other party to the contract has in good faith and without knowledge or reason to know of the misrepresentation given value in exchange for the agreement or materially changed his or her position in reliance upon it before evidence of the misrepresentation comes to light.

Exception (b) also applies to the situation where an apparently disinterested third party purports to offer "objective" advice with regard to a particular transaction, the party, in fact, having an interest in the outcome of the transaction. Because of the apparent objectivity of the speaker's opinion (apparent, not actual, because the speaker has failed to disclose his or her interest in the matter), the person receiving the advice is justified in relying upon it. It follows that he or she may avoid any resulting agreement on the grounds of fraud in the inducement.

Finally, exception (c) protects the person who is illiterate, unusually gullible, lacking in intelligence, or otherwise particularly susceptible to misrepresentation, whether of fact or opinion. A speaker who takes advantage of another's vulnerability may thus be liable for fraud in the inducement even though the misrepresentation is of opinion only, and even though the average person would not be induced to act in reliance upon it.

Before leaving the subject of justifiable reliance, a word is needed about misrepresentations of law. Generally speaking, a statement concerning law may be either fact or opinion and must be tested against the same general rules and exceptions to the rules that we have studied. Thus, in most cases, a person may justifiably rely upon another's misrepresentation of law only where the misrepresentation is factual in nature. For example, a false representation that the "state legislature yesterday passed a statute making our transaction valid" is a statement of fact concerning existing law and may give rise to fraud in the inducement. Similarly, a false, material representation as to existing foreign law may be justifiably relied upon; but a statement that "the county zoning ordinances don't affect placing the business here" is likely to be treated as a statement of opinion—a statement that, with limited exception, cannot be justifiably relied upon.

When is the reliance requirement satisfied?

The fourth element necessary for fraud in the inducement is *actual reliance* by the party hearing the misrepresentation. Sometimes referred to as the "causal" requirement, reliance demands that the party hearing the false representation enter into an agreement because of it. That is to say, the misrepresentation must cause or induce the party to enter into the intended transaction; where the party would not have entered into the transaction "but for" the misrepresentation, the reliance requirement is satisfied.

It follows that where the party hearing the misrepresentation knows of or discovers its falsity prior to entering into any agreement, there is no actual reliance and no fraud in the inducement. Once the party is aware of the statement's falsity, he or she relies upon his or her own judgment—not upon the misrepresentation of another—in deciding whether or not to enter into the transaction. For example, suppose that a party who has no duty to investigate nevertheless checks out a representation and finds it to be false. The party cannot now enter into an agreement and later successfully avoid it on the grounds of fraud in the inducement: once the party knows that the statement is false, the causal element required for fraud in the inducement cannot be satisfied.

Does concealing information or failing to provide information constitute misrepresentation for purposes of fraud in the inducement?

Up to this point, we have considered only affirmative misrepresentations made by written or spoken word. Misrepresentations may also result from *concealment* and *nondisclosure*.

Concealment. Concealment is an active effort to hide facts. It is an affirmative act intended to prevent another from learning a fact significant or relevant to a contemplated transaction, and it is equivalent to any affirmative misrepresentation made by written or spoken word. Examples of concealment include turning back the odometer (mileage meter) on an automobile, painting over defects so as to hide or cover them, and expunging (deleting) portions of relevant written records.

Nondisclosure. Ordinarily, neither party to a contemplated agreement is under any duty to disclose facts concerning the transaction, even where it is likely that one of the parties is unaware of one or more details. A party who is about to enter into an agreement is simply not expected to outline all the facts; thus, his or her failure to do so will not form the basis for fraud in the inducement. However, there are the following exceptions:

(1) *Half-truths.* A party generally has no duty to disclose any of the facts. However, if he or she chooses to assert a portion of them, he or she has a duty to disclose all relevant facts so as not to mislead the other party to the transaction. A party who fails to clarify an incomplete statement or half-truth (i. e., fails to disclose important omitted facts) may be liable for fraud in the inducement.

(2) *Fiduciary relationships.* Anyone in a fiduciary relationship or other position of trust and confidence with another is under a high duty of disclosure, and must inform the other party of all important facts pertaining to the contemplated transaction. The party's failure to disclose significant facts constitutes misrepresentation for purposes of fraud in the inducement, and any agreement induced by the nondisclosure is voidable.

(3) *Correcting statements.* Sometimes, a party's statement is not a misrepresentation at the time it is made, but it later becomes a misrepresentation because of the party's failure to make a *correcting statement* in light of a change in circumstances. While a party generally has no duty to disclose facts, the party, in this case, does have a duty to disclose facts that will correct the incorrect impression crated by his or her earlier assertion. For example, suppose that a person who truthfully asserts that he or she is in excellent financial condition later becomes insolvent. If the party to whom the representation was made is contemplating entering into an agreement on the basis of the assertion, the speaker has a duty to disclose the fact of his or her insolvency. Though the assertion of solvency was true when made, it is now false, and for the speaker to remain silent and knowingly permit another to contract in reliance upon the assertion constitutes fraud in the inducement.

Or suppose that a speaker asserts that he or she is in excellent financial condition, mistakenly believing that the assertion is true when, in fact, it is not. Upon discovering the falsity of the statement,[5] the speaker has a duty to disclose the fact of his or her insolvency to any party intending to rely upon the assertion in entering into a contract.

Finally, suppose that a person who intentionally misrepresents a fact not intending to induce reliance learns that another is, in fact, relying upon the assertion in entering into a contract. Again, a duty to disclose arises. For example, Fred Farmer might casually state in idle conversation with Nora Neighborly that the tract of land he owns south of town contains 100 acres when, in fact, it contains 92. Fred, in this case, is merely rounding off figures; he has no inten-

---

5. In most states, if the speaker fails to discover the falsity of the assertion prior to another's reliance upon it, the speaker may still be liable for fraud in the inducement if he or she was negligent in making the misrepresentation. And in some states, the speaker may be liable on a strict liability theory even where the misrepresentation was entirely innocent.

tion of defrauding Nora or inducing her to rely upon the assertion in any way. However, if Nora later contacts Fred and offers to purchase the tract of land, Fred has a duty to disclose the exact acreage. Fred's failure to disclose will be treated as a fraudulent misrepresentation.

(4) *Real property sales.* In most states, a real property seller has a duty to disclose to a prospective purchaser any facts within his or her knowledge that are material to the sales transaction. A failure to disclose constitutes fraudulent misrepresentation. Thus, a purchaser may avoid his or her purchase of a home on the basis of fraud in the inducement if he or she discovers that the seller knowingly failed to disclose prior to the sale that the basement floods every winter, that the roof leaks when it rains, or that the building is infested with termites. The same is true where the seller knowingly failed to disclose that improvements on the land violate local zoning laws or that the property is currently subject to litigation in the courts.

What legal remedies are available to a defrauded party whose agreement is voidable?

A person who is fraudulently induced to enter into a contract has what is termed a voidable agreement. This means that the party has an election of remedies: he or she may either rescind the contract and seek restitution, or he or she may affirm the contract and request money damages.

Rescission and restitution. Whenever an agreement is voidable (whether because of fraud in the inducement, duress, mistake, or undue influence), the wronged party has the option of rescinding the contract. To *rescind* is to restore the parties to the positions they were in prior to the agreement—to make it just

as though no contract had ever been entered into. A party who seeks to rescind must notify the other party of his or her intent to do so, and must tender [6] (conditionally offer to restore) anything of value received in exchange for the agreement. The injured party's tender or offer to restore is conditioned upon the other party's voluntary acceptance of rescission and willingness to restore, in turn, whatever benefits he or she has received from the contract. Whenever possible, the restoration must be *in specie*—i. e., the parties must return the actual property received rather than merely restore its value. However, if the actual property has been consumed, tender of its value will be permitted.

If, upon tender by the injured party, the other party refuses to accede to the rescission, the injured party may go to court and obtain a court order formally rescinding the agreement and ordering restitution of any benefits received by either party. For example, the court ordered restitution accompanying rescission of a land sale contract might be as follows: to the seller, recovery of possession of the land along with its fair rental value for the period of the purchaser's occupancy; to the buyer, recovery of the consideration paid plus interest, as well as recovery of any taxes paid and any expenditures made for improvements and, possibly, maintenance.

Affirmance and money damages. Rather than rescind the agreement and seek restitution, the injured party may affirm the agreement and request money damages. Rescission and affirmance are mutually exclusive alternative remedies: the injured party may do one or the other —he or she cannot do both.

Affirmance of the agreement may be either express or implied. For example,

---

6. A "tender" is simply a conditional offer to perform—a statement that "I am ready to perform if you are". The term will   arise frequently throughout our study of contracts.

if the injured party remains silent and fails to give notice of rescission and tender restoration within a reasonable period of time, the injured party will be deemed to have impliedly ratified the contract. The same is true where the injured party goes to court to recover money damages, or where the party continues to accept the benefits of the contract after discovering the fraud or other wrongful act.

To recover money damages, a party who elects to affirm a contract induced by fraud must bring a legal action in court for the tort involved. You will recall from Ch. 1 that a "tort" is any socially unreasonable conduct, and this certainly includes misrepresentation. Where the misrepresentation is intentionally made with knowledge of its falsity, either by written or spoken word or by active concealment of the truth, the tort involved is the tort of *deceit*. Where the misrepresentation is based on a careless failure to discover the falsity of the representation, the tort at issue is *negligence* (see Ch. 1). Generally speaking, only a party who is in the business of supplying information for the guidance of others (e. g., an accountant, stock broker, lawyer, or the like) will be held responsible in money damages for his or her negligent misrepresentations.

As for a completely innocent misrepresentation (one that is unintentional and nonnegligent), a growing number of courts hold the speaker liable in damages on a *strict liability* basis, particularly where the misstatement is made in connection with the sale of a chattel. The injured party in such a case is permitted to recover damages despite the absence of either intent or carelessness.

In determining the amount of *compensatory damages* [7] recoverable for fraud (whether liability is based on deceit, negligence, or strict liability), most courts use one of two damage rules: the *out-of-pocket rule* which awards the injured party the difference between the value paid and the value actually received, or the *benefit-of-the-bargain rule* which awards the injured party the difference between the value actually received and the value that would have been received had the subject matter of the agreement been as represented. The former rule compensates the injured party only for his or her actual loss; the latter rule goes beyond actual loss to take into account the party's reasonable expectations. By the way of example, suppose that Fred Farmer induces Nora Neighborly to purchase his wheat ranch for $150,000 by falsely representing to Nora that the wheat crop growing on the land is worth $30,000 when, in fact, the crop is worth $10,000. Because the fair market value of the land without the crop has been professionally appraised at $140,000, Nora believes that she is receiving $170,000 worth of property (land worth $140,000 plus a wheat crop worth $30,000) at a cost of $150,000. When Nora discovers that the crop is worth only $10,000, she affirms the contract, but seeks money damages. Applying the out-of-pocket rule, Nora will receive nothing as the difference between the value paid ($150,000) and the actual value received ($150,000) is zero. Applying the benefit-of-the-bargain rule, Nora will receive $20,000 as that is the difference between the actual value received ($150,000) and the value expected ($170,000).

Some courts apply neither rule and merely allow the injured party to recover whatever damages have been proximately caused by the fraud. This permits recovery of *consequential damages* (damages indirectly caused by the wrongful

---

7. "Compensatory" damages are damages designed to compensate or recompense the injured party for his or her loss; they are not taxable to the injured party.

act). For example, if Nora Neighborly is unable to purchase seed and fertilizer for next year's crop because this year's crop failed to yield the $30,000 promised, Nora may be able to recover consequential damages for any loss resulting to next year's crop.

Where the fraud is intentional and malicious, *punitive damages* may be recoverable in addition to compensatory damages. Whereas compensatory damages are designed to compensate the injured party for his or her loss, punitive damages are penalty damages designed to punish the wrongdoer and deter others from acting in a similar manner. Punitive damages are generally awarded by the jury (and it is always within the jury's discretion whether or not to award them) where the wrongdoer's tortious conduct is particularly outrageous or malicious.[8]

What is an unconscionable agreement?

Even in the absence of mistake, undue influence, duress, or fraud, a transaction may be so unfair and "unconscionable" (inequitable) that the courts will refuse to find mutual assent and so refuse to enforce the agreement. The doctrine of unconscionability as a factor preventing mutual assent is well over two hundred years old, having its origins in the old English case of Earl of Chesterfield v. Janssen, 28 Eng.Rep. 82 (1750). The court in the *Chesterfield* case stated that there can be no enforcement of an agreement that is so unconscionable "as no man in his senses and not under delusion would make on the one hand, and as no honest and fair man would accept on the other." Thus, the courts will refuse to enforce any contract that so takes advantage of a party that enforcement of the contract would result in tremendous hardship and unfairness. Such a contract is unconscionable.

The doctrine of unconscionability has been incorporated into the Uniform Commercial Code at *Section 2–302*, "Unconscionable Contract or Clause".[9]

The UCC provides:

(1) If the court as a matter of law finds the contract or any clause of the contract to have been unconscionable at the time it was made the court may refuse to enforce the contract, or it may enforce the remainder of the contract without the unconscionable clause, or it may so limit the application of any unconscionable clause as to avoid any unconscionable result.

(2) When it is claimed or appears to the court that the contract or any clause thereof may be unconscionable the parties shall be afforded a reasonable opportunity to present evidence as to its commercial setting, purpose and effect to aid the court in making the determination.

The *Official Comment* to Section 2–302 states as follows:

2. Under this section the court, in its discretion, may refuse to enforce the contract as a whole if it is permeated by the unconscionability, or it may strike any single clause or group of clauses which are so tainted or which are contrary to the essential purpose of the agreement, or it may simply limit unconscionable clauses so as to avoid unconscionable results.

It is clear from Section 2–302 and the *Official Comment* that any clause of any

---

8. Unlike compensatory damages, punitive damages are taxable to the recipient.

9. California and North Carolina have not adopted this particular Code Section.

contract may be found to be unconscionable. Although it is impossible to state
with precision when the rule of Section
2–302 will apply, pertinent case law in
the area provides some guidelines.

(1) Unconscionability is usually raised
as a defense. Generally, the plaintiff
(the party suing) asks the court to order
the defendant (the party being sued) to
perform his or her part of the bargain or
respond in money damages. The defendant, in turn, requests the court to
rule that all or part of the contract is unconscionable and so relieve the defendant
of his or her duty of performance.

(2) Most unconscionable contracts involve poor and otherwise disadvantaged
consumers (the courts have been particularly sympathetic to low income consumers). The courts generally refuse to apply the doctrine of unconscionability to
contracts between merchants.

(3) The agreement must be unconscionable at the time it is made. If it becomes unfair only at a later time because
future events do not turn out as predicted
by one of the parties, the agreement is
not unconscionable as that term is used
here and does not prevent the formation
of mutual assent.

(4) Many unconscionable contracts
are adhesion contracts. You will recall
that an adhesion contract is a contract in
which the offeror and offeree occupy
substantially unequal bargaining positions: the offeree, the party with inferior
bargaining strength, is forced to "adhere" to the offeror's terms in order to
acquire some essential commodity or service. In this connection, the *Official
Comment* to UCC Section 2–302 defines
the "basic test" of unconscionability in
these words.

The UCC provides:

1.   * * * The basic test is whether, in the light of the general com-

mercial background and the commercial needs of the particular
trade or case, the clauses involved
are so one-sided as to be unconscionable under the circumstances
existing at the time of the making
of the contract * * * The
principle is one of the prevention
of oppression and unfair surprise.

Thus, a contract that affords no meaningful choice to one of the parties but includes contract terms that are unreasonably favorable to the other party is an unconscionable contract that does not give
rise to mutual assent.

(5) The fact that a party had little education and could not read the language
of the contract is sometimes emphasized
by the courts in finding unconscionability, as is the fact that the seller manufactured the contract forms using fine print.

(6) Excessive price also suggests unconscionability, particularly where the
markup is two or three times the cost of
the product, or where the product is sold
at a price two or three times greater than
the average retail price elsewhere. For
example, in Kugler v. Romain, 58 N.J.
522, 279 A.2d 640 (1971), a sale of
encyclopedias to a consumer at a price
about 2½ times the reasonable market
price of the books was held to be unconscionable.

(7) Similarly, the fact that a consumer
buyer is shown the written agreement
form only after he or she has decided to
buy is strong evidence of an adhesion
contract.

(8) Finally, provisions requiring a
buyer to waive some of his or her legal
remedies or his or her right to a jury trial
in case of later controversy over the contract also indicate unconscionability.

A good example of an unconscionable
contract is found in the case of Frosti-

fresh Corp. v. Reynoso, 52 Misc.2d 26, 274 N.Y.S.2d 757 (1966). In that case, a Spanish-speaking consumer bought a freezer for a total time price of $1,145.-88. The cost of the freezer to the seller was $348. The consumer signed a contract form that was written in English, but that was neither translated for the consumer, nor explained to him. The seller advised the consumer that the freezer would actually cost him nothing because he would be paid bonuses of $25.00 for each sale that was made to his friends. Relying upon UCC Section 2–302, the court in *Frostifresh* stated that "the sale of the appliance at the price and terms indicated is shocking to the conscience." The court found the contract to be unconscionable and refused to enforce it.

Apart from UCC Section 2–302, many states have enacted legislation providing the consumer-buyer (particularly in door-to-door sales) with a "cooling off" period (usually 3 to 7 days) during which the buyer may elect to rescind or cancel the purchase upon restoring the goods to the seller. In some states, such legislation also applies to the sale of real estate.

Does the void–voidable distinction have any other significance?

Throughout the chapter, we have seen that the presence of mistake, undue influence, duress, fraud in the execution, fraud in the inducement, and unconscionability will render a transaction either completely void, partially void, or voidable. A void transaction is meaningless and of no legal effect; a voidable transaction may be either affirmed or rescinded.

There is one other important distinction between a transaction that is void and one that is voidable. A good faith purchaser (often referred to as a bona fide purchaser for value) [10] who buys property from a person who has voidable title (voidable because the person acquired it in a transaction involving mistake, duress, fraud, etc.) acquires good title to the property, while a good faith purchaser who buys property from a person who has void title acquires nothing. Void title is meaningless, and a person who holds void title because of the presence of mutual mistake, fraud in the execution, or the like, simply has nothing to transfer or sell.

CASES

CASE 1—*"The minds of the parties did not meet honestly and fairly."*

HOLLYWOOD CREDIT CLOTHING CO. v. GIBSON

District of Columbia Court of Appeals, 1963.
188 A.2d 348.

HOOD, Chief Judge.

This appeal is from a judgment denying appellant recovery of the purchase price of a television set. The testimony of appellee, largely uncontradicted and evidently accepted by the trial court, was that two days before Christmas he went to appellant's store and looked at a television, that appellant's salesman told him the price was $189 and he agreed to buy it at that price; that a conditional sales contract was filled in and he signed it; that when he arrived at home with the set he looked at his account book (apparently he was not given a copy of the conditional bill of sale) and saw that the stated price was $289, instead of $189, which with carrying charges

10. A "bona fide purchaser" is one who takes property for value (i. e., pays for it or gives other value) without knowledge or notice that there is anything wrong with the seller's title or that there are any defenses to its validity.

made a total cost to him of $354.35. As soon as the store reopened after the Christmas holidays appellee returned the set to the store, explaining that the cost was more than he agreed to pay. When the store personnel refused to take back the set, appellee left it there. He paid nothing on account and appellant brought this action for the full amount of $354.35. Trial resulted in a finding for appellee. In denying appellant's post-trial motion for judgment or a new trial, the trial court stated there had been a mutual mistake of fact as to the correct price of the set.

Appellant argues that appellee signed the contract and is bound thereby even if he failed to read it before signing it. Appellant urges us to rule that in this jurisdiction "a contract is still a contract." It is, of course, the general rule that one who signs a contract has a duty to read it and is obligated according to its terms. It is also a general rule that no relief can be afforded for a bad bargain or an extravagant purchase improvidently made. But another rule requires mutual assent or agreement as an essential element of a contract; and a contract in form may be avoided by a showing that assent was obtained by fraud or even misrepresentation falling short of fraud. If it is shown that the minds of the parties did not meet "honestly and fairly, without mistake or mutual misunderstanding, upon all the essential points involved," there is no contract.

The trial court by its finding indicated that it believed that appellee had been told that the price was $189, that this representation was a material factor in inducing him to sign the contract, and that he signed the contract believing the price to be $189. This was a sufficient basis for denying recovery to appellant.

Appellant asserts there was an error in the admission in evidence of a letter from the manufacturer of the television, stating that its suggested retail price was either $159.95 or $169.95. Possibly admission of this letter was error, but if so, it was harmless error. The letter merely showed that the price of $189, given appellee by the salesman, was not so absurdly low that appellee could not in good faith rely on it. And we note that appellant did not produce its salesman as a witness.

Affirmed.

CASE 2—*Did Columbia University falsely represent that it would teach the defendant wisdom, truth, character, understanding, courage, and beauty?*

TRUSTEES OF COLUMBIA UNIV. v. JACOBSEN

Superior Court of New Jersey, Appellate Division, 1959.
53 N.J.Super. 574, 148 A.2d 63.

GOLDMANN, S. J. A. D.

Defendant appeals * * *

Columbia brought suit in the district court against defendant and his parents on two notes made by him and signed by them as co-makers, representing the balance of tuition he owed the University. The principal due amounted to $1,049.50, * * * Defendant then sought to file an answer and counterclaim demanding, among other things, money damages in the sum of $7,016. The counterclaim was in 50 counts which severally alleged that plaintiff had represented that it would teach defendant wisdom, truth, character, enlightenment, understanding, justice, liberty, honesty, courage, beauty and similar virtues and qualities; that it would develop the whole man, maturity, well-roundedness, objective thinking and the like; and that because it had failed to do so it was guilty of misrepresentation, to defendant's pecuniary damage.

* * *

Following oral argument the Law Division judge * * * concluded that the statements attributed by defendant to plaintiff did not constitute a false representation. The judgment under appeal was then entered.

Following a successful freshman year at Dartmouth defendant entered Columbia University in the fall of 1951. He continued there until the end of his senior year in the spring of 1954, but was not graduated because of poor scholastic standing. Plaintiff admits the many quotations from college catalogues and brochures, inscriptions over University buildings and addresses by University officers cited in the schedules annexed to the counterclaim. The sole question is whether these statements constitute actionable misrepresentations.

* * *

The attempt of the counterclaim, inartistically drawn as it is, was to state a cause of action in deceit. The necessary elements of that action are by now hornbook law: a false representation, knowledge or belief on the part of the person making the representation that it is false, an intention that the other party act thereon, reasonable reliance by such party in so doing, and resultant damage to him.

We are in complete agreement with the trial court that the counterclaim fails to establish the very first element, false representation, basic to any action in deceit. Plaintiff stands by every quotation relied on by defendant. Only by reading into them the imagined meanings he attributes to them can one conclude—and the conclusion would be a most tenuous, insubstantial one—that Columbia University represented it could teach wisdom, truth, justice, beauty, spirituality and all the other qualities set out in the 50 counts of the counterclaim.

A sampling from the quotations cited by defendant will suffice as illustration. Defendant quotes from a Columbia College brochure stating that

"* * * Columbia College provides a liberal arts education.
* * * A liberal arts course * * * has extremely positive values of its own. Chief among these, perhaps, is something which has been a principal aim of Columbia College from the beginning: It develops the whole man. * * * [Columbia's] aim remains constant: to foster in its students a desire to learn, a habit of critical judgment, and a deep-rooted sense of personal and social responsibility. * * * [I]ts liberal arts course pursues this aim in five ways. (1) It brings you into firsthand contact with the major intellectual ideas that have helped to shape human thinking and the course of human events. (2) It gives you a broader acquaintance with the rest of the world. (3) It guides you toward an understanding of people and their motivations. (4) It leads you to a comprehending knowledge of the scientific world. (5) It helps you acquire facility in the art of communication. * * *"

He then cites the motto of Columbia College and Columbia University: *"In lumine tuo videbimus lumen"* ("In your light we shall see light"), and the inscription over the college chapel: "Wisdom dwelleth in the heart of him that hath understanding." He also refers to an address of the president of Columbia University at its bicentennial convocation:

"There can never have been a time in the history of the world when men had greater need of wisdom. * * * I mean an understanding of man's relationship to his fellow men and to the universe. * * * To this task of educational leadership in a troubled time and in an uncertain world, Columbia, like other great centers of learning in free societies, unhesitatingly dedicates itself. * * *"

We have thoroughly combed all the statements upon which defendant relies in his counterclaim, as well as the exhibits he handed up to the trial judge, including one of 59 pages setting out his account of the circumstances leading to the present action. They add up to nothing more than a fairly complete exposition of Columbia's objectives, desires and hopes, together with factual statements as to the nature of some of the courses included in its curricula. As plaintiff correctly observes, what defendant is seeking to do is to assign to the quoted excerpts a construction and interpretation peculiarly subjective to him and completely unwarranted by the plain sense and meaning of the language used. * * *

At the heart of defendant's counterclaim is a single complaint. He concedes that

"I have really only one charge against Columbia: that it does not teach Wisdom as it claims to do. From this charge ensues an endless number of charges, of which I have selected fifty at random. I am prepared to show that each of these fifty claims in turn is false, though the central issue is that of Columbia's pretense of teaching Wisdom."

We agree with the trial judge that wisdom is not a subject which can be taught and that no rational person would accept such a claim made by any man or institution. We find nothing in the record to establish that Columbia represented, expressly or even by way of impression, that it could or would teach wisdom or the several qualities which defendant insists are "synonyms for or aspects of the same Quality." The matter is perhaps best summed up in the supporting affidavit of the Dean of Columbia College, where he said that "All that any college can do through its teachers, libraries, laboratories and other facilities is to endeavor to teach the student the known facts, acquaint him with the nature of those matters which are unknown, and thereby assist him in developing mentally, morally and physically. Wisdom is a hoped-for end product of education, experience and ability which many seek and many fail to attain."

Defendant's extended argument lacks the element of fraudulent representation indispensable to any action of deceit. We note, in passing, that he has cited no legal authority whatsoever for his position. Instead, he has submitted a dictionary definition of "wisdom" and quotations from such works as the *Bhagavad-Gita*, the *Mundaka Upanishad*, the *Analects of Confucius* and the *Koran*; excerpts from Euripides, Plato and Menander; and references to the Bible. Interesting though these may be, they do not support defendant's indictment of Columbia. If his pleadings, affidavit and exhibits demonstrate anything, it is indeed the validity of what Pope said in his Moral Essays:

"A little learning is a dangerous thing;

Drink deep, or taste not the Pierian spring:

       * * * "

The papers make clear that through the years defendant's interest has shifted from civil engineering to social work, then to physics, and finally to English and creative writing. In college he became increasingly critical of his professors and his courses; in his last year he attended classes only when he chose and rejected the regimen of examinations and term papers. When his non-attendance at classes and his poor work in the senior year were called to his attention by the Columbia Dean of Students, he replied in a lengthy letter that "I want to learn, but I must do it my own way. I realize my behavior is non-conforming, but in these times when there are so many forces that demand conformity I hope I will find Columbia willing to grant some freedom to a student who wants to be a literary artist." In short, he chose to judge Columbia's educational system by the shifting standards of his own fancy, and now seeks to place his failure at Columbia's door on the theory that it had deliberately misrepresented that it taught wisdom.

* * *

The judgment is affirmed.

CASE 3—*"While she first exulted that she was entering the "spring of her life", she finally was awakened to the fact that there was "spring" neither in her life nor in her feet."*

VOKES v. ARTHUR MURRAY, INC.

District Court of Appeal of Florida, Second District, 1968.
212 So.2d 906.

PIERCE, Judge.

This is an appeal by Audrey E. Vokes * * *.

Defendant Arthur Murray, Inc., a corporation, authorizes the operation throughout the nation of dancing schools under the name of "Arthur Murray School of Dancing" through local franchised operators, one of whom was defendant J. P. Davenport whose dancing establishment was in Clearwater.

Plaintiff Mrs. Audrey E. Vokes, a widow of 51 years and without family, had a yen to be "an accomplished dancer" with the hopes of finding "new interest in life". So, on February 10, 1961, a dubious fate, with the assist of a motivated acquaintance, procured her to attend a "dance party" at Davenport's "School of Dancing" where she whiled away the pleasant hours, sometimes in a private room, absorbing his accomplished sales technique, during which her grace and poise were elaborated upon and her rosy future as "an excellent dancer" was painted for her in vivid and glowing colors. As an incident to this interlude, he sold her eight ½-hour dance lessons to be utilized within one calendar month therefrom, for the sum of $14.50 cash in hand paid, obviously a baited "come-on".

Thus she embarked upon an almost endless pursuit of the terpsichorean art during which, over a period of less than sixteen months, she was sold fourteen "dance courses" totalling in the aggregate 2302 hours of dancing lessons for a total cash outlay of $31,090.45, all at Davenport's dance emporium. All of these fourteen courses were evidenced by execution of a written "Enrollment Agreement—Arthur Murray's School of Dancing" with the addendum in heavy black print, "No one will be informed that you are taking dancing lessons. Your relations with us are held in strict confidence", setting forth the number of "dancing lessons" and the "lessons in rythm sessions" currently sold to her from time to time, and always of course accompanied by payment of cash of the realm.

These dance lesson contracts and the monetary consideration therefor of over $31,000 were procured from her by means and methods of Davenport and his associates which went beyond the unsavory, yet legally permissible, perimeter of "sales puffing" and intruded well into the forbidden area of * * * suggestion of falsehood, the suppression of truth, and the free exercise of rational judgment * * *. From the time of her first contact with the dancing school in February, 1961, she was influenced unwittingly by a constant and continuous barrage of flattery, false praise, excessive complements, and panegyric encomiums, to such extent that it would be not only inequitable, but unconscionable, for a Court exercising inherent chancery power to allow such contracts to stand.

She was incessantly subjected to overreaching blandishment and cajolery. She was assured she had "grace and poise"; that she was "rapidly improving and developing in her dancing skill"; that the additional lessons would "make her a beautiful dancer, capable of dancing with the most accomplished dancers"; that she was "rapidly progressing in the development of her dancing skill and gracefulness", etc., etc. She was given "dance aptitude tests" for the ostensible purpose of "determining" the number of remaining hours instructions needed by her from time to time.

At one point she was sold 545 additional hours of dancing lessons to be entitled to award of the "Bronze Medal" signifying that she had reached "the Bronze Standard", a supposed designation of dance achievement by students of Arthur Murray, Inc.

Later she was sold an additional 926 hours in order to gain the "Silver Medal", indicating she had reached "the Silver Standard", at a cost of $12,501.35.

At one point, while she still had to her credit about 900 unused hours of instructions, she was induced to purchase an additional 24 hours of lessons to participate in a trip to Miami at her own expense, where she would be "given the opportunity to dance with members of the Miami Studio".

* * *

At another point, while she still had over 1,000 unused hours of instruction she was induced to buy 151 additional hours at a cost of $2,049.00 to be eligible for a "Student Trip to Trinidad", at her own expense as she later learned.

Also, when she still had 1100 unused hours to her credit, she was prevailed upon to purchase an additional 347 hours at a cost of $4,235.74, to qualify her to receive a "Gold Medal" for achievement, indicating she had advanced to "the Gold Standard".

* * *

All the foregoing sales promotions, illustrative of the entire fourteen separate contracts, were procured by defendant Davenport and Arthur Murray, Inc., by false representations to her that she was improving in her dancing ability, that she had excellent potential, that she was responding to instructions in dancing grace, and that they were developing her into a beautiful dancer, whereas in truth and in fact she did not develop in her dancing ability, she had no "dance aptitude", and in fact had difficulty in "hearing the musical beat". The complaint alleged that such representations to her "were in fact false and known by the defendant to be false and contrary to the plaintiff's true ability, the truth of plaintiff's ability being fully known to the defendants, but withheld from the plaintiff for the sole and specific intent to deceive and defraud the plaintiff and to induce her in the purchasing of additional hours of dance lessons". It was averred that the lessons were sold to her "in total disregard to the true physical, rhythm, and mental ability of the plaintiff". In other words, while she first exulted that she was entering the "spring of her life", she finally was awakened to the fact there was "spring" neither in her life nor in her feet.

The complaint prayed that the Court decree the dance contracts to be null and void and to be cancelled, that an accounting be had, and judgment entered against the defendants "for that portion of the $31,090.45 not charged against specific hours of instruction given to the plaintiff". The Court held the complaint not to state a cause of action and dismissed it with prejudice. We disagree and reverse.

* * * Defendants contend that contracts can only be rescinded for fraud or misrepresentation when the alleged misrepresentation is as to a material fact, rather than an opinion, prediction or expectation, and that the statements and representations set forth at length in the complaint were in the category of "trade puffing", within its legal orbit.

It is true that "generally a misrepresentation, to be actionable, must be one of fact rather than of opinion". But this rule has significant qualifications, applicable here. * * *

"* * * A statement of a party having * * * superior knowledge may be regarded as a statement of fact although it would be considered as opinion if the parties were dealing on equal terms."

It could be reasonably supposed here that defendants had "superior knowledge" as to whether plaintiff had "dance potential" and as to whether she was noticeably improving in the art of terpsichore. And it would be a reasonable inference from the undenied averments of the complaint that the flowery eulogiums heaped upon her by defendants as a prelude to her contracting for 1944 additional hours of instruction in order to attain the rank of the Bronze Standard, thence to the bracket of the Silver Standard, thence to the class of the Gold Bar Standard, and finally to the crowning plateau of a Life Member of the Studio, proceeded as much or more from the urge to "ring the cash register" as from any honest or realistic appraisal of her dancing prowess or a factual representation of her progress.

* * *

Reversed.

PROBLEMS

1. Ken Lovett offers to sell Peggy Rooney "40 acres of the best farmland in Westchester County". Believing that property taxes are going to be sharply reduced by the state legislature, Peggy accepts Ken's offer and purchases the land. When the state legislature fails to cut property taxes as expected, Peggy desires to get out of the contract. She also complains that the 40 acres is not the best farmland in the county (it is not) and that the farmhouse roof leaks badly in several places (Ken had no knowledge of the leakage at the time he made the offer, but he did discover it just prior to sale). Can Peggy get out of the contract on the basis that the state legislature failed to reduce property taxes as expected? On the basis that the 40 acres is not the best farmland in the county? On the basis that the farmhouse roof leaks? Explain fully.

2. Eddie Johnson is the last surviving son of elderly widower Victor Johnson. Eddie visits Victor often, and Victor looks to Eddie for advice and assistance in dealing with his considerable properties. After much coaxing, Eddie persuades Victor to sell him his foreign sportscar for $1,000; the car is worth $15,000. Producing a written document,

Eddie tells Victor that he must sign over title to the car. Victor signs, not realizing that the writing is actually a deed of conveyance of his beachfront property to one Lucy Scruggs. Lucy, who believes that the sale is on the up-and-up, pays $60,000 for the land, giving it to Eddie as Victor's representative. Shortly thereafter, Eddie drugs Victor, and taking his hand, signs his name on a deed conveying his valuable residence to Eddie. Discuss the validity of the sale of the sportscar to Eddie, the sale of the beachfront property to Lucy, and the conveyance of the residence to Eddie. *undue influence*

3. Barbara Biggs and Wendy Hiller, salespeople representing "Lifelong Pans, Inc.", knock on Gordon Snyder's door and persuade Gordon to let them in to demonstrate the superior quality of their product. Barbara and Wendy talk fast, and Gordon, who has had little formal education, doesn't understand all the sales terms they rush through. However, he is impressed with the sheen and durable appearance of the pans and agrees to purchase them despite his limited income. The women then produce a lengthy contract form, in very small print, for Gordon to sign; Gordon does not bother reading the form before signing. When Gordon later discovers that he has agreed to pay $600 for the pans (similar pans can be purchased locally for $150), he desires to get out of the contract. Counsel him. *unconscionable act*

4. Andy Moran, the owner of "Moran's New & Used Autos" wants to sell one of his demonstrator cars. He sets the odometer back to zero and advertises it as a new (and never before used) vehicle. Jackie Barrett purchases the car, believing it to be brand new. Diane Scott then comes in looking for a used car. Andy shows her a five year old Ford and purposefully does not tell her that the car was in a major accident just over a year ago (the car has since been repaired). Diane purchases the car; she would not have purchased it had she known about the accident. Next Mike Harold inquires about a used Chevy. Andy shows him a four year old model. What he does not tell Mike is that the floorboard of the car is rotting out; just a week before, Andy put a new carpet down in the car to hide the problem. Mike purchases the car. Discuss the validity of the sale to Jackie, the sale to Diane, and the sale to Mike.

5. John Hart owns two trucks—a red pickup worth $500 and a blue pickup worth $800. Discuss the legal effect of each of the following transactions:

(a) John offers to sell his pickup to Rick Skinner for $500. Rick accepts John's offer. At the time of making the offer, John believes he is selling the red pickup; at the time of accepting the offer, Rick believes he is buying the blue pickup.

(b) John offers to sell his pickup to Rick for $500. Rick accepts John's offer, knowing that John intends to sell his red pickup. However, Rick later insists that it was the blue pickup he purchased. *latent ambiguity*

(c) John instructs the "Acme Telegram Service" to send the following message to Rick Skinner: "I offer to sell you my red pickup for $500." The Telegram Company makes an error in transmitting the message, and the offer reads: "I offer to sell you my blue pickup for $500." Rick does not know that John has two pickups. He accepts the offer.

(d) Assume the same facts as in (c) above except that, this time, the Telegram Company sends the following erroneous transmission: "I offer to sell you my red pickup for $5.00." Again, Rick accepts the offer. *no contract*

6. Bob Roberts borrows Jane Conroy's typewriter. He later refuses to return it unless Jane sells him her camera (worth $50) for $25. Jane sells Bob the camera in order to get the typewriter. Bob returns the typewriter to Jane and resells the camera for $50 to Lucy Martin who has no knowledge of how Bob obtained the camera. Jane now wants the camera returned. What are her rights, if any? Would your answer differ if Jane has sold the camera to Bob because she needed the typewriter immediately in order to type an important term paper? Explain.

7. Amy Samples offers to sell her horse to Brian Burrows for $300. Amy tells Brian that the horse is five years old and worth $400. She later discovers that the horse is really 10 years old and worth only $150. She does not pass this information on to Brian. Brian accepts Amy's offer. Upon discovering that the horse is 10 years old, what are Brian's legal rights, if any? Discuss fully. *Duty to disclose*

8. Would your answer to # 7 above differ if Brian could have discovered the horse's true age prior to the purchase by making a reasonable investigation? Explain. Would your answer to # 7 above differ if Brian would have gone through with the purchase even if he had known the horse's true age? Explain. — *not material*

no, no Duty to INVESTIGATE

9. Answer the following questions "True" or "False" and give reasons for your answers:

(a) *F* A statement of opinion can never serve as the basis for fraud in the inducement.

(b) *T* A purely unilateral mistake on the part of the offeror will not prevent the formation of mutual assent so long as the offeree neither knows nor has reason to know of the mistake.

(c) *F* A casual bystander who overhears another's misrepresentation of fact, and who relies upon the misrepresentation in entering into a contract, can generally sue the speaker for the tort of deceit.

10. Williams induced Jackson to enter into an employment contract by deliberately telling Jackson certain material facts which Williams knew were *not* true. If there are *no* other relevant facts, on what legal grounds is the contract voidable?

(a) Undue influence.

(b) Fraud.

(c) Duress.

(d) Unilateral mistake of fact.

[# 14, May 1976 CPA Exam]

Chapter 9

THE OTHER THREE REQUIREMENTS FOR A
VALID CONTRACT: CONSIDERATION,
CAPACITY AND LEGALITY

What is the scope of this chapter?

In Chapters 7 and 8, we considered mutual assent, the first of four elements necessary for a valid contract. We learned that mutual assent (offer and acceptance) is always the proper starting point for examining whether a particular agreement is a contract. If mutual assent is present, the agreement looks to be a valid contract; if mutual assent is not present, the examination need go no further as there is simply no agreement. However, it is important to realize that even though mutual assent is present because there is a valid offer and acceptance and because there is no factor preventing mutual assent (i. e., no mistake, undue influence, duress, fraud, misrepresentation, or unconscionable act), there may still be no contract because one of the other three required elements is lacking, making the agreement void or voidable. (Again, the term "agreement" rather than "contract" is appropriate because unless all four elements are present, there is no valid contract.)

Thus, even if mutual assent is present, it is necessary to further inquire whether there is consideration for the agreement, whether the parties have capacity to contract, and whether the subject matter of the contract is a legal one. Consideration, capacity, and legality are considered in detail in the chapter sections that follow.

Why does the law require consideration?

Consideration as an element required for a valid contract derives from the common law notion that not all promises should be legally enforceable. There has never been a system of law that enforced all promises. For example, Roman law took the position that an agreement was unenforceable unless a good reason for enforcing it could be established. And under our common law system, it is clearly undesirable to enforce all promises. Our courts are hardly likely to enforce (nor would we want them to enforce) a person's promise to stop smoking, to lose 20 pounds, to coach the junior high school girls' softball team, to bowl on the company team, to vote for a particular candidate, to work for another for free, or to sing in the church choir.

In fact, under our legal system, a promise that stands utterly alone is never legally enforceable. There must be something accompanying the promise that justifies enforcement. The problem has been to determine what that "something" is—to pinpoint the specific factors that will justify making a promise legally binding and enforceable. To define and limit these factors, the common law developed the rather complicated concept of *consideration*. The concept sets forth four factors or legal theories for concluding that a promise, whether express or implied, is legally binding and enforceable. In addition, the Uniform Commercial Code specifically provides that certain promises are enforceable even in the absence of common law consideration (remember that state legislative enactments can always change, qualify, or restrict common law rules).

What are the four common law theories of consideration, and when are promises enforceable under the UCC without regard to these four theories?

A promise is neither legally binding nor enforceable unless it fits within one of the four common law theories of consideration or falls within one of the Uniform Commercial Code exceptions to the common law rules. The four common law theories or justifications for enforcing promises are:

(1) *The bargain theory.* The most common basis for enforcing promises (more than 99% of all contracts entered into involve this theory), the bargain theory is what is usually meant when the term "consideration" is used.

(2) *Promissory estoppel.* Where the bargain theory of consideration does not apply, the promisor may still be held to his or her promise if the promisee has substantially changed his or her position in reliance upon the promise. This theory of consideration is referred to as promissory estoppel.

(3) *Quasi-contract.* A quasi-contract is really not a contract at all. However, unique circumstances may justify the finding of a legally binding implied promise in order to prevent unjust enrichment of the so-called promisor.

(4) *Public policy.* Sometimes, it is simply good public policy to hold a particular promise legally binding and enforceable even in the absence of (1), (2), or (3) above. Often called the "sufficient reason" theory of consideration, a promise may be enforced because there is sufficient reason and good social policy for doing so.

There are five UCC exceptions to the common law rules:

(1) *Waiver or renunciation of a claim or right after breach of contract.* Section 1–107 of the UCC provides that "any claim or right arising out of an alleged breach can be discharged in whole or in part without consideration by a written waiver or renunciation signed and delivered by the aggrieved party." This means that a party who claims that another has breached (failed to perform) a commercial contract dealing with personal property may legally waive or discharge his or her rights against that party by signing and delivering a written promise to do so *even though there is no consideration of any kind for the promise.* Suppose that a buyer breaches a sales agreement by failing to make the agreed upon payments. If the seller promises in writing to settle for one-half of what is owing on the merchandise, the seller will be legally bound by the promise upon its delivery to the buyer even though there is no consideration for the promise.

(2) *Firm offers.* You will recall from our discussion of revocability of offers in Ch. 7 that UCC Section 2–205 "Firm offers" provides as follows.

The UCC provides:

An offer by a merchant to buy or sell goods in a signed writing which by its terms gives assurance that it will be held open is not revocable, for lack of consideration, during the time stated or if no time is stated for a reasonable time, but in no event may such period of irrevocability exceed three months.

———

Thus, a merchant's written and signed promise to hold an offer open is legally binding despite the absence of consideration. A written but unsigned or completely oral promise to keep an offer open, on the other hand, is not a firm offer and is not irrevocable unless common law consideration is present.

(3) *Modification, rescission, and waiver.* Section 2–209(1) of the UCC provides that "an agreement modifying a contract within this Article (sales) needs no consideration to be binding."

This Code Section is designed to facilitate needed modifications in sales contracts by eliminating the need for common law consideration every time a change is made. The theory behind the Section is that the consideration given to support the original contract also serves to support the modified contract.

(4) *UCC Section 3–605.* This Code Section carves out an exception to the common law consideration rules in the area of negotiable instruments (checks, drafts, and notes). Discussion of the Section is left until Ch. 14.

(5) *UCC Section 5–105.* Finally, this Section deals with letters of credit and is considered in detail in Ch. 19.

In summary, the common law has developed four theories or justifications for enforcing promises, whether express or implied. The Uniform Commercial Code has specifically excepted five situations from the common law consideration requirements.

Of course, all of the Uniform Commercial Code Sections are subject to the "good faith" requirements imposed by the Code. Section 2–103 provides that the test of "good faith" between merchants or as against merchants includes "observance of reasonable commercial standards of fair dealing in the trade." Thus, the above Code Sections, particularly Sections 1–107 dealing with discharge of a claim or right and 2–209 dealing with modification of a sales contract, cannot be used in support of bad faith conduct.

What is the bargain theory of consideration?

Almost all agreements require consideration in the bargain theory sense in order to be legally binding and enforceable. Of the many thousands of contracts made daily, only a very few will fall within one of the other three theories of common law consideration or within one of the five UCC exceptions to the common law.

Bargain theory consideration requires two things:

(1) The consideration or "something" given for the promise must be bargained for between the parties—i. e., the consideration must be the motive for the promise and the promise must be the motive for the consideration.

(2) The consideration or "something" given for the promise must be legally sufficient. This is not to say that the consideration must be money or have economic value of any kind. Certainly, money or money's worth is frequently given in exchange for a promise and is legally sufficient consideration. However, just as often, the "something" given has no economic value but is still legally sufficient consideration: all that is needed is a commitment by the promisee to do something or refrain from doing something that he or she is not already obligated to do or to refrain from doing.

The motivation or bargain element. For bargain theory consideration to exist, each party must act because of what the other is giving to the agreement. That is, the promisor must make the promise because the promisee gives something by way of consideration, and the promisee must give something because the promisor makes the promise. In the examples that follow, the motivation or bargain element is clearly lacking, and, as a result, the promises made are neither legally binding nor enforceable.

(1) *Where either party intends to confer a gift upon the other.* Where either party promises to confer a gift upon the other, the motivation or bargain element is lacking because the party who promises to make the gift does not expect to receive anything in return. Because the promise of gift is not motivated by a return promise or performance, bargain theory consideration is not present, and

the promise to make the gift is legally unenforceable. (Of course, if all required elements for a completed gift are present—that is, intent coupled with delivery as explained in Ch. 3—the gift is effective to transfer ownership to the donee.)

Sometimes, however, it is difficult to determine whether a particular promise is a promise of gift or a promise motivated by a return promise or performance. For example, suppose that a man tells the children of a poor family living nearby, "If your mother says it's all right, and you want to go down to the supermarket, I promise to pay for a turkey for your Thanksgiving dinner." Is the man promising to make a gift, or is he bargaining for a return performance from the children (the act of obtaining permission and going to the store)? Most likely, the courts would conclude that the promisor intended only to make a gift of the turkey—not to bargain for the children's actions in obtaining permission and going to the store. Thus, the promise to pay for the turkey would not be legally enforceable.

But suppose that the man tells the children, "If you go to the supermarket and buy me a turkey and deliver it to my home, I will also pay for a turkey for you." In this case, the man clearly does not intend to make a gift. Rather, he is bargaining for a return performance from the children (the act of going to the store, purchasing him a turkey, and delivering it to his home). Similarly, the children's performance of the requested acts are in anticipation of and in return for the man's promise to buy them a turkey. Bargain theory consideration is present, and the promise to pay for the turkey is legally enforceable.

(2) *Where a promise is made because of some past act of the promisee.* It is often said that "past consideration is no consideration". What this means is that something done or given in the past can-

not qualify as consideration for a present promise because the essential motivation or bargain element is lacking: the past act was obviously not performed in anticipation of and in return for the present promise; and the present promise is obviously not given in anticipation of and in return for the past act. The term "past consideration" is thus a misnomer since a past act cannot qualify as valid consideration. For example, suppose that an employer promises to make a cash payment to the family of an employee who was accidentally killed on the job, the payment to be recognition of the employee's many years of service with the employer. The promise is legally unenforceable because of a failure of consideration. The essential motivation or bargain element is lacking because the employee did not perform the work in the past in anticipation of and in return for the employer's promise; and the employer did not make the promise in anticipation of and in return for the work.

(3) *Where a promise is made out of a sense of honor or moral obligation.* Where, out of a sense of honor or moral obligation, a person promises to repay another for a past favor, or to pay a good friend's debts, or to support a person he or she is not legally bound to support, etc., the promise is not legally enforceable because of the lack of motivation or bargain element. Again, the promise is not made in anticipation of and in return for some requested act or promise. Rather, it is made out a sense of honor or moral obligation. (Such promises are also unenforceable as promises to make gifts or as promises based on past acts.)

However, it should be pointed out that gratuitous promises may be enforceable, despite the lack of bargain theory consideration, on the basis of promissory estoppel, quasi contract, or public policy.

The legally sufficient or value element. Even where the motivation or bargain element is present (i. e., where the promise is given for the consideration and the consideration is given for the promise), the consideration may still not be legally sufficient. A very long time ago in the case of Currie v. Misa, 10 Exch. 153, 162 (1875), the court defined legally sufficient consideration, stating that it "may consist either in some right, interest, profit or benefit accruing to the one party, or some forbearance, detriment, loss or responsibility, given, suffered or undertaken by the other." Modernly, the court's definition has been abbreviated to the following: *Consideration is legally sufficient if it is either a benefit to the promisor or a detriment to the promisee.* (This shortened version of the *Currie* court's definition is an important statement that you will want to understand, remember, and use in explaining the element of consideration.)

The terms "benefit" and "detriment" do not refer to a monetary or economic loss or gain. The promisor legally benefits, as that term is used here, if he or she bargains for and receives a return promise or act that he or she was not previously entitled to receive. The promisee suffers a legal detriment if he or she does something or promises to do something that he or she was not previously bound to do; the promisee also suffers a legal detriment if he or she refrains from doing something or promises to refrain from doing something that he or she has a legal right to do. For example, in the case of Hamer v. Sidway, 124 N.Y. 538, 27 N.E. 256 (1891), an uncle promised his nephew that he would pay him $5,000 on his 21st birthday if the boy would refrain from drinking, smoking, swearing, and gambling until he reached that age. After the nephew had complied with the request, the uncle refused

to pay, insisting that the promise was not legally enforceable. The court, however, disagreed, holding that there was sufficient legal consideration in that the nephew (promisee) had suffered a legal detriment in limiting his otherwise free choice and action, and that the uncle (promisor) had received a legal benefit in having his nephew do so.

All that is necessary, then, for legally sufficient consideration is the creation of some kind of obligation or responsibility on the part of the promisee in return for the promisor's promise. The result must be either a benefit to the promisor, a detriment to the promisee, or both.

The fairness or adequacy of the consideration for the promise or the promise for the consideration is generally not relevant to the question of whether the consideration is legally sufficient. A mere promised change of positions by the parties will do so long as there results a benefit to the promisor or a detriment to the promisee. Along this line, a mere token or nominal consideration [1] will not result in a benefit to the promisor or in a detriment to the promisee and so cannot be termed legally sufficient. Consideration is token or nominal where the promisee is not required to do anything or promise anything of any consequence in exchange for the promise. Generally speaking, such a transaction will be viewed as a gift or as a promise to make a gift rather than as a bargained for exchange.

It might be pointed out that while fairness or adequacy of consideration has little or no bearing on the question of legal sufficiency, it may be very relevant to proving the existence of mistake, fraud, duress, undue influence, or unconscionable act.

1. Again, as with past consideration, it is actually a misnomer to say token or nominal "consideration" as such "consideration" is no consideration at all. It should be pointed out that some courts will accept a token consideration such as the payment of $1.00 so long as the $1.00 is *actually paid.* The courts will not accept a fictional statement of receipt of the consideration.

Where is bargain theory consideration found in a unilateral contract?

We learned in Ch. 7 that a unilateral contract is a promise for an act. The promisee's acceptance is found in the doing of the act—and so is the consideration for the promise. For example, if Lloyd Homeowner promises to pay Frank the Painter $1,000 to paint his house, and Frank accepts the offer by doing the act of painting the house, there exists a valid unilateral contract. It is easy to see that both essential elements of consideration are present: the promise was the motive for the act and the act was the motive for the promise (the motivation or bargain element); and the act of painting was a benefit to the promisor Lloyd and a detriment to the promisee Frank (the legal sufficiency or value element).

Whenever a transaction must be analyzed to determine if mutual assent and consideration are present, it is a good idea to begin with the first requirement of a valid contract and proceed in an orderly fashion as follows:

UNILATERAL CONTRACT ANALYSIS

Facts: Lloyd Homeowner promises to pay Frank the Painter $1,000 if Frank will paint Lloyd's house. Frank paints the house.

The Issue of Mutual Assent.

(1) *Is there apparent mutual assent?*

Yes. Lloyd Homeowner's promise to pay $1,000 is a sufficient offer, and Frank the Painter's painting of the house is a sufficient acceptance.

(2) *Is there any factor preventing mutual assent?*

No. In this case, there is no mistake, undue influence, duress, fraud in the execution, fraud in the inducement, or unconscionable act.

The Issue of Consideration.

Unilateral Contract. The first thing that must be determined is what promise is at issue i. e., what promise must be supported by consideration? In a unilateral contract, there is only one promise (here, Lloyd's promise to pay if Frank will paint the house), and so the question is always this:

WAS THERE CONSIDERATION FOR THE ONE PROMISE MADE?

In this case, was there consideration for the promise to pay the $1,000?

And more specifically   *   *   *

(1) MOTIVATION OR BARGAIN ELEMENT. *Was the promisor motivated to make the promise in anticipation of the requested act?*

In this case, was Lloyd Homeowner's promise to pay $1,000 motivated by anticipation of Frank the Painter's painting the house? The answer here is yes.

(2) THE LEGALLY SUFFICIENT OR VALUE ELEMENT. *Was the act performed by the promisee either a benefit to the promisor or a detriment to the promisee?*

In this case, was Frank the Painter's act of painting the house either a benefit to Lloyd Homeowner or a detriment to Frank?

Here, a diagram becomes especially helpful to the student.

But, first, determine who is trying to enforce what promise. In a unilateral contract, only the offeree will be trying to enforce a promise as only the offeror makes a promise. The offeree-promisee accepts the offer by doing the requested act. Doing of the act also furnishes consideration for the promise. Upon completion of the act, the offeree-promisee expects the offeror-promisor to perform his or her promise.

The consideration issue arises when the offeror refuses to perform the promise, stating that there is no consideration for the promise.

Now, diagram the situation as follows:

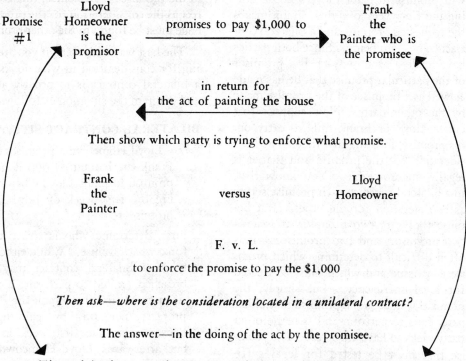

Promise #1

Lloyd Homeowner is the promisor → promises to pay $1,000 to → Frank the Painter who is the promisee

in return for
the act of painting the house

Then show which party is trying to enforce what promise.

Frank the Painter   versus   Lloyd Homeowner

F. v. L.

to enforce the promise to pay the $1,000

Then ask—where is the consideration located in a unilateral contract?

The answer—in the doing of the act by the promisee.

Then ask further—was the painting of the house a benefit to the promisor of the promise to pay $1,000 or a detriment to the promisee of that promise?

The answer—since, prior to the making of the unilateral contract, the promisor Lloyd Homeowner was not legally entitled to have Frank the Painter paint his house, nor was the promisee Frank legally obligated to do the painting, the promisor certainly receives a legal benefit from the act of painting and the promisee unquestionably suffers a legal detriment. Remember, all that is needed is either a benefit to the promisor *or* a detriment to the promisee—here, as in most cases, we have both.

Thus, there is consideration for the promise to pay $1,000, and the promise is legally enforceable.

As you can see, it is relatively easy to resolve the issue of consideration in a unilateral contract because there is only one promisor and one promisee. In a bilateral contract, each party is both a promisor and a promisee, and the issue of consideration becomes considerably more complex.

Where is bargain theory consideration found in a bilateral contract?

A bilateral contract is a promise for a promise: one party promises to do something or not to do something if another will make a requested return promise. The offeree accepts by making the return promise, and a bilateral contract springs into existence. The consideration for the contract is found in the promises made by the parties—each promise serves as consideration for the other. For example, suppose that Lloyd Homeowner promises to pay Frank the Painter $1,000 if Frank will promise to paint Lloyd's house during the first week of July. Frank makes the requested promise, and a bilateral contract comes into being. Since both parties have made a promise, each is a promisor of the particular promise that he has made as well as a promisee of the promise made by the other party. Now suppose that either Lloyd or Frank fails to carry out his promise, insisting that there is no consideration for the promise and that it is legally unenforceable. You know that, in a bilateral contract, each promise serves as consideration for the other. But because there are two promises at issue—two promisors and two promisees—it is often difficult to determine which promise is at issue and which must be treated for legal sufficiency. Put simply, the promise at issue is the promise that either party fails to perform and that the other party seeks to have enforced. The promise that must be tested for legal sufficiency is the nonbreaching party's promise, and that promise must be either a benefit to the promisor or a detriment to the promisee. (Too often, students mistak-

enly conclude that the very promise that is unperformed and at issue provides consideration for itself because it is either a benefit to the promisor or a detriment to the promisee. Of course, this is incorrect as the consideration for the promise at issue must be found in the other promise.)

The best way to proceed if you are looking for consideration in what looks to be a bilateral contract is to orderly analyze and diagram the situation as follows:

BILATERAL CONTRACT SITUATION

Facts: Lloyd Homeowner promises to pay Frank the Painter $1,000 if he will promise to paint Lloyd's house during the first week of July. Frank promises to do so.

First, determine who is trying to enforce what promise. While either party in a bilateral contract may have breached (failed to perform) a promise, assume first that Frank the Painter properly performs by painting the house during the first week in July, but, afterwards, Lloyd Homeowner refuses to pay the $1,000, stating that there is no consideration for the promise.

Diagram the situation as follows:

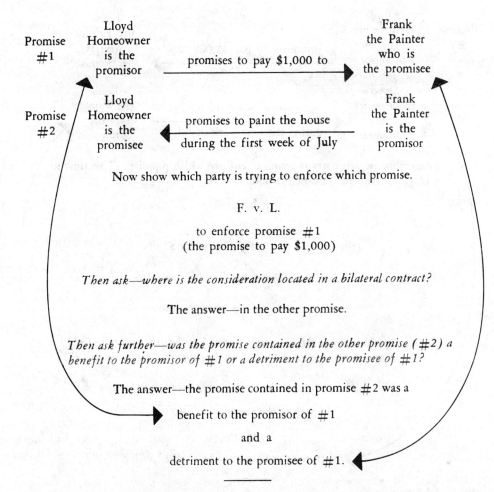

Promise #1

Lloyd Homeowner is the promisor　　promises to pay $1,000 to　　→　Frank the Painter who is the promisee

Promise #2

Lloyd Homeowner is the promisee　　←　promises to paint the house during the first week of July　　Frank the Painter is the promisor

Now show which party is trying to enforce which promise.

F. v. L.

to enforce promise #1
(the promise to pay $1,000)

Then ask—where is the consideration located in a bilateral contract?

The answer—in the other promise.

Then ask further—was the promise contained in the other promise (#2) a benefit to the promisor of #1 or a detriment to the promisee of #1?

The answer—the promise contained in promise #2 was a

benefit to the promisor of #1

and a

detriment to the promisee of #1.

Since the promisee Frank the Painter promised to do something that he was not already legally bound to do, he has suffered a legal detriment simply by making the promise to paint the house. Since he is the promisee of the promise to pay the $1,000, and since he has suffered a legal detriment, there is consideration for the promise to pay.

There is also consideration for the promise to pay $1,000 in that Lloyd Homeowner, the promisor of the promise to pay, is also the promisee of Frank's promise to paint the house and so is entitled to the legal benefits of that promise from the time of its making.

Now assume that it is Frank the Painter who fails to perform his part of the bargain. Suppose that the first week of July comes and goes but, still, Frank refuses to come and paint the house. During the last week of July, Lloyd Homeowner gives up and hires another housepainter to do the job, but it costs him $1,750. Lloyd brings an action in court against Frank the Painter to collect the $750 damages he has suffered because of Frank's failure to paint the house as promised. Frank claims that he does not have to pay any damages because there was no consideration for his promise to paint the house for the $1,000 fee.

Diagram the situation as before:

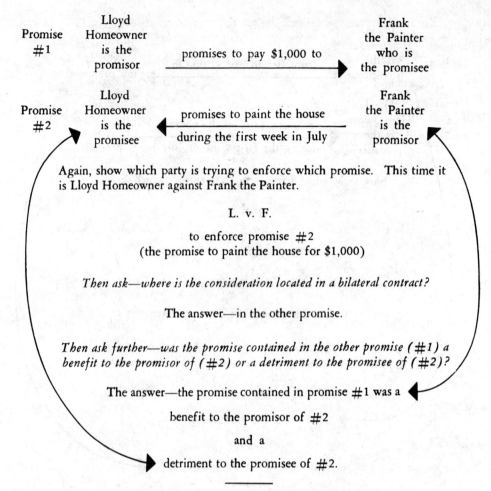

Again, show which party is trying to enforce which promise. This time it is Lloyd Homeowner against Frank the Painter.

L. v. F.

to enforce promise #2
(the promise to paint the house for $1,000)

Then ask—where is the consideration located in a bilateral contract?

The answer—in the other promise.

Then ask further—was the promise contained in the other promise (#1) a benefit to the promisor of (#2) or a detriment to the promisee of (#2)?

The answer—the promise contained in promise #1 was a

benefit to the promisor of #2

and a

detriment to the promisee of #2.

Since the promisee Lloyd Homeowner promised to do something that he was not already legally bound to do (to pay a fee of $1,000), he has suffered a legal detriment. Since Lloyd is the promisee of the promise to paint the house, and since he has suffered a legal detriment, there is consideration for Frank's promise to paint.

There is also consideration for the promise to paint the house in that Frank the Painter, the promisor of the promise to paint is also the promisee of Lloyd's promise to pay $1,000 and so is entitled to the legal benefits of that promise from the time of its making. Because Lloyd's promise has legally benefited Frank, there is consideration for the promise to paint, and Lloyd

Homeowner will be able to collect damages because of Frank's failure to carry out his promise.

Now let's change the facts. Once again, suppose that Lloyd Homeowner promises to pay Frank the Painter $1,000 if Frank will promise to paint Lloyd's house during the first week of July. Frank promises to do so, and a valid bilateral contract comes into being. On July 1st, Frank begins to paint Lloyd's house, but, that same afternoon, Frank informs Lloyd that he will not complete the job unless Lloyd promises to pay him $1,500 instead of the agreed upon $1,000. Lloyd agrees to pay the $1,500, whereupon Frank finishes painting the house. Lloyd, however, pays Frank only

$1,000, stating that there was no consideration for the promise to pay an additional $500. Frank takes his claim for the additional money to court. Is Frank legally entitled to the additional $500? Again, diagram the situation as follows:

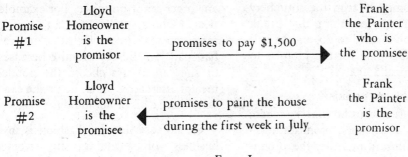

	Lloyd		Frank
Promise #1	Homeowner is the promisor	promises to pay $1,500 ⟶	the Painter who is the promisee
Promise #2	Lloyd Homeowner is the promisee	⟵ promises to paint the house during the first week in July	Frank the Painter is the promisor

F. v. L.

to enforce promise #1
(a promise to pay $1,500)

Then ask—where is the consideration located in a bilateral contract?

The answer—in the other promise.

Then ask further—was the promise contained in the other promise (promise #2) a benefit to the promisor Lloyd or a detriment to the promisee Frank?

The answer is no—there is no benefit to Lloyd nor any detriment to Frank in his promise to paint the house for $1,500

NO CONSIDERATION since Frank is already legally bound to paint the house for $1,000.

There is obviously no benefit to Lloyd in having his house painted for $1,500 when he already has a contract to have it painted for $1,000. Nor does Frank suffer any detriment in promising to paint the house for $1,500 when he has already promised to paint the house for $1,000.

Since there is no consideration for the promise to pay $1,500, Frank will not be able to collect the additional $500 in court. However, it is very important to understand that there would have been an entirely different result had the subject matter of the contract been the sale of goods. You will recall that one of the five Uniform Commercial Code exceptions to the common law consideration requirement is Section 2–209 which provides that "an agreement modifying a contract for the sale of personal property does not need consideration to be binding." UCC Section 2–209 does not come into play in the Lloyd Homeowner-Frank the Painter situation because theirs is a contract for services—not a contract for the sale of personal property. Nor does Section 2–209 apply to contracts for the sale of land. Only modifications of sales contracts are enforceable under the Section without additional consideration.

Now let's vary the facts again. Suppose that Frank the Painter promises on July 1st to trim the shrubbery in addition to painting the house if Lloyd will promise to increase his pay from $1,000 to $1,500. If Lloyd makes the requested promise, it will be legally enforceable. Here, the promise to trim the shrubbery is a promise to do something that Frank is not already obligated to do, and so will serve as consideration for the promise to pay the additional $500.

What is an illusory promise?

A promise is said to be *illusory* where the promisor, in actuality, promises nothing. In an illusory promise, the promisor undertakes no obligation and sets no limit on his or her future course of conduct. Rather, the promisor leaves himself or herself an alternative (a way out) by which to escape any contract duty whatsoever. Thus, whenever a promise is phrased in the alternative, and the promisor has the right to choose a nondetrimental alternative (one that does not require him or her to change his or her position at all), the promise is illusory and will not serve as consideration for any other act or promise. For example, a person who says, "I promise to buy your car tomorrow unless I change my mind has made an illusory promise because he or she can always choose the nondetrimental alternative (i. e., he or she can always change his or her mind).

Or suppose that Joe Fashion is in the business of manufacturing women's clothes, and Brenda Buyer is in the business of selling clothing at retail. Brenda promises to buy "whatever dresses I may wish to order" from Joe Fashion in return for Joe's promise "to sell Brenda up to 1,000 dresses during the next three months". Joe's promise is unenforceable because Brenda's promise is illusory.

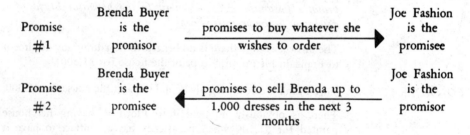

B. v. J.

to enforce promise #2
(the promise to sell the dresses)

NO CONSIDERATION

Ask—is the promise to buy whatever she wishes to order either a benefit to Joe, the promisor of promise #2, or a detriment to Brenda, the promisee of promise #2?

The answer is no. Brenda's promise does not require her to do anything at all if she chooses not to. As such, it is illusory and will not serve as consideration for Joe's promise to sell the dresses. Joe's promise is therefore unenforceable, and Joe does not have to sell the dresses to Brenda.

Now suppose that Brenda Buyer promises to buy from Joe Fashion "all the dresses I will need" or "all that I will require". Brenda's promise, in this case, will serve as consideration for Joe Fashion's promise to sell. Brenda's promise is not illusory because she has definitely restricted her freedom of action: if she "needs" or "requires" any dresses, she must buy them from Joe Fashion or not buy them at all. While Brenda has the implied alternative of no longer operating her business, that, too, would be a legal detriment. Thus, the agreement between Brenda and Joe is an enforceable *requirements* contract, and Brenda can hold Joe Fashion to his promise to sell.

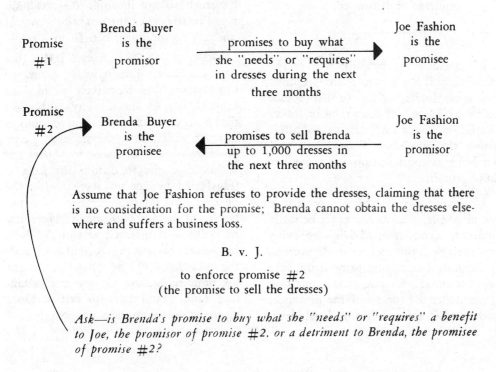

Assume that Joe Fashion refuses to provide the dresses, claiming that there is no consideration for the promise; Brenda cannot obtain the dresses elsewhere and suffers a business loss.

B. v. J.

to enforce promise #2
(the promise to sell the dresses)

Ask—is Brenda's promise to buy what she "needs" or "requires" a benefit to Joe, the promisor of promise #2, or a detriment to Brenda, the promisee of promise #2?

The answer is yes—Brenda has set some limits to her future freedom of action, thus suffering a legal detriment (if Brenda is to buy at all, she must buy from Joe). Thus, there is valid consideration present for Joe's promise to sell, and Joe must pay damages for failing to keep his part of the bargain.

In a similar manner, a seller may promise to sell to a particular buyer his or her entire output from a plant or factory, using such words as "I promise to sell all that I produce". Again, the seller's promise in such an *output* contract is not illusory becuase the seller has set some limits to his or her future course of action: the seller can sell merchandise only to the particular buyer. Obviously, the seller may circumvent selling merchandise to the buyer by closing down his or her plant or factory, but this, too, would be a legal detriment to the seller.

Of course, there are good faith limits on the demands that can be made under either "requirements" or "output" contracts. The Uniform Commercial Code at Section 2–306 "Output, Requirements and Exclusive Dealings" provides as follows.

The UCC provides:

(1) A term which measures the quantity by the output of the seller or

the requirements of the buyer means such actual output or requirements as may occur in good faith, except that no quantity unreasonably disproportionate to any stated estimate or in the absence of a stated estimate to any normal or otherwise comparable prior output or requirements may be tendered or demanded.

———

In conclusion, a promise will escape being illusory only where the promisor sets some limits on his or her future course of action. If the promisor leaves himself or herself a nondetrimental alternative, the promise is illusory and will not serve as consideration for any other act or promise.

However, this is not to say that a promised performance can never be made subject to a condition. To be sure, many promised performances are made expressly dependent upon the prior happening of a condition. So long as the condition is not under the control of the promisor, and there is a possibility of legal detri-

ment or benefit, the promise is not illusory and will serve as consideration for another act or promise. For example, a promise that "I will buy your car tomorrow on the condition that I don't change my mind" is obviously illusory as the condition is totally under the promisor's control. But a promise that "I will buy your car but only if I am first able to sell my truck" is not illusory: the condition is not totally under the promisor's control and a legal detriment benefit may result.

Or say that Lola Executive learns that her employer, Countrywide Insurance Corporation, has tentatively decided to transfer her to another city within 90 days. Lola immediately enters into a contract with Martin Homebuyer. Lola promises to sell her house to Martin for $60,000 on the condition that Lola is transferred by her employer within the next 90 days; Martin promises to buy the house for the $60,000 price. As expected, Lola is transferred within 90 days, but Martin refuses to buy her house, stating that there was no consideration for his promise because "it was not certain that Lola would have to sell". Once again, let's diagram the situation.

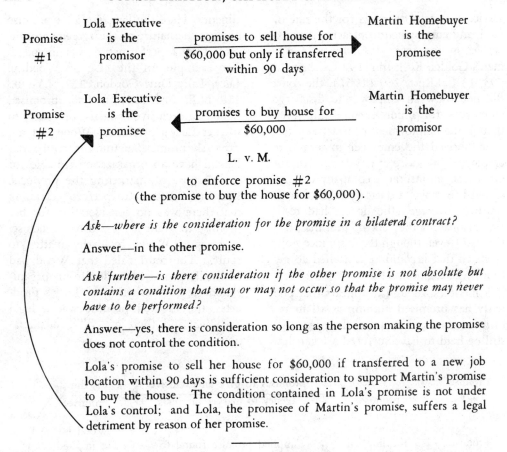

L. v. M.

to enforce promise #2
(the promise to buy the house for $60,000).

Ask—where is the consideration for the promise in a bilateral contract?

Answer—in the other promise.

Ask further—is there consideration if the other promise is not absolute but contains a condition that may or may not occur so that the promise may never have to be performed?

Answer—yes, there is consideration so long as the person making the promise does not control the condition.

Lola's promise to sell her house for $60,000 if transferred to a new job location within 90 days is sufficient consideration to support Martin's promise to buy the house. The condition contained in Lola's promise is not under Lola's control; and Lola, the promisee of Martin's promise, suffers a legal detriment by reason of her promise.

Thus, a conditional promise is not illusory and will serve as consideration for another promise or act so long as the promisor has no control over the happening of the condition and a legal detriment or benefit will result if the condition does occur (it is immaterial to the consideration issue that the condition later fails to occur, leaving both parties free of any obligation to perform).

Similarly, the fact that a promised performance is expressed in the alternative such as "I will either do this, or I will do something else" does not make the promise illusory so long as all the alternatives involve a legal detriment to the promisor or a legal benefit to the promisee. Thus, Brenda Buyer's promise that she "will buy merchandise from Joe Fashion on or before a certain date or that she will notify Joe that she is not going to buy" is not illusory and will serve as consideration for Joe's promise to sell merchandise to Brenda. Here, Brenda has a choice of alternatives, but both are detrimental. Obviously, the giving of notice is not much of a detriment or burden, but the law does not require much of one. It requires only that the party making the promise set some limits to his or her future course of action—incur some obligation, however slight, that he or she did not previously have.

And you will recall that UCC Section 1–203 stipulates that "every contract or duty within this Act imposes an obligation of good faith in its performance or enforcement." Thus, the giving of notice not to buy (i. e., to cancel or terminate the agreement) must be done in good faith and cannot be arbitrary or unreasonable. The common law imposes the same good faith duties in contracts that do not fall under the UCC, such as service contracts, contracts for the sale of land, and employment contracts. For example, in the case of Glenn v. Clearman's Golden Rock Inn, 192 Cal.App.2d 793, 13 Cal.Rptr. 769 (1961), the court did not allow an employer to discharge employees for union membership even though the employment contract expressly authorized the employer to terminate employees by notice at any time. In another case, an insurance company was not allowed to cancel a doctor's medical malpractice coverage (the doctor had testified against another doctor in a malpractice case) even though the insurance policy stated that it could be cancelled at any time by giving notice.

Sometimes, though it appears that one party has promised nothing at all in return for another's promise, the party will still be held to have suffered a legal detriment. Here the law *implies* a promise because the nature of the agreement indicates that a performance was intended. For example, in the case of Wood v. Lucy, Lady Duff-Gordon, 222 N.Y. 88, 118 N.E. 214 (1917), Lucy promised Wood an exclusive franchise or agency to market Lucy's products. Wood did not expressly promise anything in return, but he did have an organization suitable for the purpose of marketing the products. Lucy later refused to perform, claiming that there was no consideration for her promise to grant the exclusive franchise, whereupon Wood took the matter to court. The court ruled that Wood had impliedly promised to devote his organization to the marketing of Lucy's products; the implied promise was a legal detriment and, therefore, valid consideration.

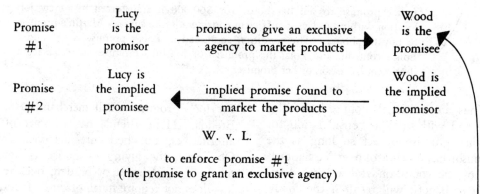

W. v. L.

to enforce promise #1
(the promise to grant an exclusive agency)

Ask—can consideration be found when no express promise to do anything is made in return for a promise?

The answer is yes—the nature of the agreement is such that it implies a promise on the part of Wood to devote his sales organization to the marketing of the products.

The implied promise constitutes a legal detriment to Wood, the promisee of Lucy's promise to grant the exclusive franchise, and therefore serves as consideration for that promise.

———

The Uniform Commercial Code has specifically adopted this rule insofar as the sale of goods is concerned. Section 2–306(2) states: "A lawful agreement by either the seller or the buyer for exclusive dealing in the kind of goods concerned imposes unless otherwise agreed an obligation by the seller to use best efforts to supply the goods and by the buyer to use best efforts to promote their sale."

Can doing what one already has an obligation to do ever serve as consideration for an act or promise?

The general rule is that doing or promising to do what one already has a legal obligation or duty to do will never serve as consideration for another act or promise. Thus, we saw in our earlier example of Lloyd Homeowner and Frank the Painter that once Frank contracted to paint Lloyd's house for $1,000, he had a legal duty to do the job, and performance of that duty could not serve as consideration for Lloyd's promise to pay Frank $1,500 rather than $1,000 for the act of painting.

Similarly, a party who is already under a legal duty to perform the very act required in a unilateral contract situation suffers no legal detriment by performing his or her duty. For example, say that Cyrus Citizen offers a $5,000 reward for the apprehension of escaped criminal Frances Fugitive. Police officer Tim Daltry, who knows about the reward, catches Frances while on duty. Tim cannot collect the $5,000. While Tim has accepted the offer by doing the requested act, he was already under a duty to catch Frances, and there is no consideration for Cyrus' promise to pay the reward.

UNILATERAL CONTRACT

Promise #1 — Cyrus Citizen is the promisor — promises to pay $5,000 reward for apprehension of Frances Fugitive → Police Officer Tim Daltry is the promisee

in return for the act of apprehending Frances

Assume that Officer Daltry catches Frances and applies for the reward, but Cyrus Citizen refuses to pay, stating that there is no consideration for the promise to pay the reward.

P. v. O.

to enforce promise #1
(promise to pay reward)

Ask—where is the consideration located in a unilateral contract?

Answer—in the doing of the act by the promisee.

Ask further—was Officer Daltry's apprehension of Frances at a time when Daltry was already under a legal duty to apprehend her either a benefit to the promisor Cyrus or a detriment to the promisee Daltry?

NO CONSIDERATION

The answer is no. Daltry has suffered no detriment because he was already under a legal obligation to perform the act of apprehending Frances. Nor has Cyrus Citizen received any benefit because he was already entitled to the receipt of Daltry's duty.

Of course, if Officer Daltry apprehends Frances while outside the scope of his duties or after working hours, there would be legal detriment to Daltry, a legal benefit to Cyrus, and consideration for Cyrus' promise to pay the reward.

Along the same line, suppose that a passenger aboard a large jumbo jet says to the airline pilot, "If you get us safely to Los Angeles, I will pay you $100." Again, the airline pilot is an employee of the airlines and is already under a legal duty to fly the jet safely to Los Angeles. In carrying out his or her duty, the pilot suffers no legal detriment, and the passenger receives no benefit since he or she is already entitled to the pilot's safe performance.

Will a promise not to sue another serve as sufficient consideration for another promise or act?

When two parties have a dispute, the law generally affords the injured party the legal remedy of taking the case to court—of bringing suit. A promise not to bring suit when there is a legitimate basis for doing so will serve as consideration for a return promise or act. The key word here is "legitimate". A promise to forego suit will constitute a legal detriment to the promisor only where the party honestly and reasonably believes in the case—i. e., where the party's claim has a reasonable possibility of success. Where the promisor simply has no basis for a legal claim, a promise to forego suit will not constitute a legal detriment, and the promise will not serve as consideration for any other promise or act. By way of example, suppose that Nancy Prudence and Stanley Caution have a car accident at a busy intersection. Nancy believes that Stanley was negligent in driving too fast at the time of the collision. Stanley is not convinced that he was careless, but he promises to pay for all repairs to Nancy's car in return for Nancy's promise not to sue him for negligence. If Stanley later refuses to pay Nancy's repair bills, claiming that there was no consideration for his promise to pay them, will Nancy be able to enforce the promise in court?

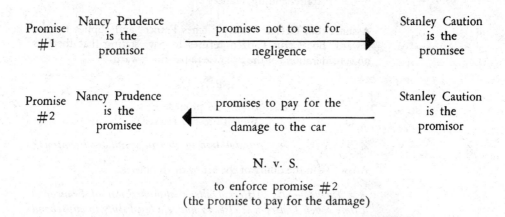

| | Nancy Prudence is the promisor | promises not to sue for negligence → | Stanley Caution is the promisee |
| Promise #1 | | | |

| Promise #2 | Nancy Prudence is the promisee | ← promises to pay for the damage to the car | Stanley Caution is the promisor |

N. v. S.

to enforce promise #2
(the promise to pay for the damage)

Ask—Does Nancy's promise not to sue constitute a legal benefit to Stanley Caution, the promisor of promise #2 or a legal detriment to Nancy Prudence, the promisee of that promise?

The answer is yes. The only exception would be where Nancy had no **legal** basis whatsoever for bringing the lawsuit (and knew she had none). In this case, Nancy would suffer no legal detriment in promising not to sue; nor would Stanley receive any legal benefit from such a promise.

Will part payment of a debt serve as consideration for a promise to forget the balance of the debt?

Two important legal terms come into play when one party claims that another has promised to forget the balance of a debt in exchange for the first party's part payment of the debt. The terms are "liquidated debt" and "unliquidated debt". The term "liquidated" means to be ascertained, determined, fixed, settled, or agreed to. *Black's Law Dictionary* defines "liquidated debt" as follows: "A debt is liquidated when it is certain what is due and how much is due." [2] *Black's Law Dictionary* defines "unliquidated debt" as "not assertained in amount; not determined; remaining unsettled * * a claim or debt will be * * * unliquidated if it is in dispute as to the proper amount." [3]

The general rule is that part payment of a liquidated debt (a settled, undisputed debt) will not serve as consideration for a promise to forget the balance of the debt (i. e., a promise to discharge the whole debt) or for any other promise. The debtor who makes part payment suffers no legal detriment because he or she is already obligated to pay the full amount owing. And the creditor who receives part payment incurs no legal benefit because he or she is already entitled to receive payment in full. By way of example, suppose that Linda Thompson goes to the J. C. Dollar Department Store and charges merchandise for $245.-00. There is no dispute about the fairness or accuracy of the charges or the quality of the merchandise, and Linda admittedly owes J. C. Dollar the full $245.-00. At the end of the month, when Linda's bill for the merchandise arrives, Linda makes out a check in the amount of $200.00 to the J. C. Dollar Department Store. On the back of the check, where the store must indorse (sign its name), Linda writes the following: "Indorsement of this check constitutes an acceptance of this check as full payment for all amounts owing and serves as consideration for a promise by the J. C. Dollar Department Store to forget the balance owing and accept $200.00 as full payment." Despite these words on the back of the check, the J. C. Dollar Department Store can indorse and cash the check, and still proceed against Linda for the balance owing. There is simply no consideration for the store's "promise" to forget the balance.

2. Henry Campbell Black, *Black's Law Dictionary*, Revised Fourth Edition, West Publishing Co., 1968, p. 1,079.

3. Ibid, p. 1,076.

UNILATERAL CONTRACT

Promise #1

| J. C. Dollar Department Store is the promisor | promises to forget → | Linda Thompson is the promisee |

the balance of $45.00 owing on a liquidated debt

in return for the act of
making a part payment
($200) of the liquidated debt

L. v. J. C. D.

to enforce promise #1
(promise to forget the balance of $45.00)

While there appears to be mutual assent because J. C. Dollar has endorsed the check, thus accepting Linda's offer to pay $200 for the $245 liquidated debt,

NO CONSIDERATION

the second element necessary for a valid contract is not present—

there is no consideration for the promise.

Part payment is no detriment to Linda (the promisee of J. C. Dollar's promise to forget the balance), nor is it a benefit to J. C. Dollar since the store is already entitled to $245.

Now suppose that, in addition to making part payment of the liquidated debt, Linda does something extra that she is not already legally obligated to do with the intent that the something serve as consideration for J. C. Dollar's promise to forget the balance of the debt. Here, Linda suffers a legal detriment, J. C. Dollar receives a legal benefit, and legal consideration for J. C. Dollar's promise exists. Obviously, the motivation or bargain element will not be present if the debtor adds something negligible and valueless (e. g., a debtor who says, "Here is part payment, and, oh, have a cigar on me"). The added "something" must be understood to constitute consideration for the creditor's promise to forget the balance of the debt owing. Additional acts that will serve as consideration include:

(1) Part payment prior to maturity of the debt (i. e., part payment ear-

lier than is called for by the terms of the credit agreement);

(2) Part payment at a different place than is called for under the terms of the agreement;

(3) Part payment coupled with the giving of something else to the creditor, such as a book, painting, tool, or other item;

(4) Part payment in a medium other than money (e. g., by transferring to the creditor corporate stock worth 2/3rds of the debt owing);

(5) Part payment at the creditor's direction to a person other than the person listed in the credit agreement; and

(6) Part payment by a person other than the debtor (this is a detriment to that person).

It should also be pointed out that one of the UCC exceptions to common law consideration may come into play in the area of part payment of a liquidated debt so as to make it impossible for the creditor to recover the balance of the debt. You will recall that Section 1–107 of the Code provides that "any claim or right arising out of an alleged breach can be discharged in whole or in part by a written waiver or renunciation signed and delivered by the aggrieved party." Thus, insofar as liquidated debts arising out of the sale of goods are concerned, if the creditor signs and delivers to the debtor a written statement promising that he or she will forget the balance of the debt in exchange for part payment, the debtor will be completely discharged by part payment even though he or she unquestionably owes the full amount of the debt. While the UCC exception applies only to debts arising out of the sale of goods, statutes and common law in a few states have extended this same result to liquidated debts of all kinds.

In contrast to the rules regarding part payment of a *liquidated* debt, part payment of an *unliquidated* debt will always serve as consideration for the creditor's promise to forget the balance of the debt. An unliquidated debt is a debt disputed in good faith by the debtor. Because there is a bona fide dispute as to the amount owing, no duty to pay arises until the dispute is settled. It follows that whenever the debtor pays even a part of the disputed amount, the debtor suffers a legal detriment, the creditor receives a legal benefit, and there is consideration for the creditor's promise to forget the balance. Of course, the dispute must be bona fide—a debtor cannot "convert" a liquidated debt into an unliquidated one by inventing a dispute. If the debtor does not truly disagree with the charges or find the merchandise or other subject matter of the contract faulty, the debt is not unliquidated.

For example, suppose that a party goes to a doctor, lawyer, CPA, plumber, or watch repairer, but later refuses to pay the bill for the services because he or she feels that the charges are too high (they appear to exceed the usual and fair market value of such services). The debt is unliquidated. If the debtor makes part payment of the debt as settlement in full, and the creditor accepts the payment, the debtor suffers a legal detriment, the creditor receives a legal benefit, and consideration exists for the creditor's promise to forget the balance of the debt. Of course, the creditor may refuse to accept part payment and go to court to obtain a judgment for the full amount of the debt. Any judgment the creditor obtains will be a liquidated debt, part payment of which will not serve as consideration for a promise by the creditor to forget the balance.

Or suppose that Linda Thompson purchases $245.00 worth of merchandise from the J. C. Dollar Department Store and later discovers that the merchandise is defective or not up to standard. Linda genuinely believes that the goods are not worth $245.00 and refuses to pay that amount. The debt is unliquidated, and any part payment accepted by J. C. Dollar as settlement in full will serve as valid consideration for the company's promise to forget the balance of the debt.

UNILATERAL CONTRACT

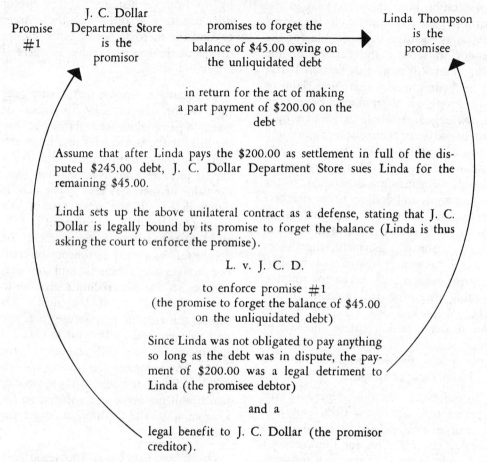

Promise #1

J. C. Dollar Department Store is the promisor

promises to forget the balance of $45.00 owing on the unliquidated debt

Linda Thompson is the promisee

in return for the act of making a part payment of $200.00 on the debt

Assume that after Linda pays the $200.00 as settlement in full of the disputed $245.00 debt, J. C. Dollar Department Store sues Linda for the remaining $45.00.

Linda sets up the above unilateral contract as a defense, stating that J. C. Dollar is legally bound by its promise to forget the balance (Linda is thus asking the court to enforce the promise).

L. v. J. C. D.

to enforce promise #1
(the promise to forget the balance of $45.00
on the unliquidated debt)

Since Linda was not obligated to pay anything so long as the debt was in dispute, the payment of $200.00 was a legal detriment to Linda (the promisee debtor)

and a

legal benefit to J. C. Dollar (the promisor creditor).

Thus, Linda will not have to pay the $45.00 balance.

What is promissory estoppel?

We stated previously that 99% plus of all contracts involve the bargain theory of consideration. Generally, if bargain theory consideration is not present, there is no consideration and no contract. Sometimes, however, an agreement will lack bargain theory consideration but still be enforceable because it meets the exact requirements of promissory estoppel, quasi contract, or public policy. Promissory estoppel is the subject matter of this section, while quasi contract and public policy are dealt with in the sections that immediately follow.

Normally, a person may reply to an assertion that he or she is bound to a par-

ticular promise with the defense that there is no consideration for the promise in the bargain theory sense. Generally, if the defense is correct, the party's promise will not be legally enforceable. But occasionally, because of the circumstances surrounding a promise, the promisor will be "estopped" from claiming that there is no consideration. To "estop" someone is to deny that person the ability to assert a particular fact. A person who is estopped from doing something is, in effect, "stopped" from acting in a particular way. To estop or stop someone from asserting a lack of consideration in the bargain theory sense is referred to in the law as *promissory estoppel*.

Promissory estoppel always involves a gratuitous promise. In other words, the party who makes the promise does not desire that the promisee accept an offer by performing an act or making a return promise. The promisor neither intends nor expects to receive anything in return for the promise, thus, neither element of bargain theory consideration is present. The motivation or bargain element is lacking because no bargain is intended; the legally sufficient or value element is also absent since the promisee is not expected to perform an act or make a return promise that will serve as valuable consideration for the gratuitous promise. Yet, because the promisee goes out and incurs a legal detriment in reliance upon the promise, the law concludes that the promisor who induced the result should be estopped from denying that there was consideration.

Generally speaking, there are four elements necessary for promissory estoppel:

(1) The promisor must make a gratuitous promise (one lacking bargain theory consideration); the promise must be such that a reasonably prudent person in the promisor's position could *foresee* that the promise might induce reliance by the promisee (i. e., the reliance must be foreseeable);

(2) The promisee must, in fact, rely upon the promise (i. e., take some action based on the promise), and the reliance must be reasonable under the circumstances;

(3) The promisee must suffer a *substantial economic* detriment as a result of the reliance (notice that the detriment required is a large monetary loss); and

(4) It must be necessary to enforce the promise to prevent injustice.

The *Restatement Second of the Law of Contracts* discusses promissory estoppel at Section 90, "Promise Reasonably Inducing Action or Forbearance".

The Restatement provides:

(1) A promise which the promisor should reasonably expect to induce action or forbearance on the part of the promisee or a third person and which does induce such action or forbearance is binding if injustice can be avoided only by enforcement of the promise. The remedy granted for breach may be limited as justice requires.

Comment: * * * This Section is often referred to in terms of "promissory estoppel," a phrase suggesting an extension of the doctrine of estoppel. Estoppel prevents a person from showing the truth contrary to a representation of fact made by him after another has relied on the representation.

* * *

Illustration:

1. A, knowing that B is going to college, promises B that A will give him $5,000 on completion of his course. B goes to college, and borrows and spends more than $5,000 for college expenses. When he has nearly completed his course, A notifies him of an intention to revoke the promise. A's promise is binding and B is entitled to payment on completion of the course without regard to whether his performance was "bargained for" * * *

* * * The principle of this Section is flexible. The promisor is affected only by reliance which he does or should foresee, and enforcement must be necessary to avoid injustice.

———

It is important to realize the if A in the above example had said to B, "I promise to give you $5,000 if you complete your college education" or "if you promise to complete you college education", there would be a valid contract supported by consideration in the bargain theory sense. B's completing his education or promising to do so would constitute legal detriment to B as the promisee of A's promise to pay. But where A states, as in the example above, "Well, I know you are going to college, and if you finish it up successfully I am going to give you $5,000," A is asking nothing in return for his or her promise, and it is a gratuitous or gift promise only. Such a promise is generally not enforceable because there is no consideration in the bargain theory sense. But where B, in foreseeable reliance upon the gift promise, incurs substantial expenses, promissory estoppel will come into play, and A will be estopped from denying a lack of bargain theory consideration in any suit by B to enforce the promise. The promise is enforceable despite the lack of bargain theory consideration because the reliance was foreseeable, it was reasonable under the circumstances, it resulted in substantial economic loss, and it can be remedied only by enforcement of the promise.

What is the meaning of quasi contract?

A *quasi contract* is really no contract at all in the sense of any mutual assent between the parties. Rather, it is an agreement implied in law to prevent unjust enrichment. The parties to a quasi contract reach no agreement and make no promises, but because one of the parties is substantially and unjustly benefited at the other's expense, the law imposes an obligation on the enriched party to restore the benefit. The typical example of a quasi contract arises where one party accidentally confers a benefit upon another who knowingly allows it to happen. For example, suppose that Lloyd Homeowner contracts with Frank the Painter to have Frank paint his house while Lloyd is gone on vacation. Frank shows up to

do the painting, but mistakenly paints the house next door to Lloyd's, a house belonging to Sheila Letithappen. The fact that Sheila observes Frank in the process of painting her house, but fails to voice any objection, places the situation into one of quasi contract. To prevent unjust enrichment of Sheila, the law will imply a promise on her part to pay for the reasonable value of the benefits received— even though there is no mutual assent and no consideration in the bargain theory sense. Of course, if Sheila is also gone on vacation and does not know that Frank is painting her house, the benefit rendered to Sheila is purely accidental, and Frank the Painter can recover nothing at all.

Quasi contract may also arise where one party mistakenly pays money to another or erroneously delivers goods to another who knows or has reason to know that a mistake has been made. Of course, if what one receives is worthless or confers no benefit, there can be no recovery to the other in quasi contract.

When will "public policy" require the performance of a promise?

In a few situations, *public policy* considerations will require the enforcement of a promise despite the lack of bargain theory consideration, promissory estoppel, quasi contract, or any of the UCC exceptions to the above. These situations include:

(1) *Debts barred by the statute of limitations.* A statute of limitations is a law passed by a legislature stating that unless a person brings his or her legal action (i. e., files the necessary papers to commence court action) within a certain period of time, the person is forever barred from suing on the case. Generally, a person must bring a tort action (an action based on socially unreasonable conduct) within two years of the injury. Contract actions must usually be initiated within five years of the making of the

contract, although the statute of limitations may be as short as three years in some states and as long as ten years in others. In some states, the type of contract entered into may determine the length of the limitations period.

Whatever the time period involved, once the statute of limitations on a contract debt has run, the creditor is forever barred from bringing legal action to enforce the debt. Occasionally, however, a debtor will promise to pay the debt even though the statute of limitations has run. The courts, in this case, generally hold that a promise to pay a contract debt barred by the statute of limitations (as opposed to a debt based on tort) is enforceable without consideration. The reasoning here is that, even though the remedy to enforce the debt may be barred, the debt itself remains. If the debtor acknowledges the debt and promises to pay it, public policy favors upholding the promise despite the lack of bargain theory consideration. And it is not necessary for the debtor to expressly promise to pay the debt in full: an enforceable promise to pay the entire debt will be inferred from any part payment accompanied by an acknowledgment of the debt. Generally, where the debtor does not make part payment, the promise to pay must be in a writing signed by the debtor or it will not be enforceable.

(2) *Debts barred by a bankruptcy proceeding.* The law of bankruptcy is discussed in detail in Ch. 26. For now, it is enough to know that when a debtor's total debts exceed his or her assets, a debtor may go through a bankruptcy proceeding and have most of his or her debts discharged. Once a debt has been discharged in bankruptcy, a debtor has no further obligation to pay it. It used to be that if the debtor expressly promised to pay the debt anyway, the promise (like an express or implied promise to pay a contract debt barred by the statute of limitations) would be enforceable without

consideration. However, that is no longer the law. The federal Bankruptcy Act of 1979 provides that a debt discharged in bankruptcy is completely extinguished, and a subsequent promise to pay the debt is not enforceable in the absence of consideration.

(3) *Promises to perform a voidable promise after a change in circumstances.* In Ch. 8, we discussed the difference between void and voidable and concluded that many promises and agreements are voidable at the option of one party. A promise or agreement may be voidable because of mistake, fraud, duress, undue influence (or, as we will learn in a later section of this chapter, because of an incapacity such as minority or insanity).

However, if the party with the option chooses to go through with the agreement after learning all the facts of the situation (e. g., after learning of the fraud or undue influence) or after attaining the age of majority (in the case of a minor), the party's promise to affirm the contract will be legally binding without new consideration. Because of the change in circumstances (the party's full knowledge or his or her reaching legal age), the reasons for voidability are no longer present, and if the party promises to go through with the agreement, public policy favors upholding the promise despite the lack of bargain theory consideration.

In contrast, a promise to go through with a void agreement is never binding in the absence of consideration (i. e., in the absence of a new, valid contract). A void agreement is a nullity and no one can be bound by it—later promises notwithstanding.

(4) *Promises to give up the benefit of a condition.* Contractual conditions are discussed in Ch. 10. However, it should be said here that where a promisor who is under a duty to perform only *if* a condition occurs (a condition precedent) or only *until* a condition occurs (a condition

subsequent) promises to forego the benefit of the condition and to perform the promise as though it were unconditional, the promisor's promise will be binding despite the lack of new consideration in the bargain theory sense. For example, in the case of Home Fire Insurance Co. v. Kuhlman, 58 Neb. 488, 78 N.E. 936 (1899), an insurance company insured a building against fire loss, promising to pay in the event of loss only on the condition that the building would not be left vacant for longer than a certain period of time. The company later agreed to forego the benefit of the condition. Its promise was held binding despite a lack of consideration when the property was subsequently damaged by fire and the stated condition had occurred.

(5) *Charitable subscriptions.* A charitable subscription is a promise to contribute or make a donation to a charity. Charities generally solicit subscriptions when undertaking special and costly projects (e. g., building a new church or charitable hospital).

The general rule is that charitable subscription promises are enforceable without consideration in the bargain theory sense. Some courts say that bargain theory consideration exists, implying that each donor's promise is given in consideration for the other donors' promises. However, most courts acknowledge that charitable subscriptions are, in fact, gratuitous —motivated, not by the hope or expectation of receiving something in return, but by simple generosity.

Of course, if the charity, in reliance upon the promise, goes out and incurs substantial expenditures or actually begins construction, there is consideration in the promissory estoppel sense. But, even without reliance, most courts hold charitable subscriptions enforceable simply on the grounds of public policy. Such promises are binding despite the lack of bargain theory consideration,

promissory estoppel, quasi contract, or UCC statutory exception.

What is meant by a contract under seal?

At early common law, most contracts had to be "formally" made. A *formal contract* is one that must comply with certain formal requirements if it is to be enforceable; it is legally binding solely because of its form and requires no consideration.

The formal contract most frequently employed was the *contract under seal.* It required three things: a sufficient writing, a seal, and delivery.

A "sufficient writing" was one that identified the parties to the agreement and contained promises sufficiently definite so as to be capable of performance by the parties. The writing did not have to be signed. In fact, the contract under seal came into existence in Medieval England primarily because widespread illiteracy made authentication of written instruments by signing a virtual impossibility.

The writings were authenticated, instead, by seal—the second requirement of a contract under seal. The first seals were wax seals: hot wax was placed on the writing and an identifiable impression was made on the wax, usually with a signet ring. As time passed, less formality was required, and, ultimately, all that was necessary for a seal was any kind of impression on the paper, including the word "seal" itself or the letters "L.S." (standing for locus sigilli and meaning "the place of the seal"). In short, almost any method of indicating that a seal was intended would do. Frequently, the party's intent to enter into a sealed agreement was evidenced by the following words: "In witness whereof I have hereunto set my hand and seal."

Delivery, the third and final requirement, demanded intent to deliver the instrument coupled with physical transfer of possession.

Modernly, the old common law rule that a contract under seal needs no consideration to be binding has been changed by statute in most states. To begin with, the seal has never had any effect in Louisiana. And nine states have made seals wholly inoperative, including Arkansas, Illinois, Indiana, Minnesota, Nebraska, New York, Ohio, Utah, and Wyoming. Similarly, the Uniform Commercial Code has rendered the seal of no effect in any transaction involving the sale of personal property. And while several states which have abolished the seal provide by statute that any written promise is presumed to be supported by consideration, this presumption is rebuttable and may be overcome by evidence to the contrary. These states include Arizona, California, Idaho, Iowa, Kansas, Kentucky, Missouri, Montana, Nevada, North Dakota, Oklahoma, Tennessee, and Texas. Finally, two states, Mississippi and New Mexico, have passed statutes providing that all written contracts are like common law sealed instruments in that they need no consideration to be binding.

Thus, in most states, a sealed instrument must be supported by consideration in order to be legally binding and enforceable. While the existence of a seal may give rise to a presumption of consideration, the presumption is rebuttable and may be dispelled by evidence to the contrary. In about one-third of the states, the common law rule regarding contracts under seal has not been changed except insofar as commercial transactions under the UCC are concerned; in these states, contracts under seal involving personal services or real property are still legally enforceable without regard to consideration.

The most important remaining effect of contracts under seal is that, in many states, such contracts enjoy a longer statute of limitations than do other contracts. Thus, a party to a contract may generally bring suit to enforce its terms for a longer period of time if the contract is under seal. For example, in Alabama, Oregon, North Carolina, and Virginia, the statute of limitations on sealed instruments is 10 years; in Maryland and the District of Columbia, it is 12 years; in New Jersey, 16 years; and in several states, including Georgia, Maine, Massachusetts, South Carolina, Florida, and Wisconsin, the statute is a lengthy 20 years.

Pennsylvania alone has adopted the "Uniform Written Obligations Act" which permits a person to bind himself or herself to a gratuitous promise as follows.

The Act provides:

A written release or promise, hereafter made and signed by the person releasing or promising, shall not be invalid or unenforceable for lack of consideration, if the writing also contains an additional express statement, in any form of language, that the signer intends to be legally bound.

What are recognizances and penal bonds?

Today, in addition to contracts under seal, we have the following formal contracts: negotiable instruments and documents, letters of credit, recognizances, and penal bonds. Negotiable instruments and documents are dealt with in Chapters 12 through 15; letters of credit are considered in Ch. 19. Recognizances and penal bonds are discussed hereafter.

A *recognizance* is a formal acknowledgment in court by a recognizor (person making the acknowledgment) that he or she is bound to make a certain payment unless a specified condition is performed. The acknowledgment is made in order to create a binding obligation that will serve as security for the specified act. Frequently, the specified act or condition is the subsequent appearance in court of a recognizor who has been charged with a crime (often referred to as releasing a person on his or her own recognizance). If the recognizor later appears as required, the debt is void. Of course, anyone can make a recognizance—not just an accused criminal. A person makes a recognizance anytime he or she appears in court and makes an oral or written acknowledgment of an indebtedness so as to create a binding obligation as security for a performance. The performance secured may be the furnishing of support to a dependent or the bringing of a civil case in court. Again, upon performance of the condition or act, the debt or obligation becomes void.

A *penal bond* is a formal contract that is similar to a recognizance. It differs from a recognizance in that the acknowledged obligation is put into writing, signed, sealed, and delivered to the court; the performance secured is that a person charged with crime will appear in court at the proper time.

Apart from contracts under seal, negotiable instruments and documents, letters of credit, recognizances, and penal bonds, contracts are considered informal agreements. They are enforceable regardless of form so long as mutual assent, consideration, capacity, and legality are present.

What is the third element necessary for a valid contract (i. e., what is contractual capacity)?

Contractual capacity refers to the power that a person normally has to enter into a contract. Occasionally, however, a person is either totally or (as is more often the case) partially incapacitated (i. e., without the power to contract). For example, a person who is so infirm or disabled that he or she cannot understand the nature of an agreement is totally incapacitated, as is a mentally disturbed person whose affairs are handled by a court appointed guardian. Any "agreement" entered into by a totally incapacitated person is void (although quasi contract is sometimes utilized in such cases to prevent unjust enrichment).

The agreement of a partially incapacitated person, on the other hand, is not void but voidable. The partially incapacitated person (a person with some, but not full understanding of the nature of the agreement) may elect either to rescind the agreement or to ratify it.

The *Restatement, Second, Law of Contracts* provides as follows at Section 18 "Capacity to Contract".

The Restatement provides:

(1) No one can be bound by contract who has not legal capacity to incur at least voidable contractual duties. Capacity to contract may be partial and its existence in respect of a particular transaction may depend upon the nature of the transaction or upon other circumstances.

(2) A natural person who manifests assent to a transaction has full legal capacity to incur contractual duties thereby unless he is

(a) under guardianship, or

(b) an infant, or

(c) mentally ill or defective, or

(d) intoxicated.

––––––––

How is capacity affected by guardianship?

A guardianship is a legal relationship created by the courts to protect and manage the person and/or property of a living person who is too young, too old, too ill, or too incompetent to handle his or her own affairs. The party with the incapacity is called the *ward*; the party appointed to look out for the ward's interests is called the *guardian*.

Generally speaking, the courts may appoint a guardian for any spendthrift or other incompetent. A *spendthrift* is a person whose excessive drinking, idleness, gambling, or debauchery so spends, wastes, or lessens his or her estate that the spendthrift's family is exposed to want or suffering. An *incompetent* is a person who is personally unable to care for his or her property for any reason, including mental illness, advanced age, or disease.

A special kind of guardian, termed a *conservator,* may be appointed upon the petition of the ward personally. Here, the ward is mentally competent but feels unable, whether for physical, mental, or emotional reasons, to properly care for his or her business or property.

A guardian's or conservator's duty is to protect, preserve, and manage the ward's estate and to apply the proceeds of the estate toward the proper care of the ward and his or her legal dependents. The guardian's duties continue so long as the ward remains incapacitated; the conservator's duties persist until the ward successfully petitions the court to permit him or her to resume management of his or her own property. Both guardians and conservators are closely supervised by the probate judge to ensure that the ward's property is adequately protected.

With regard to contractual capacity, guardianship proceedings are considered by law to give public notice of the ward's incapacity. It follows that any subsequent agreement made with the ward personally will be void even though the party dealing with the ward has no actual knowledge of the guardianship. However, the party dealing with the ward may be able to reclaim the actual merchandise or other items received by the ward if the property can be found. And if the party has furnished the ward with necessaries (e. g., food, clothing, or lodging), the party may be able to recover the fair value of the property from the ward's guardian on a quasi contract basis.

Suppose that a guardian is appointed over the ward's person only and not over his or her property. Or say that no guardian is appointed and the ward merely voluntarily commits himself or herself to a mental hospital. Here, the rules making the ward's personal agreements void do not apply. Of course, in such circumstances, the ward may be considered partially disabled such that his or her agreements will be voidable.

How does mental illness or defect affect contractual capacity in the absence of a court appointed guardian?

As we learned in Ch. 7, the first element necessary for a valid contract is mutual assent. Mutual assent requires an intent to make an agreement—unless a party can form the necessary intent, there can be no mutual assent. Obviously, a person who is extremely physically or mentally disabled may be unable to form the assent required, and so any attempted agreement by the party will be void.

Yet mental illness or defect may be far less serious than the extreme disability that renders a person unable to comprehend anything. A person may have some understanding of a transaction and some ability to form the required intent to contract and yet still not be mentally competent. If, because of mental illness or defect, such a party enters into an agreement, the agreement is voidable to the incompetent party. Generally, the test is whether the transaction and its attendant results are such that a reasonably prudent person would have entered into the agreement. If the answer is no, the agreement is voidable.

Where the agreement is voidable, the incompetent party, upon regaining full capacity, may affirm or disaffirm the contract. If the party does not regain full capacity, but instead, a guardian is appointed to care for his or her property, the guardian may affirm or disaffirm.

And if the incompetent party dies, his or her personal representative (see Ch. 30) may exercise the power of affirmance or disaffirmance.

The *Restatement, Second, Law of Contracts* states the law regarding mental illness or defect as follows.

The Restatement provides:

Section 18C. Mental Illness or Defect

(1) A person incurs only voidable contractual duties by entering into a transaction if by reason of mental illness or defect

  (a) he is unable to understand in a reasonable manner the nature and consequences of the transaction, or

  (b) he is unable to act in a reasonable manner in relation to the transaction and the other party has reason to know of his condition.

(2) Where the contract is made on fair terms and the other party is without knowledge of the mental illness, or defect, the power of avoidance under subsection (1) terminates to the extent that the contract has been so performed in whole or in part or the circumstances have so changed that avoidance would be inequitable. In such a case a court may grant relief on such equitable terms as the situation requires.

Does intoxication at the time of entering into an agreement affect contractual capacity?

As with all other guardianships, if a guardian is appointed for a habitual drunkard or drug addict, the appointment serves as public notice of the ward's incapacity, and any agreement subsequently entered into by the ward personally is void. If no guardian is appointed, but the party's drunkenness or drugged condition at the time of entering into a contract is so extreme that there is no possibility of intent to contract or mutual assent, the agreement again is void.

However, if the party is not so intoxicated (on either alcohol or narcotics) as to prevent *any* manifestation of mutual assent, the contract will be valid unless the other party knows or has reason to know that the partially intoxicated party is unable, because of his or her drunken or drugged condition, to reasonably understand the nature and consequences of the transaction or to act in a reasonable manner with regard to the transaction. If the other party knows or has reason to know these things, the agreement is voidable.

Intoxication thus renders an agreement voidable only where the other party to the contract knows or should know that intoxication has prevented the partially intoxicated party from truly understanding or consenting to the agreement. This differs from the area of mental illness or defect where the mentally incompetent party's lack of understanding will render the agreement voidable without regard to the other party's awareness of his or her mental condition. However, it should be pointed out that the competent party's equitable and quasi contract remedies are the same whether mental illness or intoxication is involved.

What are the rules regarding minors and contractual capacity?

To protect young people from the often adverse legal consequences of their actions, the law has developed a number of special rules governing minors (i. e., legal "infants") and their contracts. These special rules may be summarized as follows:

(1) *Who is an infant?* At common law, a legal infant was any person under

the age of 21 years (the age of "majority" or adulthood). Modernly, many states have lowered the age of majority by statute, commonly terminating legal infancy at the age of 18 (e. g., Kentucky and Oregon), 19 (e. g., Alaska), or 20 (e. g., Hawaii).

The chief characteristic of legal infancy or minority is that a minor has no contractual capacity. In some states, a minor who gets married acquires adult status and contractual capacity by virtue of the marriage. Generally, however, the fact that a minor is emancipated (i. e., on his or her own and outside of parental claim or control) does not confer contractual capacity or adulthood upon the minor, although a few states such as Oregon do provide a procedure whereby a child may be declared legally emancipated by a court and thereby receive contractual capacity.

(2) *What is the power of disaffirmance?* The general rule is that agreements are voidable. Again, this means that a minor may either avoid or ratify his or her contracts. It should be stressed that the power of avoidance resides only in the minor (or his or her personal representative in the case of a deceased minor): the adult who enters into the transaction with the minor has no power to avoid.

No particular language or conduct is required to disaffirm an agreement; the disaffirmance may be either oral or in writing. And the disaffirmance may be made at any time prior to ratification, even during the infancy of the minor— with one exception. Most courts hold that a minor cannot disaffirm his or her conveyance of real property until after the minor has reached the age of majority. The reason for the exception is that the transfer of the real property may be to the minor's benefit. Thus, the law seeks to protect the minor's interests by providing him or her with a longer period of time for determining whether to disaffirm or ratify.

Where a minor disaffirms a contract, the agreement is treated, for many purposes, as though it were void from the beginning. For example, suppose that a minor, upon attaining majority, disaffirms his or her transfer of real property. Even if the minor's transferee has already resold the property to a bona fide purchaser who took the land without knowledge of the minor's prior interest, the minor may still recover the property from the BFP. However, there is a different result where the subject matter of the contract is the sale of goods. The Uniform Commercial Code provides at Section 2–403 "Power to Transfer; Good Faith Purchase of Goods": "A person with voidable title has power to transfer a good title to a good faith purchaser for value."

Once made, a disaffirmance is irrevocable.

(3) *What is the power of ratification?* Ratification is the opposite of avoidance and results in a legally binding contract. A minor cannot ratify an agreement until he or she has attained the age of majority; at that time, the minor may ratify by effectively surrendering his or her power of avoidance. Where a minor attempts to ratify while still a minor, the ratification itself is subject to disaffirmance, and is therefore ineffective.

Upon reaching the age of majority, a minor may ratify a contract (i. e., surrender his or her power of avoidance) in three ways:

(a) *By failing to disaffirm within a reasonable time after reaching adulthood.* Generally, a "reasonable time" corresponds to the statute of limitations time period for bringing suit on the contract (i. e., the minor can disaffirm until all court action on the contract is barred). However, if the minor's failure to disaffirm earlier results in substantial injustice to the other party, the delay will be deemed unreasonable, and ratification of the contract will be found.

(b) *By expressly ratifying the contract.* Any words indicating the minor's intent to be bound will be a sufficient ratification. While statutes in some states require a written ratification, an oral ratification is effective in most states to make the contract binding.

(c) *By acting in a manner that amounts to ratification.* Just as ratification may be implied from a minor's failure to disaffirm within a reasonable time after reaching adulthood, ratification may also be implied from the minor's conduct upon becoming an adult. If the minor, upon attaining majority, retains, uses, and enjoys property received under the contract, he or she will be held to have impliedly ratified the contract.

A ratification, like a disaffirmance, is irrevocable.

(4) *Does a minor who disaffirms have an obligation to restore what he or she has received under the voidable transaction?* A minor who disaffirms is legally obligated to return any property still in his or her possession that he or she received under the contract. If the minor no longer has the property, or if it is impractical for the minor to return what he or she does have, the minor is not obligated to return the property or to compensate the other party to the contract in any way. This is so even where the minor has squandered the property or negligently destroyed it.

The minor's obligation is thus one of *restoration in specie* (restoration of whatever actual property is left in whatever condition it is in). The majority of courts permit the minor to recover whatever he or she has parted with under the contract simply by making restoration in specie—even where the minor returns badly damaged property or no property at all! A minority of courts offset the minor's recovery by the fair value of the minor's use of the property during his or her period of possession and/or by the amount of depreciation resulting to the property during that time. Among these states, a few offset the minor's recovery only if the minor misrepresented his or her age in entering into the contract.

(5) *Does it make any difference that a minor commits a tort by reason of his or her agreement?* While a minor is generally not obligated on his or her contracts (i. e., a minor may avoid his or her agreements), a minor is liable for his or her torts. Frequently, a minor who enters into a voidable contract commits a tort in the process.

First, a minor may in breaching a voidable agreement also commit a tort. For example, suppose that an adult takes his or her automobile to a minor who claims that he or she can service and repair the car. In the process of servicing and repairing the car, the minor negligently puts only part of the engine back together, carelessly forgetting to replace an essential part. The minor, in this case, has breached the contract; however, the minor has a legal right to disaffirm the contract and avoid liability for the breach. Yet the act of breaching the contract also constitutes the tort of negligence: the minor had a duty to repair the car properly, the minor breached the duty, and the minor's breach of duty resulted in damage to the other party's automobile. Can the minor be held liable for the tort even though he or she cannot be held liable on the contract? The answer is no. It is a rule of law that if the result of holding a minor liable for a tort is to achieve the same effect as enforcing the contract, the tort action will not be allowed. The tort, in such a case, is said to be "interwoven" with the contract and is simply not actionable. In the example, allowing the injured party to recover from the minor for his or her negligence would be tantamount to enforcing the contract. The tort is "interwoven" with the contract and is not actionable.

Second, a minor may misrepresent his or her age in order to persuade an adult to enter into an agreement (adults frequently refuse to contract with minors because of the right of minors to disaffirm). A minor who induces an adult to enter into a contract by lying about his or her age commits fraud in the inducement, which, as you know from Ch. 8, constitutes the tort of deceit. While the minor's misrepresentation of age will not prevent the minor from disaffirming the contract, nearly all courts hold that the tort of deceit is not interwoven with the contract, but is an independent, actionable tort. The reasoning here is that the tort occurred as an inducing factor prior to the making of the contract, and that the payment of damages for deceit does not result in an indirect enforcement of the contract itself. So while the minor may disaffirm the contract, he or she will still be liable for tortious deceit.

(6) *Are there any contracts that a minor cannot disaffirm?* A minor cannot disaffirm:

(a) A recognizance or penal bond;

(b) In the case of a male minor, a contract to support his illegitimate child;

(c) Frequently, educational loan contracts, life insurance contracts (to the extent that paid premiums cannot be recovered upon disaffirmance), certain banking transactions, and contracts for military enlistment.

(7) *Are there any special rules regarding a minor's necessaries?* A minor is liable in quasi contract for "necessaries" that he or she contracts for and receives. Generally, where the necessaries have yet to be furnished to the minor, he or she may still disaffirm the agreement and avoid paying for the items. This is because the nature of the minor's liability is quasi contractual: because the minor has been unjustly enriched at another's expense, the law imposes an obligation on the minor to restore whatever benefits he or she has received; if the minor has received nothing, he or she has nothing to restore.

And because the remedy is in quasi contract, the minor is not liable for the contract price of the necessaries, but only for the reasonable value of the items. Reasonable value refers to the average price in the community for such items—it does not refer to what a particular merchant or party is asking for the property. Thus, a party who furnishes necessaries to a minor may well lose a part of his or her profit.

What is a "necessary" depends upon the minor's particular circumstances in life. Generally, a minor will not be liable for a necessary unless it is a "necessary in fact", meaning that the item is essential to the minor's livelihood or well being and the minor's parent or guardian refuses to supply it. If the minor contracts for a "necessary" that his or her parent or guardian would have been willing to provide, the item is not "necessary in fact" and the minor may disaffirm the contract, the same as any other.

In addition, the minor must personally contract for the necessaries in order to be held personally liable on the contract. Obviously, an emancipated minor will personally contract for more necessaries than will a minor who lives at home with his or her parents; and a married minor will personally contract for even more. But whether the minor is emancipated or dependent, if a party furnishes necessaries to the minor on the basis of an agreement made with someone other than the minor, the minor is under no legal obligation to pay for the property.

Because each minor's necessaries differ, it is obviously impossible to inclusively list what is or is not a necessary. A few examples, however, might be helpful. Food, shelter, and clothing, for instance, are obviously necessaries; an automobile sometimes is, but usually is not; medical services usually are; legal services incurred in defense of criminal or tort charges are certainly necessaries, but legal services incurred in defense of property rights may not be (with regard to property rights, it is generally held that a guardian must be appointed to protect these rights and to contract with an attorney where necessary). With regard to education, education through the secondary level is uniformly considered necessary; a trade school education is usually deemed necessary; but a college education is generally deemed not necessary.

What is the fourth element necessary for a valid contract (i. e., what is legality of contract)?

Even where mutual assent, consideration, and contractual capacity are present, there may still be no contract because the subject matter of the agreement is illegal in light of statute or public policy. For example, suppose that Mary Embezzler enters into an agreement with Lee Hitman wherein Mary promises to pay Lee $10,000 in return for Lee's promise to kill Mary's partner, Walter. The first three elements necessary for a contract appear to be present in the example: there is a valid offer and acceptance (mutual assent); there is a change of position in the making of the promises (consideration); and both parties appear to be mentally competent and of majority age (capacity). However, if Lee carries out his promise and murders Walter, it would not only be ridiculous, but it would be terrible law to permit Lee to go to court to obtain enforcement of Mary's promise to pay him $10,000. Obviously, a fourth element—legality—must also be present if the agreement is to be a valid contract. In the example, there is a blatant absence of legality, and the agreement is invalid.

Of course, there are far more subtle forms of illegality, and we will explore many of them in the remaining sections of this chapter. However, before we move on, it should be pointed out that it is improper to refer to an illegal agreement as an illegal contract: if the agreement is illegal, there is no contract at all, thus the proper terminology is a void agreement or a void or illegal bargain.

What agreements are typically held to be illegal bargains?

The following agreements are typically held to be illegal bargains:

(1) *Crimes.* Any agreement calling for the commission of a crime is obviously an illegal bargain. Thus, any agreement to commit murder, larceny, burglary, robbery, forgery, kidnapping, etc. is void.

(2) *Obstruction of justice.* Agreements to obstruct the administration of justice are also illegal bargains. Frequently, such agreements are crimes in themselves, including agreements to commit the following offenses against the state and public order:

(a) *Bribe giving.* Generally, it is a felony (a major criminal offense) to offer to confer a pecuniary benefit upon a public servant (including a juror) with the intent to influence that servant's vote, opinion, judgment, or exercise of discretion.

(b) *Bribe receiving.* A public servant who intentionally solicits or accepts a pecuniary benefit designed to influence his or her vote, opinion, judgment, or exercise of discretion as a public servant is also guilty of a felony (usually with a possible punishment of up to 10 years in prison).

(c) *Perjury.* A person commits perjury when he or she intentionally makes a false sworn statement in regard to a material issue. Perjury is a felony and usually carries a five year prison sentence.

(d) *Escape.* An agreement to help another escape from jail is also an illegal bargain.

(e) *Interfering with the legal process.* Bribing a witness is a felony as is tampering with physical evidence or public records.

(f) *Hindering prosecution.*[4] A person hinders prosecution if, with intent to hinder the apprehension, prosecution, conviction, or punishment of a person who has committed a felony, or with intent to assist such a person in profiting or benefiting from commission of the crime, he or she:

(1) Harbors or conceals the person; or

(2) Warns the person of impending discovery or apprehension; or

(3) Provides or aids in providing the person with money, transportation, weapons, disguises, or other means of avoiding discovery or recapture; or

(4) Prevents or obstructs by force, intimidation, or deception, anyone performing an act that might lead to the person's discovery or apprehension; or

(5) Conceals, alters, destroys, or otherwise suppresses any physical evidence that might aid in the person's discovery or apprehension; or

(6) Aids the person in securing or protecting the proceeds of his or her crime.

Even where an agreement to obstruct the administration of justice does not itself constitute a crime, the agreement is invalid and will not give rise to a contract. The following examples are illustrative:

(a) *A promise not to press charges.* An employer's promise not to press criminal charges against an employee-embezzler who agrees to return the embezzled money is not legally binding. The promise not to press charges is an illegal bargain, contrary to public policy, and, even if the employee returns the money, the employer is free to cooperate in prosecution of the criminal.

(b) *Champerty.* An illegal bargain, "champerty" occurs where one person pays another's costs and expenses in bringing a case to court with the understanding that if the party bringing the case is successful, the party putting up the money will share in the proceeds. "Maintenance", an agreement to pay the costs and expenses of legal action without sharing in the proceeds is also an illegal bargain unless the agreement is entered into out of purely charitable motives or in order to answer a legal question on which a right or duty of the maintaining party depends. The rules regarding champerty and maintenance are designed to prevent people from intermeddling in other people's legal problems and encouraging them to sue.

(c) *Witness fees.* Even an agreement to pay a witness more than the regular witness fee allowed by law is an illegal bargain. The idea is that if a party is permitted to pay a witness more than is allowed by law, the witness will be encouraged to give false testimony on the party's behalf. This rule does not apply to an expert witness (one who may give his or her opinion in court) or to a witness who is outside the court's jurisdiction (such a witness must travel a greater distance and so is entitled to a higher fee). Even here, however, the witness fee must not be made contingent upon the success or outcome of the case.

(d) *Finder's fees.* A lawyer's agreement to pay someone money to find the

---

4. Hindering prosecution and obstructing justice were the major offenses that gave rise to the Watergate scandal. You will recall that officials high in the Nixon Administration made substantial efforts to cover up the break-in of the Democratic National Headquarters. Several of the officials were tried and convicted of crimes involving the "obstruction of justice".

lawyer clients is also an illegal agreement.

(e) *Contingent fees.* A contingent fee (a payment arrangement wherein an attorney takes a percentage of any recovery in a legal action) is not an illegal bargain so long as the attorney does not promise to pay the expenses of the lawsuit. However, it is illegal for a lawyer who is handling a case on a contingent fee basis to provide that his or her client cannot settle the case without the attorney's consent.

It is generally also illegal for a lawyer to handle a criminal, tax, or domestic relations (divorce, annulment, etc.) case on a contingent fee basis.

(f) *Settlement of disputes.* Usually, a provision in an agreement providing that all contract disputes must be settled in the courts of a particular state are not unlawful unless the purpose of the provision is to prevent one of the parties from being able to file suit (for example, where it would be extremely inconvenient for the party to bring suit in the state designated). Where a party accepts such a provision because of an inferior bargaining position, the provision is unlawful; and where the state designated has no real relation to the agreement (from the standpoint of either plaintiff or defendant), the provision is unconscionable.

(g) *Arbitration clauses.* Under modern statutes, a provision in a contract providing for arbitration of disputes without going to court is lawful. Earlier, such provisions were deemed unlawful because they were held to interfere with the jurisdiction of the courts.

(3) *Torts.* An agreement to commit a tort (any socially unreasonable conduct) is void as an illegal bargain. Thus, an agreement made with the intention of defrauding third parties is illegal (e. g., an agreement to use false or deceptive labels so as to deceive purchasers,

or an agreement to induce others to breach their contracts). And remember, most crimes also involve torts. Thus an agreement to commit a crime is usually an agreement to commit a tort as well.

(4) *Exculpatory clauses.* Sometimes, one party to a contract agrees as part of the contract not to hold the other party liable for his or her misconduct. Such a contract provision is called an exculpatory clause and is generally legal if it pertains only to the party's negligent misconduct, and if the party protected by the clause is other than a public service such as a common carrier (as will be seen in Ch. 16, common carriers such as trucks, trains, and jumbo jets in the business of transporting goods for the general public without discrimination and for compensation cannot exempt themselves from liability for their negligence).

However, where the exculpatory clause seeks to absolve the party from liability for his or her willful misconduct, the clause is illegal and void. The clause is also illegal and void if it is "forced" upon a person in an inferior bargaining position (e. g., where a landlord inserts such a provision into a lease agreement in an effort to escape liability for his or her negligence in maintaining the leased premises).

(5) *Usury.* Statutes in every state establish the maximum rate of interest (i. e., the highest annual rate) that may be paid on a loan at somewhere between 7 to 10%. A person who lends money at a rate of interest higher than that allowed by statute is guilty of usury, and usury is illegal.

Of course, there are many exceptions to the stated maximum rate. For example, most statutes provide that small loan associations and other financial institutions may make small loans at higher rates of interest because of the greater risk involved. And the Uniform Consumer Credit Code (UCCC), which has been adopted by approximately ten states, permits a maximum interest rate as high as 18% on home mortgages.

Originally, usury rules applied only to the loan of money and did not apply to the sale of goods or real estate on credit because there was no loan involved (of course, if the purchase was financed by a bank rather than by the credit seller, the transaction was a loan and thus subject to the usury laws). Sellers were thus free to sell to cash buyers at one price, and to installment purchasers who paid over time at a much higher price—a price that would be usurious were usury laws applied. For example, a car dealer might sell a car for $5,000 to a cash purchaser, and for $7,500 to a purchaser who paid in installments over a period of one year. As far as the installment purchaser is concerned, this is an interest charge of 50%. To remedy this situation, many states have adopted retail installment sales laws (like the UCCC) which provide that, even though there is no true loan, but rather a purchase of property on time through installments, there is still a maximum that can be charged because of the time-price differential. In most cases, the maximum is higher than the established maximum rate of interest (i. e., consumer credit sales are another exception to the stated maximum rate). For example, the UCCC permits interest up to 36% on the first $300, 21% on the next $700, and 15% annually on any excess over $1,000 *or* an alternative of 18% on the entire amount. And in the case of revolving charge accounts, the UCCC allows a maximum interest rate of 2% per month on the first $500 and 1½% per month on any excess. While most states have similar laws, the details differ, so it is essential to check the statutes in your own state.

Where the stated maximum interest rate does apply, it is not usurious for the lender to deduct all the interest in advance as a discount. Nor is it illegal usury to require the borrower to pay a penalty fee if he or she pays off the debt prior to maturity. However, service charges or placement fees are usually added to the express amount of interest in determining whether the rate of interest is usurious. And so are points (charges added to the fee at times when money is difficult to find in our economy, usually one or more percentages of the principal amount of the loan). Some courts hold that "late charges" must be included as part of interest; others do not. Again, it is essential to check your own state's laws with regard to what is included in interest and what is not.

However, there are some laws that all lenders must observe. The federal Consumer Credit Protection Act of 1968, also called "Truth in Lending", requires all lenders to spell out their finance charges. The purpose of "Truth in Lending" is to inform borrowers and customers of the cost of credit so that they may compare these costs with those of other credit sources. The federal law fixes no maximum or minimum credit charge (this is left up to the individual states), but it does require disclosure of important credit terms, including the finance charge and the annual percentage rate. These two terms tell a customer, at a glance, how much he or she will be charged for the credit, and what the relative cost of the credit is in percentage terms. The federal law applies to any individual or organization that extends or arranges credit that is repayable in more than four installments or for which a finance charge is or may be payable. The law applies to banks, savings and loan associations, department stores, credit card issuers, credit unions, automobile dealers, consumer finance companies, residential mortgage brokers, hospitals, and craftsmen (e. g., plumbers and electricians), as well as doctors, dentists, and other professionals. (See Appendix A for more information on Truth in Lending and consumer protection.)

The effect of an agreement in violation of usury statutes differs from state to state. In some states, the lender forfeits all interest on the loan; in other states, he or she forfeits only interest in excess of the lawful maximum rate. And in a few states, if the lender charges more than twice the maximum rate of interest allowable, the lender forfeits both interest and principal: not only is the borrower's debt cancelled, but the lender must return any payments the borrower has made. Finally, some states permit the borrower to recover a penalty from the lender, two to three times the amount of the usurious interest charged.

It should be pointed out prior to moving on to gambling that, in many states, corporations are not allowed to raise the defense of usury. In nearly half the states, there is no limit on the rate of interest that may be charged on loans to corporations.

(6) *Gambling.* In most states, most forms of gambling are illegal. Thus, if Abe Friendly promises to pay Charlotte Freeshooter $100 if the Los Angeles Dodgers win the National League Pennant in return for Charlotte's promise to pay Abe $100 if the Dodgers do not win the Pennant, there is no contract because the agreement is a bet and an illegal bargain. The public policy against gambling is that gambling corrupts people and prompts them to squander away their livelihoods, thus making it necessary for the gambler and his or her dependents to go on welfare. It is also believed that gambling introduces undesirable elements into the community such as organized crime.

Generally speaking, gambling requires three things: (1) a prize; (2) the taking of a chance; and (3) the giving of something of value by way of consideration. The prize aspect is satisfied if nei-

ther party has any interest apart from the gambling as to the result of the fortuitous circumstance determining whether one wins or loses. The prize aspect distinguishes gambling from an insurance contract wherein a party does have an interest in the fortuitous event prior to the making of the contract (insurance contracts are discussed in Ch. 11). Thus, if Abe Friendly buys fire insurance to protect himself against the fortuitous event of having his house burn down, the agreement is not a gambling transaction because Abe Friendly has an insurable interest in the house. However, if Abe takes out fire insurance on his neighbor's house, Abe would be gambling on the destruction of the house (having himself no insurable interest in the property), thus the agreement would be an illegal gambling transaction and not a contract.

Suppose that Abe Friendly pays a $50 entrance fee to compete for a prize in a competition of skills, such as a rodeo, bridge tournament, or golf match. Even if the competitors' entrance fees are added to the prize money to be awarded to the winner, entry in the competition is not an illegal gambling transaction so long as the prize money does not consist solely of fees paid by the competitors.

Nor is a transaction in "futures" generally considered to be a gambling agreement. A transaction in futures occurs where a person contracts to make future delivery of goods that he or she does not presently own.

Still, in many states, one or more forms of gambling are legal, including horse racing, dog racing, giveaway plans, awarding prizes (so long as participants are not required to buy anything or give anything of value to participate), and, occasionally, state sponsored public lotteries designed to raise revenue. Private lotteries and raffles, on the other hand, are almost always illegal.

And, of course, in the State of Nevada, many forms of gambling are legal.

(7) *Bargains harmful to marriage.* Basically, there are two kinds of marriage-related agreements that may be considered illegal as contrary to public policy.

(a) *Agreements in restraint of marriage.* General restraints on marriage are generally illegal following the principle that the sanctity of the marriage relation is at the foundation of the welfare of the state. A general restraint on marriage is a restriction so complete that it virtually rules out marriage for one or both parties to the agreement. Thus, Emily's promise not to marry anyone but Tom without a return promise from Tom to marry Emily is a general restraint on marriage and is void as an illegal agreement. However, where it is remarriage rather than a first marriage that is prevented, some courts uphold the agreement, finding that the restraint is reasonable.

And most courts routinely uphold the validity of partial restraints on marriage (e. g., where Abe Friendly's daughter, Cheryl, agrees not to marry until she reaches the age of 25 in exchange for Abe's promise to pay Cheryl $10,000). It is easy to understand why such agreements are upheld when it is learned that the enforceability of such agreements generally comes into play, not when one party to the contract seeks to prevent the other's marriage, but when the party who has promised not to marry, and who has, in fact, not married for the stated period, seeks to collect the other's promised payment. Along the same line, if Cheryl Friendly promises to remain single for life and to care for her father, Abe, in return for Abe's promise to pay her $25,000 (or to convey valuable real property to her), most courts will enforce the agreement if it is Cheryl who seeks enforcement, having remained single for life. Though the agreement is a general restraint on marriage, public policy favors enforcement of Abe's promise in face of Cheryl's self-imposed single life.

Just as total restraints on marriage are illegal, it is the general rule that obligations of marriage that are imposed by law cannot be avoided by agreement. Thus, an agreement relieving a husband of his obligation to support his family, and a wife of her duty to have sexual relations with her husband is an illegal bargain.

Marriage brokerage agreements (agreements to pay a fee to a third party for bringing the marriage partners together) are also illegal. Public policy favors marriage freely entered into without intermeddling by third parties.

(b) *Antenuptial agreements.* Frequently, wealthy people who have been previously married and are about to remarry enter into antenuptial agreements (premarital agreements) in an effort to control the disposition of their property in the event of divorce or death. Such agreements are usually valid, particularly where the agreement controls only the deathtime disposition of property. But where the agreement provides that a spouse will accept a stated sum in full settlement of his or her property rights in the event of divorce, the agreement is generally unlawful. While such an agreement may appear fair at the time it is entered into, it may be extremely unfair at the time of divorce, leaving a spouse and children without adequate support.

And, of course, an antenuptial agreement is also invalid if there is no mutual assent because of fraud or the like (e. g., where a wife fails to disclose her true financial position, representing her wealth to be much less than it actually is).

(8) *Bargains breaching fiduciary obligations.* It is unlawful for a person in a fiduciary relationship with another to contract to breach his or her fiduciary obligations. (As will be explained in detail in later chapters, a "fiduciary" is a person in a position of trust and confidence with another; certain duties or ob-

ligations flow from a fiduciary relationship.)

(9) *Bargains in restraint of trade.* Bargains in restraint of trade are illegal as follows:

(a) *Covenants not to compete.* Because public policy strongly favors having people work for a living, covenants not to compete are disfavored under the common law. Frequently, the seller of a business will agree not to compete with the buyer following the sale. Such a covenant not to compete is legal and enforceable only if it is reasonable both as to *time* and *area* covered. In other words, the restraint upon the seller must not exceed the extent of the business goodwill purchased ("goodwill" being the favorable position that an established and well-conducted business organization holds with the public). If the restraint is to continue for an unduly long period of time, or if it extends to territory in which the seller had no goodwill, the restraint will be unreasonable; and to the extent that it is unreasonable, it will be unenforceable. By way of example, suppose that the owner of a small grocery store in a local community sells out to a large retail chain; the grocer agrees as part of the contract of sale to never again compete in the grocery business anywhere. The restraint is obviously unreasonable as to both time and area. What would be reasonable would be a promise not to compete in the local area for a period of five years; and, to this extent, the restraint may be enforced.

Now suppose that a business with a great deal of domestic and international goodwill is sold; the buyer pays a large sum of money for the goodwill. A promise by the seller not to compete in a large area of the United States as well as in several foreign countries for a period of 25 years may well be reasonable under the circumstances.

Sometimes, an employee will agree as part of an employment contract that, upon completion of the employment, he or she will not compete with his or her former employer either by going into business personally or by working for another. Generally speaking, such covenants not to compete are illegal. They will be enforced only where the former employee is using the employer's trade secrets or secret customer lists (learned during the employment) to compete with the employer. But even absent a covenant not to compete, an employee may not after employment disclose or make use of such employment secrets—the courts will always restrain an employee from doing so. Otherwise, however, the courts are reluctant to enjoin an employee from earning his or her customary livelihood. To obtain an injunction, the former employer must generally prove that he or she has suffered substantial economic harm because of the employee's activity in soliciting customers (or in otherwise depriving the employer of goodwill); the employer must also show that the employee has other means of supporting himself or herself and his or her family.

(b) *Agreements to monopolize.* It is illegal under the law to monopolize or attempt to monopolize. This area of antitrust law is governed largely by federal and state statutes, including the federal Sherman Antitrust Act, the federal Clayton Act, and the Federal Trade Commission Act (antitrust law is presented in Ch. 25). For now, it is enough to know that any agreement to monopolize or to attempt to monopolize, including an agreement to fix prices among competitors, divide markets, boycott groups, or tie products, is illegal and unenforceable.

(10) *Licensing statutes.* All states have licensing statutes requiring people to obtain a license for the practice of certain professions, trades, and businesses, including law, medicine, accounting, real estate or stock brokering, building, plumbing, etc. Many of the statutes spe-

cifically provide that an unlicensed person who performs work requiring a license cannot recover for the value of his or her services: the unlicensed person's contracts are illegal and unenforceable. Suppose that a person licensed in one state performs work in another state where he or she is not licensed. Some states have statutes providing that a person (or business) who fails to become licensed in the state may not use the courts to recover the value of his or her services even though the person (or business) meets the licensing requirements for working in another state.

Other statutes are silent as to recovery by an unlicensed person. Whether or not an unlicensed person will be able to recover the value of his or her services will depend on whether the licensing statute is *regulatory* in nature, or whether it is designed merely to raise revenue for the government. If it is regulatory in nature (i. e., if it was enacted under the police power of the state to protect the public health, welfare, or morality against fraud and incompetence), payment is not recoverable.[5] Licensing requirements for law, medicine, and accounting, for example, are clearly regulatory: an unlicensed lawyer, doctor, or accountant cannot recover for the value of his or her services—his or her "professional" contracts are illegal and unenforceable.

If, on the other hand, the licensing requirement is designed merely to raise revenue (e. g., a license to sell newspapers), the contracts of the unlicensed person are valid and enforceable. A statute that fails to establish any standard of competence for the profession, trade, or business to be licensed looks to be a mere revenue measure.

(11) *Sunday laws.* Some states have statutes making it illegal to enter into contracts or perform contracts on Sunday (generally speaking, works of necessity and charitable operations are excluded from operation of the statutes). If work is contracted for and/or performed on Sunday in violation of the laws, the contract is illegal and unenforceable, and there can be no recovery for the performance. However, a contract entered into on Sunday may generally be "validated" by its adoption or ratification on another day of the week; of course, performance of the contract must also occur on a day other than Sunday.

Sunday laws have been repealed in many jurisdictions, and the trend in the law is to repeal them everywhere.

(12) *Discrimination.* Finally, agreements to discriminate on the basis of race, color, sex, or national origin violate the U.S. Constitution and federal civil rights legislation and are not enforceable contracts (the specifics of the civil rights laws are dealt with in Ch. 20).

What is the effect of illegality?

The effect of illegality may be summarized as follows: *First,* if an illegal agreement is severable into legal and illegal parts, and the illegal part does not go to "the essence of the bargain", then the legal portion may be enforced and the illegal part disregarded. The general rule is that an agreement is severable only if it is expressly or impliedly divisible into two or more parts. Each party's performance must be composed of installments; and each installment of a party's performance must confer an advantage or benefit on the other party so as to induce performance of the next installment (i. e., each installment of a party's perform-

---

5. An exception is made where all parties to the contract are "unlicensed"—e. g., a contract between two unlicensed dealers. The reason is that licensing requirements are designed to protect the public—not to protect one unlicensed person from another.

ance must serve as consideration for the next installment of the other party's performance).

A minority of courts hold that if a single (indivisible) promise is exchanged for one or more legal *and* one or more illegal considerations, the illegal considerations will be disregarded, and the promise will be enforced.

Second, where the agreement is not severable, and the parties are equally culpable (i. e., both have knowledge of the illegality and have willingly participated in it), the parties are in *pari delicto* ("in equal fault"), and neither will receive any help from the courts in enforcing the contract. Thus, neither party can legally require the other to perform. And it makes no difference that one party has performed, while the other has not: the performing party can neither rescind the agreement nor recover what he or she has given under quasi contract. The courts, in effect, leave the parties where they find them—in pari delicto— and neither party has any legal remedy whatsoever. (However, under the doctrine of "locus penitentiae", some courts hold that if one of the parties repents and repudiates the illegal contract before any part of it is carried out, he or she

will have a right to recover any value given under quasi contract.)

Third, if the parties are not equally culpable, but one is innocent, or relatively so, the innocent party *may* be able to recover in quasi contract for unjust enrichment. The proper word is "may" because the innocent party's recovery depends on whether the illegal agreement is *malum in se* (against good morals) or *malum prohibitum* (in violation of a statute or rule but not against good morals). A malum in se contract is void, and neither party, no matter how innocent, can obtain any help from the courts (it is just as if the parties are in pari delicto). Though the courts will not enforce a malum prohibitum contract, they will allow the innocent party to recover on the basis of quasi contract.

Fourth, sometimes, an agreement violates a statute that has been passed to protect a specific group of people. If one of the parties to the contract is a member of the protected group, that party will not be deemed in pari delicto. For example, say that a young child is employed in violation of child labor laws (laws outlawing oppressive child labor—see Ch. 20). The child employee can recover for the value of his or her work though the employment itself is illegal.

CASES

CASE 1—*"He promised his nephew that if he would refrain from drinking, using tobacco, swearing, and playing cards or billiards for money until he became 21 years of age, he would pay him the sum of $5,000."*

HAMER v. SIDWAY

Court of Appeals of New York, Second Division, 1891.
124 N.Y. 538, 27 N.E. 256.

* * * The plaintiff presented a claim to the executor of William E. Story, Sr., for $5,000 and interest from the 6th day of February, 1875. * * * The claim being rejected by the executor, this action was brought. It appears that William E. Story, Sr., was the uncle of William E. Story, 2d; that at the celebration of the golden wedding of Samuel Story and wife, father and mother of William E. Story, Sr., on the 20th day of March,

1869, in the presence of the family and invited guests, he promised his nephew that if he would refrain from drinking, using tobacco, swearing, and playing cards or billiards for money until he became 21 years of age, he would pay him the sum of $5,000. The nephew assented thereto, and fully performed the conditions inducing the promise. When the nephew arrived at the age of 21 years, and on the 31st day of January, 1875, he wrote to his uncle, informing him that he had performed his part of the agreement, and had thereby become entitled to the sum of $5,000. The uncle received the letter, and a few days later, and on the 6th day of February, he wrote and mailed to his nephew the following letter: "Buffalo, Feb. 6, 1875. W. E. Story, Jr.—Dear Nephew: Your letter of the 31st ult. came to hand all right, saying that you had lived up to the promise made to me several years ago. I have no doubt but you have, for which you shall have five thousand dollars, as I promised you. I had the money in the bank the day you was twenty-one years old that I intend for you, and you shall have the money certain. Now, Willie, I do not intend to interfere with this money in any way till I think you are capable of taking care of it, and the sooner that time comes the better it will please me. I would hate very much to have you start out in some adventure that you thought all right and lose this money in one year. The first five thousand dollars that I got together cost me a heap of hard work. You would hardly believe me when I tell you that to obtain this I shoved a jack-plane many a day, butchered three or four years, then came to this city, and, after three months' perseverance, I obtained a situation in a grocery store. I opened this store early, closed late, slept in the fourth story of the building in a room 30 by 40 feet, and not a human being in the building but myself. All this I done to live as cheap as I could to save something. I don't want you to take up with this kind of fare. I was here in the cholera season of '49 and '52, and the deaths averaged 80 to 125 daily, and plenty of small-pox. I wanted to go home, but Mr. Fisk, the gentleman I was working for, told me, if I left them, after it got healthy he probably would not want me. I stayed. All the money I have saved I know just how I got it. It did not come to me in any mysterious way, and the reason I speak of this is that money got in this way stops longer with a fellow that gets it with hard knocks than it does when he finds it. Willie, you are twenty-one, and you have many a thing to learn yet. This money you have earned much easier than I did, besides acquiring good habits at the same time, and you are quite welcome to the money. Hope you will make good use of it. I was ten long years getting this together after I was your age. * * *" The uncle died on the 29th day of January, 1887, without having paid over to his nephew any portion of the said $5,000 and interest.

* * * The defendant contends that the contract was without consideration to support it, and therefore invalid. He asserts that the promisee, by refraining from the use of liquor and tobacco, was not harmed, but benefited; that that which he did was best for him to do, independently of his uncle's promise—and insists that it follows that, unless the promisor was benefited, the contract was without consideration. * * * The exchequer chamber in 1875 defined "consideration" as follows: "A valuable consideration, in the sense of the law, may consist either in some right, interest, profit, or benefit accruing to the one party, or some forbearance, detriment, loss, or responsibility given, suffered, or undertaken by the other." Courts "will not ask whether the thing which forms the consideration does in fact benefit the promisee or a third party, or is of any substantial value

to any one. It is enough that something is promised, done, forborne, or suffered by the party to whom the promise is made as consideration for the promise made to him." * * * Pollock in his work on Contracts, (page 166,) after citing the definition given by the exchequer chamber, already quoted, says: "The second branch of this judicial description is really the most important one. 'Consideration' means not so much that one party is profiting as that the other abandons some legal right in the present, or limits his legal freedom of action in the future, as an inducement for the promise of the first." Now, applying this rule to the facts before us, the promisee used tobacco, occasionally drank liquor, and he had a legal right to do so. That right he abandoned for a period of years upon the strength of the promise of the testator that for such forbearance he would give him $5,000. We need not speculate on the effort which may have been required to give up the use of those stimulants. It is sufficient that he restricted his lawful freedom of action within certain prescribed limits upon the faith of his uncle's agreement, and now, having fully performed the conditions imposed, it is of no moment whether such performance actually proved a benefit to the promisor, and the court will not inquire into it; but, were it a proper subject of inquiry, we see nothing in this record that would permit a determination that the uncle was not benefited in a legal sense. * * * In Talbott v. Stemmons, * * * the step-grandmother of the plaintiff made with him the following agreement: "I do promise and bind myself to give my grandson Albert R. Talbott $500 at my death if he will never take another chew of tobacco or smoke another cigar during my life, from this date up to my death * * *." The [defendant] executor of Mrs. Stemmons [claimed] that the agreement was not based on a sufficient consideration. * * * In the opinion of the court it is said that "the right to use and enjoy the use of tobacco was a right that belonged to the plaintiff, and not forbidden by law. The abandonment of its use may have saved him money, or contributed to his health; nevertheless, the surrender of that right caused the promise, and, having the right to contract with reference to the subject-matter, the abandonment of the use was a sufficient consideration to uphold the promise." * * *

* * *

CASE 2—*Was the college education a "necessary" for this minor?*

JOHNSTONE v. JOHNSTONE

Appellate Court of Illinois, First District, First Division, 1965.
64 Ill.App.2d 447, 212 N.E.2d 143.

BURMAN, Presiding Justice.

This suit arises out of a claim filed by petitioner, Eloise Johnstone, against the minor's estate of her stepson, Robert B. Johnstone, Jr., for amounts expended by her and obligations incurred by her in financing his college education. She based her claim upon the contention that in modern society and under the circumstances of this case a college education falls within the legal definition of a "necessary"; and that since she furnished the only funds available for her stepson's college education he is liable to her under established principles of law. The court specifically found that petitioner's expenditures were not for "necessities", and dismissed her claim. Petitioner has appealed from this ruling.

Upon the minor's graduation from high school, he indicated his desire to continue his education at Dartmouth College in Hanover, New Hampshire. His father, Robert B. Johnstone, Sr., who was living at the time, approved of his son's plans, and in order to meet the costs of this education applied to the La Salle National Bank for a loan under the Bank's Assured College Education Plan. As an integral part of this plan, the Bank requires the Applicant Sponsor to purchase an insurance policy on his own life, naming the Bank as beneficiary. It appears from the record in this case that the poor health of the minor's father made him unable to qualify for such a policy, thereby preventing him from signing the loan as Applicant Sponsor. The application was signed by petitioner, the minor's stepmother, as Applicant Sponsor and the Minor's father signed as "Spouse of Applicant Sponsor."

Semi-annual payments of $750.00 by the Bank direct to Dartmouth College began in September of 1961, and continued through the sixth payment in December of 1963, at which time the minor's father died and payments by the Bank ceased. Prior to his death, Robert B. Johnstone, Sr., had made regular repayments to the Bank in the amount specified in the terms of the loan. At his death, the balance due the Bank was $2,101.50, for which the Bank has held petitioner responsible and which she has reduced by further payments. She seeks recovery from the minor's estate for this amount.

Two life insurance policies were left by the minor's deceased father. The first was a policy in the amount of $5,000, which named the petitioner as beneficiary. The other policy was in the amount of $10,000, and named petitioner and the minor as beneficiaries, each in the amount of $5,000. Petitioner seeks to recover against the minor's share of the proceeds of this policy. The record reveals that the father's estate is insolvent, and petitioner claims that all the monies she received from the policies will be used to pay claims against the estate.

It is well-established, as a general rule, that a minor or his estate may be liable for necessaries furnished him. As to the definition of a "necessary", our Supreme Court stated in McKanna v. Merry, 61 Ill. 177:

> There is no positive rule by means of which it may be determined what are, and what are not, necessaries. Whether articles are of a class or kind for which infants are liable, or whether certain subjects of expenditure are necessaries, are to be judged of by the court. Whether they come within the particular class, and are suitable to the condition and estate of the infant, is to be determined by the jury as a matter of fact. * * * Blackstone defines necessaries to be 'necessary meat, drink, apparel, physic,' and says that an infant may bind himself to pay 'for his good teaching and instruction, whereby he may profit himself afterwards.' The articles furnished, or money advanced, must be actually necessary, in the particular case, for use, not mere ornament, for substantial good, not mere pleasure; and must belong to the class which the law generally pronounces necessary for infants.

In Crandall v. Coyne Electrical School, 256 Ill.App. 322, the court cited the McKanna case, and went on to say:

> It is recognized that a proper education is a necessary. But what is a proper education depends on circumstances. * * * A common school education is said to be a necessary in this country.

(citing cases) In the latter case, it is said that circumstances, however, may exist where a more liberal education might properly be found a necessary as a matter of fact. (256 Ill.App. 322, at 324)

Thus, the trial judge in this case was charged with the responsibility of determining whether, on the basis of the evidence, a college education for this minor could be classified as a "necessary". But, as pointed out by Professor Williston, "What are necessaries is determined not simply by the nature of the thing, but by the need of that thing at that time by the infant in question." The evidence in this case showed the minor was at the top of his class in high school and that there was available to the minor a full tuition scholarship to the University of Chicago. The Court could have found from the evidence that the minor might have received from Dartmouth College either a scholarship or a loan on more favorable terms than the one received from La Salle National Bank. In light of these facts and the tests for "necessaries" set forth above, we cannot conclude that the Chancellor's findings were manifestly against the weight of the evidence, and therefore we cannot disturb his judgment.

Petitioner's claim is subject to a further objection. It has been the established rule in Illinois since Sinklear v. Emert, 18 Ill. 63, that a minor is liable for necessaries furnished him only if they are furnished on his credit, and not on the credit of another. Professor Williston states it thus:

It is essential to recovery that necessaries shall have been furnished on the credit of the infant. If furnished on the credit of his parent or guardian, he is not liable; * * *.

In this case, the record is clear that at the time the Johnstones entered into the loan agreement, the minor was not asked by either of them to repay the loan at any future time. Petitioner did not testify that she signed the note at the request of the minor, nor that she did so in reliance upon his credit. Indeed it appears that she obligated herself for the indebtedness at the request of her husband. The minor testified that while he knew a loan had been made he did not know, until after his father's death, that his stepmother was obligated on that loan. He further testified that his father told him that the loan was merely for the sake of convenience in view of the fact that his income fluctuated widely. Finally, the minor's father had paid regularly his tuition at a private high school, never indicating that the costs were beyond his ability to pay. In view of these facts, we conclude that petitioner has failed to prove that the funds for the minor's college education were furnished on his credit. For this reason, her appeal must fail, even assuming *arguendo* not only that the Dartmouth College education was a "necessary" in this case, but also assuming *arguendo* that petitioner is correct in her contention that a stepmother can recover for necessaries furnished despite the fact that a natural or adopting parent cannot.

Judgment affirmed.

CASE 3—*Did plaintiff have a "legal" contract (entitling her to one-half of more than one million dollars in earnings) when she gave up her singing career to become movie star Lee Marvin's "companion, homemaker, housekeeper, and cook?"*

MARVIN v. MARVIN

Supreme Court of California, In Bank, 1976.
18 Cal.3d 660, 134 Cal.Rptr. 815, 557 P.2d 106.

TOBRINER, Justice.

During the past 15 years, there has been a substantial increase in the number of couples living together without marrying. Such nonmarital relationships lead to legal controversy when one partner dies or the couple separates. Courts of Appeal, faced with the task of determining property rights in such cases, have arrived at conflicting positions: two cases held that the Family Law Act requires division of the property according to community property principles, and one decision has rejected that holding. We take this opportunity to resolve that controversy and to declare the principles which should govern distribution of property acquired in a nonmarital relationship.

We conclude: (1) The provisions of the Family Law Act do not govern the distribution of property acquired during a nonmarital relationship; such a relationship remains subject solely to judicial decision. (2) The courts should enforce express contracts between nonmarital partners except to the extent that the contract is explicitly founded on the consideration of meretricious sexual services. (3) In the absence of an express contract, the courts should inquire into the conduct of the parties to determine whether that conduct demonstrates an implied contract * * *

In the instant case plaintiff and defendant lived together for seven years without marrying; all property acquired during this period was taken in defendant's name. When plaintiff sued to enforce a contract under which she was entitled to half the property and to support payments, the trial court granted judgment on the pleadings for defendant, thus leaving him with all property accumulated by the couple during their relationship. Since the trial court denied plaintiff a trial on the merits of her claim, its decision conflicts with the principles stated above, and must be reversed.

* * *

Plaintiff avers that in October of 1964 she and defendant "entered into an oral agreement" that while "the parties lived together they would combine their efforts and earnings and would share equally any and all property accumulated as a result of their efforts whether individual or combined." Furthermore, they agreed to "hold themselves out to the general public as husband and wife" and that "plaintiff would further render her services as a companion, homemaker, housekeeper and cook to * * * defendant."

Shortly thereafter plaintiff agreed to "give up her lucrative career as an entertainer [and] singer" in order to "devote her full time to defendant * * * as a companion, homemaker, housekeeper and cook;" in return defendant agreed to "provide for all of plaintiff's financial support and needs for the rest of her life."

Plaintiff alleges that she lived with defendant from October of 1964 through May of 1970 and fulfilled her obligations under the agreement. During this period the parties as a result of their efforts and earnings acquired in defendant's name substantial real and personal property, including motion picture rights worth over $1 million. In May of 1970, however, defendant compelled plaintiff to leave his household. He continued to support plaintiff until November of 1971, but thereafter refused to provide further support.

* * *

In Trutalli v. Meraviglia (1932) 215 Cal. 698, 12 P.2d 430 we established the principle that nonmarital partners may lawfully contract concerning the ownership of property acquired during the relationship. We reaffirmed this principle in Vallera v. Vallera (1943) 21 Cal.2d 681, 685, 134 P. 2d 761, 763, stating that "If a man and woman [who are not married] live together as husband and wife under an agreement to pool their earnings and share equally in their joint accumulations, equity will protect the interests of each in such property."

* * *

Defendant first and principally relies on the contention that the alleged contract is so closely related to the supposed "immoral" character of the relationship between plaintiff and himself that the enforcement of the contract would violate public policy. He points to cases asserting that a contract between nonmarital partners is unenforceable if it is "involved in" an illicit relationship. A review of the numerous California decisions concerning contracts between nonmarital partners, however, reveals that the courts have not employed such broad and uncertain standards to strike down contracts. The decisions instead disclose a narrower and more precise standard: a contract between nonmarital partners is unenforceable only *to the extent* that it *explicitly* rests upon the immoral and illicit consideration of meretricious sexual services.

* * *

Croslin v. Scott (1957) 154 Cal.App.2d 767, 316 P.2d 755 reiterates the rule established in *Trutalli* * * *. In *Croslin* the parties separated following a three-year nonmarital relationship. The woman then phoned the man, asked him to return to her, and suggested that he build them a house on a lot she owned. She agreed in return to place the property in joint ownership. The man built the house, and the parties lived there for several more years. When they separated, he sued to establish his interest in the property. Reversing a nonsuit, the Court of Appeal stated that "The mere fact that parties agree to live together in meretricious relationship does not necessarily make an agreement for disposition of property between them invalid. It is only when the property agreement is made in connection with the other agreement, or the illicit relationship is made a consideration of the property agreement, that the latter becomes illegal."

* * *

* * * In Hill v. Estate of Westbrook, supra, 95 Cal.App.2d 599, 213 P.2d 727, the woman promised to keep house for the man, to live with him as man and wife, and to bear his children; the man promised to provide for her in his will, but died without doing so. Reversing a judgment for the woman based on the reasonable value of her services, the Court of Appeal stated that "the action is predicated upon a claim which seeks, among other things, the reasonable value of living with decedent in meretricious relationship and bearing him two children * * *. The law does not award compensation for living with a man as a concubine and bearing him children. * * * As the judgment is, at least in part, for the value of the claimed services for which recovery cannot be had, it must be reversed." (95 Cal.

App.2d at p. 603, 213 P.2d at p. 730.) Upon retrial, the trial court found that it could not sever the contract and place an independent value upon the legitimate services performed by claimant. We therefore affirmed a judgment for the estate. (Hill v. Estate of Westbrook (1952) 29 Cal.2d 458, 247 P.2d 19.)

In the only other cited decision refusing to enforce a contract, Updeck v. Samuel (1964) 123 Cal.App.2d 264, 266 P.2d 822, the contract "was based on the consideration that the parties live together as husband and wife." Viewing the contract as calling for adultery, the court held it illegal.

The decisions in the *Hill* and *Updeck* cases thus demonstrate that a contract between nonmarital partners, even if expressly made in contemplation of a common living arrangement, is invalid only if sexual acts form an inseparable part of the consideration for the agreement. In sum, a court will not enforce a contract for the pooling of property and earnings if it is explicitly and inseparably based upon services as a paramour. * * *

The principle that a contract between nonmarital partners will be enforced unless expressly and inseparably based upon an illicit consideration of sexual services not only represents the distillation of the decisional law, but also offers a far more precise and workable standard than that advocated by defendant. * * *

* * *

In summary, we base our opinion on the principle that adults who voluntarily live together and engage in sexual relations are nonetheless as competent as any other persons to contract respecting their earnings and property rights. Of course, they cannot lawfully contract to pay for the performance of sexual services, for such a contract is, in essence, an agreement for prostitution and unlawful for that reason. But they may agree to pool their earnings and to hold all property acquired during the relationship in accord with the law governing community property; conversely they may agree that each partner's earnings and the property acquired from those earnings remains the separate property of the earning partner. So long as the agreement does not rest upon illicit meretricious consideration, the parties may order their economic affairs as they choose, and no policy precludes the courts from enforcing such agreements.

In the present instance, plaintiff alleges that the parties agreed to pool their earnings, that they contracted to share equally in all property acquired, and that defendant agreed to support plaintiff. The terms of the contract as alleged do not rest upon any unlawful consideration. * * *

* * *

* * * As we have explained, the courts now hold that express agreements will be enforced unless they rest on an unlawful meretricious consideration. We add that in the absence of an express agreement, the courts may look to a variety of other remedies in order to protect the parties' lawful expectations. [24]

The courts may inquire into the conduct of the parties to determine whether that conduct demonstrates an implied contract or implied agree-

---

24. We do not seek to resurrect the doctrine of common law marriage, which was abolished in California by statute in 1895. Thus we do not hold that plaintiff and defendant were "married," * * * we hold only that she has the same rights to enforce contracts and to assert her equitable interest in property acquired through her effort as does any other unmarried person.

ment * * *. [A] nonmarital partner may recover in quantum meruit for the reasonable value of household services rendered less the reasonable value of support received if he can show that he rendered services with the expectation of monetary reward.

* * *

The judgment is reversed * * *.

PROBLEMS

1. Sidney Streeter is doing well in his retail grocery business. He tells his favorite niece Sally Streeter that he is going to give her $10,000 at the end of the year so that she can start her own business. Over the course of the year, Sally rents an office building and purchases some office machinery and supplies on credit; she is counting on the $10,000 to pay off the debts (her own salary will not cover the purchases). However, Sidney dies before the end of the year, and his personal representative refuses to pay Sally the money. Is Sally entitled to the $10,000? Explain. *yes promissory estoppel*

   Suppose that Sidney had told Sally, "I promise to give you $10,000 at the end of the year if you attend business college this term." As suming Sally attended business college, would she be entitled to the $10,000? Explain.

2. Does consideration (or an acceptable substitute for consideration) exist in the following situations? Explain your answers.

   (a) In return for Richard Klein's promise to pay her $75, Bonnie Miller promises "to shampoo Richard's carpets unless my rug shampooer breaks down." *yes*

   (b) The same as (a) above except that Bonnie promises "to shampoo Richard's carpets unless I decide I'm too busy." *N*

   (c) Grateful that Keith Robel helped her fix a flat tire last week, Jody Welty telephones Keith and promises to pay him $10 when she receives her next paycheck. *N*

   (d) Keith Robel owes a contract debt of $250 to Mike Mahoney. However, the statute of limitations has run on the contract and Mike is barred from suing on the debt. Keith nevertheless pays Mike $50 of the money and orally promises to pay the balance. *Y*

   (e) Phil Kennedy, who is in the painting business, paints Karen Spencer's fence by mistake, believing it to be that of her neighbor, Ruth Warrick. Karen is not at home at the time. *N*

   (f) The same as (e) above except that Karen is at home; she sees Phil painting the fence but does not attempt to stop him. *Y*

3. Carol Thomas contracts to purchase a used television set from Todd Ritter for $85. By the terms of the contract, Carol must make payment 30 days after delivery of the set. After the set is delivered, Carol notifies Tom that she is short on cash and has only $50 to pay him.

   (a) At Carol's insistence, and in order to get at least a part of the money owing, Todd <u>orally</u> promises "to accept payment of $50 thirty days after delivery of the set as settlement in full" of the debt. Carol pays Todd the $50, then Todd sues Carol for the $35 balance. Is there consideration for Todd's promise to accept the $50 as payment in full? Explain, using a diagram to illustrate. *No, Liquidated Debt*

   (b) Todd promises "to accept payment of $50 ten days after delivery of the set as settlement in full" of the debt, and Carol makes such payment. Is there consideration for Todd's promise to forget the balance of the debt? Explain, again using a diagram to illustrate. *y early payment*

   (c) Todd promises in writing "to accept payment of $50 thirty days after delivery of the set as payment in full"; Todd signs the writing and delivers it to Carol, whereupon Carol pays Todd $50. Todd then sues Carol for the $35 balance. Result? *written waiver*

4. Seventeen year old Steve Cassidy has a used Chevy but also wants a motorcycle. He falsely tells Archie Palmer that he is 18 (the age of majority in Steve's state) so that Archie will sell him a BMW motorcycle. A week later, Steve accidentally runs the cycle into a tree; he notifies Archie that he <u>disaffirms</u> the contract. Steve than contracts to paint Annie Hoffman's Volkswagen. Steve paints the car carelessly and <u>ruins Annie's paint job</u>. Steve notifies Annie that he disaffirms the contract. Steve then purchases some levis from "Farmer's Department Store" as well as an expensive watch and a solid gold medallion to wear around his neck. After a week, the jeans are dirty and Steve has lost the watch and medallion. Steve notifies Farmer's that he <u>disaffirms the purchases</u>. What are Steve's rights and duties vis a vis Archie, Annie, and Farmer's Department Store? Assume that Steve's parents contribute little to his support.

Archie may disaffirm ¿Return Archie sue? "tort of deceit"

Annie disaffirm tort interwoven with contract

FDS disaffirm except for FMV of levis, maybe watch

   Finally, Steve contracts to sell his beach lot (a gift from his grandfather) to Muriel Morris. A month after Muriel takes possession of the land, Steve notifies her that he disaffirms the sale; Muriel ignores the notice. Three months later, Steve turns 18. On his 19th birthday, he again notifies Muriel that he disaffirms the sale. Who is entitled to the property? Explain. *steve — can disaffirm until law of limitation runs out (?6yrs)*

5. Answer the following "True" or "False" and give reasons for your answers?

   (a) Requirement and output contracts are examples of illusory promises.

   (b) Charitable subscriptions are legally enforceable.

   (c) Modernly, a contract under seal needs no consideration to be binding.

   (d) Part payment of an unliquidated debt will serve as consideration for a promise to forget the balance.

   (e) Any contract entered into by a person who has been declared insane by a court of law is void.

   (f) A party who is partially intoxicated at the time of entering into a contract can always avoid the contract.

   (g) Antenuptial agreements providing for the deathtime disposition of property are generally illegal and invalid.

   (h) Champerty is an illegal agreement to pay the costs and expenses of a legal action without sharing in the proceeds.

   (i) An exculpatory clause in a contract is generally legal if it pertains only to a party's negligent misconduct.

   (j) Originally, usury laws applied only to loans of money and not to credit sales of goods or real estate.

6. Judge Tanner promises to dismiss Carl Cornwell's "Driving Under the Influence of Liquor" citation if Carl (who is a carpenter) will build her a solid oak desk. Carl builds the desk and delivers it to the Judge's chambers. The Judge accepts the desk, but then refuses to dismiss the citation. Can Carl legally compel dismissal of the citation? Assuming he cannot, can he obtain return of the desk? Explain your answers.

7. The basic distinction between a bilateral contract and a unilateral contract according to common law rules is

   (a) That one must be signed, sealed and delivered, whereas the other need not.

   (b) There is only one promise involved when the contract is unilateral.

   (c) The statute of frauds applies to one and not to the other.

   (d) One is assignable whereas the other is not.

   [# 38, November, 1976 CPA Exam]

8. Argot wrote Palm offering to sell him specified merchandise with the offer to remain open 30 days. Ten days later, Argot and Palm orally agreed on the terms of the sale, and Argot prepared a letter which he sent to Palm stating, "This incorporates our agreement." The letter specified the goods but failed to include the agreed price. Later, prior to the date specified for delivery Argot agreed in writing to modify the terms of the contract as requested by Palm; there was no consideration for the modification. Based on these facts

   (a) Argot's offer was revocable until accepted by Palm.

   (b) If Palm seeks to enforce the agreement, Argot may assert the Statute of Frauds as a defense since neither letter specified any price for the goods.

   (c) Lack of consideration for the modification of the agreement would not prevent its enforceability.

   (d) Neither Argot nor Palm could enforce the agreement since Palm had *not* signed any writing.

   [# 25, May, 1974 CPA Exam]

9. Martinson Services, Inc., agreed to rent two floors of office space in Jason's building for five years. An escalation clause in the lease provided for a $200 per month increase in rental in the fifth year of occupancy by Martinson. Near the end of the fourth year, during a serious economic recession, Martinson's business was doing very poorly. Martinson called upon Jason to inform him that Martinson could not honor the lease if the rent was increased in the fifth year. Jason agreed in a signed writing to allow Martinson to remain at the prior rental, and Martinson did so. At the end of the fifth year Martinson moved to another office building. Then, Jason demanded payment of $2,400 from Martinson.

   What is the legal standing of the parties involved?

   (a) A binding accord and satisfaction has resulted between the parties.

   (b) The agreed upon rent reduction is valid due to the increased burden of performance as a result of events beyond Martinson's control.

   (c) Martinson's relinquishment of the legal right to breach the contract provides the consideration for the reduction in rent.

(d) The writing signed by Jason does not bind him to the agreed reduction in rent.

[# 7, May, 1975, CPA Exam]

10. A contract effecting an unreasonable restraint of trade is invalid or void as against public policy, but a contract containing a covenant *not* to compete is valid if it is

(a) In writing.

(b) Filed with the Attorney General.

(c) Reasonable as to area and time.

(d) For services.

[# 35, May, 1977 CPA Exam]

Chapter 10

OTHER FACTORS AFFECTING THE RIGHTS OF CONTRACTING PARTIES: CONDITIONS, THE STATUTE OF FRAUDS, INTERPRETATION OF CONTRACTS, THE PAROL EVIDENCE RULE, DISCHARGE, BREACH OF CONTRACT, AND DAMAGES

Once a valid contract is present, what other factors may come into play to affect the rights of contracting parties?

In the last three chapters, we studied the four elements necessary for a valid contract: mutual assent, consideration, capacity, and legality. If all four elements are present, a valid contract exists; however, there are several other factors that may now come into play to affect the rights of the contracting parties. For example, in some cases, though a contract exists, a condition must occur before one of the parties will acquire any rights under the contract; in other cases, one of the parties will lose his or her contract rights upon the occurrence of a stated condition. Sometimes, a contract, to be enforceable, must be evidenced by a written memorandum under the Statute of Frauds. Often, a written contract contains ambiguous or conflicting terms, and the court must interpret the contract to discern the intent of the parties; occasionally, the parol evidence rule prevents the court from considering any evidence that contradicts the terms of the writing. Frequently, events occur that serve to discharge the parties from any further obligation under the contract. And, sometimes, one of the parties breaches his or her contract obligations, and the non-breaching party is entitled to money damages or other relief.

Conditions, the Statute of Frauds, interpretation of contracts, the parol evidence rule, discharge, breach of contract, and damages—all are factors that affect the rights of parties to existing contracts. Each factor is considered in detail in the following sections.

What is a condition? How does a condition differ from a covenant?

Usually, the parties to a contract perform according to the terms of the agreement, and, as a result, are "discharged" from further obligation on the contract (i. e., performance is the normal method of discharge of contracts). Sometimes, however, a party fails to perform or stops performing, and the question for determination is whether the party has breached the agreement. Generally, a breach of contract occurs where a party under an absolute and unconditional duty of performance fails to perform. An absolute and unconditional promise to perform is called a *covenant*—thus, a breach of covenant is a breach of contract.

Sometimes, however, it is difficult to determine whether a party has made a covenant (an absolute and unconditional promise) or a promise subject to a condition. A *condition* is a fact or event, the happening or nonhappening of which creates or terminates a promisor's duty of performance under a contract. Because the promisor's duty is conditional, the promisor's failure to perform in light of a "failure of condition" (the nonoccurrence of a condition giving rise to a duty) is not a breach of contract. Thus, where a party's performance is subject to the prior happening of a condition, a failure of the condition lets the party "off the hook", and he or she does not have to perform. Nor is it a breach of contract for the promisor to terminate performance upon the occurrence of a condition cutting off his or her duty to perform.

Suppose that Dora Dealer enters into a contract with Fred Farmer wherein Dora agrees to sell Fred a new tractor for $20,000, "it being understood that the tractor is to be delivered by Dora to Fred's farm on or before June 10th." Dora fails to deliver the tractor on or before June 10th, and on June 15th, Fred purchases the same kind of tractor from another dealer for $23,000 (the best price Fred can get). Was Dora's failure to deliver the tractor on or before June 10th a breach of contract enabling Fred to sue Dora for his $3,000 loss? Or was Dora's failure to perform justifiable in light of a failure of condition (Dora's failure to deliver the tractor on or before June 10th)? The answer depends upon whether the delivery provision in the contract was a covenant or a condition. There are no hard and fast rules for making this determination, but there are several guidelines:

(1) *The words used*. Words such as "on the condition that", "provided that", "if", or "when" look to be words of condition; while words such as "promises", "agrees", or "covenants" indicate that an unconditional promise (i. e., a covenant) was intended. In the example, the words "it being understood that the tractor is to be delivered" suggests an unconditional promise to deliver rather than a condition.

(2) *The reasonable prudent person test*. Again, what would a reasonable prudent person under the same or similar circumstances have thought the words to be—a covenant or a condition? In the example, a reasonable prudent person

would probably have considered the provision to be a covenant by Dora to deliver the tractor on or before June 10th.

(3) *The expectations of the parties*. Third, and most importantly, how best will the expectations of the parties be protected? In every case, the court will look at all the circumstances so as to interpret the contract in accord with the true intent of the parties. Where ambiguity remains, the court will find the language to be a covenant rather than a condition because, in most cases, the parties to a contract intend and expect their promises to be unconditionally binding. In the example, the parties probably intended the delivery provision to be unconditionally binding on Dora. Thus, the best way to protect the parties' expectations (particularly Fred's) is to rule that the provision is a covenant rather than a condition.

Because all the guidelines point to a covenant rather than a condition, Dora's failure to deliver the tractor on or before June 10th is a breach of contract, and Dora is liable in damages to Fred Farmer. Of course, there would be an entirely different result had the contract provided that "the sale of the tractor is conditioned upon its being delivered to Farmer at his farm on or before June 10th." In this situation, the provision is unquestionably a condition, the failure of which excuses Dora's duty of performance under the contract (it also excuses any duty on Fred's part to pay the $20,000).

Similarly, Dora's promise to buy Fred's farm "on the condition that financing can be obtained" is a conditional promise, and a failure to obtain financing relieves Dora of any obligation to buy the property.

Sometimes, one party's duty of performance under a contract is conditioned upon the other party's performance of his or her contract duties. Here, the same provision is both a covenant and a condition. For example, suppose that Fred Farmer promises to plow Tom Neighbor's fields by July 15th for $3,000 in return for Tom's promise to pay $3,000 upon Fred's completion of the plowing, "Tom having no obligation to pay anything until the plowing is finished." Fred Farmer has absolutely and unconditionally promised to plow Tom Neighbor's fields, and if Fred fails to do the plowing, Tom can sue Fred for breach of contract. At the same time, Fred's completion of the plowing is a condition to Tom's payment of the $3,000; and, until the plowing is finished, Tom has no duty to pay.

What kinds of conditions are there?

Conditions may be classified as either *express* conditions or *implied in fact* conditions. An *express* condition is a condition that is explicitly stated by the parties. Parties are generally free to make their contractual obligations as conditional as they desire, and the courts will give effect to the conditions. An *implied in fact* condition is an unstated condition that the parties would have expressly agreed to had they thought about it at the time of entering into the contract. For example, in the contract between Fred Farmer and Tom Neighbor, it is an implied in fact condition that Tom will allow Fred to bring his tractor through Tom's gates in order to gain access to the fields; and it is further implied in fact that neither party will act in bad faith so as to prevent the other from performing under the contract. If a party in bad faith prevents or hinders the happening of a condition, the condition is excused, and the party will be held to his or her promise even though performance of the promise was originally subject to a condition. This is called excuse of condition by *prevention*. So, if Tom Neighbor prevents Fred Farmer from coming onto his land to do the plowing, the condition that the plowing must be completed by

July 15th will be excused, and Tom's promise to pay the $3,000 will be legally enforceable despite the fact that the plowing is not completed (Fred will be allowed to recover damages based upon his lost profits).

Conditions may also be classified according to time of operation as either *precedent*, *subsequent*, or *concurrent*.

(1) *Condition precedent.* A condition precedent is a condition that must occur before a party will have an absolute duty to perform under a contract. It is the happening of the condition that gives rise to the absolute duty; if the condition never occurs (i. e., if there is a failure of condition), the party is never obligated to perform. For example, suppose that Fred Farmer promises to buy a tractor for $20,000 from Dora Dealer, but only on the condition that Fred's wheat crop produces 40 bushels to the acre and Fred is able to sell the crop for at least $50,000 by the first of December. Until and unless the condition occurs (i. e., until and unless Fred's wheat crop produces 40 bushels to the acre, and Fred sells the crop for at least $50,000 prior to December 1st), Fred has no legal obligation to buy the tractor. If the condition fails, Fred has no legal duty to perform.

The burden of proving a condition precedent is always on the plaintiff. Thus, if Fred Farmer refuses to purchase the tractor after the condition has occurred, it is up to Dora Dealer to prove in court that Fred's wheat crop produced 40 bushels to the acre, and that Fred sold the crop, prior to December 1st, for at least $50,000. (See Appendix A for civil action discovery procedures that will enable Dora to acquire the necessary evidence.)

Particularly troublesome for the courts are conditions precedent that one party must be "satisfied" with the other's performance before the first party will become obligated to perform under the contract. Generally, if the condition is that the party must be "personally" satisfied, the party will not become obligated to perform unless he or she is, in fact, personally (i. e., subjectively) pleased with the other party's performance. If the party is not pleased, he or she has no duty to perform. For example, where the contract between Fred Farmer and Tom Neighbor provides that "Tom Neighbor must be personally satisfied with the plowing done by Fred Farmer before Tom will be obligated to pay the $3,000", Tom will not have to pay, even though Fred has completed the plowing, unless Tom is personally satisfied with the job. Because the test of satisfaction is a subjective one, it makes no difference that a party's dissatisfaction is unreasonable so long as it is honest, in good faith, and not merely an attempt by the party to avoid his or her contract duties (e. g., where the party is truly pleased, but nevertheless tries to get out of the contract).

Where the condition precedent does not expressly call for "personal" satisfaction, the test applied will be either subjective or objective depending upon the subject matter of the contract. If the subject matter involves personal taste, such as works of art, medical services, tailoring services, or the like, the subjective test will apply, and the condition will be satisfied only if the party is personally satisfied. If the subject matter involves mechanical fitness or utility (e. g., a contract for repair of an automobile), an objective test will apply, and the condition will be satisfied if a reasonable person would be pleased or satisfied regardless of whether the party to the contract is personally or subjectively pleased.

(2) *Condition subsequent.* A condition subsequent is a condition the happening of which cuts off or extinguishes a previously held duty to perform or to continue performing. For example, suppose that Fred Farmer promises to plow Tom Neighbor's fields "as long as the weather holds, but if there is rain making the fields muddy, there is no further duty to plow." Because Fred is under a duty to plow until and unless the condition occurs (i. e., until and unless there is a break in the weather, and the fields become muddy), the condition is a condition subsequent: the happening of the condition will cut off or extinguish Fred's duty to perform.

In contrast to a condition precedent, the burden of proving a condition subsequent is always on the defendant. Thus, if Fred Farmer fails to plow or stops plowing, and Tom sues Fred for breach of contract, it will be up to Fred to prove that the condition subsequent occurred, extinguishing his duty of performance under the contract.

Sometimes, what looks to be a condition subsequent is, in reality, a condition precedent. Suppose, for example, that Tom Neighbor promises to pay Fred Farmer $3,000 for plowing his fields, "but my duty to pay will be extinguished if the plowing is not completed by July 15th." Though phrased as a condition subsequent, the condition is actually a condition precedent: until and unless the plowing is completed by June 15th, Tom Neighbor has no legal duty to pay the $3,000. Where a condition precedent is expressed in terms of a condition subsequent, the burden of proving the condition falls, again, on the defendant. Thus, if Fred Farmer does not finish plowing by July 15th, but finishes later and brings suit for payment, Tom Neighbor will have to prove the nonhappening of the condition precedent (i. e., that the plowing was not completed by July 15th) in order to avoid liability under the contract. Upon proof of failure of the condition, the court will not enforce Tom's promise to pay $3,000; however, the court is likely to provide Fred with some measure of relief on a quasi contract basis.

(3) *Condition concurrent.* Concurrent conditions are conditions, either express or implied by law (as opposed to being implied by fact), that must be performed at the same time. Whenever a bilateral contract explicitly conditions each party's performance upon performance by the other party, the conditions are express conditions concurrent. When a bilateral contract merely fixes the time of performance for both parties at or near the same time, and it is practicable for both parties to perform simultaneously, each party's performance is a constructive (i. e., implied by law) condition concurrent to the other party's performance. Whether express or constructive, a condition concurrent is satisfied by a tender of performance. A "tender", as you will recall, is simply a statement that "I am ready to perform if you are." Upon refusal of tender, the party tendering performance can sue for breach of contract. For example, if Fred Farmer and Dora Dealer enter into a contract wherein Fred promises to buy a tractor from Dora for $20,000 on Monday afternoon in return for Dora's promise to sell the tractor to Fred on Monday afternoon for $20,000, neither party can sue the other for breach of contract unless he or she has tendered performance to the other. Though it is nowhere expressly stated in the contract that each party's performance is conditioned upon tender of performance by the other, concurrent conditions of performance are implied by law (i. e., they are constructive conditions concurrent) to carry out the intent of the parties. Thus, if Fred wants to sue Dora for failing to deliver the tractor, Fred must first offer to pay for the tractor "if Dora will deliver it". And if Dora wants to sue Fred for failing to pay for the tractor, she must first offer to deliver the tractor "if Fred will pay for it".

What is the Statute of Frauds?

We have seen that although a valid contract exists, the promised performances of the parties may be subject to a condition precedent, a condition subsequent, or express or constructive conditions concurrent. Now we will learn that a valid contract may not be enforceable unless the party seeking to enforce the contract can produce a certain kind of written evidence. This is the subject matter of the Statute of Frauds. Every state has passed such a statute specifically providing that certain contracts are not enforceable in the absence of special written evidence.

The original "Statute of Frauds" was passed by England in 1677 to prevent fraud and perjury in litigation. The Statute was crucially needed because the courts, at that time, would not permit parties to a lawsuit to testify on their own behalf. While a party unjustly accused of breach of contract could not come to his or her own defense in court, the party could, upon the passage of the Statute of Frauds, insist upon the production of certain written evidence of the contract at issue. The Statute was also needed because the English courts had no power at that time to throw out a jury verdict even where the verdict was obviously contrary to all the evidence produced in court. With the Statute of Frauds in effect, it was much less likely that juries would reach the wrong conclusions.

Thus, the Statute of Frauds has nothing to do with fraud in the inducement or fraud in the execution. Rather, the Statute is designed to prevent fraud and perjury in the proof of certain contracts —it does so by requiring the production of special written evidence as a condition to enforcement of the contracts.

There are four "keys" to understanding and properly applying the Statute of Frauds:

(1) *Understand that most oral contracts are enforceable.* In most cases, the Statute of Frauds does not apply, and so long as there is mutual assent, considera-

tion, capacity, and legality, the contract, though completely oral, is legally enforceable.

(2) *Know that where the Statute of Frauds does apply, the contract is not void, but merely unenforceable between the original parties to the contract.* Even where the required written evidence is not available, and the contract is not enforceable, the contract is still valid for all other purposes and as to all other people. Thus, a completely oral contract to sell an automobile for $600 (contracts for the sale of goods for $500 or more fall within the Statute) is effective to transfer ownership of the property, assuming neither party reneges on his or her promise. However, if one of the parties does renege, and the other party takes him or her to court, the contract will be unenforceable because of the failure to comply with the Statute of Frauds. Of course, a person not a party to the contract cannot complain that the contract does not comply with the Statute: only one of the original parties to the agreement can set up the Statute as a defense to enforcement of the contract.

(3) *Know that the Statute of Frauds applies in only six situations.* The Statute requires special written evidence of the following: (a) promises to answer for the debt of another; (b) promises by a personal representative of a decedent's estate to answer for the decedent's debts out of the personal representative's own funds; (c) agreements made in consideration of marriage; (d) contracts for the sale of land; (e) contracts that cannot be performed within a year's time; and (f) sales of goods for $500 or more.

(4) *Appreciate that the written evidence required by the Statute is but a memo, signed by the party being sued (the defendant), that embraces certain of the essential terms of the agreement.* The contract need not be fully written; it is therefore misleading to say, as so many people do, that a contract that falls

within the Statute of Frauds must be in writing.

The four "keys" to understanding the Statute of Frauds will be enlarged upon in the sections that follow. Keep the "keys" in mind and you will have no difficulty in properly applying the Statute.

What kind of written evidence does the Statute of Frauds require?

In five of the six situations falling within the Statute of Frauds, the only way to satify the Statute is through a writing. (As will be seen later, the UCC provides a sale of goods for $500 or more will satisfy the Statute with less of a writing, and with no writing at all under some circumstances.) The writing, however, need not be a fully written integrated (unified) contract. Too often, students and laypeople mistakenly believe that a formal written contract is required to satisfy the Statute, particularly where a contract to sell real property is concerned. This is simply not so. All that is required is a written and signed *memorandum* of the essential terms of the agreement. The memo must include:

(1) The identity of the contracting parties;

(2) A description of the subject matter of the contract;

(3) The terms and conditions of the agreement;

(4) A recital of the consideration (not a requirement in all states); and

(5) The signature of the party to be charged (i. e., the defendant or party being sued).

So long as the required information is present, the memo may consist of a letter, a telegram, a mere notation on a party's books of record. The memo may even be composed of several writings so long as the writings refer to each other or to the same subject matter, or are physically attached.

The signature of the party being sued need not be a subscription (a formal signature at the end of the writing). Any symbol or mark intended by the party to authenticate the writing will do—for example, initials, a letterhead, a rubber stamp, etc. The fact that the plaintiff (the party bringing suit) did not sign the writing makes no difference whatsoever: it is the defendant's signature alone that must appear on the document.

How does the Statute of Frauds apply to "suretyship" promises (i. e., promises to answer for the debt of another)?

Black's Law Dictionary defines a contract of "suretyship" as "a contract whereby one person engages to be answerable for the debt, default, or miscarriage of another."[1] The subject of suretyship is covered in detail in Ch. 27. For now, it is enough to know that the Statute of Frauds applies to suretyship promises. You will recall that two of the situations falling within the Statute are promises to answer for the debt of another, and promises by a personal representative of a decedent's estate to answer for the decedent's debts out of the personal representative's own funds. These are suretyship promises and require a written and signed memorandum in order to be enforceable.

Promises to answer for the debt of another. A promise to discharge or answer for the debt of another (a *collateral* promise as opposed to a *primary* promise to answer for one's own debts) is legally enforceable only if the promise is supported by a written memo signed by the promisor. However, for the Statute of Frauds to apply, the promisor must not already be liable on the debt at the time he or she makes the promise; and the promise must be made to the creditor

rather than to the debtor personally. For example, suppose that Trish Kimberley promises Mike Merchant, the creditor of her brother Jim Kimberley, that she will pay the debt Jim owes to Mike if Jim fails to pay. Trish's promise, in this case, falls within the Statute of Frauds, and unless Trish has signed a written memo containing the essential terms of the agreement, the promise is not enforceable. On the other hand, if Trish promises Jim that she will pay his debt to Mike Merchant, the promise is enforceable (assuming all four elements of a valid contract are present) despite the fact that the promise is completely oral. The promise here is made to the debtor— not to the creditor—and the Statute of Frauds does not apply.

Sometimes, what looks to be a collateral promise is, in reality, a primary promise (i. e., a promise to answer for one's own debt). A primary promise does not fall within the Statute of Frauds and, therefore, does not require a signed and written memo to be enforceable. For example, suppose that Trish Kimberley telephones Mike Merchant and says, "I want to buy a pair of boots for my brother, Jim. Would you please deliver the boots to Jim and bill me." Here, though Trish is promising to pay for boots to be delivered to her brother, the promise is primary and not collateral: Trish is directly contracting with Mike on her own behalf—she is not promising to answer for a debt incurred by Jim. The Statute of Frauds does not apply, and the contract is enforceable despite the absence of any written evidence.

Similarly, the "main purpose" or "leading object" rule states that where a promisor's main purpose or leading object in making a collateral promise is to secure an advantage for himself or her-

---

1. Henry Campbell Black, *Black's Law Dictionary*, Revised Fourth Edition, West Publishing Co., 1968, p. 1611.

self or to otherwise directly benefit, the promise is not truly a promise to answer for the debt of another, and so is enforceable without written evidence. For example, suppose that Trish Kimberley hires Jim Kimberley to do the interior decorating of Trish's new home. Jim is to personally buy all the paint, wallpaper, furniture, drapes, etc., and Trish is to pay Jim a flat fee upon completion of the job. After the work is half finished, Trish learns that Jim is low on funds and is having difficulty obtaining credit at the local shops. Wanting to get her house completed on time, Trish promises Tom Merchant that she will pay off any debts incurred by Jim for the wallpaper and other furnishings if Jim fails to pay them. As the main purpose or leading object of Trish's promise is to benefit herself, the Statute of Frauds does not apply, and the promise, though oral, is enforceable.

Promises by a personal representative to answer for the decedent's debts out of the personal representative's own funds. A personal representative (an executor or administrator) is a person appointed by the probate court to administer the estate of a deceased person (see Ch. 30). A personal representative's promise to answer for the decedent's debts out of his or her own funds falls within the Statute of Frauds requiring a written memo signed by the personal representative to be enforceable. Typically, this suretyship situation arises where a son or daughter of the deceased is named as personal representative in the deceased's will; the estate contains insufficient assets to cover the deceased's debts, and the child promises to pay the debts out of his or her own funds. Although all four elements of a valid contract are present, the promise is unenforceable unless the deceased's creditor can produce a written memo signed by the child and embracing the essential terms of the agreement.

How does the Statute of Frauds apply to agreements made in consideration of marriage?

Agreements made in consideration of marriage fall within the Statute of Frauds and must be supported by a written and signed memo in order to be enforceable. Such agreements do not include mutual promises to marry exchanged between prospective spouses. Mutual promises to marry are valid contractual promises, and are enforceable even in the absence of any written evidence. Thus, if a man and woman orally exchange mutual promises to marry on a certain date, a valid, enforceable contract comes into existence assuming that all four elements of a valid contract are present. And they usually are present. Each party's acceptance of the other's offer of marriage gives rise to *mutual assent*; the agreement is normally free of *fraud, duress, mistake, undue influence,* or *unconscionable act*; each party's promise to marry serves as *consideration* for the other party's return promise; so long as each party has reached the age of consent, there is contractual *capacity;* and, of course, it is *legal* to marry so long as neither party is already married to another. Obviously, the law, in enforcing the agreement, will never require the parties to actually marry—either may back out of the wedding itself. However, if either party has incurred expenses in reliance upon the contract (e. g., in purchasing flowers for the ceremony, or in renting a reception hall), he or she will be allowed to recover compensatory money damages (damages are discussed in a following section) based upon the other party's breach of promise to marry. Again, no written evidence of the promise is necessary.

The "agreements made in consideration of marriage" that the Statute of Frauds does apply to are antenuptial or pre-nuptial property settlement agreements (i. e., pre-marital promises to transfer money or property or anything else of value in exchange for marriage or a promise of marriage). For example, suppose that Jim Kimberley promises to transfer his 500 shares of General Motors stock to Ann Malone after marriage in return for Ann's promise to marry Jim. If, after marrying Ann, Jim refuses to transfer the stock as promised, Ann can enforce the promise in court only if she can produce a written memo signed by Jim and containing the essential terms of the agreement. Although the agreement is a valid contract, it is not enforceable under the Statute of Frauds unless the special written evidence is available.

How does the Statute of Frauds apply to contracts for the sale of real property?

The Statute of Frauds states that any contract for the sale of land or an interest in land must be supported by a written memorandum signed by the party to be charged (i. e., by the party being sued to carry out the promise).

Because the transfer of *any* interest in land falls within the Statute, it is important to keep in mind the distinction between real and personal property and the many and varied interests in land that are possible. You will recall from Ch. 2 that real property and personal property sometimes mesh insofar as minerals, trees, crops, fixtures, and rentals are concerned. Where the end product of the meshing is real property, the Statute of Frauds applies to any contract for sale of the property; where the end product is personal property, the real property Statute of Frauds does not apply (although a sale of the property may nonetheless fall within the Statute as a sale of goods for $500 or more). In determining whether a particular interest in property is real or personal for purposes of the Statute of Frauds, you might find it helpful to review Chapters 2, 4, 5, and 6 (Ch. 4 de-

scribes the various interests possible in land, including fees, life estates, vested and contingent remainders, and executory interests; Ch. 5 covers incidental rights in real property; and Ch. 6 deals with easements, profits, and other transferable real property rights).

A contract to sell real property or any interest in real property is unenforceable in the absence of a written memo signed by the party to be charged. A single exception to this rule arises where there has been a transfer of possession under an oral land sale contract. The transfer of possession of the land is considered sufficient part performance of the contract to remove it from the Statute of Frauds and to make the promise to transfer the land enforceable even in the absence of a written memo signed by the promisor. The idea is that the purchaser's taking of possession with the landowner's consent provides sufficient evidence of the existence of a contract so as to diminish the likelihood of fraud or perjury. A minority of courts require something more than the mere transfer of possession to remove the contract from the Statute's operation: in some jurisdictions, the purchaser must not only receive possession of the land, but must erect permanent improvements on the property for which no adequate compensation in money damages is possible; in other jurisdictions, the purchaser must pay all or part of the purchase price in addition to receiving possession from the landowner.

How does the Statute of Frauds apply to contracts that cannot be performed within a year's time?

The Statute of Frauds provides that a contract that cannot be performed within a year's time must be supported by a written and signed memo if it is to be enforceable. This provision refers only to contracts that, by their very terms, cannot *possibly* be performed within one year from the making of the contract. The one year period commences on the date the contract is entered into—not on the date the promised performance is to begin. Thus, if, on Wednesday, Mike Merchant promises to hire Jim Kimberley to work in Mike's store for a period of one year, the year to begin next Monday, the contract falls within the Statute of Frauds and is legally unenforceable by Jim in the absence of a written memo signed by Mike. The same result follows where Jim Kimberley, on October 1st, promises to lease one-half his duplex to Jean Cherry for a period of one year, the year to begin on December 1st. Because the contract cannot possibly be performed within one year from October 1st, the contract falls within the Statute of Frauds and is unenforceable in the absence of a written memo signed by the party to be charged. (You will recall from Ch. 2 that a leasehold is not classified as real property and so does not fall within the Statute of Frauds on that basis.)

It is important to realize that the Statute of Frauds applies only to promises that cannot *possibly* be performed within a year's time. It makes no difference that performance of the contract is *likely* to continue for more than a year, or that the contracting parties *envision* a lengthier period of performance. If there is any possibility that the contract may be fully performed within a year's time, the Statute of Frauds does not apply, and the contract is enforceable without any written evidence whatsover. For example, where a promised performance is dependent upon a condition precedent or subject to a condition subsequent, the promise is enforceable though made orally if the condition can occur (however unlikely) within a year's time. Thus, an oral promise "to buy your antique car as soon as I inherit my share of my uncle's estate" is an enforceable promise despite the lack of any written evidence. Though the promisor's uncle is likely to

live for many years, it is possible that he will die within the year, and the promise could be fully performed within that time. Similarly, a promise "to take care of Sheila until she dies" could be fully performed within a year and so is not subject to the Statute of Frauds. And the "requirements" and "output" contracts discussed in Ch. 9 escape the operation of the Statute (insofar as it relates to promises capable of performance within a year's time) because the party purchasing his or her "requirements" or selling his or her "output" may go out of business within a year's time and have no further requirements or output.

Even where an oral contract truly cannot be performed within a year's time, most courts still hold the contract enforceable if one of the parties has fully performed his or her part of the bargain. Suppose, for example, that Mike Merchant orally promises to pay Jim Kimberley a $15,000 bonus if Jim will work for Mike for two more years. Here, the promise truly cannot be performed within a year's time and so is unenforceable in view of the lack of written evidence. However, if Jim works for Mike for two more years, the contract is fully performed on one side (Jim's side), and most courts will hold the contract enforceable despite the lack of written evidence.

In some states, the Statute of Frauds covers, not only promises that cannot be performed within a year, but promises that cannot be performed within the promisor's lifetime as well as agreements to make a will or leave property to a person at death. Under such an extended statute, a contract wherein the parties agree that the party who outlives the other will take care of the funeral expenses of the party who dies first is unenforceable in the absence of a written memo signed by the party to be charged. The same is true of a promise to make a will leaving a particular parcel of real property to another.

What is an "equal dignity" statute?

In Ch. 21, we will learn that one person (called a *principal*) may authorize another (called an *agent*) to contract on his or her behalf. For now, it is enough to know that most states have enacted "equal dignity" statutes providing that where a principal authorizes an agent to contract with regard to a subject matter covered by the Statute of Frauds, the agent's authority must be supported by a written memo signed by the principal or any contracts the agent enters into will not be enforceable against the principal. Thus, where Jim Kimberley orally authorizes Dan Malone to sell Jim's 50 acre ranch, and Dan sells the land to Jenny Cartwright, the land sale contract is not enforceable against Jim unless Dan or Jenny can produce a written memo signed by Jim, authorizing Dan to make the sale.

How does the Statute of Frauds apply to sales of goods for $500 or more?

We have left consideration of the sale of goods for $500 or more for last because, of the six subject matters covered by the Statute of Frauds, it is the only one that can satisfy the Statute with far less of a written memo, and in some cases, with other than a written memo. The Uniform Commercial Code tightly controls this area of the Statute of Frauds at Section 2–201 as follows.

The UCC provides:

(1) Except as otherwise provided in this section a contract for the sale of goods for the price of $500 or more is not enforceable by way of action or defense unless there is some writing sufficient to indicate that a contract for sale has been made between the parties and signed by the party against whom

enforcement is sought or by his authorized agent or broker. A writing is not insufficient because it omits or incorrectly states a term agreed upon but the contract is not enforceable under this paragraph beyond the quantity of goods shown in such writing.

(2) Between merchants if within a reasonable time a writing in confirmation of the contract and sufficient against the sender is received and the party receiving it has reason to know its contents, it satisfies the requirements of subsection (1) against such party unless written notice of objection to its contents is given within 10 days after it is received.

(3) A contract which does not satisfy the requirements of subsection (1) but which is valid in other respects is enforceable

(a) if the goods are to be specially manufactured for the buyer and are not suitable for sale to others in the ordinary course of the seller's business and the seller, before notice of repudiation is received and under circumstances which reasonably indicate that the goods are for the buyer, has made either a substantial beginning of their manufacture or commitments for their procurement; or

(b) if the party against whom enforcement is sought admits in his pleading, testimony or otherwise in court that a contract for sale was made, but the contract is not enforceable under this provision beyond the quantity of goods admitted; or

(c) with respect to goods for which payment has been made and accepted or which have been received and accepted.

The *Official Comment* to the Code clarifies Section 2–201:

The Official Comment provides:

(1) The   *   *   *   writing [required under Subsection (1)] need not contain all the material terms of the contract and such material terms as are stated need not be precisely stated. All that is required is that the writing afford a basis for believing that the offered oral evidence rests on a real transaction. It may be written in lead pencil on a scratch pad. It need not indicate which party is the buyer and which the seller. The only term which must appear is the quantity term which need not be accurately stated but recovery is limited to the amount stated. The price, time and place of payment or delivery, the general quality of the goods, or any particular warranties may all be omitted.

     *   *   *

Only three definite and invariable requirements as to the memorandum are made by this subsection: First, it must evidence a contract for the sale of goods; second, it must be "signed," a word which includes any authentication which identifies the parties to be charged; and third, it must specify a quantity.

(2) "Partial performance" as a substitute for the required memorandum can validate the contract only for the goods which have been accepted or for which payment has been made and accepted.

     *   *   *

(3) Between merchants, failure to answer a written confirmation of a contract within ten days of receipt is tantamount to a writing
     *   *   *.

(4) Failure to satisfy the requirements of this section does not render the contract void for all purposes, but merely prevents it from being judicially enforced in favor of a party to the contract   *   *   *.

     *   *   *

(6) It is not necessary that the writing be delivered to anybody. It need not be signed or authenticated by both parties but it is, of course, not sufficient against one who has not signed it. Prior to a dispute no one can determine which party's signing of the memorandum may be necessary but from the time of contracting each party should be aware that to him it is signing by the other which is important.

(7) If the making of a contract is admitted in court, either in a written pleading, by stipulation or by oral statement before the court, no additional writing is necessary for protection against fraud. Under this section it is no longer possible to admit the contract in court and still treat the Statute as a defense.

———

Thus, it is seen that while a sale of goods for $500 or more falls within the Statute of Frauds, far less of a written memo is required to prove the sale than is required to prove promises within the other five subject matter areas covered by the Statute. In the sale of goods situation, the only essential memo term is *quantity,* and even it may be misstated (although recovery, in that case, will be limited to the misstated amount). All that is required is that the writing afford a basis for believing that the oral evidence offered rests upon a real transaction. And, of course, the writing must be signed by the party to be charged.

It is also seen that, in the following instances, the Statute of Frauds may be satisfied in the sale of goods situation with other than a written memo.

(1) If the buyer *accepts and receives* all or part of the goods, the contract, though oral, is enforceable to the extent that the goods are accepted and received.

(2) If the buyer makes *part payment* for the goods, the contract, though oral, is enforceable as to the goods paid for. Obviously, there is little problem where the buyer has contracted for several items —the buyer will receive a share of the property proportionate to what he or she has paid for. The problem arises where part payment is made on a single indivisible unit (one item as opposed to several). Because the unit is indivisible, the contract cannot be partially enforced; and the question becomes whether part payment will support enforcement of the contract in its entirety. A Pennsylvania court has ruled that it will not—that payment must be made in full where a single unit item is involved. The better view, however, is to the contrary. Thus, in Lockwood v. Smigel, 18 Cal.App.3d 800, 96 Cal.Rptr. 289 (1971), the court held that a $100 down payment on an $11,000 Rolls Royce was sufficient to prove an oral promise to buy the car.

(3) If the seller is required by the terms of the contract to manufacture *special goods* for the buyer (special goods are goods unsuitable for sale to others in the ordinary course of the seller's business), and the seller has made a substantial beginning in their manufacture or has contracted for their procurement, no writing is needed to support the promise to buy the goods.

(4) If the contract is *between merchants,* and one of the merchants within a reasonable time sends a written confir-

mation of the agreement to the other merchant, and that merchant fails to object in writing to the confirmation within 10 days, the contract is enforceable against the merchant who receives the confirmation. Ordinarily, such a confirmation would serve as a valid memo against the sender who signs it, but not as against the receiving party who does not sign it. The UCC has thus created an exception to the general rule requiring production of a written memo *signed by the party to be charged.* The Code states that where a merchant fails to timely object in writing to another merchant's written confirmation of an oral agreement, the merchant's failure to object provides a sufficient basis for enforcement of the agreement.

(5) Finally, if the party to be charged admits in court or in the pleadings [2] preliminary to court that a contract does, in fact, exist, the contract will be enforceable to the extent of the party's admission.

You will recall from Ch. 9 that an agreement modifying a contract for the sale of goods needs no consideration to be binding. U.C.C. Section 2–209(17). If the modification results in a sale of goods for less than $500, the modification need not be written in order to be valid. Section 2–209(3).

Do any other promises under the UCC require a written memo to be enforceable?

Two other promises under the UCC are unenforceable in the absence of a written memo signed by the party to be charged.

(1) Section 1–206 of the Code provides that a contract for the sale of contract rights, royalties, copyrights, or other intangible personal property rights is not

---

2. The "pleadings" are the papers that must be filed with the court to commence court action. Called the "complaint", "an-

swer", and "reply", they are discussed in Appendix A.

enforceable beyond the amount of $5,000 unless it is evidenced by a written memo signed by the party to be charged. (You will recall that intangible personal property rights as defined in Chapters 1 through 3 do not fall within the Code's definition of "goods".)

(2) Section 8–319 of the Code provides that all contracts for the sale of securities (e. g., common stocks or bonds) must be supported by a written and signed memo in order to be enforceable.

What is the effect of noncompliance with the Statute of Frauds?

In nearly all states, a failure to comply with the Statute of Frauds serves merely to render the contract voidable as between the original parties to the contract. There is no question but what a valid contract was formed; and if the parties voluntarily choose to go through with the agreement, no third party may complain that the contract is oral. The author, for example, was involved in a tax case in which two taxpayers had orally agreed to transfer property rights worth many millions of dollars. The parties' agreement was based solely on a handshake—nothing was in writing. Since no written memo of the agreement could be produced, either party could have avoided the contract because the subject matter was clearly within the Statute of Frauds. Yet both parties fully performed. The government, in contesting the treatment of the transaction for tax purposes, brought up the Statute of Frauds and claimed that the agreement was unenforceable. The court, however, was quick to point out that third parties cannot raise the issue of the Statute of Frauds—only the original parties to the contract can do so. Here, the oral contract had been fully performed and was valid in every respect ("for all purposes and as to all people"). The taxing authorities had no standing to complain.

It should also be pointed out that if only one of the parties has signed a memorandum satisfying the Statute of Frauds, the contract will be enforceable only against that party and not against the other.

However, if a party has transferred property or conferred benefits upon another pursuant to an unenforceable oral promise, most courts will grant restitution to the party in quasi contract so as to prevent unjust enrichment. And if a party represents by words or conduct that he or she has reduced an oral agreement to writing, and the other party relies upon the representation to his or her substantial economic detriment, the party making the representation will be estopped from asserting the Statute of Frauds as a defense to enforcement of the contract.

Finally, if the result of allowing a party to defend against enforcement on the basis of the Statute of Frauds is to do "unconscionable injury" to the other party, the promise may be deemed enforceable even in the absence of a written memo.

What is the effect of finding that a contract does not fall within the Statute of Frauds?

Before moving on to interpretation of contracts, one final word of caution: it is very important not to make the wrong conclusion about the validity and enforceability of a contract after correctly determining that the contract does not fall within the Statute of Frauds. Too often, students correctly state that a contract does not fall within the Statute, but then turn right around and mistakenly conclude that, because it does not, the oral contract is neither valid nor enforceable. This conclusion is exactly incorrect. If a contract does not fall within the Statute of Frauds, it is valid and enforceable even though it is oral. Remember, our first "key" to understanding the Statute was to learn that most promises are oral promises, most oral promises do not fall within the Statute of Frauds, and most promises are therefore enforceable without any written evidence whatsoever. In most cases, all that is required for enforceability is the presence of mutual assent, consideration, capacity, and legality.

What rules of construction are used by the courts in interpreting contracts?

Even where a valid and enforceable contract exists, the parties sometimes disagree as to the meaning of ambiguous language used in the contract. Where this occurs, the courts are called upon to interpret the language and determine its effect using common law *rules of construction*. The following 15 rules (the first five are taken from Section 228 of the *Restatement Second of the Law of Contracts*) are commonly used in interpreting ambiguous contract language:

(1) Words and other conduct are to be interpreted in light of all the circumstances, and if the principal purpose of the parties is ascertainable, their purpose is to be given great weight.

(2) A writing is to be interpreted as a whole, and all writings that are part of the same transaction are to be interpreted together.

(3) Unless a different intention is manifested,

   (a) language is to be interpreted in accordance with any generally prevailing meaning it may have; and

   (b) technical terms and words of art are to be given their technical meaning when used in a transaction within the technical field.

(4) Where an agreement calls for repeated occasions of performance by a party, and the party performs one or more times, with the other party having knowledge of the nature of the performance and an opportunity to object to it, any course of performance accepted or acquiesced in by the party without objection is to be given great weight in interpretation of the contract.

(5) Wherever reasonable, the parties' manifestations of intent with regard to an agreement are to be interpreted as consistent with each other and with any relevant course of performance (under the same contract), course of dealing (under prior contracts between the same parties), or usage of trade (trade custom and practice).

(6) A contract is to be interpreted according to the business custom and usage prevailing in the place where the contract is made or where it is to be performed.

(7) Where printed provisions of a contract are inconsistent with written or typed provisions, the written or typed provisions are to prevail over the printed provisions.

(8) Because the policy of the law is to uphold contracts, not to render them inoperative, an interpretation that will give an agreement a lawful effect is to be preferred over an interpretation that will make all or part of the agreement unreasonable, unlawful, or of no effect.

(9) Where general provisions of a contract are inconsistent with specific provisions, the specific provisions control over the general.

(10) An interpretation that favors a public interest is to be preferred over an interpretation that favors a private interest.

(11) Where words conflict with figures or numerals, the words prevail.

(12) Where a contract is ambiguous, and two reasonable interpretations are possible, the contract is to be interpreted more strictly against the party who drafted it. (The reasoning is that the party who drafted the agreement selected the ambiguous language, so it is only fair

that the contract be interpreted against him or her and in favor of the other party. This is particularly true in the case of a printed contract such as an insurance policy: the printed form suggests that the drafter had competent legal advice while the other party may have had no alternative to accepting the form.)

(13) Where possible, an ambiguous contract is to be interpreted so that neither party gains an unreasonable advantage over the other. (This rule of construction is often used in interpreting adhesion contracts wherein a party in an inferior bargaining position must accept an offer on a "take it or leave it" basis.)

(14) A contract generally is to be governed by the law of the state having the most significant contacts with the transaction or transactions to be accomplished. It is said that the contract "gravitates" in this state.

(15) Where two or more people make a promise or promises (e. g., where Pat and Bill promise to paint Martha's house) it is presumed that the promises and resulting obligations of the parties are *joint* and not *several*. To say that parties are *jointly liable* on a contract is to say that all are liable for the entire contract obligation, and that all must be named in any court action on the contract (so long as all may be found within the area of the court's jurisdiction). If the party to whom performance is owed releases one of the jointly liable parties, all the other jointly liable parties are also released. With regard to *several liability* on the other hand, each of the parties specifically promises to be individually bound, using such language as "each of us makes this promise severally and not jointly." The result is that each party is individually bound and may be individually sued; thus, the release of one of the parties does not release the others. Sometimes, the parties use such language as, "We and each of us jointly and severally promise to be bound". The contract

in this case, is *joint and several,* and the promisee may treat the contract as either. Thus, the promisee may sue all or part of the parties jointly, or each of them individually. And a release of one does not affect the liability of the others.

What is the parol evidence rule?

The parol evidence rule comes into play only where parties to a contract have reduced their agreement to a final and complete writing. For the rule to operate, the writing must be a fully written integrated agreement, the term "integrated" meaning that the parties intended the writing to be the final and complete expression of their contract.

Assuming that the parties sign such an agreement, the parol evidence rule states that the fully written integrated contract may not be changed, altered, varied, or modified by any oral or written evidence (apart from the writing) occurring prior to or at the time of the signing of the agreement. Thus, where the rule applies, it is not permissible to contradict or vary the terms of the writing by any other evidence. The reason for the rule is that parties who have reduced their agreement to a writing intended as the final expression of their contract should be able to rely upon that expression without worry that one of the parties will later claim that something else was intended. It is a good rule for that reason.

The parties, however, must take care that all the contract terms and provisions are included in the writing before they sign it, intending it to serve as the final and complete expression of their agreement. If they carelessly leave out terms, they may find that the parol evidence rule prevents them from later offering evidence of the terms.

Usually, the parol evidence rule operates to bar the admission of evidence as follows. One of the parties to a fully written integrated contract initiates legal action against the other party for breach of contract. Either the plaintiff in proving the charge or the defendant in defending against it offers parol evidence that tends to change, alter, vary, or modify the written agreement. Strictly speaking, the term "parol evidence" refers to oral testimony, "parol" meaning "oral"; however, with regard to the parol evidence rule, the term encompasses both oral and written evidence contradictory to the fully and finally written contract. Thus, if one of the parties offers oral or written evidence that tends to change, alter, vary, or modify the written agreement the party against whom it is offered may object to its admission into evidence on grounds of the parol evidence rule. The rule will operate as a bar, preventing the court from considering the evidence.

Just as there are four "keys" to understanding the Statute of Frauds, there are three "keys" to understanding the parol evidence rule. As you will see, the rule does not often apply.

(1) *The rule applies only to fully written integrated contracts.* It does not apply to contracts that are partly oral and partly written. Nor does it apply to writings such as receipts or estimates, or to oral contracts entered into independently of a fully written integrated contract. It is not unusual for parties to enter into more than one contract at the same time—one contract may be fully reduced to writing, and a second may be oral and independent of the written contract. While the parol evidence rule operates to bar contradictory evidence about the written contract, it does not bar evidence about the independent oral agreement. For example, a party might agree to buy a movie theatre from another, all the specifics of the agreement put into a fully written and integrated contract. At the same time, the party might orally agree to hire the former owner of the theatre to work as a movie projectionist for a period of one year. The second contract is exactly that—a second and separate agreement having nothing to do with the first. Thus, while parol evidence of the first agreement is barred, parol evidence of the second is not.

(2) *The rule applies only to evidence occurring prior to or at the time of the signing of the fully written integrated contract.* Evidence that occurs after the parties have signed the agreement is not barred (e. g., the parol evidence rule never operates to prevent the showing of a subsequent change or modification of the written contract).

(3) *The rule applies only to evidence that changes, alters, varies, or modifies the terms of the fully written integrated contract.* Evidence that does not change or modify the terms is always admissible whether the evidence occurs prior to, simultaneously with, or subsequent to the signing of the written agreement. Evidence may always be offered, for example, to show the following:

(a) *That there is a condition precedent to the operation of the written contract.* Whether oral or written, the condition precedent does not alter or change the terms of the writing—it merely states that the written contract *as it is written* is not to operate until and unless a certain condition occurs.

(b) *That there was fraud, duress, mistake, undue influence, unconscionable act, forgery, incapacity, illegality, or failure of consideration (i. e., failure of a party to perform his or her obligations under the contract).* Proof of these things does not vary, alter, change, or modify the contract as it is written, but simply provides a basis for relieving the other party of his or her obligation to perform under the contract.

(c) *That the written language of the contract is ambiguous and needs to be explained or interpreted.* To explain or interpret language is not to contradict, alter, change, or modify it. Thus, the courts may use the rules of construction presented in the previous section to determine what the parties intended by their words. The parties themselves may offer evidence occurring prior to or at the time of signing the written agreement to explain away gross clerical or typographical errors, and to show that words normally having a plain or obvious meaning were used in the contract to mean something else. For example, in the case of Pacific Gas & Electric Co. v. Thomas Drayage Rigging Co., 69 Cal.2d 33, 69 Cal.Rptr. 561, 442 P.2d 641 (1968), the written contract stated that one party agreed to pay for "any injury to property." The court held that parol evidence was admissible to explain that the term "property", as used in the contract, referred only to property of third persons—not to property of the contracting parties themselves. Thus, the defendant was not responsible for injury to the plaintiff's property. The court concluded that evidence of usage or custom is admissible to define the meaning of contract terms because to define or explain is not to contradict or change.

Section 2–202 of the Uniform Commercial Code and the *Official Comment* following the Section deal with final and complete writings for the sale of goods.

The UCC provides:

Section 2–202. Final Written Expression: Parol or Extrinsic Evidence

Terms with respect to which the confirmatory memoranda of the parties agree or which are otherwise set forth in a writing intended by the parties as a final expression of their agreement with respect to such terms as are included therein may not be contradicted by evidence of any prior agreement or of a contemporaneous oral agreement but may be explained or supplemented

(a) by course of dealing or usage of trade (Section 1–205) or by course of performance (Section 2–208); and

(b) by evidence of consistent additional terms unless the court finds the writing to have been intended also as a complete and exclusive statement of the terms of the agreement.

Official Comment

Purposes: 1. This section definitely rejects:

(a) Any assumption that because a writing has been worked out which is final on some matters, it is to be taken as including all the matters agreed upon;

* * *

2. Paragraph (a) makes admissible evidence of course of dealing, usage of trade and course of performance to explain or supplement the terms of any writing stating the agreement of the parties in order that the true understanding of the parties as to the agreement may be reached. * * *

3. Under paragraph (b) consistent additional terms, not reduced to writing, may be proved unless the court finds that the writing was intended by both parties as a complete and exclusive statement of all the terms.

Section 1–205 defines "course of dealing" and "usage of trade" as follows:

(1) A course of dealing is a sequence of previous conduct between the parties to a particular transaction which is fairly to be regarded as establishing a common basis of understanding for interpreting their expressions and other conduct [e. g., a provision interpreted one way in a prior contract between the parties will likely mean the same thing in a subsequent contract].

(2) A usage of trade is any practice or method of dealing having such

regularity of observance in a place, vocation or trade as to justify an expectation that it will be observed with respect to the transaction in question [i. e., community custom and usage].

(3) A course of dealing between parties and any usage of trade in the vocation or trade in which they are engaged or of which they are or should be aware give particular meaning to and supplement or qualify terms of an agreement.

(4) The express terms of an agreement and applicable course of dealing or usage of trade shall be construed wherever reasonable as consistent with each other; but when such construction is reasonable express terms control both course of dealing and usage of trade and course of dealing controls usage of trade.

Section 2–208 adds the following regarding "course of performance".

It says:

(1) Where the contract for sale involves repeated occasions for performance by either party with knowledge of the nature of the performance and opportunity for objection to it by the other, any course of performance accepted or acquiesced in without objection shall be relevant to determine the meaning of the agreement.

What occurs where a contract is valid, enforceable, and clear in meaning?

To this point, we have learned that a valid contract exists only where there is mutual assent, capacity, consideration, and legality; that there are frequently

conditions precedent or concurrent to obligations of performance under a contract; that some contracts require special written evidence in order to be enforceable; that many contracts need interpreting or explaining; and that fully written integrated contracts cannot be changed by parol evidence. All of this brings us to the point of having a valid, enforceable contract, clear in meaning, and recognized as creating binding obligations of performance by the parties. What happens next?

Usually one of two things—either one or both parties are discharged of any further obligation of performance under the contract, or one of the parties breaches the agreement, thus incurring liability to the other party in money damages or other relief. Discharge of contract obligations and remedies for breach of contract are discussed in the following sections.

How is a party discharged from his or her contract obligations?

A party may be discharged from his or her contract obligations (i. e., freed of any further obligation to perform) in any of the following ways:

(1) *Voidable contract.* You already know that a contract may be voidable because of fraud, duress, undue influence, mistake, incapacity, or the like. When a contract is voidable, one of the parties has the option of affirming or rescinding the agreement. If the party elects to rescind or disaffirm, the party's obligations of performance under the contract are discharged.

(2) *Condition subsequent.* You know, too, that a condition subsequent is a condition the occurrence of which terminates a duty of performance under a contract. Upon occurrence of the condition, the party subject to the condition is discharged.

(3) *Complete performance.* Complete performance is the usual method of

discharge of contract obligations. In most cases, the parties completely perform without controversy, and both parties are discharged through their performances.

(4) *Impossibility of performance.* A duty of performance will also be discharged if, after a contract is entered into, the promised performance becomes *objectively impossible* to perform. The impossibility must occur *after* the contract has been entered into: if it is objectively impossible to perform at the time the parties enter into the agreement, it is a matter of mutual mistake, and there is no mutual assent and no contract. For example, suppose that Frank the Painter promises to paint Lloyd Homeowner's house for $1,000 in return for Lloyd's promise to pay him the $1,000, neither party knowing that Lloyd's house has actually burned to the ground. In this case, there is mutual mistake, no mutual assent, and no contract. Suppose, however, that the house burns to the ground a week after the parties have entered into the contract, but before Frank is to begin the painting. Painting the house is now objectively impossible, and Frank is discharged from his duty of performance under the contract.

The impossibility must be *objective* as opposed to *subjective*. *Objective impossibility* refers to the inability of anyone to perform the particular promise made; *subjective impossibility* refers to the personal inability of the promisor to perform the promise, although another person would be able to perform. While objective impossibility serves to discharge the duty of performance under the contract, subjective impossibility has no effect, leaving the obligation to perform intact. Examples of objective impossibility include a performance that becomes illegal because of a subsequent change in the law; a promise that cannot be performed because of the destruction of the subject matter of the contract through no fault of the promisor (e. g., where Lloyd Homeowner's house burns down before Frank has a chance to paint it); and a promise that cannot be carried out because of the incapacitating illness or death of a person essential to the performance. In each of these cases, no one can carry out the promised performance—to do so is objectively impossible.

In contrast, suppose that Frank the Painter cannot afford to buy the paint to carry out his promise to paint Lloyd Homeowner's house. Frank's personal inability to perform is a subjective impossibility only (others can paint the house) and does not excuse or discharge his duty of performance under the contract. Similarly, if a party promises to build a house for another, and the house burns down just prior to completion, it is not objectively impossible to reconstruct the house no matter how subjectively impossible it may be for the particular promisor to do so (e. g., because of financial or other considerations). Along the same line, if a party is unable to carry out his or her promise to provide another with 1,000 bushels of wheat because of a crop failure, the impossibility is subjective and does not discharge the party's duty of performance (the wheat may be supplied from other sources). Of course, if the promise is to provide 1,000 bushels from a designated parcel of land, the crop failure results in an objective impossibility (no one can supply 1,000 bushels from the property), and the promisor is relieved of his or her duty to perform.

Where an objective impossibility is *temporary* as opposed to *permanent,* the promisor's duty of performance is suspended rather than discharged: once the impossibility ceases, the promisor is again obligated to perform so long as the delay has not substantially changed the nature of the performance called for. Where an objective impossibility is *partial* as opposed to *total* (i. e., where only part of the contract is objectively impossible to perform), the promisor is discharged only as to the impossible part and must still perform the remainder of the contract, assuming that the nature of the performance is not substantially changed by its division into parts.

Finally, it should be pointed out that a small minority of courts allow discharge of contract duties even in the event of subjective impossibility if performance of the contract would be many times more difficult or expensive than the parties originally contemplated. Called the "doctrine of impracticability", the minority rule is recognized in but few jurisdictions. And the courts that do espouse it generally require the unexpected hardship to be extremely cumbersome—for example, a performance cost ten times as great as the anticipated cost.

Insofar as the sale of goods is concerned, the doctrine of impracticability is recognized by Section 2–615 of the Uniform Commercial Code. The Section excuses a seller from making timely delivery of goods where the seller's performance has become commercially impracticable because of unforeseen supervening circumstances not contemplated by the parties at the time of contracting. Increased cost alone is not sufficient to excuse the seller's duty of performance: some unforeseen contingency must occur to alter the essential nature of the performance (e. g., where a shortage of raw materials arises from a war, embargo, local crop failure, or the like, making it commercially impracticable for the seller to timely perform).

(5) *Frustration of purpose.* Some happening or event may so change or destroy the purpose and value of a performance that, even though the performance is still possible, the duty of performance will be discharged. The "frustration of purpose" doctrine stems from the so-called English "Coronation Cases" of 1903 wherein contracts to provide viewing points for a Coronation parade were discharged when the parade was cancelled.

(6) *Mutual rescission.* Where both parties have yet to perform under a contract, the parties may "agree" to forget the agreement. An agreement to forget an existing contract is termed a *mutual rescission.* The mutual rescission is itself a binding contract that serves to discharge all duty of performance under the agreement it rescinds or cancels: there is consideration for the mutual rescission in that each party gives up the promised performance of the other. Of course, if one party has already performed his or her part of the bargain, there would be no consideration for that party's promise to forget the performance of the other, and his or her promise to do so would not be binding.

(7) *Modified or substituted contract.* Just as parties may mutually rescind an agreement where both parties have yet to perform, the parties may also agree prior to performance to modify the original agreement or to substitute an entirely new contract in its place. So long as each party promises to do something or refrain from doing something that he or she was not previously bound to do or refrain from doing, there is consideration for the modified or substituted agreement. An agreement to modify an existing contract discharges the original contract to the extent that the terms of the original are changed or altered; an agreement to substitute an entirely new contract discharges all duty of performance under the original agreement.

However, it should be pointed out that the common law "equal dignity" rule provides that a written contract may be modified only by an instrument of "equal dignity" that is, by another writing. An exception to the rule is recognized where a written contract is modified orally, and one of the parties to the agreement substantially and detrimentally changes his or her position in reliance upon the oral modification.

(8) *Novation.* Sometimes, a third party agrees to take the place of one of the original parties to a contract, and, with the full consent of all old and new parties, the third party becomes bound on the agreement while the original party is fully discharged. The substituted contract that results in these circumstances is properly termed a *novation.* It is the agreement of all parties, both old and new, that is essential to a novation—all must agree that the new party is to fully substitute for the original party, and that the original party is to be fully discharged from any further duty of performance under the old contract.[3] For example, suppose that Frank the Painter enters into a contract with Lloyd Homeowner wherein Frank promises to paint Lloyd's house in return for $1,000. Some time later, Frank the painter, Lloyd Homeowner and Tom Olson (a nonparty) agree that Tom will substitute for Frank in performing the work, and that Lloyd will pay Tom rather than Frank. A novation (i. e., a new contract) exists between Tom and Lloyd, and Frank is completely discharged from any duty of performance under the old contract.

(9) *Release.* A release is an agreement to give up or relinquish existing rights. Generally, one party to a contract may release another from his or her contractual obligations, thereby discharging the party from any further duty to perform. Such a release is really nothing more than a form of substituted contract. In most states, a release is effective only if it is in writing and supported by consideration. In some states, an oral release supported by consideration will suffice; and, in a few states, a written release will serve to discharge contract duties with or without consideration. Insofar as the sale of goods is concerned, you will recall that Section 1–107 of the Uniform Commercial Code provides that any claim arising out of an alleged breach of contract for the sale of personal property may be discharged without regard to consideration by a written release signed and delivered by the nonbreaching party.

(10) *Accord and satisfaction.* Like a release, an accord and satisfaction is merely another form of substituted contract. It is an agreement wherein a party with an existing duty of performance under a contract promises to do something other than perform the duty as a means of discharging the contract obligation. The promise or agreement to do something different is termed an *accord*; the carrying out of the accord results in a *satisfaction* that serves to discharge both the accord itself and the contract duty which is the subject of the accord. For example, returning to our contract between Frank the Painter and Lloyd Homeowner, suppose that Frank the Painter fully performs his part of the bargain by painting Lloyd's house. Instead of paying Frank the $1,000 as promised, Lloyd promises to give Frank his boat within the next 30 days time if Frank will forego the $1,000 payment. Frank agrees, and an accord is entered into. The accord does not immediately operate to discharge Lloyd's duty to pay the $1,000: however, if the boat is delivered to Frank within the next 30 days, the delivery will operate as a satisfaction, discharging both the accord agreement and Lloyd's contract duty to pay $1,000. If Lloyd breaches the accord by failing to deliver the boat within 30 days, Frank may sue on the original promise (the promise to pay $1,000), or he may seek damages for breach of the accord agreement. In any

3. You will learn in Ch. 12 that a party may generally *assign* his or her rights in a contract regardless of the consent or lack of consent of the other parties to the contract. However, an assignment differs from a novation in that the original party is not discharged from his or her duty of performance under the contract.

event, Frank must wait the full 30 days before taking any legal action, and, if Lloyd tenders delivery of the boat within the 30 day time period, Frank must accept delivery as satisfaction in full.

(11) *Account stated.* Occasionally, a debtor and creditor who have entered into a series of transactions will agree upon an account balance, the debtor agreeing to pay the stated amount, and the creditor agreeing to accept the amount as payment in full. Such an agreement is called an *account stated,* and payment of the agreed upon amount by the debtor serves to fully discharge the debtor's obligations to the creditor.

Typically, the account stated is not express, but is implied from the conduct of the parties. Usually, one of the parties sends the other an itemized account of a series of transactions, and the other retains the itemization without objection for more than a reasonable time. The itemized account, in this instance, fixes the balance owing, and payment of that amount by the account debtor serves to discharge all obligations arising from the itemized transactions.

(12) *Statute of limitations.* A party who fails to bring legal action for breach of contract within the time period fixed by the statute of limitations will be barred from recovering money damages or obtaining other relief. While the running of the statute of limitations does not discharge the contract duty owed, it does bar any possible remedy and so frequently has the same effect as a discharge. (But remember that a new promise to pay a debt barred by the statute of limitations is enforceable without consideration.)

What is the effect of a breach of contract?

Say that a party is under a contractual obligation to perform, and nothing has discharged the party from his or her duty

of performance. A failure by the party to perform at the time and place called for in the agreement constitutes a breach of contract. Where the breach is a *major* breach—often called a material breach —the nonbreaching party is discharged from any further duty of performance under the contract and may sue immediately for breach of the *entire* contract. Where the breach is *minor* (i. e., insignificant), the nonbreaching party is not excused from further performance under the contract; however, he or she may temporarily suspend performance until the minor breach is cured, or until it becomes a major breach, in which case the party's duty of performance will be discharged. And where the breach is minor, the nonbreaching party may not sue for breach of the entire contract, but may sue only for damages arising from the minor breach itself. A good example of a minor breach of contract is an insignificant delay in performance where time is not an important factor (i. e., where time is not "of the essence"). For example, suppose that Frank the Painter agrees to paint Lloyd Homeowner's house for $1,000, Lloyd promising to pay half the amount—$500—in advance. If Lloyd fails to make the advance payment, Frank is not obligated to go ahead with the painting. Lloyd's failure to make the payment constitutes a minor breach of contract, and Frank may temporarily suspend performance until the payment is made, or until so much time has passed that the failure to pay becomes a material breach of contract. So long as the breach is minor, Frank may sue only for damages arising out of the specific breach of contract. If the breach becomes major, Frank may sue for damages based upon breach of the entire agreement.

Sometimes, complete performance by a party is an implied condition precedent to the other party's duty to perform. Thus, where Frank the Painter promises to paint Lloyd Homeowner's house for

$1,000, until and unless Frank paints the house, Lloyd is not obligated to pay any portion of the money. But suppose that Frank substantially performs (as by painting all of the house except for the window screens), and then is unable to finish performing through no fault of his own. Lloyd's duty to pay, in this case, is absolute, although Lloyd is entitled to set-off a portion of the $1,000 as damages for the minor breach of contract (Frank's failure to complete the job). The doctrine of *substantial performance* applies only where the failure to complete a performance is innocent—it never applies to a willful failure to finish a job. And with regard to the sale of goods, Section 2–601 of the Uniform Commercial Code provides that if there is any delay or deviation from the exact requirements of a sales contract, the buyer may reject the whole contract without regard to the doctrine of substantial performance. Of course, if the buyer chooses, he or she may accept the entire contract, or accept a portion of the goods under the contract and reject the rest.

What remedies does the nonbreaching party have?

Generally speaking, there are three remedies available to the nonbreaching party:

(1) *Restitution*. In prior chapters, we have considered restitution as a remedy available upon rescission of a voidable contract, and as a remedy utilized in the area of quasi contract to prevent unjust enrichment. With regard to breach of contract, restitution refers to restoring the parties, insofar as is practicable, to the positions they were in prior to entering into the contract. To restore the *status quo ante* (the pre-contract state of affairs), the courts generally order the return of specific property to the nonbreaching party, or award the nonbreach-

ing party a sum of money measured by the value of the benefit received by the breaching party.

(2) *Specific performance*. Where money damages are not an adequate remedy, the courts may order specific performance of the contract. Specific performance is performance in the exact manner specified by the contract. Thus, a breaching party who is ordered to specifically perform must actually carry out his or her contractual promise. For example, a seller who breaches a land sale contract may be ordered to specifically perform by conveying the land to the purchaser. Specific performance is always available as a remedy for a seller's breach of a land sale agreement because land, by its very nature, is unique, and money damages are never adequate. Specific performance is not available, on the other hand, as a remedy for a purchaser's breach of a land sale agreement —the nonbreaching seller, in this case, may be adequately compensated with money damages.[4]

Like land, unique chattels such as antiques, paintings, and the like may be the subject of specific enforcement. And so may common stock in a family or closed corporation (a corporation whose stock is not listed on a securities exchange and is not easily available). However, common stock in a publicly held corporation (a corporation trading on the public market) is not unique and money damages are an adequate remedy.

Of course, if it is impossible for the breaching party to perform his or her contract duty, specific performance will not be ordered. The most obvious example is where a breaching party who has contracted to convey land to the nonbreaching party has since conveyed the land to a bona fide purchaser. The bona fide purchaser, not knowing of the pre-

---

4. Nor is specific performance available where the non-performed contract duty calls for a personal service. Forcing someone to work would violate the 13th Amendment prohibition of involuntary servitude.

vious contract, will be protected, and the nonbreaching party will be able to collect money damages only.

(3) *Damages.* Usually, the nonbreaching party seeks, not restitution or specific performance, but compensatory money damages. The purpose behind compensatory money damages is to place the injured party (the nonbreaching party) in the position he or she would have been in had the contract been properly carried out. To the extent practicable, money damages compensate the injured party for his or her loss—they give the injured party the benefit of the bargain entered into. For example, suppose that a buyer or seller breaches a contract for the sale of goods. The standard measure of recovery, in this instance, is the difference between the contract price and the market price of the goods at the time and place for delivery under the contract. The same rule applies with regard to breach of a land sale agreement (assuming specific enforcement is not requested). The nonbreaching party may recover money damages based upon the difference between the contract price and the fair market value of the land in question.

Two important rules that come into play in determining the amount of money damages recoverable are the *rule of remoteness* and the rule requiring *mitigation of damages*.

What is the rule of remoteness?

An injured party's measure of recovery for breach of contract is limited by the rule of remoteness. The rule states that an injured party should be compensated only for losses that are reasonably foreseeable to the parties at the time they enter into the contract. The *Restatement, Second, Law of Contracts*, § 330, states the rule as follows:

The Restatement provides:

In awarding damages, compensation is given for only those injuries that the defendant had reason to foresee as a probable result of his breach when the contract was made. If the injury is one that follows the breach in the usual course of events, there is sufficient reason for the defendant to foresee it; otherwise, it must be shown specifically that the defendant had reason to know the facts and to foresee the injury.

The rule of remoteness was first announced in 1854 in the English case of Hadley v. Baxendale, 156 Eng.Rep. 145. The plaintiffs in that case operated a flour mill in Gloucester, England. When a crank shaft broke in an engine furnishing power to the mill, the plaintiffs decided to send the shaft to a foundry in Greenwich so that a new shaft could be made using the broken one as a model. The plaintiffs contracted with the defendants to transport the broken shaft to Greenwich, but the defendants negligently delayed delivering the shaft for several days, with the result that the plaintiffs were forced to close down the mill for an extended period of time. The plaintiffs sued the defendants for their lost profits, but the court denied recovery, stating that the lost profits were too "remote" to be recoverable. The defendants could not reasonably foresee at the time of entering into the delivery contract that a delay in delivery would force closure of the mill.

The court in *Hadley* concluded that *consequential* (remote or indirect) damages are recoverable only where both parties know of the special circumstances likely to result in the damages at the time of entering into the contract. Here, the plaintiffs would have had to inform the defendants at the time of entering into the delivery contract that a failure to timely deliver the shaft to Greenwich would result in a forced closure of the mill.

A related rule is that *speculative* (uncertain) damages are never recoverable for breach of contract (e. g., estimated lost profits where a breach of contract forces closure of a Broadway play). Nor are *punitive* (penalty) damages; and where the amount of loss is not reasonably certain of computation, any award of damages amounts to a penalty.

What is the rule requiring mitigation of damages?

The nonbreaching party is legally obligated to make a reasonable effort to mitigate (i. e., reduce or lessen) the damages flowing from the breach of contract. If the party fails to do so, his or her recovery in money damages will be reduced by the amount of loss that could have been avoided. For example, where a buyer breaches a sales contract by refusing to accept the goods contracted for, the seller must make a reasonable effort to sell the goods elsewhere—he or she cannot simply sit back and allow the goods to spoil or deteriorate. And if the seller breaches the sales agreement by refusing to deliver the goods, the buyer must make a reasonable attempt to purchase substitute goods from another seller. Suppose that a seller is manufacturing goods for a buyer who repudiates the contract. The seller, in this case, must cease manufacturing if this is the best way to mitigate the damages; however, if more loss can be avoided by completing manufacture of the goods and selling to another buyer, the seller is legally obligated to finish the job and make reasonable efforts to sell elsewhere. Similarly, if an employer breaches an employment contract by wrongfully terminating an employee, the employee is under an affirmative duty to make reasonable efforts to locate similar work in the same geographical area. If the employee's job is unique, and it is impossible to find similar work in the same area, the employee will not be required to accept a different kind of work, or similar employment, but in a different area.

Thus, a wrongfully terminated school teacher need not accept employment as a truck driver.

Of course, any expenses the injured party incurs in reasonably seeking to mitigate the damages are recoverable as *incidental* damages *regardless of whether the effort to mitigate is successful.*

What is the law regarding "anticipatory breach" (i. e., repudiation) of a contract?

If either party to an *executory bilateral* contract announces in advance of his or her promised performance that he or she will not perform (i. e., repudiates the promised performance), the other party may treat the anticipatory repudiation as a present material breach of the contract and bring legal action immediately for breach of the *entire* agreement. Anticipatory breach or repudiation applies only to executory bilateral contracts: an executory contract is a contract wherein both parties have yet to perform; a bilateral contract is a promise for a promise. If one of the parties has already fully performed at the time the other party repudiates his or her promised performance, the doctrine of anticipatory breach does not apply. Nor does it apply where the contract involved is a unilateral contract or a reverse unilateral contract. Where the doctrine does not apply, the injured party must wait until the actual breach to bring legal action upon the contract.

The doctrine of anticipatory breach or repudiation is designed to prevent hardship to the party who is told in advance that a promised performance will not be forthcoming. Certainly, it would be extremely unfair to insist that the party wait until the time for performance, remaining all the while ready and able to personally perform, after the other party has stated that he or she will not carry out his or her part of the bargain. For example, suppose that Frank the Painter enters into a contract with Lloyd Homeowner on June 1st wherein Frank promises to paint Lloyd's house in the second week of August in return for Lloyd's promise to pay Frank $1,000. On June 15th, Frank repudiates his promised performance, stating, "I am not going to do the job in August." Obviously, it would make little sense to state that there is no breach of contract until August—it would not be fair to insist that Lloyd wait until that time, all the while remaining ready and able to pay Frank the $1,000 should he come through with his promised performance. What does make sense is to hold that Frank's anticipatory repudiation of his promise constitutes a present material breach of contract that discharges Lloyd from any further duty of performance under the contract and enables him to sue immediately for money damages. Thus, immediately upon Frank's repudiation, Lloyd may hire Tom Olson to paint the house, and if Tom charges Lloyd $1,500, Lloyd may sue Frank at once to recover the $500 in damages.

Of course, the nonrepudiating party still has a duty to mitigate damages where possible.

Occasionally, the repudiating party will attempt to retract the repudiation by notifying the other party that he or she will perform the contract after all. The retraction will revive the other party's duty of counterperformance unless the party has already accepted the repudiation or has changed his or her position in detrimental reliance upon it.

With regard to the sale of goods, the Uniform Commercial Code deals with anticipatory breach at Sections 2–609, 2–610, and 2–611. The Code provides that, upon anticipatory repudiation, the nonrepudiating party may suspend his or her own performance and sue immediately for breach of contract even though he or she has urged retraction of the repudiation. However, if the repudiating party retracts before the aggrieved party has cancelled the contract or materially changed his or her position in detrimental reliance upon it, the retraction will serve to reinstate the rights of the repudiating party. Where this occurs, the aggrieved party may make a written demand for adequate assurance from the retracting party that due performance will be forthcoming at the time called for in the contract. The retracting party's failure to provide such assurance within a reasonable time, not to exceed 30 days, is itself a repudiation.

What are the rules regarding "liquidated" damages?

Frequently, a contract will expressly stipulate that a specific amount of damages (i. e., a fixed or liquidated amount) must be paid in the event of a breach of contract. The enforceability of such a provision will depend upon whether it is a valid liquidated damages clause or an unenforceable penalty provision. If the provision represents a good faith effort by the contracting parties to determine in advance what the actual damages would be upon a breach of contract, the provision will be a valid and enforceable liquidated damages clause. Thus, if the amount agreed upon by the parties bears a reasonable relationship to the amount of probable loss as measured at the time of entering into the contract, the provision will be a valid and enforceable liquidated damages clause. And where the nature of the contract is such that it is difficult to determine in advance just what the actual damages are likely to be upon a breach of contract, any determination made by the parties will be upheld so long as it is made in good faith (e. g., it might be very difficult to determine probable damages resulting from a breach of a covenant not to compete for a 10 year period.) Where a stipulated damages provision is held to be a valid liquidated damages clause, the nonbreaching party may generally recover the full stipulated amount without regard to what actual damages, if any, are suffered (a minority of courts hold that liquidated damages are not recoverable in the absence of actual damage).

Where a stipulated damages provision bears no reasonable relationship to the amount of probable loss as calculated at the time of entering into the contract, the provision is an unenforceable penalty provision. For example, suppose that Frank the Painter agrees to paint Lloyd Homeowner's house for $1,000. At the time of entering into the contract, both parties agree that if Frank does not complete the job within 10 days, liquidated damages in the amount of $50.00 a day must be paid to Lloyd until the job is finished. The $50/day liquidated damages provision may well be reasonable in light of probable loss to Lloyd in the event that his house is not completely painted within 10 days time. But where the contract provides for liquidated damages of $500/day, it is difficult to discern any reasonable relationship to probable loss, and the provision appears to be an unenforceable penalty. Where a stipulated damages provision is held to be a penalty, the nonbreaching party is not entitled to recover the stipulated amount, but must prove in court his or her actual damages.

Insofar as the sale of goods is concerned, Section 2–718 of the Uniform Commercial Code provides as follows.

It says:

(1) Damages for breach by either party may be liquidated in the agreement but only at an amount which is reasonable in the light of the anticipated or actual harm caused by the breach, the difficulties of proof of loss, and the inconvenience or nonfeasibility of otherwise obtaining an adequate remedy. A term fixing unreasonably large liquidated damages is void as a penalty.

———

Section 2–718(2) provides that, even in the absence of a valid liquidated damages provision, if the buyer of goods puts down a deposit on the purchase price, then subsequently breaches the sales agreement, with the result that the seller does not have to deliver the goods, the seller may retain the deposit up to 20% of the purchase price or $500 whichever is less.

CASES

CASE 1—*Does a $25.00 downpayment for an automobile satisfy the requirements of the Statute of Frauds?*

STARR v. FREEPORT DODGE, INC.

District Court, Nassau County, First District, 1967.
54 Misc.2d 271, 282 N.Y.S.2d 58.

Bernard TOMSON, Judge.

* * *

Plaintiff's action is for breach of contract and arises out of the attempted purchase by him of a new automobile from the corporate defendant, a car dealer, through the individual defendant, the salesman involved in the transaction. The plaintiff alleges that he signed an order form for a new automobile which described the subject matter of the sale, the price, which was in excess of $500, and the identity of both buyer and seller. The form is not signed by the dealer and bears the following printed statement, "This order is not valid unless signed and accepted by the dealer." * * *

If further appears that the plaintiff made a $25 down payment to the dealer, which was accepted by the dealer and for which deposit a credit was noted on the form. The plaintiff asserts that on the day scheduled for delivery of the car he was informed by the dealer's representative "that some error had been made" and that it would be necessary for the plaintiff to pay an additional $175 over and above the price previously agreed upon in order to obtain delivery of the car.

The defendants urge that there was no contract between the parties and that the order form, unsigned as it is by the dealer, falls within the purview of Section 2–201 of the Uniform Commercial Code as unenforceable since it was not signed by the party to be charged.

Section 2–201 of the UCC provides in part as follows.

"§ 2–201.   Formal Requirements;   Statute of Frauds

(1) Except as otherwise provided in this section a contract for the sale of goods for the price of $500 or more is not enforceable by way of action or defense unless there is some writing sufficient to indicate that a contract for sale has been made between the parties and signed by the party against whom enforcement is sought or by his authorized agent or broker. * * *

(3) A contract which does not satisfy the requirements of subsection (1) but which is valid in other respects is enforceable * * *.

(c) with respect to goods for which payment has been made and accepted or which have been received and accepted (Section 2–606)."

Had the present controversy arisen prior to the adoption of the UCC, its resolution would not have presented any unusual difficulty for at that time section 85, subd. 1, par. (c) of the Personal Property Law, since repealed, removed from the operation of the statute of frauds those transactions where part payment had been made. The law was settled on this point.

The Code now excepts from the statute of frauds those transactions "with respect to goods for which payment has been made and accepted." Noticeably lacking is the provision excepting transactions where part payment has been made.

In Williamson [Williamson v. Mantz, 11 Pa.Dist. & Co.R.2d 33 (1956)] the court, interpreting the language just quoted, stated:

"Under the law as it existed prior to the passage of the Uniform Commercial Code, namely, the Sales Act of May 19, 1915 part payment took the whole contract outside the statute of frauds. This was because the Sales Act did not discriminate between divisible and indivisible contracts, or between those providing for bulk or installment deliveries, nor did it make any distinction regarding the character of the contract. It applied to any and every class of contracts.

"The Uniform Commercial Code repealed the Sales Act of 1915. Under the code, part payment takes the case out of the statute only to the extent for which payment has been made. The code therefore makes an important change by denying the enforcement of the contract where in the case of a single object the payment made is less than the full amount."

The Williamson case is discussed in Hawkland, A Transactional Guide To the Uniform Commercial Code, as follows:

"By failing to distinguish part payment from partial accept-ance and receipt, the section does create one problem neatly illus-trated by Williamson v. Martz. Here S orally agreed to sell to B two vats for a total price of $1600, B paying $100 on account. Subsequently B refused to take the vats, and S sued for breach of contract. B set up section 2–201 of the Code as his defense, and S countered that the partial payment took the matter out of the stat-ute of frauds. The court held for B. Subsection 2–201(3)(c) re-moves the statute of frauds only to the extent of payment. Since the payment of $100 cannot be translated into one vat (worth $800), S cannot enforce the contract to the extent of one vat. There being no way to divide up a vat, S is barred completely by the Statute.

"Though this case seems to follow the plain meaning of subsection 2–201(3)(c), the result appears to be excessively re-strictive. The payment of $100 indicates a contract whose quanti-ty term must be at least one unit. The court, therefore, could safely enforce the agreement to the extent of one vat, and, thus, give the S a recovery of $800. The payment of $100, of course, does not necessarily prove a contract for two vats, and the court would not be justified in enforcing the contract for such an amount. But it is difficult to see how the contract could have con-templated less than one vat, assuming, as the court did, that vats are indivisible."

*   *   *

*   *   *   The language of section 2–201(3)(c) does not require the Williamson result. Even if subparagraph (c) validates, as the writers seem unanimously to agree, a divisible contract only for as much of the goods as have been paid for, it does not necessarily follow that such a rule invali-dates an indivisible oral contract where some payment has been made and accepted. To paraphrase Hawkland—It is difficult (here) to see how the contract could have contemplated less than one (automobile), assuming as the Court did, that (automobiles) are indivisible. Any other conclusion would work an unconscionable result and would encourage rather than dis-courage fraud if the facts as pleaded (known as "low balling" in the trade) were proven at a trial. The statute of frauds would be used to cut down the trusting buyer rather than to protect the one who, having made his bar-gain, parted with a portion of the purchase price as an earnest of his good faith. Certainly here the $25 deposit was not intended as a purchase of a portion of the automobile. It was intended as payment towards the pur-chase of the entire article if the facts alleged in the complaint are proven at the trial.

[Judgment for plaintiff].

CASE 2—*The showing of a condition precedent does not violate the parol evidence rule.*

LONG v. JONES
Court of Appeals of Kentucky, 1958.
319 S.W.2d 292.

MILLIKEN, Judge.

* * * The appellee, Mrs. Jones, recovered a judgment of $800, with interest, covering the down payment made by her on the proposed purchase of a house from the appellant, Dan Long, in Lexington. A written contract covering the terms of the proposed purchase was signed by her and by the vendor through his agent, and the $800 down payment was referred to therein "as evidence of good faith to bind this contract" and it was "to be applied on the purchase price upon passing of deed, or refunded, should title prove not merchantable, or acceptable, or if this offer is not accepted."

As an explanation of her failure to go through with the purchase within the terms of the agreement, Mrs. Jones testified that at the time she signed the printed contract form and made the $800 down payment it was understood between her and the agent of the appellant-seller that she could not complete the proposed purchase within the time allotted unless she sold her home in Flemingsburg, and the trial court accordingly instructed the jury to find for Mrs. Jones if they believed what she said. It was proper for such testimony to be admitted for the consideration of the jury, not for the purpose of varying the terms of a written agreement, but on the issue of whether a contract in fact existed. As stated in 32 C.J.S. Evidence § 935, page 857:

> "In general, parol evidence is admissible to show conditions precedent, which relate to the existence of a valid contract, but is not admissible to show conditions subsequent, which provide for the nullification or modification of an existing contract."

As summarized in 46 Am.Jur., Sales, Section 283, page 467:

> "Evidence is generally held admissible to show that the parties made an agreement before or at the time they entered into a written contract of sale that such contract of sale should become binding only on the happening of a certain condition or contingency, the theory being that such evidence merely goes to show that the writing never became operative as a valid agreement and that there is therefore no variance or contradiction of a valid written instrument."

[T]he judgment is affirmed.

CASE 3—*At 4:00 PM "workmen were all over the place, slapping on siding, laying the floors, bulldozing the yard, hooking up the utilities." Could the house have been "substantially completed" by 5:30 PM?*

SURETY DEVELOPMENT CORP. v. GREVAS

Appellate Court of Illinois, Second District, First Division, 1963.
42 Ill.App.2d 268, 192 N.E.2d 145.

SMITH, Justice.

When is a house a home? In our context a house is a home when it can be lived in. But when is that: When substantially completed or completely completed? We posit the question, because the answer is decisive.

Plaintiff sells prefabricated houses. Defendants selected one of their models, styled "Royal Countess, elevation 940". A contract was signed. The cost was $16,385.00; completion date September 27, 1961. Around 4:00 P. M. on that date defendants refused to accept the house asserting noncompletion. Plaintiff then sued for the balance due and defendants counter-claimed for their downpayment. Both alleged performance by them and non-performance by the other. The legal issue is therefore relatively simple: Who performed and who didn't. The facts are more elusive—plaintiff at times says one thing, defendants another. We narrate them briefly.

On the morning of the twenty-seventh, "Royal Countess, elevation 940" was far from being a house, let alone a home. Racing the clock, plaintiff initiated a crash program. When defendants arrived on the scene at 4:00, at plaintiff's behest for final inspection, the crash program was still crashing —workmen were all over the place, slapping on siding, laying the floors, bulldozing the yard, hooking up the utilities, and so on. Defendants' tour was not a success, to put it mildly. Instead of a home, they found, to their dismay, a hive buzzing with activity. They did not tarry, in spite of the foreman's assurances that all would be right by 5:30. Nor did they come back. They should have. Believe it or not, the foreman was right. The job *was* substantially completed by 5:30, with only a service walk, some grading and blacktopping left undone.

The trial court found that the house had been substantially completed and concluded that there had been, therefore, substantial compliance with the contract and with this we agree. But because the house was not completely completed, it found that there had not been *complete* compliance. With this, too, we agree, but such finding is beside the point. Substantial —not complete—compliance in a construction contract is all that is required. By 5:30, there had been just that, in other words, substantial performance of the contract. Plaintiff's contretemps in having inspection set for 4:00 o'clock was hardly the way to make friends and influence people, but such happenstance is of no moment in determining whether or not there had been substantial compliance, unless such can be said to indicate bad faith. We do not think that it does. What it indicates is bad timing, not bad faith.

That substantial performance or compliance is the key needs no extensive citation. In Bloomington Hotel Company v. Garthwait, 227 Ill. 613, 81 N.E. 714, it was said:

> "Literal compliance with the provisions of a contract is not essential to a recovery. It will be sufficient if there has been an

honest and faithful performance of the contract in its material and substantial parts, and no willful departure from or omission of the essential points of the contract."

In 12 Ill.Law & Practice Contracts, § 402, p. 547, it is said:

"In building contracts a literal compliance with the provisions of the particular contract, and the plans, specifications and drawings, is not necessary to a recovery by the contractor. It is sufficient that there is a substantial performance in good faith or that there is an honest and faithful performance of the contract in its material and substantial parts, with no willful departure from, or omission of, the essential points of the contract."

No substantial sum was required to complete the items left undone. Nor were they of so essential a character that defendants could not have been esconced in their new home that night if they had so desired. We have thus answered our question: A house is ready to be lived in, to become a home, when it has been substantially completed.

* * *

* * * [T]he court should have found for plaintiff and against defendants * * * Accordingly, the judgment below is reversed and remanded with directions to enter judgment for plaintiff * * * and against defendants * * * and thereafter to determine plaintiff's damages.

Reversed and remanded with directions.

PROBLEMS

1. Discuss the enforceability of each of the following contracts:

   (a) John Dolan orally contracts to purchase a farm from Jean Farlow. John makes a downpayment on the purchase price and takes possession of the property.

   (b) John Dolan contracts in writing to purchase a farm from Jean Farlow for $94,000. By the terms of the contract, John must make payment in full on September 5th, and Jean must deliver a deed to the farm on that day. Jean makes no effort to deliver a deed on the 5th, so John makes no effort to make payment. John sues Jean for breach of contract.

   (c) On October 1st, 1980, Jan Maguire orally contracts to build Tom Tucker a house by October 1st, 1983.

   (d) David Olson owns 10% of the stock of "Olson Hardware, Inc." The corporation owes a past due debt of $5,000 to supplier Jo Ann Justice. David orally promises Jo Ann that he will pay the $5,000 debt and be responsible for future deliveries if Jo Ann will continue supplying the corporation.

   (e) Edwin Hale orally contracts to purchase an $800 water heater from "Water Heaters Unlimited". Edwin makes a downpayment of $150.

2. (a) Retailer Jim Michaelson contracts in writing (on a standard purchase order form) to purchase 5,000 pairs of ladies' fashion pants from "Try Me On" Jeans, Inc. The contract specifies a total price of $25,000, payment to be made within 30 days of delivery of the

merchandise. Jim has dealt with "Try Me On" Jeans many times in the past and has always received a 10% discount for making payment at the time of delivery. Jim tenders $22,500 at the time of delivery. "Try Me On" accepts the payment and then sues Jim for the remaining $2,500. "Try Me On" insists that the written contract contains the entire agreement and cannot now be varied; that the contract does not provide for a discount; and that the prevailing practice of clothing wholesalers in the community is not to grant such a discount. Is Jim obligated to pay the $2,500? Explain.

[margin note: No of course — Past dealings prevail over trade]

(b) Suppose that the written contract is ambiguous and calls for delivery of "five thousand (4,000) pairs of ladies' fashion pants". Is "Try Me On" Jeans obligated to deliver 5,000 or 4,000 pairs of pants? Explain. *[margin note: words prevail over figures]*

3. Jake Blake contracts to reroof Harold Myer's house. What are Jake's and Harold's rights and duties in each of the following situations?

(a) After finishing 95% of the work, Jake gets bored and stops working. He demands payment for the work he has done. *[margin note: no payment]*

(b) Jake finishes the work six days after the completion date called for in the contract. The contract provides that Jake must pay $1,000 per day for every day that he is late in finishing the work. *[margin note: stipulated damages Recover only actual damages]*

(c) Before the contract time for his performance arrives, Jake tells Harold, "I am not going to do the reroofing". *[margin note: Anticipatory breach]*

(d) The same as (c) above except that Jake later changes his mind and tells Harold, "I will do the reroofing after all". *[margin note: Revives obligation unless H changed position]*

(e) Jake breaches the contract by failing to reroof the house. Harold does not hire anyone else to do the work and rain leaks through the roof causing damage to Harold's upstairs bedrooms. Harold sues Jake for the damage. *[margin note: no — mitigate damages]*

(f) Harold promises to give Jake his used stationwagon if Jake will forego the promised $1,500 payment. Jake agrees, and Harold gives him the stationwagon upon completion of the reroofing. *[margin note: no problem (accord & satisfaction)]*

(g) By the terms of the contract, Jake is obligated "to reroof the house unless and until I am called back to work in Alaska". Shortly after Jake begins working, his union notifies him that he has been called back to work in Alaska. *[margin note: Cond. subsequent]*

(h) The contract provides that "the reroofing must be done to Harold's satisfaction". Harold is not satisfied with Jake's work and refuses to pay him. *[margin note: personal satisf. — honest in good faith]*

4. Farber sold his house to Ronald. Ronald agreed among other things to pay the existing mortgage on the house. The Safety Bank, which held the mortgage, released Farber from liability on the debt. The above described transaction (relating to the mortgage debt) is

(a) Invalid in that the bank did *not* receive any additional consideration from Farber.

(b) *Not* a release of Farber if Ronald defaults, and the proceeds from the sale of the mortgaged house are insufficient to satisfy the debt.

(c) A novation.

(d) A delegation.

[# 40, November, 1976 CPA Exam]

5. Barnes agreed to purchase from Damion 1,000 shares of Excelsior Photo, Inc., stock at $100 per share. Barnes was interested in obtaining control of Excelsior, whose stock was very closely held. The stock purchase agreement contained the following clause: "This contract is subject to my (Barnes') obtaining more than 50% of the shares outstanding of Excelsior Photo stock." In this situation

   (a) The contract is *not* binding on Damion because it lacks consideration on Barnes' part, i. e., unless he obtained more than 50%, he is *not* liable.

   (b) The contract is subject to an express condition precedent.

   (c) Specific performance would *not* be available to Barnes if Damion refuses to perform.

   (d) While the contract is executory, Damion *cannot* transfer good title to a third party who takes in good faith.

   [# 10, May, 1975 CPA Exam]

6. The Johnson Corporation sent its only pump to the manufacturer to be repaired. It engaged Travis, a local trucking company, both to deliver the equipment to the manufacturer and to redeliver it to Johnson promptly upon completion of the repair. Johnson's entire plant was inoperative without this pump, but the trucking company did not know this. The trucking company delayed several days in its delivery of the repaired pump to Johnson. During the time it expected to be without the pump, Johnson incurred $5,000 in lost profits. At the end of that time Johnson rented a replacement pump at a cost of $200 per day. As a result of these facts, what is Johnson entitled to recover from Travis?

   (a) The $200 a day cost incurred in renting the pump.

   (b) The $200 a day cost incurred in renting the pump plus the lost profits.

   (c) Actual damages plus punitive damages.

   (d) Nothing because Travis is *not* liable for damages.

   [# 22, May, 1978 CPA Exam]

7. Gregor paid $100 to Henry for a thirty-day written option to purchase Henry's commercial real property for $75,000. Twenty days later Henry received an offer from Watson to purchase the property for $85,000. Henry promptly notified Gregor that the option price was now $85,000, or the option was revoked. Gregor said he would not pay a penny more than $75,000 and that he still had 10 days remaining on the option. On the 28th day of the option Gregor telephoned Henry that he had decided to exercise the option; he tendered his $75,000 check the next day which was to be held in escrow until delivery of the deed. Henry refused to accept the tender stating that he had decided not to sell and that he was going to retain the property for the present. Which of the following *best* describes the legal rights of the parties involved?

   (a) Henry effectively revoked his offer to sell because he did this prior to Gregor's acceptance.

    (b) Consideration given for the option is irrelevant because the option was in writing and signed by Henry.

    (c) Because Gregor's acceptance was *not* in writing and signed, it is invalid according to the Statute of Frauds.

    (d) Gregor's acceptance was valid, and in the event of default he may obtain the equitable remedy of specific performance.

    [# 6, May, 1975 CPA Exam]

8. Under what conditions will the statute of frauds be a defense under the Uniform Commercial Code where there is a contract for the sale of goods worth more than $500?

    (a) The seller has completed goods specially manufactured for the buyer which are *not* salable in the ordinary course of the seller's business.

    (b) The written memorandum omits several important terms but states the quantity, and it is signed by the party to be charged.

    (c) The party asserting the statute of frauds admits under oath to having made the contract.

    (d) The goods in question are fungible and actively traded by merchants in the business community.

    [# 5, November, 1976 CPA Exam]

9. Walker and White entered into a written contract involving the purchase of certain used equipment by White. White claims that there were oral understandings between the parties which are included as a part of the contract. Walker pleads the parol evidence rule. This rule applies to

    (a) Subsequent oral modifications of the written contract by the parties.

    (b) Additional consistent terms even if the contract was *not* intended as a complete and exclusive listing of all terms of the agreement.

    (c) A contemporaneous oral understanding of the parties which contradicts the terms of a written contract intended as the final expression of the agreement between the parties.

    (d) Evidence in support of the oral modification based upon the performance by Walker.

    [# 6, November, 1976, CPA Exam]

10. **Part a.** Your client, Super Fashion Frocks, Inc., agreed in writing to purchase $520 worth of coat hangers from Display Distributors, Inc., with payment terms of net/30 after delivery. Delivery was to be made within five days from the signing of the contract. Two days prior to the due date for delivery, Display Distributors called and offered a flat $25 discount if payment were made upon delivery instead of the original net/30 terms. Super Fashion Frocks agreed and tendered its check for $495 upon delivery. Display Distributors cashed the check and now seeks to enforce the original contract calling for payment of $520 (i. e., seeks to recover $25 from Super Fashion). It bases its claim upon the following arguments:

1. The Statute of Frauds applies to the contract modification.

2. The Parol Evidence Rule prohibits the introduction of oral evidence modifying the terms of a written agreement.

3. There was no consideration given for Display's promise to take a lesser amount.

Required: Discuss the validity of each argument. (See also Ch. 9)

Part b. Mark Candy Wholesalers, Inc., entered into a contract with Brown & Sons, a family partnership, which owned three small candy stores. Mark agreed to supply Brown & Sons with "its entire requirements of candy for its stores for one year" at fixed prices. Brown agreed to purchase its requirements exclusively from Mark. The price of sugar increased drastically shortly after the first month of performance. Mark breached the contract because the prices at which it was required to deliver imposed a severe financial hardship which would be ruinous. Mark asserts the following legal justifications for its actions:

1. The contract is unenforceable for want of consideration on that Brown & Sons did not agree to take any candy at all. That is, Brown & Sons were not specifically required to purchase candy if it did not require any.

2. The contract is too indefinite and uncertain as to the quantity which might be ordered and hence is unenforceable.

3. Performance is excused on the ground of legal impossibility because of the severe financial hardship imposed upon Mark as a result of the drastic rise in the price of sugar. This unforeseen event falls within the rule of implied conditions and makes the contract voidable.

Required: Discuss the validity of each of the legal justifications asserted by Mark. (See also Ch. 9 and Ch. 7)

[# 5, May, 1976 CPA Exam]

Chapter 11

THIRD PARTY BENEFICIARY CONTRACTS, LIFE INSURANCE, AND THE LAW OF INSURANCE GENERALLY

What are third party beneficiary contracts?

Many times, people will enter into a contract for the purpose of directly benefiting a third person who is not a party to the contract. Such an agreement is called a *third party beneficiary contract,* and the general rule is that the third party beneficiary may personally enforce the agreement even though he or she is not a party to it and has furnished no consideration for the promises made. This means that the third party beneficiary can sue in his or her own name to recover damages for breach of the contract.

However, the third party beneficiary must be a *direct* beneficiary as opposed to an *incidental* one who benefits but remotely or indirectly from the contract and acquires no rights of enforcement whatsoever. For example, suppose that Mark Developer contracts with Barbara Builder to erect an expensive office building on Mark's property. The fact that Tom Neighbor's land will substantially increase in value by reason of performance of the contract makes Tom Neighbor an incidental beneficiary only. The increase in value is but a remote or indirect benefit of the construction contract, and if either Developer or Builder breaches the agreement, Tom Neighbor has no legal right to complain.

Sometimes, it is difficult to determine whether a particular third party is a direct or an incidental beneficiary of a contract. Where this is so, the courts look to see whether the "primary purpose" or at least a "major purpose" of the contract is to benefit the third party. If so, the third party is a direct beneficiary with rights to enforce the agreement; if not, the third party is an incidental beneficiary with no rights of enforcement whatsoever. Generally, the fact that the promised performance is to be rendered directly to the third party indicates that the primary or major purpose of the contract is to benefit the third party. Conversely, where the promised performance is to run directly to the promisee, the third party is usually deemed a mere incidental beneficiary. Also, the fact that the contract expressly grants the third party the right to control the promisor as to the time, method, or manner of performance strongly suggests that the third party is a direct beneficiary and not an incidental one. And the more specifically the contract describes the third party, the more likely it is that the contract was made primarily for his or her benefit and not just to aid him or her indirectly.

What two kinds of third party beneficiary contracts are there?

There are two kinds of third party beneficiary contracts—*donee beneficiary* contracts and *creditor beneficiary* contracts. Where the promisee's primary purpose or intent in entering into the agreement is to confer a gift on the third party, the third party is a donee beneficiary, and the contract is a donee beneficiary contract. Where, on the other hand, the promisee's primary purpose or intent in entering into the agreement is to discharge an obligation owed or *believed to be owed* to the third party, the third party is a creditor beneficiary, and the contract is a creditor beneficiary contract.

The words "believed to be owed" are emphasized because, even if there is no legally enforceable duty owing (e. g., where the duty has been discharged in bankruptcy or is otherwise unenforceable because of the statute of limitations, the Statute of Frauds, or the like), the contract will still be a creditor beneficiary contract so long as the promisee *believes* the duty to be owing.

By way of example, suppose that Frank the Painter contracts with Lloyd Homeowner to paint Lloyd's house for $1,000. After Frank has completed the job, but before Lloyd has paid him the $1,000, Lloyd enters into a contract with Linda Thompson. Lloyd agrees to sell Linda his used Chevrolet stationwagon for the sum of $1,000, with Linda to make payment to Frank the Painter as settlement in full of Lloyd's existing duty to pay Frank $1,000. Lloyd's intent in entering into the contract with Linda is to discharge an obligation owed to Frank. Frank is thus a third party creditor beneficiary, and the contract is a third party creditor beneficiary contract.

Now let's vary the facts. Say that Lloyd contracts to sell his used stationwagon to Linda Thompson for the sum of $1,000, payment to be made to Lloyd's son, Jimmy, as a gift from his father. Jimmy is a donee beneficiary, and the contract is a donee beneficiary contract. In each case, Linda is the promisor and Lloyd the promisee of a promise that will directly benefit a third party: in each case, the benefit of the promise goes to someone other than the promisee at the express direction of the promisee.

Once a third party's rights as either a donee beneficiary or creditor beneficiary "vest" under a contract, the third party is entitled to bring legal action to enforce

the agreement made on his or her behalf. The general rule is that the third party's rights "vest" or become final when the third party (whether a donee or creditor beneficiary) acquires knowledge of the contract made for his or her benefit and assents to it. Assent is usually implied by law where the beneficiary has knowledge of the contract and fails to object to its terms. Unless and until the third party's rights vest, the parties to the contract (promisor and promisee) are free to mutually rescind the agreement, and the third party beneficiary has no legal recourse or right to complain.

It should be pointed out that some courts draw a distinction between donee beneficiaries and creditor beneficiaries insofar as the rules on vesting are concerned. In these jurisdictions, a donee beneficiary's rights vest automatically upon the making of the contract without regard to the beneficiary's knowledge of or assent to the agreement.[1] A creditor beneficiary's rights, on the other hand, do not vest automatically, but vest if and when the creditor changes his or her position in reliance on the contract or brings suit to enforce the agreement. The courts justify the distinction on the basis that if the creditor beneficiary's rights are cut off by a mutual rescission, the creditor can still go against the original debtor for payment of the debt, if the donee beneficiary's rights are cut off, the donee has no recourse against anyone.

In any case, the trend in the law is to find a vesting of the third's party's rights (whether donee or creditor beneficiary) upon the happening of any one of the following:

(1) The third party beneficiary in some way manifests assent to the contract;

1. The courts uniformly apply the "automatic" vesting rule to donee beneficiary life insurance contracts wherein the insured purchases life insurance on his or her own life, naming another as beneficiary and giving up the right to change beneficiaries.

(2) The third party beneficiary materially changes his or her position in justifiable reliance on the contract; or

(3) The third party beneficiary brings suit to enforce the contract. Vesting of the third party's rights cuts off the power of the contracting parties to mutually rescind the agreement. It confers upon the third party beneficiary a legal right to complain in the event of breach of contract.

What rights result from third party beneficiary contracts?

In a third party beneficiary contract, one party (the promisor) makes a promise to a second party (the promisee) for the benefit of a third party (the third party beneficiary). Assuming that all four elements of a valid contract are present, the following rights arise:

(1) *The beneficiary's rights against the promisor.* Once a donee or creditor beneficiary's rights vest under a contract, the beneficiary can personally sue a defaulting promisor for money damages, specific performance, or other appropriate relief. Of course, the promisor may assert against the beneficiary any defense that he or she (the promisor) could assert against the promisee. But he or she cannot assert a defense that only the promisee holds against the beneficiary.

Let's return to our previous example of Lloyd Homeowner agreeing to sell his used stationwagon to Linda Thompson for $1,000, Linda agreeing to make payment to Frank the Painter in discharge of Lloyd's existing duty to pay Frank $1,000. If after receiving the stationwagon, Linda refuses to make payment to Frank, Frank can personally sue Linda to collect the $1,000. However, any defense that Linda could assert against Lloyd she can assert against Frank. Thus, if Lloyd misrepresented the condition of the stationwagon (e. g., by setting back the odometer) so as to induce Linda to buy the ve-

hicle, Linda can assert the defense of fraud to defeat or limit Frank's recovery. But suppose that Linda discovers the misrepresentation only after she has paid Frank the $1,000. Can she legally force Frank to return the money? The answer is no. Generally, if the promisor discovers a defense justifying rescission of the contract only after he or she has fully performed to the benefit of the third party, the promisor's only relief is an action against the promisee. In the example, Linda's only legal remedy is an action against Lloyd for money damages. However, an exception arises where the third party beneficiary had knowledge of the facts justifying rescission prior to or at the time of the misrepresentation. Thus, if Frank had known about Lloyd's misrepresentation at the time Linda paid him the $1,000, Linda would have a legal right to compel return of the money.

Under no circumstances can Linda assert against Frank defenses held against him by Lloyd, the promisee. For example, if Frank used defective paint to paint Lloyd's house, and the paint is peeling, Lloyd (the promisee of Linda's promise to pay Frank) could assert this fact as a defense to payment of the promised $1,000. Linda, however, cannot assert this defense against Frank. She has received what she bargained for—the used stationwagon—and must now carry out her part of the bargain by paying Frank. It is up to Lloyd to deal personally with Frank in adjusting his loss from the paint job.

(2) *The beneficiary's rights against the promisee.* A donee beneficiary has no rights against the promisee if the promisor fails to perform as promised (it would not make sense to hold the promisee legally responsible because his or her attempted gift failed).

A creditor beneficiary, on the other hand, can generally proceed against either the promisee on the original debt or the promisor on the third party beneficiary contract or against both parties (although the third party beneficiary can recover only once). The third party beneficiary contract does not discharge the original debt, and unless the original debt is barred by the statute of limitations, bankruptcy, or the like, the creditor beneficiary has all three options available. In the example above, if Linda Thompson fails to pay Frank $1,000 as promised, Frank can sue Lloyd Homeowner on the basis of Lloyd's original promise to pay Frank $1,000 for painting his house. Or Frank can sue Linda Thompson on the basis of the third party beneficiary contract, or Frank can sue both Lloyd and Linda. Frank's recovery, in any event, will be limited to $1,000.

(3) *The promisee's rights against the promisor.* Where the promisor of a *creditor beneficiary contract* fails to pay the beneficiary as promised, the promisee may bring legal action against the promisor for either money damages or specific performance. Money damages is the appropriate remedy where the promisee personally pays the creditor beneficiary following the promisor's breach of promise to pay. Thus, if Linda Thompson fails to pay Frank the Painter, Lloyd may choose to pay Frank, then sue Linda for money damages. Or the promisee may choose not to pay the beneficiary personally, but to sue the promisor for specific performance of the promise to pay on a theory of suretyship. You will recall from Ch. 10 that a contract of "suretyship" is "a contract whereby one person engages to be answerable for the debt, default, or miscarriage of another." Upon entering into the creditor beneficiary contract, the promisor becomes the principal debtor of the money or obligation owing, and the promisee (the original debtor) becomes the surety who is

obliged to answer for the debt or obligation upon the promisor's default or miscarriage. On the basis of the surety's right of *exoneration* (his or her right to be relieved of the duty to pay by the principal debtor)[2], the surety may request the court for specific performance. If granted, the court will order the promisor to make payment as promised.

In contrast, where the promisor of a *donee beneficiary contract* fails to perform as promised, the promisee cannot recover money damages because he or she suffers no monetary loss (the promisee has no legal obligation to the donee). The promisee's exclusive remedy, in this case, is a suit for specific performance. Recall, if you will, the donee beneficiary contract between Lloyd Homeowner and Linda Thompson wherein Lloyd agrees to sell his used stationwagon to Linda in return for Linda's promise to pay $1,000 to Lloyd's son, Jimmy. If Linda fails to make the payment as promised, Jimmy, the donee beneficiary, can sue Linda for money damages as explained in (1) above. While Lloyd, the promisee, cannot sue Linda for money damages (he has suffered no economic loss having no legal obligation to Jimmy), he can request the court to order specific performance of the promise. Linda, in this case, will be ordered by the court to make payment to Jimmy, and Jimmy, the donee beneficiary, will receive what was intended by Lloyd under the contract.

When is a life insurance contract a third party beneficiary contract?

Life insurance policies are usually third party beneficiary contracts of the donee variety. Typically, the insured enters into a contract with the insurance company wherein the insured agrees to pay premiums to the company in exchange for the company's promise to pay money to a

2. Exoneration is a basic rule of suretyship and is discussed in detail in Ch. 27.

third party beneficiary upon the death of the insured. In all states, the donee beneficiary can bring legal action against the insurance company to enforce the policy; and any proceeds paid following the death of the insured belong to the beneficiary, not to the insured's estate.

While most life insurance policies are third party beneficiary contracts, this is not the case where a person having an "insurable interest" in the life of another party insures that person's life to protect his or her legally recognized interest.

In the remainder of this chapter, we will review and summarize the special laws governing insurance contracts of all varieties.

What is the nature of insurance?

Insurance is first of all a contract—a special contract that calls into play not only all the contract law rules discussed in Chapters 7 through 10 (including the requirements of mutual assent, consideration, capacity, and legality), but also a number of special rules peculiar to the law of insurance.

For insurance, in its broadest sense, is an arrangement for transferring and distributing risk. "Risk" is the key to understanding insurance; it is the factor creating the need for insurance. A businesswoman, for example, may operate her business with a maximum of planning, care, and caution, yet be unable to prevent financial losses resulting from contingencies beyond her control. Similarly, a homeowner may construct his home with flame retardant materials, eliminate all flammable wastes from his garage, instruct his children not to play with matches, yet still face fire and major destruction of his home from a defective light switch in the family room. Or a motorist may take a driver's education course, buckle up her seat belt at all times, drive carefully and cautiously, yet still be hit head-on by a drunk driver. Or a hardworking executive may jog every day, watch his diet, have a yearly checkup, yet still drop dead from an unexpected heart attack.

The risks of living go on and on. Certainly, not every risk results in loss or injury to an individual or his or her family. And, to be sure, some individuals suffer relatively little loss over the course of their lifetimes. But the risk is there, and, when disaster does strike, the loss or injury to the particular individual or his or her family may be catastrophic. The concept of insurance helps avert catastrophe by allowing a group of people to pool their risks and absorb individual losses on a group basis. Insurance is a contractual arrangement for transferring and distributing the risks of living. Usually, a company called an *insurer* contracts to pay for the loss of a person called an *insured* (or *beneficiary*) upon the happening of a specified, harmful contingency. Each insured pays *premiums* (specified monetary amounts) into a general fund: when any one insured experiences a loss, the fund covers the loss, and the individual is spared what might otherwise be an overwhelming financial setback. The insurer's promise to pay in the event of loss, and the insured's promise to pay premiums and give proper notice of the loss are set forth in a written contract called a *policy*.

What is the principle of indemnity?

The fundamental and underlying principle of insurance is the concept of indemnity—a concept which has given rise to the two important legal requirements of insurable interest and subrogation. The *World Book Dictionary* defines "indemnity" as "payment for damage, loss, or expense incurred * * *" and "indemnify" as "to compensate for damage, loss or expense incurred * * * make good; repay." [3] And *Black's Law Dictionary* defines "indemnity" as "a collateral contract assurance by which one person engages to secure another against an anticipated loss or to prevent him from being damnified by the legal consequences of an act * * * the term is also used to denote a compensation given to make the person whole from a loss already sustained * * *" [4]

The principle of indemnity thus embraces the concept of compensation for loss sustained. The principle implies that the value of the benefit paid shall not exceed the loss. In other words, the objective of insurance and of law generally is to offset and reimburse for loss by transferring the loss from insured to insurer without conferring a benefit on the insured greater than the loss. Compensation for loss sustained without further benefit (i. e., nothing beyond the loss) is the principle of indemnity. (It should be noted that the principle does not prohibit or conflict with partial reimbursement of loss—that is, compensation in an amount less than the loss.)

The reasoning behind the principle is that to permit an individual to realize gain from insurance proceeds would encourage two evils—gambling or wagering, and destruction of insured lives and property. Public policy has long been opposed to gambling on the grounds that it induces idleness, vice, poverty, and crime. And intentional destruction of lives and property in order to collect insurance proceeds is certainly not in the public interest. By limiting recovery to actual loss only, the principle of indemnity eliminates the possibility of gain and successfully protects against gambling and destruction.

The principle of indemnity has given rise to two important legal doctrines: the insurable interest doctrine and the doctrine of subrogation.

(1) *Insurable interest.* It is a general rule of insurance law that the insured must have an *insurable interest* in the subject matter of the insurance contract. If he or she does not, the insured cannot enforce the insurance agreement. The requirement of an insurable interest has its origins in 18th Century England. By the early 1740's, it had become common practice for insurers of seagoing ships and their cargoes to write insurance policies without demanding proof that the insured had any economic interest in the ship or cargo such that the insured would suffer a loss in the event of damage or destruction of the vessel. To put an end to this practice, the English Parliament passed the Statute of George II in 1746. The Statute provided that, in the absence of an insurable interest, a contract to insure property was void. The Preamble to the Statute made clear that the widespread practice of insuring without such an interest had "been productive of many pernicious practices, whereby great numbers of ships, with their cargoes [had] either been fraudulently lost and destroyed, or taken by the enemy in time of war", and had resulted in "a mischievous kind of gaming or wagering, under the pretence of assuring the risque on shipping." The Statute of George III, passed in 1774, extended the insurable interest requirement to insurance on lives or other events.

The United States has adopted the English requirement of insurable interest both as to property and human life.

(a) *Insurable interest in property.* A person possesses an insurable interest in

---

3. *The World Book Dictionary*, A Thorndike-Barnhart Publication for Field Enterprise's Educational Corporation, 1966, p. 1,000.

4. Henry Campbell Black, *Black's Law Dictionary*, Revised Fourth Edition, West Publishing Co., 1968, p. 910.

property whenever damage or destruction of the property would result in measurable economic loss (in money value) to the person. The person's interest in the property can be less than total ownership. In fact, it can be based on any one of the property interests described in the first six chapters of this text, including real property fees, life estates, remainder interests, easements, profits, covenants, licenses, water rights, support rights, mineral rights; personal property chattels; or intangible personal property interests. The interest may be held in severalty or concurrently with others. Thus, all concurrent owners of property have insurable interests in the property whether the owners are partners holding partnership property or spouses holding community property or property by the entirety. A spouse also has an insurable interest in the property of the other spouse. And a stockholder of a corporation (see Ch. 23) has an insurable interest in the property owned by the corporation. Similarly, a lessee of real estate has an insurable interest in the rental property. And a security interest holder has an insurable interest in the property serving as collateral or security for a loan (see Ch. 27)—an unsecured creditor has no such interest. Also, and very importantly, a buyer of goods has an insurable interest in goods that have been "identified to the contract of sale" (i. e., selected or set aside by the seller—see Ch. 17). The buyer's insurable interest is part and parcel of the "special property" interest created in the buyer upon identification of the goods by the seller. UCC Section 2–501. Even a person with a mere possessory interest in property has an insurable interest (e. g., a watch repairer has an insurable interest in any watch left in his or her possession for repair). And, finally, a building contractor has an insurable interest in any building under construction as the contractor is legally liable to the owner for completion of the building.

The insurable interest in the property need exist only at the time the loss occurs. For a time, some courts held that the insurable interest also had to be present at the time the insurance contract was entered into. This requirement was designed to discourage wagers by rendering them unenforceable even where the wagering party subsequently acquired an interest in the "insured" property. To require an insurable interest at the time of the loss is now considered sufficiently discouraging.

(b) *Insurable interest in life.* Every person with lawful capacity has an insurable interest in his or her own life and may insure that life, naming anyone he or she chooses as beneficiary of the insurance policy. It is not necessary for the beneficiary to have an insurable interest in the insured's life since it is the insured who is taking out the policy. At first glance, it may appear difficult to reconcile such an insurance contract with the principle of indemnity. The principle of indemnity speaks of compensation for loss sustained. Yet it is obvious that a deceased insured cannot be personally reimbursed for the loss of his or her own life. However, in reality, there is no conflict, as the loss to the insured is deemed compensated by the payment to the beneficiary.

For a person to obtain valid insurance, not on his or her own life, but on the life of another, the person taking out the policy must have an insurable interest in the life to be insured. Generally, a person has an insurable interest in the life of his or her spouse and minor children; a minor has an insurable interest in the lives of his or her parents. Decisions go both ways on whether brothers and sisters have insurable interests in one another's lives. And courts frequently hold that adult children do not have insurable interests in the lives of their parents and vice versa. With regard to the debtor-creditor relationship, a creditor generally has an insurable interest in the debtor's life since death of the debtor may mean that the creditor will not be paid. However, if the amount of the insurance greatly exceeds the debt, the excess will be declared void for lack of an insurable interest. Because the death of a partner usually results in dissolution of the partnership firm (see Ch. 22), the partnership has an insurable interest in the lives of its partners. For the same reason, each partner has an insurable interest in the life of every other partner. And a business enterprise has an insurable interest in the life of "key" employees (employees crucial to the operation of the business). The interest is present because death of the employees could result in substantial financial loss to the business.

Unless it is clear that the insurer of another's life has an insurable interest in that life (i. e., will suffer a measurable economic loss by reason of the death), the courts will rule the insurance agreement void. The courts are particularly strict in the area of life insurance because the potential abuse of the insurance agreement is so great—wagering on human life and committing murder to collect the insurance proceeds. The courts are much more likely to find that a speculative interest incident to a business relationship gives rise to an insurable interest for purposes of property insurance than for purposes of insurance on life.

Directly opposite to the insurable interest in property which must exist only at the time of loss, *the insurable interest in life must exist only at the time the policy is purchased.* The insurable interest need not be in existence at the time of the insured's death. For example, suppose that a wife purchases insurance on the life of her husband, naming herself as beneficiary. The fact that the wife

later divorces her husband and has no insurable interest in his life at the time of his death does not render the insurance agreement void. It is enough that the wife had an insurable interest in her spouse's life at the time the policy was purchased. (Of course, if the husband died owing his ex-wife alimony or child support, the ex-wife would stand in the position of a creditor and so have an insurable interest on that basis at the time of her ex-husband's death.)

As to who can raise the issue of insurable interest in life or property, only the insurance company that issues the policy can do so. Third parties cannot (e. g., a party attempting to disqualify a beneficiary so as to personally succeed to the insurance proceeds cannot question the existence of an insurable interest).

(2) Subrogation. The second legal doctrine flowing from the principle of indemnity is the doctrine of subrogation. Like the insurable interest doctrine, the doctrine of subrogation is designed to prevent an insured from realizing a net gain from insurance proceeds (i. e., a benefit beyond compensation for loss sustained). The doctrine states, at least insofar as property insurance is concerned, that an insurance company that pays for an insured's loss is *subrogated* to the legal rights of the insured against the party who caused the loss.

Black's Law Dictionary defines "subrogation" as follows.

[It is] the substitution of one person in the place of another with reference to a lawful claim, demand or right, so that he who is substituted succeeds to the rights of the other in relation to the debt or claim, and its rights, remedies, or securities.[5]

5. Henry Campbell Black, Ibid., p. 1,595.
Under liability coverage, as will be explained later in the chapter, the insurance compa-

ny pays money not to the insured, but to a claimant against the insured. The company, in this case, is subrogated to whatever

Thus, if an insured suffers a loss, he or she may look to his or her insurance company for payment. The insurance company, in turn, will receive whatever legal rights the insured may have (at least to the extent of the insurance coverage) to recover money damages in or out of court from the party who caused the loss. By transferring these rights to the insurance company, the doctrine of subrogation prevents the insured from recovering twice for the same loss (once from the insurance company and again from the party who caused the loss). The insured is thus denied a net gain from the loss, and the principle of indemnity is satisfied.

Property insurance policies are held to create a right of subrogation regardless of whether the right is mentioned in the policy. However, as a practical matter, most policies do include a subrogation clause specifically authorizing the insurance company to proceed against the party causing the loss, whether the loss arises from a breach of contract or tort. For example, suppose that a businessman deliberately sets fire to the warehouse of a competitor. If the competitor's insurance company compensates the insured for the fire damage, the insurance company will succeed to the rights of the insured to recover money damages from the wrongdoer. (Apart from his civil liability, the businessman may be convicted of criminal arson and sent to jail—see Appendix A regarding crimes and punishments.)

With regard to life and accident insurance, the insurance company is not subrogated to the rights of the insured in the absence of a specific subrogation clause (which is fairly unusual).

Automobile insurance policies, on the other hand, frequently include a subroga-tion clause, both as to liability provisions and medical payments coverage.

Does insurance cover intentional acts?

By reason of the very nature of insurance, losses are covered only if they are accidental or fortuitous as opposed to being the result of an intentional act. However, the meaning of "accidental" or "fortuitous" is determined from the point of view of the person whose interest is protected by the policy. With regard to property and accident insurance, the insured and the victim of the accident are usually one and the same. For example, if you intentionally set fire to your own house, the resulting loss will not be covered by your insurance because the loss resulted from your intentional act. With respect to liability insurance, the person whose interest is protected is the insured and not the victim of the physical harm (the insured being protected as to his or her legal liability). In some cases, a person may be liable for the intentional acts of another under what is called vicarious liability. In Chapter 20, we will study the doctrine of respondeat superior which states that an employer is liable for torts committed by his or her employees while in the scope of employment. Even where an employee commits an *intention-al* act (e. g., an assault or battery) causing injury to another, the employer *may* be liable. However, the loss is fortuitous as far as the employer is concerned, and his or her liability insurance will cover the loss. This is true even where the loss is to the employer's own property. Of course, if the intentional act is committed by or at the direction of the insured, the loss will not be covered because it is not fortuitous.

As to life insurance, it is not the interest of the insured that is being protected but rather that of his or her beneficiary. This suggests that not only homicide but

rights the insured may have to contribu-tion from others (e. g., from a person re-sponsible along with the insured for the loss).

also suicide may be accidental from the point of view of the beneficiary. Of course, a person may not commit homicide and then collect insurance on the victim's life. Also, many life insurance contracts expressly limit coverage for suicide, either not covering it at all or setting a time period during which death from suicide will not be covered (such as the first two years of the policy). Finally, many policies providing for double indemnity in the case of "accidental" death define "accidental" so as to exclude both suicide and homicide.

When should an individual buy insurance?

An individual's purchase of insurance should be based on a realistic determination of need. How great a risk is there to the individual's life or property? Is insurance necessary in the event of loss? How much money will the insurance cost? How much money does the individual have to spend on insurance?

Let's consider an example. The author is well acquainted with a local rock band that performs at high school and college dances (within a radius of perhaps 250–300 miles from their homes) an average of seven to eight times a month. The young men travel to and from their engagements in an old van, taking with them upwards of $12,000 worth of musical and amplifying equipment. Could the equipment be damaged or stolen? Certainly. The risk is considerable. Is insurance necessary in the event of loss? To be sure, it would be difficult for the young men to replace all the equipment without insurance. But is the answer for the group members to buy insurance? Looking into the situation, the young men learn first that local insurance companies are not anxious to sell insurance on the equipment for the very reason that the risks of theft and damage are so high. They learn next that, though the insurance can be purchased,

the premiums would be very high (perhaps $100 a month) in relation to the amounts of money the young men earn from their rock group (nearly any type of risk can be insured against if a person is willing to pay high enough premiums —e. g., a movie studio once insured Betty Grable's legs). Thus, while the risk is there as well as the need, the cost of the insurance is simply too high. As an alternative to purchasing insurance, the young men choose to manage the risk themselves by locking the van when transporting the equipment, keeping an eye on the property at all times, and carefully selecting the places at which they perform. Even so, the group has had six microphones and some other minor equipment stolen or "ripped off" (to use the group members' own words). But over all, as "self insurers" through what might be termed a program of "risk retention", the young men have done well and are far ahead financially of where they would have been had they purchased insurance.

In every case, then, it is a matter of determining the extent of the risk, the need for insurance, and the availability of dollars to purchase insurance. Some people say that a person can never be overinsured—but this is simply not so. A young, single person with no dependents may have little need for life insurance. The only need may be to pay for funeral expenses in the event of an untimely death (and statistically, the likelihood of such death is not great). In any case, if funeral funds are not available, society will take care of disposing of the body if for no other reason than sanitation.

On the other hand, a young person with a spouse and one or more small children dependent upon him or her for the necessities of life (e. g., a young man with a pregnant wife and three small children) generally cannot afford to go without life insurance and disability insurance. The risk of leaving the family unprotected in the event of an untimely death or disabling injury is too great.

Nor can a homeowner who has invested most of his or her lifesavings in purchasing and owning a home afford to go without fire insurance on the property: the risk is there, the need is great, and the cost is minor in comparison to the potential loss. The fact that thousands of other homeowners have the same need and pay premiums for fire loss protection permits creation of an indemnity fund to protect the few who do lose their homes to fire. (Along the same line, a renter may need "renter's" insurance to protect against loss to his or her personal property from burglary, fire, or vandalism.)

In the commercial world, a businessperson may need a variety of insurance policies to cover the risks of doing business. And a doctor, lawyer, CPA, or other professional is well advised to purchase professional liability insurance.

Finally, insurance is required by statute in some cases. For example, Oregon requires every driver of a motor vehicle to carry driver liability insurance.

How is insurance written and marketed?

The writing and marketing of insurance is best understood by consideration of the following:

(1) Government regulation of insurance;

(2) Kinds of companies that sell insurance;

(3) Individuals involved in the sale of insurance—agents versus brokers; and

(4) The writing of the policy, its interpretation, and effect.

Government regulation of insurance. The federal McCarran Act of 1945 leaves government regulation of the insurance industry to the individual states. Considering the importance of insurance,

it is not surprising that each state has a volume of statutes governing the insurance industry generally and setting forth the requirements for doing business as an insurance company within the particular state. Because each state's regulations run anywhere from 200 to 300 or more pages in length, it is not possible to list all the statutory provisions governing insurance in this chapter section. However, we can allude to a few of the more important regulations, particularly those covering the formation, licensing, supervision, and liquidation of insurance companies as well as the licensing and supervision of the individuals who sell insurance. Generally speaking, each state has the following basic provisions:

(1) Provisions creating an insurance "commissioner", "division", "administrator", or "agency" to act as the regulatory authority of insurance within the state.

(2) Provisions defining and classifying insurance companies within certain subject areas such as fire, marine, and auto insurance; life, disability, and casualty insurance; surety insurance (providing for bail bonds and guaranteeing the fidelity of persons holding positions of trust); title insurance, etc.

(3) Provisions spelling out the licensing requirements for the various classifications of insurance.

(4) Provisions setting forth factors that insurance companies must consider in determining rates, including reasonable profit margin and loss experience of the company. The objective of the law is to achieve just, reasonable, and nondiscriminatory rates without discouraging reasonable competition among the insurance companies.

(5) Provisions requiring insurance companies to file their rate schedules (i. e., what they are charging for insurance) with the regulatory authority for approval. Once the schedules have been approved, the insurance companies must

abide by the listed prices; and they may not charge higher rates for unlisted risks that pose essentially the same hazard as risks included in the schedule.

(6) Provisions requiring insurance companies to file annual financial statements with the regulatory authority showing all premiums received and all losses incurred and paid for in each class and kind of insurance.

(7) Provisions requiring insurance companies (particularly those not incorporated within the state) to maintain financial reserves in varying amounts (often hundreds of thousands of dollars) depending upon the type of insurance being sold.

(8) Provisions specifying what investments an insurance company may make with its excess funds, earnings and profits, and reserves.

(9) Provisions setting forth the licensing requirements for individuals who sell insurance. Generally, a written examination is mandatory; and any individual who purports to sell insurance without meeting the requirements of the law is subject to statutory penalties.

(10) Provisions providing for the licensing of insurance adjusters (individuals who act for the insurance company in determining the amount of the loss suffered by the insured). Again, a written exam is required, and any individual who purports to act as an insurance adjuster without meeting the statutory requirements may be penalized.

(11) Provisions allowing minors to contract for health and life insurance, and removing the minor's rights to rescind such contracts.

(12) Provisions authorizing the insurance regulatory agency of the state to examine all business operations of an insurance company every five years or so. A company that fails to cooperate with the agency in providing access to its books,

records, accounts, etc., is subject to statutory penalties, including loss of license.

(13) Provisions setting forth procedures for the liquidation of insurance companies.

Remember, these are just a few of the highlights—state statutes control, to some extent, every phase of the insurance industry.

Kinds of companies that sell insurance. Traditionally, insurance companies were classified according to the particular kind of insurance they sold. State law prohibited the companies from selling more than one major type or classification such as fire and marine, casualty, disability, title, surety, or life insurance, etc. For example, a company could sell life insurance, or it could sell casualty insurance, but it could not sell both.

Modernly, however, the trend in the law is to permit an insurer to sell or at least place (find a seller for) all kinds of insurance, including life insurance. Companies that sell life insurance as well as casualty, and fire and marine are known as "all-line" companies; companies that sell all kinds of insurance other than life are known as "multiple-line" companies. Although it is now common to find insurance companies selling more than one major type of insurance, many companies continue to specialize, particularly in the areas of title and surety insurance.

Still valid is a classification of insurance according to form of business organization. Generally speaking, an insurance company operates under one of the following forms:

(1) *Fraternal society.* A fraternal society is a nonprofit organization established for the benefit of its members. Some fraternal associations, clubs, and benevolent organizations such as the Knights of Columbus, the Lutheran Brotherhood, and the Grange, write insurance for members of their group.

Each group member is both an insurer (of the other group members) and an insured (protected by the group indemnity fund).

(2) *Lloyd's of London.* Many times when insurance cannot be purchased locally, it may be obtained through Lloyd's of London. So long as an individual is willing to pay a high enough premium, the world famous Lloyd's will write insurance (other than ordinary life) on almost any known risk. Lloyd's operates through syndicates of individuals who agree to insure particular risks, each individual being personally liable for a fraction of the risk assumed. Unlike a fraternal society which is organized for the mutual benefit of its members, Lloyd's is organized primarily for the profit of its owners—Lloyd's insureds do not participate as insurers.

(3) *Inter-insurance exchange.* Sometimes, several individuals can protect themselves against a particular risk rather inexpensively by joining together as a group or syndicate and setting up an indemnity fund to compensate group members for their losses. Such organizations are called inter-insurance exchanges or reciprocals. Like Lloyd's of London, a syndicate writes the insurance; unlike Lloyd's, each participant is both an insurer and an insured. If a surplus exists at the end of the policy period, each group member will receive a proportionate share by way of a returned premium.

(4) *Mutual corporation.* Mutual corporations generally sell more life insurance than any other kind of company. Mutual corporations are like inter-insurance exchanges but on a much larger and more permanent basis. There are no stockholders in a mutual insurance corporation, but the policyholders to elect the directors who manage the company. Again, each participant is both an insurer and an insured: any surplus of premiums over losses is returned to the members,

assuming all required reserve funds are replete.

(5) *Stock corporations.* A stock corporation is a life insurance company that is owned and controlled by stockholders. Like other business corporations, a stock corporation is operated to make a profit for its owners. The stockholders share in the earnings of the corporation through dividends declared by the board of directors and paid to the stockholders (again, assuming that all required reserve funds are filled). In contrast, the policyholders do not participate in the earnings of the stock corporation—unlike the policyholders of a mutual company, they are not both insurer and insured.

It should be pointed out that many companies modernly mix the features of mutual and stock corporations. For example, a company may have stockholders who participate in the earnings of the company through payment of dividends as well as policyholders who participate in the selection of management and who share in surplus revenue.

The individuals who sell insurance—agents versus brokers. A prospective purchaser of insurance usually deals with one of two types of individuals—an agent or a broker. As you will learn in Ch. 21, an *agent* is a person who is authorized to contract on behalf of another called a *principal.* So long as an agent remains within the scope of his or her authority, the principal is legally bound by the agent's acts and contracts. Generally speaking, the extent of an agent's authority is the sum of his or her *express, implied,* and *apparent* authority (see Ch. 21 for a complete discussion of authority). Express authority is authority specifically spelled out by the principal; implied authority is authority incidental to carrying out the agent's express powers; and apparent authority is that normal to the appearance of the agent in the position he or she has been placed in by the principal. (It is a fundamental rule of agency law that a principal is bound by the acts of an agent having apparent authority to contract.) An *insurance agent* is a person who is authorized by an insurance company, whether it be a fraternal society, a Lloyd's of London, an inter-insurance exchange, or a mutual or stock company, to negotiate and enter into insurance contracts on behalf of the company. The extent of a selling agent's authority to bind an insurance company is, again, the sum of the agent's express, implied, and apparent authority. Usually, it is not within the scope of the agent's authority to bind the company to a life insurance contract until certain conditions have been met (namely, the prospective insured must pass a physical exam and pay the first premium). However, it is generally within the agent's power to bind the company to the sale of other kinds of insurance—even before a policy has been issued (this is called a *binder* and will be explained in more detail in the next subsection).

A so called *broker*, on the other hand, is not an agent for the insurance company, nor usually an agent for the insured. Rather, he or she is an independent contractor (i. e., an independent businessperson as will be explained in Ch. 20) who is in the business of determining what a person's insurance needs are and placing those insurance needs with the appropriate companies. Typically, a prospective insured consults a broker on the basis of the broker's advertising or salesmanship. Together, broker and client discuss the client's insurance situation and pinpoint his or her insurance needs—say, auto, fire, and liability insurance. The broker then uses his or her professional contacts and abilities to place the insurance with the appropriate companies (although a broker has ready access to most companies, it should be noted that a few companies deal only through their own authorized selling agents). Usually, upon

placing the insurance, the broker collects a commission from the insurance companies; and, frequently, the broker collects the premiums from the insured and remits them to the appropriate insurer. So you see, the broker is a middleperson. Occasionally, he or she may be authorized to bind either the insured or insurer to an insurance contract (in which case, the broker is also an agent of the authorizing party), but it is best to think of the broker as an independent contractor—a middleperson not bound to any one individual or any one company (as is a selling agent).

The writing of the policy, its interpretation, and effect. The best way to approach the writing of the policy, its interpretation, and effect is to look at what happens chronologically.

Step 1—Reaching the agreement (i .e., mutual assent). As stated previously, the contract law rules discussed in Chapters 7 through 10 apply generally to the making of insurance contracts; mutual assent, consideration, capacity, and legality are all required. However, there are also some special rules that apply—rules peculiar to the law of insurance. To begin with, most states, by statute, require insurance policies to be in writing: the statutes, to some extent, specify the required contents of the policies and even the size and style of type to be used in printing them. Secondly, although minors can avoid most insurance contracts (just as they can avoid all other contracts), they generally cannot avoid contracts for life, disability, or health insurance. And, thirdly, for purposes of mutual assent, the general rule is that it is the insured who makes the offer and the insurer who makes the acceptance. With regard to the reaching of mutual assent, the following situations must be considered:

(a) *The effective moment of the insurance coverage.* Often, a substantial period of time elapses between a person's application for insurance and the insurance company's issuance of the policy. Obviously, if the insured has no insurance coverage during this time period, he or she may suffer a financially disastrous loss or undergo a change of circumstances that leaves him or her virtually uninsurable against future losses. As for the insurer, he or she may find only after spending time and money processing the insurance application that the applicant has changed his or her mind and no longer wants the insurance.

To protect both parties, insurance agents frequently agree to provide temporary insurance coverage during the time interval between application for and issuance of the policy. Insofar as life insurance is concerned, an agent often uses a *conditional binding receipt* to make the insurance effective as of the date of application. A conditional binding receipt is a written memorandum of the essential terms of the life insurance contract. The memo provides that the insurance coverage is effective as of the date of application so long as certain conditions are met (usually, that the first premium is paid at that time and that the insured is insurable). A typical conditional binding receipt might provide as follows.

It might say:

If the first full premium is paid at the time of making this application, and if at that time the applicant is insurable under the company's rules and practices (here referring to the applicant's passing of the required medical exam), for the amount and upon the plan applied for without modification, then the insurance shall be effective from the time of making application.

With regard to insurance other than life, applicant and agent frequently agree orally (often over the telephone) that the applicant will be insured temporarily during the period between application for and issuance of the policy. Such an agreement is called a *binder* and is usually followed by the agent writing, signing, and sending to the insured a memorandum stating the essential terms of the policy. For example, it is not unusual for a new car purchaser to telephone an auto insurance agent from the car dealer's office and request comprehensive automobile insurance coverage. If the agent binds coverage over the phone, the purchaser will enjoy immediate protection and may drive home in his or her new car without undue worry or concern. The binder will be effective upon the same terms and conditions as the policy; and the policy, once issued, will supersede or take the place of the binder. Of course, any defenses to coverage available to the insurer will apply both as to the binder and as to the policy (see next subsection).

In the absence of temporary insurance coverage, an insurance policy becomes effective according to the terms of the policy. Some policies call for a waiting period after delivery of the policy to the insured before the policy becomes effective; others require a prepayment of premiums coupled with delivery of the policy to the insured. Apart from such conditions, acceptance is accomplished according to the usual rules of mutual assent as outlined in Chapter 7.[6]

Also, where there is no temporary insurance provided, most courts hold that an insurer is subject to liability for negligent delay in acting on an insurance application.

6. The temporary coverage issue is of little significance with regard to the air travel trip insurance available through airport vending machines. Such insurance is effective immediately upon deposit in the machine by the insured (i. e., payment of the required premium) and issuance of the receipt or policy from the machine by the insurer. (The insured must take care not to mail the insurance policy home on the very flight that he or she is taking.)

(b) *Factors preventing operation of the insurance agreement.* Although some special terminology is used in the area of insurance law, the basic rules regarding mutual assent and the making of conditions apply with full force to insurance contracts. Like all other contracts, insurance contracts may be void or voidable on the basis of fraud, mistake, undue influence, unconscionability, etc. They may be subject to conditions precedent or subsequent, the occurrence or nonoccurrence of which will prevent the operation of the contract or discharge one or both parties from any further obligation of performance. The special terminology used in applying these general rules to insurance contracts is found primarily in the areas of *misrepresentation* and *warranty.*

Misrepresentation. If a prospective insured intentionally or innocently misrepresents a material fact that induces an insurer to enter into an insurance contract, the insurer has a right to rescind the agreement on the grounds of fraud (for intentional misrepresentation) or mistake (for innocent misrepresentation). For example, a prospective insured might misrepresent a material fact in answering questions on the insurance application form (such forms are often attached to the issued policy). The insurer, in this case, will have a right to rescind the contract upon discovering the misrepresentation. As you will recall from Ch. 10, rescission serves to place the parties in the positions they would have been in had there been no contract. Restitution is part and parcel of rescission, and the insurer must return all premiums paid by the insured in order to rescind (of course, the insurer is entitled to offset any expenses incurred by the company in processing and issuing the policy). And if the misrepresentation is intentional, the insurer may also bring suit against the insured for the tort of deceit.

Of course, to justify rescission, the misrepresentation must be as to a material fact (as opposed to an immaterial fact or an opinion). Whether or not a fact is material generally depends upon whether the insurer would have issued the policy had the truth been known.

Along the same line, an insurer may rescind an insurance agreement upon learning that the insured, in applying for the policy, intentionally failed to disclose a material fact unknown to the insurer that would have affected the insurer's willingness to accept the risk of loss. The insured's intentional failure to disclose a material fact is termed *concealment.*

Finally, insofar as life insurance is concerned, statutes generally require inclusion of what is called an *incontestable clause.* Typically, such a clause provides that, after two years time, the insurer cannot contest or challenge the validity of the life insurance policy. Thus, after two years have elapsed, the issues of misrepresentation and concealment are generally meaningless. However, it should be pointed out that most life insurance policies expressly provide that where the insured misstates his or her age in applying for the policy, the amount payable upon the insured's death will be the amount of proceeds *the premiums paid would have purchased had the insured given his or her correct age.* Generally speaking, the courts will enforce such a provision though the policy contains an incontestable clause and more than two years have elapsed.

Warranty. A *warranty* is a representation made by either insurer or insured that is contained within the insurance policy itself. Generally, a warranty operates as condition to create a duty of performance or discharge a duty of performance. For example, an automobile insurer may limit his or her liability for loss by means of the following language.

Example:

> This policy applies only to accidents, occurrences, and loss during the policy period while the automobile is within the United States of America, its territories or possessions, or Canada, or is being transported between parts thereof.

It is thus a condition precedent to recovery under the policy that the loss occur within the United States, its territories or possessions, or Canada, etc. (In face of such language, it is not surprising that most auto owners buy special insurance before venturing into Mexico.)

Similarly, a property insurer may limit his or her liability for loss by covering only the "contents" of a particular building or only the property situated at a particular location. Again, loss or damage to the particular described property is a condition precedent to recovery under the policy.

Warranties may generally be classified as either *affirmative warranties* or *promissory warranties*. An affirmative warranty is one stating a condition that must exist only at the time the contract is entered into. For example, the insured under a life insurance policy may be required to warrant as to his or her good health or lack of pre-existing disease or defect at the time of issuance of the policy. Good health is material to the risk insured against and is frequently a condition of life insurance coverage.

A promissory warranty, on the other hand, is one stating a condition that must be maintained throughout the period of the insurance policy. For example, the insured under a comprehensive property insurance policy may promise to take certain precautions against burglary or fire loss, such as hiring a nightwatchperson or installing and maintaining a sprinkler system. If the insured fails to keep his

or her promise at any time throughout the period of the policy, the warranty is breached, and the condition subsequent operates to discharge the insurer from any further duty under the contract.

In recent years, the courts have looked with increasing disfavor upon conditions subsequent that release the insurer from his or her duty to pay. The trend in the law is to permit an insurer to escape liability only where the breach of warranty is material to the risk insured against.

(c) *Changes in the contract after it is written.* Sometimes, it is necessary to change the terms of a written insurance contract to comply with changes in state law, to substitute new rates for new policy periods, to add to or restrict insurance coverage, etc. When change is required, it is generally not necessary to issue a new policy—in most cases, the change can be effected by attaching a "rider" (a separate sheet containing the change) to the policy or by "indorsing" (writing) the change directly on the policy. Where a policy has several conflicting riders or indorsements added, the last in time prevails.

(d) *Interpretation of the policy.* Most people who purchase insurance have had little or no legal training. For this reason, the rules of interpretation provide that insurance policies are to be read and construed by the courts as they would be understood by the average person or businessperson—not by the person with legal training. Because the insurer writes the insurance contract, any ambiguities in the policy are interpreted against the insurer and in favor of the insured. Thus, if it is unclear from reading the contract whether the insured had temporary coverage prior to delivery of the policy, the court will likely hold that the insured did have such coverage. If the insurer claims otherwise on the basis of statements made in the application form, the court must interpret the statements as they would be understood by a person of ordinary experience and intelligence.

This apparent "bias" of the courts in favor of the insured is not without good reason. Frequently, a person who wants insurance coverage (particularly life insurance) has little choice but to accept the policy as it is written. Confronted with an insurer whose attitude is "take it or leave it", the insured has next to no bargaining power. The contract, in this case, is one of adhesion, and the court may declare all or part of it unconscionable and unenforceable. For example, in the air travel insurance case of Lachs v. Fidelity & Cas. Co., 306 N.Y. 357, 118 N.E.2d 555 (1954), the court permitted recovery for a fatal crash occurring on a nonscheduled flight even though the vending machine and policy stated that recovery would be allowed only on scheduled flights. The provision limiting recovery was held unconscionable and unenforceable because it was couched in fine print in the policy and because the vending machine selling the insurance was placed near the airport counter where both scheduled and nonscheduled flights were processed.

Step 2—Required procedures in the event of insurance covered loss. All insurance policies contain provisions requiring the insured to give prompt notice of insurance covered loss and to furnish proof of loss. Prompt notice is essential from the insurer's point of view because it affords the insurer reasonable opportunity to protect his or her rights as well as the interests of the insured (who may, on occasion, be held to liability beyond the limits of the policy). It is extremely important for the insured to comply fully and exactly with the notice and proof of loss terms. If the insured fails to comply,

and the failure prejudices the insurance company in determining the correct amount of the loss or in proceeding against the parties responsible for the loss, the insurance company may be excused from its duty of performance under the contract.[7]

In addition to notice and proof of loss terms, liability insurance policies generally contain provisions requiring the insured to cooperate with and assist the insurer in investigating and defending insurance covered tort claims against the insured. Generally, the insured must attend trials, assist in settlement efforts, help secure evidence, obtain attendance by witnesses, etc. The insured need not, however, cooperate at his or her own expense but may look to the insurer for the costs of cooperation and assistance. Again, any failure by the insured to fully and exactly comply with these terms may result in discharge of the insurer's duty of performance under the contract. And, very occasionally, the insured's noncompliance may render him or her liable in money damages to the insurer (e. g., where the insured's failure to cooperate results in the insurance company becoming liable to a third party).

Liability insurance policies generally also contain provisions requiring the insurer to defend the insured against any insurance covered claim brought against him or her. By this is meant that the insurer must defend the insured against any allegation that the insured has caused injury or damage to another as covered by the terms of the policy. So long as the allegation is there, the insurer's duty to defend arises even where all available facts indicate that the insured cannot be held liable on any legal theory. The courts are divided on the question of whether the insurance company has a

---

7. The insurer's duty of performance may be discharged on either of two theories: (1) the insured's material breach of contract discharges the insurer's duty of per-

formance; or (2) the occurrence of the condition subsequent—failure to give proper notice and proof of loss—operates to discharge the duty.

continuing obligation to defend the insured after the company has offered the full amount of the insurance in settlement of the claim. The better view is that the obligation is a continuing one.

Along this line, it is important to realize that the fact that a person has insurance or the amount of his or her insurance is neither relevant nor admissible in court in determining the existence and extent of liability. This rule of evidence is designed to prevent the jury from arbitrarily finding for the plaintiff because his or her insurance company can easily absorb the loss. The jury must reach its decisions as to liability and as to the extent of liability without knowing whether the defendant will have to pay any or all of the judgment from his or her own pocket.

Finally, remember that if an insurance company compensates its insured for injury or damage caused by another's wrongful act, the insurance company is generally subrogated to the rights of the insured and may proceed against the wrongdoer. The insurance company, in this case, is entitled to cooperation and assistance from the insured.

Step 3—Cancellation or termination of insurance. Ultimately, the contract between insurer and insured will come to an end whether or not an insurance covered loss occurs during the period of the policy. In many cases, the policy simply expires without renewal, and the obligations of the parties are fully discharged by performance (frequently, the insured desires to renew, but the insurance company chooses not to). And, sometimes, the insurance company cancels the policy prior to the end of the policy period. Along this line, most states have statutes prohibiting insurers from refusing to write or renew policies on grounds of age, sex, race, occupation, or residency of the applicant or insured. The same statutes strictly control cancellation of poli-

cies. Generally, all policies may be cancelled for failure of the insured to pay premiums. Usually, the policy lapses if the premiums are not paid on time; however, some policies allow the insured a one month grace period in which to make up past due amounts. Liability and property insurance policies may usually be cancelled at the insurer's option. Typically, the insurer cancels such policies because the insured has a bad loss record with the company indicating that the risk of loss is too high (e. g., an insured with a bad driving record who has already cost the insurer $3,000). Where the insurance company decides to cancel, it must generally give the insured 30 days written notice of the cancellation and return all unearned premiums.

Finally, it should be noted that an insurer sometimes has the option of choosing cancellation rather than rescission as a remedy for an insured's misrepresentation. Which remedy is preferable? You already know that if the insurer rescinds the contract, the company will escape liability for any losses that have occurred, but will have to pay back all premiums, earned and unearned. On the other hand, if the insurer cancels the contract, the company will be liable for losses occurring up to the moment of cancellation, but will have to pay back only unearned premiums. Which remedy is best will thus depend upon whether a loss has occurred prior to the time the company must choose a remedy.

Are there any special rules regarding life insurance?

Life insurance could more accurately be called "death insurance" since it is a contract in which an insurer agrees to pay a stipulated sum of money upon the death of an insured. The special rules governing life insurance are summarized below.

(1) Generally speaking, there are four kinds of life insurance: term insurance,

ordinary life, limited-payment life, and endowment insurance.

Term insurance. Term insurance is insurance protection against death for a specified period of time, such as five or ten years. If the insured dies within the period of the policy, the insurer must pay a stipulated amount to the insured's beneficiary. While term insurance is the least expensive kind of life insurance (it provides the most insurance protection for the least amount of dollars), it has no investment features. The policy does not build up a cash surrender value (i. e., the insured cannot "surrender" the policy to the insurance company for cash); nor does the insured have a right to borrow from the insurer on the basis of premiums paid into the policy. However, term insurance is often renewable without regard to the health of the insured (this protects the insured who becomes uninsurable during the period of the policy because of ill health or accident). And term insurance is frequently convertible (i. e., the insured has an option to change the insurance to a "permanent" plan of ordinary life or endowment insurance).

Ordinary life. Ordinary life insurance (also called straight life) provides insurance protection against death for the entire life of the insured. Although ordinary life requires the insured to pay premiums up until the time of death, it does provide certain investment features. Unlike term insurance, ordinary life builds up a cash surrender value as well as a loan value. Thus, the insured may borrow from the insurer an amount based upon the number of premiums paid into the policy. If the insured fails to repay the loan, the insurer may deduct the amount owing along with reasonable interest from the proceeds of the policy upon the insured's death.

Because of its investment features, ordinary life costs more than term insur-

ance. In comparison, it actually affords less insurance protection for the same number of dollars. Nevertheless, many people prefer ordinary life because it guarantees the insured a certain amount of cash while he or she is still living.

Limited-payment life. Limited-payment life insurance is like ordinary life in all respects except that the payment of premiums is limited to a fixed number of years, such as 10, 20, or 30 years. Because the time of payment is shorter, the premiums are considerably higher than ordinary life premiums. However, once the period of payment has elapsed, the policy is paid up in full, and the insured can enjoy worry free insurance protection for the remainder of his or her life.

Endowment insurance. Endowment insurance is a contract wherein an insurer promises to pay an insured a lump sum of money when the insured reaches a specified age, and, if the insured fails to reach that age, to pay the lump sum to the insured's beneficiary. Like ordinary life and limited-payment life, endowment insurance offers certain investment features.

(2) Insurance companies also write annuity contracts (sometimes called retirement income insurance) containing life insurance aspects. Generally, by the terms of the annuity, the insurer must pay the annuitant (the insured) a fixed sum of money at periodic intervals (annually, quarterly, monthly, etc.) commencing upon a certain date (when the annuitant reaches a specified age) and continuing until the annuitant dies, at which time the insurer must pay a final lump sum. Payment at periodic intervals is the standard annuity feature; payment of the lump sum is the life insurance aspect.

The fixed amounts to be paid under an annuity are determined by taking the premium dollars paid by the annuitant, applying a conservative return on the money until the annuitant reaches the specified age, then dividing the total amount according to the annuitant's life expectancy. The payments begin when the annuitant reaches the required age and continue until he or she dies, whether that is one year from the beginning date of payment or 105 (i. e., the payments last as long as the annuitant lasts).[8] Obviously, if the annuitant dies soon after the payments begin, the insurance company will profit as it will have no continued obligation to pay (apart from any lump sum requirement). Of course, if the annuitant lives for many many years, it is he or she who will profit.

In either event, some part of each payment the annuitant receives under the policy will constitute a return of the annuitant's investment and will not be taxable income. For example, suppose that a person purchases an annuity policy for $24,000. According to the life expectancy tables, the annuitant will live for 20 years from the time he or she begins to receive monthly payments of $200 under the policy (the annuitant's total expected return is thus $48,000). One half of each $200 payment will constitute a return of the annuitant's investment, and the other half will be taxable income. The following formula applies:

$$\frac{cost}{expected\ return} \times payments\ received\ (annually) = nontaxable\ portion$$

$$\frac{\$24,000}{\$48,000} \times \$2,400 = \$1,200\ nontaxable\ return\ of\ investment$$

(3) For an additional premium, most life insurance policies will include a *double indemnity* clause providing that the amount of insurance will double if the insured dies as the result of an accident within ninety days of the accident. Many double indemnity clauses exempt accidental death occurring after the insured reaches a certain age such as 65 years.

(4) Insurance protection against total permanent disability of the insured is also available at an added charge. Generally, if total permanent disability occurs, the insured will receive a specified amount of money each month (many policies also waive payment by the insured of further insurance premiums).

(5) Most policies do not provide coverage for death resulting from suicide, violation of law, or execution of crime. And some policies deny coverage for death resulting from narcotics use, war activities, and operation of aircraft.

(6) As a practical matter, the beneficiary of a life insurance policy should be a named individual rather than the estate of the insured. If the insured's estate is listed as the beneficiary, the insurance proceeds will be probated upon the death of the insured and will be reduced by any outstanding debts of the estate and charges of administration. On the other hand, if a named individual is listed as the beneficiary, the full insurance proceeds will bypass probate and go directly

---

8. Of course, there are many different combinations of annuities. For example, in a "variable" annuity, the insurer promises to pay, not a fixed sum at periodic intervals, but a variable amount dependent upon the company's success at investing its annuitants' premium dollars in stocks, bonds, real estate, etc. A "cash refund" annuity guarantees that it will pay the insured at least the amount of his or her investment

in the annuity, regardless of when the insured dies. Still other annuities guarantee the annuitant a lump sum of money if he or she dies within a certain period of time, usually 10 to 20 years. And, finally, "joint and survivorship" annuities continue for the joint lives of a husband and wife (i. e., the annuity continues until the second spouse dies).

to the beneficiary. To this end, it is always a good idea for the insured to name both a primary and a contingent beneficiary to protect against the possibility of the primary beneficiary predeceasing the insured.

(7) The general rule is that a beneficiary who kills the insured is not entitled to the insurance proceeds. Most courts award the proceeds as though the beneficiary predeceased the insured—thus, if there is a contingent beneficiary, he or she will be entitled to the money. A few courts hold that the proceeds belong to the estate of the murdered insured.

(8) Most policies expressly provide that an insured may change his or her beneficiary without the beneficiary's knowledge or consent. In the absence of such a provision, the beneficiary has a vested interest in the insurance proceeds, and the insured cannot change beneficiaries so as to deprive him or her of that interest.

Remember, a life insurance policy is a third party beneficiary contract—and this is true regardless of whether the insured has the right to change beneficiaries under the policy. The named beneficiary at the time of the insured's death has the right to collect the insurance proceeds and may sue in his or her own name to enforce that right.

(9) Apart from term insurance, an insured who can no longer make the payments on his or her life insurance policy usually has the option of taking the cash surrender value of the policy and terminating the coverage, borrowing on the policy and using the money to pay as many premiums as possible, or taking a paid up policy for a smaller amount of coverage. If the insured loses coverage because of a failure to pay premiums, he or she generally has a right to have the policy reinstated (so long as he or she is still insurable) by paying all back premiums within a reasonable period of time (usually one year).

(10) Frequently the beneficiary of a policy has a choice of options upon the death of the insured. For example, instead of taking a lump sum payment, the beneficiary may commonly elect to receive the proceeds in the form of an annuity. Or he or she may choose to receive the proceeds in equal monthly installments for a certain number of years. Or he or she may simply allow the company to retain the proceeds indefinitely in return for payment of reasonable interest.

Are there any special rules regarding automobile insurance?

The special rules regarding automobile insurance may be summarized as follows.

(1) There are six basic kinds of automobile insurance that may be purchased in many combinations to afford insurance protection of varying amounts. The insurance premium, in every case, is based upon the age, sex, marital status, and driver's training of the insured, and the condition and intended use of the car (i. e., its purpose, age, and mileage).

Bodily injury liability insurance. Bodily injury liability insurance protects the insured (and those who drive the insured's car with his or her permission) against liability to third parties who suffer bodily injury as a result of the negligent operation of the insured's motor vehicle. Because statistics show that young drivers (particularly young males) have more accidents, liability insurance premiums are higher for people under 30, higher yet for people under 25, and highest of all for young males under 25.

Property damage liability insurance. Usually, a driver who purchases bodily injury liability insurance also purchases property damage liability insurance. The latter protects the insured (and, again, those who drive the insured's car with his or her permission) against liability to third parties who incur property damage as a result of the negligent operation of the insured's motor vehicle. It must be emphasized that property damage liability insurance does not cover damage to the insured's own vehicle—it pays only for damage to a third party's motor vehicle or other property.

Automobile medical payments insurance. Automobile medical payments insurance reimburses the insured and others riding in his or her automobile for personal injury resulting from an automobile accident. In most cases, the insurance also compensates the insured and his or her immediate family for auto-related personal injury suffered while riding in someone else's car or while walking as a pedestrian.

Collision insurance. Collision insurance compensates the insured for collision (i. e., contact) damage to his or her own automobile. Such insurance is designed to protect the insured who is at fault in causing the damage (if another party is at fault, the insured may generally recover from that party's insurance company). It also protects the insured who is not at fault, but whose automobile is damaged by an uninsured motorist. As a general rule, collision policies include a deductible amount, meaning that the insured must personally pay for the first $100 or $200 (or other agreed upon amount) of damage.

Comprehensive physical damage insurance. Comprehensive physical damage insurance reimburses the insured for loss or damage to his or her automobile resulting from other than collision—e. g., fire, theft, vandalism, glass breakage, windstorm, etc. Payment under the policy is based on the actual cash value of the vehicle (reflecting depreciation) at the time of the loss or damage. The policy frequently contains a deductible clause; and it often exempts from coverage losses

that are statistically likely to occur and difficult to protect against (e. g., theft of a tape deck).

Uninsured motorist coverage. Uninsured motorist coverage compensates the insured for bodily injury (as opposed to property damage) resulting from an uninsured motorist's negligent driving. For example, suppose that an uninsured driver collides with a driver carrying uninsured motorist coverage, then flees. In this case, the insured's own insurance company will pay for the insured's bodily injury. Usually, the amount of coverage is limited by statute to around $10,000. And, generally speaking, physical contact (i. e., collision) with the uninsured driver's vehicle is not a condition to recovery (the uninsured driver frequently remains unidentified).

(2) Some states issue drivers' licenses only upon proof of purchase of liability insurance. Other states have *financial responsibility laws* requiring drivers involved in accidents to furnish proof of their financial responsibility (usually by purchasing insurance or by posting a bond) as a condition to continued driving in the state. More and more states are moving toward requiring insurance for all drivers.

(3) Another legal trend is the adoption of *no fault automobile insurance.* Under a no fault plan, an insurance company pays, not for the loss of a third party bearing a lawful claim against the insured, but for the loss of its own policyholder without regard to fault of the parties. Because each party collects from his or her own insurance company, there is no need to waste time and money proving negligence in court. As a result, premiums are lower and losses are handled more quickly.

The first state to pass a no fault plan was Massachusetts in 1970. Delaware followed in 1971, and, since that time, approximately ten other states have adopted no fault auto insurance. The no fault plans generally provide coverage without regard to fault up to a certain monetary amount. If the damage suffered exceeds this amount, the injured party can still go to court and prove negligence or fault of the other party so as to collect the excess (liability insurance for such excess damage is also available).

Many other states are currently considering the adoption of no fault auto insurance as is the federal Congress. President Carter in the Summer of 1977 came out in favor of a national no fault auto insurance program that would provide no fault insurance coverage up to as high as $25,000–$50,000. Provable damage beyond this amount would be compensable under ordinary liability rules upon proof of negligence or fault. The legislation before Congress would also rule out arbitrary cancellation of a no fault policy or refusal to renew except for failure to pay premiums or revocation of driver's license.

(4) Many states require insurance companies doing business within the state to participate in an *assigned risk plan*. An assigned risk plan is a means of providing auto insurance for bad risk drivers. Often in the past, people with bad driving records (i. e., the people most in need of insurance) were unable to obtain automobile insurance from any company. To remedy this situation, many states passed statutes requiring all auto insurance companies within the state to join a pool wherein each company is assigned a proportionate share of the state's poor risk drivers.

(5) The insured under an auto policy must promptly notify the insurance company of any serious accident, claim, or lawsuit involving the insured, and must furnish the company with a detailed report of surrounding events. Also, the insured must cooperate with the insurer in defending any lawsuit brought against the insured.

(6) Finally, an insurance company that uses improper tactics in dealing with lawful claimants against its insured may be liable in tort. For example, if a company adjuster threatens or harasses a claimant, the company may be liable for the claimant's mental distress and suffering.

Are there any special rules regarding fire insurance?

It is said that a fire breaks out somewhere in the United States every ten seconds. And it is a fact that fire annually destroys many billions of dollars worth of property in this country. The special rules regarding fire insurance are important and may be summarized as follows.

(1) Fire insurance serves to compensate the insured for loss arising from fire and certain related perils. The insured need not own the property to obtain fire insurance so long as he or she has an insurable interest in the property (e. g., the holder of a mortgage on real property or the secured creditor of a chattel may insure the property against fire loss—see Ch. 27 regarding "Secured Transactions").

(2) Generally, in order for a loss to be compensable, it must arise from an actual fire (not just heat but some flame or burning), and the fire must be *hostile* as opposed to *friendly*. A hostile fire is an accidental fire or an intentional one that has escaped, broken out, or become uncontrollable. A friendly fire is an intentional fire that remains under control. For example, if a person accidentally throws some valuable jewelry into a fireplace, the loss of the jewelry arises from a friendly fire and is not normally compensable. However, coverage for loss from a friendly fire may generally be obtained by payment of a higher premium.

(3) *Extended coverage* may also be obtained at an added cost for such perils as windstorm, hail, explosion, riot, aircraft damage, vehicle damage, smoke

damage, heat damage, vandalism, etc. Many property owners purchase what is called a *homeowner's policy* which combines fire insurance with extended coverage, including coverage for theft loss, glass breakage, building collapse, accidental overflow of water or heating from plumbing or heating systems, and freezing perils. The homeowner's policy also includes liability insurance to protect the property owner against claims of bodily injury and property damage asserted by parties who come onto the insured's land.

(4) Where a loss is found to be compensable, the insurer's liability is limited to the maximum amount stated in the policy or the total amount of damages sustained by the insured, whichever is less. Even if an insured has full coverage with two different insurers, the total amount of the loss is the maximum recoverable, and the insurers will share the loss.

(5) Fire insurance coverage is based on the replacement value of the property, not on its original cost. Thus, a property owner must carefully determine how much insurance he or she needs to replace property or risk being underinsured. Premiums on fire insurance policies are generally paid annually to allow for inflation adjustment (so as to accurately reflect replacement costs).

(6) Annual premiums for fire insurance vary considerably because they depend on the construction (e. g., frame or brick), use, and location of the property as well as on the availability of firefighting facilities. In the best of conditions, an annual rate might be as low as 20 cents per $100 of insurance, while, in a high risk area, the rate might be as high as $1.50 per $100.

(7) Frequently, fire insurance policies provide that the insurer may replace or restore the property to its former condition rather than pay the insured the cash value of the loss.

(8) In most states, an insurance company may include a *co-insurance clause* in a fire policy requiring the insured to maintain a certain amount of insurance on the property (usually a percentage of the property's value such as 80%). If the insured fails to insure his or her property for the required amount, the insurer will be liable only for its proportionate share of the amount of insurance required to be carried. For example, a typical co-insurance clause might read as follows.

Example:

It is a part of the consideration of this policy, and the basis upon which the rate of premium is fixed, that the insured shall at all times maintain insurance on each item of property insured by this policy of not less than 80 percent of the actual cash value thereof, and that failing to do so, the insured shall be an insurer to the extent of such deficit, and in that event shall bear his, her or their proportion of any loss.

––––––––––

In the event that the insured fails to carry insurance amounting to 80 percent of the value of his or her property, and there is a fire, the insured must share the loss with the insurance company and can collect only that proportion of the loss which the amount of the insurance purchased bears to the amount of insurance called for under the co-insurance clause. Sound difficult? Let's get more specific. Suppose that you own a business building with a fair market value of $150,000. Under the co-insurance clause, you are required to carry insurance covering 80 percent of this value—insurance of $120,000. If you do so, any fire loss you may suffer up to $120,000 will be fully paid for by the insurance company. But if you only insure your property for $105,000, and you thereafter suffer a fire loss of $80,000, you will be able to collect only $70,000 from the insurance company. You will have to absorb the remaining $10,000 loss yourself. The following formula applies:

$$\frac{\text{Amount of insurance carried}}{\text{Amount of insurance required}} \times \text{amount of loss} = \text{amount collectible from the insurance company}$$

Using the figures from our example:

$$\frac{\$105,000}{\$120,000} \times \$80,000 = \$70,000$$

It should be pointed out that many people choose not to insure their property for the full amount required by the co-insurance clause because fires generally do not destroy property completely, but leave a part of the structure standing—at least the foundation. Other people are underinsured simply because they fail to appreciate the true replacement worth of their property.

(9) The typical fire insurance policy on business property does not permit recovery for business interruption unless there is a special indorsement covering such loss.

(10) Finally, an insured who suffers a fire loss should do the following:

(a) The insured should immediately report the loss to the insurance company (sometimes, the insurance adjuster will arrive before the fire department leaves).

(b) The insured should carefully safeguard his or her remaining property so that it is not stolen or vandalized.

(c) The insured should prepare an inventory of the damaged or destroyed property. This will be easy to do if the insured has on hand a pre-fire inventory of his or her property. To this end, a person who purchases fire insurance should always prepare a room-by-room inventory (the policy covers household and personal property) and put the inventory in a safe place outside the home (e. g., a safe deposit box). And it is a good idea to take pictures of each room and place them with the inventory.

(d) Ultimately, the insured must submit a proof of loss form supported by the inventory (including pictures if possible) and other materials such as canceled checks showing all amounts paid for replacement items. The insurance policy usually provides for payment of the loss within 60 days of submission of the proof of loss. However, as a practical matter, the insurance company generally pays much faster than this. In most cases, an insurance adjuster is sent immediately to the location of the loss to help in determining the amount of loss and whether the company wants to rebuild or pay in cash. In the event the insured and insurer cannot agree on the loss, the policy may prescribe arbitration or determination by professional appraisers.

CASES

CASE 1—*An aunt murders her 2½ year old niece after insuring her life. Insurable interest?*

LIBERTY NATIONAL LIFE INS. CO. v. WELDON

Supreme Court of Alabama, 1957.
267 Ala. 171, 100 So.2d 696.

LAWSON, Justice.

This is a suit by Gaston Weldon, who sues as the father of Shirley Dianne Weldon, deceased, his minor daughter, under § 119, Title 7, Code 1940, the so-called homicide statute, against Liberty National Life Insurance Company, a corporation; National Life & Accident Insurance Company, a corporation; and Southern Life & Health Insurance Company, a corporation.

We will sometimes hereafter refer to Gaston Weldon as the plaintiff, to his deceased child as Shirley, and to the defendant insurance companies as Liberty National, National Life and Southern Life.

Shirley died on May 1, 1952, when she was approximately two and one-half years of age. Prior to her death each of the defendant insurance companies had issued a policy wherein Shirley's life was insured. The policy of Liberty National in the amount of $500 was issued on December 1, 1951. National Life's policy in the amount of $1,000 was issued on or about April 23, 1952. The policy of Southern Life in the amount of $5,000 was issued in the latter part of March, 1952. Each of those policies was issued on an application of Mrs. Earle Dennison, who was an aunt-in-law of Shirley, that is, she was the widow of a brother of Shirley's mother. Each of the policies provided that the death benefits be paid to Mrs. Dennison. * * *

The theory on which plaintiff seeks to recover damages from the defendants is that Mrs. Dennison had no insurable interest in Shirley's life and that the defendants knew or should have known that fact; and, that by reason of the wrongful and negligent issuance of the "illegal" policies of insurance Mrs. Dennison murdered Shirley with the hope of collecting the insurance proceeds.

The case was submitted to the jury on plaintiff's amended complaint which consisted of six counts, in each of which damages were claimed in the amount of $100,000. * * * Counts 3 to 6 inclusive are grounded on negligent acts on the part of the defendants, with Counts 3 and 6 alleging that the acts of the defendants placed the insured child in a zone of danger, with unreasonable risk of harm to her and that the defendants in issuing the alleged illegal contracts of insurance knew, or by the exercise of reasonable diligence should have known, that the beneficiary, Mrs. Dennison, had no insurable interest in the life of the insured. * * * Each of the counts contains an averment to the effect that the wrongful or negligent acts of the defendant insurance companies concurred or united in proximately contributing to or causing the death of plaintiff's minor child.

* * * There were verdict and judgment for the plaintiff in the amount of $75,000. The motions for new trial filed by each of the defendant insurance companies having been overruled, each of them has appealed to this court.

* * *

Assignment of Error No. 8 of each appellant challenges the action of the trial court in overruling their motions for change of venue. In support of those motions, wherein they averred in effect that they could not get a fair and impartial trial in Elmore County, the defendants relied in the main on a newspaper story concerning this suit which appeared in the October 22, 1953, issue of the Wetumpka *Herald*, a newspaper widely circulated in Elmore County. The newspaper story pointed out the theory on which the plaintiff sought to recover damages from the defendants, the amount of damages claimed, the ruling of the trial court on the demurrers, the date the case was set for trial, and the fact that it involved questions of considerable interest to the legal profession and to the insurance business. The story also called attention to the fact, already known by most people in Alabama, that Mrs. Dennison had been electrocuted for the murder of Shirley and that she was the first white woman to be electrocuted for crime in Alabama. The newspaper account was concluded with these words in parentheses: "Not the $64,000 question but the $100,000 question."

* * * Newspaper publicity does not necessarily constitute grounds for a change of venue. Littlefield v. State, supra. We see nothing in the newspaper account which would justify us in holding that the trial court abused its discretion in denying the motions for change of venue. Nor could we put the trial court in error on the mere statement of counsel for the defendants below that the defendants could not get a fair trial in Elmore County because the people of that county were aroused over the fact that Mrs. Dennison had murdered Shirley.

* * *

The evidence in this case shows beyond peradventure that Shirley was murdered by Mrs. Dennison. We will briefly summarize the facts which tend to support that statement. In the early afternoon of May 1, 1952, Mrs. Dennison drove to plaintiff's home, in rural Elmore County, where she found the plaintiff, his wife and their two children, Orville and Shirley. Shortly after Mrs. Dennison's arrival the plaintiff and his son left the home to attend to some duties around the farm. At the time of their return home Mrs. Dennison was engaged in serving some soft drinks which she had purchased at a nearby store. Mrs. Dennison divided an orange drink between Orville and Shirley. Shirley's drink was poured into a little cup that Mrs. Dennison provided. Shortly after she consumed her drink Shirley became very nauseated. After the nausea subsided Mrs. Dennison left the room but returned in a short time shaking a partially filled bottle of Coca-Cola, from which she gave Shirley a drink. Shirley again became violently nauseated and that condition continued until she became almost unconscious. At the mother's insistence Shirley was taken to Wetumpka in search of a doctor. She was admitted to a hospital in Wetumpka shortly after her arrival there. She died within a comparatively short time after she was admitted to the hospital.

Dr. Rehling, the Director of the Department of Toxicology of this state, testified that an autopsy which he performed revealed arsenic in fatal quantities in Shirley's body and expressed the opinion that the child died as the result of arsenic taken through her mouth. He testified that he found traces of arsenic on articles of clothing worn by Shirley and by Mrs. Dennison at the time the drinks were served and he further testified that he found traces of arsenic in the cup from which Shirley drank. The appellants do not contend here that the evidence was not altogether ample to support a jury finding that Mrs. Dennison murdered the little girl.

The evidence is also clear to the effect that Mrs. Dennison murdered the child in order to collect insurance benefits payable to her upon the child's death. We will not undertake to set out all of the evidence which tends to support that statement, for the defendants do not contend that such was not the case. We simply call attention to one incident which we think clearly shows why Mrs. Dennison poisoned the child. Mrs. Dennison was a nurse in the hospital to which Shirley was admitted and she was directed by the doctor in charge of Shirley to administer aid to the patient. By late afternoon when it was apparent that Shirley was dying, Mrs. Dennison left the hospital and drove approximately twelve miles to the home of an insurance agent to pay the premium on the Liberty National policy which was about to lapse.

So it is clear that the harm which came to plaintiff's little girl was not caused by the direct act of any of the defendants, but by the intervening act of Mrs. Dennison, who has paid with her life for her horrible crime.

But as before indicated, the plaintiff says, in effect, that such harm would not have come to his little girl if the defendants had not wrongfully or negligently issued to Mrs. Dennison the alleged illegal policies covering Shirley's life.

The plaintiff has proceeded against these defendants on the theory that Mrs. Dennison did not have an insurable interest in the life of Shirley and hence the policies involved were illegal and void as against public policy; that the defendants were negligent in the issuance of the policies in that they knew there was no such interest or failed to exercise reasonable diligence to ascertain that fact before issuing the policies, although there was a duty upon them to do so; and that the failure to perform that duty was in fact the proximate cause of the child's death.

The evidence was sufficient to show a lack of insurable interest. * * * [A]n in-law relationship in and of itself does not sustain an insurable interest.

Most certainly the evidence in this case does not show as a matter of law that Mrs. Dennison had an insurable interest in Shirley because she had a reasonable expectation of possible profit or advantage to her from the continued life of Shirley. Helmetag's Adm'r v. Miller, 76 Ala. 183; Commonwealth Life Ins. Co. v. George, supra. Mrs. Dennison did not provide a home for Shirley. They lived in different towns several miles apart. Shirley lived in the home of her parents with her brother and sister and received her entire support from her parents. * * *

From the evidence presented the jury was well justified in finding that none of the defendants before issuing the policies of insurance made reasonable effort to ascertain whether Mrs. Dennison did in fact have an insurable interest in Shirley's life.

           * * *

The conclusions which we have reached above, namely, that the evidence was sufficient to show that Shirley was murdered and the policies were void because of lack of insurable interest and were, in effect, negligently issued do not, of course, determine the liability of the defendants. For all negligence is not actionable. To be actionable it must be the breach of a duty which the defendant owed the plaintiff as an individual or one of a class and the plaintiff must not only show causal connection between the negligent breach of the duty but that such negligence was the proximate cause of the injury.

* * *

The position of the defendants seems to be that if murder results the insurance companies are, of course, sorry that the insured met with such a fate, but they have no liability if there is no insurable interest although they can treat such policies as completely void. If an early death from natural causes makes the policy unprofitable, the defendants can and do refuse to pay the beneficiary for the reason that such policies are void. In other words, the defendants seem to be of the opinion that the insurable interest rule is to protect insurance companies. We do not agree. The rule is designed to protect human life. Policies in violation of the insurable interest rule are not dangerous because they are illegal; they are illegal because they are dangerous.

As we have shown, it has long been recognized by this court and practically all courts in this country that an insured is placed in a position of extreme danger where a policy of insurance is issued on his life in favor of a beneficiary who has no insurable interest. There is no legal justification for the creation of such a risk to an insured and there is no social gain in the writing of a void policy of insurance. Where this court has found that such policies are unreasonably dangerous to the insured because of the risk of murder and for this reason has declared such policies void, it would be an anomaly to hold that insurance companies have no duty to use reasonable care not to create a situation which may prove to be a stimulus for murder.

* * *

* * * [T]he wrongful or negligent acts of the three insurance companies concurred or united in proximately contributing to or causing the death of plaintiff's minor child. * * *

* * *

Section 119, Title 7, Code 1940, the statute under which this action was brought, provides that for the wrongful death of a minor child the persons there entitled to sue, if entitled to a verdict, "shall recover such damages as the jury may assess." The damages are entirely punitive, imposed for the preservation of human life. As the wording of the statute indicates, the amount of damages rests largely in the discretion of the jury. However, this discretion is not an unbridled or arbitrary one, but "a legal, sound and honest discretion." In arriving at the amount of damages which should be assessed, the jury should give due regard to the enormity or not of the wrong and to the necessity of preventing similar wrongs. The punishment by way of damages is intended not alone to punish the wrongdoer, but as a deterrent to others similarly minded.

The verdict rendered in this case is large, perhaps the largest to come before this court in a case brought under the so-called homicide statute, §§ 119 and 123, Title 7, Code 1940. But the trial court refused to disturb the amount of the verdict and we have held that when such is the case we will not order a reduction unless the verdict is so excessive as to indicate passion, prejudice, corruption or mistake. We are unwilling to say that the amount of damages awarded by way of punishment of these three appellants for wrongfully and negligently issuing illegal policies of insurance, the issuance of which the evidence clearly shows led to the murder of plaintiff's young daughter, is so excessive as to indicate passion, prejudice, corruption or mistake, and as we have heretofore shown, the jury in fixing the amount of the verdict was charged with the duty of giving consideration to the necessity of preventing the same wrongs by others similarly minded.

* * *

Affirmed.

CASE 2—*How "friendly" is a fire that causes $900.00 damage to your ring?*

YOUSE v. EMPLOYERS FIRE INS. CO., BOSTON, MASS.

Supreme Court of Kansas, 1951.
172 Kan. 111, 238 P.2d 472.

PRICE, Justice.

This was an action to recover for the loss and damage to a star sapphire ring caused by fire. Plaintiff insured prevailed in the court below and defendant company has appealed.

* * *

Both parties state the sole question for determination to be: "Is the loss resulting from damage to jewelry, by a fire intentionally kindled in and confined to a place where fire was intended to be, insured against under the terms of the fire insurance policy in question?"

The facts, which are not in dispute, are as follows:

On an occasion while the policy in question was in force the wife of insured was carrying her ring wrapped in a handkerchief in her purse. Upon arriving at her home she placed the handkerchief, together with some paper cleansing tissues (Kleenex), on the dresser in her bedroom. Later her maid, in cleaning the room, inadvertently picked up the handkerchief containing the ring, together with the cleansing tissues, and threw them into a wastebasket. Still later, another servant emptied the contents of the wastebasket, along with other trash, into a trash burner at the rear of the premises and proceeded to burn the trash so deposited. The trash burner was intended for that purpose, the fire was intentionally lighted by the servant, and was confined to the trash burner. About a week later the ring was found in the trash burner. It had been damaged to the extent of $900.

The policy, a standard form, insured household goods and personal property, usual or incidental to the occupancy of the premises as a dwelling, belonging to insured or a member of his family while contained on the premises, " * * * against all direct loss or damage by fire, except as hereinafter provided, * * * " in an amount not exceeding $2,000. The parties agree that the "exceptions" contained in the policy are immaterial to the issues in this case.

The insured also carried a "floater policy" in another company (not a party to this action) by the terms of which the ring was insured to the extent of $250. The company issuing the "floater policy" offered to pay that amount to insured, but as of the time of trial of this action such offer had not been accepted.

* * * Judgment was rendered in favor of insured in the amount of $650 (being the amount of the loss less the "floater policy" coverage), and for attorney fees in the amount of $300, to be collected as costs.

* * *

The company contends here, as it did in the court below, that the quoted insuring clause of the policy, "against all direct loss or damage by fire" covers only loss or damage resulting from a "hostile" fire as distinguished from a "friendly" fire; that here, the fire being intentionally lighted in and confined to a place or receptacle where it was intended to be, was not a hostile fire within the usual and well-established meaning of the term and therefore no recovery can be had.

The insured argues that he purchased and paid for *fire insurance*— not just for fire insurance to cover loss resulting only from so-called "hostile" fires; that the direct loss and damage to the ring by fire is undisputed; that the company would have the court write into the policy an unauthorized and unreasonable restriction; that there is no ambiguity in the terms of the policy and therefore it should be enforced according to its literal terms; and that even though there were some uncertainty as to its meaning the court is bound to construe the policy strictly against the company and favorably to the insured.

* * *

"The distinction most commonly made by courts in considering contracts of fire insurance is that drawn between 'hostile' and 'friendly' fires. If the fire burns in a place where it (is) intended to burn, although damages may have resulted where none were intended, the fire is a friendly fire, and the insurer is not liable for damages flowing therefrom. A friendly fire refers to one which remains confined within the place intended, and refers to a fire in a furnace, stove, or other usual place. A hostile fire, on the other hand, means one not confined to the place intended, or one not intentionally started; and it is generally considered to refer to such a fire which, if it had pursued its natural course, would have resulted in a total or partial destruction of the insured property. When a friendly fire escapes from the place it ought to be to some place where it ought not to be, causing damage, it becomes a hostile fire for which the insurer is liable.

"In order to recover for damages sustained, the insured must show that the fire was a hostile, rather than a friendly, fire. * * *

"The majority of courts have denied recovery for loss or damage to jewelry owned by the insured where such articles have been placed for safekeeping in a stove or thrown inadvertently into a furnace. The reason is, of course, that such a fire is considered a friendly fire, confined to its place of inception, and the primary cause of loss is the negligence of the insured or his servants. Louisiana alone seems to permit recovery in such instance."

* * *

In Reliance Ins. Co. v. Naman, 118 Tex. 21, a servant of insured, without knowledge of its contents, threw a box containing jewelry into a furnace fire. The policy in question insured " 'against all direct loss or damage by fire' ". Recovery was denied on the ground that a friendly fire was not within the undertaking of the insurance company, and that in the sense in which the word "fire" was used in the policy there had been no fire so long as it was kept within the proper and accustomed place. The holding in this case was followed by the Supreme Court of Michigan, in Harter v. Phoenix Ins. Co. of Hartford, Conn., 257 Mich. 163. In that case the insured's household servant picked up an envelope containing two rings from a desk, and, not realizing the envelope contained rings, put it in a wastebasket and later put the contents of the wastebasket, including the rings, in the furance where, when a fire was built, they were seriously damaged.   The court held the fire to be a friendly fire and denied recovery.

* * *

We think it cannot be denied that in common parlance and everyday usage one has not "had a fire" so long as it has burned only in the place where it was intended to burn, and where fire ordinarily is maintained.   By way of illustration, when a person maintains a fire in his furnace, cookstove or fireplace, or when he burns trash in his incinerator, he has not "had a fire" in the ordinary, common acceptation of the term.   On the other hand, if a fire on the roof results from sparks from fire in the furnace, cookstove or fireplace, if sparks from the latter should burn a rug or furniture or if the fire in the trash burner escapes therefrom and sets fire to the garage or fence, such person has "had a fire" for which recovery can be had, notwithstanding the fire was originally friendly.

We think it is quite true to say that when one purchases standard fire insurance he does so with the idea in mind of protecting himself from loss or damage resulting from what the law defines as a "hostile" fire, and that the word "fire," as used in fire insurance policies, has, in common parlance, such well-understood meaning.   * * *   "The meaning of the term 'loss by fire' as being a 'hostile' and not a 'friendly fire' has been so extensively and long recognized that reasonably we must consider, even under liberal interpretation that both insured and insurer contracted with such definition in mind, determinative of what losses were covered."   * * *

In our opinion there can be no question but that the fire which damaged or destroyed the sapphire ring was what in law is known as a "friendly" fire.   It was intentionally lighted, was for the usual and ordinary purpose of burning trash, and was at all times confined to the place where it was intended, and did not escape.

* * *

It follows that the court erred   * * *   in rendering judgment in favor of insured.   The judgment of the lower court is therefore reversed.

PROBLEMS

1.   Although Art Carswell has no interest in the property, he purchases fire insurance on his sister Marsha's residence.   Six months later, Art buys the house from Marsha.   One day, while burning trash in the fireplace, Art accidentally throws his wristwatch into the fire, damaging it beyond repair.   A week later, Art intentionally sets fire to the downstairs portion of the house so that he can have it rebuilt (and redecorated) at the insurance company's expense.   The following week, Art builds a fire in the upstairs fireplace; the fire goes out of control, escapes from the fireplace, and seriously damages the living and dining rooms.   The insurance company refuses to reimburse Art for any of these losses.   The company states that Art had no insurable interest at the time of purchasing the insurance, and that even if he had had such an interest, none of these particular losses would be compensable.   Discuss the validity of the insurance company's arguments.   Is Art entitled to coverage?   Explain.

2.   Answer the following "True" or "False" and give reasons for your answers:

  (a) Like all other contracts, minors can generally avoid insurance contracts for life, disability, and health insurance.

(b) In the insurance contract situation, the insured makes the offer, the insurer the acceptance.

(c) Generally, in a third party beneficiary contract, any defense that the promisor can assert against the promisee he or she can also assert against the third party beneficiary.

(d) Generally, in a third party beneficiary contract, any defense that the promisee can assert against the third party beneficiary the promisor can also assert against the third party beneficiary.

(e) Every individual should purchase life insurance.

(f) Companies that sell life insurance as well as casualty, and fire and marine are known as "all-line" companies.

(g) Inter-insurance exchanges usually sell more life insurance than any other kind of company.

(h) Unlike a fraternal society which is organized primarily for the mutual benefit of its members, Lloyd's of London is organized primarily for the profit of its owners.

(i) Insurance contracts are interpreted and construed by the courts as they would be understood by the average person with legal training.

(j) Liability and property insurance policies are generally cancellable at the insurer's option.

(k) An insurance broker is an agent for the insurance company.

(l) Fire insurance coverage is based on the original cost of the property.

(m) To make a change in an insurance contract, it is generally necessary to issue a new policy.

(n) The insured generally has a duty to cooperate with and assist the insurer in defending against covered claims.

(o) A failure to give timely notice of loss may result in no insurance coverage.

(p) With regard to property insurance, an insurer who pays for an insured's loss is generally subrogated to the legal rights of the insured against the party who caused the loss.

3. What basic types of life insurance coverage are available? What are the advantages and disadvantages of each? What basic types of automobile insurance coverage are available?

4. Items a. and b. are based on the following information:

Matson loaned Donalds $1,000 at 8% interest for one year. Two weeks before the due date, Matson called upon Donalds and obtained his agreement in writing to modify the terms of the loan. It was agreed that on the due date Donalds would pay $850 to Cranston, to whom Matson owed that amount, and pay the balance plus interest to his son, Arthur, to whom he wished to make a gift.

a. Which of the following statements is legally valid with respect to the events described above?

(1) Because Matson never received the interest on the Donalds loan, he will *not* have to include it in his gross income for federal income tax purposes.

(2) Matson has irrevocably assigned the debt to Cranston and Arthur.

(3) In the event of default by Donalds, Cranston must first proceed against him before seeking recourse against Matson.

(4) Neither of the agreements between Matson and Donalds needs to be in writing.

[# 3, May, 1975 CPA Exam]

b.   Under the modified terms of the loan, Cranston and/or Arthur have what legal standing?

(1) Cranston is a creditor beneficiary and Arthur is a donee beneficiary.

(2) Cranston has the right to prevent Matson's delegation if he gives timely notice.

(3) If Cranston is to be able to proceed against Donalds, he must have received notice of Donalds' promise to pay him the $850 prior to the due date.

(4) Arthur is an incidental beneficiary.

[# 4, May, 1975 CPA Exam]

5.   Assuming the same facts as in (4) above, answer the following:

(a) Cranston and Arthur learn of the agreement made for their benefit and assent to it. Matson and Donalds thereafter call off the agreement and return to the original payment terms (with payment to Matson). Cranston and Arthur sue to enforce the agreement made for their benefit. Result? *vest cuts off change to original agreement*

(b) Before Cranston and Arthur learn anything about the agreement, Matson and Donalds decide to return to the original payment terms. Cranston and Arthur thereafter learn about the agreement made for their benefit and sue to enforce it. Result? *NO VESTED Rights*

(c) Donalds breaches the agreement by failing to make payment to Cranston and Arthur as promised. Discuss the rights of Matson, Cranston, and Arthur against Donalds. Discuss the rights of Cranston and Arthur against Matson. *Matson → money or performance   Donee → Performance*

6.   Margo, Inc., insured its property against fire with two separate insurance companies, Excelsior and Wilberforce. Each carrier insured the property for its full value, and neither insurer was aware that the other had also insured the property. The policies were the standard fire insurance policies used throughout the United States. If the property is totally destroyed by fire, how much will Margo recover?

(a) Nothing because Margo has engaged in an illegal gambling venture.

(b) The full amount from both insurers.

(c) A ratable or pro rata share from each insurer, *not* to exceed the value of the property insured.

(d) Only 80% of the value of the property from each insurer because of the standard co-insurance clause.

[# 38, November, 1975 CPA Exam]

7.   Arthur Cox purchased a $100,000 twenty-year life insurance policy. In filling out the application, he erroneously but unintentionally answered one of the questions regarding his prior medical history incor-

rectly. The question required the applicant to list "any and all occasions within the past five years in which he was hospitalized." His response was "none." However, he had in fact been hospitalized four years previously in connection with the removal of an impacted wisdom tooth. The policy stated that all representations in the application were to be strictly enforced, constituted warranties, and were incorporated by reference into the policy. It also contained a two year incontestable clause. Less than two years after obtaining the policy, Cox suffered a fatal heart attack. The insurance company denies liability under the policy and Cox's beneficiary sues for payment. Under the circumstances, what outcome should Cox's beneficiary expect?

(a) Win because Cox lived for a period of one year after issuance of the policy.

(b) Lose because warranties are strictly construed against the warrantor.

(c) Win because the misrepresentation was unintentional and immaterial.

(d) Lose despite the fact that the misrepresentation was innocent and immaterial in that the law treats such contracts as voidable.

[# 7, May, 1977 CPA Exam]

8. Walsh owns and operates a gas station and restaurant on a highway nearby a beautiful undeveloped lake region. Clark, interested in developing the area, purchased several acres of lake-front property and contracted with Mahoney, a building contractor, to construct an elaborate hotel and ten beautiful cottages. After learning these facts from Clark, Walsh expanded his restaurant and gas station in contemplation of a substantial increase in business. Subsequently, Clark changed his plans and breached his contract with Mahoney. Clark promptly notified Mahoney not to commence construction, and Mahoney complied with Clark's instructions.

Walsh is now suing Clark for breach of contract. Walsh claims that he is a third party beneficiary under the contract between Clark and Mahoney and entitled to damages for the cost of expanding his business and the profits he would have earned had the contract been performed. In his suit against Clark, Walsh will

(a) Win in that he is a third party creditor beneficiary.

(b) Lose in that he is a third party incidental beneficiary.

(c) Win in that he is a donee beneficiary.

(d) Win in that Clark and Mahoney have acted fraudulently.

[#1, November, 1973 CPA Exam]

9. Kay owned a building valued at $100,000 when a fire occurred causing $60,000 damage. The loss was insured under an Ace Insurance Company fire insurance policy in the amount of $60,000 which contained an 80% coinsurance clause. Kay's recovery under the policy will be limited to

(a) $60,000.

(b) $48,000.

(c) $45,000.

(d) $36,000.

[#38, May, 1974 CPA Exam]

10.   Balsam was a partner in the firm of Wilkenson, Potter & Parker. The firm had a buy-out arrangement whereby the partnership funded the buy-out agreement with insurance on the lives of the partners payable to the partnership. When the insurance policies were obtained by the partnership, Balsam understated his age by three years. Eight years later, Balsam decided to sell his partnership interest to Gideon. The sale was consummated and the other partners admitted Gideon as a partner in Balsam's place. The partnership nevertheless retained ownership in the policy on the life of Balsam and continued to pay the premiums thereon. Balsam died one year later. The insurance company refuses to pay the face value of the policy claiming that the partnership is only entitled to the amount of the premiums paid. As a basis for this position, the insurance company asserts lack of an insurable interest and material misrepresentation.

Required: Answer the following, setting forth reasons for any conclusions stated.

Will Wilkenson, Potter & Parker prevail in an action against the insurance company? Give specific attention to the assertions of the insurance company.

[#6.b., November, 1977 CPA Exam]

yes – economic interest at time pol. taken out
age immaterial – reduces insurance

Chapter 12

ASSIGNMENT VERSUS NEGOTIATION

What is the scope of this chapter?

In Chapters 7 through 10, we studied the many rules governing the formation, interpretation, and discharge of contracts. In Ch. 11, we learned that contracts are frequently made for the benefit of third parties, and we looked closely at life insurance contracts as one example of third party beneficiary contracts. In this chapter, we are concerned with *assignment* of contract rights and *negotiation* of special contracts called *negotiable instruments* or *commercial paper*. Put simply, an assignment is a transfer of rights under an existing contract (e. g., Mary Smith enters into a contract with Richard Wiley, then transfers her rights under the contract to Sam Seymour). The party who transfers the rights (Mary Smith) is called the *assignor,* the party who receives the rights (Sam Seymour), the *assignee.* The general rule is that the assignee "stands in the shoes of the assignor" with respect to the transferred rights (i. e., the assignee is in the same position as the assignor and subject to the same defenses). Thus, if the other original party to the agreement (Richard Wiley) would have a defense to performance or a right to rescind the contract with the assignor, he or she will have the same right with regard to the assignee.

In this chapter, we will contrast the position of an assignee who "stands in the shoes of the assignor" with that of a person who receives a *negotiable instrument* (e. g., a check, note, or draft) through a special form of transfer called a *negotiation.* Unlike the assignee, the party receiving the negotiable instrument *may* stand in a better position than his or her transferor (i. e., even if the nontransferring original party to the instrument has a defense to performance against the transferor, the defense may not be good against the transferee). The word "may" is emphasized because the transferee of the negotiable instrument must qualify as a *holder in due course* in order to obtain rights superior to those of an assignee.

If you are confused at this point, don't worry—the significance of the prior paragraphs will become abundantly clear as you read through the following chapter sections on the law of assignments and the law of negotiability. It is important to interrelate what you learn about assignments with what you learn about negotiable instruments. As you will discover, the vast majority of contract rights are freely transferable, and the law of assignments controls in most situations. It is only occasionally that the transferee of contract rights will receive rights superior to those of his or her transferor (namely, where the transferee is a holder in due course of a negotiable instrument).

How does "assignment" of contract rights differ from novation and from third party beneficiary contracts?

You will recall from Ch. 10 that a *novation* is an agreement between the original parties to an existing contract and a nonparty wherein the nonparty is substituted for one of the original parties, and the original party is discharged. The agreement of all parties—both original and substituted—is essential to the novation; the element of discharge is its most important feature. In an *assignment,* on the other hand, one of the original parties to an existing contract transfers one or more contract rights to a third person assignee. In contrast to a novation, the assignor need not even consult the other original party to the contract before making the transfer; and the assignor is not discharged, but remains personally liable for performance under the agreement.

You will also recall from Ch. 11 that a *third party beneficiary contract* is an agreement the primary or major purpose of which is to benefit some third person who is not a party to the contract. This is the purpose of the contract from the outset. In contrast, an "assigned" contract does not contemplate a benefit to a third person at the time the contract is made, but only when the contract is assigned. If, at that time, the assignor not only assigns or transfers rights under the contract, but also delegates contract duties in exchange for consideration (delegation is dealt with in the following section), a third party beneficiary contract may come into being for the benefit of the non-transferring original party.

A few examples should be helpful.

(1) Lloyd Homeowner and Frank the Painter enter into a contract wherein Frank agrees to paint Lloyd's house during the first week of July for $1,000. On June 1st, Lloyd and Frank agree with Tom Olson that Tom will take Frank's place under the contract (i. e., Tom, not Frank, will paint Lloyd's house during the first week of July and receive the $1,000 from Lloyd). The new agreement is a novation that completely discharges Frank the Painter from any duty of performance under the original contract. As a result, neither Lloyd nor Tom can look to Frank with regard to the agreement.

(2) Lloyd Homeowner's mother-in-law, Nancy Rich, enters into a contract with Frank the Painter wherein she agrees to pay Frank $1,000 for painting her son-in-law's house during the first week of July. The agreement is a third party beneficiary contract, with Lloyd the donee beneficiary who has rights to enforce the agreement.

(3) Lloyd Homeowner contracts to pay Frank the Painter $1,000 for painting Lloyd's house during the first week of July. On June 1st, Frank assigns (transfers) his right to collect the $1,000 to his son, Robert. As an assignee, Robert "stands in the shoes" of his father—that is, he is in the same position as Frank and is subject to the same defenses. Thus, if Frank fails to paint the house during the first week of July, or does the job very poorly, the defense of failure of consideration (which would be good against Frank) will be good against Robert.

(4) In return for receiving the right to collect the $1,000, Robert promises Frank that he will paint Lloyd's house during the first week of July. Here, Frank not only assigns his right to collect the money, but he also delegates his duty to paint the house to Robert. Frank and Robert have entered into a third party beneficiary contract for the benefit of Lloyd, the creditor beneficiary (Lloyd is a creditor beneficiary because he is already entitled to performance by Frank). If Robert fails to perform, Lloyd can proceed against him on the basis of the third party contract; or Lloyd can hold Frank responsible on the original obligation (as will be explained shortly, an assignor who delegates duties is not discharged, but must stand ready to perform if the assignee does not). Of course, if Frank is held responsible, he may recover from Robert for breach of the third party beneficiary agreement.

So you see, an assignment may itself constitute a third party beneficiary contract where both rights are assigned and duties delegated. In the example above, the consideration for the assignment is found in the assignee's promise to do the painting in place of the assignor (i. e., a reverse unilateral contract).

What exactly does an assignment do?

The term "assignment" applies only to the transfer of rights under an existing contract. The transfer serves to extinguish the rights in the assignor and create the rights in the assignee: after the assignment, only the assignee may sue the nontransferring party to enforce the rights or to collect money damages for breach of contract.

The term "assignment" does not apply to and should not be used to describe an effort to transfer existing contract duties to another. Duties are not assigned—they are "delegated". To delegate a duty is to appoint another to perform the duty. Delegation does not extinguish the duties in the delegating party (the *delegant*): rather, the delegant remains liable for performance if the other party (the *delegatee*) fails to perform. Because there is no effective transfer of the duties, the term assignment does not apply.

As to whether the delegatee will be liable to the nondelegating party, this depends on the facts of the situation. In example (4) above, Frank the Painter not only assigned to Robert his right to collect $1,000 from Lloyd Homeowner, but he also delegated to Robert his duty to paint Lloyd's house during the first week of July. Here, there is both an assignment of rights and a delegation of duties. Frank is both an assignor and a delegant; Robert is both an assignee and a delegatee. Because Robert expressly assumed the contract duty in exchange for the contract right, a third party beneficiary contract came into being, and Lloyd Homeowner, the creditor beneficiary, may sue Robert to enforce the agreement.

Now suppose that Frank the Painter delegates the duty to Robert without assigning him the contract right. For example, Frank might agree to pay Robert $4.00 an hour for painting the house. In the absence of an express assumption of the contract duty by Robert (i. e., an express promise to become liable for performance in place of Frank), Robert is liable only to his father, and not to Lloyd Homeowner. This is because a delega-

tion of duties apart from an assignment of rights does not result in a third party beneficiary contract absent an express assumption of duty by the delegatee. Any benefit to the nondelegating party (Lloyd Homeowner) is considered incidental only, and an incidental beneficiary has no rights of enforcement.

How is an assignment accomplished?

Generally, any oral or written manifestation of intent by a party to *presently* transfer his or her rights under an existing contract to another person will constitute an assignment (the intent must be to transfer the interest now—not at some time in the future). No particular formality is required with limited exception. Most states have statutes requiring assignment of wages and assignment of interests in land to be in writing. Some states prohibit assignment of future wages; other states permit assignment of future wages but only upon the written consent of the employee's spouse or parent (if the employee is a minor) and only to the extent of necessaries furnished to the employee by the assignee.

An assignment need not be supported by consideration. Even a purely gratuitous assignment is valid, transferring to the assignee the rights of the assignor. However, where the assignment is gratuitous, the assignor may generally revoke the transfer by giving notice of revocation to the assignee or to the nontransferring party; by accepting performance from the nontransferring party; or by re-assigning the rights to another person (with or without consideration). And such an assignment is automatically revoked by operation of law upon the death or bankruptcy of the assignor. A single exception to revocation arises where the gratuitous assignment qualifies as a completed gift as defined in Ch. 3 (in which case the assignment is irrevocable). You will recall that a completed gift requires present intent to make the gift plus delivery to the donee. With regard to assignment of rights, a gift is considered complete upon delivery of a "token chose" (e. g., a savings account passbook or a stock certificate representing the right to be transferred) to the donee-assignee. If the right is not represented by a token chose, the donor-assignor may complete the gift by putting the assignment into writing and delivering the writing to the assignee. Signed or unsigned, the writing will serve to make the assignment irrevocable. Thus, a gratuitous oral assignment is revocable in the absence of delivery of a token chose, while a gratuitous written assignment is irrevocable so long as the writing is delivered to the donee-assignee.

Of course, any assignment supported by consideration is irrevocable, and consideration can be furnished by any one of the legal theories discussed in Ch. 9, including promissory estoppel (e. g., if an assignee detrimentally relies on a gratuitous assignment, the assignor may be estopped from revoking).

What contract rights are assignable?

We start with the proposition that all contract rights are assignable. We immediately qualify the statement by saying that, despite the strong public policy favoring the free assignability of contract rights, there are four situations where contract rights may not be assigned.

(1) *Where assignment would materially change the nontransferring party's duty.* A contract right to the personal services of another may not be assigned because it would not be fair to require the obligor (the nontransferring original party) to perform for someone other than the original party he or she contracted with. For example, suppose that, after much discussion and preliminary negotiation, a male artist agrees to paint a beautiful young woman's portrait for a fee of $3,500. The young woman then assigns her right to have the portrait

painted to her ugly older brother. The assignment is ineffective because of the personal services involved. Painting the older brother might be more difficult as well as more time-consuming than painting the young woman. And, in any case, the artist might not want to paint an ugly specimen of the opposite sex. To force him to do so would be to materially change his duty under the contract.

Personal services include not only the services of painters and authors, but the services of professionals such as doctors, lawyers, accountants, architects, and the like. In fact, any service requiring a generally recognized special talent is a personal service. Thus, an employer may generally not assign his or her right to the services of an employee hired to work under the employer's supervision and at his or her direction. Of course, the parties are always free to contract to the contrary (e. g., a professional baseball player might contract to allow the team to trade him or her to another team).

Also, the contract rights growing out of requirements and output contracts (as discussed in Chapters 7 and 9) generally cannot be assigned. Again, a requirements contract is an agreement to buy "all your requirements" from a particular factory or manufacturer; an "output" contract is an agreement to purchase "all the goods produced" by a particular factory or manufacturer. Obviously, the requirements or output of an assignee may vary greatly from those of an assignor. To permit assignment in such case would be to materially change the nontransferring party's duty under the contract.

It should also be pointed out that even an assignable contract right cannot be transferred so as to require a different performance by the nontransferring party. Thus if the nontransferring party has a duty to pay the assignor $1,000 on July 15th "at the assignor's place of business", the assignor cannot transfer the right to an assignee, payable "at the assignee's place of business". The original contract terms as to time, place, method, or manner of performance are controlling.

(2) *Where assignment would materially change the nontransferring party's risk.* An assignment that materially changes the nontransferring party's risk under the contract is also invalid. For example, in Ch. 11, you learned about insurance and insurance covered risks. You know that the particular risk insured against will vary depending upon the person or property insured under the policy. For this reason, insurance policies are generally not assignable. And this makes good sense. Certainly, it would not be fair to allow an insured to transfer his or her right to life insurance coverage to another, thereby forcing the insurance company to insure a different person (who might have a heart condition or cancer). The same is true with regard to casualty, fire, auto insurance, etc. The assignee of such a policy might well present a more serious risk to the insurer.

This is not to say that the insured cannot transfer *ownership* of the life insurance policy to another (whether the policy is term, whole life, limited payment, or endowment insurance). A policyholder will frequently transfer complete ownership of the policy to his or her beneficiary to prevent inclusion of the policy proceeds in his or her estate for purposes of death taxes. Death taxes are transfer taxes, and if the insured does not own his or her life insurance at death, there is nothing to transfer and nothing to tax. (Of course, if the insured irrevocably transfers his or her ownership of the policy with or without consideration, the insured can no longer change beneficiaries, borrow against the policy, surrender it for cash, or otherwise affect the policy without the assignee's consent.) There is no problem with assignment of ownership of the policy because such assignment does not vary the nontransferring party's risk. Assignment of the right to

be insured, on the other hand, changes the risk substantially.

Nor is there any problem with assigning the right to collect the insurance proceeds in the event of loss. Payment to an assignee rather than to the insured or his or her named beneficiary does not constitute a material change of the insurer's obligations or risk.

Similar to insurance covered risks, where personal credit serves as the basis for the nontransferring party's promise, any substitution of debtors would vary the risk. Therefore, assignment is not allowed. For example, if a bank agrees to loan $10,000 to a prosperous businessman, the businessman cannot assign his right to the loan to someone who has a poor credit rating.

(3) *Where the assignment purports to transfer future rights in a nonexistent future contract.* Only present and future rights in *existing* contracts can be assigned. If a contract has yet to come into being, there is nothing to assign, and any purported assignment of future rights in the contract is invalid. For example, suppose that Harvey Weiss enters into a contract with an employment agency; Harvey assigns his first month's wages to the agency in return for assistance in finding a job. Since Harvey does not yet have a job, he has nothing to assign, and his purported transfer of future rights in a future contract of employment is invalid. However, if the agency finds Harvey a job, the court may order specific performance of the assignment to prevent unjust enrichment.

One exception to the rule against assignment of future rights in nonexistent contracts arises under Article 9 of the Uniform Commercial Code. As you will learn in Ch. 27, Article 9 permits assignment of future rights in personal property and fixtures as security for a debt, providing that the assignment is properly recorded.

(4) *Where the contract expressly prohibits assignment.* Some contracts expressly provide that any attempted assignment will be void or will act as a condition subsequent to cut off the rights of the would be assignor. Where this is so, any attempted transfer of rights will generally be ineffective. Other contracts merely contain a promise by a party not to assign: the party, in this case, can still effectively assign rights. However, the assignment will constitute a breach of contract, giving the nontransferring party a right to sue for money damages (which should be negligible so long as the transfer causes no particular harm).

Of course, contract prohibitions against assignment will not prevent transfer of the contract rights by operation of law upon the death or bankruptcy of a party (upon death, the rights pass to the deceased's estate—see Ch. 30—and upon bankruptcy, to the creditors—see Ch. 26).

Nor is a prohibition against assignment effective to restrict the free alienation of real property. If the prohibition purports to do so, it is void as a disabling restraint (you will recall from Ch. 4 that disabling restraints are prohibited by law because the right to freely alienate or transfer property is part and parcel of fee simple ownership).

Also, it should be pointed out in connection with landlord-tenant law that a tenant's interest in the leased premises (that interest being a *chattel real*—see Ch. 2) is freely transferable in the absence of an agreement to the contrary. It is for this reason that many leases contain express prohibitions against assigning and/or subletting the leased premises. Subletting must be distinguished from assignment. A *sublease* is an agreement whereby the tenant-lessee sublets (transfers) all or part of the leased property at an agreed rental for a definite term but retains a reversionary interest in the property. In other words, the tenant-lessee

does not transfer his or her entire interest in the real property to the sublessee. Rather, the tenant transfers only a part of the property to the sublessee, or he or she transfers all of the property but for a period of time less than the period of the original lease. It is the tenant's retention of a reversionary interest that makes the transfer a sublease rather than an assignment. An *assignment* by a tenant-lessee is a transfer of his or her entire interest in the leased premises for the remainder of the lease period. In an assignment, the tenant retains no reversion in the leased premises.

With both a sublease and an assignment, the original tenant-lessee remains fully liable under the provisions of the original lease. However, with a sublease, the landlord must look to the original tenant for payment of the rent due under the lease—the subtenant pays the tenant not the landlord. With an assignment, on the other hand, the assignee becomes directly liable to the original landlord.

It should be noted that a provision in a lease prohibiting assignment will not prohibit a sublease of the property, and vice versa. Because of this, many leases expressly prohibit both assignments and subleases of the property without the lessor's express written consent. And the fact that the lessor consents to one particular assignment or sublease does not constitute consent to subsequent assignments or subleases.

Finally, most courts refuse to uphold prohibitions against assignment of contract rights to receive money only on the public policy theory that free transferability of money is good for commerce.

Are there any duties that cannot be delegated?

Although no particular words are necessary to delegate contract duties, the language used must indicate a present intent on the part of the delegant to authorize another to perform in his or her place. The phrase, "I hereby assign all rights and duties," is frequently and effectively used to appoint delegatees though the word "delegate" is not mentioned.

Just as there are contract rights that cannot be assigned, there are contract duties that cannot be delegated. The general rule is that delegation is not allowed where performance by the delegatee would vary materially from performance by the delegant. Thus, a party may not delegate a duty to perform personal services for another. As in the area of assignment, a performance by an artist, author, doctor, lawyer, teacher, accountant, etc., is simply too personal to be delegated. (Some states, including Oregon, have recently passed statutes making it illegal for a doctor to delegate the performance of surgery to another doctor— called "ghost surgery"). Of course, there are many duties that are not too personal to be transferred, such as a duty to pay money, to build or paint a building, to manufacture or transport goods. The test is whether performance by the original obligor is of the essence of the contract. If it is (e. g., where the original obligor has some special or unique talent), the nontransferring party has a substantial interest in having the original obligor perform personally, and delegation will not be allowed.

Also, if a contract specifically prohibits delegation of duties, the prohibition will be enforced. In contrast to the rules favoring the free assignment of contract rights, there are no restrictions on restraining delegation by contract.

An attempt to delegate a nondelegable duty does not in itself constitute a breach of contract since the delegant must, in any case, remain ready to perform in the event that the delegatee does not. However, if the delegant specifically states that he or she will not perform personally, this will be a repudiation of the contract as explained in Ch. 10, giving the

nontransferring party an immediate cause of action for anticipatory breach of the agreement.

What exactly does it mean to "stand in the shoes" of the assignor?

The common law rule is that an assignee takes no new rights by virtue of an assignment. He or she merely "stands in the shoes" of the assignor—that is, in the same position as the assignor and subject to the same defenses *as existed prior to the assignment.* Notice the emphasis: only defenses that are good against the assignor prior to the nontransferring party's notification of the assignment are good against the assignee. Once the other original party has been notified of the transfer, the assignee's rights under the contract "vest", and the assignor's rights are extinguished. Thus, any subsequent dealings between the two original parties to the contract are not binding on the assignee (the original parties cannot bind the assignee to "new terms") and may not be asserted against the assignee by way of defense. However, there is one exception. The defense of failure of consideration (failure by the assignor to perform his or her part of the bargain) may be asserted whether it arises before or after the assignment. Obviously, the only time the defense will arise after the assignment is where the assignor's duties under the contract are still executory (i. e., unperformed) at the time of the transfer of rights. In this case, the assignee will be deemed to take the assigned rights subject to the implied condition that the assignor will properly perform his or her part of the bargain. But apart from failure of consideration, only defenses that are in existence prior to the nontransferring party's notification of the assignment are good against the assignee, including fraud, duress, undue influence, mistake, unconscionable act, condition precedent or subsequent, incapacity, illegality, etc.

Sometimes, the nontransferring party will agree not to assert existing defenses against the assignee. This is called a *waiver of defenses* and is usually found in the original contract itself. For example, a contract might provide, "If this contract is hereafter assigned, all defenses are waived in favor of such assignee." In the absence of a contract of adhesion, such clauses are generally valid and enforceable. However, there is a special rule with regard to contracts for the sale or leasing of goods. Section 9–206 of the Uniform Commercial Code provides as follows.

It says:

> Subject to any statute or decision which establishes a different rule for buyers or lessees of consumer goods, an agreement by a buyer or lessee that he will not assert against an assignee any claim or defense which he may have against the seller or lessor is enforceable by an assignee who takes his assignment for value, in good faith and without notice of a claim or defense.

Thus, under the Code, a waiver of defenses clause is enforceable only if the assignee purchased the contract rights in good faith and without notice of any defenses that the obligor (nontransferring party) might have against the assignor. The same is true where the goods involved are consumer goods (goods used or bought primarily for personal, family, or household purposes) unless state law sets up a more stringent standard. And many states have passed statutes totally prohibiting waiver of defenses in retail installment contracts (agreements to pay over a period of time) for the purchase of consumer goods. Too often in the past, a merchant would sell an item through some form of misrepresentation, secure the purchaser's signature on a retail installment contract containing a waiver of defenses clause, then assign the contract to a third party. Because of the waiver, the assignee could collect on the contract despite the misrepresentation.

The Uniform Commercial Code also provides some special rules with regard to assignment of accounts (rights to payment for goods sold or leased). Frequently, sellers of merchandise will assign their accounts to banks or other financial institutions as a means of obtaining immediate cash (something less than the face value of the account). The assignee will then collect payment from the obligor (the account debtor) according to the terms of the contract. The problem arises where the contract is fully executory (unperformed on both sides) at the time of the assignment, and the seller and obligor thereafter desire to modify the contract terms. You already know that, under the common law, the original parties to the contract cannot bind the assignee to any new terms once the assignee's rights have "vested" (by notice to the obligor). However, under the Uniform Commercial Code, the original parties can modify the contract, even after notification to the obligor, so long as they are acting in good faith and in accordance with reasonable commercial standards. The assignee will be bound by the modification, although he or she will acquire rights under the modified or substituted contract. The pertinent Code provision is Section 9–318.

The UCC provides:

> **Section 9–318. Defenses Against Assignee; Modification of Contract After Notification of Assignment; Term Prohibiting Assignment Ineffective; Identification and Proof of Assignment**
>
> (1) Unless an account debtor has made an enforceable agreement not to assert defenses or claims arising out of a sale as provided in Section 9–206 [the waiver of de-

fenses provision] the rights of an assignee are subject to

(a) all the terms of the contract between the account debtor and assignor and any defense or claim arising therefrom; and

(b) any other defense or claim of the account debtor against the assignor which accrues before the account debtor receives notification of the assignment.

(2) So far as the right to payment or a part thereof under an assigned contract has not been fully earned by performance, and notwithstanding notification of the assignment, any modification of or substitution for the contract made in good faith and in accordance with reasonable commercial standards is effective against an assignee unless the account debtor has otherwise agreed but the assignee acquires corresponding rights under the modified or substituted contract. * * *

(3) The account debtor is authorized to pay the assignor until the account debtor receives notification that the amount due or to become due has been assigned and that payment is to be made to the assignee. A notification which does not reasonably identify the rights assigned is ineffective. If requested by the account debtor, the assignee must seasonably furnish reasonable proof that the assignment has been made and unless he does so the account debtor may pay the assignor.

(4) A term in any contract between an account debtor and an assignor is ineffective if it prohibits assignment of an account or prohibits creation of a security interest in a general intangible for money due or to become due or requires the account debtor's consent to such assignment or security interest.

In summary, the UCC carves out an exception to the common law rule that the original parties to the contract cannot bind the assignee to any new terms once the assignee's rights have vested. Under Section 9–318, the parties can modify an executory contract for the sale or leasing of goods, even after the assignee's rights have vested, so long as they do so in good faith and in accordance with reasonable commercial standards. You will also note that subsection (4) of the Code prohibits any contractual restraint on the assignment of accounts.

What are the assignee's rights against the assignor in the event that the nontransferring party fails to perform or refuses to perform?

In a purely gratuitous assignment, the assignee has no rights against the assignor in the event that the nontransferring obligor fails to perform or refuses to perform. However, where the assignment is for consideration (i. e., where it is contractual in nature), the assignee may have a cause of action against the assignor for breach of implied warranty. Even though the assignor does not expressly promise that the nontransferring party will perform, he or she is held by law to impliedly warrant (promise) the following:

(1) That the assigned right actually exists and is subject to no limitations or defenses other than those stated or apparent at the time of the assignment;

(2) That any document or paper shown to the assignee with regard to the assignment is genuine and what it purports to be; and

(3) That the assignor has the right to assign and will do nothing in the

future to defeat the assigned right (in other words, the assignor won't assign the same right to anyone else).

If the obligor's failure or refusal to perform can be traced to a breach of any of these implied warranties, the assignee may sue the assignor for money damages. If the failure or refusal to perform cannot be traced to such a breach, the assignee's only remedy is an action for breach of contract against the assignor. And you will note that the assignor does not impliedly warrant that the obligor will, in fact, perform, or that he or she is solvent and capable of performing.

How does "assignment" and "standing in the shoes" of the assignor differ from "negotiation" and having the rights of a "holder in due course"?

In the last chapter, we studied a special kind of contract—the insurance contract. We found that there are certain special rules that apply to insurance contracts, including rules on insurable interest, subrogation, concealment, and the like. In this chapter, we begin our study of another special form of contract—the *negotiable instrument*. The negotiable instrument is a contract designed to serve as a substitute for money and to help facilitate credit transactions. The basic kinds of negotiable instruments are *promissory notes, drafts* (or bills of exchange), and *checks* (a special type of draft that most of you are familiar with). Special rules apply to negotiable notes, drafts, and checks to enable them to flow freely through commerce without restriction. Obviously, if the ordinary rules of assignment were applied to such instruments, people would be unwilling to accept them in place of money or to extend credit on the basis of the instruments— the risk of a defense to payment would be too high, and the movement of the instruments through the channels of commerce would be too slow and cumbersome. Yet the commercial importance of freely flowing negotiable instruments cannot be overemphasized. Checks, drafts, and notes serve as the basic means of payment in most commercial transactions; they facilitate the payment of bills and the movement of goods and services. For this reason, negotiable instruments are frequently referred to as *commercial paper*.

Consider the fact that commercial paper is to serve as a substitute for money. Now suppose that you purchase a television set from J. C. Dollar Department Store for $750.00 cash (you pay in seven one hundred dollar bills and one fifty dollar bill). You take the TV home and find that it works on only half the channels. Obviously, J. C. Dollar has breached its part of the sales contract (buyers' remedies are discussed in Ch. 18), and your reasonable expectations have not been met. But should your remedy include the right to reacquire the exact same seven one hundred dollar bills and the exact same fifty dollar bill? By now, the bills have probably been deposited in the bank and given back out to eight individuals. Certainly, it would be both ridiculous and impossible for J. C. Dollar to have to locate the exact same bills and return them to you. The bills have moved on into the channels of commerce, and that is the way negotiable instruments are designed to move. Of course, negotiable notes, drafts, and checks will never move quite as freely as currency itself, but they can be transferred far more easily than other kinds of contracts. As you will learn in this and following chapters, if a negotiable instrument is transferred through a *negotiation* to one who qualifies as a *holder in due course,* the holder in due course will (with very limited exception) take the instrument free and clear of any defenses that the nontransferring party holds against the transferor. The instrument may thus continue to move through commerce free and clear of the defenses.

For the special rules of negotiability to come into play, the instrument involved must be a negotiable instrument. The Uniform Commercial Code, which very strictly controls negotiable instruments law, lists nine specific requirements of negotiability. Unless an instrument satisfies all nine requirements, the instrument is nonnegotiable, and the law of assignments controls (in which case, a transferee of the instrument will always "stand in the shoes" of his or her transferor).

Even where the instrument is negotiable, the law of assignments will control unless the transferee of the instrument qualifies as a holder in due course. To be a holder in due course, one must first be a "holder". Section 1–201 of the Uniform Commercial Code defines "holder" as "a person who is in possession * * * of an instrument * * * drawn, issued or indorsed to him or to his order or to bearer or in blank." The meaning of this definition will become clear as you read through this chapter and the two following. For now, realize that the kind of issuance or transfer needed to create a holder is different from an assignment. Also realize that a negotiable instrument can simply be assigned, and, if it is, the transferee will be an assignee, and not a holder. In most cases, however, a negotiable instrument is issued or transferred so as to create a holder.

Assuming that the transferee of an instrument is a holder, then he or she may also qualify as a "holder in due course". The Uniform Commercial Code defines "holder in due course" at Section 3–302 as follows.

The UCC provides:

(1) A holder in due course is a holder who takes the instrument

(a) for value; and

(b) in good faith; and

(c) without notice that it is overdue or has been dishonored or of any defense against or claim to it on the part of any person.

Unlike an assignee, a holder in due course may have rights superior to those of his or her transferor. Section 3–305 of the Uniform Commercial Code states.

The UCC provides:

Section 3–305. Rights of a Holder in Due Course

To the extent that a holder is a holder in due course he takes the instrument free from

(1) All claims to it on the part of any person; and

(2) All defenses of any party to the instrument with whom the holder has not dealt except

(a) infancy, to the extent that it is a defense to a simple contract [incapacity of a minor as discussed in Ch. 9]; and

(b) such other incapacity, or duress, or illegality of the transaction, as renders the obligation of the party a nullity [void transactions as discussed in Ch. 8]; and

(c) such misrepresentation as has induced the party to sign the instrument with neither knowledge nor reasonable opportunity to obtain knowledge of its character or its essential terms [fraud as discussed in Ch. 8]; and

(d) discharge in insolvency proceedings; and

(e) any other discharge of which the holder has notice when he takes the instrument.

The defenses listed in Subsection (2)(a) through (e) are called *real defenses* and are the only defenses that may be asserted against a holder in due course. All other defenses are *personal defenses* which cannot be asserted. Of course, as between the original parties to the contract, it makes little difference whether a defense is real or personal—if the defense exists, it can be asserted. The distinction between real and personal defenses becomes important only when the negotiable instrument is transferred to a third party. If the transferee qualifies as a holder in due course, only real defenses can be asserted against him or her; if the transferee does not qualify as a holder in due course, any defense that is good against the transferor, whether real or personal, will be good against the transferee. Of course, if the transferor of the instrument is a holder in due course, the transferee will "stand in his or her shoes" and so acquire the rights of a holder in due course (as you will learn in Ch. 13, this is a very important concept of law known as the "shelter provision").

In summary, if you are trying to determine whether the special rules of negotiability apply, ask first—*is the instrument negotiable?* If the answer is no, the law of assignments controls and you need go no further. If the answer is yes, ask a second question—*does the transferee of the instrument qualify as a holder in due course?* If the answer is yes, the rules of negotiability apply, and only real defenses will be good against the transferee. If the answer is no, the law of assignments controls, and any real or personal defenses good against the transferor will be good against the transferee. However, be sure to ask in this case—*does the transferee acquire the rights of a holder in due course under the "shelter provision"?* If so, only real defenses will be good against the transferee; personal defenses will be cut off.

After a few final comments as to the purpose and nature of negotiable instru-

ments, the remainder of the chapter will deal generally with the nine UCC requirements of negotiability. The specifics of these requirements, as well as the issues arising from the transfer of negotiable instruments, will be considered in Chapters 13 and 14.

What are the two main purposes for commercial paper?

As stated previously, negotiable instruments serve as substitutes for money in the world of commerce. Because of the special features of such instruments, people can accept them without fear that existing personal defenses will make it impossible to collect the instruments. Checks particularly are useful as monetary equivalents because they are payable on demand when presented to the bank where the drawer (the party who writes the check) keeps his or her account. Checks also permit the government to keep a much smaller supply of actual currency (money) in circulation. And using checks is safer and more convenient than using cash. People who write checks need not carry large amounts of money on their persons; and people are generally better off losing checks than they are losing cash (while lost money is nearly impossible to trace, a lost check, if unindorsed, usually cannot be converted into cash).

Negotiable instruments also serve a second purpose of helping to create credit (an important purpose in our society where most business is financed on credit). When one person pays another with a negotiable instrument that is payable at a fixed date in the future, the party who accepts the instrument is extending credit until the specified due date.

What two characteristics of negotiable instruments must always be kept in mind?

While the following chapter material will emphasize the special rules applicable to negotiable instruments, it is important to keep in mind that negotiable instruments are both contracts and forms of property. As contracts (albeit special contracts), negotiable instruments are subject to many of the rules detailed in Chapters 7 through 10. Thus, negotiable instruments require mutual assent, consideration, capacity, and legality (although, as you will learn, these defenses may be cut off by a holder in due course). Rules regarding discharge of contracts and remedies may also apply to negotiable instruments.

As property, negotiable instruments are subject to the rules and principles presented in Chapters 1 through 6, particularly the rules governing personal property and intangible personal property rights (each instrument consists of a bundle of "sticks" or rights). Thus, negotiable instruments may be transferred by sale or gift, placed into trust (see Ch. 29), or passed on at death by will or intestacy (see Ch. 30). Like other property, negotiable instruments can be stolen, lost, taxed, possessed, or converted. Of course, negotiable instruments are special forms of property, and many special rules also apply (the special rules are the subject matter of this and subsequent chapters).

What are the nine requirements of negotiability?

Because negotiable instruments serve as substitutes for money and help facilitate credit transactions, the law requires that negotiability of an instrument be determinable merely by looking at the face of the instrument. Otherwise, people would not be willing to accept the instruments as money substitutes or as instruments creating credit[1]—the risk of an existing defense to payment would be too high.

Thus, the determination of negotiability is strictly a matter of form. If an instrument fully complies with the nine requirements of negotiability set out in Section 3–104 of the Uniform Commercial Code, the instrument is negotiable. If the instrument fails to satisfy any one of the nine requirements, the instrument is nonnegotiable (in which case, the law of assignments controls). Section 3–104 of the Code, "Form of Negotiable Instruments", provides as follows.

It says:

(1) Any writing to be a negotiable instrument within this Article must

    (a) be signed by the maker or drawer;

    (b) contain an unconditional promise or order to pay a sum certain in money and no other promise, order, obligation or power given by the maker or drawer except as authorized by this Article; and

    (c) be payable on demand or at a definite time; and

    (d) be payable to order or to bearer.

Careful study of Subsection (1)(a) through (d) reveals that there are, in fact, nine requirements of negotiability:

(1) The instrument must be in writing.

(2) The instrument must be signed.

(3) The instrument must contain a promise to pay (if a note) or an order to pay (if a check or draft).

(4) The promise or order must be unconditional.

---

1. Banks, in particular, have insisted that negotiability be determinable from the face of the instrument without more.

(5) The payment required must be of a sum certain.

(6) The sum certain must be in money only.

(7) The instrument must not contain any promise or order other than the promise to pay a sum certain in money.

(8) The instrument must be payable on demand or at a definite time.

(9) The instrument must be payable "to order" or "to bearer". (Often referred to as "the magic words" of negotiability, the words "to order" or "to bearer" appear on 99.9% of all negotiable instruments. The limited exception to their use is dealt with in Ch. 14.)

Returning to the Code, Section 3–104(2) provides that a writing that complies with the nine requirements of negotiability will be one of four instruments.

The UCC provides:

(a) a "draft" (bill of exchange) if it is an order;

(b) a "check" if it is a draft drawn on a bank and payable on demand;

(c) a "certificate of deposit" if it is an acknowledgment by a bank of receipt of money with an engagement to repay it;

(d) a "note" if it is a promise other than a certificate of deposit.

In the sections that follow, each kind of negotiable instrument will be illustrated, with special emphasis given to its compliance with the nine requirements of negotiability.

What is a negotiable promissory note?

A negotiable *promissory note* is a written instrument in which one party (a *maker*) unconditionally promises to pay "to the order of" another party (a named *payee*) or "to bearer" (an unnamed *payee*) a sum certain in money upon demand or at a definite time in the future. The promissory note must be signed by the maker, and must contain no promise or order other than the promise to pay the specified sum.

As defined, a negotiable promissory note meets all nine requirements for negotiability. Where the note is made payable "to the order of" a named payee, the note is called *order paper*. The named payee must indorse the note (accomplished by signing on the back of the instrument) in order to negotiate it (i. e., transfer it so as to make the transferee a holder). Where the note is made payable "to bearer" (i. e., to any person who presents it for payment), the instrument is called *bearer paper*, and it may be freely negotiated without indorsement.

When are negotiable promissory notes used? Frequently, lenders of money require their borrowers to sign such notes; sometimes, sellers of property accept negotiable promissory notes from purchasers who cannot afford to immediately pay the full cash price of the property. And in nearly all credit real estate transactions, the purchaser is required to sign both a negotiable promissory note and a mortgage. Let's consider an example. Suppose that Larry Taylor purchases a boat from George Johnson for $10,300. Larry pays $2,000 down and gives George a negotiable promissory note (payable at any time upon demand of the payee) for the balance. The instrument, a simple promissory note, may be illustrated as follows:

February 15, 1980

ON DEMAND, the undersigned promises to pay to the order of

GEORGE JOHNSON

Eight thousand three hundred and no/100 ------------ DOLLARS

together with interest thereon from the date hereof until paid at the

rate of   9   percent per annum.

Lawrence Taylor
Lawrence Taylor

Looking at the instrument, you can see that all nine requirements of negotiability are satisfied: the instrument is in writing; it is signed by the maker, Larry Taylor; it contains an unconditional promise to pay a sum certain in money; it contains no other promise or order; and it is payable on demand to the order of a named payee, George Johnson.

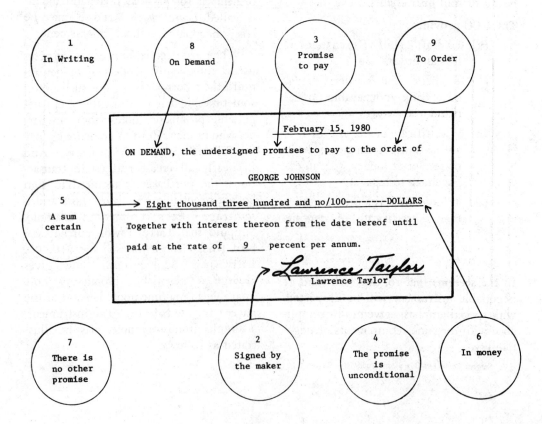

Since the promissory note is order paper made payable to the order of George Johnson, the note can be negotiated only by (1) indorsement by George and (2) delivery to a third party (the indorsee). Without George's indorsement, a third party in possession of the instrument could not be a holder (and so obviously could not be a holder in due course), but could only be an assignee subject to any and all defenses that Larry might have against George (e. g., nondelivery of the boat).

Now, let's vary the transaction so that Larry Taylor issues a promissory note payable, not on demand, but at a definite time in the future (this is more likely, in any case, since Larry does not appear to have present ability to pay the $8,300 balance). Let's also assume that Larry makes the note payable "to bearer" rather than to George Johnson. The instrument may be illustrated as follows:

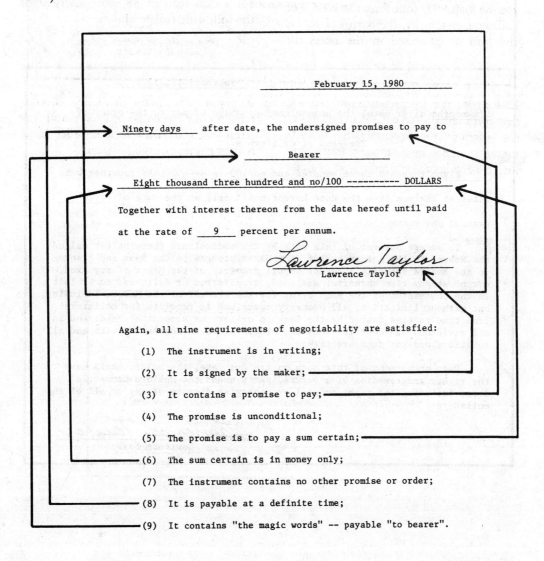

February 15, 1980

Ninety days   after date, the undersigned promises to pay to

Bearer

Eight thousand three hundred and no/100 ---------- DOLLARS

Together with interest thereon from the date hereof until paid

at the rate of   9   percent per annum.

Lawrence Taylor
Lawrence Taylor

Again, all nine requirements of negotiability are satisfied:

(1) The instrument is in writing;

(2) It is signed by the maker;

(3) It contains a promise to pay;

(4) The promise is unconditional;

(5) The promise is to pay a sum certain;

(6) The sum certain is in money only;

(7) The instrument contains no other promise or order;

(8) It is payable at a definite time;

(9) It contains "the magic words" -- payable "to bearer".

Sometimes, the maker of a promissory note is required to pledge certain personal property (usually stocks, bonds, life insurance policies with cash surrender values, sometimes jewelry) as security for his or her promise to pay a sum certain. A note secured by a pledge of personal property is called a *collateral note*. Banks, for example, will often grant a loan evidenced by a promissory note only where the borrower agrees to place certain personal property within the possession of the bank as security or collateral for the loan. If, following the *pledge* of collateral or security, the borrower repays the loan as promised in the note, the bank will return the borrower's property. If the borrower fails to repay as promised, the bank will sell the property and use the proceeds to pay the debt (returning any excess to the borrower).

Returning to our previous example, suppose that George Johnson is unwilling to accept a personal promissory note from Larry Taylor. Larry, however, owns stocks and bonds with a fair market value of $10,000, and he pledges these securities to the Bank of California in return for a cash loan of $8,300. Larry signs the following collateral note:

February 15, 1980

Six months after date, the undersigned promises to pay to the order of

_____The Bank of California_____

_____Eight thousand three hundred and no/100--------DOLLARS together with

interest thereon from the date hereof until paid at the rate of ___10___

percent per annum.

To secure payment of this note by the undersigned (hereinafter called the Maker) to the holder hereof, the Maker pledges to the Bank and grants to the Bank a security interest in all property of the Maker of any kind, now or at any time hereafter assigned, transferred or delivered to or left in the possession of the Bank by or for the account of the Maker, including, but without limitation, all property described in receipts for collateral from time to time issued by the Bank to or for the account of Maker and in all dividends and distributions on, other rights in connection with and all substitutions for such property.

Upon nonpayment of this note on its due date, the holder shall have the rights and remedies of a secured party under the Uniform Commercial Code, including the right to sell or otherwise dispose of any or all of the collateral.

Lawrence Taylor
Lawrence Taylor

As before, all nine requirements of negotiability are present. The fact that payment of the instrument is secured by collateral does not impair negotiability—rather, it makes the instrument more marketable since people are generally more willing to pay value for a note that is supported by some security. Along this line, the last paragraph of the note refers to the remedies of a secured party under the Uniform Commercial Code. These are described in detail in Ch. 27.

We have already stated that in nearly all credit real estate transactions (transactions in which the purchaser pays for the property over time), the purchaser is required to sign both a negotiable promissory note and a real estate mortgage. A home purchaser, for example, usually makes a down payment on the home,

signs a negotiable promisssory note for the balance (to be paid in monthly installments over a period of 25–30 years), and also signs a mortgage agreement in which the home serves as security for the payments. Because the promissory note calls for monthly payments, it is termed an *installment note*; the fact that the note is payable monthly does not render the note nonnegotiable.

Installment notes are also used in the sale and purchase of personal property (especially major purchases such as cars, boats, and airplanes). Thus, in our example, Larry Taylor might pay $2,000 down on the boat and sign an installment note promising to pay the $10,000[2] balance in 40 monthly payments of $250. The installment note might look like this:

February 15, 1980

The undersigned hereby promises to pay to the order of

GEORGE JOHNSON

Ten thousand and no/100 ------------------------------ DOLLARS

in ___40___ installments as follows: $250.00 on March 15, 1980

and the same amount on the same day of each successive month

thereafter until paid in full together with interest after maturity

on all unpaid principal amounts at the rate of ___9___ percent per annum.

Lawrence Taylor
Lawrence Taylor

---

2. You will note that Larry is now paying $12,000 for the boat rather than $10,300: George has upped the price because of the 40 month time span.

Many installment loans are evidenced by installment instruments called *discount notes*. In a discount note, the maker promises to pay the lender in installments a lump sum representing both loan principal and interest. The lender receives a cash amount less than the face value of the note because the interest to be paid is deducted from the face value and only the balance remaining is given to the maker. For example, suppose that Larry Taylor needs net cash of $8,300 to purchase the boat from George Johnson. To obtain that amount of cash, Larry may have to sign a discount note promising to pay a bank $10,080 in 36 monthly installments of $280. While Larry receives but $8,300 in cash, he promises to repay $10,080—a sum representing both the principal received ($8,300) and the interest on the loan for the three year payment period. The discount note may be illustrated as follows:

                                      February 15, 1980

The undersigned hereby promises to pay to the order of

        The Bank of New York

Ten thousand eighty and no/100 ---------------------- DOLLARS

in 36 installments as follows: $280.00 on March 15, 1980

and the same amount on the same day of each successive month

thereafter until paid in full together with interest after

maturity on all unpaid principal amounts at the rate of

 10 percent per annum.

                              Lawrence Taylor
                                Lawrence Taylor

Frequently, discount notes are also collateral notes. A bank, for example, will often finance the purchase of a new automobile only where the lender signs a discount note pledging the new automobile as security for repayment.

As you can see from our overview of promissory notes, the two main uses of such notes are (1) to make possible the borrowing of money, and (2) to facilitate purchase on credit. With regard to borrowing, you know that banks commonly require borrowers to sign negotiable promissory notes (frequently discount notes secured by a pledge of personal property). Where a discount note is used, the bank normally computes interest for the period of time specified in the note, deducts the interest from the note's face value, and places the balance in the maker's checking account. Many times, the bank will insist that an additional party be responsible for repaying the note. If the additional party signs on the front of the instrument at the time the loan is made, he or she will be a *co-maker* of the note along with the borrower; if the party merely indorses the back of the instrument at that time, he or she will be secondarily liable only (i. e., liable only in the event that the maker fails to repay as promised). The party who signs as an indorser is called an *accommodation party,* and the maker who receives the loan is the *accommodated party.*

Insofar as credit sales are concerned, you know that merchants sometimes require purchasers to sign negotiable promissory notes, often collateral notes, with the purchased goods themselves securing payment of the balance of the purchase price. Merchants favor negotiable notes over open accounts because notes may be negotiated to others (e. g., indorsed and

delivered in satisfaction of an existing debt) or *discounted* for immediate cash (to discount an instrument is to sell it prior to its due date for a price less than the amount stated on the face of the instrument). So long as the maker appears to be a good credit risk, discounting will enable the merchant to obtain most of his or her money immediately.

What is a negotiable certificate of deposit?

A negotiable *certificate of deposit* (a "CD") is a written instrument in which the maker (usually a bank or other financial institution) acknowledges receipt of a sum certain in money and unconditionally promises to repay the sum along with interest "to the order of" a named payee (usually the depositor) or "to bearer" on demand or at a definite time in the future and upon surrender of the certificate. The certificate of deposit must be signed by the maker, and must contain no promise or order other than the promise to repay.

Thus, a "CD" is really a form of promissory note: it not only evidences the fact that funds have been deposited, but it contains an unconditional promise to repay those funds. A "CD" is normally a better investment than an ordinary savings account because the "CD" usually earns a higher rate of interest. However, the "CD" funds must generally be left deposited for a minimum period of time. Returning to our previous example, suppose that, after receiving $10,300 for his boat, George Johnson finds that he has no immediate need for the money nor any desire to actively invest it. Rather than deposit the money in his savings account, George might be well advised to place $10,000 of it into the following certificate of deposit:

NEGOTIABLE TIME CERTIFICATE OF DEPOSIT

BANK OF PENNSYLVANIA

No. ___3542___   Philadelphia, Pennsylvania

                                  February 15, 1980

        THIS CERTIFIES THAT THERE HAS BEEN DEPOSITED

with the undersigned the sum of _____$10,000.00_____

Ten thousand . . . . Dollars

Payable to the order of _____GEORGE JOHNSON_____

on August 15, 1980 with interest only to maturity

at the rate of NINE percent (9%) per annum upon

surrender of this certificate properly indorsed.

                  BANK OF PENNSYLVANIA

        By _Abraham Banker_
               Abraham Banker
               Vice President

Once more, the instrument meets all nine requirements of negotiability: the certificate is in writing; it is signed by the maker; it contains a promise to pay; the promise is unconditional; the promise is to pay a sum certain; the sum certain is in money; the certificate contains no other promise or order; it is payable at a definite time; and it is payable "to the order of" a named payee.

What is a negotiable draft?

A *negotiable draft* is a written instrument in which one party (a *drawer*) unconditionally orders a second party (a *drawee*) to pay "to the order of" a named *payee* or "to bearer" a sum certain in money on demand or at a definite time in the future. The negotiable draft must be signed by the drawer, and must con-

tain no promise or order other than the order to pay.

Thus, whereas a promissory note is a two party (*maker* and *payee*) instrument involving a promise to pay, a draft is a three party (*drawer, drawee,* and *payee*) instrument involving an order to pay. In every draft situation, there is one important underlying relationship:

The draft presupposes a debtor-creditor relationship between the drawee and the drawer.

Obviously, a drawer cannot order a drawee to pay a sum certain in money unless the drawee is in some way indebted to the drawer. For example, most of you are familiar with one type of draft, the *check* (described in detail in a following section). The drawer of a check must deposit money in his or her checking account before writing the check ordering the drawee bank to pay "to order" or "to bearer". If the drawer fails to deposit money, the required debtor-creditor relationship does not exist (i. e., the bank is in no way indebted to the drawer), and the drawee bank is not obligated to pay upon the drawer's order. With regard to drafts other than checks, the drawee must either hold a similar account of funds belonging to the drawer, or he or she must owe the drawer money (e. g., the sale price in a purchase of goods from the drawer).

Drafts are generally classified as either time drafts or sight drafts. A *time draft* is a draft payable at a definite time in the future; a *sight draft* is a draft payable on demand (i. e., upon presentation to the drawee). Strictly speaking, a drawee incurs no liability for paying a draft until he or she has "accepted" the instrument. In the case of a time draft, the payee usually presents the draft to the drawee for acceptance well in advance of the instrument's due date. The drawee accepts the draft by writing his or her acceptance vertically across the face of the instrument as required by Section 3-410 of the Uniform Commercial Code.

The UCC provides:

(1) Acceptance is the drawee's signed engagement to honor the draft as presented. It must be written on the draft, and may consist of his signature alone. It becomes operative when completed by delivery or notification.

———

Having accepted the time draft, the *drawee-acceptor* returns the instrument to the payee who holds it until its due date (at which time the payee presents it again for payment).

Insofar as a sight draft is concerned, written acceptance is generally immaterial since the drawee accepts the draft on demand of the payee (i. e., upon the payee's presentation of the draft) simply by paying the instrument. An exception arises where the sight draft reads "payable 30 days after sight" or the like, in which case the payee must present the draft twice—once for acceptance, and, a second time, 30 days later, for payment.

As for the drawer's liability on the instrument, the drawer neither expressly promises nor expects to pay the sum certain to the payee—he or she merely orders the drawee to do so. However, there are occasions (as will be explained in Ch. 14) where the drawer will be required by law to pay according to the terms of the instrument.

Now let's return to our example. Suppose that Larry Taylor agrees to purchase George Johnson's boat for $10,300. Larry has only $2,000 to put down on the boat, but Mark Hopkins owes Larry $8,300 (due to be paid on March 15, 1980) for a parcel of real property Mark purchased from Larry. Larry puts $2,000 down on the boat and gives George the following time draft for the balance:

February 15, 1980

On March 15, 1980 pay to the order of

GEORGE JOHNSON

Eight Thousand three hundred and no/100 DOLLARS

TO: MARK HOPKINS
      228 West Rosser Avenue
      Bismarck, North Dakota

Lawrence Taylor
Lawrence Taylor

As stated before, the drawee (Mark Hopkins) is not liable on the time draft until and unless he accepts the instrument. While it is true that the draft presupposes a debtor-creditor relationship between Mark Hopkins and Larry Taylor, Mark is not obligated to assume a new form of contract for paying off the previously existing debt (i. e., Larry cannot require Mark to pay other than in accord with the terms of the original debt agreement). Thus, Mark may refuse to accept the time draft, although he will still remain liable to Larry for the $8,300.

However, it probably makes little difference to Mark whether he pays the $8,300 to Larry Taylor or George Johnson. He is therefore likely to accept the draft by writing the acceptance vertically across the face of the instrument as follows:[3]

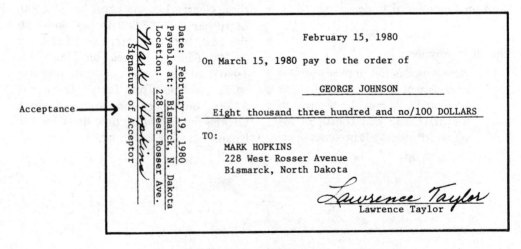

3. Remember that the drawee's signature without more constitutes sufficient acceptance under UCC Section 3–410.

By accepting the time draft in the manner illustrated, Mark Hopkins becomes liable to George Johnson in the amount of $8,300, payable March 15, 1980.

Now suppose that Larry Taylor makes out the draft to George Johnson on or after March 15, 1980, so that the $8,300 Mark Hopkins owes Larry is already due and payable. Larry, in this case, might use the following sight draft:

March 15, 1980

Pay to the order of _____ GEORGE JOHNSON _____

_____ Eight thousand three hundred and no/100 DOLLARS _____

TO: MARK HOPKINS
      228 West Rosser Avenue
      Bismarck, North Dakota

                          Lawrence Taylor
                          Lawrence Taylor

Here, written acceptance is immaterial since, on George's demand, Mark either accepts simply by paying the instrument, or he refuses to accept (and the matter is disposed of least insofar as Mark is concerned).

Both the time and sight drafts drawn by Larry Taylor upon the drawee Mark Hopkins satisfy all nine requirements of negotiability.

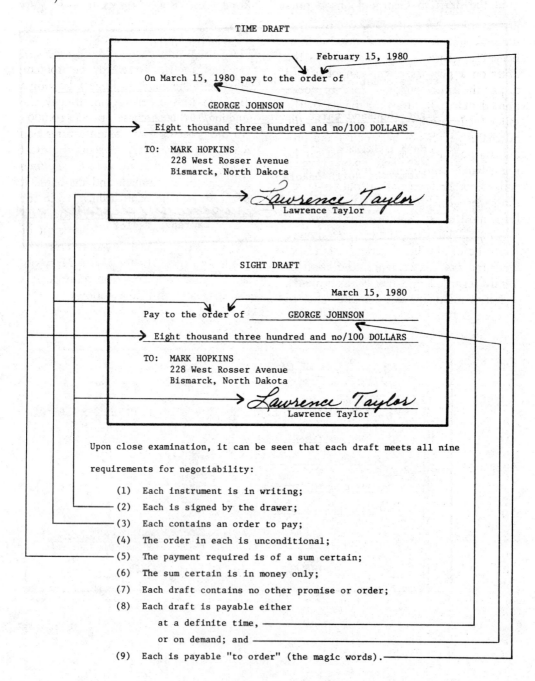

TIME DRAFT

February 15, 1980

On March 15, 1980 pay to the order of

GEORGE JOHNSON

Eight thousand three hundred and no/100 DOLLARS

TO: MARK HOPKINS
      228 West Rosser Avenue
      Bismarck, North Dakota

Lawrence Taylor
Lawrence Taylor

SIGHT DRAFT

March 15, 1980

Pay to the order of   GEORGE JOHNSON

Eight thousand three hundred and no/100 DOLLARS

TO: MARK HOPKINS
      228 West Rosser Avenue
      Bismarck, North Dakota

Lawrence Taylor
Lawrence Taylor

Upon close examination, it can be seen that each draft meets all nine requirements for negotiability:

(1)   Each instrument is in writing;

(2)   Each is signed by the drawer;

(3)   Each contains an order to pay;

(4)   The order in each is unconditional;

(5)   The payment required is of a sum certain;

(6)   The sum certain is in money only;

(7)   Each draft contains no other promise or order;

(8)   Each draft is payable either

      at a definite time,

      or on demand; and

(9)   Each is payable "to order" (the magic words).

What is a trade acceptance?

A *trade acceptance* is a special kind of draft used to finance the movement of goods in commerce. Whereas the drawer of a draft normally names some third party as payee of the instrument, the drawer of a trade acceptance (usually a seller of merchandise) names himself or herself as payee. The seller draws the draft on a purchaser who cannot afford to pay the entire purchase price of goods immediately. By drawing the draft, the seller facilitates the credit sale (i. e., the purchaser gets his or her goods) and produces a negotiable instrument that can be immediately discounted for cash to a bank or other financial institution (i. e., the seller gets his or her money—or, at least, most of it). Since, as we shall see in Ch. 14, both the drawer and drawee (once he or she has accepted) stand behind the trade acceptance, the draft is highly regarded by financial institutions, and it is relatively easy for the seller to obtain his or her money less the discount.

By way of example, assume that, on February 15, 1980, Mary Manufacturer enters into a sales contract with Roger Retailer wherein Mary agrees to manufacture and deliver 2,000 men's shirts to Roger, and Roger agrees to pay Mary $5.00 per shirt, or $10,000. The problem is that Roger is short on cash while Mary needs immediate cash to meet her own obligations. To remedy the problem, Mary sells the goods to Roger, drawing a draft on him ordering him to pay the amount of the purchase price ($10,000) "to the order of Mary Manufacturer" on April 1, 1980. Mary presents the draft to Roger for written acceptance; she then indorses the instrument and discounts it at the bank (the bank deducts from the face value of the draft a charge for interest, risk, and handling). The result of the transaction is that Roger receives the goods he needs on credit, and Mary obtains immediate cash. The trade acceptance may be illustrated as follows:

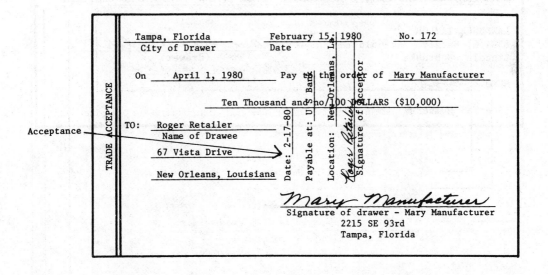

What is a check?

A *check* is a draft drawn on a bank and payable on demand; it is not only the most common kind of draft, but it is the most widely used form of commercial paper. Each year, billions of checks are processed involving trillions (thousand of billions) of dollars. Generally, a drawer orders printed checks from the bank where he or she maintains an account. The drawer's name, address, and telephone number are printed on the face of the checks. The checks are numbered or left blank for the drawer to number; and there is a "memo" space for noting the particular reason for issuing the check (e. g., rent, groceries, electric bill, etc.). Also, the checks are specially marked with numbers representing the drawer's bank and indicating a combination by which the Magnetic Ink Character Recognition check collection system (see Ch. 15) may pass the checks through a sorting computer so as to charge them to the proper account. The special numbers serve to facilitate the collection process and the movement of the checks through banking channels. Thus, Larry Taylor, might simply write George Johnson a check for $10,300 to pay for the much sought after boat. The check might look like this:

(Special Numbers)

West Slope Branch, Lincoln Nebraska
BANK OF NEBRASKA
(drawee)

February 15, 19 *80*   131

Pay to the order of *George Johnson* $ *10,300*

Ten thousand three hundred and 00/100 —————— Dollars

LAWRENCE TAYLOR
6534 E. Harney 344-6516
Lincoln, Nebraska

Lawrence Taylor
(drawer)

MEMO. *boat*

(Special Numbers)

Are there negotiable instruments apart from the promissory note, draft, CD, and check?

Negotiable notes, drafts, CD's, and checks serve as money substitutes and facilitate credit transactions. In Ch. 16, we will study about written instruments called *documents of title,* which may be either negotiable or nonnegotiable, but which serve an entirely different purpose —they evidence the ownership of goods. Documents of title are of two types: *warehouse receipts,* which evidence the ownership of goods in storage; and *bills of lading,* which evidence the ownership of goods in shipment. Warehouse receipts and bills of lading are designed not only to transfer the ownership of goods, but to represent the goods themselves. Thus, possession of the document of title may be equivalent to actual ownership: where the document is negotiable, the warehouseman or carrier (shipper) must deliver the goods to anyone in legal possession of the instrument.

While negotiable documents of title serve an entirely different function from the commercial instruments (notes, drafts, CD's, checks) discussed in this chapter, they do have similar characteristics (e.g., they may be made out "to order" or "to bearer", they may cut off defenses of prior parties, etc.). Thus, as you read through the next two chapters, bear in mind that many of the rules governing commercial paper also apply to documents of title.

CASES

CASE 1—*"I could have danced all night * * *"*

SPEELMAN v. PASCAL

Court of Appeals of New York, 1961.
10 N.Y.2d 313, 222 N.Y.S.2d 324, 178 N.E.2d 723.

DESMOND, Chief Judge.

Gabriel Pascal, defendant's intestate who died in 1954, had been for many years a theatrical producer. In 1952 an English corporation named Gabriel Pascal Enterprises, Ltd., of whose 100 shares Gabriel Pascal owned 98, made an agreement with the English Public Trustee who represented the estate of George Bernard Shaw. This agreement granted to Gabriel Pascal Enterprises, Ltd., the exclusive world rights to prepare and produce a musical play to be based on Shaw's play "Pygmalion" and a motion picture version of the musical play. The agreement recited, as was the fact, that the licensee owned a film scenario written by Pascal and based on "Pygmalion". In fact Pascal had, some time previously, produced a nonmusical movie version of "Pygmalion" under rights obtained by Pascal from George Bernard Shaw during the latter's lifetime. The 1952 agreement required the licensee corporation to pay the Shaw estate an initial advance and thereafter to pay the Shaw estate 3% of the gross receipts of the musical play and musical movie with a provision that the license was to terminate if within certain fixed periods the licensee did not arrange with Lerner and Loewe or other similarly well-known composers to write the musical play and arrange to produce it. Before Pascal's death in July, 1954, he had made a number of unsuccessful efforts to get the musical written and produced and it was not until after his death that arrangements were made, through a New York bank as temporary administrator of his estate, for the writing and production of the highly successful "My Fair Lady". Meanwhile, on February 22, 1954, at a time when the license from the Shaw estate still had two years to run, Gabriel Pascal, who died four and a half months later, wrote, signed and delivered to plaintiff a document as follows:

"Dear Miss Kingman

"This is to confirm to you our understanding that I give you from my shares of profits of the Pygmalion Musical stage version five per cent (5%) in England, and two per cent (2%) of my shares of profits in the United States. From the film version, five per cent (5%) from my profit shares all over the world.

"As soon as the contracts are signed, I will send a copy of this letter to my lawyer, Edwin Davies, in London, and he will confirm to you this arrangement in a legal form.

"This participation in my shares of profits is a present to you, in recognition for your loyal work for me as my Executive Secretary.

"Very sincerely yours,

"Gabriel Pascal."

The question in this lawsuit is: Did the delivery of this paper constitute a valid, complete, present gift to plaintiff by way of assignment of a share in future royalties when and if collected from the exhibition of the musical stage version and film version of "Pygmalion"? A consideration was, of course, unnecessary.

In pertinent parts the judgment appealed from declares that plaintiff is entitled to receive the percentages set out in the 1954 agreement, requires defendant to render plaintiff accountings from time to time of all moneys received from the musical play and the film version, and orders defendant to make the payments required by the agreement. * * *

The only real question is as to whether the 1954 letter above quoted operated to transfer to plaintiff an enforcible right to the described percentages of the royalties to accrue to Pascal on the production of a stage or film version of a musical play based on "Pygmalion". We see no reason why this letter does not have that effect. It is true that at the time of the delivery of the letter there was no musical stage or film play in existence but Pascal, who owned and was conducting negotiations to realize on the state and film rights, could grant to another a share of the moneys to accrue from the use of those rights by others. * * *

* * *

Judgment affirmed.

CASE 2—"*The assignee of contract rights stands in the shoes of the assignor * * *"*

FARMERS ACCEPTANCE CORP. v. DeLOZIER

Supreme Court of Colorado, En Banc, 1972.
178 Colo. 291, 496 P.2d 1016.

ERICKSON, Justice.

This writ of error arises out of a complaint filed by a materialman, Ladd Lumber Company, against a general contractor, Howard K. DeLozier, to recover the cost of materials which were supplied to John Diviney, a subcontractor of DeLozier. A third-party complaint was filed by DeLozier against Farmers Acceptance Corporation (hereinafter referred to as "FAC"), the assignee of Diviney's rights under the DeLozier-Diviney contract. DeLozier thereby sought to recover from FAC monies he had paid pursuant to the contract but which had not been applied in payment of the bill owed by Diviney for materials he used in performing the DeLozier contract. The trial court entered judgment in the amount of $2,865.63 in favor of Ladd Lumber Company and against DeLozier for all materials supplied to Diviney and judgment in the amount of $1,574.86 in favor of DeLozier and against FAC for the monies it had obtained pursuant to the assignment. Thereafter, FAC filed this writ of error.

The record reveals that DeLozier was engaged as the general contractor for the construction of the Lathrop Park Youth Camp. DeLozier contracted with Diviney to install drywall on the project. Before beginning work, Diviney obtained a personal loan of $1,500 from FAC * * *. As security for the loan, Diviney assigned to FAC all his right, title, and interest in his contract with DeLozier. DeLozier was notified of the assignment by FAC prior to making any payments under the contract. Thereafter, DeLozier made one payment by check in connection with the contract in the amount of $1,844. The check, which represented 35% of the total contract, was made payable to * * * FAC. FAC applied $1,574.86 [principal and interest] toward payment of Diviney's personal note and the balance of $269.14 toward Diviney's account with Ladd Lumber Company for materials used on the Lathrop Park job. Approximately one month later, DeLozier notified Diviney that he was cancelling the contract because of Diviney's failure to continue on the job. Thereafter, DeLozier received a bill from Ladd Lumber Company for materials supplied to Diviney for the Lathrop Park project. The bill was not paid, and the suit which precipitated this writ of error was instituted.

Whether or not FAC is entitled to retain the $1,574.86 which it obtained from DeLozier is wholly dependent upon the law governing assignments and FAC's status as the assignee of Diviney's contract rights with DeLozier. * * * Diviney had an absolute right to assign to FAC the money he expected to earn under his contract with DeLozier. Since the assignment was valid, the remaining question to be determined is the value of the rights assigned.

It is a general rule that an assignee of contract rights stands in the shoes of the assignor and has no greater rights against the debtor than did the assignor. The assignee is also subject to all the equities and defenses which could have been raised by the debtor against the assignor * * *.

By virtue of the assignment, FAC acquired nothing more than Diviney was entitled to under his contract with DeLozier. Diviney's right to payment under the contract was conditioned upon performance of the contract by the installation of drywall. Diviney's earnings were also subject to the burden of all the material bills incurred by Diviney in the performance of the contract. Diviney's failure to pay the material bills, coupled with their payment by DeLozier * * * subjected Diviney to a claim by DeLozier for the amount DeLozier had to pay [to] Ladd Lumber Company. Since the material bills exceeded the amount Diviney apparently earned under his contract with DeLozier, Diviney was not entitled to any money under the contract. * * * FAC's rights under the assignment to money earned by Diviney pursuant to his contract with DeLozier were also subject to claims arising out of the contract. Consequently, FAC was not entitled to any payments which were made pursuant to the underlying contract and which were conditioned upon performance.

* * *

Judgment affirmed.

CASE 3—*Title passed by oral gift.*

WATERS v. WATERS

Court of Civil Appeals of Texas, 1973.
498 S.W.2d 236.

DUNAGAN, Chief Justice.

Appellee, Patsy S. Waters, brought this suit against appellant, Jerry A. Waters, on a written agreement and contract concerning a certain promissory note whereby appellant had agreed to pay a sum certain to appellee on a certain date, bearing a specified interest and renewal of said note. The agreement was made as a part of the property settlement and division of property when the parties were divorced.

Appellant had executed a demand note payable to the order of appellee's father, Jim Still. The appellant and appellee were involved in a divorce proceeding. Appellant and appellee, by contract in writing, agreed as part of the settlement of their property rights and obligations, that the demand note would be transferred to appellee and appellant would pay a stated sum to appellee at a stated time in order not to pay the demand note at that time. Appellant obtained delayed payment of the demand note in return for his promise to pay a stipulated, specified and agreed amount to appellee at a later time. Appellant thus obtained the benefit of delaying for a substantial time, payments of a demand obligation mentioned in such agreement, and the further benefit of a fixed time of payment, as opposed to payment on demand * * *. The note referred to in the agreement was given and transferred to appellee by her father as contemplated by the agreement. * * * When the due date arrived, payment was demanded and appellant did not pay, which resulted in this suit being filed. * * *

* * *

Trial was before the court without a jury. Judgment was rendered for the appellee in the sum of $4,656.44, plus interest * * *.

* * *

Jim Still, payee in the original note described in such written instrument, was the father of plaintiff, and he died shortly after the execution of such written instrument. Prior to his death, and after the execution of such written instrument, Jim Still gave the original $5,000.00 note to plaintiff, intending to invest plaintiff with ownership thereof, and delivered such note to plaintiff. Plaintiff has had such note since such time in her possession.

* * *

Appellant contends that the trial court erred in finding that Jim Still, the payee, gave the note to appellee intending to vest appellee with ownership thereof and that such note was delivered to the appellee. * * *

* * *

Appellant contends that there was no evidence of probative force that the appellee is the owner of said note. The note does not bear the endorsement of Jim Still. However, the appellee, Mrs. Patsy Waters, testified that her father gave her the note with the statement that it was hers and she could collect same. The evidence shows that she was in possession of the note.

This evidence is before us undisputed. This evidence shows a fulfill- ment of the provisions of the settlement contract "that the note is presently payable to Jim Still, but will be transferred to Patsy A. Waters (appellee) in the future." The settlement contract did not set out or provide in what manner the note was to be transferred to the appellee, Patsy Waters, nor did it attempt to do so.

A promissory note can lawfully be transferred without a written assign- ment or an endorsement of the legal owner and holder thereof. It has been held * * * that an endorsement on note by payee or writing attached thereto was unnecessary to vest title thereto in the owner and holder.

    * * * Any person who transfers an instrument transfers whatever rights he has in it. The transferee acquires those rights even though they do not amount to "title."

    The transfer of rights is not limited to transfers for value. An instrument may be transferred as a gift, and the donee acquires whatever rights the donor had. * * *

Delivery by a donor to donee of a promissory note payable to donor with intent to invest the donee with ownership is an effective gift of the note and transfer thereof. The gift to appellee from her father did not re- quire a written transfer. Appellant by the settlement agreement and con- tract agreed for the note to be transferred to appellee and knew that such transfer was to be made and that no particular method for such transfer was provided. Title passes by oral gift. * * *

    * * *

Sec. 201:12 [of the Uniform Commercial Code] reads as follows:

    The fact that a transferee lacking a necessary indorsement is not the holder does not mean that the transferee cannot establish his right as assignee and enforce the obligation [as long as there are no defenses available against the assignor].

    * * *

The trial court's judgment is affirmed.

CASE 4—*The instrument is not negotiable so the law of assignment ap- plies.*

HAGGARD v. MUTUAL OIL & REFINING CO.

Court of Appeals of Kentucky, 1924.
204 Ky. 209, 263 S.W. 745.

CLARKE, J. The single question presented by this appeal is whether or not the following check is a negotiable instrument:
"$2,500.00. Winchester, Ky., July 10, 1920.

"The Winchester Bank, of Winchester, Ky.: Pay to Arco Refinery Con- struction Company twenty-five hundred and no/100 dollars, for a/c con- structing refinery, switch, and loading racks, Win. Ky.

"Mutual Oil & Refining Co.,

"By C. L. Bell, Pres."

Subdivision 4 of section 3720b, which is the Negotiable Instruments Act (Acts 1913, p. 213), § 1, provides that:

"An instrument to be negotiable must conform to the following requirements: * * * (4) Must be payable to the order of a specified person or to bearer."

Since, as the check itself shows, and as is admittedly true, the maker, in issuing the check, drew a line through the printed words "or bearer," we need only to examine it to ascertain whether or not it was "payable to the order of a specified person," for unless so, it lacked one of the essentials prescribed for negotiability.

Section 8 of the act (section 3720b8 of the Statutes) defines when an instrument is payable to order as follows:

"The instrument is payable to order where it is drawn payable to the order of a specified person or to him or his order."

It will be noticed that the above check is not payable to the order of the payee, nor to the payee or its order, but is payable simply to the payee. It therefore seems to us too clear for dispute that this check is not payable to order, and is therefore, as the lower court held, not negotiable.

In other words, we think it is clear that subsection 8 means, as it says, that the instrument must be payable either (1) to the order of the payee, or (2) to the payee or order * * *.

    * * *

Counsel for appellant concede that this section has been construed by this court and others in the above cases to require the use of the words "order or bearer" or other words of similar legal import in order to make a note or other bill negotiable, but they insist that there is such a material difference between a note and a check as that these cases are not applicable to one in which, as here, the bill is a check.

But in this they are clearly mistaken. Section 185 of the act (Ky.St. § 3720b185) expressly declares that a check is a bill of exchange payable on demand, and that, except as otherwise therein provided, the provisions of the act applicable to a bill of exchange payable on demand shall apply to a check, and, as it is not otherwise therein provided, it is clear that sections 1 and 8 of the act apply to a check as well as to any other bill of exchange, and to be negotiable it also must employ some such words as "order" or "bearer" indicating negotiability.

It results, therefore, that a check, just as any other bill of exchange that is made payable simply to the payee and not to his order or to bearer, is not negotiable, and that appellant, to whom this check was assigned by the payee, took same subject to all defenses which were available between the original parties.

[Defendant's defense of lack] of consideration [is a good defense against the original assignor and the assignee.]

PROBLEMS

1.   Answer the following "True" or "False" and give reasons for your answers:

   (a) A gratuitous assignment may be revoked unless it constitutes a completed gift.

   (b) Express contractual restraints on delegation are generally unenforceable.

(c) Only present and future rights in existing contracts can be assigned.

(d) An accommodation party who indorses a negotiable promissory note is primarily liable on the note as a co-maker.

(e) To discount an instrument is to sell it prior to its due date for a price greater than the amount stated on the face of the instrument.

(f) A certificate of deposit is normally a better investment than an ordinary savings account.

(g) Whereas a promissory note is a three party instrument, a draft is a two party instrument.

(h) A draft presupposes a debtor-creditor relationship between the drawer and the drawee.

(i) In trade acceptance, the drawer and the payee are one and the same.

(j) Collateral notes are the most widely used form of commercial paper.

(k) Written acceptance by the drawee is generally immaterial insofar as a time draft is concerned.

(l) Only real defenses are good against a holder in due course.

2. Is the following instrument negotiable? Explain fully, with specific reference to each of the requirements of negotiability. In your answer, identify the type of instrument at issue and name the parties involved.

December 12, 1980

ON DEMAND, pay to the order of_____Kathleen Bryant_____

Eight hundred and no/100 -----------------------------DOLLARS

TO: Mike Carpenter
332 W. Cole Street
San Francisco, California

June Jeffries
June Jeffries

---

3. On January 1st, furniture dealer Debbie Decker contracts to sell a couch and loveseat to John Walden for $1,000. By the terms of the contract, Debbie is to deliver the furniture to John on February 1st, and John is to make payment in full on February 5th. The contract contains a waiver of defenses clause. On January 5th, Debbie assigns her right to payment of the $1,000 to Hugo Green for valuable consideration; Hugo knows that Debbie fraudulently misrepresented the condition of the furniture so as to induce John to purchase it. On January 20th, Debbie and John modify the terms of the contract to provide that delivery shall be made on February 5th, and payment on February 10th (with payment in full to be $925 rather than $1,000).

    (a) Is Hugo Green bound by the contract modifications? Explain.

    (b) Assuming John asserts fraudulent misrepresentation as a defense to payment, is the defense good as against Hugo Green? Explain.

    (c) Without regard to fraud, assume that John is insolvent and cannot pay for the furniture. What are Hugo's rights, if any, against Debbie Decker? Would your answer differ if Hugo had not given value for the assignment? Explain.

4.   Unlimited Fashions, Inc., leased a store in the Suburban Styles Shopping Center for five years at $1,500 a month. The lease contained a provision which prohibited assignment of the lease. After occupying the premises for two years, Unlimited sublet the premises to Fantastic Frocks for the balance of its term, less one day, at $2,000 per month. Unlimited moved out on a Sunday and removed all its personal property and trade fixtures such as portable clothing racks, cash registers, detachable counters, etc. Which of the following *best* describes the legal status of the parties involved?

    (a) Unlimited has *not* breached its contract with Suburban.

    (b) Suburban is entitled to the additional $500 rental paid each month by Fantastic to Unlimited.

    (c) Removal of the trade fixtures in question by Unlimited was improper and it can be held liable to Suburban for their fair value.

    (d) Fantastic is a tenant of Suburban.

    [# 11, May, 1975 CPA Exam]

5.   Jane Luft, doing business as Luft Enterprises, owned a tract of land upon which she had intended to build an additional retail outlet. There is an existing first mortgage of $70,000 on the property which is held by the First County National Bank. Luft decided *not* to expand, and a buyer, Johnson, offered $150,000 for the property. Luft accepted and received a certified check for $80,000 plus a signed statement by Johnson promising to pay the existing mortgage. What are the legal rights of the indicated parties?

    (a) Luft remains liable to First County despite Johnson's promise to pay.

    (b) First County must first proceed against Johnson on the mortgage before it has any rights after Luft.

    (c) The delegation of the debt is invalid if Johnson does *not* have a credit rating roughly comparable to Luft's.

    (d) The bank is the incidental beneficiary of Johnson's promise to pay the mortgage.

    [# 29, May, 1977 CPA Exam]

6.   A typical term life insurance policy

    (a) Builds up a cash value during its duration against which the policyholder can borrow.

    (b) Is assignable.

    (c) Creates a vested interest in the named beneficiary.

(d) Does *not* require an insurable interest in the person taking out the policy as do other types of life insurance policies.

[# 31, May, 1976 CPA Exam]

7.   The usual fire insurance policy does *not*

(a) Have to meet the insurable interest test if this requirement is waived by the parties.

(b) Permit assignment of the policy prior to loss without the consent of the insurer.

(c) Provide for subrogation of the insurer to the insured's rights upon payment of the amount of the loss covered by the policy.

(d) Cover losses caused by the negligence of the insured's agent.

[# 8, May, 1977 CPA Exam]

8.   *True-False Question.* Church and Jasper, CPAs, wish to relocate their offices. The lease on their present offices is for five years with three years to run and it contains a survival clause which provides that the tenant's liability shall survive the landlord's termination of the lease for a breach by the tenant. Their landlord is not agreeable to canceling the lease which also prohibits a sublease without the landlord's consent. Church and Jasper have a financially responsible and respectable prospective subtenant but have reason to believe that the landlord will not consent to a sublease.

(a) If Church and Jasper sublease the premises without the landlord's consent, they will breach their lease and entitle the landlord to terminate the lease.

(b) If the landlord terminates the lease under the circumstances described, Church and Jasper would not be liable to the landlord for any deficiency in rent for the balance of the term of their lease.

(c) Regardless of the prohibition against subletting in their lease, Church and Jasper may assign their lease to a third party without breaching the lease.

(d) Assuming that Church and Jasper are free to assign their lease, they will not be liable to the landlord under the lease for the performance of all of their obligations as tenants.

(e) If the landlord consents to a subletting, the mere giving of such consent will relieve Church and Jasper of any further obligations under the lease.

(f) If the landlord consents to a subletting, he may collect the rent due under the lease directly from the subtenant.

(g) If Church and Jasper assign their lease, the landlord may not collect the rent due directly from the assignee.

[#3.D., May, 1971 CPA Exam]

9.   A CPA was engaged by Jackson & Wilcox, a small retail partnership, to examine its financial statements. The CPA discovered that due to other commitments, the engagement could *not* be completed on time. The CPA, therefore, unilaterally delegated the duty to Vincent, an equally competent CPA. Under these circumstances, which of the following is true?

(a) The duty to perform the audit engagement is delegable in that it is determined by an objective standard.

(b) If Jackson & Wilcox refuses to accept Vincent because of a personal dislike of Vincent by one of the partners, Jackson & Wilcox will be liable for breach of contract.

(c) Jackson & Wilcox must accept the delegation in that Vincent is equally competent.

(d) The duty to perform the audit engagement is nondelegable and Jackson & Wilcox need *not* accept Vincent as a substitute if they do *not* wish to do so.

[# 3, November, 1977 CPA Exam]

10. Your client, Robert Rose, has the following instrument in his possession.

March 1, 1976

One month from date, I Charles Wallace, do hereby promise to pay Edward Carlson seven hundred and fifty dollars ($750.00).

Charles Wallace

Edward Carlson wrote "pay to the order of Robert Rose" on the back and delivered it to Rose.

(a) Robert Rose is a holder in due course.

(b) The instrument is a negotiable promissory note.

(c) Edward Carlson is a holder in due course.

(d) All defenses, real and personal, are assertible by Wallace against Rose.

[# 39, May, 1976 CPA Exam]

Chapter 13

THE SPECIFICS OF NEGOTIABILITY, NEGOTIATION, AND THE HOLDER IN DUE COURSE DOCTRINE

What are the nine specific requirements of negotiability?

As you know from the last chapter, there are nine specific requirements of negotiability. As set forth in Section 3–104 of the Uniform Commercial Code, they are:

(1) The instrument must be in writing.

(2) The instrument must be signed by the maker or drawer.

(3) The instrument must contain a promise to pay (if a note) or an order to pay (if a check or draft).

(4) The promise or order must be unconditional.

(5) The payment required must be of a sum certain.

(6) The sum certain must be in money only.

(7) The instrument must not contain any promise or order than the promise or order to pay a sum certain in money.

(8) The instrument must be payable on demand or at a definite time.

(9) The instrument must be payable "to order" or "to bearer" (the "magic words" of negotiability).

If an instrument fully complies with all nine of these requirements, it is negotiable. If an instrument fails to comply with any one of the requirements, it is nonnegotiable, and a transferee of the instrument can have no better rights than his or her transferor (i. e., he or she will have the rights of an assignee only). Also, you will recall that negotiability must be determinable from the face of an instrument without more. Thus, by merely looking at notes, "CD's", drafts, and checks, you can determine whether the instruments are negotiable.

In this chapter, we will consider each of the nine requirements of negotiability in more detail. We will then discuss negotiation of negotiable instruments and the holder in due course doctrine. Always remember, if you conclude that an instrument is nonnegotiable, the rules of negotiation and holder in due course will not apply (with one exception to be discussed in Ch. 14).

What is meant by the requirement that the instrument must be in writing?

Generally, the first requirement of negotiability—that the instrument be in writing—poses little or no problem. Most commercial instruments are printed forms that have been carefully drafted by attorneys with an eye to satisfying the negotiability requirement. However, a printed form is not required, and any writing will suffice whether it is printed, typewritten, handwritten, engraved, photographed, or lithographed. The writing may be in pencil or ink; it may be partly printed and partly typewritten (or in any such combination). It may be placed on any material that can be easily circulated through commerce without deterioration (e. g., melting).

A written negotiable instrument is considered to be a final and complete writing for purposes of the parol evidence rule as discussed in Ch. 10. Thus, the parties to a negotiable instrument cannot change, alter, modify, or vary the terms of the writing by evidence occurring prior to or at the time of the signing of the instrument (e. g., the maker of a note cannot introduce oral or written evidence showing that he or she intended the note to be payable at a time other than that stated on the instrument). Of course, the parties can show evidence of fraud, mistake, undue influence, or duress: to do so is not to rewrite the instrument but to show that the instrument is void or voidable. Similarly, the parties can offer evidence of agreements or modifications made subsequent to the signing of the instrument; and they can generally offer oral or written evidence to explain the meaning of ambiguous terms. However, there are certain ambiguities that must be clarified and resolved according to rules of construction provided by the Uniform Commercial Code.

Section 3–118 of the Code states:

Section 3–118. Ambiguous terms and rules of construction

The following rules apply to every instrument:

* * *

(b) Handwritten terms control typewritten and printed terms, and typewritten control printed.

(c) Words control figures except that if the words are ambiguous figures control.

———

Where Section 3–118 is applicable, parol evidence is not admissible to further clarify or explain the meaning of the parties.

What is meant by the requirement that the instrument must be signed by the maker or drawer?

To say that the maker or drawer must sign the instrument is to say that he or she must affix his or her name to the writing with the intent to become bound

thereon (i. e., with the intent to assume the contractual liability growing out of the instrument). Normally, the maker or drawer does this by writing his or her name in longhand in ink on the face of the instrument, usually in the lower right hand corner. However, this is not required, and the maker or drawer can satisfy the second requirement simply by affixing a symbol representing his or her signature anywhere on the face of the instrument. The symbol may be affixed by hand or machine or by any other method (e. g., rubber stamp); it may be printed or typewritten or handwritten in pencil or ink. As Section 1–201 of the Uniform Commercial Code states: " 'Signed' includes any symbol executed or adopted by a party with present intention to authenticate a writing."

And the Official Comment to the Section states:

The inclusion of authentication in the definition of "signed" is to make clear that as the term is used in this Act a complete signature is not necessary. Authentication may be printed, stamped or written; it may be by initials or by thumbprint. It may be on any part of the document and in appropriate cases may be found in a billhead or letterhead.

———

Section 3–401 of the Code amplifies Section 1–201 as follows.

The UCC provides:

Section 3–401. Signature

(1) No person is liable on an instrument unless his signature appears thereon.

(2) A signature is made by use of any name, including any trade or assumed name, upon an instrument, or by any word or mark used in lieu of a written signature.

The Official Comment to the Section provides:

(2) A signature may be handwritten, typed, printed, or made in any other manner. It need not be subscribed, and may appear in the body of the instrument as in the case of "I, John Doe, promise to pay—" without any other signature. It may be made by mark, or even by thumbprint. It may be made in any name, including any trade name or assumed name, however false and fictitious, which is adopted for the purpose. Parol evidence is admissible to identify the signer, and when he is identified the signature is effective.

———

Note that the *Official Comment* provides that the signature may be placed on any part of the document (although, as previously stated, it is normally found in the lower right hand corner of the face of the instrument). However, unless it is clear from the signature that the party is signing as either a maker, a drawer, or an acceptor, the party will be held by law to be an indorser. This is because Section 3–402 of the Code states that "unless the instrument clearly indicates that signature is made in some other capacity it is an indorsement".

The Official Comment to Section 3–402 provides as follows:

* * * [A]ny ambiguity as to the capacity in which a signature is made must be resolved by a rule of law that it is an indorsement. Parol evidence is not admissible to show any other capacity. * * * The question is to be determined from the face of the instrument alone, and unless the instrument itself makes it clear that he has signed in some other capacity the signer must be treated as an indorser.

The indication that the signature is made in another capacity must be clear without reference to anything but the instrument. It may be found in the language used. Thus if John Doe signs after "I, John Doe, promise to pay," he is clearly a maker; and "John Doe, witness" is not liable at all. The capacity may be found in any clearly evidenced purpose of the signature, as where a drawee signing in an unusual place on the paper has no visible reason to sign at all unless he is an acceptor. Thus, by long established practice judicially noticed or otherwise established a signature in the lower right hand corner of an instrument indicates an intent to sign as the maker of a note or the drawer of a draft.

———

As to the required intent, the maker or drawer must sign the instrument, intending to become bound thereon. Obviously, if a person is tricked into signing a negotiable instrument, the required intent is not present, and the signature is not a valid one. The general rule is that anytime a person signs under a transaction that is void (as opposed to voidable), the signature is meaningless.

While it is clear that a maker or drawer can sign in almost any fashion (and in almost any place on the instrument) and still satisfy the second negotiability requirement, it is seldom a good idea to accept a negotiable instrument that has been signed in an unusual manner. This is because the burden of proving a contested signature is on the party claiming under it. While Section 3–307 of the Uniform Commercial Code provides a rebuttable presumption that all signatures are genuine, the Section also states: "When the effectiveness of a signature is put in issue (a) the burden of establishing it is on the party claiming under the signature * * *." By insisting upon a signature made "in the usual manner", it is possible to avoid difficulties of proof in the event that the signature is later contested. And it is generally much easier to discount an instrument that has been signed in the customary fashion as people feel more secure in purchasing such instruments. Of course, if the signature is not contested, the rebuttable presumption raised by Section 3–307 will operate to establish its genuineness.

May an agent sign a negotiable instrument on behalf of a maker or drawer? You will recall from Ch. 11 that an *agent* is a person who is authorized to contract on behalf of another called a *principal*. An agent enters into contracts on behalf of the principal, and the principal is bound just as though he or she had made the contracts personally. Of course, if the agent exceeds his or her authority, the principal will not be bound (the law of agency is discussed in detail in Ch. 21).

With regard to negotiable instruments, Section 3–403 of the Uniform Commercial Code provides that an agent may sign for the maker or drawer. However, Section 3–403 must be read in conjunction with Section 3–401 which states that "no person is liable on an instrument unless his signature appears thereon." Thus, if an agent signs his or her own name on a negotiable instrument without naming the principal (the maker or drawer the agent represents), the principal will not be liable on the instrument.

Section 3–403 of the Code provides:

Section 3–403. Signature by Authorized Representative

(1) A signature may be made by an agent or other representative, and his authority to make it may be established as in other cases of representation. No particular form of appointment is necessary to establish such authority.

(2) An authorized representative who signs his own name to an instrument

(a) is personally obligated if the instrument neither names the person represented nor shows that the representative signed in a representative capacity;

(b) except as otherwise established between the immediate parties, is personally obligated if the instrument names the person represented but does not show that the representative signed in a representative capacity, or if the instrument does not name the person represented but does show that the representative signed in a representative capacity.

It follows from the statement that "no particular form of appointment is necessary" that an agent's authority to sign a negotiable instrument need not be put into writing. This is so even where the instrument is given in payment of land or property falling under the Statute of Frauds: while, in most cases, the agent's authority to execute the contract would have to be in writing under the "equal dignity rules" (See Ch. 10), Section 3–403 of the Code takes precedence over such rules.

If the agent signs only the principal's name on the negotiable instrument, the principal alone is bound. If the agent signs only his or her own name without more, the agent alone is liable, and parol evidence is not admissible to identify the principal. Of course, if the agent is ultimately required to pay the instrument, he or she can sue the principal for reimbursement (including reasonable expenses).

In all other cases where the agent signs his or her own name on the negotiable instrument, the agent will be personally liable unless he or she both (1) identifies the principal on the instrument, and (2) indicates on the instrument that he or she is signing in a representative capacity. If the agent does both things, the principal again is solely liable. For example, suppose that Larry Taylor authorizes Sally Streeter to purchase George Johnson's boat for $10,300. Larry instructs Sally to put $2,000 down on the boat and sign a promissory note for the balance. If Sally signs the note—"Sally Streeter, agent for Larry Taylor"—only Larry Taylor will be bound on the instrument. If Sally signs—"Sally Streeter, Agent"— Sally will be personally liable on the instrument. However, because Sally has indicated the fact of agency without naming the principal, the instrument contains a patent ambiguity, and parol evidence is admissible to identify the principal in suits between the original parties (and/or their assignees). Once the principal is identified, he or she alone will be liable on the instrument to the original payee or his or her assignee.

Where the party suing on the instrument is not an assignee, but a holder in due course, parol evidence is not admissible, and the holder in due course can collect on the instrument from the agent. The HDC cannot collect from the principal as his or her name does not appear on the instrument as required by Section 3–401(1) of the Uniform Commercial Code. Thus, if after selling the boat to Sally Streeter, George Johnson discounts the promissory note (signed by "Sally Streeter, Agent") to a holder in due course, the HDC will be able to collect on the note from Sally. Sally will not be allowed to introduce oral or written evidence showing that Larry Taylor is her principal; and the holder in due course will not be able to proceed against Larry on the instrument.

In the event that the holder in due course cannot collect from Sally (e. g.,

where she has skipped town or is insolvent), the holder in due course can proceed against Larry Taylor—not on the negotiable instrument—but on Larry's contract to pay the $10,300 balance. By discounting the note to the holder in due course, George Johnson not only transferred his rights in the instrument, but he also assigned his rights in the underlying transaction. Thus, even though the holder in due course cannot hold Larry Taylor liable on the basis of the negotiable instrument, he or she can hold Larry liable on the basis of the assigned contract. Of course, since the sale of the boat is "for $500 or more", the holder in due course must produce a written memo signed by Larry if the contract is to be enforceable under the Statute of Frauds. If the holder in due course cannot produce such a memo, he or she will be entitled to restitution to prevent unjust enrichment.

Finally, if Sally Streeter has no authority to sign for Larry Taylor, only Sally will be liable on the instrument regardless of how and what she signs.

What is meant by the requirement that the instrument must contain a promise or order to pay?

The third requirement of negotiability is that the instrument must contain words amounting to a promise (if a note) or an order (if a draft). However, this is not to say that the word "promise" or "order" must be specifically used in the instrument. A maker who says "I engage to pay" or "I hereby contract to give" or "I certify to pay" or "the maker obliges herself to pay" (or the like) is, in effect, saying, "I promise to pay", and that is sufficient for purposes of negotiability. Similarly, a drawer who says, "Pay John Jones" (or the like) is clearly stating, "I order you to pay John Jones". On the other hand, a mere acknowledgment of a debt (e. g., "I.O.U. $10,000") does not constitute a promise to pay; nor does a mere "authorization" or "request" (e. g.,

"I request you to pay" or "I authorize you to pay") constitute an order to pay. The Uniform Commercial Code rules defining "order" and "promise" are found at Section 3–102.

The UCC provides:

Section 3–102. Definitions and index of definitions

(1) In this Article * * *

    (b) An "order" is a direction to pay and must be more than an authorization or request. It must identify the person to pay with reasonable certainty.

    (c) A "promise" is an undertaking to pay and must be more than an acknowledgment of an obligation.

———

The Official Comment to Section 3–102 provides in part:

2. * * * The prefixing of words of courtesy to the direction as "please pay" or "kindly pay"— should not lead to a holding that the direction has degenerated into a mere request. On the other hand, informal language—such as "I wish you would pay" would not qualify as an order and such an instrument would be non-negotiable [sic]. The definition of "promise" is intended to make it clear that a mere I.O.U. is not a negotiable instrument, and to change the result in occasional cases which have held that "Due Currier & Barker seventeen dollars and fourteen cents, value received," and "I borrowed from P. Shemonia the sum of five hundred dollars with four per cent interest; the borrowed money ought to be paid within four months from the above date" were promises suf-

ficient to make the instruments into notes.

———

What is meant by the requirement that the promise or order must be unconditional?

The fourth requirement of negotiability is that the promise or order to pay must be unconditional. As you will recall, negotiable instruments are designed to serve as substitutes for money and to facilitate credit transactions. If these objectives are to be accomplished, the promises and orders contained in the instruments must be unconditional. The instruments must represent obligations that are fixed and absolute—otherwise, people would not be willing to accept notes, drafts, "CD's", and checks in place of money or to extend credit on the basis of the instruments. Put simply, people must be certain that there are no strings attached to payment of negotiable instruments—that there are no contingencies or qualifications that may somehow prevent payment.

The determination of whether the promise or order is unconditional must be made by looking at the face of the instrument without more. Thus, if on the face of the instrument there is no indication of any condition to payment, the fact that the original parties agreed upon a condition is immaterial to the instrument's negotiability. Of course, the condition will be effective as between the original parties (again, the fact that an instrument is negotiable makes little or no difference to the original parties and/or their assignees). But if the instrument is transferred to a holder in due course, the condition will not operate as a defense to payment. For example, suppose that Larry Taylor signs a negotiable promissory note, unconditional on its face, designating George Johnson as payee. As Larry signs the note, he says to George,

"I will pay this money only if I am able to sell my apartment house in the next 30 days." If Larry fails to sell the apartment house within the designated time, the failure of condition will serve as a defense to payment against George or his assignee. However, it will not serve as a defense to payment against a holder in due course of the instrument. Thus, if George or his assignee has transferred the instrument to a holder in due course, Larry will have to pay though the condition precedent has failed to occur. Of course, if the condition is stated on the face of the note, the note is nonnegotiable, and a transferee of the instrument can have only the rights of an assignee (i. e., he or she will "stand in the shoes" of George Johnson).

Still, there are many items that can appear on the face of the instrument without rendering the instrument conditional. For example, a mere reference to the underlying transaction, document, or consideration upon which the instrument is based does not make the promise or order to pay conditional. Thus, a statement on the face of a promissory note that the note is executed "as per" or "in accordance with the written agreement made this date with the payee" does not impair negotiability. Nor is negotiability impaired where Larry Taylor states on the face of his promissory note that "this note is executed in consideration of the sale and delivery to me of George Johnson's boat". The Uniform Commercial Code states that conditions will not be implied or "read into" an instrument: thus, there is no implication that the consideration must be performed (i. e., that the boat must be sold and delivered) before Larry's duty to pay will arise. Again, as long as the note is in the hands of the original parties or their assignees, the defense of failure of consideration is a good one. But where the instrument has been transferred to a holder in due course, the maker (Larry Taylor) will have to pay

despite the fact that there has been no sale and no delivery (of course, the maker, in this case, can bring suit against the payee for breach of the underlying agreement).

Sometimes, however, a statement goes beyond a "mere reference" to clearly and expressly condition the promise or order on performance of the underlying transaction or consideration. Such a statement destroys negotiability. For example, a statement in a note that the instrument "IS SUBJECT TO" another document or "IS GOVERNED BY" another document or agreement is more than a mere reference—the statement clearly and expressly conditions the maker's promise to pay, and, in doing so, renders the instrument nonnegotiable.

A reference in an instrument to a particular fund from which payment is to be made does not condition the promise or order to pay unless it is stated that payment is to be made "ONLY" from that fund (in which case, the promise or order is conditioned upon the existence of the particular fund, and the instrument is nonnegotiable). Thus, the general rule is that a negotiable instrument must be based on the general credit of the obligor. However, there are two exceptions under the Uniform Commercial Code where an unstrument may be negotiable even though it is limited to payment out of certain funds or assets. The first arises where an instrument issued by a governmental agency or unit is made payable only out of certain governmental funds or accounts. Such instruments are considered negotiable because the Uniform Commercial Code says they are. Secondly, an instrument issued by a partnership (see Ch. 22), unincorporated association, trust (see Ch. 29), or estate (see Ch. 30) is considered negotiable under the Code even though it is made payable solely out of the assets of the issuing party (unincorporated associations include fraternal groups, labor unions, nonprofit associations, credit unions, professional societies, and the like).

Finally, a promise or order is not made conditional by a recital that the instrument is part of a secured transaction. Thus, a statement that "this note is secured by a mortgage on the residence located at 3516 S.W. Lansing Street, Memphis, Tennessee" does not impair negotiability. The statement merely identifies the basic underlying transaction; it does not create any implied condition that the security given must be sufficient or the duty to pay will not arise.

By way of summary, the Uniform Commercial Code rules regarding the fourth requirement of negotiability are found at Section 3–105 as follows.

The UCC provides:

Section 3–105. When Promise or Order Unconditional

(1) A promise or order otherwise unconditional is not made conditional by the fact that the instrument

(a) is subject to *implied* or *constructive* conditions;

(b) states its consideration, whether performed or promised, or the transaction which gave rise to the instrument, or that the promise or order is made or the instrument matures *in accordance with* or *"as per"* such transaction; or

(c) refers to or states that it arises out of a separate agreement or refers to a separate agreement for rights as to prepayment or acceleration ["prepayment" and "acceleration" are discussed in the chapter section entitled, "What is meant by the requirement that the instrument must be payable on demand or at a definite time?"];

(d) states that it is drawn under a letter of credit [defined and discussed in Ch. 19]; or

(e) states that it is secured, whether by mortgage, reservation of title or otherwise; or

(f) *indicates* a particular account to be debited or any other fund or source from which reimbursement is expected; or

(g) is limited to payment out of a particular fund or the proceeds of a particular source, if the instrument is issued by a government or governmental agency or unit; or

(h) is limited to payment out of the entire assets of a partnership, unincorporated association, trust or estate by or on behalf of which the instrument is issued.

(2) A promise or order *is not unconditional* if the instrument

(a) states that it is *subject to* or *governed by* any other agreement; or

(b) states that it is to be paid *only* out of a particular fund or source except as provided in this section. [Emphasis supplied.]

What is meant by the requirement that the promise or order must be to pay a sum certain?

Again, if commercial instruments are to accomplish the dual objectives of serving as money substitutes and facilitating credit transactions, the instruments must be payable on their face in a definite amount—that is, in a *sum certain*. Otherwise, people would be unable to determine the worth of the instruments; as a result, they would be unwilling to accept commercial paper in place of cash or to extend credit on the basis of the instruments.

However, this is not to say that the precise sum payable must always be stated with absolute certainty. It is enough if the party in possession of the instrument can determine the precise sum payable by looking at the face of the instrument and making whatever mathematical computations are necessary without going to any outside source. For example, a promissory note containing a promise to pay $10,000 on demand with interest at the rate of 10 percent satisfies the "sum certain" requirement. Though the amount of interest to be paid is unknown at the time the instrument is issued, it is a relatively simple matter for the party in possession of the note to compute the interest owing at the time he or she makes demand for payment. The same is true where an instrument provides for different rates of interest before and after a specified date; and where an instrument payable at a definite time provides for a fixed rate of discount if the instrument is paid prior to its due date and for a fixed rate of increase if the instrument is paid after its due date. In each case, the party in possession of the instrument can easily compute the sum certain owing at the time the payment is made.

The Uniform Commercial Code creates two exceptions to the rule that the sum certain must be ascertainable from the face of the instrument without more. The first is an instrument providing for the payment of collection costs and attorneys fees in the event that payment is not made on the due date. Though it is necessary to go beyond the face of the instrument to determine the amount of costs and fees chargeable, the Code provides that the sum certain requirement is satisfied. The second exception is an instrument payable either with or less *exchange* at the current rate. Exchange is simply the difference between the values of two currencies from different countries. Be-

cause exchange is determined by supply and demand of the currency itself, it fluctuates from day to day, and it is therefore determinable only by looking beyond the face of the instrument. Nevertheless, the Uniform Commercial Code provides that instruments payable with or less exchange at the current rate satisfy the fifth requirement of negotiability.

In all other cases, the sum certain must be determinable from the face of the instrument alone. Thus, an instrument payable "with interest at the current rate" is nonnegotiable because the current rate of interest cannot be determined without reference to outside sources. The same holds true for an instrument payable "at the bank rate": the bank rate changes from period to period and cannot be determined from the face of the instrument itself. And, finally, where the principal to be paid is "indexed" to the Consumer Price Index to offset the effects of inflation, the sum is "uncertain" (it cannot be ascertained from the face of the instrument alone), and the instrument is nonnegotiable.

The Uniform Commercial Code provisions governing the fifth requirement of negotiability are found at Section 3–106 as follows.

The UCC provides:

Section 3–106. Sum Certain

(1) The sum payable is a sum certain even though it is to be paid

  (a) with stated interest or by stated installments; or

  (b) with stated different rates of interest before and after default or a specified date; or

  (c) with a stated discount or addition if paid before or after the date fixed for payment; or

  (d) with exchange or less exchange, whether at a fixed rate or at the current rate; or

(e) with costs of collection or an attorney's fee or both upon default.

(2) Nothing in this section shall validate any term which is otherwise illegal [i. e., the Section does not make legal anything that is illegal under state usury laws prohibiting excessive rates of interest, see Ch. 9].

What is meant by the requirement that the instrument must be payable in money?

The Uniform Commercial Code adopts a formal definition of "money" at Section 1–201 as follows: " 'Money' means a medium of exchange authorized or adopted by a *domestic or foreign government* as a part of its currency." (Emphasis supplied.) And Section 3–107 (1) of the Code provides: "An instrument is payable in money if the medium of exchange in which it is payable is money at the time the instrument is made. * * *" Thus, the test of whether an instrument is payable in money is whether the instrument is payable in a medium of exchange used as currency by a domestic or foreign government at the time the instrument is issued. The fact that the domestic or foreign government thereafter stops using the medium of exchange and adopts a new currency does not impair the instrument's negotiability.

Note that the medium of exchange used in an instrument must form part of the official *government* currency of a foreign or domestic country. Unofficial "currency" in use in a particular community or by a particular group of people does not qualify as "money" for purposes of the sixth requirement of negotiability. The *Official Comment* to Code Section 3–107 makes this clear.

The Official Comment provides:

* * * [The Code] rejects the contention sometimes advanced that "money" includes any medium of exchange current and accepted in the particular community, whether it be gold dust, beaver pelts, or cigarettes in occupied Germany. Such unusual "currency" is necessarily of uncertain and fluctuating value, and an instrument intended to pass generally in commerce as negotiable may not be made payable thereon.

Thus, a promise to pay a sum certain in British sterling, French francs, Italian lira, Japanese yen, or any other recognized currency of a foreign government is a promise to pay in money. But a promise to pay "three ounces of gold" is not a promise to pay in money, and the instrument containing the promise is non-negotiable.

Even where the sum certain is stated in an officially sanctioned foreign currency, the instrument is deemed payable in an equivalent number of American dollars unless the instrument *expressly requires* payment in the foreign currency. This is the rule of UCC Section 3–107(2).

The UCC provides:

(2) A promise or order to pay a sum stated in a foreign currency is for a sum certain in money and, unless a different medium of payment is specified in the instrument, may be satisfied by payment of that number of dollars which the stated foreign currency will purchase at the buying sight rate for that currency on the day on which the instrument is payable or, if payable on demand, on the day of demand. If such an instrument specifies a foreign currency as the medium of payment

the instrument is payable in that currency.

The Official Comment to the Section states:

* * * Under subsection (2) the presumption is, unless the instrument otherwise specifies, that the obligation may be satisfied by payment in dollars in an amount determined by the buying sight rate for the foreign currency on the day the instrument becomes payable. Inasmuch as the buying sight rate will fluctuate from day to day, it might be argued that an instrument expressed in a foreign currency but actually payable in dollars is not for a "sum certain." Subsection (2) makes it clear that for the purposes of negotiability under this Article such an instrument, despite exchange fluctuations, is for a sum certain.

What is meant by the requirement that the instrument must contain no promise or order other than the promise or order to pay a sum certain in money?

An instrument is nonnegotiable if it contains any promise or order in addition to the promise or order to pay a sum certain in money. Thus, a note in which the maker promises "to pay $5,000 AND to paint the payee's house" is nonnegotiable. So is a note in which the maker promises "to pay $5,000 OR to paint the payee's house" (the fact that the promises are phrased in the alternative does not save the instrument's negotiability). The maker of a note must promise to pay money only: if, in addition to promising to pay money, he or she promises to render services, sell goods, give an option, or do anything else, the instrument, though a valid contract, is nonnegotiable.

Again, the Uniform Commercial Code carves out a number of exceptions to the general rule. The Code provides that certain promises pertaining to security for payment of the obligation and/or relating to enforcement of the obligation in the event of default (failure to pay) may be included in the instrument without destroying negotiability. For example, with regard to instruments secured by collateral (e. g., corporate stocks or bonds), the inclusion of a power to sell the collateral in the event of default does not destroy negotiability. Nor is negotiability impaired by a promise to provide additional collateral if the present collateral is deemed insufficient to cover the amount owing and to accelerate performance (i. e., make the entire debt fall due immediately) if the additional collateral is not provided. Of course, any demand by the obligee for additional collateral or for acceleration of payment or performance must be made in good faith. The Uniform Commercial Code deals with "options to accelerate at will" at Section 1–208 as follows.

The UCC provides:

A term providing that one party or his successor in interest may accelerate payment or performance or require collateral or additional collateral "at will" or "when he deems himself insecure" or in words of similar import shall be construed to mean that he shall have power to do so only if he in good faith believes that the prospect of payment or performance is impaired. The burden of establishing lack of good faith is on the party against whom the power has been exercised.

It must be emphasized that we are talking about instruments already secured by collateral. If the obligor on an unsecured instrument promises on the face of the instrument to deposit collateral on the good faith demand of the obligee, the promise is held to be a promise in addition to the promise or order to pay money, and the instrument is nonnegotiable.

Without impairing negotiability, a party issuing an instrument may promise on the face of the instrument to pay the payee's costs and attorney's fees in the event of default. The issuing party may even authorize the person in possession of the instrument to enter a confession of judgment if the instrument is not paid when due (authorizing him or her to enter a confession of judgment at any other time will destroy negotiability). *Black's Law Dictionary* defines a "confession of judgment" as "the act of a debtor in permitting judgment to be entered against him by his creditor without the institution of legal proceedings of any kind." [1]

However, it should be mentioned that some states prohibit provisions for costs and attorney's fees, and several states do not permit confession of judgment clauses in instruments arising out of consumer sales transactions. Where the provisions are illegal under state law, the Uniform Commercial Code will not serve to validate them.

What is meant by the requirement that an instrument must be payable on demand or at a definite time?

Again, if negotiable instruments are to serve as substitutes for money and facilitate credit transactions, the instruments must state on their face with certainty the time for payment. Thus, the eighth requirement of negotiability is that a negotiable instrument must be payable on demand or at a definite time.

An instrument is payable *on demand* when it states that it is so payable or when it provides no set time for payment. Thus, an instrument that states "payable on demand" or "payable at sight" or "payable upon presentation" is payable on demand. So is an instrument that contains no maturity date. Of course, checks (which set no specific time

for payment) are always payable on demand. Even a postdated check is so payable: postdating a check does not impair negotiability or prevent immediate transfer of the instrument but simply makes the check payable after the date stated on the check.

As to when an instrument is payable *at a definite time,* Section 3–109 of the Uniform Commercial Code states.

The UCC provides:

(1) An instrument is payable at a definite time if by its terms it is payable

(a) on or before a stated date or at a fixed period after a stated date;

(b) at a fixed period after sight;

(c) at a definite time subject to any acceleration;

(d) at a definite time subject to extension at the option of the holder, or to extension to a further definite time at the option of the maker or acceptor or automatically upon or after a specified act or event.

(2) An instrument which by its terms is otherwise payable only upon an act or event uncertain as to time of occurrence is not payable at a definite time even though the act or event has occurred.

———

Section 3–109 is easy to understand if you consider it subsection by subsection.

Subsection (1)(a) embraces instruments payable "on or before a stated date or at a fixed period after a stated date". Thus, an instrument payable "on December 1, 1981" or "on or before December 1, 1981" or "60 days after date" (assuming, in the latter case, that the instrument is dated) is payable at a definite time.

1. Henry Campbell Black, *Black's Law Dictionary*, Revised Fourth Edition, West Publishing Co., 1968, p. 978.

Although an instrument payable "on or before" a specified date may appear to be uncertain as to time of payment, it is really no more uncertain than a demand instrument which is payable when the party in possession decides to collect it.

Subsection (1)(b) refers to drafts payable "at a fixed period after sight". Thus, a draft payable "60 days after sight" is payable at a definite time. The party in possession of the draft must present it for acceptance to the party expected to pay; the draft will be payable 60 days following the acceptance. To a large extent, the party in possession of the sight draft controls the time of payment by deciding when to present the instrument for acceptance. (Remember, only drafts need to be presented for acceptance: the drawee of a draft has no way of knowing about the draft until the instrument is presented to him or her for acceptance or payment. The maker of a note, on the other hand, promises to pay the instrument at the time he or she signs it.)

Subsection (1)(c) deals with instruments payable "at a definite time subject to any acceleration". Thus, if the time for payment of an instrument is otherwise definite, the fact that the instrument is subject to acceleration (i. e., subject to having payment fall due sooner) does not render the time indefinite. Such an instrument is actually more certain as to time of payment than is demand paper: unlike demand paper, there is a definite time beyond which payment of the instrument cannot run (i. e., the instrument is payable "on a certain date or sooner").

Thus, an instrument made payable on a specified date subject to acceleration at the option of one of the parties (either the maker, acceptor, or party in possession of the instrument) is payable at a definite time. This would include an instrument payable "on December 1, 1981 or sooner if the party in possession so

chooses." Of course, the party in possession must exercise the option to accelerate in good faith. As noted previously, Section 1–208 of the Uniform Commercial Code states in part that "a term providing that one party * * * may accelerate payment * * * shall be construed to mean that he shall have the power to do so only if he in good faith believes that the prospect of payment * * * is impaired."

Similarly, an instrument made payable at a set time subject to acceleration automatically upon the happening of a specified event is also payable at a definite time. Frequently, for example, the full amount owing on an installment note will fall due automatically if any one installment of principal or interest is not paid on time.

Subsection (1)(d) talks of instruments payable "at a definite time subject to extension at the option of the holder, or to extension to a further definite time at the option of the maker or acceptor or automatically upon or after a specified act or event." Thus, an instrument made payable at a set date subject to extension at the option of the party in possession of the instrument is payable at a definite time. This is so even where no time limit is placed upon the extension. The reason is that the party in possession always has the right to waive the due date of the instrument regardless of whether he or she has an option to extend. To formally provide the party with such an option does not make the time for payment any more uncertain or affect negotiability in any way. However, the party in possession may never extend the time of payment over the objection of the maker or drawee. Section 3–118(f) of the Uniform Commercial Code provides: "A holder may not exercise his option to extend an instrument over the objection of a maker or acceptor or other party who * * * tenders full payment when the instrument is due." Thus, if the maker or drawee insists upon paying the instrument when it is due, and tenders full payment at that time, the instrument is discharged notwithstanding the desire of the party in possession to extend payment.

Similarly, an option on the part of the maker or acceptor (as opposed to the party in possession) to extend payment for a further *definite period* of time does not make the time for payment uncertain or otherwise interfere with negotiability. So long as the extension is for a definite period, there is an ultimate date beyond which payment cannot run (the instrument is thus similar to an instrument payable at a definite time subject to acceleration). If the instrument grants the maker or acceptor an option to extend, but fails to specify the length of extension, the time for payment is still certain as Section 3–118(f) of the Uniform Commercial Code states: "[U]nless otherwise specified consent to extension authorizes a single extension for not longer than the original period." But where the instrument expressly provides that there is no limit on the time that the maker or acceptor may extend, the instrument is not payable on demand or at a definite time and the instrument is nonnegotiable (unlike the party in possession, the maker or acceptor has no right to "waive" the due date of the instrument).

Also, an instrument made payable at a set date subject to automatic extension for a further *definite period* upon the happening of some specified event or contingency is certain as to time of payment and is negotiable. For example, a note payable "on December 1, 1981, if the maker is still working in Baltimore, Maryland, but, if he is not, this note shall be automatically extended for three months" is payable at a definite time (the note is similar to a promise to pay at a definite time subject to acceleration).

Again, if the instrument provides for automatic extension but fails to specify the length of the extension, the law will imply a single extension for not longer than the original period.

Finally, *Subsection (2)* provides that "an instrument which by its terms is otherwise payable only upon an act or event uncertain as to time of occurrence is not payable at a definite time even though the act or event has occurred." Prior to passage of the Uniform Commercial Code, an instrument payable upon the happening of an event certain to occur, though uncertain as to time of occurrence, was considered payable at a definite time. For example, in pre-Code days, an instrument payable "when the first rain begins in the fall" or "when the first frost occurs" or "when the war ends" was payable at a definite time (all these events were certain to occur though uncertain as to time of occurrence). And it was common in pre-Code days for an individual to anticipate an inheritance by borrowing money and signing a negotiable note promising to repay the money six months after the death of a relative. Thus, a note payable "six months after the death of my grandfather, John" was payable at a definite time (and therefore negotiable) because the death of the maker's grandfather was certain to occur —the fact that the time of death was uncertain was immaterial as to negotiability.

However, under Subsection (2) of the Code, an instrument payable upon the happening of an event certain to occur, though uncertain as to time of occurrence, is not payable at a definite time and is not made so payable by the fact that the act or event has already occurred. Thus, a note payable "six months after the death of my grandfather, John" is uncertain as to time of payment and is nonnegotiable. This is so even where the maker's grandfather is dead at the time the maker signs the note: negotiability must be determinable from the face of the instrument without more—it would not be fair to force a party to look outside the instrument to determine the time of payment.

Still, it is sometimes possible to accomplish the same result by making an instrument payable at a definite time subject to automatic acceleration upon the happening of a specified event. For example, a note might be made payable "ten years from today's date, or six months after the death of my grandfather, John, if that event occurs before the expiration of the ten years." Here, there is an ultimate time certain ("ten years from today's date"), and the instrument looks like any other instrument payable at a definite time subject to automatic acceleration upon the happening of an event.

Finally, it should be added that an instrument payable upon the happening of an event *uncertain* to occur is not payable at a definite time and is therefore nonnegotiable. Examples include instruments payable "when convenient" or "when I get married" or "when the corn crop is harvested" or "when my children graduate from college". As none of these events may ever occur, there is no "time certain" for payment.

What is meant by the requirement that the instrument must be payable "to order" or "to bearer"?

The ninth and last requirement of negotiability is that the instrument must be payable "to order" or "to bearer". The law requires the use of these so-called "magic words of negotiability" as proof that the parties truly intend the consequences that accompany negotiability. It is important that a party who signs a negotiable instrument realize that the instrument may be transferred to others whom he or she will have to pay even though a valid defense to payment exists against the original payee. The party's use of the words "to order" or "to bear-

er" indicates that he or she understands this and assents to it.

Although the specific words "to order" or "to bearer" appear in 99 out of 100 negotiable instruments, words clearly equivalent to these may also be used without impairing negotiability. Insofar as *order paper* is concerned, Section 3–110 of the Uniform Commercial Code provides as follows.

The UCC provides:

Section 3–110. Payable to Order

(1) An instrument is payable to order when by its terms it is payable to the order or assigns of any person therein specified with reasonable certainty, or to him or his order, or when it is conspicuously designated on its face as "exchange" or the like and names a payee.

———

Thus, an instrument that says "pay Thomas Martin or his assigns" or "pay to Thomas Martin, exchange" is just as negotiable as one that says "pay to the order of Thomas Martin". However, the words "assigns" or "exchange" are seldom used—the words "pay to the order of" appear in almost all order instruments.

Section 3–110(1) of the Code continues.

It provides:

* * * [An order instrument] may be payable to the order of

(a) the maker or drawer; or

(b) the drawee; or

(c) a payee who is not maker, drawer or drawee; or

(d) two or more payees together or in the alternative; or

(e) an estate, trust or fund, in which case it is payable to the order of the representative of such estate, trust or fund or his successors;

(f) an office, or an officer by his title as such in which case it is payable to the principal but the incumbent of the office or his successors may act as if he or they were the holder; or

(g) a partnership or unincorporated association, in which case it is payable to the partnership or association and may be indorsed or transferred by any person thereto authorized.

(2) An indorsement not payable to order is not made so payable by such words as "payable upon return of this instrument properly indorsed."

———

You will note that, under Subsection 1(d), an instrument may be payable to the order of two or more persons together (e. g., "John, Bill, and Emily") or in the alternative (e. g., "John, Bill, or Emily"). With regard to such instruments, Section 3–116 of the Code states.

The UCC provides:

An instrument payable to the order of two or more persons

(a) if in the alternative is payable to any one of them and may be negotiated, discharged or enforced by any of them who has possession of it;

(b) if not in the alternative is payable to all of them and may be negotiated, discharged or enforced only by all of them.

———

Thus, an instrument payable "to the order of John, Bill *and* Emily" is payable to and transferable by all of the parties only, while an instrument payable "to the

order of John, Bill, *or* Emily" is payable to and transferable by any one of the parties.

You will also note, that under Section 3–110(2), an instrument lacking the magic words of negotiability (or their clear equivalents) will not be made payable "to order" or "to bearer" by a statement that "this instrument is payable upon its being returned properly indorsed."

Turning to *bearer paper,* it is necessary to consider Sections 3–110(3) and 3–111 of the Uniform Commercial Code. The former provides: "An instrument made payable both to order and to bearer is payable to order unless the bearer words are handwritten or typewritten." And the latter Section states.

It says:

An instrument is payable to bearer when by its terms it is payable to

(a) bearer or the order of bearer;

(b) a specified person or bearer; or

(c) "cash" or the order of "cash", or any other indication which does not purport to designate a specific payee.

———

Thus, an instrument that says "pay to bearer" or "pay to the order of bearer" is clearly bearer paper. So is an instrument that says "pay to Thomas Martin or bearer" (the "or" makes it bearer paper) or "pay cash" or "pay to the order of cash" or "pay sundries" or the like. But what about an instrument that says "pay to the order of Thomas Martin or bearer"? Here, Section 3–110(3) of the Code controls, and unless the word "bearer" is handwritten or typewritten, the instrument is order paper. The reason for the rule is that many printed negotiable instrument forms used by the public include such language as "payable to the order of _____ or bearer". Frequently, a maker or drawer will fill in the name of a specific payee, intending the instrument to be order paper, without even realizing that the "or bearer" part of the language is present. Thus, unless the word "bearer" is handwritten or typewritten (indicating an intent that the instrument be bearer paper) the words "or bearer" will be disregarded.

While words clearly equivalent to the magic words "to order" or "to bearer" may be used without impairing negotiability, it is a good idea to use the magic words exclusively. If a dispute arises as to whether other words are clearly equivalent to the magic words, the courts are likely to find that they are not. As the *Official Comment* to Code Section 3–104 states.

The Official Comment provides:

* * * [It] is not intended to mean that the instrument must follow the language of this section, or that one term may not be recognized as clearly the equivalent of another, as in the case of "I undertake" instead of "I promise" or "pay to holder" instead of "pay to bearer." It does mean that either the language of the section or a clear equivalent must be found, and that in doubtful cases the decision should be *against negotiability*. (Emphasis added.)

———

To be safe, then, a party should use the magic words "to order" or "to bearer" and not rely on substitutes. Without the magic words or their *clear* equivalents, even an instrument that states on its face "this instrument is negotiable" may be held nonnegotiable for failing to satisfy the ninth requirement. (Some lawyers maintain that such a statement is clearly equivalent to the magic words as it indicates an unmistakable intent on the part of the maker or drawer to create

a negotiable instrument. Nevertheless, a number of courts that have considered the issue have ruled against negotiability.)

Of course, as between the original parties, it makes little difference whether the instrument is negotiable or nonnegotiable, or whether it is order paper or bearer paper. These things become important only as the instrument moves into the hands of other parties. Thus, as you will learn in the next few sections dealing with the creation of "holders" and "holders in due course", it makes a great deal of difference to a thief, finder, or transferee of an instrument whether the instrument is negotiable or nonnegotiable, and (if negotiable) whether it is order paper or bearer paper.

Assuming that all nine requirements for negotiability are satisfied (i.e., that the instrument is negotiable), what are the next important questions that must be answered?

Remember always that a negotiable instrument is a "contract" first and a "special contract" second. As stated previously, the fact that an instrument is negotiable makes little or no difference as between the original parties to the instrument. As between these parties, contract law (as studied in Chapters 7 through 10) will provide the answers to any legal questions that arise. For example, say that one party pays another in advance for work to be done in the future. Regardless of whether the party pays in cash or by negotiable check, he or she will have a right to the return of his or her money in the event of failure of consideration. And if fraud, duress, or undue influence is present, the contract, whether oral, written, or embodied in a negotiable instrument, will be void or voidable in accordance with normal contract rules.

Just like any other writing, a negotiable instrument may serve as a written memo under the Statute of Frauds, making the underlying contract enforceable against the maker or drawer of the instrument. And the instrument may constitute a final expression of the contract for purposes of the parol evidence rule (where this is so, the parties may not introduce oral or written evidence occurring prior to or at the time of the signing of the instrument to change, alter, vary, or modify the terms of the writing).

Thus, as between the original parties to a negotiable instrument, the ordinary rules of contract law are controlling. And the ordinary rules may still be controlling though the instrument has moved out of the hands of the original parties and into the hands of third parties. For example, if the original party *assigns* the instrument rather than *negotiates* it to a third party, the contract rules regarding assignment (and not the special rules of negotiability) will govern, and the assignee of the instrument will "stand in the shoes" of his or her assignor. Along this line, it should not be assumed that because an instrument is negotiable it can be transferred only through a negotiation. Like any other contract, a negotiable instrument may be assigned (although, as a practical matter, such instruments are assigned but infrequently) if the transferor clearly expresses an intent to transfer by assignment rather than by negotiation. Usually, a transferor who desires to assign will write the assignment on a separate sheet of paper unattached to the negotiable instrument itself. As you will learn shortly, an effort to assign a negotiable instrument by writing the "assignment" on the back of the instrument may well be deemed a negotiation and not an assignment in accordance with Section 3-202 of the Uniform Commercial Code.

Of course, even where an instrument is negotiated as opposed to assigned to a third party, the fact that the instrument is negotiable may make no difference whatsoever. If, as is often the case, there are

no defenses to payment good as against the original obligee, the obligor will have to pay the instrument regardless of whether the transferee is a holder in due course or merely an assignee of the instrument (i. e., where there are no defenses, the transferee of the instrument need not rely upon "special rules" or a "superior position" to collect payment—to "stand in the shoes" of the transferor is to have an unqualified right to payment.)

It is only where there is a defense to payment good as against the original obligee *and* the negotiable instrument is transferred to a third party who qualifies as a holder in due course (HDC) that the special rules of negotiability may come into play to permit the HDC to collect payment from the obligor even though the original obligee could not collect payment.

So, once it is established that an instrument is negotiable, it is important to determine (1) whether there is any defense to payment good as against the original obligee, and (2) whether the instrument has moved out of the hands of the original parties and into the hands of a holder in due course. If the answer to both questions is yes, the special rules of negotiability will govern payment of the instrument. Defenses to payment are discussed in Chapter 14; holders and holders in due course are treated in the remainder of this chapter.

How does a party become a holder?

You will recall from Ch. 12 that UCC Section 1-201 defines a "holder" as "a person who is in possession of * * * an * * * instrument drawn, issued, or indorsed to him or to his order or to bearer or in blank." Thus, for a person to qualify as a holder, (1) he or she must have possession of a negotiable instrument; and (2) the instrument must be drawn, issued, or indorsed to the person or to his or her order or to bearer or in blank.

Generally, the first requirement poses little problem since people who claim to be holders of an instrument (and therefore holders in due course) seem always to have physical possession of the instrument. It is the second requirement which demands more explanation since there are really four events that will satisfy the requirement—either an issuance, a mere taking of possession of bearer paper, a negotiation, or a mere taking of possession of order paper made payable to one's own order.

First, the instrument, whether a note, draft, or check, etc., may be originally *issued* to a named party or to bearer. Section 3–102 of the Uniform Commercial Code defines "issuance" as the first delivery of an instrument to a holder. For example, a note made payable "to the order of George Johnson" is issued by delivery of the note to George: issuance makes George, the named payee, a holder. A note made payable "to bearer" is issued by its initial delivery to anyone—thus, the first person to receive the note becomes a holder. It is a fact that a person who becomes a holder through issuance of a negotiable instrument seldom qualifies as a holder in due course. This is because of the requirement that a holder in due course must take a negotiable instrument without knowledge of any possible defense to payment. Usually, the named payee of order paper or the first person to receive bearer paper through delivery is an original party to the contract who would have such knowledge. However, there are exceptions where the payee, whether named or merely a "bearer", is not an original party and so can qualify as a holder is due course (the exceptions are dealt with in a following section).

Second, an instrument made payable "to bearer" or indorsed "in blank" (as you will learn shortly, a "blank indorsement" converts order paper into bearer paper) may be taken into possession by a party. It makes no difference how the possession is acquired, or whether the party is a purchaser, a donee, a finder, or a thief. Section 1–201 defines "holder" to include one in possession of bearer paper; thus, so long as the party has possession of the instrument, he or she is a holder.

Third, and perhaps most importantly, the instrument may be *transferred* to a party through what is termed a *negotiation.* Negotiation is primarily what is contemplated by Section 1–201 when it states that a "holder means a person who is in possession of an instrument * * * *indorsed to him or to his order or to bearer or in blank.*" (Emphasis supplied.) Whereas "issuance" refers to the original delivery of the instrument to the payee, whether named or unnamed, "negotiation" refers to the subsequent transfer of the instrument to a third party. Negotiation is accomplished in one of two ways depending on whether the instrument is bearer paper or order paper.

Bearer paper (commercial paper made payable "to bearer") is negotiated simply by delivery of the instrument. UCC Section 1–201 defines "delivery" as the voluntary transfer of possession of an instrument from one person to another. For example, suppose that Larry Taylor signs a negotiable promissory note for $10,000 to pay for the boat he is purchasing from George Johnson. Larry makes the instrument payable, not "to the order of George Johnson", but "to bearer". By issuing the note to George, the unnamed payee, Larry makes George a holder. George may now negotiate the note simply by delivering it to a third person. Thus, if George immediately discounts the note to Sally Streeter for $9,300, delivery of the note to Sally constitutes a negotiation, making Sally a holder of the instrument. (Remember, to "discount" an instrument is to sell it prior to its due date for an amount less than its face value.) If Sally, in turn, immediately discounts the note to Dick Drynan for $9,450, Sally's delivery of the note to Dick also constitutes a negotiation, and Dick becomes a holder of the note. In each case, delivery is all that is required to negotiate the bearer paper so as to make the transferee a holder.

It follows that even a thief or finder of bearer paper can negotiate the paper by delivering it to a third person who will become a holder of the instrument. (The thief or finder is also a holder, not on the basis of negotiation, but by reason of having taken possession of the bearer paper.) Because bearer paper has much of the circulation potential and risk of money, it should be handled with the same care and caution.

Order paper (commercial paper made payable "to the order of" a named payee), on the other hand, can never be negotiated by a thief or finder: to negotiate such paper requires not only delivery of the instrument, but also indorsement by the payee. The payee indorses the paper by signing his or her name on the back of the instrument. Returning to our example, suppose that Larry Taylor makes the $10,000 promissory note payable, not "to bearer", but "to the order of George Johnson". As before, George may immediately discount the note to Sally Streeter; but, this time, in order to negotiate the instrument so as to make Sally a holder, George must both *indorse* the note and *deliver* the note to Sally. Delivery alone will not suffice. Of course, if Sally has given value for the instrument, she will have a specifically enforceable right to Larry's indorsement in the event that he delivers the instrument to her unindorsed.

UCC Section 3–201 provides:

Section 3–201. Transfer: Right to Indorsement

* * *

(3) Unless otherwise agreed any transfer for value of an instrument not then payable to bearer gives the transferee the specifically enforceable right to have the unqualified endorsement of the transferor. Negotiation takes effect only when the indorsement is made and until that time there is no presumption that the transferee is the owner.

It is only upon acquiring Larry's indorsement that Sally will become a holder of the instrument.

Now whether an instrument is originally issued as order paper or bearer paper, it may be negotiated many many times before it is finally presented for payment. And a very interesting thing may occur as the instrument is transferred from party to party. Each time the paper is further negotiated, it may be changed from order paper to bearer paper, or vice versa, depending on the way the instrument is indorsed. For example, if a named payee indorses order paper *in blank* (i. e., signs only his or her name on the back of the instrument), the order paper is converted into bearer paper. Thus, before delivering the note to Sally Streeter, George Johnson might indorse the promissory note made payable to his order as follows:

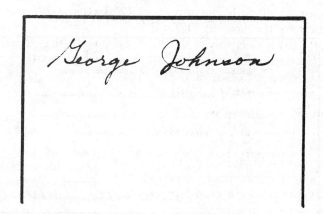

The *blank indorsement* converts the order paper into bearer paper, and Sally Streeter may further negotiate the instrument by delivery alone.

The corollary is that a *special indorsement* (i. e., one directing the maker or drawee to pay a specific named individual) changes bearer paper into order paper. This is so whether the paper is originally issued "to bearer" or merely indorsed in blank. In our example, it is clear that Sally Streeter may further negotiate the promissory note to Dick Drynan by delivery alone. Suppose, however, that Sally decides to indorse the note. If she indorses in blank, the instrument will remain bearer paper; if she indorses specially, the instrument will change into order paper, and Dick may further negotiate the instrument only by both indorsing and delivering the note. Sally's special indorsement might look like this:

Pay Dick Drynan
Sally Streeter

You will note that a special indorsement need not contain the "magic words" of negotiability—"to order" or "to bearer". The "magic words" are required only on the face of the instrument; their use in indorsements is optional.

Now let's consider a more complicated example. Suppose that Larry Taylor signs a negotiable promissory note payable "to the order of George Johnson" on demand in the amount of $10,000. Larry issues the note to George, whereafter the instrument changes hands (and changes from order paper to bearer paper and vice versa) as depicted in the following illustration.

THE FACE OF THE INSTRUMENT

February 15, 1980

ON DEMAND, the undersigned promises to pay

to the order of _____ GEORGE JOHNSON _____

Ten thousand and no/100----------------DOLLARS

Together with interest thereon from the date

hereof until paid at the rate of ___9___ per

cent per annum.

Lawrence Taylor

The following transactions occur:

THE BACK OF THE INSTRUMENT

(1) George Johnson indorses in blank and delivers the note to Sally Streeter. The blank indorsement converts the instrument into bearer paper.

(2) Though Sally may negotiate the note by delivery alone, she chooses to specially indorse and deliver the note to Dick Drynan. The special indorsement changes the instrument back into order paper.

(3) Dick must both indorse and deliver the order paper in order to negotiate it: he indorses in blank and delivers the note to Buzz Cort. Once again, the note is bearer paper.

(4) Buzz does not indorse the bearer paper. He negotiates it simply by delivering it to Martha Hiatt. (As you will learn in the next chapter, a party who indorses an instrument incurs certain contractual responsibilities by reason of the indorsement. Buzz has avoided these contractual responsibilities; however, as you will also learn in the next chapter, he has not escaped making certain implied warranties to his immediate transferee, Martha Hiatt.)

(5) Though Martha, too, may negotiate the bearer paper by delivery alone, she chooses to specially indorse the note before delivering it to Joe O'Reilly. Martha's special indorsement converts the note into order paper.

(6) Joe O'Reilly changes the note back to bearer paper by indorsing it in blank. He delivers the note to Mary Anderson.

(7) Mary negotiates the note by delivering it to Howard Hewitt.

(8) Howard holds bearer paper. However, before he can negotiate the note, the instrument is stolen by Charlie Sneakthief. Sneakthief is a holder because he has taken possession of bearer paper. He negotiates the note by delivering it to Elliott Hopson (if the note were order paper, Sneakthief could not negotiate it because of the indorsement requirement.)

(9) Rather than negotiate the bearer paper by delivery alone, Elliott specially indorses the note and delivers it to Theresa Jones.

(10) Theresa indorses the order paper in blank and delivers it to Dorothy Davis. The blank indorsement converts the order paper to bearer paper, and Dorothy can further negotiate the instrument by delivery alone. (Of course, if Dorothy chooses, she may specially indorse the note and so convert it into order paper.)

George Johnson (1)

Pay *Dick Drynan*
Sally Streeter (2)

Dick Drynan (3)

(4)

Pay *Joe O'Reilly*
Martha Hiatt (5)

Joe O'Reilly (6)

(7)

(8)

Pay *Theresa Jones*
Elliott Hopson (9)

Theresa Jones (10)

So you see, a negotiable instrument may change from order paper to bearer paper, and vice versa, any number of times before it is finally presented for payment. If the instrument is order paper, it may be negotiated only by indorsement and delivery; if the instrument is bearer paper, it may be negotiated by delivery alone.

The Uniform Commercial Code rules governing negotiation are found at Section 3–202.

The UCC provides:

Section 3–202. Negotiation

(1) Negotiation is the transfer of an instrument in such form that the transferee becomes a holder. If the instrument is payable to order it is negotiated by delivery with any necessary indorsement; if payable to bearer it is negotiated by delivery.

(2) An indorsement must be written by or on behalf of the holder and on the instrument or on a paper so firmly affixed thereto as to become a part thereof [such a paper is called an "allonge"].

(3) An indorsement is effective for negotiation only when it conveys the entire instrument or any unpaid residue. If it purports to be of less, it operates only as a partial assignment. [That is to say, a negotiable instrument cannot be negotiated in parts. Thus, indorsing an instrument "pay ⅓rd to Howard Hewitt and ⅔rd's to Elliott Hopson" will not result in making either party a holder. At best, each party will be a partial assignee; where partial assignments are not legally recognized, the parties will acquire no interests.]

(4) Words of assignment, condition, waiver, guaranty, limitation or

disclaimer of liability and the like accompanying an indorsement do not affect its character as an indorsement. [As pointed out earlier in the chapter, if one truly intends not to indorse, but to assign the instrument or provide a guaranty of payment or the like, this should be done on a separate sheet of paper not attached to the negotiable instrument. If attached to the instrument, the words of "assignment" or "guaranty" will not prevent the party's signature from serving as an indorsement for purposes of negotiation.]

————

Fourth, and finally, a party may become a holder by taking possession of an instrument made payable to his or her order or specially indorsed to him or her. For example, suppose that George Johnson discovers a negotiable promissory note made payable to his order on Larry Taylor's desk. If George takes possession of the instrument, he will become a holder of the note despite the fact that the instrument has not been issued to him. Similarly, if Sally Streeter spies the note lying on George's desk, and takes possession of it upon discovering that it's specially indorsed to her, Sally will become a holder of the note despite the fact that the instrument has not been delivered to her. In each case, the named payee has become a holder by virtue of taking possession of the note. Of course, such fact situations seldom occur, and in the vast majority of cases, the named payee of an instrument becomes a holder through either an issuance or a negotiation.

In summary, then, for a person to qualify as a holder, (1) he or she must have possession of a negotiable instrument; and (2) the instrument must be drawn, issued, or indorsed to the person or to his or her order or to bearer or in blank. The first requirement poses little problem, and the second may be satisfied by any one of four events—an issuance, a taking of possession of bearer paper, a negotiation, or a taking of possession of order paper made payable to one's self. Thus, a person is a holder anytime he or she has possession of bearer paper—period. It makes no difference how the possession is acquired: a thief who steals bearer paper, a finder who discovers it, a person who takes bearer paper through a negotiation—all are legal holders of the paper (though not all are legal owners). A person who has possession of order paper, on the other hand, will be a legal holder only if the instrument is made payable to his or her order or is specially indorsed to him or her (i. e., if the party is the named payee). Where this is the case, the party will be a holder of the instrument regardless of how he or she acquires possession (whether by theft, delivery, discovery, etc.).

Obviously, a finder or thief who qualifies as a holder has little or no rights with respect to the negotiable instrument. And even a holder who takes an instrument through a negotiation may stand in no better position than his or her transferor (i. e., he or she may have the rights of an assignee only and so stand subject to any existing defenses good against the assignor). To acquire superior rights with regard to the instrument (i. e., to cut off existing personal defenses such as mistake, fraud in the inducement, failure of consideration, and the like), a party must do more than qualify as a holder— he or she must qualify as a *holder in due course.*

When is a holder of a negotiable instrument a "holder in due course"?

A holder of a negotiable instrument is a *holder in due course* only when he or she takes the instrument:

(1) *For value;*

(2) In *good faith;* and

(3) *Without notice* that the instrument is overdue or subject to any claim or defense to payment.

Taking for value. To say that the holder of a negotiable instrument must take the instrument *for value* in order to qualify as a holder in due course is not synonymous with saying that he or she must give *consideration* for the instrument. In one respect, the concept of value is narrower than the concept of consideration; in another respect, it is broader.

You will recall from Ch. 9 that consideration sufficient to support a contract may be found simply in one's promise to do something that he or she is not already legally obligated to do. Thus, if one party promises to buy and another to sell, each party's promise, though executory (i.e., unperformed) will provide consideration for the other party's promise. This is so even where the promises are to remain executory for many months.

As between the original parties to a negotiable instrument, the instrument must be supported by consideration if it is to be a valid contract (the defense of failure of consideration is good as between the original parties and their assignees). As with all other contracts, an executory promise will furnish the required consideration. However, such a promise will not constitute "value" for purposes of making a person a holder in due course. The reasoning here is that a party who merely promises to perform in the future in return for receiving a negotiable instrument can simply refuse to perform if he or she later discovers a flaw in the transaction: the party does not need the rights of a holder in due course in order to protect his or her interests. For example, suppose that Charlie Sneakthief steals from Howard Hewitt a negotiable promissory note payable "to bearer" in the amount of $10,000. The instrument is not payable for several weeks, so Sneakthief immediately discounts it to Elliott Hopson, Hopson promising to pay Sneakthief $9,500 within 48 hours. However, before paying, Hopson discovers that the instrument has been stolen from Howard Hewitt. His promise still executory, Hopson simply refuses to pay the $9,500. He has suffered no loss, and he has no need to proceed against the maker of the note as a holder in due course.

But suppose that Hopson pays all or part of the $9,500 prior to discovering that the instrument has been stolen from Howard Hewitt. The general rule is that a holder who performs all or part of an executory promise prior to learning about a defect or defense to payment has given value and is a holder in due course but only to the extent of his or her performance. Thus, if Hopson has paid Sneakthief $4,750, Hopson has given value and is a holder in due course to the extent of $4,750.

Also, the Uniform Commercial Code provides that an executory promise will constitute value if it involves an "irrevocable commitment" to a third person. An "irrevocable commitment" is a commitment such that the promisor cannot get out of performing his or her promise. A solemn promise to carry out the executory promise is not enough—the commitment must be legally enforceable. Two examples come to mind. The first is an executory promise to pay money evidenced by a negotiable instrument. For example, suppose that, in return for the stolen note, Elliott Hopson gives Charlie Sneakthief a negotiable promissory note for the $9,500 owing. Though the promise to pay the $9,500 is executory, the negotiable note represents an irrevocable commitment: if the note is negotiated to a holder in due course, Hopson must pay the instrument despite the fact that he has received a stolen note from Sneakthief. Thus, in issuing the promis-

sory note to Sneakthief, Hopson has given value and is a holder in due course with respect to the stolen note.

The second example of an irrevocable commitment is an executory promise secured by a *letter of credit*. Letters of credit are governed by Article 5 of the Uniform Commercial Code and are discussed in Ch. 19 of the text. For now, it is enough to know that a "letter of credit" refers to the issuance by a bank (or other financial institution) of a specified amount of credit to one of its customers. The bank agrees to pay money up to the specified amount to beneficiaries designated by the customer. A party who agrees to pay for a negotiable instrument through a letter of credit at a bank makes an irrevocable commitment: once ordered to pay under the letter of credit, the bank will pay the beneficiary despite any defect or defense to payment arising on the negotiable instrument. The party has thus given value for the instrument and so qualifies as a holder in due course.

Whereas value is a narrower concept than consideration in that it generally excludes an executory promise to perform in the future, it is a broader concept in that it includes the taking of an instrument merely as security for an existing debt. Obviously, where a creditor accepts a negotiable instrument *in payment of* an existing debt, consideration exists because the creditor has given up his or her right to cash. But if the creditor takes the instrument merely as security for the existing debt (i. e., without extending the time for payment or incurring any other detriment in return for the instrument), consideration does not exist. Nevertheless, the Uniform Commercial Code provides that the creditor takes the instrument "for value" in both situations. For example, suppose that Larry Taylor contracts to buy George Johnson's boat, Larry agreeing to pay $2,000 down and the balance of $8,300 in six months time.

When six months pass and payment is not made, George takes as security for the debt a promissory note from Larry payable in six months in the amount of $8,300. Under the Code, George has given value for the note and thus qualifies as a holder in due course.

The Uniform Commercial Code provisions regarding "value" are found at Section 3–303.

The UCC provides:

Section 3–303. Taking for Value

A holder takes the instrument for value

(a) to the extent that the agreed consideration has been performed * * *; or

(b) when he takes the instrument in payment of or as security for an antecedent claim against any person whether or not the claim is due; or

(c) when he gives a negotiable instrument for it or makes an irrevocable commitment to a third person.

———

Before moving on to the good faith requirement, it should be pointed out that a donee who receives a negotiable instrument as a gift will never qualify as a holder in due course. A donee, by definition, does not take for value—at best, he or she is an assignee standing in the shoes of his or her assignor. Of course, if the donor-assignor is a holder in due course, the donee will acquire the rights of a holder in due course through the operation of the law of assignment (acquiring the rights of a holder in due course through assignment is fully discussed in the section entitled, "What is the shelter provision?").

Taking in good faith. As you know, Section 1–201(19) of the Uniform Commercial Code defines "good faith" as "honesty in fact in the conduct or transaction concerned". Thus the requirement that a holder take *in good faith* in order to qualify as a holder in due course means only that the holder must act honestly with regard to the transaction. The test of good faith is a subjective one— did the particular holder act in good faith in taking the instrument? If so, it will make no difference that a person of average shrewdness would have found the circumstances suspicious. And the fact that a holder learns of suspicious circumstances only after taking "honestly with regard to the transaction" does not destroy the good faith nature of the taking.

The good faith requirement is closely tied into the next and last requirement that a holder in due course must take "without notice" that the instrument is overdue or that it is subject to any claim or defense to payment.

Taking without notice. Though a holder acquires an instrument for value and in good faith, he or she will not be a holder in due course unless he or she also takes the instrument without notice that the instrument:

(1) Is overdue;

(2) Has been dishonored; or

(3) Is subject to any claim or defense.

A holder who knows or has reason to know any of the foregoing at the time of taking an instrument is denied holder in due course status because such knowledge puts the holder on alert that the instrument may not be enforceable—that, by taking the instrument, the holder may be getting involved in a lawsuit. Here, the test is an objective one: if, under the circumstances, the holder should realize that the instrument is overdue, has been dishonored, or is subject to a claim or defense, the holder takes "with knowledge" and does not qualify as a holder in due course. The fact that the holder does not have actual knowledge is immaterial.

A holder takes with knowledge that an instrument is *overdue* when the holder knows or has reason to know that any part of the principal amount has not been paid on time. Thus, if the instrument is payable at a definite time, the holder must acquire the instrument prior to midnight on the date set for payment. If the holder acquires the instrument later than this, he or she will have reason to know that the instrument is overdue. Where the instrument is payable in installments, the holder takes with knowledge that the instrument is overdue if he or she knows or has reason to know that the obligor has defaulted on any installment of principal (knowledge that the obligor has defaulted as to interest alone does not amount to taking with knowledge). Along the same line, where the instrument is subject to acceleration either at will or upon the happening of an event, knowledge that the previous owner accelerated the instrument, or that the event has occurred, amounts to knowledge that the instrument is overdue. Conversely, ignorance of the fact that acceleration has occurred constitutes taking without knowledge for purposes of qualifying as a holder in due course. Finally, with regard to an instrument payable on demand, a holder takes with knowledge that the instrument is overdue if the holder knows or has reason to know that demand for payment has been made. Also, where demand paper has been held for more than a reasonable time after its issuance, the paper is presumed to be overdue, and a holder who takes it is charged with such knowledge. What time is "reasonable" depends, in each case, on the nature and purpose of the instrument. The time is always shortest for checks. In fact, there is a rebuttable presumption that a "reasonable time" for

a check drawn and payable in the United States is 30 days from the date of its issue.

A holder takes an instrument with knowledge that it has been *dishonored* where the holder knows or has reason to know that demand for acceptance or payment of the instrument has been properly made upon the party expected to pay, and acceptance or payment has been refused. Usually, notation of the dishonor is made on the face of the instrument. For example, a dishonored check generally comes back stamped "insufficient funds" or "payment stopped" or "drawer has no account". Where a notation of dishonor appears on the instrument itself, the holder is put on notice of the dishonor and cannot qualify as a holder in due course. Where the dishonor does not appear on the face of the instrument, the holder may or may not qualify as a holder in due course depending on whether he or she has actual knowledge or reason to know of the dishonor.

Finally, a holder cannot qualify as a holder in due course where he or she knows or has reason to know at the time of taking a negotiable instrument that the instrument is *subject to a claim or defense* (e. g., a breach of contract between the original parties, a failure of consideration, mistake, fraud, duress, undue influence, unconscionable act, minority, illegality, or the like). While knowledge that all parties to an instrument have been discharged equals knowledge of a claim or defense,[2] knowledge that some of the parties have been discharged does not prevent the holder from taking as a holder in due course with respect to the parties who remain liable on the instrument. Uniform Commercial Code Section 3–304 provides that a holder is charged with knowledge of any claims or defenses apparent from the face of an instrument (e. g., a bungling forgery or an

2. Obviously, it seldom occurs that a person will knowingly give value for a completely discharged instrument (discharge of par-

ties is dealt with in detail in the following chapter); where it does occur, the judgment of the holder is to be questioned.

obvious alteration). Thus, if an instrument is so "incomplete, bears such visible evidence of forgery or alteration, or is otherwise so irregular as to call into question its validity, terms, or ownership, or to create an ambiguity as to the party to pay," a holder who takes the instrument cannot qualify as a holder in due course.

However, it must be emphasized that a holder is under no duty to investigate whether a claim or defense to enforcement of an instrument exists. And the Uniform Commercial Code states that knowledge of certain facts without more does not constitute knowledge of a "claim" or "defense" within the meaning of the Code. For example, knowledge that the instrument was issued or negotiated in return for an executory promise does not impair the holder's status as a holder in due course. Obviously, where a promissory note states on its face that it "is given in return for the payee's promise to deliver his boat within 60 days", a holder cannot help but realize that the executory promise to deliver the boat *may* never be carried out—that there *may* be a failure of consideration. But unless the holder knows that a breach of contract or failure of consideration has *in fact* occurred, the holder takes without knowledge of a claim or defense and so may qualify as a holder in due course. Similarly, the holder may take as a HDC despite the fact that he or she knows or has reason to know that the instrument is antedated or postdated, or that the obligee on the instrument has defaulted on interest alone. Without more, these facts do not impart knowledge of a claim or defense within the meaning of the Uniform Commercial Code.

The Uniform Commercial Code rules as to notice are found at Section 3–304 as follows:

The UCC provides:

Section 3–304. Notice to Purchaser

(1) The purchaser has notice of a claim or defense if

   (a) the instrument is so incomplete, bears such visible evidence of forgery or alteration, or is otherwise so irregular as to call into question its validity, terms or ownership or to create an ambiguity as to the party to pay; or

   (b) the purchaser has notice that the obligation of any party is voidable in whole or in part, or that all parties have been discharged.

*   *   *

(3) The purchaser has notice that an instrument is overdue if he has reason to know

   (a) that any part of the principal amount is overdue; or

   (b) that acceleration of the instrument has been made; or

   (c) that he is taking a demand instrument after demand has been made or more than a reasonable length of time after its issue. A reasonable time for a check drawn and payable within the states and territories of the United States and the District of Columbia is presumed to be thirty days.

(4) Knowledge of the following facts does not of itself give the purchaser notice of a defense or claim

   (a) that the instrument is antedated or postdated;

(b) that it was issued or negotiated in return for an executory promise or accompanied by a separate agreement, unless the purchaser has notice that a defense or claim has arisen from the terms thereof;

* * *

(d) that an incomplete instrument has been completed, unless the purchaser has notice of any improper completion;

* * *

(e) that there has been default in payment of interest on the instrument or in payment of any other instrument * * *

(5) The filing or recording of a document does not of itself constitute notice within the provisions of this Article to a person who would otherwise be a holder in due course.

(6) To be effective notice must be received at such time and in such manner as to give a reasonable opportunity to act on it.

———

It should be pointed out that though a holder may not have notice of a claim or defense within the meaning of the Code, he or she may nonetheless know facts that make taking the instrument a bad faith transaction. For example, suppose that the holder knows that his or her transferor is in bad financial straits or has a bad business reputation or has been found guilty in the past of fraud or other criminal conduct. Knowledge of any or all of these things does not amount to notice of a claim or defense. However, it may show a lack of good faith on the part of the holder in taking the instrument (i. e., in light of the knowledge, the holder may have acted dishonestly). Where, under the circumstances, the holder must have known that there was some-

thing wrong but deliberately shut his or her eyes to avoid the truth, the result is commercial bad faith. Some courts reach the same result using what is called the *cumulation doctrine*. Under this doctrine, a sufficient accumulation of suspicious circumstances, though each circumstance is in and of itself inadequate to constitute notice, will support a conclusion that the holder had notice of a claim or defense and/or was acting in bad faith.

Can a payee be a holder in due course?

The Uniform Commercial Code states at Section 3–302(2): "A payee may be a holder in due course." However, a payee seldom qualifies as a holder in due course, because, in nearly all cases, the payee is one of the original parties to the instrument and thus knows about any and all claims and defenses to payment. About the only time a payee will take for value, in good faith, and without notice (i. e., as a HDC) is where the payee is not an original party. For example, suppose that Larry Taylor, looking for a way to purchase George Johnson's boat, falsely represents to Dick Drynan that he, Larry, owns certain land that Dick wants to buy. Larry tells Dick that he still owes $10,000 on the property to George Johnson, but that he will sell the land to Dick for that amount if Dick will issue a negotiable promissory note for $10,000, payable to the order of George Johnson. Relying on the misrepresentation, Dick issues the note, and Larry delivers it to George Johnson in return for George's boat. George, the named payee, takes the instrument for value, in good faith, and without notice of any kind. He is therefore a holder in due course and can enforce the note against Dick Drynan despite Dick's personal defense of fraud in the inducement. Dick's only remedy is against Larry Taylor, who, by now, may be sailing in Mexican waters.

What is the Shelter Provision?

We stated previously that one who is not a holder in due course may still have the rights of a holder in due course by reason of taking the instrument from such a holder. This, of course, is in line with the law of assignments which provides that an assignee stands in the shoes of his or her assignor. The "Shelter Provision" (which is really simply an application of the law of assignments) states that where the assignor of a negotiable instrument is a holder in due course, the assignee of the instrument (and all subsequent transferees) will acquire the rights of such a holder. In other words, once a negotiable instrument is in the possession of a holder in due course, subsequent transferees need not worry about personally qualifying as such holders: the transferees will be effectively "sheltered" by the rights of the first holder in due course even though they take the instrument gratuitously (without giving value) and with notice of claims and defenses to enforcement. (It is sometimes helpful to think of the first HDC as holding a protective "umbrella" of rights over the heads of the subsequent transferees.)

Let's consider an example. Suppose that Larry Taylor negotiates a promissory note to Sally Streeter who qualifies as a holder in due course. Sally subsequently negotiates the note to Dick Drynan who negotiates it to Buzz Cort who negotiates it to Martha Hiatt who negotiates it to Joe O'Reilly. Under the Shelter Provision, it makes absolutely no difference whether Dick, Buzz, Martha, or Joe personally qualify as holders in due course. Each stands under Sally's protective "umbrella" and so has the rights of such a holder. (Again, the Shelter Provision is but an application of the law of assignments—each party in the example stands in the shoes of either a holder in due course or one with the rights of a holder in due course.)

The single exception to the Shelter Provision arises where a party attempts to improve his or her past or present position with respect to an instrument by taking the instrument from a holder in due course or from one with the rights of a holder in due course. Section 3–201 of the Uniform Commercial Code provides as follows.

The UCC provides:

Section 3–201. Transfer

(1) Transfer of an instrument vests in the transferee such rights as the transferor has therein, except that a transferee who has himself been a party to any fraud or illegality affecting the instrument or who as a prior holder had notice of a defense or claim against it cannot improve his position by taking from a later holder in due course.

———

Thus, a person who was party to a past fraud or illegality involving the instrument cannot better his or her position by standing under the protective umbrella held by the first holder in due course of the instrument. Nor can a prior holder with knowledge of a claim or defense better his or her position by standing under the HDC's umbrella of rights. For example, suppose that Larry Taylor fraudulently induces George Johnson to sign a promissory note, naming Larry as payee. Larry subsequently negotiates the note to Sally Streeter who qualifies as a holder in due course. Sally, in turn, transfers the note to Dick Drynan. At the time of the transfer, Dick knows about the fraud in the inducement; however, he had no part in the fraud, and thus he acquires the rights of a holder in due course under the Shelter Provision. Dick now transfers the note back to Larry Taylor, the original party to the fraud. Unlike Dick, Larry does not acquire the rights of a holder in due course. He falls within the exception to the Shelter Provision and will not be permitted to better his position by standing under Sally's protective umbrella. Now let's change the example. Suppose that Sally knows about the fraud at the time Larry transfers the note to her. Sally, in this case, takes with notice of a claim or defense and does not qualify as a holder in due course. She therefore holds no protective umbrella, and Dick Drynan, who takes the note with knowledge of the fraud, does not acquire the rights of a holder in due course under the Shelter Provision. Nor does Dick personally qualify as a HDC since he takes with notice of the defense of fraud. However, if Dick subsequently negotiates the note to Buzz Cort who qualifies as a holder in due course, and Cort transfers the note to Joe O'Reilly who also knows about the fraud, Joe will acquire the rights of a holder in due course simply by standing in Cort's shoes. But though Buzz Cort now holds a protective umbrella over subsequent transferees, it is impossible for Taylor, Streeter, or Drynan

to improve their positions by retaking the instrument. All three fall within the exception to the Shelter Provision and can never acquire the instrument with the rights of a holder in due course.

What comes next in the law of negotiable instruments?

This chapter has furnished you with all the "tools" needed for determining whether an instrument is negotiable, how it may be negotiated, and how a person may become a holder in due course of the instrument or one with rights of a holder in due course. The next chapter deals with the rights and liabilities of the parties to the instrument. What happens when the party who is expected to pay refuses to pay or is financially unable to pay? What are the legal ramifications of being a holder in due course as opposed to not being one? Does it make any difference whether an instrument is negotiated with or without an indorsement? And what are the legal effects of the various indorsements possible? These questions and more are fully explored in the following chapter.

CASES

CASE 1—*But what happens if the maker dies during the next 24 months?*

RESERVE PLAN, INC. v. SCHLEIDER

Municipal Court of the City of New York, Borough of Bronx, Second District, 1955.
208 Misc. 805, 145 N.Y.S.2d 122.

BENNETT, Justice.

* * * [T]he action was brought to recover the unpaid balance of an alleged promissory note. The plaintiff contends that it is a holder for value in due course and that as such the defenses of * * * breach of warranty and breach of agreement are not available against it. The instrument on which the action is predicated was executed by the defendant on May 5, 1954 and was given to secure payment for dental work to be performed by the payee. These payments were to be made in monthly installments of $20 each beginning June 5, 1954 for a total sum of $480. Two days after the execution of said instrument the same was negotiated to the plaintiff.

The defendant contends that the payee did not perform his agreement and that he still is in serious need of dental care which the payee has neglected and refused to furnish him; that he was not informed that the instrument he signed was a negotiable document but only a contract for instalment payments.

The question arises as to whether the agreement is in fact a negotiable instrument. If it is then the defenses asserted would not be available against this plaintiff. However, if the instrument does not conform to the requirements of the Negotiable Instruments Law of the State of New York, such defenses may be asserted against the present holder.

* * * [A negotiable instrument m]ust contain an unconditional promise or order to pay a sum certain in money * * *.

Examination of the instrument in suit discloses that the same contains this proviso, "In case of death of maker all payments not due at date of death are cancelled". Can it then be said that the form of the instrument sets forth an unconditional promise to pay a sum certain? It appears to this Court that such essential element is definitely lacking. See McClelland v. Norfolk Southern Railroad Co., 110 N.Y. 469, at page 475, wherein it was held as follows:

"If, however, these coupons contained notice to the holders of any facts or circumstances showing that the time of their payment was subject to a contingency over which the holder had no control, and which might postpone their payment indefinitely, then they could not be said to be *bona fide* holders thereof, as the negotiability of the paper would be thereby destroyed. * * * [W]hen such instruments contain special stipulations, and their payment is subject to contingencies not within the control of their holders, they are, by established rules, deprived of the character of negotiable instruments, and become exposed to any defense existing thereto as between the original parties to the instrument. It is essential by such rules that such paper should provide for the unconditional payment to a person, or order, or bearer, of a certain sum of money at a time capable of exact ascertainment."

Likewise, in Carnwright v. Gray, 127 N.Y. 92, 99, the Court of Appeals defined a promissory note in the following terms:

"A promissory note is defined to be a written engagement by one person to pay absolutely and unconditionally to another person therein named, or to the bearer, a certain sum of money at a specified time or on demand. It must contain the positive engagement of the maker to pay at a certain definite time, and the agreement to pay must not depend on any contingency, but be absolute, and at all events."

It is obvious from the foregoing that the document herein does not meet the required standards above mentioned for although the sum specified as payable is stated to be $480, such payment would be contingent on the maker continuing to live during the twenty-four months during which the installments were payable. By the terms of the said agreement, the contingency was always present during the said twenty-four months that a lesser amount would be payable in the event of death of the maker.

For the foregoing reasons the Court finds that the instrument does not constitute a negotiable promissory note and that the defendant is entitled to assert his defenses * * *.

[Judgment for defendant].

CASE 2—*"Reeking with malodorous fraud."*

NORMAN v. WORLD WIDE DISTRIBUTORS, INC.

Superior Court of Pennsylvania, 1963.
202 Pa.Super. 53, 195 A.2d 115.

WOODSIDE, Judge.

This is an appeal from a decree of the County Court of Philadelphia sitting in equity. The court declared null and void a judgment held by Peoples National Fund, Inc. against the plaintiffs, rescinded a purchase agreement for a breakfront [a type of cabinet or bookcase] and directed the plaintiffs to return the breakfront (for the purchase price of which the judgment was obtained) to State Wide or World Wide Distributors, Inc. Peoples National Fund, Inc. appealed.

This, and a companion case, grew out of transactions which the court below aptly characterized as "reeking with malodorous fraud."

Mancen, agent of defendant World Wide Distributors, Inc., called upon the plaintiffs about January 23, 1961, and outlined to them "a program for direct advertising." He represented to them that if they purchased a breakfront, he would pay them $5 for each letter they wrote to a friend requesting an appointment for World Wide's agent to explain the details of a sound advertising program and $20 for each sale made to any such person. Their friends whose names they furnished were to be given the same opportunity to profit from supplying names of their friends. He said the plaintiffs would realize sufficient money to pay for the breakfront and to enable them to send their daughter to college. He persuaded the plaintiffs to sign, without reading, a purchase agreement, an attached judgment note in blank and an "Owner's Participation Certificate." The plaintiffs were given forms by World Wide of letters to be sent to their friends and they prepared 60 of them for mailing, but received only $80. When asked for the balance due them under the contract they were told that the bookkeeper was ill, that the matter would be taken up, that the check was on the desk awaiting the treasurer's signature, and similar excuses. Under the terms of the purchase agreement, the plaintiffs agreed to "sign the attached note providing for 30 monthly installments of $35.98 or a total of $1,079.40." (It was alleged that the fair retail price of the breakfront was less than one-fifth this amount.) The first payment was to be made in 45 days.

After the note was signed and taken from the home of the plaintiffs it was filled in for $1,079.40 and made payable 3 days after date "to H. Waldran T/A State Wide Products at the office of Peoples National Fund." The note for $1,079.40, with interest, was purchased by Peoples National Fund, Inc. on January 25, 1961, for $831 and judgment was entered thereon February 7, 1961. It is hardly necessary to add that World Wide is now nowhere to be found. Within approximately a year its principals, unnamed in the record, had operated first under the name of Carpet Industries, then under State Wide, and finally under World Wide Distributors. The appellant dealt with all three companies and purchased notes from all three of them. The vice president of Peoples testified that he "had knowledge of the referral plan," although he claimed that he was not familiar with the details of the plan. Immediately after the plaintiffs received a $50 check from World Wide for the first ten names furnished under the agreement, the vice president of Peoples called the plaintiffs to inquire whether they were satisfied with the transaction. He told them Peoples had nothing to do with the referral plan.

The referral plan was a fraudulent scheme based on an operation similar to the recurrent chain letter racket. It is one of many sales rackets being carried on throughout the nation which are giving public officials serious concern. The plaintiffs introduced evidence to show that at the end of 20 months of operation, it would require *17 trillion* salesmen to carry on a referral program like World Wide described to the plaintiffs.

Peoples contend that even though World Wide may have been guilty of fraud, it can collect on the note because it was a holder in due course.

"A holder in due course is a holder who takes the instrument (a) for value; and (b) in good faith; and (c) without notice that it is overdue or has been dishonored or of any defense against or claim to it on the part of any person." § 3–302(1) of the Uniform Commercial Code.

Section 1–201(19) of the code defines "good faith" as meaning "honesty in fact in the conduct or transaction concerned." Thus, to be a holder in due course Peoples must have acted in good faith.

*   *   *

He who seeks protection as a holder in due course must have dealt fairly and honestly in acquiring the instrument as to the rights of prior parties, and where circumstances are such as to justify the conclusion that the failure to make inquiry arose from a suspicion that inquiry would disclose a vice or defect in the title, the person is not a holder in due course.

*   *   *

The appellant here had knowledge of circumstances which should have caused it to inquire concerning the payee's method of obtaining the note. Peoples knew enough about the referral plan to require it to inquire further concerning it. The fact that the appellant's vice president called the makers of the note and denied any connection with the referral plan, indicates his own suspicion concerning it. The frequency with which the principals changed the name under which they were operating—three times in approximately one year—should have added to his suspicion. Furthermore, the appellant paid $831 for a $1,079.40 note payable three days after date. Under all the circumstances, Peoples was bound to inquire further into the operation of the seller of these notes, and having made no inquiry, it is held as though it had knowledge of all that inquiry would have revealed.

*   *   *

Decree affirmed.

CASE 3—*The shelter provision.*

UNITED STATES FIDELITY & GUARANTY CO. v. WELLS

Supreme Court of Arkansas, 1969.
246 Ark. 255, 437 S.W.2d 797.

FOGLEMAN, Justice.

This case involves the liability of appellee upon a promissory note executed by him on December 21, 1959. The principal question involved is whether appellant who sued on the note was entitled to a directed verdict as a holder who had all the rights of a holder in due course. Since we agree with appellant on this point, it is unnecessary that we consider any of the other points raised.

Appellee Wells purchased a bulldozer from Kern-Limerick, Inc., on or about the date the note was executed. Appellee traded another piece of equipment as part of the down payment and gave the note in question for the remainder. This note was for $2,892.36 with interest at the rate of 8% per annum until maturity and 10% per annum after maturity. The balance of the purchase price was secured by a conditional sale contract which was assigned to Associates Discount Corporation.

The note to Kern-Limerick was negotiated to the First National Bank in Little Rock on December 23, 1959. The status of the bank as a holder in due course is undisputed. It was indicated on the face of the note that it was secured by a lien on the bulldozer. The note was payable in two installments due on June 1, 1960, and December 1, 1960, respectively. Kern-Limerick was engaged in the sale of construction equipment and handled many transactions in a similar manner. This concern filed a voluntary petition in bankruptcy and was declared bankrupt on or about May 24, 1960.

When the bank attempted to collect the note, it learned that it was not secured by a first lien on the bulldozer and that its lien was subject to the lien of the conditional sale contract. The bank then made a claim against appellant under its banker's blanket bond on this and other notes of a similar nature. [Appellant was, in effect, the insurer for the bank on such notes.] Appellant's liability was settled by the payment of $125,169.04 and the assignment of the notes upon which the claim was recognized. It appears that the payment made represented the total of the balances due on these notes on the date of assignment. While the assignment bears no date, it is undisputed that it was made well after the date of the maturity of the last installment of the note in question.

After appellee's refusal to pay the note, appellant filed suit. At the trial, a verdict in favor of the appellee was rendered by the jury and judgment entered pursuant to this verdict.

* * *

It is not contended that appellant was a party to any fraud or illegality affecting the note. * * * [A]ppellant was entitled to all of the rights of a holder in due course because it derived its title through the First National Bank in Little Rock. [This is an application of the "shelter provision" that an assignee from a holder in due course receives the rights of the holder in due course unless the assignee is an original party to the fraud] Appellee argues, however, that appellant is not entitled to the rights of a holder in due course because the note was taken by appellant as an unwilling purchaser by assignment without endorsement after maturity with full knowledge of the fraud practiced by the original payee upon appellee and the bank. We find no support for this position in the statutes and find an overwhelming weight of authority to the contrary. It is immaterial that the transferee of a note from a holder in due course took it after maturity; or without payment of value; or with notice of existing equities, infirmities or defenses. It is also immaterial that the holder in due course did not endorse the note, since transfer by assignment or by mere delivery is sufficient.

* * *

Since it is clear that appellant was entitled to a directed verdict, the judgment of the lower court is reversed and judgment entered here in favor of appellant in the sum of $2,892.36 the face amount of the note with interest * * *.

PROBLEMS

1.

> As per our agreement of March 1st, I promise to pay to Ray and Susan Martin, or their assigns
>
> Four thousand and no/100 ....DOLLARS ($5,000.00)
>
> with interest at the current rate OR deliver them a 1980 Chevrolet Monza, payment or delivery to be made on December 15, 1980, except that I reserve the right to extend the date of payment or delivery.
>
> *Cathy Carpenter*
> Cathy Carpenter, Agent
> for Carter's Autos, Inc.

Is this instrument negotiable or nonnegotiable? Discuss in detail, with specific reference to each of the requirements of negotiability. Who is liable as a maker of the instrument? Explain.

2. Dennis Barker breaks into Frank McClanahan's office and steals the following negotiable instruments: a check made payable by Frank "to the order of Frances Sweeney" in the amount of $500; a promissory note made payable by Frank "to bearer" in the amount of $1,000; and a check made payable by Mike Murphy "to the order of Frank McClanahan" in the amount of $750 (Frank has signed only his name on the back of the instrument). Dennis sells all three instruments to Betty Benson for $1,750. Betty has no idea that the instruments are stolen. She accepts delivery of the instruments, not realizing that Dennis has forged Frances Sweeney's indorsement on the check made payable to Frances' order. Was Dennis Barker a "holder" of the instruments? Is Betty Benson a "holder" of the instruments? Can Betty collect payment of the instruments despite the fact that they were stolen from Frank McClanahan? Explain your answers fully.

3. Suppose that Betty gives the $1,000 promissory note made payable to bearer to her nephew, Harley Benson. Unlike his aunt, Harley knows that the note was stolen; however, he did not participate in the theft. Harley sells the instrument for $650 to Jack Southwell who did participate in the theft with Dennis Barker. Could Harley have enforced the instrument despite the fact that it was stolen? Can Jack Southwell enforce the instrument? Explain in detail.

4. Fitz received from Gayle a negotiable instrument payable to the order of Gayle. Fitz received the instrument for value, but Gayle inadvertently did not indorse the instrument.

   a. Fitz will be treated as the holder of a bearer negotiable instrument.

   b. If Fitz later obtains Gayle's unqualified indorsement, Fitz's rights as a holder in due course are determined as of the time of indorsement.

   c. Fitz has a right to require Gayle to indorse, but Gayle may satisfy the right by a qualified indorsement.

   d. Fitz has no right after accepting the transferred instrument to require Gayle to indorse where he made no such request at the time of the transfer.

   [# 16, May, 1974 CPA Exam]

5. An instrument is nonnegotiable if it

   a. Is payable in a foreign currency.

   b. States it is secured by a mortgage.

   c. States that it is subject to any other agreement.

   d. Is issued by a partnership and limited to payment from partnership assets.

   [# 2, May, 1974 CPA Exam]

6. An otherwise valid negotiable instrument is nonnegotiable if it is

   a. Postdated.

   b. Undated.

   c. Payable thirty days after a stated date but with the right of the holder to demand immediate payment at his option.

   d. Payable only upon the happening of an event which is uncertain as to the time of occurrence.

   [# 33, May, 1976 CPA Exam]

7. Carter fraudulently misrepresented the quality and capabilities of certain machinery he sold to Dobbins. Carter obtained a check for $2,000, the amount agreed upon, at the time he made delivery. The machinery proved to be virtually worthless. Dobbins promptly stopped payment on the check. Carter negotiated the check to Marvel in satisfaction of a prior loan of $600 and received $1,400 in cash. Marvel, who had accepted the check in good faith, presented the check for payment which was refused by Dobbins' bank.

   a. Even if Marvel is a holder in due course, Dobbins has a real defense.

   b. Marvel can only collect for $1,400 cash in that he did *not* give new value beyond that amount.

   c. Marvel will be able to collect the full amount from Dobbins.

   d. Dobbins' timely stop order eliminates his liability on the check.

   [# 40, May, 1976 CPA Exam]

8. Arthur Fox purchased a large order of business supplies from Spencer
    & Company by paying 10% in cash and giving Spencer & Company the
    following instrument to cover the balance due:

Los Angeles, Calif.
February 2, 1977

For value received, I, Arthur Fox, hereby promise to pay my debt
of One thousand thirty and 26/100's dollars ($1,030.26) to Spencer
& Company or to their order. The instrument is due not later
than March 2, 1978, but the maker may at his option pay within one
month of the date of this instrument and receive a 1% discount.

Arthur Fox

   Which of the following is true with respect to this instrument?

   a. The instrument is a trade draft.

   b. Since Fox can pay earlier than the due date, the instrument is
       thereby rendered nonnegotiable.

   c. The language "For value received" is necessary in order to satisfy
       the requirements of negotiability.

   d. The instrument is negotiable.

   [# 19, May, 1977 CPA Exam]

9. Your client, Commercial Factors, Inc., purchased for $1,500 a $2,000
    promissory note payable in two years. It paid $500 initially and prom-
    ised to pay the balance ($1,000) within 10 days. Before Commercial
    Factors paid the balance, it learned that the note had been obtained
    originally by fraudulent misrepresentations which induced the maker to
    issue it. To what extent will Commercial Factors be considered a hold-
    er in due course?

   a. Commercial Factors is *not* a holder in due course because of the
       25% discount.

   b. Commercial Factors will qualify as a holder in due course for
       $2,000 if it pays the additional $1,000.

   c. Commercial Factors will only qualify as a holder in due course to
       the extent of $500 regardless of whether it pays the additional
       $1,000.

   d. Commercial Factors will qualify as a holder in due course to the
       extent of $1,500.

   [# 17, May, 1977 CPA Exam]

10. **Part a.** Magnum Enterprises, Inc., received a note from one of its major customers, Bilbo Sales, Inc., in connection with the purchase of $100,000 of merchandise. The note provided as follows:

August 1, 1974

Bilbo Sales, Inc., hereby promises to pay Magnum Enterprises, Inc., One Hundred Thousand Dollars ($100,000) within thirty days from August 1, 1974, for the purchase of goods delivered on July 26, 1974, receipt of which is hereby acknowledged. Bilbo Sales hereby confesses judgment on said note and agrees to pay any and all costs of collection in the event of wrongful default.

Walter Bilbo,
President

Magnum had promptly discounted the note with the Third National Bank. Upon examination of the merchandise, Bilbo promptly informed Magnum that the goods were not as warranted. Magnum responded by informing Bilbo that the note had been sold to Third National Bank and that whatever problems it had must first be resolved with the bank because it was the holder in due course.

Required: In the event that Bilbo was properly dissatisfied with the merchandise, can it assert the defense of breach of warranty against Third National? Explain.

[# 6.a., November, 1974 CPA Exam]

Part b. Herman Watts sold a used printing press to Marshall Offset, Inc., for two thousand dollars ($2,000). Watts requested that Marshall make the check payable to the order of the Foremost Finance Company because Watts was in arrears on a loan it owed to Foremost. That same day Watts delivered the check to Foremost which, in turn, presented the check and received payment from Marshall's bank.

Marshall subsequently discovered serious defects in the printing press purchased from Watts. The defects unquestionably represented a breach of the express warranties given by Watts in the contract of sale. Immediately upon discovery of the defect, Marshall notified his bank to stop payment but this was several days after the bank had processed the check.

Watts is hopelessly insolvent. Marshall seeks to rescind the transaction and recover the payment on the check from Foremost or its own bank.

Required: What legal remedies are available to Marshall in the situation described? Explain.

Part c. On July 1, 1974, Martin Hayes signed a promissory note which was made payable to the order of Jones Fabricating, Inc., for $10,000, plus 8% interest, payable 90 days from date. On the front of the note above his signature Hayes wrote: "Subject to satisfactory delivery of goods purchased this date. Delivery to be made no later than July 31, 1974."

Jones' president indorsed the note on behalf of the corporation and transferred it to Acme Bank in consideration of the bank's crediting $9,800 against a $20,000 debt owed to the bank by Jones Fabricating.

When the due date arrived the bank asked Hayes to pay, but Hayes refused saying that Jones had not delivered the goods he had bargained for in giving the note. Acme Bank gave notice of dishonor the next day to Jones.

Required: 1. Is the note negotiable commercial paper? Explain.

2. Assuming the note is nonnegotiable paper, can Acme Bank collect the amount due from Hayes if Hayes can prove that the goods he bargained for were not delivered? Explain.

[# 6 b. & c. (1)(2), November, 1974 CPA Exam]

Chapter 14

COLLECTING THE MONEY: LIABILITIES ON NEGOTIABLE INSTRUMENTS

Assuming a negotiable instrument has been issued, negotiated, or taken possession of, what possible situations may arise with regard to payment of the instrument?

A negotiable instrument has a life—the instrument is born, and, ultimately, it dies. Its birth may be without problems, or it may be complicated by a breach (of contract) or failure to complete the instrument (the instrument must be completed before it can lead a normal life). The lifespan of the instrument may be short and rather dull, or it may be long and full of interesting events such as thefts and alterations. Throughout the course of its life, the instrument may live with only one or two parties, or it may jump around and spend time with many (some leaving no telling mark on either the instrument's face or body). Some of the parties may be accommodating only; still others may condition and qualify their relationships with the instrument. Ultimately, however, the usefulness of the instrument will come to an end, and the instrument will be cremated or buried in the graveyard of discarded notes, drafts, and cancelled checks. Or, if life has not left the instrument too tattered, it may be reincarnated (i. e., recycled as a brown paper bag or wrapping paper for a child's Christmas present). And, occasionally, the instrument will even come back to haunt a person (e. g., when the IRS asks to see it).

At some point during the course of its life, a negotiable instrument will be presented for payment. Will the instrument be paid? Who will pay it? These questions will be answered in this chapter dealing with liabilities on negotiable instruments. As you will learn, any one of the following situations may arise:

(1) In the usual case, there are no defects or defenses to payment, and the holder of the instrument collects the sum certain from the maker or drawee.

(2) The drawee of a draft or check refuses to honor the instrument, and the holder looks to the drawer for payment.

(3) The maker or drawee refuses to pay on the grounds that the instrument was originally incomplete, that it has been materially altered, or that it is subject to a real or personal defense excusing payment.

(4) The maker or drawee is financially unable to pay, or is excused from paying because of a real or personal defense; however, a party has indorsed the instrument, and the holder may be able to collect from the party on the basis of his or her indorsement contract.

(5) The maker or drawee is financially unable to pay, or is excused from paying because of a real or personal defense; additionally, there are no indorsers liable on the instrument. Nevertheless, the holder may be able to collect from a transferor of the instrument on the basis of warranty.

We will look at these specific situations, as well as some miscellaneous problems with negotiable instruments, in the chapter sections that follow.

What usually happens when the party in possession of a negotiable instrument presents the instrument for payment?

At some point in time, the party in possession of a negotiable instrument will want to collect the sum certain in money to be paid according to the terms of the instrument. Usually, assuming payment is due, the party will present the instrument to the maker or drawee and receive payment: normally, there is no defense to payment, and the maker or drawee pays without question. Of course, in each case, the procedure for obtaining payment, and the party to look to for payment, will vary depending on whether the instrument is a promissory note, a draft, or check.

Promissory note. In a promissory note, the maker promises to pay the instrument on demand or at a definite time. Thus, at the moment of issuance of the note, the maker becomes *primarily liable* on the instrument (i. e., he or she becomes the first party to look to for payment—it being *intended* at the time of issuance of the note that the maker pay the instrument and the maker having *agreed* to pay). This, then, is the maker's contract: upon maturity of the note, he or she must pay the instrument without looking to anyone else for reimbursement. That is what the parties anticipated when the note was signed, and, barring the existence of a defense to payment or the maker's financial inability to pay, that is what will occur upon presentment of the note for payment.

The note is due either on the date it is shown to be payable or on demand in the case of a demand note. The note is deemed to show the date on which it is payable if it states that it is payable on a specific date or at a fixed period after a specific date, such as "30 days after date". In the latter case, the time for presentment for payment is determined by excluding the "specific date" from the

30 days and including the date of payment. So, if the note is dated January 15th and is payable "30 days after date", the 30 days begin to run on January 16th (January 15th, the specific date, is excluded) and end on February 14th, the date the note falls due. Section 3–122 of the Uniform Commercial Code states that "a cause of action against a maker * * * accrues * * * in the case of a time instrument on the day after maturity." Thus, if the holder presents the note for payment on February 14th, but the maker fails to pay as promised, the holder may sue the maker for payment on February 15th. However, if the note falls due on a day that is not a full business day for either the holder or the maker, presentment for payment is due on the next full business day for both parties. These same rules apply, not only to promissory notes payable at a definite time, but to all negotiable instruments so payable.

The proper time for presenting demand paper for payment is any time after issuance of the instrument. The right to sue for nonpayment also arises immediately after issue.

Draft. You will recall that a draft is a three party instrument in which a drawer orders a drawee to pay a payee. Unlike a note, there is no party immediately primarily liable on a draft: while it is *intended* from the moment of issuance of the draft that the drawee pay the instrument, the drawee has not *agreed* to do so. In fact, the drawee usually has no knowledge of the order at the time of issuance, and he or she generally acquires none until the draft is presented for acceptance. It is only by accepting the draft (i. e., by writing the "acceptance" on the face of the draft as explained and illustrated in Ch. 12) that the drawee becomes primarily liable on the instrument. Thereafter, the drawee is called the *acceptor*.

Of course, the drawee is not legally obligated to accept the draft. While a draft presupposes a debtor-creditor relationship between the drawee and drawer (i. e., that the drawee owes the drawer money), the law will not require the drawee to pay anyone other than the drawer personally. In the event that the drawee refuses to accept and pay the instrument, the drawer may have to pay the draft. Even so, the drawer will not qualify as a primarily liable party: it was not intended from the moment of issuance of the draft that the drawer pay the instrument—it was intended that the drawee do so.

Thus, only makers and acceptors are classified as primarily liable parties (or "primary parties"). Like a maker, a drawee-acceptor of a draft contracts to pay the instrument according to its terms. Again, barring a defense to payment or insolvency of the drawee-acceptor, this is what will take place upon presentment of the accepted draft for payment. But remember, a draft made payable on demand rather than at a definite time is generally not presented for formal acceptance. Usually, demand for payment is made immediately, and the drawee simply pays the draft without writing anything on the face of the instrument. Once paid, the draft has no further legal effect. Thus, it is technically improper to say that there is an "acceptor" of the demand draft or a party "primarily liable" on the instrument.

Check. You will also recall from Ch. 12 that a check is a special kind of draft drawn on a bank and payable on demand. The drawer, who has an account with the bank, gives the check to the payee who presents the check to the bank for payment (sometimes, the payee does this indirectly by depositing the check in his or her own checking or savings account). Like other demand drafts, checks are seldom accepted prior to payment; thus, there is usually no "acceptor" or "primary party" on a check. However, as will be discussed in Ch. 15, it is possible to present a check for acceptance or "certification" rather than for immediate payment. A bank that certifies (accepts) a check will immediately take sufficient funds to cover the check from the drawer's account. The bank does this to protect itself—by certifying the check, the bank has become primarily liable on the instrument.

To summarize, in a promissory note, there is always a primary party (the maker) from the moment of issuance of the note. In a draft, there is never a primary party from the moment of issuance; however, the drawee may become a primary party by accepting the draft. Finally, in a check, there is usually no primary party, although the drawee-bank may become one by certifying the check. Primary parties are thus makers or acceptors only. As a primary party, a maker or acceptor is bound by his or her contract to pay the instrument on demand (where demand paper) or upon the due date of the instrument (where payable at a definite time). The primary party's liability is unconditional. As Section 3–413 of the Uniform Commercial Code states: "The maker or acceptor engages that he will pay the instrument according to its tenor at the time of his engagement * * *."

As stated previously, the maker of a negotiable note will usually pay the instrument without question upon its presentment for payment. The drawee of a draft payable at a definite time will generally accept and pay the draft; and the drawee of a demand draft, such as a check, will usually simply pay the instrument.

Still, two problems may arise. The first occurs where the holder of a negotiable instrument makes no effort to collect payment even though the instrument is payable on demand or is due to be paid, and the maker or acceptor of the instrument desires to make payment. Being unconditionally liable, the maker or acceptor will have to pay the demand paper or the past due instrument whenever it is presented for payment so long as it is presented prior to the running of the statute of limitations. (Each state has a statute specifying a time period—e. g., 5 years—within which a suit to enforce a negotiable instrument must be brought or the holder will be forever barred from collecting.) The problem is that the stated interest on the note or draft may also continue to run for the statutory period, with the maker or acceptor liable for the interest. To protect the maker or acceptor in this situation, Section 3–604 of the Uniform Commercial Code provides as follows.

The UCC provides:

Section 3–604. Tender of Payment

(1) Any party making tender of full payment to a holder when or after it is due is discharged to the extent of all subsequent liability for interest, costs and attorney's fees.

(3) Where the maker or acceptor of an instrument payable otherwise than on demand is able and ready to pay at every place of payment specified in the instrument when it is due, it is equivalent to tender.

Subsection (1) provides that an actual tender of payment will stop the running of interest both as to demand instruments and instruments payable at a definite time. A tender, you will recall, is simply an offer to do something if the other party will perform in return: here, the maker or acceptor must offer to pay the instrument in full on condition that the holder of the instrument accept payment and discharge the maker or acceptor. Of course, to actually tender payment, the maker or acceptor must know where to find the holder of the instrument. If the holder cannot be found, the maker or acceptor may be liable for interest for the full statutory period.

Subsection (3) applies only to instruments payable at a definite time. Thus, if an instrument with a definite due date is payable at a *special place* (such an instrument is called "domiciled" paper), and the maker or acceptor is able and ready to pay at that place when the instrument is due, the maker or acceptor has effectively tendered payment, and the running of interest is stopped. Thereafter, the holder of the instrument can collect only the principal amount owing and interest to the due date. What is a "special place" for purposes of Subsection (3)? It is a place specific in nature, such as "the Main Branch of the First National Bank of California located in Sacramento". An instrument payable merely in "Sacramento, California" or in "Pittsburgh, Pennsylvania", on the other hand, is not payable at a special place.

But remember, unless an instrument is both domiciled *and* payable at a definite time, an actual tender is required to stop the running of interest. To avoid the interest problem, a party might combine a domiciled instrument with an acceleration provision, thus giving the payee the principal advantage of a demand instrument without the risk of interest liability for the statute of limitations period. For example, the maker or drawer might make the instrument payable at a special place and on a fixed date (within the maximum time limits acceptable to the maker or acceptor) but with a provision giving the holder the right to accelerate payment upon demand.

The second problem arises where a party deposits funds with a bank or other drawee to cover payment of a note, draft, or check, and the funds are fully or partially lost through the subsequent insolvency of the bank or other drawee. If the holder of the instrument has contributed to the loss by failing to present the instrument for acceptance or payment within a reasonable time, the depositor of the funds may discharge his or her liability on the instrument by assigning to the holder his or her rights against the insolvent bank or other drawee. The pertinent Code provision is Section 3–502.

The UCC provides:

Section 3–502. Unexcused delay

* * *

(1) Where without excuse any necessary presentment * * * is delayed beyond the time when it is due [note: Section 3–502 applies to unexcused delay in any necessary presentment, whether for payment or for acceptance]

* * *

(b) any drawer or the acceptor of a draft payable at a bank or the maker of a note payable at a bank who because the drawee or payor bank becomes insolvent during the delay is deprived of funds maintained with the drawee or payor bank to cover the instrument may discharge his liability by written assignment to the holder of his rights against the drawee or payor bank in respect of such funds, but such drawer, acceptor or maker is not otherwise discharged.

Upon assignment to the holder, the depositor is discharged, and the holder's only remedy, for what it is worth, is against the insolvent bank or other drawee (the holder "stands in the shoes" of the depositor and can collect from the insolvent party only if the depositor could have collected).

Section 3–503 of the Uniform Commercial Code defines "reasonable time" for purposes of presentment; and Section 3–511 outlines circumstances where a delay in presentment will be excused. These sections also apply to the liability of drawers and indorsers (secondary parties) and will be reproduced later in the chapter following a discussion of secondary liability.

What is the liability of the drawer when the drawee of a draft refuses to accept or pay the instrument?

A drawer issues a draft, but, unlike a maker of a note, does not expect to pay the instrument. Rather, the drawer is ordering the drawee to pay. The drawer, in effect, is stating to the payee, "Go to the drawee and ask for payment. If the drawee does not pay, come back to me and I will pay the draft." Thus, the drawer of a draft is not a primary party but is secondarily liable only—that is, the drawer's liability is backup liability in the event that the drawee fails to pay as ordered. Section 3–413(2) of the Uniform Commercial Code defines the contract of the drawer as follows.

The UCC provides:

The drawer engages that upon dishonor of the draft and any necessary notice of dishonor or protest he will pay the amount of the draft to the holder or to any indorser who takes it up. The drawer may disclaim this liability by drawing without recourse.

As you can see, there are generally three conditions precedent to the drawer's liability on the draft:

(1) The holder of the draft must *present* the instrument for acceptance or payment;

(2) The drawee-acceptor must dishonor the instrument (i. e., refuse to accept or pay the instrument because of a real or personal defense or because of financial inability to pay); and

(3) The holder must *notify* the drawer of the dishonor.

You know that, in the usual case, the drawee accepts and pays the instrument without question. The draft is based on a debtor-creditor relationship between the drawee and drawer: the drawee simply pays all or part of the money he or she owes the drawer to the payee. Where the drawee accepts and pays the draft, the drawer's secondary liability does not come into play.

Sometimes, however, the drawee dishonors the draft, and this is where the drawer's secondary liability becomes important. So long as all three conditions precedent are met (or excused as will be explained in a later section), the drawer must pay the draft upon its dishonor by the drawee. Generally, this is true even where the holder has unreasonably delayed in presenting the draft for acceptance or payment, or in notifying the drawer of the dishonor. An exception arises where the bank or other drawee goes insolvent during the holder's delay, and the drawer loses funds deposited with the drawee to cover the draft. As you will recall from the previous section, where the holder's delay in presentment has contributed to the loss, the drawer may discharge his or her secondary liability by assigning to the holder his or her rights against the insolvent party. The drawer may discharge his or her liability in the same manner where it is the holder's delay in notifying the drawer that has made the loss possible (by depriving the drawer of the opportunity to proceed immediately against the insolvent drawee so as to protect his or her rights). Once more, Section 3–502(1) is the relevant Uniform Commercial Code provision.

It provides:

(1) Where without excuse any necessary presentment or *notice of dishonor* is delayed beyond the time when it is due

(b) any drawer * * * who because the drawee * * * becomes insolvent during the delay *is deprived of funds* maintained with the drawee * * * to cover the instrument may discharge his liability by written assignment to the holder of his rights against the

drawee * * * [Emphasis supplied.]

Note that the holder's failure to make presentment within a reasonable time or to give timely notice must be to the prejudice of the drawer if the drawer is to escape liability on the instrument. If the drawer has lost nothing by reason of the holder's failure to act timely—either in presenting the draft for payment or acceptance or in notifying the drawer of the dishonor—the drawer will remain secondarily liable on the instrument. Let's consider an example. Suppose that Larry Taylor writes out a check payable "to the order of George Johnson" in the amount of ten-thousand and no/100 dollars. The check is drawn on Larry's account at the First National Bank. Upon receiving the check, the payee George Johnson immediately presents the instrument to the bank for payment, whereupon the check is dishonored because of insufficient funds (Larry has nowhere near $10,000 in his account). As drawer of the instrument, Larry Taylor is secondarily liable and must pay the $10,000 check.

Would the result differ if George Johnson had unreasonably delayed in either presenting the check for payment or in notifying Larry Taylor of the dishonor? The answer is no. It is not the drawee who is insolvent here—it is the drawer Larry Taylor who has insufficient funds in his account to cover the check. Because a failure by George to act timely would not deprive Larry of any funds on deposit with the bank, Larry cannot escape liability on the instrument.

Remember, the drawer can escape his or her secondary liability on the basis of the holder's failure to act timely only where the drawer is deprived of funds on deposit with the drawee, the drawee having gone insolvent during the holder's delay. This seldom occurs, and, in most cases, the drawer will be required to pay the draft upon its dishonor by the drawee.[1]

Two other terms used in UCC Section 3–413(2) with regard to the drawer's secondary liability must also be explained. As you will recall, the Section states in part: "[The] drawer engages upon dishonor of the draft and any necessary notice of dishonor or *protest* he will pay the amount of the draft to the holder or to any indorser who takes it up. The drawer may disclaim this liability by drawing *without recourse*." (Emphasis supplied.) The terms "protest" and "without recourse" are words with special meaning.

A "protest" is a formal notice of dishonor required *only* when dealing with *drafts* (and including checks) drawn or payable in a *foreign country*. It is frequently referred to as "a notice of dishonor with trimmings" because it is a formal certificate of notice (sometimes annexed to the instrument itself) certifying to the fact of presentment and dishonor. Usually, the protest is notarized by a notary public or made under the hand and seal of a United States consul or vice consul. Section 3–502(2) of the Uniform Commercial Code states that

"where without excuse a necessary protest is delayed beyond the time when it is due any drawer or indorser is discharged." Thus, if a holder unreasonably delays in protesting the dishonor of a draft drawn or payable in a foreign country, the drawer is completely discharged of all liability on the instrument. And this is so whether or not the drawer is prejudiced by the holder's delay—if the holder has failed to make timely protest, the drawer is discharged, period. Apart from drafts drawn or payable in a foreign country, notice of dishonor may generally be given informally (even orally) as long as the notice sufficiently describes the negotiable instrument and states the facts of presentment and dishonor. Section 3–508(3) of the Code states that notice sent by mail is effective when sent regardless of whether the notice is received. And Sections 4–302, 3–508(2), and 3–509(4) of the Code provide that any necessary protest or notice of dishonor must be given by a bank before midnight of the next banking day following dishonor, and by any other person before midnight of the third business day after dishonor or receipt of notice of dishonor.

If a drawer uses the term "without recourse" in signing a draft or check, the drawer's secondary liability will be completely eliminated (i. e., the drawer will not be liable in the event the drawee fails to accept or pay the instrument). A draft signed by a drawer "without recourse" might look like this:

1. Of course, like the maker or acceptor, the drawer may be financially unable to pay the instrument, or he or she may have a real or personal defense to payment. In this case, the holder may have to look to indorsers or other transferors of the draft for payment.

February 15, 1980

On March 15, 1980 pay to the order of

GEORGE JOHNSON

Eight-thousand three hundred and no/100 DOLLARS

TO: Mark Hopkins
228 West Rosser Avenue
Bismarck, North Dakota   *Lawrence Taylor, Without Recourse*

However, it is very unusual for a drawer to sign without recourse. Generally, the drawer is ordering the drawee to pay the payee because the drawer is indebted to the payee on the basis of an underlying transaction. In our example, for instance, Larry Taylor owes George Johnson $10,300 for the boat he purchased from George. By signing "without recourse", Larry can eliminate his secondary liability on the draft; however, he cannot escape his liability on the underlying transaction. That is to say, if Mark Hopkins fails to accept or pay the draft, George can always sue Larry for the $10,300 on the basis of the sales contract even if he cannot hold Larry on the instrument itself. Larry thus gains little or nothing by signing "without recourse" and is unlikely to do so.

Before moving on, let's summarize where we are on the collecting of negotiable instruments:

(1) In the usual case, there are no defects or defenses to payment: the holder of the instrument presents it when due to the maker or acceptor who pays without question (the maker and drawee-acceptor are primary parties who have unconditionally contracted to pay the instrument).

(2) Sometimes, the maker, drawer, or acceptor of an instrument suffers a loss of funds on deposit with a bank or other drawee because the holder of the instrument has unreasonably delayed in making presentment or giving notice of dishonor, during which time the bank or other drawee has gone insolvent. Where this occurs, the maker, drawer, or acceptor may discharge his or her liability by assigning his or her rights against the insolvent party to the holder who delayed.

(3) Subject to (2) above, the drawer is secondarily liable on a draft or check and must pay if the drawee does not. The three conditions precedent to the drawer's liability are *presentment, dishonor,* and *notice* of dishonor.

(a) The drawer's liability is completely discharged if the holder of a draft drawn or payable in a foreign country unreasonably delays in making protest of dishonor.

(b) The holder may eliminate his or her secondary liability by signing the draft or check without recourse.

Can a maker or acceptor (i. e., a primary party) rightfully refuse to pay an instrument on grounds that it was originally incomplete, has been materially altered, or is subject to a defense?

We now consider the situation where the holder of an instrument presents the instrument to the primary party for payment, but the primary party refuses to pay on the basis of some defense. As you read through the section, bear in mind that secondarily liable parties (i. e., drawers and indorsers) and parties liable on the basis of warranty will also be able to assert these defenses in appropriate cases. (The indorser's contract and warranty liability are considered later in the chapter.)

Incomplete instrument. On occasion, a maker or drawer will sign an instrument but leave portions of it blank. For example, the name of the payee may be left off the instrument, such as "Pay to the order of _____"; the sum certain amount may be left blank; the instrument, though undated, may state that it is payable "90 days after date", etc. In each case, the instrument is incomplete and, therefore, nonnegotiable.

To be complete, an instrument must sufficiently identify the parties to the contract and fully comply with the nine requirements of negotiability. If blanks are left in any material portion of the instrument, the instrument is incomplete and cannot be enforced until it is completed. Where the maker or drawer completes the instrument, the instrument will be enforced accordingly; where someone other than the maker or drawer fills in the blanks, the instrument will be enforced if it is completed in the manner intended by the maker or drawer. The legal presumption is that, by signing the incomplete instrument, the maker or drawer has authorized another to fill in the gaps in the intended manner.

A holder who takes an incomplete instrument is held to take with knowledge of a possible claim or defense and so cannot qualify as a holder in due course. However, if the instrument is subsequently completed in the manner intended by the maker or drawer and presented to the primary party for payment, the primary party cannot refuse to pay on the basis that the instrument, when issued, was incomplete. It is only where the instrument is completed in a manner *not intended or authorized* by the maker or drawer that the primary party will have a defense to payment good as against all but a holder in due course (e. g., where the sum certain blank is completed as $10,000 rather than the $1,000 intended by the maker or drawer). The Uniform Commercial Code rules regarding incomplete instruments are found at Section 3–115 as follows.

The UCC provides:

Section 3–115. Incomplete Instruments

(1) When a paper whose contents at the time of signing show that it is intended to become an instrument is signed while still incomplete in any necessary respect it cannot be enforced until completed, but when it is completed in accordance with authority given it is effective as completed.

(2) If the completion is unauthorized the rules as to material alteration apply (Section 3–407), even though the paper was not deliv-

ered by the maker or drawer; but the burden of establishing that any completion is unauthorized is on the party so asserting.

———

As you can see from Subsection (2), unauthorized completion of instruments is governed by the rules of "material alteration" to be explained immediately following.

Material alteration. The holder of an instrument may find that the maker or acceptor (i. e., the primary party) refuses to pay on the grounds that the instrument has been altered. Alteration may take the form of an addition, change, or deletion of terms, or, in the case of an incomplete instrument, an unauthorized completion. Section 3–407 of the Uniform Commercial Code defines "alteration" in this manner.

The UCC provides:

(1) Any alteration of an instrument is material which changes the contract of any party thereto in any respect, including any such change in

(a) the number or relations of the parties; or

(b) an incomplete instrument, by completing it otherwise than as authorized; or

(c) the writing as signed, by adding to it or by removing any part of it.

———

Whether an alteration will serve as a defense to payment depends upon the nature of the alteration and the kind of holder trying to collect payment. The following rules prevail:

(1) With regard to all holders other than holders in due course, a *fraudulent* and *material* alteration *made by a holder* of an instrument will discharge from lia-

bility any party whose contract is changed thereby. To result in discharge, the alteration must be made by a holder or his or her confederate—"spoliation" (i. e., alteration by a meddling stranger) will not affect anyone's rights. Also, the alteration must be material: if the addition, change, deletion, or unauthorized completion in no way affects the contract of a previous signer, it is immaterial and will not result in discharge. But if the alteration effects a change, however slight, in the contract of a party, the requirement of materiality is satisfied (e. g., adding one cent to the amount payable or advancing the due date of the instrument by one day). Finally, the alteration must be fraudulent. An addition, change, or deletion made with a benevolent motive as opposed to a fraudulent one (e. g., lowering an interest rate so as to confer a gift or benefit upon a party) will not serve to discharge anybody.

(2) To say that an alteration that is immaterial, nonfraudulent, or made by one other than a holder will not discharge a party is not to say that the alteration will be given effect. The altered instrument will be enforced but only according to its "original tenor" (i. e., according to the original terms of the instrument).

(3) A subsequent holder in due course may in all cases enforce the altered instrument according to its original tenor —even where the alteration is fraudulent, material, and made by a holder. And where the maker or drawer has negligently and substantially contributed to the alteration, the holder in due course may enforce the instrument in its altered form (e. g., where the maker or drawer leaves numerous blanks in the instrument, making it easy for someone to change the figures).

(4) Finally, where the alteration is an unauthorized completion of an incomplete instrument, a subsequent holder in due course may enforce the instrument ei-

ther as intended or as completed. (Compare—as to all other fraudulent and material alterations made by a holder, a subsequent HDC can enforce the instrument only according to its original tenor with the exception of alterations substantially induced by the negligence of the maker or drawer.)

The above rules are set forth in Sections 3–407 and 3–406 of the Uniform Commercial Code as follows.

The UCC provides:

Section 3–407. Alteration

(2) As against any person other than a subsequent holder in due course

(a) alteration by the holder which is both fraudulent and material discharges any party whose contract is thereby changed unless that party assents or is precluded from asserting the defense;

(b) no other alteration discharges any party and the instrument may be enforced according to its original tenor, or as to incomplete instruments according to the authority given.

(3) A subsequent holder in due course may in all cases enforce the instrument according to its original tenor and when an incomplete instrument has been completed, he may enforce it as completed.

Section 3–406. Negligence Contributing to Alteration * * *

Any person who by his negligence substantially contributes to a material alteration of the instrument * * * is precluded from asserting the alteration against a holder in due course or against a drawee or other payor who pays the instrument in good faith and in accordance with the reasonable commercial standards of the drawee's or payor's business.

———————

Of course, it should be realized that a purchaser who takes an instrument with knowledge of its material alteration takes with notice of a claim or defense and cannot qualify as a holder in due course.

Personal defenses. The maker or acceptor of an instrument may also refuse to pay on the basis of some *personal defense.* A personal defense is a defense that is good against all but a holder in due course; it is "personal" in the sense that it arises out of a breach of agreement between former parties to the instrument. The rule is that transfer of a negotiable instrument to a holder in due course "cuts off" personal defenses—anyone other than a holder in due course takes the instrument subject to the defenses. Personal defenses include:

(1) *Fraud in the inducement.* You will recall from Ch. 8 that fraud in the inducement refers to misrepresentation of a material fact. For example, suppose that George Johnson falsely represents to Larry Taylor that he paid $18,000 for his boat one year ago when, in fact, George paid only $10,000 for the boat. Relying on the misrepresentation, Larry purchases the boat, giving George a negotiable promissory note for $10,300. George's misrepresentation constitutes fraud in the inducement. If George or his assignee later tries to collect the note from Larry, Larry has a good defense to payment. However, the defense is personal, and if the note is subsequently transferred to a holder in due course, the holder in due course may enforce the note against Larry. And so may an assignee with the rights of a holder in due course under the Shelter Provision. Larry's only remedy, in this case, is to sue George for fraud— that is, if Larry can find George and George has enough money to make a suit worthwhile.

(2) *Failure of consideration.* Failure of consideration is also a personal defense. Say that Larry Taylor gives George Johnson a promissory note in payment for the boat, but George never delivers the boat to Larry. Here, there is a failure of consideration, and if George or his assignee tries to collect the note, Larry has a good defense to payment. But the personal defense will not be good as against a subsequent holder in due course of the instrument (or one with the rights of such a holder).

(3) *Nondelivery of the instrument.* Nondelivery of the instrument to the payee is also a personal defense good against all but a holder in due course. For example, suppose that Larry Taylor makes the promissory note out "to bearer", but the note is stolen before Larry can deliver it to George Johnson. Because the note is bearer paper, the thief can negotiate it by delivery alone: if he or she negotiates it to a holder in due course, the holder in due course will "cut off" the personal defense of nondelivery.

As will be explained later under the heading of "mixed defenses", there are several defenses that are sometimes personal and sometimes real (a "real" defense is a defense that is good even against a holder in due course) depending on the circumstances involved.

And it should be pointed out that several state legislatures have passed consumer protection statutes abolishing the "holder in due course doctrine" with regard to consumer goods financing. Too often in the past, an unscrupulous merchant would use fraudulent means to induce a buyer to purchase consumer goods, taking a negotiable instrument in return for the goods. The merchant would then sell the instrument to a holder in due course, and the buyer would have to pay despite the fraud in the inducement. The same thing resulted in cases of failure of consideration: the merchant who failed to perform would sell the buyer's negotiable instrument to a holder in due course, and the buyer would have to pay despite the fact that he or she received defective merchandise or no merchandise at all. Understandably, many state legislatures found this to be unacceptable. They enacted laws providing that, in the case of a negotiable instrument arising out of the sale of consumer goods, personal defenses such as fraud in the inducement and failure of consideration are not "cut off" by transfer of the instrument to a holder in due course.

Even in states without consumer statutes, the courts have held that if the holder of the instrument is *closely connected* to the seller of the consumer goods (e. g., where the holder is the finance company that finances all of the merchant's credit sales), the holder is charged with knowledge of the fraud or other defense and cannot qualify as a holder in due course. This is referred to as the "close connection" doctrine.

Real defenses. Sometimes, the maker or acceptor of an instrument will refuse to pay on the basis of a *real defense.* Unlike a personal defense, a real defense is good against everyone, including a holder in due course (the defense goes to a defect so serious and so substantial that not even a holder in due course can cut it off). Real defenses include:

(1) *Fraud in the execution.* You will recall that fraud in the execution (also called fraud in the factum) usually involves the surreptitious substitution of one document for another. Thus, where the maker or drawer is tricked into signing an instrument without realizing that it is even a contract (e. g., signing an "autograph" that turns out to be a check), the maker or drawer will have a real defense to payment good against even a holder in due course.

(2) *Forgery.* Forgery (i. e., unauthorized signature) is also a real defense with one exception. Generally speaking, a forgery creates no legal obligation on the part of the party whose signature has been forged. That party—whether the maker, drawer, drawee, or indorser

—will not have to pay even where the instrument has been transferred to a holder in due course. The exception arises where the party has negligently and substantially contributed to the forgery. Section 3–406 of the Code states the exception as follows.

The UCC provides:

Section 3–406. Negligence Contributing to * * * Unauthorized Signature

Any person who by his negligence substantially contributes to * * * the making of an unauthorized signature is precluded from asserting the * * * lack of authority against a holder in due course or against a drawee or other payor who pays the instrument in good faith and in accordance with the reasonable commercial standards of the drawee's or payor's business.

———

In contrast, forgery always creates obligation on the part of the wrongdoer who has forged the signature. Section 3–404 of the Code provides: "[Whereas] any unauthorized signature is wholly inoperative as that of the person whose name is signed unless he * * * is precluded from denying it * * * it operates as the signature of the unauthorized signer in favor of any person who in good faith pays the instrument or takes it for value." Thus, as to parties who in good faith pay the instrument or take it for value, the forger is fully liable on the instrument in the capacity in which he or she signed (e. g., if he or she forged the maker's signature, he or she will be primarily liable; if he or she forged an indorsement, he or she will be liable on the indorsement contract, etc.). Of course, the forger's liability will be of little practical value if the forger cannot be found, or if he or she has insufficient funds to pay the instrument.

(3) *Infancy.* Infancy, too, is a real defense good as against even a holder in due course. You will recall from Ch. 9 that a minor's contracts are generally voidable. To the same extent that a minor may rescind his or her agreements, he or she may rescind negotiable instruments arising out of the agreements. For example, if, under local law, a minor has the right to rescind a contract for purchase of a stereo, he or she also has the right to refuse to pay a negotiable note signed to pay for the stereo. This is so even where the note has been transferred to a holder in due course. And where local law provides that a minor is liable for the fair value of necessaries, the minor cannot refuse to honor a note signed to pay for the necessaries. Infancy or minority is thus a defense to payment of an instrument only where it would justify the minor in rescinding the underlying transaction.

Mixed defenses. As stated previously, some defenses are sometimes personal and sometimes real depending on the circumstances involved. They are called *mixed defenses*, and include duress, incapacity (other than infancy), illegality, and discharge of contract duties. As you will recall from Chapters 8 and 9, the first three of these defenses will make a contract either void or voidable. If the duress, incapacity (other than infancy), or illegality is such as to make the contract void, the defense is a real defense good as against even a holder in due course. If the defense merely makes the contract voidable, the defense is personal and is cut off by a holder in due course.

(1) *Duress.* Again, duress is any physical or mental coercion used to deprive a person of his or her free will and force him or her to act in a manner contrary to his or her free will. Duress used to force a person to enter into a contract renders the agreement void or voidable.

It renders the agreement void where it reduces its victim to a mere mechanical instrument or automaton who is *physically* compelled to enter into the contract (e. g., hypnotizing or drugging the victim so that he or she will sign the agreement, or taking the victim's hand and physically forcing him or her to sign). If such duress results in a negotiable instrument, the victim of the duress will have a real defense to payment—a defense good against even a holder in due course.

Where the duress falls short of reducing the victim to an automaton, the duress renders the contract merely voidable. This is the situation where the victim intentionally, rather than mechanically, enters into the agreement because of the threat or force employed (e. g., where the victim signs the contract because a gun is pointed at him or her or because of a threat such as "I will tell your spouse if you don't sign"). If this kind of duress results in a negotiable instrument, the victim of the duress will have but a personal defense to payment—the defense will not be effective against a holder in due course (or one with the rights of such a holder). Of course, if the victim (i. e., the maker or acceptor) has to pay the instrument, he or she will have a right to recover damages from the perpetrator of the duress—that is, if he or she can find the party and prove the duress in court.

(2) *Incapacity other than infancy.* In Ch. 9, you learned that capacity refers to the normal power that a person has to enter into a contract. People who lack this power because of mental or physical disability are "incapacitated". Sometimes, incapacity is total (e. g., where a person needs a guardian to handle all his or her affairs, or where a person is so completely physically or mentally disabled that he or she is incapable of understanding a simple agreement). An agreement made by a totally incapacitated person is void: if the agreement results in a negotiable

instrument, the primary party's total incapacity will serve as a real defense good against even a holder in due course.

Often, however, incapacity is only partial. Although a person is not completely mentally competent, he or she may have some understanding of a transaction, and, where this is so, any contract that results will be voidable only. It follows that, if a negotiable contract results, the partial incapacity of the primary party will operate as a personal defense to payment. Thus, if the instrument is transferred to a holder in due course, the primary party will have to pay despite his or her lack of full capacity. Again, if the incapacitated party is required to pay the instrument, he or she may be able to recover the loss by avoiding the transaction against the other original party to the instrument—that is, if the other party can be found, and if that party has sufficient financial resources.

(3) *Illegality.* You will also recall from Ch. 9 that if the parties to an agreement are in pari delicto (i. e., in equal fault), neither will receive any help from the courts in enforcing the agreement. This is because the agreement is not a contract but a void and illegal bargain. Assuming that a negotiable instrument results in such circumstances, the defense of illegality is a real defense, and anyone (including a holder in due course) who takes the instrument takes it subject to the defense.

Sometimes, however, one of the parties is not in pari delicto, and the agreement is not *malum in se* (i. e., against good morals) but only *malum prohibitum* (i. e., against a statute). In this case, the party who is not in pari delicto may be able to enforce the agreement on the basis of quasi contract. Here, if a negotiable instrument results, the illegality is but a personal defense and is cut off by a holder in due course.

(4) *Discharge.* Discharge of an instrument is frequently encountered as a defense. One type of discharge—discharge in bankruptcy—is a real defense and is good against everyone, including a holder in due course. (You will learn in Ch. 26, "Creditors and Bankruptcy", that most of a bankrupt individual's debts are discharged in a bankruptcy proceeding, including debts represented by negotiable instruments.)

Discharge by payment of the negotiable instrument is a personal defense *unless* the payment is noted on the instrument (or unless the party who pays takes up the instrument and destroys it, in which case the problem of subsequent transfer is altogether eliminated). Of course, where the payment or other discharge of parties is apparent on the instrument itself, any holder who takes the instrument takes "with notice" of the discharge and so cannot qualify as a holder in due course with respect to the discharged party or parties.

Section 3–305 of the Uniform Commercial Code summarizes the rights of a holder in due course as follows.

The UCC provides:

Section 3–305. Rights of a Holder in Due Course

To the extent that a holder is a holder in due course he takes the instrument free from

(1) all claims to it on the part of any person; and

(2) all defenses of any party to the instrument with whom the holder has not dealt except

    (a) infancy, to the extent that it is a defense to a simple contract; and

    (b) such other incapacity, or duress, or illegality of the transaction, as renders the obligation of the party a nullity [void]; and,

(c) such misrepresentation as has induced the party to sign the instrument with neither knowledge nor reasonable opportunity to obtain knowledge of its character or its essential terms [fraud in the execution]; and,

(d) discharge in insolvency proceedings; and

(e) any other discharge of which the holder has notice when he takes the instrument.

———

Section 3–404 of the Code adds that "any unauthorized signature [i. e., forgery] is wholly inoperative as that of the person whose name is signed."

What are the responsibilities of indorsers?

To this point, you have seen that the party who is primarily liable on an instrument (i. e., the maker or acceptor) usually pays without question. Sometimes, however, the primary party is financially unable to pay or has a real or personal defense to payment. Insofar as a dishonored draft or check is concerned, you know that the drawer is secondarily liable and must pay the instrument upon notice of the dishonor. But what about a dishonored note? And who will pay if the drawer of a dishonored draft is financially unable to pay or has a real or personal defense to payment? Are there any other parties secondarily liable on the instruments?

The answer is yes—secondary liability usually goes to any *indorser* of a negotiable instrument. By indorsing (signing) the instrument, the indorser assumes contractual liability thereon. This is so even where the indorsement is not required to negotiate the instrument (e. g., where the party chooses to indorse bearer paper in blank or specially). Section 3–414 of the Uniform Commercial Code defines the contract of the indorser as follows.

The UCC provides:

Section 3–414. Contract of Indorser; Order of Liability

(1) Unless the indorsement otherwise specifies (as by such words as "without recourse") every indorser engages that upon dishonor and any necessary notice of dishonor and protest he will pay the instrument according to its tenor at the time of his indorsement to the holder or to any subsequent indorser who takes it up, even though the indorser who takes it up was not obligated to do so.

(2) Unless they otherwise agree indorsers are liable to one another in the order in which they indorse, which is presumed to be the order in which their signatures appear on the instrument.

———

Thus, the indorser is secondarily liable only: like the drawer, the indorser says, "I will pay but only if the primary party does not pay." The indorser's contract is to pay according to the tenor of the instrument *at the time of the indorsement.* Thus, if the instrument is altered prior to the indorsement, the indorser must pay according to the altered terms. If the instrument is altered after the indorsement, the indorser is not liable, and, in fact, may be discharged if the alteration changes the terms of his or her contract. The indorser's contract runs not only to the immediate indorsee (the party to whom he or she indorses the note) but also to any subsequent holder who takes the instrument (and who may have to pay upon the instrument's dishonor).

However, as with the drawer, there are three conditions precedent to the indorser's liability:

(1) The holder of the instrument must present it to the primary party for acceptance or payment *within a reasonable time* after the indorsement;

(2) The primary party must dishonor the instrument; and

(3) The holder must protest the dishonor (in the case of a draft drawn or payable in a foreign country) or notify the indorser of the dishonor *within a reasonable time* after the dishonor.

Note that these conditions are very similar to the conditions precedent to the drawer's liability—however, there is one major difference. You know that a holder's failure to act timely in presenting a draft or in notifying the drawer of the instrument's dishonor will not affect the drawer's liability (except where the drawer loses funds on deposit with a drawee who goes insolvent during the delay). However, a holder's failure to present an instrument *within a reasonable time* after its indorsement or to notify the indorser of the instrument's dishonor *within a reasonable time* after dishonor will serve to completely discharge the indorser. A "reasonable time" is measured from the time each indorser signs the instrument. A presentment for payment may be prompt enough to bind the last indorser but too slow to bind a prior indorser who is discharged as a result.

Also note that there is no condition precedent that the holder of a dishonored draft or check must first seek payment from the drawer before seeking it from the indorser. Once the instrument is dishonored, the holder may proceed against any or all of the parties secondarily liable (i. e., the drawer and/or indorsers).

Quite often, there are several indorsements on an instrument. Since, upon dishonor and notice, the holder may proceed against any one of the indorsers without proceeding against the others, it becomes important to know whether an indorser who is required to pay has any rights against the other indorsers. The rule is that the indorsers are liable to each other in the order in which their signatures appear on the instrument: each indorser may hold his or her prior indorser, back to the first indorser (barring untimely presentment or notice by the holder which has discharged some or all of the indorsers). Thus, in most cases, the first indorser is ultimately required to pay the instrument, although he or she, in turn, may collect from the drawer if the drawer is financially solvent and has no defense to payment good as against the indorser. Let's take an example. Suppose that John Henry is the holder of a dishonored draft drawn by Sandy Johnson and indorsed by Fred Stoner, Pete Dawkins, and Nancy Freeman, in that order. All conditions precedent to the indorser's liability having been met, John Henry collects payment from Pete Dawkins (Henry chose to proceed against Pete because there was no question but what Pete had sufficient financial resources to pay). Pete, in turn, may collect from Fred Stoner, or, possibly, from Sandy Johnson. However, Pete cannot collect from Nancy Freeman—an indorser can hold only his or her prior indorsers on the instrument, not subsequent indorsers.

The Uniform Commercial Code provisions setting forth the conditions precedent to the indorser's liability are found at Sections 3–501 through 3–508 and Section 3–511 as follows.

The UCC provides:

Section 3–501. When Presentment, Notice of Dishonor, and Protest Necessary or Permissible

(1) Unless excused (Section 3–511) presentment is necessary to charge secondary parties as follows:

(a) presentment for acceptance is necessary to charge the drawer and indorsers of a draft where the draft so provides, or is payable elsewhere than at the residence or place of business of the drawee, or its date of payment depends upon such presentment. The holder may at his option present for acceptance any other draft payable at a stated date;

(b) presentment for payment is necessary to charge any indorser * * *

(2) Unless excused

(a) notice of any dishonor is necessary to charge any indorser;

(b) in the case of a drawer * * * notice of dishonor is necessary * * *

Section 3–502. Unexcused delay; discharge

(1) Where without excuse any necessary presentment or notice of dishonor is delayed beyond the time when it is due

(a) any indorser is discharged;
* * *

(3) Where without excuse a necessary protest is delayed beyond the time when it is due any drawer or indorser is discharged.

Section 3–503. Time of Presentment

(1) Unless a different time is expressed in the instrument the time for any presentment is determined as follows:

(a) where an instrument is payable at or a fixed period after a stated date any presentment for acceptance must be made on or before the date it is payable;

(b) where an instrument is payable after sight it must either be presented for acceptance or negotiated within a reasonable time after date or issue whichever is later;

(c) where an instrument shows the date on which it is payable presentment for payment is due on that date;

(d) where an instrument is accelerated presentment for payment is due within a reasonable time after the acceleration;

(e) with respect to the liability of any secondary party presentment for acceptance or payment of any other instrument is due within a reasonable time after such party becomes liable thereon.

(2) A reasonable time for presentment is determined by the nature of the instrument, any usage of banking or trade and the facts of the particular case. In the case of an uncertified check which is drawn and payable within the United States and which is not a draft drawn by a bank the following are presumed to be reasonable periods within which to present for payment or to initiate bank collection:

(a) with respect to the liability of the drawer, thirty days after date or issue whichever is later; and

(b) with respect to the liability of an indorser, seven days after his indorsement.

(3) Where any presentment is due on a day which is not a full business day for either the person making presentment or the party to pay or accept, presentment is due on the next following day which is a full business day for both parties.

(4) Presentment to be sufficient must be made at a reasonable hour, and if at a bank during its banking day.

Section 3–504. How Presentment Made

(1) Presentment is a demand for acceptance or payment made upon the maker, acceptor, drawee or other payor by or on behalf of the holder.

(2) Presentment may be Made

  (a) by mail, in which event the time of presentment is determined by the time of receipt of the mail; or

  (b) through a clearing house; or

  (c) at the place of acceptance or payment specified in the instrument or if there be none at the place of business or residence of the party to accept or pay. If neither the party to accept or pay nor anyone authorized to act for him is present or accessible at such place presentment is excused.

* * *

(4) A draft accepted or a note made payable at a bank in the United States must be presented at such bank.

Section 3–505. Rights of Party to Whom Presentment is Made

(1) The party to whom presentment is made may without dishonor require

  (a) exhibition of the instrument; and

  (b) reasonable identification of the person making presentment and evidence of his authority to make it if made for another, and

  (c) that the instrument be produced for acceptance or payment at a place specified in it, or if there be none at any place reasonable in the circumstances; and

  (d) a signed receipt on the instrument for any partial or full payment and its surrender upon full payment.

Section 3–506. Time Allowed for Acceptance or Payment

(1) Acceptance may be deferred without dishonor until the close of the next business day following presentment. The holder may also in a good faith effort to obtain acceptance and without either dishonor of the instrument or discharge of secondary parties allow postponement of acceptance for an additional business day.

Section 3–507. Dishonor; Holder's Right of Recourse; Term Allowing Re-Presentment

(1) An instrument is dishonored when

  (a) a necessary or optional presentment is duly made and due acceptance or payment is refused or cannot be obtained within the prescribed time * * *

  (b) presentment is excused and the instrument is not duly accepted or paid.

(2) Subject to any necessary notice of dishonor and protest the holder has upon dishonor an immediate right of recourse against the drawers and indorsers.

(3) Return of an instrument for lack of proper indorsement is not dishonor.

Section 3–508. Notice of Dishonor

(1) Notice of dishonor may be given to any person who may be liable on the instrument by or on behalf of the holder or any party who has himself received notice, or any other party who can be compelled to pay the instrument * * *

(2) Any necessary notice must be given by a bank before its midnight deadline and by any other person before midnight of the third business day after dishonor or receipt of notice of dishonor.

(3) Notice may be given in any reasonable manner. It may be oral or written and in any terms which identify the instrument and state that it has been dishonored * * *

(4) Written notice is given when sent although it is not received.

Section 3–511. Waived or Excused Presentment, Protest or Notice of Dishonor or Delay Therein

(1) Delay in presentment, protest or notice of dishonor is excused when the party is without notice that it is due or when the delay is caused by circumstances beyond his control and he exercises reasonable diligence after the cause of the delay ceases to operate.

(2) Presentment or notice or protest as the case may be is entirely excused when

(a) the party to be charged has waived it expressly or by implication either before or after it is due; or

(b) such party has himself dishonored the instrument or has

countermanded payment or otherwise has no reason to expect or right to require that the instrument be accepted or paid; or

(c) by reasonable diligence the presentment or protest cannot be made or notice given.

(3) Presentment is also entirely excused when

(a) the maker, acceptor or drawee of any instrument * * * is dead or in insolvency proceedings instituted after the issue of the instrument or

(b) acceptance or payment is refused but not for want of proper presentment.

What does all of this mean? The following brief summary should be helpful:

First—presentment for payment is not a condition precedent to the liability of a maker or acceptor (i. e., a primary party); presentment for acceptance, on the other hand, is required to create the acceptor (by accepting, the drawee becomes a primary party).

Second—presentment and notice of dishonor are conditions precedent to the liability of secondary parties (i. e., drawers and indorsers). A holder's failure to act timely in making presentment or in giving notice of dishonor will discharge an indorser; however, it will not affect the drawer's liability (again, with the exception of the situation where the drawer loses funds on deposit with a drawee who goes insolvent during the holder's delay).

Third—time of presentment is governed by Section 3–503 of the Code. With regard to the liability of a drawer, a check is presented within a "reasonable time" if presented within 30 days after date or issue of the check. With regard to the liability of an indorser, a "reasonable time" for presentment is "within 7 days" of the indorsement. If the liability of secondary parties is not to be impaired, notice of dishonor of an instrument must be given by a bank by midnight of the next banking day following dishonor, and, by any other person, by midnight of the third business day following dishonor.

Fourth—as outlined in UCC Section 3–511, presentment of notice of dishonor, or delay in presentment or notice may be excused in certain circumstances (e. g., presentment is entirely excused where the maker, acceptor, or drawee waives presentment, is dead, or is involved in insolvency proceedings).

Thus, it should be concluded that presentment and notice are conditions precedent to secondary liability. Any unreasonable delay in presentment or notice will discharge an indorser, but will not affect the drawer's liability (subject to the exception previously mentioned).

You already know that a drawer may avoid secondary liability by signing without recourse. So may an indorser avoid secondary liability by indorsing without recourse. Such an indorsement is called a *qualified indorsement* because the indorser who signs "without recourse" disclaims liability on the indorsement contract. The indorser, in effect, states, "I do not agree to pay the instrument upon dishonor by the primary party even if timely presentment is made and notice of dishonor given." Words other than "without recourse" may be used to accomplish a qualified indorsement if the words clearly indicate an intent to disclaim the indorsement contract. However, an indorser seldom uses other words, because if there is any question as to the indorser's intent, the words will be considered a regular and not a qualified indorsement. The only safe way to make a

qualified indorsement is to indorse "without recourse". (As you will learn in the next section, a person who indorses without recourse may still be liable on the basis of warranty.)

In direct contrast to a qualified indorsement is an indorsement with words of guaranty added. Here, the indorser does more than engage to pay the instrument upon its dishonor (assuming all conditions precedent have been met)—he or she guarantees payment. The practical effect of the guaranty depends on the words used by the indorser. If the indorser adds words like *"payment guaranteed"* to his or her indorsement, the indorser's liability is like that of a comaker: the indorser promises that if the instrument is not paid when due, he or she will immediately pay it without any conditions precedent. Unlike the usual unqualified indorser, this indorser has no right to insist upon presentment to the maker or drawee or notice of dishonor.

An indorser who adds words like *"collection guaranteed"*, on the other hand, merely guarantees the solvency of the principal obligor. Like the indorser who guarantees *payment,* this indorser waives the conditions precedent of presentment and notice of dishonor. However, the indorser creates several new conditions to liability. The indorser, in effect, states, "I will pay the instrument if it is not paid when due *provided that* (1) the holder reduces his or her claim against the maker or acceptor to judgment, and the judgment is returned unsatisfied; or (2) the maker or acceptor has become insolvent; or (3) it is otherwise apparent that it is useless to proceed against the maker or acceptor." The Uniform Commercial Code provisions regarding indorsements with words of guaranty are found at Section 3–416 as follows.

The UCC provides:

Section 3–416. Contract of Guarantor

(1) "Payment guaranteed" or equivalent words added to a signature mean that the signer engages that if the instrument is not paid when due he will pay it according to its tenor without resort by the holder to any other party.

(2) "Collection guaranteed" or equivalent words added to a signature mean that the signer engages that if the instrument is not paid when due he will pay it according to its tenor, but only after the holder has reduced his claim against the maker or acceptor to judgment and execution has been returned unsatisfied, or after the maker or acceptor has become insolvent or it is otherwise apparent that it is useless to proceed against him.

*   *   *

(5) When words of guaranty are used presentment, notice of dishonor and protest are not necessary to charge the user.

Will a party other than an original party (i. e., a party other than a maker, drawer, or drawee-acceptor) ever be liable on an instrument that he or she has not indorsed, has indorsed but without recourse, or has indorsed but has been discharged because of improper presentment or notice?

Throughout this chapter, we have considered the efforts of a holder to collect the sum certain payable on a negotiable instrument. To this point, we have learned the following:

(1) Usually, the holder goes to the maker or acceptor (i. e., the primary party) who pays the sum certain without question.

(2) Sometimes, however, the maker, drawer, or acceptor of an instrument suffers a loss of funds on deposit with a bank or other drawee because the holder has unreasonably delayed in making presentment or in giving notice of dishonor, during which time the bank or other drawee has gone insolvent. Where this occurs, the maker, drawer, or acceptor may discharge his or her liability on the instrument by assigning his or her rights against the insolvent party to the holder who delayed.

(3) Sometimes, the primary party is financially unable to pay or refuses to pay on the basis of a real or personal defense to payment. A real defense is good against everyone, including a holder in due course; a personal defense is good against everyone except a holder in due course (or one with the rights of such a holder).

(4) If the primary party is financially unable to pay or has a good defense against the holder, the holder will have to look to secondary parties (i. e., drawers and indorsers) for payment. Presentment, dishonor, and notice of dishonor are conditions precedent to the liability of secondary parties. Whereas the holder's unexcused failure to act timely in making presentment or in giving notice will discharge an indorser, it will not affect a drawer's liability (with the exception noted in (2) above). However, the holder's failure to make timely protest, where required, will discharge both drawers and indorsers.

(5) Both drawers and indorsers may avoid secondary liability by drawing or indorsing without recourse. On the opposite side of the coin, both drawers and indorsers may guarantee payment or collection, thus dispensing with the conditions precedent to their liability of presentment and notice of dishonor.

Now we move to the situation where the primary party and all secondary parties (i. e., drawer and indorsers) are financially unable to pay, have a good defense to payment, or are discharged from liability. Or the drawer and indorsers have drawn or indorsed without recourse so as to avoid secondary liability. Can the holder collect payment from anyone in this situation? On what basis?

The holder may be able to collect payment from a party on the basis of breach of *implied warranty of transfer*. Apart from an original party (i. e., a maker, drawer, or drawee), any party who transfers an instrument for value, whether through an assignment or a negotiation, is held to make certain implied warranties. If the party indorses the instrument prior to transfer, the warranties run to all subsequent good faith holders of the instrument. If the party does not indorse prior to transfer (e. g., where the party transfers bearer paper by delivery alone), the warranties run only to the party's immediate transferee. The idea is that a negotiable instrument is "property", and a purchaser of "property" is entitled to certain basic protections (i. e., the purchaser should have legal recourse in the event the property turns out to be something other than what it appears to be).

Warranty liability exists independently of secondary liability (irrespective of indorsement). A party who indorses an instrument prior to transferring it may be liable both on his or her indorsement contract (assuming he or she is financially solvent and has no defense to payment) and on the basis of breach of implied warranty. However, as to the party's warranty liability, there are no conditions precedent of presentment, dishonor, protest, or notice of dishonor: the party is liable immediately upon breach of any one of the five warranties set forth in Section 3–417 of the Uniform Commercial Code. Section 3–417 provides as follows.

The UCC provides:

Section 3–417. Warranties on Presentment and Transfer

* * *

(2) Any person who transfers an instrument and receives consideration warrants to his transferee and if the transfer is by indorsement to any subsequent holder who takes the instrument in good faith that

(a) he has a good title to the instrument or is authorized to obtain payment or acceptance on behalf of one who has a good title and the transfer is otherwise rightful; and

(b) all signatures are genuine or authorized; and

(c) the instrument has not been materially altered; and

(d) no defense of any party is good against him; and

(e) he has no knowledge of any insolvency proceeding instituted with respect to the maker or acceptor or the drawer of an unaccepted instrument.

(3) By transferring "without recourse" the transferor limits the obligation stated in subsection (2)(d) to a warranty that he has no knowledge of such a defense.

Thus, there are five specific warranties implied in the areas of title, signatures, alteration, defenses, and insolvency proceedings.

(1) *Warranty of title*. By transferring an instrument, a party impliedly warrants that he or she has good title (or is authorized to obtain payment or acceptance on behalf of one who has good title) and that the transfer is otherwise rightful. The warranty of title is de-

signed to protect the transferee who ultimately discovers that his or her transferor did not own the instrument. This may occur, for example, where an instrument is stolen and transferred with or without a forged indorsement. In the case of order paper, suppose that Larry Taylor makes out a negotiable promissory note payable "to the order of George Johnson". After Larry delivers the note to George, Charlie Sneakthief steals the instrument, forges George's blank indorsement, and sells the note to Sally Streeter. Sally, in turn, transfers the "bearer paper" by delivery alone to Mark Hopkins who takes the note for value and in good faith. Mark presents the note to Larry Taylor for payment; however, Larry has been informed of the theft by George Johnson and refuses to pay. Larry's personal defense of nondelivery is good against Mark who does not qualify as a holder in due course (indorsement by George is required to negotiate the note so as to make someone a holder, and, therefore, a holder in due course). Looking to secondary parties, can Mark collect from anyone on the basis of indorsement? You know that he cannot collect from George Johnson (forgery is a real defense), and he cannot collect from Sally Streeter who did not indorse. While he could collect from Charlie Sneakthief who is liable in the capacity in which he signed, Charlie has left town and has little or no money to boot. However, Mark can hold Sally Streeter liable for breach of implied warranty of title: by transferring the note without an indorsement, Sally impliedly warranted good title to Mark, her immediate transferee. Of course, Charlie Sneakthief is also liable for breach of implied warranty of title both as to Sally (his immediate transferee) and as to Mark (Charlie's forged indorsement is effective to make the warranty run to subsequent good faith holders). But again, Charlie has left town, so the remedies are of little

practical value. Thus, it is Sally Streeter who must bear the loss here, and that is only fair, since it was Sally who first dealt with forger Charlie Sneakthief.

Would the result differ if the instrument involved were bearer paper? Yes—only Charlie Sneakthief would be liable for breach of implied warranty of title, and only as to his immediate transferee. Remember, a holder in due course who receives bearer paper from a thief obtains good title and can pass good title to another. Thus, Sally Streeter has good title at the time of her transfer to Mark Hopkins and so has not breached the warranty of title.

(2) *Warranty that all signatures are genuine or authorized.* One who transfers an instrument for value also warrants that all signatures on the instrument are genuine or authorized. Where it is the signature of a payee or indorsee that is forged, the transferor breaches both the warranty of title and the warranty of genuine signatures (e. g., Sally Streeter breaches both warranties when she sells the note containing George Johnson's forged indorsement to Mark Hopkins).

(3) *Warranty against material alteration.* A party who purchases a negotiable instrument assumes that he or she will be able to enforce the instrument according to its tenor at the time of the purchase. Yet, if the instrument has been materially altered, the liability of previous signers may be limited to the tenor of the instrument at the time of their signature, or their liability may be altogether discharged. To protect the transferee in this situation, the Uniform Commercial Code provides that a party who transfers an instrument for value warrants that the instrument has not been materially altered. Thus, even if the transferor has a good defense to secondary liability, he or she may still be liable on the basis of warranty.

(4) *Warranty against defenses.* This is the only transfer warranty that differs in the case of a qualified indorsement. Any transferor for value other than a qualified indorser (i. e., one who indorses "without recourse") warrants absolutely that no defenses of any party are good against him or her. A qualified indorser warrants merely that *he or she has no actual knowledge of any defense good as against him or her.* To protect the transferee, qualified indorsers are sometimes asked to make express warranties against defenses.

(5) *Warranty against knowledge of insolvency proceedings.* Finally, a transferor for value warrants that he or she has no knowledge of any insolvency proceeding (e. g., bankruptcy) instituted with respect to the maker or acceptor (or drawer of an unaccepted instrument). This warranty goes no further than what it says. The transferor does not warrant that the maker, acceptor, or drawer is a good credit risk or that he or she is in good shape financially—the transferor merely states, "I have no knowledge of any formal insolvency proceeding instituted with respect to the party."

Thus, you have the basic procedure for collecting the sum certain on a negotiable instrument. Start by going against the primary party, and, if he or she pays the instrument, that is the end of it. If the primary party is financially unable to pay or sets up a good defense to payment (remember, a holder in due course cuts off personal defenses), proceed against any secondarily liable parties (drawer and indorsers). Of course, the secondary parties may also be financially unable to pay or may have good defenses to payment; or the drawer and indorsers may have avoided secondary liability by drawing or indorsing without recourse. In this case, look to see whether any transferor for value of the instrument is liable on the basis of breach of warranty (whether title, signatures, alterations, defenses, or

insolvency). If the transferor for value has indorsed the instrument, the warranties will run to all subsequent good faith holders of the instrument; if the transferor has not indorsed, the warranties will run only to his or her immediate transferee.

What other principles about negotiable instruments must be understood to complete the picture?

While you are now familiar with the basic procedure for collecting a negotiable instrument, a few miscellaneous principles [2] must be added to complete the picture. They are considered in this section under the following headings:

(1) Warranties on presentment;

(2) Accommodating parties;

(3) Instruments lacking only the magic words of negotiability;

(4) Acceptance by the drawee that varies the terms of the draft;

(5) Conversion of an instrument by a drawee or other party;

(6) Restrictive indorsements; and

(7) Cancellation and renunciation.

Warranties on presentment. A party who presents an instrument for payment or acceptance makes certain implied warranties to the party who pays or accepts. Prior transferors of the instrument are held to make the same warranties to the party (these presentment warranties are separate from and in addition to the transfer warranties they make). Section 3–417 of the Uniform Commercial Code provides as follows.

---

2. There are also many special rules dealing with checks, banks, and bank-customer relations. All aspects of the bank collection process and banking laws generally are dealt with in Ch. 15.

The UCC provides:

Section 3–417. Warranties on Presentment * * *

(1) Any person who obtains payment or acceptance and any prior transferor warrants to a person who in good faith pays or accepts that

(a) he has a good title to the instrument or is authorized to obtain payment or acceptance on behalf of one who has good title; and

(b) he has no knowledge that the signature of the maker or drawer is unauthorized, except that this warranty is not given by a holder in due course acting in good faith

(i) to a maker with respect to the maker's own signature; or

(ii) to a drawer with respect to the drawer's own signature, whether or not the drawer is also the drawee; or,

(iii) to an acceptor of a draft if the holder in due course took the draft after the acceptance or obtained the acceptance without knowledge that the drawer's signature was unauthorized; and

(c) the instrument has not been materially altered; except that this warranty is not given by a holder in due course acting in good faith

(i) to the maker of a note; or

(ii) to the drawer of a draft whether or not the drawer is also the drawee; or

(iii) to the acceptor of a draft with respect to an alteration made prior to the acceptance if the holder in due course took the draft after the acceptance even though the acceptance provided "payable as originally drawn" or equivalent terms; or

(iv) to the acceptor of a draft with respect to an alteration made after the acceptance.

———

As you can see, there are three presentment warranties (as opposed to the five transfer warranties); they deal with title, signature of the issuing party, and material alteration.

(1) *Warranty of title.* Any prior transferor and any party who obtains payment or acceptance of an instrument warrants to the paying or accepting party that he or she has good title to the instrument or is authorized to obtain payment or acceptance on behalf of one who has good title. The warranty is designed to protect the paying or accepting party in the event that he or she pays to or accepts from the wrong party. By way of example, suppose again that Larry Taylor makes out a negotiable note payable "to the order of George Johnson". After Larry delivers the note to George, Charlie Sneakthief steals the instrument, forges George's blank indorsement and sells the note to Sally Streeter. Without indorsing, Sally transfers the note to Mark Hopkins who takes the instrument for value and in good faith. This time, however, when Mark presents the note to Larry Taylor for payment, Larry pays the instrument, believing George's forged indorsement to be valid. Hopkins, in this case, has breached his presenter's warranty of good title; and, as prior transferors, Charlie Sneakthief and Sally Streeter have also breached the warranty. Larry may thus recover the payment from Hopkins (or from Sally or Charlie if Hopkins

is unable to pay and Larry can find Sally and Charlie). If required to pay, Hopkins' best remedy as before is against Sally Streeter for breach of transfer warranty of title. Again, it is Sally who must ultimately bear the loss, assuming she cannot locate Charlie Sneakthief, or Charlie is financially unable to pay. But this is only fair as Sally was the first party to actually deal with the thief.

(2) *Warranty against knowledge that the issuing party's signature (i. e., the signature of the maker or drawer) is unauthorized.* Any prior transferor and party making presentment also warrants that he or she has no knowledge that the signature of the maker or drawer is unauthorized. You will note that this differs from the transfer warranty wherein a transferor for value warrants *absolutely* against unauthorized signature of *any party*—here, the prior transferor and party making presentment warrant only that they have no *knowledge* of an unauthorized *issuing party's* signature. While the second presentment warranty does not extend to an indorser's signature, forged indorsements are protected against by the presenter's warranty of title. And, finally, it should be noted that a holder in due course generally does not give the second warranty of presentment.

(3) *Warranty against material alteration.* Nor does a holder in due course generally give the third warranty that there has been no material alteration of the instrument.

Along this line, it should be pointed out that, even apart from breach of warranty of presentment, a party who pays to or accepts from the wrong party usually has the right to demand return of his or her money or to cancel the acceptance. However, this is limited by the "doctrine of finality" as stated at Section 3–418 of the Uniform Commercial Code.

The UCC provides:

Section 3–418. Finality of Payment or Acceptance

* * * [E]xcept for liability for breach of warranty on presentment * * * payment or acceptance of any instrument is final in favor of a holder in due course, or a person who has in good faith changed his position in reliance on the payment.

———

Thus, ~~unless a breach~~ of warranty of presentment can be shown (and often it cannot be as a holder in due course generally makes only one of the three presenter's warranties), a mistaken payment is final if made in favor of a holder in due course or one who has in good faith changed his or her position in reliance on the payment or acceptance. The reasoning here is that it is usually better to end the transaction upon payment or acceptance rather than set aside a whole string of transactions to rectify the mistake.

Accommodating parties. Usually, a party who signs a negotiable instrument does so because of personal involvement in the underlying transaction (e. g., the party is buying or selling something). An *accommodation* party, on the other hand, signs only to support some other party to the instrument. For example, a merchant may extend credit to a party who is a bad credit risk only if the party produces an accommodation party with good credit to sign with him or her—usually, as an indorser (secondary party) or co-maker (primary party). The accommodation party is liable in whatever capacity he or she signs. And it makes no difference whether the accommodation party signs before or after the instrument is transferred, or whether all the parties are aware that an accommodation was intended.

Generally speaking, lack of consideration is no defense to the accommodation party's liability. The Uniform Commercial Code provides that consideration need not move to the accommodation party to make him or her bound on the instrument (usually, consideration moves to the accommodated party, i. e., the party who needs the support). This is so even where the accommodation party signs the instrument *after* it has been taken by the creditor in payment for the goods or services: so long as the creditor took the instrument for value before it was due, the accommodation party will become bound despite the lack of new or additional consideration.

Finally, the accommodation party is always a *surety* (see Ch. 27). Thus, he or she is not liable to the accommodated party; and, if he or she is required to pay the instrument, he or she will have a right to reimbursement from the accommodated party.

The Uniform Commercial Code deals with the contract of the accommodation party at Section 3–415 as follows.

The UCC provides:

Section 3–415. Contract of Accommodation Party

(1) An accommodation party is one who signs the instrument in any capacity for the purpose of lending his name to another party to it.

(2) When the instrument has been taken for value before it is due the accommodation party is liable in the capacity in which he has signed even though the taker knows of the accommodation.

* * *

(5) An accommodation party is not liable to the party accommodated, and if he pays the instrument has a right of recourse on the instrument against such party.

Instruments lacking only the magic words of negotiability. You will recall that an instrument must satisfy all nine requirements of negotiability in order to be a negotiable instrument. If an instrument lacks any one of the nine requirements, the instrument is nonnegotiable, and the special rules of negotiability do not come into play *with one exception.* The exception arises where the instrument satisfies all but the ninth requirement of negotiability—that is, where an instrument lacks only the magic words "to order" or "to bearer". Section 3–805 of the Uniform Commercial Code provides that such an instrument, while nonnegotiable, is still governed by all the special rules of negotiability found in Article 3 of the Code except that there can be no holder in due course of the instrument. Section 3–805 states as follows.

The UCC provides:

Section 3–805. Instrument Not Payable to Order or to Bearer

This Article applies to any instrument whose terms do not preclude transfer and which is otherwise negotiable within this Article but which is not payable to order or to bearer, except that there can be no holder in due course of such an instrument.

Thus, an instrument lacking only the magic words of negotiability may be negotiated, and, if negotiated, will give rise to all the rights and duties that accompany secondary and warranty liability. The only difference between this kind of instrument and a negotiable one is that there can be no holder in due course of the instrument. For example, there can be no holder in due course of a check that says "pay Lawrence Taylor" because the check does not say "pay to the *order* of Lawrence Taylor" or "pay Lawrence Taylor or *bearer*". Nevertheless, the check may be negotiated by indorsement and delivery; the indorser will be secondarily liable unless he or she indorses without recourse; the indorser will be entitled to timely presentment and notice of dishonor; the rules as to alteration and completion will apply, etc.

An instrument that is nonnegotiable for any reason other than or in addition to lack of the magic words is treated like any other contract and is governed by the rules presented in Chapters 7 through 11. The special rules unique to Article 3 of the Uniform Commercial Code simply do not apply (including laws relating to the drawee's acceptance, the drawer's secondary liability, indorsements, presentment, dishonor, and notice of dishonor). Thus, one who signs such an instrument assumes only the responsibilities of an assignor—the term "indorsement" as a contract creating secondary liability has no meaning insofar as the instrument is concerned.

Acceptance by the drawee that varies the terms of the draft. Sometimes, the drawee of a draft agrees to accept the instrument only if one or more terms are changed (e. g., the amount payable or the time of payment). The holder, in this case, may treat the drawee's refusal to accept the draft as drawn as dishonor of the instrument: the holder may notify the drawer and indorsers of the dishonor and rely on secondary and warranty liability to recover. Or the holder may accept the draft as altered by the drawee's acceptance. However, if the holder does so, each drawer and indorser who does not affirmatively assent to the variance will be discharged from liability on the instrument. This is only fair as the drawer and indorsers agreed to be liable on one contract and should not be held liable on another in the absence of assent to the changed terms. Section 3–412 of the Uniform Commercial Code deals with acceptance of a varying draft as follows.

The UCC provides:

Section 3–412. Acceptance Varying Draft

(1) Where the drawee's proffered acceptance in any manner varies the draft as presented the holder may refuse the acceptance and treat the draft as dishonored in which case the drawee is entitled to have his acceptance cancelled.

(2) The terms of the draft are not varied by an acceptance to pay at any particular bank or place in the United States, unless the acceptance states that the draft is to be paid only at such bank or place.

(3) Where the holder assents to an acceptance varying the terms of the draft each drawer and indorser who does not affirmatively assent is discharged.

———

Conversion of an instrument by a drawee or other party. In Ch. 1, you learned that the concept of property is the underlying element of all commercial law. You will recall from that chapter that any unreasonable interference with another's real or personal property constitutes a legal "tort"—a "tort" being any socially unreasonable conduct that causes personal or property loss to another. You will also recall that a person who seriously interferes with another's personal property (goods, documents, stock certificates, etc.) may be forced by a court of law to purchase the property at its fair market value. Such a serious interference is called a *conversion*, and always results in a forced sale of the goods to the interfering party.

As with other property, recovery may be had for conversion of a negotiable instrument (a negotiable contract is intangible personal property evidenced by a document—a note, draft, or check—the possession of which gives control over the intangible property rights). Thus, if a drawee refuses to return a draft after dishonoring it, he or she will be liable for conversion of the instrument. The same is true of a maker, drawer, acceptor, or indorser who dishonors an instrument, then refuses to return it, and also of a party who pays an instrument upon a forged indorsement. Section 3–419 of the Uniform Commercial Code defines "conversion of instruments" as follows.

The UCC provides:

Section 3–419. Conversion of Instrument * * *

(1) An instrument is converted when

   (a) a drawee to whom it is delivered for acceptance refuses to return it on demand; or

   (b) any person to whom it is delivered for payment refuses on demand either to pay or to return it; or

   (c) it is paid on a forged indorsement.

(2) In an action against a drawee under subsection (1) the measure of the drawee's liability is the face amount of the instrument. In any other action under subsection (1) the measure of liability is presumed to be the face amount of the instrument.

The Official Comment to the Section provides:

* * *

(2) A negotiable instrument is the property of the holder. It is a mercantile specialty which embodies rights against other parties, and a thing of value. This section adopts the generally recognized rule that a refusal to return it on demand is a conversion.

The provision is not limited to drafts presented for acceptance, but extends to any instrument presented for payment, including a note presented to the maker. The action is not on the instrument, but in tort for its conversion.

The detention of an instrument voluntarily delivered is not wrongful unless and until there is demand for its return. Demand for a return at a particular time may, however, be made at the time of delivery; or it may be implied under the circumstances or understood as a matter of custom. If the holder is to call for the instrument and fails to do so, he is to be regarded as extending the time. "Refuses" is meant to cover any intentional failure to return the instrument, including its intentional destruction. It does not cover a negligent loss or destruction, or any other unintentional failure to return. In such a case the party may be liable in tort for any damage sustained as a result of his negligence, but he is not liable as a converter under this section.

(3) Subsection (1)(c) * * * adopts the prevailing view of decisions holding that payment on a forged indorsement is not an acceptance, but that even though made in good faith it is an exercise of dominion and control over the instrument inconsistent with the rights of the owner, and results in liability for conversion.

(4) Subsection (2) * * * adopts the rule generally applied to the conversion of negotiable instrument, that the obligation of any party on the instrument is presumed * * * to be worth its face value. Evidence is admissi-

ble to show that for any reason such as insolvency or the existence of a defense the obligation is in fact worthless, or even that it is without value. In the case of the drawee, however, the presumption is replaced by a rule of absolute liability.

Restrictive indorsements. To this point, we have dealt with three kinds of indorsements—*blank, special,* and *qualified* (versus *unqualified*) indorsements. You will recall that a blank indorsement (the indorser's signature alone) converts order paper into bearer paper, and a special indorsement (indorsement to a named payee) converts bearer paper into order paper. A qualified indorsement (one "without recourse") eliminates the indorser's secondary liability and somewhat limits his or her warranty liability.

Now we move to yet another kind of indorsement—a *restrictive* (versus *nonrestrictive*) indorsement. Section 3–205 of the Uniform Commercial Code defines "restrictive indorsement" as follows.

The UCC provides:

Section 3–205. Restrictive Indorsements

An indorsement is restrictive which either

(a) is conditional; or

(b) purports to prohibit further transfer of the instrument; or

(c) includes the words "for collection", "for deposit", "pay any bank", or like terms signifying a purpose of deposit or collection; or

(d) otherwise states that it is for the benefit or use of the indorser or of another person.

Section 3–206. Effect of Restrictive Indorsement

(1) No restrictive indorsement prevents further transfer or negotiation of the instrument.

* * *

(3) Except for an intermediary bank, any transferee under an indorsement which is conditional or includes the words "for collection", "for deposit", "pay any bank", or like terms . . . must pay or apply any value given by him for or on the security of the instrument consistently with the indorsement and to the extent that he does so he becomes a holder for value. In addition such transferee is a holder in due course if he otherwise complies with the requirements of Section 3–302 on what constitutes a holder in due course.

Several important conclusions may be drawn from the above Code provisions:

(1) An indorsement expressly prohibiting further transfer of an instrument will not prevent further transfer. Thus, an indorsement "pay Sally Streeter only" will be treated the same as the special indorsement "pay Sally Streeter".

(2) Whereas the promise or order on the face of the instrument must be unconditional, an indorsement on the back of the instrument may be restrictive (i. e., conditional or for a special purpose only). Usually, the purpose of a *conditional indorsement* is to make certain that the indorsee will perform a duty owed to the indorser. For example, George Johnson might indorse a note payable to his order, "Pay Sally Streeter but only if she fully harvests the corn crops located on my ranch by the 15th of September." Such a condition does not prevent further

transfer of the instrument. However, the instrument is enforceable only to the extent that any transferee (other than an intermediary bank merely handling the instrument in the normal course of collection—see Ch. 15) pays or applies any value given for the instrument consistently with the indorsement. Suppose, for instance, that Sally Streeter sells the conditionally indorsed note to Mark Hopkins, then fails to fulfill the condition (i. e., harvest the corn crops). Hopkins, in this case, will not only be unable to collect the note from the maker, but he will be personally liable to George Johnson, the restrictive indorser. Hopkins' only remedy, in this event, is to sue Sally Streeter for the value given—that is, if he can find Sally, and if Sally has sufficient financial resources.

So you see, it is Hopkins, the transferee, who may end up bearing the loss here. Anyone who gives value for an instrument subject to a conditional indorsement must appreciate the risk of the condition not occurring and the funds not being applied consistently with the condition.

(3) Indorsements for deposit or collection (e. g., "for deposit", "for collection", or "pay any bank" followed by the signature of the indorser) are also restrictive. Again, the indorsee or his or her transferee must deal with the instru-

ment according to the terms of the restriction (i. e., the indorsee must credit the indorser's account accordingly or collect the amount of the sum certain and remit it to the indorser). If the funds are not so applied, the indorsee or his or her transferee will be liable for any loss resulting to the indorser.

(4) Finally, an indorsement to one person for the benefit of another is restrictive (e. g., "pay Sally Streeter for the benefit of Mark Hopkins"). However, unlike other restrictive indorsements, only the original indorsee takes subject to the restriction: subsequent holders take free of the restriction *unless they have actual knowledge that the instrument is being negotiated in breach of the restriction.* For example, suppose that Sally Streeter transfers the instrument to Fritz Fitzmaurice. Sally is legally obligated to apply whatever value Fritz gives for the instrument for the benefit of Mark Hopkins. But even where Sally uses the funds to benefit one other than Hopkins, Fritz takes the instrument free and clear of the restriction unless he has actual knowledge of the improper use.

In conclusion, each and every indorsement will be *blank* or *special,* and *qualified* or *unqualified,* and *restrictive* or *nonrestrictive.* The following illustration shows how to accurately and completely describe any particular indorsement.

(1) *George Johnson*

Blank, unqualified, nonrestrictive (converts the order paper into bearer paper).

(2) *George Johnson Without Recourse*

Blank, qualified, nonrestrictive (converts the order paper into bearer paper).

(3) *For deposit, George Johnson*

Blank, unqualified, restrictive (converts the order paper into bearer paper).

(4) *For collection,*
George Johnson
Without Recourse

Blank, qualified, restrictive (converts the order paper into bearer paper).

(5) *Pay Mark Hopkins,*
George Johnson

Special, unqualified, nonrestrictive (remains order paper).

(6) *Pay Mark Hopkins,*
George Johnson
Without Recourse

Special, qualified, nonrestrictive (remains order paper).

(7) *Pay Mark Hopkins,*
For collection only,
George Johnson

Special, unqualified, restrictive (remains order paper).

(8) *Pay Sally Streeter*
For the benefit of
Mark Hopkins,
George Johnson
Without Recourse

Special, qualified, restrictive (remains order paper).

Cancellation and renunciation. The holder of an instrument may discharge a party in any manner apparent on the face of the instrument or indorsement. Thus, the holder may cancel the entire instrument by marking it "paid" on its face, or he or she may discharge a single indorser by striking out the party's signature. In each case, the *cancellation* or discharge must be intentional to be effective.

The holder may also discharge a party by expressly or impliedly renouncing his or her rights against the party. Express *renunciation* is accomplished in a separate writing signed and delivered by the holder; implied renunciation is achieved by surrendering the negotiable instrument to the party to be discharged. However, because the renunciation does not appear on the instrument itself, it is possible for a party to subsequently take the instrument without knowledge of the renunciation. If the party qualifies as a holder in due course, he or she will cut off the personal defense of discharge.

The Uniform Commercial Code treats cancellation and renunciation at Section 3–605 as follows.

The UCC provides:

Section 3–605. Cancellation and Renunciation

(1) The holder of an instrument may even without consideration discharge any party

(a) in any manner apparent on the face of the instrument or the indorsement, as by intentionally cancelling the instrument or the party's signature by destruction or mutilation, or by striking out the party's signature; or

(b) by renouncing his rights by a writing signed and delivered or by surrender of the instrument to the party to be discharged.

However, it should be pointed out that if, in discharging a party, the holder of an instrument impairs the right of recourse of any other party to the instrument, the party whose rights have been impaired will also be discharged.

UCC 3–606 provides:

Section 3–606. Impairment of Recourse or of Collateral

(1) The holder discharges any party to the instrument to the extent that without such party's consent the holder

(a) without express reservation of rights releases or agrees not to sue any person against whom the party has to the knowledge of the holder a right of recourse or agrees to suspend the right to enforce against such person the instrument or collateral or otherwise discharges such person, except that failure or delay in effecting any required presentment, protest or notice of dishonor with respect to any such person does not discharge any party as to whom presentment, protest or notice of dishonor is effective or unnecessary; or

(b) unjustifiably impairs any collateral for the instrument given

by or on behalf of the party or any person against whom he has a right of recourse.

Thus, striking out the signature of a prior indorser with intent to discharge the party generally discharges any subsequent indorser who has a right of recourse against the discharged party. This is only fair as the subsequent indorsers relied upon the credit of the prior indorsers in agreeing to be secondarily liable on the instrument.

An exception to discharge arises where the holder who strikes out the signature or otherwise discharges the prior indorser *expressly reserves* his or her rights against one or more of the subsequent indorsers.

UCC 3–606(2) provides:

(2) By express reservation of rights against a party with a right of recourse the holder preserves

(a) all his rights against such party as of the time when the instrument was originally due; and

(b) the right of the party to pay the instrument as of that time; and

(c) all rights of such party to recourse against others.

So where, in discharging a prior indorser, a holder expressly reserves his or her rights against one or more subsequent indorsers, the prior indorser is discharged as to the holder (and subsequent holders who take with knowledge of the discharge), but not as to the subsequent indorsers who remain liable on the instrument by express reservation.

CASES

CASE 1—*The "holder in due course" has "super plaintiff" status.*

ILLINOIS VALLEY ACCEPTANCE CORP. v. WOODARD

Court of Appeals of Indiana, First District, 1973.
304 N.E.2d 859.

ROBERTSON, Presiding Judge.

The plaintiff-appellant (Acceptance) is appealing the denial of its attempt to collect upon a trade acceptance made by the defendant-appellee (Woodard). The primal issue raised concerns Acceptance's status as a holder in due course of a negotiable instrument.

Woodard was a part time salesman for Moody Manufacturing Company (Moody), a manufacturer of grain bins and grain handling equipment. In May of 1966, Moody, as "borrower", had entered into a Finance Agreement with Acceptance listed as "the lender". This agreement made provision, among other things, for Moody to sell acceptable accounts to Acceptance for face value with 15% being reserved for deductions, expenses, accumulated interest, etc. On the 24th of December, 1968, Woodard signed, as acceptor, the trade acceptance which is the subject of this litigation. Moody was the drawer and payee. At that time it was in blank with the face value subsequently being filled in for the face amount of $8,815.62. In the four or five years prior to 1968, Woodard had signed several trade acceptances in blank for Moody for the purposes of covering the purchase of materials which he sold. The face amount was ultimately to be filled in when it was determined how much he had ordered. The December, 1968, trade acceptance was endorsed by Moody's secretary and given to Acceptance several days after Woodard had signed it. Between February and April, 1970, and several months past the due date, Moody went bankrupt. When Acceptance presented the instrument for payment it was refused by Woodard. Additionally, Woodard never received the materials presented by the trade acceptance, nor was he aware it had been negotiated by Moody to Acceptance.

Acceptance filed its complaint for collection of the trade acceptance against Woodard. * * * Woodard * * * raised the defenses of fraud and want of consideration. Acceptance filed a response alleging itself to be a holder in due course, which would defeat Woodard's professed defenses. Acceptance then filed a motion for summary judgment with an affidavit made by the vice-president of Acceptance in support thereof. The pertinent parts of the affidavit read:

"4. That since May 17, 1966, Illinois Valley Acceptance Corp. would periodically purchase from Moody Manufacturing Company trade acceptances, promissory notes or other negotiable instruments.

5. That on or about December 26, 1968, Illinois Valley Acceptance Corp., for the cash consideration of Seven Thousand Four Hundred Ninety-Three Dollars and Twenty-Eight Cents ($7,493.-28), purchased from Moody Manufacturing Company a certain trade acceptance shown as 'No. Inv. # 302', dated December 24, 1968, due November 30, 1969 and accepted on December 24, 1968

by ROBERT WOODARD, the same being payable at PEOPLES STATE BANK, Fairbanks, Indiana. * * *

* * *

7. That on December 26, 1968, Affiant knew of no reason or fact which would indicate to him that the trade acceptance attached to the Complaint in this cause was anything other than a valid and enforceable trade acceptance, issued by Moody Manufacturing Company, and accepted by ROBERT WOODARD in the ordinary course and scope of their respective businesses, and that same was a valid, legitimate and enforceable negotiable instrument."

The affidavit concluded with statements to the effect that the trade acceptance had been refused and that Acceptance was the lawful owner and holder of the trade acceptance.

Woodard filed no response. The trial court overruled the motion for summary judgment and some time thereafter proceeded to trial with subsequent judgment against Acceptance. Acceptance's overruled motion to correct errors raises two issues; whether the trial court erred in overruling its motion for summary judgment, and whether the judgment is contrary to the evidence and the law. As previously indicated, the answer to both is tied to Acceptance's classification as a holder in due course of the questioned trade acceptance.

* * *

This case is to be decided under the provisions of the Uniform Commercial Code * * * Acceptance's acknowledged status as a holder was not sufficient for it to recover because Woodard raised the defenses of fraud and failure of consideration, each a valid defense. These defenses, however, may have been cut off if Acceptance was a holder in due course. The holder in due course takes the instrument "free from all defenses of any party to the instrument with whom the holder has not dealt," subject to several exceptions. To avail itself of this "super-plaintiff" status, Acceptance had the burden of establishing by a preponderance of the evidence that it was "in all respects a holder in due course." "In all respects" means that Acceptance had to establish the existence of each of the elements set forth in IC 1971, 26–1–3–302, Ind.Ann.Stat. § 19–3–302. It provides:

"(1) A holder in due course is a holder who takes the instrument

(a) for value; and

(b) in good faith; and

(c) without notice that it is overdue or has been dishonored or of any defense against or claim to it on the part of any person."

The evidence, when examined with the foregoing requisites in mind, establishes Acceptance as a holder in due course. Briefly summarized that evidence shows the trade acceptance being endorsed over to Acceptance by Moody. Moody in turn received a draft for 85% of the face value of the trade acceptance. There was nothing irregular with the appearance of the trade acceptance and the transaction was similar to other prior transactions between the parties. At that time Acceptance had no knowledge that the trade acceptance had been signed in blank and that the goods had not been delivered.

A portion of Woodard's arguments appears to be directed to the questions of good faith and notice. Both are statutorily defined:

"(19) 'Good faith' means honesty in fact in the conduct or transaction concerned."

Notice, insofar as applicable, is defined as:

"(1) The purchaser has notice of a claim or defense if

(a) the instrument is so incomplete, bears such visible evidence of forgery or alteration, or is otherwise so irregular as to call into question its validity, terms or ownership or to create an ambiguity as to the party to pay; or

(b) the purchaser has notice that the obligation of any party is voidable in whole or in part, or that all parties have been discharged."

The gist of Woodard's cross examination of Acceptance's vice-president was directed to when Acceptance became aware of Moody's bankruptcy and to the Finance Agreement between Moody and Acceptance. We believe that the bankruptcy has no relevancy because of its nonexistence at the time the trade acceptance was endorsed over to Acceptance. The Finance Agreement, introduced into evidence by Woodard, may have been an attempt to establish something akin to the doctrine of close connectedness, characterized by Woodard as the lack of an arms-length transaction, for the purpose of showing that Acceptance was so closely related to Moody commercially that it knew, or should have known, either Moody was in poor financial shape or that it had not delivered the goods represented by the trade acceptance. Acceptance's summary judgment affidavit as well as the testimony given at the trial belies such a relationship.

Woodard further argues that there was no value given for the trade acceptance and that the Finance Agreement between Moody and Acceptance was merely a borrowing agreement. The evidence shows that Acceptance paid Moody 85% of the face value of trade acceptance and held the remainder in reserve. There can be little question that the value concept was satisfied. * * *

Woodard also argues that Acceptance failed to show the instrument was negotiated because the evidence is in conflict as to whether there was delivery of the instrument. Delivery is an element required by IC 1971, 26–1–3–202, Ind.Ann.Stat. § 19–3–202, and is defined as a voluntary transfer of possession. We fail to find any conflicting evidence on delivery of the trade acceptance from Moody to Acceptance.

Woodard's affirmative defense of want of consideration is not available against a holder in due course.

Turning next to the question of fraud § 19–3–305(2)(c) allows a defense against a holder in due course based upon "such misrepresentation as has induced the party to sign the instrument with neither knowledge nor reasonable opportunity to obtain knowledge of its character or its essential terms." The comments subsequent to this statute state that fraud in the essence or fraud in the factum is a valid defense against a holder in due course with the theory being that the "signature is ineffective because he did not intend to sign such an instrument at all." Woodard's past conduct in signing blank trade acceptances for Moody negates a defense based on the foregoing. Woodard testified he was familiar with the forms and knew they constituted a promise to pay.

In determining whether a verdict is contrary to the law the proper rule is:

> " * * * only where the evidence is without conflict and can lead to but one conclusion, and the trial court has reached an opposite conclusion, that the decision of the trial court will be set aside on the ground that it is contrary to law."

It is our conclusion that the evidence conclusively demonstrated Acceptance to be a holder in due course. We, accordingly, reverse and remand for judgment to be entered for the plaintiff-appellant Illinois Valley Acceptance Corp., and against the defendant-appellee Robert Woodard.

Reversed and remanded.

CASE 2—*Unreasonable delay will discharge an indorser.*

HANE v. EXTEN

Court of Appeals of Maryland, 1969.
255 Md. 668, 259 A.2d 290.

SINGLEY, Judge.

John B. Hane is the assignee of the note of Theta Electronic Laboratories, Inc. (Theta) in the stated amount of $15,377.07, with interest at six per cent per annum. The note was dated 10 August 1964; stipulated that the first monthly payment of $320.47 would be due five months from date, or on 10 January 1965; and that "In the event of the failure to pay the interest or principal, as the same becomes due on this Note the entire debt represented hereby shall at the end of thirty (30) days become due and demandable * * *." The note was assigned without recourse to Hane by George B. and Marguerite F. Thomson, the original payees, on 26 November 1965. A default having occurred in the making of the monthly payments, Hane * * * [sued] Theta and * * * individuals, Gerald M. Exten * * * and [his wife], who had endorsed Theta's note. * * * From a judgment for the Extens for costs, Hane has appealed.

This case raises the familiar question: Must Hane show that the Extens were given notice of presentment and dishonor before he can hold them on their endorsement?

The court below, in finding for the Extens, relied on the provisions of Uniform Commercial Code.

> "Unless the indorsement otherwise specifies (as by such words as 'without recourse') every indorser engages that upon dishonor and any necessary notice of dishonor and protest he will pay the instrument according to its tenor at the time of his indorsement to the holder or to any subsequent indorser who takes it up, even though the indorser who takes it up was not obligated to do so."

§ 3–501(1)(b) provides that "Presentment for payment is necessary to charge any indorser" and § 3–501(2)(a) that "Notice of any dishonor is necessary to charge any indorser," in each case subject, however, to the provisions of § 3–511 which recite the circumstances under which notice of dishonor may be waived or excused, none of which is here present. § 3–502(1)(a) makes it clear that unless presentment or notice of dishonor is waived or excused, unreasonable delay will discharge an indorser.

There was testimony from which the trier of facts could find as he did that presentment and notice of dishonor were unduly delayed.

It is clear that Hane held the note from November, 1965, until some time in April 1967 before he made demand for payment. U.C.C. § 3–503(1)(d) provides that "Where an instrument is accelerated presentment for payment is due within a reasonable time after the acceleration." "Reasonable time" is not defined in § 3–503, except that § 3–503(2) provides, "A reasonable time for presentment is determined by the nature of the instrument, any usage of banking or trade and the facts of the particular case." But § 1–204(2) characterizes it: "What is a reasonable time for taking any action depends on the nature, purpose and circumstances of such action."

Reasonableness is primarily a question for the fact finder. We see no reason to disturb the lower court's finding that Hane's delay of almost 18 months in presenting the note "was unreasonable from any viewpoint."

As regards notice of dishonor, § 3–508(2) requires that notice be given by persons other than banks "before midnight of the third business day after dishonor or receipt of notice of dishonor." Exten, called as an adverse witness by Hane, testified that his first notice that the note had not been paid was * * * on 7 June 1967. Hane's brother testified that demand had been made about 15 April 1967. He was uncertain as to when he had given Exten notice of dishonor, but finally conceded that it was "within a week." The lower court found that the ambiguity of this testimony, coupled with Exten's denial that he had received *any* notice before 7 June fell short of meeting the three day notice requirement of the U.C.C. * * *

In the absence of evidence that presentment and notice of dishonor were waived or excused, Hane's unreasonable delay discharged the Extens, § 3–502(1)(a)

      * * *

Hane makes much of the fact the he is a holder in due course. * * * Whether Hane was or was not a holder in due course has no relevance to the issue here presented. In either case timely presentment and notice of dishonor were required to hold the Extens. Whether Hane was or was not a holder in due course is of no significance * * *.

Judgment affirmed, costs to be paid by appellant.

CASE 3—A *"without recourse" indorsement does not eliminate all obligations.*

HARTFORD LIFE INS. CO. v. TITLE GUARANTEE CO.

United States Court of Appeals, District of Columbia Circuit, 1975.
520 F.2d 1170.

WEIGEL, District Judge.

This case turns upon facts which are somewhat complicated and include prior litigation before this Court. In In re Parkwood, Inc., 149 U.S.App.D. C. 67, 461 F.2d 158 (1971), we invalidated a loan entered into in violation of the District of Columbia Loan Shark Law, D.C.Code § 26–601 et seq. The effect of the decision was to render uncollectable the unpaid balance of approximately $79,000.00. * * *

In October, 1960, Walker & Dunlop, a real estate broker and mortgage banker, loaned $100,000 to Suburban Motors, Inc. The loan, evidenced by a promissory note, was to bear interest at an annual rate of 6½% and was secured by a deed of trust on real property owned by Suburban.   *   *   * In January, 1961, pursuant to an understanding reached before the loan was made, Walker & Dunlop transferred the note and deed of trust to Hartford, endorsing the note "without recourse".

In March, 1962, Suburban sold the property, subject to the deed of trust, to Adams Properties, Inc., a subsidiary of Parkwood, Inc. In July, 1966, these companies filed petitions for reorganization under the Bankruptcy Act. Later that year, Hartford filed a proof of claim as a secured creditor of Adams for the balance due on the note—some $79,000.00.

In May, 1968, the Trustee appointed for Adams objected to the claim on the ground that the loan had been made in violation of the Loan Shark Act, Section 601. That statute makes it unlawful to charge yearly interest on a secured loan at a higher rate than 6% unless a license has been procured to charge the higher rate. [I]n In re Parkwood, supra, this Court found * * * that the loan was subject to the Act, and that the loan and accompanying deed of trust were void. Hartford's proof of claim was disallowed.

Hartford instituted this action in December, 1972. In its amended complaint, Hartford seeks to recover its loss from Walker & Dunlop on * * * breach of warranty * * *.

The District Court held that the causes of action against Walker & Dunlop * * * were barred * * * by the "without recourse" endorsement on the note which Walker & Dunlop had transferred to Hartford. * * *

                  *   *   *

The District Court * * * erred in ruling that Hartford's claims against Walker & Dunlop were barred by the "without recourse" endorsement on the note transferred by Walker & Dunlop to Hartford.

The legal effect of a "without recourse" endorsement is defined by the Uniform Commercial Code. D.C.Code § 28:3–417(3), (2)(d). Thus, whether or not this endorsement bars Hartford's claims against Walker & Dunlop must be determined with reference to the principles of commercial law established therein.

A "without recourse" endorsement is a qualified endorsement; it does not eliminate all obligations owed by the transferor of an instrument to his transferee. By endorsing the note "without recourse", Walker & Dunlop still warranted to Hartford that it had no knowledge of any fact which would establish the existence of a good defense against the note. Walker & Dunlop breached this warranty. At all times it was fully aware of the facts relevant to our later determination that the note was unenforceable because of the illegality of the underlying loan. * * *
                  *   *   *

     *   *   *   [W]e hereby reverse the order granting * * * judgment in favor of Walker & Dunlop * * *.

CASE 4—*The renunciation was not delivered.*

GREENE v. COTTON

Court of Appeals of Kentucky, 1970.
457 S.W.2d 493.

DAVIS.

The critical question is whether a writing by decedent S. R. Jones legally accomplished the cancellation and release of a promissory note which B. C. Cotton and his wife, appellees, had executed to Jones. The circuit court held that it did. * * *

On August 17, 1955, the Cottons executed and delivered to S. R. Jones their promissory note in the sum of $72,000 bearing 5% interest and secured by mortgage on real estate in Grant County owned by the Cottons. Various payments on the note had reduced the principal due to $38,400 at the date of the death of Jones on May 2, 1967.

The appellants, executors of the will of Jones, found among Jones' effects a key to a lockbox at Citizens Bank of Dry Ridge. Upon inspecting the contents of that lockbox, they found an envelope bearing the typewritten address:

"To admrs. of my estate

"S. R. Jones"

Within the envelope was found a typewritten paper signed by S. R. Jones, which recited:

"I, S. R. Jones hereby request that if B. C. Cotton be living at the time of my death and if there is an unpaid balance on his note and mortgage to me that same be released and the note and mortgage returned to him marked paid.

Dated July 7, 1966

/s/ S. R. Jones"

* * *

KRS 355.3–605(1)(b), in treating the legal requirements for cancellation and renunciation of a note, provides that the result may be achieved:

"(b) by renouncing his rights by a writing signed *and delivered* or by surrender of the instrument to the party to be discharged." (Emphasis supplied.)

* * *

It follows that the court erred in entering judgment for appellees and dismissing appellants' counterclaim on the note.

The judgment is reversed for proceedings consistent with the opinion.

PROBLEMS

1. Nancy Bagley draws a negotiable draft on Margie Davis payable "to the order of Jonathan Beal" in the amount of $300. Jonathan skillfully changes the "3" into an "8" so that the draft appears to be payable in the amount of $800. The following transactions occur:

(1) Jonathan indorses the draft in blank without recourse and delivers it to Lorna Roberts in satisfaction of an $800 debt he owes Lorna.

(2) Lorna, who is unaware of the alteration, gives the draft to her niece, Myrna, who needs the money for college.

(3) Myrna presents the draft to Margie for payment; Margie pays Myrna the $800, and Myrna uses the money to pay her college tuition.

> (1) *Johnathan Beal*
>   Without Recourse
>
> (2) (no indorsement)
>
> (3) (no indorsement)

Margie thereafter discovers that the draft has been altered. What are Margie's rights, if any, against Myrna Roberts, Lorna Roberts, and Jonathan Beal? Explain fully.

Suppose that Margie is insolvent and cannot pay when Myrna presents the draft to her for payment. What are Myrna's rights, if any, against Nancy Bagley? Would your answer differ if Nancy had negligently and substantially contributed to the alteration (e.g., by writing the monetary amount in pencil so that it could be easily changed)? Would it differ if Margie had gone insolvent during an unreasonable delay by Myrna in presenting the draft for payment? Explain your answers.

Assuming that Nancy Bagley is also insolvent or has a good defense to payment, what are Myrna's rights, if any, against Lorna Roberts and Jonathan Beal? Explain fully.

Is Myrna required to proceed against Nancy before proceeding against Lorna and Jonathan? Explain.

2. Answer the following "True" or "False" and give reasons for your answers:

T (a) There is no party immediately primarily liable on a draft.

F (b) An actual tender of payment is required to stop the running of interest on an instrument that is both domiciled and payable at a definite time.

T (c) Several states have abolished the "holder in due course" doctrine with regard to consumer goods financing.

T (d) A forger is liable on an instrument in the capacity in which he or she signs.

F (e) Indorsers are liable to each other in the reverse order in which their signatures appear on the instrument.

T (f) A holder's failure to act timely in making presentment or giving notice of dishonor will discharge an indorser, but will generally not affect the drawer's liability.

Payment – comaker

F (g) The liability of an indorser who signs "collection guaranteed" is like that of a co-maker.

T (h) A drawee who refuses to return a draft after dishonoring it will be liable for conversion of the instrument.

F (i) Generally speaking, only the original indorsee takes an instrument subject to a restrictive indorsement.

3.

> ON APRIL 15th, 1978, I promise to pay to the order of
> DOUGLAS CRENSHAW
>
> One thousand one hundred fifty DOLLARS ($1,150.00)
>
> *Julie Bradley*
> Julie Bradley

(1) Doug indorses in blank and delivers the note to Mary O'Connall for $850.

(2) Mary specially indorses to Ron Weiss and delivers the note to Ron in payment for a used car.

(3) Ron indorses in blank and gives the note to his son, Howard.

(4) Howard specially indorses to Jean Peacock and delivers the note to her in exchange for $950.

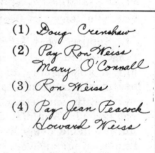

(1) *Doug Crenshaw*
(2) *Pay Ron Weiss*
   Mary O'Connall
(3) *Ron Weiss*
(4) *Pay Jean Peacock*
   Howard Weiss

Who is primarily liable on this instrument? Explain. Who is secondarily liable? Explain. Who is liable on the basis of warranty? Explain. What would be the effect of Jean Peacock striking out Doug Crenshaw's indorsement on the back of the instrument (with intent to discharge him) while at the same time notifying Mary O'Connall that she expressly reserves all her rights against Mary? Explain.

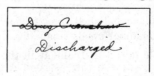

Doug Crenshaw
Discharged

4. Price has in his possession an otherwise negotiable instrument which reads:

> "I, Waldo, hereby promise to pay to the order
> of Mark or bearer * * *"

Which of the following is true with respect to the above instrument?

a.   Mark's signature is required to negotiate the instrument.

b.   The instrument is non-negotiable.

c.   If Mark indorses the instrument, Mark assumes potentially greater liability to subsequent transferees than if Mark transfers it by mere delivery.

d.   Since the instrument is payable to Mark's order, it is a draft.

[# 25, May 1977 CPA Exam]

5.

	No. 111

DIANA DAVIDSON
21 West 21st Street
Toronto, Canada

April 1, 1977

Pay to the
order of   Stanley Stark $1,000.00

One thousand & no/100's Canadian Dollars

Diana Davidson
Diana Davidson

FIRST NATIONAL TRUST
Buffalo, New York

For Finder's Fee

After examining the above instrument, which of the following conclusions is correct?

a.   It is non-negotiable because it is payable in Canadian money.

b.   It is a demand instrument but does *not* qualify as a negotiable instrument, because it is drawn in Canada and payable by a bank in the United States.

c.   The instrument is a negotiable foreign check (draft), and in the event of dishonor a formal protest must be made by the party seeking recovery.

d.   Diana Davidson is the maker of the instrument and as such is primarily liable thereon.

[# 20, May, 1977 CPA Exam]

6. One who signs as an accommodation party to a negotiable instrument

a.   Has the same liability on the instrument whether he signs as an accommodation maker or as an accommodation indorser.

b.   Has a right of recourse against the party he accommodated.

   c. *Cannot* be held liable against a subsequent holder in due course if the party he accommodated has a contract (personal) defense against the party to whom the instrument was originally issued.

   d. Has *no* liability to any subsequent taker who knew of the accommodation.

[# 34, May, 1976 CPA Exam]

7. During the course of your audit you discover a dispute concerning one of your client's checks. The check had been sent to a supplier but without indicating the sum on the face of the instrument. The supplier fraudulently filled in the check for $500 more than the amount indicated in the letter which accompanied the check. A subsequent holder in due course is asserting the right to recover the full amount stated in the completed instrument.

   a. Alteration is a complete defense against all parties.

   b. The holder in due course can only collect an amount equal to the authorized amount.

   c. The holder in due course may enforce the instrument as completed.

   d. The holder in due course must first proceed against the fraudulent supplier.

[# 35, May, 1976 CPA Exam]

8. The transferor of a bearer negotiable instrument who transfers without indorsing but for full consideration

   a. Is liable to all subsequent holders if there exists a personal defense to the instrument maintainable by the primary party and the transferor was aware of the defense.

   b. Warrants to his immediate transferee that he has good title.

   c. Makes no warranty that prior signatures are genuine or authorized.

   d. Engages that he will pay the instrument if his immediate transferor is unable to obtain payment upon due presentment and dishonor because of insufficient funds and due notice is given the transferor.

[# 3, May 1974 CPA Exam]

9. When the holder of a negotiable instrument transfers it for consideration by indorsing "without recourse", he

   a. Makes *no* warranty as to title as to any subsequent holder.

   b. Prevents further negotiability.

   c. Makes the same warranties as an unqualified indorser except that he warrants that he does *not* have knowledge of a defense of any party good as against him rather than that there is *no* such defense.

   d. Becomes immune from recourse to him by a subsequent holder.

[# 4, May, 1974 CPA Exam]

10.   **Part a.**   Your CPA firm was engaged to audit the Meglo Corporation.   During the audit you examined the following instrument:

April 2, 1977

Charles Noreen
21 West 21st Street
St. Louis, Missouri

I, Charles Noreen, do hereby promise to pay to Roger Smith, Two Thousand Dollars ($2,000) one year from date, with 8% interest upon due presentment.

FOR: Payment for used IBM typewriters.

Charles Noreen

Meglo purchased the instrument from Smith on April 10, 1977, for $1,700.   Meglo received the instrument with Smith's signature and the words "Pay to the order of Meglo Corporation" on the back.   Upon maturity, Meglo presented the instrument to Noreen, who refused to pay.   Noreen alleged that the typewriters were defective and did not satisfy certain warranties given in connection with the purchase of the used IBM typewriters which were guaranteed for one year.   Noreen had promptly notified Smith of this fact and had told him he would not pay the full amount due.

Required: Answer the following, setting forth reasons for any conclusions stated.

1.   Is the instrument in question negotiable commercial paper? *NO*

2.   Assuming that the instrument is negotiable, does Meglo qualify as a holder in due course entitled to collect the full $2,000? *yes*

3.   Assuming that the instrument is negotiable, is Noreen's defense valid against a holder in due course? *no*

4.   Assuming that the instrument is nonnegotiable, what is the legal effect of the transfer by Smith to Meglo?

Part b.   Marvin Farber cashed a check for Harold Kern which was made to the order of Charles Walker by Marglow Investments & Securities.   The check had the following indorsements on the back:

1.   *Charles Walker*

2.   without recourse
     Doris Williamson

3.   Pay to the order of Harold Kern
     Jack Dixon

4.   Pay to the order of Marvin Farber

Kern neglected to sign his indorsement when he gave the check to Farber, and Farber did not notice this until the following day. Before Farber could locate Kern and obtain his signature, Farber learned that Walker had fraudulently obtained the check from Marglow (the drawer). Farber finally located Kern and obtained his signature. Farber promptly indorsed the check in blank and cashed it at National Bank. National Bank presented the check for payment through normal banking channels, but it was dishonored by Marglow's bank pursuant to a valid stop order. National Bank contacted Farber and informed him of the situation. Farber repaid the amount and the check was returned to him with National Bank's blank indorsement on the back.

Required: Answer the following, setting forth reasons for any conclusions stated.

1. Identify the type of indorsement and indicate the liability for each indorsement numbered 1, 2, and 3 above.

2. Will Farber prevail in a legal action seeking payment of the check by Marglow?

[# 2, May, 1978 CPA Exam]

Fraud in execution — Real Def
" " inducement — personal Def

Chapter 15

BANKING: NEGOTIABLE INSTRUMENTS AND BANK CUSTOMERS

When and how did checks come into existence?

History does not record exactly when the first checks came into existence; however, it is clear that such instruments were being used in Italy by the 15th Century, and in England by the 17th. The first English checks resulted from the widespread practice of using "goldsmith notes". Fearful of keeping gold on their persons or in their homes, the English would deposit their gold with a goldsmith for safekeeping. The goldsmith, who charged a modest fee for the service, would give the depositor a paper receipt —called a "goldsmith note"—whereon the goldsmith promised to pay the sum certain in gold to the depositor or to the "bearer" of the note on demand. The depositor would then use the note like paper money (yet to come into existence) to make payments to others. For example, to pay all of the gold to a specific creditor or payee, the depositor would simply deliver the goldsmith note to the party; to pay part of the gold, the depositor would issue a written "order" directing the goldsmith to pay the specified part to the creditor or payee on demand. After paying the note or order (by handing over the proper amount of gold), the goldsmith would mark the instrument "paid" and return it to the depositor.

Sound familar? It should—the goldsmith notes and orders of 17th Century England had all the basic characteristics of our modern checks. While we no longer deposit gold with goldsmiths, we do deposit money with banks whereupon we acquire the right to order the banks through checks to pay our money to others. After paying our checks, the banks (like goldsmiths) mark the instruments "cancelled" and return them to us.

Modernly, our use of checks has three important consequences. First, as with the goldsmith notes and orders of long ago, checks make it possible for us to meet our financial obligations without keeping large amounts of cash on hand (with all its attendant risks). Second, checks permit us to pay the exact amount required by a transaction and to send the amount through the mails with little risk of loss. And, third, checks provide us with an automatic receipt (the "cancelled" check) that can be preserved and used to prove payment.

How are banks regulated in the United States?

Volumes could be written on the nature and regulation of the banking industry in the United States. Here, we point out but a few of the highlights. The most important fact to remember is that almost all banks in the United States are regulated by the federal government, at least to a considerable extent. The three major federal agencies responsible for regulating the banking industry are the Comptroller of the Currency, the Federal Reserve System, and the Federal Deposit Insurance Corporation.

The Comptroller of the Currency charters and regulates national banks. In the United States, a bank cannot operate and do business unless it first receives permission from the government through what is called a "charter". The history of the United States has been one of dual government (state and federal), with continued emphasis on the distinctions between state and federal government powers.

The result has been a dual banking system under which a bank can be chartered as either a state bank (under state laws and regulations) or a national bank (under federal laws and regulations). National banks operate not on a national level but within particular state boundaries, like state banks.

The Federal Reserve System was created by the Federal Reserve Act of 1913. The FRA divided the country into twelve districts, established a Federal Reserve Bank in each district, and set up a Federal Reserve Board to formulate regulations and supervise the entire system. National banks were compelled to join the system, and state banks were allowed to become members (however, most state banks have failed to join). The Federal Reserve System is important because it establishes monetary and credit policy throughout the United States, thereby affecting all banks (whether members or nonmembers of the System) as well as the entire economy.

The third major agency—the Federal Deposit Insurance Corporation—was established by the Banking Act of 1933. More than 500 banks a year had failed financially during the 1920's, and more than 2,000 a year during the early 1930's. The FDIC was established to restore public confidence in banks by providing federal insurance coverage for deposits up to a maximum of $2,500 per bank account. The per account maximum was raised to $5,000 in 1934; $10,000 in 1950; $15,000 in 1966; $20,000 in 1969; and $40,000 in 1974. All national banks and most state banks —some 15,000 banks in all—have found it necessary to join the FDIC: without federal insurance coverage, it is almost impossible to attract depositors. However, to qualify for FDIC coverage, the banks must meet federal banking regulations designed to prevent the banks from failing financially. The regulations are very similar to those of the Comptroller of the Currency and the Federal Reserve Board; thus, even state banks that escape regulation by the Comptroller of the Currency and the Federal Reserve Board (because they have not joined the FRS) are subject to substantially similar regulation by the FDIC. By restoring public confidence in the banking system, the FDIC has dramatically reduced the number of bank failures—as few as five banks a year now fail financially in the United States.

How does the Federal Reserve System control monetary and credit policy in the United States?

The Federal Reserve System controls U.S. monetary and credit policy in three ways:

(1) By buying or selling government bonds;

(2) By lowering or raising the interest rate on loans to member banks; and

(3) By lowering or raising the reserve requirements of member banks.

Buying or selling government bonds on the open market. From time to time, the federal Congress authorizes the issuance of government bonds for sale on the open market. By trading in government bonds, the Federal Reserve System can sharply affect the availability of money in this country. If the System buys bonds, it will make more money available to the economy; if it sells bonds, it will reduce the amount of available money. For example, if the Federal Reserve Board feels that the economy needs bolstering (with additional amounts of money made available to business and others), the Board may decide to purchase 1 billion dollars worth of government bonds. Ultimately, the 1 billion dollars used to purchase the bonds will be deposited into the nation's banks by the sellers of the bonds. The result of making 1 billion dollars in new deposits available to the banks is to pump some 5 billion dollars into the economy. This occurs because banks are not required to keep in reserve 100% of the deposits made, but can lend a considerable portion of the deposits back out into the community. The exact percentage of deposits (called "reserves") that must be kept on hand is determined by the Federal Reserve Board and is subject to change by the Board. Typically, the Board requires banks to maintain reserves of 20% of deposits. Thus, if you deposit $1,000 in your bank account, the bank must keep only $200.00 of the money in reserve, and may lend or otherwise invest $800.-00 of the money (e. g., in bonds or securities). Ultimately, the $800.00 which goes back into the economy will be deposited in a second bank; again, 20% of the money will be placed in reserve, and 80% or $640.00 will be used for loans or other investments. The $640.00 will, in turn, be deposited in a third bank, the bank retaining 20% or $128.00 and placing 80% or $512.00 back into the economy. A fourth bank will loan or invest $409.60 of the $512.00 and reserve $102.40; a fifth will loan or invest $327.68 and retain $81.92; and so on. The process will continue until, after 25 deposits, a total of $5,000 has been deposited in 25 banks; a total of $1,000 (20% of $5,000) has been retained in reserve; and a total of $4,000 (80% of $5,000) has been put back into the economy through loans and other investments. The effect is summarized below:

Bank	Deposit Made to Bank	Loan or Investment Made by Bank	Amount of Deposit Retained (Reserves)
Bank 1	$1,000.00	$800.00	$200.00
Bank 2	800.00	640.00	160.00
Bank 3	640.00	512.00	128.00
Bank 4	512.00	409.60	102.40
Bank 5	409.60	327.68	81.92
Bank 6	327.68	262.14	65.54
Bank 7	262.14	209.72	52.42
Banks 8 through 25	1,048.58	838.86	209.72
Total deposits made to all 25 banks	$5,000.00		
Total loans or other investments made by all 25 banks—new money created from original deposit		$4,000.00	
Total amount of deposits retained as reserves by all 25 banks			$1,000.00

The 20% reserve-80% investment process works because it seldom happens that all bank customers want to withdraw their money at one time (in fact, in many banks, new deposits balance withdrawals). Of course, if this should occur, the banks simply would not have enough money to pay their customers. That is why it is so important that the government stand behind the banks and guarantee the deposits. Remember, the FDIC insures customer accounts. If there was ever a panic (i. e., a "run on the banks"), with everyone wanting to withdraw his or her money at the same time, the Congress, the President and the Federal Reserve Board would act to insure that enough cash money was available to pay each customer in full. Because of this, it is highly unlikely that such a panic would occur.

It follows that if the Federal Reserve Board buys 1 billion dollars worth of government bonds, the 1 billion dollars paid for the bonds will ultimately be deposited in the banking system. The banks will hold 20% of the money or 200 million dollars in reserve, and will loan or otherwise invest 800 million dollars. The 800 million dollars will, in turn, be deposited, with 20% or 160 million dollars retained and 80% or 640 million dollars put back into the economy. The 640 million dollars will then be deposited, with 128 million dollars retained and 512 million dollars loaned or invested, etc., etc., etc., until a total of 5 billion dollars has been deposited—all as a result of the 1 billion dollar expenditure by the Federal Reserve Board. Of course, the effect of placing 5 billion dollars into the economy is to stimulate economic growth and expansion.

To achieve the opposite effect (i. e., to stem economic growth and expansion), the Federal Reserve Board can sell government bonds. For example, the FRB may feel that inflation is too high and want to initiate a curb. If the FRB sells 1 billion dollars worth of government bonds, the buyers will pay for the bonds by withdrawing 1 billion dollars from the banks. Again, the effect is 5 to 1, and the result of pulling 1 billion dollars out of the banks is to reduce the money supply to the economy by 5 billion dollars (without the 1 billion dollars in reserve, the banks cannot loan or otherwise

invest 4 billion dollars). The net result is that money is much "tighter" (harder to get), and there is less growth, less development, and less inflation.

Lowering or raising the interest rate on loans to member banks. The Federal Reserve Board loans money to its member banks, charging interest on the loans. If the FRB wants to pump money into the economy, it will lower its interest rates so as to encourage banks to borrow more money (with more money in reserve, the banks can loan more money and make more investments).

To slow down the economy, the FRB will raise its interest rates so as to discourage loans to its members. With less money in reserve, the member banks will have to cut back on customer loans and other investments, and will have to raise their own interest rates. An increase in the prime rate (the rate charged preferred corporate borrowers) will deter business growth and expansion. Less preferred borrowers will have to pay still higher rates, and may, in fact, be unable to borrow at all because there is not enough money available. Throughout the country, money will be "tight" and economic growth slow or halted.

Lowering or raising the reserve requirements of member banks. Finally, the Federal Reserve Board has the power to change the reserve ratio requirements of its member banks (again, the reserve ratio being the percentage of deposits that must be retained by the banks). If the FRB lowers the reserve requirements (say, from 20% to 18%), member banks will have more money to loan or otherwise invest, and the economy will be stimulated. Conversely, if the FRB raises the reserve requirements (say, from 20% to 22%), member banks will have less money to loan or invest, and the result will be a "tight" money economy.

What are the two most important functions of a bank for its customers?

Frequently, banks make loans; sometimes, they act as trustees to manage the property of others (see Ch. 29 "Trusts"); occasionally, they serve as personal representatives in charge of probating a decedent's estate (see Ch. 30 "Wills"). As important as these bank functions are, they do not directly affect most of us very often. However, there are two other bank functions that do affect most of us, if not on a daily basis, at least several times monthly:

(1) Banks *collect* the checks that we deposit into our accounts; and

(2) Banks *pay* the checks that we order paid from our accounts.

These two bank functions—collection and payment—are the crux of the relationship between a bank and its customers. The importance of these two functions—both as to our national economy and as to our individual economies—cannot be overemphasized. For example, the owner of a small grocery store might receive 300 to 400 checks a month from his or her customers. If the owner had to go from bank to bank and personally collect each check, the owner would have little time to conduct his or her business.

Thus, bank collection and payment are the two most important functions of a bank for its customers. As stated in the *Official Comment* to UCC Section 4–103, they are functions that affect virtually everyone in the country.

The Official Comment provides:

* * * [I]t is recognized that banks handle probably 25,000,000 items every business day and that the parties interested in each item include the owner of the item, the drawer (if it is a check), all non-bank indorsers, the payor bank and from one to five or more collecting banks * * *. En masse, the interested parties constitute virtually every adult person and business organization in the United States.

What is the basis of the legal relationship between a bank and its customer?

A party who opens a checking account with a bank enters into a contract with the bank wherein it is agreed that the bank will provide collection and payment services for the party in return for a service charge and use of the depositor's money. The contractual relationship is one of debtor-creditor: the bank becomes a debtor of the depositor by virtue of receiving the deposited funds; the depositor becomes a creditor of the bank by reason of depositing the funds.[1] Both bank and depositor benefit substantially from the relationship. The bank charges for its services and acquires the use of the depositor's money. The depositor receives the benefit of the two most important bank functions—collection and payment. The bank's duty is to collect checks presented by the depositor for deposit and to pay from the depositor's account only according to the order of the depositor.

The contract itself is entered into with a minimum of formality. Usually, the customer discusses the account with a bank employee and then signs a *signature card* containing *some* of the terms of the contract. Most of the contract terms are found, not on the signature card, but in the rules of the bank and in prevailing law and custom regarding bank accounts.

---

1. However, the individual deposits made by a customer become part of the general assets of the bank. This means that if the bank goes insolvent and the customer must sue the bank for the balance of his or her account, the customer will have no preferred position over other bank creditors (see Ch. 26 for a discussion of creditors' rights). Of course, in most cases, the customer's account will be insured up to $40,000 by the FDIC.

To a considerable extent, Article 4 of the Uniform Commercial Code, "Bank Deposits and Collections", is controlling.

While the signature card does not contain the entire contract of the parties, it is important to read the card before signing —particularly as the terms of the card may vary from bank to bank. Too often, however, the terms are in very small print, and, despite the warning at the top of the card to "read before signing", the bank customer does not read the card. A typical signature card might contain the following provisions.

It might say:

ACCOUNT AGREEMENT—PLEASE READ BEFORE SIGNING

1. All transactions are governed by contract as printed on Bank's deposit slips and other forms, including as respects savings account any amendments to savings rules as posted in Bank's lobby.

2. This account is subject to Bank service charges existing at any time. Bank is authorized to mail statements and vouchers to any of the signers at their risk, unless otherwise directed by any of them.

3. Bank may apply any funds, in whole or in part, in this account to any matured obligation of the owner of this account to the Bank whether held at the Branch at which this account is held or at any other Branch.

4. It is agreed that all transactions between said Bank and the signers shall be governed by contract as printed on this signature card, deposit slips and other forms; that said account is subject to Bank's services charges in effect at any time; that statements, cancelled vouchers and other entries may be mailed to the signer's address as shown on the bank's records; that signer will examine the statement of account, cancelled vouchers and other entries within 30 days after delivery or mailing date; and that signer will notify the Bank in writing within 30 days of the delivery or mailing of any statement of account, cancelled vouchers, or other entries of any forgeries or other apparent discrepancies; or, failing to do so, the said statement of account, cancelled vouchers and other entries will be considered correct for all purposes and signer will hold the Bank, its officers and employees, harmless from any and all liability whatsoever.

*   *   *

The undersigned hereby agrees to the terms and conditions of the *   *   * account agreement, receipt of which is hereby acknowledged.

          ——————————————
               Signature

          ——————————————

Any signature card provision or bank rule that conflicts with Article 4 of the Uniform Commercial Code is invalid. Let's look at Paragraph 4 above. The Paragraph provides that if the customer fails to notify the bank within 30 days of any forgery or other apparent discrepancy in a cancelled check or statement of account, the customer will be forever barred from holding the bank liable for wrongful payment. In other words, the customer must inspect his or her cancelled checks and statements of account and make any complaints about them within 30 days or lose all rights. This provision probably conflicts with Section 4–103 of the Uniform Commercial Code. While the parties to the contract (the bank and its customer) are free to determine many of the specifics of their agreement, Section 4–103 of the Code expressly provides that no bank can effectively disclaim responsibility for its lack of good faith or failure to exercise ordinary care; nor can any bank limit the measure of damages for such lack of good faith or failure to exercise ordinary care. Section 4–103 provides as follows.

The UCC provides:

> **Section 4–103. Variation by Agreement; Measure of Damages; Certain Action Constituting Ordinary Care**
>
> (1) The effect of the provisions of this Article may be varied by agreement except that no agreement can disclaim a bank's ordinary care or can limit the measure of damages for such lack or failure; but the parties may by agreement determine the standards by which such responsibility is to be measured if such standards are not manifestly unreasonable.
>
> *   *   *
>
> (5) The measure of damages for failure to exercise ordinary care in handling an item is the amount of the item reduced by an amount which could not have been realized by the use of ordinary care, and where there is bad faith it includes other damages, if any, suffered by the party as a proximate consequence.

———

Of course, the bank may well argue that the "30 day period" of Paragraph 4 merely sets a standard for measuring responsibility within the meaning of Section 4–103(1), and that the standard is not manifestly unreasonable. The courts, in this case, must determine whether the provision does, in fact, conflict with the Code. However, in light of the fact that such provisions are generally in small print, on cards prepared by the bank and neither read nor understood by the customer, the provision will likely be held invalid.

As to Section 4–103(5), it is clear that the bank cannot limit the measure of damages by agreement. However, the maximum amount recoverable by the customer is the amount of the item concerned unless bad faith on the part of the bank can be shown.

What is the bank collection process?

As stated previously, collection and payment are the two most important banking functions for the average bank customer. What does the collection process entail? Almost all of you deposit checks or other deposit items in your checking accounts. You may deposit a single paycheck once a month or perhaps 40 to 50 business checks every week to ten days. The drawee of the checks may be your own bank, a bank down the street, or one many thousands of miles away. In any case, your bank will accept the deposit, credit your account with the amount of the deposit, and initiate the *bank collection process* whereby the checks are presented to the drawee bank for payment, the drawee bank charging the account of the drawer for the amount designated on the checks.

It should be noted that the initial crediting of a check on the day of deposit to the customer's account is a "provisional settlement" only. That is to say, if the customer's bank is for some reason unable to collect the check (e. g., where the drawee bank dishonors the check because the drawer has insufficient funds in his or her account to cover the item), the bank may charge back the item against the customer's account. Section 4–212 of the Uniform Commercial Code provides as follows.

The UCC provides:

> **Section 4–212. Right of Charge-Back or Refund**
>
> (1) If a collecting bank has made provisional settlement with its

customer for an item and itself fails * * * to receive settlement for the item * * * the bank may revoke the settlement given by it, charge back the amount of any credit given for the item to its customer's account or obtain refund from its customer * * *.

———

If the customer has already withdrawn or otherwise used the amount provisionally credited to his or her account, the bank's remedy is refund rather than charge-back. The question might arise—why make "provisional settlement" at all? Why not simply wait until the check is paid by the drawee bank before crediting it to the customer's account?

The Official Comment to Section 4–212 (1) explains:

1. Under current bank practice, in a major portion of cases banks make provisional settlement for items when they are first received and then await subsequent determination of whether the item will be finally paid. This is the principal characteristic of what are referred to in banking parlance as "cash items." Statistically, this practice of settling provisionally first and then awaiting final payment is justified because more than ninety-nine percent of such cash items are finally paid, with the result that in this great preponderance of cases it becomes unnecessary for the banks making the provisional settlements to make any further entries. In due course the provisional settlements become final simply with the lapse of time. However, in those cases where the item being collected is not finally paid or where for various reasons the bank making the provisional settlement does not itself receive final payment, * * * provision is made for the reversal of the provisional settlement, charge-back of provisional credits, and the right to obtain refund.

———

A typical deposit slip looks like this:

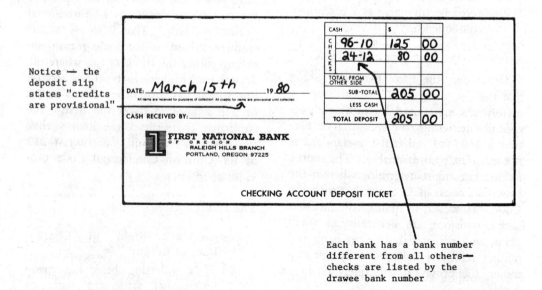

Notice → the deposit slip states "credits are provisional"

Each bank has a bank number different from all others— checks are listed by the drawee bank number

It should be pointed out that a provisional settlement by a bank does not itself constitute the giving of "value" within the meaning of the requirement for becoming a holder in due course (as discussed in Ch. 13). The bank "gives value" only when the customer withdraws or uses the provisionally credited amount, or when the provisional credit becomes final. By way of example, suppose that Joe Depositor makes the following deposits (starting with an account balance of $500.00):

Monday—Checks and notes payable to his order totalling $900.00.

Tuesday—Checks and notes payable to his order totalling $200.00.

Wednesday—Checks and notes payable to his order totalling $1,800.00.

Joe now has a total of $3,400.00 in his account. On Thursday, Joe withdraws $1,600.00. On the theory that the first money in is the first money out ("FIFO" —meaning "First In, First Out"), the bank is deemed to have paid value to Joe insofar as the $500 beginning balance and the Monday and Tuesday deposits are concerned. As to those checks and notes, the bank satisfies the "value" requirement for purposes of being a holder in due course. As to the checks and notes deposited on Wednesday, the provisional credit to Joe's account does not constitute the giving of value, and the bank could not be a holder in due course as yet.

Now assuming that deposit and "provisional settlement" have been made, how is the bank collection process completed? The process varies depending on the relationship between the *depositary bank* (the bank where the check is deposited) and the *payor bank* (the drawee bank).

(1) *Where the depositary bank is also the payor bank.* It sometimes occurs that the depositary bank is also the payor bank. For example, if both you and your

employer have accounts in the same bank, your paychecks will be drawn on the bank where you will deposit the checks. Such checks are referred to by banks as "on us" items. After determining that an "on us" item is in proper form (complete and without forgeries) and that there are sufficient funds in the drawer's account to cover the item, the depositary-payor bank will pay the check by deducting the proper amount from the drawer's account and crediting the amount to the payee-depositor's account. The provisional credit given to the payee-depositor upon deposit now becomes final.

(2) *Where the depositary bank and payor bank are different banks but are located in the same city or vicinity.* More frequently, it occurs that the depositary bank and payor bank are different banks but are located in the same city or vicinity. The checks, in this case, are called "city" or "clearinghouse" items. Usually, if two banks in the same city or vicinity regularly receive items drawn on each other, the banks will have a system of forwarding the checks on a daily basis. As between the banks, provisional settlement is made by striking a balance (i. e., making the appropriate debit or credit) in running accounts maintained by the banks. For example, if Bank C receives checks totalling $190,000 all drawn on Bank A, and Bank A receives checks totalling $240,000 all drawn on Bank C, the two banks will forward the checks, and strike a $50,000 balance in their records of account (Bank C owing $50,000 to Bank A). Payment is accomplished by making the appropriate entry on the accounts, the balances changing from day to day.

Where several banks in the same city or vicinity share this kind of relationship (i. e., each regularly receives for collection checks drawn on the other banks), the same collection procedure is followed with one major difference. Instead of forwarding the checks to the individual payor banks, the depositary banks forward them to a "clearing house" (a central gathering place) where all transfers are made and all account balances determined. The "clearing house" approach is a natural outgrowth of early collection procedures. Originally, collecting banks employed messengers to take bundles of sorted checks to the individual drawee banks and collect the cash. Before long, the collecting banks realized that this was a very inefficient way of doing things. They directed their messengers to take all the sorted bundles to one central "clearing house" where all the bundles could be exchanged at one time. A clearing house manager kept a set of accounts so that payment could be accomplished through bookkeeping entries rather than with actual cash. The use of the clearing house is still basic to collection procedure today. Of course, the efficiency of the system has greatly improved with the availability of modern data processing equipment.

(3) *Where the depositary bank and payor bank are different banks and are located in different cities or vicinities.* Often, the depositary bank is located in one city or vicinity and the payor bank in another. How is the check or other deposit item (promissory note or trade acceptance) collected? The Federal Reserve System, through its Federal Reserve Banks, provides a countrywide clearing house for such items; any bank can become a member of the collection system without joining the Federal Reserve System itself. For example, suppose that a Florida resident purchases merchandise from a Washington resident, mailing a check drawn on a Florida bank in payment. The Washington resident deposits the check in a Tacoma bank which forwards the instrument to the Federal Reserve Bank of Seattle. The Federal Reserve Bank of Seattle, in turn, forwards the check to the Federal Reserve Bank of Atlanta which finally presents the instru-

ment for payment to the payor bank in Florida.

What obligations do banks have in the collection process?

The *Official Comment* to Section 4–213 of the Uniform Commercial Code describes the collection process.

The Official Comment provides:

2. If an item being collected moves through several states, e. g., is deposited for collection in California, moves through two or three California banks to the Federal Reserve Bank of San Francisco, to the Federal Reserve Bank of Boston, to a payor bank in Maine, the collection process involves the eastward journey of the item from California to Maine and the westward journey of the proceeds from Maine to California.

The banks involved in the collection process are defined by Section 4–105 of the Code as follows.

The UCC provides:

Section 4–105. In this Article unless the context otherwise requires:

(a) "Depositary bank" means the first bank to which an item is transferred for collection even though it is also the payor bank.

(b) "Payor bank" means a bank by which an item is payable as drawn or accepted;

(c) "Intermediary bank" means any bank to which an item is transferred in course of collection except the depositary or payor bank;

(d) "Collecting bank" means any bank handling the item for collection except the payor bank;

(e) "Presenting" bank means any bank presenting an item except a payor bank * * *

The responsibilities of a collecting bank (including depositary banks) are set forth in Section 4–202 of the UCC as follows.

The UCC provides:

Section 4–202. Responsibility for Collection; Where Action Seasonable

(1) A collecting bank must use ordinary care in

(a) presenting an item or sending it for presentment; and

(b) sending notice of dishonor or non-payment or returning an item * * * after learning that the item has not been paid * * *

(c) settling for an item when the bank receives final settlement; and

(d) making or providing for any necessary protest; and

(e) notifying its transferor of any loss or delay in transit within a reasonable time after discovery thereof.

(2) A collecting bank taking proper action before its midnight deadline following receipt of an item, notice or payment acts seasonably; taking proper action within a reasonably longer time may be seasonable but the bank has the burden of so establishing.

(3) Subject to subsection (1)(a), a bank is not liable for the insolvency, neglect, misconduct, mistake or default of another bank or person or for loss or destruction of an item in transit or in the possession of others.

Under Section 4–202, a collecting bank is responsible for using ordinary care in selecting the proper route for collection; in selecting properly qualified intermediary banks; and in properly instructing the intermediary banks. A collecting bank must also use ordinary care in giving notice of dishonor or in returning an unpaid item. If a collecting bank uses ordinary care with regard to these particulars, the bank will not be liable for any other bank's negligence or misconduct in the collection process.

You will note that Section 4–202(2) provides that a collecting bank takes proper action (meaning timely action) if the bank acts (forwards the item, presents it, gives notice of dishonor, or returns it, etc.) before its midnight deadline. Section 4–104(h) of the Code defines "midnight deadline" in the following manner: " 'Midnight deadline' with respect to a bank is midnight on its next banking day following the banking day on which it receives the relevant item or notice * * *." Thus, if a collecting bank receives an item on Monday, the bank acts timely if it acts before midnight on Tuesday. However, two other Code provisions must be added to complete the picture. Section 4–107 permits a bank to cut off its banking day for collection purposes as of 2:00 p.m. or later; any items received after that time are treated as being received at the opening of the next banking day. The effect is to extend the midnight deadline by one day.

Section 4–107 reads:

Section 4–107. Time of Receipt of Items

(1) For the purpose of allowing time to process items, prove balances and make the necessary entries on its books to determine its position for the day, a bank may fix an afternoon hour of 2 P.M. or later as a cut-off hour for the

handling of money and items and the making of entries on its books.

(2) Any item or deposit of money received on any day after a cut-off hour so fixed or after the close of the banking day may be treated as being received at the opening of the next banking day.

The Official Comment to the Section provides:

Purposes:

1. After an item has been received by a bank it goes through a series of processes varying with the type of item that it is. It moves from the teller's window, branch office, or mail desk at which it is received through settlement and proving departments until it is forwarded or presented to a clearing house or another bank, if it is a transit item, or until it reaches the book-keeping department, if the bank receiving it is the payor bank. In addition, in order that the books of the bank always remain in balance while items are moving through it, the amount of each item is included in lists or proofs of debits or credits several times as it progresses through the bank. The running of proofs, the making of debit and credit entries in subsidiary and general ledgers and the striking of a general balance for each day requires a considerable amount of time. If these processes are to be completed on any particular day during normal working hours without the employment of night forces, a number of banks have found it necessary to establish a "cut-off hour" to allow time to obtain final figures to be incorporated into the bank's position for the day.

Unless otherwise instructed by the customer, a collecting bank may also extend the midnight deadline by one day if it does so in a good faith effort to secure payment of the item. And any delay is excused if brought about by a blizzard, flood, hurricane, wreck, or other disaster. The relevant Code provision is Section 4–108.

The UCC provides:

Section 4–108. Delays

(1) Unless otherwise instructed, a collecting bank in a good faith effort to secure payment may, in the case of specific items and with or without the approval of any person involved, waive, modify or extend time limits imposed by this Act for a period not in excess of an additional banking day without discharge of secondary parties and without liability to its transferor or any prior party.

(2) Delay by a collecting bank or payor bank beyond time limits prescribed or permitted by this Act or by instructions is excused if caused by interruption of communication facilities, suspension of payments by another bank, war, emergency conditions or other circumstances beyond the control of the bank provided it exercises such diligence as the circumstances require.

Is notice of final payment by the payor bank sent back through the collection chain to all intermediary banks and the depositary bank?

Each collecting bank (depositary and intermediary bank) makes a "provisional settlement" as the item moves through the collection process. You will recall that 98% of all items are paid by the payor bank, at which time all "provisional settlements" become final. Two questions arise. *First*, is notice of final payment by the payor bank sent back through the collection chain to all intermediary banks and the depositary bank? *Second*, what constitutes "final payment" by the payor bank?

In answer to the first question, no notice is sent back if the item is paid—notice is sent back only if the item is not paid (in other words, "no news is good news"). Thus, if no notice is received within the prescribed time limits of the Code (the midnight deadline as qualified), final payment is assumed. The time period may be very short as where the item is sent directly from the depositary bank to the payor bank. Or it may be a long week to ten days as where there are several intermediary banks involved (each bank has a successive midnight deadline). Once final payment can be assumed, the customer who deposited the item will be permitted to withdraw or write checks against the amount—that is, if he or she has not already been given that right. Banks frequently permit their regular customers to immediately withdraw or write checks against provisionally settled amounts: if the provisionally settled item is ultimately dishonored, the bank will have a right to refund of any amount withdrawn or otherwise used.

What constitutes "final payment" by the payor bank?

Remember, a payor bank's duty is to pay *only according to the customer's order*. Both aspects of this duty—paying when the bank should pay and not paying when the check is not "according to the customer's order" (e. g., a forged check)—will be considered in subsequent sections. Here, we are concerned merely with what constitutes "final payment" by the payor bank: final payment of a check or other deposit item makes all provisional settlements final and brings the collection process to an end. Section 4–213 of

the Uniform Commercial Code provides as follows.

It says:

Section 4–213. Final Payment by Payor Bank * * *

(1) An item is finally paid by a payor bank when the bank has done any of the following, whichever happens first;

    (a) paid the item in cash; or

    (b) completed the process of posting the item to the indicated account of the drawer, maker or other person to be charged therewith; or

    (c) make a provisional settlement for the item and failed to revoke the settlement in the time and manner permitted by statute, clearing house rule or agreement.

———

Subsection (b) states that payment is final when the "process of posting" is completed. UCC Section 4–109 defines this process as follows.

The UCC provides:

Section 4–109. Process of Posting

The "process of posting" means the usual procedure followed by a payor bank in determining to pay an item and in recording the payment including one or more of the following or other steps as determined by the bank:

    (a) verification of any signature;

    (b) ascertaining that sufficient funds are available;

    (c) affixing a "paid" or other stamp;

    (d) entering a charge or entry to a customer's account;

    (e) correcting or reversing an entry or erroneous action with respect to the item.

———

And payment is final under Section 4–213(c) if the payor bank makes provisional settlement upon receiving the item, then fails to revoke the settlement (as by sending notice of dishonor or returning the item) within the time limits prescribed by the Code (i. e., by midnight of the next banking day following receipt of the item). While the failure to revoke makes the collection process complete (i. e., makes all provisional settlements final), it does not serve to deprive the payor bank of any rights that it may have against its customer or any other party.

In conclusion, final payment is important because it is the end of the line in the collection process. Final payment of even a forged check makes all provisional settlements final; the payor bank cannot revoke the settlement, but can proceed only against the forger (assuming no one else is liable for breach of presentment warranty). This is so even though, as will be seen shortly, the bank cannot charge the amount of the check to the drawer's account.

What is the liability of the payor bank when it fails to pay as promised according to the order of the drawer-customer?

Having completed our study of collection, we turn now to the second most important banking function—payment. Under the bank-customer contract, the bank has a primary duty to honor the customer's checks (i. e., orders to pay) so long as the customer has sufficient funds in his or her account to cover the items. If the bank fails to pay an item that it should pay, the bank will be liable to the customer in damages.

However, it seldom occurs that a bank intentionally or with hostile motive dishonors a good check. Usually, the bank simply acts out of mistake. Section 4–402 of the Uniform Commercial Code provides that where a bank *mistakenly*

fails to pay an item that it should have paid, the bank's liability is limited to *actual* damages proved.[2] Actual damages may include damages for injury to the customer's credit or credit rating, or damages stemming from arrest or prosecution for writing bad checks. Section 4–402 states as follows.

The UCC provides:

Section 4–402. Bank's Liability to Customer for Wrongful Dishonor

A payor bank is liable to its customer for damages proximately caused by the wrongful dishonor of an item. When the dishonor occurs through mistake liability is limited to actual damages proved. If so proximately caused and proved damages may include damages for an arrest or prosecution of the customer or other consequential damages. Whether any consequential damages are proximately caused by the wrongful dishonor is a question of fact to be determined in each case.

Is it proper for the payor bank to charge the drawer's account when it pays a materially altered check or a check bearing a forged drawer's signature or forged indorsement?

Again, the bank's contractual duty is to pay *only* according to the customer's order. Obviously, materially altered items or items containing forgeries are not *according to the customer's order* and are not "properly payable" (an exception, to be explained shortly, arises where the drawer has negligently and substantially contributed to the forgery or alteration). Thus, if a drawee bank makes "final payment" (i. e., cash payment, posting, or unrevoked provisional settlement) of a materially altered check (say, one on which the sum certain has been raised from $100 to $1,000), the bank cannot

---

2. In no case will the bank incur liability to the holder of the item who presents it for payment (not even to a HOC).

charge the altered amount to the drawer's account: the bank can charge against the account only to the extent of the check's original tenor ($100). Nor can the drawee bank charge a paid check bearing a forged drawer's signature to the drawer's account, nor a paid check bearing a forged indorsement, with two exceptions. The exceptions are known as the fictitious payee and imposter problems.

Fictitious payees. As an exception to the general rule, the payor bank may charge against the drawer's account an instrument bearing a forged indorsement of a *fictitious payee*. The fictitious payee situation arises where a trusted employee of the drawer secures the drawer's signature on a check made out to the order of a nonexistent or actual person not intended by the employee to have any interest in the check proceeds. For example, the employee may be in charge of making up the monthly payroll. He or she simply adds to the payroll the name of a fictitious payee who is really not an employee at all. The drawer, who signs perhaps 100 to 200 employee paychecks a month, signs the check made payable to the fictitious payee without even realizing it. The "trusted" employee then forges the fictitious payee's indorsement, and the bank pays the check. Section 3–405 of the Uniform Commercial Code provides that the bank may charge the check against the employer-drawer's account. The theory is that the employer-drawer should bear the loss resulting from his or her employment of a person who cheats and pads the payroll. The employer-drawer's only recourse is against the employee who cheated him or her.

Imposters. Similarly, it is the drawer who must bear the loss where he or she is fooled into issuing a check to an imposter who pretends to be the named or intended payee. If the imposter forges the payee's indorsement and cashes the check, the check will be chargeable against the drawer's account.

The Uniform Commercial Code deals with fictitious payees and imposters at Section 3–405 as follows.

The UCC provides:

Section 3–405. Impostors; Signature in Name of Payee

(1) An indorsement by any person in the name of a named payee is effective if

(a) an imposter by use of the mails or otherwise has induced the maker or drawer to issue the instrument to him or his confederate in the name of the payee; or

(b) a person signing as or on behalf of a maker or drawer intends the payee to have no interest in the instrument, or,

(c) an agent or employee of the maker of drawer has supplied him with the name of the payee intending the latter to have no such interest.

(2) Nothing in this section shall affect the criminal or civil liability of the person so indorsing.

———

Apart from the fictitious payee and imposter exceptions, a forged or altered instrument may be charged to a drawer's account only where the drawer has negligently and substantially contributed to the forgery or alteration. Two Uniform Commercial Code Sections are pertinent. As you will recall, Section 3–406 provides as follows.

The UCC provides:

Section 3–406. Negligence Contributing to Alteration or Unauthorized Signature

Any person who by his negligence substantially contributes to a material alteration of the instrument or to the making of an unauthorized signature is precluded from asserting the alteration or lack of authority against a holder in due course or against a drawee or other payor who pays the instrument in good faith and in accordance with the reasonable commercial standards of the drawee's or payor's business.

Thus, if a drawer negligently leaves large gaps in a check with the result that the instrument is easily altered, the altered check will be chargeable against the drawer's account. However, the negligence must substantially contribute to the alteration. If the payee chemically erases all the writing and writes an entirely new check, the drawer's negligence in leaving gaps is immaterial, and the drawer is not liable on the instrument as altered. Other examples of negligence include failing to look after a signature stamp or other automatic signature device with the result that someone uses the device to "manufacture" checks; and carelessly mailing a check to someone other than the payee but with the same name as the payee who indorses the check and cashes it.

The second Code provision dealing with the drawer's negligence is Section 4–406. As you know, banks furnish checking account customers with periodic statements of account transactions at which time cancelled checks are also returned. Section 4–406 of the Code imposes certain duties upon bank customers upon their receipt of the bank statements and cancelled checks. The Section is designed to protect banks against losses that could be avoided by prompt customer inspection for forgeries and alterations.

Section 4–406 provides:

(1) When a bank sends to its customer a statement of account accompanied by items paid in good faith in support of the debit entries or holds the statement and items pursuant to a request or instructions of its customer or otherwise in a reasonable manner makes the statement and items available to the customer, the customer must exercise reasonable care and promptness to examine the statement and items to discover his unauthorized signature or any alteration on an item and must notify the bank promptly after discovery thereof.

(2) If the bank establishes that the customer failed with respect to an item to comply with the duties imposed on the customer by subsection (1) the customer is precluded from asserting against the bank

(a) his unauthorized signature for any alteration on the item if the bank also establishes that it suffered a loss by reason of such failure; and

(b) an unauthorized signature or alteration by the same wrongdoer on any other item paid on good faith by the bank after the first item and statement was available to the customer for a reasonable period not exceeding fourteen calendar days and before the bank receives notification from the customer of any such unauthorized signature or alteration.

Thus, the customer-drawer must do two things:

(1) He or she must promptly examine the statement and cancelled checks; and

(2) He or she must promptly notify the bank of any apparent forgery or alteration.

If the customer-drawer fails to exercise the required care, the forged or altered instrument may be charged to his or her account. And so may any other item subsequently forged or altered by the same wrongdoer and paid by the bank within fourteen days of the customer's receipt of the bank statement. These rules are only fair as the customer's failure to act promptly deprives the bank of reasonable opportunity to catch the wrongdoer and to be on the alert for additional forgeries or alterations by the same party.

However, Section 4–406(1)–(2) is qualified in that the bank cannot hold the customer liable for negligence where the bank itself has failed to exercise ordinary care in paying the check. Section 4–406(3) states that "the preclusion under subsection (2) does not apply if the customer establishes lack of ordinary care on the part of the bank paying the item."

And, finally, Section 4–406(4) provides.

It says:

> (4) Without regard to care or lack of care of either the customer or the bank a customer who does not within one year from the time the statement and items are made available to the customer discover and report his unauthorized signature or any alteration on the face or back of the item or does not within 3 years from that time discover and report any unauthorized indorsement is precluded from asserting against the bank such unauthorized signature or indorsement or such alteration.

In other words, even where the customer is entirely blameless and the bank completely negligent, the customer must assert an unauthorized drawer's signature or alteration within one year of receipt of the statement containing the forgery or alteration or forever lose his or her right to do so. With regard to a forged indorsement, the customer-drawer has up to three years to assert the defense. The time limit is shorter in the first instance because the drawer has little excuse for not realizing that his or her own signature has been forged or his or her own instrument altered. It is more reasonable that the drawer should be unaware of a forged indorsement.

In the event that the payor bank pays a forged or altered check but cannot charge the drawer's account, is there anyone else the bank can hold liable?

You will recall from Ch. 14 the presentment and transfer warranties of UCC Section 3–417. Basically the same presentment warranties are made with regard to checks presented for payment or acceptance. Section 4–207(1) of the Uniform Commercial Code provides.

It says:

> (1) Each customer or collecting bank who obtains payment or acceptance of an item and each prior customer and collecting bank warrants to the payor bank or other payor who in good faith pays or accepts the item that
>
> (a) he has a good title to the item or is authorized to obtain payment or acceptance on behalf of one who has a good title; and
>
> (b) he has no knowledge that the signature of the maker or drawer is unauthorized, except that this warranty is not given by any customer or collecting bank that is a holder in due course and acts in good faith
>
> > (i) to a maker with respect to the maker's own signature; or
> >
> > (ii) to a drawer with respect to the drawer's own sig-

nature, whether or not the drawer is also the drawee; or

(iii) to an acceptor of an item if the holder in due course took the item after the acceptance or obtained the acceptance without knowledge that the drawer's signature was unauthorized; and

(c) the item has not been materially altered, except that this warranty is not given by any customer or collecting bank that is a holder in due course and acts in good faith

(i) to the maker of a note; or

(ii) to the drawer of a draft whether or not the drawer is also the drawee; or

(iii) to the acceptor of an item with respect to an alteration made prior to the acceptance if the holder in due course took the item after the acceptance, even though the acceptance provided "payable as originally drawn" or equivalent terms; or

(iv) to the acceptor of an item with respect to an alteration made after the acceptance.

———

Basically the same transfer warranties are also made; however, the warranties run to the transferor's immediate transferee *and* to any subsequent collecting bank regardless of indorsement by the transferor (under Section 3–417, the warranties run beyond the transferor's immediate trans-

feree only if the transferor indorses the instrument). The warranties in no case run to the payor bank.

Section 4–207(2) states:

(2) Each customer and collecting bank who transfers an item and receives a settlement or other consideration for it warrants to his transferee and to any subsequent collecting bank who takes the item in good faith that

(a) he has a good title to the item or is authorized to obtain payment or acceptance on behalf of one who has a good title and the transfer is otherwise rightful; and

(b) all signatures are genuine or authorized; and

(c) the item has not been materially altered; and

(d) no defense of any party is good against him; and

(e) he has no knowledge of any insolvency proceeding instituted with respect to the maker or acceptor or the drawer of an unaccepted item.

———

What is the result of these warranties? Suppose that the payor bank pays an instrument bearing a forged drawer's signature and cannot charge it to the drawer's account. Since the transfer warranties do not run to the payor bank, the bank must look to the presentment warranties for relief. However, not all parties make the presentment warranties, and even those who do warrant only that they have no knowledge of an unauthorized drawer's signature (as you will recall from Ch. 14, the warranty of good title encompasses only forged indorsements). Thus, in most cases, the bank's only recourse will be against the forger (assuming the forger can be found).[3]

Where the bank has paid an instrument bearing a forged indorsement, on the other hand, the bank can proceed against most parties in the chain of collection following the forgery on the basis of breach of presentment warranty of good title. Again, this warranty applies only to forged indorsements—it does not apply to a forged drawer's signature.

The same is true of a material alteration. While the *transfer* warranties as to material alteration do not apply, the payor bank can proceed against most parties in the chain of collection following the alteration on the basis of breach of *presentment* warranty against material alteration.

To summarize:

(1) The general rule is that the drawer's account may not be charged where the bank has paid a forged instrument; nor may the account be charged beyond the original tenor of an altered instrument. To charge the account would be to pay other than according to the customer's order.

(2) As an exception to the general rule, the drawer's account may be charged in the case of (a) a fictitious payee; (b) an imposter; or (c) negligence on the part of the drawer that has substantially contributed to the forgery or alteration.

(3) In most cases, if the drawee bank pays an instrument bearing a forged drawer's signature, the bank's only remedy is against the forger.

(4) If the drawee bank pays an altered instrument or an instrument bearing a forged indorsement, the bank can recover from most anyone in the chain of collection following the alteration or forgery on the basis of breach of presentment warranty against material alteration or good title.

Can a customer-drawer "stop payment" of a check?

Occasionally, a bank customer writes a check, then discovers that he or she has been defrauded by the payee, or that the check has been lost or stolen. The customer, in this case, will want to order the bank to "stop payment" of the check. Section 4–403 of the Uniform Commercial Code provides for stop payment orders as follows.

It says:

Section 4–403. Customer's Right to Stop Payment; Burden of Proof of Loss

(1) A customer may by order to his bank stop payment of any item payable for his account but the order must be received at such time and in such manner as to afford the bank a reasonable opportunity to act on it.

* * *

(2) An oral order is binding upon the bank only for fourteen calendar days unless confirmed in writing within that period. A written order is effective for only six months unless renewed in writing.

(3) The burden of establishing the fact and amount of loss resulting from the payment of an item contrary to a binding stop payment order is on the customer.

———

The customer-drawer (or his or her personal representative in the case of a deceased customer-drawer) is the only

---

3. Where the bank discovers the forgery before making final payment, and dishonors the instrument, the item will be sent back through the chain of collection with the result that the party who actually dealt with the forger will bear the loss (i. e., unless he or she can find the forger and collect from him or her).

person who can order payment stopped. The payee cannot do so. The customer-drawer must give the order at such time as to afford the bank reasonable opportunity (usually, two hours at maximum) to act before "final payment" of the item is made. Note that under Subsection (2), an oral stop payment order is binding for only 14 days. Usually, the customer-drawer will call the bank and give the stop payment order orally: there is a need for haste so as to prevent the check from being cashed. But unless the customer-drawer follows up with a written stop payment order, the order will cease to be binding after 14 days. A written order, on the other hand, is binding for six months, and may be renewed for additional periods of time.

Of course, stopping payment of an item affects only the relationship between the drawer and the bank (it keeps the bank from charging the check against the drawer's account). It does not affect the underlying transaction which gave rise to the check. Thus, if the payee is entitled to payment because of underlying contract or other rights, the payee can successfully sue upon dishonor of the instrument and hold the drawer for the amount owing. And if the check is dishonored while in the hands of a holder in due course, the drawer will have to pay the HDC unless the drawer has a real as opposed to a personal defense to payment.

It must be emphasized that a bank is obligated to follow a timely given stop payment order. If it disregards the order and pays the check, the bank will be liable to the customer-drawer for any loss he or she suffers as a result. The bank, in turn, will be subrogated to the customer-drawer's rights against the payee or other party.

The bank itself will never become liable to the payee by reason of following the stop payment order. If there is a dispute regarding the underlying transaction, it must be settled between the customer and the payee without involvement by the bank.

What is a stale check?

A check that has been outstanding (i. e., issued but not presented for payment) for more than six months is considered to be "stale". Banks are not required to pay stale checks and usually will not pay them without first consulting the customer-drawer of the check. However, such consultation is not required, and if the bank pays the stale check in good faith, it can still charge the drawer's account. These rules are found in Section 4–404 of the Uniform Commercial Code: "A bank is under no obligation to a customer having a checking account to pay a check * * * which is presented more than six months after its date, but it may charge its customer's account for a payment made thereafter in good faith."

What happens if a drawer-customer dies or becomes legally incompetent?

Obviously, it would be extremely difficult for a bank to try to keep up-to-date and accurate information on whether its customers are alive or dead, competent or incompetent. Thus, the Uniform Commercial Code provides that a bank may legally pay the checks of a dead or incompetent drawer until such time as the bank learns of the death or incompetency, and in the case of a dead drawer, for ten days thereafter (unless ordered to stop payment by a person claiming an interest in the decedent's account). These rules are designed to protect the bank which must pay according to the drawer's order or face liability for wrongful dishonor. The rules also serve to expedite probate of a deceased drawer's estate (allowing checks to be paid for a reasonable time after the drawer's death cuts down on the number of creditors filing claims against the decedent's estate—see Ch. 30 "Wills"). The Uniform Commercial

Code provisions as to death and incompetency are found at Section 4–405 as follows.

The UCC provides:

Section 4–405. Death or Incompetence of Customer

(1) A payor or collecting bank's authority to accept, pay or collect an item or to account for proceeds of its collection if otherwise effective is not rendered ineffective by incompetence of a customer of either bank existing at the time the item is issued or its collection is undertaken if the bank does not know of an adjudication of incompetence. Neither death nor incompetence of a customer revokes such authority to accept, pay, collect or account until the bank knows of the fact of death or of an adjudication of incompetence and has reasonable opportunity to act on it.

(2) Even with knowledge a bank may for 10 days after the date of death pay or certify checks drawn on or prior to that date unless ordered to stop payment by a person claiming an interest in the account.

What is a certified check?

After writing a check, but before issuing it, the drawer may have his or her bank *certify* the instrument. Similarly, the payee or subsequent holder of a check may present the instrument to the drawee bank, not for payment, but for *certification*. Certification is the drawee bank's signed engagement to honor the check when it is presented for payment; certification constitutes formal acceptance by the bank making the bank primarily liable on the instrument (ordinarily, checks are not accepted but are paid on demand as are other demand drafts). At the very moment of certification, the bank charges the amount of the check against the drawer's account. The result—the bank has its money, and the holder of the check is secure in the knowledge that the bank's assets stand behind the instrument. And certification constitutes "final payment" by the bank—once a check is certified, the drawer can no longer stop payment on the check. Where it is the payee or subsequent holder who presents the check for certification, the drawer and all prior indorsers of the instrument are discharged; where it is the drawer who presents the check, the drawer remains secondarily liable on the instrument. UCC Section 3–411.

Certified checks are useful, particularly in transactions where a party is reluctant to accept a regular drawer's check (e. g., because of fear of insufficient funds in the drawer's account). Say that you put an ad in the paper to sell your used Chevrolet for $900.00. A shabby looking buyer comes along and gives you his or her personal check for that amount. You take the check, the buyer takes the car, the check bounces, and you are out both car and money. If you had demanded a certified check in payment, this could not have happened.

Thus, it is often prudent to require payment by certified check, and, in fact, many contracts do require payment by either certified check or *cashier's check*. A cashier's check is a check issued by the bank itself; unlike a certified check, it is not drawn on a customer's account. Anyone can go into a bank and purchase a cashier's check—the cost is the amount of money for which the check is to be drawn plus an amount charged by the bank for the service of providing the check. Obviously, the issuing bank is primarily liable on the cashier's check. There is no secondary liability in the purchaser.

Who will prevail if more than one person has a legitimate claim to the proceeds of a check?

A customer-drawer has only so much money deposited in his or her bank account. Sometimes, the customer-drawer writes checks against the deposited amount, then other events occur and two or more parties are claiming the same deposited funds. Who will prevail as between a checkholder and other claimant? Generally speaking, a checkholder's claims may be cut off by any one of the following (called the "four legals"):

(1) Knowledge or notice of the customer's death, incompetency, or bankruptcy;

(2) The customer's stop payment order;

(3) Legal process such as garnishment;

(4) Set-off by the drawee-payor bank.

Knowledge or notice of the customer's death, incompetency, or bankruptcy. Suppose that the court appointed guardian of an incompetent drawer claims the deposited funds so as to use them to care for the drawer? Or say that the legal representative of a deceased drawer claims the money as part of the decedent's estate. You already know that, as to incompetency, the checkholder will prevail only if "final payment" of the check is made before the bank learns of the incompetency. (Remember, "final payment" is defined by the Code to include cash payment, completion of the posting process, and provisional settlement accompanied by failure to revoke in the time and manner prescribed by statute.) As to a deceased customer-drawer, you know that the checkholder will prevail if "final payment" is made either before the bank learns of the death or within ten days thereafter. Again, the bank has a right to make final payment of an item for ten days following notice of the drawer's death unless instructed to the

contrary by the decedent's legal heir or representative (in which case, the checkholder will prevail only if final payment precedes notice of the legal heir's or representative's claim to the money).

Now suppose that the customer-drawer has gone into bankruptcy, and the trustee in bankruptcy claims the bank account balance as part of the bankrupt's assets to be distributed to his or her creditors (see Ch. 26 for a complete description of bankruptcy). Again, if the bank makes final payment of an item before being notified of the bankruptcy with reasonable time to react to the notice, the checkholder will prevail over the trustee in bankruptcy (conversely if notice and time to react precede final payment).

The customer's stop payment order. The customer may personally claim the deposited funds on the basis of a stop payment order. The customer will prevail over the checkholder only if the bank receives the order and has time to react to it before final payment is made.

Legal process such as garnishment. A creditor of the drawer may also claim the funds that the checkholder claims. For example, the creditor may be trying to reach the customer's bank account balance through a "garnishment" proceeding. In a garnishment, the court orders the bank (the garnishee) to disclose any assets of the debtor (the customer-drawer) in its possession and to hold the assets to pay off the creditor (see Ch. 26 for a discussion of garnishment). If the bank disregards the order, it will become personally liable to the creditor. Garnishment is always available to a creditor who has gone to court and obtained a judgment against the debtor; it is sometimes available to a creditor who has yet to reduce his or her claim to judgment. Who prevails as between the creditor and the checkholder? Once again, if the check is finally paid within the meaning of the Code before the bank is notified of the garnishment and has time to react to it, the checkholder will prevail. But if the notice of garnishment comes first, with reasonable time to react, the garnishment order will prevail and the creditor will be paid.

Set-off by the drawee-payor bank. Finally, the drawee bank itself may claim the funds. This occurs where the customer not only has a checking account with the bank but has also borrowed money from the bank in a separate transaction. If the customer fails to repay the loan as promised, the bank has a contract right to offset the amount owing against the drawer's bank account. If the offset occurs before final payment of a particular check is made, the bank will prevail over the checkholder. Conversely, if final payment precedes the set-off, the checkholder will prevail over the drawee-payor bank.

What is the Financial Institutions Regulatory and Interest Rate Control Act of 1978?

In 1978, the federal Congress passed the Financial Institutions Regulatory and Interest Rate Control Act, the first major "bank reform" measure to be passed in almost a decade. With a 1979 effective date, the Act was designed to put a halt to a number of banking abuses and to protect the confidentiality of customer banking records. Among other things, the Act:

(1) Prohibits overdrafts by bank insiders (officers, directors, controlling shareholders, etc.).

(2) Limits the amount of loans a bank can make to its officers and directors to not more than 10% of the bank's capital (and provides that insider loans must be made on a nonpreferential basis).

(3) Provides federal bank regulators (the Federal Reserve Board, Comptroller of the Currency, Federal Deposit Insurance Corporation, etc.) with increased supervisory powers; the right to fine individuals for banking law violations; the authority to obtain cease-and-desist orders against unsafe and unsound banking practices and to remove bank directors and officers who engage in such practices; and the power to block changes in bank ownership that endanger the safety of the financial institution.

(4) Bars interlocking directorates (see Ch. 23 for a discussion of "interlocking directorates") among large financial institutions and among smaller ones in the same market area.

(5) Requires full disclosure by financial institutions of all terms and conditions of "electronic fund transfers" (a transfer initiated through an electronic terminal, telephonic instrument, or computer or magnetic tape, including automated teller machine transactions); requires the financial institution to make available for the consumer written documentation of the transfer; and defines and limits the consumer's liability for unauthorized transfers.

(6) Limits access of most federal authorities (not including the Internal Revenue Service) to a customer's bank records by requiring that the customer be notified and given an opportunity to challenge the records request in court (this portion of the Act is referred to as the "Right to Financial Privacy Act of 1978").

Section 1117(a) of the Act provides:

(a) Any agency or department of the United States or financial institution obtaining or disclosing financial records or information contained therein in violation of this title is liable to the customer to whom such records relate in an amount equal to the sum of—

(1) $100 without regard to the volume of records involved;

(2) any actual damages sustained by the customer as a result of the disclosure;

(3) such punitive damages as the court may allow, where the violation is found to have been willful or intentional; and

(4) in the case of any successful action to enforce liability under this section, the costs of the action together with reasonable attorney's fees as determined by the court.

* * *

CASES

CASE 1—*The depositor has a duty to examine his or her checks and report forgeries to the bank.*

HUBER GLASS CO. v. FIRST NAT. BANK OF KENOSHA

Supreme Court of Wisconsin, 1965.
29 Wis.2d 106, 138 N.W.2d 157.

WILKIE, Justice.

The law concerning the duty of a bank towards it depositor was summarized in Wussow v. Badger State Bank. Since their relationship is grounded in contract, a bank can only make payments from a depositor's account in accordance with proper authorization and is bound to restore any amount paid out on forged checks. A bank can only avoid this strict liability where the "depositor is in equity estopped to assert that the bank is absolutely liable." To do this successfully, the bank must show (1) that it was without fault in failing to detect the forgeries, and (2) that the depositor was negligent in causing the money to be paid. In the instant case the trial court found as a matter of fact that (1) the bank "was negligent in not detecting the forgeries," and (2) that the depositor "was not negligent." To enable the bank to prevail against the depositor's claim it must, on this appeal, demonstrate that both of these findings are against the great weight and clear preponderance of the evidence.

Thus, the two issues presented on this appeal are:

1. Is the finding of negligence on the part of the bank against the evidence?

2. Is the finding of no negligence on the part of the depositor against the evidence?

The Bank's Negligence.

Two bank officials, George Gehring and Rudolph Scuglik, explained the procedures employed by the bank when a check was presented for payment. When checks come in, they are totaled, listed, and sorted alphabetically in the proof department and are then routed to the bookkeeping department. There an employee, who is responsible for a particular alphabetical segment of accounts, examines each check for signature, date, amount, payee, and endorsement, and posts it to the appropriate account. The checks are then photographed, perforated, filed with others charged against the same account, and, at the end of the month, returned to the depositor. Every bookkeeping department employee has a file containing signature cards for each of their depositors and are trained to recognize the various signatures. The checks are actually compared with the cards until the employee becomes sufficiently familiar with the signature. The head of the bookkeeping department is notified in case of a discrepancy. Scuglik, who was in charge of the bookkeeping department, could not say that each of the checks in question was processed according to the prescribed manner, but he assumed that this was done as a matter of routine. There was no testimóny which would even suggest that there was a breakdown of this system in regard to the checks in question. As to the forgeries themselves, an examination of the bogus checks, respondent's signature card, and several genuine checks which were introduced into evidence, demonstrates that "each forged signature was a reasonable facsimile of the genuine signature."

The record establishes that the bank used a reasonable method to inspect and process the checks presented to it, and that the forgeries were not palpable or flagrant, as was the case in Wussow, where the bank was found to be negligent for failing to detect the obvious discrepancy in signatures. Thus, unless the mere fact that the forgeries did escape detection of itself raises an inference of negligence, the bank, in the absence of any affirmative evidence to the contrary, has sustained the burden of showing that it acted reasonably and with "due diligence." Consequently there is no evidence to support the finding that the bank was negligent.

Negligence of Depositor.

Even if the bank is not guilty of negligence in failing to uncover the forgery, the depositor is nonetheless entitled to a restoration of the funds paid out in the absence of negligence on its own part. Thus, the crucial question here is whether or not the depositor was negligent.

A depositor is bound to examine the checks and statements returned by the bank, and this duty is violated when it neglects to do those things dictated by ordinary business customs and which, if done, would have prevented the wrongdoing.

In Wussow, the court held that the depositor had a duty
> "to examine his checks and the statement and discover whether
> the balance stated was correct and whether any forgeries were
> included and report any discrepancies in balance and any forgeries
> to the bank at once."

It has been held that the reconciliation should include, as a minimum, the following steps: (1) A comparison of the cancelled checks with the check stubs, (2) a comparison of the statement balance with the checkbook balance, and (3) a comparison of the returned checks with the checks listed on the statement.

There is no question that in the case at bar the procedure employed by the respondent in checking the returned checks and bank statements did not comply with these suggested steps. On the contrary, the undisputed evidence showed that the checks returned to respondent by appellant were received by Miller who made a preliminary examination of the statement. Presumably, the forged checks were removed from the others at this point. Then another employee of the bookkeeping department listed the checks numerically and determined the ones that were outstanding. After this, Miller would reconcile the bank statement with the check ledger. Huber got the checks at this point, but he testified that he never attempted to reconcile the bank statement with the books but left this task entirely up to Miller.

When asked:

"Q. * * * You could have yourself taken the number of checks that were there, taped them, and added to it the outstanding checks and subtracted that from your total deposit and determined whether there was any discrepancy, could you not?"

Huber replied:

"A. I could have, but this is what I hired Mr. Miller to do."

Miller advised Huber that the accounts were in balance. Between April 2, 1962, and April 19, 1963, respondent's account was overdrawn on 14 different occasions. Although appellant mailed respondent a notice of overdraft each time, Huber did not recall having seen any of them. However, he did learn of the overdrafts from the monthly statement.

Miller's methods were such that a comparison of the statement balance with the checkbook balance or a matching of the cancelled checks with the actual charges on the statement would have quickly disclosed a discrepancy. Likewise, a perusal of the cancelled checks, which were numbered consecutively, would have revealed that certain checks were missing and had been missing for some time. Yet Huber admittedly never complied with any of the suggested reconciliation practices, and, in fact, left full responsibility to Miller.

No other employee was assigned to verify Miller's work. That there were 14 overdrafts in a year should have prompted Huber to investigate the state of his books even if ordinary business practices did not so persuade him. Under the circumstances, entrusting Miller alone with the job of reconciling the statements for three years, when a simple spot check of the records would have uncovered the forgeries, was unreasonable and the trial court's finding of no negligence is contrary to the great weight and clear preponderance of the evidence. Huber, however, takes the position that the president of a company which employs between 50 and 75 people, and which writes almost 13,000 checks a year, cannot be expected to personally examine and/or reconcile the books. But the president himself is not required to do this; the task can be delegated to another employee. Modern business practice dictates at least some semblance of internal control. Estoppel from claiming against the bank is the price of blind reliance on a single employee.

The earliest checks forged on the depositor's account by Miller appeared in August of 1960. Respondent's negligence in failing to employ proper reconciliation methods preceded the one-year period—April, 1962–1963—embraced by the depositor's claim and he is estopped from asserting a claim against the bank for any check embraced in the lower court's judgment.

Other courts have arrived at the same conclusion upon similar facts. In Clarke v. Camden Trust Co. the depositor never made an attempt to reconcile his bank statement himself but left this job entirely to his trusted secretary. After the secretary mysteriously disappeared, it was learned that she had forged 41 checks over a four-year period. The depositor was precluded from recovering from the bank because "any kind of reasonable examination" would have detected the forgeries. * * *.

Judgment reversed.

CASE 2—*A dishonest employee forged endorsements of fictitious payees*

MAY DEPT. STORES CO. v. PITTSBURGH NAT. BANK

United States Court of Appeals, Third Circuit, 1967.
374 F.2d 109.

Before HASTIE, GANEY and SEITZ, Circuit Judges.

OPINION OF THE COURT

This is an appeal from summary judgment entered for the defendant after these facts were established without contradiction. An employee of the plaintiff, May Department Stores Co., fraudulently caused the plaintiff to draw its checks payable to fictitious suppliers. The wrongdoing employee then forged the endorsements of the fictitious payees, cashed the checks at the defendant bank and converted the proceeds. The bank charged the sums thus paid against the plaintiff's account.

The plaintiff then sued the bank for illegally charging its account with amounts paid on forged endorsements. On the record before it, and in the absence of any allegation or showing of countervailing circumstances by the plaintiff, the district court properly concluded that the bank was protected by the following provision of the Uniform Commercial Code as in force in Pennsylvania.

"(1) An indorsement by any person in the name of a named payee is effective if

* * *

(c) an agent or employee of the drawer has supplied him with the name of the payee intending the latter to have no such interest." 12A P.S. § 3–405(1)(c).

The judgment will be affirmed.

CASE 3—*"Rockford Tom Plunkett * * * a fast thinking, old time horse trader."*

PARK STATE BANK v. ARENA AUTO AUCTION, INC.

Appellate Court of Illinois, Second District, 1965.
59 Ill.App.2d 235, 207 N.E.2d 158.

PETERSEN, Justice.

This case comes into Court by reason of certain mistakes made by employees of the involved parties following the normal routine of customary business details so characteristic of the rapidly changing society and world in which we live.

Defendant-Appellant, Arena Auto Auction, Inc., created the problem brought to court by the issuance of its check dated December 17, 1963, and by the mailing of it to Plunkett Auto Sales, Rockford, Illinois. For clarity's stake, we will refer to the Rockford Plunkett and the Alabama Plunkett by these geographic designations rather than by their corporate names which, to this Court, are almost identical. Rockford Tom Plunkett might well have felt, upon receiving said check, that he was the recipient of some give-away or promotional scheme, for it later appears that he had sold no merchandise, a fact of which he was well aware, to the Defendant-Appellant. We might visualize Rockford Tom Plunkett as a fast-thinking, old-time horse trader, now engaged in the business of buying and selling used automobiles. He, being well known to the Plaintiff-Appellee Bank by reason of his borrowing and having cashed one previous check of the Defendant-Appellant, after holding this check from December 17th or 18th until January 3rd, 1964, and after due reflection on his part, signed his name to the check and presented it for payment to Charlotte Parish, head teller, who, promptly and without question, turned over to him the check-designated sum of $1,435.00.

On January 9, 1964, the said check was returned to the Plaintiff-Appellee Bank by reason of a stop-payment order by the maker, and came into the hands of the Assistant Vice-President, Mr. Marconi, whose duties are to assist in the operation of a financial institution, to know its customers, and, equally, to earn a profit for the Plaintiff-Appellee. Vice-President Marconi promptly called his personal friend, Jack Clark of the Arena Auto Auction, Inc., who, to cover the shortcomings of his secretary, called at the Plaintiff-Appellee Bank on January 10, 1964, to make explanation. Now, Jack Clark, being in the business of operating an automobile auction and using the speed of their operation to explain the error, commented thus: "This guy here (meaning Rockford Tom Plunkett) wasn't supposed to get the check. It was another Plunkett in Alabama. But Alabama Plunkett wasn't on our books, so that's why our gals sent the check to Rockford Plunkett, and that's why we stopped payment on our check."

But, to put the frosting on the cake, or as Counsel put it, to add insult to injury, Defendant-Appellant, Arena Auto Auction, Inc., issued their second check in the same amount to the same payee, and again sent the check to Rockford Tom Plunkett. Again we can visualize quick-thinking Rockford Tom Plunkett's surprise, for this truly must come from the money tree. He loses no time in going to the same financial institution as before. Not so fortunate on this second occasion, poor Rockford Tom Plunkett, as he tendered the second check, is questioned as to why payment was stopped on the first one. In his effort to secure quick payment he stated, "This check is to replace the first. Cash this check, give me back the first one, and I will return it to the Arena Auto Auction."

Mindful of the first experience, the Vice-President was reluctant to follow this advice and informed poor Tom that he was in difficulty. Rockford Tom Plunkett, seeing that the Vice-President could be right, promptly left the State of Illinois and established his abode in a more sunny climate. This is verified by Vice-President Marconi, who stated that he held a telephone conversation with Mr. Plunkett who was then in a restaurant in Amory, Mississippi. Despite the Vice-President's appeal to Tom to come home and correct his mistake, which is again borne out by the testimony as follows: "All I can tell you is you'd better come up here and make this good." It was to no avail. Rockford Tom Plunkett said, "You will never find me." Sad, but true; Vice-President Marconi tried: "Rockford Tom Plunkett wasn't there and I don't know where he is now."

So now we find the Plaintiff-Appellee Bank in the embarrassing position of having cashed a check and having had payment of that check stopped. Desirous of not losing money, they start suit to recover from the Arena Auto Auction. Judge Dusher of the Circuit Court of Winnebago decided in favor of the Plaintiff and against the Arena Auto Auction, Inc., who appeals to this Court.

From a purely legal point of view, there are two questions raised. First, did Rockford Tom Plunkett commit a forgery by signing his own name to a check ostensibly issued to him. Without passing on the very technical question of whether or not these facts constitute a forgery, this is apparently admitted by all parties concerned, for they cite cases in the Trial Court and in this Court, holding that a forgery passes no title by which one can recover as a bar to the Plaintiff-Appellee recovering. The Plaintiff-Appellee Bank relies upon Chapter 26, Illinois Revised Statutes, 1963, Section 3–406; which, being a new section of our Commercial Code, is as follows:

> "Any person who by his negligence substantially contributes to a material alteration of the instrument or to the making of an unauthorized signature is precluded from asserting the alteration or lack of authority against a holder in due course or against a drawee or other payor who pays the instrument in good faith in accordance with the reasonable commercial standards of the drawee's or payor's business." * * *

Without repeating the various errors previously recited, it appears to this Court presumptuous on the part of Arena Auto Auction, Inc., Defendant-Appellant, to insist that they did nothing for which they should be held accountable. We point out the interval of lapsed time before they, in their fast-thinking, fast-operating business, decide first to stop payment.

Secondly, bearing in mind the erroneous sending of a second check to the same payee, and considering the custom of the trade as set forth by the testimony of the several gentlemen of the financial world as to the routine handling of checks in banking institutions, it is our considered conclusion that to require the recipient Bank to stop and question persons known to that Bank and presenting checks in routine business and issued by makers likewise known to the Bank, would be placing cogs in the wheels of business, which, in turn, would bring those wheels of the banking business to an astounding and abrupt halt. This, as we see it, was neither the intent nor the purpose of our legislators in passing the section in our Commercial Code to which reference was made.

We, therefore and accordingly, do conclude that the Trial Court was correct in holding that the Defendant-Appellant, by their own negligence, substantially assisted in making it possible that an unauthorized person's signature passed title to the funds represented by said check.

Judgment of the Trial Court is affirmed.

PROBLEMS

1. Answer the following "True" or "False" and give reasons for your answers:

   (a) State banks are required to join the Federal Reserve System.

   (b) Most banks in the United States have joined the Federal Deposit Insurance Corporation.

   (c) To slow down the economy and achieve a "tight" money situation, the Federal Reserve Board can purchase government bonds.

   (d) Collection and payment are the two most important functions of a bank for its customers.

   (e) Any signature card provision or bank rule that conflicts with Article 4 of the Uniform Commercial Code is invalid.

(f) A provisional settlement by a bank constitutes the giving of "value" within the meaning of the requirement for becoming a holder in due course.

(g) Notice of final payment by the payor bank is generally sent back through the collection chain to all intermediary banks and the depositary bank.

(h) A bank that pays a stale check without first consulting with the drawer of the check cannot charge the check to the drawer's account.

(i) A collecting bank may generally extend the midnight deadline by one day if it does so in a good faith effort to secure payment of an item.

(j) It is the drawer who must bear the loss if he or she is fooled into issuing a check to an imposter who pretends to be the named or intended payee of the check.

2. Charlie Waters draws a check on First State Bank payable "to the order of Chris Foster" in the amount of $500 (the check given in payment for Chris' day care services for Charlie's daughter, Sara). Charlie mails the check to Chris, but a neighbor, Mike Pratt, rummages through Chris' mailbox and steals the instrument. Mike forges Chris' blank indorsement and delivers the check to Robin Richards in exchange for a color television set. Robin, who has no knowledge of the forgery, delivers the check to Ida Wilson in satisfaction of an existing debt.

Ida, who also takes the instrument in good faith, presents the check to her own bank—U. S. National—and receives $500 cash for the instrument (because Ida is a regular customer, the bank allows her to "cash" the check immediately). As between U. S. National and First State Bank, the check is provisionally settled at the clearinghouse; then a final entry is made in the books of account between the banks. First State Bank charges the $500 check to Charlie Waters' account and mails Charlie a statement of account. By this time, Chris has reported the theft to Charlie, and Charlie notifies the bank that the indorsement is forged and that the check should not be charged to his account.

Chris Foster
(No other indorsements)

(a) Can First State Bank charge the $500 check to Charlie's account? Explain.

(b) Assuming First State Bank cannot charge the check to Charlie's account, what are the bank's rights, if any, against U. S. National Bank, Ida Wilson, Robin Richards, and Mike Pratt? Explain.

(c) Assuming First State Bank can recover from U. S. National Bank, what are U. S. National's rights, if any, against Ida Wilson, Robin Richards, and Mike Pratt? Explain.

3. Assume the same facts as in (2) above except that Mike does not steal the check from Chris, but rather breaks into Charlie's house and steals a blank check form, makes the check out payable to his own order in the amount of $500, and forges Charlie's signature as drawer of the instrument. Mike indorses in blank and again transfers the check to Robin, Robin to Ida, Ida to U. S. National, and U. S. National to First State Bank which charges the check to Charlie's account. Upon receiving his statement of account, Charlie notifies First State Bank that his signature has been forged and that the check should not be charged to his account.

> (a) Can First State Bank charge the $500 check to Charlie's account? Explain.
>
> (b) Assuming First State Bank cannot charge the check to Charlie's account, what are the bank's rights, if any, against U. S. National Bank, Ida Wilson, Robin Richards, and Mike Pratt? Explain.
>
> (c) Assuming First State Bank can recover from U. S. National Bank, what are U. S. National's rights, if any, against Ida Wilson, Robin Richards, and Mike Pratt? Explain.

Mike Pratt

(No other indorsements)

4. Suppose that Charlie receives his bank statement containing the cancelled check bearing his forged drawer's signature, but does not examine the statement until six weeks have passed. At that time, he informs the bank that his signature has been forged and that the check should not be charged to his account. Charlie then learns that a second check also forged by Mike Pratt was charged to his account six days after he received the bank statement containing the first forged instrument. Can First State Bank charge the first forged check to Charlie's account? Can it charge the second forged check to his account? Explain.

14 days

5. Liz Becker, an employee of First State Bank, mistakenly concludes that Stewart Ackerman has insufficient funds in his checking account to cover a $350 check and so dishonors the instrument. The same day, the federal Bureau of Land Management (through its employee Mike McCormack) asks to see the bank's records regarding Stewart's account, and Liz allows him full access to the records. Stewart is not notified of the records request and has no opportunity to challenge it in court. What are Stewart's rights, if any, against First State Bank? Against the federal Bureau of Land Management? Explain.

6. Certification of a check by the drawee bank
>   (a) Is obligatory if demanded by a holder in due course.
>   (b) Is the drawee's signed engagement to honor it when presented.
>   (c) Where procured by a holder discharges all prior indorsements, but does *not* affect the drawer's liability.

(d) Is ineffective regarding any indorsement made after certification and creates *no* liability for the subsequent indorser.

[# 37, May, 1976, CPA Exam]

The following two questions are based on this fact situation.

Marlin ordered merchandise from Plant to be delivered that noon and delivered a check payable to the order of Plant and drawn on Marlin's account in First Bank. The goods were *not* delivered and Marlin exercised his rights to rescind. Plant negotiated the check for full value to Rose who took in good faith and without notice of any defense; Rose then negotiated it for full value to Quirk who knew of Plant's breach of his agreement.

7. If, after rescission, Marlin notified First Bank to stop payment on the check, First Bank

   (a) Will incur *no* liability by paying the check if *no* written notification was received prior to payment.

   (b) Is liable for any loss suffered by Marlin as a result of First Bank's payment after receiving a written stop-payment order regardless of the time interval between receipt of the order and payment.

   (c) Is *not* required to pay even if a valid presentment is made by a holder in due course.

   (d) Is liable to Marlin for any loss suffered by Marlin where it had issued its cashier's check in payment of Marlin's check before receipt of the stop-payment order but paid the cashier's check three days after receipt of the stop-payment order.

   [# 14, May, 1974 CPA Exam]

8. If First Bank pays the check five days after Marlin gave it to Plant

   (a) Without prior knowledge of Marlin's death, the bank would be liable to Marlin's estate if Marlin had had a defense to payment of the check.

   (b) Payment by First Bank to Quirk after First Bank received an effective stop-payment order would require First Bank to credit Marlin's account for the amount of the check.

   (c) Payment by First Bank would require the bank to credit Marlin's account if prior to payment First Bank had learned that Marlin had a valid defense against Plant on the check.

   [# 15, May, 1974 CPA Exam]

9. During your initial examination of the payroll procedures and transactions of Fox Burglar Alarm, Inc., you discover the following facts. Martin Goodson is employed as a payroll officer. Some time ago he became addicted to narcotics, and in order to support his drug habit, he began preparing payroll checks made out to fictitious parties. Fox's treasurer, unaware of the fraud, signed the checks in the ordinary course of his duties. After signature, Goodson would pick up the checks to distribute to the employees. In the process, Goodson removed the checks payable to the fictitious parties. He would then cash the checks at various check-cashing agencies, forging the names of the payees appearing on each check.

Required: What rights, if any, does Fox Burglar Alarm have against its own bank which paid the checks, the check-cashing agencies, and Goodson? Explain.

[# 5.b., November, 1973 CPA Exam]

10.   John Ford signed a check for $1,000 on January 25, 1975, payable to the order of Charles Benson Manufacturing, a sole proprietorship. The check was dated February 1, 1975. Benson indorsed the check to Francis Factoring, Inc., by writing on the back of the check: "Pay only to Francis Factoring, Inc., Charles Benson." After Benson delivered the check to Francis Factoring, Francis Factoring immediately took the check to First National Bank, the drawee, and had the check certified. Francis Factoring then indorsed the check in blank to Hills Brokerage Corporation in payment of materials purchased.

Required: a.   Did the indorsement, "Pay only to Francis Factoring, Inc.," stop the negotiability of the check and legally require the drawee bank to pay the proceeds of the check to Francis Factoring only? Explain.

b.   Can Hills Brokerage qualify as a valid holder of the check with all the rights of a holder in due course? Explain.

c.   Assuming Hills Brokerage qualifies as a holder in due course, can it successfully sue First National Bank if the bank refuses to honor the check on February 1? Explain.

d.   Assuming Hills Brokerage qualifies as a holder in due course, can it successfully sue Ford for the proceeds of the check if the bank refuses to honor it on February 1? Explain.

e.   Assuming Hills Brokerage qualifies as a holder in due course, can it successfully sue Benson for the proceeds of the check if the bank refuses to honor it on February 1? Explain.

f.   Assuming Hills Brokerage qualifies as a holder in due course, can it successfully sue Francis Factoring for the proceeds of the check if the bank refuses to honor it on February 1? Explain.

[# 7.c., May, 1975 CPA Exam]

Chapter 16

BAILMENTS, CARRIERS, WAREHOUSEMEN, AND
DOCUMENTS OF TITLE

What is a bailment?

A *bailment* may be defined as:

The rightful possession of another's personal property. The owner of the property is called the *bailor*, the party in possession the *bailee*. There are four "keys" to understanding bailments.

First, realize that only personal property can be bailed. It is not possible to create a bailment with real property (land or fixtures as explained in Ch. 2). Only books, clothes, cars, stock certificates, promissory notes, money, and other personal property can be bailed.

Second, appreciate that the bailee's possession must be "rightful" (a party in wrongful possession of stolen property is *not* a bailee).

Third, understand that legal possession demands two things: actual physical control over the property plus intent to assume or exercise control. The intent to possess (i. e., to assume custody and control over the property) is essential to a bailment. A person who exercises physical control over personal property without *intending* to possess it has mere "custody" and not "possession". And custody is not sufficient to create a bailment. For example, suppose that Susie Customer is shopping at Super Value Department Store. If Susie picks up a silk scarf to examine it, Susie has custody only; she lacks the intent to assume control that is necessary for a bailment. Similarly, if John Clerk of the Super Value Store carries items of merchandise from place to place in the store as part of his job, he has custody only (though John has physical possession, like Susie he lacks the intent to control required for a bailment).

Now suppose that Susie decides to try on a new coat in the store. John helps Susie remove her coat, and he places it on a counter from which it disappears. Here, the Super Value Store, through its employee John Clerk, has manifested an intent to exercise control over the coat, and a bailment exists. If, on the other hand, Susie takes off her own coat and lays it on the counter, with the result that the coat disappears, there is no physical possession by the store, no intent, and no bailment. The same is true where Susie personally hangs her coat on a hook in a restaurant—the restaurant is not a bailee of the coat. However, if Susie forgets her coat at the restaurant, and the restaurant owner or his or her employee puts the coat away for Susie, a bailment comes into being. And, of course, if the restaurant provides a hat and coat check room staffed by an employee of the restaurant, the restaurant manifests the required intent to assume control and is a bailee of any checked item, including Susie's coat. Now suppose that, on her way home, Susie sees a billfold lying in the street. Again, if Susie merely picks up the billfold, examines it, and throws it back down to the street, Susie has custody only and a bailment relationship does not come into being. But if, after examining the billfold, Susie takes it home with her, Susie holds the property as a finder and bailee for the true owner (see Ch. 3 regarding "finders").

Fourth and finally, recognize that the possession must be of a chattel belonging to someone else. The bailee must realize that he or she has possession of another person's personal property or a bailment relationship will not exist.

You can see from the finder example that a contract is not required for a bailment although, as a practical matter, contracts often give rise to bailment relationships. For example, if Susie Customer rents a car from Skimpy Budget Car Rental, or takes her watch in for repairs or her clothes in to the laundry, there is in each case a contract creating a bailment. The bailments arising from express and implied contracts may be distinguished from bailments which are *gratuitous* (not supported by consideration). Gratuitous bailments may be *voluntary* (the bailor intentionally delivers personal property to the bailee), *involuntary* (the bailor unintentionally turns over possession of the property as where Susie forgets her coat in the restaurant and the restaurant owner—the involuntary bailee—takes possession of it), or *constructive* (the bailor loses the property and the finder—the constructive bailee—takes possession of it).

Whether a bailment is contractual or gratuitous, certain rights and duties arise by law for both the bailor and bailee.

What are a bailee's rights?

Suppose that a bailor *gratuitously* agrees to deliver a chattel to a bailee for a certain period of time. If the bailor fails to deliver the chattel as promised, the bailee has no legal remedy. But if the bailor *contractually* agrees to deliver the chattel, the bailee may sue the bailor for any damages that result from nondelivery of the chattel. Or if the chattel is unique (i. e., cannot be obtained elsewhere), the bailee may ask the court for specific performance of the contract (i. e., ask the court to order the bailor to deliver the chattel—see Ch. 10 on "specific performance"). For example, say that Audrey Artist contracts to provide Martin Art-Dealer with 50 original paintings for exhibition at Martin's gallery. If Audrey later refuses to deliver the paintings, Martin is entitled to specific performance

of the contract. As originals, the paintings are unique, and money damages are not an adequate remedy. Along the same line, the bailor may be obligated under the terms of the bailment contract to furnish the bailee with specific goods or chattels of a particular quality or nature. The bailee, in this case, has a right to receive goods that comply with the contract description and that are fit for the purposes of the bailment. If such goods are not provided, the bailee may sue the bailor for money damages or for specific performance where appropriate.

Once the bailor has contractually or gratuitously delivered the personal property to the bailee, the bailee has the right to the exclusive use and control of the item during the term of the bailment. Of course, the use must be consistent with the conditions of the bailment. If there is a contract between the parties, the contract terms control. If there is no contract, or if the contract terms do not expressly provide as to use, the bailee's right is to "reasonable" use of the item —"reasonable" use being what the parties as reasonable people would have assented to under the circumstances had the matter been brought to their attention. For example, where a particular use would be to the benefit of the bailed property (e. g., milking a bailed cow or exercising a bailed horse), it is reasonable to assume that the bailor would have assented to the use had he or she given the matter thought. Such use will be permitted as a "reasonable" use of the item. With regard to an involuntary bailment, reasonable use encompasses any legitimate means designed to compensate the involuntary bailee for expenses incurred in caring for the chattel. For example, in the case of Alvord v. Davenport, 43 Vt. 30 (1870), a stranger left a horse with the defendant livery stable owner and never returned for the animal. The defendant ultimately concluded that the horse was stolen; however, he had no way to find the true owner, so he kept the animal for three years, using it in his business to pay for the cost of its care and upkeep. Eventually, the true owner discovered his horse in the defendant's possession. The true owner claimed that the defendant's commercial use of the animal constituted a conversion (see Ch. 1). The court, however, held that a gratuitous bailment existed, and that the defendant—the involuntary bailee—had the right to use the horse so as to pay for the cost of its maintenance.

Where a bailment contract provides for a specific term of bailment (e. g., 24 hours, 6 months, or 3 years), the bailee is entitled to exclusive possession and use of the chattel for the stated period. The bailee's right to exclusive possession and use during this time is good as against the whole world, including the bailor. Thus, if the bailor wrongfully interferes with the bailee's possession or use of the chattel during the term of bailment (as by wrongfully retaking the chattel or preventing its proper use), the bailee may sue for an injunction or for money damages.

Whether a bailment is contractual or gratuitous, if a third person interferes with the bailee's use and possession of the bailed property (as by injuring or destroying the property), the bailee may sue in his or her own name for money damages. Although the bailee can recover up to the full value of the chattel, the bailee must account to the bailor for any recovery in excess of the value of the bailee's bailment interest. And it should be realized that while the bailee *may* bring legal action against the interfering third party, he or she is not legally obligated to do so, and the bailor cannot force him or her to do so. If the bailee refuses to bring suit, the bailor can always sue for damages in his or her own right as the owner of the chattel.

Where a specific term of bailment is provided by contract, the bailee's right to

exclusive possession and use extends not only to the bailed chattel itself but also to any increases or profits that flow from the chattel during the term of the bailment. The bailee does not acquire ownership of the increases or profits—he or she obtains possession only. For example, suppose that a bailor contractually bails 20 head of cattle with a bailee for a period of two years. If the cattle give birth to a dozen calves during the two year period, the bailee has the exclusive right to possess and use the calves (for proper bailment purposes). However, the bailee's right continues only until the end of the bailment period, at which time all the cattle, including the calves, must be returned to the bailor.

Ordinarily, creditors of the bailee may not reach the bailed chattels because the bailee does not own the chattels—the bailor does. However, if the bailment itself has value because of the right to use the chattels (e. g., a 3 year bailment of a fleet of taxicabs), the bailee's creditors can reach the bailee's interest and succeed to the bailee's right to exclusively possess and use the property (of course, the creditors must use the property in accord with the terms of the bailment). An exception arises where the bailed property is special in nature and cannot be used properly by anyone other than the bailee (e. g., a thoroughbred horse bailed to a particular jockey); the bailee's creditors, in this case, will not be allowed to reach the bailee's interest.

What are a bailee's duties?

A bailee has three basic duties with regard to the bailed personal property.

First, the bailee has a duty to use the chattel only in accord with the bailment contract, and, if there is no contract, only in a manner that is fair and reasonable under the circumstances. In other words, the bailee must use the chattel for proper bailment purposes only. If the bailee uses the property for an improper purpose (i. e., uses it in any manner inconsistent with and in defiance of the bailor's ownership rights), the bailee will be liable to the bailor for misuse of the chattel (and for any damage or destruction resulting from the misuse) and breach of the bailment relationship. For example, suppose that Bill Bradley bails a television set to Randy Johnson for storage only. If Randy willfully destroys the set or uses it for his own purposes (as opposed to storing it), Randy will be liable in damages for misuse of the goods and breach of the bailment relationship. Or suppose that Susie Customer rents a car from Skimpy Budget Car Rental for commuting to and from work and for other normal driving purposes. In derogation of the bailment contract, Susie uses the car to compete in organized, competitive drag racing. If the car is damaged as a result of the misuse, Susie will be liable to Skimpy Budget Car Rental for the damage. Again whenever a bailee uses bailed property for an improper purpose, the risk of damage or destruction resulting from the misuse is on the bailee.

Second, the bailee has a duty to exercise care over the bailed chattel. Apart from liability for misuse the bailee is not liable for damage or destruction of the chattel in the absence of negligence (as you will recall from Ch. 1, negligence demands four things—a duty, a breach of duty, a causal connection between the breach and the damage, and actual damage measurable in dollar terms). So long as the bailee uses the chattel for a proper purpose and exercises care over the chattel, the risk of damage or destruction is entirely on the bailor. However, if the bailee is negligent (i. e., violates his or her duty of care), and the chattel is damaged or destroyed as a result of the negligence, the bailee will again be liable to the bailor. For example, suppose that Susie Customer uses the rented car for normal driving purposes only. If the car is struck by

lightning or is stolen without any fault on Susie's part, Susie will not be liable for the damage; the risk of loss is entirely on the bailor. But if Susie drives the car while intoxicated, and, as a result, runs it into a telephone pole, Susie will be liable; Susie's negligence has shifted the risk of damage or destruction back to the bailee.

The bailee's duty is to exercise the degree of care that a reasonable person under the same or similar circumstances would exercise. The circumstances include the nature of the bailed chattel, its apparent value, its proper uses, the location of the bailment, etc. To help in determining whether a bailee has exercised reasonable care, some courts have classified bailments into three categories, each requiring a different degree of care and imposing liability for a variant degree of negligence. The three traditional classifications are as follows:

(1) *A bailment for the mutual benefit of both the bailor and the bailee (frequently referred to as a "mutual benefit bailment", a "bailment for hire", or a "commercial bailment").* Where both parties benefit from the bailment relationship, the bailment is referred to as a *mutual benefit bailment.* For example, where Susie Customer rents a car from Skimpy Budget Car Rental, Susie (the bailee) benefits by reason of having a car to drive, and Skimpy Budget Car Rental (the bailor) benefits by virtue of receiving the rental payment. The bailment is properly termed a mutual benefit bailment.

The bailee in a mutual benefit bailment is required to exercise *ordinary care* and is liable for *ordinary negligence.* Courts frequently define "ordinary care" as "what a reasonable person would do in caring for his or her own goods of a similar kind under similar circumstances"; "ordinary negligence" is a failure to exercise ordinary care. Thus, if Susie Customer parks the rented car in front of her house instead of in her garage, and a hit-and-run driver damages the vehicle, Susie is not liable to the bailor. Susie has exercised ordinary care (a reasonable person would park his or her own car on the street); therefore, her actions do not amount to ordinary negligence. On the other hand, if Susie leaves the keys to the rented car in the ignition with the result that the car is stolen, Susie is liable to the bailor. Susie has failed to exercise ordinary care (a reasonable person would not leave ignition keys in his or her car) and is liable for ordinary negligence.

What constitutes ordinary care necessarily varies with the circumstances of the particular bailment (e. g., a bailee is obviously expected to use more care for a chattel of great value than for a relatively inexpensive chattel).

(2) *A bailment for the sole benefit of the bailee.* Here, the bailee alone benefits from the bailment relationship (typically, the mere loan of a chattel to the bailee). The bailee is required to exercise *extraordinary* or *great care* (as opposed to ordinary care) and is liable for *slight negligence* (as opposed to ordinary negligence). But not even a borrower-bailee is an insurer of the bailed goods. Some negligence, however slight, must be shown if the bailee is to be held liable. For example, suppose that Susie Customer borrows a friend's car and leaves it parked in the street instead of parking it in her garage. If the car is damaged by a hit-and-run driver, Susie may well be liable for failure to use extraordinary care. At most, Susie has been slightly negligent in leaving the car parked in the street; however, slight negligence is all that is necessary for liability where the bailment is for the sole benefit of the bailee. Still, Susie is not an insurer of the car. If she locks the car in her garage, and the garage is struck by lightning, destroying the vehicle, Susie will not be liable because she has not been negligent.

(3) *A bailment for the sole benefit of the bailor.* This kind of bailment is frequently referred to as a "gratuitous bailment" [1] since only the bailor benefits —the bailee holds the property gratuitously (i. e., without receiving anything in return). For example, a finder of lost property is a gratuitous bailee who holds the property for the sole benefit of the true owner. Similarly, where Susie Customer gratuitously stores Bill Bradley's car in her garage while Bill is vacationing in Europe, Susie holds the car solely for the benefit of Bill Bradley. The general rule (by court decision and by statute in some states, such as California) is that a gratuitous bailee who cares for another's goods or chattels without receiving payment or other benefit in return must exercise only *slight care* (as opposed to ordinary or great care) and is liable only for *gross negligence* (as opposed to slight or ordinary negligence). Courts have met with considerable difficulty in trying to define the term "gross negligence". One court defined it in this way.

It stated:

Gross negligence is substantially and appreciably higher in magnitude than ordinary negligence. It is materially more want of care than constitutes simple inadvertence. It is an act or omission respecting legal duty of an aggravated character as distinguished from a mere failure to exercise ordinary care. It is very great negligence, or the absence of slight diligence, or the want of even scant care. It amounts to indifference to present legal duty and to utter forgetfulness of legal obligations so far as other persons may be affected. It is a heedless and palpable vio-

---

1. As you already know, any bailment not supported by consideration is a gratuitous bailment; a bailment for the sole benefit of the bailor is merely one kind of gratuitous bailment.

lation of legal duty respecting the rights of others.

———

Altman v. Aronson, 231 Mass. 588, 121 N.E. 505 (1919).

But such definitions are not very helpful when dealing with actual fact situations. For example, we concluded that Susie Customer's conduct in leaving the keys to the rented car in the ignition (with the result that the car was stolen) amounts to ordinary negligence. But does Susie's conduct constitute gross negligence? You can appreciate the problem. Because of it, modern authorities have tended to stop analyzing bailments—particularly mutual benefit bailments and bailments for the sole benefit of the bailor —in terms of degrees of care and negligence. Instead, the courts now state that "negligence in such cases is nothing more than a failure to bestow the care which the property in its situation demands; the omission of the reasonable care required is the negligence which creates the liability; and whether this existed is a question of fact for the jury to determine * * *." Preston v. Prather, 137 U.S. 604, 11 S.Ct. 162, 34 L.Ed. 788 (1891). The Court in the *Preston* case went on to say.

The reasonable care which persons should take of property entrusted to them for safekeeping without reward will necessarily vary with its nature, value and situation, and the bearing of the surrounding circumstances upon its security. The business of the bailee will necessarily have some effect upon the nature of the care required of him, as, for example, in the case of bankers and banking institutions having special arrangements by vaults and other guards to protect property in their custody.

Nevertheless, it would seem that the circumstance of whether or not the bailee received a benefit from the bailment should not be ignored in instructing a jury concerning the care required of the bailee. One finds it hard to deny the appeal of the statement of the Massachusetts court to the effect that "justice requires that the one who undertakes to perform a duty gratuitously should not be under the same measure of obligation as one who enters upon the same undertaking for pay."

———

Thus, under the modern approach, the fact that a bailee receives no payment or other benefit for taking care of the bailed property is but one of the many circumstances to be considered in determining how much care is required of the bailee and whether he or she has been negligent in causing injury or loss to the chattel.

Sometimes, the parties to a bailment desire to vary the duty of "reasonable care under the circumstances" imposed by law upon the bailee. The parties, by contract, may generally impose a lesser or greater duty of care. For example, a bailee will frequently insert a contract provision limiting his or her liability to a fixed amount in the event of damage or loss; or the bailee will insert a provision exempting himself or herself from liability. The limitation or exemption may apply to all kinds of loss or damage, or it may be limited to a few specific kinds such as loss or damage resulting from "leakage, freezing, or flooding" (e. g., where the parties anticipate that "leakage, freezing, or flooding" is likely to occur despite any reasonable precautions taken). Most courts uphold such provisions so long as they are clearly called to the bailor's attention or are placed so that a reasonable person in the position of the bailor would notice them. Thus, a large sign stating "not responsible for theft or damage to articles checked" is effective to disclaim liability for negligence when placed at the entrance to a restaurant hat and coat check room. However, the same statement in small print on the back of a standard claim check is not effective to disclaim liability for negligence unless it is clearly called to the customer's attention.

Of course, a bailee can never limit his or her liability for willful or intentional injury to the bailed chattel. Nor can the bailee exempt himself or herself from such liability. Any provision purporting to do so is contrary to public policy and, thus, unenforceable. Along the same line, many courts prohibit a bailee from limiting or exempting his or her liability for gross negligence. And some courts prohibit any and all limitation or exemption of liability as being contrary to public policy.

Finally, the parties to a bailment may choose to increase the bailee's responsibility by contract. For example, a bailee might agree, in return for consideration, to assume absolute responsibility for goods —to become, in effect, an insurer of the property. The "insurer" bailee has a duty to return the goods in an undamaged condition under all circumstances; he or she is liable for any loss or damage no matter what the cause. Contract provisions imposing a greater duty of care upon the bailee are generally upheld unless they are unconscionable as defined in Ch. 8.

In any event, a bailee may purchase liability insurance to protect against liability for loss or damage of the bailed goods. The bailee in every case has an insurable interest in the bailed property; however, he or she is under no obligation to the bailor to insure the goods.

Third, the bailee has a duty to redeliver the chattel to the bailor (or his or her

appointee). The bailee's duty is absolute.[2] No reasonable care standard is applied; if the bailee improperly delivers the chattel to one other than the bailor (or his or her appointee), the bailee will be liable regardless of how much care he or she has exercised.

However, the bailee will not be liable if, knowing that a third person claims ownership of the chattel, the bailee delivers the chattel into the "custody of the law" (i. e., takes the chattel to court for a determination of who is entitled to the property). The bailee will, in fact, be liable to the third person if the bailee redelivers the chattel to the bailor and it later turns out that the third person and not the bailor owns the item.

The bailee's duty is to redeliver the *identical* goods bailed to him or her. The single exception is where the goods are "fungible" goods as defined in Ch. 3.

"Fungible" goods are goods of the same quality and value, any one unit of which is the same as any other unit, which are customarily sold by weight and measure. Examples are grain, oil, or minerals of the same grade. So long as each party knows how much he or she has contributed to the mass, it makes no difference that different goods are in fact returned to each owner—all the goods are identical.

In other words, each fungible unit is the equivalent of any other like unit. Frequently, when a bailor deposits fungible goods with a bailee, the bailee places the goods in a common mass of like fungibles. The bailee agrees to redeliver not the identical goods deposited but merely an equal amount of like goods taken from the common mass. The bailor depositors of the goods making up the common mass own the property as tenants in common (see Ch. 5 on "tenants in common"). Any individual depositor may

---

2. A bailee has no power to transfer the bailed goods to a 3rd party. The bailor will prevail over a transferee even where the transferee is a bona fide purchaser (but see Ch. 19, "sales of goods by nonowners.")

have an option to sell his or her deposit and receive back cash rather than the deposited fungibles; such an option does not impair the bailment relationship.

How does the bailor prove that the bailee was negligent?

You know that if bailed goods are lost, damaged, or destroyed while in the possession of the bailee, the bailor can recover from the bailee only if the bailee has been negligent. Yet, in many situations, it is difficult, if not impossible, for the bailor to prove any lack of care on the bailee's part (where the bailee fails to return the bailed chattel, or returns it in a damaged condition, how is the bailor to know, much less prove, what happened to the property?). If required to prove negligence, the bailor would seldom recover.

For this reason, the law does not require the bailor to prove that the bailee was negligent. It requires only that the bailor establish the existence of the bailment (possession in the bailee) along with the bailee's failure to return the goods on demand or his or her return of the property in a damaged state. This is called making out a *prima facie* case against the bailee. The effect of making out a *prima facie* case is to establish a rebuttable presumption that the bailee was negligent and that his or her negligence caused the loss or damage. If the bailee fails to rebut the presumption (i. e., fails to prove that he or she was not negligent), judgment will be entered on behalf of the bailor.

For example, suppose that Susie Customer leaves a car rented from Skimpy Budget Car Rental in her garage while she goes on vacation. While Susie is away, a fire breaks out in the garage, and the car is destroyed. Though there is no evidence as to how the fire started or whether Susie was to blame, Skimpy Budget Car Rental can make out a *prima facie* case against Susie by proving that

the car was rented and not returned. Since Susie cannot disprove negligence, she will lose the case. On the other hand, if Susie can prove that the fire was caused by lightning striking the garage, Susie will rebut the presumption of negligence and win the case.

Is a bailment created when a person pays to leave his or her car in a parking lot?

The answer is—it depends. There are three possible fact situations:

(1) *Rented space.* Here, a car owner drives into a parking lot, parks his or her own car, keeps his or her car keys, and pays a charge for the parking space. The lot owner makes little or no effort to provide security for the car. There is no bailment as the parking lot owner does not have legal possession of the car (physical control plus intent to assume control). The car owner has merely rented the space: he or she has a license to use the land for parking purposes (see Ch. 6 for a definition of "license"). The rental may be for a few hours (e. g., where a person rents parking space from the owner of vacant land so as to attend a sporting event or other special activity), or it may be on a monthly basis (e. g., where a person rents a particular parking space by the month from a commercial rental lot).

(2) *Bailment relationship.* Here, the car owner leaves his or her car with a parking lot attendant who assumes control over the vehicle and parks it for the owner. The owner pays a fee for the service and receives a claim check to be used for purposes of reclaiming the car. In this situation, a bailment clearly exists: the lot attendant not only has physical control of the car but intends to assume control. The bailment is for the mutual benefit of both parties. In the event that the car is stolen or damaged while in the bailee's possession, the bailor can make out a *prima facie* case against the bailee

by establishing the existence of the bailment along with the bailee's failure to return the car in the condition in which it was bailed.

Frequently, in the parking lot bailment situation, the bailee attempts to limit his or her liability by posting signs or printing disclaimers on the back of the claim check. The validity of these attempts is determined by the limitation of liability rules as discussed previously in the chapter.

(3) *The problem of possession.* The third situation falls somewhere in between situations (1) and (2) (i. e., there is a mixture of facts from both situations). For example, a car owner may park his or her own car and keep his or her keys, yet the parking lot owner may still provide security for the car. Or the parking lot attendant may park the car, return the keys to the car owner, yet charge no fee for the service.

Whether or not a bailment exists in such a case depends on whether the parking lot owner has legal possession of the car (again, physical control of the vehicle plus intent to assume control). Possession is the key to finding a bailment. Thus, the fact that a party parks his or her own car and retains his or her keys does not necessarily preclude a bailment (auto thieves frequently start cars without ignition keys). If the parking lot owner holds himself or herself out as providing security for the car and makes an effort to keep the car safe and under his or her exclusive control, a bailment will exist regardless. Along this line, the cases generally hold that there is both physical control and manifested intent to assume control where the parking lot is constructed so that it is impossible for any unauthorized person to enter or leave the lot except through the parking lot owner's failure to provide the promised security. (The rules are the same for anyone who promises to furnish security for goods. Obviously, there is no bail-

ment where you merely rent space to dock your boat, and the dock owner makes no promise and no effort to physically control and look after the boat. But if you store your boat at a moorage that offers and furnishes protection for the boat, a bailment relationship exists).

Similarly, if a restaurant parking lot attendant parks your car as a matter of courtesy and convenience to restaurant customers, a bailment will exist though no fee is charged for the service. Again, it is "possession" that is the key to finding a bailment, and the parking lot attendant has both physical control of the car plus intent to assume control.

What is the bailment container rule?

When the bailed chattel is a closed container or other item containing property not visible to the bailee, the bailee is responsible for the chattel's contents only where he or she knows or should know as a reasonable person (e. g., because of the nature of the container) that the contents are present. For example, suppose that you park your car with a bailee, and the car is stolen or damaged as a result of the bailee's negligence. Obviously, the bailee will be liable for the loss of the car. But will he or she be liable for the loss of property contained in the trunk of the car? As to ordinary automobile accessories such as a jack and a spare tire, the answer is yes, because the bailee should reasonably expect such items to be present in the trunk. But the bailee will not be responsible for the loss of golf clubs contained in the trunk unless you informed him or her of their presence and he or she took possession of the car anyway.

What are the bailment responsibilities of a safe deposit box company?

A safe deposit box company (usually a bank or other financial institution) that "rents" safe deposit boxes to customers is a bailee of the property contained in any particular box. Though the transaction is referred to as a box "rental", the safe deposit box company is responsible as a bailee because of the high degree of control that it exercises in preventing unauthorized access to the box. Typically, the company maintains two keys for each box; the customer holds one key, the safe deposit box company the other. The use of both keys is required to unlock the box.

As a bailee of the contents of the box, the safe deposit box company must exercise reasonable care under the circumstances. Almost always, this means a high degree of care since it is reasonable to expect that items of great value will be placed in the box.

Under the container rule, the company should reasonably anticipate that the box will contain any kind of valuable that will fit into it. Of course, in order to make out a *prima facie* case against the company, the bailor must establish that the valuable was in fact placed in the box and was not there when the bailor returned. This may well be difficult to prove if the bailor alone purports to have knowledge of the specific deposit, and there appears to have been no lapse in security by the safe deposit box company. For example, in the case of Henderick v. Uptown Safe Deposit Box Co., 21 Ill. App.2d 515, 159 N.E.2d 58 (1959), an 80 year old depositor-bailor claimed that she had placed some $89,000 in cash in a safe deposit box and that, when she returned, only $51,000 was there. In holding that there was no negligence or breach of duty on the part of the safe deposit box company, the court stated the following with regard to the company's security procedures.

The Court said:

Whenever a box holder desires entry to his box, he is required to sign an entrance ticket pertaining to his box. This he presents to the counterman at the business office who checks the signature, and if it is found to be that of the renter, the ticket is initialed and time-stamped. The counterman then admits the renter to the vault by releasing the lock on the day gate at the front door by means of a buzzer. He is met by a custodian who examines the ticket; if it is found in proper order the custodian, using the customer's key and his own guard key, unlocks the cubicle in which the box is locked.

If a box holder takes his box to one of the booths in the booth lobby, the door of the cubicle is opened and the custodian gives him back the key with the box. The door to the booth locks behind the customer after he has entered, and when he comes out the booth door automatically locks again. The custodian then examines the booth to ascertain if anything has been left there; any articles found are turned over to the manager and returned to the owner if he can be traced. The vault is cleaned daily by a maintenance man in the presence of the manager or a custodian. The vault mechanism is inspected every two months * * *. It appears that during the past eighteen years no burglaries or hold-ups have occurred * * *. In the present case there was no mark on the face of the door of the cubicle which showed any tampering; the original lacquer was still on it.

There is, in the instant case, nothing more than plaintiff's testimony * * that $37,750 in cash was missing from her safe deposit box. Plaintiff, a woman about eighty at the time of the trial, commented herself that she couldn't "remember so good any more" * * *

The principle underlying all the cases to which our attention has been called and in which the plaintiff prevailed is that the receipt of the bailed article was admitted or established by a fair degree of proof * * *

———

What are the bailment responsibilities of a hotel or motel owner?

The term "hotelkeeper" ("innkeeper" at common law) is used in law to describe a person who operates a hotel or motel or the like—i. e., anyone in the business of providing living accommodations for transient persons. The *World Book Dictionary* defines "transient" as "passing quickly or soon * * * not lasting * * * fleeting * * * passing through and not staying long." [3] Thus, a hotel *guest* or transient person is one who takes up quarters at a hotel or motel, intending to live there but temporarily. A guest may stay for a few hours, for several days, or even for several months and still be "passing through" as a transient. However, a person who enters a hotel merely to attend a dance or banquet, or eat lunch or dinner in the hotel restaurant is not a guest.

It is important to distinguish a hotel "guest" from a "tenant" and "permanent lodger". As you will recall from Ch. 2, a *tenant* who rents premises from a landlord receives exclusive possession of the rented real property; not even the owner of the land may interfere with the tenant's possession. It follows that the landlord is not a bailee of the tenant's personal property on the rented premises and has no duty of care with regard to the property.

A *permanent lodger* is a person who takes up residence at a hotel or boarding house, intending to stay there permanently. The permanent lodger is a mere licensee who has bare use of the premises as opposed to exclusive possession (see Ch. 6 for a discussion of "licensees"). The boarding house operator may provide such services as cleaning the room, making the bed, furnishing meals, etc. As to any of the lodger's personal property that comes under his or her control,
the boarding house operator is a mutual benefit bailee and must exercise ordinary care over the property.

The hotel guest is like the permanent lodger in that he or she is a mere licensee with bare use of the hotel or motel premises. However, under the common law, the hotelkeeper owes a much higher duty to the guest than the boarding house operator owes to the permanent lodger: the hotelkeeper is strictly liable as an insurer of the safety of the guest's personal property. If the guest's goods are stolen or damaged while the guest is staying at the hotel, the hotelkeeper will be liable period without regard to negligence. At common law, there are only five exceptions to the hotelkeeper's strict liability (of course, even where one of the five exceptions applies, the hotelkeeper will still be liable if he or she negligently contributes to the loss):

(1) *Act of God*. As used in the law, an "act of God" is any sudden, violent, natural phenomenon such as an earthquake, a hurricane, lightning, or a flood that causes damage to the bailed property. Normal weather conditions, even where unusually severe, do not fall within the definition of an act of God; however, weather that is unusual for a particular area might qualify (e. g., a snowstorm in a normally snow free climate).

(2) *Act of a public enemy*. A "public enemy" refers to the military force of a hostile nation, not to common criminals or FBI "public enemy #1" figures. Thus, a hotelkeeper is strictly liable for loss or damage to a guest's property caused by mob violence, robbers, thieves, or rioters. But a hotelkeeper is not strictly liable for loss or damage caused by a military take-over of the hotel, terrorist activities forming part of an international conspiracy against recognized

3. *The World Book Dictionary*, Field Enterprises Educational Corporation, 1967, p. 329.

governmental powers, pirate forces of a hostile nation (in the case of a passenger cruise ship or other "moving" hotel or motel), etc.

(3) *Act of a public authority.* Similarly, a hotelkeeper is not responsible for loss resulting from the act of a state, federal, or local governmental agency. Frequently, for example, agencies administering food and drug and public health laws have power to inspect goods or quarantine them, which may cause loss or damage to the goods.

(4) *The inherent nature of the property.* Sometimes, goods spoil or deteriorate simply because of the passage of time. The loss or damage stems from the inherent nature of the goods, and the hotelkeeper is not liable.

(5) *The fault of the guest.* Finally, the hotelkeeper is not liable where the guest himself or herself causes the loss (e. g., where the guest leaves the door to his or her room wide open with the result that his or her luggage is stolen).

It is important to realize that statutes in most states have substantially modified the hotelkeeper's common law strict liability. Generally, the statutes provide that the hotelkeeper may limit his or her liability by providing a safe where guests may deposit their money and other valuables. The hotelkeeper must post notice of the availability of the safe either in the individual hotel rooms or at the hotel front desk. If, after notice, a guest chooses not to utilize the safe, the hotelkeeper will not be liable beyond a certain minimal amount set by statute for loss or damage to the guest's valuables. The same minimal amounts will apply to property not normally kept in a safe (e. g., a wedding ring or a personal wristwatch).

By strictly complying with the statutory requirements, the hotelkeeper can greatly reduce his or her potential liability. Of course, the statutory limitation does not apply to the hotelkeeper's own negligence, and where the hotelkeeper or his or her employee is at fault in causing the loss, the hotelkeeper will be liable for the full amount of the damage.

The hotelkeeper is not responsible for a guest's automobile unless the hotelkeeper provides parking facilities and a bailment relationship comes into being as discussed previously under parking lot bailments.

In any event, the hotelkeeper's duty to a guest comes to an end when the guest leaves the hotel or ceases to be transient (as by becoming a permanent boarder or lodger).

Finally, the federal Civil Rights Act of 1964 prohibits the hotelkeeper from discriminating against guests on the basis of race, color, religion, or national origin. If the hotelkeeper refuses to accommodate a person on any of these grounds, the hotelkeeper will be liable to the party in damages, including punitive damages. However, the law does not prevent the hotelkeeper from excluding as a guest any person who is unfit because he or she is intoxicated, criminally violent, or improperly dressed (i. e., not dressed in accordance with reasonable hotel regulations uniformly applied to all people who come into the hotel or motel).

What are the bailment responsibilities of a common carrier of goods?

A person who is in the business of transporting goods for others (whether by truck, plane, ship, etc.) is called a *carrier*. If a carrier holds himself or herself out to transport goods for any and all members of the public, he or she is a *common carrier:* a common carrier is one engaged in transporting goods for the general public without discrimination and for compensation. If a carrier does not hold himself or herself out to transport goods for the general public, but merely agrees to carry goods for a limited number of customers under contract, the carrier is a *private contract carrier.*

Both common carriers and private contract carriers are bailees (both are in possession of another's personal property during the carriage); however, their responsibilities are very different. A private contract carrier is in the position of a mutual benefit bailee and is responsible for loss or damage to the goods only if he or she fails to exercise reasonable care under the circumstances. A common carrier, on the other hand, is like the hotelkeeper under the common law, and is strictly liable for the goods once they have been delivered to the carrier and have been accepted by him or her for immediate transportation. As with the common law hotelkeeper, there are five exceptions to the common carrier's strict liability:

(1) *Act of God.* Again, this is any sudden, violent, natural phenomenon that damages or destroys goods in the custody of the carrier. The force must be natural, extraordinary, and unforeseeable (e. g., a fire caused by lightning). A force of human origin is not an act of God (e. g., a fire resulting from arson). If the carrier knows of the natural force's approach, the carrier has a duty to exercise reasonable care to protect the shipper's goods. And if the carrier in any way contributes to the loss caused by the act of God (whether a flood, tornado, earthquake, etc.), the carrier will be liable for the full value of the loss or destruction.

(2) *Act of a public enemy.* If a public enemy (i. e., a military force of a hostile nation) causes loss or damage to goods in possession of a common carrier, the carrier will not be liable in the absence of negligence. As before, "public enemy" does not encompass common criminals: an ordinary hijacker of a carrier truck, cargo plane, or vessel is not a public enemy; nor is a rioting mob. However, "public enemy" does include a hijacker or pirate involved in an international conspiracy against a recognized governmental power.

(3) *Act of a public authority.* Similarly, a carrier is not strictly liable for loss or damage caused by an act of a state, federal, or local government agency. For example, a public health agency might halt the carrier to inspect the goods; the delay might result in loss or damage for the shipper. Or a county sheriff might seize the goods to satisfy a judgment obtained by a creditor of the shipper (as you will see in Ch. 26, if a creditor goes to court and obtains a judgment against a debtor, the government will help the creditor enforce the judgment by seizing and selling the debtor's nonexempt property). In any case, the carrier has a duty to notify the shipper of any potentially injurious action by the state so that the shipper can take steps to protect his or her interest.

(4) *The inherent nature of the goods.* The carrier also escapes strict liability where the loss or damage stems from the inherent nature of the bailed goods. Fruits and vegetables, for example, may spoil or deteriorate while being transported without any fault on the part of the carrier—the carrier is not liable for this natural, normal spoilage. Nor is a carrier of live animals responsible if the animals die of fright or refuse to eat and starve to death because they are highly strung and nervous creatures.

Of course, if the carrier in any way contributes to the loss or destruction, the carrier will be liable on the basis of negligence. For example, if the carrier can tell by seeing the goods that they will spoil during the carriage, the carrier is under a duty to refuse to transport the property. If the carrier accepts the goods, and they spoil en route, the carrier will be liable. Similarly, the carrier of live animals will be liable if he or she fails to provide the animals with proper food and water and proper shelter from the elements. All perishables must be properly carried to prevent deterioration.

To protect themselves, most common carriers provide special refrigerated and heated cars which are available to shippers at a higher rate. A shipper who fails to take advantage of the special cars, but ships his or her goods in ordinary cars so as to pay the lower charge cannot later recover from the carrier on the basis that special cars should have been provided.

(5) *The fault of the shipper-bailor.* Finally, if the shipper himself or herself causes the loss, the carrier will not be liable. The most common example is where a shipper defectively packages goods, and the goods spoil or deteriorate as a result. Of course, if the defect in packaging is apparent, the carrier is under a duty to refuse to transport the goods; if the carrier accepts the goods, and the goods spoil or deteriorate as a result of the packaging, the carrier will be liable.

A second example is where a shipper gives faulty directions to a carrier. Unless the carrier knows or should know that the directions are incorrect, the carrier will not be liable for any delay or damage that results.

Because common carriers deal with the public, they are closely regulated by government agencies. The federal Interstate Commerce Commission (ICC) regulates common carriers engaged in interstate transportation; state and local agencies regulate intrastate carriers. Under the law, a shipper is entitled to demand that a common carrier accept and carry his or her goods at a reasonable rate (subject to regulation and approval by the regulatory agencies) and subject to the insurer's liability. A common carrier must accept and carry goods without discrimination. However, a carrier is not bound to accept and carry:

(1) Goods beyond the capacity of the carrier;

(2) Goods of a kind which the carrier does not normally carry and has no facilities to carry;

(3) Goods injurious to person or property;

(4) Goods that have been defectively packed or loaded; or

(5) High risk goods requiring unusual care in transport.

Also, the common carrier may limit his or her strict liability by contract with the shipper. While the carrier may not enter into a valid agreement to absolve himself or herself of negligence, the carrier may lawfully contract to exempt himself or herself from liability for accidental loss or certain specific hazards (e. g., employee strikes, fires resulting from causes other than an act of God or carrier negligence).

The common carrier may also contract to limit his or her liability to a certain fixed amount or percentage of the value of the goods. Notice that, in each case, the word "contract" has been used: a carrier's limited liability agreement with a shipper is enforceable only if the carrier gives consideration for the agreement in the form of a reduced rate for the shipment with limited liability. In other words, the agreement will be upheld only if the carrier offers the shipper a choice between limited and unlimited liability, and gives the shipper a decrease in rate for the former. A carrier who offers only one rate of coverage cannot escape strict liability. Along this line, the Interstate Commerce Act and many state statutes require or authorize carriers to file *tariffs* (books or tables of rates and limitations) with the appropriate federal (the ICC) and state regulatory agencies. Air carriers file tariffs with the Civil Aeronautics Board (CAB). A shipper is held to be on notice of any rate or limitation contained in a published tariff filed by a carrier and approved by the appropriate federal or state agency.

Sometimes, a common carrier takes freight for shipment, then ships the goods over more than one line or through connecting carriers. The law provides that the original ("originating") carrier may not limit his or her strict liability for losses occurring on the other lines or carriers. By accepting the freight for shipment, the originating carrier assumes responsibility for its entire transport. The liability of a connecting carrier, on the other hand, is limited to the period of the carrier's possession of the goods (of course, if the originating carrier is held liable for a connecting carrier's portion of the transport, the originating carrier may be able to recover from the connecting carrier).

Finally, the common carrier is under an absolute duty to deliver the goods to the right person (remember, a bailee's third duty is to redeliver the bailed goods only to the bailor or his or her appointee). If the carrier delivers the goods to the wrong person, the carrier will be liable for any loss or damage that results.

What are the responsibilities (including bailment responsibilities) of a common carrier of passengers?

Similar to a common carrier of goods, a common carrier of passengers is a person who holds himself or herself out as being willing to carry all members of the public for compensation (e. g., the owner-operator of a passenger bus, train, plane, ship, etc.). Because of his or her public calling, the common carrier must accept all passengers without discrimination; the carrier does not violate this duty by refusing carriage to one who would endanger other passengers on board the carrier (e. g., an ill or violent person).

The common carrier is not an insurer of the safety of his or her passengers. However, the carrier is required to exercise the highest degree of care, skill, and diligence in providing for their safety.

It follows from this extremely high duty of care that the carrier is liable for the slightest negligence resulting in loss or damage to a passenger. For example, if the owner-operator of a passenger bus fails to provide safe areas for boarding and alighting from the vehicle, and a passenger is injured while getting on or off the bus, the carrier will be liable.

It must be stressed that the carrier owes this high duty of care to *passengers* only. A "passenger" is a person who comes upon the carrier's premises with the intention of traveling using the carrier's facilities under contract with the carrier. The high degree of care applies though the contract is not yet consummated at the time the injury or loss occurs: it is sufficient that the party has come on the carrier's premises with the intention of purchasing a ticket and boarding the carrier vehicle. Obviously, the carrier's employees are not passengers during working hours (they can be outside of working hours); while the high duty of care does not apply, the carrier does have a duty to maintain reasonably safe working conditions for the employees (see Ch. 20 regarding employees). As to a stowaway or other trespasser who sneaks aboard the carrier without paying the fare, the carrier's only duty is to warn the trespasser about hidden dangers on board the carrier. The duty arises upon the carrier's discovery of the trespasser. If the trespasser becomes obnoxious or violent, the carrier may take whatever steps are necessary to protect his or her passengers.

The common carrier of passengers is under a duty to accept and carry without extra charge a reasonable amount of a passenger's baggage. Like the common carrier of goods, the common carrier of passengers is strictly liable (subject to the same five exceptions) for any loss or damage to the baggage. But also like the common carrier of goods, the carrier of passengers may contract to limit his or her liability to a certain maximum amount or to the amount declared by the passenger, whichever is less. Along this line, the Carmack Amendment to the Interstate Commerce Act provides that a common carrier of passengers may limit his or her liability for baggage as to the amount of loss and as to the type of hazard. And again, passengers are on notice of any limitations contained in published tariffs filed by the carrier and approved by the appropriate federal or state agency.

"Baggage" includes only those items that a passenger takes on the carrier for his or her personal use and convenience either during the journey or afterwards. Items intended for exhibit or sale do not fall within the meaning of baggage; nor do items of exceptional value such as fine jewelry or large amounts of cash. Such items must be shipped on a common carrier of goods so that appropriate fees may be charged for the high risk carriage. To transport such items on a carrier of passengers so as to avoid payment of regular freight charges is to misuse the carrier's duty to carry baggage. The carrier in such case will not be strictly liable for loss or damage to the property.

Finally, it should be pointed out that if the passenger retains control over his or her baggage while on the carrier (e. g., carries a travel bag on the shoulder rather than in the luggage compartment of the carrier), the carrier will not be responsible as a bailee of the property. The possession required for a bailment is not present. However, the carrier may be liable for damage to the property on the basis of simple negligence (i. e., failure to render the high duty of care required in protecting the passenger and his or her personal effects and clothing).

What are the bailment responsibilities of a warehouseman?

A *warehouseman* is a person who is in the business of storing the goods of oth-

ers for compensation. A public warehouseman holds himself or herself out generally to serve the public without discrimination. Because of their public calling, warehousemen are subject to special statutory regulation as to rates, storage facilities, and proper safety precautions.

Unlike a common carrier, a warehouseman is not strictly liable for the goods in his or her possession. Rather, the warehouseman is deemed to be an ordinary mutual benefit bailee and must exercise only ordinary care and is liable for ordinary negligence.

Like a common carrier, a warehouseman may limit his or her liability to a specified maximum. To do so, the warehouseman must offer the customer a choice between full liability for the storage at one rate and limited liability at a lower rate. The warehouseman must state the limitation for each item or each unit of weight (e. g., "our maximum liability for this fur coat will be $500" or "our maximum liability for each bushel of corn will be $50") rather than use a blanket limitation, such as "our maximum liability will be $1,500".

It should be pointed out that a common carrier of goods may have only a warehouseman's liability at certain times. You will recall that the carrier's strict liability arises when goods have been *delivered* to the carrier and *accepted* by the carrier for *immediate transportation*. If the goods are delivered to the carrier, but are not yet ready for immediate carriage because something remains to be done by the shipper (e. g., the shipper must deliver more goods or give further instructions, etc.), the carrier will be liable only as a warehouseman until the goods are ready for shipment. The case of London & Lancashire Fire Ins. Co. v. Rome, W. & O. R. Co., 144 N.Y. 200, 39 N.E. 79 (1894) well describes the transition from warehouseman's liability to that of strict insurer.

It states:

The liability of a railroad company as common carrier of goods delivered to it attaches only when the duty of immediate transportation arises. So long as the shipment is delayed for further orders as to destination of the goods, or for the convenience of the owners, the liability of the company is that of warehousemen. The liability of a common carrier for goods received by him begins as soon as they are delivered to him, his agents or servants, at the place appointed or provided for their reception when they are in a fit and proper condition and ready for immediate transportation. If a common carrier receives goods into his own warehouse for the accommodation of himself and his customers, so that the deposit there is a mere accessory to the carriage and for the purpose of facilitating it, his liability as a carrier will commence with the receipt of the goods. But on the contrary, if the goods when so deposited are not ready for immediate transportation, and the carrier cannot make arrangements for their carriage to the place of destination until something further is done or some further direction is given or communication made concerning them by the owner, the deposit must be considered to be in the meantime for his convenience and accommodation, and the receiver until some change takes place will be responsible only as a warehouseman.

———

It should also be mentioned that a common carrier's strict liability may terminate at a point in time prior to the actual receipt of the goods by the party (called the "consignee") to whom they are shipped. Where an express company or other common carrier delivers the goods to the consignee's residence or place of business, the carrier's strict lia-

bility naturally continues until the moment of delivery. But where a carrier completes transporting the goods, then puts the goods in storage for the consignee, the carrier's liability again becomes that of a warehouseman. For example, a railroad company generally transports goods to the point of destination, then deposits the goods in the station or warehouse for delivery to the consignee. Once the consignee is notified that the goods are ready for delivery, and has reasonable time to react to the notification, the carrier's liability changes from that of strict insurer to mutual benefit bailee.

How are the written contracts used by warehousemen (warehouse receipts) and common carriers of goods (bills of lading) unique, and when are these "documents of title" negotiable?

Without warehousemen and common carriers, there could be little business or commerce. Each year, literally billions of dollars worth of goods have to be stored and/or transported. On the one hand, there are goods that must be aged or cured in storage; many crops must be stored after harvest to await delivery to the consumer; goods pledged as loan collateral must be stored until the loans are repaid. On the other hand, raw materials must be sent to both foreign and domestic processing and manufacturing plants; and manufactured goods must be shipped to retailers both at home and abroad.

The warehousing and transporting of goods is essential to the working of our national economy. While these functions are largely governed by the law of bailments, the economy's need for a free flow of goods demands the ability to pass ownership (title) of the goods even while they are in the possession of the warehouseman or common carrier. This is where the special written contracts of the warehouseman and common carrier come into play. Called "warehouse receipts" when issued by a warehouseman and "bills of lading" when issued by a common carrier, these written contracts are properly designated *documents of title*. When issued in negotiable form, the documents of title can be used to transfer ownership of the goods though the goods remain in the possession of the warehouseman or carrier bailee. Negotiable documents of title have similar characteristics to the negotiable notes, drafts, and checks discussed in Chapters 12 through 15. Just as a negotiable note, draft, or check may be transferred to a *holder in due course* who acquires superior rights in the instrument, a negotiable document of title may be transferred to a *bona fide purchaser* who acquires superior rights both in the document itself and in the goods covered by the document. The bona fide purchaser (bfp) succeeds to ownership without having to worry about the claims of prior parties.

And both negotiable and nonnegotiable documents of title can be pledged as security or collateral for a loan though the goods remain in the warehouseman's or carrier's possession.

The use of documents of title is an important legal concept and is summarized below under the following six headings:

(1) Definition of document of title;

(2) The difference between a negotiable and nonnegotiable document of title;

(3) Purchaser's rights (his or her rights vary depending on whether the document is negotiable or nonnegotiable);

(4) Pledgee's rights;

(5) Document of title delivery requirements; and

(6) Misdescription of goods and related problems.

Definition of document of title. Section 1–201 of the Uniform Commercial Code defines the terms "document of title", "bill of lading", and "warehouse receipt" as follows.

The UCC provides:

Section 1–201.

(15) "Document of Title" includes bill of lading, dock warrant, dock receipt, warehouse receipt or order for the delivery of goods, and also any other document which in the regular course of business or financing is treated as adequately evidencing that the person in possession of it is entitled to receive, hold, and dispose of the document and the goods it covers. To be a document of title a document must purport to be issued by or addressed to a bailee and purport to cover goods in the bailee's possession which are either identified or are fungible portions of an identified mass.

Section 1–201.

(6) "Bill of lading" means a document evidencing the receipt of goods for shipment issued by a person engaged in the business of transporting or forwarding goods, and includes an airbill. "Airbill" means a document serving for air transportation as a bill of lading does for marine or rail transportation, and includes an air consignment note or air waybill.

Section 1–201.

(45) "Warehouse receipt" means a receipt issued by a person engaged in the business of storing goods for hire.

———

Thus, a warehouseman who stores goods for a price issues a "warehouse receipt" to the owner-bailor of the property. The receipt is first of all a written contract between the parties wherein the bailor promises to pay the storage charge, and the bailee acknowledges receipt of the goods and promises to properly care for the goods and deliver them according to the bailor's direction. The warehouse receipt is second of all a "document of title" which may be used to transfer ownership of the goods though the goods never leave the bailee's warehouse.

A common carrier also issues a written contract called a "bill of lading" to the bailor-shipper of goods. A bill issued by an originating carrier and specifying one or more connecting carriers is called a *through bill* of lading. Like the warehouse receipt, the bill of lading evidences the contract between the parties: the bill is an order for delivery of the goods in which the shipper promises to pay the carriage charge, and the carrier promises to properly care for the goods and transport and deliver them as provided by the shipper. The bill of lading also serves as a receipt for the goods to be transported; the bill describes the condition, quantity, and weight of the goods and names the party to whom they are to be delivered (the consignee). Finally, the bill of lading is a document of title which may be used to transfer ownership of the goods even while the goods are in transit (i. e., while they are being transported by the carrier).

The difference between a negotiable and nonnegotiable document of title. A negotiable document of title represents legal ownership of the goods covered by the document—the owner of a negotiable warehouse receipt or negotiable bill of lading is entitled to the goods. When is a warehouse receipt or bill of lading negotiable? You will recall from Chapters 12 through 15 that notes, drafts, and checks must satisfy nine requirements if they are to be negotiable instruments that serve as money substitutes. A "money instrument" must be in writing; it must

contain an unconditional promise or order to pay a sum certain in money on demand or at a definite time; it must be signed by the maker or drawer; and it must be made payable to "order" or to "bearer".

With regard to negotiable documents of title, Article 7 of the Uniform Commercial Code entitled "Warehouse Receipts, Bills of Lading and Other Documents of Title" provides as follows at Section 7–104.[4]

The UCC provides:

(1) A warehouse receipt, bill of lading or other document of title is negotiable

    (a) if by its terms the goods are to be delivered to bearer or to the order of a named person

        * * *

(2) Any other document is non-negotiable.

Thus, like "money instruments", negotiable documents of title ("goods instruments") must contain the magic words to "order" or to "bearer". However, unlike money instruments, goods instruments need satisfy no other requirements in order to be negotiable. If a warehouse receipt or bill of lading makes the goods deliverable to "bearer" or to the "order" of a named person, the document of title is negotiable. If the warehouse receipt or bill of lading does not contain the magic words, the document is nonnegotiable. It is as simple as that.

Negotiable documents of title are negotiated in much the same manner as negotiable notes, drafts, and checks. "Or-

---

4. With regard to interstate or foreign commerce, Article 7 is expressly subject to applicable federal laws including the Interstate Commerce Act, the federal Bills of Lading Act, the Harter Act of 1893 (which regulates offshore ocean commerce), the

Carriage of Goods by Sea Act, and the U. S. Warehouse Act. It is interesting to note that the *uniform bills of lading* promulgated by the ICC are used as standard forms in both interstate and intrastate commerce.

der" documents of title are negotiated by indorsement and delivery; "bearer" documents are negotiated by delivery alone. As with money instruments, a blank indorsement (signature alone) of an "order" document converts it to bearer paper. A special indorsement (indorsement to a specified person) of a "bearer" document converts it to order paper. Other kinds of indorsements (e. g., conditional and qualified do not apply to documents of title. The provisions of Uniform Commercial Code Section 7–501 are applicable.

The UCC provides:

(1) A negotiable document of title running to the order of a named person is negotiated by his indorsement and delivery. After his indorsement in blank or to bearer any person can negotiate it by delivery alone.

(2) (a) A negotiable document of title is also negotiated by delivery alone when by its original terms it runs to bearer.

(3) Negotiation of a negotiable document of title after it has been indorsed to a specified person requires indorsement by the special indorsee as well as delivery.

And Section 7–506 states:

Section 7–506.   Delivery Without Indorsement: Right to Compel Indorsement

The transferee of a negotiable document of title has a specifically enforceable right to have his transferor supply any necessary indorsement but the transfer becomes a negotiation only as of the time the indorsement is supplied.

As you know, the result of negotiating a money instrument is to transfer the

right to payment of the sum certain: negotiation of the instrument to a *holder in due course* cuts off all personal defenses to payment such as fraud in the inducement, failure of consideration, and the like. The result of duly negotiating a negotiable document of title, on the other hand, is to transfer the right to delivery of the goods covered by the document, and, along with this right, ownership of the goods themselves. Like negotiation of a money instrument to a HDC, due negotiation of a negotiable document of title may create rights in the purchaser of the document superior to those of his or her transferor. Uniform Commercial Code Section 7–501(4) states:

(4) A negotiable document of title is "duly negotiated" when it is negotiated * * * to a holder who purchases it in good faith without notice of any defense against or claim to it on the part of any person and for value, *unless it is established that the negotiation is not in the regular course of business or financing or involves receiving the document in settlement or payment of a money obligation.* [Emphasis added.]

A purchaser who takes a goods instrument through a negotiation in good faith, without notice, for value, and in the regular course of business or financing and not in settlement or payment of a money obligation is referred to as a *bona fide purchaser.* With limited exception, a bona fide purchaser acquires ownership (title) both of the document of title and of the goods covered by the document. The bfp's ownership (title) is good as against the whole world. This is so notwithstanding that the transferor had no right to negotiate the document to the bona fide purchaser (e. g., where the transferor had rightful possession of the document but no authority to negotiate it, or where the transferor obtained the document by defrauding the true owner). Like the holder in due course who acquires superior rights in a money instrument, the bona fide purchaser of the document may acquire rights superior to those of his or her transferor—the bfp's rights are good even against the true owner.

As far as the requirements of a bfp are concerned, you already know how documents of title are negotiated. And you are familiar with the requirements of taking in good faith, without notice, and for value—these are the same requirements for a holder in due course of a money instrument. However, the last requirement of a bona fide purchaser—*taking in the regular couse of business of financing and not in settlement or payment of a money obligation*—is new and requires some explanation. To begin with, the law regarding bona fide purchasers is designed to facilitate the speedy flow of goods in commerce. A bfp who acquires superior rights in bailed goods can further negotiate the document of title covering the goods, and the transferee will succeed to ownership free of the claims of prior parties. Because the objective of the law is to protect only commercial transactions, the law requires that the bfp take the document in the regular course of business or financing and not in settlement or payment of a money obligation. In other words, the bfp must acquire the document in a usual and ordinary commercial transaction, the purpose of which is to move the goods in commerce. A transfer out of the regular course of business (including a transfer of a document merely to pay off or settle a money debt) is not protected by UCC Section 7–501, and the transferee cannot qualify as a bona fide purchaser. The *Official Comment* to Section 7–501 provides an example.

It states:

No commercial purpose is served by allowing a tramp or a professor to "duly negotiate" an order bill of lading for hides or cotton not his own, and since such a transfer is obviously not in the regular course of business, it is excluded from the scope of the protection of subsection (4).

———

To summarize:

(1) There is only one requirement of negotiability for a document of title: the document must contain the magic words to "order" or to "bearer".

(2) "Goods" instruments are negotiated in much the same manner as "money" instruments. "Order" documents are negotiated by indorsement and delivery; "bearer" documents are negotiated by delivery alone. But remember, negotiable documents of title can be changed from bearer paper to order paper and vice versa by using blank and special indorsements. Other kinds of indorsements do not apply to documents of title.

(3) A bona fide purchaser of a document of title is like a holder in due course of a money instrument in that he or she must take the document for value, in good faith, and without notice of any claim or defense. Unlike a holder in due course (and because the law intends to protect only commercial transactions), the bona fide purchaser must also take the document in the regular course of business or financing and not in settlement or payment of a money obligation. With limited exception (to be considered in the following section), a bona fide purchaser who meets the above requirements will obtain ownership (title) of the document of title and of the goods covered by the document, good as against the whole world.

Purchaser's rights (his or her rights vary depending on whether the document is negotiable or nonnegotiable). The only way that title to goods covered by a negotiable document of title can be effectively transferred is by negotiation of the document. With limited exception, a bona fide purchaser who takes a negotiable document of title through a negotiation cuts off claims of prior parties both as to the negotiable document and as to the goods covered by the document. For example, a bona fide purchaser of a bearer document of title acquires complete ownership rights to the document and to the goods covered by the document even though the true owner has already sold the document or the goods to another. The same is true where the true owner is deprived of the bearer document through misrepresentation, fraud, accident, mistake, duress, loss, or conversion; if a bona fide purchaser takes the document through a negotiation (delivery alone), the bfp acquires title good as against the whole world, including the true owner or his or her transferor.

Of course, if the document is order paper, a thief or finder cannot negotiate it (indorsement as well as delivery is required), and any subsequent purchaser or transferee cannot qualify as a bona fide purchaser. The fact that the thief or finder has forged the required signature does not improve the transferee's position: the transferee is an assignee who "stands in the shoes" of his or her transferor. The transferee's only remedy, for what it is worth, is against the forger.

Suppose that a thief steals goods (as opposed to stealing a bearer document of title) and takes the goods to a warehouseman or common carrier who issues the thief a negotiable warehouse receipt or bill of lading. The law provides that the thief cannot divest the true owner of title to the goods by now negotiating the "goods instrument" to a bona fide purchaser. This is like a "real defense" good as against a holder in due course: though a purchaser qualifies as a bfp (i. e., takes the negotiable document of title through a negotiation, in good faith, without notice, for value, and in the regular course of business), he or she does not acquire paramount title to the property.

Another "real defense" arises where fungible goods covered by a negotiable warehouse receipt are sold and delivered by a warehouseman (who is also in the business of buying and selling such fungibles) to a buyer in the ordinary course of business. Though the warehouse receipt has been duly negotiated to a bfp, the bfp will not prevail against the buyer in the ordinary course of business.

UCC Section 7–205 states:

Section 7–205. Title Under Warehouse Receipt Defeated in Certain Cases

A buyer in the ordinary course of business of fungible goods sold and delivered by a warehouseman who is also in the business of buying and selling such goods takes free of any claim under a warehouse receipt even though it has been duly negotiated.

———

Of course, the warehouseman who wrongfully sells the fungibles will be liable to the bailor or his or her transferee (bfp or otherwise) who holds the warehouse receipt. Generally, the problem is compounded by the fact that the warehouseman had the fungibles stored in a common mass of like fungibles belonging to other bailors. Ordinarily, warehoused goods under a particular warehouse receipt must be kept separate to permit easy identification and delivery but fungibles may be commingled.

UCC Section 7–207 states:

Section 7–207. Goods Must Be Kept Separate; Fungible Goods

(1) Unless the warehouse receipt otherwise provides, a warehouseman must keep separate the goods covered by each receipt so as to permit at all times identification and delivery of those goods except that different lots of fungible goods may be commingled.

Assuming the warehouseman-bailee who wrongfully sells the bailed fungibles has insufficient fungibles remaining in the common mass to cover every bailor's interest, the bailors (or their transferees) are entitled to their proportionate share of the common mass as tenants in common.

But apart from the "stolen goods" and "sale of fungibles" exceptions and a few other limited exceptions not within the scope of this text, the bona fide purchaser of a document of title acquires paramount title to the document and to the goods covered by the document. The bona fide purchaser's title is good as against the whole world, including the true owner.

In contrast, the purchaser of a nonnegotiable warehouse receipt or bill of lading receives only the rights of his or her transferor (the purchaser is an assignee "standing in the shoes" of his or her transferor). For example, suppose that Jake Howard fraudulently induces Mary Smith to part with goods, then warehouses the goods so as to create a nonnegotiable warehouse receipt. Jake subsequently sells the receipt to Jean Kent, whereupon Mary finds and claims her goods. As between Jean and Mary, Mary prevails: her defense of fraud is good not only against Jake but also against his assignee, Jean, and Mary is entitled to the return of her property. (Of course, if Jake had obtained a negotiable warehouse receipt and

duly negotiated it to Jean—a bfp—Jean, and not Mary, would prevail.)

Pledgee's rights. A "pledge" is a special kind of bailment. As you will recall, a pledge is the placement of personal property in the possession of another as security or collateral for some act by the bailor. Usually, the act secured is the repayment of a loan: the bailee makes the loan because the bailor deposits personal property with the bailee as collateral; the pledged property secures repayment of the money. The bailee-pledgee of the personal property must exercise the ordinary care of a mutual benefit bailee. He or she has the right to exclusive possession of the property during the term of the pledge and can use the property in any manner contemplated by the pledge agreement (any substantial misuse will constitute a conversion of the property). Once the pledgor has performed the required act (e. g., has repaid the loan), the pledge automatically terminates, and the pledgor is entitled to the return of his or her property. In the event that the pledgor fails to perform as promised (e. g., fails to repay the loan), the pledgee has the right to sell the pledged personal property and collect the money owing.

In the usual bailment pledge, there is actual delivery of possession of the personal property. But where the goods are represented by a document of title, delivery of the document is sufficient. For example, when warehouse receipts are pledged as security for a loan, the borrower simply deposits the receipts with the bank or other lending institution. Generally, if a warehouseman has goods in his or her actual possession at the warehouse, he or she will issue a negotiable warehouse receipt. A security interest in a negotiable document of title carries over into the goods covered by the document. The lender who has possession of the negotiable document has title to the document and to the goods themselves—of course, once the loan is repaid, the pledge terminates, and the goods go back to the pledgor. (But don't forget the "stolen goods" exception. If the goods are stolen and warehoused so as to create the negotiable receipt, the lender in possession of the document will not prevail as against the true owner. Nor will the lender prevail if he or she has possession of an order document containing forged indorsements.)

Sometimes, the owner of goods wants to use the goods as security for a loan but it is not feasible to transfer the goods to a warehouse. You will understand the problem if you imagine thousands of logs piled in the forest, or vast quantities of raw materials sitting in a manufacturing yard, or a large inventory of automobiles held by a dealer for sale to retailers. Obviously, it would be very difficult to pledge the goods if they first had to be placed in a warehouse. Most lenders do not have warehouse facilities available, yet they are willing to lend on such goods if their security interest in the goods can be protected. The solution is a procedure known as *field warehousing*. Rather than move the goods to a warehouse, the "warehouse" is set up in the "field" (i. e., where the goods are located). Generally, part of the owner's plant or yard is blocked off and put under the control of the warehouseman; sometimes, only a fence is placed around the goods. What is essential is that the warehouseman have control over the property so that the lender can be assured that his or her security interest is protected. Once control is established, the warehouseman can issue a warehouse receipt; the receipt can be pledged as security for the loan, and the owner of the goods can receive the needed cash from the lending institution.

Usually, where the warehouseman does not have the goods in his or her warehouse but controls them only in the field, he or she will issue a nonnegotiable warehouse receipt. It is not desirable to issue

a negotiable receipt because the debtor-owner-bailor will frequently need to have part of the warehoused goods released to him or her so as to be able to continue business operations—for example, the logs will have to be milled, the raw materials manufactured, the automobiles sold. With a negotiable receipt, the warehouseman has a duty to collect the receipt at the time of delivery of the goods; in the case of partial delivery, the warehouseman must conspicuously note the extent of delivery on the face of the receipt (this protects the parties from subsequent transfer of a collected document to a bfp). Thus, the warehouseman cannot rightfully deliver part of the goods to the owner-bailor without asking the pledgee to physically hand over the document of title and risk losing his or her security. With a nonnegotiable receipt, the lender can retain possession of the document and simply authorize the warehouseman to release goods in the desired quantity. Also, with a nonnegotiable receipt, additional inventory can be added to the field warehoused goods as it is purchased or as it arrives for use in the business.

Bills of lading are also pledged as security for cash loans. Sellers of goods frequently enter into transactions where the buyer is to pay cash for goods only upon their arrival at the buyer's place of business. The goods may not arrive for many days or even weeks—yet, the seller needs the cash immediately for business or other reasons. The seller can obtain the money (less a discount) at the time of shipment by pledging the bill of lading covering the goods with a lender. The procedure is as follows. The seller directs the carrier to issue a negotiable bill of lading to the "order" of the seller covering the goods to be transported to the buyer. The seller also draws a draft on the buyer for the amount of the purchase price. The seller then specially indorses both the negotiable bill of lading and the draft to the "order" of the lender. The lender, in turn, pays the seller an amount of money equal to the purchase price of the goods minus a discount reflecting the lender's profit. The lender then forwards the draft and the bill of lading to his or her representative in the area where the buyer is located. After the goods arrive in the area, the lender's representative presents the draft and the bill of lading and collects the purchase price.

So you see, documents of title are used not only to transfer ownership of goods, but also to finance business and business transactions.

Document of title delivery requirements. A warehouseman or common carrier is absolutely liable for misdelivery of goods (i. e., if a warehouseman or carrier delivers goods to the wrong person, the warehouseman or carrier will be liable without regard to negligence). However, there is no misdelivery and no liability where the warehouseman or carrier delivers goods to "a person entitled under the document". Section 7-403(4) of the Uniform Commercial Code defines such a person as a "holder in the case of a negotiable document, or the person to whom delivery is to be made by the terms of or pursuant to written instructions under a nonnegotiable document." Obviously, the holder of a negotiable document of title may be a wrongdoer—for example, a thief who has stolen the goods and warehoused or shipped them so as to create a negotiable warehouse receipt or bill of lading. Yet, as a holder, the thief or other wrongdoer is "a person entitled under the document", and if the warehouseman or carrier redelivers the goods to the party in good faith and without knowledge that the goods have been stolen, the warehouseman or carrier will not be liable to the true owner. As Uniform Commercial Code Section 7-404 states.

A bailee who in good faith including observance of reasonable commercial standards has received goods and delivered or otherwise disposed of them according to the terms of the document of title or pursuant to this Article is not liable therefor. This rule applies even though the person from whom he received the goods had no authority to procure the document or to dispose of the goods and even though the person to whom he delivered the goods had no authority to receive them.

Of course, if the warehouseman or carrier discovers the theft, he or she is protected in delivering the goods to the true owner rather than to the thief. Section 7-403(1)(a) provides: "The bailee must deliver the goods to a person entitled under the document * * * unless the bailee establishes delivery of the goods to a person whose receipt was rightful [the true owner] as against the claimant [the thief] * * *"

If the warehouseman or carrier knows that more than one party is claiming the goods, but does not know whose claim is rightful (or does not want to risk deciding incorrectly), the warehouseman or carrier should deliver the goods into the custody of the court for judicial determination of the matter.

Also, you will recall that a bill of lading is a written contract issued by a carrier to a shipper. The bill acknowledges the carrier's receipt of the goods, it describes the bailed property, and it states the terms of transport and delivery of the goods including the agreed upon destination. If the bill of lading is nonnegotiable (i. e., if it is not made deliverable to "bearer" or to the "order" of a named person), it is termed a *straight bill of lading.* A straight bill of lading specifies a consignee to whom the goods are to be delivered—the carrier is contractually obligated to deliver the goods to that person only. Unlike a bona fide purchaser of a negotiable bill of lading, a party in possession of a straight bill has no paramount claim to title of the document or to the goods covered by the document. If the carrier delivers the goods to a person in possession of the bill other than the named consignee, the carrier will be liable for conversion of the bailed property. And it is not necessary for the named consignee to present or surrender the straight bill of lading in order to pick up the goods. The consignee has a right to receive the goods, and the carrier has an obligation to deliver them, without surrender of the document.

With a negotiable bill of lading, the rules are entirely different. Here, the carrier undertakes to deliver the goods, not to a named consignee, but to anyone who qualifies as a holder of the document. Again, the carrier is protected only if he or she complies with the terms of the bill: in the case of a "bearer" bill, the carrier must deliver the goods to any person in possession of the document; where the document is an "order" bill, the carrier must deliver the goods to any person in possession of the bill properly indorsed. And where the bill of lading is negotiable, the carrier is also obligated to take up and cancel the bill upon delivery of the goods. If the delivery is partial, the carrier must conspicuously note the amount of the delivery upon the face of the bill. If the carrier fails to do so, the consignee may thereafter sell the bill to a bona fide purchaser, and the carrier will again be liable though he or she has already delivered the goods covered by the instrument. To protect himself or herself, the carrier must take possession of the negotiable bill and cancel it to the extent of the delivery made.

Suppose that a carrier accepts goods for shipment, issues a bill of lading covering the goods, then is subsequently instructed to deliver the goods to a person or destination other than that stated in the bill (e. g., when perishable items are sold after they have been placed on the carrier at which time the seller instructs the carrier to deliver them to a particular buyer). Diversion is a very common commercial practice, and a carrier will be protected in following a change of instructions (e. g., a change of consignee) according to the terms of UCC Section 7–303.

The UCC provides:

Section 7–303. Diversion: Reconsignment; Change of Instructions

(1) Unless the bill of lading otherwise provides [i. e., expressly disallows a change of instructions], the carrier may deliver the goods to a person or destination other than that stated in the bill or may otherwise dispose of the goods on instructions from

(a) the holder of a negotiable bill; or

(b) the consignor on a non-negotiable bill notwithstanding contrary instructions from the consignee; or

(c) the consignee on a non-negotiable bill in the absence of contrary instructions from the consignor, if the goods have arrived at the billed destination or if the consignee is in possession of the bill; or

(d) the consignee on a non-negotiable bill if he is entitled as against the consignor to dispose of them.

(2) Unless such instructions are noted on a negotiable bill of lading, a

person to whom the bill is duly negotiated can hold the bailee according to the original terms.

And Section 7–504(3) states:

(3) A diversion or other change of shipping instructions by the consignor in a non-negotiable bill of lading which causes the bailee not to deliver to the consignee defeats the consignee's title to the goods if they have been delivered to a buyer in ordinary course of business and in any event defeats the consignee's rights against the bailee.

In the event that a document of title is lost, stolen, or destroyed, a court may order delivery of the goods or issuance of a substitute document, and the bailee (carrier or warehouseman) may comply with the order without liability to any party. UCC § 7–601.

Misdescription of goods and related problems. Sometimes, a warehouseman or common carrier issues a document of title for goods that do not exist (or issues duplicate documents for the same goods), or issues a document that misdescribes the covered goods.

The general rule is that a warehouseman or carrier who issues a document of title for nonexistent goods (i. e., goods that the warehouseman or carrier has not received) is liable for any damages that result. Such a document is invalid from its inception. For example, in the case of Chicago & N.W. Ry. Co. v. Stephens Nat. Bank, 75 F.2d 398 (8th Cir. 1935), a bank bought and paid for bills of lading purporting to cover eggs. The facts showed that the eggs were never loaded, and that the carrier never transported the cars named in the bills. When the shipper-seller went bankrupt, and the bank

lost the $5,200 that it had paid for the documents, the bank successfully sued the common carrier for issuing documents of title covering goods it had not received.

A warehouseman or carrier is also liable for any misdescription of goods on a document of title unless the warehouseman or carrier conspicuously disclaims such liability on the document itself. A disclaimer by a warehouseman such as "contents, condition and quality unknown" or "the issuer does not know whether the goods in fact conform to the description" is generally effective to eliminate liability on the part of the warehouseman where the warehoused goods do not conform to the description on the warehouse receipt. As for a common carrier, he or she can effectively disclaim liability for misdescription on a bill of lading by making the same statements or by stating that "the goods are according to the shipper's load and count". If it is obvious that the carrier has no first-hand knowledge of the contents of the shipment (e. g., where the shipper provides sealed cartons and misdescribes their contents), the carrier will not be liable even absent a disclaimer on the bill of lading. A valid disclaimer on a warehouse receipt or bill of lading puts a bona fide purchaser on notice, and the warehouseman or carrier will not be liable in the absence of negligence.

Finally, it should be pointed out that the holder of a document issued for nonexistent goods or issued containing misdescriptions may be able to successfully sue and recover from his or her transferor on the basis of warranty liability.

UCC Section 7–507 provides:

Section 7–507. Warranties on Negotiation or Transfer of Receipt or Bill

Where a person negotiates or transfers a document of title for value * * * he warrants to his immediate purchaser * * *

(a) that the document is genuine; and

(b) that he has no knowledge of any fact which would impair its validity or worth; and

(c) that his negotiation or transfer is rightful and fully effective with respect to the title to the document and the goods it represents.

What liens result from bailment relationships?

A "lien" is a claim on property that arises because of a debt owing to the claimant from the property owner. The property subject to the lien serves as security for payment of the debt. For example, a pledge of property is a *consensual lien* (i. e., a lien that arises by *agreement* of the parties).

Liens also arise in bailment situations by operation of law. Such liens are called *possessory liens* because they arise against property in the bailee's possession; the bailee is entitled to retain the property as security for the payment of some debt. A good example of a possessory lien is a "work" lien. The law provides that a bailee has a possessory lien upon any chattel bailed to him or her for work or services performed on the chattel at the bailor's request. The lien is a *special* lien in that it secures payment only for the work or service performed on the particular chattel. (In contrast, a *general* lien secures payment of any and all debts owed by the bailor to the bailee). The possessory lienholder is entitled to exclusive possession of the bailed chattel until the indebtedness (for which the lien is security) is paid. Thus, if you take your watch in for repairs, your clothes in for cleaning, or your car in for painting, and you fail to pay for the services rendered, the bailee may hold your property—the watch, the clothes, or the car—until you do pay.

As long as a bailee holds property subject to a possessory lien, the bailment continues, and the bailee must exercise reasonable care to protect and preserve the item. However, the possessory lienholder has no right to use the chattel, and if he or she does so without the bailor-owner's consent, the lienholder will be liable for conversion.

Also, the bailee-lienholder loses his or her possessory lien by voluntarily redelivering the bailed chattel to the property owner. Ordinarily, the lien does not "revive" upon a subsequent reacquisition of possession. However, an exception is made where the lienholder is tricked into redelivering the chattel: the lien, in this case, will revive upon a subsequent reacquisition of possession subject only to the claim of intervening bona fide purchasers (good faith purchasers for value).

At common law, a possessory lien is a bare right to hold the property until the debt is paid: unlike the pledgee of personal property, the possessory lienholder cannot sell the property to enforce the lien. If the bailor-debtor refuses to pay, the possessory lienholder must go to court and obtain a judgment against the party. The lienholder may then "execute" the judgment against the bailed property (as you will learn in Ch. 26, this involves the sheriff selling the property at a public sale pursuant to a court order to enforce the judgment).

Modernly, statutes in most states have changed the common law to give the possessory lienholder the right to sell the bailed property in satisfaction of the lien. Some statutes providing for the seizure and sale of the property without notice or judicial hearing have been declared unconstitutional by the courts as violating the Due Process Clause of the 14th Amendment.

In any case, a possessory lien is a mere personal right, and, in most jurisdictions, cannot be assigned.

Some specific possessory liens include:

(1) *Common carrier's lien.* A common carrier has a lien for the value of the transportation charges on any goods carried at a shipper's request. The carrier's possessory lien encompasses "demurrage charges" (charges for unreasonable detention of the carrier's cars or other equipment by either the shipper or the consignee) as well as any costs incurred in preserving the goods or in selling them to enforce the lien. The carrier's lien is a specific lien. That is to say, it attaches only to goods shipped under the particular contract (however, it includes all of the shipment, even though shipped in installments). Not having a general lien, the carrier cannot lay claim to goods subsequently shipped by the same shipper under a different contract (i. e., the goods cannot be seized to secure payment of the earlier shipment).

(2) *Warehouseman's lien.* A warehouseman has a possessory lien upon any chattel delivered for storage, the lien securing payment of the storage charge. As provided by Section 7–209 of the Uniform Commercial Code, the warehouseman's lien is both specific and general. It is "specific" in that it covers charges for the storage, protection, and preservation of the particular bailed chattel; it is "general" in that, if the warehousing contract so provides, it also covers charges owing from the bailor to the warehouseman for the storage of other goods.

(3) *Innkeeper's lien.* A hotelkeeper has a lien on all chattels brought on the hotel or motel premises by a guest, with the exception of necessary wearing apparel and personal effects on the guest's person. The hotelkeeper's lien secures payment of all charges owed by the guest for the particular hotel or motel lodging.

(4) *Landlord's lien.* At common law, if a tenant defaults in payment of rent, and the landlord enters and retakes possession of the premises, the landlord has a possessory lien to secure unpaid rent on all chattels in the tenant's possession. Modernly, most states have greatly restricted the landlord's lien to protect the tenant (e. g., by exempting "necessaries" from the lien); and some states have completely eliminated it (see Ch. 2, "landlord-tenant law").

What is the difference between a bailment and a sale?

As you know, a *bailment* is the rightful possession of another's personal property. A bailment is a transfer of possession only—not a transfer of ownership: when the bailment comes to an end, the bailee must return the identical property bailed to the bailor. A *sale,* on the other hand, is the transfer of ownership of goods from a seller to a buyer for a consideration known as a price. A sale can be effected (i. e., ownership or title can be transferred) with or without a transfer of possession.

So in a bailment, possession—not ownership—is transferred; in a sale, ownership is transferred, sometimes with and sometimes without a transfer of possession.

What is a consignment?

The term "consignee" has been used to describe the person to whom goods are shipped by a common carrier. The term "consignment" also describes a bailment arrangement in which the owner of goods delivers them to a bailee along with authority to sell the goods on behalf of the owner. Ownership (title) remains in the bailor-consignor; the bailee-consignee has possession plus authority to sell. When the bailee-consignee sells the goods as instructed by the bailor-consignor, ownership passes to the purchaser just as though the owner himself or herself had made the sale.

Where a consignee is in the business of selling goods on consignment, he or she is called a *factor* or *commission merchant*. Most states have what are called "factors acts" (or "traders acts") providing that if goods are entrusted with a factor, the factor has authority to sell or otherwise transfer the goods as though they are his or her own. Thus, if the factor sells or transfers the property contrary to the bailor-consignor's instructions, the innocent purchaser or transferee is protected, and the bailor-consignor's only remedy is against the factor. As you will see in the chapters on "sales", the Uniform Commercial Code goes even further in protecting the rights of an innocent purchaser for value by providing that if goods are "entrusted" to a merchant who ordinarily deals in goods of that kind, the merchant is deemed to have the power to transfer the entruster's rights in the goods to a buyer in the ordinary course of business.

CASES

CASE 1—*The automobile was stolen from a self-service parking lot.*

WALL v. AIRPORT PARKING CO. OF CHICAGO

Supreme Court of Illinois, 1969.
41 Ill.2d 506, 244 N.E.2d 190.

HOUSE, Justice.

Defendant, Airport Parking Company of Chicago, operator of a self-parking lot at O'Hare Airport as lessee of the city of Chicago, appealed to the Appellate Court, First District, from a judgment against it in favor of the insurer of an automobile stolen from the lot. The Appellate Court reversed, and we granted leave to appeal.

The cause was submitted on an agreed statement of facts. The lot is wholly enclosed, well lighted, paved and marked into parking spaces. Motorists enter through automatic gates and there receive a ticket bearing the date and time of arrival. They park in any available parking space, lock their automobiles, and retain the keys. When ready to depart they walk into the lot, pick up their vehicle and leave via an exit where the ticket is handed to an attendant to compute and collect the parking charges.

This is a case of first impression in this court although there is a great variety of holdings in the area of the liability of operators of parking-lot facilities, mostly by courts of intermediate jurisdiction. From this welter of decisions there emerge two principal classes of relationship between the automobile owner and the lot operator. One is that of the leasing of a parking space with no bailment being created. The other is a delivery of the vehicle into the possession and control of the lot operator thereby creating a bailment.

Typical of the first class of cases is where the owner parks his own car either at a place designated by an attendant or chosen by himself, retains the keys, and does not actually deliver the car to the lot operator. In the second class of cases, a bailment is usually created where the keys are left in the parked vehicle (at the request of the parking-lot attendant to permit moving it for the entrance or exit of other vehicles on the lot) and where tickets are issued identifying the car for redelivery. In final analysis, however, parking-lot cases do not readily lend themselves to precise categorization of whether the motorist is leasing space on the one hand, or whether delivery of the vehicle onto a parking lot creates a *prima facie* bailment. As was said by the Court of Appeals of New York in Osborn v. Cline, 263 N.Y. 434, 189 N.E. 483, 484: "Whether a person simply hires a place to put his car or whether he has turned its possession over to the care and custody of another depends on the place, the conditions and the nature of the transaction." In a case very similar to this, except that parking was in an enclosed parking garage and valuables in the car rather than the car itself were stolen, the Pennsylvania Supreme Court said: "Since here plaintiffs reserved possession of the car at all times by retaining the keys thereto, defendant acquired no dominion over the vehicle nor any right to control removal of it; hence there was no bailment." Taylor v. Philadelphia Parking Authority, 398 Pa. 9, 156 A.2d 525, 527.

In recent years a new type of self-service vehicular parking lot has developed, particularly at the larger airports of this country. The one here involved is typical. A motorist gains admission to the lot through one or more automatic entrance gates, which open when he takes a machine dispensed ticket from an automatic dispenser. The ticket is stamped with the day and hour of arrival, but it does not identify any particular automobile or owner. No attendant is present nor is the motorist directed where to park, except that he is expected to park within the lines marking individual parking spaces. The motorist retains the keys. There is nothing to prevent him from moving the car from place to place within the confines of the lot as often as he chooses. He may not have (and probably has not) seen an attendant until he re-enters his car and proceeds to an exit where an attendant computes and collects the charges for the period of time the vehicle has been on the lot. This checking-out process is his only necessary contact with the lot operator or attendants.

In order to establish a bailor-bailee relationship there must be either an express agreement (there is none here) or an agreement by implication, which may be gathered from the circumstances surrounding the transaction, such as the benefits to be received by the parties, their intentions, the kind of property involved, and the opportunities of each to exercise control over the property. There must not only be a delivery of possession, but there must also be an acceptance, either actual or constructive, before there can be a bailment. Applying these criteria to the facts here we find that the self-parking-lot operator primarily offers spaces for parking with a minimum amount of labor, which presumably is reflected in the fees charged for use of the facilities. There undoubtedly is more protection to the users of the facilities than is afforded by street parking in that the parking lot is fenced, well lighted, attended around the clock by one to five attendants, and is patrolled by the Chicago police squad cars from time to time. But space rather than security is the primary purpose of a self-service parking lot. The motorist is, of course, benefited by having parking space reasonably close to the airport.

By its very nature a self-service parking lot must be open at all times to the public and the operator has no control over who uses the lot. True, temporary possession in the sense that the motorist leaves a vehicle on the lot may be said to have been given up, but actual control is retained by the act of locking the vehicle and taking the keys, thereby preventing its movement. There is no acceptance of the vehicle by the lot owner. Plaintiff asserts that National Safe Deposit Co. v. Stead, 250 Ill. 584, 95 N.E. 973, is analogous. There, the safe deposit company held itself out as safeguarding valuables, and security was that which was being bought by the public. Valuables were stored in vaults and entry was through iron gates manned by armed guards. It was inherent in the nature of the service offered that the primary objective was to safeguard customers. That case is not persuasive.

We are of the opinion that use of self-service parking lots, such as the one here involved, does not create a bailor-bailee relationship and the lot operator is not subject to the liability imposed by the rules relating to bailments.

* * *

Judgment affirmed.

CASE 2—*Is a truck hijacker a "public enemy"?*

DAVID CRYSTAL INC. v. EHRLICH–NEWMARK TRUCKING CO.

Civil Court of the City of New York, New York County, Trial Term, 1970.
64 Misc.2d 325, 314 N.Y.S.2d 559.

Bentley KASSAL, Judge.

* * *

Defendant, as a common carrier for hire in interstate commerce, concededly received and failed to deliver a property shipment received from plaintiff. The defense, in essence, is that the loss resulted from a hijacking on the streets of New York City of the defendant's truck, containing this shipment. Defendant contends that the loss resulted by reason of the act of a "public enemy" and that it therefore is not responsible for such loss.

The general rule is that a common carrier is an insurer against the loss of property received by it for transportation. The only exceptions are losses arising from an act of God or from acts of the public enemy.

Defendant contends that a truck hijacker is a "public enemy" and, therefore, falls within the exception to the general rule.

However, the Court decides to the contrary. In its general usage, the phrase "public enemy" connotes the existence of an actual state of war and refers to the government of a foreign nation at war with the carrier's government. It has also been expanded to include pirates on the high seas (who are considered enemies of all civilized nations) and in some instances, rebels in insurrection against their own government.

Thieves, rioters and robbers, although at war with social order, are not to be classed as "public enemies" in a legal sense, but are merely depredators for whose acts the carrier remains liable.

The Court is of the opinion that despite the enormous increase in crimes generally and hijacking specifically, domestic criminals, whether or not they have achieved the status of having been singled out by the F.B.I. so that they become numbered public enemies, do not fall within the scope of "public enemies" for purposes of being an exception to the insurer liability of a common carrier for its shipments.

* * * [J]udgment in favor of plaintiff against defendant. * * *.

PROBLEMS

1. Blackburn Trucking Company accepts a truckload of mandarin oranges for delivery to Little Rock. Explain whether the Company is liable for loss or damage to the oranges in each of the following situations:

    (a) An escaped convict hijacks the truck and runs it off the road with the result that the oranges are badly squashed and damaged.

    (b) The oranges are overripe when they're delivered to the carrier and they spoil en route. (In your answer, assume first that the Trucking Company knew that the oranges were overripe when it accepted them for shipment, and second that it did not know.)

    (c) Lightning strikes the truck which bursts into flame, destroying all of the oranges.

    (d) Joe Gibbs, the driver for Blackburn Trucking, is drunk and carelessly runs the truck into a ditch. While Joe is waiting for help, a tornado strikes, destroying the truck and what's left of the oranges.

    (e) A state health inspector delays shipment and half the oranges spoil before they arrive in Little Rock.

2. Edie Evans delivers three carloads of onions to Great Lincoln Railroad for shipment to Newberg. The Railroad issues Edie a negotiable bill of lading covering the onions. Edie indorses the bill in blank and forwards it to John Johanson who has purchased the onions. When the onions arrive in Newberg, John presents the bill of lading to the Railroad, and the Railroad delivers the onions to John. However, the Railroad neither takes up the bill of lading nor marks it "delivered in full", and John subsequently sells the bill to Paula Kern, a produce wholesaler who is unaware that delivery has been made under the bill. In a suit by Paula against Great Lincoln Railroad, who will prevail? Explain. Would your answer differ if the bill were nonnegotiable? Explain.

3. Kevin McBride stores 30 portable TV sets with Farrell Storage, Inc. Farrell issues Kevin a negotiable warehouse receipt covering the sets made deliverable to Kevin's order. James Denny breaks into Kevin's office and steals the receipt, forges Kevin's blank indorsement, and presents the receipt to Farrell Storage which delivers the sets to Denny. In a suit by Kevin against Farrell Storage, who will prevail? Explain. Would your answer differ if the warehouse receipt were originally made deliverable "to bearer"? Explain.

    Now suppose that James Denny steals 30 portable TV sets from Kevin McBride and warehouses them so as to obtain a negotiable warehouse receipt. Denny later delivers the receipt to the warehouseman and recollects the sets. What rights, if any, does Kevin McBride have against the warehouseman? Explain fully. Assuming Denny does not recollect the sets, but, instead, transfers the warehouse receipt to Ann Pringle who pays value for the receipt and takes without knowledge of the theft, what are Ann's rights, if any, to the TV sets? Explain fully.

4. Nellie Harrold checks into the Cooper Hotel for a six day stay. Though the hotel provides a safe for the deposit of valuables (and advertises this fact at the front desk), Nellie chooses to keep her diamond necklace in her room on top of her dresser. One day while Nellie is out,

the hotel maid comes in to clean the room. The maid forgets to lock the door when she leaves, and a thief enters and steals Nellie's necklace. Nellie sues the Cooper Hotel for the full value of the necklace. Result? Would your answer differ if it had been Nellie who had forgotten to lock the door? Would it differ if the thief had forced the lock to gain entrance? Explain fully.

5. (a) Dave Tuggle loans his car to Frank Zimmer so that Frank can take his girlfriend to dinner. Frank has too much to drink at dinner, and, on the way home, he carelessly runs the car into a truck. Dave's car is "totalled" and two expensive stereo speakers in the trunk of the car are damaged beyond repair. Frank did not know that the speakers were in the trunk. What are Dave's rights, if any, against Frank Zimmer? Explain fully.

(b) Dave Tuggle stores $10,000 worth of furniture with Farrell Storage, Inc. A fire in a nearby building spreads to the Farrell warehouse and completely destroys Dave's furniture. In a suit by Dave against Farrell for the full value of the furniture, who will prevail? Explain fully.

(c) Dave Tuggle persuades Margie Owen to do him a favor—take his camera in for repairs. On her way to the repair shop, Margie stops to do some shopping and she places Dave's camera down on a store counter and forgets it there. When Margie returns for the camera, the camera is gone. What are Dave's rights, if any, against Margie Owen? Explain fully.

(d) Dave Tuggle purchases a one-way ticket from Reedsport to Newberg from the Fastway Buslines. Dave checks two suitcases to be carried in the luggage compartment of the bus—one contains Dave's clothes and toilet articles—the other contains valuable watch samples for Dave's sales promotion activity. On the way to Newberg, the bus hits an icy spot in the road, and the driver loses control of the vehicle. In the wreck that follows, Dave's two suitcases are completely destroyed and Dave is seriously injured. Who will prevail in a suit by Dave against Fastway Buslines to recover for his personal injuries and the loss of his two suitcases and their contents? Explain fully.

6. Answer the following "True" or "False" and give reasons for your answers:

(a) Both real and personal property can be bailed.

(b) Custody is synonymous with legal possession.

(c) A contract is required for bailment.

(d) The bailee of property has the right to the exclusive use and control of the bailed property during the term of the bailment.

(e) If a third person interferes with the bailee's use and possession of the bailed property, the bailee may sue in his or her own name for money damages.

(f) Whenever a bailee uses bailed property for an improper purpose, the risk of damage or destruction resulting from the misuse is on the bailee.

(g) The law requires the bailor to prove that the bailee was negligent in order to recover for loss or damage to the bailed goods.

F (h) There is no difference between a "guest", a "tenant", and a "permanent lodger".

T (i) A hotelkeeper may refuse to accommodate an intoxicated, criminally violent, or improperly dressed person.

T (j) A common carrier may contract to limit his or her liability to a certain fixed amount or percentage of the value of goods.

T (k) A warehouseman may contract to limit his or her liability to a specified maximum.

T (l) A common carrier of goods may have only a warehouseman's liability at certain times.

T (m) A warehouseman or carrier is liable for any misdescription of goods in a document of title unless the warehouseman or carrier conspicuously disclaims such liability on the document itself.

T (n) Modernly, the holder of a possessory lien may sell the bailed property to enforce the lien.

F (o) A possessory lien is lost upon voluntary redelivery of possession of the bailed chattel to the property owner, but it generally revives upon a subsequent reacquisition of possession by the bailee.

T (p) A transfer of possession is required for a bailment but not for a sale.

7. Field warehousing is a well-established means of securing a loan. As such, it resembles a pledge in many legal respects. Which of the following is correct?

(a) The field warehouseman must maintain physical control of and dominion over the property.

(b) A filing is required in order to perfect such a financing arrangement.

(c) Temporary relinquishment of control for any purpose will suspend the validity of the arrangement insofar as other creditors are concerned.

(d) The property in question must be physically moved to a new location although it may be a part of the borrower's facilities.

[# 24, November, 1977 CPA Exam]

8. Safekeeping, Inc., a public warehouse operator, issued negotiable warehouse receipts to the owner of whiskey stored in the warehouse. As required by law each receipt set forth the storage and other charges for which Safekeeping claimed liens on the whiskey. Safekeeping then became bankrupt and the warehouse was sold to another warehouse operator at a judicial foreclosure sale. The foreclosure sale was for the benefit of all creditors who held claims against Safekeeping. Which of the following is a correct legal conclusion?

(a) The judicial foreclosure sale extinguished the legal and equitable interest of the holder of the warehouse receipts in the whiskey held for storage by Safekeeping.

(b) The trustee in bankruptcy appointed for Safekeeping was immediately vested with legal title to the whiskey upon the filing of the bankruptcy petition.

(c) The negotiable warehouse receipts represent legal ownership of the whiskey, and the owner of the receipts is entitled to the property.

(d) The successor warehouse operator is *not* entitled to the whiskey and can *not* collect the storage and other charges against the owner.

[# 25, November, 1977 CPA Exam]

9. Pierre, owner of Ritz Restaurant, Inc., had in his possession several valuable items which wealthy patrons had lost or left in the restaurant. The total value of these items was in excess of $5,000.

Ritz Restaurant's financial position was poor. Consequently, Pierre decided to pledge the items in question as collateral for a loan. He took the items to Friendly Finance Company and obtained a loan of $3,500 on the property pledged.

Required: 1. What is the legal relationship and duty of Pierre of Ritz Restaurant, Inc. to the original owners of the property in question? Explain.

2. As between the original owners of the property and Friendly Finance Company, who is entitled to the property? Explain.

[# 8.b., May, 1968 CPA Exam]

(See also Chapter 3)

10. During the course of an audit of Acme Produce Company you learn the following:

Acme warehoused 1,000 pounds of beans with Baker Warehouse and Trading Company and received Baker's nonnegotiable warehouse receipt. In addition to being a licensed public warehouse, Baker also regularly bought and sold beans. When Acme delivered its beans to the warehouse, Baker commingled the beans with beans being warehoused for other owners. Then, running short of its own beans, Baker removed 1,000 pounds of beans from its public warehouse and sold them in the normal course of its business as part of its regular stock to Cory Company. Shortly thereafter Baker became insolvent. Acme was the last firm to warehouse beans with Baker prior to Baker's becoming insolvent.

Required: a. Describe the legal relationship between Acme and Baker in connection with the warehousing of the beans.

b. Define the terms "fungible goods" and "warehouse receipt".

c. Did Baker have a right to commingle the beans delivered by Acme with beans warehoused for other customers? Explain.

d. May Acme successfully sue Cory to recover the beans bought from Baker? Explain.

e. How will the beans remaining in Baker's warehouse be distributed among owners who delivered beans for warehousing?

f. Would your answers to question "c", "d" or "e" vary if Acme had received a negotiable warehouse receipt from Baker? Explain.

[# 5, May, 1968 CPA Exam]

Chapter 17

THE LEGAL SETTING OF A SALE OF GOODS, THE LEGAL RESULT OF IDENTIFYING THE GOODS TO BE SOLD, AND THE RULES DETERMINING WHEN THE RISK OF LOSS REGARDING THE GOODS PASSES FROM THE SELLER TO THE BUYER

What is a "sale"?

A "sale" of goods is a contract by which the ownership of goods is transferred from a seller to a buyer. As you will note, there are several elements to this definition—a sale is a "contract"— its subject matter is "goods"—its result is to transfer "ownership" of goods (as opposed to mere possession) from a seller to a buyer. Looking at these elements, it should be clear that many of the rules and principles discussed in previous chapters will come into play whenever there is a sale of goods. For example, in determining whether an enforceable sales contract exists, ordinary contract law (including several special rules unique to sales transactions) governs. Often, the goods purchased in a sale are shipped by common carrier from the seller's location to the buyer's location; or the goods are stored with a warehouseman for a period of time. Where this is the case, the special bailments of the common carrier and warehouseman come into play along with the use of documents of title, which may or may not be negotiable. Negotiable notes, drafts, or checks may be used to pay for the goods. And the Uniform Commercial Code may create in the buyer a special insurable interest in the property. And so on.

In addition to these familiar rules and principles, there are a number of special rules that are unique to the concept of sales; most are provided by the Uniform Commercial Code and come into play when certain "fact situations" or "events" disrupt the usual sales transaction. In this chapter and the next, we will first review some of the familiar rules that form the legal setting of the sales transaction, then we will consider the special rules that control in specific fact situations.

What is the legal setting of the sales transaction? [1]

A sale is a contract by which the ownership of goods is transferred from a seller to a buyer. The legal setting of the sales transaction thus involves the concept of *ownership*. You will recall the following definition of "ownership" from Ch. 3.

Ownership of property (real or personal) is generally referred to as "title". And it is important to realize that title is not a written paper. It is a legal concept indicating ownership— that is, a legally protected interest in property good as against the whole world. Ownership of title may be evidenced by a written "document of

---

1. In describing the legal setting of the "sales transaction", reference will be made to previous chapters of the text, and brief summaries of the material will be provided. By way of review, and for a full understanding of the material on sales, you should go back and reread the entire chapter section from which each summary is excerpted.

title" or "title certificate" (and usually is in the case of large items such as cars, boats, and airplanes), but these papers are merely evidence of ownership and are not required. The owner of a book, a table, or a TV set may possess nothing in writing to indicate ownership, but he or she will possess title (a legally protected interest in the property) nonetheless.

Title or ownership is important because it confers upon the owner of the property the exclusive right to use, possess, and dispose of the property owned. Disposition encompasses lifetime transfers as well as distribution to heirs and beneficiaries upon the owner's death.[2]

The legal setting of a sale also encompasses the concept of *goods*: a sales transaction results in the transfer of ownership of "goods".

The Uniform Commercial Code definition of "goods" encompasses both "goods" and "goods and chattels" as defined in Black's Law Dictionary, excluding only rental terms for years (i. e., chattels real).

The UCC provides:

> **Section 2–105. Definitions:** * *
>
> (1) "Goods" means all things (including specially manufactured goods) which are movable at the time of identification to the contract for sale * * * "Goods" also includes the unborn young of animals and growing crops and other identified things attached to realty as described in the section on goods to be severed from realty (Section 2–107).

As a result of the UCC definition, "goods", which are always and without exception classified as personal property, will always include animals as well as their unborn young, growing crops, timber, and other things to be severed from land or realty.

The timing of when crops, timber, minerals, structures, and the like change from real estate to personal property is controlled by Section 2–107 of the Uniform Commercial Code as follows.

The UCC provides:

> **Section 2–107.**
>
> (1) A contract for the sale of minerals or the like (including oil or gas) or a structure or its materials to be removed from realty is a contract for the sale of goods within this Article if they are to be *severed by the seller* * * * (emphasis added).
>
> (2) A contract for the sale apart from the land of growing crops or other things attached to realty and capable of severance without material harm thereto but not described in subsection (1) or of timber to be cut is a contract for the sale of goods within this Article *whether the subject matter is to be severed by the buyer or by the seller* even though it forms part of the realty at the time of contracting, and the parties can by identification effect a present sale before severance.[3]

As you will recall from Ch. 10, the Statute of Frauds imposes less stringent requirements for a sale of "goods" than for a sale of "land".

It provides:

> The Statute of Frauds states that any contract for the sale of land or an in-

---

2. Ch. 3, "What is the most common way to acquire ownership of personal property?", p. 51.

3. Ch. 2, "When, under the law, do minerals, trees, crops, and the like change from real property to personal property"?, p. 23.

terest in land must be supported by a written memorandum signed by the party to be charged (i. e., by the party being sued to carry out the promise).

Because the transfer of *any* interest in land falls within the Statute, it is very important to keep in mind the distinction between real and personal property and the many and varied interests in land that are possible. You will recall from Ch. 2 that real property and personal property sometimes mesh insofar as minerals, trees, crops, fixtures, and rentals are concerned. Where the end product of the meshing is real property, the Statute of Frauds applies to any contract for sale of the property; where the end product is personal property, the real property Statute of Frauds does not apply (although a sale of the property may nonetheless fall within the Statute as a sale of goods for $500 or more).

* * * [T]he sale of goods for $500 or more * * * is the only [subject matter covered by the Statute of Frauds] that can satisfy the Statute with far less of a written memo, and in some cases, with other than a written memo. The Uniform Commercial Code tightly controls this area of the Statute of Frauds at Section 2–201 * * *

* * *

* * * [I]t is seen that while a sale of goods for $500 or more falls within the Statute of Frauds, far less of a written memo is required to prove the sale than is required to prove promises within the other five subject matter areas covered by the Statute. In the sale of goods situation, the only essential memo term is *quantity,* and even it may be misstated (although recovery, in that case, will be limited to

the misstated amount). All that is required is that the writing afford a basis for believing that the oral evidence offered rests upon a real transaction. And, of course, the writing must be signed by the party to be charged.

It is also seen that, in the following instances, the Statute of Frauds may be satisfied in the sale of goods situation with other than a written memo.

(1) If the buyer *accepts and receives* all or part of the goods, the contract, though oral, is enforceable to the extent that the goods are accepted and received.

(2) If the buyer makes *part payment* for the goods, the contract, though oral, is enforceable as to the goods paid for.

* * *

(3) If the seller is required by the terms of the contract to manufacture *special goods* for the buyer (i. e., goods that are unsuitable for sale to others in the ordinary course of the seller's business), and the seller has made a substantial beginning in their manufacture or has contracted for their procurement, no writing is needed to support the promise to buy the goods.

(4) If the contract is *between merchants,* and one of the merchants within a reasonable time sends a written confirmation of the agreement to the other merchant, and that merchant fails to object in writing to the confirmation within 10 days, the contract is enforceable against the merchant who receives the confirmation.

(5) Finally, if the party to be charged admits in court or in the pleadings preliminary to court that a contract does, in fact, exist, the contract will be enforceable to the extent of the party's admission.[4]

---

4. Ch. 10, "How does the Statute of Frauds apply to contracts for the sale of real property?" and "How does the Statute of Frauds apply to sales of goods for $500 or more?", pp. 304–306.

Because a sale of goods is first and foremost a *contract,* it is important in discussing the legal setting of a sales transaction to review the definition of a contract.

As stated in Ch. 7:

"Contracts" * * * *[are] legally recognized promises or bargains made by two or more persons, including all rights and duties resulting from the promises or bargains.*

The law generally requires four elements for a valid contract: (1) mutual assent, (2) consideration, (3) capacity, and (4) legality. Lacking any one of these four elements, the promises or bargains between parties will usually not create rights and duties, and will not result in a valid contract.[5]

Like any other contract, a contract of sale requires the four elements of mutual assent, consideration, capacity, and legality. Insofar as these requirements are concerned, sales transactions are subject to the ordinary contract law principles discussed in Chapters 7 through 10, including some special rules that apply only to sales.

The rules provide:

Mutual assent. Mutual assent is usually manifested by one party making an offer and another party making an acceptance of the offer.

An offer may be succinctly defined as a "definite conditional undertaking": it is a *definite* proposal made by one party (the "offeror") to another party (the "offeree") indicating the offering party's present intent to enter into a contract * * * *conditioned* upon the offeree's completion of the contract by acceptance * * *

An offer * * * need only be "reasonably" definite—that is, sufficiently definite that the court can determine the essential terms of the agreement as intended by the parties so as to meet the reasonable expectations of either party in damages * * *.

* * * It is also important to realize that the Uniform Commercial Code has liberalized the requirement of definiteness insofar as contracts for the *sale of goods* are concerned * * *.

As a result of Code sections designed to liberalize the definiteness requirement, any offer for the sale of "goods" may give rise to mutual assent upon acceptance by the offeree even though the same offer and acceptance would fail for lack of definiteness in the case of a subject matter other than goods (e. g., contracts for personal services such as those of a plumber or lawyer, or sales of insurance or real estate) Section 2–204 of the UCC provides as follows:

(1) A contract for [the] sale of goods may be made in any manner sufficient to show agreement, including conduct by both parties which recognizes the existence of such a contract.

(2) An agreement sufficient to constitute a contract for sale may be found even though the moment of its making is undetermined [this provision particularly applies to situations where there is an exchange of correspondence indicating a binding obligation, but failing to disclose the exact time when the contract came into existence.]

(3) Even though one or more terms are left open a contract for sale

---

5. Ch. 7, "What is a contract?", p. 170.

does not fail for indefiniteness if the parties intended to make a contract and there is a reasonably certain basis for giving an appropriate remedy.

* * *

In recognition of the fact that "open price terms" are frequently necessary and desirable in business transactions, UCC Section 2–305, "Open Price Terms" provides as follows:

(1) The parties if they so intend can conclude a contract for sale even though the price is not settled. In such a case the price is a reasonable price at the time for delivery if

(a) nothing is said as to price; or

(b) the price is left to be agreed by the parties and they fail to agree; or

(c) the price is to be fixed in terms of some agreed market or other standard as set or recorded by a third person or agency and it is not so set or recorded.

* * *

* * * Where either a commercial or private sale of goods fails to specify the place of delivery, the transactions will not fail for lack of definiteness because of UCC Section 2–308 * * *:

Unless otherwise agreed

(a) the place for delivery of goods is the seller's place of business or if he has none, his residence; but

(b) in a contract for sale of identified goods which to the knowledge of the parties at the time of contracting are in some other place, that place is the place for their delivery.

* * *

* * * If the buyer and seller do not agree either expressly or impliedly on the time for delivery of the goods, UCC Section 2–309 provides that the time for delivery shall be a "reasonable time".

* * *

* * * Where the time for payment is not specified by the parties, payment is due under UCC Section 2–310 at the time and place where the buyer receives the goods.

* * *

* * * [Under Section 2–306], a transaction for "output" or "requirements" is not too indefinite as it is held to mean the "actual good faith" output or requirements of the party.

* * *

By way of summary * * * "definiteness" is required because it is essential that offers * * * be clearly understandable * * *

Insofar as the sale of goods is concerned, the Uniform Commercial Code has liberalized the "definiteness" requirement with provisions designed to "fill in the gaps" where essential terms such as price, quantity, or place of delivery are left open.[6]

* * *

In the case of a sale of goods, the Uniform Commercial Code also liberalizes the common law requirement that an "acceptance" to an offer be unequivocal, unconditional, and exact: in the sales situation, an acceptance stating different or additional terms will not necessarily constitute a rejection of the offer.

The UCC provides:

* * * [With regard to the sale of goods], Section 2–207 of the Code provides that the offeree's injection of

6. Ch. 7, "How is mutual assent usually manifested?" and "How definite does a statement have to be in order to constitute an offer?", pp. 179–181.

different terms will not necessarily constitute a rejection of the original offer, nor a counteroffer that serves to terminate the original offer. Unless the original offer expressly limits acceptance to its terms, the additions to the offer will not prevent acceptance by the offeree, but will be treated merely as proposals for addition to the contract. And where the transaction is between merchants, the new terms will automatically become part of the contract unless the new terms materially alter the contract, or unless the offeror objects to the terms within a reasonable period of time.[7]

As for the consideration requirement, Ch. 9 of the text provides.

It states:

Consideration * * * [U]nder our system of law, a promise that stands utterly alone will probably never be legally enforceable. There must be something accompanying the promise that justifies enforcement. * * * A promise is neither legally binding nor enforceable unless it fits within one of the four common law theories of consideration or unless it falls within one of the UCC exceptions to the common law rules. * * *
[The UCC exceptions include:]

Firm offers * * * UCC Section 2–205, "Firm offers" provides as follows:

An offer *by a merchant to buy or sell goods* in a signed writing which by its terms gives assurance that it will be held open *is not revocable for lack of consideration, during the time stated* or if no time is stated for a reasonable time, but in no

event may such period of irrevocability exceed three months.
* * *

Modification, rescission, and waiver. Section 2–209(1) of the UCC provides that "an agreement modifying a contract within this Article (sales) needs no consideration to be binding." This Section of the Code is designed to facilitate necessary and desirable modifications of sales contracts by eliminating the need for common law consideration in the case of each and every change. * * * *[8]

The legal setting of a sales transaction also includes the concept of *insurable interest* as defined in Ch. 11. In many situations, both the buyer and the seller of goods have an insurable interest in the property which is the subject matter of the sale. "Insurance" and "insurable interest" are defined in Ch. 11 as follows:

It provides:

Insurance is first of all a contract * * *. [It] is an arrangement for transferring and distributing risk. "Risk" is the "key" to understanding insurance; it is the factor creating the need for insurance. A businesswoman, for example, may operate her business with a maximum of planning, care, and caution, yet be unable to prevent financial losses resulting from contingencies beyond her control. * * *

* * * [T]he objective of insurance and of law generally is to offset and reimburse for loss by transferring the loss from insured to insurer without conferring a benefit on the insured greater than the loss. Compensation for loss sustained without further ben-

---

7. Ch. 7, "What possible responses are there to an offer?", p. 191.

8. Ch. 9, "Why does the law require consideration?" and "What are the four common law theories of consideration, and when are promises enforceable under the UCC without regard to these four theories?", pp. 243–244.

efit (i. e., nothing beyond the loss) is the principle of indemnity. * * *

The reasoning behind the principle is that to permit an individual to realize gain from insurance proceeds would encourage two evils—gambling or wagering, and destruction of insured lives and property. * * *

* * * It is a general rule of insurance law that the insured must have an *insurable interest* in the subject matter of the insurance contract. If he or she does not, the insured cannot enforce the insurance agreement. * * *

* * * A person possesses an insurable interest in property whenever damage or destruction of the property will result in measurable economic loss (in money value) to the person. * * * [9]

———

As will be explained in detail later in the chapter, Section 2–501 of the Uniform Commercial Code creates an "insurable interest" in the buyer of goods upon "identification" of the goods to the contract (i. e., upon selection of the specific goods to be sold). The "insurable interest" arises though the goods remain in the seller's possession and await long distance shipment to the buyer.

Because goods are often shipped to buyers, a discussion of the legal setting of a sales transaction would not be complete without mention of the legal concept of *bailment* (particularly as it includes the special bailments of the warehouseman and common carrier). As you will recall from Ch. 16, a "bailment" is "the rightful possession of another's personal property." The fact that goods are bailed to a warehouseman (for storage) or to a common carrier (for shipment) may have

significant consequence in the law of sales, as may the fact that the goods are covered by a negotiable or nonnegotiable document of title.

In conclusion, a sale of goods brings into operation many of the legal concepts that you are familiar with. There are literally millions of commercial sales transactions daily. In most cases, the buyer orders the goods from the seller, receives the goods and pays for them, and there are no legal problems. Sometimes, however, problems do arise—certain fact situations occur—and the special rules of sales are needed to resolve the conflict. In this chapter and the next, we will consider the "disrupting events" that may upset a sales transaction and the special rules that govern in such events. But first we will look at one event—"identification" of the goods—that must always occur in order to complete a sale. "Identification" has important legal consequences for the buyer.

What is the effect of "identification" of the goods to the contract of sale?

A sale is a contract by which the ownership of goods is transferred from a seller to a buyer. Obviously, if a sale is to occur, the specific goods to be sold must at some point be identified. The process of selecting or setting aside the specific goods is referred to as "identification" of the goods to the contract. Identification requires two things: first, the goods must be in existence; and, second, the specific chattel or chattels to be transferred from the seller to the buyer must be singled out. Other than this, no specific procedure is required—it is sufficient that the specific goods be in some way earmarked for the buyer.

Occasionally, goods are identified at the time the contract is entered into.

---

9. Ch. 11, "What is the nature of insurance?" and "What is the principle of indemnity?", p. 337.

Here, both buyer and seller have in mind certain specific goods that are to be sold, and the buyer bargains for the specific goods. More often, however, identification takes place after the contract is entered into. At the time of the sale, the seller merely agrees to furnish a specified number of items from his or her general inventory; the seller segregates the specific items to be sold at a later point in time. For example, suppose that Susan Seller agrees to sell 50 TV sets from her general stock of 1,000 such sets to Barry Buyer. At the time of entering into the contract, Susan makes no effort to single out or set aside the specific sets to be sold to Barry; thus, identification does not occur at this point. It occurs later when Susan segregates the 50 sets to be delivered to Barry. Of course, if, at the time of contracting, Susan gives Barry a list of 50 serial numbers identifying the specific sets that he will receive, identification takes place at that time.

Identification of the goods to the contract has important legal consequences for the buyer. Section 2–501 of the Uniform Commercial Code provides that the buyer acquires a "special property and insurable interest" in the goods at the time they are identified. The buyer's "special property" consists of three rights: the right to inspect the identified goods [UCC Section 2–513(1)], the right to replevin the goods [UCC Sections 2–502 and 2–716], and the right to recover damages from any third party who converts the goods or otherwise interferes with the property [UCC Section 2–722]. These rights of the buyer do not exist absent identification (they are considered in detail in Ch. 18 along with the other rights and remedies of the buyer).

As for the buyer's "insurable interest" in the goods, you will recall that a person must have an insurable interest in property in order to purchase insurance on the property. The Uniform Commercial Code creates an insurable interest in the buyer upon identification of the goods on the rationale that as soon as the buyer knows or can determine which specific goods he or she will receive, the buyer can enter into other contracts regarding the goods requiring insurance protection. For example, Barry Buyer may contract to provide the 50 identified TV sets for a new motel operation or local retail dealer.

UCC Section 2–501 which creates the "special property and insurable interest" provides as follows.

Section 2–501. Insurable Interest in Goods; Manner of Identification of Goods

(1) The buyer obtains a special property and an insurable interest in goods by identification of existing goods as goods to which the contract refers even though the goods so identified are nonconforming and he has an option to return or reject them. Such identification can be made at any time and in any manner explicitly agreed to by the parties. In the absence of explicit agreement identification occurs

(a) when the contract is made if it is for the sale of goods already existing and identified;

(b) if the contract is for the sale of future goods other than those described in paragraph (c), when goods are shipped, marked or otherwise designated by the seller as goods to which the contract refers;

(c) when the crops are planted or otherwise become growing crops or the young are conceived if the contract is for the sale of unborn young to be born within twelve months after contracting or for the sale of crops to be harvested within twelve months or the next normal harvest season after contracting whichever is longer.

* * *

(3) Nothing in this section impairs any insurable interest recognized under any other statute or rule of law.

The *Official Comment* to Section 2–501 points out that "undivided shares in an identified fungible bulk, such as grain in an elevator or oil in a storage tank, can be sold. The mere making of the contract with reference to an undivided share in an identified fungible bulk is enough * * * to effect an identification if there is no explicit agreement otherwise."

It should be realized that the buyer's "special property and insurable interest" is far less than the complete ownership of the goods that the buyer will acquire upon completion of the sale: the "special property and insurable interest" exists independently of ownership (title) which is almost certain to remain in the seller (along with the risk of loss for damage or destruction of the goods) for a period of time after identification. The seller-owner retains his or her own insurable interest in the property until such time as ownership passes to the buyer. And if the seller retains a *security interest* in the goods (see Ch. 27), his or her insurable interest will continue until the goods are paid for. Section 2–501(2) is the relevant Code provision.

The UCC provides:

(2) The seller retains an insurable interest in goods so long as title to or any security interest in the goods remains in him and where the identification is by the seller alone he may until default or insolvency or notification to the buyer that the identification is fi-

nal substitute other goods for those identified.

As between the buyer and the seller, who must bear the loss if the goods are lost, damaged, or destroyed?

Obviously, goods start out at the risk of the seller. A seller may have a whole warehouse full of inventory that he or she intends to sell. If the warehouse burns to the ground, destroying the goods, the seller will have to absorb the loss and look to insurance coverage for reimbursement. Potential but as yet unknown buyers would not share in the loss.

At some point, however, a buyer enters into the picture. And, at some point, the risk of loss may pass from the seller to the buyer. If the goods to be sold under the contract are lost, damaged, or destroyed while the risk is in the seller, the seller must bear the loss; but if the risk has passed to the buyer, the buyer must bear the loss. As to when the risk of loss passes, the Uniform Commercial Code provides that title is not determinative: the fact that ownership of the goods has not yet passed to the buyer does not mean that risk of loss has not yet passed, and vice versa. Rather, the Uniform Commercial Code deals with risk of loss from an event or situation standpoint. One of the parties—either buyer or seller—may be at fault in causing the loss. Or, as is more often the case, neither party may be at fault—as where the loss or damage results from an act of God (e. g., a flood, earthquake, tornado, or the like), an unavoidable accident (e. g., a fire that starts without negligence of any kind), or a negligent or wrongful act of a third party (e. g., a delay in shipment by a common carrier). The seller may have fulfilled all his or her duties with regard to shipment of the goods; or he or she may have duties remaining. And either party, buyer or seller, may have breached the contract of sale, etc.

The possible events or situations governing whether risk of loss has passed from the seller to the buyer are categorized and discussed below under the following headings:

(1) The goods are lost, damaged, or destroyed through fault of one of the parties.

(2) The goods are lost, damaged, or destroyed through no fault of the parties but before the risk of loss has passed from the seller to the buyer.

(3) The goods are lost, damaged, or destroyed through no fault of the parties but after the risk of loss has passed from the seller to the buyer.

The goods are lost, damaged or destroyed through fault of one of the parties. Where either the buyer or the seller is "at fault" in causing the loss or damage, the party at fault bears the risk of loss and is liable to the other party for any loss that he or she suffers. The *Official Comment* to Section 2–613 of the Uniform Commercial Code states that " 'fault' is intended to include negligent and not merely willful wrong."

The goods are lost, damaged, or destroyed through no fault of the parties but before the risk of loss has passed from the seller to the buyer. More often, the goods are lost, damaged, or destroyed through no fault of the parties. If the loss or damage occurs before the risk of loss has passed from the seller to the buyer, the seller will be liable to the buyer unless his or her inability to perform (i. e., to deliver the goods in the condition promised) constitutes an "objective impossibility" or is "commercially impracticable" within the meaning of UCC Section 2–615. You will recall the following discussion of "objective impossibility" and "commercial impracticability" from Ch. 10 of the text.

It provides:

(4) *Impossibility of performance.* A duty of performance is also discharged where, after a contract is entered into, the promised performance becomes *objectively impossible* to perform. * * * The impossibility must be objective as opposed to subjective. Objective impossibility is impossibility of anyone to perform the particular promise made; subjective impossibility is the personal inability of the promisor to perform the promise, although another person would be able to perform. While objective impossibility serves to discharge the duty of performance under the contract, subjective impossibility has no effect, leaving the obligation to perform intact.

* * * [I]f a party is unable to carry out his or her promise to provide another with 1,000 bushels of wheat because of a crop failure, the impossibility is subjective and does not discharge the party's duty of performance (the wheat may be supplied from other sources). Of course, if the promise is to provide 1,000 bushels from a designated parcel of land, the crop failure results in an objective impossibility (no one can supply 1,000 bushels from the property) and the promisor is relieved of his or her duty to perform.[10]

* * *

* * * [I]t should be pointed out that a small minority of courts al-

---

10. Ch. 10, "How is a party discharged from his or her contract obligations?", p. 314.

low discharge of contract duties even in the event of subjective impossibility if performance of the contract would be many times more difficult or expensive than the parties originally contemplated. Called the "doctrine of impracticability", the minority rule is recognized in but few jurisdictions.

* * * Insofar as the sale of goods is concerned, the doctrine of impracticability is recognized by Section 2–615 of the Uniform Commercial Code. The section excuses a seller from timely delivery of goods contracted for where the seller's performance has become commercially impracticable because of unforeseen supervening circumstances not within the contemplation of the parties at the time of contracting. Increased cost alone is not sufficient to excuse the seller's duty of performance: some unforeseen contingency must occur to alter the essential nature of the performance (e. g., where a shortage of raw materials arises from a war, embargo, local crop failure, or the like, making it "commercially impracticable" for the seller to timely perform).

* * *

And Section 2–615 of the Code states: "Delay in delivery or non-delivery in whole or in part by a seller * * * is not a breach of his duty under a contract for sale if performance as agreed [upon] has been made impracticable by the occurrence of a contingency the non-occurrence of which was a basic assumption on which the contract was made. * * *"

In almost all cases where the goods are lost, damaged, or destroyed prior to identification (as where the seller's entire inventory is destroyed by fire), or after identification, where identification takes place after the contract is entered into

(the usual situation), it is only subjectively impossible for the seller to perform (the goods could be obtained from other sources). Unless the seller can establish "commercial impracticability" within the meaning of Section 2–615, the seller will be liable to the buyer in damages.

Occasionally, however, the goods are identified to the contract at the time the contract is entered into. Here, as you will recall, both buyer and seller have certain specific goods in mind as the subject matter of the sale at the time the contract is entered into. The buyer bargains for the specific goods, and, if the goods are lost, damaged, or destroyed, it will be objectively impossible for the seller to perform (no one could deliver the specific goods bargained for). The contract will thus be avoided, and the seller will be excused from performance (however, both buyer and seller may be protected by insurance as both have insurable interests in the property, the buyer by virtue of his or her "special property and insurable interest", the seller by virtue of his or her ownership).

Returning to our earlier example, suppose that Susan Seller segregates the 50 TV sets to be sold to Barry Buyer at the time of entering into the contract with Barry. If the 50 sets are subsequently damaged or destroyed without fault of either party, and before the risk of loss has passed to Barry Buyer, the contract will be avoided and both parties will be excused from further performance. Assuming both parties have insured the TV sets, each can recover from his or her respective insurance company. On the other hand, if the TV sets are not identified at the time the contract is entered into, and the sets are thereafter damaged or destroyed (again, without fault of the parties and before the risk of loss has passed to Barry Buyer), Susan will be liable to Barry unless she can show "commercial impracticability" within the terms of Section 2–615.

Where goods *identified when the contract is entered into* are not totally, but are only partially lost or destroyed (again, without fault of the parties and before the risk of loss has passed to the buyer), the buyer has the right under Section 2–613 of the Code to demand inspection of the goods and at his or her option either avoid the contract or accept the goods in their damaged state with due allowance from the contract price for the damage or deterioration. So if only 22 of the 50 TV sets identified at the time of contracting are destroyed by fire, Barry Buyer can demand inspection of the goods (all 50 sets) and then either avoid the sale completely or take the remaining 28 sets with due allowance from the contract price for the sets that have been destroyed.

Section 2–613 of the Code states:

Section 2–613. Casualty to Identified Goods

Where the contract requires for its performance goods *identified when the contract is made,* and the goods suffer casualty without fault of either party before the risk of loss passes to the buyer, or in a proper case under a "no arrival, no sale" term (section 2–324) then

(a) if the loss is total the contract is avoided; and

(b) if the loss is partial or the goods have so deteriorated as no longer to conform to the contract the buyer may nevertheless demand inspection and at his option either treat the contract as avoided or accept the goods with due allowance from the contract price for the deterioration or the deficiency

in quantity but without further right against the seller. [Emphasis supplied.]

The Official Comment to the Section provides:

Purposes of Changes:

1. Where goods whose continued existence is presupposed by the agreement are destroyed without fault of either party, the buyer is relieved from his obligation but may at his option take the surviving goods at a fair adjustment. * * * The buyer is expressly given the right to inspect the goods in order to determine whether he wishes to avoid the contract entirely or to take the goods with a price adjustment.

2. The section applies whether the goods were already destroyed at the time of contracting without the knowledge of either party or whether they are destroyed subsequently but before the risk of loss passes to the buyer. Where under the agreement * * * the risk has passed to the buyer before the casualty, the section has no application.

You will note that Section 2–613 makes reference to a "no arrival, no sale" term. *Black's Law Dictionary* defines "no arrival, no sale" as follows: "If goods do not arrive at destination buyer acquires no property therein and does not become liable for price." [11] Section 2–324 of the Uniform Commercial Code

----

11. Henry Campbell Black, *Black's Law Dictionary*, Revised Fourth Edition, West Publishing Co., 1968, p. 1197.

provides:

Section 2–324. "No Arrival, No Sale Term"

Under a term "no arrival, no sale" or terms of like meaning, unless otherwise agreed,

(a) the seller must properly ship conforming goods and if they arrive by any means he must tender them on arrival but he assumes no obligation that the goods will arrive unless he has caused the non-arrival; and

(b) where without fault of the seller the goods are in part lost or have so deteriorated as no longer to conform to the contract or arrive after the contract time, the buyer may proceed as if there had been casualty to identified goods (Section 2–613.)

Thus, in a "no arrival, no sale" contract, the seller makes no promise that the goods will arrive. There is obviously some risk that they will not arrive, and the seller contracts to protect himself or herself from liability. However, this is not to say that the seller has an option not to ship the goods: he or she must ship the goods, and the goods must conform to the contract. But if the goods do not arrive, the seller will not be liable to the buyer and will have no further obligation under the contract. The risk of loss in a "no arrival, no sale" contract remains on the seller until the goods are delivered to the buyer. Usually, a seller will utilize a "no arrival, no sale" term when shipping goods overseas or when reselling goods purchased from one who retains possession of the property and will ship the goods to the seller's buyer.

Under Section 2–324(b), if goods being sold under a "no arrival, no sale" contract are partially lost or damaged without fault of the parties, the buyer has the right to demand inspection of the goods and at his or her option either avoid the agreement or take the remaining goods with a reduction in purchase price—just as though there had been a casualty to identified goods under Section 2–613.

The goods are lost, damaged, or destroyed through no fault of the parties but after the risk of loss has passed from the seller to the buyer. Once the risk of loss has passed from the seller to the buyer, it becomes the buyer's problem if the goods are lost, damaged, or destroyed: the buyer will have to pay the seller the full contract price for the goods even though they arrive in a damaged or deteriorated condition or don't arrive at all. Of course, the buyer, in turn, may be able to recover from a third party (e. g., a common carrier) who is strictly liable or at fault in causing the loss.

As to *when* the risk of loss passes from the seller to the buyer, the Uniform Commercial Code very specifically controls according to the following situations or events:

(1) Where there is no carrier or other bailee involved, and the parties have made no agreement as to risk of loss (the usual situation).

(2) Where the goods are to be shipped to the buyer by a common carrier.

(3) Where the goods are in the possession of a bailee and are to be "delivered" to the buyer without being moved.

(4) Where the parties have made an agreement as to risk of loss.

(5) Where the goods are transferred in a "sale on approval" or a "sale or return".

(6) Where either the buyer or the seller has breached the contract of sale.

(1) *Where there is no common carrier or other bailee involved, and the parties have made no agreement as to risk of loss—the usual situation.* In most sales contracts, there is no common carrier or other bailee involved, and the parties make no agreement as to risk of loss. The seller simply delivers the goods to the buyer. For example, if you purchase a pair of shoes from a department store, the store employee will hand you the shoes, and you will take them home with you. If you purchase a refrigerator-freezer from the store, the store will deliver the appliance to you in a company truck (as opposed to a common carrier). If you buy a used set of dishes at a neighborhood garage sale, the seller will relinquish possession of the dishes, and you will take possession.

At some point in time, the risk of loss for damage or destruction of the shoes, the refrigerator-freezer, or the dishes passes to you, the buyer. If the seller is a *merchant,* the risk of loss passes to you upon your *receipt* of the goods, "receipt" meaning physical possession. If the seller is a *nonmerchant,* the risk of loss passes to you upon the seller's *tender of delivery* of the goods without regard to your actual receipt of the goods (as you will recall, a "tender" is simply a conditional offer to perform—a statement that "I am ready to perform if you are"). Thus, if the nonmerchant seller tenders delivery of the goods (says "here they are, take them"), and you, the buyer, refuse to accept delivery, the risk of loss will nevertheless pass to you at the moment of tender.

Returning to our examples, suppose that you accidentally leave your new shoes on a counter in the same department store while making another purchase. If the shoes are stolen from the counter, you must bear the loss. The risk of loss passed to you at the time you received actual possession of the shoes from the department store merchant seller.

Now suppose that the department store delivery truck arrives at your home and the driver of the truck tenders delivery of the refrigerator-freezer. You refuse delivery. The truck leaves to return to the store, but is in an accident on the way back, and the refrigerator-freezer is badly damaged. Here, the department store merchant seller must bear the loss—you, the buyer, have not *received* the goods, and receipt is necessary for the risk of loss to pass to you from the merchant seller. (Of course, the merchant seller is likely to sue you for breach of contract if you have no valid reason for refusing delivery.)

On the other hand, suppose that the nonmerchant neighborhood seller brings the used dishes to your home in his or her stationwagon and there "tenders delivery" to you. Again, you refuse delivery, the seller is in an accident on the way home, and the dishes are destroyed. Here, you must bear the loss. The seller being a nonmerchant, the risk of loss passed to you upon tender of delivery without regard to your actual receipt of the goods.

So you see, it makes a great deal of difference with regard to risk of loss whether the seller is a merchant or nonmerchant. But remember, these risk of loss rules apply only where there is no common carrier or other bailee involved, and the parties have made no contrary agreement as to risk of loss.

(2) *Where the goods are to be shipped by a common carrier.* Most *business* contracts for the sale of goods call for the goods to be shipped to the buyer by common carrier. Here, the risk of loss passes to the buyer at one of two times depending on whether the contract is a "shipment" contract or a "destination" contract. In a *shipment contract,* the seller is required to deliver the goods merely to a carrier at the place of shipment rather than to a particular destination. The risk of loss passes to the buyer

when the goods are "duly delivered" to the carrier.[12] Goods to be "duly delivered" must meet the following requirements of UCC Section 2–504.

The UCC provides:

Section 2–504. Shipment by Seller

Where the seller is required or authorized to send the goods to the buyer and the contract does not require him to deliver them at a particular destination, then unless otherwise agreed he must

(a) put the goods in the possession of such a carrier and make such a contract for their transportation as may be reasonable having regard to the nature of the goods and other circumstances of the case; and

(b) obtain and promptly deliver or tender in due form any document necessary to enable the buyer to obtain possession of the goods or otherwise required by the agreement or by usage of trade; and

(c) promptly notify the buyer of the shipment.

The *Official Comment* to Section 2–504 adds by way of explanation.

It states:

In the absence of agreement, the provision of this Article on options and cooperation respecting performance gives the seller the choice of any reasonable carrier, routing and other arrangements. Whether or not the shipment is at the buyer's expense the seller must see to any arrangements, reasonable in the circumstances, such as refrigeration, watering of livestock, protection against cold, the sending along of any necessary help, selection of specialized cars and the like for paragraph (a) is intended to cover all necessary arrangements whether made by contract with the carrier or otherwise. There is, however, a proper relaxation of such requirements if the buyer is himself in a position to make the appropriate arrangements and the seller gives him reasonable notice of the need to do so. It is an improper contract under paragraph (a) for the seller to agree with the carrier to a limited valuation below the true value and thus cut off the buyer's opportunity to recover from the carrier in the event of loss, when the risk of shipment is placed on the buyer. * * *

If the seller "duly delivers" the goods to the carrier (i. e., delivers them to the carrier in the condition contracted for and makes proper arrangements for their carriage), the goods will be "conforming" (i. e., in accord with the terms of the contract). The goods being conforming, the buyer will have no right to reject them even if they arrive in a spoiled or damaged condition. The risk of loss has passed to the buyer (upon due delivery of the goods to the carrier), and the buyer will have to pay the full contract price for the goods and seek recovery from the carrier or other third party. Of course, if the goods are not in the condition contracted for when delivered to the carrier (e. g., if they are already spoiled or damaged), the goods are *nonconforming* (i. e., not in accord with the terms of contract), and there is no due delivery. The risk of loss remains in the seller, and the buyer has the right to reject the goods upon their arrival in the spoiled or damaged state.

---

12. This is so even where the seller retains a "security interest" in the goods. As you will learn in Ch. 27, a security interest is a means of securing payment or performance by the buyer; a seller may ship goods with "reservation" of such an interest.

Let's consider an example. Suppose that Barry Buyer orders 50 TV sets from Susan Seller, the sets to be shipped to Barry by common carrier train. As Susan is required merely to deliver the sets to the carrier at the place of shipment (rather than to a particular destination), the contract is a shipment contract. Assuming Susan delivers 50 sets in A-1 condition to the carrier, and makes proper arrangements for their carriage, there is due delivery of the goods, and the risk of loss passes to Barry Buyer at the time of delivery to the carrier. If the goods are thereafter destroyed by an act of God (e. g., a tornado), the loss will be Barry's, not Susan's. Nor will Barry be able to recover from the common carrier as an act of God is one of the five exceptions to the carrier's strict liability. (Of course, if the goods are perishable and spoil en route because of a delay in shipment, Barry will be entitled to reimbursement from the carrier.)

In a *destination contract,* on the other hand, the seller must deliver the goods to a particular destination: the risk of loss does not pass to the buyer until the goods are there *duly tendered* to the buyer. Remember, a tender is a conditional offer. Under UCC Section 2–503, tender of delivery demands that the seller, at a reasonable hour, put and hold conforming goods (i. e., goods in accord with the terms of the contract) at the buyer's disposal and provide the buyer with such notice and documents as are reasonably necessary to enable the buyer to take possession of the goods. Upon due tender, the risk of loss passes to the buyer—this is so whether or not the buyer takes actual delivery of the goods (as where the buyer is unwilling to accept delivery).

Sale contracts calling for shipment to the buyer by common carrier are presumed to be shipment and not destination contracts unless the contract expressly provides to the contrary. The fact that a seller is required to pay freight to the point of destination does not in and of itself make a contract a destination contract; nor does the fact that goods are to be delivered "C.O.D." (meaning "collect on delivery", with the buyer required to pay for the goods and their transportation before delivery will be made).

However, the use of other commercial shipment terms such as "F.O.B.", "F.A. S.", or "C.I.F." may be controlling as to whether a particular contract is a shipment or destination contract. Remember always that in a shipment contract, the risk of loss passes to the buyer upon due delivery of the goods to the carrier; in a destination contract, the risk of loss passes to the buyer upon due tender of delivery at the specified destination point.

F.O.B. The term "F.O.B.", standing for "free on board", is used as a delivery term rather than a price term. When the contract calls for the seller to ship the goods "F.O.B. place of shipment," the agreement is a shipment contract governed by U.C.C. Section 2–504, and the seller is required only to bear the risk and expense of putting the goods into the possession of the carrier; the seller is not obligated to bear the expense of loading. As in other shipment contracts, the risk of loss passes to the buyer once the goods are duly delivered to the carrier. So if the contract is "F.O.B. the seller's place of business" or "F.O.B. the seller's factory" or "F.O.B. Chicago (where Chicago is the point of shipment)", the contract is a shipment contract and the risk of loss passes to the buyer upon due delivery of the goods to the carrier.

In contrast, if the language used is "F.O.B. place of destination" (e. g., "F.O.B. buyer's place of business"), the contract is a destination contract, and the risk of loss does not pass to the buyer until the seller makes proper tender of delivery (as required by Section 2–503) at the destination point.

Section 2–319 of the Uniform Commercial Code states these rules as follows.

The UCC provides:

(1) Unless otherwise agreed the term F.O.B. (which means "free on board") at a named place, even though used only in connection with the stated price, is a delivery term under which

   (a) when the term is F.O.B. the place of shipment, the seller must at that place ship the goods in the manner provided in this Article (Section 2–504) and bear the expense and risk of putting them into the possession of the carrier; or

   (b) when the term is F.O.B. the place of destination, the seller must at his own expense and risk transport the goods to that place and there tender delivery of them in the manner provided in this Article (Section 2–503);

   (c) when under either (a) or (b) the term is also F.O.B. vessel, car or other vehicle, the seller must in addition at his own expense and risk load the goods on board. *   *   *

———

F.A.S. The letters "F.A.S." mean "free alongside" and are generally used in maritime shipping contracts (i. e., in contracts calling for the goods to be shipped over the water on oceangoing or other vessels). A seller who agrees to ship "F.A.S." must deliver the goods free of expense to the buyer alongside (on the dock next to) the vessel on which they are to be loaded (the buyer bears the expense of loading); the seller must there tender a receipt for the goods in exchange for which the carrier is under a duty to issue a bill of lading. The risk of loss passes to the buyer when the goods are duly delivered alongside the vessel. UCC Section 2–319(2) is the applicable provision.

The UCC provides:

(2) Unless otherwise agreed the term F.A.S. vessel (which means "free alongside") at a named port, even though used only in connection with the stated price, is a delivery term under which the seller must

   (a) at his own expense and risk deliver the goods alongside the vessel in the manner usual in that port or on a dock designated and provided by the buyer; and

   (b) obtain and tender a receipt for the goods in exchange for which the carrier is under a duty to issue a bill of lading.

———

C.I.F. and C. & F. "C.I.F." and "C. & F." contracts are also maritime shipment contracts. The letters "C.I.F." stand for "cost, insurance, and freight", the letters "C. & F." for "cost and freight". Under a "C.I.F." contract, the buyer promises to pay a price for the goods that includes not only the cost of the goods, but also all freight charges to the named destination, as well as all insurance costs in providing for safe delivery of the shipment. The seller, in turn, must at his or her own expense and risk put the goods into the possession of the carrier at the port of shipment; obtain negotiable bills of lading to cover their transportation to the named destination; have the goods loaded; pay the costs of loading; obtain a receipt from the carrier showing that the freight has been paid or provided for; obtain an appropriate certificate of insurance on behalf of and for the benefit of the buyer; prepare an invoice and procure any other necessary document and forward and tender the documents, properly indorsed, to the buyer. The risk of loss passes to the buyer upon due delivery of the goods to the carrier.

Under a "C. & F." contract, the buyer promises to pay a price including the cost of the goods and all freight charges to the named destination—the price does not include the cost of insurance. With the exception of duties relating to insurance, the seller has the same duties under a C. & F. contract that he or she has under a C.I.F. contract. Again, the risk of loss passes to the buyer upon due delivery of the goods to the carrier.

With regard to both C.I.F. and C. & F. contracts, when all proper documents, including the negotiable bill or bills of lading, have been tendered to the buyer, the buyer is obligated to pay the full purchase price of the goods though the goods themselves have not arrived. (Remember, a person in possession of a bearer bill or a properly indorsed order bill is a "person entitled" under the document.) In fact, a tender of the actual goods without a tender of the document would not constitute full performance by the seller and the buyer would not be obligated to accept or pay for the goods. (This is true in any case where documents are needed to take possession of the goods, whether the contract is F.A.S., F.O.B. vessel, etc.)

The above rules are provided by Section 2–320 of the Uniform Commercial Code as follows.

The UCC provides:

Section 2–320.　C.I.F. and C. & F. Terms

(1) The term C.I.F. means that the price includes in a lump sum the cost of the goods and the insurance and freight to the named destination. The term C. & F. or C.F. means that the price so includes cost and freight to the named destination.

(2) Unless otherwise agreed and even though used only in connection with the stated price and destination, the term C.I.F. destination or its equivalent requires the seller at his own expense and risk to

(a) put the goods into the possession of a carrier at the port for shipment and obtain a negotiable bill or bills of lading covering the entire transportation to the named destination; and

(b) load the goods and obtain a receipt from the carrier (which may be contained in the bill of lading) showing that the freight has been paid or provided for; and

(c) obtain a policy or certificate of insurance, including war risk insurance, of a kind and/on terms then current at the port of shipment in the usual amount, in the currency of the contract, shown to cover the same goods covered by the bill of lading and providing for payment of loss to the order of the buyer or for the account of whom it may concern; but the seller may add to the price the amount of the premium for any such war risk insurance; and

(d) prepare an invoice of the goods and procure any other documents required to effect shipment or to comply with the contract; and

(e) forward and tender with commercial promptness all the documents in due form and with any indorsement necessary to perfect the buyer's rights.

(3) Unless otherwise agreed the term C. & F. or its equivalent has the same effect and imposes upon the seller the same obligations and risks as a C.I.F. term except the obligation as to insurance.

(4) Under the term C.I.F. or C. & F. unless otherwise agreed the buyer must make payment against tender of the required documents and the seller may not tender nor the buyer demand delivery of the goods in substitution for the documents.

Ex-Ship. Finally, an "ex-ship" contract is a destination contract. A seller who agrees to deliver goods "ex-ship" agrees to bear full risk and expense until the goods leave the ship's tackle (i. e., until they are unloaded). The risk of loss passes to the buyer when the goods are unloaded. As always, the seller must furnish the buyer any documents that are required to enable the buyer to take possession of the goods. Uniform Commercial Code Section 2–322 is the relevant Code provision.

The UCC provides:

Section 2–322. Delivery "Ex-Ship"

(1) Unless otherwise agreed a term for delivery of goods "ex-ship" (which means from the carrying vessel) or in equivalent language is not restricted to a particular ship and requires delivery from a ship which has reached a place at the named port of destination where goods of the kind are usually discharged.

(2) Under such a term unless otherwise agreed

* * *

(b) the risk of loss does not pass to the buyer until the goods leave the ship's tackle or are otherwise properly unloaded.

---

(3) *Where the goods are in the possession of a bailee and are to be "delivered" to the buyer without being moved.*

Sometimes, the goods are in the possession of a bailee and are to be delivered into the buyer's ownership without being moved (i. e., after the sale is complete, the goods will still be in the bailee's possession, but will be owned by the buyer rather than by the seller). Section 2–509 of the Uniform Commercial Code provides that the risk of loss passes to the buyer in this situation, upon the buyer's receipt of any document of title covering the goods (usually, the goods are in the hands of a professional warehouseman and are covered by a warehouse receipt), or, if there is no document, upon the bailee's acknowledgment of the buyer's right to possession of the goods.

An exception arises where the seller himself or herself is the bailee. It is generally held that if the seller retains possession of the goods after the sale, Section 2–509 will not apply, and the risk of loss will pass according to the "usual" rule discussed in (1) above (i. e., upon delivery in the case of a merchant seller, or upon tender of delivery in the case of a nonmerchant seller).

(4) *Where the parties have made an agreement as to risk of loss.* Rules (a), (b), and (c) above may be altered by agreement of the parties. The *Official Comment* to Section 2–509 of the Code states in part that "the buyer and seller are left free to readjust their rights and risks as declared by this section in any manner agreeable to them."

Section 2–509 summarizes the risk of loss rules in the absence of breach of contract as follows.

The UCC provides:

Section 2–509. Risk of Loss in the Absence of Breach

(1) Where the contract requires or authorizes the seller to ship the goods by carrier

(a) if it does not require him to deliver them at a particular destination, the risk of loss passes to the buyer when the goods are duly delivered to the carrier even though the shipment is under reservation [i. e., even though the seller retains a security interest in the goods] but

(b) if it does require him to deliver them at a particular destination and the goods are there duly tendered while in the possession of the carrier, the risk of loss passes to the buyer when the goods are there duly so tendered as to enable the buyer to take delivery.

(2) Where the goods are held by a bailee to be delivered without being moved, the risk of loss passes to the buyer

(a) on his receipt of a negotiable document of title covering the goods; or

(b) on acknowledgment by the bailee of the buyer's right to possession of the goods; or

(c) after his receipt of a non-negotiable document of title or other written direction to deliver. . .

(3) In any case not within subsection (1) or (2), the risk of loss passes to the buyer on his receipt of the goods if the seller is a merchant; otherwise the risk passes to the buyer on tender of delivery.

(4) The provisions of this section are subject to contrary agreement of the parties and to the provisions of this Article on sale on approval and the effect of breach on risk of loss.

———

(5) *Where the goods are transferred in a "sale on approval" or a "sale or re-*

turn". In a *sale on approval*, goods are delivered to a buyer for a stated period of time, or, if no time is stated, for a reasonable time, during which the buyer may use the goods for the purpose of determining whether or not to purchase them. Ownership and risk of loss remain in the seller until the buyer accepts the goods. Generally, the buyer accepts by notifying the seller that he or she "approves" the sale. And the buyer will be deemed to accept if he or she fails to return the goods to the seller within a reasonable time (or to notify the seller of their return), or if he or she exercises dominion over the goods inconsistent with the purpose of determining approval (e. g., selling the goods to another). Upon acceptance, title and risk of loss pass to the buyer, and the buyer becomes liable for the purchase price of the goods.

In a *sale or return*, on the other hand, goods are delivered to a buyer who has an option to return them to the seller. Here, ownership and risk of loss pass to the buyer according to rules (1) through (4) above. However, in a sale or return, the buyer can revest ownership and risk of loss in the seller by returning the goods. The return is at the buyer's risk and expense.

The above rules are found at Section 2–327 of the Uniform Commercial Code.

The UCC provides:

Section 2–327. Special Incidents of Sale on Approval and Sale or Return

(1) Under a sale on approval unless otherwise agreed

(a) although the goods are identified to the contract the risk of loss and the title do not pass to the buyer until acceptance; and

(b) use of the goods consistent with the purpose of trial is not acceptance but failure seasonably to notify the seller of election to return the goods is acceptance, and if the goods conform to the contract acceptance of any part is acceptance of the whole; and

(c) after due notification of election to return, the return is at the seller's risk and expense but a merchant buyer must follow any reasonable instructions.

(2) Under a sale or return unless otherwise agreed

(a) the option to return extends to the whole or any commercial unit of the goods while in substantially their original condition, but must be exercised seasonably; and

(b) the return is at the buyer's risk and expense.

———

The *Official Comment* to Section 2–327 adds that "in the case of a sale on approval the risk rests on the seller until acceptance of the goods by the buyer, while in a sale or return the risk remains throughout on the buyer."

Sometimes, it is difficult to determine whether a particular contract is a sale on approval or a sale or return. To aid in such situations, Section 2–326 of the Uniform Commercial Code provides that if the goods are delivered primarily for the buyer's use, the transaction is a sale on approval, but if the goods are delivered primarily for resale by the buyer, the transaction is a sale or return. For example, in a "sale on consignment", a seller transfers goods to a buyer for purposes of resale; the seller purports to retain ownership of the goods and any goods that go unsold must be returned to the seller. Under Section 2–326, a sale on consignment is a sale or return (the goods are delivered primarily for resale by the buyer) and ownership and risk of loss pass to the buyer accordingly. (A sale on consignment is considered a sale or return primarily to protect creditors of the buyer who have no way of knowing that the goods "belong" to another.)

Section 2–326 provides:

Section 2–326. Sale on Approval and Sale or Return; Consignment Sales and Rights of Creditors

(1) Unless otherwise agreed, if delivered goods may be returned by the buyer even though they conform to the contract, the transaction is

(a) a "sale on approval" if the goods are delivered primarily for use, and

(b) a "sale or return" if the goods are delivered primarily for resale.

(2) Except as provided in subsection (3), goods held on approval are not subject to the claims of the buyer's creditors until acceptance; goods held on sale or return are subject to such claims while in the buyer's possession.

(3) Where goods are delivered to a person for sale and such person maintains a place of business at which he deals in goods of the kind involved, under a name other than the name of the person making delivery, then with respect to claims of creditors of the person conducting the business the goods are deemed to be on sale or return. The provisions of this subsection are applicable even though an agreement purports to reserve title to the person making delivery until payment or resale or uses such words as "on consignment" or "on memorandum." However, this subsection is not applicable if the person making delivery

(a) complies with an applicable law providing for a consignor's interest or the like to be evidenced by a sign, or

(b) establishes that the person conducting the business is generally known by his creditors to be substantially engaged in selling the goods of others, or

(c) complies with the filing provisions of the Article on Secured Transactions (Article 9) [see Ch. 27].

---

(6) *Where either the buyer or the seller has breached the contract of sale.* There are three situations where the risk of loss rules discussed in (1) through (5) above do not apply because one of the parties—either buyer or seller—has breached the contract of sale.

The first situation arises where the seller breaches the contract by sending *nonconforming* goods, and the buyer rejects the goods. Uniform Commercial Code Section 2–601 states in part that "if the goods or the tender of delivery fail in any respect to *conform* to the contract, the buyer may (a) reject the whole; or (b) accept the whole; or (c) accept any commercial unit or units and reject the rest." (Emphasis supplied.) And Section 2–106(2) of the Code states that goods or conduct, including any part of a performance, are "conforming" or "conform to the contract" when they are in accordance with the terms of or obligations under the contract; goods or conduct are nonconforming when they are not in accord with the terms of or obligations under the contract. Thus, in a shipment contract, if the seller puts goods in A–1 condition in the possession of the carrier, the goods conform to the contract (i. e., are in the condition contracted for) at the time the risk of loss passes to the buyer. The fact that the goods are later damaged or destroyed through no fault of the seller does not make the goods nonconforming (i. e., not in accord with the terms of the contract), and the buyer has no right to reject the goods upon receiving them in the spoiled or damaged state. On the other hand, if the goods deviate, however slightly, from the terms of the contract at the time the seller puts them in the carrier's possession, the goods are nonconforming, and the buyer has a right to reject them. As for the risk of loss, Uniform Commercial Code Section 2–510(1) states that "where a tender or delivery of goods so fails to conform to the contract as to give a right of rejection the risk of their loss remains on the seller until cure or acceptance." Thus, where goods are nonconforming, the risk of loss remains in the seller until he or she "cures" the nonconformity by sending conforming goods (the seller's right to "cure" is discussed in detail in Ch. 18), or until the buyer accepts the nonconforming goods (the buyer, in this case, may set off a reasonable amount from the purchase price, or may pay the full purchase price and sue the seller for breach of contract of sale).

The second situation occurs where the seller breaches the contract by sending nonconforming goods, and the buyer accepts the goods before discovering the nonconformity. If the nonconformity is "substantial" (i. e., if it substantially impairs the value of the goods to the buyer), the buyer may upon discovering it revoke his or her acceptance under UCC Section 2–608 and treat the risk of loss as being in the seller to the extent that the buyer does not have insurance covering the loss. For example, suppose that auto manufacturer Paula Pontiac agrees to sell ten cars to auto retailer Junior Samples. The cars arrive in apparently good order, and Junior accepts the cars. However, as it turns out, each car has 100 minor defects that "substantially" impair the value of the cars to Junior. Upon discovering the defects, Junior can revoke his acceptance. It follows that if the cars are destroyed in Junior's parking lot by an unexpected flood, Junior can treat the risk of loss as being in Paula Pontiac to the extent that Junior has no insurance coverage for the loss. As Section 2–510(2) states: "Where the buyer rightfully revokes acceptance he may to the extent of any deficiency in his effective insurance coverage treat the risk of loss as having rested on the seller from the beginning."

However, it should be realized that the buyer must notify the seller of his or her intention to revoke within a reasonable time after discovering the nonconformity. If the buyer unreasonably delays in notifying the seller and continues to use the goods, the buyer will lose the right to revoke.

The third and final situation arises where the buyer *wrongfully* repudiates or otherwise breaches the contract of sale after the goods have been identified to the contract, but before the risk of loss has passed to the buyer. To the extent that the seller is uninsured for loss or damage to the property, the seller may treat the risk of loss as being in the buyer for a "commercially reasonable time" after the repudiation or other breach.

Uniform Commercial Code Section 2–510(3) provides.

Where the buyer as to conforming goods already identified to the contract for sale repudiates or is otherwise in breach before risk of their loss has passed to him, the seller may to the extent of any deficiency in his effective insurance coverage treat the risk of loss as resting on the buyer for a commercially reasonable time.

——————

Assume, for example, that Paula Pontiac has the ten cars ready for shipment to Junior Samples. The day prior to ship-

ment, Junior wrongfully repudiates the contract by informing Paula that he will not accept or pay for the cars. That night the cars are destroyed in Paula's parking lot by an unexpected flood. Though the risk of loss has not yet passed to Junior Samples (the cars have not been delivered to the carrier), Paula can treat the risk of loss as being in Junior to the extent that Paula's insurance does not cover the loss.

Now suppose that the cars are destroyed by flood, not on the night of Junior's wrongful repudiation, but six months later. Six months is not a "commercially reasonable time" as prescribed by Section 2–510(3), and Junior will not be liable for any part of the loss.

To summarize the rules as to risk of loss:

(1) Usually, there is no carrier or other bailee involved, and the parties have made no agreement as to risk of loss. In this situation, the risk of loss passes to the buyer upon delivery of the goods, in the case of a merchant seller, and upon tender of the goods, in the case of a nonmerchant seller.

(2) Sometimes, the goods are to be shipped to the buyer by common carrier. In a shipment contract (e. g., "C.O.D.", "F.O.B. place of shipment", "C.I.F.", "C. & F.", etc.), the risk of loss passes to the buyer upon due delivery of the goods to the carrier; in a destination contract (e. g., "F.O.B. destination"), the risk of loss passes to the buyer upon due tender of the goods to the buyer at the point of destination. "F.A.S." is a shipment contract with the risk of loss passing to the buyer when the goods are delivered alongside the vessel. "Ex ship" is a destination contract with the risk of loss passing to the buyer when the goods are unloaded.

(3) Sometimes, goods in the possession of a bailee are to be delivered to the

buyer without being moved. The risk of loss passes to the buyer upon his or her receipt of the document of title covering the goods, or, if there is no document, upon the bailee's acknowledgment of the buyer's right to possession.

(4) Rules (1) through (4) may be altered by agreement of the parties.

(5) In a "sale on approval" (where the goods are delivered primarily for the buyer's use), the risk of loss remains in the seller until the buyer gives approval. In a "sale or return" (where the goods are delivered primarily for resale by the buyer), the risk of loss passes to the buyer according to rules (1) through (4) above; the risk of loss revests in the seller upon return of the goods unsold to him or her.

(6) The above rules as to risk of loss do not apply where the buyer or seller breaches the contract as follows. *First,* if the seller breaches by sending nonconforming goods, and the buyer rejects the goods, the risk of loss remains in the seller. *Second,* if the seller sends substantially nonconforming goods, and the buyer accepts the goods before discovering the nonconformity, the buyer may revoke his or her acceptance and treat the risk of loss as being in the seller to the extent that the buyer does not have insurance covering the loss. *Third,* if the buyer wrongfully repudiates or otherwise breaches the contract before the risk of loss has passed to him or her, the seller may treat the risk of loss as being in the buyer (to the extent that the seller is uninsured) for a commercially reasonable time.

CASES

CASE 1—*The "special property" interest.*

DRAPER v. MINNEAPOLIS–MOLINE, INC.

Appellate Court of Illinois, Third District, 1968.
100 Ill.App.2d 324, 241 N.E.2d 342.

CULBERTSON, Justice.

This appeal presents questions concerning the Uniform Commercial Code, * * * and stems from a judgment entered in favor of the plaintiff, Robert Draper, against the defendant, Minneapolis-Moline, Inc., * * *.

On December 30, 1966, plaintiff entered into a written contract with Larry Meiners, a farm equipment dealer who handled defendant's products, for the purchase of a new Minneapolis-Moline tractor and a new six bottom plow for use on plaintiff's farm. By the terms of the contract various extras, including a cab and radio, were to be installed on the tractor by the dealer; plaintiff was to trade in an old tractor and an old plow; and delivery was to be "by" April 1, 1967. The net purchase price of $5,300.00 was to be paid on delivery. Subsequently, on a date not entirely clear from the record, the old and the new plows were exchanged but nothing was paid on the contract.

At the time the contract was entered into, the dealer did not have the required tractor in stock, but received one from defendant on or about January 26, 1967. This machine was delivered under * * * agreement * * * which gave Meiners the right to sell the tractor at retail in the ordinary course of business, and provided that * * * the machine could be repossessed if the dealer defaulted in the terms for payment.

Shortly after the dealer received the machine, plaintiff came to the store and was shown the tractor and was told that it was his. At the trial plaintiff recalled that the last three digits of the serial number on the tractor shown to him were "804," and this coincided with the number shown on the purchase agreement between the dealer and defendant. The dealer had not as yet received the cab called for by the contract and this appears to have delayed delivery of the tractor to the plaintiff. On one occasion, apparently in February, 1967, the dealer offered to let plaintiff take the tractor without the cab but plaintiff refused the offer.

During the last week of February, 1967, the completion of a routine audit disclosed the dealer to be greatly in arrears for substantial sums of money owed to defendant. When it became apparent that he was not financially able to correct or alleviate the situation, defendant repossessed all of its products on the store premises for which it had not been paid, including the tractor plaintiff had been told would be delivered to him under his contract. At the time plaintiff had neither turned in his old tractor nor had he paid anything to the dealer. Plaintiff then negotiated directly with defendant to complete the deal, but the negotiations fell through because defendant, as a manufacturer, was in no position to accept a trade-in or to provide and install the contract extras. It is undisputed that plaintiff thereafter did his spring plowing with his old tractor, and that he incurred expenses of $396.70 he would not have had if the new tractor had been available to him. This action against defendant for damages soon followed.

The authority for plaintiff's action is found in Section 2–722 of Article 2 of the Uniform Commercial Code which, in substance, gives to one having a special property interest in goods a right of action against a third party who "so deals with goods which have been identified to a contract for sale as to cause actionable injury to a party to that contract." The quoted language, we believe, intends that a third party would be liable for conversion, physical damage to the goods, or interference with the rights of a buyer in the goods. Section 2–103(1)(a) of Article 2 states that in such Article: " 'Buyer' means a person who buys *or contracts to buy goods,*" and it is thereafter provided in Section 2–501(1) in pertinent part:

> "The buyer obtains a special property and an insurable interest in goods by identification of existing goods as goods to which the contract refers *even though the goods so identified are non-conforming* and he has an option to return or reject them. Such identification can be made at any time and in any manner explicitly agreed to by the parties. In the absence of explicit agreement identification occurs
>
>   (b) if the contract is for the sale of future goods * * * when goods are shipped, marked or otherwise designated by the seller as goods to which the contract refers.

While defendant makes a mild argument that the tractor did not conform to the contract because the extras had not been installed when it was pointed out by the dealer, we think it manifest from the evidence that there was a complete and sufficient identification of the tractor to the contract within the purview of Section 2–501(1). It is apparent, too, that defendant's conduct made it impossible for the dealer to deliver the tractor to plaintiff, and that defendant so dealt with the goods as to interfere with plaintiff's special property interest.

* * *

* * * [J]udgment * * * affirmed * * * for the plaintiff in the amount of $396.70.

CASE 2—*The Revel Craft Playmate Yacht was destroyed by fire.*

HAYWARD v. POSTMA

Court of Appeals of Michigan, Div. 3, 1971.
31 Mich.App. 720, 188 N.W.2d 31.

V. J. BRENNAN, Judge.

From a judgment in favor of the plaintiff buyer in an action to determine risk of loss under a sales contract, defendant appeals.

On February 7, 1967, the plaintiff agreed to purchase a 30-foot Revel Craft Playmate Yacht for $10,000. The total purchase price included a number of options which the dealer was to install after he received the boat from the manufacturer. The parties agreed that defendant would deliver the boat to a slip on Lake Macatawa in or about April, 1967.

On March 1, 1967, shortly after the boat arrived at the dealer's showroom, plaintiff executed a security agreement in favor of the defendant seller along with a promissory note in the amount of $13,095.60. The note was subsequently assigned to Michigan National Bank. Clauses 7 and 8 of the security agreement provided:

"(7) Buyer will at all times keep the Goods in first class order and repair, excepting any loss, damage or destruction which is fully covered by proceeds of insurance;

"(8) Buyer will at all times keep the Goods fully insured against loss, damage, theft and other risks, in such amounts and companies and under such policies * * * satisfactory to the secured party, which policies shall specifically provide that loss thereunder shall be payable to the secured party as its interest may appear * * *."

In April of 1967, prior to delivery of the boat, a fire on defendant's premises destroyed part of his inventory of boats including the Revel Craft Playmate. Neither party had obtained insurance although both the seller and the buyer had an insurable interest in the boat. Plaintiff requested the defendant to pay off the promissory note or reimburse him for payments made, and when he refused, the plaintiff started suit in Kent county circuit court. The lower court held that the seller bore the risk of loss and entered judgment for plaintiff.

There is little dispute as to the facts of this case; the entire controversy centers around a single provision of the Uniform Commercial Code. Under the Code, risk of loss is no longer determined by which party has title to the goods at the time of the loss. It is determined, instead, by rules in the Code covering specific fact situations independent of title. The question of risk of loss in the absence of breach of the sale contract is covered in § 2509 which provides in subsection (3):

> "* * * risk of loss passes to the buyer on his receipt of the goods if the seller is a merchant; otherwise the risk passes to the buyer on tender of delivery."

But for the next subsection of the Code, the solution to this case would be clear, since it is undisputed that the seller was a merchant and that the buyer had not received the goods.

The Code further provides at § 2509(4) that:

> "The provisions of this section are subject to contrary agreement of the parties and to the provisions of this article on sale on approval (section 2327) and on effect of breach on risk of loss (section 2510)."

It is the seller's claim that clause 8, supra, in the security agreement declaring that the buyer must "at all times keep the Goods fully insured" is equivalent to a contrary agreement of the parties. We do not agree.

The general approach of Article 2 of the code is that freedom of contract prevails; the greater part of it is concerned with detailing what happens where the contract is silent on a particular point. Such is the purpose of § 2509(3). This provision was meant to cover the common situation where parties have not agreed on who shall bear the risk of loss. In deciding that the seller should bear the risk of loss while the goods are still in his hands, the drafters give the following explanation in Code Comment # 3:

> "The underlying theory of this rule is that a merchant who is to make physical delivery at his own place continues meanwhile to control the goods and can be expected to insure his interest in them. The buyer, on the other hand, has no control of the goods and it is *extremely unlikely* that he will carry insurance on goods not yet in his possession." (Emphasis supplied.)

The code drafters correctly observe that it would be highly unusual for the average consumer to carry insurance on an item of personal property weeks or even months before it is delivered to him. The question in our case, then, is whether boilerplate language in a security agreement to the effect that the buyer agrees to keep the goods insured at all times is sufficient to apprise the buyer that he bears the risk of loss on goods he has contracted for, but has not yet received. We think not.

On the contrary, we feel that a contract which shifts the risk of loss to the buyer before he receives the goods is so unusual that a seller who wants to achieve this result must make his intent very clear to the buyer. Fine print in a security agreement concerning insurance does not achieve this result. Clause 8 is entirely vague when it states that insurance is to be carried "at all times. " Common experience would dictate that the words "at all times" mean "at all times after one gets possession." This interpretation of the clause is borne out if we consider the language immediately preceding it:

> "(7) Buyer will at all times keep the Goods in first class order and repair, excepting any loss, damage or destruction which is fully covered by proceeds of insurance; "

Clause 7, including its mention of insurance which is later expanded upon in clause 8, apparently assumes that the buyer (debtor) is in possession of the collateral. One cannot keep in repair what he does not have. Finally, risk of loss is nowhere mentioned in clause 8, and under the circumstances it cannot readily be inferred. We, therefore, hold that the parties to this contract had not agreed that the buyer would bear the risk of loss prior to his receipt of the goods and that the seller bears the loss under § 2509(3).

      *   *   *

We do not mean to say that parties may not validly agree on who bears the risk of loss; rather, we hold that if they intend to shift that burden to the buyer before his receipt of the goods, they must do so in clear and unequivocal language.

For the foregoing reasons, the judgment of the lower court is affirmed.

Affirmed.

PROBLEMS

1. Answer the following "True" or "False" and give reasons for your answers:

  (a) In a "no arrival, no sale" contract, the seller has an option not to ship the goods.

  (b) Sales contracts calling for shipment to the buyer by common carrier are presumed to be shipment and not destination contracts unless the contract expressly provides to the contrary.

  (c) In a "sale or return", the buyer has an option to return the goods to the seller.

  (d) If the place of delivery is not specified in a sale of goods, the transaction will fail for lack of definiteness.

  (e) The buyer's "special property and insurable interest" is far less than the complete ownership of the goods that the buyer will acquire upon completion of the sale.

  (f) The general rule is that risk of loss passes to the buyer at the same time as title passes to him or her.

  (g) An "ex-ship" contract is a shipment contract.

  (h) A sale on consignment is considered to be a sale on approval.

  (i) CIF and C&F contracts are shipment contracts.

  (j) If goods being sold under a "no arrival, no sale" contract are partially lost or damaged without fault of the parties, the buyer has the right to inspect the goods and either avoid the agreement or take the remaining goods with a reduction in purchase price.

2. Debra Warren contracts in writing to purchase two prize-winning, registered Hereford bulls from Hank Turner, a Texas rancher. By the terms of the contract, Hank must ship the bulls "F.O.B. Pendleton, Oregon" where Debra owns a cattle ranch. Hank ships the two registered bulls via West Central Railroad; he procures a negotiable bill of lading covering the animals from the Railroad and forwards it to Debra in Oregon. While the West Central train carrying the bulls is passing through Utah, an unexpected flashflood causes the train to derail, and one of the bulls is killed (the other escapes injury).

  (a) As between Debra and Hank, who bears the risk of loss regarding the bulls during the shipment to Oregon? Explain.

(b) Following the derailment, what are Debra's rights, if any, against Hank Turner? Explain fully.

(c) How would your answers to (a) and (b) differ if the contract had called for shipment "F.O.B. Dallas, Texas"?

3. Jack Buell, a radio dealer in Miami, Florida telephones radio manufacturer Ron Fletcher in Detroit, Michigan on June 1st and orders 500 Z–Mac radios at a cost of $10,000, the radios to be shipped to Jack in September "F.O.B. Central Atlantic Railroad, Detroit, Michigan". On June 5th, Ron sends the following note to Jack:

DEAR JACK:

This is to confirm that per our agreement of June 1st, I will ship 500 radios to you in September via the Central Atlantic Railroad, the total contract price for the radios to be $10,000.

Yours truly,

Ron Fletcher

Jack does not respond to the note. In September, Ron delivers the 500 Z–Mac radios to the carrier and obtains a negotiable bill of lading from the Railroad which he forwards to Jack in Miami. The carrier, however, is negligent in loading the radios, and more than half of them arrive in Miami in a damaged condition.

(a) As between Jack and Ron, who bears the risk of loss regarding the radios during shipment to Miami? Explain. Would your answer differ if Ron had shipped 500 T–Mac radios instead of the Z–Mac models ordered by Jack? Explain.

(b) Assuming Jack bears the risk of loss, can he avoid paying for the radios because (to quote him) "the contract is oral and therefore unenforceable"? Explain.

(c) Suppose that Jack orders the radios because he needs them for the Christmas trade and cannot obtain them elsewhere. The contract calls for Ron to deliver the radios "F.O.B. Miami, Florida". What action can Jack take even before the radios leave Detroit to protect himself from the possibility of loss or destruction of the radios during shipment?

4. As between the buyer and the seller, who must bear the loss in each of the following situations:

(a) Peggy Newman contracts to purchase a baby grand piano from Overmyer's Music Shop. The store's delivery truck arrives at Peggy's home on Saturday and employees of the store attempt to deliver the piano. Though the piano is conforming in all respects, Peggy refuses delivery. The delivery truck is involved in an accident on its way back to the store, and the piano is destroyed.

(b) David Bushey contracts to purchase Alan Jensen's old snow skis. As per the terms of the contract, Alan brings the skis over to David's house and attempts to deliver them. However, David is not home at the time so Alan takes the skis back home with him. That night, a fire breaks out in Alan's garage, and the skis, which are stored there, are totally destroyed.

(c) Retailer Marian McKinney contracts to purchase 150 occasional chairs from Comfort Furniture, Inc., the chairs to be shipped to Marian "F.A.S. The Voyager". Comfort Furniture delivers the chairs alongside "The Voyager" and the crew of the ship begins to *Buyer* load the goods. The crew is careless in loading and some of the chairs are damaged.

(d) Again, Marian McKinney contracts to purchase 150 occasional chairs from Comfort Furniture. This time, however, the chairs *Buyer* are in the possession of Waterman Storage Company, and Comfort Furniture merely delivers to Marian a negotiable warehouse receipt covering the chairs. After Marian receives the receipt, but before she notifies the Storage Company of her right to the chairs, the chairs are destroyed in a warehouse explosion.

5. In connection with risk and expense associated with the delivery of goods to a destination under a sales contract, the term "F.O.B. place of destination" means that

    a. The seller bears the risk and expense.

    b. The buyer bears the risk and expense.

    c. The seller bears the risk but *not* the expense.

    d. The buyer bears the risk but *not* the expense.

    [# 47, May 1977 CPA Exam]

6. In connection with a contract for the sale of goods, the term "C.I.F." means that the price includes

    a. The cost of the goods exclusive of insurance and freight.

    b. The cost of the goods plus freight but exclusive of insurance.

    c. The cost of the goods plus insurance but exclusive of freight.

    d. The cost of the goods, freight, and insurance.

    [# 48, May 1977 CPA Exam]

7. An oral contract for the sale of goods for a price in excess of $500 is enforceable by the seller if

    a. The goods are generally suitable for sale to others in the ordinary course of the seller's business.

    b. The buyer admits in court that the contract was made.

    c. Payment has not yet been made by the buyer.

    d. The goods have been received but *not* accepted by the buyer.

    [# 3, November 1975 CPA Exam]

8. Under a contract for sale on approval, unless otherwise agreed, what happens to "risk of loss" and "title" upon delivery to the buyer?

    a. Risk of loss but *not* title passes to buyer.

    b. Title but *not* risk of loss passes to buyer.

    c. Risk of loss and title pass to buyer.

    d. *Neither* risk of loss *nor* title pass to buyer.

    [# 42, May 1977 CPA Exam]

9. Wexford Furniture, Inc., is in the retail furniture business and has stores located in principal cities in the United States. Its designers created a unique cocktail table. After obtaining prices and schedules, Wexford ordered 2,000 tables to be made to its design and specifications for sale as a part of its annual spring sales promotion campaign.

Which of the following represents the earliest time Wexford will have an insurable interest in the tables?

a.   At the time the goods are in Wexford's possession.

b.   Upon shipment of conforming goods by the seller.

c.   When the goods are marked or otherwise designated by the seller as the goods to which the contract refers.

d.   At the time the contract is made.

[# 14, May 1978 CPA Exam]

10.   On July 14, 1976, Seeley Corp. entered into a written agreement to sell to Boone Corp. 1,200 cartons of certain goods at $.40 per carton, delivery within 30 days. The agreement contained no other terms. On July 15, 1976, Boone and Seeley orally agreed to modify their July 14 agreement so that the new quantity specified was 1,500 cartons, same price and delivery terms. What is the status of this modification?

a.   Enforceable.

b.   Unenforceable under the statute of frauds.

c.   Unenforceable for lack of consideration.

d.   Unenforceable because the change is substantial.

[# 43, May 1977 CPA Exam]

Chapter 18

THE RIGHTS OF THE BUYER AND SELLER WHEN THE SALES CONTRACT IS BREACHED

What are the rights of the nonbreaching party when either the buyer or seller refuses to perform his or her part of the sales contract?

Each year, countless millions of sales transactions go without a "hitch" (i. e., the sales agreement is made and the goods are transferred to the buyer without problem). Sometimes, however, an "event" or "situation" occurs that disrupts the normal sales transaction—it is then that the special sales laws provided by the Uniform Commercial Code come into play. Thus, in Ch. 17, we saw that the goods which are the subject matter of the sales contract may be lost, damaged, or destroyed before the sales transaction is completed. Where this "disrupting event" takes place (and there are many possible fact situations), the Uniform Commercial Code rules as to risk of loss are controlling.

Or, as we will see in this chapter, one of the parties—either buyer or seller—may refuse to carry out his or her part of the sales agreement. Section 2–301 of the Uniform Commercial Code, entitled, "General Obligations of Parties", states that "the [basic] obligation of the seller is to *transfer and deliver* [the goods] and that of the buyer is to *accept and pay* [for the goods] in accordance with the contract." (Emphasis added.) Yet, sometimes, the seller fails to "transfer and deliver" the goods, or the buyer fails to "accept and pay" for them. Does the party's failure to perform constitute a breach of contract? If so, what are the nonbreaching party's remedies? In this chapter, we will answer both questions, again according to the specific disrupting situation or event.

What are the seller's rights, if any, in the event that the buyer refuses to accept or pay for the goods unless he or she is first allowed to inspect them?

In almost all cases, the buyer has a right to inspect the goods prior to accepting or paying for them—the seller has no basis for objection if the buyer refuses to accept or pay until inspection is made. The Uniform Commercial Code at Section 2–513 provides that the buyer may inspect the goods at any reasonable time and place, and in any reasonable manner, either before or after delivery. However, if the buyer fails to inspect within a reasonable time after receipt of the goods, the buyer will lose the right to inspect. Sometimes, it is impossible to tell from a mere visual inspection (by simply looking at the goods) whether the goods are conforming or nonconforming. The buyer, in this case, also has a right to test a reasonable amount of the goods in any manner reasonable under the circumstances. The expenses of inspection must be borne by the buyer; however, he or she can recover the expenses from the seller if the goods do not conform and the buyer rejects them.

On occasion, the buyer is obligated under the terms of the contract to pay for the goods upon receipt of the shipping documents (as opposed to receipt of the goods themselves). This is referred to as "paying against documents of title"— usually, bills of lading. The buyer, in this situation, generally has no right to demand inspection of the goods prior to making payment: this makes sense as the shipping documents commonly arrive and are tendered to the buyer while the goods are still in transit. However, if the goods, by the terms of the contract, are to be "available for inspection" at the time the payment falls due, the buyer will have a right to inspect before making payment.

Similarly, in a "C.O.D." contract (meaning "collect on delivery"), the buyer has no right of inspection prior to payment unless the agreement expressly provides for such a right.

Nor does a buyer who is obligated to pay "against documents" or "C.O.D." have any right to possession of the goods prior to making payment in full. However, payment under these circumstances does not constitute acceptance of the goods, and if the goods turn out to be nonconforming, the buyer may still reject them and recover from the seller any payment made along with damages incurred.

The Uniform Commercial Code provides for the buyer's right to inspect at Section 2–513 as follows.

The UCC provides:

Section 2–513. Buyer's Right to Inspection of Goods

(1) Unless otherwise agreed and subject to subsection (3), where goods are tendered or delivered or identified to the contract for sale, the buyer has a right before payment or acceptance to inspect them at any reasonable place and time and in any reasonable manner. When the seller is required or authorized to send the goods to the buyer, the inspection may be after their arrival.

(2) Expenses of inspection must be borne by the buyer but may be recovered from the seller if the goods do not conform and are rejected.

(3) Unless otherwise agreed * * * the buyer is not entitled to inspect the goods before payment of the price when the contract provides

(a) for delivery "C.O.D." or on other like terms; or

(b) for payment against documents of title, except where such payment is due only after the goods are to become available for inspection.

(4) A place or method of inspection fixed by the parties is presumed to be exclusive but unless otherwise expressly agreed it does not postpone identification or shift the place for delivery or for passing the risk of loss. If compliance becomes impossible, inspection shall be as provided in this section unless the place or method fixed was clearly intended as an indispensable condition failure of which avoids the contract.

The *Official Comment* to Section 2–513 adds by way of explanation.

* * *

3. The buyer may exercise his right of inspection at any reasonable time or place and in any reasonable manner. It is not necessary that he select the most appropriate time, place, or manner to inspect or that his selection be the customary one in the trade or locality. Any reasonable time, place or manner is available to him and the reasonableness will be determined by trade usages, past practices between the parties and the other circumstances of the case. * * *

4. Expenses of an inspection made to satisfy the buyer of the seller's performance must be assumed by the buyer in the first instance. Since the rule provides merely for an allocation of expense there is no policy to prevent the parties from providing otherwise in the agreement. Where the buyer

would normally bear the expenses of the inspection but the goods are rightly demonstrable and reasonable costs of the inspection are part of his incidental damage caused by the seller's breach.

* * *

5. In the case of payment against documents, subsection (3) requires payment before inspection, since shipping documents against which payment is to be made will commonly arrive and be tendered while the goods are still in transit. This Article recognizes no exception in any peculiar case in which the goods happen to arrive before the documents. However, whereby the agreement payment is to await the arrival of the goods, inspection before payment becomes proper since the goods are then "available for inspection."

* * *

6. Under subsection (4) an agreed place or method of inspection is generally held to be intended as exclusive. However, where compliance with such an agreed inspection term becomes impossible, the question is basically one of intention. If the parties clearly intend that the method of inspection named is to be a necessary condition without which the entire deal is to fail, the contract is at an end if that method becomes impossible. On the other hand, if the parties merely seek to indicate a convenient and reliable method but do not intend to give up the deal in the event of its failure, any reasonable method of inspection may be substituted under this Article.

What are the buyer's rights, if any, in the event that the seller fails to perform his or her part of the sales bargain?

Sometimes, the seller does not properly perform his or her part of the sales bargain (i. e., does not carry out his or her primary duty to transfer and deliver the goods). For example, the seller may send nonconforming goods to the buyer or no goods at all. The seller may partially perform, then become insolvent (financially unable to perform) and stop performing. Or the seller may repudiate the contract by informing the buyer in advance that he or she will not perform. Assuming that it is neither objectively impossible nor commercially impracticable for the seller to perform (as you will recall from Ch. 17, UCC Section 2–615 excuses the seller from any performance that is objectively impossible or commercially impracticable), the seller's failure to "transfer and deliver" the goods as promised constitutes a breach of contract, and the buyer has recourse to one or more legal remedies depending on the specific circumstances of the breach (default).

The possible circumstances ("disrupting events") of the seller's breach include:

(1) The seller delivers nonconforming goods to the buyer;

(2) The seller becomes insolvent and cannot perform;

(3) The seller simply fails to deliver the goods;

(4) He or she repudiates the contract. Depending on the specific circumstance or event of breach, the buyer will have one or more of the following legal remedies:

(1) Rejection of the goods (as opposed to acceptance);

(2) Revocation of acceptance;

(3) Sale of the goods to recover pre-payments made on the purchase price;

(4) Cover (the purchase of substitute goods);

(5) Action in court for breach of warranty;

(6) Set-off (deduction from the purchase price for damages incurred);

(7) Capture (obtaining the identified goods from the seller without going to court);

(8) Action in court for money damages;

(9) Possessory action in court to obtain the goods, such as replevin or specific performance.

In the remainder of this section, we will discuss each possible circumstance of the seller's breach along with the buyer's legal remedies in each situation.

The Circumstance of the Seller Sending Nonconforming Goods

(1) *The buyer's right to reject the goods.* As stated in Ch. 17, UCC Section 2–601 provides that "if the goods or the tender of delivery fail *in any respect to conform* to the contract, the buyer may * * * reject the whole * * * or * * * accept any commercial unit and reject the rest." (Emphasis supplied.) You will recall that "to conform" means to be in accordance with the terms of the contract: UCC Section 2–106 states that "goods conform to the contract when they are in accordance with the obligations under the contract." Thus, if the goods sent by the seller are not in accordance with the terms of or obligations under the contract, the buyer may reject the goods—that is, refuse to keep them. The buyer must notify the seller of his or her decision to reject within a reasonable time after delivery or tender of the goods. As UCC Section 2–602(1) states: "Rejection of goods must be within a reasonable time after their delivery or tender. It is ineffective unless the buyer seasonably notifies the seller." And the notification must be specific: the buyer must disclose the nature of the defect if it is curable (the seller's right to cure is discussed hereafter) or he or she will be barred from asserting the defect as a reason for rejecting the goods.

UCC Section 2–605 states:

Section 2–605. Waiver of Buyer's Objections by Failure to Particularize

(1) The buyer's failure to state in connection with rejection a particular defect which is ascertainable by reasonable inspection precludes him from relying on the unstated defect to justify rejection or to establish breach

(a) where the seller could have cured it if stated seasonably; or

(b) between merchants when the seller has after rejection made a request in writing for a full and final written statement of all defects on which the buyer proposes to rely.

* * *

_____

The buyer who rejects all the goods tendered or delivered because all or part of the goods are nonconforming, in effect, cancels (i. e., puts an end to) the contract of sale. This is a significant remedy in that the buyer is freed from all obligation under the contract and may recover from the seller any part of the purchase price paid along with any damages incurred by reason of the nonconforming delivery. For example, suppose that New England Produce Company orders 2,000 crates of Grade A apples from Hood River Apple Company. When the apples arrive, 25 of the crates contain Grade C apples. Under Section 2–601, New England Produce can rightfully reject the entire shipment. If the market price for Grade A apples has fallen since the time of contracting, New England Produce may be able to save hundreds of dollars by buying the apples elsewhere in the market. On the other hand, if the market price of Grade A apples has substantially increased, the buyer will be better off accepting the 1,975 crates of conforming apples and rejecting only the 25 nonconforming crates. The buyer who accepts part of the goods and rejects the rest "cancels" only a portion of the contract; the buyer may "set-off" (i. e., deduct) from the purchase price owing on the accepted goods any damages incurred by reason of the nonconformity. The buyer's right to "set-off" is provided by Section 2–717 of the Uniform Commercial Code:

The UCC provides:

Section 2–717. Deduction of Damages from the Price

The buyer on notifying seller of his intention to do so may deduct all or any part of the damages resulting from any breach of contract from any part of the price due under the same contract.

_____

The Official Comment to the Section states:

1. This section permits the buyer to deduct from the price damages resulting from any breach by the seller and does not limit the relief to cases of breach of warranty [the buyer's right to accept the nonconforming goods and sue for breach of warranty is discussed later in the section] * * *

2. The buyer, however, must give notice of his intention to withhold all or part of the price * * *.

No formality of notice is required and any language which reasonably indicates the buyer's reason for holding up his payment is sufficient.

_____

Thus, the remedy of "set-off" applies any time a buyer owing money under a contract of sale suffers damages by reason of the seller's breach of contract.

Generally, delivery of the goods means delivery in a single lot; any other manner of delivery will be nonconforming, giving the buyer a right of rejection.

UCC Section 2–307 provides:

Section 2–307. Delivery in Single Lot or Several Lots

Unless otherwise agreed all goods called for by a contract for sale must be tendered in a single delivery and payment is due only on such tender but where the circumstances give either party the right to make or demand delivery in lots the price if it can be apportioned may be demanded for each lot.

_____

And the Official Comment to the Section provides:

* * * The "but" clause of this section goes to the case in which it is not commercially feasible to deliver or to receive the goods in a single lot as for example, where a contract calls for the shipment of ten carloads of coal and only three cars are available at a given time. Similarly, in a contract involving brick necessary to build a building the buyer's storage space may be limited so that it would be impossible to receive the entire amount of brick at once. * * *

In such cases, a partial delivery is not subject to rejection for the defect in quantity alone. * * * However, in such cases the undelivered balance of goods under the contract must

be forthcoming within a reasonable time and in a reasonable manner.
* * *

The buyer who rejects goods may have certain duties with regard to the goods. If, prior to rejection, the buyer has taken physical possession of the goods, the buyer must exercise reasonable care over the property for a time sufficient for the seller to remove the goods. UCC Section 2–602(b) states: "If the buyer has before rejection taken physical possession of goods * * * he is under a duty after rejection to hold them with reasonable care at the seller's disposition for a time sufficient to permit the seller to remove them. * * *" If the buyer is a merchant, and the seller has no business representative or place of business at the place of rejection, the buyer must follow the seller's reasonable instructions with regard to the goods, and, in the absence of such instructions, must sell the goods for the seller's account if they are "perishable or threaten to decline in value speedily." Of course, the buyer may deduct from the sales proceeds or otherwise collect from the seller his or her expenses in caring for and selling the goods. Section 2–603 is the relevant Code provision.

The UCC provides:

Section 2–603. Merchant Buyer's Duties as to Rightfully Rejected Goods

(1) * * * [W]hen the seller has no agent or place of business at the market of rejection a merchant buyer is under a duty after rejection of goods in his possession or control to follow any reasonable instructions received from the seller with respect to the goods and in the absence of such instruction to make reasonable efforts to sell them for the seller's

account if they are perishable or threaten to decline in value speedily. Instructions are not reasonable if on demand indemnity for expenses is not forthcoming.

(2) When the buyer sells goods under subsection (1), he is entitled to reimbursement from the seller or out of the proceeds for reasonable expenses of caring for and selling them, and if the expenses include no selling commission then to such commission as is usual in the trade or if there is none to a reasonable sum not exceeding ten per cent on the gross proceeds.

(3) In complying with this section the buyer is held only to good faith and good faith conduct hereunder is neither acceptance nor conversion nor the basis of an action for damages.

The buyer's right to reject nonconforming goods is subject to modification by agreement of the parties.

Section 2–719 of the UCC provides:

(1) * * * (a) The agreement may provide for remedies in addition to or in substitution for those provided in this Article and may limit or alter the measure of damages recoverable under this Article, as by limiting the buyer's remedies to return of the goods and repayment of the price or to repair and replacement of nonconforming goods or parts; and

(b) resort to a remedy as provided is optional unless the remedy is expressly agreed to be exclusive, in which case it is the sole remedy.

(2) Where circumstances cause an exclusive or limited remedy to fail of its essential purpose, remedy

may be had as provided in this Act.

_____

The parties, by agreement, may thus limit the remedies of either buyer or seller, or may provide for an "exclusive" remedy for either party. In the event that such an "exclusive" or "limited" remedy fails of its essential purpose, the several remedies discussed in this chapter may be utilized. For example, suppose that the buyer and seller agree as part of the sales contract that the buyer may not reject the goods if they arrive nonconforming, but must resell them and recover any net loss from the seller. If the goods arrive totally spoiled or damaged so that it is not feasible to resell them, the remedy of resale "fails of its essential purpose", and the buyer may resort to the other remedies provided by the Uniform Commercial Code, including the remedy of rejection.

The buyer's right to reject is also subject to the seller's right to "cure" (i. e., remedy) the nonconformity. So long as the contract time for performance has not yet expired, the seller who makes an improper tender or delivery has a right to cure the nonconformity by delivering conforming goods. And even where the contract time for performance has expired, the seller will have a reasonable time to effectuate cure if the seller had "reasonable grounds to believe" that the goods would be acceptable.

Obviously, to effectuate cure, the seller must know of the nonconformity: it is for this reason that UCC Section 2–602 requires the buyer to seasonably notify the seller of his or her intention to reject the goods, and UCC Section 2–605 requires the buyer to specifically list the defects prompting the rejection. Upon cure by the seller, the buyer loses his or her right of rejection.

Section 2–508 of the UCC provides for the seller's right to cure as follows:

Section 2–508. Cure by Seller of Improper Tender or Delivery; Replacement

(1) Where any tender or delivery by the seller is rejected because nonconforming and the time for performance has not yet expired, the seller may seasonably notify the buyer of his intention to cure and may then within the contract time make a conforming delivery.

(2) Where the buyer rejects a nonconforming tender which the seller had reasonable grounds to believe would be acceptable with or without money allowance the seller may if he seasonably notifies the buyer have a further reasonable time to substitute a conforming tender.

_____

As to what constitutes "reasonable grounds to believe" under Subsection (2), the *Official Comment* to Section 2–508 states in part.

The Official Comment provides:

2. Subsection (2) seeks to avoid injustice to the seller by reason of a surprise rejection by the buyer. However, the seller is not protected unless he had "reasonable grounds to believe" that the tender would be acceptable. Such reasonable grounds can lie in prior course of dealing, course of performance or usage of trade as well as in the particular circumstances surrounding the making of the contract. The seller is charged with commercial knowledge of any factors in a particular sales situation which require him to comply strictly with his obligations under the contract as, for example, strict conformity of documents in

an overseas shipment or the sale of precision parts or chemicals for use in manufacture. Further, if the buyer gives notice either implicitly, as by a prior course of dealing involving rigorous inspections, or expressly, as by the deliberate inclusion of a "no replacement" clause in the contract, the seller is to be held to rigid compliance. If the clause appears in a "form" contract evidence that it is out of line with trade usage or the prior course of dealing and was not called to the seller's attention may be sufficient to show that the seller had reasonable grounds to believe that the tender would be acceptable.

———

Returning to our New England Produce/Hood River Apple Company example, it is likely that Hood River Apple would "cure" the 25 crate nonconformity by sending 25 additional crates of Grade A apples. While it is not clear under the Code whether a mere reduction in sales price constitutes an effective cure, the better view is that it does in the case of a minor nonconformity. Thus, Hood River Apple Company could cure the 25 crate defect merely by giving New England Produce a reasonable reduction in the purchase price of the apples.

(2) *Following acceptance, the buyer's right to revoke acceptance.* Sometimes, the buyer accepts the goods, and only afterwards discovers that they are nonconforming. Section 2–606 of the Uniform Commercial Code defines "acceptance of goods" as follows.

The UCC provides:

Section 2–606. What Constitutes Acceptance of Goods

(1) Acceptance of goods occurs when the buyer

(a) after a reasonable opportunity to inspect the goods signifies to the seller that the goods are conforming or that he will take or retain them in spite of their non-conformity; or

(b) fails to make an effective rejection * * * but such acceptance does not occur until the buyer has had a reasonable opportunity to inspect them; or

(c) does any act inconsistent with the seller's ownership; but if such act is wrongful as against the seller it is an acceptance only if ratified by him.

———

Usually, where nonconforming goods are accepted, the acceptance occurs by virtue of Subsection (1)(b)—i. e., the buyer "fails to make an effective rejection". Remember, the buyer must reject the goods within a reasonable time after their tender or delivery, and must give timely notice of the rejection to the seller. A failure to effectively reject results in acceptance of the goods.

Under certain circumstances, a buyer who accepts goods, then subsequently discovers the goods to be nonconforming, may revoke his or her acceptance. However, revocation of acceptance is not as easily accomplished as rejection of the goods in the first instance. Whereas a buyer may reject goods that are nonconforming *in any respect,* the buyer may revoke acceptance of goods only if the goods are *substantially nonconforming.* In other words, to justify revocation, the nonconformity must substantially impair the value of the goods to the buyer. Where this is the case, the buyer may revoke his or her acceptance as to all the goods or any commercial unit of the goods,[1] whereupon the buyer will be in

---

1. Remember, the buyer has a right under UCC Section 2–601 to accept any commercial unit of the goods and reject the rest.

the same position as though he or she had rejected the goods from the outset. The Uniform Commercial Code provides for revocation of acceptance at Section 2–608 as follows.

The UCC provides:

Section 2–608. Revocation of Acceptance in Whole or in Part

(1) The buyer may revoke his acceptance of a lot or commercial unit whose non-conformity substantially impairs its value to him if he has accepted it.

    (a) on the reasonable assumption that its non-conformity would be cured and it has not been seasonably cured; or

    (b) without discovery of such non-conformity if his acceptance was reasonably induced either by the difficulty of discovery before acceptance or by the seller's assurances.

(2) Revocation of acceptance must occur within a reasonable time after the buyer discovers or should have discovered the ground for it and before any substantial change in condition of the goods which is not caused by their own defects. It is not effective until the buyer notifies the seller of it.

(3) A buyer who so revokes has the same rights and duties with regard to the goods involved as if he had rejected them.

Note under Subsection (c) that the buyer who revokes has the same rights and duties with regard to the goods as if he or she had rejected the goods. Thus, the buyer who revokes his or her acceptance as to all the goods, in effect, cancels the sale, and is freed from all obligation under the contract; the buyer may recover from the seller any damages suffered by reason of the nonconforming delivery.

The buyer who revokes his or her acceptance as to part of the goods "cancels" only that portion of the contract, and must pay for the goods accepted; however, the buyer may "set-off" from the purchase price owing any damages incurred because of the nonconformity.

Like the buyer's right of rejection, the buyer's right of revocation of acceptance is subject to the seller's right to "cure" the defect. Since the buyer who revokes is in the same position as if he or she had rejected the goods, it follows that the seller has a right to "cure" under UCC Section 2–508. If the contract time for performance by the seller has not yet expired, the seller has an absolute right to "cure"; if the contract time for performance has expired, the seller has a right to cure only if he or she had "reasonable grounds to believe" at the time of performing that the goods would be acceptable to the buyer.

Finally, if the buyer who revokes has "physical possession" of the goods at the time of revocation of acceptance, the buyer will have the same duties with regard to the goods as if he or she had rejected them. Thus, under UCC Section 2–602, the buyer must hold the goods for a time sufficient for the seller to remove them. And under UCC Section 2–603, if the seller has no business representative or place of business at the place of revocation, and the buyer is a merchant in possession of the seller's goods, the buyer must follow the seller's reasonable instructions as to disposition of the property. In the absence of such instructions, the buyer must sell the goods for the seller's account if the goods are "perishable or threaten to decline in value speedily." Of course, the buyer may deduct from the sales proceeds or otherwise collect from the seller an amount reflecting his or her expenses in caring for and selling the goods.

By way of example, suppose that Hood River Apple Company ships 2,000 crates of apples to New England Produce. Eight hundred of the crates are nonconforming Grade C apples; however, all the nonconforming crates are piled at the bottom of the stack, and New England Produce accepts the apples based on its inspection of the Grade A apples on top. Later, while removing the apples from the siding for sale and delivery to retailers, New England Produce discovers the nonconforming crates. The nonconformity "substantially impairs" the value of the apples to New England Produce, and the Company justifiably revokes its acceptance of the 800 crates. After so notifying Hood River Apple Company (which has no business representative or place of business at the location of revocation) and receiving no instructions, New England Produce must sell the rejected apples as they are "perishable" and turn over the sales proceeds (less any expenses of storage and sale) to Hood River Apple Company.

(3) *Following rejection or revocation of acceptance, the buyer's right of resale to recover prepayments made on the purchase price.* Following cancellation of all or part of the contract of sale, the buyer has a right to recover any prepayments made on the purchase price. Where the buyer cancels but a portion of the sale, the buyer may generally "recover" the prepayments simply by "setting-off" the prepaid amounts from the monies still owing under the contract. Sometimes, however, this is insufficient to reimburse the buyer; and, where the buyer has prepaid all of the purchase price, or has cancelled the entire contract, the remedy of "set-off" has no application.

Short of going to court, how is the buyer in this situation to recover his or her prepayments? In demanding repayment, the buyer has one very important "bargaining tool"—he or she has physical possession of the nonconforming goods. Under UCC Sections 2–711

(3) and 2–706(6), a buyer who has prepaid all or part of the purchase price may offer to restore the nonconforming shipment to the seller in return for repayment of the monies paid; if the seller refuses, the buyer may sell the goods to recover his or her prepayments. The buyer must remit to the seller any resale proceeds in excess of the buyer's prepayments and costs in selling the goods.

Sections 2–711(3) and 2–706(6) provide:

Section 2–711

(3) * * * On rightful rejection or justifiable revocation of acceptance a buyer has a security interest in goods in his possession or control for any payments made on their price and any expenses reasonably incurred in their inspection, receipt, transportation, care and custody and may hold such goods and resell them. * * *

Section 2–706

(6) * * * [A] buyer who has rightfully rejected or justifiably revoked acceptance must account for any excess over the amount of his security interest. * * *

———

The *Official Comment* to Section 2–711 states in part.

* * * [It is clear from] Subsection (3) that the buyer may hold and resell rejected goods if he has paid a part of the price or incurred expenses of the type specified. "Paid" as used here includes acceptance of a draft or other time negotiable instrument or the signing of a negotiable note * * * [T]he buyer may not keep any profit resulting from the resale and is limited to retaining only the amount of the price paid and the costs involved in the inspection and handling of the goods * * * [T]he buyer is not permitted to retain such funds as he might

believe adequate for his damages. The buyer's right * * * to have damages for non-delivery is not impaired by his exercise of his right of resale.

———

For example, suppose that New England Produce has prepaid $2,500 for 2,000 crates of Grade A apples. Hood River Apple Company ships nonconforming apples to New England Produce (800 of the crates are Grade C apples), and New England Produce rejects all the goods. Having prepaid $2,500 for the apples, New England Produce has a right to demand repayment of its money. If New England offers to return the apples in exchange for repayment, and Hood River refuses to cooperate, New England may resell the apples to recover its money. Assuming New England obtains $4.00 per crate for the Grade A apples, and $1.50 per crate for the Grade C apples, for a total of $6,000, New England will have to remit to Hood River Apple Company a balance of $3,500 ($6,000 minus $2,500) less any expenses incurred by New England in reselling the apples.

Of course, the buyer's right of resale is subject to the seller's right to cure the defect. If the contract time for performance by Hood River has not yet expired, Hood River will have a right to cure the defect by sending conforming apples. If the time for performance has expired, Hood River will have no right to "cure" as the Company can hardly purport to have had "reasonable grounds to believe" that the 800 crates of Grade C apples would be acceptable.

Finally, remember that the risk of loss for damage or destruction of the apples remains in the Hood River Apple Company: the apples being nonconforming at the time of their delivery to the carrier, the risk of loss did not pass to New England Produce. Thus, if the apples are lost, damaged, or destroyed before New England Produce returns or resells them, the Hood River Apple Company must bear the loss.

(4) *Following rejection or revocation of acceptance, the buyer's right to "cover" or sue for money damages for nondelivery.* A buyer who rightfully rejects nonconforming goods or justifiably revokes acceptance of the goods has a right to effect "cover" under Section 2–712 of the Uniform Commercial Code. To effect "cover" means to go out into the market and purchase substitute goods. So long as the buyer acts reasonably and in good faith, the buyer may recover from the seller any excess of the cover price over the contract price (along with any incidental or consequential damages, less expenses saved by reason of buying in another market).

Section 2–712 of the UCC provides as follows:

(1) * * * [On rightful rejection or justifiable revocation of acceptance] the buyer may "cover" by making in good faith and without unreasonable delay any reasonable purchase of or contract to purchase goods in substitution for those due from the seller.

(2) The buyer may recover from the seller as damages the difference between the cost of cover and the contract price together with any incidental or consequential damages * * * but less expenses saved in consequence of the seller's breach.

(3) Failure of the buyer to effect cover within this section does not bar him from any other remedy.

———

The *Official Comment* to Section 2–712 explains.

The Official Comment provides:

1. This section provides the buyer with a remedy aimed at enabling him to obtain the goods he needs

thus meeting his essential need
* * *.

2. The definition of "cover" under
subsection (1) envisages a series
of contracts or sales, as well as a
single contract or sale; goods not
identical with those involved but
commercially usable as reasonable
substitutes under the circumstances
of the particular case; and contracts on credit or delivery terms
differing from the contract in
breach, but again reasonable under
the circumstances. The test of
proper cover is whether at the
time and place the buyer acted in
good faith and in a reasonable
manner, and it is immaterial that
hindsight may later prove that
the method of cover used was not
the cheapest or most effective.
The requirement that the buyer
must cover "without unreasonable
delay" is not intended to limit the
time necessary for him to look
around and decide as to how he
may best effect cover. * * *

3. Subsection (3) expresses the policy that cover is not a mandatory
remedy for the buyer. The buyer
is always free to choose between
cover and damages for non-delivery. * * *

4. This section does not limit cover
to merchants, in the first instance.
It is the vital and important remedy for the consumer buyer as well.
Both are free to use cover; the domestic or non-merchant consumer
is required only to act in normal
good faith while the merchant
buyer must also observe all reasonable commercial standards of fair
dealing in the trade, since this
falls within the definition of good
faith on his part. [UCC Section
2–103 provides that "good faith
in the case of a merchant means

honesty in fact and the observance
of reasonable commercial standards of fair dealing in the
trade."]

Thus, both merchant and nonmerchant
buyers have a right to effect "cover" following rightful rejection of goods or justifiable revocation of acceptance (as will
be seen in a later section, merchant and
nonmerchant buyers have the same right
where the seller fails to deliver the goods
or repudiates the contract in advance—
called "anticipatory repudiation").

Of course, there can be a problem if
the buyer, following rejection or revocation of acceptance, notifies the seller and
immediately effects cover, only then to
receive notice from the seller that the
seller intends to cure the defect under U
CC Section 2–508. It would appear
that the buyer must be careful not to cover until he or she is certain that the seller
cannot cure the nonconformity under Section 2–508.

Returning to our example, suppose
that Hood River Apple Company delivers 2,000 crates of apples to New
England Produce, 800 crates of which
are nonconforming Grade C apples.
New England rejects the 800 nonconforming crates, and notifies Hood
River of its intention to effect cover for
the apples. Assuming Hood River cannot cure the nonconformity, New England may purchase 800 crates of Grade A
apples on the open market. If the company has to pay $1.00 more per crate
than it had contracted to pay Hood River,
the Company can recover the $800.00
from Hood River along with any incidental or consequential damages incurred,
less expenses saved by purchasing in another market.

As an alternative to cover, a buyer who
has rightfully rejected goods or justifiably revoked acceptance of them has a
right under UCC Section 2–713 to sue

for money damages for nondelivery (as you will learn in later sections, the buyer has the same right where the seller fails to deliver the goods or repudiates the contract in advance).

Section 2–713 of the UCC states:

Section 2–713. Buyer's Damages for Non-Delivery * * *

(1) Subject to the provisions of this Article with respect to proof of market price (Section 2–723), the measure of damages for non-delivery * * * by the seller is the difference between the market price *at the time when the buyer learned of the breach* and the contract price together with any incidental and consequential damages provided in this Article (Section 2–715), but less expenses saved in consequence of the seller's breach.

(2) Market price is to be determined *as of the place for tender,* or, in cases of rejection after arrival or revocation of acceptance, *as of the place of arrival.* (Emphasis supplied.)

___

And the Official Comment to the Section provides:

1. The general baseline adopted in this section uses as a yardstick the market in which the buyer would have obtained coverage had he sought that relief. So the place of measuring damages is the place for tender (or the place of arrival if the goods are rejected or their acceptance is revoked after reaching their destination) and the crucial time is the time at which the buyer learns of the breach.

* * *

5. The present section (2–713) provides a remedy which is completely alternative to cover * * * and

applies only when and to the extent that the buyer has not covered.

___

Thus, the buyer's measure of damages for nondelivery is the difference between the market price at the time when the buyer learned of the breach and the contract price (together with any incidental or consequential damages less expenses saved in consequence of the seller's breach). The market price is determined as of the place of arrival where the goods are rejected after arrival or acceptance of them is revoked; in all other cases, market price is determined as of the place for tender. With respect to proof of market price, Section 2–723 provides.

Section 2–723. Proof of Market Price: Time and Place
* * *

(2) If evidence of a price prevailing at the times or places described in this Article is not readily available the price prevailing within any reasonable time before or after the time described or at any other place which in commercial judgment or under usage of trade would serve as a reasonable substitute for the one described may be used, making any proper allowance for the cost of transporting the goods to or from such other place.

___

Frequently, the buyer's measure of damages for nondelivery will be the same as his or her measure of damages following cover. However, this is not always so: market price for purposes of nondelivery is determined as of the time the buyer learns of the breach, for purposes of cover, at the time of cover. Obviously, the market price may differ at these two times, particularly where the buyer waits several days or even weeks after learning of the breach to effect cover (remember, though the buyer must cover within a reasonable time, he or she is free to shop around for a good bargain). For example, suppose that New England Produce decides to sue for money damages for nondelivery rather than effect cover and sue for the excess of the cover price over the contract price. New England's measure of damages under Section 2–713 will be the difference between the market price of 800 crates of Grade A apples at the time and place of rejection (or revocation of acceptance) and the contract price (again, plus any incidental or consequential damages and less any expenses saved because of the breach). If the market price at the time and place of rejection (or revocation of acceptance) is $1.00 more per crate than the contract price (the same as in the previous example where New England effected cover for the 800 crates), the measure of damages for nondelivery will be the same as the measure of damages following cover. But if the market price when New England learns of the breach is less than $1.00 more per crate (the market price going up shortly thereafter), or greater than $1.00 more per crate (the market price declining thereafter), New England's measure of damages for nondelivery will obviously differ from its measure of damages following cover (in the first instance, it will be less, in the second, greater).

In any case, whether the buyer covers and sues for damages, or sues for money damages for nondelivery, the buyer is entitled as part of his or her measure of damages to any *incidental* or *consequential damages* incurred (less expenses saved because of the seller's breach). Such damages are defined at Section 2–715 of the Uniform Commercial Code as follows.

It provides:

Section 2–715. Buyer's Incidental and Consequential Damages

(1) Incidental damages resulting from the seller's breach include expenses reasonably incurred in inspection, receipt, transportation and care and custody of goods rightfully rejected, any commercially reasonable charges, expenses or commissions in connection with effecting cover and any other reasonable expense incident to the delay or other breach.

(2) Consequential damages resulting from the seller's breach include

    (a) any loss resulting from general or particular requirements and needs of which the seller at the time of contracting had reason to know and which could not reasonably be prevented by cover or otherwise * * *

    * * *

———

Thus, under Subsection (1), the buyer is entitled to recover any reasonable expense *incident* to the seller's breach. For example, suppose that New England Produce hires someone to inspect the 2,000 crates of apples sent by Hood River Apple Company. Upon discovering that 800 of the crates are nonconforming, New England rejects all the apples, whereupon it incurs expenses in storing and selling the apples for Hood River. New England is entitled to recover the reasonable expenses of inspection, storage, and sale as incidental damages within the meaning of Subsection (1).

Subsection (2) deals with *consequential* damages. You will recall the following discussion of such damages from the Ch. 10 section, "What is the rule of remoteness?".

An injured party's measure of recovery for breach of contract is limited by the rule of remoteness which states that an injured party should be compensated only for losses that are reasonably foreseeable to the parties at the time they enter into the contract. The *Restatement of the Law of Contracts,* Section 330, states the rule as follows:

> In awarding damages, compensation is given for only those injuries that the defendant had reason to foresee as a probable result of his breach when the contract was made. If the injury is one that follows the breach in the usual course of events, there is sufficient reason for the defendant to foresee it; otherwise, it must be shown specifically that the defendant had reason to know the facts and to foresee the injury.

> * * * [C]onsequential (remote or indirect) damages are recoverable only where both parties know of the special circumstances likely to result in the damages at the time of entering into the contract.

Section 2–715(2)(a) provides for the rule of remoteness, stating that consequential damages may be recovered for "any loss resulting from * * * requirements * * * which the seller at the time of contracting had reason to know and which could not reasonably be prevented by cover or otherwise."

The Official Comment to the Section states:

> * * * [T]he seller is liable for consequential damages in all cases where he had reason to know of the buyer's general or particular requirements at the time of contracting. It is not necessary that there be a conscious acceptance of an insurer's liability on the seller's part, nor is his obligation for consequential damages limited to cases in which he fails to use due effort in good faith.

Thus, the test for recovery of consequential (remote or indirect) damages is whether the loss was reasonably foreseeable by the seller at the time of contracting. However, there is no requirement that the loss be actually foreseen by the seller. In the case of Lewis v. Mobil Oil Corp., 438 F.2d 500, 510 (8th Cir. 1971), the court stated with regard to the buyer's lost profits.

> Where a seller provides goods to a manufacturing enterprise with knowledge that they are to be used in the manufacturing process, it is reasonable to assume that he should know the defective goods will cause a disruption of production, and loss of profits is a natural consequence of such disruption. Hence, loss of profits should be recoverable under these circumstances.

In addition to lost profits, consequential damages might include such items as legal expenses, repair expenses, amounts paid to third parties as a result of the seller's breach, etc.

The rule that any reasonably foreseeable loss is recoverable is subject to one qualification: consequential damages will not be allowed where the buyer could have prevented the loss by cover or other action. For example, lost profits will not be allowed as consequential damages where the buyer could have avoided the loss by effecting cover (i. e., by purchasing substitute goods on the open market). This qualification stems from the rule of mitigation of damages which requires the aggrieved party in a breach of contract situation to do whatever is reasonable to "mitigate" the damages. As was stated in Ch. 10.

The injured party is legally obligated to make a reasonable effort to mitigate (i. e., reduce or lessen) the damages flowing from the breach of contract. If the party fails to do so, his or her recovery in money damages will be reduced by the amount of loss that could have been avoided. * * * If the seller breaches the sales agreement by refusing to deliver the goods, the buyer must make a reasonable attempt to purchase substitute goods from another seller. * * * Of course, any expenses the injured party incurs in reasonably seeking to mitigate the damages are recoverable as *incidental* damages *regardless of whether the effort to mitigate is successful.*

---

(5) *Following acceptance of the goods, the buyer's right to damages for breach of express or implied warranty.* In nearly all sales, the seller makes express and/or implied "warranties" to the buyer. As you will recall from Chapters 6 (dealing with "warranty" deeds for the transfer of land) and 11 ("warranties" in connection with insurance policies), a "warranty" is simply a promise that a proposition of fact is true. With regard to sales of goods, the seller warrants (promises) as true certain facts about the character, quality, or title of the goods. Frequently, the seller's warranties are express—i. e., stated either orally or in writing. For example, the seller or his or her salesperson may make oral warranties to the buyer, or place the warranties right in the contract of sale. And all of you are familiar with the "warranty" cards that accompany the purchase of small appliances, sporting equipment, and other items. The cards contain the seller's express warranties as to the goods; generally, the buyer is asked to fill out the cards and return them either to the seller or manufacturer (some special rules which apply only to "consumer

product" warranties are discussed at the end of this section under the heading "The Magnuson-Moss Act"). The Uniform Commercial Code deals with express warranties at Section 2–313 as follows.

The UCC provides:

Section 2–313. Express Warranties by Affirmation, Promise, Description, Sample

(1) Express warranties by the seller are created as follows:

   (a) Any affirmation of fact or promise made by the seller to the buyer which relates to the goods and becomes part of the basis of the bargain creates an express warranty that the goods shall conform to the affirmation or promise.

   (b) Any description of the goods which is made part of the basis of the bargain creates an express warranty that the goods shall conform to the description.

   (c) Any sample or model which is made part of the basis of the bargain creates an express warranty that the whole of the goods shall conform to the sample or model.

(2) It is not necessary to the creation of an express warranty that the seller use formal words such as "warrant" or "guarantee" or that he have a specific intention to make a warranty, but an affirmation merely of the value of the goods or a statement purporting to be merely the seller's opinion or commendation of the goods does not create a warranty.

The Official Comment to the Section provides:

5.   * * *   A description need not be by words. Technical specifica-

tions, blueprints and the like can afford more exact description than mere language and if made part of the basis of the bargain goods must conform with them. Past deliveries may set the description of quality, either expressly or impliedly by course of dealing.

* * *

6. The basic situation as to statements affecting the true essence of the bargain is no different when a sample or model is involved in the transaction. This section includes both a "sample" actually drawn from the bulk of goods which is the subject matter of the sale, and a "model" which is offered for inspection when the subject matter is not at hand and which has not been drawn from the bulk of the goods. * * *

7. The precise time when words of description or affirmation are made or samples are shown is not material. The sole question is whether the language or samples or models are fairly to be regarded as part of the contract. If language is used after the closing of the deal (as when the buyer when taking delivery asks for and receives an additional assurance), the warranty becomes a modification, and need not be supported by consideration if it is otherwise reasonable and in order (Section 2–209).

———————

You will note that no special words or intent are required to create an express warranty. Thus, the statement that an item is an "air conditioner" will operate as an express warranty though the words "warrant" or "promise" are not used.

However, to constitute an express warranty, the statement must be one of fact, and not merely a statement of "opinion" or "puffing" of wares. As you will recall from Ch. 8,[2] it is sometimes difficult to distinguish between statements of fact and puffing. A statement that "this car is the best on the market" is obviously "puffing" and not an express warranty, while a statement that "this car is mechanically perfect" may well be a statement of fact constituting an express warranty.

You will also note that express warranties may arise from the seller's use of samples or models. Also, the timing of the affirmation of fact (the express warranty) is immaterial so long as the language, the sample, or the model is fairly to be regarded as "part of the basis of the bargain".

In our example, Hood River Apple Company expressly warranted that the 2,000 crates of apples would be Grade A. Upon receipt and acceptance of the 2,000 crates, 800 of which are Grade C, New England Produce may sue Hood River Apple for damages for breach of express warranty.

In addition to express warranties, the seller may make certain *implied warranties* regarding title[3] or quality of the goods, or implied warranties against infringement of patents or trademarks. An implied warranty is one that arises by operation of law without regard to any express affirmation of fact made by the seller: whether or not the seller makes

———————

2. You may find it helpful at this point to review the Ch. 8 discussion on the differences between statements of fact and statements of opinion or puffing. The differences were there explained in connection with "fraud in the inducement" (misstatements of a material fact made with the intention of inducing detrimental reliance by another, and, in fact, inducing such reliance). Of course, if the elements of fraud are present in a sales transaction, this is yet another remedy for the buyer.

3. The implied warranty of title will be discussed in Ch. 19 dealing with the sale of goods by one lacking title to the property.

any express warranties, he or she is held to imply certain promises simply by virtue of making the sale. Thus, a seller who sends nonconforming goods may breach an express warranty, an implied warranty, or both. A breach of either kind of warranty will provide the buyer with a complete remedy for the nonconforming delivery.

Two implied warranties—the *implied warranty of merchantability* and the *implied warranty against infringement*—apply only to merchants. Section 2–104(1) of the Uniform Commercial Code defines "merchant" in general terms as follows.

The UCC provides:

"Merchant" means a person who deals in goods of the kind or otherwise by his occupation holds himself out as having knowledge or skill peculiar to the practices or goods involved in the transaction or to whom such knowledge or skill may be attributed by his employment of an agent or broker or other intermediary who by his occupation holds himself out as having such knowledge or skill.

———

Insofar as the implied warranties are concerned, however, the term "merchant" is restricted to the first part of the Section 2–104(1) definition: for purposes of the implied warranties, a "merchant" is "a person who deals in goods of the kind" period.

The Official Comment to UCC Section 2–314 explains:

[I]n Section 2–314 on the warranty of merchantability, such warranty is implied only "if the seller is a merchant with respect to goods of that kind." Obviously this qualification restricts the implied warranty to a much smaller group than everyone who is engaged in business and [the warranty] requires a professional status as to particular kinds of goods.

———

Thus, a plumber, electrician, or carpenter who installs parts as part of his or her services makes no implied warranties about those parts. And statutes in more than half the states provide that blood donors make no implied warranties about the quality or "merchantability" of their blood. Only those who are actually in the business of selling "goods of that kind"—department stores, grocery stores, hardware stores, etc.—qualify as "merchants" for purposes of making the implied warranties.

The implied warranty of merchantability is provided for by Section 2–314 of the Uniform Commercial Code as follows.

The UCC provides:

Section 2–314. Implied Warranty; Merchantability; Usage of Trade

(1) Unless excluded or modified (Section 2–316), a warranty that the goods shall be merchantable is implied in a contract for their sale if the seller is a merchant with respect to goods of that kind. Under this section the serving for value of food or drink to be consumed either on the premises or elsewhere is a sale.

(2) Goods to be merchantable must be at least such as

(a) pass without objection in the trade under the contract description; and

(b) in the case of fungible goods, are of fair average quality within the description; and

(c) are fit for the ordinary purposes for which such goods are used; and

(d) run, within the variations permitted by the agreement, of even kind, quality and quantity within each unit and among all units involved; and

(e) are adequately contained, packaged, and labeled as the agreement may require; and

(f) conform to the promises or affirmations of fact made on the container or label if any.

(3) Unless excluded or modified (Section 2–316) other implied warranties may arise from course of dealing or usage of trade.

———

Thus, the delivery by Hood River Apple Company of 800 crates of Grade C apples constitutes a breach of the implied warranty of merchantability. The Grade C apples obviously cannot "pass without objection in the trade under the contract description" and are not "fit for the ordinary purposes" of Grade A apples.

It should be realized that the implied warranty of merchantability applies to the sale of used goods as well as new goods. The *Official Comment* to Section 2–314 states: "A contract for the sale of second-hand goods, however, involves only such obligation as is appropriate to such goods for that is their contract description." (In other words, the older and more used the goods are, the less of a warranty there will be). In the case of Overland Bond and Investment Corp. v. Howard, 9 Ill.App.3d 348, 292 N.E.2d 168 (1972), the plaintiff purchased a used 1965 automobile in June of 1970. The day after the plaintiff purchased the car, the transmission fell out of the automobile and had to be repaired. A week later, the brakes went out. Upon suit by the buyer, the court held that the defendant seller had breached the implied warranty of merchantability: The used car could not "pass without objection in the used car trade" and was not "fit for the ordinary purposes" for which used cars are utilized. The car was, therefore, unmerchantable, and the merchant seller liable.

The second implied warranty applying only to merchants—the implied warranty against patent or trademark infringement (see Ch. 2 for patents and trademarks)—is found at Section 2–312(3) the Uniform Commercial Code.

The UCC provides:

Unless otherwise agreed a seller who is a merchant regularly dealing in goods of the kind warrants that the goods shall be delivered free of the rightful claim of any third person by way of infringement or the like but a buyer who furnishes specifications to the seller must hold the seller harmless against any such claim which arises out of compliance with the specifications.

———

The Official Comment to the Section explains:

* * * 3. When the goods are part of the seller's normal stock and are sold in his normal course of business, it is his duty to see that no claim of infringement of a patent or trademark by a third party will mar the buyer's title. A sale by a person other than a dealer, however, raises no implication in its circumstances of such a warranty. Nor is there such an implication when the buyer orders goods to be assembled, prepared or manufactured on his own specifications. If, in such a case, the resulting product infringes a patent or trademark, the liability will run from buyer to seller. There is, under such circumstances, a tacit representation on the part of the buyer that the seller will be safe in manufacturing according to the specifications, and the buyer is under an obligation in good faith to indemnify him for any loss suffered.

———

The implied warranty against patent or trademark infringement is unique in that, where the buyer furnishes the plans or specifications for the goods to be assembled, prepared, or manufactured, the warranty is imposed on the buyer rather than on the seller. The buyer, in such case, is held to impliedly warrant that the manufacture or assembly of the items will not infringe on another's patent or trademark rights.

A third implied warranty—the *implied warranty of fitness for a particular purpose*—applies to both merchant and nonmerchant sellers. Uniform Commercial Code Section 2–315 provides: "Where the seller at the time of contracting has reason to know any particular purpose for which the goods are required and that the buyer is relying on the seller's skill or judgment to select or furnish suitable goods, there is an implied warranty that the goods shall be fit for such purpose." Thus, there are three conditions required for the warranty to arise:

(1) The seller must know or have reason to know of the buyer's particular purpose;

(2) The seller must know or have reason to know that the buyer is relying on the seller's skill or judgment to select suitable or proper goods;

(3) The buyer must, in fact, rely upon the seller's skill and judgment in selecting the goods.

The *Official Comment* to Section 2–315 further clarifies these requirements.

The Official Comment provides:

1. Whether or not this warranty arises in any individual case is basically a question of fact to be determined by the circumstances of the contracting. Under this section the buyer need not bring home to the seller actual knowledge of the particular purpose for which the goods are intended or of his reliance on the seller's skill and judgment, if the circumstances

are such that the seller has reason to realize the purpose intended or that the reliance exists. The buyer, of course, must actually be relying on the seller.

2. A "particular purpose" differs from the ordinary purpose for which the goods are used in that it envisages a specific use by the buyer which is peculiar to the nature of his business whereas the ordinary purposes for which goods are used are those envisaged in the concept of merchantability and go to uses which are customarily made of the goods in question. For example, shoes are generally used for the purpose of walking upon ordinary ground, but a seller may know that a particular pair was selected to be used for climbing mountains.

A contract may of course include both a warranty of merchantability and one of fitness for a particular purpose.

The implied warranty of merchantability assures the buyer of goods "fit for the *ordinary* purpose for which such goods are used"; the implied warranty of fitness for a particular purpose assures the buyer of goods fit for a "particular" or "special" purpose. Again, the former warranty applies only to merchant sellers while the latter applies to all sellers, merchants and nonmerchants alike.

By way of example, suppose that New England Produce orders 2,000 crates of apples "appropriate for the Halloween caramel apple trade" from Hood River Apple Company. Here, Hood River Apple knows of the buyer's particular purpose (using the apples for caramel apples), and the Company also knows that the buyer is relying on the Company's skill and judgment in selecting the right size and grade of apple for the purpose intended. (The same would be true if New England Produce ordered 2,000 crates of apples "appropriate for making applesauce".) It follows that Hood River Apple Company makes an implied warranty of fitness for the particular purpose, and if the apples (though merchantable) are not fit for that purpose, the Hood River Apple Company will be liable for breach of warranty.

In the event that the seller breaches an express or implied warranty by sending nonconforming goods, the buyer upon *acceptance* of the goods may bring legal action against the seller to recover money damages. As far as the buyer's measure of damages is concerned, it makes no difference whether one warranty is breached or five are breached, or whether the warranties are express or implied—the buyer's measure of damages is the same in any case.

Section 2–714 of the UCC provides as follows: [4]

Section 2–714. Buyer's Damages for Breach in Regard to Accepted Goods

(1) Where the buyer has accepted goods and given notification (subsection (3) of Section 2–607) he may recover as damages for any non-conformity of tender the loss resulting in the ordinary course of events from the seller's breach as determined in any manner which is reasonable.

(2) The measure of damages for breach of warranty is the difference at the time and place of acceptance between the value of the goods accepted and the value they would have had if they had been as warranted, unless special circumstances show proximate damages of a different amount.

(3) In a proper case any incidental and consequential damages under the next section may also be recovered.

Subsection (1) provides that, before the buyer can recover damages for breach of warranty, he or she must give notice to the seller as required by UCC Section 2–607(3). Section 2–607(3) states: "Where * * * a tender has been accepted * * * the buyer must within a reasonable time after he discovers or should have discovered any breach notify the seller of breach or be barred from any remedy * * *".

The Official Comment to the Section adds:

* * * The time of notification is to be determined by applying commercial standards to a merchant buyer. "A reasonable time" for notification from a retail consumer is to be judged by different standards so that in his case it will be extended, for the rule of requiring notification is designed to defeat commercial bad faith, not to deprive a good faith consumer of his remedy.

* * * The content of the notification need merely be sufficient to let the seller know the transaction is still troublesome and must be watched. There is no reason to require that the notification which saves the buyer's rights under this section must include a clear statement of all the objections that will be relied on by the buyer * * *. Nor is there reason for requiring the notification to be a claim for damages or of any threatened litigation or other resort to a remedy. The notification which saves the buyer's rights under this Article need only be such as informs the seller that the transaction is claimed to involve a

---

4. Remember, we are talking here about the breach of warranty remedy of a buyer who has *accepted* the goods. Section 2–714 does not apply where the buyer rejects the goods or revokes his or her acceptance of them.

breach, and thus opens the way for normal settlement through negotiation.

———

Thus, all that is required is that the buyer notify the seller within a "reasonable time" that there may be a breach of warranty. What is a "reasonable time" varies, depending on the circumstances. In the case of a merchant buyer, commercial standards are controlling; in the case of a consumer buyer, less stringent standards are applied, with the result that the consumer buyer has a longer period of time for giving notice.

Under Section 2–714(2), the buyer's measure of damages for breach of warranty is the difference between the "value of the goods accepted and the value they would have had if they had been as warranted". Very often, the value of the goods "as warranted" is the same as the purchase price set in the contract of sale. But this is not always the case. For example, suppose that the fair market value of 2,000 crates of Grade A apples is $10,000 at the time and place of acceptance by New England Produce. While $10,000 is the value of the apples as warranted, the apples delivered are nonconforming (800 of the crates are Grade C apples), and their fair market value at the time and place of acceptance is only $6,000. Thus, New England Produce's measure of damages for breach of warranty is $4,000 ($10,000–$6,000). And this is so whether the purchase price set by the contract of sale is $5,000, $6,000, or $12,000, etc. Obviously, where the purchase price is less than the value of the goods as warranted, the buyer will benefit from the bargain. Assuming the purchase price is $5,000, and the buyer has already paid the seller, the buyer can sell the nonconforming apples for $6,000 and collect $4,000 from the seller for breach of warranty. Where, on the other hand, the purchase price is greater than the value of the goods as warranted, the buyer will suffer the result of his or her

bad bargain. Assuming the purchase price is $12,000 (the buyer, again, having already paid the seller), the buyer will end up with a net loss of $2,000 ($12,000 minus [$6,000 plus $4,000]).

A better remedy for the buyer in the latter situation is to reject all the apples. As you will recall, the effect of rejecting all the goods is to cancel the contract: the buyer escapes the bargain completely, and, where it is a bad bargain, this is to the buyer's great advantage. Thus, by rejecting all the apples, or revoking acceptance of them, New England Produce can avoid paying any part of the $12,000 purchase price. (If New England has already paid the $12,000, it can exercise its right of resale to recover prepayments and hold Hood River Apple Company for any part of the prepayment unrecovered.) Since New England Produce can effect cover for $10,000 (this being the current fair market value of 2,000 crates of Grade A apples), the Company will escape the $2,000 net loss effect of its bad bargain. Remember, cover, following rejection of the goods or revocation of acceptance, is often a better remedy than bringing an action for damages for breach of warranty. And it can be accomplished without going to court.

Frequently, it is possible to determine the measure of damages for breach of warranty simply by looking at the cost of repair. For example, if the buyer orders a television set and receives one with a faulty tuner, the difference between the value of the goods as warranted and their value as received is the price of a new tuner together with installation cost less the value, if any, of the defective tuner. Of course, where the entire set is defective and cannot be repaired, the measure of damages is the replacement cost of the set (the market value of the item at the time and place of acceptance) less any scrap or salvage value the set may have.

In any case, where the buyer in the breach of warranty situation still owes the seller any or all of the purchase price of the accepted goods, the buyer may "set-off" (i. e., deduct) from the amount owing any damages incurred by reason of the breach of warranty. As explained previously, the "set-off" remedy is not confined to any particular situation, but applies any time a buyer owing money under a contract of sale suffers damages by reason of the seller's breach of contract.

Finally, Section 2–714(3) provides that the buyer's measure of damages for breach of warranty includes any incidental or consequential damages that are recoverable under UCC Section 2–715 (Section 2–715 was discussed previously in relation to the buyer's right to effect cover or sue for damages for nondelivery following rejection or revocation of acceptance). It should be pointed out that Section 2–715(2)(b) states that consequential damages may be recovered for "injury to person or property proximately resulting from any breach of warranty." Whereas consequential damages are generally recoverable only where they are reasonably foreseeable by the seller at the time of contracting, there is no foreseeability requirement insofar as Section 2–715(2)(b) is concerned. Thus, if the buyer accepts nonconforming goods, and is subsequently injured as a result of the defective condition of the property, the buyer will be able to recover from the seller under Section 2–715(2)(b) though the injury was not foreseeable at the time of contracting. This provision of the Code is considered in detail in Ch. 19 under "product liability".

One special problem for the buyer in the warranty area is "disclaimer" of warranty liability by the seller. You will recall from Ch. 7 that the common law of contracts (remember always that a sale is first of all a contract) has a twofold purpose: (1) *not* to hold parties to their promises or agreements in the absence of evidence that the parties truly intended or agreed to be bound; and (2) *to* ensure

that parties who do make promises and enter into agreements, desiring to be bound, are met with their reasonable expectations. In other words, there should be "freedom of contract": parties should become bound only where they freely intend to become bound; parties should be free to set contract terms in any manner they desire so long as the terms are legal.

To some extent, this principle of freedom of contract allows the seller of goods to avoid liability based on warranty. However, the Uniform Commercial Code, which modifies the common law in places, does not permit the seller complete freedom in avoiding or disclaiming warranty liability. Also, the courts tend to construe disclaimers as strictly as possible so as to protect the buyer.

The following disclaimer situations may arise:

(1) *Written disclaimer of an express warranty contained in the same written agreement.* Sometimes, an express warranty is found in a written form that also contains a disclaimer of warranties. For example, a provision that an air conditioner is free from all defects might be found on a form disclaiming all express warranties. Or a handwritten or typewritten statement that "this air conditioner shall be guaranteed against all defects for the next one year" may be found on a printed form stating that "there are no guarantees or express warranties made by the seller." Even a written statement that "this machine is an air conditioner" is an express warranty that the machine will function as such machines are designed to do; a statement in the same writing that "there are no express warranties" contradicts the description of the machine as an air conditioner.

Whenever an express warranty within a writing is contradicted by a disclaimer of warranty in the same writing, Uniform Commercial Code Section 2–316(1) applies.

The UCC provides:

Section 2–316. Exclusion or Modification of Warranties

(1) Words or conduct relevant to the creation of express warranty and words or conduct tending to negate or limit warranty shall be construed wherever reasonable as consistent with each other; but * * * negation or limitation is inoperative to the extent that such construction is unreasonable.

The Official Comment to the Section provides:

1. This section is designed principally to deal with those frequent clauses in sales contracts which seek to exclude "all warranties, express or implied." It seeks to protect a buyer from unexpected and unbargained language of disclaimer by denying effect to such language when inconsistent with language of express warranty. * * *

The result of UCC Section 2–316 is that it is very difficult to disclaim in writing an express warranty contained in the same writing. The language of disclaimer and warranty would appear, in every case, to be inconsistent, rendering the disclaimer inoperative. (The same would be true where an oral express warranty is subsequently disclaimed orally.) This conclusion is bolstered by the fact that the courts have always been hostile to disclaimers of express warranties and hold them invalid wherever possible (the courts are particularly hostile to such disclaimers today in light of the heavy emphasis on consumer protection).

(2) *Written disclaimer of an oral express warranty made prior to the written sales agreement containing the disclaimer.* In this situation, though the oral express warranty and written disclaimer

may conflict, the buyer may not be protected. This follows from the *parol evidence rule* (studied in Ch. 10) which states that a fully written integrated contract (i. e., a final writing intended by the parties as their complete agreement) may not be changed, varied, altered, or modified by any oral or written evidence occurring prior to or at the time of the signing of the agreement. The parol evidence rule is incorporated into the Uniform Commercial Code at Section 2–202.

The UCC provides:

Section 2–202. Final Written Expression: Parol or Extrinsic Evidence

Terms with respect to which the confirmatory memoranda of the parties agree or which are otherwise set forth in a writing intended by the parties as a final expression of their agreement with respect to such terms as are included therein may not be contradicted by evidence of any prior agreement or of a contemporaneous oral agreement but may be explained or supplemented

(a) by course of dealing or usage of trade * * * or by course of performance; * * * and

(b) by evidence of consistent additional terms unless the court finds the writing to have been intended also as a complete and exclusive statement of the terms of the agreement.

The UCC "parol evidence rule" is designed to protect the seller from false allegations that he or she made oral warranties prior to preparing and signing the written contract containing a disclaimer of such warranties. In order to overcome the rule so as to introduce evidence of the oral express warranty, the buyer must prove that the written agreement was not intended by the parties as the complete and/or final expression of their sales agreement. If the buyer can show either of these things, he or she will be allowed to introduce evidence of the oral express warranty which, being inconsistent with the disclaimer, will render the disclaimer inoperative under UCC Section 2–316.

As to when a writing is the complete and final expression of the parties' agreement, even a statement in the writing that "this is the complete and final statement of the terms of the agreement" will not make the writing so if it is not. But where from all the circumstances it is clear that both buyer and seller intended the written sales contract to be the complete and final expression of their agreement, and the writing contains a disclaimer of all warranties not contained in the writing, there is an effective disclaimer of any and all oral warranties made prior to and apart from the writing.

For example, sellers frequently insert the following language into written sales agreements to protect themselves from statements made by their salespeople.

> Any statements made by seller's salespeople in describing the goods which are the subject matter of this contract do not constitute warranties and cannot be relied upon by the buyer because they are not part of the contract. This contract is the final agreement of the parties and states all of its terms, there being no others.

The buyer's only hope of setting such a disclaimer aside is to assert that the disclaimer is unconscionable (as discussed in Ch. 8). If the buyer can show a disparity of bargaining positions such that he or she was taken advantage of by the seller, the disclaimer will be set aside by the courts. The *Official Comment* to UCC Section 2–719 explains: "[A]ny clause purporting to modify or limit the remedial provisions of this Article in an unconscionable manner is subject to deletion and in that event the remedies made available by this Article are applicable as if the stricken clause had never existed."

(3) *Disclaimer of the implied warranties of merchantability and fitness for a particular purpose.* Often, the seller disclaims implied warranties as well as express. Because implied warranties are not made intentionally, but arise by operation of law, the law allows the seller more latitude in disclaiming or limiting them (however, you will see under the Magnuson-Moss Act that it may be impossible for a seller to disclaim or limit any implied warranty to a consumer with regard to a consumer product). Uniform Commercial Code Section 2–316 provides for disclaimer of the implied warranties of merchantability and fitness for a particular purpose as follows.

The UCC provides:

Section 2–316. Exclusion or Modification of Warranties

(2) Subject to subsection (3), to exclude or modify the implied warranty of merchantability or any part of it the language must mention merchantability and in case of a writing must be conspicuous, and to exclude or modify any implied warranty of fitness the exclusion must be by a writing and conspicuous. Language to exclude all implied warranties of fitness is sufficient if it states, for example, that "There are no warranties which extend beyond the description on the face hereof."

(3) Notwithstanding subsection (2)

(a) unless the circumstances indicate otherwise, all implied warranties are excluded by expressions like "as is", "with all faults" or other language which in common understanding calls the buyer's attention to the exclusion of warranties and makes plain that there is no implied warranty; and

(b) when the buyer before entering into the contract has examined the goods or the sample or model as fully as he desired or has refused to examine the goods there is no implied warranty with regard to defects which an examination ought in the circumstances to have revealed to him; and

(c) an implied warranty can also be excluded or modified by course of dealing or course of performance or usage of trade.

The following conclusions may be drawn:

First, if the goods contain patent (i. e., obvious) defects, and the buyer inspects the goods prior to sale, the buyer waives the implied warranties with respect to the patent defects. The same is true where the buyer refuses to inspect the goods following a demand by the seller that he or she do so: by making the demand, the seller puts the buyer on notice that there may be patent defects; by not inspecting, the buyer assumes the risk of the defects.

Second, if the parties by their course of performance or previous dealings have excluded or modified the implied warranties, or if the warranties are excluded or modified by custom or usage within the particular trade, the implied warranties will be excluded or modified accordingly.

Third, and closely related to the second, the seller may effectively disclaim the implied warranties by using "catch-all" terms such as "as is", "as they stand", "with all faults", etc.

The Official Comment to UCC Section 2–316 states:

7. Paragraph (a) of subsection (3) deals with general terms such as "as is", "as they stand", "with all faults", and the like. Such terms in ordinary commercial usage are understood to mean that the buyer takes the entire risk as to the quality of the goods involved. The terms covered by paragraph (a) are in fact merely a particularization of paragraph (c) which provides for exclusion or modification of implied warranties by usage of trade.

Thus, the use of "catch-all" language to disclaim implied warranties is but an application of exclusion of warranty by usage of trade. While the use of "catch-all" language is the easiest way to disclaim implied warranties, the language has no effect upon express warranties. And one court has held that such language applies only to used goods, not new. The case in point is Gindy Mfg. Corp. v. Cardinale Trucking Corp., 111 N.J.Super. 383, 268 A.2d 345 (1970). The plaintiff buyer in the case purchased 20 new semi-trailers from the defendant seller. The contract of sale provided for sale of the semis "as is", the defendant using the same contract forms for both new and used vehicles. In ruling that the "as is" clause was ineffective to disclaim the seller's implied warranty liability, the court stated that it was not the custom of the trade for "as is" language to be found in contracts for the sale of new vehicles—only in contracts for the sale of used vehicles.

While UCC Section 2–316 does not specifically require that "catch-all" words of disclaimer be "conspicuous" (as is required for "merchantability" or "fitness for a particular purpose"), the courts in interpreting the Section have nonetheless held this to be a necessary requirement. Thus, in the case of Osborne v. Genevie, 289 So.2d 21 (Fla.App.1974), a fine-print "as is" clause was held ineffective to disclaim implied warranty liability.

Fourth, apart from using "catch-all" language, the seller may specifically disclaim the implied warranties of merchantability and fitness for a particular purpose as follows:

Disclaimer of the implied warranty of merchantability. The implied warranty of merchantability may be disclaimed by the seller either orally or in writing. Whether oral or written, the disclaimer must specifically mention the word "merchantability"; if in writing, the disclaimer must be conspicuous.

These two requirements are very strictly enforced by the courts. If the word "merchantability" is not found in the disclaimer, the disclaimer will be ineffective to exclude the implied warranty. Thus, a statement that "any claim for defects is waived unless made within 10 days" does not serve to disclaim or limit the implied warranty of merchantability because the word "merchantability" is nowhere found in the disclaimer.

Similarly, though a written disclaimer specifically mentions the word "merchantability", the disclaimer is ineffective to exclude or limit the implied warranty unless it is conspicuous. Section 1–201(10) of the Uniform Commercial Code defines "conspicuous" as follows.

The UCC provides:

A term or clause is conspicuous when it is so written that a reasonable person against whom it is to operate ought to have noticed it. A printed heading in capitals (as: NON–NEGOTIABLE BILL OF LADING) is conspicuous. Language in the body of a form is "conspicuous" if it is in larger or other contrasting type or color. But in a telegram any stated term is "conspicuous". Whether a term or clause is "conspicuous" or not is for decision by the court.

———

Thus, a term is "conspicuous" only if it is written in such a manner that a reason-

able person against whom it is to operate would notice it. Language set off in unusual or contrasting type or color, or set off in capitals, is conspicuous; language in fine-print or regular size type on the back of a contract is inconspicuous. The courts have so strictly enforced the "conspicuous" requirement as to rule invalid a disclaimer admittedly read by the buyer because it failed to meet the requirements of Section 1–201(10).

And don't forget, even a technically valid disclaimer may be set aside by the courts if it is unconscionable.

Disclaimer of the implied warranty of fitness for a particular purpose. Unlike the implied warranty of merchantability which may be disclaimed either orally or in writing, the implied warranty of fitness for a particular purpose may be disclaimed *only* in writing, and the disclaimer must be *conspicuous.* Unlike the word "merchantability", the word "fitness" need not appear in the disclaimer. A conspicuous written statement that "there are no warranties which extend beyond the description on the face hereof" is sufficient to disclaim the implied warranty of fitness for a particular purpose even though it would be insufficient to disclaim merchantability.

Remember, the implied warranty of fitness is made by both merchant and nonmerchant sellers; the disclaimer requirements apply equally to both. Remember, too, that a disclaimer of the implied warranty will be stricken by the courts if it is found to be unconscionable.

(4) *Disclaimer of the implied warranty against patent or trademark infringement.* UCC Section 2–312(2) provides that the implied warranty against patent or trademark infringement may be disclaimed only by specific wording or by circumstances giving the buyer reason to know that such infringement may exist (as you will see in Ch. 19, the same rule applies to disclaimer of the implied war-

ranty of good title). Thus, while "catch-all" language such as "with all faults" or "as is" will be effective to disclaim the implied warranties of merchantability and fitness for a particular purpose, it will not be effective to disclaim the implied warranty against patent or trademark infringement absent knowledge of possible infringement on the part of the buyer.

The Magnuson-Moss Warranty Federal Trade Commission Improvement Act of 1975. Our discussion of warranty would not be complete without mention of the "Magnuson-Moss Warranty Federal Trade Commission Improvement Act of 1975". Merchant buyers, who purchase goods on a large scale, have enough bargaining power to demand that sellers provide them with adequate warranty protection. Consumers, on the other hand, generally have little bargaining power and are easily confused by deceptive or misleading warranty advertising. In 1975, to provide increased protection for consumers, Congress passed the "Magnuson-Moss Warranty Federal Trade Commission Improvement Act".

Section 2302(a) of the Act provides:

In order to improve the adequacy of information available to consumers, prevent deception, and improve competition in the marketing of consumer products any warrantor warranting a consumer product to a consumer by means of a written warranty shall, to the extent required by rules of [the Federal Trade Commission] fully and conspicuously disclose in simple and readily understood language the terms and conditions of such [warranty].

———

Under the Act, the term "consumer product" means any tangible personal property which is purchased primarily for personal, family, or household purposes. The term "consumer" means a buyer

(other than for purposes of resale) of a consumer product, and any subsequent transferee of the product during the duration of any written or implied warranty covering the product. Section 2301(6) defines "written warranty" as follows.

It says:

(A) Any written affirmation of fact or written promise made in connection with the sale of a consumer product by a supplier [manufacturer or retailer] to a buyer *which relates to the nature of the material and workmanship and affirms or promises that such material is defect free or will meet a specified level of performance over a specified period of time, or*

(B) Any undertaking in writing in connection with the sale by a supplier of a consumer product *to refund, repair, replace, or take other remedial action* with respect to such product in the event that such product fails to meet the specifications set forth in the undertaking *which written affirmation, promise, or undertaking becomes part of the basis of the bargain* between a supplier and a buyer for purposes other than resale of the product. (Emphasis added.)

———

As used here, the term "written warranty" has a restricted meaning. For example, certain written representations such as energy efficiency ratings for electrical appliances, care labeling of wearing apparel, and other product information disclosures might well constitute express written warranties under UCC Section 2–313. However, they probably would not constitute written warranties under the Magnuson-Moss Act unless they related to a specified period of time.

Empowered by Section 2302, the Federal Trade Commission (FTC) has set down certain minimum disclosure requirements with regard to written warranties of consumer products.

FTC Regulation 16 CFR 701.3 states:

(a) Any warrantor warranting to a consumer by means of a written warranty a consumer product costing the consumer more than $15.00 shall clearly and conspicuously disclose in a single document in simple and readily understood language, the following items of information:

   (1) The identity of the party or parties to whom the written warranty is extended, if the enforceability of the written warranty is limited to the original consumer or is otherwise limited to persons other than every consumer owner during the term of the warranty;

   (2) A clear description and identification of products, or parts, or characteristics, or components or properties covered by and where necessary for clarification, excluded from the warranty;

   (3) A statement of what the warrantor will do in the event of a defect, malfunction or failure to conform with the written warranty, including the items or services the warrantor will pay for or provide, and, where necessary for clarification, those which the warrantor will not pay for or provide;

   (4) The point in time or event in which the warranty term commences, if different from the purchase date, and the time or other measurement of warranty duration;

   (5) A step-by-step explanation of the procedure which the consumer should follow in order to obtain performance of any warranty obligation * * *;

   (6) Information respecting the availability of any informal dispute settlement mechanism elected by the warrantor [a "mechanism" being any informal, independent dispute settlement procedure incorporated into the terms of a written warranty];

   (7) Any limitations on the duration of implied warranties, disclosed on the face of the warranty * * * accompanied by the following statement:

"Some states do not allow limitations on how long an implied warranty lasts, so the above limitation may not apply to you."

   (8) Any exclusions of or limitations on relief such as incidental or consequential damages, accompanied by the following statement:

"Some states do not allow the exclusion of or limitation of incidental or consequential damages, so the above limitation or exclusion may not apply to you."

   (9) A statement in the following language:

"This warranty gives you specific legal rights, and you may also have other rights which vary from state to state."

———

The FTC has no power under the Magnuson-Moss Act to require sellers to warrant their products or to prescribe the duration of written warranties. However, if a seller does give a written warranty, the warranty must contain all the information in (1) through (9) above, and the seller must make the warranty information available to the buyer prior to sale.

Section 2303 of the Magnuson-Moss Act further requires the warrantor of consumer goods costing the consumer more than $10.00 to clearly and conspicuously designate any written warranty covering the goods as either a "full (statement of duration, e. g., 1 year) warranty" or a "limited warranty". To be labeled a "full warranty", a written warranty must meet the following minimum federal standards:

(1) The warrantor must agree to remedy the consumer product (repair or replace it, or, if this is not possible, refund the consumer's money) within a reasonable time and without charge in the case of defect, malfunction, or other breach of the written warranty;

(2) The warrantor may not limit the duration of any implied warranty covering the product;

(3) The warrantor may not exclude or limit consequential damages for breach of any written or implied warranty unless the exclusion or limitation conspicuously appears on the face of the warranty;

(4) If the product still contains a defect or malfunction after a reasonable number of attempts by the warrantor to remedy the defects, the warrantor must allow the customer to elect a refund or replacement of the article without charge.

A warrantor who gives a "full" written warranty may not impose upon the consumer any condition precedent to repair, replacement, or refund other than notification of the breach of warranty (e. g., the warrantor may not require as a condition precedent return of a "warranty registration card"). A warrantor who labels a written warranty as a "full warranty"

will be bound by the minimum federal standards.

No warrantor of a consumer product may condition his or her written or implied warranty of the product on the consumer's use (in conjunction with the product) of an article or service identified by brand, trade, or corporate name unless that article or service is provided free of charge to the consumer.

As to disclaimer or modification of implied warranties, Section 2308 of the Magnuson-Moss Act states:

The Act says:

(a) No supplier may disclaim or modify (except as provided in subsection (b) of this section) any implied warranty to a consumer with respect to such consumer product if (1) such supplier makes any written warranty with respect to such consumer product, or (2) at the time of sale, or within 90 days thereafter, such supplier enters into a service contract with the consumer which applies to such consumer product. [A "service contract" being a contract in writing to perform over a fixed period of time or for a specified duration services relating to the maintenance or repair, or both, of a consumer product.]

(b) For purposes of this chapter * * * implied warranties may be limited in duration to the duration of a written warranty of reasonable duration, if such limitation is conscionable and is set forth in clear and unmistakable language and prominently displayed on the face of the warranty [but remember, a warrantor who gives a "full warranty" may not limit the duration of implied warranties].

(c) A disclaimer, modification, or limitation made in violation of this section shall be ineffective for purposes of this chapter and State law.

———

Thus, if a manufacturer or retailer gives a written warranty (as defined by the Magnuson-Moss Act) covering consumer goods, the manufacturer or retailer cannot exclude any implied warranty covering the goods. However, if the written warranty is a "limited" one, the manufacturer or retailer can limit the duration of the implied warranty.

Finally, the Magnuson-Moss Act authorizes the FTC to investigate and enjoin violations of the Act (including deceptive warranty advertising). And the Act provides a civil action remedy for any consumer who is injured by a warrantor's failure to comply with the Magnuson-Moss Act or with any written or implied warranty thereunder. The consumer may sue in state court (and in certain cases in federal court) and recover damages as well as the costs and expenses of the action.

The Circumstance of the Seller Becoming Insolvent and Being Unable to Perform Because of the Insolvency —The Buyer's Right to "Capture"

To this point, we have considered one way in which the seller may fail to perform his or her part of the sales contract: he or she may send nonconforming goods to the buyer. We have learned that the buyer's possible remedies in this situation include rejection of the goods, revocation of acceptance, resale to recover prepayments, cover, damages for nondelivery, breach of warranty action, and set-off.

Now we turn to a second way in which the seller may fail to perform—he or she may become insolvent and be unable to deliver the goods because of the insolvency. The Uniform Commercial Code defines "insolvency" at Section 1–201(23) as follows: "A person is 'insolvent' who either has ceased to pay his debts in the

ordinary course of business or cannot pay his debts as they become due or is insolvent within the meaning of the federal bankruptcy law." A person is "insolvent" within the meaning of the federal Bankruptcy Act if his or her liabilities exceed his or her assets (see Ch. 26, "Creditors and Bankruptcy").

Where the buyer becomes insolvent and is unable to deliver the goods to the buyer, the buyer will have a right under certain circumstances to "capture" the goods (i. e., demand and obtain them from the seller). Section 2–502 of the Uniform Commercial Code provides for this right as follows.

The UCC provides:
Section 2–502. Buyer's Right to Goods on Seller's Insolvency

(1) * * * [E]ven though the goods have not been shipped a buyer who has paid a part or all of the price of the goods in which he has a special property * * * may on making and keeping good a tender of any unpaid portion of their price recover them from the seller if the seller becomes insolvent within ten days after receipt of the first installment on their price.

———

Thus, there are three specific requirements for the right of capture to exist:

(1) The goods must be *identified* to the contract of sale. As you will recall from Ch. 17, identification of the goods creates in the buyer a "special property and insurable interest" in the goods. Identification also gives the buyer the right to capture the goods so long as the other two requirements are met.

(2) The buyer must have *prepaid* all or part of the purchase price of the goods. Where the buyer has prepaid only part of the price, he or she must ten-

der to the seller the balance owing and keep the tender open.

(3) Finally, the seller must have become *insolvent within ten days after receiving the first installment* on the purchase price.

The *Official Comment* to Section 2–502 summarizes:

The Official Comment provides:

[Section 2–502] gives an additional right to the buyer as a result of identification of the goods to the contract in the manner provided in Section 2–501. The buyer is given a right to the goods on the seller's insolvency occurring within 10 days after he receives the first installment on their price.

————

The right of capture allows the buyer to demand and obtain the goods without going to court. However, the right does not carry with it a right to use force or self-help in claiming the property. If the seller refuses to recognize the buyer's right and deliver over the property, the buyer must go to court to *replevin* the goods (as you will recall from Ch. 1, a suit to "replevin" is a "request to the court for specific goods"). For example, suppose that Hood River Apple Company identifies the 2,000 crates of Grade A apples to be sold to New England Produce. Within ten days of receiving the first installment of the purchase price, Hood River Apple becomes insolvent and is unable to deliver the goods. New England Produce has a right under UCC Section 2–502 to capture the apples. If Hood River Apple refuses to permit capture, New England Produce may go to court to replevin the goods (probably not a good remedy since the apples are likely to spoil).

Of course, where the seller is unable to deliver goods because of insolvency, the buyer will have other possible remedies in addition to capture or replevin—most

notably, the right to effect cover or sue for money damages for nondelivery (these remedies are dealt with in the following section). However, these other remedies are generally of little value to the buyer since they involve seeking money damages: where the seller is insolvent, money damages are unlikely to be forthcoming.

The Circumstance of the Seller Failing to Deliver the Goods For Any Reason—The Buyer's Right to "Cover" or "Specific Performance" or "Money Damages For Nondelivery" or "Capture"

The seller, for whatever reason (including insolvency) may fail to transfer and deliver the goods to the buyer. If the specific insolvency situation contemplated by UCC Section 2–502 is not present, the buyer will have to resort to one of the following legal remedies:

(1) Cover;

(2) Suit for specific performance;

(3) Suit for money damages for non-delivery; or

(4) Capture (under UCC Section 2–711(2)(a).

As you will recall, a buyer "covers" by purchasing substitute goods on the open market; the buyer may recover from the seller any excess of the cover price over the contract price. Cover is a very effective remedy and the remedy most frequently used because satisfactory substitute goods are almost always available, with the result that the buyer can obtain the goods he or she needs despite the seller's breach of contract.

Occasionally, however, the buyer cannot cover because adequate substitute goods are not available on the open market. In this unusual situation, the goods are deemed "unique", and the buyer may sue for specific performance—that is, for replevin of the specific goods. (You will recall from Ch. 10 that specific performance is granted by the courts only where money damages are not an adequate remedy.)

Sometimes, though the goods are unique, the buyer prefers not to sue for specific performance. Or perhaps cover is possible but not desirable (e. g., where the buyer no longer needs the goods). The buyer, in this case, may simply sue the seller for money damages for nondelivery of the goods. This remedy is an alternative to cover and to specific performance—that is, the buyer can cover *or* sue for specific performance *or* sue for damages for nondelivery. Again, the buyer's measure of damages for nondelivery is the difference between the market price at the time when the buyer learns of the breach and the contract price (plus allowable incidental and consequential damages less expenses saved because of the breach).

Finally, where the goods have been identified to the contract, the buyer has another alternative: he or she may "capture" the goods under UCC Section 2–711(2)(a). Unlike the buyer's right of capture under UCC Section 2–502 (requiring part payment and seller's insolvency within ten days of the payment), the only requirements under Section 2–711(2)(a) are identification and nondelivery (or repudiation as discussed in the following section). To assert his or her right of capture, the buyer must tender the full purchase price of the goods (and keep the tender open) and demand their immediate delivery. Again, the buyer may not use force or self-help in claiming the goods. If the seller refuses to honor the buyer's demand for capture, the buyer must seek replevin in court under UCC Section 2–716—only here (unlike under UCC Section 2–502 where replevin is automatically granted), replevin will be granted only if the goods are not otherwise available on the open market. That is to say, the goods must be unique and unavailable through cover. Where replevin is denied, the buyer must either cover or sue for money damages for nondelivery.

UCC Section 2–711 provides as follows:

(1) Where the seller fails to make delivery * * * the buyer may cancel and whether or not he has done so may in addition to recovering so much of the price as has been paid

(a) "cover" * * * or

(b) recover damages for non-delivery * * *

(2) * * * [Or] the buyer may * * *

(a) if the goods have been identified recover them as provided in this Article (Section 2–502); or

(b) in a proper case obtain specific performance or replevy the goods as provided in this Article (Section 2–716).

———

Section 2–716 states:

Section 2–716. Buyer's Right to Specific Performance or Replevin

(1) Specific performance may be decreed where the goods are unique or in other proper circumstances.

(2) The decree for specific performance may include such terms and conditions as to payment of the price, damages, or other relief as the court may deem just.

(3) The buyer has a right of replevin for goods identified to the contract if after reasonable effort he is unable to effect cover for such goods or the circumstances reasonably indicate that such effort will be unavailing * * *.

———

Consider the following example. Suppose that Hood River Apple Company fails to deliver the 2,000 crates of Grade A apples to New England Produce. New England may cover by purchasing substitute goods on the open market. If the cover price is greater than the contract price, New England may recover the excess from Hood River Apple. Assuming cover is not a desirable remedy (e. g., where New England no longer wants or needs the apples), New England Produce may sue Hood River for money damages for nondelivery. Where cover is desirable but cannot be accomplished (because substitute apples are not available), New England Produce may sue for specific performance of the contract (however, the likelihood that the apples will spoil makes this an impractical remedy); or New England may sue for money damages for nondelivery. Assuming the 2,000 crates of apples have been identified to the contract of sale, New England Produce may choose instead to assert its right of capture under UCC Section 2–711(2)(a) by tendering the full purchase price of the apples and demanding their immediate delivery. If Hood River Apple Company refuses to deliver the apples—that is, refuses to honor New England's right of capture—New England may sue to replevin the apples. However, replevin will be granted only if the goods are otherwise unavailable on the open market.

The Circumstance of the Seller Repudiating in Advance His or Her Obligation to Perform According to the Contract of Sale—The Buyer's Right to Treat the Repudiation as a Breach of Contract

In Ch. 10, we described the doctrine of anticipatory breach or repudiation as follows.

If either party to an executory bilateral contract announces in advance of his or her promised performance that he or she will not perform (i. e., repudiates the promised performance), the other party may treat the anticipatory repudiation as a present material breach of the contract and bring legal action immediately for breach of the *entire* agreement. Anticipatory breach or repudiation applies only to executory bilateral contracts: an executory contract is a contract wherein both parties have yet to perform; a bilateral contract is a promise for a promise. * * * The doctrine of anticipatory breach or repudiation is designed to prevent hardship to the party told in advance that a promised performance will not be forthcoming. Certainly, it would be extremely unfair to insist that the party wait until the time for performance, remaining ready and able to personally perform, after the other party has stated that he or she will not carry out his or her part of the bargain.

———

Insofar as the sale of goods is concerned, the Uniform Commercial Code extends the doctrine of anticipatory breach or repudiation to include any contract of sale in which there remains some duty of performance owing by at least one of the parties: in other words, the Code (a statute modifying the common law in places) has eliminated the requirement that the contract of sale be fully executory.

The Code provides for the doctrine of anticipatory breach or repudiation at Section 2–610, which states.

Section 2–610. Anticipatory Repudiation

When either party repudiates the contract with respect to a performance not yet due the loss of which will substantially impair the value of the contract to the other, the aggrieved party may

(a) for a commercially reasonable time await performance by the repudiating party; or

(b) resort to any remedy for breach * * * even though he has notified the repudiating party that he would await the latter's performance and has urged retraction; and

(c) in either case suspend his own performance * * *.

The *Official Comment* to the Section states: "Anticipatory repudiation centers upon an overt *communication* of intention or an *action* which renders performance impossible or demonstrates a clear determination not to continue with performance." (Emphasis supplied.) Thus, a seller may repudiate a contract by words or by actions. For example, Hood River Apple Company repudiates its contract with New England Produce where, prior to the contract time for performance, Hood River informs New England that it will not deliver the 2,000 crates of apples. The same is true where Hood River, after contracting to sell 2,000 crates of Grade A apples to New England, sells all of its Grade A apples to another company, making it impossible for Hood River to fulfill its contract obligations to New England. In each case, Hood River repudiates a performance not yet due the loss of which will "substantially impair" the value of the contract to New England Produce. New England may treat the repudiation as a breach of contract and suspend its own promised performance under the contract.

Many times, however, it is not clear whether the particular words or acts of a party constitute a repudiation of the sales contract. An oral or written communication from the party may be ambiguous as to the party's intent or ability to perform. Or the party may appear to be insolvent and incapable of performing. If the oth-

er party, believing there has been a repudiation of the contract, suspends his or her own performance (or indicates an intent to do so), that party, if mistaken, will himself or herself be liable for breach of contract or anticipatory repudiation. To prevent this from happening, the Uniform Commercial Code provides a method for determining whether a repudiation has, in fact, occurred. Under Section 2–609, if one party has a reasonable basis for feeling insecure about the other's performance, he or she may demand *adequate assurance* of due performance. If the other party fails to provide such assurance within a reasonable time not exceeding 30 days, that party will be deemed to have repudiated the contract.

Section 2–609 provides:

Section 2–609. Right to Adequate Assurance of Performance

(1) A contract for sale imposes an obligation on each party that the other's expectation of receiving due performance will not be impaired. When reasonable grounds for insecurity arise with respect to the performance of either party the other may in writing demand adequate assurance of due performance and until he receives such assurance may if commercially reasonable suspend any performance for which he has not already received the agreed return.

(2) Between merchants the reasonableness of grounds for insecurity and the adequacy of any assurance offered shall be determined according to commercial standards.

(3) Acceptance of any improper delivery or payment does not prejudice the aggrieved party's right to demand adequate assurance of future performance.

(4) After receipt of a justified demand failure to provide within a reasonable time not exceeding thirty days such assurance of due performance as is adequate under the circumstances of the particular case is a repudiation of the contract.

————————

The *Official Comment* to Section 2–609 explains.

The Official Comment provides:

(1) The section rests on the recognition of the fact that the essential purpose of a contract between commercial men is actual performance and they do not bargain merely for a promise, or for a promise plus the right to win a lawsuit and that a continuing sense of reliance and security that the promised performance will be forthcoming when due, is an important feature of the bargain. If either the willingness or the ability of a party to perform declines materially between the time of contracting and the time for performance, the other party is threatened with the loss of a substantial part of what he has bargained for.

(2) Three measures have been adopted to meet the needs of commercial men in such situations. First, the aggrieved party is permitted to suspend his own performance and any preparation therefor, with excuse for any resulting necessary delay, until the situation has been clarified.

* * *

Secondly, the aggrieved party is given the right to require adequate assurance that the other party's performance will be duly forthcoming.

* * *

Third, and finally, this section provides the means by which the aggrieved party may treat the contract as broken if his reasonable grounds for insecurity are not cleared up within a reasonable time. This is the principle underlying the law of anticipatory breach, whether by way of defective part performance or by repudiation.

————————

Once it is established that the seller has, in fact, repudiated the contract, the buyer has a right under UCC Section 2–610 to resort immediately to "any remedy for breach". The buyer's remedies, in the case of repudiation by the seller, are summarized at UCC Section 2–711 as follows.

The UCC provides:

(1) Where the seller * * * repudiates * * * then with respect to any goods involved, and with respect to the whole if the breach goes to the whole contract * * * the buyer may cancel and whether or not he has done so may in addition to recovering so much of the price as has been paid

(a) "cover" and have damages * * * as to all the goods affected whether or not they have been identified to the contract; or

(b) recover damages for non-delivery as provided in this Article (Section 2–713).

(2) Where the seller * * * repudiates the buyer may also

(a) if the goods have been identified recover them as provided in this Article (Section 2–502); or

(b) in a proper case obtain specific performance or replevy the goods as provided in this Article (Section 2–716).

———

Thus, upon repudiation by the seller, the buyer may immediately "cancel" the contract (i. e., put an end to the contract) and recover any portion of the purchase price already paid. In addition, the buyer may either cover *or* sue for money damages for nondelivery. Or, where appropriate, the buyer may capture the goods (if the goods have been identified) *or* sue for specific performance or replevin of the goods. All of these buyer's remedies have been discussed in detail previously in the chapter.

However, a few special rules insofar as anticipatory repudiation and Section 2–713 are concerned should be pointed out. As you will recall, Section 2–713 provides that the buyer's measure of damages for nondelivery or repudiation is "the difference between the market price at the time when the buyer learned of the breach and the contract price together with any incidental and consequential damages * * * but less expenses saved in consequence of the seller's breach." The market price, in the case of repudiation by the seller, is determined as of the place for "tender" of the goods.

The question arises—when does the buyer *learn of the breach* for purposes of determining market price? At the time he or she learns of the repudiation? When the contract time for performance arrives and the seller fails to perform? The Uniform Commercial Code is not clear on this question. However, it appears that the buyer will *learn of the breach* as of the time of repudiation only where the case against the seller comes to court before the contract time for performance falls due; in all other cases, the buyer will *learn of the breach* as of the contract time for performance. This conclusion is bolstered by UCC Section 2–723(1), "Proof of Market Price: Time and Place", which states.

The UCC provides:

If an action based on anticipatory repudiation comes to trial before the time for performance with respect to some or all of the goods, any damages based on market price * * * shall be determined according to the price of such goods prevailing at the time when the aggrieved party learned of the repudiation.

———

Again, if evidence of the market price prevailing at this time is not readily available, evidence of any other reasonable market price may be used under Section 2–723(2).

By way of example, suppose that Hood River Apple Company informs New England Produce on August 1st (two months in advance of the contract time for performance) that it will not deliver the 2,000 crates of Grade A apples. Hood River has repudiated the contract, and New England has a right to resort immediately to any remedy for breach: New England decides to sue for money damages for nondelivery. Assuming the case comes to court before October 1st (the contract time for performance), the market price will be determined as of August 1st. If the contract price is $5.00 per crate, and the market price on August 1st at the place for tender is $8.00, New England's measure of damages for nondelivery will be $6,000 (the difference between the $16,000 market price and the $10,000 contract price) plus any incidental or consequential damages incurred less expenses saved.

Where, on the other hand, the case comes to court after October 1st, the market price will be determined as of October 1st. If the contract price is $5.00 per crate, and the market price on October 1st at the place for tender is $7.00 per crate (the market price having dropped $1.00 since August 1st), New England's measure of damages for nondelivery will be $4,000 (the difference between the $14,000 market price and the $10,000 contract price) plus any incidental or consequential damages incurred less expenses saved.

While the aggrieved buyer has a right to resort immediately to any remedy for breach in the case of repudiation by the seller, the buyer is not required to do so. So long as the buyer takes no action, the seller is free to retract (i. e., withdraw) his or her repudiation under UCC Section 2–611 and reinstate his or her rights under the contract. In other words, an anticipatory repudiation is revocable unless and until the aggrieved party has (1) cancelled the contract; (2) changed his or her position materially in response to the repudiation; or (3) indicated in some other way that he or she has accepted the repudiation as final.

Section 2–611 states:

Section 2–611. Retraction of Anticipatory Repudiation

(1) Until the repudiating party's next performance is due he can retract his repudiation unless the aggrieved party has since the repudiation cancelled or materially changed his position or otherwise indicated that he considers the repudiation final.

(2) Retraction may be by any method which clearly indicates to the aggrieved party that the repudiating party intends to perform, but must include any assurance justifiably demanded under the provisions of this Article (Section 2–609).

(3) Retraction reinstates the repudiating party's rights under the contract with due excuse and allowance to the aggrieved party for any delay occasioned by the repudiation.

Under Subsection (2), the retraction may be by "any method" indicating the repudiating party's intention to perform—the party may retract by words (oral or written) or by conduct. For example, suppose that Hood River Apple Company repudiates (in writing) its contract with New England Produce two months in advance of the contract time for performance. Hearing nothing from New England, Hood River ultimately ships the 2,000 crates of apples before the contract time for performance has expired. Assuming New England Produce has not materially changed its position in the interim, Hood River Apple has effectively retracted the repudiation and reinstated its rights under the contract.

Finally, before moving on to the seller's remedies in the event of breach by the buyer, it is a good idea to summarize the remedies available to the buyer upon breach by the seller.

Uniform Commercial Code Section 2–711 provides as follows:

Section 2–711. Buyer's Remedies in General * * *

(1) Where the seller fails to make delivery or repudiates or the buyer rightfully rejects or justifiably revokes acceptance then with respect to any goods involved, and with respect to the whole if the breach goes to the whole contract * * * the buyer may cancel and whether or not he has done so may in addition to recovering so much of the price as has been paid

(a) "cover" and have damages * * * as to all the goods affected whether or not they have been identified to the contract; or

(b) recover damages for non-delivery as provided in this Article (Section 2–713).

(2) Where the seller fails to deliver or repudiates the buyer may also

(a) if the goods have been identified recover them as provided in this Article (Section 2–502); or

(b) in a proper case obtain specific performance or replevy the goods as provided in this Article (Section 2–716).

———

And, of course, the buyer who accepts nonconforming goods may sue the seller for breach of express and/or implied warranty.

As for the buyer's measure of damages for cover, nondelivery, and breach of warranty, there are three rules:

First—damages following cover. In the event of rightful rejection, justifiable revocation of acceptance, failure by the seller to deliver the goods, or repudiation by the seller, the buyer may cover (i. e., purchase substitute goods on the open market) and recover from the seller any excess of cover price over contract price. In addition, the buyer may recover any incidental or consequential damages less expenses saved by reason of purchasing in another market.

Second—damages for nondelivery. In the same circumstances, the buyer may choose the alternative remedy of suing for money damages for nondelivery. The buyer's measure of damages for nondelivery is the difference between the market price when the buyer learned of the breach and the contract price, together with any incidental or consequential damages less expenses saved because of the seller's breach. The market price is determined as of the place for tender, or. in the case of rejection or revocation of acceptance after the goods have arrived, as of the place of arrival.

Third—damages for breach of warranty. The buyer who accepts nonconform-

ing goods may sue the seller for breach of express or implied warranty. The buyer's measure of damages is the difference at the time and place of acceptance between the value of the goods as warranted and their value as received. The buyer may also recover incidental or consequential damages, where appropriate.

What are the seller's rights, if any, in the event that the buyer fails to perform his or her part of the sales bargain?

Having completed our study of the buyer's remedies in the event of breach by the seller, we turn now to the seller's remedies in the event of breach by the buyer. As you will recall, UCC Section 2–301 provides that the buyer's basic duty is to "accept and pay for" the goods in accordance with the sales contract. The buyer sometimes fails in this duty as follows:

(1) He or she fails to pay for the goods;

(2) He or she becomes insolvent and cannot perform;

(3) He or she wrongfully refuses to accept the goods;

(4) He or she repudiates the contract of sale.

Barring objective impossibility or "commercial impracticability" within the meaning of UCC Section 2–615, the buyer's failure to carry out his or her basic duty constitutes a breach of contract. Depending upon the specific event or circumstance of the buyer's breach, the seller will have access to one or more of the following legal remedies:

(1) Withhold delivery of the goods to the buyer;

(2) Refuse credit to the buyer and demand cash before delivery;

(3) Reclaim the goods from the buyer without court action;

(4) Replevin the goods in court;

(5) Stop the goods in transit and re-take possession of them;

(6) Identify (or finish identifying) the goods to the contract and re-sell them to another, recovering from the buyer the difference between the contract price and the resale price;

(7) With regard to incomplete goods still in the manufacturing process, sell or salvage the goods in their incomplete form or complete the goods and resell them, again recovering from the buyer the difference between the contract price and the resale price;

(8) Cancel the contract;

(9) Bring legal action in court for the full purchase price of the goods;

(10) Bring legal action in court for money damages.

The Circumstance of the Buyer Failing to Make a Payment Due Under the Contract or Repudiating the Contract, the Seller Not Yet Having Delivered the Goods to the Buyer— The Seller's Right to Withhold Delivery of the Goods

If the buyer fails to make a payment due on or before delivery, or repudiates the contract in advance of delivery, the seller may withhold delivery of the goods. To withhold delivery in no way affects any other remedies available to the seller. UCC Section 2–703 provides: "Where the buyer * * * fails to make a payment due on or before delivery or repudiates with respect to a part or the whole * * * the aggrieved seller may * * * withhold delivery of the goods."

The Official Comment to the Section states:

In addition to the typical case of refusal to pay or default in payment, the language in the preamble, "fails to make a payment due," is intended to cover the dishonor of a check on due presentment, or the non-acceptance of a draft * * *.

———

For example, suppose that New England Produce is required by the terms of its contract with Hood River Apple to make a down payment on the 2,000 crates of apples 30 days before delivery. New England pays by check, and the check is dishonored for lack of sufficient funds. Hood River Apple may withhold delivery of the apples and proceed with any other available remedy for the breach.

Or suppose it appears that New England Produce is insolvent. Hood River Apple may suspend delivery and demand adequate assurance of performance under UCC Section 2–609. If such assurance is not forthcoming, Hood River Apple may treat the failure to respond as a repudiation of the contract and withhold delivery of the apples; the Company may then proceed with any other available remedy for the breach.

The Circumstance of the Seller Learning of the Buyer's Insolvency Before Delivery (or After Partial Delivery) Under a Contract of Sale on Credit to the Buyer—The Seller's Right to Demand Cash Payment and to Withhold (Further) Delivery Until Cash Payment is Made

If a seller who has contracted to sell goods on credit to a buyer discovers prior to delivery that the buyer is insolvent,[5]

5. As you will recall, a person is "insolvent" who cannot pay his or her debts as they fall due, who has ceased to pay his or her debts in the ordinary course of business, or who is "insolvent" within the meaning of the federal Bankruptcy Act (i. e., his or her liabilities exceed his or her assets).

the seller may demand payment in cash for the goods and withhold delivery until cash payment is made. If the seller has already delivered part of the goods at the time of learning of the buyer's insolvency, he or she may demand payment in cash for all the goods (both those delivered and those to be delivered) and withhold further delivery until such payment is made. UCC Section 2–702(1) provides: "Where the seller discovers the buyer to be insolvent he may refuse delivery except for cash including payment for all goods theretofore delivered under the contract, and stop delivery * * *." Demanding payment in cash and withholding delivery does not affect any of the seller's other rights and remedies against the defaulting buyer.

By way of example, suppose that Hood River Apple Company agrees to sell 2,000 crates of Grade A apples on credit to New England Produce. After delivering 500 of the crates, Hood River Apple discovers that New England Produce is insolvent. Hood River may demand payment in cash for the 500 crates delivered as well as for the 1,500 to be delivered and withhold further delivery until the cash payment is made.

The Circumstance of the Buyer Receiving Goods on Credit While Insolvent—The Seller's Right of Reclamation

Sometimes, the seller does not discover that the buyer is insolvent until after he or she has delivered the goods on credit to the buyer. Obviously, the remedy of withholding delivery is not available to the seller in this case. But if the buyer was insolvent at the time of receipt of the goods, the seller may *reclaim* the property as provided by Section 2–702 of the Uniform Commercial Code.

The UCC provides:

Section 2–702. Seller's Remedies on Discovery of Buyer's Insolvency

* * *

(2) Where the seller discovers that the buyer has received goods on credit while insolvent he may reclaim the goods upon demand made within ten days after the receipt, but if misrepresentation of solvency has been made to the particular seller in writing within three months before delivery the ten day limitation does not apply. Except as provided in this subsection the seller may not base a right to reclaim goods on the buyer's fraudulent or innocent misrepresentation of solvency or of intent to pay.

(3) The seller's right to reclaim under subsection (2) is subject to the rights of a buyer in ordinary course or other good faith purchaser * * *. Successful reclamation of goods excludes all other remedies with respect to them * * *.

The Official Comment to the Section provides:

Subsection (2) * * * [is based on] the proposition that any receipt of goods on credit by an insolvent buyer amounts to a tacit business misrepresentation of solvency and therefore is fraudulent as against the particular seller. This Article makes discovery of the buyer's insolvency and demand with a ten-day period a condition of the right to reclaim goods on this ground. The ten-day limitation period operates from the time of receipt of the goods.

An exception to this time limitation is made when a written misrepresentation of solvency has been made to the particular seller within three months prior to the delivery. To fall within the exception the statement of solvency must be in writing, addressed to the particular seller and dated within three months of the delivery.

———

Thus, to reclaim the goods, the seller must demand their return within ten days after the buyer receives them. The ten-day limitation does not apply where the buyer misrepresented his or her solvency in writing to the seller within three months prior to delivery. For example, suppose that Hood River Apple Company delivers 2,000 crates of Grade A apples on credit to New England Produce. Five days after delivery, Hood River discovers that New England was insolvent at the time of receipt of the goods and cannot now pay for the apples. Hood River may reclaim the goods by making demand for their return within the next five days (i. e., within ten days after their receipt by New England).

Now let's change the facts. Suppose that Hood River does not learn of New England's insolvency (at the time of receipt of the apples) until fifteen days after delivery. Hood River may reclaim the apples only if New England misrepresented to the Company in writing that it was solvent within three months prior to the delivery. Of course, considering the distances involved (Hood River Apple on the West Coast and New England Produce on the Eastern Seaboard) and the perishable nature of the commodity (apples), reclamation may be impracticable in any case.

Just as an aggrieved buyer may not use force or self-help to *capture* goods, an aggrieved seller may not use force or self-help to *reclaim* goods. If the buyer refuses to honor the seller's right of reclamation, the seller must go to court to replevin the goods. Successful reclamation (whether the goods are given up voluntarily by the buyer or obtained through replevin) excludes all other remedies with respect to the property, although the

seller is still entitled to incidental damages. UCC Section 2–710 states: "Incidental damages to an aggrieved seller include any commercially reasonable charges, expenses or commissions incurred in * * * connection with return * * * of the goods."

Finally, as pointed out in Section 2–702(3), the transfer of the goods to a bona fide purchaser for value (i. e., one who buys the goods for value without notice of the seller's rights) cuts off the seller's right of reclamation: the bfp prevails over the seller as to possession of the goods, and the seller must resort to some other remedy. For example, suppose that New England Produce immediately sells the 2,000 crates of Grade A apples to Boston Farmers Market. The latter pays full value for the goods and takes without knowledge of New England's insolvency. The transfer by New England to Boston Farmers Market—a bfp—cuts off Hood River's right to reclaim the goods, and Hood River must resort to another remedy.

The Circumstance of the Seller Learning of the Buyer's Insolvency After the Goods Have Been Shipped But Before They Have Been Delivered to the Buyer—The Seller's Right of Stoppage in Transit

If the seller learns of the buyer's insolvency after delivering the goods to a carrier for shipment, the seller may "stop" the goods while they are in transit and retake possession of them. The seller may thereafter withhold delivery of the goods pending cash payment, and, if such payment is not forthcoming, may resort to any other available remedy. Referred to as the right of *stoppage in transit,* this seller's remedy is provided by Section 2–705 of the Uniform Commercial Code (which also extends the right to situations where the goods are in the possession of a bailee other than a carrier—e. g., a warehouseman).

The UCC provides:

Section 2–705. Seller's Stoppage of Delivery in Transit or Otherwise

(1) The seller may stop delivery of goods in the possession of a carrier or other bailee when he discovers the buyer to be insolvent

* * *

(2) As against such buyer the seller may stop delivery until

(a) receipt of the goods by the buyer; or

(b) acknowledgment to the buyer by any bailee of the goods except a carrier that the bailee holds the goods for the buyer; or

(c) such acknowledgment to the buyer by a carrier by reshipment [at the buyer's direction] or as warehouseman; or

(d) negotiation to the buyer of any negotiable document of title covering the goods.

(3)(a) To stop delivery the seller must so notify as to enable the bailee by reasonable diligence to prevent delivery of the goods.

(b) After such notification the bailee must hold and deliver the goods according to the directions of the seller but the seller is liable to the bailee for any ensuing charges or damages.

(c) If a negotiable document of title has been issued for the goods the bailee is not obliged to obey a notification to stop until surrender of the document.

(d) A carrier who has issued a non-negotiable bill of lading is not obliged to obey a notification to stop received from a person other than the consignor.

Thus, the seller may stop delivery until one of the following occurs:

(1) The buyer receives possession of the goods from the carrier or other bailee;

(2) The bailee (other than a carrier) acknowledges to the buyer that he or she is holding the goods for the buyer;

(3) The carrier makes such an acknowledgment by agreeing to reship the goods for the buyer or to warehouse the goods for him or her following transport. The *Official Comment* to Section 2–705 provides: "Acknowledgment by the carrier as a 'warehouseman' within the meaning of this Article requires a contract of a truly different character from the original shipment, a contract not in extension of transit but as a warehouseman." Thus, the seller may stop delivery though the carrier has agreed to hold the goods at destination for a few days until the buyer picks them up; the seller may not stop delivery where the carrier has agreed to store the goods in his or her warehouse at destination for several months time.

(4) A negotiable document of title (bill of lading or warehouse receipt) covering the goods is negotiated to the buyer. As you will recall from Ch. 16, a carrier or other bailee is not protected in surrendering goods covered by a negotiable document of title unless the document is presented for cancellation.

Where none of the above has occurred, the seller may exercise his or her right of stoppage in transit by notifying the carrier or other bailee to stop delivery. The notice must be such as to give the carrier or other bailee sufficient time to locate the goods and prevent their delivery. Upon receiving a timely "stop" notice, the carrier must hold and deliver the goods according to the seller's direction. If the goods are covered by a negotiable document of title, the carrier is not obliged to obey the "stop" order until the seller surrenders the document. By way of example, suppose that after shipping the 2,000 crates of Grade A apples, Hood River Apple Company learns that New England Produce is insolvent. Though New England is in possession of a straight bill of lading covering the goods, Hood River Apple exercises its right of stoppage in transit and orders the carrier to return the apples to Hood River (the straight bill of lading has no effect upon Hood River's right to stop delivery). If, on the other hand, the apples are covered by a negotiable bill of lading which has been negotiated to the buyer, Hood River has no right of stoppage in transit.

A carrier or other bailee who refuses to comply with a timely given "stop" order will be liable to the seller for conversion of the goods. Conversely, if the carrier or other bailee stops delivery, and it turns out that the seller did not have the right of stoppage in transit, the carrier or other bailee will be liable to the buyer for failure to deliver the goods. Of course, the carrier will be protected in acting in accordance with UCC Section 7–303 (see Ch. 16 regarding "diversion, reconsignment, and change of instructions" to a carrier). And even if the carrier is found liable, UCC Section 2–705(3)(b) gives him or her a right of indemnity against the seller. In any event, to protect himself or herself from liability where the buyer disputes the seller's right to stop delivery, the carrier or other bailee may bring an *interpleader* action in court. In an interpleader action, the issue of who is entitled to the goods is placed before the court, and the carrier or other bailee is relieved of responsibility in the matter.

Where goods "stopped" in transit are returned to the seller, the seller must bear the expense of redelivery. Ultimately, the seller can recover the expense from the buyer as incidental damages under UCC Section 2–710. The Section states: "Incidental damages to an ag-grieved seller include any commercially reasonable charges, expenses or commissions incurred in stopping delivery * * * in connection with return * * * of the goods * * *."

Finally, it should be pointed out that if the buyer sells the goods while they are in transit to a bona fide purchaser, the bfp will cut off the seller's right of stoppage in transit. The same is true where the buyer obtains a negotiable document of title covering the goods and negotiates it to a bona fide purchaser. This is so whether the document is negotiated to the bfp *before* or *after* the seller has notified the carrier to stop delivery. UCC Section 7–502(2). The buyer's creditors, however, do not qualify as bona fide purchasers for purposes of cutting off the seller's right of stoppage in transit.

The Circumstance of the Seller Shipping a "Big Shipment" and the Buyer Thereafter Repudiating the Contract, Failing to Make a Payment Due on or Before Delivery, or Otherwise Seriously Breaching the Agreement—Again, the Seller's Right of Stoppage in Transit

UCC Section 2–705(1) also provides that the seller "may stop delivery of carload, truckload, planeload or larger shipments of express or freight when the buyer repudiates or fails to make a payment due before delivery or if for any other reason the seller has a right to withhold or reclaim the goods."

The Official Comment to the Section provides:

* * * [Section 2–705] expands the remedy [of stoppage in transit] to cover * * * situations * * * in addition to buyer's insolvency * * * But since stoppage is a burden in any case to carriers, and might be a very heavy burden to them if it covered all small shipments in all these situations, the right to stop for reasons other than insolvency is limited to car-

load, truckload, planeload or larger shipments.

All the rules discussed in the previous section apply to stoppage of "big shipments" upon breach or repudiation by the buyer. Thus, if Hood River Apple Company ships the 2,000 crates of Grade A apples (certainly a "big shipment" within the meaning of Section 2–705), and New England Produce thereafter repudiates the contract of sale, Hood River may notify the carrier to stop delivery and return the goods to Hood River.

The Circumstance of the Buyer Refusing to Accept the Goods (Wrongfully Rejecting Them or Unjustifiably Revoking Acceptance of Them), Failing to Make a Payment Due on or Before Delivery, or Repudiating the Contract, the Seller Being in Possession of the Goods— The Seller's Right to Resell the Goods or Sue for Money Damages For Nonacceptance or Repudiation

Probably the easiest thing for the seller to do when the buyer wrongfully refuses to accept the goods, fails to make a payment due on or before delivery of the goods, or repudiates the contract in advance of the time for performance is simply to resell the goods to another party. Section 2–706 of the Uniform Commercial Code provides for the buyer's right of resale as follows.

The UCC provides:

Section 2–706. Seller's Resale Including Contract for Resale

(1) * * * [Where the buyer wrongfully refuses to accept the goods or fails to make a payment due on or before delivery or repudiates the contract of sale] the seller may resell the goods * * *. Where the resale is made in good faith and in a commercially reasonable manner the seller may recover the difference between the resale price and the contract price together with any incidental damages allowed * * * but less expenses saved in consequence of the buyer's breach.

(2) Except as otherwise provided in subsection (3) or unless otherwise agreed resale may be at public or private sale including sale by way of one or more contracts to sell or of identification to an existing contract of the seller. Sale may be as a unit or in parcels and at any time and place and on any terms but every aspect of the sale including the method, manner, time, place and terms must be commercially reasonable. The resale must be reasonably identified as referring to the broken contract, but it is not necessary that the goods be in existence or that any or all of them have been identified to the contract before the breach.

(3) Where the resale is at private sale the seller must give the buyer reasonable notification of his intention to resell.

(4) Where the resale is at public sale
    * * *
    (b) it must be made at a usual place or market for public sale if one is reasonably available and except in the case of goods which are perishable or threaten to decline in value speedily the seller must give the buyer reasonable notice of the time and place of the resale; and

    (c) if the goods are not to be within the view of those attending the sale the notification of sale must state the place where the goods are located and provide for their reasonable inspection by prospective bidders; and

(d) the seller may buy.

(5) A purchaser who buys in good faith at a resale takes the goods free of any rights of the original buyer even though the seller fails to comply with one or more of the requirements of this section.

(6) The seller is not accountable to the buyer for any profit made on any resale * * *.

———

Thus, the seller's right of resale arises where the buyer wrongfully refuses to accept the goods, fails to make a payment due on or before delivery, or repudiates the contract in advance. So long as the seller resells the goods "in good faith" and in a "commercially reasonable manner", the seller may recover from the buyer the difference between the resale price and the contract price together with any allowable incidental or consequential damages, less expenses saved by reason of the buyer's breach. In the event the resale price is greater than the contract price, the seller may keep the excess proceeds, having no obligation to account to the buyer for profits made on the resale.

If, at the time of the breach, the goods have not yet been identified to the contract, the seller may generally identify the goods and then resell them. UCC Section 2–704(1)(a) provides: "An aggrieved seller * * * may * * * identify to the contract conforming goods not already identified if at the time he learned of the breach they are in his possession or control * * *."

Unless the parties provide to the contrary, the seller may resell the goods at either a public or private sale. A "public" sale is a sale by auction (see Ch. 7 for a discussion of the special auction rules that are designed to further protect the buyer's interests). Section 2–706(4)(d), permitting the seller to "buy" at a "public" sale, thus makes

sense. The *Official Comment* to Section 2–706 points out: "The provision of paragraph (d) of subsection (4) permitting the seller to bid, and, of course, to become the purchaser, benefits the original buyer by tending to increase the resale price and thus decreasing the damages he will have to pay." A "private" sale is any sale other than a public auction; the sale may be negotiated directly with the purchaser or through a broker. Whether the sale is public or private, the seller must give the buyer in default reasonable notice of his or her intention to resell. An exception arises in the case of a public sale where the goods are perishable or threaten to decline in value rather quickly.

By way of example, suppose that New England Produce fails to make an advance payment called for under its contract with Hood River Apple Company. At the time of the breach by New England, Hood River Apple has not yet identified the specific 2,000 crates of apples to be delivered to the Company. Under UCC Section 2–704(1)(a), Hood River may identify the crates subsequent to the breach, and, under Section 2–706, may resell the apples to another purchaser. Because the apples are perishable, public sale without reasonable notice to New England is permissible. Assuming the contract price is $5.00 per crate and the resale price is $4.00 per crate, Hood River's measure of damages following resale is the difference between the contract price and resale price ($5.00 x 2,000 − $4.00 x 2,000 = $2,000) together with any allowable incidental or consequential damages, less expenses saved because of the breach.

Sometimes, however, the seller is unable to resell the goods, or prefers not to resell them. As an alternative to resale, the seller may bring legal action for *money damages for nonacceptance or repudiation* (this remedy is the seller's counterpart to the buyer's right to sue for money damages for nondelivery under UCC Section 2–713).

UCC Section 2–708 provides as follows:

Section 2–708. Seller's Damages for Non-acceptance or Repudiation

(1) Subject to * * * the provisions of this Article with respect to proof of market price (Section 2–723), the measure of damages for nonacceptance or repudiation by the buyer is the difference between the market price at the time and place for tender and the unpaid contract price together with any incidental damages * * * but less expenses saved in consequence of the buyer's breach.

Again, UCC Section 2–723 provides:

(1) If an action based on anticipatory repudiation comes to trial before the time for performance with respect to some or all of the goods, any damages based on market price * * * shall be determined according to the price of such goods prevailing at the time when the aggrieved party learned of the repudiation.

Thus, the market price for purposes of damages for nonacceptance or repudiation is determined as of the time and place for tender. If the action is based on anticipatory repudiation, and the case comes to trial before the time for tender, the market price is determined as of the time the seller *learned of the breach.*

As you will recall, in a "shipment" contract, the place for tender is the seller's location; in a "destination" contract, it is the buyer's location. Returning to our example, suppose that the contract calls for Hood River Apple to deliver the goods "F.O.B. Hood River". Again, New England Produce fails to make an advance payment due under the contract. This time, rather than resell the apples, Hood River Apple sues New England for money damages under UCC Section 2–708(1). Hood River's measure of damages is the difference between the market price at the time and place for tender (Hood River under the "F.O.B." shipment contract) and the unpaid contract price (plus, of course, incidental damages less expenses saved). Assuming the contract price is $5.00 per crate and the market price in Hood River at the time for tender is $3.50 per crate, Hood River may recover $1.50 per crate in damages or $3,000 ($5.00 x 2,000 − $3.50 x 2,000).

If, on the other hand, the contract calls for Hood River to deliver the apples "F. O.B. New England", New England is the place for tender (the contract being a destination contract). If the contract price is $5.00 per crate, and the market price in New England at the time and place for tender is $4.00 per crate, Hood River's measure of damages will be $1.00 per crate or $2,000 ($5.00 x 2,000 − $4.00 x 2,000).

Just as the buyer's measure of damages for nondelivery may differ from his or her measure of damages following cover, the seller's measure of damages for nonacceptance or repudiation may differ from his or her measure of damages following resale. Suppose that Hood River decides to resell the apples rather than sue for damages for nonacceptance or repudiation. While the market price at the time and place for tender is $4.00 per crate, Hood River is unable to resell the apples until several days after the time for tender when the market price has dropped to $3.00 per crate. Hood River's measure of damages, in this case, is the difference between the $6,000 resale price ($3.00 x 2,000) and the $10,000 contract price ($5.00 x 2,000) for total damages of $4,000. Had Hood River sued for damages for nonacceptance or repudiation, the Company's total damages would be only $2,000 ($10,000 contract price — $6,000 market price at the time and place for tender).

Often, neither Section 2–706 (damages following resale) nor Section 2–708(1) (damages for nonacceptance or repudiation) provides a fair or adequate remedy for the seller. This is particularly true where the contract of sale deals with standard priced items in unlimited supply (e. g., toothbrushes). For example, suppose that a buyer contracts to buy 5,000 toothbrushes at 50 cents each. As it costs the seller only 30 cents to manufacture each brush, he or she stands to make a profit of $1,000 on the sale (20¢ x 5,000). The buyer, however, wrongfully rejects the toothbrushes, whereupon the seller resells them at 50 cents each. The new buyer would have purchased 5,000 brushes in any case, yielding the seller another $1,000 profit. The seller should thus have $2,000 in profit; because of the first buyer's breach, he or she has only $1,000. Yet, under Section 2–706, the seller has suffered no damages, there being no difference between the resale price and the contract price. The same is true where the seller sues for damages for nonacceptance under Section 2–706: the toothbrushes are standard priced items in unlimited supply, and the market price at the time and place for tender is 50 cents each—the same as the contract price. Again, there are no damages under the relevant Code Section, yet the seller has lost profits of $1,000!

To aid the seller in this situation, the Uniform Commercial provides that he or she may sue for nonacceptance or repudiation using an altered measure of damages.

UCC Section 2–708(2) states:

(2) If the measure of damages provided in subsection (1) is inadequate to put the seller in as good a position as performance would have done then the measure of damages is the profit (including reasonable overhead) which the seller would have made from full performance by the buyer, together with any incidental damages * * * due allowance for costs reasonably incurred and due credit for payments or proceeds of resale.

The *Official Comment* adds: "The normal measure there would be list price less cost to the dealer or list price less manufacturing cost to the manufacturer. It is not necessary to a recovery of 'profit' to show a history of earnings, especially if a new venture is involved."

The purpose of Section 2–708(2) is to restore the seller to the position he or she would have been in had the buyer not breached the contract. Thus, the seller may recover lost profits on the particular contract (including lost profits on specially manufactured goods—i. e., goods made to order for the buyer—that are not resaleable in the usual market). Under the "overhead" provision of Subsection (2), the seller may also recover for loss of profitability on other parts of his or her operation (e. g., where the contract with the buyer required the seller to add additional space or equipment, thus increasing the seller's overall manufacturing costs).

The Circumstance of the Buyer Failing to Make a Payment Due on or Before Delivery or Repudiating the Contract of Sale, the Seller Being in the Process of Manufacturing the Goods Which Are Still Incomplete—The Seller's Right to Sell

the Goods in Their Unfinished State for Scrap or Salvage Value or Finish the Goods and Then Resell Them

Where the seller is in the process of manufacturing the goods at the time the buyer breaches the contract (by failing to make an advance payment or repudiating the contract), the seller may do one of two things. *First,* he or she may cease manufacturing and identify the goods though they are still incomplete; it must be clear that the goods were intended for the particular contract with the buyer. The seller may then sell the identified goods for their scrap or salvage value.

Or, *second,* the seller may complete the manufacturing process if such is commercially reasonable, and then identify the goods for resale. The seller may recover from the buyer the difference between the resale price and the contract price.

The Uniform Commercial Code provides for this seller's remedy at Section 2–704 as follows.

The UCC provides:

Section 2–704. Seller's Right to Identify Goods to the Contract Notwithstanding Breach or to Salvage Unfinished Goods

(1) An aggrieved seller   *   *   * may

    *   *   *

    (b) treat as the subject of resale goods which have demonstrably been intended for the particular contract even though those goods are unfinished.

(2) Where the goods are unfinished an aggrieved seller may in the exercise of reasonable commercial judgment for the purposes of avoiding loss and of effective realization either complete the manufacture and wholly identify the goods to the contract or cease

manufacture and resell for scrap or value or proceed in any other reasonable manner.

The *Official Comment* to the Section provides that "the burden is on the buyer to show the commercially unreasonable nature of the seller's action in completing manufacture."

The Circumstance of the Buyer Failing to Pay the Purchase Price Where (1) the Buyer Has Accepted the Goods; (2) the Goods Are Lost or Damaged After the Risk of Loss Has Passed to the Buyer; or (3) the Seller is Unable to Resell the Identified Goods Following a Breach By the Buyer—The Seller's Right to Maintain an Action for the Price (i. e., Recover the Full Purchase Price)

In just three situations, the seller may recover the full purchase price that the buyer was obligated to pay under the contract:

    (1) Where the buyer has, in fact, accepted the goods;

    (2) Where the goods are lost or damaged after the risk of loss has passed to the buyer; or

    (3) Where, following the buyer's breach, the seller is unable to resell the identified goods through reasonable efforts.

First, the Uniform Commercial Code provides that the buyer must pay the full purchase price of goods if the buyer has, in fact, accepted the goods. Thus, if New England Produce accepts the 2,000 crates of Grade A apples, but fails to pay for them, Hood River Apple Company may go to court and recover the full purchase price.

Second, though the buyer has not received or accepted the goods, he or she must pay the full purchase price if the goods are lost or damaged after the risk of loss has passed to him or her. You will recall the risk of loss rules from Ch. 17 of the text. For example, in a "shipment" contract, the risk of loss passes from the seller to the buyer upon delivery of conforming goods to the carrier. If Hood River Apple Company must ship the apples "F.O.B. Hood River", the risk of loss passes to New England Produce when the 2,000 crates of Grade A apples are delivered to the carrier. If the apples are thereafter lost or damaged, New England must still pay the full purchase price to Hood River Apple Company. Of course, if the loss occurs while the apples are in the possession of the carrier, New England will be able to recover from the carrier barring one of the five exceptions to the carrier's strict liability (e. g., an act of God).

Third, where the buyer has breached the contract, he or she must pay the full purchase price of the identified goods if the seller is unable to resell them at a reasonable price through reasonable efforts. For example, say that New England Produce repudiates its promise to pay for the apples. Hood River Apple Company makes a reasonable effort to resell the apples but is unsuccessful. Hood River may recover the full purchase price from New England. Usually, however, the seller has no trouble reselling a commodity like Grade A apples; more often, it is specially manufactured goods that cannot be resold.

This seller's remedy is provided at UCC Section 2-709 as follows.

The UCC provides:

Section 2-709. Action for the Price

(1) When the buyer fails to pay the price as it becomes due the seller may recover, together with any incidental damages * * * the price

    (a) of goods accepted or of conforming goods lost or damaged

* * * after risk of their loss has passed to the buyer; and

    (b) of goods identified to the contract if the seller is unable after reasonable effort to resell them at a reasonable price or the circumstances reasonably indicate that such effort will be unavailing.

(2) Where the seller sues for the price he must hold for the buyer any goods which have been identified to the contract and are still in his control except that if resale becomes possible he may resell them at any time prior to the collection of the judgment. The net proceeds of any such resale must be credited to the buyer and payment of the judgment entitles him to any goods not resold.

(3) After the buyer has wrongfully rejected or revoked acceptance of the goods or has failed to make a payment due or has repudiated * * * a seller who is held not entitled to the price under this section shall nevertheless be awarded damages for nonacceptance under * * * [Section 2-708].

The Circumstance of the Buyer Wrongfully Rejecting or Revoking Acceptance of the Goods, Failing to Make a Payment Due on or Before Delivery, or Repudiating the Contract of Sale—The Seller's Right to Cancel the Contract

Under Section 2-703(f) of the Uniform Commercial Code, the seller has a right to cancel (i. e., put an end to) the contract of sale whenever the buyer wrongfully rejects or revokes acceptance of the goods, fails to make a payment due on or before delivery, or repudiates the contract. Cancellation serves to terminate any further obligation on the part of the seller; however, it does not prevent him or her from using any other available remedy for the buyer's breach.

Finally, to summarize the seller's remedies in the event of breach by the buyer, Uniform Commercial Code Section 2–703 provides as follows.

The UCC provides:

Section 2–703. Seller's Remedies in General

Where the buyer wrongfully rejects or revokes acceptance of goods or fails to make a payment due on or before delivery or repudiates with respect to a part or the whole, then with respect to any goods directly affected and, if the breach is of the whole contract * * * then also with respect to the whole undelivered balance, the aggrieved seller may

(a) withhold delivery of such goods;

(b) stop delivery by any bailee as * * * provided [by] Section 2–705;

(c) proceed under * * * [Section 2–704] respecting goods still unidentified to the contract;

(d) resell and recover damages as * * * provided [by] Section 2–706;

(e) recover damages for nonacceptance (Section 2–708) or in a proper case the price (Section 2–709);

(f) cancel.

May the buyer and seller agree to remedies and/or damages not provided by the Uniform Commercial Code?

As stated previously in the chapter, the parties, by agreement, may provide for remedies in addition to or in place of those provided by the Uniform Commercial Code. The parties may designate such remedies as "exclusive" remedies for either the buyer or seller. The parties may also limit or alter the measure of damages recoverable to return of the goods and repayment of the price or to repair and replacement of nonconforming goods or parts.

UCC Section 2–719 provides:

Section 2–719. Contractual Modification or Limitation of Remedy

(1) Subject to the provisions of subsections (2) and (3) of this section and of the preceding section on liquidation and limitation of damages

    (a) the agreement may provide for remedies in addition to or in substitution for those provided in this Article and may limit or alter the measure of damages recoverable to return of the goods and repayment of the price or to repair and replacement of non-conforming goods or parts; and

    (b) resort to a remedy as provided is optional unless the remedy is expressly agreed to be exclusive, in which case it is the sole remedy.

(2) Where circumstances cause an exclusive or limited remedy to fail of its essential purpose, remedy may be had as provided in this Act.

(3) Consequential damages may be limited or excluded unless the limitation or exclusion is unconscionable.

The *Official Comment* to Section 2–719 provides in part.

The Official Comment provides:

(1) Under this section parties are left free to shape their remedies to their particular requirements and reasonable agreements limiting or modifying remedies are to be given effect.

However, it is of the very essence of a sales contract that at least minimum adequate remedies be available. If the parties intend to conclude a contract for sale within this Article they must accept the legal consequence that there be at least a fair quantum of remedy for breach of the obligations or duties outlined in the contract. Thus any clause purporting to modify or limit the remedial provisions of this Article in an unconscionable manner is subject to deletion and in that event the remedies made available by this Article are applicable as if the stricken clause had never existed. Similarly, under subsection (2), where an apparently fair and reasonable clause because of circumstances fails in its purpose or operates to deprive either party of the substantial value of the bargain, it must give way to the general remedy provisions of this Article.

Along the same line, Section 2–718 of the Code permits the parties to set *liquidated damages*. You will recall the following discussion of liquidated damages from Ch. 10 of the text.

It says:

Frequently, a contract will include a provision stipulating a specific amount of damages (i. e., a fixed or liquidated amount) that must be paid in the event of a breach of contract. The enforceability of such a provision depends upon whether it is held to be a valid liquidated damages clause or an unenforceable penalty provision. If the provision represents a good faith effort by the contracting parties to determine in advance what the actual damages would be upon a breach of contract, the provision is likely to be held a valid and enforceable liquidated damages clause. * * * Where a stipulated damages provision is held to be a valid liquidated damages clause, the nonbreaching party may generally recover the full stipulated amount without regard to what actual damages, if any, are suffered. * * *

Where a stipulated damages provision bears no reasonable relationship to the amount of probable loss as calculated at the time of entering into the contract, the provision is not a valid liquidated damages clause, but is an unenforceable penalty provision.

UCC Section 2–718 states:

Section 2–718. Liquidation or Limitation of Damages * * *

(1) Damages for breach by either party may be liquidated in the agreement but only at an amount which is reasonable in the light of the anticipated or actual harm caused by the breach, the difficulties of proof of loss, and the inconvenience or nonfeasibility of otherwise obtaining an adequate remedy. A term fixing unreasonably large liquidated damages is void as a penalty.

* * *

Even in the absence of a liquidated damages provision, if the seller justifiably withholds delivery of the goods because of a breach by the buyer, the seller may retain any deposit made on the purchase price up to 20 percent of the price, or $500, whichever is less.

Section 2–718 goes on to state:

(2) Where the seller justifiably withholds delivery of goods because of the buyer's breach, the buyer is entitled to restitution of any amount by which the sum of his payments exceeds

(a) the amount to which the seller is entitled by virtue of terms liquidating the seller's damages in accordance with subsection (1), or

(b) in the absence of such terms, twenty per cent of the value of the total performance for which the buyer is obligated under the contract or $500, whichever is smaller.

(3) The buyer's right to restitution under subsection (2) is subject to the offset to the extent that the seller establishes

(a) a right to recover damages under the provisions of this Article other than subsection (1), and

(b) the amount or value of any benefits received by the buyer directly or indirectly by reason of the contract.

Section 2–718(2) is designed to help the buyer who has defaulted after making an advance payment on goods recover at least a portion of the advance payment. For example, suppose that New England Produce contracts to buy 2,000 crates of Grade A apples from Hood River Apple Company at $5.00 per crate for a total contract price of $10,000. New England Produce makes an advance payment of $2,500 on the purchase price, then defaults. Hood River justifiably withholds delivery of the apples and resells the goods at $6.00 a crate for a total price of $12,000. If there is a valid liquidated damages clause (say, in the amount of $1,500), that clause controls, and Hood River may deduct from the advance payment the amount of the liquidated damages. This is so though Hood River suffered no actual damages: though the Company was able to resell the apples for $2,000 more than the contract price, it was reasonable to anticipate at the time of contracting that a breach by New England would result in $1,500 damages. If there is no liquidated damages clause, Hood River may retain the advance up to 20 percent of the purchase price or $500, whichever is less. Since 20 percent of the $10,000 purchase price is $2,000, Hood River may retain $500, and must return the remaining $2,000 to New England Produce. This is a fair result as Hood River suffered no damages by reason of the breach.

Of course, where the seller can prove actual damages, he or she is not limited to the 20 percent or $500 rule. Thus, if the market price for Grade A apples has declined substantially with the result that Hood River takes a $1,000 loss in reselling the 2,000 crates, Hood River may deduct $1,000 from the $2,500 advance notwithstanding Section 2–718(2).

**REMEDIES OF BUYER & SELLER WHEN SALES CONTRACT
IS BREACHED**

CIRCUMSTANCES OF THE
SELLER'S BREACH

BUYER'S
REMEDIES

SELLER SENDS NONCONFORMING GOODS

1. Reject and cancel, 2–601—Subject to seller's cure, 2–508
2. Revoke acceptance, 2–608
3. Sell goods to recover prepayments, 2–711(3)
4. Cover, 2–712
5. Damages for nondelivery, 2–713
6. Damages for breach of warranty, 2–714
7. Set-off, 2–717

SELLER FAILS TO DELIVER THE GOODS BECAUSE OF INSOLVENCY OR OTHER REASON

8. Capture, 2–502
9. "Capture", 2–711(2)(a)
10. Specific performance, 2–716
    * Plus (4) and (5) above

SELLER REPUDIATES THE CONTRACT

11. Demand adequate assurance of performance, 2–609
    —Subject to seller's retraction, 2–611
    * Plus (4), (5), (8), (9), and (10) above

CIRCUMSTANCES OF THE
BUYER'S BREACH

SELLER'S
REMEDIES

BUYER'S INSOLVENCY

1. Withhold delivery until cash payment, 2–702(1)
2. Reclaim goods, 2–702(2)
   —Subject to bfp's rights, 2–702(3)
3. Stoppage in transit, 2–705

BUYER FAILS TO MAKE PAYMENT DUE ON OR BEFORE DELIVERY

4. Cancel, 2–703(f)
5. Withhold delivery, 2–703
6. Stoppage of "big shipment" in transit, 2–705(1)
7. Resale, 2–706
8. Damages for nonacceptance or repudiation, 2–708
   * Possibly lost profits, 2–708(2)
9. Identify unfinished goods and sell for scrap or salvage or finish goods and then identify and resell, 2–704

BUYER WRONGFULLY REFUSES TO ACCEPT GOODS

(4), (7), and (8) above

BUYER REPUDIATES THE CONTRACT

10. Demand adequate assurance of performance, 2–609
    —Subject to buyer's retraction, 2–611
    * Plus (4), (5), (6), (7), (8), and (9) above

BUYER FAILS TO PAY PURCHASE PRICE (1) AFTER ACCEPTING THE GOODS (2) AFTER RISK OF LOSS HAS PASSED TO HIM OR HER AND GOODS ARE LOST OR DAMAGED, OR (3) WHERE SELLER IS UNABLE TO RESELL AFTER BREACH BY THE BUYER

11. Action for the price, 2–709

* The buyer and seller may add or substitute remedies by agreement, 2–719, or provide for liquidated damages, 2–718 (so long as not unconscionable). And don't forget the 20%/$500 rule where the buyer defaults after making prepayments, 2–718(2).

CASES

CASE 1—*There is nothing unique about these lipsticks.*

HILMOR SALES CO. v. HELEN NEUSHAEFER DIVISION OF SUPRONICS CORP.

New York Supreme Court, Queens County, Special Term, Part I.
New York Law Journal, 6 U.C.C.Rept.Serv. 325.
1969.

CRISONA, J. Plaintiff moves by order to show cause for an order (1) enjoining the defendant from disposing of goods which the defendant has allegedly contracted to sell to plaintiff, and (2) directing that the defendant specifically perform its contract.

The subject matter of the contract in dispute here is a substantial quantity of lipsticks and containers of nail polish. The only claim made by plaintiff with respect to these chattels being unique is that they were purchased at close-out prices and cannot be replaced at the contract price.

Section 2–716(1) of the Uniform Commercial Code provides with respect to a buyer's right to specific performance that it may be decreed "where the goods are unique or in other proper circumstances." Plaintiff has failed to establish that there is anything unique about these chattels. It appears to the court that plaintiff can be adequately compensated for any breach of the contract herein by an award of money damages. In such a situation, "there should be no specific performance". Finally, plaintiff has failed to demonstrate that it will be irreparably damaged if the injunction which it seeks is not granted.

For the foregoing reasons, the motion is denied.

CASE 2—*Is there a breach of implied warranty with "good tobacco" merely because the effects of smoking it may be harmful?*

GREEN v. AMERICAN TOBACCO CO.

United States Court of Appeals, Fifth Circuit, En Banc, 1968.
391 F.2d 97.

Action for breach of implied warranty. [Upon its first hearing of the case, the majority decided the plaintiff could recover damages for the death of her husband resulting from lung cancer caused from smoking cigarettes. The Court was composed of three judges, and one judge (Simpson) dissented. The other two held that the American Tobacco Company had breached its implied warranty of merchantability, i. e. an implied warranty that the cigarettes were fit and wholesome for consumption by the public. On rehearing of the case, the entire court (all eleven judges of the United States Court of Appeals for the Fifth Circuit) reversed the holding of the two judges and adopted as its holding (with only three judges dissenting) the dissenting opinion of Judge Simpson. Judge Simpson's opinion follows.]

SIMPSON, Circuit Judge (dissenting):

With deference, I dissent from the majority opinion. *   *   *

I.

I understand Part I of the majority opinion to hold the trial judge in error for refusing to strike the testimony of the defendant's expert witnesses * * * to the general effect that they did not know the cause of cancer, and that they did not believe there was a causal connection between smoking and lung cancer. This line of testimony was opened up by and in direct response to testimony by the plaintiffs' experts to the effect that cigarette smoking causes lung cancer in a sizeable part of the smoking population, that one out of nine or ten heavy cigarette smokers die of lung cancer, that 30,000 or 35,000 deaths yearly in the United States are caused by lung cancer caused by cigarette smoking and that there is a much greater incidence of lung cancer in the half of the adult population that smokes. The jury was left to draw the inference that defendant's cigarettes are not reasonably fit for human consumption.

It should be noted that *plaintiffs'* expert witnesses testified either on direct or cross-examination to similar lack of knowledge as to the cause of cancer.

That long, costly and intensive research in depth aimed at discovering the cause or causes of cancer by both public and private agencies is continuing, and is so far unsuccessful is a matter of general, practically universal knowledge. It is a fact of our daily life as well known to laymen as to doctors or judges. Of course it was known to the members of this jury. The receipt of this intelligence could hardly have come as a shock to them.

In his jury instructions the trial judge made it abundantly clear that "in a previous determination it was determined that one of the proximate causes of his (Edwin Green's) death was the smoking of these cigarettes." Earlier the jury had been instructed: "It has been determined that Green smoked cigarettes and one of the proximate causes of his death was lung cancer caused by cigarettes. But now we are not concerned particularly with Green. We are concerned with whether or not cigarettes are reasonably fit and wholesome for the use of the general public to whom they are sold."

It was iterated and reiterated by the instructions that the sole factual issues were (1) whether cigarettes are reasonably fit and wholesome for consumption by the public and (2) if they are not, what were plaintiffs' proven damages. * * *

There is simply no basis for the majority's conclusion * * *.

* * *

In substance, my position is that the majority has failed to recognize the uniqueness of the situation presented. We are not dealing with an obvious, harmful, foreign body in a product. Neither do we have an exploding or breaking bottle case wherein the defect is so obvious that it warrants no discussion. Instead, we have a product (cigarettes) that is in no way defective. They are exactly like all others of the particular brand and virtually the same as all other brands on the market. The statement of Judge Goodrich, in a concurring opinion in Pritchard v. Liggett and Myers Tobacco Co., 295 F.2d 292, 302 (3 Cir. 1961), is equally applicable here:

> "If a man buys whiskey and drinks too much of it and gets some liver trouble as a result I do not think the manufacturer is liable *unless* (1) the manufacturer tells the customer the whiskey will not hurt him or (2) the whiskey is adulterated—made with

methyl alcohol, for instance. The same is surely true of one who churns and sells butter to a customer who should be on a nonfat diet. The same is true, likewise, as to one who roasts and sells salted peanuts to a customer who should be on a no-salt diet. Surely if the butter and the peanuts are pure there is no liability if the cholesterol count rises dangerously." (Emphasis added).

It is significant to note that in the instant case there has never been even an attempt to prove either of the two above listed exceptions. Inability to prove a specific defect would not preclude liability if there was proof the product was unreasonably dangerous without a defect.

Even under the new strict liability in tort (as opposed to an action in warranty) theory found in Section 402A of the Restatement of Torts (Second), Comment i provides: "Good tobacco is not unreasonably dangerous merely because the effects of smoking may be harmful * * *.

"There is a clear distinction between a product which is not adulterated—one which meets all the standards established for a particular product but which is attended with a known risk to the consumer—and a product which is, in fact, adulterated and defective—that is, which does not meet the standards established for this particular product—and which would, because of such unknown and undetectable defect, produce a harmful effect upon *any* consumer thereof." 196 So.2d at 120.

* * *

It has been firmly established by the prior panel for purposes of this case that the cigarettes are not adulterated:

"There has never been presented by the evidence any contention that Lucky Strike cigarettes were more dangerous or had a greater propensity to cause lung cancer than cigarettes bearing other brand names. Nor has there been any contention that the cigarettes which Mr. Green smoked contained any foreign substance, or any spoiled, contaminated or other substandard ingredient which caused his injury and death. Instead, plaintiffs' contention from the beginning has been that cigarettes—not Lucky Strike cigarettes alone—cause lung cancer." 325 F.2d at 676.

My research has not revealed any Florida decision finding a manufacturer liable in which there was not some defect or adulteration in the product. For the majority now to decide that proof of a defect or adulteration * * * is no longer necessary, as a matter of law, goes far beyond anything yet decided or even foreshadowed in the Florida decisions.

* * *

* * * [T]he Florida court refers to Section 25 of Frumer and Friedman, Products Liability, wherein cases are collected involving products whose contents are sufficiently repulsive so as to require no proof of unwholesomeness. Such cases include those where the product contained mice, flies, slime, mud, bugs, roaches and worms. Little doubt exists that the presence of such articles in a product intended for human consumption renders said product unwholesome or unmerchantable as a matter of law.

* * *

[T]he Florida Supreme Court quotes with approval Frumer and Friedman's analysis of a Wisconsin case to the effect that: ' " 'What is to be *reasonably expected* by the consumer is a *jury question in most cases;*

*   *   *   This test as applied to an action for breach of the implied warranty is keyed to what is *"reasonably fit" ' " '*. (Emphasis added)

*   *   *   [T]he scope and nature of the implied warranty here is one of "reasonable wholesomeness and fitness for use by the public."

*   *   *

Respectfully, but vehemently, I dissent from the holding of both Part I and Part II of the majority opinion. I would affirm the trial court and write "FINIS" to this long and troublesome litigation.

CASE 3—*The Old Colony truck driver refused to deliver the merchandise inside the door of defendant's store.*

NINTH STREET EAST, LTD. v. HARRISON

Connecticut Circuit Court, First Circuit, 1968.
5 Conn.Cir.Ct. 597, 259 A.2d 772.

Norton M. LEVINE, J. This is an action to recover the purchase price of merchandise sold to defendant by plaintiff. Plaintiff is a manufacturer of men's clothing, with a principal place of business in Los Angeles, California. Defendant is the owner and operator of a men's clothing store, located in Westport, Connecticut, known as "The Rage."

Pursuant to orders received by plaintiff in Los Angeles on November 28, 1966, defendant ordered a variety of clothing items from plaintiff. On November 30, 1966, plaintiff delivered the merchandise in Los Angeles to a common carrier known as Denver-Chicago Trucking Company, Inc., hereinafter called Denver, and received a bill of lading from the trucker. Simultaneously, plaintiff mailed defendant four invoices, all dated November 30, 1966, covering the clothing, in the total sum of $2216. All the invoices bore the notations that the shipment was made "F.O.B. Los Angeles" and "Via Denver-Chicago." Further, all four invoices contained the printed phrase, "Goods Shipped at Purchaser's Risk." Denver's bill of lading disclosed that the shipment was made "collect," to wit, that defendant was obligated to pay the freight charges from Los Angeles to Westport. Denver subsequently transferred the shipment to a connecting carrier known as Old Colony Transportation Company, of South Dartmouth, Massachusetts, hereinafter called Old Colony, for ultimate delivery at defendant's store in Westport. The delivery was attempted by Old Colony at defendant's store on or about December 12, 1966. A woman in charge of the store, identified as defendant's wife, requested the Old Colony truck driver to deliver the merchandise inside the door of defendant's store. The truck driver refused to do so. The dispute not having been resolved, Old Colony retained possession of the eight cartons comprising the shipment, and the truck thereupon departed from the store premises.

Defendant sent a letter, dated December 12, 1966, and received by plaintiff in Los Angeles on December 20, 1966, reporting the refusal of the truck driver to make the delivery inside defendant's store. This was the first notice to plaintiff of the nondelivery. The letter alleged that defendant needed the merchandise immediately for the holidays but that defendant nevertheless insisted that the merchandise must be delivered inside his store, as a condition of his acceptance. Plaintiff tried to reach defendant by phone, but without success. Similarly, its numerous attempts to locate the shipment were fruitless. Plaintiff filed a claim against Denver for the lost merchandise, but up to the date of trial had not been reimbursed, in whole or in part, by the carrier. Defendant never recovered possession of the merchandise at any time following the original refusal.

The sole special defense pleaded was, "The Plaintiff refused to deliver the merchandise into the Defendant's place of business." Therefore defendant claimed that he is not liable for the subsequent loss or disappearance of the shipment, or the purchase price thereof, and that the risk of loss remained with plaintiff.

The basic problem is to determine the terms and conditions of the agreement of the parties as to transportation, and the risks and hazards incident thereto. The court finds that the parties had originally agreed that the merchandise would be shipped by common carrier F.O.B. Los Angeles, as the place of shipment, and that the defendant would pay the freight charges between the two points. The notations on the invoices, and the bill of lading, previously described, make this clear. The use of the phrase "F. O.B.," meaning free on board, made this portion of the agreement not only a price term covering defendant's obligation to pay freight charges between Los Angeles and Westport but also a controlling factor as to risk of loss of the merchandise upon delivery to Denver and subsequently to Old Colony as the carriers. * * * [A]n F.O.B. term must be read to indicate the point at which delivery is to be made unless there is specific agreement otherwise and therefore it will normally determine risk of loss."

* * *

The arrangements as to shipment were at the option of plaintiff as the seller. § 2–311(2). Plaintiff duly placed the goods in possession of a carrier, to wit, Denver, and made a reasonable contract for their transportation, having in mind the nature of the merchandise and the remaining circumstances. Notice of the shipment, including the F.O.B. provisions, was properly given to defendant, as required by law, pursuant to the four invoices. 2–504; Uniform Commercial Code § 2–504, comment 5.

The law erects a presumption in favor of construing the agreement as a "shipment" contract, as opposed to a "destination" contract. § 2–503; Uniform Commercial Code § 2–503, comment 5. Under the presumption of a "shipment" contract, plaintiff's liability for loss or damage terminated upon delivery to the carrier at the FO.B. point to wit, Los Angeles. The court finds that no persuasive evidence was offered to overcome the force of the statutory presumption in the instant case. Thus, as § 2–509(1) indicates, "[w]here the contract requires or authorizes the seller to ship the goods by carrier (a) if it does not require him to deliver them at a particular destination, the risk of loss passes to the buyer when the goods are duly delivered to the carrier." Accordingly, at the F.O.B. point, when the risk of loss shifted, Denver and Old Colony, as carriers, became the agents or bailees of defendant. The risk of subsequent loss or delay rested on defendant, and not plaintiff. A disagreement arose between defendant's wife and the truck driver, resulting in nondelivery of the merchandise, retention thereof by the carrier, and, finally, disappearance of the shipment. The ensuing dispute was fundamentally a matter for resolution between defendant and the carriers, as his agents. Nothing in the outcome of that dispute could defeat or impair plaintiff's recovery against defendant.

Defendant has urged that, since plaintiff pressed a damage claim against the carrier, this constitutes an assertion of an ownership interest by plaintiff, and responsibility for loss thereof, inconsistent with plaintiff's present claim against defendant. The court does not agree. Even though the risk of loss, subsequent to delivery to the carrier, had passed to defendant, plaintiff nevertheless had the privilege of pressing the damage claim against the trucker. Any recovery on the claim would, however, be held by plaintiff, subject to its own interest, as a fiduciary for defendant. § 2–722(b). In this connection, the evidence demonstrated that plaintiff first made an effort to secure defendant's cooperation in asserting the damage claim but was unsuccessful.

*   *   *

In view of defendant's wrongful rejection, following the shifting of the risk of loss to him, he is liable to plaintiff for the entire purchase price of the merchandise. Thus, § 2–709 provides in part: "(1) When the buyer fails to pay the price as it becomes due the seller may recover . . . the price (a) * * * of conforming goods lost or damaged within a commercially reasonable time after risk of their loss has passed to the buyer."
*   *   *

The issues are found for plaintiff. Judgment may therefore enter for plaintiff to recover of defendant the sum of $2216, plus taxable costs.

PROBLEMS

1. Sporting goods retailer Amy Burrows contracts to purchase 150 fishing rods for $2,500 from Wiseman Fish-Outfitters, Inc. What are Amy's legal rights and remedies in each of the following situations?

   (a) By the terms of the contract, Amy must pay the $2,500 in two equal installments of $1,250—the first installment due prior to delivery of the fishing rods, the second due at the time of delivery. Five days after Amy pays the first installment, Wiseman Fish-Outfitters, Inc. goes insolvent; and although the Company has already set aside the 150 rods to be sent to Amy, it does not deliver the rods.

   (b) Amy does not prepay any part of the purchase price (by the terms of the contract, she must pay the $2,500 within 30 days after delivery of the goods). Again, Wiseman, Inc. goes insolvent after "earmarking" the specific rods to be sent to Amy, and the Company fails to deliver the rods.

   (c) The same facts as in (b) above except that Wiseman, Inc. never "earmarks" the specific rods to be sent to Amy. Assume that substitute rods are readily available on the open market.

   (d) Wiseman, Inc. ships 100 fishing rods to Amy (instead of the 150 called for in the contract). Amy has prepaid $500 on the purchase price.

   (e) Wiseman, Inc. ships 150 fishing rods to Amy, but the rods are poorly constructed and not at all like the samples that Wiseman showed to Amy before she entered into the contract.

   (f) Three months before delivery is due under the contract, Amy hears rumors that Wiseman, Inc. is insolvent. The rumors come from a reliable source and Amy fears that the fishing rods may not be delivered.

2. Dale Fitzsimmons contracts to purchase a truckload of Idaho potatoes from Sara McCracken for $1,200. What are Sara's legal rights and remedies in each of the following situations?

(a) The contract calls for Sara to sell the potatoes to Dale on credit. Before delivering the potatoes to the carrier for shipment, Sara learns that Dale is insolvent.

(b) The same as in (a) except that Sara has already delivered the potatoes to the carrier when she learns of Dale's insolvency; the carrier is en route to Dale's place of business.

(c) Sara delivers a truckload of conforming Idaho potatoes to Dale; Dale refuses to accept the potatoes.

(d) Sara sells the potatoes to Dale on credit. Five days after she delivers the goods, Sara discovers that Dale was insolvent at the time of receiving the potatoes and cannot pay for them. This surprises Sara as Dale assured her in writing prior to delivery that he was financially solvent.

(e) The same as in (d) except that Dale has already resold the potatoes to Joseph Roberts who paid $1,500 for them and took them without knowledge of Dale's financial problems.

(f) By the terms of the contract, Dale is obligated to pay $500 of the purchase price in advance of delivery of the potatoes. Dale fails to make the $500 payment when due. Sara, at this time, has not yet set aside the specific potatoes to be sent to Dale.

(g) Thirty days before Sara is to ship the potatoes, Dale notifies her that he no longer wants the potatoes and will not accept them if they are delivered.

3. Answer the following "True" or "False" and give reasons for your answers:

(a) A buyer generally has a right to inspect goods prior to accepting or paying for them.

(b) A buyer may revoke acceptance of goods if the goods are nonconforming in any respect.

(c) Whether a buyer sues for damages following cover, or sues for nondelivery, the test for recovery of consequential damages is whether the loss was reasonably foreseeable to the seller at the time of contracting.

(d) Anything constituting a warranty under UCC Section 2–313 also constitutes a warranty under the Magnuson-Moss Act.

(e) Only merchants give an implied warranty of fitness for a particular purpose.

(f) Cover, following rejection of goods or revocation of acceptance, is often a better remedy than bringing an action for damages for breach of warranty.

(g) A buyer who refuses to inspect goods following a demand by the seller that he or she do so waives implied warranties with respect to patent defects.

(h) The implied warranty of fitness for a particular purpose may be disclaimed either orally or in writing.

(i) A manufacturer or retailer who gives a written warranty regarding a consumer product to a consumer may disclaim implied warranties regarding the product so long as the disclaimer is in writing and is conspicuous.

T (j) A manufacturer or retailer who gives a written warranty regarding a consumer product to a consumer must make the warranty information available to the consumer prior to sale.

F (k) It makes little difference whether a written warranty covering a consumer product is labeled a "full warranty" or a "limited warranty".

T (*l*) Generally, an anticipatory repudiation of a sales contract is revocable.

F (m) The buyer's measure of damages is the same whether he or she sues for damages following cover, or sues for nondelivery, or sues for breach of warranty.

F (n) Under UCC Section 2–705, an aggrieved seller may stop goods in transit even though a negotiable document of title covering the goods has been negotiated to the buyer.

F (*o*) No matter what the size of the shipment, the seller may stop the goods in transit if the buyer, though solvent, fails to make a payment due before delivery.

F (p) The seller's measure of damages is the same whether he or she sues for damages following resale or sues for nonacceptance or repudiation.

T (q) In some cases, a seller who sues for nonacceptance or repudiation will be allowed to recover lost profits.

T (r) Even in the absence of a liquidated damages provision, a seller who justifiably withholds delivery of the goods because of a breach by the buyer may retain any deposit made on the purchase price up to 20% of the price, or $500, whichever is less.

T (s) The parties to a sale may, by agreement, add to or subtract from the remedies provided by the UCC.

4. Wilcox Manufacturing repudiated its contract to sell 100 radios to Ready Stores, Inc. What recourse does Ready Stores have?

    a. It can obtain specific performance by the seller.

    b. It can recover punitive damages.

    c. It can "cover", that is, procure the goods elsewhere and recover any damages.

    d. It must await the seller's performance for a commercially reasonable time after repudiation if it wishes to recover anything.

[# 37 May 1978 CPA Exam]

5. Badger Corporation sold goods to Watson. Watson has arbitrarily refused to pay the purchase price. Under what circumstances will Badger *not* be able to recover the price if it seeks this remedy instead of other possible remedies?

    a. If Watson refused to accept delivery and the goods were resold in the ordinary course of business.

    b. If Watson accepted the goods but seeks to return them.

    c. If the goods sold were destroyed shortly after the risk of loss passed to the buyer.

    d. If the goods were identified to the contract and Badger made a reasonable effort to resell them at a reasonable price but was unable to do so.

[# 39, May 1978 CPA Exam]

6. Carter purchased goods from Dunn for $450. Dunn orally made an express warranty of fitness of the goods for the particular purpose described by Carter. In addition, Dunn orally disclaimed "all warranty protection." The express warranty of fitness

   a. Is irrelevant in any event, because it is superceded by the Uniform Commercial Code section which creates an implied warranty of fitness.

   b. Is valid even though *not* in writing.

   c. Is effectively negated by the general disclaimer clause assuming both the warranty and disclaimer are in writing.

   d. Coupled with the disclaimer, effectively negates all Carter's implied warranty protection.

   [# 34, May 1975 CPA Exam]

7. On February 1, 1975, Colonial Industries ordered 10,000 feet of two-inch pipe in 20-foot lengths from the Eire Steel Company. Delivery was to be made on or before March 15, time being of the essence, FOB buyer's loading platform, cash on delivery. Eire Steel accepted the order. On February 15, Eire informed Colonial that its biggest customer had just purchased and taken delivery of its entire stock of two-inch pipe and that it would be impossible for Eire to deliver the pipe until May 15, at the earliest. Colonial demanded that Eire perform as agreed; Eire apologized but reiterated its prior position that it was now impossible for them to perform until the middle of May.

   a. Eire's action of February 15 constituted an anticipatory repudiation of the contract.

   b. Colonial must "cover" (procure the same or similar goods elsewhere) within a reasonable time in order to determine the damages recoverable.

   c. If Colonial waits for performance by Eire and tenders the amount due on March 15, it can recover damages of the difference between the contract price and the market value on March 15.

   d. Because Eire had sold and delivered all its supply of two-inch pipe, it can successfully plead impossibility of performance in order to avoid liability.

   [# 43, May 1975 CPA Exam]

8. In connection with a contract for the sale of goods, in which of the following ways can the implied warranty of merchantability be excluded by the seller?

   a. By an oral statement which mentions merchantability.

   b. By a written statement without mentioning merchantability.

   c. By an oral statement which does *not* mention merchantability.

   d. By an inconspicuous written statement which mentions merchantability.

   [# 45, May 1977 CPA Exam]

9. Kent, a wholesale distributor of cameras, entered into a contract with Williams. Williams agreed to purchase 100 cameras with certain optional attachments. The contract was made on October 1, 1976, for delivery by October 15, 1976; terms: 2/10, net 30. Kent shipped the cameras on October 6, and they were delivered on October 10. The

shipment did *not* conform to the contract, in that one of the attachments was *not* included. Williams immediately notified Kent that he was rejecting the goods. For maximum legal advantage Kent's most appropriate action is to

a. Bring an action for the price less an allowance for the missing attachment.

b. Notify Williams promptly of his intention to cure the defect and make a conforming delivery by October 15.

c. Terminate his contract with Williams and recover for breach of contract.

d. Sue Williams for specific performance.

[# 9, November 1976 CPA Exam]

10. **Part a.** Your annual examination of the financial statements of Mars Distribution Corporation revealed that Colossal Computer Co. sold Mars 1,000 desk computers. The contract stated in bold type:

The buyer hereby purchases these computers with all faults, and all warranties are hereby expressly excluded.

After Mars had sold approximately 200 of the computers, [two] significant problems arose.

● [First], B.M.I. Computers has indicated that the computers in question infringe its existing patents. & Title still implied

● [Second], 90% of the computers sold have proven to be defective.

Mars' customers have claimed that the computers are nonmerchantable. Colossal, when informed of the various problems encountered by Mars, said, "That's your tough luck, we rely on the disclaimer in the contract."

Required: What are the rights of Mars against Colossal? Explain.
Part b. During an examination of the financial statements of Menlow Shoe Company, a receivable-confirmation exception brought to your attention a dispute concerning an order of 2,000 boys' and men's canvas play shoes. Menlow had received the order to manufacture the shoes from Mid-West Department Stores. Menlow had set up its machines to fill the order and was approximately two-thirds finished with the manufacture of the shoes when it received a letter from Mid-West cancelling the order. Since the remaining work only involved completion of the stitching and cutting the eyelets, Menlow disregarded the cancellation order and completed the shoes. Mid-West claims it is only liable for the cost at the time of the receipt of the cancellation order, plus the profit which Menlow would have obtained under the terms of the contract. Menlow seeks to hold Mid-West liable for the difference between the proceeds from the sale of the goods at the prevailing market price and the amount Mid-West was obligated to pay under the terms of the contract.

Required: What are the rights of <del>Mars</del> Menlow against <del>Colossal</del> Mid-West? Explain. Mid-West? Explain.

[# 6.a. & b., November 1973 CPA Exam]

Chapter 19

PRODUCT LIABILITY, SALES OF GOODS BY NONOWNERS, AND LETTERS OF CREDIT

What is the scope of this chapter?

In the last chapter, we considered the various remedies available to the buyer upon a breach of sales contract by the seller, and vice versa. We learned that, where the seller fails in his or her basic duty to transfer and deliver the goods by sending nonconforming goods, the buyer, rather than reject the goods, may accept the goods and sue for breach of warranty—express or implied. What we did not consider is that the defective or nonconforming goods sent by the seller may result in far more serious damage to the buyer than a mere breach of contract (i. e., a mere failure to fulfill the buyer's contract expectations in providing him or her with conforming goods). The defective or nonconforming goods may result in personal injury or property damage to the buyer and/or third parties. The area of law involved here is *product liability* —it is the first subject matter we deal with in this chapter.

We turn next to the *sale of goods by a nonowner.* Sometimes, a party will purport to sell property that he or she does not own. In this chapter, we will look at the rights and liabilities of the "purported" owner, the buyer who "purchases" under such circumstances, and the true owner of the goods.

Finally, we conclude our study of the law of sales by examining the use of *letters of credit.* Letters of credit (governed by Article 5 of the Uniform Commercial Code) are special devices used often in sales transactions (particularly international sales) both as a method of payment and as a means of financing the sale.

What is the law regarding product liability?

On February 6, 1978, a Superior Court jury in Santa Ana, California ordered the Ford Motor Company to pay damages of $127,800,000 to a teenager who suffered severe burns over 95 per cent of his body when the gasoline tank of a 1972 Ford Pinto exploded (the young man was required to undergo some 52 operations).[1] The jury determined that the young man's extensive injuries were caused by a defective product (the Pinto) manufactured by the Ford Motor Company. The evidence at the trial (which lasted seven months) showed that the Pinto was hit in the rear by another vehicle moving at only about 35 miles per hour. Because of faulty welding, the gas tank of the car was punctured on impact, with the result that ignited gasoline leaked into the passenger compartment. The compartment was entirely engulfed by flames, and the plaintiff was severely burned. The evidence also showed that the Ford Motor Company had prior knowledge of the defect: before putting the particular Pinto model on the market, the company had conducted crash tests on the car, and the car had failed the tests. In August of 1977, consumer advocate Ralph Nader charged that Ford had allowed the sale of the Pintos in a defective condition. The

1. Following the decision, Ford appealed the amount of the award; as of the time of this writing, no final decision has been made.

attorney for the injured plaintiff was quoted after the jury verdict as saying:

"We were charging that Ford Motor Co. had consciously, knowing that those tests had failed, put out that model to save 10 bucks a car at the risks of hundreds of more injuries like the plaintiff's * * *.

This is probably the loudest noise that the jury has made in any civil suit in American jurisprudence."

Like the young man in the Pinto, all of us buy, use, or are exposed to consumer products that are manufactured and sold by others. Many of the products turn out to be defective in some way. The National Commission of Product Safety reports that 20 million Americans are injured annually, 30,000 are killed, and 110,000 are permanently disabled in their own homes as a result of incidents connected with consumer products. To be sure, not all the injuries and deaths are a result of "defective" products, but numbers are.

A person injured by a defective product may sue for money damages on any one of three theories of liability:

(1) Negligence;

(2) Breach of warranty; or

(3) Strict liability in tort.

(1) *Negligence.* The tort theory of negligence was explained in Ch. 1 in the following words:

Any unreasonable interference with another's personal or property interests is called a legal "tort". Simply put, a "tort" is socially unreasonable conduct —conduct society will not tolerate— that adversely affects another's interests, causing personal loss or property loss. The legal concept of tort law is designed to measure the amount of

loss sustained, and to equitably "adjust" the loss by providing compensation for the tort victim.

Thus, the law of tort allows a person to recover money damages for sustaining what are termed "intentional" torts (in tort law, a person is said to intend the reasonable, natural, or probable consequences of his or her acts—a malicious or harmful intent is not required.)

* * *

In addition to intentional torts * * * is the tort of negligence which requires no intent on the part of the tortfeasor (person committing the tort), but simply carelessness. Negligence is perhaps best defined as unintentional conduct that falls below the standard established by law for the protection of others against unreasonably great risk of harm to either person or property. To constitute negligence, the risk must be foreseeable at the time the conduct occurs, and, in light of that risk, the defendant's actions must be unreasonable. For example, many negligence cases arise out of automobile accidents in which one party's careless driving has resulted in personal injury or property loss for another party. However, where the accident is unforeseen and unavoidable (e. g., where a child unexpectedly darts out in front of an automobile, and the driver has no time or opportunity, to miss hitting the child) there is no negligence * * * and no liability.

How do courts determine whether any particular conduct is negligent? Most apply what is called the "reasonable prudent person" test and define negligence as the failure to do what a reasonable prudent person would do under the same or similar circumstances. In an emergency situation, for example, it might be "reasonable" to react with panic or confusion. In addition, the plaintiff (the party who brings the lawsuit) must establish four elements to prove negligence:

(1) The plaintiff must show that the defendant had a duty to act according to a certain standard of conduct. This duty varies with the situation and circumstances. While a doctor has a high duty of care to a patient, a landowner has very little duty to a trespassing adult. In later chapters * * * we will be particularly concerned with the duties of various kinds of bailees, common carriers, and warehousemen.

(2) Once duty is established, the plaintiff must prove that the defendant breached the duty—that he or she failed to conform to the required standard of conduct.

(3) The plaintiff must also prove that the defendant's duty caused the injury. The defendant's conduct causes the injury only where it is a material element or substantial factor in bringing the injury about.

(4) Finally, the plaintiff must prove that he or she suffered actual loss or damage.

Negligence is a very important tort concept, and it will become particularly relevant to our study of commercial law in the areas of insurance, banking, bailments, agency, and property.

———

Back in 1916, in the famous case of MacPherson v. Buick Motor Co., 217 N. Y. 382, 111 N.E. 1050, Judge Cardozo held that an automobile manufacturer owes a duty of care and vigilance to thoroughly inspect a car before offering it to the public for sale. In that case, Buick Motor Company was held liable for negligence for failing to inspect a wooden wheel that turned out to be defective, its spokes crumbling and causing injury to the plaintiff. Judge Cardozo stated that

"irrespective of contract, the manufacturer of this thing of danger is under a duty to make it carefully."

It is still the law that a manufacturer is under a duty to make his or her products carefully. It is still the law that a person injured by reason of a defective product may bring an action against the manufacturer of the product for the tort of negligence. However, the tort of negligence is frequently an unsatisfactory remedy as it is often difficult or imposssible for the injured party to prove the four elements of negligence: the manufacturer alone may know what was done in making the product; the product itself may be so deteriorated (following the accident) that it is impossible to tell whether it was defectively made. For this reason, the courts, since 1916, have looked increasingly to two additional theories of liability—a contract theory based on warranty, and a second tort theory based, not on negligence, but on strict liability.

(2) *Warranty.* In the last chapter, we dealt with warranties only as they relate to a buyer's remedies when the seller sends him or her nonconforming goods. As you will recall, the buyer may accept the nonconforming goods and sue the seller for breach of express and/or implied warranty. Again, a warranty is simply a promise that a proposition of fact is true. In sales of goods, warranties have reference to the character, quality, or title of goods, the seller promising that certain facts about the goods are as he or she represents them to be. Frequently, the warranties are express; some are implied by law. Thus, absent a valid disclaimer, a merchant impliedly warrants that the goods he or she sells are "merchantable", meaning, among other things, that the goods are fit for the ordinary purposes for which such goods are used.

You will also recall that the buyer's measure of damages for breach of warranty in sending nonconforming goods is the difference at the time and place of acceptance between the value of the goods received and their value as warranted. Obviously, this measure of damages is of little use or consequence where the buyer or a third party suffers personal injury or property damage as a result of a defective product. For example, suppose that a person buys a new furnace for his or her home. The furnace is defective (i. e., it does not conform to the contract of sale), with the result that it blows up shortly after it is installed, injuring the occupants of the house, and severely damaging the building itself. Clearly, the difference in value between the furnace received and the furnace as warranted would be of little help in paying for the damage caused by the defective product. Or say that a person purchases a power lawn mower with a defective shield. While in use, the mower kicks a rock across the street into a neighbor's yard, taking out a small child's eye. Again, the difference in value between the mower received and the mower as warranted would have little relevancy in measuring the damages to the injured child. The same is true of a defective automobile that causes injury to the buyer or other parties: with regard to the young man severely burned in the Ford Pinto, the difference in value between the Pinto received and the Pinto as warranted certainly had no bearing on the 127.8 million dollars awarded to the injured plaintiff.

Yet, there is no question but what a seller's breach of warranty may result in personal injury or property damage to the buyer and/or third parties. While the ordinary measure of damages for breach of warranty has little application in this "product liability" area, Uniform Commercial Code Section 2–714(3) states: "In a proper [breach of warranty] case any incidental and consequential damages under * * * Section [2–715] may

also be recovered." And Section 2–715(2) provides: "Consequential damages resulting from the seller's breach include * * * injury to person or property proximately resulting from any breach of warranty."

Thus, breach of warranty is a second basis for holding a manufacturer (or retailer) liable for damages resulting from defective products. We left consideration of this aspect of breach of warranty until now because it is more properly a part of product liability law. For example, in the case of Henningsen v. Bloomfield Motors, Inc., 32 N.J. 358, 161 A. 2d 69 (1960), a New Jersey driver slammed a new car into a brick wall, the steering wheel apparently being defective. Though the trial judge was unable to find evidence of negligence by the manufacturer, he nevertheless held the manufacturer liable on the basis of breach of implied warranty.

While, at first glance, damages for breach of warranty would appear to encompass any personal injury or property damage caused by a defective product, this is not always the case. Like the tort of negligence, a contract action for breach of warranty is often an unsatisfactory remedy—the defendant manufacturer or seller may have any one of the following three defenses to such an action:

(1) Failure to give proper notice to the defendant;

(2) Lack of privity of contract; or

(3) Disclaimer of warranty.

Failure to give proper notice. You will recall from Ch. 18 that before a buyer can recover damages for breach of warranty, he or she must give notice of the breach to the seller.

UCC Section 2–607 provides in part:

(3) Where a tender has been accepted

(a) the buyer must within a reasonable time after he discovers or should have discovered any breach notify the seller of breach or be barred from any remedy.

You will further recall that a consumer generally has a longer period of time for giving notice than does a merchant. The *Official Comment* to Section 2–607 states: "The rule of requiring notification is designed to defeat commercial bad faith, not to deprive a good faith consumer of his remedy." Thus, a consumer injured by a defective product may have a substantial "reasonable time" for giving notice to the seller (this makes sense as the consumer may be in the hospital for many weeks or even months following the injury). However, if a "reasonable time" passes without notice being given, the injured consumer may not proceed on the basis of breach of warranty, but must look to another remedy for relief.

Lack of privity of contract. Breach of warranty is a contract theory of liability. Whereas a tort action for negligence requires no underlying agreement between the parties (a tort simply being any kind of socially unreasonable conduct), a breach of warranty action, being based on contract, demands an underlying agreement meeeting all four requirements discussed in Chapters 7 through 9.

Thus, the general rule is that in order to sue for breach of warranty (i. e., for breach of contract), the plaintiff must have entered into a contract of sale with the party to be sued. Parties who have contracted with each other are said to be in "privity" of contract; parties who have not contracted with each other lack privity of contract. And lack of privity of contract is a defense to a breach of warranty action. For example, the neighbor child injured by the defective lawn mower may not sue the manufacturer or retailer of the mower on the basis of breach of warranty—the child lacks privity of contract with both parties.

The same is true of a neighbor whose property is damaged by the defective furnace, and of a pedestrian who is injured by a defective automobile. The injured party, in each case, lacks privity of contract with the manufacturer or retailer of the product.

However, to some extent, the Uniform Commercial Code relaxes the strict privity requirement and extends the liability of sellers for breach of warranty. At Section 2–318, the Code provides three alternatives for states to choose from:

The UCC provides:

Section 2–318. Third Party Beneficiaries of Warranties Express or Implied

Alternative A

A seller's warranty whether express or implied extends to any natural person who is in the family or household of his buyer or who is a guest in his home if it is reasonable to expect that such person may use, consume or be affected by the goods and who is injured *in person* by breach of the warranty. A seller may not exclude or limit the operation of this section. [Emphasis supplied.]

Thus, Alternative A eliminates the privity requirement for members of the buyer's family or household, or guests in the buyer's home, if it is reasonable to expect that they will use, consume, or be affected by the particular product. Alternative A applies only to personal injury, not property damage. States having adopted Alternative A include Florida, Idaho, Illinois, Indiana, Iowa, Kentucky, Massachusetts, Michigan, Mississippi, New Mexico, New York, North Carolina, Ohio, Oklahoma, Oregon, Pennsylvania, South Dakota, Tennessee, Virgin Islands, Washington, West Virginia, and Wisconsin.

The UCC provides:

Alternative B

A seller's warranty whether express or implied extends to any natural person who may reasonably be expected to use, consume or be affected by the goods and who is injured *in person* by breach of the warranty. A seller may not exclude or limit the operation of this section. [Emphasis supplied.]

Unlike Alternative A, Alternative B does not limit recovery to members of the buyer's family of household, or guests in the buyer's home. So long as it is foreseeable that a person will use, consume, or be affected by a particular product, the seller of the product may be liable to the party for breach of warranty. Like Alternative A, Alternative B applies only to personal injury, not property damage. This second alternative has been enacted by Alabama, Kansas, Maryland, and Vermont.

The UCC provides:

Alternative C

A seller's warranty whether express or implied extends to any person who may reasonably be expected to use, consume or be affected by the goods and who is injured by breach of the warranty. A seller may not exclude or limit the operation of this section with respect to injury to the person of an individual to whom the warranty extends.

Under Alternative C, any person who may reasonably be expected to use, consume, or be affected by a particular product and who is injured by a breach of warranty may recover from the seller for both the *personal injury and property damage* resulting. Alternative C is by far and away the broadest of the three alternatives. It has been adopted by Arkansas, Hawaii, North Dakota, Colorado, Delaware, Minnesota, Rhode Island, and Wyoming.

It should be noted that Georgia, Maine, South Carolina, and Virginia have enacted still a different version of Section 2–318 which extends liability in much the same manner as Alternative C. California and Utah have omitted Section 2–318 entirely, and the Texas Legislature has expressly left the issue up to the courts for determination.

Still, in some cases, and in some states, an injured consumer will be denied recovery for breach of warranty because of lack of privity of contract.

Disclaimer of warranty. Finally, a party who suffers personal injury and/or property damage because of a defective product may be unable to recover for breach of warranty because the seller has effectively disclaimed warranty responsibility. You will recall from Ch. 18 that the UCC permits a seller to disclaim warranty liability so long as the disclaimer complies with all Code requirements (see Ch. 18) and is not unconscionable. Along this line, Section 2–719(3) of the Code specifically states.

The UCC provides:

Consequential damages may be limited or excluded unless the limitation or exclusion is unconscionable. Limitation of consequential damages for injury to the person in the case of consumer goods is prima facie unconscionable.

Section 2–719(3) makes clear that any effort to provide a warranty but "limit" the amount of damages recoverable for personal injury caused by a defective product is unconscionable.

However, the Section does not prevent the seller from completely disclaiming warranty liability under UCC Section 2–316: so long as the buyer is fully aware of the disclaimer, and the disclaimer complies with all the requirements of Section 2–316, it will be very difficult for the buyer (or a third party) to prove unconscionability. Assuming the disclaimer is held valid, the injured party (whether it is the buyer himself or herself or a third party under Section 2–318) will be unable to recover for breach of warranty. (But remember, a manufacturer or retailer who warrants a consumer product to a consumer by means of a written warranty cannot disclaim any implied warranty covering the product—see Ch. 17, the Magnuson-Moss Act.)

(3) *Strict liability in tort.* Because negligence and breach of warranty are often unavailable or unsatisfactory remedies for a person injured by a defective product, the law has developed still a third basis for recovery—strict liability in tort. As you know, tort liability is generally based on either *intentional* or *negligent* conduct. However, a party may also be liable in tort for *unintentional* conduct that he she has taken every precaution to prevent. Such liability is called "strict liability", meaning liability without fault. The three traditional areas of strict liability include animals, abnormally dangerous things, and food and drink.

Animals. A person who owns *trespassing* animals (i. e., animals likely to roam and cause damage such as cattle) is strictly liable for any harm the animals inflict while wandering. Similarly, a person who keeps a *dangerous* animal is strictly liable for any harm the animal causes. Dangerous animals include naturally wild animals (e. g., a tiger, bear, or monkey) as well as particular animals known to be vicious (e. g., a dog known to bite, a horse with a propensity to kick).

Abnormally dangerous things. Certain activities are so dangerous that they pose a serious risk of harm to people even when utmost care is exercised. Strict liability, in this case, will be imposed on the person directing the activity if two requirements are met: first, the activity must be ultra-hazardous (i. e., abnormally dangerous); and, second, it must be unnatural to its surroundings. Examples include using or storing explosives in a city, crop dusting, drilling oil wells in a populated area, etc.

Food and drink. At the turn of the century, the sale of defective food was a considerable problem in this country. Because negligence in the preparation of food and drink was difficult to prove (particularly where the food and drink was purchased from wholesale or retail sellers), the common law imposed strict liability on sellers of food and drink.

Beyond food and drink, strict liability for the sale of other defective products is a rather new legal development, coming into play only since 1960. It was a needed development because of the difficulty of proving negligence or establishing breach of warranty. Generally speaking, strict liability is now imposed on any seller (in the business of selling such goods) who sells a defective product that is unreasonably dangerous to those who may come into contact with it. Strict liability is imposed because the law has determined that it is socially unreasonable—that is to say, a tort—to sell defective products. Because strict liability is based on tort rather than contract, the defenses of lack of notice or privity, and disclaimer of warranty liability are not available to the seller.

The landmark case recognizing strict liability in tort for the sale of a dangerously defective product is Greenman v. Yuba Power Products, Inc., 59 Cal.2d 57, 27 Cal.Rptr. 697, 377 P.2d 897 (1963). In that case, the plaintiff's wife purchased a combination power tool from the defendant retailer and gave it to her husband. The plaintiff was using the tool as a lathe for turning a large piece of wood (to be made into a chalice) when, suddenly, a chunk of the wood flew out of the machine and struck the plaintiff in the head causing serious injury. In sustaining damages of $65,000 against the manufacturer, the appellate court stated.

———

* * * [T]o impose strict liability on the manufacturer under the circumstances of this case, it was not necessary for the plaintiff to establish * * * warranty. * * * A manufacturer is strictly liable in tort when an article he places on the market, knowing that it is to be used without inspection for defects, proves to have a defect that causes injury to a human being.

———

The court went on to criticize the use of warranty as a basis for recovery for injury due to defective products.

———

* * * [T]he abandonment of the requirement of a contract between [the parties] * * * the recognition that the liability is not assumed by agreement but imposed by law, and the refusal to permit the manufacturer to define the scope of its own responsibility for defective products make clear that the liability is not one governed by the law of contract warranties but by the law of strict liability in tort.

* * * [T]he purpose of such liability is to insure that the costs of injuries resulting from defective products are borne by the manufacturers that put such products on the market rather than by the injured persons who are powerless to protect themselves. Sales warranties serve this purpose fitfully at best.

———

Following the *Greenman* decision, all the impediments of a warranty action—failure to give notice, lack of privity, and disclaimer—were swept aside by the courts, and strict liability in tort was firmly established as a basis for recovery for injury caused by defective products. In 1965, the American Law Institute incorporated the rule of strict liability in the *Restatement, Second Torts* § 402A as follows.

The Restatement provides:

(1) One who sells any product in a defective condition unreasonably dangerous to the user or consumer or to his property is subject to liability for physical harm thereby caused to the ultimate user or consumer, or to his property, if

   (a) the seller is engaged in the business of selling such a product, and

   (b) it is expected to and does reach the user or consumer without substantial change in the condition in which it is sold.

(2) The rule stated in Subsection (1) applies although

   (a) the seller has exercised all possible care in the preparation and sale of his product, and

   (b) the user or consumer has not bought the product from or entered into any contractual relation with the seller.

———

Thus, under Section 402A, a manufacturer who places a defective product on the market is strictly liable for any damage the product causes. The same is true of any other seller of the product so long as the seller is *in the business of selling such goods* (e. g., a retailer). Subsection 2(a) provides for liability without regard to fault; Subsection 2(b) dispenses with the requirement of a contract, thus eliminating the problems of notice, privity, and disclaimer. In order to recover, the injured plaintiff need prove only the following:

(1) That the defendant seller sold the product in a defective condition making the product unreasonably dangerous to the user or consumer or his or her property;

(2) That the defective product reached the user or consumer without substantial change in its condition; and

(3) That the plaintiff suffered personal injury or property damage as a result of the defect.

Obviously, not all products that are dangerous to use are "defective". A knife, though perfectly constructed, might easily cut a finger; a hammer might smash a thumb. Roller skates, though sturdy, might increase one's risk of falling (of course, if the skates fall apart on first use, they are probably defective, in which case the seller will be liable for any injury that results).

While the early strict liability decisions limited recovery to loss for personal injury, the modern rule is that strict liability encompasses both personal and property loss (including damage to the defective product itself). Thus, if a defective furnace explodes, injuring the neighbors and burning up their property, all the personal injury and property damage will be part of the manufacturer's strict liability.

The early strict liability cases also limited recovery to "users" and "consumers" of the defective product—bystanders injured by the product were not protected. Again, the majority of jurisdictions now extend protection even to bystanders, stating that industry is responsible for all foreseeable harm caused by their defective products. For example, in Piercefield v. Remington Arms Co., 375 Mich. 85, 133 N.W.2d 129 (1965), a bystander was injured when a defective shotgun discharged. The decision was in favor

of the bystander. Similarly, in Sills v. Massey-Ferguson, Inc., 296 F.Supp. 776 (N.D.Ind.1969), a bystander was awarded damages after being hit by an object thrown some 150 feet by a defective power lawn mower manufactured by the defendant.

By way of defense, the seller may show that his or her product was not used in the normal way: the seller will not be liable if the product was put to some abnormal or unforeseeable use. Thus, an automobile driver who is recklessly speeding when a defective tire blows out on his car cannot recover for his personal injuries on the basis of strict liability. And in Meche v. Farmers Drier & Storage Co., 193 So.2d 807 (La.App.1967), the court ruled against liability where an elevator proved to be defective only after it had been improperly installed.

However, it is no defense to a seller's liability that a long period of time elapsed before the defect in the product came to light—it frequently takes a long time for a defect to result in injury, particularly where the defect is in the design of the product. At the same time, a consumer is held by law to know that certain products have a normal life expectancy and will ultimately wear out (e. g., a consumer is expected to realize that automobile tires will wear out and become dangerous if they are not replaced after a reasonable time).

Nor may a manufacturer of a completed product escape liability by tracing the defect to a component part supplied by another (although the manufacturer would certainly be able to recover from the supplier for providing him or her with the defective product). The manufacturer is liable for the defect regardless of its source. It follows that the manufacturer remains strictly liable though he or she delegates the final steps of the manufacturing process to a retailer, and the defect is traced to the retailer's part in the process (here, or course, the manufacturer will be able to recover from the retailer).

Finally, it should be pointed out that a retailer, too, is strictly liable for any defective product he or she sells though the retailer has nothing to do with the manufacturing process. If the injured party chooses to sue the retailer, the retailer may generally recover from the manufacturer. The reasoning here is that the cost of protection for the consumer can be adjusted by contract between the manufacturer and retailer in the course of their continuing business relationship.

What happens when a person purports to sell goods that he or she does not own?

It has been pointed out several times in previous chapters that the question of when ownership (title) passes from a seller to a buyer is not very important under the Uniform Commercial Code. Risk of loss problems, buyer's and seller's remedies for breach of contract, liability for personal injury or property damage to the buyer or third parties—all are specifically controlled by the Uniform Commercial Code without regard to who has title to the goods or when or whether title passes from the seller to the buyer. Insofar as most issues and disputes regarding the contract of sale are concerned, title is simply not a consideration.

Yet at some point in the sales transaction (assuming there is no problem or dispute) the seller has complete title (ownership) to the goods and, through the sale, transfers this title (ownership) to the buyer. UCC Section 2–401 provides the rules for passing of title, stating that once the goods are identified, title passes from the seller to the buyer at whatever time the parties intend that title should pass. If the parties have not explicitly agreed as to the time of passage of title, the Code provides that title passes when the seller has completed what-

ever performance is required of him or her with respect to physical delivery of the goods. Thus, in a "shipment" contract, title passes to the buyer upon shipment; in a "destination" contract, title passes upon proper tender of the goods at destination. If delivery is to be made without moving the goods, and the seller is to deliver a document of title, title passes at the time and place of delivery of the document; if the goods are already identified at the time of contracting, and no document of title is involved, title passes at the time of contracting. Of course, if a negotiable document of title is involved, title to the goods will pass whenever the document of title is negotiated to a bona fide purchaser.

Title, however, cannot pass until the goods are in existence. So if future goods are specified—for example, an agreement to sell "all the apples produced by Hood River Apple Company over the next 3 years"—title to the goods cannot pass until the goods are grown regardless of any contrary expression of intent by the buyer and seller.

UCC Section 2–401 provides:

Section 2–401.   Passing of Title   *   *

Each provision of this Article with regard to the rights, obligations and remedies of the seller, the buyer, purchasers or other third parties applies irrespective of title to the goods except where the provision refers to such title. Insofar as situations are not covered by the other provisions of this Article and matters concerning title become material the following rules apply:

(1) Title to goods cannot pass under a contract for sale prior to their identification to the contract (Section 2–501), and unless otherwise explicitly agreed the buyer acquires by their identification a special property as limited by this Act.   *   *   *   Title to goods

passes from the seller to the buyer in any manner and on any conditions explicitly agreed on by the parties.

(2) Unless otherwise explicitly agreed title passes to the buyer at the time and place at which the seller completes his performance with reference to the physical delivery of the goods. * * *

(a) if the contract requires or authorizes the seller to send the goods to the buyer but does not require him to deliver them at destination, title passes to the buyer at the time and place of shipment; but

(b) if the contract requires delivery at destination, title passes on tender there.

(3) Unless otherwise explicitly agreed where delivery is to be made without moving the goods,

(a) if the seller is to deliver a document of title, title passes at the time when and the place where he delivers such documents; or

(b) if the goods are at the time of contracting already identified and no documents are to be delivered title passes at the time and place of contracting.

(4) A rejection or other refusal by the buyer to receive or retail the goods, whether or not justified, or a justified revocation of acceptance revests title to the goods in the seller. Such revesting occurs by operation of law and is not a sale.

The *Official Comment* to Section 2–401 adds: " 'Future' goods cannot be the subject of a present sale. Before title can pass the goods must be identified in the manner set forth in Section 2–501. The parties, however, have full liberty to ar-

range by specific terms for the passing of title to goods which are existing."

Though title is generally not a consideration in most sales disputes, it becomes a crucial factor when someone purports to sell goods he or she does not own. There are always three parties involved: (1) the *purported seller* who does not have title (ownership) to the goods; (2) the *buyer* who believes he or she is acquiring title from the seller; and (3) the *true owner* of the property who does have title. The various rights, duties, and liabilities of the parties will depend on the circumstances. Sometimes, the "buyer" will prevail against the true owner even though the seller had no title to transfer; other times, the true owner will prevail. In any event, one of the parties —either buyer or true owner—will have a cause of action against the purported seller, the true owner on the basis of conversion of the property, the buyer on the basis of breach of warranty of title.

Four situations must be considered:

(1) *The purported seller is a thief, finder, or nonmerchant bailee of the goods; the goods are not covered by a negotiable document of title.* Regardless of his or her good faith, a person who purchases goods (not covered by a negotiable document of title) from a thief, finder, or nonmerchant bailee of the goods, acquires no rights or title whatsoever. The thief, finder, or nonmerchant bailee (e. g., one who borrowed the goods) simply has no ability to transfer any rights in the property. It follows that the true owner may replevin the goods from the buyer, or even sue the buyer for conversion of the goods. You will recall the following discussion of conversion from Ch. 1:

A person who seriously interferes with another's personal property (goods, things, documents, stock certificates, etc.) may be forced by a court of law to purchase the property from its lawful owner at its fair market value. Such a serious interference is called a conversion, and always results in a forced sale of the goods to the interfering party. The interfering party, however, must intend to convert the property (again, a hostile intent is not required, but simply an intent to exercise control over the property inconsistent with the true owner's rights). Thus, if the interfering party intentionally steals someone's property, destroys it, or seriously damages it, there will be liability for the tort of conversion. But if the damage results from the party's carelessness, then the tort action must be based on negligence, not on conversion.

Suppose you want the "converted" item returned? For example, if someone intentionally carries off your TV set and you sue the party for conversion bringing about a forced sale of the property to the converter, you will receive the TV set's fair market value in cash, but the converter will be allowed to keep your former property. If you prefer to keep the TV, rather than "sell" it to the converter, you should not bring an action for conversion, but should ask the court for a decree requiring the interfering party to return the item to you. A request to the court for the return of specific goods is called a suit to replevin the goods.

A person who buys goods from a thief, finder, or nonmerchant bailee "intends" to exercise control over the property inconsistent with the true owner's rights; thus, the party is liable for conversion. Rather than replevin the goods, the true owner may "force" their sale to the buyer, requiring him or her to pay the fair market value of the property. It is no defense to payment that the buyer has already paid once—to the purported seller.

Where the true owner cannot find the buyer, he or she may, of course, sue the purported seller for conversion.

Assuming the true owner recovers from the buyer—either by way of a conversion action or a suit to replevin the goods—the buyer may, in turn, recover from the purported seller on the basis of breach of warranty of title. Section 2–312 of the Uniform Commercial Code provides that a seller impliedly warrants that he or she conveys good title and that his or her transfer is rightful. Like other warranties, the implied warranty of title may be specifically excluded or disclaimed by the seller.

Section 2–312 provides:

Section 2–312. Warranty of Title
* * *

(1) Subject to subsection (2) there is in a contract for sale a warranty by the seller that

(a) the title conveyed shall be good, and its transfer rightful; and

(b) the goods shall be delivered free from any security interest or other lien or encumbrance of which the buyer at the time of contracting has no knowledge.

(2) A warranty under subsection (1) will be excluded or modified only by specific language or by circumstances which give the buyer reason to know that the person selling does not claim title in himself or that he is purporting to sell only such right or title as he or a third person may have.

The *Official Comment* to Section 2–312 states in part.

The Official Comment provides:

1. Subsection (1) makes provision for a buyer's basic needs in respect to a title which he in good faith expects to acquire by his pur-

chase, namely, that he receive a good, clean title transferred to him also in a rightful manner so that he will not be exposed to a lawsuit in order to protect it.

* * *

2. The provisions of this Article requiring notification to the seller within a reasonable time after the buyer's discovery of a breach apply to notice of a breach of the warranty of title where the seller's breach was innocent. However, if the seller's breach was in bad faith he cannot be permitted to claim that he has been misled or prejudiced by the delay in giving notice. In such case the "reasonable" time for notice should receive a very liberal interpretation.

———

To sue on the basis of breach of warranty of title, the aggrieved buyer must give "reasonable notice" to the purported seller. However, as stated in the *Official Comment,* if the purported seller knew that he or she did not have title (e. g., where the seller is a thief), the requirement of "reasonable notice" is to be very liberally interpreted.

(2) *The goods are entrusted to a merchant who regularly deals in goods of that kind, and the merchant, in the regular course of his or her business, wrongfully sells the goods to a good faith purchaser for value ("bona fide purchaser")—the entruster rule.* Section 2–403(2) of the Uniform Commercial Code provides that if the goods are "entrusted" to a merchant who deals in goods of that kind, the merchant automatically acquires the power to transfer all the rights of the entruster of the goods to a buyer in the ordinary course of business.

The UCC provides:

(2) Any entrusting of possession of goods to a merchant who deals in

goods of that kind gives him the power to transfer all rights of the entruster to a buyer in ordinary course of business. The Code defines "buyer in ordinary course of business" as "a person who in good faith and without knowledge that the sale to him is in violation of the ownership rights or security interest of a third party in the goods buys in ordinary course from a person in the business of selling goods of that kind but [a buyer in the ordinary course of business] does not include a pawnbroker."

———

Generally speaking, to "entrust" is to acquiesce in any retention of possession of the goods by the merchant. For example, if you leave your watch at a jeweler's place of business for repair (i. e., you entrust it to the jeweler for repair), and the jeweler sells the watch to a customer in the regular course of business, the buyer will acquire title (ownership) to the watch.

Or if you take your car into a car dealer for servicing, and the dealer wrongfully (whether intentionally or mistakenly) sells the car in the ordinary course of business, the buyer again will acquire full ownership and title to the car. This would appear to hold true even though the car dealer could not and did not provide the buyer with a motor vehicle registration certificate. Although many states have passed the Uniform Motor Vehicle Anti-Theft Act providing for registration of motor vehicles, the Act is not deemed to be the exclusive method of transferring ownership. Thus, under the entruster rule, title would pass to a good faith purchaser for value despite the fact that he or she received no certificate of registration. To perfect his or her title, the good faith purchaser would have a right to demand (in court if necessary) a motor vehicle registration certificate from the true owner.

In other states, strict compliance with local vehicle registration laws is required by statute: ownership of automobiles may not be transferred in any other way. While it is not made clear under the Uniform Commercial Code, it is believed that the entruster rule would prevail even in these states. The Uniform Commercial Code at Section 10–103 provides that all acts inconsistent with the Code are repealed. As a result of this provision, the entruster rule would appear to take priority even over a statute requiring mandatory compliance with motor vehicle registration laws and the use of motor vehicle registration certificates to transfer title. Again, to perfect his or her title, the bfp would have a right to demand (in court if necessary) a motor vehicle registration certificate from the true owner.

Note well that the entruster rule provides that the merchant has the power to transfer all the rights *of the entruster.* Thus, if the entruster is not the owner of the goods but is only a bailee (not authorized by the owner to entrust the goods), a finder, or a thief, the merchant can transfer only the rights of the bailee, finder, or thief—the bfp in this case will not obtain full ownership (title). It is only where the true owner entrusts the goods (or authorizes another to entrust them) that the merchant will acquire power to transfer complete ownership (title).

Also, the entruster rule applies only to a merchant who deals regularly in goods of the kind entrusted to him or her. And it applies only if the entrusted goods are sold by the merchant "in the ordinary course of business"—not in some unusual situation or isolated transaction.

Where the entruster rule operates to transfer title, the true owner may neither replevin the goods from the buyer nor bring an action for conversion against him or her. However, the true owner may certainly bring an action for conversion against the merchant who sold the entrusted goods.

(3) *A finder, thief, or other non-owner negotiates a regularly issued negotiable document of title covering goods (i. e., a negotiable bill of lading or warehouse receipt) to a bona fide purchaser for value.* As you will recall from Ch. 16, where a regularly issued negotiable document of title covering goods—either a negotiable bill of lading or a negotiable warehouse receipt—is negotiated to a bona fide purchaser for value, the bfp obtains title to the document (and to the goods covered by the document) good as against the whole world including the true owner.

Of course, for a thief, finder, or other nonowner to be able to negotiate a document of title, the document must be in "bearer" form. As you will recall, a document is in bearer form if it is issued as bearer paper and contains no special indorsement; or if it is issued as order paper but is indorsed in blank.

A bfp who takes such a document through a negotiation acquires complete ownership (title) of the document and of the goods covered by the document. This is so though the seller lacked title to the document or had only voidable title (e. g., where the seller obtained the document through fraud, duress, or mistake).

Of course, the negotiable document of title must be *regularly issued.* If the document is a forgery, or if the document was issued to a thief who shipped or warehoused stolen goods so as to create the document (here, the thief steals *goods* as opposed to a regularly issued negotiable document of title), no rights can be created in the goods by transfer of the document. A person who buys such an instrument receives no interest (no title) in the goods, and his or her only recourse is against the person who sold him or her the document.

Finally, where the document of title is nonnegotiable, transfer of the document (a mere receipt for the goods) has no effect on ownership of the property.

(4) *A person with voidable title to the goods sells them to a bona fide purchaser for value.* A person is said to have *voidable* title where he or she acquires goods in such a way that the transferor has power to rescind the transaction and reacquire ownership. Thus, a person has voidable title where he or she obtains ownership of goods through fraud, trick, imposture, or use of bad checks. The defrauded party in each case has a right to avoid the sale because of the deception.[2]

Suppose, however, that the party with voidable title sells the goods to an innocent purchaser for value before the defrauded party avoids. Section 2–403 of the Uniform Commercial Code provides that sale to a bfp transfers complete and valid title to the purchaser though it is clear that the seller's title was voidable at the time of the sale.

By way of example, say that Floyd Fraud visits Sea Scape Art Gallery and buys a painting for $1,000 paying with a worthless check. Floyd immediately turns around and sells the painting for $800 to Roberta Collector, who takes the painting without knowledge of the bad check. Under UCC Section 2–403, Roberta receives full title to the painting even though Floyd Fraud had only voidable title. The same would be true had Floyd acquired ownership in any of the following ways:

(1) Floyd impersonated another so as to induce Sea Scape Art Gallery to part with the painting; fooled by Floyd's impostering, Sea Scape transferred the painting to Floyd.

(2) Sea Scape specified that the sale was to be "strictly cash", then took a check from Floyd in payment; the check was later dishonored.

(3) Floyd otherwise fraudulently induced Sea Scape Art Gallery to part with the painting; Floyd's conduct was larcenous under the criminal law.

Again, Section 2–403 is the relevant Code provision.

The UCC provides:

Section 2–403. Power to Transfer; Good Faith Purchase of Goods
* * *

(1) A purchaser of goods acquires all title which his transferor had or had power to transfer * * *. A person with voidable title has power to transfer a good title to a good faith purchaser for value. When goods have been delivered under a transaction of purchase the purchaser has such power even though

  (a) the transferor was deceived as to the identity of the purchaser, or

  (b) the delivery was in exchange for a check which is later dishonored, or

  (c) it was agreed that the transaction was to be a "cash sale", [and it was not], or

  (d) the delivery was procured through fraud punishable as larcenous under the criminal law.

———

Remember, a "good faith purchaser for value" (also called a "bona fide purchaser") is a person who purchases goods for value, in good faith, and without notice of any defect in the seller's title or of any adverse claim to the goods. To give

———

2. You might find it helpful at this point to review the Ch. 8 discussion of voidable contracts, with emphasis on the remedies available to the defrauded party.

"value" means to provide any consideration sufficient to support a simple contract (see Ch. 9 for a definition of bargain theory consideration). Whether a person takes "in good faith" (i. e., without notice of any claim or defect) is to be determined subjectively. Thus, the fact that a reasonable person would have discovered a particular claim or defect is immaterial if the buyer did not discover it. At the same time, if the claim or defect is so patent (i. e., obvious) that the buyer could not have missed it, the buyer will be held to have taken "with knowledge" though he or she claims otherwise.

What are letters of credit?

We conclude our study of "sales" with a description of *letters of credit*. A letter of credit is a special device used often in sales transactions both as a method of payment and as a means of financing the sale. We have left our discussion of letters of credit until now because to understand such "letters" requires a knowledge of contract law generally, the law of negotiable instruments (as drafts are used in connection with letters of credit), the law of documents of title (as bills of lading are used in conjunction with such letters), and the law of sales (as usually, though not always, letters of credit involve a sale of goods, and, if the transaction breaks down, the remedies of buyer and/or seller may control the outcome of the dispute).

Letters of credit originated in international trade to reduce the sales risks of both the buyer and seller of goods. Today, such letters are widely used internationally, and they are used increasingly in domestic trade (frequently, in transactions not even involving the sale of goods, such as the construction of apartment houses or manufacturing plants).

Before defining letters of credit, let's look at a hypothetical international sale to determine why the ordinary methods of payment and/or financing may not be acceptable to the buyer and seller. Suppose that Rita Retailer is a new, but so far successful new car dealer in Denver, Colorado. George Nikota is a Japanese businessman who has been manufacturing "Nikota" brand cars for only a few months; the "Nikota", which sells for $7,000 in Japan, will sell for $8,500 in the American market. Rita Retailer believes (backed by some good marketing statistics) that she can easily sell 500 "Nikota" cars in the Denver market during the upcoming year. Rita writes to George, offering to buy 500 of the automobiles on credit, but George rejects the offer, feeling that Rita has insufficient business experience to warrant such a credit sale. Rita looks for a new solution. She does not want to pay for the cars in advance (even assuming she could afford to do so) because she wants assurance they will arrive in the Denver market in early July—crucial if the "Nikotas" are to be put on the market before the new car releases of the American manufacturers in early fall. Rita thus proposes to pay cash for the cars when they arrive in Denver and ownership is transferred to her; she suggests using a document of title (bill of lading) and a sight draft to facilitate the sale (the sale would be a "documentary sale" with Rita obligated to "pay cash against documents"). Should George agree to Rita's terms, he would place 500 "Nikotas" on board a carrier (obviously, a ship) for shipment by sea and rail to Denver, Colorado. He would demand and receive from the carrier a negotiable bill of lading drawn to his order (with a negotiable bill, the carrier will be liable for misdelivery if it delivers the goods to anyone not in possession of the bill). George would then draw a sight draft on Rita Retailer (the drawee) ordering her to pay the sum of $3,500,000 (i. e., $7,000 x 500) to the order of Nikota Motor Company. The draft would look like this:

July 1, 1980

Pay to the order of   <u>Nikota Motor Company,</u>

<u>Three million five hundred thousand and no/100 dollars</u>

TO: Rita Retailer
        1500 S.W. Canyon Drive
        Denver, Colorado

<u>*George Nikota*</u>
       Nikota Motor Company
       by: George Nikota
            Vice-President

You will note that George Nikota is both the drawer and payee of the draft; Rita Retailer is the drawee.

George would next forward both the negotiable bill of lading and the sight draft to his representative in Denver. (If George has no representative there, he will send one from Japan or appoint a local bank to represent him.) The representative would deliver the negotiable bill of lading properly indorsed to Rita only if she first pays the sight draft. Upon paying the draft, Rita would receive the bill of lading which, being negotiable, would give her ownership of the automobiles.

While the above transaction is less risky than a sale on open credit, it still presents considerable risk for both the seller and buyer. For George Nikota, the risks are these:

(1) Rita Retailer may be insolvent when the negotiable bill of lading and sight draft are presented to her. The cars, at this time, may be half-way between Japan and the United States, or they may already be in Denver. Though resale is a possibility, George may find it difficult to resell the cars in the Denver market; reshipment to Japan will be costly.

(2) Rita Retailer may refuse to accept or pay for the cars because she believes them to be nonconforming. Whether or not Rita is justified in refusing to accept or pay, George is again faced with disposing of the autos in a market he is unfamiliar with.

(3) Rita may decide to back out of the contract of sale because she no longer believes she can make a profit on the "Nikotas". Though this is clearly a breach of contract entitling George to all the seller's remedies described in Ch. 18, George is in an unfamiliar market and may have difficulty dealing with the U.S. courts and legal procedures.

For Rita Retailer, the risk is that the automobiles will be nonconforming when they arrive. In most documentary sales, the documents arrive before the goods, and the buyer is faced with paying cash against the documents without first being able to inspect the goods. Thus, it is likely that the negotiable bill of lading and sight draft will arrive before the 500

Nikotas: Rita will pay the draft, receive the bill of lading, and only later get a chance to inspect the goods. If the cars are nonconforming when they arrive, Rita (having paid $3,500,000 for defective merchandise) will have to seek redress through the courts of Japan.

To reduce the risks for both George and Rita, a "letter of credit term" could be added to the contract of sale requiring Rita to obtain a letter of credit from a bank or other reputable financial institution (the "letter" to be used along with the nogotiable bill of lading and sight draft). Generally speaking, the buyer (called the "bank customer") applies for the letter of credit from a bank (the "issuer") paying whatever deposit and/or service charge is required. The bank issues the letter in favor of the seller (the "beneficiary" designated by the buyer). In the letter, the bank agrees to pay a draft drawn by the beneficiary upon the customer (or the issuer bank) when the beneficiary presents the draft to the bank and shows compliance with any and all conditions stated in the letter of credit. A typical letter of credit might provide in part:

> We hereby agree with the drawers, indorsers and bona fide holders of drafts drawn under and in compliance with the terms of this credit that such drafts will be duly honored on presentation to the drawee * * *

"Conditions" of the letter might include that the beneficiary present certain documents to the bank along with the draft —usually, a bill of lading describing the goods as they are described in the letter of credit, a certificate or policy of insurance covering the goods, and a certificate of inspection (issued by a disinterested inspection agency) certifying that the goods have arrived, have been inspected, and are without defect.

A letter of credit is not a "negotiable instrument": the letter is conditional by nature, and the beneficiary must comply with the conditions before he or she has a right to payment. Article 5 of the Uniform Commercial Code deals with letters of credit.

Section 5–102 provides:

(1) This Article applies

    (a) to a credit issued by a bank if the credit requires a documentary draft or a documentary demand for payment; and

    (b) to a credit issued by a person other than a bank if the credit requires that the draft or demand for payment be accompanied by a document of title; and

    (c) to a credit issued by a bank or other person if the credit is not within subparagraphs (a) or (b) but conspicuously states that it is a letter of credit or is conspicuously so entitled.

———

Section 5–103 states:

(1) In this Article unless the context otherwise requires

    (a) "Credit" or "letter of credit" means an engagement by a bank or other person made at the request of a customer and of a kind within the scope of this Article (Section 5–102) that the issuer will honor drafts or other demands for payment upon compliance with the conditions specified in the credit. A credit may be either revocable or irrevocable. The engagement may be either an agreement to honor or a statement that the bank or other person is authorized to honor.

    (b) A "documentary draft" or a "documentary demand for payment" is one honor of which is conditioned upon the presentation of a document or documents. "Document" means any paper including document of title, security, invoice, certificate, notice of default and the like.

(c) An "issuer" is a bank or other person issuing a credit.

(d) A "beneficiary" of a credit is a person who is entitled under its terms to draw or demand payment.

*   *   *

(g) A "customer" is a buyer or other person who causes an issuer to issue a credit.

And Sections 5–104 and 5–105 provide:

(1) Except as otherwise required in subsection (1)(c) of 5–102 on scope, no particular form of phrasing is required for a credit. A credit must be in writing and signed by the issuer *   *   *.

*   *   *

No consideration is necessary to establish a credit or to enlarge or otherwise modify its terms. [As a practical matter, however, banks generally require payment of a deposit and a service charge to establish a credit.]

You will note that a letter of credit may be either revocable or irrevocable. However, Section 2–325(3) of the Uniform Commercial Code states.

The UCC provides:

Unless otherwise agreed the term "letter of credit" or "banker's credit" in a contract for sale means an irrevocable credit issued by a financing agency of good repute and, where the shipment is overseas, of good international repute.

Thus, unless the parties agree otherwise, a contract of sale calling for a "letter of credit" means an *irrevocable* letter of credit (i. e., one that the bank *must* honor so long as all conditions of the letter are met). This makes sense as the seller is not protected with a revocable letter: where the letter is irrevocable, and all conditions of the letter have been satisfied, the buyer cannot "stop payment" by the bank on the grounds that the goods are nonconforming or that the contract has otherwise been breached. An irrevocable letter of credit is independent of the underlying contract between the buyer and the seller. So long as all conditions of the letter are satisfied, the issuer must pay the draft regardless of what happens between the customer and beneficiary as regards the contract of sale. For example, suppose that the only condition of a letter of credit is that the beneficiary present along with the draft a bill of lading properly describing the goods—a certificate of inspection is not required. If the beneficiary duly presents the draft and bill of lading (i. e., meets the condition of the letter), the issuer will be obligated to pay the draft though the buyer complains that the goods are nonconforming.

On the other hand, though the letter is irrevocable, if the beneficiary fails to fully and exactly comply with the conditions of the letter, the issuer is obligated *not* to pay the draft and will be liable to the customer if it does so (e. g., the issuer will be liable for paying the draft where the goods described in the bill of lading are not the same as those described in the letter of credit).

Let's return to our example. George Nikota is worried that he may not be paid when the cars arrive in Denver; Rita Retailer is concerned that the cars may arrive nonconforming after she has paid the $3,500,000 draft. By adding a letter of credit to the transaction, both parties may reduce their risks. Suppose that George insists as a part of the contract of sale that Rita obtain an irrevocable letter of credit from a reputable bank naming George as beneficiary. Rita applies for the letter, depositing $2,000,000 (as security for repayment) and paying a small service charge. The bank issues the letter in favor of George. The conditions of the letter are that George (or his representative) present the draft along with a bill of lading properly describing the goods, a certificate or policy of insurance covering the goods, and a certificate of inspection certifying that the goods have arrived, have been inspected, and are without defect (this, of course, is to protect Rita). Obviously, the letter of credit represents a contract between Rita and the issuer bank. Because the letter is irrevocable, the bank must pay the draft so long as George complies with all the requirements of the letter—regardless of what happens between George and Rita as regards the contract of sale!

But suppose that the issuer bank *wrongfully dishonors* the draft (i. e., fails to pay though George has met all the requirements of the letter). As you will recall, the bank has demanded but a $2,000,000 deposit. If Rita Retailer dies before payment is made, the bank may refuse payment, fearing that it will not be immediately reimbursed for the additional $1,500,000 (the 500 Nikotas along with Rita's other assets are likely to be tied up in court for some time.) Of course, George Nikota, in this case, will have available to him all the seller's remedies described in Ch. 18, including the rights of stoppage in transit and resale. However, to the extent that these remedies do not place George in the position he would have been in had the contract been carried out, George may sue the issuer of the credit for the face amount of the draft plus incidental damages and interest.

Now assume in the alternative that the bank *wrongfully honors* the draft (i. e., pays the draft though George has failed to fully and exactly meet all the requirements of the letter). U.C.C. Section 5–109 states that "an issuer must examine the documents with care so as to ascertain that on their face they appear to comply with the terms of the credit * * *." Because this may take some time, the Code provides that the issuer has until the close of the third banking day following receipt of the documents to make this determination. Say that George presents to the issuer a bill of lading showing shipment of only 300 Nikotas—not the 500 specified in the letter of credit. The issuer pays the draft despite George's failure to meet all the conditions of the letter (namely, to present a bill of lading properly describing the goods). Upon receiving only 300 cars, Rita may sue the bank for wrongful honor of the draft and recover compensatory damages. The issuer, in turn, may sue the beneficiary for breach of warranty that all conditions of the letter have been complied with.

Section 5–111 of the Code states:

Section 5–111. Warranties on Transfer and Presentment

(1) Unless otherwise agreed the beneficiary by transferring or presenting a documentary draft or demand for payment warrants to all interested parties that the necessary conditions of the credit have been complied with.

Obviously, the issuer may have some difficulty collecting from a foreign beneficiary—however, it should be pointed out that most countries have a substantial and sophisticated body of law similar to Article 5 on letters of credit.

The result of using a letter of credit, then, is to reduce the sales risks of both seller and buyer: the seller is assured of payment so long as he or she complies with all the conditions of the letter; the buyer can reduce the risk of nonconforming goods by demanding a certificate of inspection.

Although letters of credit are most widely used in international sales transactions, they are used increasingly in domestic sales as well. Returning to last chapter's example, suppose that Hood River Apple Company agrees to sell 2,000 crates of Grade A apples to New England Produce Company for $10,000. Hood River might insist that New England obtain a letter of credit from its bank in Boston, naming Hood River as the beneficiary. In the letter, the bank would agree to honor a $10,000 draft drawn on it by Hood River assuming certain conditions were met. Most likely, the condition of the letter would be that Hood River (through its representative in Boston) present a negotiable document of title (bill of lading) covering the 2,000 crates of apples to the bank along with the draft. New England might also demand as a condition of the letter that Hood River present a certificate of inspection (of course, Hood River might refuse to accept such a condition and choose not to deal on this basis). Assuming Hood River complies with all the conditions of the letter, the bank would pay the $10,000 draft and use the bill of lading to secure reimbursement from New England.

Of course, as stated previously, letters of credit may contain any kind of condition and may be used for purposes other than sales. A letter of credit, for example, might be used in connection with the building of an apartment house. Say the beneficiary of the letter is building the apartment house for the bank customer. The condition of the letter is that the beneficiary present construction certificates showing that certain progress has been made toward completion of the complex. Perhaps the foundation must be completed before the first draft is honored; then the framing must be finished; then the roofing, etc.

Thus, we conclude our study of the law of sales. The subject of letters of credit is a fitting ending point for, in using a letter of credit in a sales transaction, all the many Uniform Commercial Code rules we have dealt with (and struggled with) are tied together as part of one unified commercial transaction— the sale. As Professor Bradford Stone points out in his text on the UCC.

The UCC provides:

"The concept of the Uniform Commercial Code is that 'commercial transactions' is a single subject of the law notwithstanding its many facets." This is best illustrated by the commercial transaction made pursuant to a letter of credit, the subject of Article 5. * * * In this letter of credit transaction the goods are sold per Article 2. A draft is used per Article 3 and collected per Article 4. A bill of lading is issued per Article 7 * * *. Thus, "every phase of commerce involved is but a part of one transaction, namely, the sale of and payment for goods." [3]

---

3. Bradford Stone, *Uniform Commercial Code in a Nutshell*, West Publishing Co., 1975, p. 497.

CASES

CASE 1—*A 38-foot pleasure boat—the RIVER QUEEN.*

GALLAGHER v. UNENROLLED MOTOR VESSEL RIVER QUEEN

United States Court of Appeals, Fifth Circuit, 1973.
475 F.2d 117.

Before COLEMAN, MORGAN and RONEY, Circuit Judges.

Plaintiffs sued to recover possession of their 38-foot pleasure motor boat, RIVER QUEEN, which one defendant, a marina operator, had sold to the other defendants. Judgment was entered for plaintiff against the purchasers on the finding that the marina operator had no right to sell the plaintiff's vessel, and against the marina operator in favor of the purchasers who had paid for the boat which they could not keep.

The purchasers appeal on the ground that they acquired all rights to RIVER QUEEN under Section 2.403(b) of the Uniform Commercial Code which provides:

"(b) Any entrusting of possession of goods to a merchant who deals in goods of that kind gives him power to transfer all rights of the entruster to a buyer in ordinary course of business."

We find no error in the District Court's conclusion that

"* * * Plaintiffs did not entrust the vessel River Queen to Defendant Smith as a merchant within the meaning of Section 2.-403 of the Uniform Commercial Code. Plaintiffs rented a stall at Defendant Smith's marina to keep this vessel. This defendant operated several businesses at this one location. His business of renting stalls for vessels was separate and apart from his business as a boat repair. [By inference, the Court concluded that the renting of stalls was also separate and apart from his business as a boat merchant.] The River Queen was kept at this marina pursuant to a verbal rental contract."

* * *

Affirmed.

CASE 2—*Was there a breach of warranty of title when the police impounded the antique pistol?*

TRIAL v. McCOY

Texas Court of Civil Appeals, El Paso, 1977, rehearing denied, 1977.
553 S.W.2d 199.

PRESLAR, C. J. The question presented * * * involves the proof necessary to show a breach of warranty of title.

Appellee bought an antique pistol from appellant for $1,000.00 and brought this action for breach of warranty of title when the gun was taken from appellee by police officers as being a stolen gun and was returned to a third party. The trial court granted appellee's motion for summary judgment * * * We affirm * * *.

Appellee sought recovery for breach of warranty of title under Tex.Bus. & Comm Code Ann § 2.312, which conforms to § 2–312 of the Uniform Commercial Code promulgated by the American Law Institute and the National Conference of Commissioners on Uniform State Laws. The section provides that, in a contract of sale, there is a warranty by the seller that the title conveyed shall be good and its transfer rightful * * *. The question here presented is whether there has been a breach of the warranty of title, and the answer to that question is dependent on whether there must be proof that the gun was stolen, or may the breach of warranty be established by the fact that there was a disturbance of quiet possession in appellee.

The summary judgment evidence that the gun was stolen cannot be considered since it was hearsay. That leaves the evidence to be that the gun was taken from appellee's possession by police officers on their information that it was stolen property, and it was never returned to appellee. Appellee notified appellant of the loss and appellant subsequently refused to refund appellee's money. If there is a duty to prove that the gun was stolen for breach of warranty of title, then appellee's failure to do so would require a reversal of the summary judgment. We are of the opinion, however, that the proof made was sufficient under § 2.312. The official comment to that section provides:

> "The warranty of quiet possession is abolished. Disturbance of quiet possession, although not mentioned specifically, is one way, among many, in which the breach of the warranty of title may be established."

Cases from other jurisdictions have found breach of warranty of title in the loss of the buyer's property where it was impounded by law enforcement officials. American Container Corp. v. Hanley Trucking Corp., 111 NJ Super 322. In American Container, the property was possessed by the police for ninety days and afterwards was returned to a third party. Such is the substance of the proof before us, and we think it sufficient to show that there was a breach of the warranty of title. The trial court properly found that appellee was entitled to recover under Tex Bus & Comm Code Ann § 2.312, and that would entitle him to his actual damages —loss of the purchase price. * * *.

CASE 3—*The "Blue-Grass" hammer chipped, and he lost the sight of his right eye.*

DUNHAM v. VAUGHAN & BUSHNELL MFG. CO.

Supreme Court of Illinois, 1969.
42 Ill.2d 339, 247 N.E.2d 401.

SCHAEFER, Justice.

A jury in the circuit court of Macoupin County returned a verdict in the sum of $50,000 in favor of the plaintiff, Benjamin E. Dunham, and against the defendants, Vaughan & Bushnell Mfg. Co. and Belknap Hardware and Mfg. Co. * * *.

The injury that gave rise to this action occurred while the plaintiff was fitting a pin into a clevis to connect his tractor to a manure spreader. He had made the connection on one side, using a hammer to insert the pin. To insert the second pin he lay on his right side underneath the tractor and used the hammer extended about two and one-half feet above his head. The hammer moved through an arc which he described as about 8 inches. He testified that as he undertook to "tap" the pin into the clevis a chip from the beveled edge of the hammer, known as the chamfer, broke off and struck him in the right eye. He lost sight of that eye.

The hammer in question is a claw hammer of the best grade manufactured by the defendant Vaughan & Bushnell Mfg. Co. It bore the "Blue-Grass" trademark of its distributor, the other defendant, Belknap Hardware and Manufacturing Co. The plaintiff had received the hammer from a retailer, Heyen Implement Company, located near his home. He received it as a replacement for another "Blue-Grass" hammer, the handle of which had been broken. Before the accident occurred the plaintiff had used the hammer for approximately 11 months in connection with his farming and custom machine work. He had used it in repairing a corn crib and had also used it in working upon his farming implements and machinery.

Each party offered the testimony of an expert metallurgist. Neither expert found any flaws due to the forging of the hammer, or any metallurgical defects due to the process of manufacture. The experts agreed that the hammer was made of steel with a carbon content of "1080". The plaintiff's expert testified that such a hammer was more likely to chip or shear than one made of steel with a lower carbon content of "1040", which would not be so hard. The defendant's expert disagreed; it was his opinion that a hammer made of harder steel, with the higher carbon content, would be less likely to chip or shear than one made of steel with a lower carbon content. Both experts testified that use of a hammer produced a condition described as "work hardening" or "metal failure", which made a hammer more likely to chip or shear.

The defendants apparently suggest that the plaintiff should not have used a claw hammer to tap the pin into the clevis, because the mushroom head of the pin was made of steel of a "Rockwell" test hardness of C57, which was harder than the head of the hammer, which tested Rockwell C52. But as the appellate court pointed out, the specifications of the General Service Administration used by all Federal agencies, call for a Rockwell "C" hardness of 50–60 in carpenter's claw hammers and a Rockwell "C" hardness of 50–57 for machinist's ball-peen hammers. Those specifications also require that sample carpenter's claw hammers and sample ball-peen hammers be subjected to identical tests, by striking them against another hammer and against a steel bar, to determine their tendency to "chip, crack or spall". The specifications thus negate the defendant's suggestion that the plaintiff should have used a ball-peen hammer, rather than the hammer in question, in tapping the pin into the clevis.

The basic theory of the defendants in this court is that the requirements of strict liability, as announced in Suvada v. White Motor Co., 32 Ill.2d 612, 210 N.E.2d 182, were not established, because the testimony of the experts showed that the hammer contained no defect. *Suvada* required a plaintiff to prove that his injury resulted from a condition of the product which was unreasonably dangerous, and which existed at the time the product left the manufacturer's control. But the requirement that the defect must have existed when the product left the manufacturer's control does not mean that the defect must manifest itself at once. The defective "aluminum brake linkage bracket," with which the court was concerned in ruling upon the legal sufficiency of the complaint in *Suvada*, was alleged to have been installed in the tractor not later than March of 1957; it did not break until June of 1960.

Although the definitions of the term "defect" in the context of products liability law use varying language, all of them rest upon the common premise that those products are defective which are dangerous because they fail to perform in the manner reasonably to be expected in light of their nature and intended function. So, Chief Justice Traynor has suggested that a product is defective if it fails to match the average quality of like products. The Restatement emphasizes the viewpoint of the consumer and concludes that a defect is a condition not contemplated by the ultimate consumer which would be unreasonably dangerous to him. Dean Prosser has said that "the product is to be regarded as defective if it is not safe for such a use that can be expected to be made of it, and no warning is given." Dean Wade has suggested that apart from the existence of a defect "the test for imposing strict liability is whether the product is unreasonably dangerous, to use the words of the Restatement. Somewhat preferable is the expression 'not reasonably safe.' "

The evidence in this case, including both the General Services Administration specifications and tests and the testimony of the experts as to "work hardening" or "metal failure," shows that hammers have a propensity to chip which increases with continued use. From that evidence it would appear that a new hammer would not be expected to chip, while at some point in its life the possibility of chipping might become a reasonable expectation, and a part of the hammer's likely performance. The problems arise in the middle range, as Chief Justice Traynor has illustrated: "If an automobile part normally lasts five years, but the one in question proves defective after six months of normal use, there would be enough deviation to serve as a basis for holding the manufacturer liable for any resulting harm. What if the part lasts four of the normal five years, however, and then proves defective? For how long should a manufacturer be responsible for his product?"

The answers to these questions are properly supplied by a jury, and on the record that is before us this case presents only the narrow question whether there is sufficient evidence to justify the jury's conclusion that the hammer was defective. The record shows that it was represented as one of "best quality" and was not put to a use which was regarded as extraordinary in the experience of the community. The jury could properly have concluded that, considering the length and type of its use, the hammer failed to perform in the manner that would reasonably have been expected, and that this failure caused the plaintiff's injury.

Strict liability, applied to the manufacturer of the hammer, Vaughan & Bushnell, extends as well to the wholesaler, Belknap Hardware and Mfg. Co., despite the fact that the box in which this hammer was packaged passed unopened through Belknap's warehouse. The strict liability of a retailer arises from his integral role in the overall producing and marketing enterprise and affords an additional incentive to safety.   *   *   *
    *   *   *

Judgment affirmed.

CASE 4—*The letter of credit related to the shipment of 5,000 long tons, more or less, of Guatemalan Bulk Raw Centrifugal Sugar.*

ASOCIACION DE AZUCAREROS DE GUATEMALA v. UNITED STATES NAT. BANK OF OREGON

United States Court of Appeals, Ninth Circuit, 1970.
423 F.2d 638.

MERRILL, Circuit Judge. By this * * * action appellee Association seeks recovery of sums allegedly due under an irrevocable letter of credit issued by appellant Bank. From judgment in favor of the Association the Bank has taken this appeal.

On June 7, 1966, the Bank issued an Irrevocable Commercial Letter of Credit to the Association. The letter related to a shipment of sugar sold by the Association to one Greenberg and consigned to him. By the letter the Bank agreed to pay 90 per cent of the invoice value of the sugar upon presentation of documents evidencing August shipment of "5,000 Long Tons * * * more or less, Guatemalan Bulk Raw Centrifugal Sugar of the 1965/66 Crop, F.O.B. Stowed Guatemalan port/ports, basis 96 degrees minimum polarization." [2]

On August 15, 1966, the Association shipped the sugar on the S. S. Gardenia and immediately dispatched the shipping documents to the Bank. The documents evidenced shipment in accordance with the requirements of the letter of credit.

Greenberg had arranged for resale of the sugar and a back-to-back letter of credit had been issued in his favor (with the Bank acting on his behalf) by J. Henry Schroder Banking Corp., acting for the ultimate purchaser. Accordingly when the Bank received the shipping documents from the Association it forwarded them to Schroder Corp. On August 26th it received payment in full from Schroder on the back-to-back letter of credit.

The sugar arrived and was unloaded at Gramercy, Louisiana, on August 24th.

* * *

On August 26th Greenberg advised the Bank that the sugar on testing failed to meet contract standards; that he had so advised the Association and that the Association had agreed to modify the letter of credit to provide payment of 75 per cent rather than 90 per cent of the invoice value. Greenberg asked the Bank to cable the Association's representative to the effect that polarization was "below credit requirements" and to ask authorization to modify the letter of credit. The Bank accepted Greenberg's representations without verification and cabled the Association as requested. The Association read the cable as a representation that the sugar polarized

2. "Polarization," as explained in the trial testimony, has reference to the purity or polarity of sugar. In the international sugar trade to constitute "raw sugar" the product must polarize between 94 and 98 degrees. Polarization thus serves a definitional purpose. It also serves, by trade custom, to provide a basis for adjustment of sale price in accordance with the purity of the sugar delivered. "Basis 96 degrees polarization" has reference to 96 degrees as the standard of purity for the agreed sale price. Sugar polarizing at lower than 96 degrees is subject to penalties or deductions from the agreed price. Sugar polarizing at higher than 96 degrees is subject to premiums. Penalties and premiums are established by the By-Laws of the New York Coffee & Sugar Exchange.

below 94 degrees. In fact, the shipment's polarization averaged out at 95.-176358 degrees, well within the trade's definitional standard.

Upon receipt of the Bank's cable the Association agreed to reduce the letter of credit from 90 per cent to 75 per cent. The Bank paid the Association the reduced amount out of the Schroder payment. It retained $75,000 to apply against debts of Greenberg to the Bank. The balance was turned over to Greenberg, who subsequently dissipated most of it.

The District Court found that the Bank's cable was a false statement upon which the Association relied in agreeing to modification of the letter of credit; that this misrepresentation entitled the Association to rescission of its agreement to reduce the letter of credit from 90 per cent to 75 per cent and accordingly that the Bank remained obligated in accordance with the terms of the original letter.

The court granted judgment in favor of the Association for the difference between 75 per cent and 90 per cent of the invoice value—$55,866.38 plus interest.

*   *   *

We find no error in the court's finding of misrepresentation.

*   *   *

The letter of credit, unlike the classic surety undertaking, is a primary obligation between the issuer and the beneficiary. Uniform Commercial Code, § 5–114(1), comment 1. The agreement, as here, is to pay on presentation of shipping documents and may well arise even before the buyer receives the goods. The issuer is not concerned with the state of affairs between the buyer and seller. He is concerned only with the evidence of shipment and is bound to honor his promise "regardless of whether the goods or documents conform to the underlying contract for sale or other contract between the customer and the beneficiary." If it were otherwise, letters of credit could not safely be honored until after delivery of the goods. No issuer could safely accept the risk of paying against documents. The unique commercial usefulness of the letter of credit as a vehicle of rapid and guaranteed payment in commercial transactions would be destroyed.

The Uniform Commercial Code, § 5–106(2), provides that "once an irrevocable credit is established as regards * * * the beneficiary it can be modified or revoked only with his consent." In the interests of certainty and stability, we hold that any modification or revocation of the underlying agreement between buyer and seller (or of the rights of the parties springing from it) cannot be permitted to affect the letter of credit unless the beneficiary explicitly consents to the alteration or revocation of the letter.
*   *   *

*   *   *

Judgment affirmed.

PROBLEMS

1. Sharon Steinberg makes the following purchases at "Costless" Variety Store: a five-speed "Eatwell" brand electric mixer; a "Foreversharp" brand chef's knife; and a spray bottle of "Cleanwell" brand glass and window cleaner. Sharon's daughter, Shelley, is using the mixer to beat up a chocolate cake mix when one of the beaters flies out of the mixer and strikes Shelley in the eye, injuring her. The cake mix splatters on Shelley's new dress, ruining it. The same day, Sharon cuts her hand on

the blade of the chef's knife while removing it from the package. And Sharon's husband, Bob, mistakes the glass and window cleaner for hairspray and sprays it on his hair, with the result that a goodly portion of his hair falls out.

(a) What are Shelley's rights, if any, against "Eatwell", Inc., the manufacturer of the mixer? Against "Costless" Variety Store? Discuss all possible bases of liability. Would your answer differ if Shelley waited until six months after her injury to bring the matter to the attention of Eatwell and Costless? Explain. Would your answer differ if the package containing the mixer stated in bold print: "All warranties, whether express or implied, are disclaimed." Explain.

(b) What are Sharon's rights, if any, against "Foreversharp", the manufacturer of the chef's knife? Against "Costless" Variety Store?

(c) What are Bob's rights, if any, against "Cleanwell", the manufacturer of the glass and window cleaner? Against "Costless" Variety Store?

2. Professional thief Ben Boggs breaks into the home of wealthy widow Gertrude Lents and steals Gertrude's fine diamond brooch. Ben sells the brooch to Judith Corbin (who is unaware that the brooch is stolen) for $1,500. Boggs then purchases a used car from Fred Fisher for $750; Boggs pays by check, and Fred accepts the check though the sale was to be "strictly cash". Ultimately, the check is dishonored and returned to Fred, but, by that time, Boggs has resold the car to Eunice Byers who paid $700 cash for the car. Eunice took without knowledge of the prior transaction or the bad check.

(a) Upon discovering that her brooch has been sold to Judith Corbin, what are Gertrude's rights, if any, against Judith? Assuming that Judith must return the brooch to Gertrude, what are Judith's rights, if any, against Ben Boggs? Explain fully.

(b) What are Fred Fisher's rights, if any, against Eunice Byers? Assuming that Eunice must return the car to Fred, what are Eunice's rights, if any against Ben Boggs? Explain fully.

3. Julie Benson borrows an expensive camera from Paul Cotton to take with her on vacation. While photographing some bears in Yellowstone Park, Julie accidentally drops the camera and the lens is broken. Julie decides to repair the camera before returning it to Paul. She takes it to Tyler's Camera Shop and leaves it there for repair along with her own less expensive camera which is also broken. Ted Tyler, the shop proprietor, repairs the cameras and then sells them to Glenn Davies, a customer who sees the cameras on the shelf and thinks they are part of Ted's inventory. When Paul and Julie learn of the sale, they are incensed. What are their rights, if any, against Glenn Davies? Against Ted Tyler? Discuss fully. What are Glenn Davies' rights, if any, against Ted Tyler? Discuss fully.

4. Andrew Cross, a San Francisco clothing retailer, contracts in writing to purchase 10,000 ladies' tops at a total contract price of $30,000 from Mike Korasu, a Hong Kong based clothing manufacturer. The contract contains a letter of credit term requiring Andrew to obtain an irrevocable letter of credit from First State Bank in San Francisco, naming

Mike as beneficiary. Andrew applies for the letter, depositing $17,000 as security for repayment. The bank issues the letter in favor of Mike. The conditions of the letter are that Mike (or his representative) present to the bank a draft drawn on Andrew Cross for $30,000 along with a negotiable bill of lading properly describing the goods. Mike's San Francisco representative presents the draft and bill of lading to the issuer bank. Although the bill of lading describes only "6,000 ladies' tops", the bank nonetheless honors the $30,000 draft. What are Andrew's rights, if any, against First State Bank? What are First State Bank's rights, if any, against Mike Korasu?

5. Assume that Mike Korasu's representative presents the draft and bill of lading properly describing the "10,000 ladies' tops". Does Andrew have any right to "stop payment" of the draft in the event that the tops arrive nonconforming? Explain. What contract provision could Andrew have insisted upon to prevent such a problem?

6. What is a "letter of credit"? What are the advantages of using one?

7. Carol Kraft purchases a new automobile from Burnside Motors. One year after Carol makes the purchase, her neighbor Beverly Leggett offers to buy the car and Carol agrees to sell it to Beverly. A few weeks later, while Beverly is driving the car, a defect in the steering mechanism causes her to lose control of the vehicle, and Beverly is injured in the accident that results. What are Beverly's rights, if any, against the manufacturer of the automobile? Against Burnside Motors? Against Carol Kraft? Explain fully.

8. Answer the following "True" or "False" and give reasons for your answers:

F (a) A bystander who is injured by a defective product cannot recover on the basis of strict liability in tort.

T (b) The tort of negligence is frequently an unsatisfactory remedy for a person who is injured by a defective product.

F (c) It is a defense to a strict liability in tort action that that seller exercised all possible care in preparation and sale of the product.

T (d) Title is generally not a consideration in most sales disputes.

F (e) A letter of credit is a negotiable instrument.

T (f) Unless otherwise agreed, the term "letter of credit" in a contract for sale means an irrevocable letter of credit issued by a financing agency of good repute.

T (g) Letters of credit may be used for purposes other than sales.

F (h) Title to future goods passes at the time of contracting.

9. Assuming the parties have made no express agreement as to passage of title, when does title to the goods pass in each of the following situations:

(a) The goods are identified at the time of contracting; they are to be delivered without being moved and without transfer of any document of title.

(b) The contract requires the seller to deliver the goods "F.O.B. destination."

(c) The contract requires the seller to deliver the goods "F.O.B. place of shipment."

(d) The contract requires the seller to deliver the goods "F.O.B. place of shipment." Upon arrival of the goods at destination, the buyer rightfully rejects the goods as being nonconforming.

(e) The goods are to be delivered without being moved; the seller is to deliver a document of title to the buyer.

10. A claim has been asserted against Ajax Motors for $7,000 arising out of the sale of a used 1975 automobile. Knox purchased the automobile in February 1977 and subsequently learned that it was a stolen car. The serial numbers had been changed, but it has been conclusively determined that the car belongs to Watts who has duly repossessed it. The contract contained a disclaimer which read as follows: "Ajax Motors hereby disclaims any and all warranties, express or implied, which are not contained in the contract." Knox has brought a legal action against Ajax Motors alleging breach of warranty.

Required: Answer the following, setting forth reasons for any conclusions stated.

What is the probable outcome of such a legal action? Discuss fully the legal basis upon which Knox is relying and any defense that Ajax Motors may assert.

[# 7 b., November 1977 CPA Exam]

Chapter 20

EMPLOYERS, EMPLOYEES, AND INDEPENDENT CONTRACTORS

What is the difference between an employee and an independent contractor?

What is modernly called the employer-employee relationship was referred to, in old common law terminology, as the relationship of "master-servant". The use of these terms—master and servant—is still legally correct; and judges, lawyers, and law students frequently and correctly describe what the layman thinks of as "employer-employee" in terms of "master-servant".

A servant is a person employed to render services of any type to a master who retains control or the right to control the servant in how he or she renders the services. And this is the essential feature of the master-servant relationship: the master, at all times, retains control or the right to control the physical activities of the servant in the performance of his or her required employment duties. The master is said to have the right to direct both the method and the mode of the service; and the servant is said to be entirely under the control of the master and without independent discretion. Still, this does not mean that the master must actually stand by and constantly observe and supervise the work. Rather, it means merely that the relationship presupposes a right on the part of the master to have the work performed in such manner as he or she directs, and a correlative duty on the part of the servant to perform in the manner directed. The crucial element of the relationship is the "right to control".

As used here, the term "servant" includes all persons of whatever rank or position who are subject to the right of control. The term "servant" is therefore synonymous with "employee". Almost everyone is an employee at one time or another, working subject to the control of an employer.

An employee (servant) is to be distinguished from an independent contractor in that, while the independent contractor works physically for the employer, the employer has no right to control the contractor in how he or she performs the work. The independent contractor exercises an independent occupation or calling. He or she contracts with the employer only as to the results to be accomplished—not as to the method, mode, or means whereby the work is to be done. The independent contractor, it is often stated, is hired to do a job for a price. While the finished job must meet certain specifications, the manner and method of doing the work is left entirely up to the contractor. The independent contractor usually works for a lump sum, while the employee is paid by the hour. In addition, the independent contractor generally possesses a high degree of skill or expertise that the employer lacks—thus it would not make sense for the employer to have a right to control the contractor in how the work is done. And while the independent contractor usually owns his or her own business, uses his or her own tools, and furnishes his or her own place to work, the employee generally relies upon the employer to provide these things.

Still, the "right to control" test is the most important consideration in determining whether a particular worker is an employee or an independent contractor. Even the specially skilled man or woman who provides his or her own tools and works for a lump sum is still an employee and not an independent contractor where the employer retains the right of control.

A worker's classification as either an employee or an independent contractor has several important legal consequences in the areas of tort liability and taxation.

First—tort liability. The most important reason for distinguishing between an employee and an independent contractor is that the doctrine of "respondeat superior" applies only to the former. The doctrine of respondeat superior means simply that the master or employer must respond in damages for all torts committed by his or her employees while acting within the scope of their employment. Thus, whenever an employee tortiously injures a third person while acting within the scope of his or her employment, the injured party may bring an action at law against either the employee or the employer or both (however, the injured party may collect damages only once). The employee is directly liable for his or her wrongful act, and the employer is vicariously liable under the legal doctrine of respondeat superior.

Of common law origin, this doctrine developed at a time when the servant was viewed as the property of his or her master. Since the master had absolute control over the servant's acts, it was considered only fair to hold the master responsible for any injury that resulted from those acts. Of course, the servant or employee is no longer considered the property of his or her master or employer, but the doctrine of respondeat superior still makes sense as a matter of good social policy. The doctrine is justified under two theories: (1) the "deep pocket" doctrine which states that public policy is furthered if an injured person is present-

ed with the most effective relief available —as the employee's financial resources are extremely limited in comparison with those of the employer, the injured party should be able to proceed against the employer who, in terms of finances, has the "deeper pocket"; and (2) the "entrepreneur theory" which says that, since the employer created the risk of harm by hiring the employee, the employer should assume full financial responsibility if the employee's tortious, scope of employment conduct causes injury to a third party. The employer can protect himself or herself against this risk by passing the cost of liability (along with the other costs of doing business) on to the consumers who use his or her products or services. This is good social policy because it "forces" employers to regulate and supervise their employees' work more closely. And with closer employee supervision, the risk of injury to the public is substantially reduced.

The employer is liable for torts committed by his or her employee while acting within the scope of employment notwithstanding the employer's exercise of due care in hiring the employee and in supervising his or her acts. The only requirements for liability are that the person committing the tort is, in fact, an employee (i. e., subject to the employer's control), and that the employee is acting within the scope of his or her employment at the time he or she commits the tort. An employee is acting within the scope of his or her employment if, at the time of committing the tort, he or she is intending to serve the master, and is doing the work in the usual and normal way. For example, suppose that an employee truckdriver drives the company truck negligently while delivering the employer's goods and injures a third party. The employee, at the time of the injury, is intending to serve the master by delivering the goods; and he or she is delivering the goods in the usual and normal way

—by transporting them in the employer's truck. The employee's negligent driving is a risk of doing business, and the employer is thus liable in damages to the injured third party. The result is to the contrary, however, where the employee "borrows" the truck to take his or her family on a weekend outing and negligently drives the vehicle into an unfortunate pedestrian. The employee, in this case, is not intending to serve the master, and he or she is not within the scope of employment. The employer is therefore not liable to the injured pedestrian.

The scope of employment requirement is a necessary limitation on employer liability: it ensures that an employer will be held liable only for torts that his or her employee commits while engaged in work of the type he or she was hired to perform during hours he or she was hired to perform it in.

In determining whether a particular employee was acting within the scope of employment (intending to serve the employer and doing the work in the usual and normal way) at the time of commission of a tort, the following factors are taken into account: (1) Was the act authorized, or was it incidental to an act authorized by the employer? (2) The time, place, and purpose of the act. (3) Is the act one commonly done by employees on behalf of their employers? (4) To what extent were the employer's interests advanced by the act that resulted in the tort? (5) To what extent were the private interests of the employee involved? (6) Did the employer furnish the means or the instrumentality with which the injury was inflicted (the truck, machine, tool, etc.)? (7) Did the employer have reason to know that the employee would do the act in question? (8)

Had the employee ever done this act before while employed by this employer? (9) Did the act involve crime as well as tort? (10) Was the act a way of doing what the employee was hired [1] to do, or was it totally unrelated to his or her duties, and no way of doing the job at all?

Under these rules, an employer is seldom held responsible for his or her employee's intentional torts (as opposed to a negligent tort or trespass tort). This is because most employers do not hire employees to fight with customers or to commit intentional assaults and batteries upon them. Still, there are exceptions. An employee hired to keep order in a cocktail lounge, for example, may commit a battery upon a customer while trying to calm him or her down. Since the employee is intending to serve the master in keeping order, and since the employee is doing his or her job in the usual and normal way (with physical force, where necessary), the employee is within the scope of employment, and the employer is liable for the customer's injuries.

Generally, an employer is not liable for the crimes of his or her employees unless he or she has in some way directed, participated in, or approved the criminal act. Exceptions to this rule arise, however, where the illegal sale of liquor is involved, or where the purity and branding of foods, or the accuracy and range of prices and weights, is at issue.

In summary, two elements must be shown in order to establish vicarious liability on the part of an employer for the torts of any particular employee.

(1) The "master-servant" (employer-employee) relationship must be shown to exist between the party whose act caused the injury and the person being sued for

---

1. However, it should be understood that "hired" does not require any payment of money or other compensation. A person will be a servant so long as there is a *right to control* in the employer. Thus, a son or daughter at the wheel of the family car will make his or her parents liable under the doctrine of respondeat superior if the child is negligent while carrying out family business for the parents.

damages for the injury (the right to control).

(2) And it must be shown that the employee's wrongful act was committed within the scope of his or her employment (i. e., while the employee was intending to serve the employer, and doing the job in the usual and normal way).

The doctrine of respondeat superior does not apply where tortious acts are committed by an independent contractor. Thus an employer is not vicariously liable for injuries to third persons caused by the independent contractor's negligent acts. Again, the following factors are generally taken into account in determining whether an individual is an employee or an independent contractor:

(1) How much control the employer may exercise over the details of the work (according to the agreement with the person performing the work);

(2) Whether or not the party doing the work has his or her own occupation or business distinct from that of the employer;

(3) Whether the kind of work at issue is usually done under direction, or by a specialist without any supervision;

(4) Whether the person doing the work furnishes his or her own tools and his or her own place to work;

(5) How long the person has been employed—for one job or for a continuous period of time;

(6) The method of payment—by the hour or by the job;

(7) How much skill is required to accomplish the work.

While the employer is never vicariously liable for the independent contractor's tort, there are situations in which the employer may be held liable for his or her own negligence in permitting the contractor to come onto the employer's premises to do dangerous work that results in injury to the general public—injury that could have been avoided if the employer had taken the proper precautions.

For example, suppose an employer hires an independent contractor to wash the windows on his or her building. While performing the job, the contractor drops a bucket on a customer's head from some six stories up. If the employer failed to warn his or her customers with signs, or by roping off the area beneath the contractor, he or she will be liable for the customer's injury. But this is not vicarious liability—this is liability for the employer's own negligence.

Also, where the work contracted is of a highly dangerous nature, the employer will be held liable for any injuries that result. The employer cannot avoid or delegate the potential liability involved with such work by contracting to have it done by an independent contractor. In application, this generally involves some kind of ultra-hazardous activity for which strict liability is imposed under the law of torts (see Ch. 19 for ultrahazardous activities including the transport of highly volatile chemicals, crop-spraying, drilling oil wells, blasting, etc.). Thus, if an employer hires an independent contractor in the blasting business to blast some stumps out of his or her land, and the blast (though set off carefully) hurls a large piece of rock onto the plaintiff's roof, damaging his or her house, the employer will be strictly liable for the damage even though both the employer and the independent contractor acted carefully and without negligence.

Finally, the employer will be liable for injuries caused by an independent contractor where the employer is negligent in selecting the particular contractor or in permitting him or her to undertake the activity in question.

The second significant legal difference between the employee and the independent contractor is in the area of taxation. The tax consequences resulting from a worker's classification as either an employee or an independent contractor vary in three areas: (1) withholding for Social Security purposes; (2) withholding for income tax purposes; and (3) income tax deductions.

What are the Social Security requirements for employees versus independent contractors?

Social Security law provides for three kinds of benefits for nearly all workers in the United States. These are *retirement, survivors,* and *disability* benefits, and all three are paid for through the Social Security tax. Thus, if you retire at the age of 62, you will receive monthly retirement benefits if you are fully insured. In the event of your death at any age, certain members of you family will receive insurance payments if you are insured at the time of your death under the Social Security system. And if you become totally disabled and are unable to work, you may be eligible for monthly payments if you have been covered under the Social Security program for the required period of time.

Both employees and independent contractors must pay Social Security tax. But it makes substantial difference to employers, employees, and independent contractors just what classification they find themselves in.

Under the Federal Insurance Contributions Act (FICA), all employers are required to pay Social Security tax on their employees' wages (including bonuses and commissions) up to a certain fixed amount. The employee must pay an equal amount of tax, but his or her payment is automatically deducted and withheld from each salary or wage payment made by his or her employer. The employer must then file a quarterly return (Form 941) by the last day of the month following the quarter covered by the return, and he or she must deposit the Social Security taxes (both his or her share

and the tax withheld from the employees' wages) into an authorized bank with Federal Tax Deposit Form 501. Large employers deposit the tax funds weekly, and small employers pay them every quarter when they file their quarterly return.

It must be emphasized that an employer is liable for payment of the tax that must be withheld from employee wages —even where the employer fails to withhold the tax and pays what should have been withheld to the employees. The employer, in this case, will still have to pay both the *employer* and *employee* shares. Of course, the employer will have a right to reimbursement from the employees. And an employer may also be liable for penalties and interest for failure to collect a tax, failure to file a return, failure to deposit taxes, nonpayment of tax, fraud in connection with withholding statements, or failure to supply taxpayer identification numbers.

As you can see, it is essential for employers to keep accurate records of all wages paid to employees. While no particular form of accounting is prescribed, the system used must show that the employer's tax liability was correctly figured, and that the proper amount of tax was paid.

So if you made $22,900 of wages in 1979, 6.13% of your wages (for a total of $1,403.77) was deducted from your salary for Social Security tax. Your employer matched this amount (making the total 12.26%) and paid the total tax to the federal government.

Independent contractors pay a higher Social Security tax than do employees. But, in their case, there is no "matching" payment by employers—employers pay Social Security tax only on behalf of employees. Again, the tax is levied on the same fixed amount of the independent contractor's income as on the employee's income; the independent contractor's income is called *self-employment* income under the Social Security system. For example, in 1979, a self-employed person (e. g., a doctor, lawyer, or other independent businessperson) paid 8.1% of his or her first $22,900 of self-employment income to the federal government for Social Security taxes (a total tax of $1,854.-90). The independent contractor must file an annual return of his or her self-employment income on the same date as he or she files his or her regular income tax return. And even if the contractor has no income tax to pay on his or her self-employment income (because of high medical expense deductions, charitable deductions, and the like), he or she will still have to pay Social Security tax.

Both the Social Security earnings base and tax rates for employees and independent contractors are scheduled to go up in future years (the earnings base to as high as $29,700). Congress frequently changes these amounts to ensure adequate Social Security coverage.

How do you distinguish between an employee and an independent contractor for purposes of Social Security law?

Generally, the common law "right of control" test is used to distinguish between employees and independent contractors for purposes of Social Security law. However, special provisions in the law provide that the following workers are "employees" regardless of who has the right of control so long as the workers perform services for pay in the prescribed circumstances.

(1) A full-time traveling or city salesperson is an employee if he or she solicits orders for one employer for merchandise and business supplies from wholesalers, retailers, contractors, hotels, restaurants, and the like. The salesperson's entire or principal business activity must be devoted to solicitation for one employer (the multiple-line salesperson is thus not an "employee" under this Social Security

law). Of course, if the employer has the right to control the salesperson's manner or method of doing his or her job, the salesperson is an employee under the common law "right of control" test. But even where he or she fails this test, the salesperson is still an "employee" for Social Security purposes if he or she works full-time for one employer.

(2) An agent-driver or commission-driver is an "employee" if he or she distributes meats, vegetables, fruits, bakery goods, or beverages (except milk), or if he or she handles laundry or dry-cleaning for his or her employer. This includes the person who operates his or her own truck or the company's truck, who serves customers designated by the company as well as those solicited on his or her own, and whose pay is either a commission on sales or simply the difference between the price he or she charges customers and the price he or she pays to the company for the product or service.

(3) A full-time life insurance salesperson is an "employee" for Social Security purposes regardless of who has the right to control so long as the salesperson's entire or principal business activity is devoted to soliciting life insurance for one insurance company.

(4) A homeworker is an employee if he or she meets the common law test, or if he or she satisfies each of the following requirements:

(a) The homeworker performs work according to specifications furnished by the person for whom the services are performed. The homeworker's materials are furnished by that person, and they must ultimately be returned to that person or his or her designee; and

(b) The homeworker is paid at least $50 cash in any calendar quarter.

These four exceptions to the common law test do not apply where the worker in question has a substantial investment in the facilities used in connection with his or her job (other than facilities for transportation), or where the services are in the nature of a single transaction and not part of a continuing relationship with the employer.

Social Security law also specifically includes "any officer" of a corporation as an employee. Partners, on the other hand, are not employees of the partnership, and their shares of partnership earnings are subject, not to the employ-er-employee tax, but to the self-employment tax on independent contractors.

What are the income tax withholding requirements for employees vs. independent contractors?

Every employer who pays wages to an employee must withhold from the wages for federal income tax purposes an amount determined according to government tables like the one presented in the following illustration.

SINGLE Persons — MONTHLY Payroll Period

And the wages are—		And the number of withholding allowances claimed is—										
At least	But less than	0	1	2	3	4	5	6	7	8	9	10 or more
		The amount of income tax to be withheld shall be—										
$0	$120	$0	$0	$0	$0	$0	$0	$0	$0	$0	$0	$0
120	124	.60	0	0	0	0	0	0	0	0	0	0
124	128	1.20	0	0	0	0	0	0	0	0	0	0
128	132	1.80	0	0	0	0	0	0	0	0	0	0
132	136	2.40	0	0	0	0	0	0	0	0	0	0
136	140	3.00	0	0	0	0	0	0	0	0	0	0
140	144	3.60	0	0	0	0	0	0	0	0	0	0
144	148	4.20	0	0	0	0	0	0	0	0	0	0
148	152	4.80	0	0	0	0	0	0	0	0	0	0
152	156	5.40	0	0	0	0	0	0	0	0	0	0
156	160	6.00	0	0	0	0	0	0	0	0	0	0
160	164	6.60	0	0	0	0	0	0	0	0	0	0
164	168	7.20	0	0	0	0	0	0	0	0	0	0
168	172	7.80	0	0	0	0	0	0	0	0	0	0
172	176	8.40	0	0	0	0	0	0	0	0	0	0
176	180	9.00	0	0	0	0	0	0	0	0	0	0
180	184	9.60	0	0	0	0	0	0	0	0	0	0
184	188	10.20	0	0	0	0	0	0	0	0	0	0
188	192	10.80	0	0	0	0	0	0	0	0	0	0
192	196	11.40	0	0	0	0	0	0	0	0	0	0
		* * *			* * *			* * *				
1,760	1,800	415.00	386.70	358.40	330.00	301.70	276.20	251.20	226.20	204.00	182.30	160.60
1,800	1,840	428.60	400.30	372.00	343.60	315.30	288.20	263.20	238.20	214.40	192.70	171.00
1,840	1,880	442.20	413.90	385.60	357.20	328.90	300.60	275.20	250.20	225.20	203.10	181.40
1,880	1,920	457.10	427.50	399.20	370.80	342.50	314.20	287.20	262.20	237.20	213.50	191.80
1,920	1,960	472.70	441.10	412.80	384.40	356.10	327.80	299.40	274.20	249.20	224.20	202.20
1,960	2,000	488.30	455.80	426.40	398.00	369.70	341.40	313.00	286.20	261.20	236.20	212.60
2,000	2,040	503.90	471.40	440.00	411.60	383.30	355.00	326.60	298.30	273.20	248.20	223.20
2,040	2,080	519.50	487.00	454.50	425.20	396.90	368.60	340.20	311.90	285.20	260.20	235.20
2,080	2,120	535.10	502.60	470.10	438.80	410.50	382.20	353.80	325.50	297.20	272.20	247.20
2,120	2,160	550.70	518.20	485.70	453.20	424.10	395.80	367.40	339.10	310.80	284.20	259.20
2,160	2,200	566.30	533.80	501.30	468.80	437.70	409.40	381.00	352.70	324.40	296.20	271.20
2,200	2,240	581.90	549.40	516.90	484.40	451.90	423.00	394.60	366.30	338.00	309.60	283.20
2,240	2,280	597.50	565.00	532.50	500.00	467.50	436.60	408.20	379.90	351.60	323.20	295.20
2,280	2,320	613.10	580.60	548.10	515.60	483.10	450.60	421.80	393.50	365.20	336.80	308.50
2,320	2,360	628.70	596.20	563.70	531.20	498.70	466.20	435.40	407.10	378.80	350.40	322.10
2,360	2,400	644.30	611.80	579.30	546.80	514.30	481.80	449.30	420.70	392.40	364.00	335.70
2,400	2,440	659.90	627.40	594.90	562.40	529.90	497.40	464.90	434.30	406.00	377.60	349.30
2,440	2,480	675.50	643.00	610.50	578.00	545.50	513.00	480.50	448.00	419.60	391.20	362.90
2,480	2,520	691.10	658.60	626.10	593.60	561.10	528.60	496.10	463.60	433.20	404.80	376.50
2,520	2,560	706.70	674.20	641.70	609.20	576.70	544.20	511.70	479.20	446.80	418.40	390.10
2,560	2,600	722.30	689.80	657.30	624.80	592.30	559.80	527.30	494.80	462.30	432.00	403.70
2,600	2,640	737.90	705.40	672.90	640.40	607.90	575.40	542.90	510.40	477.90	445.60	417.30
2,640	2,680	753.50	721.00	688.50	656.00	623.50	591.00	558.50	526.00	493.50	461.00	430.90
2,680	2,720	769.10	736.60	704.10	671.60	639.10	606.60	574.10	541.60	509.10	476.60	444.50
2,720	2,760	784.70	752.20	719.70	687.20	654.70	622.20	589.70	557.20	524.70	492.20	459.70
		39 percent of the excess over $2,760 plus—										
$2,760 and over		792.50	760.00	727.50	695.00	662.50	630.00	597.50	565.00	532.50	500.00	467.50

As with Social Security taxes, the employer is required to withhold income taxes only if the legal relationship of employer-employee exists: the employer need not withhold income taxes from wages paid to an independent contractor. Again, the same common law tests control. There is generally an employer-employee relationship when the person for whom services are performed has the right to control and direct the individual who performs the services not only as to the result to be accomplished, but also as to the details and means of performance. The employer does not have to actually direct or control the way the services are performed—it is enough that he or she has the right to do so. Individuals who are in fact partners, independent contractors, or sole proprietors of a business are not subject to withholding on their drawings or earnings.

How do income tax deductions differ between an employee and an independent contractor?

Deductions are important to all of us. This is because every deduction an individual is permitted to take under the law reduces his or her amount of income; and since the income tax rate is applied against the amount of income, the lower the income, the lower the tax.

An employee can take only limited deductions with respect to his or her employment. Only those expenses required for the job are allowed. Thus, the cost and maintenance of uniforms and work clothes are deductible if the clothes are required as a condition of employment and are not suitable for regular wearing apparel off duty or away from work. Labor union dues paid as a condition of employment are also deductible. But expenses of training for a career, securing a license, or commuting expenses to and from work are not.

An independent contractor, on the other hand, can deduct any expense incurred in carrying on his or her trade, business, or profession. Only two requirements must be met: (1) the expense must be directly connected with the taxpayer's trade, business, or profession; and (2) it must be reasonable in amount. Expenses incurred for repairs, rent, advertising, insurance, travel, and entertainment, for example, are all included within this category.

By now it should be apparent that the classification of a worker as either an employee or an independent contractor has important consequences in the areas of vicarious liability for the worker's torts, withholding for Social Security and income tax purposes, and income tax deductions.

Consider the following situation. Your author once had a friend and client who was a high school music and band teacher in a small town some 40 or 50 miles away from a very large city. When an out-of-town minister asked the teacher to act as the organist and choir director at his church in the city, the teacher sought your author's advice. The job would require the teacher to make one trip into the city each week on a Tuesday night to practice with the choir and to remain there all Sunday morning to lead the choir and play the organ. The church minister offered to pay the teacher $150 a month for this service.

Now is the teacher an employee or an independent contractor if he accepts this job as choir director? And does his classification make a difference? All parties agree that, if possible, the teacher should be classified as an independent contractor. The minister, in that case, would not have to withhold income taxes from the $150 a month fee. And the church would not face liability if its new choir director negligently struck some choir member in the eye while directing the choir. Also, as an independent contractor, the "choir director" could deduct the expenses he incurred in commuting to the city twice a week to practice and lead the choir.

A contract was drafted specifically stating that the choir director would be in complete charge of the practices—he alone would decide what music he would use and what and when he would play on Sundays. The director was further described in the contract as an independent contractor and not an employee. It was specifically agreed in writing that he was hired to do a job for a price and that the minister would have no right to control his manner and method of performance. Finally, a lump sum payment of $450.00 was agreed upon and inserted into the contract to cover a three month period of time.

Today, the minister and the choir director continue to use this contract, entering into a new one every quarter. Since the minister has no right of control, the choir director is clearly an independent contractor. This saves the minister all the trouble of withholding, and it eliminates his potential liability under the doctrine of respondeat superior. And it makes for greater cash income for the choir director who can claim additional deductions against his income.

What happens if a worker is injured on the job?

We have already seen that where an employee injures some member of the public while acting within the scope of his or her employment, the employer is liable under the doctrine of respondeat superior.

But who must bear the loss if the *employee* is injured while on the job?

This is the subject of Workmen's Compensation. By 1900, industrial accidents were at an all-time high in this country. An enormous number of workers were injured on the job every year. Some were injured as a result of their employer's carelessness in providing un-

safe working conditions. But many other accidents were simply unavoidable and not due to any negligence on the part of the employer. Where the injured employee could prove that the accident resulted from the employer's negligence, he or she could recover damages. But negligence was extremely difficult to prove since the employer had available an "unholy trio" of defenses—the fellow-servant rule, assumption of risk, and contributory negligence. The fellow-servant rule provided that respondeat superior did not apply where an employee injured a *fellow employee* as opposed to a member of the general public. The injured employee, in this case, could not recover damages from the employer, but was left to his or her remedies against the frequently penniless fellow servant. The employer could also assert, to bar recovery, that the employee "assumed the risk" of unsafe working conditions by accepting the employment. This defense was especially effective where the employee knew of the unsafe condition and nevertheless remained on the job. And, finally, where the employee's own carelessness contributed to or increased his or her injury, the employer could plead "contributory negligence" and successfully prevent recovery. Negligence was not only a difficult charge to prove, it was timely and expensive as well. Even where the injured employee had a good claim, the expense and delay of litigation often prompted the employee to accept a compromise settlement for a fraction of the full value of his or her claim. And where the accident was unavoidable, the employee could not recover at all.

But was it fair to expect the injured worker to shoulder his or her own accident costs? Obviously not, as the average worker seldom has sufficient savings to tide him or her over in the event of serious injury. Someone else had to assume this burden. The only question was who—the worker's relatives? The state or federal government? Some organized charity? Or the employer (even though not negligent)? Ultimately, it was decided that the employer should bear the cost since he or she created the risk. Of course, the cost can be anticipated and passed on to the public by means of higher prices. Or the employer can spread the cost by purchasing liability insurance.

Workmen's Compensation thus rests upon the economic principle that those persons who enjoy the product of a business should ultimately bear the cost of industrial accidents incident to the manufacture, preparation, and distribution of the product or service. It makes no difference who is at fault. The injured employee is guaranteed under his or her state Workmen's Compensation statute at least a minimum sum to use for medical expense and support after each and every accident.

Workmen's Compensation statutes provide for the injured worker to receive a monetary amount worked out in advance by a state agency. The agency predetermines specific amounts for varying injuries and additionally grants limited amounts of compensation for periods of time depending on the extent and length of disability. The worker who receives an award is not entitled to further compensation. And he or she cannot bring suit against the employer for additional recovery. In other words, the employee will recover Workmen's Compensation no matter who is at fault in the injury, but his or her recovery will be limited to an amount deemed proper by the state administrative agency for the particular kind of injury and period of disability involved. (However, it should be pointed out that if a third party is at fault in causing the injury, the worker can sue the third party and recover further.) This system of Workmen's Compensation protects all workers in America and handles

over 2 million worker injuries each year (it is interesting to note that there is a growing movement to place auto-accidents under a similar type of no-fault provision throughout the country).

The purpose of this limited, no-fault recovery is to mitigate the disastrous economic effects of a work-related injury by providing for payments of money (called *benefits* to or for the benefit of an injured employee. Each state has its own schedule of benefit payments. All states furnish medical aid for injured employees, including the cost of the services of physicians and nurses, hospitalization expenses, the cost of recuperation equipment such as crutches, and the cost of prosthetic devices such as artificial arms, false teeth, and similar aids. More than a billion dollars of medical expenses are paid each year under Workmen's Compensation statutes.

The amount of disability benefits granted depends on whether the disability is partial or total, and whether it is temporary or permanent. Maximum weekly benefits for total disability range from less than $100.00 a week in some states to over $500.00 a week in others. A number of states provide for payment of a percentage of lost wages (from 50 to 90%); others set maximum dollar amounts. And while some states cover the injured employee for as long as he or she is disabled, still others have maximum periods of payment. The present trend is to extend coverage for the entire period of disability.

Certain types of injuries involving permanent partial disability are specifically covered in state statutes and are commonly referred to as *scheduled injuries*. A scheduled injury is one listed on a schedule in the law and a predetermined amount of compensation is made payable for the injury. Typical scheduled injuries include loss of an arm, an eye, a leg, or other bodily member.

Death benefits are also payable to cover burial expenses and to take care of the deceased worker's family.

Methods of providing the money for the injured worker vary from state to state. Some states require the employer to obtain insurance protection from a private insurance company. In other states, the employer must contribute money for each employee into a state insurance fund which serves as the exclusive source for payment of compensation claims. Still other states permit the employer at his option to either participate in the state fund, to secure protection from a private insurer, or to establish himself or herself as a self-insurer.[2]

Again, it is important to distinguish between the employee who is covered under the Workmen's Compensation statutes and the independent contractor who is not. Statutes generally exclude from coverage workers who are not regular employees but are hired only as "casual" laborers—i. e. for an isolated job of a temporary nature. Statutes throughout the states, however, vary greatly on this subject.

It is also important to note than an injury is compensable only where it arises "out of and in the course of employment." An employee who is injured Sunday afternoon while at home fixing his or her TV set is not injured on the job, and Workmen's Compensation is not available. Still, there is often a fine line between what is in the course and what is out. For example, an employee who takes his or her meals off work premises on his or her own time is generally regarded as outside the course of his or her employment both while eating the meal and while proceeding to and from the eating place. But an employee who is injured in an organized recreational activity or sporting event that has been acquiesced in by the employer and that takes place on the employer's premises

during a period of rest or recreation is considered to be within the scope of his or her employment and thus covered by Workmen's Compensation.

In summary, Workmen's Compensation statutes (which have been enacted in all our states) provide limited, no-fault recovery for any covered employee who is injured or killed while on the job. Whereas under the old common law, the employer could escape all liability by asserting the fellow-servant rule, assumption of risk, or contributory negligence, these three defenses are not available to the employer under Workmen's Compensation statutes. In most states, the injured employee will receive benefits even where the injury is a result of his or her own negligence, stupidity, drunkenness, intentional disregard of safety standards, or fight with a fellow worker (a few states, however, do deny or limit recovery where the injury results from the employee's willful misconduct).

What is unemployment compensation?

Injury is not the only risk of employment. Perhaps as great a risk is the possibility of becoming unemployed. In terms of numbers, for example, it certainly affects more of our working population. Less than 20 workers per 100,000 suffer disabling injuries each year in this country. But in some recent years, the unemployment rate has been running 5 to 8% and higher with over 8,000 per 100,000 workers out of work. Even in prosperous times, when our unemployment rate stabilizes at a low 4%, 4,000 out of every 100,000 workers are still out of a job. And a growing proportion of our unemployed are teenagers and young women in the 20 to 24 year old age bracket.

The unemployment compensation system is a complicated combination of federal and state law designed to protect the worker against complete loss of income when he or she is out of work and suit-

---

2. An employer who fails to obtain the required Workmen's Compensation coverage may be sued by the employee, and the employer cannot assent the "unholy trio" of defenses. In some states, the state will pay the employee's claim and bring suit against the employer for reimbursement.

able replacement work is not available. Only the worker with a history of working experience will qualify for unemployment compensation, because only he or she can suffer a "wage loss" within the meaning of the unemployment legislation.

Basically, what is required under the federal law is the payment of a 3.2% tax on the payrolls of all employers who either have in any year one employee for 20 weeks (for at least one day each week) in industrial and commercial employments, or who pay wages of $1,500 or more in a calendar year for such employment. For agricultural or domestic labor, the requirements are different.

Section 3306 of the federal Unemployment Tax Act provides:

Section 3306.　Definitions

(a) *Employer.* For purposes of this chapter—

(1) *In general.* The term "employer" means, with respect to any calendar year, any person who—

(A) during any calendar quarter in the calendar year or the preceding calendar year paid wages of $1,500 or more, or

(B) on each of some 20 days during the calendar year or during the preceding calendar year, each day being in a different calendar week, employed at least one individual in employment for some portion of the day.

(2) *Agricultural labor.* In the case of agricultural labor, the term "employer" means, with respect to any calendar year, any person who—

(A) during any calendar quarter in the calendar year or the preceding calendar year paid wages of $20,000 or more for agricultural labor, or

(B) on each of some 20 days during the calendar year or during

the preceding calendar year, each day being in a different calendar week, employed at least 10 individuals in employment in agricultural labor for some portion of the day.

(3) *Domestic service.* In the case of domestic service in a private home, local college club, or local chapter of a college fraternity or sorority, the term "employer" means, with respect to any calendar year, any person who during any calendar quarter in the calendar year or the preceding calendar year paid wages in cash of $1,000 or more for such service.

* * *

(c) *Employment.* * * * the term "employment" means any service * * * except * * *

(B) service performed in the employ of a school, college or university, if such service is performed (i) by a student who is enrolled and is regularly attending classes at such school, college or university, * * *.

(C) service performed by an individual under the age of 22 who is enrolled at a nonprofit or public educational institution which normally maintains a regular faculty and curriculum and normally has a regularly organized body of students in attendance at the place where its educational activities are carried on as a student in a full-time program, taken for credit at such institution, which combines academic instruction with work experience, if such service is an integral part of such program, * * * or

(D) service performed in the employ of a hospital, if such service is performed by a patient of such hospital * * *.

The tax applies to the first $6,000 of the employee's wages. And it is paid by the employer—not by the employee (i. e., it is not withheld from the employee's salary as is the income tax and part of the Social Security tax). The unemployment compensation tax is properly considered an expense of doing business.

To be eligible for unemployment compensation benefits, an unemployed worker must qualify under his or her own state statute. Generally, he or she must be unemployed, have filed a claim for benefits, be able and available for work, and have been previously employed for a specified period of time. While unemployment statutes vary somewhat from state to state, the following language is typical of such statutes.

The Statutes provide:

TYPICAL LANGUAGE OF STATE UNEMPLOYMENT COMPENSATION LAW
from Or.Rev.Stat. 657.000

657.150

(2) To qualify for benefits an individual must have had at least 18 weeks of work with an average of $20 per week in subject employment in his base year. However, to qualify for benefits, his total base year wages must be $700 or more, and in addition thereto he must have earned wages equal to six times his weekly benefit amount in employment, * * *.

(4) An eligible individual's weekly benefit amount shall be 1.25 percent of the total wages paid him in his base year. However, such amount shall not be less than the minimum, nor more than the maximum weekly benefit amount.

(a) The minimum weekly benefit amount shall be 15 percent of the state average weekly covered wage for the preceding calendar year, * * * [minimum benefits may run at something around $35 a week]

(b) The maximum weekly benefit amount shall be 55 percent of the state average weekly covered wage for the preceding calendar year, * * * [maximum benefits may run at something around $125 a week]

* * *

(d) For the purposes of this subsection, the state average weekly covered wage means an amount determined by the Employment Division by dividing the total wages paid by subject employers during the year by 52 times the average monthly employment reported by subject employers for the year.

(5) Benefits paid to an eligible individual in a benefit year shall not exceed 26 times his weekly benefit amount, or one third of his base year's wages paid, whichever is the lesser.

657.155

(1) An unemployed individual shall be eligible to receive benefits with respect to any week only if the assistant director finds that:

(a) He has registered for work at and thereafter has continued to report at an employment office in accordance with such rules as the assistant director may prescribe.

(c) He is able to work, is available for work, and is actively seeking and unable to obtain suitable work.

657.176

(1) An authorized representative designated by the assistant director shall promptly examine each claim to determine whether an individual is subject to disqualification as a result of his separation, termination, leaving, or disciplinary suspension from work, or as a result of the individual's failure to apply for or accept work and shall promptly enter an assistant director's

decision [of disqualification] if
* * *

(a) The individual has been discharged for misconduct connected with his work, or

(b) the individual has been suspended from work for misconduct connected with his work, or

(c) The individual voluntarily left work without good cause, or

(d) The individual failed without good cause to apply for available suitable work when referred by the employment office or the assistant director, or

(e) The individual failed without good cause to accept suitable work when offered to him, * * *.

657.430

The assistant director shall, for each calendar year determine the tax rate applicable to each employer on the basis of his actual experience with respect to benefits paid to unemployed individuals on account of wages for services performed in the employ of such employer during the base years of such unemployed individuals * * *.

What are the rules regarding wages, hours, and working conditions?

The following exchange took place in 1911 between a Pennsylvania judge and a little girl named Helen Susscak who was an 8 year old textile mill employee:

Judge.   "Helen, what time do you go to work?"

Helen.   "Half after 6 evenin's."

Judge.   "When do you come home from the mill?"

Helen.   "Half after 6 mornin's."

Judge.   "How far do you live from the mill?"

Helen.   "I don't know. I guess it mostly takes an hour to git there."

Judge.   "And the inspector tells me it's across lonely fields exposed to storms that sweep down the valley. What's your pay, Helen?"

Helen.   "I gits 3 cents an hour, sir."

Judge.   "If my arithmetic is good that is almost 36 cents for a night's work. Well, now, we do indeed find the flesh and blood of little children coined into money."

The above incident was recounted by Senators Javits of New York and Williams of New Jersey at the time the 1966 Amendments to the Fair Labor Standards Act were being considered. The original Fair Labor Standards Act was the product of the "New Deal" of the 1930's. In May of 1937, President Franklin Roosevelt sent to Congress a wage-hour proposal stressing the necessity of conserving "our primary resources of manpower by controlling maximum hours, minimum wages, the evil of child labor and the exploitation of unorganized labor." Senator Hugo L. Black of Alabama (who became Justice of the Supreme Court in 1938 where he served some 35 years before his death in 1972) introduced an appropriate bill in the Senate, where the bill was ultimately passed as the Fair Labor Standards Act of 1938. The purpose of the Act was to guarantee certain minimum working conditions, particularly a minimum wage and a maximum length work week. The 1977 amendments passed by Congress provided for a minimum hourly wage of $2.90 an hour beginning January 1, 1979, $3.10 beginning January 1, 1980, and $3.35 beginning January 1, 1981.

The Fair Labor Standards Act (FLSA) is primarily a wage and hour law. The following are its most important substantive provisions.

The Act provides:

Sec. 6

(a) Every employer shall pay to each of his employees who in any workweek is engaged in commerce or in the production of goods for commerce, * * * wages at the following rates:

(1) not less than $2.65 an hour during the year beginning January 1, 1978, not less than $2.90 an hour during the year beginning January 1, 1979; not less than $3.10 an hour during the year beginning January 1, 1980; and not less than $3.35 an hour after December 31, 1980, * * *.

Sec. 7

(a)(1) Except as otherwise provided in this section, no employer shall employ any of his employees who in any workweek is engaged in commerce or in the production of goods for commerce, * * * for a workweek longer than forty hours unless such employee receives compensation for his employment in excess of the hours above specified at a rate not less than one and one half times the regular rate at which he is employed.

* * *

EXEMPTIONS

Sec. 13

(a) The provisions of sections 6 * * * and 7 [wages and hours] shall not apply with respect to—

(1) any employee employed in a bona fide executive, administrative, or professional capacity (including any employee employed in the capacity of academic administrative personnel or teacher in elementary or secondary schools) or in the capacity of outside salesman * * *; or

(2) any employee employed by any retail or service establishment * * * if more than 50 per centum of such establishment's annual dollar volume of sales of goods or services is made within the State in which the establishment is located * * *; [This exemption applies only to establishments doing $275,000 or less worth of business annually. They are exempt from all the requirements of the Fair Labor Standards Act. Under the 1977 amendments, the test for coverage of employees of enterprises comprised of retail or service establishments is raised to $325,000 on July 1, 1980 and to $362,500 on December 31, 1981.] or

(3) any employee employed by an establishment which is an amusement or recreational establishment, organized camp, or religious or nonprofit educational conference center, if (A) it does not operate for more than seven months in any calendar year * * *; or

* * *

(5) any employee employed in the catching, taking, propagating, harvesting, cultivating, or farming of any kind of fish, shellfish, crustacea, sponges, seaweeds, or other aquatic forms of animal and vegetable life, or in the first processing, canning, or packing such marine products at sea as an incident to, or in conjunction with, such fishing operations, * * *; or

(6) any employee in agriculture (A) if such employee is employed by an employer who did not, during any calendar quarter during the preceding calendar year, use more than five hundred man-days of agricultural labor, (B) if such employee is the parent, spouse, child, or other member of his employer's immediate family, (C) if such employee (i) is employed as a

hand harvest laborer and is paid on a piece rate basis in an operation which has been, and is customarily and generally recognized as having been, paid on a piece rate basis in the region of employment, (ii) commutes daily from his permanent residence to the farm on which he is so employed, and (iii) has been employed in agriculture less than thirteen weeks during the preceding calendar year, (D) if such employee (other than an employee described in clause (C) of this subsection) (i) is sixteen years of age or under and is employed as a hand harvest laborer, is paid on a piece rate basis in an operation which has been, and is customarily and generally recognized as having been, paid on a piece rate basis in the region of employment, (ii) is employed on the same farm as his parent or person standing in the place of his parent, and (iii) is paid at the same piece rate as employees over age sixteen are paid on the same farm, or (E) if such employee is principally engaged in the range production of livestock; or

* * *

(8) any employee employed in connection with the publication of any weekly, semiweekly, or daily newspaper with a circulation of less than four thousand the major part of which circulation is within the county where published or counties contiguous thereto; or

* * *

(10) any switchboard operator employed by an independently owned public telephone company which has not more than seven hundred and fifty stations; or

* * *

(15) any employee employed on a casual basis in domestic service employment to provide babysitting services or any employee employed in domestic service employment to provide

companionship services for individuals who (because of age or infirmity) are unable to care for themselves.

(b) The provisions of section 7 [hours only] shall not apply with respect to * * *

(2) any employee of an employer engaged in the operation of a common carrier by rail and subject to the provisions of Part I of the Interstate Commerce Act, or

(3) any employee of a carrier by air subject to the provisions of title II of the Railway Labor Act, or

* * *

(5) any individual employed as an outside buyer of poultry, eggs, cream, or milk, in their raw or natural state; or

(6) any employee employed as a seaman; or

* * *

(9) any employee employed as an announcer, news editor, or chief engineer by a radio or television station the major studio of which is located (A) in a city or town of one hundred thousand population or less, * * *; or

(10)(A) any salesman, partsman, or mechanic primarily engaged in selling or servicing automobiles, trucks, or farm implements, if he is employed by a nonmanufacturing establishment primarily engaged in the business of selling such vehicles or implements to ultimate purchasers; or

(B) any salesman primarily engaged in selling trailers, boats, or aircraft, if he is employed by a nonmanufacturing establishment primarily engaged in the business of selling trailers, boats, or aircraft to ultimate purchasers; or

(11) any employee employed as a driver or driver's helper making local

deliveries, who is compensated for such employment on the basis of trip rates, or other delivery payment plan, . . . ; or

(12) any employee employed in agriculture or in connection with the operation or maintenance of ditches, canals, reservoirs, or waterways, not owned or operated for profit, or operated on a sharecrop basis, and which are used exclusively for supply and storing of water for agricultural purposes; or

* * *

(15) any employee engaged in the processing of maple sap into sugar * * * or syrup; or

(16) any employee engaged (A) in the transportation and preparation for transportation of fruits or vegetables, whether or not performed by the farmer, from the farm to a place of first processing or first marketing within the same State, or (B) in transportation, whether or not performed by the farmer, between the farm and any point within the same State of persons employed or to be employed in the harvesting of fruits or vegetables; or

(17) any driver employed by an employer engaged in the business of operating taxicabs; or

* * *

(20) any employee of a public agency who in any workweek is employed in fire protection activities or any employee of a public agency who in any workweek is employed in law enforcement activities (including security personnel in correctional institutions), if the public agency employs during the workweek less than 5 employees in fire protection or law enforcement activities, as the case may be; or

(21) any employee who is employed in domestic service in a house-

hold and who resides in such household; or

* * *

(24) any employee who is employed with his spouse by a nonprofit educational institution to serve as the parents of children—(A) who are orphans or one of whose natural parents is deceased, or (B) who are enrolled in such institution and reside in residential facilities of the institution, while such children are in residence at such institution, if such employee and his spouse reside in such facilities, receive, without cost, board and lodging from such institution, and are together compensated, on a cash basis, at an annual rate of not less than $10,000; or

* * *

(27) any employee employed by an establishment which is a motion picture theater; or

(28) any employee employed in planting or tending trees, cruising, surveying, or felling timber, or in preparing or transporting logs, or other forestry products to the mill, processing plant, railroad, or other transportation terminal, if the number of employees employed by his employer in such forestry or lumbering operations does not exceed eight; or

(29) any employee of an amusement or recreational establishment located in a national park or national forest or on land in the National Wildlife Refuge System if such employee (A) is an employee of a private entity engaged in providing services or facilities in a national park or national forest, or on land in the National Wildlife Refuge System, under a contract with the Secretary of the Interior or the Secretary of Agriculture, and (B) receives compensation for employment in excess of fifty-six hours in any workweek at a rate not less than one

and one-half times the regular rate at which he is employed.

DEFINITIONS

Sec. 3

As used in this Act—

* * * (1) "Oppresive child labor" means a condition of employment under which (1) any employee under the age of sixteen years is employed by an employer (other than a parent) * * * in any occupation, or (2) any employee between the ages of sixteen and eighteen years is employed by an employer in any occupation which the Secretary of Labor shall find and by order declare to be particularly hazardous for the employment of children between such ages or detrimental to their health or well-being; * * *. The Secretary of Labor shall provide by regulation or by order that the employment of employees between the ages of fourteen and sixteen years in occupations other than manufacturing and mining shall not be deemed to constitute oppressive child labor if and to the extent that the Secretary of Labor determines that such employment is confined to periods which will not interfere with their schooling and to conditions which will not interfere with their health and well-being.

CHILD LABOR PROVISIONS

Sec. 12

(a) No producer, manufacturer, or dealer shall ship or deliver for shipment in commerce any goods produced in an establishment situated in the United States in or about which within thirty days prior to the removal of such goods therefrom any oppressive child labor has been employed: Provided, That any such shipment or delivery for shipment or sale of such goods by a purchaser who acquired them in good faith in reliance on written assurance from the producer, manufacturer, or dealer that the goods were produced in compliance with the requirements of this section, and who acquired such goods for value without notice of any such violation, shall not be deemed prohibited by this subsection. * * *

* * * (c) No employer shall employ any oppressive child labor in commerce or in the production of goods for commerce or in any enterprise engaged in commerce or in the production of goods for commerce.

(d) In order to carry out the objectives of this section, the Secretary may by regulation require employers to obtain from any employee proof of age.

Sec. 13

(c)(1) Except as provided in paragraph (2), the provisions of section 12 relating to child labor shall not apply to any employee employed in agriculture outside of school hours for the school district where such employee is living while he is so employed, if such employee—

(A) is less than twelve years of age and (i) is employed by his parent, or by a person standing in the place of his parent, on a farm owned or operated by such parent or person, or (ii) is employed with the consent of his parent or person standing in the place of his parent, on a farm, none of the employees of which are [because of section 13 (a)(6)(A)] required to be paid at the wage rate prescribed by section 6 (a)(5). [Section 6 (a)(5) states that agricultural workers must be covered by the regular minimum wage rate after January 1, 1978— before this time there had been a special minimum wage rate for agricultural workers.]

(B) is twelve years or thirteen years of age and (i) such employment is with the consent of his parent or person standing in the place of his parent, or (ii) his parent or such person is employed on the same farm as such employee, or

(C) is fourteen years of age or older.

(2) The provisions of section 12 relating to child labor shall apply to an employee below the age of sixteen employed in agriculture in an occupation that the Secretary of Labor finds and declares to be particularly hazardous for the employment of children below the age of sixteen except where such employee is employed by his parent or by a person standing in the place of his parent on a farm owned or operated by such parent or person.

(3) The provisions of section 12 relating to child labor shall not apply to any child employed as an actor or performer in motion pictures or theatrical productions, or in radio or television productions.

(4)(A) An employer or group of employers may apply to the Secretary for a waiver of the application of section 12 to the employment for not more than eight weeks in any calendar year of individuals, who are less than twelve years of age, but not less than ten years of age, as hand harvest laborers in an agricultural operation which has been, and is customarily and generally recognized as being, paid on a piece rate basis in the region in which such individuals would be employed. The Secretary may not grant such a waiver unless he finds, based on objective data submitted by the applicant, that—

(i) the crop to be harvested is one with a particularly short harvesting season and the application of section 12 would cause severe economic disruption in the industry of the employer or group of employers applying for the waiver;

(ii) the employment of the individuals to whom the waiver would apply would not be deleterious to their health or well-being;

(iii) the level and type of pesticides and other chemicals used would not have an adverse effect on the health or well-being of the individuals to whom the waiver would apply;

(iv) individuals aged twelve and above are not available for such employment; and

(v) the industry of such employer or group of employers has traditionally and substantially employed individuals under twelve years of age without displacing substantial job opportunities for individuals over sixteen years of age.

(B) Any waiver granted by the Secretary under subparagraph (A) shall require that—

(i) the individuals employed under such waiver be employed outside of school hours for the school district where they are living while so employed;

(ii) such individuals while so employed commute daily from their permanent residence to the farm on which they are so employed; and

(iii) such individuals be employed under such waiver (I) for not more than thirteen weeks between June 1 and October 15 of any calendar year, and (II) in accordance with such other terms and conditions as the Secretary shall prescribe for such individuals' protection.

(d) The provisions of sections 6, 7, and 12 shall not apply with respect to any employee engaged in the delivery of newspapers to the consumer or to any homeworker engaged in the making of wreaths composed principally of natural holly, pine, cedar, or other evergreens (including the harvesting of the evergreens or other forest products used in making such wreaths).

LEARNERS, APPRENTICES, AND HANDICAPPED WORKERS

Sec. 14

* * * (b)(3) The Secretary to the extent necessary in order to prevent curtailment of opportunities for employment, shall by special certificate issued under a regulation or order provide for the employment by an institution of higher education at a rate not less than 85 per centum of the otherwise applicable wage rate in effect under section 6 or not less than $1.60 an hour, whichever is the higher, * * * of full time students (regardless of age but in compliance with applicable child labor laws) who are enrolled in such institution.

* * *

(c)(2) The Secretary, pursuant to such regulations as he shall prescribe and upon certification of the State agency administering or supervising the administration of vocational rehabilitation services, may issue special certificates for the employment of—

(A) handicapped workers engaged in work which is incidental to training or evaluation programs, and

(B) multihandicapped individuals and other individuals whose earning capacity is so severely impaired that they are unable to engage in competitive employment, at wages which are less than those required * * * and which are related to the worker's productivity.

PENALTIES

Sec. 16

(a) Any person who willfully violates any of the provisions of section 15 shall upon conviction thereof be subject to a fine of not more than $10,000, or to imprisonment for not more than six months or both.

———

As you can see, the Fair Labor Standards Act strictly regulates "child labor". Minors may not be employed in "oppressive" labor—i. e., occupations particularly hazardous for them or detrimental to their health and well-being. Notice that the Statute prohibits a wholesaler from delivering goods to a dealer in another state where the wholesaler knows that oppressive child labor was used in manufacturing the goods.

For minors between the ages of 16 and 18, prohibited jobs include logging, roofing, meat packing or slaughtering, and building demolition. For persons between 14 and 16, some employment is permitted under regulations provided by the Secretary of Labor. Employment in occupations other than mining or manufacturing, for example, is allowed so long as it does not interfere with the schooling, health, or well-being of the 14 to 16 year old. Permissible categories include office and clerical work, retailing, price marking and shelving, deliveries by foot or on bicycle, garden work, and gasoline station work as long as the minor does not work in the pits or racks.

Are there laws prohibiting job discrimination on grounds of race, color, religion, sex, national origin, and age?

The answer is yes. Job discrimination on grounds of race, color, religion, sex, national origin, and age is unlawful under federal law. Various state laws expand this list and include other characteristics such as creed and ancestry. Title

VII of the Civil Rights Act of 1964 is the most important federal law designed to eliminate discriminatory employment practices. Section 703 of Title VII states:

Sec. 703

(a) It shall be an unlawful employment practice for an employee—

(1) to fail or refuse to hire or to discharge any individual or otherwise to discriminate against any individual with respect to his compensation, terms, conditions, or privileges of employment, because of such individual's race, color, religion, sex or national origin; or

(2) to limit, segregate, or classify his employees or applicants for employment in any way which would deprive any individual of employment opportunities or otherwise adversely affect his status as an employee, because of such individual's race, color, religion, sex, or national origin.

On October 31, 1978, President Carter signed into law a pregnancy disability amendment to Title VII. The change in the law expands the definition of "sex" discrimination to include discrimination on the basis of "pregnancy, childbirth, or related medical conditions". The following new subsection was added to Section 701 of Title VII.

It says:

(k) The terms "because of sex" or "on the basis of sex" include, but are not limited to, because of or on the basis of pregnancy, childbirth or related medical conditions; and women affected by pregnancy, childbirth, or related medical conditions shall be treated the same for all employment-related purposes, including receipt of benefits under fringe benefit programs, as other persons not so af-

fected but similar in their ability or inability to work, and nothing in this section 703(h) of this title shall be interpreted to permit otherwise. This subsection shall not require an employer to pay for health insurance benefits for abortion, except where the life of the mother would be endangered if the fetus were carried to term, or except where medical complications have arisen from an abortion: Provided, That nothing herein shall preclude an employer from providing abortion benefits or otherwise affect bargaining agreement in regard to abortion.

Among other things, the amendment does the following:

—requires employers to treat pregnancy and childbirth the same as other causes of disability under fringe benefit plans;

—prohibits terminating or refusing to hire or promote a woman solely because she is pregnant;

—bars mandatory leaves for pregnant women arbitrarily set at a certain time in their pregnancy and not based on their inability to work; and

—protects the reinstatement rights of women on leave for pregnancy-related reasons, including credit for previous service and accrued retirement benefits, and accumulated seniority.

The types of practices that are outlawed by Title VII are outlawed with respect to age discrimination by the Age Discrimination in Employment Act of 1967. Originally, the provisions of the Act were limited to individuals who were at least 40 years of age but less than 65. However, the Age Discrimination in Employment Act Amendments of 1978 raised the upper age limit on coverage from 65 to 70 and prohibited the forced retirement based on age of employees below the age of 70. The law applies only to employers of twenty or more workers. The Amendments (a) forbid a seniority system or employee benefit plan to require or permit the involuntary retirement of an employee under the age of 70; (b) permit the compulsory retirement at age 65 of employees employed in a bona fide executive or high policymaking position and entitled to a pension of at least $27,000 per year; (c) allow colleges and universities to retire tenured employees at age 65 until July 1, 1982; and (d) eliminate the maximum age for retirement of 70 that presently applies to U.S. Government employees.

The 1978 Amendments do not preclude an employer from terminating an employee for cause. Any employee, including an older person, who is incompetent or unable to perform his or her job is not protected under the Act from being discharged or retired. This fact may prompt the firing of some older workers who would have been kept on the job prior to the passage of the Amendments. Many employers have tolerated less than acceptable work performance from older employees simply because they were near retirement age (on the other hand, prior to passage of the Amendments, many capable persons were forced to retire simply because of their age). Of course, in terminating employees for cause, the same performance standards must be applied to all employees—not special standards for older employees—or this itself will violate the Act as being age discrimination.

The Age Discrimination in Employment Act does not prevent discrimination on the basis of age where age is a bona fide occupational qualification reasonably necessary to the normal operation of the business (as in piloting a plane or playing professional ball). But where it is not an occupational qualification (e. g., where a flight attendant is concerned), a person cannot be hired or fired because of his or her age.

Along the same line, Title VII, Section 706(g) of the Civil Rights Act of 1964 authorizes federal district courts to correct unlawful discriminatory practices by enjoining them and ordering such "affirmative action as may be appropriate." The Statute especially provides for the "reinstatement or hiring of employees, with or without back pay," and adds the additional ability to give "any other equitable relief as the court deems appropriate."

The Civil Rights Act of 1968 also provides:

(b) Whoever, whether or not acting under color of law, by force or threat of force willfully injures, intimidates or interferes with, or attempts to injure, intimidate or interfere with

(2) any person because of his race, color, religion, or national origin and because he is or has been—

(C) applying for or enjoying employment, or any perquisite thereof, by any private employer or any agency of any State or subdivision thereof, or joining or using the services or advantages of any labor organization, hiring hall, or employment agency;

* * * shall be fined not more than $1,000 or imprisoned not more than one year or both; and if bodily injury results shall be fined not more than $10,000, or imprisoned not more than ten years, or both; and if death results shall be subject to imprisonment for any term of years or for life.

———

Discrimination in pay and other employment practices is still permitted under these laws if it is done in conformance with a bona fide (a) seniority system; (b) merit system; (c) a system that measures earnings by quantity or quality of production; (d) a system that distinguishes among employees who work in different locations; or (e) a system based on the results of a professionally developed ability test related to the work in question.

What is meant by "Affirmative Action?"

"Affirmative Action" is a program initiated by the federal government to eliminate discrimination in employment against women and minorities. By threatening to terminate supply and research contracts, the federal government (particularly the Department of Health, Education and Welfare) has pressured employers to take specific steps to hire and promote minorities and women in percentages roughly equal to their representation in the local community. Though "affirmative action" results in reverse discrimination against white male employees and white male applicants, the justification for the program is found in the conclusion that such white males can find other jobs more easily than can women and minorities—if necessary, in firms where federal contracts have not been entered into, and where the government does not have this corrective weapon available. Some opponents of the program maintain that there should be no discrimination against anyone, and that the Civil Rights Act should be administered with neutrality. These opponents believe that employment and promotion should be based on merit. Proponents, on the other hand, believe that steps should be taken to catch women and minorities up even at the expense of reverse discrimination.

CASES

CASE 1—*The mechanic was an independent contractor.*

NAWROCKI v. COLE

Supreme Court of Washington, Department 2, 1952.
41 Wash.2d 474, 249 P.2d 969.

OLSON, Justice.

A jury returned a verdict in favor of plaintiff for damages incurred in an automobile collision. * * * [D]efendant has appealed. J. T. Cole is the sole defendant, his wife having died before the trial.

His appeal presents two principal questions: (1) Was a mechanic he employed to repair his car, and who was testing it on the highway when the collision occurred, an independent contractor, and (2) was defendant himself negligent in having his car driven on the highway when, as plaintiff alleges, "he knew that said automobile had serious motor trouble and might be stalled on said highway"?

During the evening in question, defendant and two guests were returning to Tacoma from Wilbur in defendant's automobile. As they approached Ellensburg, the motor ceased to function properly. It operated jerkily, and the car could be driven only at slow speeds, estimated by defendant to be from five or ten miles an hour to thirty or thirty-five miles an hour. It did not stop entirely, nor was it necessary to drive the car in low gear.

Defendant arrived at a garage in Ellensburg late in the evening. He told the mechanic how the car had operated and asked him to find the trouble and repair it. The mechanic proceeded to work on the motor, and it was running smoothly when he presented a bill for his services. Defendant did not pay the bill or accept the car, but asked the mechanic to take it out on the highway and test it to be sure that it was operating properly.

The mechanic, accompanied by one of defendant's guests, then drove the car onto the main traveled highway leading out of Ellensburg. After he had gone about one mile, the motor again ceased to function properly, and it was impossible to accelerate the car. He then decided that the fuel pump was the source of the trouble, and, as he was returning to the garage, plaintiff, going in the same direction, drove his automobile into the rear of defendant's car. Plaintiff testified that, before the collision, defendant's car was stopped on the highway and that he saw no lights on it. Some rain had fallen during the evening, and the pavement was wet. Visibility was poor because of haze or fog in the vicinity of the collision.

An independent contractor is one who, in the pursuit of an independent business, undertakes to perform a specified piece of work or to render a particular service for another, without submitting to control in the manner of performance. The principal question is, who has the right to control the manner of doing the work? The independence of the relation is not affected by a reservation, by the one ordering the work, of a right to supervise it merely to determine whether or not it is done according to the contract.

      *   *   *

The evidence   *   *   *   establishes that the mechanic was engaged in an independent business, that of repairing automobiles. He undertook a specified piece of work, the repair oi defendant's car. Defendant did not know what had to be done, and the mechanic was free from his direction or control regarding the details or the manner of repair. Defendant was concerned only with the result of the work and did not supervise it, except to request that the car be tested to determine whether the work of repair was completed. Neither defendant nor his guest, who rode with the mechanic during the test, specified or controlled the exact place or kind of test to be made. The test became part of the work of repair, and the mechanic did what he determined, from the test, was necessary to finish his job. Not until then did he complete his work, deliver the car to defendant, and receive his pay.

Upon these facts the mechanic became an independent contractor, as a matter of law, when he accepted defendant's car for repair. Defendant's request that the car be tested did not change this relationship, as plaintiff contends, and it prevailed until the car was redelivered to defendant. * * *

Therefore, because the negligence, if any, of the mechanic, an independent contractor, cannot be imputed to defendant, if the judgment can be sustained, it must be upon the alleged negligence of defendant himself.

An automobile is not *per se* a dangerous instrumentality. It may become such if it is so mechanically defective as to render it liable to become uncontrollable on the highway.

The case at bar is not pleaded on a theory of strict or absolute liability. It is rested upon the alleged negligence of defendant. The standard of conduct required of defendant upon this theory of the case may be defined by stating the essential elements of plaintiff's proof, if he is to recover. They are that, at the time defendant's automobile went upon the highway, (1) it was defective, (2) defendant knew or, as a reasonable man, should have known of the defect and of the reasonable likelihood that it would cause injury, (3) the defect proximately caused the injury to plaintiff, and (4) the damages he sustained.

Upon this issue, the evidence is undisputed that defendant's car did not stop on the highway, nor did its lights cease to function, before he delivered it to the garage for repair. The motor was operating smoothly, and all of the lights, both front and rear, were burning when the mechanic drove the car out of the garage to test it. * * * [W]e find no fact or reasonable inference from the facts or circumstances in this case, to sustain a verdict adverse to defendant upon the second essential element of plaintiff's proof.

Neither of the issues we have discussed should have been submitted to the jury. The judgment is reversed, and the cause is remanded to the trial court for the entry of judgment in favor of defendant, notwithstanding the verdict of the jury.

CASE 2—*There are without doubt a substantial number of women who could lift over 50 pounds and a large number of men who could not.*

LOCAL 246, UTILITY WORKERS UNION v. SOUTHERN CALIFORNIA EDISON CO.

United States District Court, C.D.California, 1970.
320 F.Supp. 1262.

DAVID W. WILLIAMS, District Judge.

* * *

Plaintiff Brunhilde Blossfeld is a woman employed by defendant Southern California Edison Company. Since October 8, 1964, she has held the position of clerk-typist in the Clerical and Technical working unit of the company.

In October of 1968, a vacancy occurred in the company in the position of junior clerk. Plaintiff Blossfeld made a timely application for the position. Under the collective bargaining agreement in force between Edison and plaintiff's union, it was required that "where ability and qualifications are sufficient * * * seniority shall be observed in promotions and transfers." Nevertheless, on about November 8, 1968, Edison posted a notice that there were no qualified bidders for the junior clerk position and thereafter appointed a male employee with less seniority than plaintiff to the position.

Edison based its conclusion that plaintiff was unqualified solely on the facts that the job of junior clerk requires lifting objects in excess of 50 pounds on a regular basis, that plaintiff Blossfeld is a woman, and that Section 1251 of the California Labor Code provides that "No female employee shall be requested or permitted to lift any object weighing 50 pounds or over."

Plaintiffs contend that Section 1251 cannot justify Edison's conduct. They contend that the weight lifting restrictions of the California Labor Code are invalid because inconsistent with Title VII of the Equal Opportunities in Employment Act of 1964. The Act makes it unlawful for an employer

"(1) to fail or refuse to hire or to discharge any individual, or otherwise to discriminate against any individual with respect to his compensation, terms, conditions, or privileges of employment, because of such individual's * * * sex * * * ; or

"(2) to limit, segregate, or classify his employees in any way which would deprive or tend to deprive any individual of employment opportunities or otherwise adversely affect his status as an employee, because of such individual's * * * sex * * *." 42 U.S.C. § 2000e–2(a).

* * *

Defendants * * * argue that the California statute upon which Edison relied is valid because sex is a bona fide occupational qualification for weight lifting. Section 703(e) (42 U.S.C. § 2000e–2(e)) of the Civil Rights Act creates an exception to Section 703(a)'s general prohibition against discrimination in employment on the basis of sex. It permits an employer to employ "any individual * * * on the basis of sex * * * in those certain instances where * * * sex * * * is a bona fide occupational qualification reasonably necessary to the normal operation of that particular business or enterprise." This Court has carefully considered the issue of whether the California statute creates a bona fide occupational qualification (BFOQ) and is forced to conclude that it does not.

Section 703(e) creates a very narrow exception to the Act; it refers to a particular business or enterprise rather than to broad categories of employment such as industrial or technological occupations. Secondly, it refers to employing any individual on the basis of sex and does not permit discrimination on the basis of groups. Finally, it permits discrimination on the basis of sex when this is a reasonably necessary qualification. The California statute in question is much broader than Section 703(e) would permit. It applies not to a "particular business", but to any occupation. It applies not to an "individual", but to a class which comprises over half the population of the state. Finally, in order to establish a BFOQ it must be shown that the criterion in issue is a "reasonably necessary" prerequisite to satisfactory performance of the employment in question. It could be said that in order to operate an authentically atmospheric Chinese restaurant, it is reasonably necessary to have the waiters and waitresses be Chinese. Similarly, in order for a play to be communicative and effective, it must be reasonably necessary to have all female roles played by women and all male roles played by men. There is no such relationship between the requirement of being male and lifting over 50 pounds. On the contrary, there are without doubt a substantial number of women who could lift over 50 pounds and a large number of men who could not. Therefore, it does not appear at all necessary, let alone reasonably necessary, that a position requiring such lifting be filled by a male.

We conclude that the classification and discrimination authorized by Section 1251 does not constitute a BFOQ. Since the California statute consequently permits discrimination prohibited by Title VII, it unavoidably conflicts with that Title and is invalid under the Supremacy Clause of the Constitution. Defendant Edison's conduct pursuant to the invalid statute constitutes an unlawful employment practice in violation of the Act.

By its decision, this Court does not mean to suggest that all rules restricting certain types of employment to one sex are invalid under Title VII of the Equal Employment Opportunities Act. Such restrictions can be made where sex is relevant. State laws or private employer policies imposing weight lifting restrictions would be permissible under Title VII if they applied the same limits to men as to women or if they provided that every individual lift no more than is safe or he is capable of, that amount to be determined on an individual basis. Had Edison felt that Plaintiff Blossfeld, for example, could not safely lift over 50 pounds on a regular basis (an argument which defendants never raise), it would have been lawful for the company to deny her the position of junior clerk. However, weight lifting restrictions applicable only to the broad category of women, such as provided by § 1251 of California Labor Code, are not permissible under the Act.

* * *

In Richards v. Griffith Rubber Mills, 300 F.Supp. 338 (D.Ore., 1969), plaintiff Diana Richards applied for each of two openings as a "Press Operator B". The jobs were given to two men with less seniority. Employer Griffith justified its conduct by reference to the union contract which required that females get two ten-minute rest periods and Order No. 8 of the Wage and Hours Commission which prohibited consistent lifting of over 30 pounds by women. In response to the contention that the Order and defendant's conduct violated Section 703(a) of the Equal Employment Opportunities Act, the Court stated: "the law no longer permits either employers or the states to deal with women as a class in relation to employment."

* * *

[I]n Bowe v. Colgate-Palmolive Co., 416 F.2d 711 (7th Cir., 1969) * * * Colgate had a company policy which restricted women to jobs which did not require lifting more than 35 pounds. The Circuit Court reversed the trial court, holding that the defendant "may if it so desires, retain its 35-pound weight-lifting limit as a general guideline for *all* of its employees, male and female. However, * * * [e]ach employee who is able to so demonstrate (that he can lift larger amounts) must be permitted to bid on and fill any position."

* * *

[Judgment for plaintiff.]

CASE 3—*The Allan Bakke case.*

REGENTS OF UNIVERSITY OF CALIFORNIA v. BAKKE

Supreme Court of the United States, 1978.
438 U.S. 265, 98 S.Ct. 2733, 57 L.Ed.2d 750.

Mr. Justice BRENNAN, Mr. Justice WHITE, Mr. Justice MARSHALL and Mr. Justice BLACKMUN filed an opinion concurring in the judgment in part and dissenting.

Mr. Justice WHITE filed a separate opinion.

Mr. Justice MARSHALL filed a separate opinion.

Mr. Justice BLACKMUN filed a separate opinion.

Mr. Justice STEVENS concurred in the judgment in part and dissented in part and filed an opinion in which Mr. Chief Justice BURGER, Mr. Justice STEWART and Mr. Justice REHNQUIST joined.

Mr. Justice POWELL announced the judgment of the Court.

This case presents a challenge to the special admissions program of the petitioner, the Medical School of the University of California at Davis, which is designed to assure the admission of a specified number of students from certain minority groups. The Superior Court of California sustained respondent's challenge, holding that petitioner's program violated the California Constitution, Title VI of the Civil Rights Act of 1964, 42 U.S.C.A. § 2000d, and the Equal Protection Clause of the Fourteenth Amendment. The court enjoined petitioner from considering respondent's race or the race of any other applicant in making admissions decisions. * * * The Supreme Court of California affirmed * * * and directed the trial court to order his [Bakke's] admission.

For the reasons stated in the following opinion, I believe that so much of the judgment of the California court as holds petitioner's special admissions program unlawful and directs that respondent be admitted to the Medical School must be affirmed. For the reasons expressed in a separate opinion, my Brothers THE CHIEF JUSTICE, Mr. Justice STEWART, Mr. Justice REHNQUIST and Mr. Justice STEVENS concur in this judgment.

I also conclude for the reasons stated in the following opinion that the portion of the court's judgment enjoining petitioner from according any consideration to race in its admissions process must be reversed. For reasons expressed in separate opinions, my Brothers Mr. Justice BRENNAN, Mr. Justice WHITE, Mr. Justice MARSHALL, and Mr. Justice BLACK-MUN concur in this judgment.

Affirmed in part and reversed in part.

The Medical School of the University of California at Davis opened in 1968 with an entering class of 50 students. In 1971, the size of the entering class was increased to 100 students, a level at which it remains. No admissions program for disadvantaged or minority students existed when the school opened, and the first class contained three Asians but no blacks, no Mexican-Americans, and no American Indians. Over the next two years, the faculty devised a special admissions program to increase the representation of "disadvantaged" students in each medical school class. The special program consisted of a separate admissions system operating in coordination with the regular admissions process.

Under the regular admissions procedure, a candidate could submit his application to the medical school beginning in July of the year preceding the academic year for which admission was sought. Because of the large number of applications,[2] the admissions committee screened each one to select candidates for further consideration. Candidates whose overall undergraduate grade point averages fell below 2.5 on a scale of 4.0 were summarily rejected. About one out of six applicants was invited for a personal interview. Following the interviews, each candidate was rated on a scale of 1 to 100 by his interviewers and four other members of the admissions committee. The rating embraced the interviewers' summaries, the candidate's overall grade point average, grade point average in science courses, and scores on the Medical College Admissions Test (MCAT), letters of recommendation, extracurricular activities, and other biographical data. The ratings were added together to arrive at each candidate's "benchmark" score. Since five committee members rated each candidate in 1973, a perfect score was 500; in 1974, six members rated each candidate, so that a perfect score was 600. The full committee then reviewed the file and scores of each applicant and made offers of admission on a "rolling"

---

2. For the 1973 entering class of 100 seats, the Davis medical school received 2,464 applications. For the 1974 entering class, 3,737 applications were submitted.

basis.[3] The chairman was responsible for placing names on the waiting list. They were not placed in strict numerical order; instead, the chairman had discretion to include persons with "special skills."

The special admissions program operated with a separate committee, a majority of whom were members of minority groups. On the 1973 application form, candidates were asked to indicate whether they wished to be considered as "economically and/or educationally disadvantaged" applicants; on the 1974 form the question was whether they wished to be considered as members of a "minority group," which the medical school apparently viewed as "Blacks," "Chicanos," "Asians," and "American Indians." If these questions were answered affirmatively, the application was forwarded to the special admissions committee. No formal definition of "disadvantage" was ever produced, but the chairman of the special committee screened each application to see whether it reflected economic or educational deprivation. Having passed this initial hurdle, the applications then were rated by the special committee in a fashion similar to that used by the general admissions committee, except that special candidates did not have to meet the 2.5 grade point average cut-off applied to regular applicants. About one-fifth of the total number of special applicants were invited for interviews in 1973 and 1974.[5] Following each interview, the special committee assigned each special applicant a benchmark score. The special committee then presented its top choices to the general admissions committee. The latter did not rate or compare the special candidates against the general applicants, but could reject recommended special candidates for failure to meet course requirements or other specific deficiencies. The special committee continued to recommend special applicants until a number prescribed by faculty vote were admitted. While the overall class size was still 50, the prescribed number was eight; in 1973 and 1974, when the class size had doubled to 100, the prescribed number of special admissions also doubled, to 16.

From the year of the increase in class size—1971—through 1974, the special program resulted in the admission of 21 black students, 30 Mexican-Americans, and 12 Asians, for a total of 63 minority students. Over the same period, the regular admissions program produced one black, six Mexican-Americans, and 37 Asians, for a total of 44 minority students.[6] Although disadvantaged whites applied to the special program in large numbers, see n. 5, supra, none received an offer of admission through that pro-

3. That is, applications were considered and acted upon as they were received, so that the process of filling the class took place over a period of months, with later applications being considered against those still on file from earlier in the year.

5. For the class entering in 1973, the total number of special applicants was 297, of whom 73 were white. In 1974, 628 persons applied to the special committee, of whom 172 were white.

6. The following table provides a year-by-year comparison of minority admissions at the Davis Medical School:

Special Admissions Program				General Admissions				Total
	Blacks	Chicanos	Asians	Total	Blacks	Chicanos	Asians	Total	
1970	5	3	0	8	0	0	4	4	12
1971	4	9	2	15	1	0	8	9	24
1972	5	6	5	16	0	0	11	11	27
1973	6	8	2	16	0	2	13	15	31
1974	6	7	3	16	0	4	5	9	25

Sixteen persons were admitted under the special program in 1974, but one Asian withdrew before the start of classes, and the vacancy was filled by a candidate from the general admissions waiting list.

cess. Indeed, in 1974, at least, the special committee explicitly considered only "disadvantaged" special applicants who were members of one of the designated minority groups.

Allan Bakke is a white male who applied to the Davis Medical School in both 1973 and 1974. In both years Bakke's application was considered by the general admissions program, and he received an interview. His 1973 interview was with Dr. Theodore H. West, who considered Bakke "a very desirable applicant to [the] medical school." Despite a strong benchmark score of 468 out of 500, Bakke was rejected. His application had come late in the year, and no applicants in the general admissions process with scores below 470 were accepted after Bakke's application was completed. There were four special admissions slots unfilled at that time however, for which Bakke was not considered. After his 1973 rejection, Bakke wrote to Dr. George H. Lowrey, Associate Dean and Chairman of the Admissions Committee, protesting that the special admissions program operated as a racial and ethnic quota.

Bakke's 1974 application was completed early in the year. His student interviewer gave him an overall rating of 94, finding him "friendly, well tempered, conscientious and delightful to speak with." His faculty interviewer was, by coincidence, the same Dr. Lowrey to whom he had written in protest of the special admissions program. Dr. Lowrey found Bakke "rather limited in his approach" to the problems of the medical profession and found disturbing Bakke's "very definite opinions which were based more on his personal viewpoints than upon a study of the total problem." Dr. Lowrey gave Bakke the lowest of his six ratings, an 86; his total was 549 out of 600. Again, Bakke's application was rejected. In neither year did the chairman of the admissions committee, Dr. Lowrey, exercise his discretion to place Bakke on the waiting list. In both years, applicants were admitted under the special program with grade point averages, MCAT scores, and benchmark scores significantly lower than Bakke's.[7]

---

7. The following table compares Bakke's science grade point average, overall grade point average, and MCAT scores with the average scores of regular admittees and of special admittees in both 1973 and 1974. Record 210, 223, 231, 234:

Class Entering in 1973

| | | | | MCAT (Percentiles) | | |
	SGPA	OGPA	Verbal	Quantitative	Science	Gen. Infor.
Bakke	3.44	3.51	96	94	97	72
Average of Regular Admittees	3.51	3.49	81	76	83	69
Average of Special Admittees	2.62	2.88	46	24	35	33

Class Entering in 1974

| | | | | MCAT (Percentiles) | | |
	SGPA	OGPA	Verbal	Quantitative	Science	Gen. Infor.
Bakke	3.44	3.51	96	94	97	72
Average of Regular Admittees	3.36	3.29	69	67	82	72
Average of Special Admittees	2.42	2.62	34	30	37	18

Applicants admitted under the special program also had benchmark scores significantly lower than many students, including Bakke, rejected under the general admissions program, even though the special rating system apparently gave credit for overcoming "disadvantage." Record 181, 388.

After the second rejection, Bakke filed the instant suit in the Superior Court of California. He sought mandatory, injunctive, and declaratory relief compelling his admission to the Medical School. He alleged that the Medical School's special admissions program operated to exclude him from the school on the basis of his race, in violation of his rights under the Equal Protection Clause of the Fourteenth Amendment,[9] Art. I, § 21 of the California Constitution,[10] and § 601 of Title VI of the Civil Rights Act of 1964, 42 U.S.C.A. § 2000d.[11] The University cross-complained for a declaration that its special admissions program was lawful. The trial court found that the special program operated as a racial quota, because minority applicants in the special program were rated only against one another and 16 places in the class of 100 were reserved for them. Declaring that the University could not take race into account in making admissions decisions, the trial court held the challenged program violative of the Federal Constitution, the state constitution and Title VI. The court refused to order Bakke's admission, however, holding that he had failed to carry his burden of proving that he would have been admitted but for the existence of the special program.

Bakke appealed from the portion of the trial court judgment denying him admission, and the University appealed from the decision that its special admissions program was unlawful and the order enjoining it from considering race in the processing of applications. * * * [T]he California court held that the Equal Protection Clause of the Fourteenth Amendment required that "no applicant may be rejected because of his race, in favor of another who is less qualified, as measured by standards applied without regard to race."

Turning to Bakke's appeal, the court ruled that since Bakke had established that the University had discriminated against him on the basis of his race, the burden of proof shifted to the University to demonstrate that he would not have been admitted even in the absence of the special admissions program. * * * [T]he University conceded its inability to carry that burden. The California court thereupon amended its opinion to direct that the trial court enter judgment ordering Bakke's admission to the medical school. We granted certiorari to consider the important constitutional issue.

* * *

B

The language of § 601 [The Civil Rights Act of 1964], like that of the Equal Protection Clause, is majestic in its sweep:

"No person in the United States shall, on the ground of race, color, or national origin, be excluded from participation in, be denied the

---

9. "* * * [N]or shall any State . . . deny to any person within its jurisdiction the equal protection of the laws."

10. "No special privileges or immunities shall ever be granted which may not be altered, revoked, or repealed by the Legislature: nor shall any citizen, or class of citizens, be granted privileges, or immunities which, upon the same terms, shall not be granted to all citizens.

This section was recently repealed and its provisions added to Art. 1, § 7 of the state constitution.

11. Section 601 of Title VI provides as follows:

"No person in the United States shall, on the ground of race, color, or national origin, be excluded from participation in, be denied the benefits of, or be subjected to discrimination under any program or activity receiving Federal financial assistance."

benefits of, or be subjected to discrimination under any program
or activity receiving Federal financial assistance."

The concept of "discrimination," like the phrase "equal protection of the
laws," is susceptible to varying interpretations, for as Mr. Justice Holmes
declared, "[a] word is not a crystal, transparent and unchanged, it is the
skin of a living thought and may vary greatly in color and content according to the circumstances and the time in which it is used." We must,
therefore, seek whatever aid is available in determining the precise meaning
of the statute before us. Train v. Colorado Public Interest Research Group,
426 U.S. 1, 10, 96 S.Ct. 1938, 1942, 48 L.Ed.2d 434 (1976), quoting United
States v. American Trucking Assns., 310 U.S. 534, 543–544, 60 S.Ct. 1059,
1063–1064, 84 L.Ed. 1345 (1940). Examination of the voluminous legislative history of Title VI reveals a congressional intent to halt federal funding of entities that violate a prohibition of racial discrimination similar to
that of the Constitution. Although isolated statements of various legislators taken out of context, can be marshalled in support of the proposition
that § 601 enacted a purely color-blind scheme, without regard to the reach
of the Equal Protection Clause, these comments must be read against the
background of both the problem that Congress was addressing and the
broader view of the statute that emerges from a full examination of the legislative debates.

The problem confronting Congress was discrimination against Negro
citizens at the hands of recipients of federal moneys. Indeed, the color-
blindness pronouncements cited in the margin at n. 19, generally occur in
the midst of extended remarks dealing with the evils of segregation in federally funded programs. Over and over again, proponents of the bill detailed
the plight of Negroes seeking equal treatment in such programs. There
simply was no reason for Congress to consider the validity of hypothetical
preferences that might be accorded minority citizens; the legislators were
dealing with the real and pressing problem of how to guarantee those citizens equal treatment.

In addressing that problem, supporters of Title VI repeatedly declared
that the bill enacted constitutional principles. For example, Representative
Celler, the Chairman of the House Judiciary Committee and floor manager
of the legislation in the House, emphasized this in introducing the bill:

"The bill would offer assurance that hospitals financed by Federal
money would not deny adequate care to Negroes. It would prevent
abuse of food distribution programs whereby Negroes have been
known to be denied food surplus supplies when white persons were
given such food. It would assure Negroes the benefits now accorded only with students in programs of higher education financed by
Federal funds. It would, in short, *assure* the existing right to
equal treatment in the enjoyment of Federal funds. It would not
destroy any rights of private property or freedom of association."
110 Cong.Rec. 1519 (1964) (emphasis added).

Other sponsors shared Representative Celler's view that Title VI embodied
constitutional principles.

* * * Senator Humphrey noted the relevance of the Constitution:

"As I have said, the bill has a simple purpose. That purpose is to
give fellow citizens—Negroes—the same rights and opportunities
that white people take for granted. This is no more than what

was preached by the prophets, and by Christ Himself. It is no more than what our Constitution guarantees."

In view of the clear legislative intent, Title VI must be held to proscribe only those racial classifications that would violate the Equal Protection Clause or the Fifth Amendment.

[T]he special admissions program is undeniably a classification based on race and ethnic background. To the extent that there existed a pool of at least minimally qualified minority applicants to fill the 16 special admissions seats, white applicants could compete only for 84 seats in the entering class, rather than the 100 open to minority applicants. Whether this limitation is described as a quota or a goal, it is a line drawn on the basis of race and ethnic status.

* * * Racial and ethnic distinctions of any sort are inherently suspect and thus call for the most exacting judicial examination.

* * * Petitioner urges us to adopt for the first time a more restrictive view of the Equal Protection Clause and hold that discrimination against members of the white "majority" cannot be suspect if its purpose can be characterized as "benign." * * * [T]here are serious problems of justice connected with the idea of preference * * *. First, it may not always be clear that a so-called preference is in fact benign. Courts may be asked to validate burdens imposed upon individual members of particular groups in order to advance the group's general interest. * * * Second, preferential programs may only reinforce common stereotypes holding that certain groups are unable to achieve success without special protection based on a factor having no relationship to individual worth. Third, there is a measure of inequity in forcing innocent persons in respondent's position to bear the burdens of redressing grievances not of their making.

By hitching the meaning of the Equal Protection Clause to these transitory considerations, we would be holding, as a constitutional principle, that judicial scrutiny of classifications touching on racial and ethnic background may vary with the ebb and flow of political forces. Disparate constitutional tolerance of such classifications well may serve to exacerbate racial and ethnic antagonisms rather than alleviate them.

* * *

We have never approved a classification that aids persons perceived as members of relatively victimized groups at the expense of other innocent individuals in the absence of judicial, legislative, or administrative findings of constitutional or statutory violations.

* * *

Petitioner does not purport to have made and is in no position to make, such findings. Its broad mission is education, not the formulation of any legislative policy or the adjudication of particular claims of illegality. For reasons similar to those stated in Part III of this opinion, isolated segments of our vast governmental structures are not competent to make those decisions, at least in the absence of legislative mandates and legislatively determined criteria.[45]

---

45. For example, the University is unable to explain its selection of only the three favored groups—Negroes, Mexican-Americans, and Asians—for preferential treatment. The inclusion of the last group is especially curious in light of the substantial numbers of Asians admitted through the regular admissions process. See also n. 37, supra.

Hence, the purpose of helping certain groups whom the faculty of the Davis Medical School perceived as victims of "societal discrimination" does not justify a classification that imposes disadvantages upon persons like respondent, who bear no responsibility for whatever harm the beneficiaries of the special admissions program are thought to have suffered. To hold otherwise would be to convert a remedy heretofore reserved for violations of legal rights into a privilege that all institutions throughout the Nation could grant at their pleasure to whatever groups are perceived as victims of societal discrimination. That is a step we have never approved.

Petitioner identifies, as another purpose of its program, improving the delivery of health care services to communities currently underserved. It may be assumed that in some situations a State's interest in facilitating the health care of its citizens is sufficiently compelling to support the use of a suspect classification. But there is virtually no evidence in the record indicating that petitioner's special admissions program is either needed or geared to promote that goal. The court below addressed this failure of proof:

> "The University concedes it cannot assure that minority doctors who entered under the program, all of whom express an 'interest' in participating in a disadvantaged community, will actually do so. It may be correct to assume that some of them will carry out this intention, and that it is more likely they will practice in minority communities than the average white doctor. Nevertheless, there are more precise and reliable ways to identify applicants who are genuinely interested in the medical problems of minorities than by race. An applicant of whatever race who has demonstrated his concern for disadvantaged minorities in the past and who declares that practice in such a community is his primary professional goal would be more likely to contribute to alleviation of the medical shortage than one who is chosen entirely on the basis of race and disadvantage. In short, there is [sic] no empirical data to demonstrate that any one race is more selflessly socially oriented or by contract that another is more selfishly acquisitive."

Petitioner simply has not carried its burden of demonstrating that it must prefer members of particular ethnic groups over all other individuals in order to promote better health care delivery to deprived citizens. Indeed, petitioner has not shown that its preferential classification is likely to have any significant effect on the problem.[47]

The fourth goal asserted by petitioner is the attainment of a diverse student body. This clearly is a constitutionally permissible goal for an institution of higher education. Academic freedom, though not a specifically enumerated constitutional right, long has been viewed as a special concern of the First Amendment. The freedom of a university to make its own judgments as to education includes the selection of its student body. Mr.

---

47. It is not clear that petitioner's two-track system, even if adopted throughout the country, would substantially increase representation of blacks in the medical profession. That is the finding of a recent study by Sleeth & Mishell, Black Under-Representation in United States Medical Schools, New England J. of Med. 1146 (Nov. 24, 1977). Those authors maintain that the cause of black under-representation lies in the small size of the national pool of qualified black applicants. In their view, this problem is traceable to the poor premedical experiences of black undergraduates, and can be remedied effectively only by developing remedial programs for black students before they enter college.

Justice Frankfurter summarized the "four essential freedoms" that comprise academic freedom:

"'* * * It is the business of a university to provide that atmosphere which is most conducive to speculation, experiment and creation. It is an atmosphere in which there prevail "the four essential freedoms" of a university—to determine for itself on academic grounds who may teach, what may be taught, how it shall be taught, and who may be admitted to study.' "

Our national commitment to the safeguarding of these freedoms within university communities was emphasized in Keyishian v. Board of Regents, 385 U.S. 589, 603, 87 S.Ct. 675, 683, 17 L.Ed.2d 629 (1967):

"Our Nation is deeply committed to safeguarding academic freedom which is of transcendent value to all of us and not merely to the teachers concerned. That freedom is therefore a special concern of the First Amendment. * * * The Nation's future depends upon leaders trained through wide exposure to that robust exchange of ideas which discovers truth 'out of a multitude of tongues, rather than through any kind of authoritative selection.' United States v. Associated Press, D.C., 52 F.Supp. 362, 372."

The atmosphere of "speculation, experiment and creation"—so essential to the quality of higher education—is widely believed to be promoted by a diverse student body. As the Court noted in *Keyishian*, it is not too much to say that the "nation's future depends upon leaders trained through wide exposure" to the ideas and mores of students as diverse as this Nation of many peoples.

Thus, in arguing that its universities must be accorded the right to select those students who will contribute the most to the "robust exchange of ideas," petitioner invokes a countervailing constitutional interest, that of the First Amendment. In this light, petitioner must be viewed as seeking to achieve a goal that is of paramount importance in the fulfillment of its mission.

It may be assumed that the reservation of a specified number of seats in each class for individuals from the preferred ethnic groups would contribute to the attainment of considerable ethnic diversity in the student body. But petitioner's argument that this is the only effective means of serving the interest of diversity is seriously flawed. In a most fundamental sense the argument misconceives the nature of the state interest that would justify consideration of race or ethnic background. It is not an interest in simple ethnic diversity, in which a specified percentage of the student body is in effect guaranteed to be members of selected ethnic groups, with the remaining percentage an undifferentiated aggregation of students. The diversity that furthers a compelling state interest encompasses a far broader array of qualifications and characteristics of which racial or ethnic origin is but a single though important element. Petitioner's special admissions program, focused *solely* on ethnic diversity, would hinder rather than further attainment of genuine diversity.

* * *

The experience of other university admissions programs, which take race into account in achieving the educational diversity valued by the First Amendment, demonstrates that the assignment of a fixed number of places to a minority group is not a necessary means toward that end. An illuminating example is found in the Harvard College program: * * * See Appendix hereto.

This kind of program treats each applicant as an individual in the admissions process. The applicant who loses out on the last available seat to another candidate receiving a "plus" on the basis of ethnic background will not have been foreclosed from all consideration for that seat simply because he was not the right color or had the wrong surname. It would mean only that his combined qualifications, which may have included similar nonobjective factors, did not outweigh those of the other applicant. His qualifications would have been weighed fairly and competitively, and he would have no basis to complain of unequal treatment under the Fourteenth Amendment. [52]

It has been suggested that an admissions program which considers race only as one factor is simply a subtle and more sophisticated—but no less effective—means of according racial preference than the Davis program. A facial intent to discriminate, however, is evident in petitioner's preference program and not denied in this case. No such facial infirmity exists in an admissions program where race or ethnic background is simply one element —to be weighed fairly against other elements—in the selection process. * * *

In summary, it is evident that the Davis special admission program involves the use of an explicit racial classification never before countenanced by this Court. It tells applicants who are not Negro, Asian, or "Chicano" that they are totally excluded from a specific percentage of the seats in an entering class. No matter how strong their qualifications, quantitative and extracurricular, including their own potential for contribution to educational diversity, they are never afforded the chance to compete with applicants from the preferred groups for the special admission seats. At the same time, the preferred applicants have the opportunity to compete for every seat in the class.

The fatal flaw in petitioner's preferential program is its disregard of individual rights as guaranteed by the Fourteenth Amendment. Shelley v. Kraemer, 334 U.S. 1, 22, 68 S.Ct. 836, 846, 92 L.Ed.2d 1161 (1948). Such rights are not absolute. But when a State's distribution of benefits or imposition of burdens hinges on the color of a person's skin or ancestry, that individual is entitled to a demonstration that the challenged classification is necessary to promote a substantial state interest. Petitioner has failed to carry this burden. For this reason, that portion of the California court's judgment holding petitioner's special admissions program invalid under the Fourteenth Amendment must be affirmed.

In enjoining petitioner from ever considering the race of any applicant, however, the courts below failed to recognize that the State has a substantial interest that legitimately may be served by a properly devised admissions program involving the competitive consideration of race and ethnic origin. For this reason, so much of the California court's judgment as enjoins petitioner from any consideration of the race of any applicant must be reversed.

52. The denial to respondent of this right to individualized consideration without regard to his race is the principal evil of petitioner's special admissions program. Nowhere in the opinion of Mr. Justice BRENNAN, Mr. Justice WHITE, Mr. Justice MARSHALL, and Mr. Justice BLACKMUN is this denial even addressed.

With respect to respondent's entitlement to an injunction directing his admission to the Medical School, petitioner has conceded that it could not carry its burden of proving that, but for the existence of its unlawful special admissions program, respondent still would not have been admitted. Hence, respondent is entitled to the injunction, and that portion of the judgment must be affirmed.

APPENDIX

Harvard College Admissions Program

For the past 30 years Harvard College has received each year applications for admission that greatly exceed the number of places in the freshman class. The number of applicants who are deemed to be not "qualified" is comparatively small. The vast majority of applicants demonstrate through test scores, high school records and teachers' recommendations that they have the academic ability to do adequate work at Harvard, and perhaps to do it with distinction. Faced with the dilemma of choosing among a large number of "qualified" candidates, the Committee on Admissions could use the single criterion of scholarly excellence and attempt to determine who among the candidates were likely to perform best academically. But for the past 30 years the Committee on Admissions has never adopted this approach. The belief has been that if scholarly excellence were the sole or even predominant criterion, Harvard College would lose a great deal of its vitality and intellectual excellence and that the quality of the educational experience offered to all students would suffer. Consequently, after selecting those students whose intellectual potential will seem extraordinary to the faculty —perhaps 150 or so out of an entering class of over 1,100—the Committee seeks—

> variety in making its choices. This has seemed important * * * in part because it adds a critical ingredient to the effectiveness of the educational experience [in Harvard College] * * * *The effectiveness of our students' educational experience has seemed to the Committee to be affected as importantly by a wide variety of interests, talents, backgrounds and career goals as it is by a fine faculty and our libraries, laboratories and housing arrangements.*

The belief that diversity adds an essential ingredient to the educational process has long been a tenet of Harvard College admissions. Fifteen or twenty years ago, however, diversity meant students from California, New York, and Massachusetts; city dwellers and farm boys; violinists, painters and football players; biologists, historians and classicists; potential stockbrokers, academics and politicians. The result was that very few ethnic or racial minorities attended Harvard College. In recent years Harvard College has expanded the concept of diversity to include students from disadvantaged economic, racial and ethnic groups. Harvard College now recruits not only Californians or Louisianans but also blacks and Chicanos and other minority students. Contemporary conditions in the United States mean that if Harvard College is to continue to offer a first-rate education to its students, minority representation in the undergraduate body cannot be ignored by the Committee on Admissions.

In practice, this new definition of diversity has meant that race has been a factor in some admission decisions. When the Committee on Admissions reviews the large middle group of applicants who are "admissible" and deemed capable of doing good work in their courses, the race of an applicant may tip the balance in his favor just as geographic origin or a life spent on a farm may tip the balance in other candidates' cases. A farm boy from Idaho can bring something to Harvard College that a Bostonian cannot offer. Similarly a black student can usually bring something that a white person cannot offer. The quality of the educational experience of all the students in Harvard College depends in part on these differences in the background and outlook that students bring with them.

In Harvard College admissions the Committee has not set target-quotas for the number of blacks, or of musicians, football players, physicists or Californians to be admitted in a given year. At the same time the Committee is aware that if Harvard College is to provide a truly heterogenous environment that reflects the rich diversity of the United States, it cannot be provided without some attention to numbers. It would not make sense, for example, to have 10 or 20 students out of 1,100 whose homes are west of the Mississippi. Comparably, 10 or 20 black students could not begin to bring to their classmates and to each other the variety of points of view, backgrounds and experiences of blacks in the United States. Their small numbers might also create a sense of isolation among the black students themselves and thus make it more difficult for them to develop and achieve their potential. Consequently, when making its decisions, the Committee on Admissions is aware that there is some relationship between numbers and achieving the benefits to be derived from a diverse student body, and between numbers and providing a reasonable environment for those students admitted. But that awareness does not mean that the Committee sets a minimum number of blacks or of people from west of the Mississippi who are to be admitted. It means only that in choosing among thousands of applicants who are not only "admissible" academically but have other strong qualities, the Committee, with a number of criteria in mind, pays some attention to distribution among many types and categories of students.

The further refinements sometimes required help to illustrate the kind of significance attached to race. The Admissions Committee, with only a few places left to fill, might find itself forced to choose between A, the child of a successful black physician in an academic community with promise of superior academic performance, and B, a black who grew up in an inner-city ghetto of semi-literate parents whose academic achievement was lower but who had demonstrated energy and leadership as well as an apparently abiding interest in black power. If a good number of black students much like A but few like B had already been admitted, the Committee might prefer B; and vice versa. If C, a white student with extraordinary artistic talent, were also seeking one of the remaining places, his unique quality might give him an edge over both A and B. Thus, the critical criteria are often individual qualities or experience not dependent upon race but sometimes associated with it.

Opinion of Mr. Justice BRENNAN, Mr. Justice WHITE, Mr. Justice MARSHALL, and Mr. Justice BLACKMUN, concurring in the judgment in part and dissenting.

The Court today, in reversing in part the judgment of the Supreme Court of California, affirms the constitutional power of Federal and State Government to act affirmatively to achieve equal opportunity for all. The difficulty of the issue presented—whether Government may use race-conscious programs to redress the continuing effects of past discrimination—and the mature consideration which each of our Brethren has brought to it have resulted in many opinions, no single one speaking for the Court. But this should not and must not mask the central meaning of today's opinions: Government may take race into account when it acts not to demean or insult any racial group, but to remedy disadvantages cast on minorities by past racial prejudice, at least when appropriate findings have been made by judicial, legislative, or administrative bodies with competence to act in this area.

THE CHIEF JUSTICE and our Brothers STEWART, REHNQUIST, and STEVENS, have concluded that Title VI of the Civil Rights Act of 1964, prohibits programs such as that at the Davis Medical School. On this statutory theory alone, they would hold that respondent Allan Bakke's rights have been violated and that he must, therefore, be admitted to the Medical School. Our Brother POWELL, reaching the Constitution, concludes that, although race may be taken into account in university admissions, the particular special admissions program used by petitioner, which resulted in the exclusion of respondent Bakke, was not shown to be necessary to achieve petitioner's stated goals. Accordingly, these Members of the Court form a majority of five affirming the judgment of the Supreme Court of California insofar as it holds that respondent Bakke "is entitled to an order that he be admitted to the University."

We agree with Mr. Justice POWELL that, as applied to the case before us, Title VI goes no further in prohibiting the use of race than the Equal Protection Clause of the Fourteenth Amendment itself. We also agree that the effect of the California Supreme Court's affirmance of the judgment of the Superior Court of California would be to prohibit the University from establishing in the future affirmative action programs that take race into account. See ante, at 2738 n.**. Since we conclude that the affirmative admissions program at the Davis Medical School is constitutional, we would reverse the judgment below in all respects. Mr. Justice POWELL agrees that some uses of race in university admissions are permissible and, therefore, he joins with us to make five votes reversing the judgment below insofar as it prohibits the University from establishing race-conscious programs in the future.[1]

* * *

Mr. Justice MARSHALL.

I agree with the judgment of the Court only insofar as it permits a university to consider the race of an applicant in making admissions decisions. I do not agree that petitioner's admissions program violates the Constitution. For it must be remembered that, during most of the past 200 years, the Constitution as interpreted by this Court did not prohibit the most ingenious and pervasive forms of discrimination against the Negro. Now, when a State acts to remedy the effects of that legacy of discrimination, I cannot believe that this same Constitution stands as a barrier.

* * *

Mr. Justice BLACKMUN.

I participate fully, of course, in the opinion, that bears the names of my Brothers BRENNAN, WHITE, MARSHALL, and myself. I add only some general observations that hold particular significance for me, and then a few comments on equal protection.

1. We also agree with Mr. Justice POWELL that a plan like the "Harvard" plan, see ante, at 2760–2762, is constitutional under our approach, at least so long as the use of race to achieve an integrated student body is necessitated by the lingering effects of past discrimination.

I

At least until the early 1970's, apparently only a very small number, less than 2%, of the physicians, attorneys, and medical and law students in the United States were members of what we now refer to as minority groups. In addition, approximately three-fourths of our Negro Physicians were trained at only two medical schools. If ways are not found to remedy that situation, the country can never achieve its professed goal of a society that is not race conscious.

I yield to no one in my earnest hope that the time will come when an "affirmative action" program is unnecessary and is, in truth, only a relic of the past. I would hope that we could reach this stage within a decade at the most. But the story of Brown v. Board of Education, 347 U.S. 483, 74 S.Ct. 686, 98 L.Ed. 873 (1954), decided almost a quarter of a century ago, suggests that that hope is a slim one. At some time, however, beyond any period of what some would claim is only transitional inequality, the United States must and will reach a stage of maturity where action along this line is no longer necessary. Then persons will be regarded as persons, and discrimination of the type we address today will be an ugly feature of history that is instructive but that is behind us.

The number of qualified, indeed highly qualified, applicants for admission to existing medical schools in the United States far exceeds the number of places available. Wholly apart from racial and ethnic considerations, therefore, the selection process inevitably results in the denial of admission to many *qualified* persons, indeed, to far more than the number of those who are granted admission. Obviously, it is a denial to the deserving. This inescapable fact is brought into sharp focus here because Allan Bakke is not himself charged with discrimination and yet is the one who is disadvantaged, and because the Medical School of the University of California at Davis itself is not charged with historical discrimination.

* * *

Programs of admission to institutions of higher learning are basically a responsibility for academicians and for administrators and the specialists they employ. The judiciary, in contrast, is ill-equipped and poorly trained for this. The administration and management of educational institutions are beyond the competence of judges and are within the special competence of educators, provided always that the educators perform within legal and constitutional bounds. For me, therefore, interference by the judiciary must be the rare exception and not the rule.

* * *

I am not convinced, as Mr. Justice POWELL seems to be, that the difference between the Davis program and the one employed by Harvard is very profound or constitutionally significant. The line between the two is a thin and indistinct one. In each, subjective application is at work. Because of my conviction that admission programs are primarily for the educators, I am willing to accept the representation that the Harvard program is one where good faith in its administration is practiced as well as professed. I agree that such a program, where race or ethnic background is only one of many factors, is a program better formulated than Davis' two-track system. The cynical, of course, may say that under a program such as Harvard's one may accomplish covertly what Davis concedes it does openly. I need not go that far, for despite its two-track aspect, the Davis program, for me, is within constitutional bounds, though perhaps barely so. It is surely free of stigma, and, I am not willing to infer a constitutional violation.

It is worth noting, perhaps, that governmental preference has not been a stranger to our legal life. We see it in veterans' preferences. We see it in the aid-to-the-handicapped programs. We see it in the progressive income tax. We see it in the Indian programs. We may excuse some of these on the ground that they have specific constitutional protection or, as with Indians, that those benefited are wards of the Government. Nevertheless, these preferences exist and may not be ignored. And in the admissions field, as I have indicated, educational institutions have always used geography, athletic ability, anticipated financial largess, alumni pressure, and other factors of that kind.

* * *

Mr. Justice STEVENS, with whom THE CHIEF JUSTICE, Mr. Justice STEWART, and Mr. Justice REHNQUIST join, concurring in the judgment in part and dissenting in part.

It is always important at the outset to focus precisely on the controversy before the Court.[1] It is particularly important to do so in this case because correct identification of the issues will determine whether it is necessary or appropriate to express any opinion about the legal status of any admissions program other than petitioner's.

I

This is not a class action. The controversy is between two specific litigants. Allan Bakke challenged petitioner's special admissions program, claiming that it denied him a place in medical school because of his race in violation of the Federal and California Constitutions and of Title VI of the Civil Rights Act of 1964. The California Supreme Court upheld his challenge and ordered him admitted. If the state court was correct in its view that the University's special program was illegal, and that Bakke was therefore unlawfully excluded from the medical school because of his race, we should affirm its judgment, regardless of our views about the legality of admissions programs that are not now before the Court.

* * *

It is clear that the question whether race can ever be used as a factor in an admissions decision is not an issue in this case, and that discussion of that issue is inappropriate.

* * *

Section 601 of the Civil Rights Act of 1964 provides:

> "No person in the United States shall, on the ground of race, color, or national origin, be excluded from participation in, be denied the benefits of, or be subjected to discrimination under any program or activity receiving Federal financial assistance."

The University, through its special admissions policy, excluded Bakke from participation in its program of medical education because of his race. The University also acknowledges that it was, and still is, receiving federal financial assistance. The plain language of the statute therefore requires affirmance of the judgment below. * * *

* * *

1. Four Members of the Court have undertaken to announce the legal and constitutional effect of this Court's judgment. See opinion of Justices BRENNAN, WHITE, MARSHALL, and BLACKMUN, ante, at 2766–2767. It is hardly necessary to state that only a majority can speak for the Court or determine what is the "central meaning" of any judgment of the Court.

Accordingly, I concur in the Court's judgment insofar as it affirms the judgment of the Supreme Court of California. To the extent that it purports to do anything else, I respectfully dissent.

CASE 4 *The Brian Weber Case.*

UNITED STEELWORKERS v. WEBER

Supreme Court of the United States, 1979.
— U.S. —, 99 S.Ct. 2721, 61 L.Ed.2d 480.

Mr. Justice BRENNAN delivered the opinion of the Court.

Challenged here is the legality of an affirmative action plan—collectively bargained by an employer and a union—that reserves for black employees 50% of the openings in an in-plant craft training program until the percentage of black craft workers in the plant is commensurate with the percentage of blacks in the local labor force. The question for decision is whether Congress, in Title VII of the Civil Rights Act of 1964 as amended, 42 U.S.C.A. § 2000e, left employers and unions in the private sector free to take such race-conscious steps to eliminate manifest racial imbalances in traditionally segregated job categories. We hold that Title VII does not prohibit such race-conscious affirmative action plans.

In 1974 petitioner United Steelworkers of America (USWA) and petitioner Kaiser Aluminum & Chemical Corporation (Kaiser) entered into a master collective-bargaining agreement covering terms and conditions of employment at 15 Kaiser plants. The agreement contained, *inter alia,* an affirmative action plan designed to eliminate conspicious racial imbalances in Kaiser's then almost exclusively white craft work forces. Black craft hiring goals were set for each Kaiser plant equal to the percentage of blacks in the respective local labor forces. To enable plants to meet these goals, on-the-job training programs were established to teach unskilled production workers—black and white—the skills necessary to become craft workers. The plan reserved for black employees 50% of the openings in these newly created in-plant training programs.

This case arose from the operation of the plan at Kaiser's plant in Gramercy, La. Until 1974 Kaiser hired as craft workers for that plant only persons who had had prior craft experience. Because blacks had long been excluded from craft unions, few were able to present such credentials. As a consequence, prior to 1974 only 1.83% (five out of 273) of the skilled craft workers at the Gramercy plant were black, even though the work force in the Gramercy area was approximately 39% black.

Pursuant to the national agreement Kaiser altered its craft hiring practice in the Gramercy plant. Rather than hiring already trained outsiders, Kaiser established a training program to train its production workers to fill craft openings. Selection of craft trainees was made on the basis of seniority, with the proviso that at least 50% of the new trainees were to be black until the percentage of black skilled craft workers in the Gramercy plant approximated the percentage of blacks in the local labor force.

During 1974, the first year of the operation of the Kaiser-USWA affirmative action plan, 13 craft trainees were selected from Gramercy's production work force. Of these, 7 were black and 6 white. The most junior black selected into the program had less seniority than several white production workers whose bids for admission were rejected. Thereafter one of those white production workers, respondent Brian Weber, instituted this class action in the United States District Court for the Eastern District of Louisiana.

The complaint alleged that the filling of craft trainee positions at the Gramercy plant pursuant to the affirmative action program had resulted in junior black employees receiving training in preference to more senior white employees, thus discriminating against respondent and other similarly situated white employees in violation of §§ 703(a)[2] and (d)[3] of Title VII. The District Court held that the plan violated Title VII, entered a judgment in favor of the plaintiff class, and granted a permanent injunction prohibiting Kaiser and the USWA "from denying plaintiffs, Brian F. Weber and all other members of the class, access to on-the-job training programs on the basis of race." A divided panel of the Court of Appeals for the Fifth Circuit affirmed, holding that all employment preferences based upon race, including those preferences incidental to bona fide affirmative action plans, violated Title VII's prohibition against racial discrimination in employment. We granted certiorari. We reverse.

We emphasize at the outset the narrowness of our inquiry. Since the Kaiser-USWA plan does not involve state action, this case does not present an alleged violation of the Equal Protection Clause of the Constitution. Further, since the Kaiser-USWA plan was adopted voluntarily, we are not concerned with what Title VII requires or with what a court might order to remedy a past proven violation of the Act. The only question before us is the narrow statutory issue of whether Title VII *forbids* private employers and unions from voluntarily agreeing upon bona fide affirmative action plans that accord racial preferences in the manner and for the purpose provided in the Kaiser-USWA plan. That question was expressly left open in McDonald v. Santa Fe Trail Trans. Co., 427 U.S. 273, 281 n. 8 (1976) which held, in a case not involving affirmative action, that Title VII protects whites as well as blacks from certain forms of racial discrimination.

Respondent argues that Congress intended in Title VII to prohibit all race-conscious affirmative action plans. Respondent's argument rests upon a literal interpretation of §§ 703(a) and (d) of the Act. Those sections make it unlawful to "discriminate * * * because of * * * race" in hiring and in the selection of apprentices for training programs.

2. Section 703(a), 42 U.S.C.A. § 2000e-2(a), provides:

"(a) It shall be an unlawful employment practice for an employer—

"(1) to fail or refuse to hire or to discharge any individual, or otherwise to discriminate against any individual with respect to his compensation, terms, conditions, or privileges of employment, because of such individual's race, color, religion, sex, or national origin; or

"(2) to limit, segregate, or classify his employees or applicants for employment in any way which would deprive or tend to deprive any individual of employment op-

portunities or otherwise adversely affect his status as an employee, because of such individual's race, color, religion, sex, or national origin."

3. Section 703(d), 42 U.S.C.A. § 2000e-2(d), provides:

"It shall be an unlawful employment practice for any employer, labor organization, or joint labor-management committee controlling apprenticeship or other training or retraining, including on-the-job training programs to discriminate against any individual because of his race, color, religion, sex, or national origin in admission to, or employment in, any program established to provide apprenticeship or other training."

Since, the argument runs, McDonald v. Santa Fe Trail Trans. Co., supra, settled that Title VII forbids discrimination against whites as well as blacks, and since the Kaiser-USWA affirmative action plan operates to discriminate against white employees solely because they are white, it follows that the Kaiser-USWA plan violates Title VII.

Respondent's argument is not without force. But it overlooks the significance of the fact that the Kaiser-USWA plan is an affirmative action plan voluntarily adopted by private parties to eliminate traditional patterns of racial segregation. In this context respondent's reliance upon a literal construction of § 703(a) and (d) and upon *McDonald* is misplaced. It is a "familiar rule that a thing may be within the letter of the statute and yet not within the statute, because not within its spirit nor within the intention of its makers." The prohibition against racial discrimination in §§ 703(a) and (d) of Title VII must therefore be read against the background of the legislative history of Title VII and the historical context from which the Act arose. Examination of those sources makes clear that an interpretation of the sections that forbade all race-conscious affirmative action would "bring about an end completely at variance with the purpose of the statute" and must be rejected.

Congress' primary concern in enacting the prohibition against racial discrimination in Title VII of the Civil Rights Act of 1964 was with "the plight of the Negro in our economy." 110 Cong.Rec. 6548 (remarks of Sen. Humphrey). Before 1964, blacks were largely relegated to "unskilled and semi-skilled jobs." Id., at 6548 (remarks of Sen. Humphrey); id., at 7204 (remarks of Sen. Clark); id., at 7279–7280 (remarks of Sen. Kennedy). Because of automation the number of such jobs was rapidly decreasing. See 110 Cong.Rec., at 6548 (remarks of Sen. Humphrey); id., at 7204 (remarks of Sen. Clark). As a consequence "the relative position of the Negro worker [was] steadily worsening. In 1947 the non-white unemployment rate was only 64 percent higher than the white rate; in 1962 it was 124 percent higher." Id., at 6547 (remarks of Sen Humphrey). Congress considered this a serious social problem. As Senator Clark told the Senate:

> "The rate of Negro unemployment has gone up consistently as compared with white unemployment for the past 15 years. This is a social malaise and a social situation which we should not tolerate. That is one of the principal reasons why this bill should pass." Id., at 7220.

Congress feared that the goals of the Civil Rights Act—the integration of blacks into the mainstream of American society—could not be achieved unless this trend were reversed. And Congress recognized that that would not be possible unless blacks were able to secure jobs "which have a future." As Senator Humphrey explained to the Senate.

> "What good does it do a Negro to be able to eat in a fine restaurant if he cannot afford to pay the bill? What good does it do him to be accepted in a hotel that is too expensive for his modest income? How can a Negro child be motivated to take full advantage of integrated educational facilities if he has no hope of getting a job where he can use that education?" Id., at 6547.

> * * *

> "Without a job, one cannot afford public convenience and accommodations. Income from employment may be necessary to further a man's education, or that of his children. If his children have

no hope of getting a good job, what will motivate them to take advantage of educational opportunities?" Id., at 6552.

* * *

Accordingly, it was clear to Congress that "the crux of the problem [was] to open employment opportunities for Negroes in occupations which have been traditionally closed to them," id., at 6548 (remarks of Sen. Humphrey), and it was to this problem that Title VII's prohibition against racial discrimination in employment was primarily addressed.

* * *

Given this legislative history, we cannot agree with respondent that Congress intended to prohibit the private sector from taking effective steps to accomplish the goal that Congress designed Title VII to achieve. * * * It would be ironic indeed if a law triggered by a Nation's concern over centuries of racial injustice and intended to improve the lot of those who had "been excluded from the American dream for so long" 110 Cong.Rec., at 6552 (remarks of Sen. Humphrey), constituted the first legislative prohibition of all voluntary, private, race-conscious efforts to abolish traditional patterns of racial segregation and hierarchy.

Our conclusion is further reinforced by examination of the language and legislative history of § 703(j) of Title VII.[5] Opponents of Title VII raised two related arguments against the bill. First, they argued that the Act would be interpreted to *require* employers with racially imbalanced work forces to grant preferential treatment to racial minorities in order to integrate. Second, they argued that employers with racially imbalanced work forces would grant preferential treatment to racial minorities, even if not required to do so by the Act. See 110 Cong.Rec. 8618–8619 (remarks of Sen. Sparkman). Had Congress meant to prohibit all race-conscious affirmative action, as respondent urges, it easily could have answered both objections by providing that Title VII would not require or *permit* racially preferential integration efforts. But Congress did not choose such a course. Rather Congress added § 703(j) which addresses only the first objection. The section provides that nothing contained in Title VII "shall be interpreted to *require* any employer * * * to grant preferential treatment * * * to any group because of the race * * * of such * * * group on account of" a defacto racial imbalance in the employer's work force. The section does *not* state that "nothing in Title VII shall be interpreted to *permit*" voluntary affirmative efforts to correct racial imbalances. The natural inference is that Congress chose not to forbid all voluntary race-conscious affirmative action.

---

5. Section 703(j) of Title VII, 42 U.S.C.A. § 2000e–2(j), provides:

"Nothing contained in this subchapter shall be interpreted to require any employer, employment agency, labor organization, or joint labor-management committee subject to this subchapter to grant preferential treatment to any individual or to any group because of the race, color, religion, sex, national origin of such individual or group on account of an imbalance which may exist with respect to the total number or percentage of persons of any race, color, religion, sex, or national origin employed by any employer, referred or classified for employment by any employment agency or labor organization, admitted to membership or classified by any labor organization, or admitted to, or employed in, any apprenticeship or other training program, in comparison with the total number or percentage or persons of such race, color, religion, sex, or national origin in any community, State, section, or other area, or in the available work force in any community, State, section, or other area."

* * * In view of this legislative history and in view of Congress' desire to avoid undue federal regulation of private businesses, use of the word "require" rather than the phrase "require or permit" in § 703(j) fortifies the conclusion that Congress did not intend to limit traditional business freedom to such a degree as to prohibit all voluntary, race-conscious affirmative action.

We therefore hold that Title VII's prohibition in §§ 703(a) and (d) against racial discrimination does not condemn all private, voluntary, race-conscious affirmative action plans.

We need not today define in detail the line of demarcation between permissible and impermissible affirmative action plans. It suffices to hold that the challenged Kaiser-USWA affirmative action plan falls on the permissible side of the line. The purposes of the plan mirror those of the statute. Both were designed to break down old patterns of racial segregation and hierarchy. Both were structured to "open employment opportunities for Negroes in occupations which have been traditionally closed to them."

At the same time the plan does not unnecessarily trammel the interests of the white employees. The plan does not require the discharge of white workers and their replacement with new black hires. Nor does the plan create an absolute bar to the advancement of white employees; half of those trained in the program will be white. Moreover, the plan is a temporary measure; it is not intended to maintain racial balance, but simply to eliminate a manifest racial imbalance. Preferential selection of craft trainees at the Gramercy plant will end as soon as the percentage of black skilled craft workers in the Gramercy plant approximates the percentage of blacks in the local labor force.

We conclude, therefore, that the adoption of the Kaiser-USWA plan for the Gramercy plant falls within the area of discretion left by Title VII to the private sector voluntarily to adopt affirmative action plans designed to eliminate conspicious racial imbalance in traditionally segregated job categories. Accordingly, the judgment of the Court of Appeals for the Fifth Circuit is

Reversed.

Mr. Justice REHNQUIST, with whom THE CHIEF JUSTICE joins, dissenting.

In a very real sense, the Court's opinion is ahead of its time: it could more appropriately have been handed down five years from now, in 1984, a year coinciding with the title of a book from which the Court's opinion borrows, perhaps subconsciously, at least one idea. Orwell describes in his book a governmental official of Oceania, one of the three great world powers, denouncing the current enemy, Eurasia, to an assembled crowd:

> "It was almost impossible to listen to him without being first convinced and then maddened. * * * The speech had been proceeding for perhaps twenty minutes when a messenger hurried onto the platform and a scrap of paper was slipped into the speaker's hand. He unrolled and read it without pausing in his speech. Nothing altered in his voice or manner, or in the content of what he was saying, but suddenly the names were different. Without words said, a wave of understanding rippled through the crowd. Oceania was

at war with Eastasia!   *   *   *   The banners and posters with which the square was decorated were all wrong!   *   *   *

"[T]he speaker had switched from one line to the other actually in mid-sentence, not only without a pause, but without even breaking the syntax."   G. Orwell, Nineteen Eighty-Four, 182–183 (1949).

Today's decision represents an equally dramatic and equally unremarked switch in this Court's interpretation of Title VII.

The operative sections of Title VII prohibit racial discrimination in employment *simpliciter*.   Taken in its normal meaning, and as understood by all Members of Congress who spoke to the issue during the legislative debates, this language prohibits a covered employee from considering race when making an employment decision, whether the race be black or white. Several years ago, however, a United States District Court held that "the dismissal of white employees charged with misappropriating company property while not dismissing a similarly charged Negro employee does not raise a claim upon which Title VII relief may be granted."   McDonald v. Santa Fe Trail Transp. Co.   This Court unanimously reversed, concluding from the "uncontradicted legislative history" that "[T]itle VII prohibits racial discrimination against the white petitioners in this case upon the same standards as would be applicable were they Negroes   *   *   *."

We have never waivered in our understanding that Title VII "prohibits *all* racial discrimination in employment, without exception for any particular employees."   In Griggs v. Duke Power Co., 401 U.S. 424, 431 (1971), our first occasion to interpret Title VII, a unanimous court observed that "[d]iscriminatory preference, for any group, minority or majority, is precisely and only what Congress has proscribed."   And in our most recent discussion of the issue, we uttered words seemingly dispositive of this case: "It is clear beyond cavil that the obligation imposed by Title VII is to provide an equal opportunity for *each* applicant regardless of race, without regard to whether members of the applicant's race are already proportionately represented in the work force."   Furnco Construction Corp. v. Waters, 438 U.S. 567, 579.[1]

Today, however, the Court behaves much like the Orwellian speaker earlier described, as if it had been handed a note indicating that Title VII would lead to a result unacceptable to the Court if interpreted here as it was in our prior decisions.   Accordingly, without even a break in syntax, the Court rejects "a literal construction of § 703(a)" in favor of newly discovered "legislative history," which leads it to a conclusion directly contrary to that compelled by the "uncontradicted legislative history" unearthed in *McDonald* and our other prior decisions.   Now we are told that the legislative history of Title VII shows that employers are free to discriminate on the basis of race: an employer may, in the Court's words, "trammel the interests of white employees" in favor of black employees in order to eliminate "racial imbalance."

Our earlier interpretations of Title VII, like the banners and posters decorating the square in Oceania, were all wrong.

As if this were not enough to make a reasonable observer question this Court's adherence to the oft-stated principle that our duty is to construe

1. Our statements in *Griggs* and *Furnco Construction*, patently inconsistent with today's holding, are not even mentioned, much less distinguished, by the Court.

rather than rewrite legislation, the Court also seizes upon § 703(j) of Title VII as an independent, or at least partially independent, basis for its holding. Totally ignoring the wording of that section, which is obviously addressed to those charged with the responsibility of interpreting the law rather than those who are subject to its proscriptions, and totally ignoring the months of legislative debates preceding the section's introduction and passage, which demonstrate clearly that it was enacted to prevent precisely what occurred in this case, the Court infers from § 703(j) that "Congress chose not to forbid all voluntary race-conscious affirmative action."

Thus, by a *tour de force* reminiscent not of jurists such as Hale, Holmes, and Hughes, but of escape artists such as Houdini, the Court eludes clear statutory language, "uncontradicted" legislative history, and uniform precedent in concluding that employers are, after all, permitted to consider race in making employment decisions. It may be that one or more of the principal sponsors of Title VII would have preferred to see a provision allowing preferential treatment of minorities written into the bill. Such a provision, however, would have to have been expressly or impliedly excepted from Title VII's explicit prohibition on all racial discrimination in employment. There is no such exception in the Act. And a reading of the legislative debates concerning Title VII, in which proponents and opponents alike uniformly denounced discrimination in favor of, as well as discrimination against, Negroes, demonstrates clearly that any legislator harboring an unspoken desire for such a provision could not possibly have succeeded in enacting it into law.

Kaiser opened its Gramercy, La., plant in 1958. Because the Gramercy facility had no apprenticeship or in-plant craft training program, Kaiser hired as craft workers only persons with prior craft experience. Despite Kaiser's efforts to locate and hire trained black craftsmen, few were available in the Gramercy area, and as a consequence, Kaiser's craft positions were manned almost exclusively by whites. In February 1974, under pressure from the Office of Federal Contract Compliance to increase minority representation in craft positions at its various plants,[2] and hoping to deter the filing of employment discrimination claims by minorities, Kaiser entered into a collective-bargaining agreement with the United Steelworkers of America (Steelworkers) which created a new on-the-job craft training program at 15 Kaiser facilities, including the Gramercy plant. The agreement

---

2. The Office of Federal Contract Compliance (OFCC), subsequently renamed the Office of Federal Contract Compliance Programs (OFCCP), is an arm of the Department of Labor responsible for ensuring compliance by government contractors with the equal employment opportunity responsibilities established by Executive Order 11246, 30 Fed.Reg. 12319 (1965).

Executive Order 11246 requires all applicants for federal contracts to refrain from employment discrimination and to "take affirmative action to ensure that applicants are employed, and that employees are treated during employment, without regard to their race, color, religion, sex or national origin." The Executive Order empowers the Secretary of Labor to issue rules and regulations necessary and appropriate to achieve its purpose. He, in turn, has

delegated most enforcement duties to the OFCC.

The affirmative action program mandated by 41 CFR 60–2 (Revised Order No. 4) for nonconstruction contractors requires a "utilization" study to determine minority representation in the work force. Goals for hiring and promotion must be set to overcome any "underutilization" found to exist.

The OFCC employs the "power of the purse" to coerce acceptance of its affirmative action plans. Indeed, in this case, "the district court found that the 1974 collective bargaining agreement reflected less of a desire on Kaiser's part to train black craft workers than a self-interest in satisfying the OFCC in order to retain lucrative government contracts."

required that no less than one minority applicant be admitted to the training program for every nonminority applicant until the percentage of blacks in craft positions equaled the percentage of blacks in the local work force.[3] Eligibility for the craft training programs was to be determined on the basis of plant seniority, with black and white applicants to be selected on the basis of their relative seniority within their racial group.

Brian Weber is white. He was hired at Kaiser's Gramercy plant in 1969. In April 1974 Kaiser announced that it was offering a total of nine positions in three on-the-job training programs for skilled craft jobs. Weber applied for all three programs, but was not selected. The successful candidates—five black and four white applicants—were chosen in accordance with the 50% minority admission quota mandated under the 1974 collective bargaining agreement. Two of the successful black applicants had less seniority than Weber.[4] Weber brought the instant class action in the United States District Court for the Eastern District of Louisiana, alleging that use of the 50% minority admission quota to fill vacancies in Kaiser's craft training programs violated Title VII's prohibition on racial discrimination in employment. The District Court and the Court of Appeals for the Fifth Circuit agreed, enjoining further use of race as a criterion in admitting applicants to the craft training programs.

Were Congress to act today specifically to prohibit the type of racial discrimination suffered by Weber, it would be hard pressed to draft language better tailored to the task than that found in § 703(d) of Title VII:

"It shall be an unlawful employment practice for any employer, labor organization, or joint labor-management committee controlling apprenticeship or other training or retraining, including on-the-job training programs to discriminate against any individual because of his race, color, religion, sex, or national origin in admission to, or employment in, any program established to provide apprenticeship or other training."

Equally suited to the task would be § 703(a)(2), which makes it unlawful for an employer to classify his employees "in any way which would deprive or tend to deprive any individual of employment opportunities or otherwise adversely affect his status as an employee, because of such individual's race, color, religion, sex, or national origin."

Entirely consistent with these two express prohibitions is the language of § 703(j) of Title VII, which provides that the Act is not to be interpreted

3. * * * Contrary to the Court's assertion, it is not at all clear that Kaiser's admission quota is a "temporary measure * * * not intended to maintain racial imbalance." Dennis E. English, industrial relations superintendent at the Gramercy plant, testified at trial:

"Once the goal is reached of 39 percent, or whatever the figure will be down the road, I think it's subject to change, once the goal is reached in each of the craft families, at that time, we will then revert to a ratio of what that percentage is, if it remains at 39 percent and we attain 39 percent someday, we will then continue placing trainees in the program at that percentage. The

idea, again, being to have a minority representation in the plant that is equal to that representation in the community work force population."

4. In addition to the April programs, the company offered three more training programs in 1974 with a total of four positions available. Two white and two black employees were selected for the programs, which were for "Air Conditioning Repairman" (one position), "Carpenter-Painter" (two positions), and "Insulator" (one position). Weber sought to bid for the insulator trainee position, but he was not selected because that job was reserved for the most senior qualified black employee.

"to require any employer * * * to grant preferential treatment to any individual or to any group because of the race ˣ ˣ ˣ of such individual or group" to correct a racial imbalance in the employer's work force. 42 U. S.C.A. § 2000e–2(j). Seizing on the word "require," the Court infers that Congress must have intended to "permit" this type of racial discrimination. Not only is this reading of § 703(j) outlandish in the light of the flat prohibitions of §§ 703(a) and (d), but, as explained Part III, it is totally belied by the Act's legislative history.

Quite simply, Kaiser's racially discriminatory admission quota is flatly prohibited by the plain language of Title VII. This normally dispositive fact, however, gives the Court only momentary pause. An "interpretation" of the statute upholding Weber's claim would, according to the Court, " 'bring about an end completely at variance with the purpose of the statute.' " To support this conclusion, the Court calls upon the "spirit" of the Act, which it divines from passages in Title VII's legislative history indicating that enactment of the statute was prompted by Congress' desire "to open employment opportunities for Negroes in occupations which [had] been traditionally closed to them." But the legislative history invoked by the Court to avoid the plain language of §§ 703(a) and (d) simply misses the point. To be sure, the reality of employment discrimination against Negroes provided the primary impetus for passage of Title VII. But this fact by no means supports the proposition that Congress intended to leave employers free to discriminate against white persons. In most cases, "[l]egislative history * * * is more vague than the statute we are called upon to interpret." United States v. Public Utilities Comm'n, 345 U.S. 295, 321 (1954) (Jackson, J., concurring). Here, however, the legislative history of Title VII is as clear as the language of §§ 703(a) and (d), and it irrefutably demonstrates that Congress meant precisely what it said in §§ 703(a) and (d)—that *no* racial discrimination in employment is permissible under Title VII, not even preferential treatment of minorities to correct racial imbalance.

* * *

Introduced on the floor of the House of Representatives on June 20, 1963, the bill—H.R. 7152—

* * * the opening speech in support of its passage was delivered by Representative Celler, Chairman of the House Judiciary Committee and the Congressman responsible for introducing the legislation. A portion of that speech responded to criticism "seriously misrepresent[ing] what the bill would do and grossly distort[ing] its effects":

"[T]he charge has been made that the Equal Employment Opportunity Commission to be established by title VII of the bill would have the power to prevent a business from employing and promoting the people it wished, and that a 'Federal inspector' could then order the hiring and promotion only of employees of certain races or religious groups. This description of the bill is entirely wrong

* * *.

* * *

"Even [a] court could not order that any preference be given to any particular race, religion or other group, but would be limited to ordering an end of discrimination. The statement that a Federal inspector could order the employment and promotion only of members of a specific racial or religious group is therefore patently erroneous.

* * *

"* * * The Bill would do no more than prevent * * * employers from discriminating against *or in favor* of workers because of their race, religion, or national origin.

"It is likewise not true that the Equal Employment Opportunity Commission would have power to rectify existing 'racial or religious imbalance' in employment by requiring the hiring of certain people without regard to their qualifications simply because they are of a given race or religion. Only actual discrimination could be stopped." 110 Cong.Rec. 1518 (1964) (emphasis added).

Representative Celler's construction of Title VII was repeated by several other supporters during the House debate.[13]

* * * Supporters of H.R. 7152 in the House ultimately prevailed by a vote of 290 to 130, and the measure was sent to the Senate to begin what became the longest debate in that body's history.

* * * Senator Humphrey, perhaps the primary moving force behind H.R. 7152 in the Senate, was the first to state the proponents' understanding of Title VII. Responding to a political advertisement charging that federal agencies were at liberty to interpret the word "discrimination" in Title VII to require racial balance, Senator Humphrey stated: "[T]he meaning of racial or religious discrimination is perfectly clear. * * * [I]t means a distinction and treatment given to different individuals because of their different race, religion, or national origin." Stressing that Title VII "does not limit the employer's freedom to hire, fire, promote, or demote for any reasons—or no reasons—so long as his action is not based on race," Senator Humphrey further stated that "nothing in the bill would permit any official or court to require any employer or labor union to give preferential treatment to any minority group."

In the opening speech of the formal Senate debate on the bill, Senator Humphrey addressed the main concern of Title VII's opponents, advising that not only does Title VII not require use of racial quotas, *it does not permit* their use. "The truth," stated the floor leader of the bill, "is that this

---

13. Representative Lindsay had this to say: "This legislation * * * does not, as has been suggested heretofore both on and off the floor, force acceptance of people in * * * jobs * * * because they are Negro. It does not impose quotas or any special privileges of seniority or acceptance. There is nothing whatever in this bill about racial balance as appears so frequently in the minority report of the Committee.

"What the bill does do is prohibit discrimination because of race * * *." 110 Cong. Rec. 1540 (1964).

Representative Minish added: "Under title VII, employment will be on the basis of merit, not of race. This means that no quota system will be set up, no one will be forced to hire incompetent help because of race or religion, and no one will be given a vested right to demand employment for certain jobs." Id., at 1600. Representative Goodell, answering the charge that Title VII would be interpreted "to requir[e] a racial balance," id., at 2557, responded: "There is nothing here as a matter of legislative history that would require racial balancing. * * * We are not talking about a union having to balance its membership or an employer having to balance a number of employees. There is no quota involved. It is a matter of an individual's rights having been violated, charges having been brought, investigation carried out, and conciliation having been attempted and then proof in court that there was discrimination and a denial of rights on the basis of race or color."

title forbids discriminating against anyone on account of race. This is the simple and complete truth about title VII." 110 Cong.Rec. 6549 (1964). Senator Humphrey continued:

> "Contrary to the allegations of some opponents of this title, there is nothing in it that will give any power to the Commission or to any courts to require hiring, firing, or promotion of employees in order to meet a racial 'quota' or to achieve a certain racial balance.

> "That bugaboo has been brought up a dozen times; but it is nonexistent. In fact, *the very opposite is true. Title VII prohibits discrimination.* In effect, it says that race, religion, and national origin are not to be used as the basis for hiring and firing. Title VII is designed to encourage hiring on the basis of ability and qualifications, not race or religion." Ibid. (emphasis added).

At the close of his speech, Senator Humphrey returned briefly to the subject of employment quotas: "It is claimed that the bill would require racial quotas for all hiring, when in fact it provides that race shall not be a basis for making personnel decisions."

Senator Kuchel delivered the second major speech in support of H.R. 7152. In addressing the concerns of the opposition, he observed that "[n]othing could be further from the truth" than the charge that "Federal inspectors" would be empowered under Title VII to dictate racial balance and preferential advancement of minorities. Senator Kuchel emphasized that seniority rights would in no way be affected by Title VII: "Employers and labor organizations could not discriminate *in favor of or against* a person because of his race, his religion, or his national origin. In such matters * * * the bill now before us * * * is color-blind."

A few days later the Senate's attention focused exclusively on Title VII, as Senators Clark and Case rose to discuss the title of H.R. 7152 on which they shared floor "captain" responsibilities. In an interpretative memorandum submitted jointly to the Senate, Senators Clark and Case took pains to refute the opposition's charge that Title VII would result in preferential treatment of minorities. Their words were clear and unequivocal:

> "There is no requirement in title VII that an employer maintain a racial balance in his work force. On the contrary, any deliberate attempt to maintain a racial balance, whatever such a balance may be, would involve a violation of title VII because maintaining such a balance would require an employer to hire or to refuse to hire on the basis of race. It must be emphasized that discrimination is prohibited as to any individual."

Of particular relevance to the instant case were their observations regarding seniority rights. As if directing their comments at Brian Weber, the Senators said:

> "Title VII would have no effect on established seniority rights. Its effect is prospective and not retrospective. Thus, for example, if a business has been discriminating in the past and as a result has an all-white working force, when the title comes into effect the employer's obligation would be simply to fill future vacancies on a nondiscriminatory basis. He would not be obliged—*or indeed permitted*—to fire whites in order to hire Negroes, *or to prefer Negroes for future vacancies, or, once Negroes are hired, to give them spe-*

cial seniority rights at the expense of the white workers hired earlier."

Thus with virtual clairvoyance the Senate's leading supporters of Title VII anticipated precisely the circumstances of this case and advised their colleagues that the type of minority preference employed by Kaiser would violate Title VII's ban on racial discrimination. To further accentuate the point, Senator Clark introduced another memorandum dealing with common criticisms of the bill, including the charge that racial quotas would be imposed under Title VII. The answer was simple and to the point: "Quotas are themselves discriminatory."

* * * Senators Smathers and Sparkman, while conceding that Title VII does not in so many words require the use of hiring quotas, repeated the opposition's view that employers would be coerced to grant preferential hiring treatment to minorities by agencies of the Federal Government. Senator Williams was quick to respond:

> "Those opposed to H.R. 7152 should realize that to hire a Negro solely because he is a Negro is racial discrimination, just as much as a 'white only' employment policy. Both forms of discrimination are prohibited by title VII of this bill. The language of that title simply states that race is not a qualification for employment. * * * Some people charge that H.R. 7152 favors the Negro, at the expense of the white majority. But how can the language of equality favor one race or one religion over another? Equality can have only one meaning, and that meaning is self-evident to reasonable men. Those who say that equality means favoritism do violence to common sense."

Senator Williams concluded his remarks by noting that Title VII's only purpose is "the elimination of racial and religious discrimination in employment." Ibid. On May 25, Senator Humphrey again took the floor to defend the bill against "the well-financed drive by certain opponents to confuse and mislead the American people." Id., at 11846. Turning once again to the issue of preferential treatment, Senator Humphrey remained faithful to the view that he had repeatedly expressed:

> "The title does not provide that any preferential treatment in employment shall be given to Negroes or to any other persons or groups. It does not provide that any quota systems may be established to maintain racial balance in employment. In fact, *the title would prohibit preferential treatment for any particular group,* and any person, whether or not a member of any minority group, would be permitted to file a complaint of discriminatory employment practices."

* * *

The Court draws from the language of § 703(j) primary support for its conclusion that Title VII's blanket prohibition on racial discrimination in employment does not prohibit preferential treatment of blacks to correct racial imbalance. Alleging that opponents of Title VII had argued (1) that the act would be interpreted to require employers with racially imbalanced work forces to grant preferential treatment to minorities and (2) that "employers with racially imbalanced work forces would grant preferential treatment to racial minorities, even if not required to do so by the Act," ante, at 9, the Court concludes that § 703(j) is responsive only to the opponents' first objection and that Congress therefore must have intended to permit voluntary, private discrimination against whites in order to correct racial imbalance.

Contrary to the Court's analysis, the language of § 703(j) is precisely tailored to the objection voiced time and again by Title VII's opponents. Not once during the 83 days of debate in the Senate did a speaker, proponent or opponent, suggest that the bill would allow employers *voluntarily* to prefer racial minorities over white persons. In light of Title VII's flat prohibition on discrimination "against any individual * * * because of such individual's race," § 703(a), 42 U.S.C.A. § 2000e–2(a), such a contention would have been, in any event, too preposterous to warrant response. Indeed, speakers on both sides of the issue, as the legislative history makes clear, recognized that Title VII would tolerate no *voluntary* racial preference, whether in favor of blacks or whites. The complaint consistently voiced by the opponents was that Title VII, particularly the word "discrimination," would be *interpreted* by federal agencies such as the Equal Employment Opportunity Commission to *require* the correction of racial imbalance through the granting of preferential treatment to minorities. Verbal assurances that Title VII would not require—indeed, would not permit—preferential treatment of blacks having failed, supporters of H.R. 7152 responded by proposing an amendment carefully worded to meet, and put to rest, the opposition's charge. Indeed, unlike §§ 703(a) and (d), which are by their terms directed at entities—e. g., employers, labor unions—whose actions are restricted by Title VII's prohibitions, the language of § 703(j) is specifically directed at entities —federal agencies and courts—charged with the responsibility of interpreting Title VII's provisions.

In light of the background and purpose of § 703(j), the irony of invoking the section to justify the result in this case is obvious. The Court's frequent references to the "voluntary" nature of Kaiser's racially discriminatory admission quota bear no relationship to the facts of this case. Kaiser and the Steelworkers acted under pressure from an agency of the Federal Government, the Office of Federal Contract Compliance, which found that minorities were being "underutilized" at Kaiser's plants. See n. 2, supra. That is, Kaiser's work force was racially imbalanced. Bowing to that pressure, Kaiser instituted an admissions quota preferring blacks over whites, thus confirming that the fears of Title VII's opponents were well founded. Today § 703(j), adopted to allay those fears, is invoked by the Court to uphold imposition of a racial quota under the very circumstances that the section was intended to prevent.

 * * * In a lengthy defense of the entire civil rights bill, Senator Muskie emphasized that the opposition's "torrent of words * * * cannot obscure this basic, simple truth: Every American citizen has the right to equal treatment—not favored treatment, not complete individual equality—just equal treatment." With particular reference to Title VII, Senator Muskie noted that the measure "seeks to afford to all Americans equal opportunity in employment without discrimination. Not equal pay, not 'racial balance.' Only equal opportunity."

 * * *

On June 9, Senator Ervin offered an amendment that would entirely delete Title VII from the bill. In answer to Senator Ervin's contention that

Title VII "would make the members of a particular race special favorites of the laws," Senator Clark retorted:

"The bill does not make anyone higher than anyone else. It estabilies no quotas. It leaves an employer free to select whomever he wishes to employ. * * *

"All this is subject to one qualification, and that qualification, is to state: 'In your activity as an employer * * * you must not discriminate because of the color of a man's skin * * *.'

"That is all this provision does. * * * It merely says, 'When you deal in interstate commerce, you must not discriminate on the basis of race * * *.'"

The Ervin amendment was defeated * * *.

* * * Senator Moss in a speech delivered on the day that the civil rights bill was finally passed, had this to say about quotas:

"The bill does not accord to any citizen advantage or preference— it does not fix quotas of employment or school population—it does not force personal association. What it does is to prohibit public officials and those who invite the public generally to patronize their businesses or to apply for employment, to utilize the offensive, humiliating, and cruel practice of discrimination on the basis of race. In short, the bill does not accord special consideration; it establishes *equality*."

Later that day, June 19, the issue was put to a vote, and was passed.

* * *

Reading the language of Title VII, as the Court purports to do, "against the background of [its] legislative history * * * and the historical context from which the Act arose," ante, at 6, one is led inescapably to the conclusion that Congress fully understood what it was saying and meant precisely what it said. Opponents of the civil rights bill did not argue that employers would be permitted under Title VII voluntarily to grant preferential treatment to minorities to correct racial imbalance. The plain language of the statute too clearly prohibited such racial discrimination to admit of any doubt.

* * * § 703(j) simply enjoins federal agencies and courts from interpreting Title VII to require an employer to prefer certain racial groups to correct imbalances in his work force. The section says nothing about voluntary preferential treatment of minorities because such racial discrimination is plainly proscribed by §§ 703(a) and (d). Indeed, had Congress intended to except voluntary, race-conscious preferential treatment from the blanket prohibition on racial discrimination in §§ 703(a) and (d), it surely could have drafted language better suited to the task than § 703(j). It knew how. Section 703(i) provides:

"Nothing contained in [title VII] shall apply to any business or enterprise on or near an Indian reservation with respect to any publicly announced employment practice of such business or enterprise under which a preferential treatment is given to any individual because he is an Indian living on or near a reservation." § 703 (i), 42 U.S.C.A. § 2000e–2(i).

Our task in this case, like any other case involving the construction of a statute, is to give effect to the intent of Congress. To divine that intent, we traditionally look first to the words of the statute and, if they are unclear, then to the statute's legislative history. Finding the desired result hopelessly foreclosed by these conventional sources, the Court turns to a third source —the "spirit" of the Act. But close examination of what the Court proffers as the spirit of the Act reveals it as the spirit animating the present majority, not the Eighty-eighth Congress. For if the spirit of the Act eludes the cold words of the statute itself, it rings out with unmistakable clarity in the words of the elected representatives who made the Act law. It is *equality*. Senator Dirksen, I think, captured that spirit in a speech delivered on the floor of the Senate just moments before the bill was passed:

"[T]oday we come to grips finally with a bill that advances the enjoyment of living; but, more than that, it advances the equality of opportunity.

"I do not emphasize the word 'equality' standing by itself. It means equality of opportunity in the field of education. It means equality of opportunity in the field of employment. It means equality of opportunity in the field of participation in the affairs of government * * *.

"That is it.

"Equality of opportunity, if we are going to talk about conscience, is the mass conscience of mankind that speaks in every generation, and it will continue to speak long after we are dead and gone."

There is perhaps no device more destructive to the notion of equality than the *numerus clausus*—the quota. Whether described as "benign discrimination" or "affirmative action," the racial quota is nonetheless a creator of castes, a two-edged sword that must demean one in order to prefer another. In passing Title VII Congress outlawed *all* racial discrimination, recognizing that no discrimination based on race is benign, that no action disadvantaging a person because of his color is affirmative. With today's holding, the Court introduces into Title VII a tolerance for the very evil that the law was intended to eradicate, without offering even a clue as to what the limits on that tolerance may be. We are told simply that Kaiser's racially discriminatory admission quota "falls on the permissible side of the line." By going not merely *beyond*, but directly *against* Title VII's language and legislative history, the Court has sown the wind. Later courts will face the impossible task of reaping the whirlwind.

———

Mr. Chief Justice BURGER, dissenting.

The Court reaches a result I would be inclined to vote for were I a Member of Congress considering a proposed amendment of Title VII. I cannot join the Court's judgment, however, because it is contrary to the explicit language of the statute and arrived at by means wholly incompatible with long-established principles of separation of powers. Under the guise of statutory "construction," the Court effectively rewrites Title VII to achieve what it regards as a desirable result. It "amends" the statute to do precisely what both its sponsors and its opponents agreed the statute was *not* intended to do.

When Congress enacted Title VII after long study and searching debate, it produced a statute of extraordinary clarity, which speaks directly to the issue we consider in this case. In § 703(d) Congress provided:

> "It shall be an unlawful employment practice for any employer, labor organization, or joint labor-management committee controlling apprenticeship or other training or retraining, including on-the-job training programs to discriminate against any individual because of his race, color, religion, sex, or national origin in admission to, or employment in, any program established to provide apprenticeship or other training." 42 U.S.C.A. § 2000e-2(d).

Often we have difficulty interpreting statutes either because of imprecise drafting or because legislative compromises have produced genuine ambiguities. But here there is no lack of clarity, no ambiguity. The quota embodied in the collective-bargaining agreement between Kaiser and the Steelworkers unquestionably discriminates on the basis of race against individual employees seeking admission to on-the-job training programs. And, under the plain language of § 703(d), that is "an *unlawful* employment practice."

Oddly, the Court seizes upon the very clarity of the statute almost as a justification for evading the unavoidable impact of its language. The Court blandly tells us that Congress could not really have meant what it said, for a "literal construction" would defeat the "purpose" of the statute—at least the congressional "purpose" as five Justices divine it today. But how are judges supposed to ascertain the *purpose* of a statute except through the words Congress used and the legislative history of the statute's evolution? One need not even resort to the legislative history to recognize what is apparent from the face of Title VII—that it is specious to suggest that § 703(j) * * * permits employers to do what §§ 703(a) and (d) unambiguously and unequivocally *forbid* employers from doing. Moreover, as MR. JUSTICE REHNQUIST's opinion—which I join—conclusively demonstrates, the legislative history makes equally clear that the supporters and opponents of Title VII reached an agreement about the statute's intended effect. That agreement expressed so clearly in the language of the statute that no one should doubt its meaning, forecloses the reading which the Court gives the statute today.

Arguably, Congress may not have gone far enough in correcting the effects of past discrimination when it enacted Title VII. The gross discrimination against minorities to which the Court adverts—particularly against Negroes in the building trades and craft unions—is one of the dark chapters in the otherwise great history of the American labor movement. And, I do not question the importance of encouraging voluntary compliance with the purposes and policies of Title VII. But that statute was conceived and enacted to make discrimination against *any* individual illegal, and I fail to see how "voluntary compliance" with the no-discrimination principle that is the heart and soul of Title VII as currently written will be achieved by permitting employers to discriminate against some individuals to give preferential treatment to others.

Until today, I had thought the Court was of the unanimous view that "[d]iscriminatory preference for any group, minority or majority, is precisely and only what Congress has proscribed" in Title VII. Griggs v. Duke Power Co., 401 U.S. 424, 431 (1971). Had Congress intended otherwise, it very easily could have drafted language allowing what the Court permits today. Far from doing so, Congress expressly *prohibited* in §§ 703(a) and (d) the discrimination against Brian Weber the Court approves now. If "affirmative action" programs such as the one presented in this case are to be permitted, it is for Congress, not this Court to so direct.

* * *

PROBLEMS

1. Clyde Markum, a California farmer, produces an annual crop of blackberries and peaches. Clyde is in need of workers to harvest his fruit so he runs the following advertisement in the local paper:

   Wanted: Able bodied young men under the age of 25 to pick blackberries and peaches.

   Nellie Johnson, who is 23 years old, applies for work, but Clyde refuses to consider her application because she is a woman. Clyde also turns away 42 year old Arthur Chandler because (in Clyde's words) "he's too old for the job". Clyde ultimately persuades a group of migrant farm workers to move into temporary living quarters on his land and start picking the blackberries and peaches. However, the workers soon grow dissatisfied with their wages ($2.00 an hour no matter how many hours they work), and they pick up and leave the farm. Clyde, who is beginning to grow desperate, sends his own children, Mark, 10, and Karen, 13, out into the field to pick berries. He also runs an ad asking local school children ages 8 to 15 to come out and help with the harvest—they will be paid $3.00/flat for blackberries and $2.50/bushel for peaches. Some local citizens complain that it is unlawful for Clyde to use school children in the fields (particularly as pesticide was sprayed on the bushes and trees) or to allow his own children to help with the harvest. Clyde, however, pays no heed to the citizens. He is having trouble with the tractor he purchased from Farm Supply, Inc., and he calls the Company to repair the tractor. The Company sends its top mechanic, Gwen Grover, out to look at the tractor. While she is there, Gwen complains to Clyde that she works 10-12 hours a day but is never paid more than $4.85 an hour. Answer the following:

   (a) What legal rights, if any, do Nellie Johnson and Arthur Chandler have against Clyde Markum? Explain.

   (b) The migrant farm workers complain to the Secretary of Labor about their wages and hours while employed by Clyde. Do they have any legal cause to complain? Explain.

   (c) Is is unlawful for Clyde to send his own children into the fields to work? To send the 8 to 15 year old school children into the fields and pay them as described? Explain.

   (d) Does Gwen Grover have any legal cause to complain about her wages and hours as an employee of Farm Supply, Inc.? Explain.

2. For several years, Clyde Markum has had an arrangement with Ralph Hoy whereby Ralph is to sell Clyde's fresh eggs and vegetables to local produce markets. Ralph uses his own truck to pick up the produce and make the deliveries; he is paid on a commission basis, and he works hard to solicit new customers. He does his job as he sees fit without direction from Clyde Markum. One day while Ralph is on his way to the Markum farm to pick up a truckload of eggs and vegetables, he carelessly runs his truck into a car driven by Libby Connors. Libby's

car is damaged beyond repair, and Libby herself is seriously injured. Libby sues both Ralph Hoy and Clyde Markum for money damages for her injuries. Result? Explain.

Ralph Hoy is also injured in the accident and will be permanently disabled. Can Ralph recover under Workmen's Compensation? Explain. Can Ralph recover unemployment compensation for any portion of the six month period he spends in the hospital? Explain. Can he recover Social Security disability benefits? Explain. For purposes of Social Security law, is Ralph an employee or an independent contractor? Explain. Does his classification for Social Security purposes make a difference? Explain.

3. Erica Becker performs secretarial work (typing and filing) for Lawson Furniture Store. Erica works Monday through Friday from 8 a.m. to 5 p.m.; she is paid $225/week for her services. Erica's supervisor, Carol Landis, rates Erica as one of the best secretaries around. To improve her shorthand skills, Erica signs up for a nightclass at the local business college. She also joins the employee union, paying $10 a month in union dues. One day at work, Carol tells Erica to hand deliver an important written contract to Mrs. Ferguson who lives across town. Erica takes the company car, and, on her way to Mrs. Ferguson's, she negligently runs the car into Maurice Lambert, a young bicycle rider. After seeing Maurice off to the hospital, Erica delivers the contract to Mrs. Ferguson. Though it is only 3:30 p.m., Erica takes the company car and goes to visit her sister, Ginny. At 4:30 p.m., Erica leaves Ginny's house and starts home (Erica plans to return the company car the following day). Erica, however, is still a little shaken up from her earlier accident, and she negligently runs the company car into a parked truck belonging to Jerry Ellis.

(a) Maurice Lambert sues both Erica Becker and Lawson Furniture for his injuries. Result? Explain.

(b) Jerry Ellis sues both Erica and Lawson Furniture for the damage to his truck. Result? Explain.

(c) Assuming Erica is injured in the first accident, can she recover from Lawson Furniture for her injuries under modern law? Under common law? Explain.

(d) Assuming Erica is injured in the second accident, can she recover from Lawson Furniture for her injuries under modern law? Under common law? Explain.

(e) Can Erica deduct the cost of the nightclass and the union dues from her gross income for purposes of federal income tax? Explain.

4. Lawson Furniture Company hires Richard Robel to come out to the office and repair the photocopy machine. The Company agrees to pay Richard, who makes a living out of repair work, $75 for his efforts. Richard arrives at the office with his own tools and sets to work on the machine. Before long, Anna Lawson, the owner of the Company, asks Richard if he will help load some furniture on the company truck. Richard agrees and follows the foreman's direction in loading the cof-

fee tables, lamps, and other furniture items. While helping with the loading, Richard carelessly drops a heavy coffee table right on the foot of Mary Overmyer, a visitor to the Company. Mike Oliphant, a company employee, calls Richard a "stupid fool", and Richard socks him in the nose. Richard then apologizes and returns to repairing the photocopy machine. The machine is located on the second floor near an open railing. While working on the machine, Richard carelessly drops a heavy wrench on the head of Myra Parker, a business customer downstairs on the second floor. Myra was not aware that repair work was going on upstairs; she is seriously injured. The Lawson Company immediately fires Mike Oliphant and Richard Robel for causing trouble. It also fires 60 year old Simon Rider because his work production has fallen below company standards. And it hires Candy Harris because she is a female, and there are more males than females working at the plant; Sam Johnson, who is just as qualified as Candy, complains when she is hired instead of him.

(a) Mary Overmyer sues both Richard Robel and Lawson Furniture for damages for her injuries. Result? Explain.

(b) Myra Parker sues both Richard Robel and Lawson Furniture for damages for her injuries. Result? Explain.

(c) Can Mike Oliphant recover for injury to his nose from Lawson Furniture under modern law? Under common law? Explain.

(d) Can Mike recover unemployment compensation until he finds another job? Can Richard Robel do so? Explain.

(e) Simon Rider claims that he was the victim of age discrimination. A valid contention? Explain.

(f) Sam Johnson claims that he was the victim of sex discrimination. A valid contention? Explain.

5. During the 1976 examination of the financial statements of Viscount Manufacturing Corporation, the CPAs noted that although Viscount had 860 full-time and part-time employees, it had completely overlooked its responsibilities under the Federal Insurance Contributions Act (FICA). Under these circumstances, which of the following is true?

   a. *No* liability under the act will attach if the employees voluntarily relinquish their rights under the act in exchange for a cash equivalent paid directly to them.

   b. If the union which represents the employees has a vested pension plan covering the employees which is equal to or exceeds the benefits available under the act, Viscount has *no* liability.

   c. Since employers and employees owe FICA taxes at the same rate and since the employer must withhold the employees' tax from their wages as paid, Viscount must remit to the government a tax double the amount assessed directly against the employer.

   d. The act does *not* apply to the part-time employees.

[# 13, November 1977 CPA Exam]

6. The Federal Social Security Act

    a. Applies to self-employed businessmen.

    b. Excludes professionals such as accountants, lawyers, and doctors.

    c. Provides for a deduction by the employee against his federal income tax.

    d. Applies to professionals at their option.

    [# 47, November 1976 CPA Exam]

7. Jackson is a junior staff member of Stutz & Harris, CPAs. He has been with the firm for one year working with the audit staff.

    a. If Jackson is injured while auditing one of the firm's clients, the client's workmen's compensation insurance will cover him.

    b. The federal wage and hour laws do *not* apply to Jackson.

    c. Stutz & Harris will be liable for the torts committed by Jackson within the scope of his employment.

    d. Clients will be liable for the torts committed by Jackson since he and his principal (Stutz & Harris) were engaged by them.

    [# 45, May 1976 CPA Exam]

8. Workmen's compensation laws

    a. Are uniform throughout the United States with the exception of Louisiana.

    b. Have *not* been adopted by all states except where required by federal law.

    c. Do *not* preclude an action against a third party who has caused an injury.

    d. Do *not* cover employees injured outside the jurisdiction.

    [# 35, May 1975 CPA Exam]

9. Joe Walters was employed by the Metropolitan Department Store as a driver of one of its delivery trucks. Under the terms of his employment he made deliveries daily along a designated route and brought the truck back to the store's garage for overnight storage. One day instead of returning to the garage as required, he drove the truck twenty miles north of the area he covered expecting to attend a social function unrelated to his employment or to his employer's affairs. Through his negligence in operating the truck while enroute, Walters seriously injured Richard Bunt. Walters caused the accident and was solely at fault. Bunt entered suit in tort against the store for damages for personal injuries, alleging that the store, as principal, was responsible for the tortious acts of its agent. Under these circumstances

    a. Metropolitan is *not* liable because Walters was an independent contractor.

    b. Metropolitan is *not* liable because Walters had abandoned his employment and was engaged in an independent activity of his own.

    c. Metropolitan is liable based upon the doctrine of *respondeat superior*.

    d. Bunt can recover damages from both Walters and Metropolitan.

    [# 14, November 1974 CPA Exam]

10. Markum was grossly negligent in the operation of a forklift. As a result he suffered permanent disability. His claim for workmen's compensation will be

a. Denied.

b. Limited to medical benefits.

c. Reduced by the percentage share attributable to his own fault.

d. Paid in full.

[# 48, November 1976 CPA Exam]

Chapter 21

AGENCY

What is an agent?

An *agent* is a person who is authorized to make contracts on behalf of another called a *principal*.[1] A properly authorized agent enters into contracts on behalf of the principal, and the principal is bound just as though he or she had made the contracts personally.

Ordinarily, anything a person can do legally himself or herself, he or she can also do through an agent (however, the subject of the agency must not be illegal or contrary to public policy). In the business world, the concept of agency is essential: rather than enter into each and every contract personally, a businessperson can authorize others to contract for him or her. Imagine the difficulties, for example, if the owner of a large department store or supermarket had to wait personally on each and every customer. The business would have little chance to survive, much less expand. Under the concept of agency, the store owner can authorize salesclerks to sell goods to customers (on the owner's behalf) and can authorize a general business manager to purchase inventory from wholesalers (again on the owner's behalf). With agency, it makes no difference what kind of contract is involved—it can be a sale of goods, a purchase of land, an agreement to perform services, etc.

Of course, this is not to say that agency is without risks. So long as an agent acts within the scope of his or her authority, the principal will be "stuck" (i. e., bound) by the agent's contracts even if the principal does not like the contracts (in some cases, the agent will also be bound by the contracts).

The "key" to understanding the concept of agency is one word—*authority*. An agent exists only because of the *authority* given to him or her by the principal. As used in the law of agency, the term *authority* has a very special meaning.

What is meant by the term "authority"?

For an agent to bind a principal in contract, the agent must have "authority" to do so. Many times, the authority is created by contract. Suppose, for example, that Ray Chamberlain owns a sporting goods store in which he sells fishing, hunting, skiing, football, basketball, baseball, golf, and other sports equipment. Ray employs several people to sell merchandise in the store. Here, the employment contract creates the agency relationship and provides the "authority" for Ray's clerks to bind him in contract when selling inventory. If the clerks mistakenly sell skis at 25% less than cost, Ray is bound by the contracts the same as if he had made them personally. (The fact that Ray's clerks are also his employees is irrelevant to the agency issue. Frequently, a person is both an employee and an agent at the same time. Most retail salesclerks, for example, are "servants" when arranging inventory and cleaning up the store; they are "agents" when selling inventory.)

While authority is often created by contract, a contract is not required to establish an agency relationship. Authority

---

1. The concept of agency has been mentioned previously in Chapters 11 ("insur-ance agents") and 13 (the liability of an agent who signs a negotiable instrument).

rests, not on contract, but on the *consent* of the principal. It is *consent* that is the basis of authority. Say you tell your 15 year old daughter that she can use your credit card to do some shopping at the local department store. Your daughter clearly has no contract right to use the card: neither of you intend to create a contract; and there is no mutual assent, consideration, or capacity (your daughter being only 15). Yet your daughter has your *consent* to use the card, and, as your agent, she can bind you to pay for her charges. The same would be true if you told her to fill up your car with gas and charge it to your account at the local service station. Again, there would be no "breach of contract" if your daughter did not purchase the gas; at the same time, she has your *consent* (i. e., your authority) to purchase it, and, as your agent, can bind you to pay for it.

And it makes no difference that your daughter is a minor or otherwise lacks capacity to contract. Contractual capacity on the part of the agent is not required —the agent binds the principal in contract, not himself or herself. The general rule is that anyone can be an agent who is capable of performing the functions involved. (Thus it is that many 16 and 17 year olds work in gas stations selling gas, and in fast food restaurants selling hamburgers.) Of course, an agent cannot be so bereft of mind that he or she cannot perform the work of the agency.

As for the principal's capacity, anyone can be a principal who is not fully and completely incapacitated. Where the principal is partially incapacitated, his or her agent's contracts will be void or voidable according to the ordinary rules of contract law. For example, if a minor contracts through an agent, he or she can

disaffirm the contracts just as if he or she had made them personally.

Generally speaking, no formality is required to create authority: the authority may be given orally, in writing, or even by conduct. However, there is an exception. You will recall from Ch. 10 that certain kinds of contracts must be evidenced by a writing in order to be enforceable under the Statute of Frauds.[2] "Equal dignities" statutes, in effect in most states, provide that an agent's authority to enter into contracts subject to the Statute of Frauds must also be in writing. If the agent's authority is not in writing, the principal will not be bound by the contract; nor will he or she have any right to enforce the contract. (Along the same line, where sealed instruments are still used, an agent's authority to execute a sealed instrument must also be in writing—see Ch. 10 regarding "sealed instruments".)

While no formality is generally required to create authority, it is often prudent to specify in writing exactly what authority is being given. If nothing else, this lets the agent know what is expected of him or her (often, the agent does not know, and, as a result, enters into contracts not intended by the principal).

Whether or not a principal will be bound by any particular contract entered into by his or her agent depends on whether *authority* for the contract can be found. The two general classifications of authority are *real authority* and *apparent authority*. So long as the agent had either kind of authority for entering into the contract, the principal will be "stuck" —period. Real authority and apparent authority may be defined as follows:

(1) *Real authority.* Real authority is authority manifested by the principal to

2. As you will recall, the Statute of Frauds requires written evidence of six kinds of contracts: (1) contracts for the sale of any interest in land; (2) promises to answer for the debt of another; (3) promises by a

personal representative to pay personally for the decedent's debts; (4) promises that cannot be performed within one year; (5) promises in consideration of marriage; and (6) sales of goods for $500 or more.

the agent either expressly or by implication. There are four kinds of real authority:

(a) *Express authority.* A principal confers express authority upon an agent when he or she explicitly authorizes the agent, either orally or in writing, to contract on his or her behalf.

(b) *Incidental authority.* It is not necessary for a principal to spell out every detail of an agent's authority. By virtue of giving an agent express authority to contract, a principal also consents to any authority that is normally incidental to carrying out the contracting. Incidental authority is thus "extra" authority that enables the agent to carry out his or her express agency duties. For example, suppose that college professor John Jensen accepts a two-year teaching post in Europe. John gives express authority to Greta Powers to rent his house while he is away. Greta not only has express authority to bind John to a rental contract, but she also has incidental authority to sign the lease and collect the monthly rent (though neither item was expressly mentioned).

(c) *Implied authority.* Even in the absence of express oral or written authority to contract, real authority may be implied by the conduct of the principal. Implied authority is not incidental to express authority, but, rather is part of the basic consent itself—found in conduct rather than words. For example, say that John Jensen sends Greta Powers a note stating, "I am off to Europe for two years—do what you can with the house." John encloses the keys to the house along with the note. Though John's written expression of authority is incomplete at best, John's conduct in enclosing the keys along with the note impliedly authorizes Greta to lease the house. Greta's authority, in this case, is partly express and partly implied.

(d) *Authority by necessity.* In a narrow category of cases, the courts recognize a type of real authority known as authority by necessity. The courts state that, in an emergency situation where someone is injured, a "servant" (employee) may have real authority (by necessity) to summon medical aid on behalf of his or her employer, binding the employer to pay for the aid. Usually, the cases involve either a bus or train accident occurring in a remote area where it is impossible for the servant to contact either his or her employer or any other person with express authority to summon aid (if it is possible for the servant to communicate with someone who is expressly authorized, no authority by necessity arises). In such a situation, the highest ranking servant on the scene (e. g., the bus driver or train conductor) is held to have real authority by necessity to summon medical aid and bind the employer to pay for it. The servant's authority by necessity ends when the emergency ends or when anyone with express authority takes over, whichever occurs first.

(2) *Apparent authority.* Though a person has no real authority (express, incidental, implied, or by necessity) to act as another's agent, he or she may nevertheless have apparent authority to do so. Apparent authority is authority that results from an appearance of authority *created by the principal;* it is authority that is normal to the appearance created.

Apparent authority is based on the objective theory of contracts as explained in Ch. 7: the secret or hidden intentions of a party (here, the principal) will not control over what is objectively manifested to others (here, the third parties who deal with the agent). Regardless of a principal's private intentions, if he or she creates in a party an appearance of authority, the principal will be bound by acts of the party that are normal to that appearance. The test of apparent authority is thus twofold:

First, what appearance did the principal create?

Second, was the agent's effort to bind the principal normal to that appearance? Let's return to our previous example. John Jensen sends Greta Powers a note stating, "I am off to Europe for two years—do what you can with the house." Again, John encloses the keys to the house along with the note. This time, however, John telephones Greta and instructs her as follows: "I don't want you to rent the house while I'm gone—just take care of it, and hire someone to mow the lawn and spray the trees, etc." Greta rents the house anyway, showing the tenant the letter from John and handing over the keys. John is bound by the lease agreement notwithstanding his private intentions and the fact that he specifically instructed Greta not to rent the house. John has created an appearance of authority in Greta by giving her the letter and keys. The appearance is to take charge of the house and "do what she can with it" for two years; the act of renting the house is normal to that appearance.

And so it is in most cases. The apparent agent generally has *some* real authority, but not all the powers usually associated with the particular job or position (the principal having "secretly" limited the agent's powers in some way). Let's look at another example. A salesclerk of merchandise customarily has authority to relinquish possession of the goods and accept payment of the purchase price.[3] While Ray Chamberlain may privately instruct sales clerk Tom Parker that he cannot accept payment of the purchase price, third parties who deal with Tom have no reason to question Tom's authority to ac-

cept their money. Such authority is normal to the appearance of a salesclerk, and Tom has apparent authority to accept payment (of course, this would not be the case if Ray had posted notice in the store that salesclerks have no authority to accept payment). Similarly, if Ray places a security guard behind the sales counter and instructs him or her not to make any sales, but simply to "watch out for shoplifters", Ray will nonetheless be bound by any sales the guard does make. By placing the guard behind the counter, Ray has created an appearance of authority (the authority of a salesclerk) and will be bound by acts of the guard that are normal to that appearance.

It seldom occurs that an apparent agent has no real authority of any kind. However, it does happen occasionally. For example, in Kanelles v. Locke, 12 Ohio App. 210 (1919), the defendant principal owned a hotel in Cleveland, Ohio. The plaintiff checked into the hotel late one night, registering with a man who went behind the counter and signed the plaintiff in as a guest. The plaintiff left some valuables with the man to be placed in the hotel safe. The next day both the man and the valuables had disappeared. When the plaintiff sued the defendant hotel owner, the defendant disclaimed any knowledge of the man, stating that he certainly was not her agent. The court, however, ruled in favor of the plaintiff, stating that the defendant had negligently created the appearance of agency by permitting the man to go behind the counter and "take charge". It held that the man had apparent authority to bind the defendant to the contract for care of the plaintiff's valuables. The court also concluded that the agency was created by estoppel.

It should be emphasized that the appearance of authority *must be created by*

---

3. However, such a clerk does not normally have power to accept payment for goods previously sold on credit to the customer—

credit payments must be made directly to the principal's bookkeeping department.

the principal—either giving the agent some secretly limited express authority, or by intentionally or negligently placing the unauthorized person in an apparent position of authority. It follows that a person who fraudulently "manufacturers" evidence to prove that he or she represents another has no authority (either real or apparent) and no ability to bind the principal in contract. It would not make sense to hold otherwise: the purported principal (who may not even know the purported agent) has neither authorized the party to act nor in any way contributed to creating the appearance of authority. A third party who deals with such an "agent" will have no legal recourse against the "principal" (it is a risk we all face—the risk of being fooled by others).

One problem in the area of apparent authority is that it is frequently difficult to determine just what is "normal" to a particular appearance or occupation. Where the matter is disputed in court, expert witnesses in similar positions of authority may be called to testify. In the next section, we will look at several occupations that have been "court-tested"; in each case, detailed conclusions have been drawn as to what is normal to the appearance of the occupation.

What are some "court-tested" examples of apparent authority?

The courts have established what authority is "normal to the appearance" of the following occupations and professions:

(1) *A business manager.* A business manager has authority to do what is normally done in similar businesses in carrying out the day-to-day business operation. This includes authority to buy and sell (e. g., inventory), to purchase equipment and supplies for normal business operations, to employ counsel, and to hire and fire daily employees. It does not include authority to mortgage business property, to make any negotiable paper on behalf of the company (e. g., as to borrow money from a bank), or to expand or terminate the business or alter it in any way.

(2) *A real estate dealer or broker.* A prospective buyer or seller of land usually employs a real estate dealer or broker to find a willing seller or buyer for the property. Generally speaking, a real estate dealer or broker is not an agent at all, but is an independent contractor who is paid a commission for doing a job. It follows that the dealer or broker has no apparent authority to bind his or her employer in any way: he or she cannot bind the employer to a contract of sale or purchase; nor can he or she accept payment of all or part of the purchase price of the property on behalf of the employer. The dealer's or broker's only job is to find a willing buyer or seller—period. Upon successful completion of the job, he or she is entitled to his or her commission regardless of whether a contract of sale or purchase is ultimately concluded.

(3) *A loan agent.* With one exception, an agent who is authorized to negotiate a loan of money to a third party has no apparent authority to collect repayment of either the loan principal or interest (even if the agent has real authority to collect interest, he or she has no apparent authority to collect principal). The exception arises where the agent retains possession of the promissory note evidencing the loan. The debtor, here, is protected in making repayment to the agent.

Authority (real or apparent) to accept repayment means authority to accept *money only*—not goods, land, checks, promissory notes, etc. Of course, an agent may always have real authority to accept other than money: an agent who is authorized to accept a check in repayment has no apparent authority to indorse the check and present it for payment.

(4) *A traveling salesperson of goods.* A salesperson who travels from "door to

door" in an effort to sell his or her company's products normally does not carry the goods with him or her, but simply takes orders for the goods. The goods themselves are delivered later, independent of the salesperson's selling activity. A traveling salesperson who carries no goods has no apparent authority to accept the purchase price of the goods. Say that a saleswoman visits your home and takes your order for a 12 piece cutlery set. The saleswoman has no apparent authority to receive the purchase price. If you pay her, and she absconds with the money, you will have to pay a second time to the principal. (The fact that the saleswoman had samples with her is immaterial—a traveling salesperson has no apparent authority to sell a principal's samples.)

On the other hand, a traveling salesperson who carries goods (not just samples) with him or her and delivers them over to the buyer at the time of purchase has apparent authority to accept the purchase price. Paying the salesperson, in this case, is the same as paying the principal. If the salesperson absconds with the money, it is the principal who will suffer the loss. (Even here, however, the salesperson does not have apparent authority to accept payment for goods sold previously to the buyer on a credit basis— again, the buyer must make credit payments directly to the principal's bookkeeping department.)

(5) *An agent authorized to take full charge of land.* An agent who is authorized to take full charge of land has apparent authority to insure the land and any buildings on the land against fire loss and other hazards. If it is rental property, the agent has apparent authority to rent the land for such periods of time and at such rates of rental as are customary. If it is farming property, the agent has apparent authority to farm the land (or rent it out for farming) and sell the farm products; the agent also has ap-

parent authority to purchase whatever equipment is needed to operate the farm.

In no case, however, does the agent have apparent authority to sell the land or mortgage the property (see Ch. 28 on "mortgages").

(6) *An attorney-at-law.* An attorney who represents a client has apparent authority to use whatever legal procedures will best protect the client's interests (along this line, the client will be bound to pay for the attorney's necessary expenses). However, an attorney has no apparent authority to release (i. e., relinquish) any of the client's legal rights—only the client may do so. For example, say that an insurance company offers a $5,000 settlement in exchange for release of the client's right to sue its insured for negligence. The attorney cannot bind the client to the settlement, but must permit the client to make his or her own decision. Assuming the client accepts the settlement, the attorney must forward the settlement check or draft to the client for indorsement and presentment for payment (frequently, the attorney must indorse the check or draft along with the client).

Of course, it should be realized that a principal is always free to give an agent *more* authority than what is normal to the appearance of a particular occupation or profession. What a principal cannot do without running the risk of being held liable on the basis of apparent authority is to give the agent *less* authority than what is normal. A principal who gives less authority should make it very clear to third parties that the agent's authority has been restricted.

Does marriage create authority in a spouse?

When a man and a woman get married, neither party, by virtue of the marriage, becomes an agent of the other—i. e., the marriage relationship in and of itself provides no authority for either party to contract for the other.

However, under the law of domestic relations ("family law"), a husband owes certain support obligations to his wife and children. The husband is liable under the law for his family's *necessaries*. This means that the husband must provide the family with food, clothing, shelter, and such "necessaries" as medical and dental care. If the husband fails to do so, the wife may purchase the necessaries without his permission and charge them in his name. However, the husband is not liable for "unnecessary" items, and a merchant who extends credit to a wife risks finding out later that the items purchased were not necessary (in which case the merchant can hold the husband liable only if the wife was, in fact, acting as the husband's agent).

But, again, the support laws are based, not on agency, but on domestic relations or family law. These laws reflect the past, traditional roles of husband and wife: the husband was the family "provider" whose job it was to provide the family with food, clothing, and shelter; the wife was charged with keeping the house in order and caring for the children. In about half the states, "Family Expense Acts" now impose the burden of family support on both the husband and wife. Yet, even in these states, the husband is not absolved of his duty to support his wife and children. So while a person who furnishes necessaries to the family can recover their cost from the wife under the Family Expense Act, the wife, in turn, can seek reimbursement from her husband.

While marriage in and of itself does not establish any agency relationship, the longterm conduct of the spouses in mixing incomes and accounts, and in paying each other's bills often results in one or both parties having real authority to contract for the other. In other words, a large amount of authority is usually creat-

ed in a marriage after a time. A husband and wife may have joint bank accounts, joint charge accounts, jointly owned property, and so forth. The wife may charge her husband's account for luxury items as well as for household supplies, and the husband may pay the bills over a long period of time. If the wife is an income producer, she may pay her husband's bills over a long period of time. Through such conduct, real authority (for the most part implied) will result, and one or both parties will be an agent of the other.

What is the difference between a general and a special agent?

It is sometimes useful to classify an agent as either a *general agent* or a *special agent*. A general agent is one who is authorized to contract regarding more than a single transaction and/or for a continuing period of time. A special agent is one who is authorized to conduct but a single transaction not involving any continuity of service. For example, if you authorize an agent to sell your car, the party is a special agent—the sale is one transaction involving only a short period of service. On the other hand, if you employ an agent to manage your business, the party is a general agent: he or she will represent you in many transactions over a considerable length of time.

A general agent has much more by way of implied, incidental, and apparent authority than does a special agent. And, as will be explained later in the chapter, there are special requirements for terminating a general agent's (as opposed to a special agent's) authority.

Can an agent delegate his or her authority to another party?

It is a general rule of agency law that, absent real authority to do so, an agent may not delegate the performance of his or her duties to another party or parties (i. e., the agent may not use agents of his or her own in performing the duties of the agency). If the agent does so, he or she will be liable to the principal for any damages that result. Frequently, of course, the principal authorizes such delegation either expressly or by implication. For example, the principal impliedly authorizes delegation where he or she employs an agent to do more contracting than is possible for one person to accomplish. Say the principal (the owner of a national insurance business) employs a party as his or her general agent for the City of Chicago or the State of North Carolina. Obviously, one person cannot handle all the negotiation and contracting for so large an area: the principal has given real authority (though implied) to the agent to delegate.

Where authorized, the agent's delegatees (i. e., the parties to whom the agent delegates his or her authority) are designated *subagents* to underline the fact that they are agents of the agent—not agents of the principal. Subagents are paid by the agent; and the agent is liable to the principal for any loss or damage caused by the subagents. At the same time, the principal is bound by acts of the subagents to the same extent that he or she would be bound by acts of the agent. It is the agent himself or herself acting through the subagents, and both the agent and his or her delegation of authority have been authorized by the principal.

The fact that an agent is not authorized to delegate his or her authority does not mean that the agent must personally carry out every detail of the agency. An agent may always employ others to perform the mechanical or ministerial functions of the job—e. g., typing, mailing, running errands, etc. What the agent may not delegate is the actual skill and discretion involved—the principal's intent is that the agent alone exercise this skill and discretion. Thus, so long as the agent carries out his or her duties with

regard to negotiation and execution of the contract, it makes little difference who actually types the agreement or delivers it to the post office for mailing.

Finally, it should be pointed out that an agent's job may simply be to hire other agents for the principal. Where this is the case, the agents hired are not subagents at all. They are agents of the principal employed on his or her behalf by one expressly authorized to make the selection. There is no delegation involved.

What are the duties of an agent to a principal?

An agent is a *fiduciary* of his or her principal—i. e., an agent is in a position of trust and confidence with the principal. *Black's Law Dictionary* defines "fiduciary" in this way.

It says:

A person having duty, created by his undertaking, to act primarily for another's benefit in matters connected with such undertaking * * *. As an adjective it means * * * relating to or founded upon a trust or confidence * * *.

[A] relationship implying and necessitating great confidence and trust on the one part and a high degree of good faith on the other part * * *.

A relation subsisting between two persons in regard to a business contract, or piece of property, or in regard to the general business or estate of one of them, of such a character that each must repose trust and confidence in the other and must exercise a corresponding degree of fairness and good faith.

Out of such a relation, the law raises the rule that neither party may exert influence or pressure upon the other, take selfish advantage of his trust, or deal with the subject matter of the trust in such a way as to benefit himself or prejudice the other except in the exercise of the utmost good faith and with the full knowledge and consent of that other, business shrewdness, hard bargaining, and astuteness, to take advantage of the forgetfulness or negligence of another being totally prohibited as between persons standing in such a relation to each other. Examples of fiduciary relations are those existing between attorney and client, guardian and ward, principal and agent, executor and heir, trustee and *cestui que trust,* landlord tenant * * *.[4]

As a fiduciary, an agent owes a high duty of care and responsibility to the principal. The agent's fiduciary duties include:

(1) *The duty of loyalty.* An agent has a duty to act with complete and utmost loyalty and fidelity regarding his or her responsibilities to the principal. The law very strictly enforces this duty; it will not allow the agent to have any conflict of interest with the principal.

Thus, an agent may not represent one whose interests conflict with those of the principal (e. g., a party looking to contract with the principal). The law has long recognized that "no man can serve two masters". An agent cannot properly (and loyally) represent the interests of his or her principal if, at the same time and with regard to the same transaction, the agent is trying to represent another's interests. An exception is made where both principals, being fully informed of the agent's dual representation, consent that he or she act for both of them.

The duty of loyalty also prohibits an agent from secretly acting for himself or herself in the transaction (called "self-dealing"). For example, an agent who

is authorized to sell a car for his or her principal cannot sell the car to himself or herself; an agent authorized to buy a car cannot buy from himself or herself. Again, an exception is made where the principal is fully informed and consents to the transaction.

It is also "self-dealing" for an agent to use information acquired during the course of the agency to make a profit for himself or herself at the principal's expense—the agent may not compete with his or her principal.

Anytime an agent breaches the duty of loyalty by self-dealing, the principal has a right to avoid the transaction even though he or she has not been injured. Say that a principal employs an agent to sell her car for $5,000; the agent buys the car at the stated price for himself. Upon discovering that the agent is the buyer, the principal may avoid the contract of sale or let it stand at her option. The fact that the principal received $5,000 for the car—all that she asked for —is immaterial.

Similarly, if an agent profits at the principal's expense by reason of a breach of loyalty, the courts will impose a "constructive trust" (see Ch. 29) on the profits, meaning that the agent must hold the profits for the principal's account and ultimately turn them over to the principal.

An agent who breaches his or her duty of loyalty also forfeits any fee, commission, or other compensation provided for by the terms of the agency. And the agent is liable for any damages incurred by the principal by reason of the breach (e. g., where the agent sells the principal's property at less than a fair value to an innocent third party who is entitled to keep the property).

4.　Henry Campbell Black, *Black's Law Dictionary,* Revised Fourth Edition, West Publishing Co., 1968, p. 753.

(2) *The duty to obey the principal's instructions.* An agent also has a fiduciary duty to comply exactly with any instructions given by the principal; the agent will be liable to the principal for any loss resulting from a failure to follow instructions. For example, suppose that an agent who is instructed to sell goods "for cash only" sells the goods on credit. If the principal suffers a loss because of the credit sale, the agent will be liable. Or suppose that an agent who is instructed to insure property against fire loss or other hazard fails to do so. Again, if the principal suffers a loss because of the agent's failure to follow instructions, the agent will be liable. And it is no defense that the agent's intentions were good or that the agency was gratuitous (i. e., the agent was serving without compensation). (Obviously, where the agency is gratuitous, the agent is not obligated to perform at all. But if the gratuitous agent undertakes the work of the agency, he or she owes the same fiduciary duties to the principal that a contractual agent owes).

It should be noted that there are a few exceptions where an agent may deviate from the principal's instructions without incurring liability. In an emergency situation demanding immediate action, an agent who is unable to communicate with his or her principal may deviate from the principal's instructions to the extent reasonably necessary to protect the principal's interests. Also, where the principal's instructions are not entirely clear, an agent will be protected in making a reasonable interpretation of the instructions though the principal had another meaning in mind. And, of course, an agent has no obligation to follow instructions calling for illegal activity.

(3) *The duty to exercise reasonable care.* An agent has a duty to exercise reasonable care and skill in carrying out his or her agency duties. In other words, an agent must take the steps and precautions that any reasonable person in his or her position would take. Thus, an agent who is authorized to sell a car must use reasonable care and skill in making the sale. If the agent sells the car to a transient, taking a bad check in return for delivery of the automobile, the agent breaches his or her duty and is liable to the principal for the damages.

Sometimes, an agent holds himself or herself out as having special expertise or skill (e.g., an attorney or stockbroker). The principal, in this case, is entitled to have the agent exercise the care and skill usual to such occupation or capacity. This is so whether the agent serves gratuitously or for hire.

(4) *The duty to account.* An agent has a duty to carefully (and timely) account for any money, property, or profits in his or her possession belonging to the principal. To say that the accounting must be "timely" means that the agent must notify the principal of actual receipts and expenditures within a reasonable time after they occur. Formal books of account are not required as long as the agent can produce vouchers or other evidence showing the receipts and expenditures.

The agent also has a duty not to mix any of his or her own money or property with that of the principal. If the agent does commingle funds or property, and the principal suffers a loss, the agent will be liable. And, of course, if the property is so intermixed that the separate monies or properties cannot be identified and separated, the agent will lose the whole of the property to the principal under the law of "confusion" (see Ch. 2 on "confusion").

Sometimes, a sales agent is a factor, i. e., a commercial agent employed by a principal to sell merchandise. The principal consigns goods to the factor for sale; the factor is a bailee of the property (see Ch. 16). The factor is paid on a commission basis for any goods that are sold (the commission is called a "factorage"). Sometimes, when selling consigned goods on credit, the factor, for an additional commission, will guarantee the solvency of the purchaser and his or her performance under the contract. The factor, in this case, is called a *del credere agent*. A *del credere agent* is liable to his or her principal only in cases where the purchaser defaults.

(5) *The duty to disclose.* Finally, an agent has a duty to inform the principal of any and all facts within his or her knowledge that relate to the principal's interests. The duty to disclose is far-reaching: the facts to be disclosed may concern the agent's duty of loyalty, his or her care of the principal's property, the intentions of third parties who may threaten the principal's interests, etc.

What are the duties of a principal to an agent?

A principal, in turn, owes the following duties to his or her agent:

(1) *The duty of good conduct.* Just as an agent must act with loyalty and special care regarding his or her relationship with the principal, the principal must act with good conduct toward the agent. It follows that the principal must not injure the agent's personal or business reputation in any way, nor abuse or insult the agent or treat him or her with other than respect while the agency relationship continues.

(2) *The duty to cooperate with the agent in performance of the agency.* Where the agency is based on a contract between the principal and agent, the principal has a duty to cooperate with the agent in performing the agency duties. That is to say, the principal must not interfere with the agent's performance, but must aid the agent in carrying out his or her duties. For example, if Ray Chamberlain hires a clerk to sell goods in his sporting goods store, Ray must provide the clerk with sufficient opportunity to make sales and reasonable access to the store's inventory.

Where the agency is gratuitous (not based on contract), the principal has no duty of cooperation (of course, it is unlikely that a gratuitous agent would persist where the principal is uncooperative).

(3) *The duty to compensate the agent for services rendered.* Again, whether the principal has a duty to pay the agent for his or her services will depend on whether the agent has a contract right to payment. As you know, many agents are also servants: frequently, such agents receive one weekly or monthly salary payment encompassing both their physical work as a servant and their contract work as an agent. In contrast, one who acts as an agent alone often works on a commission basis. Ray Chamberlain, for example, might employ an agent to sell his car for $5,000 with a 10% commission to the agent. When and if the agent sells the car, Ray will be obligated to pay the agent 10% of the sales price or $500.

Where the principal and agent make no express provision as to compensation, the courts will ordinarily imply a promise to pay unless circumstances indicate otherwise (e. g., a close family relationship between the parties). The amount to be paid will be the "customary rate" or what the services are "reasonably worth" (taking into account the agent's skill and reputation, and the importance of the work).

(4) *The duty of indemnity.* A principal has a duty to indemnify (i. e., reimburse) his or her agent for any expenses or liabilities incurred in carrying out the agency duties. Of course, the principal and agent are always free to contract to the contrary. Frequently, for example, an agent who works on a commission basis agrees to bear expenses out of his or her commission.

(5) *The duty to maintain accounts.* An agent who has a right to payment and/or indemnification, but no way of knowing just what is owing, also has a right to a careful and timely accounting from the principal. Say that an agent is to be compensated by the number of hours worked or the amount of goods sold; the principal keeps all the pertinent records. The agent is entitled to an accounting from the principal, and the principal must make the records available to the agent for verification.

Is the principal ever liable for torts committed by his or her agent?

In the previous chapter, we learned that a "master" (employer) is liable under the doctrine of respondeat superior for torts committed by his or her "servant" (employee) while in the scope of employment. Remember, a servant is one who works physically, subject to the master's right of control. An independent contractor, on the other hand, is a person hired to do a job for a price; though the independent contractor works physically for his or her employer, he or she is not subject to the employer's right of control. Unlike a servant or an independent contractor, an agent does not work physically for an employer, but, rather, enters into contracts on behalf of a principal. If a person is both an agent and a servant, the doctrine of respondeat superior applies to the person only in his or her capacity as a servant—the doctrine does not apply to agents.

Thus, the general rule is that a principal is not liable for torts committed by his or her agent. However, there is one major exception. If an agent who is authorized to make true representations about the subject matter of the agency (in most cases, such authority is implied or apparent) makes a fraudulent misrep-

resentation, the principal will be liable for the tort of deceit.[5] It is just as though the principal personally made the misrepresentation. (In other words, so long as an agent is authorized to make true representations, the principal is bound by the agent's unauthorized misrepresentations—though the principal had no knowledge of the fraud and certainly would not have approved of it!) The injured third party may avoid the contract because of the misrepresentation and hold the principal liable in damages.

By way of example, suppose that Ray Chamberlain's salesclerk falsely tells customer Sue Sailer that the wholesale price of a 20 foot cabin cruiser is $23,000 (the wholesale price is actually $12,000). Relying on the misrepresentation, Sue purchases the boat for $21,000. Eighteen months later, Sue discovers the deception: not only may she rescind the sale on the basis of fraud in the inducement, but she may hold Ray Chamberlain liable for the salesclerk's tort of deceit (the salesclerk had at least apparent authority to make true representations about the boat). Sue's damages for deceit will include the loss of interest on her money for the 18 month period.

Is an agent obligated to inform third parties that he or she represents a principal—or may the agency remain "undisclosed"?

In our discussions to this point, we have assumed a *disclosed agency* situation —i. e., the third party who deals with the agent has knowledge of the *existence* of the agency and of the *identity* of the principal (e. g., the agent signs the contract with the third party, "Tom Parker, agent for Ray Chamberlain"). Where the agency is disclosed, the principal alone is liable on the contract; the agent can neither sue nor be sued on the agree-

---

5. See Ch. 8 for a complete discussion of fraudulent misrepresentation (i. e., the tort of deceit).

ment (unless the contract specifically provides to the contrary, as where the agent guarantees performance by the principal).

Sometimes, however, the third party has no knowledge of the existence of the agency (and ergo no knowledge of the principal's identity). The third party truly believes that the agent represents only himself or herself. In this situation, the agency is said to be *undisclosed*.

An undisclosed agency is perfectly legal and proper (assuming, of course, that the subject of the agency is legal and not contrary to public policy). The law has long recognized that a party may have sound business reasons for dealing "behind the scenes" as an undisclosed principal. For example, say that a successful real estate developer wants to buy all the land in a particular downtown block; ultimately, the developer wants to construct a 20 story office building upon the property. The land is currently rundown with old buildings, and its market value is quite low. By using an undisclosed agent, the developer will be able to purchase the land at its current market value. In contrast, if the agency is disclosed, and the lot owners learn that a successful developer wants to buy the property, the land values may soar, and the development may not occur.

The examples go on and on. A businessperson in a small town might want to expand his or her commercial interests or holdings without drawing attention to the fact. A public figure (e. g., a television personality) might want to invest in a business or property development without public knowledge of the investment. In each case, an undisclosed agency will make the transaction possible (and there is nothing "deceitful" or "evil" about it!)

Thus, the general rule is that an undisclosed agent has no duty to inform the third party about the agency. Once the undisclosed principal comes forward, the principal's rights under the contract are the same as those of a disclosed principal. In other words, the principal may sue in his or her own name and right, and the third party is obligated to treat him or her as the other contracting party in all respects. And this is not unfair to the third party. In most cases, it makes no difference that there is an undisclosed principal involved. If a third party contracts to sell a house or car to an agent representing an undisclosed principal, the third party loses nothing by accepting the purchase price from the undisclosed principal and transferring title to him or her (rather than to the agent). Thus, the general rule is that it is no defense to performance that the third party had no knowledge of the agency and would not have dealt with the undisclosed principal had he or she had knowledge. There are only two exceptions to this rule:

(1) *Where the contract is personal in nature.* An undisclosed principal has no right or ability to enforce a contract that is personal in nature. For example, a contract may call for personal services. Say that undisclosed agent Elton John contracts to perform musically for a third party. Undisclosed principal Dolly Parton cannot later demand to perform on the basis that she is the real party to the contract.

Or a contract may be based on personal credit. Say that a third party banker agrees to loan $50,000 to undisclosed agent Molly Millionaire. Undisclosed principal Bill Bankrupt has no right to demand a personal loan of $50,000 from the banker.

In each case, the third party, if he or she chooses, may enforce the contract against the agent.

(2) *Where the undisclosed agent falsely asserts that he or she does not represent an undisclosed principal.* Any false assertion by the agent that the real

principal has no interest in the transaction will serve as the basis for fraud in the inducement. Thus, if the third party asks the undisclosed agent whether he or she represents a principal, and the agent says "no", the agent's misrepresentation will constitute fraud, permitting the third party to rescind the contract. (Of course, to constitute fraud, the misrepresentation must be material: if the third party really does not care whether an agency relationship exists, the misrepresentation is immaterial and nonfraudulent.)

In some cases, it is so apparent that the third party would not deal with a particular undisclosed principal that the agent has an affirmative duty to disclose the existence of the agency (even though not asked). The agent's failure to make disclosure constitutes fraud, again justifying rescission of the contract.

As to who is liable on the contract in the undisclosed agency situation, both the principal *and* the agent are liable. It follows that, in the event of breach of contract, the third party may sue either the principal (once disclosed) *or* the agent *or* both. However, in most states, a judgment against one of the parties precludes a judgment against the other (i. e., the third party may complete the court process against only one of the parties). A few states provide that if a judgment against one is uncollectible (for example, because of the party's insolvency), the third party may obtain a judgment against the other.

In nearly all states, if the third party obtains a judgment against the agent *before* learning of the principal's existence, the judgment against the agent will not bar a second judgment against the principal. After the agency is disclosed, the third party may sue the principal and obtain a judgment against him or her as well. However, the third party may collect only one of the judgments: collection of one bars collection of the other. (Of course, the party who ultimately pays may be able to obtain reimbursement from the other depending on the circumstances of the case and the underlying agency contract, if any.)

Where the third party elects to sue the undisclosed principal, the principal may assert in defense any and all defenses that would be available to the agent, including fraud, duress, failure of consideration, objective impossibility, etc.

Additionally, if there is a negotiable instrument involved (a negotiable note, draft, or check) the undisclosed principal may assert as a defense to payment that his or her name does not appear on the instrument. As you will recall from Ch. 13, U.C.C. Section 3–401(1) provides: "No person is liable on an instrument unless his signature appears thereon." The *Official Comment* to Section 3–401 states in part.

The Official Comment provides:

1. No one is liable on an instrument unless and until he has signed it. The chief application of the rule has been in cases holding that a principal whose name does not appear on an instrument signed by his agent is not liable on the instrument even though the payee knew when it was issued that it was intended to be the obligation of one who did not sign.

———

Of course, if the third party is forced to collect payment from the agent, the agent may, in turn, seek reimbursement from the principal based, not on the negotiable instrument (the principal's name does not appear on the instrument), but on the underlying agreement between the parties.[6]

6. For a detailed discussion of the liability of an agent who signs a negotiable instrument, see Ch. 13, p. 408.

One final defense available to an undisclosed principal is that, prior to the third party's knowledge of the principal's existence, the principal completely settled his or her accounts with the agent in reasonable reliance upon the third party's conduct. By way of example, suppose that Ray Chamberlain hires Tom Parker to go out and buy him a new delivery truck. Ray tells Tom not to disclose that he is acting for Ray because Ray believes that Tom will get a better deal if the seller does not know Ray is really the buyer. Tom goes out and talks to several dealers and finally enters into an agreement to purchase a truck for $12,500. Though payment is to be made in 30 days, the dealer mistakenly gives Tom a receipt showing that the truck has been paid for in full; the dealer delivers the truck to Tom. Tom, in turn, delivers the truck along with the receipt to Ray Chamberlain who pays Tom not only his commission for making the purchase, but also the $12,500 it appears Tom has paid the dealer. Tom subsequently disappears with the money; the dealer learns of Ray's identity as the principal and brings an action against him for the purchase price. Ray has a good defense to payment in that he settled his accounts with Tom in reasonable reliance upon the dealer's conduct in providing Tom with a receipt marked "paid in full". The dealer's only remedy is to locate Tom and bring legal action against him.

What is a "partially disclosed" principal?

A principal is "undisclosed" where his or her agent does not reveal the existence of the agency relationship. Where the agent reveals the existence of the relationship, but does not identify the principal, the principal is said to be *partially disclosed*.

The partially disclosed principal is treated much the same under the law as the undisclosed principal. Upon learning of the partially disclosed principal's identity, the third party (who has dealt with the agent) may hold either the agent or the principal liable on the contract. Again, the third party must elect to hold either one or the other: he or she cannot recover from both. Also, the same defenses are available to both partially disclosed and undisclosed principals, including full settlement of accounts with the agent in reasonable reliance upon the third party's conduct.

Does an agent make any warranties to third parties?

One who purports to be an agent impliedly warrants to third parties that he or she has authority to represent the principal with regard to the particular transaction. If the agent's authority does not extend to the transaction, or if he or she has no authority at all, the agent breaches the *implied warranty of authority* and is liable to the third party in damages.

An agent (real or purported) does not impliedly warrant, however, that the principal is honest or solvent, or that he or she (the principal) will perform the contract. Nor does the agent impliedly warrant that the principal has full capacity (an exception arises where the agent knows for a fact that the principal is incapacitated, and that the third party is ignorant of the fact). However, the agent does impliedly warrant that the principal is alive (not dead) and has, at least, partial capacity.

The third party's measure of damages for breach of warranty is the amount of money it will take to place the party in the position he or she would have been in had there been no breach. Thus, an agent who breaches the implied warranty of authority may escape paying damages because the purported principal is insolvent and incapable of performing: even if the "agent" had authority, the third party would be in no better position—remember, the agent does not warrant the principal's solvency.

What is ratification?

Sometimes, an agent exceeds his or her authority and attempts to bind a principal to a contract that is clearly unauthorized. Less often, a person who is not an agent at all purports to bind a "principal" to a contract. Though, in each case, the "agent" clearly has no authority to bind the "principal", the principal may still be bound on the basis of *ratification*. Ratification means acceptance, express or implied, of the contract. It comes into play *only where no authority of any kind— real or apparent—can be found with regard to the particular transaction* (where there is authority, the principal is bound because of the authority, and it is incorrect to talk of ratification).

Ratification is an "all or nothing" proposition. A purported principal is not free to ratify portions of a contract and reject the rest. He or she must accept the entire contract or none of it. If the purported principal ratifies, he or she becomes bound on the contract, and acquires full rights to enforce the agreement against the third party. The effect of ratification is to treat the transaction as though the agent had authority from the outset (the purported agent is thus off the hook insofar as the implied warranty of authority is concerned).

Ratification is possible, however, only where the purported agent was, in fact, attempting to contract on the purported principal's behalf. If the agent was actually trying to contract on his or her own behalf, the principal cannot ratify (remember, offers are not assignable— one person may not accept another's offer by purporting to be a "principal"). For the same reason, an undisclosed principal can never ratify a contract. The law says

that it is simply going too far to state, first, that an undisclosed agency relationship exists; second, that the agent had no authority to bind the undisclosed principal with regard to the particular transaction; and, third, and on top of it all, that the undisclosed principal has ratified the unauthorized contract.

Generally speaking, ratification occurs in one of two ways:

1. *The principal wants to ratify the contract and does so either expressly or by implication.* The purported principal may like the terms of the unauthorized contract and want to ratify it. Upon learning of the contract, the purported principal is in the position of an offeree, with the third party as the offeror. (As you will recall from Ch. 7, an offeree is the party to whom an offer is made.) Like any other offeree, the purported principal has a reasonable time to either accept or reject the offer; however, up until the moment of acceptance, the third party may revoke the offer. Suppose, for example, that Tom Parker, without real or apparent authority of any kind, contracts to purchase a truck for $12,500, purportedly on behalf of Ray Chamberlain. Clearly, Ray has not authorized Tom to make the purchase and is not bound by the contract. Nevertheless, upon learning of the purchase, Ray is in the position of an offeree—he may either accept or reject the offer. If Ray accepts the offer (i. e., "ratifies" the contract), he will be bound just as though he had authorized the purchase from the outset. And Tom will be off the hook insofar as the implied warranty of authority is concerned. If Ray rejects the offer, or if the dealer revokes the offer before Ray accepts,[7] the dealer's only remedy is against the purported agent Tom on the basis of breach of the implied warranty of authority.

7. And all the rules studied in Chapters 7 and 8 are applicable, including the "deposited acceptance" rule, counteroffers, inquiries, factors preventing mutual assent, etc.

A purported principal who wants to ratify may do so expressly (by giving oral or written notice to the third party) or impliedly by conduct (e. g., by retaining and using the subject matter of the contract or otherwise accepting the contract benefits).

2. *The principal does not want to ratify the contract but has done something resulting in ratification.* It happens far more often that the purported principal wants to escape liability on the contract but is estopped (prevented) from denying the agent's authority. Typically, this occurs where the principal has accepted some benefit from the contract without immediately informing the third party of the purported agent's lack of authority. Thus, where the purported principal accepts delivery of the subject matter of the contract and retains and uses it for a period of time, the principal will be held to have ratified the contract by his or her conduct.

Returning to our previous example, if Ray Chamberlain accepts delivery of the truck and uses it for three or four weeks, Ray will be deemed to have ratified the contract and will be estopped from denying that Tom had authority. Another example is found in Wilkins v. Waldo Lumber Co., 130 Me. 5, 153 A. 191 (1931). In that case, a party purporting to be an agent for a lumber company (but clearly lacking any real or apparent authority from the company) entered into a contract to buy standing timber from a third party. On learning of the contract, the lumber company not only contracted to sell part of the timber to another party, but actually milled some of the timber into lumber and delivered it to the party. The lumber company then tried to get out of the original contract on the grounds that the purported agent had no authority to contract on the company's behalf. Understandably, the court held that the lumber company had, by its con-

duct, ratified the contract and was bound by its terms.

It follows from the rule that ratification must be all or nothing that there can be no ratification unless the purported principal has full knowledge of all facts relevant to the contract. This goes back to Ch. 7 where it was stated.

It says:

The requirement of mutual assent is part and parcel of the twofold purpose of the law of contracts: (1) *not* to hold parties to their promises or agreements in the absence of evidence that the parties truly intended or agreed to be bound; and (2) *to* ensure that parties who make promises and enter into agreements, desiring to be bound, are met with their reasonable expectations. This is an important purpose, for parties should not be bound to unintended promises, or promises they were forced to make, or promises that arose out of a mutual mistake about the facts of the situation; and, yet, parties should be obliged to follow through on intended agreements or promises so that the reasonable expectations of the party or parties relying upon the promised performance can be met. The notion that parties should be bound only to their intended agreements and promises is the underlying reason for the many rules regarding the formation of mutual assent.

––––––––

The principle of ratification rests upon the same premise. A purported principal who, with full knowledge of the facts, expressly or impliedly ratifies the contract should be bound though the purported agent had no authority at the time of contracting. At the same time, if the purported principal lacks full knowledge of the facts, he or she should not be bound even though he or she has ostensibly approved the contract. Without full knowledge, ratification is impossible.

For example, suppose that Ray Chamberlain knows that Tom Parker has, without authority, contracted to purchase a truck on his behalf. What Ray does not know is that Tom has promised the dealer (as part of the contract) that Ray will use the truck for one year, then trade it in to the dealer for a new truck for an additional $5,000. Ray accepts delivery of the truck and uses it for three weeks. Ray has not ratified the contract. (Of course, equitable considerations will not permit the unjust enrichment of Ray who has received a benefit in retaining and using the truck. At the least—and most likely—the courts will order Ray to pay the dealer a fair amount for his use of the truck; at most, the courts will find ratification and simply hold invalid the "one year, trade-in and purchase provision".)

How is the agency relationship terminated?

The agency relationship, which is created through the consent of the principal, may be terminated in one of two ways: (1) by operation of law; or (2) by act of the parties.

Termination by operation of law. The principal-agent relationship automatically and instantly ends by operation of law when any of the following occurs:

(1) *The death of the principal or agent.* The agent's authority automatically terminates by operation of law upon the principal's death; the deceased principal's personal representative (see Ch. 30) is responsible for carrying on the principal's business affairs after death. The agent's authority also ends instantly upon the agent's death; it does not pass to the agent's heirs or personal representative.

(2) *The insanity of the principal or agent.* The agency relationship also terminates instantly by operation of law at any time either party—principal or agent —is formally adjudged insane by a court of law. If the principal becomes insane but has not been declared so by a court, the principal's contracts (including those entered into by the agent) are voidable, the principal lacking capacity to contract. And remember, the agent does not warrant the principal's capacity. The agent is liable for failing to inform the third party of the principal's incapacity only where the agent knows for a fact that the principal is incapacitated, and that the third party has no knowledge of the incapacity.

While the agent himself or herself need not have capacity to contract in order to contract on behalf of the principal, the agent cannot be so bereft of mind as to be incompetent to do the act required of the agency. Where the agent becomes so bereft of mind, the agency terminates by operation of law.

(3) *Bankruptcy of the principal or agent.* Similarly, the agency terminates automatically and instantly at any time bankruptcy proceedings begin for either principal or agent. With the commencement of such proceedings, the bankrupt's assets are turned over to the trustee in bankruptcy who is authorized to look after the bankrupt's affairs (see Ch. 26 on "bankruptcy").

(4) *War between the countries of the principal and agent.* In nearly all cases where the principal and agent are residents or nationals of different countries, the outbreak of war between the two countries makes it impossible or illegal for the agency relationship to continue; the agency terminates by operation of law.

(5) *Destruction of the subject matter of the agency.* If the agency pertains to specific property, and the property is lost or destroyed, the agency terminates as a matter of necessity.

Termination by act of the parties.
The parties may themselves terminate the agency relationship as follows:

(1) *The original agreement may provide for a fixed term of agency or for termination upon the happening of a certain event.* The parties being free to contract, they may provide in their original agreement (assuming they have one) that the agency relationship will terminate in one year, in 18 months, at the end of the "fishing season", etc.

(2) *Accomplishment of the object of the agency.* Where the agent is authorized to do a particular thing—e. g., to sell a car—the agency will end when the task is accomplished.

(3) *Mutual assent of both parties.* The parties may at any time mutually agree to end the relationship.

(4) *Renunciation by the agent.* The agent may teminate the agency relationship at any time by giving oral or written notice of termination to the principal. Of course, if the agency is contractual in nature, the agent's renunciation may constitute a breach of contract, allowing the principal to bring an action for damages against the agent.

(5) *Revocation of authority by the principal.* Conversely, the principal may at any time revoke the agent's authority. Again, if the agency is contractual, the revocation may constitute a breach of contract, allowing the agent to sue the principal for money damages.

When is notice required to prevent an agent from continuing to bind the principal in contract following termination of the agency relationship?

Where a disclosed, general agency is terminated *by the act of the parties,* the general agent continues to have apparent authority to bind the principal in contract unless and until notice of termination is given to third parties. Remember, a general agent is one who is authorized to contract for a principal with regard to more than a single transaction and/or for a continuing period of time; a special agent is one authorized to conduct but a single transaction not involving any continuity of service.

Notice is required in the case of a general agent (and not a special agent) because a general agent is likely to establish a pattern or course of dealing with third parties. Absent notice that the principal has fired the agent or that the agent has quit the agency, etc., the third parties have no reason to suspect that the agent's authority has been terminated. Thus, the law operates to protect the third parties at the expense of the principal who fails to give notice. For example, say that Ray Chamberlain has employed the same traveling salesman for five years. The salesman has regularly covered a three-state area, dealing with a sizeable number of steady customers. It makes sense that if Ray fires the salesman, he had better notify the salesman's customers that the agency relationship has come to an end. If Ray does not, the salesman will continue to have apparent authority to bind Ray in contract.

The required notice consists of the following:

(1) Individual notice to each of the agent's steady customers (their names and addresses will be found in Ray Chamberlain's books of record); and

(2) Public notice of termination of the agency (typically, the notice is placed in a local newspaper, but any reasonable method of giving public notice will do).

Additionally, the principal must make a reasonable effort to recover from the agent any company stationery, forms, business cards, etc., that would indicate a continuing authority on the part of the agent to contract in the principal's behalf (a failure to recover such items may give rise to apparent authority in the agent).

To summarize, notice to third parties is required only where a *disclosed, general* agency is terminated *by act of the parties.* Notice is not required where the agency is undisclosed (an undisclosed agent, even where general, establishes no pattern or course of dealing on behalf of a principal); where the agent is special as opposed to general; or where the agency is terminated by operation of law (e. g., the death, insanity, or bankruptcy of the principal or agent).

Is an agent's authority ever irrevocable?

Only one type of agency authority cannot be revoked—"an agency power coupled with an interest" (sometimes called "an agency coupled with security"). Here, the agency power is given to the agent to enable him or her to protect an interest that is separate from the subject of the agency. Typically, the interest stems from some prior relationship or dealings between the principal and agent. For example, the agent may have advanced or loaned money to the principal some months prior to the agency—the agent's "interest", here, is repayment of the money. Or the agent may have performed work for the principal at a prior date—the agent's "interest" being compensation for the work performed. The principal gives the agent an unrelated agency power (e. g., authority to sell the principal's house or car) so that the agent can protect his or her interest (i. e., collect payment of the monies owing). Because the agency is coupled with an interest, the principal cannot revoke it, and it will not terminate even upon the death, insanity, or bankruptcy of the principal or agent.

A good example of an agency coupled with an interest is found in Chrysler Corp. v. Blozic, 267 Mich. 479, 255 N. W. 399 (1934). There, a hospitalized and dying principal had only life insurance proceeds with which to pay his hospital bill. Before he died, the principal authorized the hospital to collect the insurance money and apply it to his bill. Of course, in the ordinary agency situation, the agency would terminate by operation of law upon the principal's death. Here, however, the agency was coupled with an interest (the hospital's right to payment of the bill) and was not revoked by the death of the principal. The hospital needed the agency power to secure payment of the bill.

An agency coupled with an interest must be distinguished from the situation where an agent is to be paid a commission for doing the work of the agency. Obviously, the agent has an "interest" in receiving his or her commission. But it is not an interest separate from the subject of the agency, and the agency is not one coupled with an interest (i. e., the agency is not irrevocable).

CASES

CASE 1—*Is an "Authorized Ford Dealer" an agent of Ford Motor Company?*

WASHINGTON v. COURTESY MOTOR SALES, INC.

Appellate Court of Illinois, First District, First Division, 1964.
48 Ill.App.2d 380, 199 N.E.2d 263.

MURPHY, Presiding Justice.

This is an action of fraud and deceit. * * *

In substance, the fraud alleged is that while plaintiff negotiated and paid for a new car, the automobile which was delivered to her had been previously used, and its speedometer had been set back. Charging fraud and deceit in the sale, plaintiff seeks damages totaling $50,018—being $1,018 compensatory and $49,000 exemplary.

The determinative question is whether the amended complaint alleges sufficient facts in law to support plaintiff's allegation that, for the purpose of selling a new Ford automobile to plaintiff, defendant Courtesy Motor Sales was an agent of the defendant Ford Motor Company.

The amended complaint alleges that defendant Courtesy is a "duly authorized franchised dealer for selling and distributing the products of Defendant, Ford Motor Company" and "acting as a franchised agent of the Ford Motor Company * * * executed a contract of sale and purchase with the Plaintiff on Courtesy Motor Sales New Car Division order blanks. * * * upon delivery of the automobile, Ford Motor Company, by and through its franchised agent, Courtesy Motor Sales, warranted the 1962 Ford Fairlane * * * to be new by giving Plaintiff a New Car Warranty."

Plaintiff contends that the allegations of a principal-agent relationship between defendants, the admission of an agreement between defendants ("the terms and provisions of which agreement are unknown to the Plaintiff"), and "the delivery to the Plaintiff of new car warranties of the Ford Motor Company by Courtesy Motor Sales, its franchised dealer," meet the test for a complaint against defendant Ford sufficient in law within the limits outlined in City of Evanston v. Piotrowicz, 20 Ill.2d 512, at p. 518, 170 N.E.2d 569, at p. 573 (1960):

> "Agency may be established and its nature and extent shown by parol evidence, whether direct or circumstantial, and reference may be had to the situations of parties and property, acts of parties, and other circumstances germane to the question, and if the evidence shows one acting for another under circumstances implying knowledge on the part of the supposed principal of such acts, a *prima facie* case of agency is established."

Of the exhibits attached to the amended complaint, plaintiff contends that Exhibits "D" and "E" meet the foregoing agency test as to defendant Ford. Exhibit "D" is a printed form, headed in bold type with: "This is your Ford Dealer's NEW CAR WARRANTY," and opens with the statement: "Ford Motor Company has warranted to the Dealer who, pursuant to his sales agreement with the Company, hereby, on his own behalf, warrants to the Purchaser each part of this 1962 Ford Fairlane to be free under normal use and service from defects in material and workmanship * * *." All other references are to "the Dealer" or "any Authorized Ford Dealer." Exhibit "E" is a series of blank service coupons, each of which is headed in bold type: "NEW CAR WARRANTY SERVICE ACKNOWLEDGMENT COUPON." The terms refer to "your Ford Dealer's New Car Warranty * * * the selling dealer * * * any Authorized Ford Dealer * * *."

     * * *

We think it is a matter of common knowledge that the term "Authorized Ford Dealer" is in the nature of a trade-mark sign, which is used by independent dealers and means nothing more than a dealer who sells products which have a trade name carrying substantial good will. As stated in Westerdale v. Kaiser-Frazer Corp., 6 N.J. 571, 80 A.2d 91, 94 (1951):

> "Nor does the fact that when a sale is made by a dealer to the ultimate purchaser a manufacturer's warranty goes with the auto-

mobile spell out the dealer as the agent of the manufacturer. It is merely incidental to the sale and in no wise by itself gives apparent authority or agency to the dealer. * * * The owner's service policy simply provided that defective material or workmanship would be replaced free by an authorized Frazer dealer or distributor without charge. This was an undertaking of the distributor, not the Kaiser-Frazer Corporation, and spelled out no agency existing between them."

We conclude that * * * plaintiff has failed to allege facts to show in law that an "authorized" or "franchised" dealer, in the sale of a new car, is an agent of the manufacturer rather than an independent merchant.

CASE 2—*Appellant's wife had neither express nor implied authority to draw on her husband's trading account.*

TAYLOR v. MERRILL LYNCH, PIERCE, FENNER & SMITH, INC.

District of Columbia Court of Appeals, 1968.
245 A.2d 426.

MYERS, Associate Judge.

Appellee is a securities dealer with whom appellant kept a trading account, in his name only. Appellant's estranged wife, residing in the state of Washington, who was not authorized to draw on the account, wrote to appellee saying that an emergency had arisen and asked to withdraw $1,000.00. At that time the account contained a balance of $1,072.14. Appellee drew a check for $1,000.00, payable to appellant, mailed it to his wife at her residence, and debited appellant's account. Apparently the wife signed appellant's name as endorser and cashed the check. Upon learning of the withdrawal, appellant filed suit alleging that appellee owed him $1,072.14. Appellee answered and admitted owing $72.14, but argued that it had paid $1,000.00. From a trial finding in appellee's favor, the present appeal is taken. The only question before us is whether, as a matter of law, the established facts make out the affirmative defense of payment.

Generally, payment of a debt so as to extinguish it may be made only to the creditor or to someone to whom the creditor directs payment to be made. One making payment to an agent has the burden of showing that the latter had express or apparent authority to receive such payment on behalf of a creditor. * * *

In the instant case, it is not contended that appellant's wife had either express or implied authority to draw on her husband's trading account. The only question is whether making the check payable to appellant under the present circumstances constituted payment to him. We hold that it did not.

Appellee drew the check on the instructions of a person who had no authority to give that instruction. In addition, appellee mailed the check to appellant's wife at an address different from the address at which it had been corresponding with appellant. Furthermore, appellee did not inform appellant of its action, and it was not until appellant received a periodic statement that he was apprised of the withdrawal. Under the circumstances, we are of the opinion that appellee's actions do not amount to payment, despite its issuance of the check payable to appellant.

Reversed with directions to enter judgment for appellant in the amount of $1,072.14.

CASE 3—*If there was no authority, was there ratification?*

STUDLEY, INC. v. GULF OIL CORP.

United States District Court, S.D. New York, 1968.
282 F.Supp. 748.

OPINION

POLLACK, District Judge.

Gulf Oil Corp. leased space in the Sperry Rand Building in New York City for a ten year period with renewal options. It was represented in the negotiations for the lease by the brokerage firm of Cushman & Wakefield to where the landlord has paid brokerage commissions.

The plaintiff in this case, a real estate brokerage firm, asserted that it was improperly deprived of a brokerage commission on the lease by the misconduct of Gulf Oil Corp. and brought suit against Gulf Oil Corp. for damages.

This case was submitted to a jury together with special questions and it rendered a verdict in favor of the plaintiff for $25,000. The defendant, Gulf Oil Corp. has moved to set the damage verdict aside * * *.

* * *

The plaintiff's * * *

* * * claim—for breach of contract—was that the defendant employed the plaintiff as its real estate agent to locate office space for it in New York City with the understanding that, if the plaintiff procured an acceptable lease for it, "defendant would enter into a lease * * * and * * * plaintiff would be the broker in the transaction", and thereby become eligible for payment of a commission by the owner of the property or the landlord.

The plaintiff alleged that the contract with it was made by one Burkhiser, the director of defendant's department of General Services stationed in Pittsburgh, Pennsylvania.

The plaintiff further contended that if Burkhiser was not authorized either actually or apparently to commit the defendant to the alleged agreement made on its behalf, the defendant had ratified the agreement by accepting the services of the plaintiff with full knowledge of the alleged agreement.

The plaintiff contended that the defendant breached the agreement by failing to act in good faith and by failing to designate the plaintiff as broker upon entering into a lease with the landlord, Rock-Uris and by failing to advise Rock-Uris of the plaintiff's role in the transaction resulting in a lease of space in the Sperry Rand Building. The plaintiff claimed that it would have received a commission from Rock-Uris, but for Gulf's breach and sought as damages the amount of the compensation it would have earned.

* * *

With respect to the * * * claim the case was submitted to the jury on the following special questions:

1. "Did Gulf authorize Burkhiser to enter into an agreement with Studley binding it to represent to Rock-Uris that Studley was responsible for the lease to Gulf in the Sperry Rand Building?"

The jury's answer to this first question was "No".

2. *"Did Gulf ratify with knowledge thereof any arrangements made by Burkhiser with Studley pertaining to the lease to Gulf in the Sperry Rand Building?"*

3. "Did Gulf breach any agreement with Studley made with Gulf's authority or ratified by it with knowledge thereof?"

The jury answered each of the second and third questions "Yes".

6. "To what award, if any, is plaintiff entitled from Gulf?"

The jury's answer to the sixth question was "$25,000."

The defendant contends that there is no evidence whatsoever in the record of a ratification of the unauthorized arrangement made by Burkhiser.

* * *

Consideration of the question raised is aided by a brief review of the facts including the scope and nature of the services rendered by Studley.

In September, 1962 Gulf Oil Corp. was seeking office space in New York City. In response to a request by Burkhiser, Studley furnished Burkhiser with a list of buildings in the Rockefeller Center area in which there was space for rent; the list gave the rentals being requested. The data identified buildings that were completed or in the process of construction and nearing completion. One of the buildings included in Studley's list was the Sperry Rand Building at 1290 Avenue of the Americas, which was nearing completion.

The data supplied by Studley was essentially the information circulated publicly by renting agents of the buildings involved. None of the data involved any special or confidential information; it was all of the type which building owners and their renting agents circulate generally to lists of brokers and to business organizations generally or to those known to be interested in leasing commercial space. In addition to furnishing such a list Studley walked with Burkhiser to inspect the Pan American Building at 200 Park Avenue which was then completed and walked to the site of the Sperry Rand Building which was still in process of construction. There also were telephone calls between Studley and Burkhiser which kept the contact alive during the ensuing weeks.

Unknown to Burkhiser, a senior officer of the defendant stationed in its New York Office, one Cadman, had independently been negotiating for space through another broker, Cushman & Wakefield. The existing lease which the defendant had on space in Canada House was about to terminate; either it had to be renewed by October 31, 1962 or other space procured. Cushman & Wakefield were the renting agents for Canada House and were also the renting agents for the Sperry Rand Building. Although the emphasis was on attempting to work out a renewal of the space arrangement at Canada House, according to defendant, Cushman & Wakefield had, prior to Burkhiser's contacts with Studley, already called to the attention of Mr. Cadman the Sperry Rand Building and the possibilities of acquiring space therein for the defendant.

The defendant's determination to move its quarters crystallized at a meeting of Gulf Oil executives in Florida during the week of October 22, 1962. Shortly before that date or during that week Mr. Cadman notified Cushman & Wakefield that it desired to proceed actively with the consideration of space in the Sperry Rand Building.

*   *   *

Thereafter, on October 30, 1962, a meeting was called in Mr. Cadman's office in New York attended by a representative of Cushman & Wakefield and by the technical staff of the defendant whose function it was to plan the specifications and layout and furnishing of space rented by the defendant. Included in the latter group was Burkhiser, who as the director of General Services Administration, was concerned with such problems.

It was at this meeting of October 30, 1962 that Burkhiser made the first disclosure to Cadman of his arrangements with Studley which the jury has stamped as forming an unauthorized contract. *   *   *

Mr. Cadman then told Burkhiser that he agreed to go along with Cushman & Wakefield because he believed that Gulf was exposed first by Cushman & Wakefield to the Sperry Rand Building.

*   *   *

No act or statement of the defendant or any authorized person on its behalf thereafter gives any indication that the defendant adopted or made use of any of the services rendered by Studley or recognized or intended to recognize or adopt the unauthorized arrangements as obligations of the defendant. Due to the generality of the services it cannot be said realistically that Gulf *thereafter* utilized Studley's services or reports, or derived benefits therefrom.

In the ensuing weeks, Studley did not attempt to or speak with any authorized officer of Gulf and Gulf gave no indication to Studley of any intention or willingness to adopt its services or any obligation for its services or any obligation to request the landlord to consider or recognize Studley as the representative of Gulf in the matter of the lease of space in the Sperry Rand Building.

The plaintiff has failed to point to any evidence of ratification on which to impose an obligation on Gulf herein. *   *   *

*   *   *

"Ratification is a form of subsequent authorization and is based upon the principle of approval with knowledge of the facts to be ratified. If a principal with such knowledge that there is an agreement outstanding and with knowledge of what that agreement is then accepts the benefits of an agent's action, the principal is responsible for agreement of the agent whether originally authorized or not." *   *   *

" *   *   * ratification is the affirmance by a principal of a prior act or commitment which does not bind him but which was done or professedly done on his account, and the ratification occurs when the principal learns of the commitment and then affirmatively elects to adopt it as if originally authorized by him."

*   *   *

Thus, ratification exists upon the concurrence of three elements: (1) acceptance by the principal of the benefits of the agent's act, (2) with full knowledge of the facts, and (3) circumstances or an affirmative election indicating an intention to adopt the unauthorized arrangement.

The knowledge required of the principal must be full and complete. If the principal's knowledge of the facts is partial or imperfect he will not be held to have ratified the unauthorized act, and the proof of adequate knowledge should be reasonably clear and certain.

The affirmative election to adopt must be evidenced by either express or implied intention to adopt.

"A ratification of the unauthorized act of an agent or of a stranger who claims to act as such, if it exists, must be found in the intention of the principal, either express or implied. If that intention cannot be shown, no ratification can be held to have been established. * * * Where one who has assumed to act as an agent for another has no authority to do so, but is a mere volunteer, a failure to disavow his acts will not amount to a ratification, unless under such circumstances as indicate an intention to do so."
* * *

The earliest occasion which presents any possibility of knowledge of the contract on the part of Gulf was the October 30 meeting between Cadman * * * and Burkhiser. * * * There was no evidence that Cadman either acknowledged Burkhiser's authority or adopted the alleged contract with Studley for Gulf. Indeed, it would be unreasonable for the triers of fact to find and conclude that Cadman at one and the same time intended to ratify the alleged contract for Gulf and yet sought to have the commission paid to another broker. * * *

The evidence adequately supports the jury's finding on the first special question, that Burkhiser's arrangement with Studley lacked authority. However, there is no support for the finding of a ratification.

There is only one reasonable conclusion with respect to the question of ratification, which conclusion is reached without weighing the credibility of the evidence. There is a total absence of evidence on which to find ratification expressly or by implication, or of an intent to ratify, or of an election to adopt the unauthorized arrangement, or of a ratification by estoppel.

Plaintiff, having failed to establish the alleged contract, is not entitled to the award of damages.

The jury's findings of a ratification and a breach of a ratified but unauthorized contract and its damage verdict in plaintiff's favor are set aside; * * *.

So ordered.

CASE 4—*The company clothed Mrs. Chaffee with the attributes of agency enabling her to sell without arousing the defendant's suspicions.*

CALIFORNIA LIFE INS. CO. v. MULTNOMAH COUNTY SCHOOL DIST.

#40, Civil No. 63–130, Memorandum Opinion, Oct. 27, 1964.

SOLOMON, Judge.

Plaintiff, the California Life Insurance Company, issues policies that insure schools and school districts against loss or damage resulting from injury to students and faculty while engaged in various school activities. The company sells its insurance through general agents, one of whom was National Scholastic Underwriters, Inc. (National). This controversy concerns the sale of insurance to the defendant, Multnomah County School District (School District), by an employee of National, Sara Ann Chaffee, a duly authorized representative of the Company and licensed to sell insurance by the State of Oregon. Mrs. Chaffee issued a policy to the School District for the 1962–63 school year containing altered endorsements to which the Company contends it never consented. The Company brings this action to have the altered endorsements declared void.

Mrs. Chaffee, as an agent for the company, wrote a policy for the School District for the 1962–1963 year which contained substantially the same coverage as the 1961–62 policy, which she had also written. The Company claims that it notified Mrs. Chaffee that she could not write any policies for the 1962–1963 period, but the School District was not notified of that fact, and she was permitted to retain supplies containing policy forms and endorsements. The School District purchased its insurance from Mrs. Chaffee, unaware of her lack of authority.

Where the authority of an insurance agent is terminated, it is the duty of the insurance company to notify those who are dealing with this person of such termination. If the insureds continued to deal with such person as an agent, not knowing of the termination, the company will be bound by his acts. * * *

Here the company terminated Mrs. Chaffee's authority to write policies some six months prior to her having written the 1962–1963 policy. Defendant was not notified of the termination and was unaware of it. In addition, the Company, by permitting Mrs. Chaffee to retain all the supplies, clothed her with the attributes of agency and enabled her to sell these policies without arousing the defendant's suspicions. * * *

Judgment is for the defendant.

PROBLEMS

1. Answer the following "True" or "False" and give reasons for your answers:

   (a) A contract is required to establish an agency relationship.

   (b) An agent must have capacity to contract.

   (c) An agent who is authorized to negotiate a loan of money to a third party generally has apparent authority to collect payment of both loan principal and interest.

   (d) Marriage in and of itself does not establish any agency relationship between the spouses.

   (e) An undisclosed principal has no right or ability to enforce a contract that is personal in nature.

   (f) To ratify a contract, a purported principal must have full knowledge of all facts relevant to the contract.

   (g) There is no such thing as an irrevocable agency.

   (h) An agent who is authorized to sell property for a principal may generally purchase the property for himself or herself.

   (i) An agent's authority to sell land must be put into writing.

   (j) Consent is the basis of authority.

   (k) A real estate broker or dealer is generally not an agent at all.

(*l*) A principal has a duty to indemnify the agent for any expenses incurred in carrying out the agency duties.

(m) Apparent authority is based on the subjective theory of contracts.

(n) In an emergency situation demanding immediate action, an agent may deviate from the principal's instructions to the extent reasonably necessary to protect the principal's interests.

(*o*) An agent impliedly warrants that his or her principal is solvent.

(p) An agent impliedly warrants that he or she has authority to contract on behalf of the principal.

(q) If an agency pertains to specific property, and the property is lost or destroyed, the agency terminates as a matter of necessity.

2. Sullivan Products hires Molly Taylor to act as its traveling salesperson in the small and sparsely populated Harrow County. Molly travels from "door to door" taking orders for goods; she carries only samples with her (the company sends the goods later by company truck). Without informing Sullivan Products, Molly also agrees to sell goods in Harrow County for Wyler Products; Wyler's goods directly compete with those of the Sullivan Company. One day, while traveling through Harrow County, Molly persuades Nancy Homer to purchase a Sullivan food processor. To obtain the order, Molly falsely tells Nancy that the processor is manufactured by Hytone, Inc. (a highly respected producer of good quality products) and simply sold under the Sullivan label. The processor is actually manufactured by the Sullivan Company. The same day, Molly sells an electric meat slicer to Harvey Mix who knows that the product is manufactured by Sullivan Products. Molly accepts Harvey's $150 check as payment for the meat slicer. Molly cashes the check and pockets the proceeds. She then delegates her sales duties for the Sullivan Company to Harry Owen and skips town.

(a) Was Molly within her rights in agreeing to represent Wyler Products? Explain.

(b) Who, if anyone, can Nancy hold liable for Molly's false assertion about the food processor? Explain.

(c) Sullivan Products delivers a meat slicer to Harvey Mix and demands payment of $150. In a suit by the Company against Harvey to recover payment, who will prevail? Explain.

(d) Did Molly have authority to delegate her sales duties to Harry Owen? Explain.

3. An agency relationship

   a. Must be in writing if it is to be legally enforceable.

   b. Creates a fiduciary duty on the principal's part.

   c. Can be created by estoppel, i. e., implied as a matter of law.

   d. Is normally delegatable as a matter of law.

   [# 28, May 1975 CPA Exam]

4. The ratification doctrine

   a. Is not applicable to situations where the party claiming to act as the agent for another has *no* express or implied authority to do so.

   b. Is designed to apply to situations where the principal was originally incompetent to have made the contract himself, but who, upon becoming competent, ratifies.

    c. Requires the principal to ratify the entire act of the agent and the ratification is retroactive.

    d. Applies only if the principal expressly ratifies in writing the contract made on his behalf within a reasonable time.

    [# 30, May 1975 CPA Exam]

5. An agent for an undisclosed principal

    a. Has less express authority than would be the case if he were acting as an agent for a disclosed principal.

    b. Has liability on a contract he made with a third party, if the third party elects to hold him liable thereon.

    c. Must derive whatever authority he may have from a written power of attorney.

    d. Must disclose his principal's identity prior to performance.

    [# 10, November 1974 CPA Exam]

6. An agent's power to bind his principal to a contract is generally terminated

    a. Automatically upon the commission of a tort by the agent.

    b. Instantly upon the death of the principal.

                   *   *   *

    d. Without further action by the principal upon the resignation of the agent.

    [# 11, November 1974 CPA Exam]

7. The ratification doctrine with respect to principal and agent

    a. Does *not* apply to real estate contracts.

    b. Requires that a written notice of ratification be sent to the third party and the agent in order to create an enforceable contract.

    c. Does *not* apply to torts committed by the agent.

    d. Requires that the agent or purported agent indicates to the third party that he is acting for and on behalf of the person subsequently ratifying.

    [# 16, November 1975 CPA Exam]

8. Winter is a sales agent for Magnum Enterprises. Winter has assumed an obligation to indemnify Magnum if any of Winter's customers fail to pay. Under these circumstances, which of the following is correct?

    a. Winter's engagement must be in writing regardless of its duration.

    b. Upon default Magnum must first proceed against the delinquent purchaser-debtor.

    c. The above facts describe a del credere agency relationship and Winter will be liable in the event his customers fail to pay Magnum.

    d. There is *no* fiduciary relationship on either Winter's or Magnum's part.

    [# 4, May 1978 CPA Exam]

9. Under which of the following circumstances will an agent acting on behalf of a disclosed principal *not* be liable to a third party for his actions?

    a. He signs a negotiable instrument in his own name and does *not* indicate his agency capacity.

b. He commits a tort in the course of discharging his duties.

c. He is acting for a non-existent principal which subsequently comes into existence after the time of the agent's actions on the principal's behalf.

d. He lacks specific express authority but is acting within the scope of his implied authority.

[# 29, November 1976 CPA Exam]

10. In examining the financial statements of Plover Corporation, you learn that Plover hired Amber to manage its farm and gave him authority to purchase seed up to a maximum of $500 per year. Amber was also given authority to hire employees to help operate the farm. Plover also gave Amber authority to buy for Plover a forty-acre tract, adjacent to the farm, if it became available, and to collect the monthly rental of a house located on the farm.

     Amber purchased seed from Supplee as authorized but exceeded his authority by contracting in Plover's name with Supplee for fertilizer in the amount of $600. Amber hired Mans to operate a farm tractor. While operating the tractor in a negligent manner, Mans destroyed a boundary fence belonging to Naybor. Meanwhile, Amber had entered into a contract to purchase the forty acres from Honer, its owner, without revealing that he was purchasing for Plover.

     Plover, on learning of the Mans incident, discharged Amber. Amber, who had been collecting the rents on the house, promptly collected the rent then due for the current month from the lessee and disappeared. The lessee did not know of Amber's discharge.

Required: 1. Discuss Plover's liability to Supplee on the order for fertilizer.

           2. To what extent, if any, is Plover liable to Naybor for Mans' actions?

           3. What are Plover's rights under the agreement for the forty acres?

           4. Discuss Plover's liability on the contract for the purchase of the land if it wishes to avoid the obligations.

           5. Discuss Plover's rights to recover from the tenant of the house for the last rental payment made to Amber.

[# 6.a., May 1974 CPA Exam]

Chapter 22

THE FIRST TWO METHODS OF DOING BUSINESS:
THE SOLE PROPRIETORSHIP AND
THE PARTNERSHIP

What does it mean "to do business"?

Interestingly, *Black's Law Dictionary* begins its definition of "business" with these words.

It says:

> The term "business" has no definite or legal meaning.[1]

Yet we call this text "a complete *business law text*", and all of us talk about "doing *business*", being in *business*, dealing with *business people*, and taking *business* courses in college. A doctor, lawyer, or CPA might refer to his or her practice as his or her *business*. The owner of a service station, TV repair shop, variety store, or grocery store might designate the operation his or her business. Even an employee might refer to his or her occupation as his or her business (e. g., a chef might describe himself or herself as being in the "restaurant business").

Thus, while the term "business" may have no "definite" or "legal" meaning, it is a word of very common usage. All of the above examples are proper uses of the term. *Black's Law Dictionary* continues its definition, stating.

> The term [business] may mean or embrace:
>
> * * * commercial or industrial establishment or enterprise * * *; employment, occupation, or profession engaged in for gain or livelihood * * *; enterprise in which person engaged shows willingness to invest time and capital on future outcome * * *; occasional, single, or isolated activities do not constitute business * * * labor, business and work are not synonyms.[2]

And *Webster's Student Dictionary* defines "business" as "a commercial or industrial enterprise of any kind; as, a grocery business."[3]

However, none of these definitions (and certainly not all of the examples) are narrow enough for our purpose in discussing the methods or ways of doing business. Our discussion will be restricted to those who are the *owners* of the business enterprise. Only those who actually own the business (and therefore participate in its profits and losses) are "doing business" within our meaning. Thus, a doctor who owns and operates a medical practice is "in business". So is a plumber who owns and runs a plumbing service. The same is true of an owner of a grocery store, variety store, automobile dealership, restaurant, factory, cannery, lumber mill, insurance company, etc. And it makes no difference whether the company is a large operation doing millions of dollars worth of business annually or a small concern barely supporting a single owner or even operating at a loss.

1. Henry Campbell Black, *Black's Law Dictionary*, Revised Fourth Edition, West Publishing Co., 1968, p. 248.

2. Ibid.

3. *Webster's Student Dictionary* (American Book Co.), G. & C. Merriam Co., 1962, p. 112.

A business agent or employee, on the other hand, is not "doing business" unless, apart from his or her job, he or she owns a part of the business enterprise. Absent such an interest, an agent or employee has no concern and no "say so" about either the structure of the business or its internal operation. It is the business owners who are concerned with these things: they are interested in the possible ways of doing business, and in the legal ramifications of each method. For it is they—the owners—who must make the determination as to the form of business organization to be used.

What are the three main methods or ways of doing business?

The three main methods or ways of doing business are:

(1) A sole proprietorship;

(2) A partnership; or

(3) A corporation.

A *sole proprietorship* is a "one person" operation: one person (the "sole proprietor") owns and operates the business. Generally speaking, any kind of business may be operated as a sole proprietorship —a grocery store, hardware store, law practice, plumbing company, auto-body shop, etc.

A sole proprietorship is the least complicated form of business organization with no body of law directly governing it (i. e., there is no "sole proprietorship law" as there is contract law, tort law, negotiable instruments law, sales law, agency law, and the like). The result is that there are no formal requirements for going into business as a sole proprietor. However, a sole proprietorship, like any other form of business organization (including partnerships and corporations), is subject to regulation by city, county, state, and federal governments. For example, a sole proprietor generally has to obtain a city, county, and/or state business license in order to operate his or her business. Zoning laws (see Ch. 6) may prevent the proprietor from locating his or her business in a particular area; the proprietor's operation will be subject to environmental laws, consumer protection laws (see Appendix A), antitrust and labor laws (see Ch. 25). And if the sole proprietor hires employees or agents to work or contract for him or her, all the rules of employer-employee law and agency law will apply. (But again, all forms of business organization are subject to these rules.)

In contrast to the sole proprietorship, there is a great body of law governing the partnership method of doing business. A *partnership* is an association of two or more persons ("partners") to carry on as co-owners a business for profit. A partnership is based on a contract (written, oral, or implied) between the partners, specifying how the business is to be operated, and how the profits and losses are to be divided.

In 47 out of the 50 states, partnerships are subject to the Uniform Partnership Act (UPA).[4] The UPA was passed to codify and replace in part the extensive common law on partnership. The Act is divided as follows:

Uniform Partnership Act

Part I.   Preliminary Provisions

Part II.   Nature of Partnership

Part III.   Relations of Partners to Persons Dealing with the Partnership

Part IV.   Relations of Partners to One Another

Part V.   Property Rights of a Partner

Part VI.   Dissolution and Winding Up

Part VII.   Miscellaneous Provisions

---

4. Only Georgia, Louisiana, and Mississippi have not passed the UPA.

A sole proprietorship and a partnership have one important element in common—unlimited risk. By this is meant that, for purposes of liability, the personal assets of a sole proprietor or partner [5] are lumped together with his or her business assets. It follows that if a sole proprietor or partner incurs a large contract debt or is held liable for the negligent act of his or her employee under the doctrine of respondeat superior, every nonexempt asset (see Ch. 26) the sole proprietor or partner owns may be taken to pay the debt or to satisfy the liability judgment. Of course, to a large extent, the risks of liability can be covered by insurance (see Ch. 11). Still, the cost of insurance may be prohibitive, and the insurance coverage inadequate. For example, say that a small town druggist (a sole proprietor) is sued for 1.5 million dollars because his employee-pharmacist misfilled a prescription. The druggist's insurance coverage is far less than 1.5 million dollars; and the drugstore's total assets amount to less than $100,000. All the druggist's personal assets will be at stake in the case.

Limited liability is one of the major attractions of the corporate method of doing business. As will be explained in detail in Ch. 23, a *corporation* is an "artificial person"—i. e., a legal entity that is separate and distinct from its owners. A corporation enables its owners to limit their liability to the amount of their investment in the corporation.

As with partnerships, there is a large body of law (partly common and partly statutory) governing corporations. The Model Business Corporation Act has been passed in whole or in part by 34 states. In addition to providing limited liability, the corporate method of doing business

offers the advantages of "perpetual life" (whereas sole proprietors and partners eventually die, corporations, being "artificial" persons, are immune from death), and easy growth and expansion (capital may be raised by selling stock in the corporation).

In the remainder of this chapter, we will consider the sole proprietorship and partnership methods of doing business. In Ch. 23, we will take an indepth look at corporations.

How does a sole proprietor report his or her profits and losses for federal income tax purposes?

Again, a sole proprietorship is a "one person" operation: one person (the sole proprietor) owns and operates the business, and receives all the profits (and losses) from the business. Because of the sole proprietor's complete ownership and control, a sole proprietorship is a very popular method of doing business.

People frequently start out working as employees with the objective of saving enough money to begin a business of their own. Consider the hypothetical case of Ray Chamberlain. An All-American football player in college, Ray is drafted by a National Football League team after college and plays professional football for nearly a dozen seasons at a high salary. Ray manages to save a considerable portion of what he earns so that when he retires from football at the age of 34, he has sufficient funds to invest in a business. Ray decides to go into the sporting goods business, and returns to his home town in Oregon to find a good location for a sporting goods store. On January 1st, Ray opens a bank account in an Oregon bank in the name of "Ray Chamberlain

---

5. The single exception is for a partner who qualifies as a "limited partner" under the Uniform Limited Partnership Act. As will

be seen later in the chapter, a "limited partner" is liable only to the extent of his or her investment in the partnership.

Sports"; Ray deposits savings of $120,-000 in the account. The first balance sheet for "Ray Chamberlain Sports" looks like this:

RAY CHAMBERLAIN SPORTS

Balance Sheet

January 1, Year #1

Assets

Cash	$120,000	
Total Assets		$120,000

Liabilities and Ownership

Liabilities		$ 00.00
Ownership		
Ray Chamberlain's investment		$120,000.00
Total liabilities and ownership		$120,000.00

A balance sheet shows what a business owns ("assets") and owes ("liabilities") on a particular day. The difference between the assets and liabilities represents the book value of the business (the owner's "equity") on that day. On January 1st, Ray Chamberlain Sports has assets of $120,000 cash, and no liabilities. Ray's equity in the business on January 1st is $120,000.

On January 2nd, Ray purchases a building (and the land it is on) for use as a store for $150,000. He pays $80,000 down and signs a contract to pay the balance ($70,000) in ten annual $7,000 installments, due on December 30th each year, with interest of 8% on the unpaid balance. The same day, Ray purchases an initial inventory of sporting goods, including fishing equipment, skiing equipment, bats, gloves, balls, racquets, shoes, golf clubs, etc. The cost of the inventory is $30,000. Before the day is over, Ray moves the merchandise into the new store, and hires one employee to work for him. The business is ready to operate.

Ray's balance sheet for January 2nd looks like this:

RAY CHAMBERLAIN SPORTS

Balance Sheet

January 2, Year #1

Assets

Cash	$ 10,000.00
Inventory (merchandise available for sale)	30,000.00
Building	150,000.00
Total Assets	$190,000.00

Liabilities and Ownership

Liabilities

Balance owing on purchase of the building $ 70,000.00

Ownership

Ray Chamberlain's investment   120,000.00

Total Liabilities and Ownership $190,000.00

During the first year of operations, Ray's business records show the following transactions:

(1) Purchased additional inventory costing $82,000.00 (this figure represents the total additional inventory purchased in many transactions over the course of the year).

(2) Paid employee wages of $750.00 a month for a total of $9,000.-00.

(3) Paid advertising expenses of $2,875.00.

(4) Paid utility bills (heat, light, water) of $1,120.00.

(5) Paid insurance expenses (to protect against loss from burglary, fire, etc. as well as liability expenses for any injury happening in the store) in the amount of $1,850.00.

(6) Paid total telephone bills of $785.00.

(7) Paid accounting and legal expenses of $530.00.

(8) Paid total taxes of $2,830.00 (including social security taxes on inventory; a license tax to operate the business; real estate taxes on the land and building).

(9) On December 30th, paid the first installment of $7,000.00 on the balance of the building.

(10) Paid interest in the amount of $5,600.00 on the unpaid balance ($70,000 owing for one year at $8\% = \$5,600.$).

(11) Had total cash sales of merchandise for the year of $132,400.00 (about $11,000 a month).

(12) Each month, Ray Chamberlain took out $1,500.00 for his personal living expenses for a total of $18,000.00.

At the end of the year—on December 31st—Ray counts his inventory. He finds after pricing all the unsold sporting goods in the store, that his remaining inventory totals $34,300 in cost.

Ray has been operating as a sole proprietor for one year now. Has he made a profit? What is his cash balance? Ray's cash balance may be determined as follows:

DETERMINATION OF CASH BALANCE

Cash balance at the beginning of the year
  (taken from the January 2nd balance sheet) $ 10,000.00

Add: Total cash received from all sales
        (Transaction #11—i. e., "T #11")   132,400.00

This gives the total cash available for use
  during the year $142,400.00

How the cash was used:

Purchases of merchandise (T #1)	$ 82,000.00	
Wages paid (T #2)	9,000.00	
Advertising expenses (T #3)	2,875.00	
Utility expenses (T #4)	1,120.00	
Insurance expenses (T #5)	1,850.00	
Telephone bills (T #6)	785.00	
Accounting and legal expenses (T #7)	530.00	
Taxes paid (T #8)	2,830.00	
Interest expenses (T #10)	5,600.00	
Principal paid on purchase price of building (T #9)	7,000.00	
Monthly allotment for Ray Chamberlain's personal living expenses (T #12)	18,000.00	
total cash used during the year	$131,590.00	131,590.00
Cash balance at the end of the year		$ 10,810.00

The $10,810.00 cash balance should agree with the bank account balance Ray shows for Ray Chamberlain Sports.

However, the cash balance does not reflect the actual profits and losses of the sole proprietorship for the one year period. Some of the cash that went out during the year went out for other than actual business operations (e. g., Transactions #9 and #12).

The profits and losses must be determined in order to compute the amount of income tax and social security self-employment tax Ray owes. While we know that Ray had sales of $132,400, this figure does not represent Ray's profit: Ray obviously had to pay for the merchandise to begin with, and he incurred many expenses in running the business. To determine his profits and losses, Ray must compute the *cost of goods sold*; deduct this figure from total sales to arrive at *gross profit;* and, finally, from gross profit, subtract the operating expenses of the business to reach *net (i. e., taxable) profit.*

The *cost of goods sold* may be determined in the following manner:

DETERMINATION OF COST OF GOODS SOLD

Inventory on January 2nd (from the balance sheet of that date)	$ 30,000.00
Add to the purchases of merchandise during the year (T #1)	82,000.00
Total merchandise available for sale	$112,000.00
Subtract the cost of the merchandise that remains unsold at the end of the year (this was the value resulting when Ray took inventory on December 31st)	34,300.00
The balance gives us the cost of the merchandise actually sold during the year	$ 77,700.00

Deducting $77,700 (the cost of goods sold) from total sales of $132,400, we arrive at a *gross profit* of $54,700.

Total sales	$132,400.00
Cost of goods sold	77,700.00
Gross profit	$ 54,700.00

Ray's business operating expenses must now be subtracted from the $54,700 figure in order to reach *net profit*. All but one of the expenses are reflected in cash payments made by Ray throughout the course of the year. The exception is *depreciation* expense (depreciation being the estimated yearly decrease in value of a business asset from normal wear and tear). As you will recall, Ray purchased a building (for use as a store) at a total cost of $150,000.00. The building will not last forever; ultimately, it will wear out and have to be replaced. If profits and losses are to be expressed accurately, the depreciation or "wearing out" process must be taken into account. Depreciation is held to be an expense of doing business, and Ray may deduct from gross profit a proportionate part of the expense each year over the life of the building. Assuming the building has an estimated "life" of 30 years, ⅟30th of the cost of the building may be deducted each year (for 30 years) to determine net profit. Taking ⅟30th of the $150,000, we arrive at a depreciation deduction of $5,000 a year. Knowing this, a profit and loss statement may be prepared:

RAY CHAMBERLAIN SPORTS

Profit and Loss Statement

For the year ending December 31st

Sales		$132,400.00
Less cost of goods sold		77,700.00
Gross profit		$ 54,700.00
Less operating expenses		
Depreciation expense	$ 5,000.00	
Wages paid	9,000.00	
Advertising expense	2,875.00	
Utility expense	1,120.00	
Insurance expense	1,850.00	
Telephone bills	785.00	
Accounting and legal expense	530.00	
Taxes paid	2,830.00	
Interest expense	5,600.00	
Total expenses	$29,590.00	29,590.00
Net profit		$ 25,110.00

Ray's net profit of $25,110.00 is reflected in the following:

First,   Ray took out $18,000 for his personal living expenses $18,000.00

Second,   the cash on hand at the beginning of the year was $10,000; the cash on hand at the end of the year is $10,810—there is an increase of cash in the business in the amount of $810.00   810.00

Third,   Ray paid the first $7,000 installment on the real property contract—there is a reduction of debt in the amount of $7,000   7,000.00

Fourth,   the beginning of the year inventory was $30,000; the end of the year inventory is $34,300—Ray owns an additional $4,300 worth of assets   4,300.00

Total profit reflected $30,110.00

Fifth,   the $5,000 depreciation expense must be deducted from the total profit figure. The building, once worth $150,000.00 is now worth only $145,000—there has been a $5,000 reduction in the value of Ray's asset   5,000.00

Total net profit $25,110.00

Ray must thus compute his income and social security self-employment taxes on a net profit of $25,110.00. Ray must report and pay the taxes on or before April 15th of the coming year, using "Form 1040 U.S. Individual Income Tax Return", along with "Schedule C Profit or (Loss) from Business or Profession" and "Schedule SE Computation of Social Security Self-Employment Tax". Ray's returns would, in part, look like this:

Schedule C (Form 1040)   Page 2

SCHEDULE C-1.—Cost of Goods Sold and/or Operations
(See Schedule C Instructions for Line 2)

1 Inventory at beginning of year (if different from last year's closing inventory, attach explanation)	1	30,000 00
2 Purchases $............ Less: cost of items withdrawn for personal use $............ Balance ▶	2	82,000 00
3 Cost of labor (do not include salary paid to yourself)	3	
4 Materials and supplies	4	
5 Other costs (attach schedule)	5	
6 Add lines 1 through 5	6	112,000 00
7 Inventory at end of year	7	34,300 00
8 Cost of goods sold and/or operations (subtract line 7 from line 6). Enter here and on page 1, line 2	8	77,700 00

SCHEDULE C-2.—Depreciation (See Schedule C Instructions for Line 6)
If you need more space, use Form 4562.

a. Description of property	b. Date acquired	c. Cost or other basis	d. Depreciation allowed or allowable in prior years	e. Method of computing depreciation	f. Life or rate	g. Depreciation for this year
1 Total additional first-year depreciation (do not include in items below) ⟶						
2 Other depreciation:						
Store building	Jan 2, 19--	150,000.00	00.00	SL*	30 yrs	5,000 00

*SL stands for straight line depreciation, meaning that the cost of the asset ($150,000) is divided by the number of years of life of the asset (30 years) to determine the amount of depreciation for the year. If the asset will have any salvage value at the end of its life, this amount must be deducted from the cost before dividing by the number of years of life. We have assumed no salvage value in this case. (It should be noted that there are other methods of depreciation allowing the cost of the asset to be deducted at a faster rate--these methods are permitted for certain assets only in limited situations.)

Total depreciation for the year

3 Totals		150,000.00				5,000 00
4 Depreciation claimed in Schedule C-1, above						
5 Balance (subtract line 4 from line 3). Enter here and on page 1, line 6						5,000 00

SCHEDULE C-3.—Expense Account Information (See Schedule C Instructions for Schedule C-3)

Enter information with regard to yourself and your five highest paid employees. In determining the five highest paid employees, expense account allowances must be added to their salaries and wages. However, the information need not be submitted for any employee for whom the combined amount is less than $25,000, or for yourself if your expense account allowance plus line 21, page 1, is less than $25,000.

	Name	Expense account	Salaries and Wages
Owner			
1			
2			
3			
4			
5			

Did you claim a deduction for expenses connected with:

(1) Entertainment facility (boat, resort, ranch, etc.)? ☐ Yes ☒ No   (3) Employees' families at conventions or meetings? ☐ Yes ☒ No

(2) Living accommodations (except employees on business)? ☐ Yes ☒ No   (4) Employee or family vacations not reported on Form W-2? ☐ Yes ☒ No

	Profit or (Loss) From Business or Profession	
SCHEDULE C **(Form 1040)** Department of the Treasury Internal Revenue Service	(Sole Proprietorship) Partnerships, Joint Ventures, etc., Must File Form 1065. ▶ Attach to Form 1040. ▶ See Instructions for Schedule C (Form 1040).	**19**

Name of proprietor		Social security number
Ray Chamberlain		540 21 2215

A Principal business activity (see Schedule C Instructions) ▶ .....Sales..... ; product ▶ Sporting Goods

B Business name ▶ .....Ray Chamberlain Sports.....

C Employer identification number ▶ ....06359213....

D Business address (number and street) ▶ .....221 N. Chemeketa.....

City, State and ZIP code ▶ .....Salem, Oregon 97203.....

C

	Yes	No
E Indicate method of accounting: (1) ☒ Cash (2) ☐ Accrual (3) ☐ Other ▶		
F Was an Employer's Quarterly Federal Tax Return, Form 941, filed for this business for any quarter in 19 ?	X	
G Did you own the business at the end of 19 ?	X	
H How many months in 19 did you own this business? ▶ ...12...		
I Check valuation method(s) used for total closing inventory: ☒ cost, ☐ lower of cost or market, ☐ other (if "other," attach explanation).		
Was there any substantial change in determining quantities, costs, or valuations between opening and closing inventory? If "Yes," attach explanation.		X

Income

1 Gross receipts or sales $ ..132,400... Less: returns and allowances $.................... Balance ▶	1	132,400	00
2 Less: Cost of goods sold and/or operations (Schedule C–1, line 8)	2	▶ 77,700	00
3 Gross profit	3	54,700	00
4 Other income (attach schedule)	4		
5 Total income (add lines 3 and 4)	5	54,700	00

Deductions

6 Depreciation (explain in Schedule C–2)	6	▶ 5,000	00
7 Taxes on business and business property	7	2,830	00
8 Rent on business property	8		
9 Repairs	9		
10 Salaries and wages not included on line 3, Schedule C–1 (exclude any paid to yourself) .	10	9,000	00
11 Insurance	11	1,850	00
12 Legal and professional fees	12	530	00
13 Commissions	13		
14 Amortization (attach statement)	14		
15 a Pension and profit-sharing plans (see Schedule C Instructions)	15a		
b Employee benefit programs (see Schedule C Instructions)	b		
16 Interest on business indebtedness	16	5,600	00
17 Bad debts arising from sales or services	17		
18 Depletion	18		
19 Other business expenses (specify):			
a .....Advertising expense..... 2,875 00			
b .....Utility expense..... 1,120 00			
c .....Telephone bills..... 785 00			
d			
e			
f			
g			
h			
i			
j			
k			
l			
m			
n			
o			
p Total other business expenses (add lines 19a through 19o)	19p	4,780	00
20 Total deductions (add lines 6 through 19p)	20	29,590	00
21 Net profit or (loss) (subtract line 20 from line 5). Enter here and on Form 1040, line 13. ALSO enter on Schedule SE, line 5a . . . . ▶	21	25,110	00

NET PROFIT

Did you claim a deduction for expenses of an office in your home? . . . . ☐ Yes ☒ No

SCHEDULE SE
(Form 1040)
Department of the Treasury
Internal Revenue Service

Computation of Social Security Self-Employment Tax

▶ Each self-employed person must file a Schedule SE. ▶ Attach to Form 1040.
▶ See Instructions for Schedule SE (Form 1040).

19

● If you had wages, including tips, of $16,500 or more that were subject to social security or railroad retirement taxes, do not fill in this schedule (unless you are eligible for the Earned Income Credit). See Instructions.

● If you had more than one business, combine profits and losses from all your businesses and farms on this Schedule SE.

Important.—The self-employment income reported below will be credited to your social security record and used in figuring social security benefits.

NAME OF SELF-EMPLOYED PERSON (AS SHOWN ON SOCIAL SECURITY CARD)	Social security number of self-employed person ▶
Ray Chamberlain	540 : 21 : 2215

● If you have only farm income complete Parts I and III.   ● If you have only nonfarm income complete Parts II and III.
● If you have both farm and nonfarm income complete Parts I, II, and III.

Part I   **Computation of Net Earnings from FARM Self-Employment**

You may elect to compute your net farm earnings using the OPTIONAL METHOD, line 3, instead of using the Regular Method, line 2, if your gross profits are: (1) $2,400 or less, or (2) more than $2,400 and net profits are less than $1,600. However, lines 1 and 2 must be completed even if you elect to use the FARM OPTIONAL METHOD.

REGULAR METHOD	**a** Schedule F, line 54 (cash method), or line 72 (accrual method)	1a	
1 Net profit or (loss) from:	**b** Farm partnerships	1b	
2 Net earnings from farm self-employment (add lines 1a and b)		2	
FARM OPTIONAL METHOD			
3 If gross profits from farming¹ are:	**a** Not more than $2,400, enter two-thirds of the gross profits . .		
	b More than $2,400 and the net farm profit is less than $1,600, enter $1,600	3	

¹ Gross profits from farming are the total gross profits from Schedule F, line 28 (cash method), or line 70 (accrual method), plus the distributive share of gross profits from farm partnerships (Schedule K–1 (Form 1065), line 14(b)) as explained in instructions for Schedule SE.

4 Enter here and on line 12a, the amount on line 2, or line 3 if you elect the farm optional method .	4	

Part II   **Computation of Net Earnings from NONFARM Self-Employment**

	a Schedule C, line 21. (Enter combined amount if more than one business.)	5a	25,110	00
	b Partnerships, joint ventures, etc. (other than farming)	5b		
REGULAR METHOD	**c** Service as a minister, member of a religious order, or a Christian Science practitioner. (Include rental value of parsonage or rental allowance furnished.) If you filed Form 4361, check here ▶ ☐ and enter zero on this			
5 Net profit or (loss) from:	line	5c		
	d Service with a foreign government or international organi-	5d		
	e Other (See Form 1040 instructions for line 20.) Specify ▶	5e		

6 Total (add lines 5a through e)	6	25,110	00
7 Enter adjustments if any (attach statement)	7		
8 Adjusted net earnings or (loss) from nonfarm self-employment (line 6, as adjusted by line 7) . .	8	25,110	00

If line 8 is $1,600 or more **OR** if you do not elect to use the Nonfarm Optional Method, omit lines 9 through 11 and enter amount on line 8 on line 12b, Part III.

Note: You may use the nonfarm optional method (line 9 through line 11) only if line 8 is less than $1,600 and less than two-thirds of your gross nonfarm profits,² and you had actual net earnings from self-employment of $400 or more for at least 2 of the 3 following years: 1974, 1975, and 1976. The nonfarm optional method can only be used for 5 taxable years.

SE

NONFARM OPTIONAL METHOD

9 a Maximum amount reportable, under both optional methods combined (farm and nonfarm) . .	9a	$1,600	00
b Enter amount from line 3. (If you did not elect to use the farm optional method, enter zero) .	9b		
c Balance (subtract line 9b from line 9a)	9c		
10 Enter two-thirds of gross nonfarm profits² or $1,600, whichever is smaller	10		
11 Enter here and on line 12b, the amount on line 9c or line 10, whichever is smaller	11		

² Gross profits from nonfarm business are the total of the gross profits from Schedule C, line 3, plus the distributive share of gross profits from nonfarm partnerships (Schedule K–1 (Form 1065), line 14(b)) as explained in instructions for Schedule SE. Also, include gross profits from services reported on line 5c, d, and e, as adjusted by line 7.

Part III   **Computation of Social Security Self-Employment Tax**

12 Net earnings or (loss): **a** From farming (from line 4)	12a		
b From nonfarm (from line 8, or line 11 if you elect to use the Nonfarm Optional Method) . . .	12b	25,110	00
13 Total net earnings or (loss) from self-employment reported on line 12. (**If line 13 is less than $400, you are not subject to self-employment tax. Do not fill in rest of schedule.**)	13	25,110	00
14 The largest amount of combined wages and self-employment earnings subject to social security or railroad retirement taxes for 19 is	14	$16,500	00
15 a Total "FICA" wages (from Forms W–2) and "RRTA" compensation .			
b Unreported tips subject to FICA tax from Form 4137, line 9 or to RRTA			
c Total of lines 15a and b	15c		
16 Balance (subtract line 15c from line 14)	16		
17 Self-employment income—line 13 or 16, whichever is smaller	17	$16,500	00
18 Self-employment tax. (If line 17 is $16,500, enter $1,303.50; if less, multiply the amount on line 17 by .079.) Enter here and on Form 1040, line 48 .	18	1,303	50

These figures will go up in future years

Social Security Self-employment Tax

NET PROFIT

Form **1040** Department of the Treasury—Internal Revenue Service **U.S. Individual Income Tax Return** **19** |

For the year January 1–December 31, 19 , or other taxable year beginning , 19 ending , 19 .

Use IRS label. Otherwise, print or type.	First name and initial (if joint return, give first names and initials of both) Ray	Last name Chamberlain	Your social security number 540 : 21 : 2215
	Present home address (Number and street, including apartment number, or rural route) 200 S. Liberty Street	For Privacy Act Notice, see page 3 of Instructions.	Spouse's social security no. :
	City, town or post office, State and ZIP code Salem, Oregon 97203	Occupation Yours ▶ Sporting Goods Spouse's ▶	

Presidential Election Campaign Fund ▶ Do you want $1 to go to this fund? . . . . X Yes No

If joint return, does your spouse want $1 to go to this fund? . Yes No

Note: Checking "Yes" will not increase your tax or reduce your refund.

Filing Status

Check Only One Box

1 X Single
2 ___ Married filing joint return (even if only one had income)
3 ___ Married filing separately. If spouse is also filing, give spouse's social security number in the space above and enter full name here ▶
4 ___ Unmarried Head of Household. Enter qualifying name ▶ .... See page 7 of Instructions.
5 ___ Qualifying widow(er) with dependent child (Year spouse died ▶ 19). See page 7 of Instructions.

Exemptions

Always check the "Yourself" box. Check other boxes if they apply.

6a X Yourself ☐ 65 or over ☐ Blind | Enter number of boxes checked on 6a and b ▶ 1
b ☐ Spouse ☐ 65 or over ☐ Blind
c First names of your dependent children who lived with you ▶ .... | Enter number of children listed ▶

d Other dependents: (1) Name	(2) Relationship	(3) Number of months lived in your home.	(4) Did dependent have income of $750 or more?	(5) Did you provide more than one-half of dependent's support?

Enter number of other dependents ▶

7 Total number of exemptions claimed . . . . | Add numbers entered in boxes above ▶ 1

Income

Please Attach Copy B of Forms W-2 Here

8 Wages, salaries, tips, and other employee compensation. (Attach Forms W-2. If unavailable, see page 5 of Instructions.) . . . . | 8
9 Interest income. (If over $400, attach Schedule B.) . . . . | 9
10a Dividends (If over $400, attach Schedule B) ....:........, 10b less exclusion ....:........, 8a (See pages 9 and 17 of Instructions)

(If you have no other income, skip lines 11 through 20 and go to line 21.)

11 State and local income tax refunds (does not apply if refund is for year you took standard deduction) . | 11
12 Alimony received . . . . | 12
13 Business income or (loss) (attach Schedule C) . . . . | 13 | 25,110 | 00
14 Capital gain or (loss) (attach Schedule D) . . . . | 14
15 50% of capital gain distributions not reported on Schedule D . . . . | 15
16 Net gain or (loss) from Supplemental Schedule of Gains and Losses (attach Form 4797) . . | 16
17 Fully taxable pensions and annuities not reported on Schedule E . . . . . . | 17
18 Pensions, annuities, rents, royalties, partnerships, estates or trusts, etc. (attach Schedule E) . | 18
19 Farm income or (loss) (attach Schedule F) . . . . | 19
20 Other (state nature and source—see page 9 of Instructions) ▶ .... | 20
21 Total income. Add lines 8, 9, and 10c through 20 . . . . ▶ | 21

(handwritten, pointing to line 13:) Business income reported from Schedule C

Adjustments to Income *(If none, skip lines 22 through 27 and enter zero on line 28.)*

Please Attach Check or Money Order Here

22 Moving expense (attach Form 3903) . . . . | 22
23 Employee business expenses (attach Form 2106) . . . . . . | 23
24 Payments to an individual retirement arrangement (from attached Form 5329, Part III) . . . . | 24
25 Payments to a Keogh (H.R. 10) retirement plan . . . . . . | 25
26 Forfeited interest penalty for premature withdrawal . . . . . | 26
27 Alimony paid (see page 11 of Instructions) . . . . | 27
28 Total adjustments. Add lines 22 through 27 . . . . ▶ | 28
29 Subtract line 28 from line 21 . . . . | 29
30 Disability income exclusion (sick pay) (attach Form 2440) . . . . | 30
31 Adjusted gross income. Subtract line 30 from line 29. Enter here and on line 32. If you want IRS to figure your tax for you, see page 4 of the Instructions . . . . ▶ | 31

Having reported his first year's income for tax purposes, Ray now prepares a balance sheet for the beginning of Year #2. The balance sheet looks like this:

RAY CHAMBERLAIN SPORTS

Balance Sheet

January 1, Year #2

Assets

Cash (end of year balance)	$ 10,810.00
Inventory (from end of year count)	34,300.00
Building (original cost $150,000 less $5,000 depreciation)	145,000.00
Total Assets	$190,110.00

Liabilities and Ownership

Liabilities:

Balance owing on purchase price of the building	$ 63,000.00

Ownership:

Owner's investment (the amount of money Ray originally put into the business)		$120,000	
Add: Net profit	$25,110		
Less what owner took out for personal needs	18,000	7,110	
Total value of ownership at beginning of second year		$127,110	127,110.00
Total Liabilities and value of Ownership			$190,110.00

Comparing this balance sheet with the January 2nd balance sheet of Year #1, we see that Ray's ownership interest has increased from $120,000 (the amount of his original investment) to $127,000. And his liabilities have decreased from $70,000 to $63,000 (Ray paid the first $7,000 installment on the building). And, though it doesn't appear on the balance sheet, don't forget that Ray took out $18,000 for his personal living expenses.

Beginning with the January 1, Year #2 balance sheet, the entire process will be repeated during the next year.

How are partnership profits and losses reported for tax purposes?

As stated previously, a *partnership* is an association of two or more persons to carry on as co-owners a business for profit. More than one person owns the business, and more than one shares in the profits and losses of the business.

With regard to taxes, the partnership itself pays no taxes. Rather, it files a mere *information* return with the government ("Form 1065 U.S. Partnership Return of Income"), specifying how much income the partnership had for the year, and what each partner's share of the income is. The reporting and payment of taxes on the income is left to the individual partners: each must report his or her share of the partnership income on his or her personal income tax return (Form 1040 plus appropriate schedules). Each partner will be taxed on his or her share whether or not it was actually distributed to him or her during the course of the year.

By way of example, suppose that Ray Chamberlain, after retiring from the NFL, wants to invest in a sporting goods store, but does not want to spend all his time managing the business. Ray enters into a partnership agreement with Lola Forthright, whereby Ray will put up the necessary cash (the $120,000 capital) for the two to go into business, and Lola will do most of the day-to-day managing of the business. The two partners agree that Ray will receive 25% of the profits (and losses), and Lola will receive 75% (as you will learn later, partners may divide profits and losses as they see fit). They decide to call the business Ray Chamberlain Sports.

Over the course of the year, the partnership enters into the same transactions as were entered into by the sole proprie-

torship. In other words, the partnership makes the same purchases, incurs the same expenses, and hires the same number of employees (one). The only difference is that Lola, not Ray, takes out the $18,000 for her personal living expenses. Ray takes nothing out of the partnership during the first year of operations. The result is that the ending inventory, cash balance, and profit and loss statement are all the same. It is only the tax reporting that differs. The partnership itself must file an information return (Form 1065), and each partner must report his or her share of the partnership income on his or her personal income tax return (Form 1040). The returns, in part, would look like this (note that Form 1065 contains much the same information as was found on Schedule C of sole proprietor Ray's personal return):

Form 1065 — U.S. Partnership Return of Income

FOR CALENDAR YEAR 19 , or other taxable year beginning .... 19 , and ending .... , 19 ......   **19**

Department of the Treasury — Internal Revenue Service

A Principal business activity (See page 10 of instructions) **Sales**

B Principal product or service (See page 10 of instructions) **Spt. Goods**

C Business code no. (See page 10 of instructions)

Use IRS label. Otherwise, print or type.

Name **Ray Chamberlain Sports**

Number and street **221 N. Chemeketa**

City or town, State, and ZIP code **Salem, Oregon 97203**

D Employer identification no. **06359213**

E Date business commenced **January 1**

F Enter total assets from line 13, column (D), Schedule L **$ 190,110.00**

G Was this partnership in business at the end of 19 ? . . . . ▶ [x] Yes ☐ No

H How many months in 19 was this partnership in business? . . . . ▶ 12

IMPORTANT—Fill in all applicable lines and schedules. If the space provided is not sufficient, see Instruction Q. Enter any items specially allocated to the partners on Schedule K, line 15, instead of on the numbered lines on this page or in Schedules D through J. (See General Instruction P.)

INCOME

1a Gross receipts or sales $ 132,400.00 1b Less returns and allowances $ .... Balance ▶	1c	132,400 00
2 Less cost of goods sold and/or operations (line 34, Schedule A)	2	77,700 00
3 Gross profit	3	54,700 00
4 Ordinary income (loss) from other partnerships and fiduciaries (attach statement)	4	
5 Nonqualifying dividends (attach list—see Instruction 5)	5	
6 Interest	6	
7 Rents (Schedule H)	7	
8 Royalties (attach schedule)	8	
9 Net farm profit (loss) (attach Schedule F (Form 1040))	9	
10 Net gain (loss) (Form 4797, line 9)	10	
11 Other income (attach schedule)	11	
12 TOTAL income (add lines 3 through 11)	12	54,700 00

DEDUCTIONS

13 Salaries and wages (other than to partners)	13	9,000 00
14 Guaranteed payments to partners (see Instruction 14)	14	
15 Rent	15	
16 Interest (attach schedule)	16	5,600 00
17 Taxes (attach schedule)	17	2,830 00
18 Bad debts (Schedule I if you use reserve method)	18	
19 Repairs	19	
20 Depreciation (see Instructions for Schedule J)	20	5,000 00
21 Amortization (attach schedule)	21	
22 Depletion (attach schedule—see Instruction 22)	22	
23a Retirement plans, etc. (see Instruction 23a). (Enter number of plans ▶ ....) . . .	23a	
23b Employee benefit programs (see Instruction 23b)	23b	
24 Other deductions (attach schedule)	24	7,160 00
25 TOTAL deductions (add lines 13 through 24)	25	29,590 00
26 Ordinary income (loss) (subtract line 25 from line 12) (see General Instruction G)	26	25,110 00

Schedule A—COST OF GOODS SOLD AND/OR OPERATIONS (See Instruction 2)

27 Inventory at beginning of year (if different from last year's closing inventory, attach explanation)	27	30,000 00
28a Purchases $ 82,000 ...... 28b Less cost of items withdrawn for personal use $ .... Balance ▶	28c	82,000 00
29 Cost of labor	29	
30 Material and supplies	30	
31 Other costs (attach schedule)	31	
32 Total of lines 27 through 31	32	112,000 00
33 Less inventory at end of year	33	34,300 00
34 Cost of goods sold. Enter here and on line 2, above	34	77,700 00

35(a) Check valuation method(s) used for total closing inventory: ☒ Cost ☐ Lower of cost or market ☐ Other (if "other," attach explanation)

(b) Check if this is the first year LIFO inventory method was adopted and used ☐. If checked, attach Form 970.

(c) If you are a manufacturer, check if you valued your inventory in accordance with regulation section 1.471–11. ☐

(d) Was there any substantial change in determining quantities, cost, or valuations between opening and closing inventory? ☐ Yes ☒ No If "Yes," attach explanation.

Under penalties of perjury, I declare that I have examined this return, including accompanying schedules and statements, and to the best of my knowledge and belief, it is true, correct, and complete. Declaration of preparer (other than taxpayer) is based on all information of which preparer has any knowledge.

▶ Paid preparer's signature and Identifying number (see Instructions)

▶ Your signature   Date   ▶ Paid preparer's address (or employer's name, address, and identifying number)

The net profit of $25,110.00 reported on line 26 of Form 1065 is exactly the same as the net profit of the sole proprietorship. Here, however, the net profit must be divided between Ray and Lola according to the terms of the partnership agreement. Remember, by the terms of the agreement, Ray is to receive only 25% of the profit, and Lola is to receive the remaining 75%.

Ray Chamberlain's share

$ 25,110.00 x 25% = $ 6,277.50

Lola Forthright's share

$ 25,110.00 x 75% = $ 18,832.50

Total income $ 25,110.00

Each partner's share of the income must be reported on a Schedule K-1 (one for each partner) to be filed along with Form 1065. Ultimately, the information contained on the K-1 will be compared with the partner's personal income tax return.

SCHEDULE K–1 (Form 1065) Department of the Treasury Internal Revenue Service	Partner's Share of Income, Credits, Deductions, etc.—19 For Calendar year 19　or fiscal year beginning ...., 19 , ending ...., 19........ (Complete for each partner—See instructions on back of Copy C)	Copy A (File with Form 1065)

Partner's identifying number ▶ Ray's Social Sec. #	Partnership's identifying number ▶　06359213
Partner's name, address, and ZIP code	Partnership's name, address, and ZIP code
Ray Chamberlain	Ray Chamberlain Sports

	Yes	No	
A Date(s) partner acquired any partnership interest during the year ▶　January 1			**G** IRS Center where partnership return filed ▶...............................

B Is partner a nonresident alien? . . . .　|　X

C Is partner a limited partner (see General Instruction S(2))? .　|　X

D (i) Did partner ever contribute property other than money to the partnership (if "Yes," complete line 20)? . . .　|　X

(ii) Did partner ever receive a distribution other than money from the partnership (if "Yes," complete line 21)? .　|　X

(iii) Was any part of the partner's interest ever acquired from another partner? . . . .　|　X

E (i) Did partnership interest terminate during the year? . .　|　X

(ii) Did partnership interest decrease during the year? . .　|　X

H Partner's share of liabilities (see instructions):

	(i) Incurred prior to 1/1/	(ii) Incurred after 12/31/
Nonrecourse . .	$...............	$...............
Other . . . $	....	$...............

I Enter total amount of liabilities other than nonrecourse in respect of which the partner is protected against loss through guarantees, stop loss agreements, or other similar arrangements to which the partnership is a party or has knowledge:

Incurred prior to 1/1/ . . . . . $...............

Incurred after 12/31/ . . . . . $...............

J Partner's share of any pre-19 loss(es) resulting from a section 465 activity for which there existed a corresponding amount of nonrecourse liability at the end of the year in which loss(es) occurred $...............

F Enter Partner's percentage of:

	(i) Prior to decrease or termination	(ii) End of year
Ownership of capital . . . . %		100 %
Profit sharing . . . . %		25 %
Loss sharing . . . . %		25 %
Time devoted to business . . . . %		5 %

K Reconciliation of partner's capital account:

a. Capital account at beginning of year	b. Capital contributed during year	c. Ordinary income (loss) from line 1(b)	d. Income not included in column c, plus non-taxable income	e. Losses not included in column c, plus unallowable deductions	f. Withdrawals and distributions	g. Capital account at end of year
$120,000	00.00	6,277.50			00.00	126,277.50 ◀

c. 1040 filers enter col. b amount as shown. All others enter on corresponding line of that form.

Ray's share ➤

a. Distributive share item	b. Amount	
1 (a) Guaranteed payments to partner: (1) Deductible by the partnership .		Sch. E, Part III
(2) Capitalized by the partnership		Sch. E, Part III
(b) Ordinary income (loss)	6,277.50	Sch. E, Part III
2 Additional first-year depreciation		Sch. E, Part III
3 Dividends qualifying for exclusion		Sch. B, Part II, line 3
4 Short-term capital gain (loss)		Sch. D, line 2 (See Form 4625 Instr.)
5 Long-term capital gain (loss)		Sch. D, line 9
6 Involuntary conversions gain (loss)—casualty and theft		Form 4797, line 1
7 Other gain (loss)—from property under section 1231 .		Form 4797, line 3
8 Net earnings (loss) from self-employment	6,277.50	Sch. SE, Part I or Part II
9 Charitable contributions: 50% ...., 30% ...., 20%		Sch. A, line 21 or 22
10 Expense account allowance		
11 New jobs credit		Form 5884, line 19
12 Taxes paid by regulated investment company . . .		Line 61, add words "from 1065"
13 (a) Payments on behalf of partner to a Keogh Plan		Line 25
(b) Payments on behalf of partner to an Individual Retirement Arrangement		Line 24
14 (a) Other income, deductions, etc. (specify) ▶..........................		(Enter on applicable lines of your return)
(b) Other information (specify) ▶		
(c) Oil and gas depletion. Enter amount (not for partner's use) ▶		
15 Specially allocated items: **(a)** Short-term capital gain (loss)		Sch. D, line 2 (See Form 4625 Instr.)
(b) Long-term capital gain (loss)		Sch. D, line 9
(c) Ordinary gain (loss)		Form 4797, line 8
(d) Other		Sch. E, Part III
16 Tax preference items: **(a)** Itemized deductions		(See Form 4625 Instructions)
(b) Accelerated depreciation on real property: **(1)** Low-income rental housing		Form 4625, line 1(b)(1)
(2) Other real property . .		Form 4625, line 1(b)(2)
(c) Accelerated depreciation on personal property subject to a lease . . .		Form 4625, line 1(c)
Amortization: **(d)**............, **(e)**............, **(f)**............, **(g)**		Form 4625, line 1(d) thru (g)
(h) Reserves for losses on bad debts of financial institutions		Form 4625, line 1(h)
(i) Depletion		Form 4625, line 1(j)
(j) (1) Excess intangible drilling costs ...., (2) Net income (loss)		(See Form 4625 Instructions)

See balance sheet

Ray took nothing out during the course of the year

See balance sheet

SCHEDULE K-1 (Form 1065) Department of the Treasury Internal Revenue Service	Partner's Share of Income, Credits, Deductions, etc.—19 For Calendar year 19 or fiscal year beginning ...., 19 , ending ...., 19........ (Complete for each partner—See instructions on back of Copy C)	Copy A (File with Form 1065)

Partner's identifying number ▶ Lola's Social Sec. #	Partnership's identifying number ▶ 06359213
Partner's name, address, and ZIP code Lola Forthright	Partnership's name, address, and ZIP code Ray Chamberlain Sports

A Date(s) partner acquired any partnership interest during the year ▶ January 1

G IRS Center where partnership return filed ▶ ....

B Is partner a nonresident alien? — No X
C Is partner a limited partner (see General Instruction S(2))? — No X
D (i) Did partner ever contribute property other than money to the partnership (if "Yes," complete line 20)? — No X
(ii) Did partner ever receive a distribution other than money from the partnership (if "Yes," complete line 21)? — No X
(iii) Was any part of the partner's interest ever acquired from another partner? — No X
E (i) Did partnership interest terminate during the year? — No X
(ii) Did partnership interest decrease during the year? — No X

H Partner's share of liabilities (see instructions):
(i) Incurred prior to 1/1/ — Nonrecourse $; Other $
(ii) Incurred after 12/31/ — $; $

F Enter Partner's percentage of:
	(i) Prior to decrease or termination	(ii) End of year
Ownership of capital	%	0 %
Profit sharing	%	75 %
Loss sharing	%	75 %
Time devoted to business	%	100 %

I Enter total amount of liabilities other than nonrecourse in respect of which the partner is protected against loss through guarantees, stop loss agreements, or other similar arrangements to which the partnership is a party or has knowledge:
Incurred prior to 1/1/ $
Incurred after 12/31/ $
J Partner's share of any pre-19 loss(es) resulting from a section 465 activity for which there existed a corresponding amount of nonrecourse liability at the end of the year in which loss(es) occurred $

K Reconciliation of partner's capital account:

a. Capital account at beginning of year	b. Capital contributed during year	c. Ordinary income (loss) from line 1(b)	d. Income not included in column c, plus nontaxable income	e. Losses not included in column c, plus unallowable deductions	f. Withdrawals and distributions	g. Capital account at end of year
00.00	00.00	18,832.50			18,000.00	832.50

Lola's share — a. Distributive share item — What she took out — b. Amount — c. 1040 filers enter col. b amount as shown. All others enter on corresponding line of that form.

		Amount	
1 (a) Guaranteed payments to partner: (1) Deductible by the partnership			Sch. E, Part III
(2) Capitalized by the partnership			Sch. E, Part III — See
(b) Ordinary income (loss)		18,832.50	Sch. E, Part III — balance sheet
2 Additional first-year depreciation			Sch. E, Part III
3 Dividends qualifying for exclusion			Sch. B, Part II, line 3
4 Short-term capital gain (loss)			Sch. D, line 2 (See Form 4625 Instr.)
5 Long-term capital gain (loss)			Sch. D, line 9
6 Involuntary conversions gain (loss)—casualty and theft			Form 4797, line 1
7 Other gain (loss)—from property under section 1231			Form 4797, line 3
8 Net earnings (loss) from self-employment		18,832.50	Sch. SE, Part I or Part II
9 Charitable contributions: 50% ...., 30% ...., 20%			Sch. A, line 21 or 22
10 Expense account allowance			
11 New jobs credit			Form 5884, line 19
12 Taxes paid by regulated investment company			Line 61, add words "from 1065"
13 (a) Payments on behalf of partner to a Keogh Plan			Line 25
(b) Payments on behalf of partner to an Individual Retirement Arrangement			Line 24
14 (a) Other income, deductions, etc. (specify) ▶			Enter on applicable lines of your return
(b) Other information (specify) ▶			
(c) Oil and gas depletion. Enter amount (not for partner's use) ▶			
15 Specially allocated items: (a) Short-term capital gain (loss)			Sch. D, line 2 (See Form 4625 Instr.)
(b) Long-term capital gain (loss)			Sch. D, line 9
(c) Ordinary gain (loss)			Form 4797, line 8
(d) Other			Sch. E, Part III
16 Tax preference items: (a) Itemized deductions			(See Form 4625 Instructions)
(b) Accelerated depreciation on real property: (1) Low-income rental housing			Form 4625, line 1(b)(1)
(2) Other real property			Form 4625, line 1(b)(2)
(c) Accelerated depreciation on personal property subject to a lease			Form 4625, line 1(c)
Amortization: (d)........, (e)........, (f)........, (g)........			Form 4625, line 1(d) thru (g)
(h) Reserves for losses on bad debts of financial institutions			Form 4625, line 1(h)
(i) Depletion			Form 4625, line 1(j)
(j) (1) Excess intangible drilling costs , (2) Net income (loss)			(See Form 4625 Instructions)

As you can see from looking at the K-1's, Ray Chamberlain must report $6,277.50 as his share of partnership income for both income tax and social security self-employment tax purposes; Lola Forthright must report $18,832.50. Like sole proprietor Ray, both Ray and Lola must file Form 1040 on or before April 15th of the year following. However, rather than attach "Schedule C" as sole proprietor Ray did, Ray and Lola must attach "Schedule E Supplemental Income Schedule": The partnership income shown on line 13 of Schedule E must be carried forward to page one of Form 1040, line 18.

To report their social security self-employment income, Ray and Lola must also attach Schedule SE (listing the income on line 5b, Part II "partnerships"—see previous illustration of Schedule SE).

The Internal Revenue Service can easily check the accuracy of the partners' personal returns by comparing the amounts listed on the two Schedule E's with the amounts listed on the two information return K-1's (the partnership identification number—in our case, 06359213—is found on both Schedule E and K-1, facilitating a computer check).

SCHEDULE E
(Form 1040)
Department of the Treasury
Internal Revenue Service

Supplemental Income Schedule

(From pensions and annuities, rents and royalties, partnerships, estates and trusts, etc.)
▶ Attach to Form 1040.   ▶ See Instructions for Schedule E (Form 1040).

19

Name(s) as shown on Form 1040	Your social security number
Lola Forthright	

Part I   **Pension and Annuity Income.** If fully taxable, do not complete this part. Enter amount on Form 1040, line 17. For one pension or annuity not fully taxable, complete this part. If you have more than one pension or annuity that is not fully taxable, attach a separate sheet listing each one with the appropriate data and enter combined total of taxable portions on line 5.

1 Name of payer

2 Did your employer contribute part of the cost? . . . . ☐ Yes ☐ No

If "Yes," is your contribution recoverable within 3 years of the annuity starting date? . . . . ☐ Yes ☐ No

If "Yes," show: Your contribution $........................, Contribution recovered in prior years . . .   **2**

3 Amount received this year   **3**

4 Amount excludable this year **4**

5 Taxable portion (subtract line 4 from line 3) **5**

Part II   **Rent and Royalty Income.** If you need more space, use Form 4831.

Have you claimed expenses connected with your vacation home rented to others? ☐ Yes ☐ No

(a) Kind and location of property If residential, also write "R"	(b) Total amount of rents	(c) Total amount of royalties	(d) Depreciation (explain below) or depletion (attach computation)	(e) Other expenses (Repairs, etc.— explain below)

6 Totals . . . .

7 Net income or (loss) from rents and royalties (column (b) plus column (c) less columns (d) and (e)) .   **7**

8 Net rental income or (loss) (from Form 4831) **8**

9 Net farm rental profit or (loss) (from Form 4835) **9**

10 Total rent and royalty income (add lines 7, 8, and 9) **10**

Part III   **Income or Losses from Partnerships, Estates or Trusts, Small Business Corporations.**

Enter in column (b): P for Partnership, E for Estate or Trust, or S for Small Business Corp.

(a) Name	(b)	(c) Employer identification number	(d) Your share of gross farming or fishing income	(e) Income or (loss)	(f) Additional 1st year depreciation (applicable only to partnerships)
Ray Chamberlain Spts	P	06359213		18,832.50	

11 Totals . . . . | | | | 18,832.50 | |

12 Income or (loss). Total of column (e) less total of column (f) **12** 18,832 50

13 TOTAL (add lines 5, 10, and 12). Enter here and on Form 1040, line 18 . . . . ▶   **13** 18,832 50

Explanation of Column (e), Part II

Item	Amount	Item	Amount	Item	Amount

Schedule for Depreciation Claimed in Part II above. If you need more space use Form 4562.

(a) Description of property	(b) Date acquired	(c) Cost or other basis	(d) Depreciation allowed or allowable in prior years	(e) Method of computing depreciation	(f) Life or rate	(g) Depreciation for this year
1 Total additional first-year depreciation (do not include in items below) ────────▶						
2 Totals						

| SCHEDULE E
(Form 1040)
Department of the Treasury
Internal Revenue Service | **Supplemental Income Schedule**
(From pensions and annuities, rents and royalties, partnerships, estates and trusts, etc.)
▶ Attach to Form 1040.   ▶ See Instructions for Schedule E (Form 1040). | 19 |

Name(s) as shown on Form 1040   Ray Chamberlain   **Your social security number**

Part I   **Pension and Annuity Income.** If **fully taxable**, do not complete this part. Enter amount on Form 1040, line 17. For one pension or annuity not fully taxable, complete this part. If you have more than one pension or annuity that is not fully taxable, attach a separate sheet listing each one with the appropriate data and enter combined total of taxable portions on line 5.

1 Name of payer.
2 Did your employer contribute part of the cost? . . . . ☐ Yes ☐ No
  If "Yes," is your contribution recoverable within 3 years of the annuity starting date? . . . . ☐ Yes ☐ No
  If "Yes," show: Your contribution $..................., Contribution recovered in prior years . . . **2**
3 Amount received this year **3**
4 Amount excludable this year **4**
5 Taxable portion (subtract line 4 from line 3) **5**

Part II   **Rent and Royalty Income.** If you need more space, use Form 4831.
Have you claimed expenses connected with your vacation home rented to others? ☐ Yes ☐ No

(a) Kind and location of property If residential, also write "R"	(b) Total amount of rents	(c) Total amount of royalties	(d) Depreciation (explain below) or depletion (attach computation)	(e) Other expenses (Repairs, etc.— explain below)

6 Totals . . . .
7 Net income or (loss) from rents and royalties (column (b) plus column (c) less columns (d) and (e)) . **7**
8 Net rental income or (loss) (from Form 4831) **8**
9 Net farm rental profit or (loss) (from Form 4835) **9**
10 Total rent and royalty income (add lines 7, 8, and 9) **10**

Part III   **Income or Losses from Partnerships, Estates or Trusts, Small Business Corporations.**
Enter in column (b): P for Partnership, E for Estate or Trust, or S for Small Business Corp.

(a) Name	(b)	(c) Employer identification number	(d) Your share of gross farming or fishing income	(e) Income or (loss)	(f) Additional 1st year depreciation (applicable only to partnerships)
Ray Chamberlain Spts	P	06359213		6,277.50	

11 Totals 6,277.50
12 Income or (loss). Total of column (e) less total of column (f) . . . . **12** | 6,277|50
13 **TOTAL** (add lines 5, 10, and 12). Enter here and on Form 1040, line 18 . . . . ▶ **13** | 6,277|50

Explanation of Column (e), Part II

Item	Amount	Item	Amount	Item	Amount

Schedule for Depreciation Claimed in Part II above. If you need more space use Form 4562.

(a) Description of property	(b) Date acquired	(c) Cost or other basis	(d) Depreciation allowed or allowable in prior years	(e) Method of computing depreciation	(f) Life or rate	(g) Depreciation for this year	E
1 Total additional first-year depreciation (do not include in items below) ——————————————▶							
2 Totals				. . . .			

☆U.S. GOVERNMENT PRINTING OFFICE 1977—0-235-062—87-032-1919

Form **1040** Department of the Treasury—Internal Revenue Service
U.S. Individual Income Tax Return **19**

For the year January 1–December 31, 19 , or other taxable year beginning   , 19   ending   , 19   .

First name and initial (if joint return, give first names and initials of both)	Last name	Your social security number
Lola	Forthright	

Present home address (Number and street, including apartment number, or rural route)

501 Park Avenue

For Privacy Act Notice, see page 3 of Instructions.   Spouse's social security no.

City, town or post office, State and ZIP code

Salem, Oregon 97203

Occu-pation   Yours ▶ Sporting goods
Spouse's ▶

Use IRS label. Otherwise, print or type.

Presidential Election Campaign Fund

Do you want $1 to go to this fund? . . . .   X Yes   No
If joint return, does your spouse want $1 to go to this fund? . .   Yes   No

Note: Checking "Yes" will not increase your tax or reduce your refund.

Filing Status

Check Only One Box

1 X Single
2   Married filing joint return (even if only one had income)
3   Married filing separately. If spouse is also filing, give spouse's social security number in the space above and enter full name here ▶ . . . .
4   Unmarried Head of Household. Enter qualifying name ▶ . . . . See page 7 of Instructions.
5   Qualifying widow(er) with dependent child (Year spouse died ▶ 19   ). See page 7 of Instructions.

Exemptions

Always check the "Yourself" box. Check other boxes if they apply.

6a X Yourself   65 or over   Blind   Enter number of boxes checked on 6a and b ▶ 1
b   Spouse   65 or over   Blind
c First names of your dependent children who lived with you ▶ . . . .   Enter number of children listed ▶

d Other dependents: (1) Name	(2) Relationship	(3) Number of months lived in your home.	(4) Did dependent have income of $750 or more?	(5) Did you provide more than one-half of dependent's support?

Enter number of other dependents ▶

7 Total number of exemptions claimed . . . .   Add numbers entered in boxes above ▶ 1

Income

8	Wages, salaries, tips, and other employee compensation. (Attach Forms W–2. If unavailable, see page 5 of Instructions.)	8
9	Interest income. (If over $400, attach Schedule B.)	9
10a	Dividends (If over $400, attach Schedule B) . . . . , 10b less exclusion . . . . , Balance ▶	10c

(See pages 9 and 17 of Instructions)

(If you have no other income, skip lines 11 through 20 and go to line 21.)

11	State and local income tax refunds (does not apply if refund is for year you took standard deduction) . .	
12	Alimony received	
13	Business income or (loss) (attach Schedule C)	
14	Capital gain or (loss) (attach Schedule D)	
15	50% of capital gain distributions not reported on Schedule D	15
16	Net gain or (loss) from Supplemental Schedule of Gains and Losses (attach Form 4797) . .	16
17	Fully taxable pensions and annuities not reported on Schedule E . . .	17
18	Pensions, annuities, rents, royalties, partnerships, estates or trusts, etc. (attach Schedule E) .	18 18,832 50
19	Farm income or (loss) (attach Schedule F)	19
20	Other (state nature and source—see page 9 of Instructions) ▶	20
21	Total income. Add lines 8, 9, and 10c through 20 . . . . ▶	21

Lola's share of partnership income

Adjustments to Income   *(If none, skip lines 22 through 27 and enter zero on line 28.)*

22	Moving expense (attach Form 3903)	22
23	Employee business expenses (attach Form 2106)	23
24	Payments to an individual retirement arrangement (from attached Form 5329, Part III)	24
25	Payments to a Keogh (H.R. 10) retirement plan	25
26	Forfeited interest penalty for premature withdrawal	26
27	Alimony paid (see page 11 of Instructions)	27
28	Total adjustments. Add lines 22 through 27 . . . . ▶	28
29	Subtract line 28 from line 21	29
30	Disability income exclusion (sick pay) (attach Form 2440)	30
31	Adjusted gross income. Subtract line 30 from line 29. Enter here and on line 32. If you want IRS to figure your tax for you, see page 4 of the Instructions . . . . ▶	31

Please Attach Copy B of Forms W–2 Here

Please Attach Check or Money Order Here

Form **1040**   Department of the Treasury—Internal Revenue Service   **U.S. Individual Income Tax Return** **19**

For the year January 1–December 31, 19 , or other taxable year beginning   , 19   ending   , 19

Use IRS label. Otherwise, print or type.

First name and initial (if joint return, give first names and initials of both)	Last name	Your social security number
Ray	Chamberlain	

Present home address (Number and street, including apartment number, or rural route)
200 South Liberty Street

For Privacy Act Notice, see page 3 of Instructions.

Spouse's social security no.

City, town or post office, State and ZIP code
Salem, Oregon 97203

Occupation   Yours ▶ sporting goods
Spouse's ▶

Presidential Election Campaign Fund ▶
Do you want $1 to go to this fund? . . . .   X Yes ▨ No
If joint return, does your spouse want $1 to go to this fund? .   Yes ▨ No

Note: Checking "Yes" will not increase your tax or reduce your refund.

Filing Status
Check Only One Box

1   X   Single
2   Married filing joint return (even if only one had income)
3   Married filing separately. If spouse is also filing, give spouse's social security number in the space above and enter full name here ▶
4   Unmarried Head of Household. Enter qualifying name ▶ . . . . See page 7 of Instructions.
5   Qualifying widow(er) with dependent child (Year spouse died ▶ 19). See page 7 of Instructions.

Exemptions

Always check the "Yourself" box. Check other boxes if they apply.

6a   X Yourself   ☐ 65 or over   ☐ Blind   Enter number of boxes checked on 6a and b ▶ **1**

b   ☐ Spouse   ☐ 65 or over   ☐ Blind

c   First names of your dependent children who lived with you ▶ . . . .   Enter number of children listed ▶

d Other dependents: (1) Name	(2) Relationship	(3) Number of months lived in your home.	(4) Did dependent have income of $750 or more?	(5) Did you provide more than one-half of dependent's support?

Enter number of other dependents ▶

7   Total number of exemptions claimed . . . . Add numbers entered in boxes above ▶ **1**

Income

(Please Attach Copy B of Forms W-2 Here)

8	Wages, salaries, tips, and other employee compensation. (Attach Forms W-2. If unavailable, see page 5 of Instructions.)	8	
9	Interest income. (If over $400, attach Schedule B.)	9	
10a	Dividends (If over $400, attach Schedule B), 10b less exclusion , Balance ▶	10c	
	(See pages 9 and 17 of Instructions)		

(If you have no other income, skip lines 11 through 20 and go to line 21.)

11	State and local income tax refunds (does not apply if refund is for year you took standard deduction) . .		
12	Alimony received		
13	Business income or (loss) (attach Schedule C)		
14	Capital gain or (loss) (attach Schedule D)		
15	50% of capital gain distributions not reported on Schedule D	15	
16	Net gain or (loss) from Supplemental Schedule of Gains and Losses (attach Form 4797) . .	16	
17	Fully taxable pensions and annuities not reported on Schedule E	17	
18	Pensions, annuities, rents, royalties, partnerships, estates or trusts, etc. (attach Schedule E) . .	18	6,277 50
19	Farm income or (loss) (attach Schedule F)	19	
20	Other (state nature and source—see page 9 of Instructions) ▶	20	
21	**Total income.** Add lines 8, 9, and 10c through 20 . . . . ▶	21	

Ray's share of partnership income ↘

Adjustments to Income   *(If none, skip lines 22 through 27 and enter zero on line 28.)*

(Please Attach Check or Money Order Here)

22	Moving expense (attach Form 3903)	22		
23	Employee business expenses (attach Form 2106)	23		
24	Payments to an individual retirement arrangement (from attached Form 5329, Part III)	24		
25	Payments to a Keogh (H.R. 10) retirement plan	25		
26	Forfeited interest penalty for premature withdrawal	26		
27	Alimony paid (see page 11 of Instructions)	27		
28	**Total adjustments.** Add lines 22 through 27 . . . . ▶		28	
29	Subtract line 28 from line 21		29	
30	Disability income exclusion (sick pay) (attach Form 2440)		30	
31	**Adjusted gross income.** Subtract line 30 from line 29. Enter here and on line 32. If you want IRS to figure your tax for you, see page 4 of the Instructions . . . . ▶		31	

Having filed their taxes, Ray and Lola draw up a balance sheet for January 1, Year #2. With one exception, the balance sheet reflects the same assets, liabilities, and ownership as were found in the January 1, Year #2 balance sheet for the sole proprietorship. The exception is that the partners share the *ownership* (capital) interest.

RAY CHAMBERLAIN SPORTS

Balance Sheet

January 1, Year #2

(Partnership between Ray Chamberlain and
Lola Forthright with 25% profits and losses to
Ray, 75% profits and losses to Lola.)

Assets

Cash (balance from end of year)	$ 10,810.00
Inventory (from end of year count)	34,300.00
Building (original cost of $150,000 less $5,000 depreciation)	145,000.00
Total assets	$190,110.00

Liabilities and Ownership

Liabilities

Balance owing on purchase price of the building	$ 63,000.00

Ownership

Ray Chamberlain

Original investment	$120,000.00	
25% of net profit	6,277.50	$126,277.50

Lola Forthright

Original investment	$ 00,000.00	
75% of net profit	18,832.50	
less actual cash paid out to Lola Forthright	18,000.00	832.50
Total owner's equity		$127,110.00
Total liabilities and ownership		$190,110.00

How will our study of partnership law be divided?

In the remainder of the chapter, we will study partnership law in the following six parts:

(1) The nature of a partnership;

(2) The formation of a partnership;

(3) The legal relationship existing between partners;

(4) The legal relationship existing between partners and third parties (i. e., nonpartners);

(5) Dissolution of a partnership; and

(6) Limited partnerships.

In our study, we will emphasize the Uniform Partnership Act (in effect in all states but Georgia, Louisiana, and Mississippi) and the Uniform Limited Partnership Act (enacted by all states except Louisiana and Delaware).

What is the nature of a partnership?

The Uniform Partnership Act defines a "partnership" at Section (6)(1) as follows: "A partnership is an association of two or more persons to carry on as co-owners a business for a profit." Note that there are four elements to the definition of a partnership:

(1) There must be *at least two persons* (or partners);

(2) Each must have an *ownership* interest (not necessarily equal) in the business;

(3) The parties must intend to *carry on the business together*; and

(4) They must associate in order to make a *profit* (parties who associate for nonprofit purposes are not partners).

The requirement of co-ownership distinguishes a partnership from a single agency relationship: unlike a partner, an agent is not required to have any ownership interest in the business he or she represents. For example, if Ray Chamberlain authorizes Lola Forthright to sell sporting goods in his store, Lola is Ray's agent whether or not she owns a part of the business. But she is Ray's partner only if she is a co-owner of the sporting goods store. (Still, the law of agency has considerable application to partnerships—as will be explained later, every partner is deemed to be an agent of the partnership with respect to ordinary partnership business.)

At the same time, co-ownership of a business or property does not in and of itself establish a partnership. Section 7 of the Uniform Partnership Act provides.

The Act says:

Section 7. Rules for Determining the Existence of a Partnership

* * *

(2) Joint tenancy, tenancy in common, tenancy by the entireties, joint property, common property, or part ownership does not of itself establish a partnership, whether such co-owners do or do not share any profits made by the use of the property. [Concurrent ownership of property is discussed in detail in Ch. 5.]

———

Nor does the sharing of gross income from concurrently held property in and of itself establish a partnership. Again, Section 7 is the relevant UPA provision.

It says:

* * *

(3) The sharing of gross returns does not of itself establish a partnership, whether or not the persons sharing them have a joint or common right or interest in any property from which the returns are derived.

———

In other words, even though two or more persons concurrently own income producing property, and share the profits or gross returns from the property, there may still be no partnership. For a partnership to exist, the co-owners must also intend to *carry on a business together for profit*. The word "together" is crucial—the co-owners must intend to manage and control the business together.

The fact that a person receives a share of the profits from an unincorporated business is considered prima facie evidence that the person is a partner in the business. Section 7(4) of the Uniform Partnership Act states.

Section 7. Rules for Determining the Existence of a Partnership

* * *

(4) The receipt by a person of a share of the profits of a business is prima facie evidence that he is a partner in the business, but no such inference shall be drawn if such profits were received in payment:

(a) As a debt by installments or otherwise:

(b) As wages of an employee or rent to a landlord;

(c) As an annuity [see Ch. 11] to a widow or representative of a deceased partner;

(d) As the consideration for the sale of goodwill of a business or other property by installments or otherwise. [Goodwill is the intangible value in a business beyond its book value; a buyer is willing to purchase goodwill because it represents future potential earnings based on the previous record of the business.]

———

Black's Law Dictionary defines "prima facie" as follows.

It says:

Prima Facie. Lat. At first sight; on the first appearance; on the face of it; so far as can be judged from the first disclosure; *presumably; a fact presumed to be true unless disproved by some evidence to the contrary* [6] [Emphasis added.]

———

Thus, the effect of showing that a person has received profits from an unincorporated business is to raise a rebuttable presumption of partnership (barring any one of the four exceptions in (a) through (d) above). If the party who has received the profits does not introduce evidence to the contrary, he or she will be held liable as a partner.

Again, for a partnership to exist, the co-owners must intend to carry on together a *business* for profit. As used here, "business" means an enterprise involving continuous and on-going activity for an indefinite period of time. It does not refer to a single business transaction or ownership of property requiring a limited management. The latter type of activity is properly termed a "joint venture" (or "joint adventure"), and is a much more informal arrangement than a partnership. For example, if three people (joint venturers) with separate, full-time occupations get together for the purpose of building an apartment house (which they intend to co-own and co-manage), the arrangement is a joint venture and not a partnership. However, it should be realized that for all intents and purposes, a joint venture is treated the same under the law as a partnership. Partners and joint venturers have much the same rights and liabilities, and where appropriate, the courts will apply the Uniform Partnership Act to issues arising from joint venture arrangements. The only practical difference between a partner and joint venturer is that the latter does not file a partnership tax return, but instead shows his or her profits on his or her personal return as investment earnings or other income. Also, joint ventures seldom operate under firm names, so some parts of the UPA are not applicable.

Under the common law, a partnership (and also a joint venture) is considered to be an *aggregate* of individuals rather than a separate *entity* (as you will learn

———

6. Henry Campbell Black, *Black's Law Dictionary*, Revised Fourth Edition, West Publishing Co., 1968, p. 1353.

in Ch. 23, a corporation is deemed to be an entity—an artificial person—existing separate and distinct from the shareholders who own it). The "aggregate theory" is a very important aspect of the partnership form of business organization.

Generally speaking the Uniform Partnership Act and other partnership statutes follow the "aggregate theory" of partnerships; however, the UPA also applies an "entity theory" to a limited extent for purposes of convenience.[7] The "entity theory" is apparent in the statute as follows:

(1) The common law rule is that a partnership, being an aggregate of individuals, can neither sue nor be sued in the partnership name—suits must be brought and defended in the names of the individual partners. The UPA changes this rule, allowing a partnership to both sue and be sued as an entity (i. e., in the partnership name). However, in some states, a judgment obtained against the partnership alone is enforceable only against partnership assets and not against the personal assets of the individual partners. For this reason, suit is usually brought against *both* the partnership and the individual partners.

(2) Under Section 8(3) of the Uniform Partnership Act, a partnership can hold and convey real property as an entity (i. e., in its own name). The Section states: "Any estate in real property may be acquired in the partnership name. Title so acquired can be conveyed in the partnership name." Where real property is acquired in the partnership name, it must be conveyed in the partnership name, and not in the names of the individual partners.

(3) For accounting purposes, partnership assets, liabilities, and ownership, as well as all business transactions, are accounted for separately and distinct from the personal assets and liabilities of the individual partners.

(4) A partnership may go through bankruptcy as an entity, without involving the personal assets of the individual partners. But, remember, the individual partners are liable for the partnership debts, and every partner (with the exception of a limited partner) exposes all of his or her personal assets to liability for the debts. So if partnership debts exceed partnership assets, the creditors of the partnership may look to the individual assets of each partner.

(5) Sometimes, the partners' personal assets are brought into court along with the partnership assets, and creditors of the partnership and creditors of the individual partners both claim an interest in all the assets. Under Section 40(h) of the UPA, the partnership creditors are given a prior right to the partnership assets, while the creditors of the individual partners are given a prior right to the personal assets of their individual debtors. This is referred to as the *marshaling* of partnership and individual assets (*marshaling* being the arranging or ranking of assets in a certain order toward payment of debts).

Section 40(h) of the Act reads:

Section 40.　Rules for Distribution

* 　* 　*

(h) When partnership property and the individual properties of the partners are in possession of a court for distribution, partnership creditors shall have priority on partnership property and separate creditors on individual property.

* 　* 　*

———————

7. Louisiana (which has not passed the UPA) is the only state which treats a partnership as a complete legal entity.

To summarize, a partnership is an aggregate of individuals (treated as an entity for limited purposes) who have agreed to own, manage, and control a business together for profit.

How is a partnership formed?

A partnership is formed by *contract* between or among the partners. A person who is not a partner (because he or she has not entered into any partnership contract) may nevertheless be held liable as a partner on the basis of *estoppel*.

Partnership by contract. A partnership contract is an agreement between two or more persons to carry on as co-owners a business for profit. Like any other contract, a partnership agreement require mutual assent (the partners must associate voluntarily); consideration (usually found in the partners' mutual promises to place money, labor, and/or skill into the business); capacity (any person with capacity to contract has capacity to become a partner); and legality (the purpose or object of the partnership must be legal and not contrary to public policy). The common law rule is that a corporation has no capacity to become a partner (a number of states have changed this rule by statute—see Ch. 23). A minor has voidable capacity; thus, a minor who enters into a partnership contract may disaffirm the contract.

As with most contracts, there are no special formalities required for entering into a partnership: the agreement may be written, oral, or even implied. However, it is often prudent to put the agreement in writing so as to prevent subsequent problems and controversy. And, of course, if the partnership falls within the Statute of Frauds (e. g., where the partnership is to continue for more than a year), written evidence of the contract is required if the agreement is to be enforceable. Along this line, it is generally held that an agreement between partners to deal in real property does not fall within the Statute of Frauds provision requiring written evidence of any contract involving the sale or transfer of an interest in land. But a contract whereby real property is to be transferred to or by the partnership does fall within the Statute.

Where partners do sit down and write out a formal partnership agreement, the agreement is referred to as the *articles of partnership* or *articles of copartnership*. The articles usually include the following specifics:

(1) The name of the partnership and the identity of the partners;

(2) The nature and scope of the partnership business;

(3) The duration of the partnership;

(4) The capital contributions of each partner (specifying whether they are made in cash or specifically described property);

(5) A plan for division of profits and losses among the partners;

(6) The amount of time to be devoted to the business by each partner, and each partner's management duties;

(7) A provision for withdrawals of money by the partners, whether in the form of salaries or otherwise;

(8) Any restrictions upon the partners in acting for the partnership;[8]

(9) The rights, if any, of the partners to withdraw from the partnership; and the terms, conditions, and notice requirements for withdrawal;

---

8. However, as will be explained later, a partner has apparent authority to act on behalf of the partnership with respect to ordinary partnership business. The partner's contracts will thus be binding on the partnership notwithstanding any secret limitation on the partner's authority unless the third party who dealt with the partner had knowledge of the limitation.

(10) In the event of dissolution of the partnership (dissolution is discussed in detail in a later section), a method for the remaining partners to form a new partnership, if desired; and

(11) A provision for determining the value of a partner's "interest in the partnership" upon the partner's death or withdrawal from the partnership.

It should be pointed out that most partnerships have firm names—usually, the name of one or more of the partners (e. g., Ray Chamberlain Sports or Chamberlain and Forthright Sports) or an assumed (fictitious) name (e. g., Executive Sports or Happy Time Sports). There are few restrictions on names other than that a partnership name may not be the same as or deceptively similar to the name of an already existing partnership. Nor may a partnership name include a term or phrase that is likely to mislead the public into thinking the business is a corporation (e. g., "Ray Chamberlain Sports, Inc." would not be acceptable). Also, any business operating under an assumed name (whether a sole proprietorship or partnership) is generally required to file a certificate with the state setting forth the assumed name of the business along with the true names and addresses of the owners of the business. If ownership of the business subsequently changes hands (e. g., where the business is sold, or a partner is added or withdrawn), a new certificate must be filed. This protects the public by providing an up-to-date record of all people doing business in the state under assumed names. Failure to file the required certificate may result in fine, imprisonment, or both; and the business itself may be disallowed from using the courts to enforce its contract rights against third parties (some states allow the business to "cure" the defect by filing the certificate prior to initiating any legal action).

With regard to duration of a partnership, the partnership agreement may provide for a fixed term of partnership (e. g., 1 year, 5 years, 18 months), or for duration until a certain project is complete. The partnership, in this case, is a *partnership for term,* and any partner who dissolves it (or causes it to dissolve) prior to the expiration of the term or before the completion of the project is liable to his or her co-partners for breach of contract.

A *partnership at will*, on the other hand, has no fixed or determinable period of duration, and any partner can dissolve it at any time without violating the partnership agreement.

Partnership by estoppel. The principle of estoppel has come up several times in previous chapters. As you will recall, the principle states that a party may be estopped (in effect—stopped) from asserting a position that is true because the party has led another to believe that something else was true. The principle applies with full force to partnership law. Suppose that a person who is not a partner purports to be one or knowingly allows another to misrepresent that he or she is a partner. If a third party extends credit or other consideration in reliance on the misrepresentation, the purported partner will be estopped from denying the existence of a partnership.

By way of example, suppose that sole proprietor Ray Chamberlain, in an effort to obtain a bank loan, falsely tells the loan officer that Lola Forthright, who is a wealthy businesswoman in the community, is his partner in the business. Lola has knowledge of the misrepresentation, but does not advise the bank to the contrary, with the result that the bank makes the loan to Ray. If Ray is unable to repay the loan, Lola will have to repay it: she will be estopped from denying that she is Ray's partner because she allowed the bank to believe that she is.

Lola, however, is not a partner in fact (estoppel does not establish an actual partnership) and has no right to interfere in Ray's business or assist in its management.

Section 16 of the Uniform Partnership Act provides:

Section 16. Partner by Estoppel

(1) When a person, by words spoken or written or by conduct, represents himself, or consents to another representing him to any one, as a partner in an existing partnership or with one or more persons actual partners, he is liable to any such person to whom such representation has been made, who has, on the faith of such representation, given credit to the actual or apparent partnership, and if he has made such representation or consented to its being made in a public manner he is liable to such person, whether the representation has or has not been made or communicated to such person so giving credit by or with the knowledge of the apparent partner making the representation or consenting to its being made.

    (a) When a partnership liability results, he is liable as though he were an actual member of the partnership.

    (b) When no partnership liability results, he is liable jointly with the other persons, if any, so consenting to the contract or representation as to incur liability, otherwise separately.

Suppose that one or more partners in a firm falsely represent that a third party is also a partner in the firm. By virtue of the misrepresentation, the partners make the nonpartner their agent with power to bind them to contracts just like any other partner (the partners will be estopped from denying that the nonpartner is their agent). It must be stressed, however, that only the partners who actually made or consented to the misrepresentation will be bound by the nonpartner's acts. Section 16(2) of the UPA states.

(2) When a person has been thus represented to be a partner in an existing partnership, or with one or more persons not actual partners, he is an agent of the persons consenting to such representation to bind them to the same extent and in the same manner as though he were a partner in fact, with respect to persons who rely upon the representation. Where all the members of the existing partnership consent to the representation, a partnership act or obligation results, but in all other cases it is the joint act or obligation of the person acting and the persons consenting to the representation.

What legal relationship exists between the partners themselves?

The legal relationship existing between or among the partners themselves may be broken into the following parts:

    (1) Partners as fiduciaries;

    (2) Rights and duties regarding management;

    (3) Rights and duties regarding books, records, and other information;

    (4) Division of profits and losses;

    (5) Property rights in the partnership; and

    (6) Rights to a formal accounting.

(1) *Partners as fiduciaries.* Each partner is a fiduciary of every other partner. As you will recall from Ch. 21, a fiduciary is a person in a position of trust and confidence with another. A partner is in a position of trust and confidence with his or her co-partners because of the special nature of the partnership relation-

ship (each partner is a co-owner of the business), and because each partner is an agent of the partnership with respect to ordinary partnership business. Just as an agent must act with utmost loyalty and care regarding his or her relationship with the principal, a partner may not compete with the partnership (e. g., by engaging in a competitive business) or "self-deal" in partnership transactions without the consent of *all* the partners. If the partner does so, he or she will have to account to the partnership for any profits derived. And if a partner has agreed (in the partnership agreement) to devote his or her full time to the partnership business, the partner may not work for any other employer, even though the work does not compete with the partnership business. Again, any salary derived from such employment will belong to the partnership.

Section 21 of the Uniform Partnership Act describes the fiduciary responsibilities of a partner as follows.

The Act provides:

Section 21. Partner Accountable as a Fiduciary

(1) Every partner must account to the partnership for any benefit, and hold as trustee for it any profits derived by him without the consent of the other partners from any transaction connected with the formation, conduct, or liquidation of the partnership or from any use by him of its property.

(2) This section applies also to the representatives of a deceased partner engaged in the liquidation of the affairs of the partnership as the personal representatives of the last surviving partner.

———

Note the use of the term "trustee"—a partner holds as "trustee" for the partnership any profits he or she derives personally from the partnership business.

In other words, though the partner may have actual possession of the profits, he or she holds them for the benefit and ownership of all the partners (see Ch. 29 for a discussion of "trusts" and "trustees").

And note that, if all the partners have died and the personal representative of the last surviving partner is liquidating the partnership, the personal representative is a fiduciary as to the survivors of the deceased partners and their interests.

(2) *Rights and duties regarding management.* Start out by realizing that the partners are free to apportion management rights and responsibilities in any manner they desire in the partnership agreement. Thus, one partner may be given much more responsibility than another (e. g., in most large law firms, one partner is designated the "management partner" and given most of the responsibility for the day-to-day operation of the firm—this allows the other partners to concentrate on the practice of law).

Where the partnership agreement is silent as to the specifics of management and control, UPA Section 18 governs, and the partners are deemed to have equal rights. This is so even though the partners are entitled to different percentages of the profits. In the event of a disagreement as to operations, a majority vote of the partners will be decisive with one exception: if the proposed act is contrary to a specific provision of the partnership agreement, *all* the partners must consent to the act or it cannot be done.

Section 18 of the UPA provides:

Section 18. Rules Determining Rights and Duties of Partners

The rights and duties of the partners in relation to the partnership shall be determined, *subject to any agreement between them,* by the following rules

* * *

(e) All partners have equal rights in the management and conduct of the partnership business.

* * *

(h) Any difference arising as to ordinary matters connected with the partnership business may be decided by a majority of the partners; but no act in contravention of any agreement between the partners may be done rightfully without the consent of all the partners. [Emphasis added.]

---

(3) *Rights and duties regarding books, records, and other information.* Upon demand by a co-partner, a partner must give full and accurate information on all matters affecting the partnership business. And each partner has a right to access to the partnership books and records at all times (a deceased partner's personal representative has the same right of access to the partnership books and records).

Sections 19 and 20 of the UPA state:

Section 19. Partnership Books

The partnership books shall be kept, subject to any agreement between the partners, at the principal place of business of the partnership, and every partner shall at all times have access to and may inspect and copy any of them.

Section 20. Duty of Partners to Render Information

Partners shall render on demand true and full information of all things affecting the partnership to any partner or the legal representative of any deceased partner or partner under legal disability.

---

(4) *Division of profits and losses.* In almost all cases, the partnership agreement provides a plan for division of profits and losses among the partners (e. g., Ray Chamberlain 25%, Lola Forth-

right 75%). In the absence of such a plan, the partners are held to share profits and losses equally. Section 18(a) of the UPA states: "[S]ubject to any agreement between them * * * each partner shall * * * share equally in the profits * * * and must contribute toward the losses * * * according to his share in the profits."

(5) *Property rights in the partnership.* Three aspects must be considered:

(a) Each partner's ownership interest in specific partnership property;

(b) Each partner's "interest in the partnership" (i. e., his or her right to partnership profits and surplus); and

(c) Each partner's right as to distributions by the partnership.

Specific partnership property. Section 8(1) of the Uniform Partnership Act provides as follows.

[A]ll property originally brought into the partnership stock or subsequently acquired, by purchase or otherwise, *on account of the partnership,* is partnership property. [Emphasis added.]

The intent of the partners controls: if the partners bought or acquired the property with the intention of devoting it to partnership business, the property is partnership property.

Frequently, however, the intent of the partners is not clear, and a dispute arises between an individual partner and the partnership over whether certain specific property belongs to the partner personally or is partnership property (e. g., a car, typewriter, piece of real property, etc.). In resolving the dispute, the court will look carefully at the following factors:

First, who paid for the property? UPA Section 8(2) states: "Unless the contrary intention appears, property acquired with partnership funds is partnership property." Conversely, the fact that the individual partner paid personally for the property is persuasive (though not conclusive) evidence that the partner owns the property.

Second, who holds title to the property? Whoever holds title is likely to own the property. However, title is not determinative—it is simply one factor to consider. Property that belongs to the partnership may be held in the name of an individual partner purely as a matter of convenience.[9]

Third, is the property necessary to the business operation of the partnership? If it is, the property is likely to be partnership property and not property belonging to the individual partner. The partnership has an even stronger position if it is actually *using* the property (although it is possible that the individual partner loaned the property to the partnership). And if the partnership lists the property as a firm asset on its record books, and treats the property as a partnership asset for tax purposes, there is little likelihood of the individual partner establishing personal ownership. Thus, where Ray Chamberlain lists the building (purchased for use as a store) as an asset of the partnership, and deducts depreciation expense on the building from the partnership income, Ray would have considerable difficulty proving that the building belongs to him personally and not to the partnership.

A special rule applies to "cross" life insurance policies (i. e., policies purchased by partners on each other's lives). Partners frequently purchase such policies in order to have ready cash (in the form of insurance proceeds) with which to "buy out" the interest of a deceased partner (this will be explained in more detail in the section on termination of partnerships). Although an individual partner is listed as the owner and beneficiary of

each policy, all the policy premiums are paid with partnership funds. The question arises—do the insurance proceeds belong to the individual partner or to the partnership?

Unless the partnership agreement provides to the contrary, most courts hold that the proceeds belong to the surviving partner and not to the partnership. By way of example, say that Ray Chamberlain and Lola Forthright purchase insurance on each other's lives, using partnership funds to pay the policy proceeds. Ray is listed as the owner and beneficiary of the insurance on Lola; Lola is listed as the owner and beneficiary of the policy on Ray. If Ray dies, the life insurance proceeds will belong to Lola, not to the partnership. If there are partnership losses to be paid in excess of partnership assets, the losses will be shared by Ray's estate and Lola Forthright according to the terms of the partnership agreement.

Where there are more than two partners and each partner owns a life insurance policy on more than one partner, it is common to provide in a "buy out" agreement that, upon the death of a partner, his or her estate will transfer all life insurance policies on the surviving partners to the surviving partners.

What are each partner's rights in specific partnership property? Each partner has an ownership interest in the property as a *tenant in partnership.* You will recall the following discussion of *tenancy in partnership* from Ch. 5 of the text.

The Chapter states:

As to ownership of partnership property, each partner has equal rights to the property in the form of concurrent ownership called *tenancy in partnership.* The legal "unity" required for this form of ownership is the partnership method of doing business.

9. If partnership property that is held in the name of an individual partner is transferred to a bona fide purchaser, the bfp will prevail over the partnership as to the property even if the partner had no authority to make the transfer.

The incidents of ownership are as follows:

(1) Each partner has an equal right to possession of partnership property for partnership purposes (as opposed to private purposes or interests of the individual partners);

(2) All partners must join in any transfer of an interest in partnership property;

(3) Partnership property is subject only to the claims of creditors of the partnership—not to claims of creditors of the individual partners;

(4) Partnership property is not considered community property, and is not subject to any property interests of spouses or families;

(5) Partnership property is not part of the deceased partner's estate; upon the death of a partner, the remaining partners automatically receive the decedent's interest in the partnership property until the last surviving partner owns the property in severalty.

———

Survivorship is perhaps the most important feature of a tenancy in partnership: when a partner dies, the remaining partners automatically acquire his or her interest in the partnership property. Of course, the surviving partners have a duty to account to the deceased's estate for the value of the deceased's "interest in the partnership" (explained below). In so doing, the survivors will, in effect, pay over the full value of the deceased's interest in the specific partnership property —however, the survivors will be able to keep the specific assets in case they want to continue the business as a new partnership.

Finally, it should be pointed out that each individual partner has an insurable interest in partnership property even though title to the property is in the partnership name.

A partner's "interest in the partnership" (i. e., his or her interest in partnership profits and surplus). This brings us to the second property right of each partner—his or her *interest in the partnership* (i. e., his or her share of partnership profits and surplus as of any given date).

A partner's interest in the partnership is figured from the partner's capital account as reflected by the partnership balance sheet. It includes any capital contributions and advances made by the partner to the partnership (an "advance" is a capital contribution beyond the amount the partner agreed to contribute in the partnership agreement). Looking back to the January 1, Year #2 balance sheet for Ray Chamberlain Sports, we see that Ray has a partnership interest of $126,277.50 as of January 1st; Lola Forthright has an interest of $832.50. Assuming Ray dies on January 1st, Lola (as the last surviving tenant in partnership) will become the sole owner of the partnership assets, including the cash, inventory, and building worth a total of $190,110.00. However, Lola will be obligated to account to Ray's estate for the value of Ray's interest in the partnership —$126,277.50.

A partner's interest in the partnership is always classified as *personal property* even where all the partnership assets are real property. UPA Section 26 sttaes: " real property. UPA Section 26 states: "A partner's interest in the partnership is his share of the profits and surplus, and the same is personal property." The classification of the interest as personal property can make a difference, particularly where a decedent partner leaves all his or her personal property to one beneficiary and all his or her real property to another.

A partner is free to assign his or her interest in the partnership: the assignee does not become a partner by virtue of the assignment, but merely succeeds to the partner's rights as to profits and surplus.

A judgment creditor of an individual partner, though he or she may not reach specific partnership property, may obtain a *charging order* against the partner's interest in the partnership. Under the charging order, future distributions in respect of the partner's interest must be paid to the creditor until the judgment is satisfied. In some cases, the courts will even order sale of the partner's interest to satisfy the judgment.

Section 28 of the Uniform Partnership Act provides:

Section 28. Partner's Interest Subject to Charging Order

(1) On the due application to a competent court by any judgment creditor of a partner, the court which entered the judgment, order, or decree, or any other court, may charge the interest of the debtor partner with payment of the unsatisfied amount of such judgment debt with interest thereon.

* * *

Rights as to distributions. In any particular year, a partner may or may not receive his or her share of profits by way of cash or property distributions. As you already know, a partner is taxed on his or her share of profits whether or not he or she actually receives them. In our example, Ray Chamberlain was entitled to 25% of the profits of the sporting goods store, and Lola Forthright 75%. In Year #1, Lola received nearly all of her share of the profits (she took out $18,000 for her personal living expenses), while Ray received none of his (Ray's share went into his interest in the partnership as reflected in Ray's capital account). Both parties were taxed on their share of the profits.

When a partnership is dissolved, any partner who has not actually received his

or her full share of profits is entitled to payment in full of the share as part of his or her interest in the partnership (however, as will be seen in the section on termination of partnerships, partnership debts and liabilities must be satisfied first).

Upon dissolution, a partner is also entitled to the return of his or her capital investment (part of his or her interest in the partnership) along with any advances made to the partnership (again, an "advance" being a capital contribution by a partner beyond the amount the partner agreed to contribute in the partnership agreement). Section 18(a) of the Uniform Partnership Act states in part: "[S]ubject to any agreement between them . . . each partner shall be repaid his contributions, whether by way of capital or advances to the partnership property."

In our example, Ray Chamberlain contributed $120,000 capital to the partnership (Lola Forthright contributed no capital, offering instead her management skills to the business). The $120,000 is reflected in Ray's capital account on the balance sheet for Ray Chamberlain Sports. When the partnership comes to an end, Ray or his estate is entitled to repayment of the $120,000, along with interest from the date when repayment should have been made (in other words, if the partnership agreement provided for repayment at an earlier date, and repayment was not made at that time, Ray will be entitled to interest from that date). In the case of an advance, interest is payable from the date of the advance. Section 18 of the UPA provides in part.

It says:

* * *

(c) A partner, who in aid of the partnership makes any payment or advance beyond the amount of capital which he agreed to contribute, shall be paid interest from the date of the payment or advance.

(d) A partner shall receive interest on the capital contributed by him only from the date when repayment should be made.

———

As to remuneration, the general rule is that a partner is not entitled to any salary or wage for working for the partnership unless all the partners have consented to such payment. However, a partner is entitled to reimbursement for expenses incurred by him or her in the ordinary conduct of the partnership business. Section 18 of the UPA, Subsections (b) and (f) state:

(b) The partnership must indemnify every partner in respect of payments made and personal liabilities reasonably incurred by him in the ordinary and proper conduct of its business, or for the preservation of its business or property.

*   *   *

(f) No partner is entitled to remuneration for acting in the partnership business, except that a surviving partner is entitled to reasonable compensation for his services in winding up the partnership affairs.

———

(6) *A partner's right to a formal accounting.* Usually, a breach of the partnership agreement by one partner results in dissolution of the partnership. If the breaching partner refuses to cooperate in dissolving the business, the other partners may go to court to obtain a decree of dissolution and a formal accounting of the partnership assets.

Under Section 22 of the Uniform Partnership Act, a partner is entitled to a formal accounting if he or she is wrongfully excluded from the partnership business,

or other circumstances render an accounting just and reasonable. Generally speaking, a demand in court for a formal accounting will result in dissolution of the partnership even where the party seeking the accounting does not request a dissolution (the other partners usually choose to dissolve the partnership under such circumstances). Section 22 of the Uniform Partnership Act provides:

Section 22. Right to an Account

Any partner shall have the right to a formal account as to the partnership affairs:

(a) If he is wrongfully excluded from the partnership business or possession of its property by his co-partners,

(b) If the right exists under the terms of any agreement,

(c) As provided by Section 21 (Partner Accountable as a Fiduciary),

(d) Whenever other circumstances render it just and reasonable.

———

Where legal relationship exists between the partners and third parties (i. e., nonpartners)?

We move now to the legal relationship existing between the partners and third parties (i. e., nonpartners). This is an important area of partnership law as the purpose of a partnership is to do business with third parties. There are two aspects to the relationship that must be considered:

(1) The authority of partners as agents to contract with third parties; and

(2) The liability of partners to third parties.

Authority of partners as agents. Every partner is an agent of the partnership with respect to ordinary partnership business. It follows that any routine business contract entered into by a partner with a third party is binding on the partnership. Any nonbusiness-related contract or contract outside the ordinary scope of the business is not binding on the partnership. For example, it may be routine for partners to transfer or sell real property belonging to the partnership; more often, however, such a transfer or sale is outside the scope of ordinary business matters, and will not be binding on the partnership.

Because it is normal to the appearance of a partner to be able to bind the partnership in ordinary business matters, a partner will have apparent authority to do so notwithstanding any secret limitation on his or her authority. Of course, if the third party who deals with the partner has knowledge of the limitation, the partner will have no apparent authority, and the partnership will not be bound.

Section 9 of the Uniform Partnership Act provides as follows.

Section 9. Partner Agent of Partnership as to Partnership Business

(1) Every partner is an agent of the partnership for the purpose of its business, and the act of every partner, including the execution in the partnership name of any instrument, for apparently carrying on in the usual way the business of the partnership of which he is a member binds the partnership, unless the partner so acting has in fact no authority to act for the partnership in the particular matter, and the person with whom he is dealing has knowledge of the fact that he has no such authority.

(2) An act of a partner which is not apparently for the carrying on of the business of the partnership in the usual way does not bind the partnership unless authorized by the other partners.

* * *

(4) No act of a partner in contravention of a restriction on authority shall bind the partnership to persons having knowledge of the restriction.

However, there are certain things that a partner has no apparent authority to do.

UPA Section 9(3) states:

(3) Unless authorized by the other partners or unless they have abandoned the business, one or more but less than all [10] the partners have no authority to:

(a) Assign the partnership property in trust for creditors or on the assignee's promise to pay the debts of the partnership,

(b) Dispose of the good-will of the business,

(c) Do any other act which would make it impossible to carry on the ordinary business of a partnership,

(d) Confess a judgment,

(e) Submit a partnership claim or liability to arbitration or reference.

It should be pointed out that a partner's power to bind the partnership cannot be terminated by the act of another partner short of dissolution of the partnership (dissolution is discussed in detail in the following section).

Liability of partners to third parties. The liability of partners to third parties

10. In other words, *all* the partners can get together to do these things, but less than all cannot do so absent express authorization.

varies depending on whether it is contract liability or tort liability.

Contract liability. Partners are *jointly* liable on all partnership contracts. By this is meant that they are liable *together as a group* on contracts; they are not liable individually. It follows that all partners are "necessary parties" to any action involving a contract—if one partner is named in a suit to enforce a contract, all must be named.

Of course, a creditor of the partnership may always proceed against the partnership itself by filing suit in the partnership name. But if the creditor names only the partnership, and not the individual partners, any judgment obtained will bind only the partnership assets (together with the personal assets of any individual partner who is actually served with a summons—see Appendix A on use of a summons to obtain jurisdiction over a person).

The fact that partners are jointly liable does not mean they each must pay an equal amount and no more of any judgment obtained against them. If there are ten partners, and only two have assets (the others being bankrupt), the two with assets will have to pay the entire judgment (beyond whatever the partnership assets will cover). This is so though all the partners are jointly liable, and all are named in the contract action. Of course, any partner who pays more than his or her share of the losses as set by the partnership agreement will have a right to contribution from the other partners.

The rule of joint liability applies even to a partner whose identity has been kept secret (called a "dormant" partner). A dormant partner is bound by the acts of his or her co-partners in the same manner as an undisclosed principal is bound by the acts of his or her agents.

The rule of joint liability also applies to an incoming partner who is held liable even for debts that existed before he or she came into the partnership. However, the incoming partner is liable for such pre-existing debts only to the extent of his or her investment in the partnership (in other words, his or her liability must be satisfied out of partnership assets). This is provided by Section 17 of the Uniform Partnership Act as follows.

Section 17. Liability of Incoming Partner

A person admitted as a partner into an existing partnership is liable for all the obligations of the partnership arising before his admission as though he had been a partner when such obligations were incurred, except that this liability shall be satisfied only out of partnership property.

———

Because the contract liability of partners is *joint,* a release of one partner by a creditor serves to release all partners (a "release" is a contract not to hold the partner liable on the debt).

Tort liability. In contrast to their *joint* liability on contract obligations, partners are *jointly and severally* liable for partnership torts. That is to say, the partners are liable not only *together as a group,* but also *individually.* Thus, the tort victim may sue all the partners together, or a single partner (without joining the other partners).

Each partner is held to assume liability for torts committed by his or her co-partners within the ordinary scope of the partnership business. This is a rule of partnership law, and is not based on the doctrine of respondeat superior. However, if the particular tort requires proof of malice or bad intent (e. g., fraud or misrepresentation), each partner who is held liable must be shown to have had the specific intent or malice. Of course, negligence, which is the most common tort, has no specific intent requirement, and each partner is jointly and severally liable without regard to intent. The following UPA provisions are relevant.

Section 13. (Partnership Bound by Partner's Wrongful Act)

Where, by any wrongful act or omission [i. e., a tort] of any partner acting in the ordinary course of the business of the partnership or with the authority of his co-partners, loss or injury is caused to any person, not being a partner in the partnership, or any penalty is incurred, the partnership is liable therefor to the same extent as the partner so acting or omitting to act.

Section 14. (Partnership Bound by Partner's Breach of Trust)

The partnership is bound to make good the loss:

(a) Where one partner acting within the scope of his apparent authority receives money or property of a third person and misapplies it [i. e., converts it]; and

(b) Where the partnership in the course of its business receives money or property of a third person and the money or property so received is misapplied [i. e., converted] by any partner while it is in the custody of the partnership.

Section 15. (Nature of Partner's Liability)

All partners are liable:

(a) Jointly and severally for everything chargeable to the partnership under Sections 13 and 14.

(b) Jointly for all other debts and obligations of the partnership; but, any partner may enter into a separate obligation to perform a partnership contract.

Partners may even be held liable for torts inflicted on one of their own members. So if one partner negligently injures another while acting within the scope of ordinary partnership business, the remaining partners are liable for the tort. However, if a third person injures a partner, the partnership has no right to recover damages—remember, a partnership is an aggregate of individuals, not an entity.

Finally, the release of one partner by the victim of the tort does not serve to release any other partner. The partners, in this case, are jointly and severally liable, and each may be held without regard to the liability of any other partner.

How is a partnership terminated?

The term "dissolution" has a special meaning in the law of partnership. It refers, not to the actual termination of the partnership, but to the beginning of the "winding up" of the partnership business preliminary to termination. Section 29 of the Uniform Partnership Act defines "dissolution" in these words: "The dissolution of a partnership is the change in the relation of the partners caused by any partner ceasing to be associated in the carrying on as distinguished from the winding up of the business." Note the distinction—prior to dissolution, a partnership is "carrying on" business; after dissolution, it is "winding up" business. And UPA Section 30 states: "On dissolution the partnership is not terminated, but continues until the winding up of partnership affairs is completed [at which time the dissolved partnership goes out of existence]."

The "winding up" process may be lengthy and cumbersome, as where all the partners disband, all the assets are sold, and all business operations cease. Or it may be short and rather easily accomplished, as where only one partner leaves, and the others continue the business as a new partnership—the "winding up" here being simply to account to the withdrawing partner for the value of his or her interest in the partnership. Once the "winding up" is complete, the dissolved partnership is terminated.

In all cases, the following events will trigger dissolution of a partnership, although the "winding up" process will vary depending on the circumstances:

(1) *The express will of a partner.* Any partner may, at any time, dissolve the partnership. This is so even in the case of a *partnership for term* (i. e., one with a fixed or determinable period of duration). A partnership is considered a highly personal relationship, and it is a rule of law that no person can be forced to become a partner or to remain one against his or her will.

Of course, a partner who prematurely dissolves a partnership for term breaches the partnership agreement and is liable in damages to the other partners. And though the original partnership is dissolved, the other partners have a right under UPA Section 38(2)(b) to continue the business *in the partnership name* [11] (but as a new partnership, upon payment to the breaching partner of the value of his or her partnership interest less any recoverable damages). Here, "winding up" is a relatively easy matter.

(2) *Expulsion of a partner.* A partnership dissolves if the partners expel one of their members; to continue in business, the remaining partners must effect a new partnership agreement. Whether the expulsion will constitute a breach of contract, entitling the expelled partner to damages, depends on the partnership agreement. If the agreement makes no provision for expulsion, or if the expulsion was made in bad faith, the expelled partner will be allowed to recover.

(3) *Death or bankruptcy of a partner.* The personal services and credit of each partner are considered essential to a part-

nership. It follows that the death or bankruptcy of a partner dissolves the partnership. Any surviving, nonbankrupt partners have the right to "wind up" the partnership affairs.

Though some events are a cause for dissolution, the partners may waive dissolution and continue with the partnership (in 1 through 3 above, the partners cannot waive dissolution because at least one of their members is actually leaving the partnership).

(4) *Expiration of the partnership term.* Generally speaking, a partnership for term dissolves upon the expiration of the term or upon the completion of the project. However, the partners may waive the dissolution and proceed as a partnership at will.

(5) *Illegality.* Similarly, a partnership usually dissolves if its operations becomes illegal (e. g., where a court decision or a statute makes the partnership business unlawful). But again, the partners may waive dissolution and simply return to a legal business activity.

In most cases, the partners look ahead at the time of forming the partnership and include a "buy out" plan in the partnership agreement which provides for continuing the business in the event of dissolution by act of a partner, by expulsion, or by death or bankruptcy of a partner. Again, in this case, "winding up" is usually limited to settling accounts with the withdrawing, expelled, or deceased partner.

Finally, a partnership has no choice but to dissolve if it is ordered to do so by *judicial decree.* Section 32 of the Uniform Partnership Act provides that, upon application by or for a partner, the courts will order dissolution whenever:

(a) A partner has been declared *insane* in any judicial proceeding or is otherwise shown to be of unsound mind;

---

11. This is also true whenever the partnership is dissolved by judicial decree be-

cause of one **partner's** improper conduct which adversely affected the partnership.

(b) A partner is *incapable of performing* his or her partnership duties;

(c) A partner is guilty of *improper conduct* which adversely affects the partnership business or the interests of the partners. Examples would include a partner acting to further his or her own interests at the expense of the partnership, or wrongfully excluding his or her co-partners from the partnership business;

(d) The partnership can *continue operating only at a loss;* and

(e) Dissolution is the only way to protect the interests of an assignee of a partner or a judgment creditor with a charging order against a partner's interest in the partnership. However, if the partnership is for term, dissolution must await expiration of the term or completion of the project.

(f) Other circumstances render *dissolution the equitable thing to do.*

In determining how extensive a "winding up" will be required, the courts will look at all the circumstances, including the partnership agreement and the wishes of the partners. Say that some of the partners want to continue the business as a new partnership. If the interests of all parties can be protected by allowing the business to continue absent a partner or two, the courts will order a limited "winding up" (i. e., the partners who want to stay in business will be allowed to "buy out" the dissatisfied, deceased, or objectionable partners).

But if the interests of the parties demand a complete liquidation of the partnership, the courts will not hesitate to so require. The courts will order that all partnership assets be sold, and that all proceeds be applied to partnership debts and liabilities. Any excess proceeds will be used, first, to repay each partner's capital account, and, next, to pay profits as provided by the partnership agreement.

In the event that partnership debts and liabilities exceed assets, the partners will be ordered to contribute according to their share in the profits. If any partner is insolvent, the remaining partners will have to make up his or her share, again sharing the loss proportionately according to the partnership agreement.

These distribution rules are set forth in Section 40 of the Uniform Partnership Act as follows:

Section 40.   Rules for Distribution

In settling accounts between the partners after dissolution, the following rules shall be observed, subject to any agreement to the contrary:

(a) The assets of the partnership are:

I.   The partnership property,

II. The contributions of the partners necessary for the payment of all the liabilities specified in clause (b) of this paragraph.

(b) The liabilities of the partnership shall rank in order of payment, as follows:

I.   Those owing to creditors other than partners,

II. Those owing to partners other than for capital and profits;

III. Those owing to partners in respect of capital,

IV. Those owing to partners in respect of profits.

(c) The assets shall be applied in order of their declaration in clause (a) of this paragraph to the satisfaction of the liabilities.

(d) The partners shall contribute, as provided by Section 18(a) [12] the

---

12. Again, Section 18(a) provides that "each partner * * * must contribute toward the losses * * * sustained by the partnership according to his share in the profits."

amount necessary to satisfy the liabilities; but if any, but not all, of the partners are insolvent, or, not being subject to process, refuse to contribute [in other words, if there is no way to obtain jurisdiction over them so as to bring them into court and make them pay—see Appendix A on jurisdiction over the person of the defendant], the other partners shall contribute their share of the liabilities, and, in the relative proportions in which they share the profits, the additional amount necessary to pay the liabilities.

As to the effect of dissolution upon a partnership, it may be summarized as follows:

(1) Upon dissolution, any nonbankrupt partner who has not wrongfully dissolved (or the legal representative of the last surviving nonbankrupt partner) has the right to "wind up" the partnership affairs. This is provided by Section 37 of the Uniform Partnership Act.

(2) The general rule is that dissolution terminates all authority of any partner to act for the dissolved partnership except to the extent necessary to wind up the partnership affairs (of course, if some of the partners are continuing the business as a new partnership, they will have authority to act as agents on behalf of the new partnership). An exception arises where the dissolution is caused by the act, death, or bankruptcy of a partner. The other partners, in this case, have power to bind the partnership until they have knowledge of the dissolution.

A second exception arises where the dissolved partnership fails to give public notice of the dissolution (e. g., by advertising in a newspaper of general circulation) as well as specific notice to persons who have previously dealt with the partnership. If a third party, with prior

knowledge of the partnership and no knowledge of the dissolution, enters into a contract with one of the partners, the dissolved partnership and all of its members will be bound by the contract. For this reason, partners who withdraw from a firm generally publish notice of their withdrawal and give specific notice to previous clients and customers. And if the remaining partners continue on in business as a new partnership, they will want to make certain that proper notice is given so that the withdrawing partners will have no apparent authority to bind the partnership.

(3) Under UPA Section 41, if a new partnership is formed to carry on the business of the dissolved partnership, the new partnership will be liable for the old partnership's debts (i. e., creditors of the dissolved partnership will be creditors of the new partnership). This is so whether or not any of the old members are members of the new firm. Old partners who are members will have unlimited liability for debts of the old partnership. New members (incoming partners) will be liable only to the extent of their investment in the new partnership—they will not be personally liable.

(4) Where the dissolution is triggered by the death of a partner, the surviving partners (as tenants in partnership) are entitled to possession of the partnership assets. The survivors are responsible for "winding up" the partnership affairs (of course, if the survivors choose to continue in business as a new partnership, "winding up" will be little more than settling accounts with the decedent's estate).

As fiduciaries of the deceased partner's estate, the survivors must account to the estate, without delay, for the value of the decedent's interest in the partnership. If the survivors fail to make timely accounting and continue to do business without the consent of the estate, the survivors will be liable for reasonable interest on the decedent's interest in the partnership, or for an appropriate share of any profits earned after the decedent's death, whichever amount is greater. If, by reason of the delay, the value of the business (and thus the value of the decedent's interest) declines, the survivors will be accountable for the value of the deceased's interests as of the date of his or her death. See UPA Section 42. (Of course, many of these problems can be avoided by having the partners enter into a "buy out" agreement which anticipates the death or withdrawal of any partner and establishes values in advance.)

Finally under UPA Section 18(f), the surviving partner who actually performs the work of "winding up" the partnership is entitled to reasonable compensation for his or her efforts as well as reimbursement for any costs incurred in the winding up process.

What is a "limited" partnership?

Early in the chapter, we discussed the unlimited liability of a partner. We saw that, for purposes of liability, a partner's personal assets are lumped together with his or her partnership assets, and all are subject to the claims of partnership creditors. Thus, a partner may lose the proverbial "shirt off his or her back" if the partnership enters into a series of financially disastrous contracts, or incurs liability under the doctrine of respondeat superior for the negligent act of an employee (e. g., where an employee truck driver negligently hits a school bus, injuring several children).

To enable a person to become a partner without risking total financial ruin, the law developed the concept of limited partnership. A *limited partnership* is a partnership consisting of one or more *general (regular) partners* and one or more *limited partners*. Unlike a general partner who has unlimited liability, a limited partner is liable only to the extent of his or her investment in the partnership—the limited partner's personal assets are not subject to liability. However, in exchange for limited liability, the limited partner forfeits the right to act as an agent of the partnership and to participate in the partnership management.

Limited partnerships are governed by the Uniform Limited Partnership Act (ULPA), which has been adopted by 48 states (not including Louisiana and Delaware) since it was first written in 1916. A revised version of the statute has recently been drafted and made available to the state legislatures for consideration.

Section 1 of the ULPA defines "limited partnership" as follows:

A limited partnership is a partnership formed by two or more persons * * * having as members one or more general partners and one or more limited partners. The limited partners as such shall not be bound by the obligations of the partnership.

Under the Uniform Limited Partnership Act, general partners assume full management responsibility along with unlimited liability. Limited partners invest cash or other property (but not services) in the partnership, are not active in management, and have only limited liability (a limited partner's maximum loss is the amount of his or her investment). If a limited partner takes part in management of the partnership, he or she will become liable as a general partner.

ULPA Section 7 provides:

Section 7. (Limited Partner Not Liable to Creditors)

A limited partner shall not become liable as a general partner unless, in addition to the exercise of his rights and powers as a limited partner, he takes part in control of the business.

Apart from the fact that a limited partner may not participate in management or act as an agent of the partnership, the limited partner's rights are much the same as those of a general partner.

Section 10 of the ULPA states:

> **Section 10. (Rights of a Limited Partner)**
>
> (1) A limited partner shall have the same rights as a general partner to
>
> (a) Have the partnership books kept at the principal place of business of the partnership and at all times to inspect and copy any of them,
>
> (b) Have on demand true and full information of all things affecting the partnership, and a formal account of partnership affairs, whenever circumstances render it just and reasonable, and
>
> (c) Have dissolution and winding up by decree of court.
>
> (2) A limited partner shall have the right to receive a share of the profits or other compensation by way of income, and to the return of his contribution. * * *

Under Section 13 of the ULPA, a limited partner may loan money to the partnership or otherwise transact business with the partnership. A limited partner who does so will be treated the same as any other partnership creditor.

The Act provides:

> **Section 13. (Loans and Other Business Transactions with Limited Partner)**
>
> (1) A limited partner also may loan money to and transact other business with the partnership, and, unless he is also a general partner, receive on account of resulting claims against the partnership, with general creditors, a pro rata share of the assets. * * *

Whereas there are no prescribed formalities for entering into a regular partnership, the ULPA requires parties forming a limited partnership to prepare and execute a certificate setting forth, among other things, the name of the partnership; the character or kind of business involved; the location of the principal office; the names and addresses of all partners and their capital contributions; and the designation of each partner as either "general" or "limited". The purpose of the certificate is to put potential creditors of the partnership on notice that some of the partners have limited liability. The certificate must be filed with the appropriate state and/or county official in the location where the business is to operate. If the certificate contains false information, anyone who suffers a loss in reliance on the misrepresentation will be able to recover from any partner—general or limited—who had knowledge of the statement's falsity.

The ULPA demands at least "substantial compliance in good faith" on the part of the parties filing the certificate: anything less will result in the partnership being a regular rather than a limited partnership. Where this occurs, a person who erroneously and in good faith believed himself or herself to be a limited partner may escape liability as a general partner by immediately renouncing his or her interest in the profits of the business or any other partnership income. The filing requirements are set forth in Section 2 of the ULPA as follows:

> **Section 2. (Formation)**
>
> (1) Two or more persons desiring to form a limited partnership shall
>
> (a) Sign and swear to a certificate, which shall state

I. The name of the partnership [generally speaking, the name may not include the surname of any limited partner—if it does, the limited partner will be liable as a general partner],

II. The character of the business,

III. The location of the principal place of business,

IV. The name and place of residence of each member; general and limited partners being respectively designated,

V. The term for which the partnership is to exist,

VI. The amount of cash and a description of and the agreed value of the other property contributed by each limited partner,

VII. The additional contributions, if any, agreed to be made by each limited partner and the times at which or events on the happening of which they shall be made,

VIII. The time, if agreed upon, when the contribution of each limited partner is to be returned,

IX. The share of the profits or the other compensation by way of income which each limited partner shall receive by reason of his contribution,

X. The right, if given, of a limited partner to substitute an assignee as contributor in his place, and the terms and conditions of the substitution,

XI. The right, if given, of the partners to admit additional limited partners,

XII. The right, if given, of one or more of the limited partners to priority over other limited partners, as to contributions or as to compensation by way of income, and the nature of such priority,

XIII. The right, if given, of the remaining general partner or partners to continue the business on the death, retirement or insanity of a general partner, and

XIV. The right, if given, of a limited partner to demand and receive property other than cash in return for his contribution.

Note that in XIII above, reference is made to the right of the remaining general partners to continue the business on the death, retirement, or insanity of a *general partner*. In other words, unless the partnership agreement expressly provides to the contrary, the death, retirement, or insanity of a general partner dissolves the partnership.

The death of a limited partner, on the other hand, does not of itself dissolve the partnership. Rather, the partnership continues, and the personal representative of the deceased limited partner is given the right of a limited partner for purposes of settling the deceased's estate. Thus, the personal representative may have a right to demand a return of capital under VIII above (the time for return may be "upon the death of a partner, general or limited"); or he or she may have a right to appoint a substituted limited partner under X above. Absent an express provision authorizing substitution, substitution will be allowed only with the consent of *all* the partners. If the partners withhold consent, the personal representative may demand and obtain a judicial decree of dissolution, whereupon the value of the decedent's interest in the partnership will be distributed to his or her estate when the "winding up" of the partnership is complete.

The following provisions of the ULPA are relevant.

Section 21. (Death of Limited Partner)

(1) On the death of a limited partner his executor or administrator [see Ch. 30 on "wills"] shall have all the rights of a limited partner for the purpose of settling his estate, and such power as the deceased had to constitute his assignee a substituted limited partner.

Section 19. (Assignment of Limited Partner's Interest)

* * *

(2) A substituted limited partner is a person admitted to all the rights of a limited partner who has died or has assigned his interest in a partnership.

* * *

(4) An assignee shall have the right to become a substituted limited partner if all the members (except the assignor) consent thereto or if the assignor, being thereunto empowered by the certificate, gives the assignee that right.

———

In conclusion, the concept of limited partnership allows a person to become a partner without assuming the full responsibility and unlimited liability of a general partner. Apart from the special rules discussed in this section, a limited partnership operates in much the same way as a regular partnership. Liabilities are the same. Relations between the partners are the same. Dissolution is the same. And so is the "winding up" of the partnership business. However, on distribution of assets, limited partners are paid first before general partners.

Section 23 of the ULPA states:

Section 23. (Distribution of Assets)

(1) In settling accounts after dissolution the liabilities of the partnership shall be entitled to payment in the following order:

(a) Those to creditors, in the order of priority as provided by law * * * [remember that a limited partner who makes bona fide loans to a partnership is treated the same as other creditors as to those loans],

(b) Those to limited partners in respect to their share of the profits and other compensation by way of income on their contributions,

(c) Those to limited partners in respect to the capital of their contributions,

(d) Those to general partners other than for capital and profits,

(e) Those to general partners in respect to profits,

(f) Those to general partners in respect to capital.

———

It should be pointed out that, unless the partnership agreement provides to the contrary, a limited partner may rightfully demand the return of his or her contribution upon dissolution of the partnership or anytime after he or she has given six months notice in writing to all other partners. However, the limited partner shall not receive any part of his or her contribution until all liabilities, except liabilities to partners, have been paid, or there remains sufficient partnership property with which to pay them.

CASES

CASE 1—*Partner Dooley made it clear that he was "voting no."*

SUMMERS v. DOOLEY

Supreme Court of Idaho, 1971.
94 Idaho 87, 481 P.2d 318.

DONALDSON, Justice.

This lawsuit tried in the district court, involves a claim by one partner against the other for $6,000. The complaining partner asserts that he has been required to pay out more than $11,000 in expenses without any reimbursement from either the partnership funds or his partner. The expenditure in question was incurred by the complaining partner (John Summers, plaintiff-appellant) for the purpose of hiring an additional employee. The trial court denied him any relief except for ordering that he be entitled to one half $966.72 which it found to be a legitimate partnership expense.

The pertinent facts leading to this lawsuit are as follows. Summers entered into a partnership agreement with Dooley (defendant-respondent) in 1958 for the purpose of operating a trash collection business. The business was operated by the two men and when either was unable to work, the non-working partner provided a replacement at his own expense. In 1962, Dooley became unable to work and, at his own expense, hired an employee to take his place. In July, 1966, Summers approached his partner Dooley regarding the hiring of an additional employee but Dooley refused. Nevertheless, on his own initiative, Summers hired the man and paid him out of his own pocket. Dooley, upon discovering that Summers had hired an additional man, objected, stating that he did not feel additional labor was necessary and refused to pay for the new employee out of the partnership funds. Summers continued to operate the business using the third man and in October of 1967 instituted suit in the district court for $6,000 against his partner, the gravamen of the complaint being that Summers has been required to pay out more than $11,000 in expenses, incurred in the hiring of the additional man, without any reimbursement from either the partnership funds or his partner. After trial before the court, sitting without a jury, Summers was granted only partial relief and he has appealed. He urges in essence that the trial court erred by failing to conclude that he should be reimbursed for expenses and costs connected in the employment of extra help in the partnership business.

The principal thrust of appellant's contention is that in spite of the fact that one of the two partners refused to consent to the hiring of additional help, nonetheless, the non-consenting partner retained profits earned by the labors of the third man and therefore the non-consenting partner should be estopped from denying the need and value of the employee, and has by his behavior ratified the act of the other partner who hired the additional man.

The issue presented for decision by this appeal is whether an equal partner in a two man partnership has the authority to hire a new employee in disregard of the objection of the other partner and then attempt to charge the dissenting partner with the costs incurred as a result of his unilateral decision.

The State of Idaho has enacted specific statutes with respect to the legal concept known as "partnership." Therefore any solution of partnership problems should logically begin with an application of the relevant code provision.

In the instant case the record indicates that although Summers requested his partner Dooley to agree to the hiring of a third man, such requests were not honored. In fact Dooley made it clear that he was "voting no" with regard to the hiring of an additional employee.

An application of the relevant statutory provisions and pertinent case law to the factual situation presented by the instant case indicates that the trial court was correct in its disposal of the issue since a majority of the partners did not consent to the hiring of the third man. I.C. § 53–318(8) provides:

> "Any difference arising as to ordinary matters connected with the partnership business may be decided by a *majority of the partners* * * *." (emphasis supplied)

*   *   *   A careful reading of the statutory provision indicates that subsection 5 bestows *equal rights in the management and conduct of the partnership business* upon all of the partners. The concept of equality between partners with respect to management of business affairs is a central theme and recurs throughout the Uniform Partnership Law, I.C. § 53–301 et seq., which has been enacted in this jurisdiction. Thus the only reasonable interpretation of I.C. § 53–318(8) is that business differences must be decided by a majority of the partners provided no other agreement between the partners speaks to the issues.

A noted scholar has dealt precisely with the issue to be decided.

> " *   *   *   if the partners are equally divided, those who forbid a change must have their way." Walter B. Lindley, A Treatise on the Law of Partnership, Ch. II, § III, ¶ 24–8, p. 403 (1924). See also, W. Shumaker, A Treatise on the Law of Partnership, § 97, p. 266.

In the case at bar one of the partners continually voiced objection to the hiring of the third man. He did not sit idly by and acquiesce in the actions of his partner. Under these circumstances it is manifestly unjust to permit recovery of an expense which was incurred individually and not for the benefit of the partnership but rather for the benefit of one partner.

Judgment affirmed.

CASE 2—*Was the continuation of the newspaper after the death of the partners an act of winding up the partnership?*

KING v. STODDARD

Court of Appeal, First District, Division 3, 1972.
28 Cal.App.3d 708, 104 Cal.Rptr. 903.

Harold C. BROWN, Associate Justice.

This is an appeal from a judgment in the sum of $12,370 rendered in favor of respondents, Harley King and Stanford White, for accounting services performed for the Walnut Kernel, a newspaper. The action was brought against the executors of two deceased partners who owned the newspaper.

The question presented on this appeal is whether the continuation of the newspaper after the death of the partners was an act of winding up the partnership under Corporations Code section 15035 so as to render the estate of the partners liable for an accountant's bill incurred subsequent to the death of the partners.

The facts: Prior to 1962, the newspaper, Walnut Kernel, was operated as a general partnership in which Lyman E. Stoddard, Sr., and Alda S. Stoddard owned a 51 percent interest as community property, and their son, Lyman E. Stoddard, Jr., owned 49 percent. On January 3, 1963, Alda S. Stoddard died and her daughter, Nancy Gans, was appointed executrix. After the death of Alda S. Stoddard, no formal winding up of the partnership took place. On February 13, 1964, Lyman E. Stoddard, Sr., died, and his son, John L. Stoddard, was appointed executor.

The operation of the business continued after the death of Lyman E. Stoddard, Sr.; Lyman E. Stoddard Jr., operated it as the sole surviving partner. John L. Stoddard, who was then acting on behalf of both estates, considered his duty was to obtain the winding up of partnership affairs as quickly as possible. He was not satisifed with the continuation of the business and when his brother, Lyman, Jr., did not wind up the business, John made some unsuccessful attempts to sell it himself. In 1965 he brought an action against his brother, Lyman, Jr., to force an accounting and liquidation of the assets of the partnership. The case was dismissed before trial upon agreement of the parties which became effective September 6, 1966. In the written agreement, the parties settled their accounts with each other. Lyman E. Stoddard, Jr., agreed to be responsible for all debts arising out of the business since February 13, 1964. The agreement was approved by the probate court. The business was in a weak financial condition after Lyman E. Stoddard, Sr.'s, death and was eventually discontinued.

For approximately 10 years prior to the death of Alda S. Stoddard, the respondents, King and White, and their predecessors had been accountants for the Walnut Kernel. They continued to do the accounting after the deaths of Alda and Lyman, Sr. The appellants were aware that respondents were continuing their work. One of the respondents, King, testified that he understood that respondents would be paid at such time as the estates were in a liquid condition allowing payment and that he would not have continued to render the services had he known that the estates would not be responsible.

John L. Stoddard and Nancy Gans, the executors, did not individually participate in the operation of the partnership business in any manner. The court concluded they were not individually liable.

The court found the estate of Alda S. Stoddard liable for the accounting services rendered by appellants during the period of time following her death—1963 to 1968. The court also found the estate of Lyman E. Stoddard, Sr., jointly liable with the estate of Alda S. Stoddard for the accounting services rendered by appellants following his death—1964 to 1968. * * * The estate's liability was predicated upon the court's finding that the services were rendered during the process of winding up the partnership operation of the Walnut Kernel newspaper. We have concluded that the trial court erred and that the continuation of the business was not a winding up of the affairs of the partnership.

The partnership was dissolved by operation of law upon the deaths of Alda and Lyman E. Stoddard, Sr. Corporations Code section 15029 provides that dissolution of a partnership is "* * * caused by any partner ceasing

to be associated in the carrying on as distinguished from the winding up of
the business." Death is one of the causes of dissolution. Dissolution, however, does not terminate the partnership which " * * * continues until
the winding up of partnership affairs is completed." (Corp. Code, § 15030.)

"In general a dissolution operates only with respect to future transactions; as to everything past the partnership continues until all pre-existing
matters are terminated." Although the general rule is that a partner has
no authority to bind his copartners to new obligations after dissolution section 15035 of the Corporations Code provides that "[a]fter dissolution a
partner can bind the partnership * * * (a) By any act appropriate for
winding up partnership affairs * * * ."

It is this latter provision upon which the court based its decision that
the estates of the deceased partners were liable for the accounting services
performed after dissolution. The court found that "LYMAN STODDARD,
JR.'S continuation of the WALNUT KERNEL business was an appropriate
act for winding up the partnership, since the assets of the business would
have substantial value only if it was a going business. It was to the advantage of the partnership that the business be maintained as a going business."

Respondents, as accountants, had performed services both before and
after the dissolution. The services, however, were a continuation of the accounting services pursuant to the ordinary course of the operation of the
business. Respondent King testified that he was " * * * doing work for
the activity of the newspaper, the financial activity of the newspaper" and
that he was doing the same type of work as he had always performed for
the Walnut Kernel. The exhibits which support his bill for services indicate that he did not, or was not able to, break down his services into categories which would separate ordinary accounting services from those related
to a winding up of the partnership. The court, however, found that the
continuation of the business itself was an "act appropriate for winding up
partnership affairs."

We disagree with this finding. It is probably true that there might
have been advantages to the partnership to sell the business as a going
business, but the indefinite continuation of the partnership business is contrary to the requirement for winding up of the affairs upon dissolution. In
Harvey v. Harvey, 90 Cal.App.2d 549, 554, 203 P.2d 112, 115–116, the court
disapproved a finding that the business and assets of a partnership were of
such character as to render its liquidation impracticable and inadvisable
until a purchaser could be found. The court stated: "In effect it [the
finding] authorizes the indefinite continuation of the partnership after
the death of a partner, a procedure not in accordance with section 571 of
the Probate Code. Respondents counter with the argument that the
business is such that it cannot be wound up profitably, and the estate
given its share. But this argument overlooks the distinction between
winding up a business and winding up the partnership interest in that
business."

There are few cases which illustrate acts approved as "appropriate for
winding up partnership affairs" under either the California Corporations
Code or the identical section 35 of the Uniform Partnership Act. (See
Stump v. Tipps, 120 Cal.App.2d 418, 261 P.2d 315 [assignment of partnership property to repay partnership debt]; Cooley v. Miller & Lux, 168 Cal.
120, 142 P. 83 [disposition of partnership property]; Leh v. General Petro-
leum Corporation, 165 F.Supp. 933 (S.D.Cal.1958) [maintenance of action

for damages on behalf of the partnership]; In re Heller's Estate, 319 Pa. 135, 178 A. 681 [execution of renewal notes after death of partner].)

Even if we assume that a situation might exist where continuation of the business for a period would be appropriate to winding up the partnership interest, such a situation did not exist here. The record reflects the fact that the surviving partner was not taking action to wind up the partnership as was his duty under Probate Code section 571, nor did the estates consent in any way to a delay. Rather, their insistence on winding up took the form of an effort to sell the business and a suit to require an accounting. There is nothing in the record upon which to base the argument made by respondents that appellants consented to their continued employment. The fact that they did not object is of no relevance. They had no right to direct and did not participate in the operation of the business. Therefore, the determination that the acts of the accountants were rendered during a winding up process is not based upon substantial evidence.

* * *

We conclude that the services of respondents were rendered after the dissolution resulting from the deaths of the partners, Lyman, Sr., and Alda Stoddard, and do not constitute services during the "winding up" processes of the partnership within the meaning of section 15031 of the Corporations Code. The claim for those services, therefore, are not chargeable to the partnership.

The judgment is reversed.

CASE 3—*Russell and Andrews took part in the control of the business—limited or general partners?*

HOLZMAN v. DE ESCAMILLA

District Court of Appeal, Fourth District, California, 1948.
86 Cal.App.2d 858, 195 P.2d 833.

MARKS, Justice.

This is an appeal by James L. Russell and H. W. Andrews from a judgment decreeing they were general partners in Hacienda Farms, Limited, a limited partnership, from February 27 to December 1, 1943, and as such were liable as general partners to the creditors of the partnership.

Early in 1943, Hacienda Farms, Limited, was organized as a limited partnership (Secs. 2477 et seq., Civil Code) with Ricardo de Escamilla as the general partner and James L. Russell and H. W. Andrews as limited partners.

The partnership went into bankruptcy in December, 1943, and Lawrence Holzman was appointed and qualified as trustee of the estate of the bankrupt. On November 13, 1944, he brought this action for the purpose of determining that Russell and Andrews, by taking part in the control of the partnership business, had become liable as general partners to the creditors of the partnership. The trial court found in favor of the plaintiff on this issue and rendered judgment to the effect that the three defendants were liable as general partners.

The findings supporting the judgment are so fully supported by the testimony of certain witnesses, although contradicted by Russell and Andrews, that we need mention but a small part of it. * * *

De Escamilla was raising beans on farm lands near Escondido at the time the partnership was formed. The partnership continued raising vegetable and truck crops which were marketed principally through a produce concern controlled by Andrews.

The record shows the following testimony of de Escamilla:

"A. We put in some tomatoes.

"Q. Did you have a conversation or conversations with Mr. Andrews or Mr. Russell before planting the tomatoes? A. We always conferred and agreed as to what crops we would put in. * * *

"Q. Who determined that it was advisable to plant watermelons? A. Mr. Andrews. * * *

"Q. Who determined that string beans should be planted? A. All of us. There was never any planting done—except the first crop that was put into the partnership as an asset by myself, there was never any crop that was planted or contemplated in planting that wasn't thoroughly discussed and agreed upon by the three of us; particularly Andrews and myself."

De Escamilla further testified that Russell and Andrews came to the farms about twice a week and consulted about the crops to be planted. He did not want to plant peppers or egg plant because, as he said, "I don't like that country for peppers or egg plant; no, sir," but he was overruled and those crops were planted. The same is true of the watermelons.

Shortly before October 15, 1943, Andrews and Russell requested de Escamilla to resign as manager, which he did, and Harry Miller was appointed in his place.

Hacienda Farms, Limited, maintained two bank accounts, one in a San Diego bank and another in an Escondido bank. It was provided that checks could be drawn on the signatures of any two of the three partners. It is stated in plaintiff's brief, without any contradiction * * * that money was withdrawn on twenty checks signed by Russell and Andrews and that all other checks except three bore the signatures of de Escamilla, the general partner, and one of the other defendants. The general partner had no power to withdraw money without the signature of one of the limited partners.

Section 2483 of the Civil Code provides as follows:

"A limited partner shall not become liable as a general partner, unless, in addition to the exercise of his rights and powers as a limited partner, he takes part in the control of the business."

The foregoing illustrations sufficiently show that Russell and Andrews both took "part in the control of the business." The manner of withdrawing money from the bank accounts is particularly illuminating. The two men had absolute power to withdraw all the partnership funds in the banks without the knowledge or consent of the general partner. Either Russell or Andrews could take control of the business from de Escamilla by refusing to sign checks for bills contracted by him and thus limit his activities in the management of the business. They required him to resign as manager and selected his successor. They were active in dictating the crops to be planted, some of them against the wish of Escamilla. This clearly shows they took part in the control of the business of the partnership and thus became liable as general partners.

Judgment affirmed.

PROBLEMS

1. Kelly Mertens has been employed by the federal government for several years. Upon the death of her great aunt, Kelly inherits $35,000 cash and decides to quit her job with the government in order to buy and operate a local greeting card and curio shop which is for sale for $30,000. On January 1st, Kelly pays $30,000 cash for the business and receives in return an inventory worth $28,000 and used fixtures (shelving and the like) worth $2,000 (these will last four years and have no value after that time). She also opens a bank account in the name of the new business (Kelly's Cards and Curios) depositing $5,000 as the initial deposit. The next day, Kelly enters into a new lease for the store building, agreeing to pay rent of $200 a month—the rent being due on the 5th day of each month. During the next twelve months, Kelly has total cash sales of merchandise of $94,000. During this time, she buys additional merchandise to sell at a cost of $59,000. She also pays twelve months of rent. She has utility bills for heat, light, and water in the amount of $1,700 for the year. Insurance expenses are $325, and advertising expenses amount to $490. All of Kelly's other cash expenses for the year total $1,115. She takes $750 a month out of the business for her personal expenses. At the end of the year, Kelly counts her inventory and finds that it has a cost value of $24,000. Prepare Kelly's opening balance sheet. Figure her end of the year cash balance. Determine whether she made a profit. Prepare her balance sheet for the beginning of the next year. How must she report her income for tax purposes? For Social Security purposes?

   What different results if Kelly and her brother Bart had together inherited the $35,000 and operated the business as equal partners each taking $750 a month for personal expenses?

2. Answer the following "True" or "False" and give reasons for your answers:

   (a) A partnership is a separate and distinct legal entity.

   (b) The sharing of gross returns from concurrently held property does not in and of itself establish a partnership.

   (c) A partnership can hold and convey real property in its own name.

   (d) A limited partner may participate in management to the same extent as a general partner.

   (e) Both partners and sole proprietors have unlimited liability.

   (f) A partner is taxed on his or her share of partnership income whether or not he or she actually receives the share during the taxable year.

   (g) Dissolution refers to the actual termination of a partnership.

   (h) A partnership is the least complicated form of business organization with no body of law directly governing it.

   (i) The effect of showing that a person has received profits from an unincorporated business is to raise a conclusive presumption of partnership.

   (j) A joint venture is treated the same under the law as a partnership.

   (k) A partnership is treated as an entity for purposes of taxation.

3. Executive Office Supply, Co. is a limited partnership consisting of three general partners (Mike Miller, Bob Bishop, and Jean Carpenter) and two limited partners (Dick Pierce and Vera Vaughn). On March 1st, Vera agrees to work full-time managing the partnership; she immediately begins making important management decisions. On March 3rd, in order to obtain a $25,000 bank loan for the business, Mike and Bob falsely tell First State Bank that Peter Hunter, a well known and prosperous businessman, is a general partner in the firm. Though Peter knows that Mike and Bob are wrongfully using his name, he does not inform the bank, and the bank makes the loan in reliance on the misrepresentation. On March 5th, Sara Carter, an employee of Executive Office Supply, negligently runs the company delivery truck into an auto driven by Fred Jensen. Fred is seriously injured and his claim against the company amounts to $85,000. On March 10th, Jean Carpenter withdraws from the partnership in order to go into the office supply business on her own. Purportedly acting on behalf of Executive Office Supply, Jean purchases $25,000 worth of inventory on credit from Martex Manufacturing Company. Jean has dealt with the Martex Company on behalf of Executive Office Supply many times in the past; Martex has no knowledge that Jean has withdrawn from the partnership. Meanwhile, Bob Bishop feels that he is being unfairly excluded from management decisions, and that he is not receiving his full share of partnership income. He demands a formal accounting.

(a) Who is liable on the $25,000 bank loan from First State Bank? To what extent is each person liable? Explain.

(b) Who is liable to Fred Jensen for Sara Carter's negligence? To what extent is each person liable? Explain.

(c) What is the effect of Jean Carpenter's withdrawal from the partnership?

(d) Who, if anyone, is bound by Jean's contract with Martex Manufacturing Company? To what extent are they bound? Explain.

(e) Does Bob Bishop have a right to a formal accounting? Explain.

(f) Assuming that the whole matter is taken to court, and that creditors of both the partnership and the individual partners are claiming the partnership assets and the assets of the individual partners, how will the court determine priorities among creditors?

4. A general partner will *not* be personally liable for which of the following acts or transactions committed or engaged in by one of the other partners or by one of the partnership's employees?

a. The gross negligence of one of the partnership's employees while carrying out the partnership business.

b. A contract entered into by the majority of the other partners but to which the general partner objects.

c. A personal mortgage loan obtained by one of the other partners on his residence to which that partner, without authority, signed the partnership name on the note.

d. A contract entered into by the partnership in which the other partners agree among themselves to hold the general partner harmless.

[# 12, November 1977 CPA Exam]

5. Martin Cosgrove induced Harold Watts, Charles Randall, and James Howard to join him in a partnership venture. Cosgrove is a sophisticated investor. He proposed that Watts, Randall, and Howard each contribute $100,000 cash to a limited partnership which would consist of himself as general partner and the others as limited partners. Cosgrove was to contribute $50,000, but he was to share equally in all profits and assume all losses in excess of $50,000 upon dissolution. Under these circumstances

   a. The purported creation of a limited partnership is invalid because there must be at least two general partners.

   b. Creditors of the limited partnership would have to sue Cosgrove for any deficiency of assets in liquidation in excess of $50,000 before being able to resort to limited-partnership property above this amount.

   c. If one of the limited partners agreed in the certificate to contribute $100,000 cash but instead contributed $90,000 in cash and $10,000 in services, he may be held liable to the partnership creditors for $10,000.

   d. The limited partnership can properly be called the Cosgrove, Watts, Randall & Howard Investing Company, Limited Partnership.

   [# 18, May 1975 CPA Exam]

6. Kimball, Thompson, and Darby formed a partnership. Kimball contributed $25,000 in capital and loaned the partnership $20,000; he performed no services. Thompson contributed $15,000 in capital and part-time services, and Darby contributed only his full-time services. The partnership agreement provided that all profits and losses would be shared equally. Three years after the formation of the partnership, the three partners agreed to dissolve and liquidate the partnership. Firm creditors, other than Kimball, have bona fide claims of $65,000. After all profits and losses have been recorded there are $176,000 of assets to be distributed to creditors and partners. When the assets are distributed

   a. Darby receives nothing since he did not contribute any property.

   b. Thompson receives $45,333 in total.

   c. Kimball receives $62,000 in total.

   d. Each partner receives one-third of the remaining assets after all the firm creditors, including Kimball, have been paid.

   [# 19, May 1975 CPA Exam]

7. James Quick was a partner in the Fast, Sure and Quick Factors partnership. He subsequently died. His will left everything to his wife including a one-third interest in the land and building owned by Fast, Sure, and Quick.

   a. Mrs. Quick is a one-third owner of Fast, Sure, and Quick's land and building.

   b. The real property in question was held by the partnership as a tenancy in common.

   c. Mrs. Quick automatically becomes the partner of Fast and Sure upon her husband's death.

d. Mrs. Quick has the right to receive a settlement for her husband's interest in the partnership.

[# 39, November 1973 CPA Exam]

8. Eric, Steve, and John are partners. John was recently admitted to the partnership and is relatively inexperienced. If the partners have made *no* agreement to the contrary

a. John's role in the management of the partnership is subordinated to Eric and Steve because of his inexperience.

b. Each partner must contribute to losses according to his share of profits.

c. John is *not* entitled to interest on money he loans the partnership.

d. Profits will be divided in proportion to the amount of each partner's capital investment in the partnership.

[# 44, November 1973 CPA Exam]

9. Braudy and Jones are partners and wish to admit Halsey to the partnership. If Halsey is admitted

a. He is liable for preexisting obligations of the partnership to the same extent as Braudy and Jones.

b. Only Braudy and Jones are liable for preexisting obligations of the partnership.

c. The old partnership is dissolved.

d. The old partnership must be wound up and liquidated.

[#45, November 1973 CPA Exam]

10. **Part a.** Elwynn, Mitchell, and Grady formed a partnership to assemble and market lamps. After renting delivery trucks for several years the partnership was able to accumulate sufficient cash to purchase three delivery trucks. The title to the trucks was placed in the partnership name. Six months after the trucks were purchased, Grady sold one of the trucks and retained the proceeds on the basis that one of the three trucks belonged to him. The other partners disagreed and sought to regain title to the truck from the buyer or recover the proceeds from Grady.

Required: Answer the following, setting forth reasons for any conclusions stated.

1. Discuss the distinction between "partnership property" and a "partnership interest." Include in your discussion reasons for the legal importance of the distinction.

2. Under what circumstances will the partnership succeed in regaining title to the truck from the buyer?

3. If the partnership does not regain title to the truck from the buyer, may it recover the proceeds from Grady?

Part b. The Minlow, Richard, and Jones partnership agreement is silent on whether the partners may assign or otherwise transfer all or part of their partnership interests to an outsider. Richard has assigned his partnership interest to Smith, a personal creditor, and as a result the other partners are furious. They have threatened to remove Richard as a partner, not admit Smith as a partner, and bar Smith from access to the firm's books and records.

Required: Answer the following, setting forth reasons for any conclusions stated.

Can Minlow and Jones successfully implement their threats? Discuss the rights of Richard and Smith and the effects of the assignment on the partnership.

[#5.a. & b., May 1977 CPA Exam]

Chapter 23

THE THIRD WAY OF DOING BUSINESS: THE CORPORATION

A corporation is an artificial being, invisible, intangible and existing only in contemplation of law. Being the mere creature of law, it possesses only those properties which the charter of its creation confers upon it. * * * Among the most important are immortality, and * * * individuality.[1]

What are the characteristics of a corporation?

The corporate form of business organization offers certain advantages that the sole proprietorship and partnership methods do not. Operating a business as a corporation may not only be desirable, it may be essential. For, unlike a sole proprietorship or partnership, a corporation is a separate legal entity existing independently and apart from the people who own it (the owners are called "shareholders" or "stockholders"). A corporation is recognized as an artificial "person" within the meaning of the Due Process Clauses of the fifth and Fourteenth Amendments of the U.S. Constitution.

Being a legal entity, a corporation has rights and liabilities that are separate and distinct from those of its shareholder-owners: the assets and liabilities of a corporation belong to the corporation—not to the shareholders. The legal entity offers the following five advantages:

(1) Limited liability;

(2) Separation of ownership from management;

(3) Ease of transferring ownership interests;

(4) Perpetual life; and

(5) Ease of raising capital.

Limited liability. A person who invests in a corporation (i. e., purchases corporate stock) becomes an owner of the corporation and is called a *shareholder* or *stockholder.* Unlike a sole proprietor or partner, a shareholder enjoys *limited liability*—i. e., a shareholder is liable only to the extent of his or her investment in the corporation: his or her personal assets are not subject to liability. The corporation as an entity is responsible for its own debts. (In contrast, all the personal assets of a sole proprietor or partner—with the exception of a limited partner—may be taken to satisfy business debts or judgments.)

Returning to our example from the previous chapter, suppose that partners Ray Chamberlain and Lola Forthright hire C. Harold as a part-time clerk and delivery girl. While making a delivery in the company truck, C. Harold negligently speeds through a crosswalk, injuring several school children and other pedestrians. As you know, partners Ray and Lola are liable for C. Harold's negligence under the doctrine of respondeat superior; their liability is unlimited. Not only their business assets, but all their nonexempt personal assets (see Ch. 26 regarding exempt property) as well may be taken to satisfy a liability judgment. Even if Ray and Lola have some liability insurance, a judgment in the many hundreds of thousands of dollars is likely to bankrupt both of them.

But suppose that Ray and Lola are doing business, not as a partnership, but as a corporation. In this case, their liability for C. Harold's negligence is limited to the amount of their investment in

---

1. Chief Justice John Marshall speaking for the U.S. Supreme Court in the *Dartmouth* *College* case, 4 Wheat. (17 U.S.) 518, 4 L. Ed. 629 (1819).

the corporation. Their personal assets are not at stake.

Of course, Ray could always limit his liability by becoming a limited partner, or Lola could limit hers by becoming one. But both partners could not do so—at least one of them must remain a general partner, completely liable personally. And, in any case, a limited partner forfeits the right to participate in management of the business. While shareholders as such have no right to participate in management of the corporation, they can serve as corporate directors and officers who do have such a right.

Separation of ownership from management. Another important advantage of a corporation is that ownership is completely separable from management (important because many people want to invest in a business, but have no desire or ability to participate in management). As stated previously, shareholders have no right by virtue of being shareholders to participate in management of the corporation. However, they do have a right to elect a board of directors, which, in turn, chooses corporate officers. It is the directors and officers who are responsible for corporate management.

Of course, if they choose, the shareholders may serve as directors and officers (assuming they can get elected or appointed). But the important thing is that not a single one of them *need* participate in business management.

Take the case of Ray Chamberlain and Lola Forthright. Assuming Ray and Lola incorporate, they can elect themselves as directors and appoint themselves as officers of the corporation. Or they can take a less active role in management, electing themselves as directors, but appointing others as officers. Or they can eschew corporate management altogether by electing a board of nonshareholder directors, and declining appointment as officers.

Ease of transferring ownership interests. The corporate form of business organization also makes for ease of transferring ownership interests. Think about the problems involved when a sole proprietor sells his or her business. He or she personally owns every item of business inventory and other property. The sole proprietor must attach a value to each item of personal property and transfer each item according to the law of sales as studied in Chapter 17 through 19; any real property must be transferred by use of a deed. Where the total inventory or a major part of it is to be sold, the rules on "bulk sales" also apply (see Ch. 27). Observing these legal formalities takes time, and weeks or even months may elapse before the new owner can take over the business. At least for a time, business operations will cease or slow down considerably.

The same is true when a partner withdraws from a partnership. Remember, while a partner may freely transfer his or her *interest in the partnership,* he or she cannot transfer his or her interest in specific partnership property or his or her right to participate in management of the business without the consent of all the partners. If a partner leaves the partnership, a dissolution and winding up is required, which in many cases will halt or slow down business operations, at least for a time.

Now think about the situation where a sole proprietor or partner dies. The sole proprietorship or partnership comes to an end (although the remaining partners may choose to continue the business as a new partnership). And the interest of the deceased sole proprietor or partner must be probated. As you will learn in Ch. 30, "probate" is the process by which a decedent's property is listed, valued, taxed (death taxes), and distributed to the decedent's rightful heirs or beneficiaries. Thus, every item of the deceased sole proprietor's inventory must be listed and valued for probate purposes—in Ray Chamberlain's case, skis, balls, bats, shoes, golf clubs, etc. Similarly, the deceased partner's *interest in the partnership* must be probated, and the partnership wound up. In each case, the business will either cease to exist, or its operations will be slowed or halted temporarily.

In contrast to both a sole proprietor and a partner, a shareholder of a corporation can easily transfer his or her ownership interest inter vivos or at death without disrupting the corporate operations in any way. This is because a shareholder owns—not an interest in any specific corporate property (remember, the corporation as an entity owns its own property) or a right to participate in corporate management—but an intangible personal property interest in the entire corporation. The shareholder's interest is represented by a stock certificate which evidences the number of corporate shares owned. Thus, during his or her lifetime, a shareholder may transfer all or part of his or her stock (e. g., by sale or gift) without affecting the corporate operations. The shareholder merely indorses the stock certificate over to the transferee (there is a place on back of the certificate for the transferor-owner to sign); the certificate is then delivered to the corporation which issues a new stock certificate to the new owner. Obviously, this is much easier than worrying about the individual business assets. And it does not halt or slow down business operations. Furthermore, if the transferor has held the stock long enough to qualify for long term capital gain treatment (one year), sale of the stock may result in a tax advantage to the seller (generally only 50% of long term capital gain is taxed for income tax purposes). The sale of the individual assets held in a sole proprietorship or partnership may well result in higher taxes.

Suppose that a shareholder dies? Certainly, his or her stock must be valued and listed for probate purposes. But this is much simpler than valuing and listing individual business assets. Moreover, it does not disrupt the corporate business operations, which brings us to the fourth advantage of the corporate method of doing business—perpetual life.

Perpetual life. Because a corporation is a legal entity and not an aggregate of its individual shareholders, it is capable of perpetual life. In other words, a corporation, being an artificial person, is immune from death. Unless the Articles of Incorporation provide for a limited period of duration or the shareholders vote to dissolve the corporation, the corporation will live forever, unaffected by the deaths of its shareholder owners. And it may have many generations of different shareholders.

Ease of raising capital. Finally, a corporation does not have the limited financial resources of a sole proprietorship or partnership. If a corporation wants to raise capital (e. g., to start or expand the business), it can offer stock for sale. And it can have literally thousands of shareholders. (The fact that management is completely separable from ownership makes it possible for a corporation to raise capital without risking automatic interference in its management.)

However, it should be pointed out that the issuance and sale of corporate stock is strictly controlled by state and federal statutes called "Blue Sky Laws"—these are considered in detail in Ch. 24 of the text dealing with "securities regulations".

Is the corporate form always effective to limit the liability of the shareholders?

The rights and liabilities of a corporation are separate and distinct from those of its shareholders. The corporate entity is said to be like a "veil" in that it shields the shareholders from corporate debts and other obligations. Thus, if a judgment is entered against the corporation, the shareholders will be liable only to the extent of their investment in the corporation; their personal assets will not be subject to liability.

However, the "corporate veil" operates only if the business is conducted in good faith. It was stated in the case of United States v. Milwaukee Refrigerator Transit Co., 142 F. 247, 255 (C.C.E. D.Wis. 1905).

If any general rule can be laid down * * * it is that a corporation will be looked upon as a legal entity * * * until sufficient reason to the contrary appears; but, when the notion of legal entity is used to defeat public convenience, justify wrong, protect fraud, or defend crime, the law will regard the corporation as an association of persons.

Thus, the general rule is that the corporate entity protects the shareholders from liability beyond their investments. However, if the corporate entity is being used to defraud people or to achieve other injustice, the courts will "pierce" (set aside) the corporate veil, and hold the shareholders personally liable for the corporate debts and other obligations. (It is sometimes said that since the shareholders themselves have in effect disregarded the corporate entity, they are estopped from asserting the entity as a defense to actions brought against them personally.) Generally, the courts will pierce the corporate veil only where the following two factors are present:

(1) The corporation is not operating as a true legal entity, but is really the "alter ego" of its shareholders who are using the corporate form as a "shell" or "vehicle" to control private interests and assets, or debts. A corporation looks to be the alter ego of its shareholders when no corporate stock is issued following formation of the corporation, no directors are elected, or no corporate records kept.

(2) Failure to pierce the corporate veil would result in fraud or other injustice. By way of example, suppose that a corporation is being used to defraud creditors: the shareholders invest little money in the corporation; the corporation incurs debts far in excess of the investments. A failure to pierce the corporate veil and hold the shareholders personally liable would work an injustice on the creditors.

Usually, the corporate veil is pierced only where there are very few shareholders (small corporations with few shareholders are more likely to be conducted in close association with the personal assets of the owners). But the fact that a corporation has few shareholders or even just one shareholder does not mean that its entity status will be disregarded and its corporate veil pierced. So long as the corporation is adequately financed; complies with all formation and recordkeeping requirements; conducts itself on a corporate and not on a personal basis; and has a legal purpose and objective, its shareholders will certainly enjoy limited liability. This is so even though it is a one shareholder or family corporation.

How is a corporation formed?

Every state has a general corporation statute governing the formation and operation of corporations. Though the statutory provisions vary somewhat from state to state, the basic requirements are the same. Generally, one or more incorporators (people desiring to form a corporation—some states require only one, others require at least three) must prepare written *Articles of Incorporation* and file them with the state corporation commissioner (or other designated official). A small filing fee, typically under

$100, is charged. If the Articles are in order (i. e., if they comply with the requirement of the general corporation statute), the corporation commissioner will issue a *corporate charter,* which is a written instrument in certificate form creating the corporation and permitting it to operate. The charter certificate should become part of the permanent records of the corporation.

As a general rule, the Articles of Incorporation must include the following:

(1) *The name of the corporation.* In some states, the corporate name must include the word "corporation", "company", or "incorporated", or an abbreviation thereof, to put the public on notice that the business is incorporated. In most states, the name may not be the same as or deceptively similar to the name of an existing corporation doing business in the state.

(2) *The period of duration of the corporation (which may be perpetual).* In some states, if the period of duration is not stated, it will be deemed perpetual.

(3) *The purpose of the corporation.* In all states, the Articles of Incorporation must set forth the corporate purpose or purposes. Generally, this may be in the form of a statement of specific purpose (the main business actually contemplated by the corporation) or a general statement that the corporation will pursue "any and all lawful purposes". (It is usually good practice to state both the specific purpose contemplated and to provide that the corporation will pursue any and all lawful purposes.)

In the past, it was unlawful for a corporation to practice certain learned professions such as law, medicine, accounting, and the like. Because individuals engaged in such professions have to meet specific education and licensing requirements and are subject to continuing regulation in areas of professional responsibility and ethics, it was considered contrary

to public policy to allow them to limit their liability by incorporating. Today, most states allow such "professional corporations" so as to permit professionals to take advantage of the various benefits available only to corporate employees under the federal tax laws—most notably, pension and profit-sharing plans with deferred compensation aspects (i. e., some income taxation is postponed to a later time, such as when the employee retires). However, the professionals, though they are incorporated, retain *unlimited liability* for their own acts, as well as for the professional acts of those who perform under their supervision. Thus it is that accountants, lawyers, doctors, dentists, architects, nurses, engineers, etc. who incorporate will continue to have unlimited personal liability for their malpractice.

A professional corporation is incorporated in much the same manner as any other corporation. However, the Articles of Incorporation must identify the business as a professional corporation; and only licensed members of the particular profession may own its shares. The corporate name is restricted in that it must consist of the names of some or all of the shareholders, followed by the initials "P. C.", to indicate its professional status. Where the corporation has only one or two shareholders, it is limited to the same number of directors and officers.

(4) *The address of the initial corporate office and agent.*

(5) *The number of directors making up the original board of directors; and the name and address of each director (some states require only 1, others require at least 3).*

(6) *The number of authorized shares of stock; whether the stock is to be par value or no-par value; the different classes of stock, and the number of shares of each class.*

A corporation sells its ownership by issuing shares of stock. The Articles of

Incorporation must state how many shares *can* be issued (i. e., how many are authorized by the corporation). Say that a corporation is authorized to issue 1,000 shares of stock. It issues all the shares; you buy 200. You own 20 percent of the corporation (but remember, you have no interest in the specific corporate property—the corporation as an entity owns this—you own a 20% intangible personal property interest in the entire corporation). It is usually a good idea for a corporation to issue only a part of its authorized stock. The corporation may want to expand at a later time and add other shareholders; if all authorized stock has already been issued, the Articles of Incorporation will have to be amended to provide for a new issue.

The Articles must also state whether the stock is to be *par value* or *no-par value*. Par value stock is stock that is assigned a specific value (such as $100 a share or $10 a share) which is stated on the stock certificate. The initial board of directors determines what the par value should be. Par value shares cannot legally be issued unless the corporation receives consideration for the shares equal to the par value (i. e., the value stated on the certificate). However, as will be seen in a later section dealing with "promoters" (people who help in the creation or organization of a new corporation), par value stock is not always issued for cash—it is sometimes issued for property or services. Thus, even at the outset of the business, the actual value of the corporate assets may be less than the par value of the issued stock (e. g., where stock is issued in return for services). And if the corporation is unsuccessful, the value of a shareholder's interest (the difference between corporate assets and liabilities times the shareholder's percentage share) will decrease and become far smaller than the par value stated on the certificate.

No-par value stock is stock that is issued without any stated value on the certificate. The board of directors determines what amount of cash or other consideration is to be accepted for what number of shares. Say that a corporation issues 100 shares of no-par value stock. One investor contributes $25,000 capital for 25% (25 shares) of the stock; so do two other investors. An inventor who has patented a new machine gives the patent to the corporation for the remaining 25% of its shares. The intangible personal property right represented by the patent is treated as having a value equal to the cash contributions of the other investors even though its actual value cannot be ascertained.

Whether stock is par value or no-par value, its *book value* is determined by dividing the value of the corporate assets less liabilities by the number of shares of stock issued by the corporation. In the example above, there are corporate assets of $75,000 and no liabilities (three investors contributed $25,000 capital each; the inventor contributed a patent, but it has no established market value and therefore should be listed on the corporate balance sheet as having zero value). The $75,000 divided by the 100 shares of issued stock yields a book value of $750 a share.

Obviously, the book value of stock changes constantly, reflecting the profits and losses of the business. And it often differs substantially from the *market value* of the stock. The market value is the price that a willing buyer would pay a willing seller for the stock, neither party being under any compulsion to buy or sell. For example, though the book value of the inventor's stock is $750 a share, a willing buyer might be eager to pay $1,200 or even $2,000 a share if the patent (and hence the corporation) has great potential. On the other hand, if there is little hope for a marketable product from the patent, the market value of the inventor's stock might be as little as $100 a share or even less.

Finally, the Articles of Incorporation must specify the *classes* of stock to be issued, and the number of shares of each class. A corporation may issue two basic classes of stock: *common stock* and *preferred stock.*

Common stock is the ordinary stock of a corporation. If only one class of stock is authorized, it will, in effect, be common, and the common stockholders will have complete, unrestricted voting rights. They will also be entitled to share ratably in any dividends that are distributed, and in such net assets as are distributed upon dissolution of the corporation.

If more than one class of stock is authorized, the Articles must set forth the preferences, limitations, and relative rights of each class. Shares with a preference as to earnings (dividends) or net assets (liquidation) or both are termed *preferred stock.* Shares with no preference as to earnings and/or net assets are termed *common stock. Except as otherwise provided by the Articles of Incorporation*, all classes of stock enjoy equal rights as to voting, dividends, and net assets. The Articles typically provide otherwise as follows:

Voting rights. At least one class of shares must have complete, unrestricted voting rights. Usually, the Articles provide that the common stock is the "voting stock" (i. e., that the common stockholders have the right to elect the board of directors; the preferred stock has no voting rights.) However, there is nothing to prevent the Articles from making the preferred stock voting, the common nonvoting, or authorizing two classes of common stock or preferred stock, one of which is voting and one of which is nonvoting.

Dividends. Dividends are the means by which shareholders participate in corporate earnings (net profit). A dividend is a distribution of cash or other property (sometimes stock) made by a corporation to its shareholders. The board of directors determines whether or not a dividend should be declared in any particular year, and in a nonprofit year, the decision is likely to be against paying one.

Some corporations pay dividends every year, while others seldom pay dividends. However, the fact that a corporation pays few dividends does not necessarily make the company a bad investment. People invest in corporations, not only for dividends, but also to share in growth of the company. If a corporation, rather than pay dividends, reinvests its income profitably (e. g., by adding more factories, or purchasing more inventory), the stockholders will be able to watch the value of their stock go up and up.

Most dividends are cash dividends. A corporation generally pays cash dividends from the preceding year's net profits. But realize that the net profits of a corporation are subject to federal income taxation. In this way, a corporation differs from a partnership. Because a corporation is a legal entity and not an aggregate of individuals (like a partnership), a corporation must report and pay taxes on its net income. The first $25,000 of corporate income is taxed at the rate of 17 percent; its income over $25,000 is taxed at a rate up to 46 percent.[2] Thus, if a corporation has $100,000 of net income, the following federal taxes are payable:

$25,000 x 17% = $ 4,250.00
25,000 x 20% =   5,000.00
25,000 x 30% =   7,500.00
25,000 x 40% = 10,000.00

total federal tax $26,750.00

2. As of January 1, 1979 the corporate tax rate was changed by Congress to a graduated tax rate of 17% on the first $25,000 of income, 20% on the next $25,000, 30% on the next $25,000, 40% on the next $25,000 and 46% on income over $100,000.

And there may be state tax on the corporate income as well. It is only the balance—what is left after taxes (in our example, $73,250 of income)—that may be paid to the shareholders as dividends.

Though it may seem inequitable, the corporate income is then taxed a second time as each shareholder must report his or her dividends as income on his or her personal income tax return. This "double taxation" is one disadvantage of using the corporate form of business organization (as you will learn in a later section, some corporations may escape double taxation by electing to be taxed as partnerships under Subchapter S of the Internal Revenue Code).[3]

A stock dividend refers to the distribution of additional stock to each shareholder. The immediate result of such a dividend is to make all issued stock decline in book value. For example, suppose that a corporation has 1,000 shares of stock outstanding; the book value of the stock is $100.00 a share. The corporation declares a stock dividend of one share for every ten outstanding (i. e., for every ten shares of stock a shareholder owns, he or she receives an additional one share). Though there are now 1,100 shares of stock outstanding, the assets of the corporation have not increased, and the book value of the stock is down to just under $91.00 a share. Why did the corporation declare the dividend? In many cases, a stock dividend, though it reduces the book value of the stock, has little or no effect on the stock's market value. Obviously, if you own 100 shares of stock with a market value of $100.00 each, and after a stock dividend, you own 110 shares with a market value of $97.00 each, your position is substantially improved.

The Articles of Incorporation generally give preferred stockholders a prefer-

ence (i. e., a preferred position) on dividends, the "preference" being that the preferred stockholders will be paid a stated annual rate of dividend (e. g., 6%) before any dividend is paid to the common stockholders. Suppose that the board of directors does not declare a dividend for a particular year. If the stock is *cumulative preferred,* the preferred stockholders' right to the dividend will carry over to the next year (and subsequent years) until it is paid (and it must be paid before the common stockholders receive any dividend). If the stock is *noncumulative preferred,* the stockholders' right to the dividend will not carry over (in other words, if no dividend is declared for the particular year, the preferred dividend will not have to be paid).

Following payment of preferred dividends, the common stockholders may generally receive a dividend of any amount (e. g., the preferred stockholders might receive 6%, the common stockholders 10%). However, if the preferred stockholders own what is called *participating preferred stock,* they are entitled to participate (share) in any dividends paid to the common stockholders beyond the preferred shareholders' own annual rate. For example, the holders of 6% participating preferred are entitled to a 6% dividend before the common stockholders receive anything. Following payment of the 6%, the common stockholders may also receive 6%. As to any remaining surplus distributed, the preferred and common stockholders have equal rights. Let's get more specific. Say that a corporation has issued 1,000 shares of $100 par value 6% participating preferred stock, and 2,000 shares of no-par value common stock. The board of directors votes to distribute a $30,000 cash dividend. The first $6,000 goes to

3. There is some serious consideration being given by Congress to eliminating this double taxation.

the preferred stockholders (1,000 shares x 6% of $100); the next $12,000 goes to the common stockholders (2,000 shares x $6.00—the same dividend as the preferred stockholders received). The $12,000 balance is divided equally between the preferred and common stockholders (the preferred stockholders receive $4,000, the common $8,000). The net result is that each shareholder, whether preferred or common, receives a $10.00 dividend.

Distribution of net assets on dissolution of the corporation. A second preference common to preferred stock is one on the assets of a corporation in the event of dissolution. Typically, the preference states that after creditors have been paid, but before the common stockholders receive anything, the preferred stockholders must receive the par value of their stock from the corporate assets, or the par value plus a premium. The common stockholders are entitled to any surplus remaining.

While the preferred stockholders are guaranteed a specific sum of money upon liquidation of the corporation, that is the *maximum* amount they will receive. It is the common stockholders who, by receiving the surplus, will participate in growth of the corporation. And some corporations have increased in value many hundreds of times since they first came into existence. To enable preferred stockholders to share in corporate growth, they are often given *conversion rights*—i. e., rights to convert their stock to common stock at certain times or under certain circumstances.

To summarize, common stock generally carries the voting power, and allows the investor to participate in corporate

growth and hedge against inflation. Preferred stock usually provides more security (i. e., more likelihood of a fixed return on the investment).

(7) *Some states require a minimum of paid-in capital ($1,000) before a corporation may begin business. If such a minimum is required, the Articles must state receipt of the capital.*

(8) *Any provisions the incorporators may choose to insert regarding internal operations of the corporation.* Usually, however, such specifics are included in the corporate by-laws rather than in the Articles.

(9) *The name and address of each incorporator.*

(10) *The signature of each incorporator.*

Assuming the Articles are in order, the state will issue a corporate charter, and the corporation will become a legal entity.[4] The initial board of directors will meet and elect officers to carry out the day-to-day business operations. Usually, a president, vice-president, secretary, and treasurer will be elected, and sometimes, many more officers. The directors will also adopt corporate by-laws. *By-laws* are written rules (usually many pages long) governing corporate activities and operations. The by-laws typically include:

(1) The duties of each corporate officer;

(2) The time, place, and notice requirements for meeting of directors and shareholders; also, rules of procedure for the meetings (e. g., voting and quorum requirements);

---

4. To do business in another state, a corporation must file the appropriate papers in that other state to qualify for doing business there. Failure to file the appropriate papers may result in fines, penalties, or injunction proceedings to prohibit the corporation's carrying on of business in the state. Also, the corporation may be denied the right of access to the courts of the state.

(3) A plan for corporate recordkeeping;

(4) A list of the sole powers of the board of directors (i. e., actions the board may take without shareholder approval) and a list of acts requiring shareholder approval; and

(5) Provisions regarding the issurance and transfer of corporate stock.

Returning to our example, suppose that Ray Chamberlain and Lola Forthright decide to incorporate. They prepare the following Articles of Incorporation:

ARTICLES OF INCORPORATION
OF

Ray Chamberlain Sports, Incorporated

KNOW ALL MEN BY THESE PRESENTS, That Ray Chamberlain and Lola Forthright

a natural person, or if more than one, each a natural person of the age of eighteen years or more, do hereby incorporate a corporation under and pursuant to the laws of the State of Oregon relative to private corporations and hereby do adopt, execute and verify, in duplicate, the following ARTICLES OF INCORPORATION thereof:

ARTICLE I.

The name of the corporation is Ray Chamberlain Sports, Incorporated

and the duration thereof shall be perpetual.

ARTICLE II.

The purpose or purposes for which the corporation is organized shall be:

(1) To engage in any lawful activity for which corporations may be organized under Chapter 57 of Oregon Revised Statutes;

(2) To engage in retail sales of sporting goods equipment and apparel.

Lastly, to do any and all other acts and things necessary, incident, proper, desirable or convenient for carrying out the purposes of this corporation or any of them, and generally to engage in any or all of the foregoing enterprises, businesses and occupations, either within or without the State of Oregon or the United States.

The foregoing enumeration of powers is not intended and shall not be held to limit or restrict in any manner the general powers of this corporation under the laws of the State of Oregon.

ARTICLE III.

The address of said corporation's initial registered office is 221 N. Chemeketa

_____, Salem , Oregon, 97203

(Do not use post office box number; use street address only)   (City)   (Zip)

and the name of its initial registered agent at said address is: Ray Chamberlain

ARTICLE IV.

The number of directors constituting the initial board of directors is............two................and the names and addresses of the persons who are to serve as directors until the first annual meeting of the shareholders or until their successors be elected and qualified are:

NAME	ADDRESS	(INCLUDE CITY, STATE, ZIP)
Ray Chamberlain	200 South Liberty	Salem, Oregon 97203
Lola Forthright	501 Park Avenue	Salem, Oregon 97203

ARTICLE V.

The name and address (including street and number, if any) of each of the incorporators of said corporation are:

NAME	ADDRESS	(INCLUDE CITY, STATE, ZIP)
Ray Chamberlain	200 South Liberty	Salem, Oregon 97203
Lola Forthright	501 Park Avenue	Salem, Oregon 97203

ARTICLE VI.

The aggregate number of shares which the corporation shall have authority to issue is............200................ Unless otherwise hereinafter stated, all said shares shall be of one class: Common.

ARTICLE VII.

ARTICLE VIII.

IN WITNESS WHEREOF, we, the undersigned incorporators, declare under penalties of perjury that we have examined the foregoing document and to the best of our knowledge and belief, it is true, correct and complete.

Dated.......(today's date)........................, 19.........

Ray Chamberlain
Lola Forthright

NOTE:
See the Oregon Business Corporation Act in Chapter 57 of Oregon Revised Statutes, which provides that one or more natural persons of the age of eighteen years or more, may act as incorporator or incorporators of a coporation by signing, verifying and delivering, in duplicate, to the Corporation of the State of Oregon, Salem, Oregon, articles of incorporation for such corporation (ORS 57.306) and that one or more directors are required. (ORS Section 57.185).
Space is provided in Article VI of the form for setting forth the par value of each share of stock or the fact that shares are without par value, as well as information as to different classes of stock if there are to be more than one, and in Article VIII for setting forth any provision not inconsistent with law for the regulation of the internal affairs of the corporation.

Ray files the Articles of Incorporation with the State Corporation Commissioner and pays the appropriate filing fee (about $25.00). The Articles being in proper order, the Corporation Commissioner issues the corporate charter, which looks like this:

State of Oregon

Department of Commerce
Corporation Division

Certificate of Incorporation

OF

RAY CHAMBERLAIN SPORTS, INCORPORATED

The undersigned, as Corporation Commissioner of the State of Oregon, hereby certifies that duplicate originals of Articles of Incorporation, duly signed and verified pursuant to the provisions of the Oregon   Business   Corporation Act, have been received in this office and are found to conform to law.

Accordingly, the undersigned, as such Corporation Commissioner, and by virtue of the authority vested in him by law, hereby issues this Certificate of Incorporation and attaches hereto a duplicate original of the Articles of Incorporation.

In Testimony Whereof, I have hereunto set my hand and affixed hereto the seal of the Corporation Division of the Department of Commerce of the State of Oregon this day of , 19 .

Frank J. Healy
Corporation Commissioner

By _Shirley Smith_
Chief Clerk

C-11-B/N/C
4-75

The Articles of Incorporation for "Ray Chamberlain Sports, Inc." authorizes issuance of 200 shares of common stock (see Article VI). The directors, Ray and Lola, issue 100 shares of the stock, Ray taking 80% (80 shares), and Lola 20% (20 shares). Ray's stock certificate looks like this:

Lola's stock certificate looks the same, with the exception that hers is made out for 20 shares.

Can a corporation ever elect not to be taxed as a corporation for federal income tax purposes?

As explained previously, a corporation is taxed on its net income at a rate of 17% on the first $25,000 of income and up to 46% on income over $25,000. Let's take an example. Suppose that the first year of operations for Ray Chamberlain Sports, Incorporated is identical to the first year of sole proprietor Ray's or partner Ray's business. The corporate profit and loss statement for Year #1 looks like this.

RAY CHAMBERLAIN SPORTS, INCORPORATED

Profit and Loss Statement

For the First Year of Operations

Sales		$132,400.00
Less cost of goods sold		77,700.00
Gross profit		$ 54,700.00
Less operating expenses		
Depreciation expense	$ 5,000.00	
Wages paid	9,000.00	
Advertising expense	2,875.00	
Utility expense	1,120.00	
Insurance expense	1,850.00	
Telephone bills	785.00	
Accounting and legal	530.00	
Taxes paid	2,830.00	
Interest expense	5,600.00	
total expenses	$29,590.00	29,590.00
Net profit		$ 25,110.00

The corporation must report and pay taxes on its net profit (income) of $25,110.00: the taxes amount to $4,272.00 (17% of $25,000 plus 20% of $110.00).[5]

Net profit	$25,110.00
Corporate taxes	4,272.00
Balance remaining after corporate tax	$20,838.00

5. The corporate return (Form 1120 S) looks much like Schedule C of Form 1040 (individual income tax return) and Form 1065 (partnership information return).

Thus, there is a balance of $20,838.00 available for the payment of dividends. Of course, any dividends paid to Ray and Lola will also be taxed: each shareholder must report his or her dividends as income on his or her personal income tax return (remember, "double taxation" is one disadvantage of a corporation). The rate of tax will vary depending on each party's tax bracket.

If, on the other hand, no dividends are paid, the $20,838.00 will go on the books as "earned surplus", and the balance sheet for January 1, Year #2 will look like this:

RAY CHAMBERLAIN SPORTS, INCORPORATED

Balance Sheet

January 1, Year #2

Assets

Cash (end of year balance)	$ 24,538.00 [6]
Inventory	34,300.00
Building	145,000.00
total assets	$203,838.00

Liabilities and Capital

Liabilities

Balance owing on purchase of the building	$ 63,000.00

Capital

Stated capital

200 shares of no par common stock authorized	
100 shares issued	$120,000.00

Earned surplus

(1st year profit after taxes)	20,838.00	
total capital	$140,838.00	140,838.00
Total liabilities and capital		$203,838.00

In our example, Ray Chamberlain Sports, Incorporated can easily avoid any corporate tax by paying salaries to Ray and Lola so as to eliminate corporate profit. Say that the corporation pays Ray $7,500, and Lola $18,000, for a total of $25,500. The wages are deductible from gross profit as an expense of doing business; instead of a net profit of $25,110.00, there is a net loss of $390.-00. Obviously, since there is no corporate profit, there is no corporate tax.

---

6. This is a much larger cash balance than the $10,810.00 cash balance found on the partnership balance sheet for January 1, Year #2 in Ch. 22. The difference is accounted for in that Lola Forthright took nothing out of the corporation during the first year of operations, while she took $18,000 out of the partnership. Of course, the corporate cash balance was reduced by federal income tax in the amount of $4,272.-00.

Of course, the salaries must be "reasonable" to be deductible under the law. A high salary looks to be unreasonable anytime there exists a relationship between the parties in addition to that of employer and employee (e. g., in the sole proprietorship situation, where the employee is a son or daughter of the sole proprietor; in the corporate situation, where the employee is a shareholder of the corporation). There is no precise rule as to what is reasonable: the test is the amount of compensation that like enterprises would ordinarily pay for like services. Obviously, if a shareholder has nothing to do with corporate operations, a salary to the shareholder is unjustified. And where a corporation has a history of paying little or no dividends, a high salary paid even to a working shareholder may be declared unreasonable (in which case the excessive portion of the salary will be disallowed as a deduction).

Assuming the salaries to Ray and Lola are reasonable (i. e., that both parties perform work in the sporting goods store commensurate with their salaries), the corporation will escape payment of any corporate tax. Of course, Ray and Lola must report their wages as income on their personal income tax returns; and the corporation must withhold income and social security taxes from their wages (see Ch. 20 for the tax aspects of the employer-employee relationship). The advantage is that there is $25,110.00 of profit to distribute to the owners as taxable wages, whereas there would be only $20,838.00 of profit to distribute as taxable dividends.

However, it is sometimes impossible for a corporation to avoid paying corporate tax simply by paying salaries to employees. There may be too much net profit, and high salaries may not be justified. Even so, it may be possible for the corporation to escape payment of corporate tax by electing to be taxed, not as a corporation, but as a partnership under Subchapter S of the federal Internal Revenue Code (the IRC, the basic tax law of the United States, is divided into many chapters and subchapters). Subchapter S provides that certain "small business corporations" may elect to be taxed as partnerships. (As you will recall, a partnership pays no taxes, but files a mere information return—Form 1065 plus attached K-1's. Each partner must report his or her share of the partnership income on his or her personal tax return; each is taxed on his or her share whether or not he or she actually received it during the course of the year.)

For a corporation to qualify as a Subchapter S corporation, it must meet the following specific requirements:

(1) The corporation must have no more than ten shareholders. A single exception is recognized for a corporation that has been a Subchapter S corporation for at least five consecutive years. Such a corporation may add up to five extra shareholders, but only by reason of people acquiring the stock through inheritance; at no time may the number of shareholders exceed fifteen.

Where stock is held concurrently (see Ch. 5 regarding "concurrent ownership"), each joint tenant or tenant in common is counted as one shareholder. An exception is made for a husband and wife who own stock concurrently (as joint tenants, tenants in common, or as community property owners)—they are together counted as one shareholder. (Where a husband and wife own stock individually, each is counted as one shareholder.)

(2) Each shareholder of the corporation must be an individual (or the estate of a deceased individual) and not a corporation, partnership, or trust (with the exception of a "grantor trust" or a trust receiving the stock of a deceased shareholder under a will for a period not to exceed 60 days—see Ch. 29 on "trusts").

(3) The corporation must have no more than one class of stock (e. g., it cannot have both common and preferred).

(4) The corporation must not obtain more than 80 percent of its gross receipts from sources outside the United States.

(5) The corporation must not obtain more than 20 percent of its gross receipts from interest, dividends, rents, royalties, annuities, and gains from sales or exchanges of items such as stocks, bonds, or other securities. In other words, the corporation must be an "operation business" as opposed to one designed to hold investments—a hotel operation would qualify whereas an apartment house would not.

A corporation that meets all five requirements can elect to be taxed as a partnership under Subchapter S. However, all the shareholders must consent to the election, including *both* husband and wife, even though they own stock concurrently and are counted as only one shareholder.

Like a partnership, a Subchapter S corporation pays no taxes, but files a mere information return (Form 1120 S), reporting each individual shareholder's share of the corporate income on special, attached K–1 Schedules. And like partners, each shareholder must report his or her share of the corporate income on his or her personal income tax return (see illustration of Schedule E in Ch. 22). Also like partners, each is taxed on his or her share whether or not it was distributed to him or her during the course of the year.

By way of example, say that a Subchapter S corporation with $100,000 of net income has five shareholders: Mary owns 28% of the stock; Tom owns 25%; Jane 22%; Dick 15%; and Harry 10%. The shareholders must report and pay taxes on the following shares of the corporate income: Mary $28,000;

Tom $25,000; Jane $22,000; Dick $15,000; and Harry $10,000. Each shareholder will be taxed on his or her share regardless of whether he or she actually received it during the course of the year. Of course, if the income is distributed in a later year, the shareholders will not be taxed on it again at that time.

Electing under Subchapter S, then, serves to eliminate the double taxation that results when the corporate income is taxed, first, up to 46% (for income over $25,000), and, then again, as income to the individual shareholders when dividends are paid. However, Subchapter S does not eliminate any of the other characteristics or advantages of the corporate form of doing business. Limited liability, ease in transferring ownership interests, perpetual life, corporate deferred compensation plans—the Subchapter S corporation enjoys all of these.

In summary, what are the differences between a partnership and a corporation?

The differences between a partnership and a corporation may be summarized as follows:

(1) *Formation of the business.* A partnership is formed by a contract between the partners. No particular formality is required, and (with the exception of a limited partnership) nothing need be filed with the state.

A corporation, on the other hand, comes into existence only upon issuance of a corporate charter by the state: the charter is issued on the basis of Articles of Incorporation filed with the state by one or more incorporators.

(2) *Status as a legal entity.* A partnership is an aggregate of its individual partners, while a corporation is a complete legal entity (an artificial person) existing separate and distinct from its shareholders.

(3) *Ownership of the business property.* Partners own partnership assets concurrently as tenants in partnership. Shareholders have no ownership interest in the specific corporate assets, but have an intangible personal property interest in the entire corporation.

(4) *Limitation of liability.* With the exception of limited partners, partners are subject to unlimited liability for partnership debts and obligations.

In contrast, shareholders have limited liability: they are liable for corporate debts and obligations only to the extent of their investment in the corporation (i. e., their personal assets are not at stake —but remember, the "corporate veil" may be pierced if necessary to prevent fraud or injustice).

(5) *Taxation.* Being an aggregate of individuals, a partnership pays no taxes, but files a mere information return. Each partner reports and pays taxes on his or her own share of the partnership income.

A corporation, being a legal entity, is taxed at a rate of 46% (on income over $100,000). The corporate income is taxed again to the individual shareholders when dividends are paid. "Small business corporations" can avoid this double taxation by electing to be taxed as partnerships under Subchapter S of the Internal Revenue Code.

(6) *Transferability of interests.* A partner may freely transfer his or her *interest in the partnership* (giving the transferee the right to receive the partner's share of profits and surplus as distributed). However, a partner may not transfer his or her interest in specific partnership property or his or her right to participate in management without the consent of all the partners.

A shareholder, on the other hand, may freely transfer his or her shares in the corporation either inter vivos (e. g., lifetime gift or sale) or at death.

(7) *Duration of the business.* Whereas a partnership has a limited existence (e. g., it is dissolved by the death, bankruptcy, or withdrawal of a partner), a corporation is capable of perpetual life (i. e., it may live forever, unaffected by the deaths, bankruptcies, or other problems of its shareholders.)

(8) *Management of the business.* Unless the partnership agreement provides to the contrary, all partners have an equal voice in management of the partnership.

Shareholders have no direct voice in corporate management, but elect a board of directors to manage the day-to-day business affairs.

(9) *Role of partner or shareholder.* Each partner is an agent of every other partner and can bind the partnership with respect to ordinary partnership business.

Unless a shareholder is also a director and/or officer, he or she is not an agent of any other shareholder or of the corporation.

(10) *Court actions.* Under modern procedure statutes, a partnership may generally sue and be sued in the firm name. However, the personal assets of the partners will not be bound by a judgment against the partnership unless the partners are also named in the suit.

Being a legal entity, a corporation sues and is sued in its own name.

What is the Model Business Corporation Act?

In contrast to the Uniform Partnership Act, there is no uniform corporation act. However, the American Bar Association drafted and proposed a Model Business Corporation Act in 1950. The Model Act was revised in 1969 and has had considerable influence in many states. The Act reflects the basic corporation law rules, principles, and standards generally accepted throughout the United States.

Some 35 states have adopted portions of the Act as their basic corporation code. However, state corporation law is by no means uniform (as is partnership law in 47 states under the UPA). The state codes provide varying language to control the creation and continuing regulation of the corporate method of doing business. For example, the Model Act requires only one incorporator to incorporate a business—some states require as many as three. Some states prohibit a corporation from beginning business until a specified amount has been paid into the corporation; the Model Act makes no such requirement. Under the Model Act, corporate existence begins upon the issuance of the certificate of incorporation. Some states require an organizational meeting before corporate existence begins. Still others require local recording of the certificate of incorporation.

In summary, it may be said that the Model Business Corporation Act is exactly that—a very good model that reflects much of the statutory corporation law of the various states. At the same time, state corporate law is not uniform, and it is necessary to look to the specific language of each state's particular corporation code for the detail of the law.

Does a valid corporation always result when Articles of Incorporation are filed?

Incorporators may or may not comply with all statutory requirements in filing Articles of Incorporation. Depending on the degree of compliance, the corporation will be valid or invalid, and will be classified as either:

(1) A de jure corporation;

(2) A de facto corporation;

(3) A less than de facto corporation; or

(4) A corporation by estoppel.

De jure corporation. A *de jure* corporation is one that is organized in compliance with the statutory requirements for incorporation. "Compliance" means literal compliance with all "mandatory" requirements as opposed to "directory" provisions of the statute. For example, if a statute states that the Articles *must* give the "business" addresses of the incorporators, and *should* give their "home" addresses, the first part of the language is mandatory while the second is merely directory. Thus, if the Articles list the business addresses of the incorporators, the Articles are in compliance with the statutory requirements even though the incorporators' home addresses are not given.

A de jure corporation is valid in all respects. No one—not even the state—may attack it as being invalid on the basis of its formation. (However, this does not mean that the corporate veil cannot be pierced and the shareholders held personally liable if this is necessary to prevent fraud or injustice.)

De facto corporation. Though a corporation is not organized in compliance with all statutory requirements (i. e., de jure), it may still be valid insofar as all parties other than the state are concerned. So long as the incorporators made a *good faith* attempt to comply with the statute, and made some *actual use* of the corporation (as by contracting in the corporate name), the corporation will be considered *de facto,* and only the state will have a right to declare it invalid. Thus, if the incorporators forget to pay the filing fee, or one of the incorporators fails to sign the Articles of Incorporation, the corporation will be a de facto corporation, assuming some actual use of the corporation has been made.

The effect of de facto status is that creditors of the corporation cannot assert the defect in formation as a basis for holding the shareholders personally liable for corporate debts and other liabilities. That is to say, limited liability is not lost because of the noncompliance with the organization statute. (However, the fact that a corporation is organized de facto, and not de jure, may be pertinent in establishing that the corporation is merely the alter ego of its shareholders and that the corporate veil should be pierced.)

Less than de facto corporation. A *less than de facto* corporation results when the incorporators make less than a good faith attempt to comply with the statutory requirements. For example, if the incorporators leave required information completely out of the Articles of Incorporation, or if no one signs the Articles, there is simply no corporation even if a charter is mistakenly issued. Any "shareholders" who participate actively in management of the venture after this time will be held liable as partners—i. e., they will have unlimited liability. "Shareholders" who do not participate actively in management will be liable only to the extent of their investment in the "corporation".

Corporation by estoppel. Generally speaking, a party who deals with a corporation as if it is valid will be estopped from claiming later that the corporation was defectively formed. Usually, the estopped party is trying to get out of good faith bargain by reason of having discovered a technicality (the fact that the corporation was not organized in compliance with state law). For example, suppose that a person who sells land to a corporation discovers later that the corporation is less than de facto. The land having gone up considerably in value since the time of the sale, the seller decides to "rescind" the transaction on the grounds that the buyer was not a valid corporation. To permit rescission would be unfair; thus, the seller is estopped from denying the validity of the corporation. As to the sale, the buyer is a corporation by estoppel.

Finally, it should be pointed out that the corporation itself may never assert by way of defense that it was improperly formed.

What are the functions of corporate promoters?

A great many corporations are formed from existing sole proprietorships or partnerships needing no extra capital to convert over into the corporate form. Still others are organized by individuals who plan to own all the corporate stock themselves: the incorporators neither want nor need any other shareholders. A lesser number of corporations are started from scratch by individuals who do need to raise capital—or at least obtain the promise of capital—in order to go into business as a corporation. In the latter case, the people who participate in forming the corporation, selling its stock and organizing its initial business activities are referred to in law as corporate *promoters*.

Prior to formation of the corporation, promoters are considered to be joint venturers (see Ch. 22). It follows that they are fiduciaries and owe each other full disclosure regarding all their activities in forming the business. As between or among themselves, they are held to a high standard of fair dealing.

Promoters are also fiduciaries of the corporation they form. If a promoter sells his or her own property to the corporation for cash or stock, he or she must disclose to the corporation (1) what property is being sold; (2) the fact that he or she owns the property; and (3) the amount of profit that he or she stands to make from the sale. A failure to disclose these things constitutes a fraud on the corporation. The disclosure must be made either to an *independent* board of directors (meaning a majority of the board's directors who are disinterested) or to all existing stockholders plus any people then known to be planning to become stockholders.

Where a promoter fails to make full disclosure in contracting with the corporation for stock, the corporation may rescind the contract (by returning the promoter's property and cancelling any shares of stock issued to him or her), or, if the stock is par value,[7] may sue the promoter for money damages. For example, suppose that a promoter sells real property having a fair market value of $30,000 to the corporation in exchange for $50,000 of par value stock. The promoter, who originally paid $15,000 for the property, fails to disclose the land's true value. Upon discovering the nondisclosure, the corporation may rescind the sale, or it may sue the promoter for money damages. In most states, the corporation's measure of damages is the difference between the par value of the stock and the fair market value of the property ($50,000–$30,000=$20,000). However, the courts in some states penalize the promoter by denying him or her any profit whatsoever: here, the corporation's measure of damages is the difference between the par value of the stock and the original cost of the property ($50,000–$15,000 = $35,000). Usually, the "penalty" is applied only where the promoter makes affirmative misstatements about the value of the property as opposed to merely failing to disclose its value.

Suppose that the promoters take all the stock themselves. If they have made full disclosure to each other as joint venturers, no further disclosure will generally be required. This is so even where the promoters later sell their stock (the purchasers will buy based on values at the time of purchase). However, an exception is made where the promoters plan at the time of formation of the corporation to issue additional stock to others who are unaware of the promoters' sale of

property to the corporation. Under the so-called "Massachusetts Rule", the original capitalization of the corporation is considered to be a single transaction requiring full disclosure to all who end up with shares though the shares are issued at different times over a period of several weeks or even months. The subsequent issue of stock is thus part of the original capitalization of the corporation, and the promoters must make full disclosure to all who purchase shares.

It should be pointed out that disclosure problems have been obviated to a great extent by state and federal statutes regulating the issuance of securities (see Ch. 24). These statutes require complete disclosure of all factors affecting the value of property received by a corporation in exchange for its stock. The laws also require that a corporation receive full value for its shares (this is the issue of "watered stock" which is dealt with in a later section). There are criminal penalties for violation of the statutes; also, the corporation, as well as any injured shareholders, may bring legal action to recover any damages incurred.

In organizing a corporation, promoters often enter into contracts on behalf of the business prior to issuance of the corporate charter. For example, the promoters might negotiate to purchase an office building for use as the main place of business. Or they might negotiate contracts to purchase inventory. To what extent is the corporation liable on these contracts?

The corporation is liable only if it ratifies or adopts the contracts after issuance of the corporate charter. The ratification may be express (e. g., where the board of directors passes a resolution ratifying the contract), or it may be implied (e. g., where the corporation moves into the office building or accepts delivery of the

---

7. Where the stock is no-par value, the corporation's only remedy is to rescind the

transaction, the stock having no specific per share value.

inventory). Following ratification, the corporation may enforce the contract against the third party.

As for the promoters, they have no personal liability on pre-incorporation contracts so long as they make it clear at the time of contracting that they are contracting *on behalf of the corporation only and not for themselves personally.* The third party, in this case, relies solely on the credit of the proposed corporation and has no claim against the promoters personally (e. g., the third party cannot hold the promoters liable if the corporation is never formed, or if it otherwise fails to ratify or carry out the contract). It follows that the promoters have no ability to enforce the contract against the third party if the corporation is not formed.

If, on the other hand, the promoters fail to make it clear that they are contracting solely on behalf of the corporation, they will be liable personally on the contract. In this case, the promoters will have a right to enforce the contract against the third party if the corporation is not formed.

What is the law regarding stock subscriptions?

A *stock subscription* is an agreement by a party called a "subscriber" to purchase a certain amount of capital stock of a corporation. If the corporation is in existence at the time of the subscription, the agreement is an enforceable contract (assuming mutual assent, consideration, capacity, and legality are present). It should be pointed out that if the corporation fraudulently misrepresents the state of its finances or business affairs to induce the subscriber to enter into the subscription agreement, the fraud will justify rescission of the contract by the subscriber. Most state "blue sky" laws (securities regulations) specifically define what

constitutes fraud in a public stock offering by an existing corporation, and provide that the defrauded subscriber may revoke the stock subscription.

Promoters of a corporation frequently arrange for stock subscriptions before the corporation comes into existence. The majority rule is that a pre-incorporation stock subscription is a mere offer by the subscriber and not an enforceable contract: the corporation is not yet in existence and, hence, cannot accept the offer. The subscription becomes an enforceable contract only at such time as the corporation is formed and accepts the offer. This is assuming the offer is still outstanding. As you will recall from Ch. 7, an offer is revocable until it is accepted. Thus, up until the corporation is formed and accepts the offer, the subscriber may revoke the subscription. And like any other offer, the subscription will be revoked by operation of law upon the subscriber's death or insanity.

A minority of courts feel that revocability of pre-incorporation stock subscriptions is contrary to public policy. They point out that other shareholders rely on the subscriptions in subscribing for their own shares, and that revocation often results in undercapitalization of the corporation. Accordingly, the minority courts hold that a pre-incorporation stock subscription is more than a mere offer to purchase shares when the corporation is formed—it is also a contract between or among the subscribers, and, as such, is binding. If a subscriber fails to go through with his or her stock subscription following formation of the corporation, the other subscribers may sue him or her and recover money damages.

Statutes in other states simply make pre-incorporation stock subscriptions irrevocable for a certain period of time (e. g., 90 days or six months).[8]

---

8. Six months under the Model Business Corporation Act.

There are three implied conditions precedent to enforcement of a pre-incorporation stock subscription. They are as follows:

(1) *The full issue of stock must be subscribed.* Where the stock subscription states that a certain amount of stock will be offered, such as "5,000 shares of $50.00 par value", the entire amount must be subscribed or the subscriber will have no obligation to buy the stock. Full subscription is an implied condition precedent to his or her purchase.

(2) *The corporation must be organized "de jure" and not merely "de facto".* A "de jure" corporation is also an implied condition precedent to the subscriber's agreement to buy the stock. (Remember, a "de jure" corporation is one organized in compliance with the incorporation requirements set by state statute.) If the corporation is but "de facto", the subscriber does not have to go through with the purchase (a "de facto" corporation is one that does not comply with the statutory requirements, but can be "attacked" only by the state because of the incorporator's good faith attempt to comply).

(3) *The stock offering must meet all the legal requirements of state and federal securities laws (see Ch. 24).* Exact compliance with state and federal securities regulations is the third implied condition precedent to performance by the subscriber. If the laws are violated in any way, the subscriber does not have to buy the stock.

Assuming the corporation has accepted the subscription offer, and all three conditions precedent have occurred, the corporation is entitled to the full subscription price from the subscriber upon tender of the stock certificates. If the corporation becomes insolvent before the subscriber pays for his or her shares, the creditors of the corporation can enforce the subscription agreement, and the sub-scriber will have to pay full value for their benefit.

Suppose that a promoter fraudulently induces a subscriber to enter into a prein-corporation subscription agreement. Up until the time the corporation comes into existence and accepts the subscription offer, the subscriber can revoke the offer on the basis of fraud (under the majority rule, the subscriber may revoke for any reason). But once the corporation accepts the offer, the subscriber cannot revoke (assuming all conditions precedent have been met), even though the subscription was fraudulently obtained. The promoter cannot be considered the agent of a nonexistent principal (the corporation was not in existence at the time of the fraud). Thus, the fraud is no defense to enforcement of the contract. Of course, the subscriber can always bring a legal action against the promoter to recover money damages.

What is an "ultra vires" act by a corporation?

As you will recall, the Articles of Incorporation must state the corporate purpose or purposes. Once the corporate charter is issued, the corporation has express power to perform any legal act required to carry out its purposes. The corporation also has whatever power is conferred upon corporations generally by the state corporation statute—e. g., power to own property, to buy and sell, to sue and be sued, etc.

An "ultra vires" act is one that goes beyond the powers of the corporation (the term "ultra vires" obviously has little meaning where the corporation's stated purpose is "to engage in any lawful activity"). Often in the past, a corporation would try to assert a plea of ultra vires as a defense to a contract action brought against the corporation. Generally, the corporation would enter into a contract beyond the scope of its powers (i. e., an ultra vires contract). Later, wanting to get out of the contract, the corporation would assert that the agreement was ultra vires and, hence, not binding on the corporation. Understandably, the argument held little water. Today, most corporation statutes expressly provide that ultra vires may not be raised as a defense to an existing contract. If what would be an ultra vires contract is still in the negotiating stage, the shareholders may go to court to enjoin (stop) the corporation from entering into it. But once the corporation has entered into the contract, neither the corporation itself nor the shareholders may set it aside on the grounds that it is ultra vires. However, the corporation (or the shareholders themselves in a "derivative action" as will be explained in a later section) may bring an action against the directors and/or officers who authorized the ultra vires act to recover any loss that results to the corporation.

Along the same line, a corporation may not assert ultra vires as a defense to a tort action brought against the corporation on the basis of respondeat superior. As you know from Ch. 20, the doctrine of respondeat superior states that an employer is vicariously liable for torts committed by his or her employees while acting within the scope of employment. If a corporate employee is directed to perform an ultra vires act, the corporation will be liable for any torts committed by the employee while engaged in the ultra vires activity notwithstanding that the activity is beyond the corporate powers.

What is "watered stock"?

A corporation that issues par value stock must receive consideration for the stock equal to the amount of the "par". If the corporation issues no par value stock, it may sell the stock at whatever price the board of directors determines is "reasonable" (if the corporation is issuing stock for the first time, and the corporation has little or no assets, any price will be reasonable).

The issuance of stock by a corporation for less than full and adequate consideration is an ultra vires act. Such stock is called *watered stock,* and usually results when par value stock is issued in return for property (other than cash) or services having a fair value less than the par or stated value of the stock. Along this line, statutes generally provide that stock may be issued for money, property, or past services rendered; it may not be issued for services to be performed in the future (i. e., future services).

Though it is less common, it is also possible to have watered no par value stock. By way of example, suppose that ten people each pay $10,000 for 25 shares of no par value stock. Unknown to the ten, an eleventh person exchanges property worth only $3,000 for the same amount of stock. The latter shareholder's stock is watered to the extent of $7,000. The corporation, or the shareholders on behalf of the corporation, may go to court to set aside the issuance.

However, this is not to say that a corporation cannot issue no par value stock for property or services having a doubtful present value, but promising a high, though speculative, return. This is one of the very purposes for which no par value stock is designed. So long as full disclosure is made, a corporation may gamble on a high future return. Again, suppose that ten people each pay $10,000 for 25 shares of no par value stock. An eleventh person, an inventor, contributes his or her as yet unproved but highly promising patent right to the corporation for the same amount of no par value stock. Full disclosure of the transaction is made. The fact that the patent right has questionable present value does not make the inventor's stock watered.

It is sometimes difficult to determine whether shares of stock have been issued for less than adequate consideration. How are property and services to be valued? A minority of courts apply the "true value rule" which states that stock is watered whenever the fair market value of the property or services received for the stock substantially varies from the stock's par or stated value; the good faith of the shareholder (the transferor of the property or services) is immaterial.

A majority of courts follow the "good faith rule" which provides that stock is watered only where (1) the fair market value of the property or services received substantially varies from the stock's par or stated value, and (2) the shareholder (transferor of the property or services) fraudulently misrepresented the value of the property or services (i. e., intentionally overvalued it) when transferring it to the corporation. Here, the good faith of the shareholder-transferor is all important.

The most frequent issue before the courts in watered stock cases is whether creditors of an insolvent corporation can collect the amount of the "water" (i. e., the difference between the consideration given and the par or stated value of the stock) from the shareholder who transferred the property or services to the corporation in exchange for the stock. Most courts provide that only creditors who extended credit *after* issuance of the watered shares can collect the amount of the "water" from the shareholder; creditors who extended credit *before* issuance of the shares cannot.

In any event, before proceeding against the shareholder, a creditor must first reduce his or her claim against the corporation to judgment, and then try to collect the judgment. An exception arises where the corporation has been declared brankrupt by a federal bankruptcy court: the creditor, in this case, may proceed directly against the shareholder without first going against the corporation.

Suppose that the shareholder has sold or otherwise transferred the watered stock. The transferee is not liable for the amount of the water unless he or she had knowledge of it at the time of the transfer.

Finally, it should be pointed out that watered stock problems seldom arise anymore. State and federal securities statutes prohibit the issuance of such stock and require full disclosure in the sale of securities. The result is that little watered stock is issued. Where the problem does arise, it is usually in the formation of small corporations where the securities laws have the least impact.

How is a corporation managed and controlled?

The shareholders. As stated previously, the shareholders of a corporation have no right or power by virtue of being shareholders to participate directly in management of the corporation. However, they do exercise indirect control over corporate management through their voting rights. To begin with, the shareholders elect the board of directors which is directly responsible for managing the corporation. While the shareholders cannot command the directors to act in any particular way, they can remove a director—or the entire board for that matter—at any time by majority vote.

The shareholders can also vote to amend the Articles of Incorporation or the corporate by-laws, or to dissolve the corporation, etc. And though the board has sole power to manage the day-to-day business affairs of the corporation (and to contract on behalf of the corporation), the board cannot make major changes in corporate structure or business operations without shareholder approval. This would include, for example, a decision to merge with another corporation, or to dissolve the corporation. (Shareholders' voting rights are considered in detail in a later section).

The board of directors. The initial board of directors of a corporation is named in the Articles of Incorporation. Often, the initial board holds its position only until the first meeting of the shareholders at which time a new board is elected to serve for a given period of time as specified in the corporate by-laws (usually one year). Whatever their term of office, directors serve "until their successors are elected and have accepted their appointment as directors". The by-laws will provide for an annual meeting of the shareholders at which time a new board of directors will be elected. Note that the term of a director does not automatically end, but terminates only when a new director has been elected and accepts the position.

Unless the by-laws provide to the contrary, directors do not have to be shareholders of the corporation. And they are not entitled to any salary for serving on the board. However, many directors double as officers (particularly in small corporations) and officers do receive salaries.

The board of directors is responsible for managing the corporation. The directors are fiduciaries of the corporation, and, as such, are held to high standards of good faith; they must exercise reasonable care and diligence in all matters relating to corporate management. Because directors often have many business interests in addition to their directorship, they are not held to an impossible standard—rather, the "business judgment rule" is applied. The rule states that a director is personally liable for an erroneous business judgment that results in loss to the corporation only if the director acted fraudulently or in bad faith. Thus, the standard of care required is one of honest judgment. So long as a director makes an honest judgment, he or she will not be personally liable even if the judgment proves to be in error. However, a director who makes no effort to acquire sufficient facts on which to base his or her judgment does not act honestly and

in good faith, and will be personally liable to the corporation for any loss that results from the judgment. Examples of "bad faith" judgments include the reckless hiring of dishonest employees and the failure to purchase adequate insurance to provide against foreseeable casualty. And it is generally considered a "bad faith" judgment for a director to authorize a corporate loan to a director, officer, or shareholder of the corporation. In most states, a director who does so without approval of at least two-thirds of the shareholders is held to guarantee repayment of the loan.

In making business judgments, a director is entitled to rely on statements and reports made to him or her by corporate officers and employees; the director does not have to make independent investigations.

Directors function through meetings of the board. Generally speaking, there are no particular formalities (e. g., place of meeting) required. Unless the by-laws provide to the contrary, a simple majority of the directors constitutes a "quorum", and a quorum vote is sufficient to bind the corporation to actions within the ordinary scope of corporate business (the Articles or by-laws may require a higher percentage for certain actions or decisions —and don't forget, the shareholders must approve major changes in corporate structure and business operations).

If a majority of the directors cannot agree, and the board becomes deadlocked on a decision, the courts may appoint a "provisional director" to break the deadlock. A provisional director has the same powers and responsibilities as the other directors until such time as the deadlock is broken. Resolutions passed by the board are entered into the minute books of the corporation, which form a permanent part of the corporate records.

To aid in carrying out its duties, the board of directors frequently appoints an executive committee of its own members to carry on the day-to-day management between board meetings. Such a committee is generally prohibited by statute from making major business decisions such as declaring dividends or amending by-laws—only the board as a whole can do these things. Along the same line, the board can never eliminate board meetings completely nor delegate board responsibilities to one who is not a member of the board.

Finally, it should be pointed out that statutes in every state make it a crime to knowingly be a party to a false statement or entry in corporate records presenting a false financial picture of the corporation. A director who violates such a statute is subject to fine, imprisonment, or both.

A director may resign his or her position at any time. In addition, the shareholders can remove a director—or the entire board for that matter—at any time by majority vote. The board itself can remove any member who has been declared legally insane by a court of law or has been convicted of a felony. And a court can remove a director upon petition of a minority of shareholders (usually at least 10%) if it is established that the director has acted fraudulently or otherwise failed in his or her duties as a director.

The officers. The officers of a corporation are elected by the board of directors which also sets their terms of office and salaries. As stated previously, the officers generally include a president, vice-president, secretary, and treasurer; however, there are sometimes many more officers. The officers are agents of the corporation, and as such, have real and apparent authority to operate the business on a day-to-day basis. The officers have power to bind the corporation to contracts within the ordinary scope of the corporate business.

Like directors, officers are fiduciaries of the corporation, and have fiduciary duties of good faith, loyalty, and honesty.

Because of their day-to-day familiarity with the corporate affairs, officers are generally held to a higher standard of care than are directors.

The board of directors may remove the officers at any time without shareholder approval (this falls squarely within the meaning of corporate management).

What are the rules regarding conflicts of interest?

As fiduciaries, directors and officers have a duty of loyalty requiring them not to take advantage of the corporation for their own interests. In other words, directors and officers must not use their positions within the corporation to gain personally. When their personal interests conflict with those of the corporation, there is said to be a *conflict of interest*. There are five major areas where a conflict of interest may arise:

(1) Where a director or officer enters into a personal business transaction with the corporation;

(2) Where a director serves on the boards of two corporations that deal with each other (called an "interlocking directorate");

(3) Where a director or officer personally takes advantage of a business opportunity that would be advantageous to the corporation (the "corporate opportunity doctrine");

(4) Where a director or officer acquires an ownership interest in a competing business; and

(5) Where a director, officer, or other "insider" uses his or her "inside information" to make a personal profit (called "insider profits").

A director or officer enters into a personal business transaction with the corporation. A director or officer who contracts personally with the corporation is in much the same position as a promotor who does so. If the director or officer fails to make full disclosure regarding the contract to an independent board of directors, the corporation will have a right to rescind the contract or sue the director or officer for money damages (the corporation's measure of damages being the amount of unfair profit made on the transaction by the director). Where the contract is fundamentally unfair and unreasonable, the corporation will have the same right though full disclosure is made.

A director serves on the boards of two corporations that deal with each other (called an "interlocking directorate"). Obviously, a person who serves on two boards owes fiduciary duties to two corporations (the director has a responsibility to make the best contracts possible for each corporation). And if the corporations deal with each other, there is a possible conflict of interest. However, it is "possible" only. Most courts hold that contracts between such corporations are valid unless one of the corporations took undue advantage of the other or acted fraudulently by reason of having its director on the board of the other corporation.

A director or officer personally takes advantage of a business opportunity that would be advantageous to the corporation (the "corporate opportunity doctrine"). The *corporate opportunity doctrine* states that a director or officer must offer the corporation a "right of first refusal" on any business opportunity that he or she learns of that would be of benefit to the corporation. For example, say that a director learns that a large warehouse is up for sale. Though the corporation would have many uses for such a warehouse, the director fails to disclose the opportunity and purchases the warehouse for himself or herself. The corporation, in this case, may legally force the director to convey the property to the corporation at the director's expense (the courts will impose a "constructive trust" on the property in favor of the corporation—see

Ch. 29). Or, if the director has already sold the property to another, the corporation may sue the director for money damages and collect all the profits the director made on the transaction.

It is generally held that a director or officer may dispense with the "right of first refusal" if the corporation would be clearly unable to take advantage of the opportunity (e. g., because of insufficient finances). However, the better view is that this is not a decision for the director or officer to make on his or her own, and he or she should disclose the opportunity regardless.

And some courts hold that a director or officer may dispense with disclosure and take personal advantage of any transaction that would be ultra vires (beyond the powers of the corporation). Other courts state that the director or officer must make disclosure and give the corporation an opportunity to amend its Articles so as to make the transaction "intra vires" (within its powers).

A director or officer becomes an owner of a competing business. Anytime a director or officer becomes an owner of a competing business, there is a conflict of interest. The director or officer may not continue to serve as a director or officer. If he or she does so, he or she breaches his or her fiduciary duties and may be held accountable to the corporation for any loss that results.

A director, officer, employee, or other "insider" uses inside information to make "insider profits". Directors, by virtue of sitting on the board, often acquire information affecting the value of the corporation and its stock. Officers, employees, and large shareholders of the corporation may also have access to such "insider information". At common law, the rule varied as to whether an insider could buy or sell stock in the corporation without disclosing his or her inside information to the buyer or seller of the stock. Some courts held that insiders were free to buy and sell stock without disclosure of any kind. Other courts required full disclosure of any information affecting the value of the stock. Still others said that disclosure was necessary only where the insider had knowledge of "special facts" affecting stock value, such as an imminent merger, special dividends to be paid, a huge lawsuit facing the corporation, etc. (From a practical standpoint, the "special facts" approach would seem to require disclosure whenever there is an insider issue).

Today, the common law rules regarding insider profits have been largely superseded by statute. To begin with, most states have statutes controlling or prohibiting insider trading. And the federal Securities Exchange Act of 1934 (which is discussed in detail in Ch. 24) provides for the recovery of insider profits as follows:

Rule 10(b)-5. Rule 10(b)-5 (promulgated pursuant to Section 10(b) of the Securities Exchange Act of 1934) states that it is unlawful to use a "manipulative or deceptive device" including a "misstatement or *omission* of any material fact in connection with the purchase or sale of any security in interstate commerce [emphasis added]."

Rule 10(b)-5 applies to every sale or resale of securities, including the first such sale. It applies whether or not the securities must be registered under the Securities Exchange Act of 1934 (the Act requires registration of securities of any corporation engaged in interstate commerce having at least 500 shareholders of equity securities and total assets of at least $1,000,000—see Ch. 24).

By reason of its reference to any "omission", Rule 10(b)-5 clearly applies to any failure to disclose material "inside" information. (Examples of "material" inside information would include knowledge of imminent merger, changes in dividend rates, new product develop-

ment, discovery of new resources, anticipated legal action, etc.) Under the Section, *anyone* who possesses such inside information must disclose it. Thus, a broker who receives inside information from someone in the corporation must disclose the information when buying or selling the corporate stock.

The "interstate commerce" requirement means only that some instrumentality of interstate commerce must be used in connection with the purchase or sale—e. g., the mail, a telegraph. Even a purely intrastate telephone call (a call made entirely within one state) will do.

Any buyer or seller—even a member of the investing public—who is injured by an insider's violation of Rule 10(b)-5 may sue to rescind the purchase or sale or to recover money damages. If several people have been injured, they may bring a single class action to recover damages for the entire group (see Appendix A regarding "class actions").

Rule of Section 16. Section 16 of the Securities Exchange Act of 1934 applies only to securities that must be registered under the Act (again, those of any corporation engaged in interstate commerce having at least 500 shareholders of equity securities and total assets of $1,000,000). Section 16 requires an insider of a covered corporation (i. e., one whose securities must be registered) to disclose any short term profits he or she makes on the corporate stock. The Section defines "short term" or "short swing" profits as any profits made by an insider as the result of the purchase and sale of the covered corporation's stock within six months of each other. For purposes of the Section, an "insider" includes not only a director or officer of the corporation, but also any shareholder who owns at least 10% or more of the corporate stock at the time of the purchase and sale. Each insider must report his or her holdings in the corporation along with his or her transactions in the corporate stock.

Under Section 16, all short swing profits made by an insider belong to the corporation—there are no exceptions. The law raises a conclusive presumption that the profits resulted from inside information; no evidence to the contrary will be considered. Thus, it makes no difference that the profits resulted from normal market conditions only, that the insider had good motives, *or even that he or she had no inside information at all!*

Short swing profits belong to the corporation, not to the shareholders. However, if the corporation refuses to bring legal action to recover the profits, the shareholders may bring action on behalf of the corporation (this is a "derivative suit" as will be explained in a later section).

In determining whether short swing profits have been made, any pair of transactions occurring within a six month period may be looked to; losses from other transactions occurring within the same period may be disregarded. (In other words, though the insider's dealings show an overall loss, any profit made from a particular pair of transactions will still be short swing profits belonging to the corporation.) By way of example, suppose that the following insider transactions occur:

(1) On January 15th, an insider buys 200 shares of covered stock at $50.00 a share.

(2) On February 15th, the insider sells 100 shares at $75.00 a share.

(3) On March 15th, he or she sells 100 shares at $25.00 a share.

(4) On April 15th, he or she buys 100 shares at $15.00 a share.

(5) On May 15th, he or she sells 50 shares at $35.00 a share.

(6) On June 15th, he or she buys 50 shares at $25.00 a share.

(7) On July 15th, he or she sells 50 shares at $20.00 a share.

The insider has made "short swing" profits of $3,750 on the following pairs of transactions: $2,500 on transactions (1) and (2), $1,000 on transactions (4) and (5), and $250 on transactions (4) and (7). All the profits belong to the corporation, not to the insider. The fact that the insider has incurred losses —$2,500 if transactions (1) and (3) are paired and $250 if transactions (6) and (7) are paired—is immaterial. The losses belong to the insider alone. After all the transactions, the insider is considered to own the 50 shares he or she purchased on June 15th for $25.00 a share.

What are the rights and responsibilities of shareholders?

The owners of a corporation (i. e., the "shareholders" or "stockholders") have no interest in specific corporate property; nor do they have any direct voice in corporate management. However, shareholders do have certain basic rights and duties which may be summarized under the following headings:

(1) Dividends;

(2) Redemption of shares;

(3) Pre-emptive rights;

(4) Inspection of corporate records;

(5) Voting rights;

(6) Rights of minority stockholders; and

(7) Court actions or suits by shareholders.

(1) *Dividends.* Shareholders have no legal right to dividends. The declaring of dividends is a matter within the discretion of the board of directors. However, if a large surplus has accumulated and the directors refuse to declare a dividend, their refusal may be held in violation of their fiduciary duties (in which case the courts may order payment of a dividend upon petition of the shareholders).

Dividends may be declared and paid only out of *current profits* (the profits of the year) or *earned surplus* (undistributed profits from previous years). They may not be declared and paid out of *stated capital*. Stated capital refers to the total par value of all issued par value shares plus the total value received for all no-par value shares. Any amount paid for par value stock over and above its par value is called *capital surplus*. Generally, dividends may be paid out of capital surplus only if (1) there is no earned surplus available, and (2) the distribution will not render the corporation insolvent. For purposes of declaring and paying dividends, a corporation is insolvent when it is unable to meet its debts as they fall due. Sometimes, the board of directors will set aside a portion of "earned surplus" for special purposes (e. g., to retire a specific debt, acquire specific property, or maintain a fund required by a creditor as a condition to the granting of credit). Such surplus is referred to as *restricted surplus* and is not available for the payment of dividends.

Most states prohibit the payment of dividends, even out of current profits, where the result would be to impair the stated capital of the corporation. For example, a corporation's capital may already be impaired because of losses occurring in prior years (the corporation having to use capital to cover its expenses during those years). The corporation must refrain from declaring dividends and retain its earnings until the deficit has been recovered.

Other states expressly allow the payment of what are called "nimble dividends" even though payment will impair the corporation's capital account. Statutes in Delaware, Maryland, Virginia, and Wyoming provide that dividends may be paid out of the current year's earnings and/or the preceding year's earnings even though the corporation is operating under a capital impairment. Thus, though the total corporate operations reflect a loss, dividends may be declared and paid so long as there are earnings either in the current year or in the year prior. They are called "nimble dividends" because the corporation must act quickly within the current year to take advantage of the profits made in the preceding year.

No dividends of any kind (including nimble dividends) may be paid if the corporation is insolvent or would become so by payment of a dividend.

Nor may dividends be paid where the result would be to jeopardize the preferred stock's preference on net assets when the corporation is dissolved (an exception is made where the dividend is paid to the preferred stockholders only). A corporation must retain the full amount necessary to pay off its preferred shareholders on liquidation of the corporation (assuming such shares have a liquidation preference).

Where dividends are paid unlawfully, any directors who voted for the dividends will be personally liable to any creditors or preferred stockholders who are adversely affected. Directors who voted against the dividends will not be liable.

It should be noted that the foregoing rules do not apply to the payment of stock dividends. As you will recall, a stock dividend is simply a distribution of stock to the shareholder—each shareholder receiving a ratable share according to his or her holdings. A stock dividend has no effect on the assets or net worth of a corporation. However, it does reduce the amount of earned surplus available for future dividends: a bookkeeping entry is made to reflect the new shares added to stated capital, and the earned surplus account is reduced by whatever value is given to the stock dividend (depending on whether it is par value or no-par value stock).

Sometimes, the board orders, not a stock dividend, but a *stock split*. A stock split is no dividend at all, but simply an increase in the number of shares of stock outstanding. In the usual split, each share of outstanding stock is split into a larger number of shares; the split has no effect on the corporate capital or surplus accounts. For example, suppose that the board of directors of a corporation having 1,000 shares of stock outstanding with a stated capital value of $200,000 orders a 2 for 1 stock split. A shareholder owning 100 shares of stock will own 200 after the split. And there will be a total of 2,000 shares of stock outstanding with a stated capital value of $200,000. Clearly, this does not reduce earned surplus at all. A corporation often orders a stock split when the market value of the corporate stock goes so high that investors shy away from purchasing it. By increasing the number of shares on the market, the value of each share immediately declines, encouraging more active trading in the stock.

(2) *Redemption of shares.* A corporation *redeems* shares when it purchases shares of its stock from shareholders and cancels the shares. A corporation has no power to redeem absent express authorization in the Articles of Incorporation. And redemption is never allowed where a corporation has only one class of stock such as common (to permit redemption in such a case would be to allow the directors to eliminate the very shareholders to whom they are responsible for managing the corporation).

The right to redeem is often built into preferred stock to enable the corporation to ultimately eliminate that class of stock (and its dividend and liquidation preferences) for the benefit of the common stockholders. Generally, where the Articles provide for redemption of preferred stock, it is completely discretionary with the board of directors; occasionally, it is mandatory. Sometimes, the preferred stockholders, by the terms of the Articles, have a right to redemption of their stock at certain times and under certain circumstances (in this way, the preferred stockholders are guaranteed a "buyer" for their stock). Where the preferred stockholders have such a right, the corporation is obliged to maintain a reserve fund for the purpose of redeeming the stock. Generally, the corporation may use either earned surplus or stated capital to redeem shares.

Corporate *redemption* should not be confused with corporate *repurchase* of shares. A corporation repurchases shares when it buys shares of its stock from shareholders, but does not cancel the shares. Though the stock remains authorized and issued, it is no longer outstanding (i. e., held by shareholders); rather, it is held by the corporation itself, and is known as *treasury stock*. Treasury stock cannot be voted, it does not participate in dividends, and it has none of the other rights of stock held by the shareholders. However, it can be reissued by the corporation at a later time (redeemed shares, on the other hand, are cancelled and cannot be reissued). Moreover, treasury stock can be resold without worrying about receiving full consideration for the shares: the stock will not be considered "watered" so long as the original issue complied with the requirement that full value be received.

Unlike the power to redeem shares, the power to repurchase exists independently of the Articles of Incorporation: a corporation is deemed to have inherent power to repurchase its own shares. Because the same number of shares remain issued, repurchase has no effect on the stated capital of the corporation.

As with the payment of dividends, neither redemption nor repurchase of shares is legal if the result is to leave the corporation insolvent or without sufficient funds to cover preferences on liquidation.

(3) *Pre-emptive rights.* It is possible for a corporation to change the proportionate interests of its shareholders by issuing new shares of stock to new owners, or by issuing new shares to old shareholders but in amounts disproportionate to their ownership interests. To enable shareholders to prevent a decrease in

their proportionate ownership interest, all states recognize what are called "pre-emptive rights" of shareholders. Most states provide that if the Articles of Incorporation do not mention pre-emptive rights, the shareholders will have them. A few states (including California, Delaware, Indiana, Massachusetts, Oklahoma, and Pennsylvania) provide that pre-emptive rights must be expressly provided for in the Articles of Incorporation or they will not exist. And in all states, the Articles of Incorporation may expressly deny pre-emptive rights.

A "pre-emptive" right is a shareholder's right to "pre-empt" his or her share of any new issue of corporate stock. In other words, the shareholders must be given the opportunity to purchase an amount of the new issue equal to his or her present holdings; in this way, the shareholder can prevent a decrease in his or her proportionate ownership interest. A pre-emptive right is a right of first refusal only, and if the shareholder does not purchase his or her share of the stock, it may be sold to others.

The resale of treasury stock is not subject to pre-emptive rights.[9]

(4) *Inspection of corporate records.* In most states, the shareholders have a statutory right to make a reasonable inspection of the corporate records (financial reports, minutes of meetings, and any other records reflecting the corporate business and management). That is to say, a shareholder has a right to inspect the corporate records at a reasonable time and for a purpose related to the shareholder's interests as an owner of the corporation. A shareholder has no right to inspect at an unreasonable time or for any purpose adverse to the corporate interest. For example, a shareholder may not inspect the corporate records to ac-

quire information allowing him or her to go into a competing business. However, it is generally accepted that a shareholder may inspect shareholder lists for the purpose of contacting the shareholders to undertake a change in control of the corporation. Under the law, a shareholder who requests inspection is presumed to be acting properly, and it is up to the corporation to prove an improper motive.

A shareholder may inspect personally or through an agent such as an attorney or CPA. The right to inspect usually includes the right to make copies of the corporate records.

It should be pointed out that, in some states (and, in some cases, under the federal securities laws—see Ch. 24), a corporation must provide the shareholders with an annual report of the corporate operations. The report must include a profit and loss statement and a balance sheet.

(5) *Voting rights.* As stated previously, the shareholders exercise indirect control over corporate management through their voting rights. The corporate by-laws generally provide for an annual meeting of the shareholders, at which time the shareholders elect a new board of directors and vote on any other business matters within their power—e. g., to amend the Articles or by-laws, dissolve the corporation, etc.

The general rule is that the shareholder vote can *only* be exercised at *duly called* shareholder meetings, meaning that each shareholder entitled to vote receives proper notice of the meeting. Some states permit the shareholders to take action without a meeting if they do so by unanimous written consent of all shareholders entitled to vote (in Delaware, majority consent of the shareholders is sufficient).

9. Also not subject to pre-emptive rights are shares issued for consideration other than money; shares to be issued upon exercise of options or warrants; shares issued upon merger or consolidation; shares

originally authorized; shares issued within a specified time of incorporation; shares needed to initiate the business; or shares issued as a stock dividend.

A simple majority of the shareholders entitled to vote constitutes a quorum, and a quorum vote is sufficient to elect or remove directors. Generally, a quorum (majority) vote is also sufficient to amend the Articles of Incorporation or the corporate by-laws (certain kinds of amendments require a higher percentage —see section on amendment of the Articles).

To merge with another corporation or to dissolve the corporation, on the other hand, requires at least a two-thirds vote of all shareholders affected by the proposal. This, again, is to protect the minority shareholders.

And don't forget, the directors of the corporation have no power to order major changes in corporate structure or business operation (e. g., merger, dissolution) without shareholder approval (usually by a two-thirds vote).

Straight voting. Each common stockholder generally has the right to cast one vote for each share of stock that he or she owns. This is called *straight voting.* In all matters other than the election of directors, straight voting is the method used. (Sometimes, where there is more than one class of voting shares, a class will be given multiple votes—e. g., two votes for each share—this is called *weighted voting.*)

Cumulative voting. Obviously, if straight voting is used to elect the board of directors, any group of shareholders with at least 51% of the shares will be able to elect all the directors. To ensure shareholders with less than 51% some representation on the board, all states now require or at least allow the use of *cumulative voting.* Under cumulative voting, each share of common stock has as many votes as there are directors to be elected. And a shareholder can distribute his or her votes among the candidates in any way that he or she chooses. That is to say, he or she may "cumulate" his or her votes: he or she may cast them all for one director; or half for one and half for another, or in any other desired combination. For example, suppose that a five person board of directors is to be elected. The majority shareholders (having 51% or more of the stock) want to choose every member of the board, and, under straight voting, could do so. The majority supports the election of Tom, Dick, Harry, John, and Mark. The minority shareholders (having less than 51% of the vote) would like to elect at least two members of the board—they support the election of Ann and Mary as directors. The total number of voting shares is 2,000; cumulative voting is required. The question is, how many shares of stock must the minority own in order to elect at least two members of the board? The following formula applies:

$$X = \frac{ac}{b + 1} + 1$$

Where X = the number of shares needed to elect the number of directors the minority wants to elect

a = the number of shares voting

b = the number of directors to be selected

c = the number of directors the minority wants to elect

In our example,

$$a = 2,000$$
$$b = 5$$
$$c = 2$$

so $X = \frac{2,000 \times 2}{5 + 1} + 1$ or $\frac{4,000}{6} + 1$ or 668

Thus, if the minority shareholders own 668 shares of stock, they can assure the election of Ann and Mary as directors. The majority shareholders will be able to control the election of the other three members of the board. Bearing in mind that it will take 334 shares of stock to elect one director, the minority will cast their 668 shares, and the majority their 1,332 shares (2,000–668) as follows:

The minority will cast:	334 shares for Ann
	334 shares for Mary
	and Ann and Mary are elected
The majority will cast:	334 shares for Tom
	334 shares for Dick
	334 shares for Harry
	and they are elected
And the majority has	330 shares left to cast for John or Mark, but this is not enough to elect either.
Total shares cast	2,000

As stated, cumulative voting may be mandatory or merely permissive, depending on the state statute. Where it is merely permissive, the Articles of Incorporation may provide exclusively for straight voting.

Proxy voting. In all states, shareholders have a right to vote by proxy. A *proxy* is a power of attorney given by a shareholder to another party authorizing the party to exercise the voting rights of the shares. The use of proxies enables minority shareholders to obtain enough votes to gain representation on the board of directors; majority shareholders frequently solicit proxies as well.

Generally, a proxy must be in writing, and must be filed with the corporation before the shareholder meeting at which it is to be voted. If the proxy is given for a specific length of time, it will be valid for the time stated or for five years, whichever is less. If given for an indefinite period, the proxy will become invalid after a period of time set by statute, typically one year. Like any other agency authority, a proxy may be revoked at any time unless it is coupled with an interest (e. g., where the shareholder receives consideration for the proxy).

To prevent abuse of proxies, the federal Securities Exchange Commission has adopted certain proxy rules pursuant to authority conferred by Section 14 of the Securities Exchange Act of 1934. Rule 14(a) states that anyone who is soliciting proxies covering registered securities must set forth complete information regarding the matters to be voted on and must identify all the participants involved in the proxy solicitation. Where the proxy is being solicited in an effort to remove the current directors of the corporation, the soliciting party must also provide the shareholders with a complete corporate financial report.

If corporate management is soliciting proxies, it must also include an opposition statement of up to 200 words from any minority interest that wants to make one. And if the minority wants to make an independent solicitation, management must cooperate by supplying a list of the corporate shareholders or by mailing the solicitations for the minority.

Where any of the above rules are violated, the Securities Exchange Commission can enjoin the solicitation and/or prevent the use of any proxies obtained. And injured minorities may seek rescission of any actions approved following the improper proxy solicitation.

(6) *Additional protection of minority shareholders.* To this point, we have seen that minority shareholders find protection in cumulative voting and pre-emp-

tive rights. Now we find that they are further protected by reason of their fiduciary relationship with the majority.

The majority shareholders are fiduciaries of the minority. As fiduciaries, they have a duty to use their power in the interests of all the shareholders—not to use it to produce a profit for themselves at the expense of the minority (by paying dividends, setting salaries, and otherwise controlling the corporation in their favor). For example, say that a majority shareholder takes advantage of his or her controlling interest to purchase property from the corporation at less than its fair market value. The majority shareholder has breached his or her fiduciary duty to the minority (by dealing in his or her own favor at the minority's expense), and is liable to the minority in damages.

Similarly, the majority breaches its fiduciary duty to the minority where it attempts to amend the Articles or by-laws so as to decrease minority representation. The same is true where the majority dissolves the corporation in an effort to "freeze out" the minority (here, the majority's plan is to get rid of the minority shareholders, then continue the business with the majority only—the minority's damages include a part of the new business' profits).

There may even be a breach of fiduciary duty where the majority sells its shares to outsiders who take over control of the corporation. Ordinarily, the majority (like any other seller) is entitled to sell its shares so as to make the best deal possible for itself. But the majority breaches its fiduciary duty to the minority if it makes the sale notwithstanding its knowledge of "special facts" indicating that the minority's interest will sharply decline in value as a result of the sale (e. g., where the majority knows that the buyer plans to limit expansion of the corporation by confining his or her sales to a single buyer under his or her control).

Some courts go so far as to state that whenever control of the corporation is material, the majority must exercise "inherent fairness" and give the minority shareholders an "equal opportunity" to sell their shares on the same terms as the majority. For example, suppose that the majority works out a deal whereby it may sell and exchange its shares for shares in a corporation having a public market for its stock. The minority is excluded from the deal, and after the transaction, is left with relatively unmarketable shares. Under the inherent fairness doctrine, the minority may sue the majority for failing to provide it with an equal opportunity to exchange its shares for shares in the other corporation.

Finally, the majority breaches its fiduciary duty to the minority where it takes advantage of inside information to purchase minority shares.

(7) *Court actions or suits by shareholders.* As discussed above, shareholders sometimes find it necessary to bring legal action against directors, officers, or majority shareholders who have injured them personally (e. g., where the majority breaches its fiduciary duty to the minority). If several shareholders have been injured, they may use a single class action to recover for the entire group.

Occasionally, however, it is not the shareholders who have been injured by the actions of others, but the corporation itself. For example, a director who takes personal advantage of a corporate opportunity, or makes swing profits, or violates the proxy rules promulgated by the Securities and Exchange Commission, breaches his or her fiduciary duties to the *corporation*. And, as you know, a corporation may sue in its own name to recover damages.

But suppose that the corporation refuses to sue. The directors, who are responsible for bringing suit for the corporation, may well refuse to take legal action if it means suing one of their own members or a corporate officer for mismanagement. The shareholders, in this case, cannot sue as individuals because they have not been damaged as individuals. However, one or more shareholders can bring an action *on behalf of the corporation to recover damages for the corporation.* Such a proceeding is called a *derivative suit* because it derives from the corporation's cause of action.

A shareholder may bring a derivative suit only after he or she has made written demand upon the directors to take legal action, and the directors either refuse or fail to take action within a reasonable time. That is to say, a shareholder must give the corporation an opportunity to bring legal action before taking it upon himself or herself to sue on behalf of the corporation.

Where a shareholder brings a derivative suit against directors or officers of the corporation, and the shareholder loses the suit, the defendant directors or officers are entitled to reimbursement from the corporation for their personal costs and expenses (including attorneys fees) in defending the action. If, on the other hand, the shareholder wins the suit, the corporation may not indemnify the losing officers or directors. Some corporations have tried to get around this rule by purchasing indemnity insurance for its officers and directors (the reasoning being that it is the insurance company and not the corporation that reimburses the insured). Most states expressly prohibit such indirect reimbursement, finding it as reprehensible as direct payment. Other states permit it except in cases involving fraud, other intentional wrongdoing, or violations of state or federal securities laws.

Are there any special rules regarding the transfer of shares?

In Ch. 13, we learned that negotiable notes, drafts, and checks serve as substitutes for money: the transfer of a "money instrument" to a holder in due course cuts off all existing personal defenses to payment of the instrument. In Ch. 16, we learned that common carriers and warehousemen frequently issue negotiable documents of title (negotiable bills of lading and negotiable warehouse receipts); the transfer of such a document serves to transfer ownership of the goods.

Now we find that there is yet another form of negotiable instrument—the corporate stock certificate. A corporate stock certificate is fully negotiable. By this is meant that a *valid transfer* of the certificate serves to transfer ownership of the shares in the corporation. In many ways, the rules for valid transfer of a stock certificate are like the rules for negotiation of negotiable money instruments; in other ways, they are markedly different. For stock certificates are governed, not by Article 3 of the Uniform Commercial Code, but by Article 8, entitled "Investment Securities".

Section 8–102 provides:

Section 8–102. Definitions and Index of Definitions

(1) In this Article unless the context otherwise requires

    (a) A "security" is an instrument which

        (i) is issued in bearer or registered form; and

        (ii) is of a type commonly dealt in upon securities exchanges or markets or commonly recognized in any area in which it is issued or dealt in as a medium for investment; and

(iii) is either one of a class or series or by its terms is divisible into a class or series of instruments; and

(iv) evidences a share, participation or other interest in property or in an enterprise or evidences an obligation of the issuer.

*   *   *

(c) A security is in "registered form" when it specifies a person entitled to the security or to the rights it evidences and when its transfer may be registered upon books maintained for that purpose by or on behalf of an issuer or the security so states.

(d) A security is in "bearer form" when it runs to bearer according to its terms and not by reason of any indorsement.

___

Generally speaking, stock certificates are issued in what Article 8 terms "registered form". By this is meant that a stock certificate is issued in the name of a specific person whose name appears on the face of the certificate itself. The corporation lists the named party as the owner of the stock on the corporate stock register (hence the term "registered owner"). The stock register provides the corporation with a list of shareholders to whom dividends can be paid, notice and voting rights given, and net assets distributed upon dissolution of the corporation.

The first "valid transfer" of a registered stock certificate demands (1) *delivery* of the certificate, and (2) *indorsement* by the registered owner of the stock. (The certificate is thus like "order" paper: it is made out to a specific person, and requires both delivery and indorsement for transfer.) The registered owner (and subsequent transferors) may indorse specially (i. e., in the

name of a specific person) or in blank (i. e., sign his or her name and nothing more)—this, of course, is like converting the certificate from order paper to bearer paper, and vice-versa. Where the last indorsement is special, both delivery and indorsement by the special indorsee are required for further transfer of the certificate. Where the last indorsement is blank, delivery alone will suffice to transfer ownership of the shares. Thus, a thief or finder of a stock certificate that is indorsed in blank can transfer the certificate (by delivery alone) to a bona fide purchaser who will prevail even as against the true owner.

Where indorsement is required, it may be placed on the back of the certificate itself, or on a separate sheet of paper, called a *stock power*. Uniform Commercial Code Section 8–308 is pertinent.

The UCC provides:

Section 8–308. Indorsement, How Made; Special Indorsement * *

(1) An indorsement of a security in registered form is made when an appropriate person signs on it or on a separate document an assignment or transfer of the security or a power to assign or transfer it or when the signature of such person is written without more upon the back of the security.

(2) An indorsement may be in blank or special. An indorsement in blank includes an indorsement to bearer. A special indorsement specifies the person to whom the security is to be transferred, or who has power to transfer it. A holder may convert a blank indorsement into a special indorsement.

___

Suppose that the transferor forgets to indorse the certificate. The transferee can compel indorsement under U.C.C. Section 8–307.

The UCC provides:

Section 8–307. Effect of Delivery Without Indorsement; Right to Compel Indorsement

Where a security in registered form has been delivered to a purchaser without a necessary indorsement he may become a bona fide purchaser only as of the time the indorsement is supplied, but against the transferor the transfer is complete upon delivery and the purchaser has a specifically enforceable right against the transferor to have any necessary indorsement supplied.

Once the transfer is complete, the transferee should surrender the certificate (along with any stock power) to the corporation. The corporation will substitute the new owner's name for the old owner's on the stock register, cancel the old stock certificate, and issue a new certificate to the new owner.

A person who presents a stock certificate to a corporation for registration of transfer makes the following warranties to the corporation.

The UCC provides:

Section 8–306. Warranties on Presentment * * *

(1) A person who presents a security for registration of transfer or for payment or exchange warrants to the issuer that he is entitled to the registration, payment or exchange. But a purchaser for value without notice of adverse claims who receives a new, reissued or re-registered security or registration of transfer warrants only that he has no knowledge of any unauthorized signature * * * in a necessary indorsement.

Suppose that a corporation discovers after issuing a transferee a new certificate that a necessary indorsement on the old certificate was forged. Ordinarily, a forged indorsement has no adverse effect on the true owner's rights. However, if a certificate containing a forgery is transferred to a bona fide purchaser for value who registers the transfer with the corporation, the bona fide purchaser will prevail as against the true owner. The true owner can recover from the corporation for improper registration; and the corporation will have no recourse against the bfp (the bfp warranted only that he or she had no *knowledge* of any unauthorized signature). If possible, the corporation must issue equivalent stock to the true owner; where this would result in over-issue (remember, a corporation is authorized to issue just so many shares of stock), the corporation must pay the true owner the monetary value of his or her transferred shares. Uniform Commercial Code Sections 8–311 and 8–104 are relevant.

The UCC provides:

Section 8–311. Effect of Unauthorized Indorsement

Unless the owner has ratified an unauthorized indorsement or is otherwise precluded from asserting its ineffectiveness

(a) he may assert its ineffectiveness against the issuer or any purchaser other than a purchaser for value and without notice of adverse claims who has in good faith received a new, reissued or re-registered security on registration of transfer; and

(b) an issuer who registers the transfer of a security upon the unauthorized indorsement is subject to liability for improper registration.

* * *

Section 8–104. Effect of Overissue; "Overissue"

(1) The provisions of this Article which validate a security or compel its issue or reissue do not apply to the extent that validation, issue or reissue would result in overissue; but

  (a) if an identical security which does not constitute an overissue is reasonably available for purchase, the person entitled to issue or validation may compel the issuer to purchase and deliver such a security to him against surrender of the security, if any, which he holds; or

  (b) if a security is not so available for purchase, the person entitled to issue or validation may recover from the issuer the price he or the last purchaser for value paid for it with interest from the date of his demand.

(2) "Overissue" means the issue of securities in excess of the amount which the issuer has corporate power to issue.

To avoid the forged indorsement problem, most corporations insist that all signatures on the certificate be guaranteed by a bank or other responsible party, such as a stock brokerage house. Then, if the signature proves to be a forgery, the corporation can go against the signature guaranty to recoup its losses.

Section 8–312 of the Code provides:

Section 8–312. Effect of Guaranteeing Signature or Indorsement

(1) Any person guaranteeing a *signature* of an indorser of a security warrants that at the time of signing

  (a) the signature was genuine; and

  (b) the signer was an appropriate person to indorse; and

  (c) the signer had legal capacity to sign.

But the guarantor does not otherwise warrant the rightfulness of the particular transfer.

(2) Any person may guarantee an *indorsement* of a security and by so doing warrants not only the signature (subsection (1)) but also the rightfulness of the particular transaction in all respects. But no issuer may require a guarantee of indorsement as a condition to registration of transfer * * * however, a guarantee of *signature* can be required.

(3) The foregoing warranties are made to any person taking or dealing with the security in reliance on the guarantee and the guarantor is liable to such person for any loss resulting from breach of the warranties.

[Emphasis added.]

As to the indorser's liability on the stock certificate, he or she has none in the sense that an indorser of a negotiable money instrument is secondarily liable on the basis of an indorsement contract. Uniform Commercial Code Section 8–308(4) states: "Unless otherwise agreed the indorser by his indorsement assumes no obligation that the security will be honored by the issuer." The *Official Comment* to the Section provides.

Official Comment:

The indorser of a security is relieved from liability insofar as honor of the instrument by the issuer is concerned. In view of the nature of investment securities and the circumstances under which they are normally transferred an indorser cannot be held to warrant as to the issuer's actions.[10]

However, all transferors for value of stock certificates make certain warranties, and an indorser, as a transferor of stock, may be liable on the basis of breach of warranty.

UCC Section 8–306(2) provides:

(2) A person by transferring a security to a purchaser for value warrants * * * that

(a) his transfer is effective and rightful; and

(b) the security is genuine and has not been materially altered; and

(c) he knows no fact which might impair the validity of the security.

As to the rights acquired by the purchaser of the stock, Uniform Commercial Code Section 8–301 states.

Section 8–301. Rights Acquired by Purchaser; "Adverse Claim"; Title Acquired by Bona Fide Purchaser

(1) Upon delivery of a security the purchaser acquires the rights in the security which his transferor had or had actual authority to convey except that a purchaser who has himself been a party to any fraud or illegality affecting the security or who as a prior holder had notice of an adverse claim cannot improve his position by taking from a later bona fide purchaser. "Adverse claim" includes a claim that a transfer was

or would be wrongful or that a particular adverse person is the owner or has an interest in the security. [Note—this provision is like the "shelter provision" discussed in Ch. 14.]

(2) A bona fide purchaser in addition to acquiring the rights of a purchaser also acquires the security free of any adverse claim. [In this respect, the purchaser is like a holder in due course of commercial paper who takes free of existing personal defenses.]

Sometimes, particularly with regard to small corporations, the shareholders attempt to restrict transfer of shares so as to keep outsiders out of the corporate ownership. However, the law will not permit an absolute restraint on transfer: as you will recall from Ch. 1, free transferability is one of the fundamental rights of property ownership. To be valid, the restraint on transfer must be reasonable (e. g., it is reasonable to require a shareholder to give the corporation and other shareholders a "right of first refusal" on stock before offering it to outsiders for sale). And to be enforceable against a transferee of the stock, the restraint must appear on the face of the stock certificate. Section 8–204 is the relevant Uniform Commercial Code provision.

The UCC provides:

Section 8–204. Effect of Issuer's Restrictions on Transfer

Unless noted conspicuously on the security a restriction on transfer imposed by the issuer even though otherwise lawful is ineffective except against a person with actual knowledge of it.

----

10. Thus, qualified and restrictive indorsements have no meaning insofar as stock certificates are concerned—indorsement serves merely to facilitate transfer of the certificate.

If the restriction, though reasonable, does not appear on the face of the certificate, a transferee of the stock will acquire full ownership rights. Of course, the transferor, in this case, may well be liable to the corporation and the other shareholders for breach of contract.

Similarly, if stock is issued for partial payment, the corporation's assessment or lien against the original shareholder for the remainder of the purchase price does not carry over to an innocent purchaser of the stock unless the lien appears on the face of the stock certificate. Section 8–103 of the Uniform Commercial Code provides: "A lien upon a security in favor of an issuer thereof is valid against a purchaser only if the right of the issuer to such lien is noted conspicuously on the security."

Are there any special rules on corporate mergers and consolidations?

A *merger* takes place when an existing corporation absorbs one or more existing corporations: the absorbing corporation survives the merger; the absorbed corporations cease to exist.

A *consolidation* occurs when a new corporation is formed from one or more existing corporations: the new or consolidated corporation absorbs the existing corporations which cease to exist as separate entities.

The mechanics of merger and consolidation are similar—the surviving or consolidated corporation issues its shares to the shareholders of the absorbed corporations in exchange for their shares. The absorbed corporations then dissolve (dissolution is treated in the final section of this chapter).

The effect of each is also similar—with limited exception, the surviving or consolidated corporation succeeds to all the rights and liabilities of the absorbed corporations. After the merger or consolidation, the shareholders of the absorbed corporations own stock in the surviving or new corporation.

To protect the rights of minority shareholders, all states place certain restrictions on mergers and consolidations. Most states require shareholder approval of a proposed merger or consolidation by at least two-thirds of the shareholders of each corporation involved in the transaction. And, in most states, minority shareholders who vote against a proposed merger or consolidation have a statutory remedy: the dissenters can require the corporation in which they own stock to purchase their shares at fair market value as a condition precedent to merger or consolidation. For a minority shareholder to take advantage of this remedy, he or she must (1) file an objection to the proposed merger or consolidation before the shareholders meeting at which the proposal is to be considered; (2) vote against the proposal; and (3) make written demand upon the corporation to purchase his or her shares at a price to be determined by appraisal.

Are there any alternatives to merger or consolidation?

In a merger or consolidation, the surviving or consolidated corporation acquires the *stock* of the absorbed corporations. As an alternative to merger or consolidation, an existing corporation may simply purchase the *assets* of another corporation. Only a majority of the shareholders of the selling corporation must consent to the purchase; shareholders of the purchasing corporation need not approve. And, in most states, dissenters have no rights to be bought out as they do in a merger or consolidation.

Or a corporation may gain voting control of another corporation by purchasing at least 51% of its stock. In this case, the controlled corporation will continue to operate as a subsidiary of the controlling corporation. No shareholder approval is required.

How are the Articles of Incorporation amended?

Sometimes, because of changing conditions, a corporation will want to expand, change its operations, issue new stock, etc. If these things are not authorized by the Articles of Incorporation, amendment of the Articles will be required. The Articles of Incorporation cannot validly prohibit amendment.

All amendments to the Articles must be approved by the shareholders, generally by a simple majority vote (although the Articles can require a higher percentage). However, in most states, an amendment that would adversely affect a particular class of stock (e. g., an amendment to reduce the dividend rate for preferred stock) must be approved by at least two-thirds of the shareholders of that class. An amendment to reduce the number of directors to less than five must be approved by at least two-thirds of all shareholders. And 100% shareholder approval is required to levy an assessment from all shareholders on fully paid shares.

Once approved, the amendment must be filed with the state corporation commissioner (or other designated official, such as the secretary of state).

As for corporate by-laws, there is usually no prescribed formality for amending them—they can generally be amended by a simple majority vote of the shareholders.

What are the rules on dissolution and liquidation of a corporation?

Like a partnership, a corporation may at some point dissolve and begin the process of "winding up" its affairs preliminary to termination. The winding up process—paying the bills, distributing the net assets, etc.—is referred to as liquidation of the business. The directors of a dissolved corporation are responsible for liquidating the business as quickly and fairly as possible.

Dissolution of a corporation may be voluntary or involuntary. A corporation voluntarily dissolves when its directors meet and pass a resolution to dissolve and liquidate; the resolution must be ratified by a majority of the shareholders who are entitled to vote. Following ratification, the directors must file a certificate of dissolution with the proper state official, usually the corporation commissioner. (A corporation that is absorbed through merger or consolidation also dissolves by filing such a certificate.)

The state itself may force the corporation into involuntary dissolution by bringing what is called a "quo warranto" action to require forfeiture of the corporate charter. Usually, the state will do this only where the corporation engages in ultra vires activity or fails to properly organize and operate following issuance of the charter. As an alternative to dissolution, the corporation may simply be suspended from operation until it clears up its problems—typical of such problems as failure to pay state corporation taxes. A suspended corporation may not do business in the state or use the courts (the corporate officers and directors will be personally liable for any business undertaken during the suspension). However, on clearing up its problems, the suspended corporation will be reinstated.

The directors or shareholders of the corporation may also force an involuntary dissolution under certain circumstances. Statutes generally provide that, upon petition of at least one-half of the directors or at least one-third of the shareholders, involuntary dissolution will be ordered whenever any of the following occurs:

(1) A deadlock in corporate management and control (although here, the court may simply appoint a provisional director to break the deadlock);

(2) Abandonment of the corporate business for a long period of time (usually, a minimum of one year);

(3) Fraud or mismanagement on the part of the directors or officers, or other illegal activity or abuse of authority;

(4) Continued waste of the corporate assets and resources by the corporate management; or

(5) Expiration of the term of the corporation as set by the Articles of Incorporation (remember, the Articles may provide for a fixed period of duration).

Where minority shareholders petition the court for involuntary dissolution, the majority may be allowed to purchase the minority's stock and thereby prevent the dissolution.

Creditors of a corporation cannot force the corporation into involuntary dissolution. But once dissolution has begun, the creditors' interests are protected. To begin with, the corporation must notify the creditors of the dissolution and liquidation activity. It must carry out any existing contracts with the creditors (dissolution does not excuse performance of existing contracts). And the corporation must pay the creditors in full before paying the shareholders anything. But, remember, the shareholders of the corporation have limited liability and are not responsible for corporate debts. If the corporation has insufficient assets to pay all its creditors, the creditors cannot look to the individual shareholders for payment. However, if the corporation pays the shareholders first before paying the creditors, the creditors can trace the assets into the hands of the shareholders and require their return for distribution to the creditors.

After all creditors have been paid in full, the shareholders are entitled to their proportionate shares of the net assets of the corporation. Preferred shareholders with liquidation preferences must be paid before the common shareholders receive anything; if their stock is cumulative preferred, they are generally entitled to all cumulative dividends in arrears.[11] The final distribution to shareholders may be in the form of cash or other property. Where property other than cash is transferred to the shareholders, they become tenants in common as to the property (see Ch. 6).

Finally, the interest of any shareholder (or shareholder's heir or beneficiary) who cannot be located will escheat to the state (see Ch. 30).

CASES

CASE 1—*"Perfect candor, full disclosure, the utmost good faith, and the strictest honesty are required of promoters."*

FRICK v. HOWARD

Supreme Court of Wisconsin, 1964.
23 Wisc.2d 86, 126 N.W.2d 619.

Action to foreclose a mortgage on real estate. Plaintiff-respondent is the assignee of the promoter of a corporation. The * * * mortgage being foreclosed was executed by the corporation in favor of the promoter and his wife when they sold certain real estate located in the city of Milwaukee to the corporation. Defendant-appellant is the receiver of the corporation. * * *

---

11. It should be pointed out that preferred stockholders are not creditors of the corporation, and are not entitled to any payment before all creditors' claims have been satisfied.

On January 24, 1958, Michael D. Preston, an attorney, entered into a contract to purchase real estate located at 3816 West Wisconsin Avenue, Milwaukee. The purchase price was $240,000. Preston agreed to pay $5,000 down, $65,000 on the date of closing, and the vendor agreed to take back a purchase money mortgage for $170,000. On April 1, 1958, Preston organized Pan American Motel, Inc. He subscribed to one share of capital stock of the corporation. The stated value of this one share of stock was $1,000.

* * *

On September 1, 1958, Pan American Motel, Inc. offered to purchase the real estate in question from Preston and his wife for $350,000. The terms of the offer were $70,000 on closing; that the corporation would assume the outstanding mortgage of $170,000; and that the corporation would execute a note and mortgage in the sum of $110,000 to make up the balance of the purchase price. * * * The offer was accepted and carried out according to its terms. * * *

In order to construct a motel on the premises the corporation negotiated a $550,000 construction loan with First Federal Savings and Loan Association. A mortgage securing this loan was recorded on July 2, 1959. Preston recorded his mortgage on September 17, 1959.

* * * On December 8, 1961 * * * the mortgage of April 1, 1959 was assigned by Preston and his wife to the plaintiff. The plaintiff paid $72,500 for the mortgage * * *. On September 15, 1961 an appraisal of the assets of the corporation was made by the American Appraisal Company * * *. A letter from the American Appraisal Company * * * stated that the fair value for investment purposes of the property was $1,200,000. At this time a motel had been erected on the real estate and Pan American Motel, Inc. was a going concern. On January 16, 1962 the defendant was appointed receiver of the corporation * * * [the corporation being in financial difficulty]. On July 10, 1962 plaintiff recorded his mortgage assignment from Preston.

In his complaint plaintiff * * * asked for foreclosure of the 1959 mortgage and a deficiency judgment against the corporation. The defense was violation of a fiduciary duty to the corporation on the part of plaintiff's assignor and a contention that the mortgage was a fraudulent conveyance.

* * *

From a judgment of foreclosure in favor of the plaintiff for the amount of $77,159.57 defendant appeals.

BEILFUSS, Justice.

* * *

Did Preston, as a promoter, breach a fiduciary duty to the corporation? It appears without dispute that Preston was the organizer and promotor of the Pan American Motel, Inc.

He entered into the contract to purchase land for $240,000 on January 24, 1958. The terms were,—$5,000 down payment, $65,000 at the closing of the sale and purchase money mortgage back in the amount of $170,000. He borrowed the $5,000 down payment * * *. He organized the corporation April 1, 1958 and was its sole stockholder until September 3, 1958. * * * To pay for the land he withdrew at least $61,000 of the $65,000 closing payment from the corporation and gave the mortgage for $170,000. Three days later, September 1, 1958, the corporation offered him $350,000 for the land. The offer was accepted and the corporation paid Preston $70,000 by cancellation of his debt of $35,000 to the corporation, issuing 35 shares of its stock to him, assuming the $170,000 mortgage, and giving him a note and mortgage for $110,000. The offer was signed by Preston as seller and Frank J. Mack for the corporation. At the time the offer to purchase was made by the corporation Preston was, as far as the record reveals, the sole stockholder and completely dominated the affairs of the corporation. There was a board of directors consisting of Preston and two others but the record does not show they owned any stock or that they were in any way independent of Preston. On April 1, 1959 the note of $110,000 and mortgage were signed by Preston as president of the corporation and by Frank J. Mack as secretary payable to Preston and his wife.

The trial court found that Preston committed a fraud upon the corporation but that the transaction was not secret.

The fact that the transaction was not secret does not in all instances relieve a promoter of his fiduciary obligation to the corporation.

"The promoters may deal with the corporation, but they must deal fairly, the burden of proof of fairness being on them. When they deal with the corporation, it must have independent directors; and the promoters cannot also be directors or dominate them as representatives of the other adversely interested parties.

"Perfect candor, full disclosure, good faith, in fact, the utmost good faith, and the strictest honesty are required of promoters, and their dealings must be open and fair, or without undue advantage taken.

"It is the duty of the promoters to retain in their hands the property which is to constitute corporate assets until the corporation is formed, to cause it to be formed within a reasonable time, and then to turn over to it the assets so held * * *." * * *

"As a result of the fiduciary relation or relation of trust and confidence sustained by a promoter, an unfair advantage taken or secret profit gained thereby is a fraud. * * *"

"*Conditions Requisite to Valid Sale.*   A promoter cannot act as both seller and buyer. Hence, where he seeks to sell property to the corporation, he must, if he wishes to retain his profit, provide the corporation with an independent board of directors in no wise under his control and make a full disclosure to the corporation through them, or make a full disclosure of all material facts to each original subscriber for stock in the corporation, or procure a ratification of the sale, after disclosure of its circumstances, by the completely established corporation. * * *"

"From the foregoing we deduce this: If one or more persons acquire property, intending to promote the organization of a corporation to purchase it from them at a profit to themselves and effect such purpose, limiting the membership to interested parties till the transaction is completed between them and the corporation, intending thereafter to cause the balance of the capital stock to be sold to outsiders, they being kept in ignorance of the true nature of such transaction, and effecting such intent, they are guilty of actionable fraud upon the corporation and responsible to it for the gains made. *   *   *

It is clear that at the time of the sale of the land to the corporation, and the execution of the note and mortgage, that the corporation had no independent board of directors. The actions of the corporation were completely dominated by Preston. The transaction to sell the land held for a very short period of time was controlled by Preston both as buyer and seller. This was not an agreement between an independent buyer and seller dealing at arm's length. Preston as an individual selling the property had a personal financial interest to obtain the highest price available; Preston as the alter ego of Pan American Motel, Inc. had a financial interest to purchase the property at the lowest price available. There could be no meeting of the minds.

The fact that the land may or may not have been worth more than $240,000 cannot override Preston's fiduciary obligation as a promoter of the corporation. In this instance where he completely dominated the corporation at the time of the transaction it was his fiduciary obligation to give the corporation the benefit of his bargain, if it was one. If Preston had provided the corporation with a board of directors who could have acted independently and at arm's length the situation might have been different. For Preston to obtain a profit of $110,000 for himself under the circumstances herein is unconscionable and a violation of his fiduciary obligation and as such a fraud upon the corporation.

*   *   *

Frick, the assignee of Preston, contends that the land sale transaction was subsequently ratified by the corporation and, therefore, the defense of constructive fraud by the promoter is no longer available. The burden of proof to show ratification and to show that it was the act of an independent board of directors was upon Preston's assignee. He has not met this burden. In any event the creditors cannot be bound by a ratification in which they had no voice.

Judgment reversed with directions to dismiss the complaint.

CASE 2—*The doctrine of ultra vires is designed to protect the share-holders' interest, but here the corporate veil must be pierced.*

LURIE v. ARIZONA FERTILIZER & CHEMICAL CO.

Supreme Court of Arizona, In Division, 1966.
101 Ariz. 482, 421 P.2d 330.

McFARLAND, Justice.

Appellants bring this appeal from a directed verdict and judgment against them in the lower court. Melvin Lurie, Alan Lurie, Tolbert Lurie, and Meyer Lurie, hereinafter designated the Luries, were engaged in the hotel and construction business in Washington, California, Arizona, and several other States. The Luries controlled or were the sole stockholders of over twenty separate corporations, one of which was Allied Yuma Farms, Inc., a Washington corporation licensed to do business in Arizona. Allied Yuma Farms, Inc., was engaged in farming operations in Arizona, producing primarily vegetable and truck crops. Due to harvesting difficulties with regard to a melon crop that farming operation lost money during the 1958 season.

A neighboring grower, Jay Chapman, persuaded the Luries to continue their farming activities in the area, and to enter into a joint farming venture with Arizona Desert Farms, a limited partnership with which Chapman was connected. The joint venture was formed, and it was agreed that profits and losses be shared on a 50–50 basis. Although the joint venture agreement was never reduced to writing the joint venture commenced farming during the 1959 growing season. Due to market and growing conditions, the return from the sale of the venture's farm products fell well below growing costs.

During this operation, Arizona Fertilizer and Chemical Co., hereinafter designated plaintiff, furnished $11,453.38 worth of chemical fertilizers to the joint venture on an open account. The bill was not paid, and plaintiff brought suit against the Luries individually, and as partners in the Lurie Construction Co. Also joined as defendants were Jay Chapman and the various interests with which he was connected. As this appeal is brought solely on behalf of the defendants Luries, it is unnecessary to discuss the rather complicated structure of the Chapman interests.

At the close of the presentation of all the evidence, the trial court directed a verdict in favor of plaintiff and against the Luries individually, and as partners in the Lurie Construction Company. It is from the judgment entered on this verdict that the Luries appeal.

The Luries admit that the debt is owing to plaintiff, and that their corporation—Allied Yuma Farms, Inc.—would be liable for it. The Luries' sole contention is that they are not liable personally—or as partners. The theory on which plaintiff seeks to hold the Luries personally liable is that the contract for plaintiff's fertilizer was ultra vires as to Allied Yuma Farms, Inc., and the directors of the corporation—the Luries—should be held personally liable for their ultra vires acts.

The proposition that the contract was ultra vires is based on the corporation's actions in entering into a joint venture and into farming operations generally, where neither act was within the powers granted by the articles of incorporation.

Although it has not been decided in this jurisdiction, the general rule is, in the absence of statute or charter provision, that a corporation is without legal authority to enter into a partnership. A joint venture differs from a partnership principally in that while a partnership is usually formed for the transaction of a general business of a particular kind, a joint venture is usually, but not necessarily, limited to a single transaction, although the business of conducting it may continue for a number of years.

Plaintiff cites the case of Brand v. Fernandez (Tex.Civ.App.) 91 S.W. 2d 932, as authority for its contention that joint ventures should be treated as partnerships insofar as the validity of corporate involvement is concerned. The Brand case found a joint-venture agreement resulting in the surrender of control of a substantial part of the corporation's assets to be invalid, reasoning that the agreement deprived the corporate officers of their elected authority. In that case, however, the corporation was a bank, and its affairs were more closely connected with the public interest than in the instant case.

The legal effect of corporate embarkation on a joint venture should be distinguished from entry into a partnership. Although the corporation may subject itself to debts other than those contracted by its directors and officers, the directors divest themselves of their sole controlling authority only as to one transaction in a joint venture, and not of the entire corporate business as in a partnership. The prevailing view is to hold corporate joint ventures valid, either directly—or by implication.

As applied to corporate entry into partnerships and joint ventures, the doctrine of ultra vires is designed to protect the shareholders' interest. In the instant case, the shareholders were all directors, and were cognizant of the joint venture. The entire assets of the corporation were not committed to the venture, but only a portion thereof, and the co-adventurer had no control over those assets left out of the venture other than the power to subject them to the venture's debts. The claim of ultra vires is not being brought on behalf of the shareholders or any one with a genuine interest in the retention of director control, but by a creditor who placed no reliance on the corporate structure. The doctrine of ultra vires, and its resultant legal effect, should not be applied on this ground.

The other theory on which plaintiff seeks to invoke the doctrine is that the articles of incorporation of Allied Yuma Farms, Inc., do not expressly authorize the business of farming. The articles of incorporation provide for construction and management of hotels, dwellings, etc., the acquisition and sale or lease of personal and real property, and to further engage in any and all general business or activities as are permitted corporations under the laws of the State of Washington. That these articles may be more broadly interpreted under the Washington law is of no import, as Art. 14, § 5, of the constitution of Arizona, A.R.S., provides that foreign corporations may stand in no better position than Arizona corporations when doing business in Arizona.[1]

The law of Arizona relating to scope of corporate business is set out in Article 14, Sec. 4 of the constitution of Arizona, which provides:

> "No corporation shall engage in any business other than that expressly authorized in its charter or by the law under which it may have been or may hereafter be organized."

This provision is implemented by A.R.S. § 10–171, which states:

> "No corporation shall engage in any business other than that expressly authorized in its articles of incorporation or by the law under which it is organized."

These limitations were thoroughly considered by this court in Trico Electric Cooperative v. Ralston, 67 Ariz. 358, 196 P.2d 470, wherein it was held that a corporation could not lawfully contract outside the object of its creation as defined in the law of its organization. In that case, we laid down the following fundamental rules of law:

> "A corporation has only such powers as are expressly or impliedly conferred by its charter. Unlike a natural person, if [sic] may not do all things not expressly or impliedly prohibited, but must draw from its charter the power to act in any given respect, and can do only that which is expressly or impliedly authorized therein. A corporate charter is the index to the objects for which it was created and to the powers with which it has been endowed. The enu-

1. Constitution of Arizona, Art. 14, § 5: "No corporation organized outside of the limits of this State shall be allowed to transact business within this State on more favorable conditions than are prescribed by law for similar corporations organized under the laws of this State; * * *"

meration of certain powers operates as a limitation on such objects only as are embodied therein, and is an implied prohibition of the exercise of other and distinct powers, except such incidental powers as are reasonably necessary to accomplish the purposes for which it was organized. The charter of a corporation organized under general legislation consists of the provisions of the state constitution, the particular statute under which it is organized, and all other general laws which are made applicable to the corporation formed thereunder and its articles of incorporation. With respect to matters to which statutes do not apply, the articles of incorporation of the corporation control and are its fundamental and organic law. * * *

Although the Luries argue that farming may be necessarily incident to the charter power to acquire and sell real property, they do not contend that this property was held for resale or that it was acquired for a valid charter purpose. In the absence of any evidence showing farming to be an incidental business reasonably necessary under the charter powers, we find the farming transaction and the contract for fertilizer which arose from it to be ultra vires.

The contract being ultra vires, it is plaintiff's contention, and presumably the theory on which the trial court granted the directed verdict, that the Luries should be personally liable as directors. The proposition that the directors will be held personally liable for acts done in behalf of the corporation which were outside of its charter powers finds support in the case of Mandeville v. Courtright, 3 Cir., 142 F. 97. In that case, the corporation was incorporated in New Jersey, and practiced dentistry in Pennsylvania under the corporate name. The corporation was forbidden by Pennsylvania law to so practice. The plaintiff was a dental patient who was injured by improper treatment. The Circuit Court of Appeals, 3d Circuit, held the directors and managing officers liable for the tortious acts of their agents, reasoning that the directors could not act under the guise of their corporate entity when that corporation could not conduct such a business and they knew it.

In the instant case, Allied Yuma Farms, Inc., was not permitted to carry on farming operations nor to enter into the fertilizer contract under the law of Arizona as implemented by the corporate charter. There were only four stockholders, all of whom were directors in the corporation and knew the nature of the business in which the corporation was engaged. The corporation was undercapitalized, and funds were diverted to it from other Lurie corporations and the Lurie partnership, as needed. The corporation had no separate offices, no stationery, and little other outward indicia of corporate existence. These facts tend to point up to the conclusion that the corporation was merely a means of avoiding personal liability while using the financial standing and good will of the Luries as individuals in their dealings with others.

Plaintiff did not know the Luries intended to engage in the joint venture solely through their corporation, and was led to believe by Chapman that they were acting as individuals. It was never made clear to their co-adventurers that the Luries intended to act only as a corporation, as the venture agreement was not reduced to writing, and it was only after the venture had failed and the liabilities accrued that the corporate entity was brought out.

The question then is whether this ultra vires act is binding on the Luries personally. The result is, in effect, a piercing of the corporate veil.

In Whipple v. Industrial Commission, 59 Ariz. 1, 121 P.2d 876, Whipple and Brady, as partners, or individually, sought by the use of a corporation to evade any liability on their part under the compensation act. In holding them individually liable, we said:

"A corporation is merely a legal fiction created for the convenience of conducting business, the true human entity behind it being the stockholders who, in reality, own it and all its property, though the legal title may stand in the name of the corporation. It is now well settled as a general rule that when this fiction of the law is urged and carried on for an intent not within the reason and purpose for which it is allowed by the law, the form should be disregarded and the corporation should be considered merely as an individual or an aggregation of persons both in equity and in law.

The leading case of Wenban Estate, Inc. v. Hewlett, 193 Cal. 675, 227 P. 723, states the rule as follows:

"While it is the general rule that a corporation is an entity separate and distinct from its stockholders, with separate, distinct liabilities and obligations, nevertheless there is a well-recognized and firmly settled exception to this general rule, that, when necessary to redress fraud, protect the rights of third persons, or prevent a palpable injustice, the law and equity will intervene and cast aside the legal fiction of independent corporate existence, as distinguished from those who hold and own the corporate capital stock, and deal with the corporation and stockholders as identical entities with identical duties and obligations."

The facts in the instant case are similar in many respects to the facts in Whipple v. Industrial Commission, supra. In the instant case, Alan Lurie stated in his deposition:

"There might have been a tax reason but basically I would say that is the reason, so that if the crops lost the money the corporation would be stuck with the bill and we wouldn't have to pick it up personally.

*   *   *

"We didn't want to be personally responsible for anything."

The Luries, in this ultra vires act, were attempting to use the corporation to make money as individuals without incurring individual liability, as stated above. In the Whipple v. Industrial Commission case, Whipple and Brady were attempting to make money in the sawmill business without the liability imposed by statute under the compensation act. As set forth herein, the acts of the Luries were ultra vires in that they were not within the reason and purpose for which the corporation was ostensibly formed and were clearly for the purpose of their own personal benefit. In the light of the Luries' total disregard of the corporate entity, both in their actions and representations in conducting this venture, and in disregard of the charter which they now attempt to stand behind, the law and equity must intervene to protect the rights of third persons as the corporate fiction has been urged to an extent not within its reason and purpose.

These considerations, taken in conjunction with the premise that the Luries were bound by law to know the invalidity of their ultra vires transactions, prohibited by the law of the corporation which they now attempt to stand behind, are sufficient to warrant the personal liability imposed by the trial court.

Judgment affirmed.

CASE 3—*Could the minority shareholder compel payment of dividends?*

DOHERTY v. MUTUAL WAREHOUSE

United States Court of Appeals, Fifth Circuit, 1958.
255 F.2d 489.

RIVES, Circuit Judge.

This action is by a minority shareholder against a corporation to compel declaration and payment of dividends. * * *

* * *

In Alabama, the law is well settled that a court of equity will not interfere with the internal business management of corporate affairs by the board of directors so long as they keep within the scope of the charter powers, and are not guilty of fraud, maladministration, or abuse of discretion.

The district court made the following among other findings of fact:

"3. The original capital of the corporation was $15,000.00, and as of the end of the year 1955 the surplus of the corporation was $188,738.38.

"4. Prior to the year 1955, the management of the corporation had determined that for sound business reasons the corporation should accumulate a surplus of $200,000.00. At the end of the year 1956 the surplus of the corporation, for the first time exceeded $200,000.00; the surplus being $206,314.30. Early in 1957 the directors of the corporation declared a dividend of $6,000.00 to stockholders of record—being a $40.00 dividend for each share of outstanding stock.

"5. The decision not to declare a dividend for the year 1955 and to use the profits of the corporation in the business was not an abuse of discretion, and such refusal to declare a dividend was not arbitrary, nor was there any bad faith, or fraud or maladministration destructive or injurious to the corporation. The decision not to declare a dividend for 1955 and to accumulate surplus was consistent with the character and needs of the business. At all times here material the directors, officers and management of the corporation have acted fairly and in the utmost good faith in the handling of the business, management and corporate affairs of the corporation in the interest of the corporation."

This Court should not set aside those findings of fact unless it determines that they are clearly erroneous. After carefully reading and studying the record in the light of the briefs and oral argument, we find ourselves in entire agreement with the district court. No good purpose would be served by a more detailed discussion of the evidence. The judgment was right, and it is

Affirmed.

PROBLEMS

1. Answer the following "True" or "False" and give reasons for your answers:

   (a) Corporation law is uniform in all the states.

   (b) It is usually a good idea for a corporation to issue only a part of its authorized stock.

   (c) The book value of stock is always the same as its market value.

   (d) Most corporation statutes expressly provide that "ultra vires" can not be raised as a defense to an existing contract.

   (e) The shareholders can remove a director—or even the entire board— at any time by majority vote.

   (f) Shareholders have a legal right to dividends.

   (g) Dividend may be declared and paid out of current profits, earned surplus (including restricted surplus), and stated capital.

   (h) A stock split has no effect on the corporate capital or surplus accounts.

   (i) A corporation has inherent power to redeem shares.

   (j) In all states, shareholders have a right to vote by proxy.

   (k) A corporate stock certificate is fully negotiable.

   (l) A restraint on transfer of stock is enforceable against a transferee of the stock only if the restraint appears on the face of the stock certificate.

   (m) Any person who fails to disclose inside information about a security in connection with the purchase or sale of the security is liable in damages under the federal securities laws.

   (n) Double taxation is one disadvantage of the corporation method of doing business.

   (o) Any corporation, whatever its size, can elect to be taxed under Subchapter S of the IRS.

2. (a) What five advantages does the corporate method of doing business offer? Explain.

   (b) *Define:* quo warranto action; de jure corporation; de facto corporation; less than de facto corporation; straight voting; weighted voting; cumulative voting; merger; consolidation.

   (c) Discuss the relative roles of corporate directors, officers, and shareholders with regard to the corporate form of business organization.

   (d) A stock certificate representing 25 shares in Coleman, Inc. is issued in the name of Carol Judd. Carol specially indorses the certificate to Mike Robel and delivers it to Mike. Francine Warren steals the certificate from Mike, forges his indorsement, then transfers the certificate to Barbara Franklin who takes the certificate for value, in good faith, and without knowledge that it is stolen. Barbara presents the certificate to Coleman, Inc. for registration of transfer. The Corporation cancels the old certificate and issues Barbara a new one. As between Mike Robel and Barbara Franklin, who will prevail as to the 25 shares? What are

Coleman, Inc.'s rights, if any, against Barbara Franklin? Against Francine Warren? What are Mike Robel's rights, if any, against Coleman, Inc.? Explain fully.

(e) Creditors of the insolvent Maxwell, Inc. have discovered that, in November of 1979, Maxwell issued Alice Rockney 200 shares of $100 par value Maxwell common stock in exchange for real property having a fair market value of $11,000. Assuming that some of the creditors extended credit to Maxwell prior to November of 1979, and some after, what are the creditors' rights, if any, against Alice Rockney? (Answer without regard to federal securities laws.)

3. Delray Corporation has a provision in its corporate charter as follows: "Holders of the noncumulative preferred stock shall be entitled to a fixed annual dividend of 8% before any dividend shall be paid on common stock." There are *no* further provisions relating to preferences or statements regarding voting rights. The preferred stock apparently

(a) Is noncumulative, but only to the extent that the 8% dividend is *not* earned in a given year.

(b) Is nonvoting unless dividends are in arrears.

(c) Has a preference on the distribution of the assets of the corporation upon dissolution.

(d) Is *not* entitled to participate with common stock in dividend distributions beyond 8%.

[# 33, November 1974 CPA Exam]

4. Smith, a promoter, entered into a contract with Ace Equipment, Inc., for the purchase of equipment of $23,500. Smith contracted for the equipment on behalf of a yet-to-be-formed corporation, Eastern Machinery Co. No mention of Smith's intent or the planned incorporation appeared in the contract. The incorporation has been completed. Smith is

a. *Not* liable for the $23,500 because of his role as agent for the corporation.

b. Jointly liable with the corporation for the $23,500.

c. Primarily liable for the $23,500.

d. Relieved of liability on the contract when it is ratified by Eastern.

[# 19, November 1973 CPA Exam]

5. Seymore was recently invited to become a director of Buckley Industries, Inc. If Seymore accepts and becomes a director, he along with the other directors will not be personally liable for

a. Lack of reasonable care.

b. Honest errors of judgment.

c. Declaration of a dividend which the directors know will impair legal capital.

d. Diversion of corporate opportunities to themselves.

[# 20, November 1973 CPA Exam]

6. The separate corporate entity will be disregarded if

a. One man owns all the shares of stock.

   b. It was used to effect a fraud.

   c. There is a parent-subsidiary relationship between two corporations.

   d. It is used for the purpose of obtaining limited liability.

[# 21, November 1973 CPA Exam]

7. Randolph Corporation would like to pay cash dividends on its common shares outstanding. Under corporate law, Randolph may *not* pay these dividends if it is insolvent or would be rendered so by the payment. For this purpose, an insolvent corporation is one which

   a. Is unable to pay its debts as they become due in the usual course of its business.

   b. Has an excess of liabilities over assets.

   c. Has an excess of current liabilities over current assets.

   d. Has a deficit in earned surplus.

[# 15, May 1977 CPA Exam]

8. Coe Corporation is authorized to issue 15,000 shares of $100 par value common stock of which 10,000 shares are issued and, of these, 500 shares are held as treasury stock. The treasury stock was appropriately acquired under applicable state law. The treasury stock held by Coe

   a. Is treated as issued and outstanding stock.

   b. May be resold without regard to preemptive rights.

   c. May be voted by management.

   d. Normally entitles a purchaser at a later date to an amount equal to all dividends per share paid while the shares were held by the corporation as treasury stock.

[# 49, May 1974 CPA Exam]

9. While examining the financial statements of Fesmore Industries, Inc., for the fiscal year ended October 31, 1974, Dey & Co., CPAs, discovered that J. Parker Dilmore, executive vice president of Fesmore, was actively involved in trading Fesmore's common stock. While Dilmore has always owned at least 100,000 shares of Fesmore's common stock, he executed the following specific transactions during the year under examination.

Transaction	Number of Shares	Date	Price per Share
Purchased	15,000	March 1, 1974	$24
Sold	15,000	June 5, 1974	40
Purchased	5,000	June 7, 1974	35
Sold	5,000	September 3, 1974	30
Purchased	5,000	October 2, 1974	25

The stock sold on June 5 and September 3, 1974, was the same stock purchased on March 1 and June 7, 1975, respectively.

Required: Discuss the legal implications of the facts discovered by Dey & Co.

[# 5.b., November 1974 CPA Exam]

10. **Part a.** Grace Dawson was actively engaged in the promotion of a new corporation to be known as Multifashion Frocks, Inc. On January 3, 1978, she obtained written commitments for the purchase of shares totaling $600,000 from a group of 15 potential investors. She was also assured orally that she would be engaged as the president of the corporation upon the commencement of business. Helen Banks was the principal investor, having subscribed to $300,000 of the shares of Multifashion. Dawson immediately began work on the incorporation of Multifashion, made several contracts for and on its behalf, and made cash expenditures of $1,000 in accomplishing these goals. On February 15, 1978, Banks died and her estate has declined to honor the commitment to purchase the Multifashion shares. At the first shareholders' meeting on April 5, 1978, the day the corporation came into existence, the shareholders elected a board of directors. With shareholder approval, the board took the following actions:

1. Adopted some but not all of the contracts made by Dawson.

2. Authorized legal action, if necessary, against the Estate of Banks to enforce Banks' $300,000 commitment.

3. Declined to engage Dawson in any capacity (Banks had been her main supporter).

4. Agreed to pay Dawson $750 for those cash outlays which were deemed to be directly beneficial to the corporation and rejected the balance.

Required: Answer the following, setting forth reasons for any conclusions stated.

Discuss the legal implications of each of the above actions taken by the board of directors of Multifashion.

Part b. Duval is the chairman of the board and president of Monolith Industries, Inc. He is also the largest individual shareholder, owning 40 percent of the shares outstanding. The corporation is publicly held, and there is a dissenting minority. In addition to his position with Monolith, Duval owns 85 percent of Variance Enterprises, a corporation created under the laws of the Bahamas. During 1977 Carlton, the president of Apex Industries, Inc., approached Duval and suggested that a tax-free merger of Monolith and Apex made good sense to him and that he was prepared to recommend such a course of action to the Apex board and to the shareholders. Duval studied the proposal and decided that Apex was a most desirable candidate for acquisition. Duval informed the president of Variance about the overture, told him it was a real bargain, and suggested that Variance pick it up for cash and notes. Not hearing from Duval or Monolith, Carlton accepted an offer from Variance and the business was sold to Variance. Several dissenting shareholders of Monolith learned the facts surrounding the Variance acquisition and have engaged counsel to represent them. The Variance acquisition of Apex proved to be highly profitable.

Required: Answer the following, setting forth reasons for any conclusions stated.

Discuss the rights of the dissenting Monolith shareholders and the probable outcome of a legal action by them.

[# 4.a. & b., May 1978 CPA Exam]

Chapter 24

LAWS REGULATING THE SALE OF SECURITIES AND THE SALE OF LAND: FEDERAL SECURITIES STATUTES, STATE "BLUE SKY" LAWS, AND THE FEDERAL INTERSTATE LAND SALES FULL DISCLOSURE ACT

What are "securities"?

The federal Securities Act of 1933, Section 2(1), defines the term "security" in these words.

The Act provides:

[A "security" is] any note, stock, treasury stock, bond, debenture, evidence of indebtedness, certificate of interest or participation in any profit-sharing agreement, collateral-trust certificate, preorganization certificate or subscription, transferable share, investment contract, voting-trust certificate, certificate of deposit for a security, fractional undivided interest in oil, gas, or other mineral rights, or in general, any interest or instrument commonly known as a "security", or any certificate of interest or participation in, temporary or interim certificate for, receipt for, guarantee of, or warrant or right to subscribe to or purchase, any of the foregoing.

The Securities Act definition has been given a very expansive interpretation by the courts. Before getting down to specifics, realize that securities are *intangibles*. You will recall the following definition of an "intangible" from Ch. 3.

It says:

Personal property rights may be further classified into "tangibles", called choses in possession and "intangibles",
called choses in action * * *. An intangible * * * has no material substance. It is called a chose in "action" because, in the event of a dispute, it is necessary to bring a legal action in court to effectuate the right— since the chose in action has no material substance, it would be impossible to enforce the right in any other way (e. g., by taking possession of the property). Intangible personal property rights include patents, copyrights, common stock rights, bonds, accounts receivable, business goodwill, and any other transferable contract right.

Perhaps the most common form of security is the share of stock that a person owns in a corporation. A share is an intangible that is evidenced by a stock certificate (the certificate itself has no material or intrinsic value as it merely represents rights in something else).

The term "security" not only covers "equity" (ownership) interests, but also "debt" interests—money loans made in the form of promissory notes (see Ch. 13), bonds, debentures, etc. A *bond* is simply a borrower's written promise given in return for money (or its equivalent) to pay a fixed sum of money (the face value of the bond or bond "principal") at a specified future time (the "maturity" date), with stated interest payable at fixed intervals. Corporations and governmental bodies issue bonds to raise revenue.[1] Corporate bonds are frequently "convertible"—i. e., they may be exchanged for a stated number of common shares at certain times and under certain circumstances. *Debentures* are bonds that are not secured by specific assets.

But the term "security" is not restricted to shares, notes, bonds, and debentures. It covers any offering that constitutes an "investment" regardless of its form, and regardless of whether it is oral or written. In 1946, the U.S. Supreme Court stated in Securities and Exchange Comm. v. W. J. Howey Co., 328 U.S. 293, 66 S.Ct. 1100, 90 L.Ed. 1244, that the basic test of whether something is a security is whether "the person *invests* his money in a common enterprise and is led to expect profits solely from the efforts of the promoter or a third party." (Emphasis added.) The Court in the case held the sale of individual rows of orange trees, along with a service contract under which the seller was to cultivate, harvest, and market the orange crop, to be a security within the meaning of the 1933 federal Securities Act.

Under the so-called *Howey* test, assignments of fractional interests in oil and gas royalties, percentages of patent rights, investments in real estate condominiums and warehouse receipts—all have been held to fall within the meaning of "securities". Whenever an investor turns his or her funds over to another for the purpose of obtaining profits based on the efforts of others, the investment is a security.

For many years, the *Howey* test prevented a conclusion that an investment in which the investor takes an active part (as opposed to expecting profits solely from the efforts of others) constitutes a security. More recently, however, the courts have held an investment to be a security though the investor was personally required to make some effort to solicit others to participate in the investment. Such holdings allow the regulation of "pyramid" sale schemes in which an investor-buyer is obligated to persuade others to buy before he or she can receive any return on his or her investment (e. g., the typical "chain letter" scheme). And some states have concluded that an investment is a security even where the investor takes an active role in the enterprise as long as the funds he or she contributes are part of the "risk capital" for the initial development of the enterprise.

Why is it necessary to regulate securities?

Because securities are intangibles, they are peculiarly susceptible to abuse and may be used to defraud naive and unsophisticated investors. The value of a share of corporate common stock, for example, depends on the value of the corporation. The value of a note depends on the ability of the maker to pay the note. If inaccurate or incomplete information regarding the securities is provided to the investing public, investors can be easily misled or defrauded.

To prevent this, the securities laws require full disclosure of all material facts surrounding the initial issuance ("primary offering") of securities and their subsequent resale in "secondary offerings" (many shares of publicly held cor-

1. Unlike shares, which are generally issued in "registered form" (see Ch. 23), bonds are frequently issued by corporations and governmental bodies in "bearer form" (UCC Section 8–102 provides that "a security is in 'bearer form' when it runs to bearer according to its terms and not by reason of indorsement"—in other words, when it is originally issued to bearer). UCC Section 8–310 states that the concept of indorsement applies only to securities issued in registered form: thus, the "special indorsement" of a bearer form bond does not convert the bond into "order paper"—the bond remains a bearer instrument throughout its lifetime. The original owner and each subsequent owner of the bond "registers" his or her ownership interest with the bond issuer.

porations are traded thousands of times in the stock market[2]). The latter is accomplished by requiring a continuous flow of information about the issuer of the securities. Anti-fraud provisions in the laws provide a civil action remedy for investors who are defrauded in the purchase or sale of securities.

The securities laws also extensively regulate the individuals and firms that are in the business of buying and selling securities for customers. Regulation is needed here because billions of dollars of securities are bought and sold every year, making the potential for fraud and abuse overwhelming.

In this chapter, we will first examine some of the reasons why a closely held corporation might want to offer its shares to the public. Next, we will study the federal securities laws—the federal Securities Act of 1933 and the federal Securities Exchange Act of 1934—and then look at the state ("Blue Sky") securities legislation. Finally, we will turn our attention to the federal Interstate Land Sales Full Disclosure Act—an Act patterned largely after the federal Securities Act of 1933.

Why would a closely held corporation decide to sell its shares to the public?

A closely held corporation might decide to sell its shares to the public for any or all of the following reasons:

(1) The corporation needs additional money in order to expand or diversify. Returning to our example from the previous chapter, suppose that Ray Chamberlain Sports, Inc. has become a very successful business with a net value of more than a million dollars. Ray Chamberlain and Lola Forthright, the owners and "managers" of the corporation, believe

that the corporation could be even more successful if it could open additional stores in other locations. By offering part of their stock to the public, Ray and Lola can raise enough money to expand the business.

(2) The shareholders of the corporation want to convert a portion of their stock to money so as to be able to invest in other companies (they don't want all of their investment income dependent on the earnings of a single enterprise). Establishing a public market for their shares allows the shareholders to sell and liquidate their holdings at most any time. Again, with regard to Ray Chamberlain Sports, Inc., Ray and Lola may want to liquidate some of their (million dollar) holdings in the corporation and reinvest so as not to have all their "eggs in one basket".

(3) The shareholders anticipate estate tax problems when one or more of their number pass away. By selling some of their holdings to the public, the shareholders will not only establish a share value for estate tax purposes, but will generate some liquidity (cash) with which to pay the taxes (see Ch. 30 for a discussion of probate problems, including wills and estate taxes).

(4) Having publicly owned shares establishes a share value for purposes of merger or consolidation and makes a corporation more attractive for such purposes (many closely held corporations will merge only with publicly owned corporations so as to be sure of receiving readily marketable shares).

(5) Having publicly owned shares makes it easier for a corporation to attract and hold key management people. One way that a corporation tries to attract and keep key management is by giving key executives and employees stock options.

2. A "publicly held" corporation is one whose shares have been offered and sold to the public; a "closely held" corporation is one whose stock has not been offered

and sold to the public, but is held by a relatively small group of private shareholders.

A stock option is simply a right to purchase so many shares of stock at a certain price. An executive or employee can exercise a stock option after the stock has gone up in value and thus share in the results of his or her successful management efforts. Stock options are particularly attractive to business executives when the stock has a public market and the executives can see its value going up on a daily basis.

(6) Finally, a corporation with publicly owned securities generally has an easier time borrowing funds at low interest rates. Financial institutions prefer to make loans to such corporations because the public market for the corporation's shares provides the corporation with an additional source of equity capital, reducing the risk that the corporation will be unable to meet its loan commitments.

So you see, there are many reasons why a closely held corporation might want to sell its shares to the public. However, to make a "public offering", a corporation must strictly comply with all applicable state and federal securities laws.

What federal law controls "public offerings" of securities?

The federal Securities Act of 1933 controls "public offerings" of securities (i. e., initial offerings of securities for sale to the public). Often called the "truth in securities" law, it is essentially a "disclosure" statute. Section 5 of the Act states that no security may be offered or sold to the public unless the security is first *registered* with the Securities and Exchange Commission—the "SEC" (however, as will be discussed in a later section, certain securities and securities transactions are exempt from the registration requirements of the Act). The purpose of the registration is to provide full and fair disclosure of all material facts regarding the securities to be offered for sale. While the Securities Act does not give the SEC any power to prohibit public offerings of securities, it does give the Commission power to require the issuer of securities to make full disclosure of all material facts regarding the securities. The Statute states in part:

SECURITIES ACT OF 1933
AN ACT

[PURPOSE] To provide full and fair disclosure of the character of securities sold in interstate and foreign commerce and through the mails, and to prevent frauds in the sale thereof, and for other purposes.

Section 1.   This act may be cited as the Securities Act of 1933.   * * *

Section 5.   (a) Unless a registration statement is in effect as to a security, it shall be unlawful for any person, directly or indirectly—

(1) to make use of any means or instruments of transportation or communication in interstate commerce or of the mails to sell such security through the use or medium of any prospectus or otherwise; or

(2) to carry or cause to be carried through the mails or in interstate commerce, by any means or instruments of transportation, any such security for the purpose of sale or for delivery after sale.

Our study of the Securities Act of 1933 will be broken into the following parts:

(1) The requirements of the registration statement;

(2) The registration process with the Securities and Exchange Commission;

(3) The exemptions under the Securities Act of 1933; and

(4) The civil liability of people who fail to make full disclosure.

(1) *The requirements of the registration statement.* An issuer of securities "registers" the securities by filing a registration statement with the Securities and Exchange Commission. The statement consists of two parts: first, a *prospectus* or pamphlet summarizing the key information contained in the registration statement (a copy of the prospectus must be furnished to every purchaser of the securities); and, second, *Part II* of the statement which must set forth extensive information about the securities and the issuer of the securities (Part II remains on file with the SEC but is available for public inspection).

The Securities Act specifically requires 32 items of information in the registration statement, and it authorizes the Securities and Exchange Commission to require whatever additional information it deems necessary for full disclosure. To facilitate the filing of the registration statement, the SEC has promulgated Form S–1 [3] as the basic form for use in registering a proposed securities offering. Form S–1 runs to more than 50 pages of instructions and usually results in many times that number of pages when the registration statement is complete. Page one of the form looks like this.

SECURITIES AND EXCHANGE COMMISSION

Washington, D.C.   20549

FORM S–1

Registration Statement

Under

The Securities Act of 1933

_____

(Exact name of registrant as specified
in charter)

_____

(Address of principal executive offices)

_____

(Name and address of agent for service)

Approximate date of commencement of proposed sale to the public

_____

* * *

_____

The remainder of Form S–1 is divided into the following main parts:

General Instructions

Part I.   Information required in prospectus (with 21 parts)

Part II.   Other required information (with 9 parts)

Undertakings

Signatures

Instructions as to Financial Statements

Instructions as to Exhibits

Instructions as to Summary Prospectuses

Obviously, we cannot reproduce the entire 50 pages of disclosure requirements. However, we can set forth some of the most important elements.

They include:

General Instructions
* * *

C.   The registration statement shall consist of the facing sheet of the form, the prospectus containing the information specified in Part I, the Information called for by Part II, the undertaking to file reports, the required signatures, consents of experts, financial statements and exhibits and any other prospectus, information, undertakings or documents which are required or which the regis-

_____

3.   In addition to the basic Form S–1, the SEC has prepared a number of specialized registration forms, including Form S–2 (for companies still in what is considered a "development" stage); S–5 (for mutual funds); S–8 (where the offering is to include employees); and S–7 (for companies having a certain record of earnings).

trant may file as a part of the registration statement.

D.　Form and Content of Prospectus.

(a) The purpose of the prospectus is to inform investors. Hence, the information set forth in the prospectus should be presented in clear, concise, understandable fashion. Avoid unnecessary and irrelevant details, repetition or the use of unnecessary technical language. The prospectus shall contain the information called for by all of the items of Part I of the form * * *

G.　Preparation of Part II.

(a) Part II of the registration statement shall contain the numbers and captions of the items in Part II of the form, but the text of the items may be omitted provided the answers are so prepared as to indicate to the reader the coverage of the items without the necessity of referring to the text of the items or the instructions thereto. If the information required by any item of Part II is completely disclosed in the prospectus, reference may be made to the specific page or caption of the prospectus which contains such information.

Part I.　Information Required in Prospectus

Item 1.　Distribution Spread

The information called for by the following table shall be given, in substantially the tabular form indicated, on the outside front cover page of the prospectus as to all securities being registered which are to be offered for cash * * *

	Price to Public	Underwriting discounts and commissions	Proceeds to registrant or other persons
Per Unit _____			
Total _____			

Item 2.　Plan of Distribution

(a) If the securities being registered are to be offered through underwriters, give the names of the principal underwriters, and state the respective amounts underwritten. * * * State briefly the nature of the underwriters' obligation to take the securities.

Instruction

All that is required as to the nature of the underwriters' obligation is whether the underwriters are or will be committed to take and to pay for all of the securities if they are taken, or whether it is merely an agency or "best efforts" arrangement under which the underwriters are required to take and pay for only such securities as they may sell to the public.

———

Here, it should be pointed out that an issuer may or may not use an *underwriter* in making a securities offering to the public. In broad terms, an "underwriter" is a financing specialist (frequently a stock brokerage house) who is paid to offer advice regarding the need for public financing, the best types of securities to offer, the best time to offer them, and the best offering price. Usually, the underwriter determines the manner of distributing the securities and participates in the distribution.[4] The actual distribution is often accomplished through a *syndicate* (i. e., an association of brokerage firms with each member firm offering the securities to its customers).

Underwriting compensation is strictly regulated by the National Association of Securities Dealers and typically runs from 6 to 15% of the aggregate proceeds received from the public. Of course, unless the underwriter sells the whole offering "in-house" (to his or her own customers only and not through a syndicate), the other brokerage firms will share in the underwriting commissions.

By not using an underwriter, an issuer obviously saves the commission expense. However, this is the only expense that he or she saves—accounting, legal, and printing expenses are still incurred. And these expenses are always substantial. Remember, the issuer must furnish a prospectus to every customer—the printing cost of the prospectus alone may run as high as $30,000 to $40,000. The legal and accounting expenses may also run into many thousands of dollars. And there are registration fees with the Securities and Exchange Commission (1/50th of 1% of the securities registered) and miscellaneous expenses for the new certificates, and for postage and envelopes. On top of this, it is much more difficult (particularly for small corporations) to sell securities without the assistance of an underwriter. It always sounds easier to sell securities "to customers and friends" than it actually is. For a corporation that is badly in need of funds, incurring all the costs of a public offering without

being able to sell the stock may well signal the end of the corporation.

Now continuing with the prospectus disclosure requirements from Form S–1.

It further provides:

Item 3.   Use of Proceeds to Registrant

State the principal purposes for which the net proceeds to the registrant from the securities to be offered are intended to be used, and the approximate amount intended to be used for each such purpose.

1. Details of proposed expenditures are not to be given; for example, there need be furnished only a brief outline of any program of construction or addition of equipment * * *

2. Include a statement as to the use of the actual proceeds if they are not sufficient to accomplish the purposes set forth and the order of priority in which they will be applied * * *

3. * * * If any material part of the proceeds is to be used to discharge a loan, * * * state the proceeds are to be used to discharge the indebtedness created by the loan.

4. If any material amount of the proceeds is to be used to acquire assets, otherwise than in the ordinary course of business, briefly describe the assets and give the names of the person from whom they are to be acquired. State the cost of the assets to the registrant and the principle followed in determining such cost.

Item 9.   Description of Business

(a) Describe the business done and intended to be done by the regis-

---

4. The term "underwriter" is defined in its strictest sense in a later section dealing with the "casual sales" exemption to the

registration requirements of the Securities Act of 1933.

trant * * * and the general development of such business during the past five years, or such shorter period as the registrant may have been engaged in business. The description shall include information as to matters such as the following:

1. Competitive conditions in the industry or industries involved and the competitive position of the registrant, if known * * *. If several products or services are involved, separate consideration shall be given to the principal products or services or classes of products or services.

2. If a material part of the business is dependent upon a single customer or a few customers, the loss of any one or more of whom would have a materially adverse effect on the business of the registrant, the name of the customer or customers, their relationship, if any, to the registrant and material facts regarding their importance to the business of the registration.

3. The principal products produced and services rendered by the registrant, the principal markets for, and methods of distribution of, such products and services, including any significant changes in the kinds of products produced or services rendered, or in the markets or methods of distribution, during the past three fiscal years.

5. The sources and availability of raw materials essential to the business.

6. The importance to the business and the duration and effect of all material patents, trade marks, licenses, franchises and concessions held.

7. * * * The estimated dollar amount spent during each of the last two fiscal years on material research activities relating to the development of new products or services or the improvement of existing products or services.

8. The number of persons employed by the registrant.

9. The extent to which the business of the registrant or a material portion thereof is or may be seasonal.

Item 10. Description of Property

State briefly the location and general character of the principal plants, mines and other materially important physical properties of the registrant and its subsidiaries. If any such property is not held in fee or is held subject to any major encumbrance, so state and briefly describe how held.

Item 11. Organization within 5 years

If the registrant was organized within the past 5 years, furnish the following information:

(a) State the names of the promoters, the nature and amount of anything of value (including money, property, contracts, options or rights of any kind) received or to be received by each promoter directly or indirectly from the registrant, and the nature and amounts of any assets, services or other consideration therefore received or to be received by the registrant.

Item 12. Legal Proceedings

Briefly describe any material legal proceedings * * * to which the registrant * * * is a party or of which any of their property is the subject.

* * *

Item 17.   Remuneration of Directors and Officers

(a) Furnish the following information * * * as to all direct remuneration paid by the registrant and its subsidiaries during the registrant's last fiscal year to the following persons for services in all capacities:

(1) Each director, and each of the three highest paid officers * * *

* * *

Item 21.   Financial Statements

Include in the prospectus all financial statements called for by the Instructions as to Financial Statements for this form * * *

* * *

1.   Balance Sheets of the Registrant.

(a) The registrant shall file a balance sheet as of a date within 90 days prior to the date for filing the registration statement.

(b) If the balance sheet * * * is not certified, there shall be filed in addition a certified balance sheet as of a date within one year * * *

2.   Profit and Loss and Source and Application of Funds Statements.

The registrant shall file profit and loss and source and application of funds statements for each of the three fiscal years preceding the date of the latest balance sheet filed and for the period, if any, between the close of the latest of such fiscal years and the date of the latest balance sheet filed. These statements shall be certified up to the date of the latest certified balance sheet filed.

———

The financial statements contained in the registration statement (and provided to the public in the prospectus) must be certified by an independent certified or public accountant. This guarantees an independent evaluation of the validity of the statements. The absence of proper certification constitutes an omission of a material fact and is a violation of the Securities Act of 1933. Furthermore, the Securities and Exchange Commission has taken the position that an accountant is not "independent" for purposes of certifying financial statements included in a registration statement if he or she is (or was during the period under review) a director or officer of the issuer-corporation or if he or she holds a significant ownership interest in the corporation (significant with respect to the total capital of the corporation *or* the accountant's own personal fortune). This is not to say that an accountant may not own any stock in the corporation—however, even a small amount may put him or her in a suspect position.

An accountant must base his or her independent certification on a thorough and detailed analysis of the issuer's financial records. If the accountant's investigation reveals information that casts (or tends to cast) suspicion upon the financial statements, the accountant must reveal this information in his or her certification (this subject is dealt with in more detail in Ch. 28 under "accountant's professional responsibilities").

As you can see, the preparation of a registration statement is a very substantial undertaking. Remember that the objective of the Securities Act is to provide prospective investors with all the information they need to make intelligent, informed decisions about investing in securities. This is a difficult goal to accomplish because the issuer may resist telling all (to do so may guarantee that no one will invest). Also, many investors are financially unsophisticated and do not understand complex financial terminology or financial statements.

(2) *The registration process with the Securities and Exchange Commission.* Once prepared, the registration statement must be filed with the main office of the Securities and Exchange Commission. The Securities and Exchange Commission was created by the Securities Exchange Act of 1934. The Commission is charged with the responsibility of enforcing and administering the federal securities laws, including the 1933 Securities Act. The SEC consists of five members appointed by the president for five-year terms (the term of one commissioner expires each year); no more than three of the commissioners may be members of the same political party. The main office of the SEC is located in Washington, D.C. However, the Commission has nine regional and eight branch offices in financial centers around the United States. The SEC has a large staff of lawyers and nonlawyers who work reviewing registration statements to determine if proper disclosure has been made. The SEC is also engaged in fraud prevention and in regulation of the securities industry (brokers and dealers who make a living buying and selling stocks, bonds, and other securities for the investing public).

Unless the SEC orders to the contrary, a registration statement becomes effective automatically 20 days after it is filed with the Commission. While Section 5(c) of the Securities Act prohibits any offers to sell or to buy securities before the registration statement is filed, the Act permits offers, but not sales, during the 20 day "waiting period" between filing and effectiveness. There are no restrictions on oral offers made during this pe-

riod. However, written offers may be made only through a "preliminary prospectus" containing all the information discussed above with limited exception. You know that the final prospectus must state the offering price of the security to the public and the amount that will go by way of discount or commission to the underwriters or dealers. Usually, at the time the registration statement is filed, the offering price and details of the arrangement with the underwriters or dealers have not been set. The Securities Act therefore allows the issuer to file initially a "preliminary prospectus" omitting the offering price and related information. The preliminary prospectus may be used in making written offers during the 20 day waiting period. Securities Act Rule 433 states that the outside front cover page of the preliminary prospectus must bear, in red ink, and printed in type as large as that generally found in the body of the prospectus, the title "preliminary prospectus", the date of its issuance, and the following legend (inscription):

A REGISTRATION STATEMENT RELATING TO THESE SECURITIES HAS BEEN FILED WITH THE SECURITIES AND EXCHANGE COMMISSION BUT HAS NOT YET BECOME EFFECTIVE. INFORMATION CONTAINED HEREIN IS SUBJECT TO COMPLETION OR AMENDMENT. THESE SECURITIES MAY NOT BE SOLD NOR MAY OFFERS TO BUY BE ACCEPTED PRIOR TO THE TIME THE REGISTRATION STATEMENT BECOMES EFFECTIVE. THIS PROSPECTUS SHALL NOT CONSTITUTE AN OFFER TO SELL OR THE SOLICITATION OF AN OFFER TO BUY NOR SHALL THERE BE ANY SALES OF THESE SECURITIES IN ANY STATE IN WHICH SUCH OFFER, SOLICITATION OR SALE WOULD BE UN-

LAWFUL PRIOR TO REGISTRA-
TION OR QUALIFICATION UN-
DER THE SECURITIES LAWS OF
ANY SUCH STATE.

A preliminary prospectus is often called a
"red herring" prospectus because of the
requirement that the legend be printed in
red ink.

Also during the waiting period, the issuer may advertise that a public offering
is going to be made so that interested parties can obtain a preliminary prospectus
and become informed about the securities. Generally, the advertisements must
state the name and business of the issuer,
the amount of securities being offered,
the approximate date when the offering
will be made, and the price of the securities if known at that time. Because of
the black borders customarily placed
around such advertisements, they are
known as "tombstone ads".

By using a "red herring" prospectus
and one or more "tombstone ads" during
the waiting period, the issuer can put the
public on notice that a public offering is
to be made and thus facilitate the offering once the registration statement becomes effective.

The Securities and Exchange Commission uses the 20 day waiting period to review the registration statement. If it is
readily apparent that the statement fails
to accomplish the basic purpose of the Securities Act—that is, assure the public of
adequate reliable information about the
securities offered for sale—the SEC will
notify the issuer in writing that it will
spend no further time reviewing the
statement and that no detailed comments
about the statement will be forthcoming.
(Generally, this occurs only where the
statement is very poorly prepared or has
glaring gaps in disclosure of required
material.) Such written notice from the
SEC is called a "bed-bug" letter.

**A typical "bed-bug" letter might pro-
vide:**

It is our opinion that under the disclosure standards of the Securities Act
of 1933 the registration statement as
filed is inadequate as a means for conveying to prospective investors a fair
presentation of the material characteristics of the Company and that the
general effect of the prospectus as a
whole could create a misleading impression.

We have noted many deficiencies in
the prospectus which are such as to
make impractical any detailed discussion of the registration statement.
Under the circumstances, we recommend that a request for withdrawal of
the registration statement be submitted
or that it be rewritten to be in full
compliance with the Securities Act of
1933 and understandable to potential
investors.

An issuer who receives a "bed-bug"
letter must either re-write the registration
statement or forego the public offering.

If the statement is not rewritten, the
Securities and Exchange Commission will
issue an order preventing the statement
from becoming effective. Section 8(b)
of the Securities Act authorizes the Commission to issue an order "refusing to
permit   *   *   *   a registration statement to become effective   *   *   *   if
the statement [on its face] is incomplete
or inaccurate in any material respect"
(after 10 days notice and opportunity for
a hearing). And Section 8(d) of the
Act authorizes the Commission to issue a
"stop order" suspending the effectiveness
of any registration statement found to
contain a misrepresentation or omission
of a material fact (after 15 days notice
and opportunity for a hearing).

Where the registration statement complies in most, but not all respects with

the statutory requirements, the SEC will issue detailed comments as to how the statement can be brought into full conformity with the requirements. The Commission may require supplemental information, including letters from the issuer's chief executive officer, accountants, and managing underwriter (where the issue is being handled by underwriters) acknowledging that the parties are aware of their statutory responsibilities under the Securities Act. As to their responsibilities, it makes no difference to what extent the SEC reviews the registration statement—the statutory burden of full disclosure remains on the issuer, the issuer's directors, the underwriter, the accountants, and any other experts named in the registration statement. *The burden never shifts to the Securities and Exchange Commission.* Even after the registration statement has become effective, there must be printed on the outside front cover page of the prospectus, in boldface at least as large as 10-point modern type, the following statement:

THESE SECURITIES HAVE NOT BEEN APPROVED OR DISAPPROVED BY THE SECURITIES AND EXCHANGE COMMISSION NOR HAS THE COMMISSION PASSED UPON THE ACCURACY OR ADEQUACY OF THIS PROSPECTUS. ANY REPRESENTATION TO THE CONTRARY IS A CRIMINAL OFFENSE.

———

Once a registration statement becomes effective, the securities covered by the statement may be sold, but a copy of the final prospectus must be delivered to each purchaser.

Of course, the securities may not immediately sell after the registration statement becomes effective. Occasionally, the securities never sell (this is easy to understand after reading a prospectus or two providing full disclosure about a company in extremely dire straits). Along this line, the Securities Act of 1933 provides that any prospectus that is still in use more than nine months after its effective date must be updated so that the information contained in the prospectus is not more than 16 months old. And even without regard to the "nine month" provision, the seller of securities must take care that the information contained in the prospectus is accurate at all times. The delivery of a prospectus that has become inaccurate with the passage of time is a violation of the Securities Act though the prospectus was completely accurate at the time of its effective date. The issuer or dealer, in this case, will be liable in damages to the purchaser.

An issuer can modify or change a prospectus by filing ten copies of the modified document with the Securities and Exchange Commission prior to use of the document.

It should be pointed out that willful violations of the Securities Act are criminal offenses punishable by fine, imprisonment, or both. The SEC does not itself prosecute criminal cases, but turns the evidence over to the Justice Department for prosecution.

(3) *Exemptions under the Securities Act of 1933.* Certain securities and securities transactions are exempt from the registration requirements of the Securities Act of 1933. They include:

(a) *Securities issued or guaranteed by the government.* The Securities Act of 1933 specifically exempts from its registration requirements any security issued by the United States, or by any state or political subdivision of a state, such as a county or city. This would include, for example, a government bond issue, the proceeds of which are to be used for such things as sewage or parking facilities, airports, docks, or sports facilities, etc.

(b) *Securities issued by banks.* The Securities Act also expressly exempts banks from its registration statement requirements (as you will recall from Ch. 15, banks are regulated by other agencies).

(c) *Short-term commercial paper.* Negotiable promissory notes and drafts (see Ch. 13) that arise out of current business transactions or the proceeds of which are to be used for current operations are exempt so long as they will mature within nine months of their issuance date. Not included within the exemption are notes and drafts the proceeds of which are to be used to construct a plant, purchase equipment, or fund real estate development (this would be longterm capital investment as opposed to current operations).

(d) *Securities issued by nonprofit organizations.* Securities that are issued by religious, educational, or other charitable, nonprofit organizations are exempt. However, to qualify for the exemption, an organization must be totally nonprofit, and no member may receive any part of its net earnings.

(e) *Securities issued by savings and loan associations.* Like banks, savings and loan and building and loan associations are supervised by other state and federal agencies and are exempt from the registration provisions of the Securities Act. The same is true of farmers' co-operative associations.

(f) *Securities issued by common carriers.* Common carriers (see Ch. 16) are regulated by the Interstate Commerce Commission and are exempt from the registration requirements of the Securities Act of 1933.

(g) *Insurance policies.* Insurance policies issued by insurance companies (see Ch. 11) are not considered securities within the meaning of the 1933 Securities Act, and are therefore not subject to the federal registration requirements.

(Of course, stock or other securities issued by insurance companies are subject to the registration requirements.)

(h) *Securities exchanged with existing security holders.* Securities that are exchanged by an issuer with the issuer's existing security holders exclusively are exempt from federal registration requirements so long as no commissions are made or given on the exchange. For example, stock dividends, stock splits, the exchange of one class of stock for another—all fall within the exemption. However, if any part of the new issue goes to someone other than an existing security holder, the entire issue will be disqualified from the exemption.

(i) *Intrastate offerings of securities.* Intrastate offerings of securities are also exempt from the registration requirements of the 1933 Act. An *intrastate offering* is an issue that is offered and sold only to residents within one state by an issuer who resides and does business within the state, or, in the case of a corporation, is incorporated in and doing business in the state. One sale or even one offer to sell to a nonresident will render the entire issue ineligible for the exemption. And once the exemption is lost, it is lost forever and cannot be regained though the nonresident offers or sales are completely discontinued.

If an issue qualifies as intrastate, the fact that the issuer used the mails intrastate in making the offering will not destroy the exemption. Nor will the fact that the issuer delivered securities by mail outside of the state to a resident purchaser who left the state temporarily or permanently destroy the exemption.

But realize that even though no registration is required for an intrastate offering under the *federal* Securities Act of 1933, state "Blue Sky" laws may well require registration before the intrastate offering can be made ("Blue Sky" laws are discussed later in the chapter).

(j) *Transactions by any person other than an issuer, underwriter, or dealer (also called the "casual sales" exemption).* The Securities Act specifically exempts from its registration requirements transactions by any person other than an *issuer, underwriter,* or *dealer.* The exemption is frequently referred to as the "casual sales" exemption because it permits investors to make casual sales of their securities without registration. The exemption is limited to what are termed "routine trading transactions" (as opposed to distributions of securities).

To qualify for the exemption, a person must not be an issuer, underwriter, or dealer. An *issuer* is any person who issues or proposes to issue a security (e. g., this would include corporate promoters). Under Section 11 of the Securities Act (an anti-fraud provision), the term "issuer" includes any person who directly or indirectly controls the issuer (e. g., a dominant shareholder). Section 11 is discussed in a later section.

In strict terms, an *underwriter* is any person who (1) has purchased or participated in the purchase of securities from an issuer with a view to distributing any security; (2) offers or sells securities for an issuer in connection with the distribution of any security; or (3) participates in underwriting the distribution of any security. More briefly, *an underwriter is any person who has purchased securities from an issuer with a view toward, or offers or sells for an issuer in connection with, the distribution of any security.* For purposes of the underwriter definition, the term "issuer" includes any person who directly or indirectly controls or is controlled by the issuer, or any person under direct or common control with the issuer. Excluded from the definition of "underwriter" is any person whose interest is limited to a commission from an underwriter or dealer not in excess of usual or customary distributor's or seller's commissions (in other words, the typical

"broker's transaction" does not render the broker liable as an underwriter—brokers' transactions are defined under (n) below). Anyone who participates in an underwriting is an "underwriter" whether or not he or she is the principal underwriter. For example, corporate directors or officers who participate in the distribution of securities may be deemed underwriters if they receive commissions or payments over and above their regular salaries.

Under the 1933 Act, a *dealer* is any person who is engaged in the business of offering, selling, dealing, or otherwise trading in securities issued by another (see (n) below with regard to dealer and broker transactions).

Generally, the issue that arises under the casual sales exemption is whether the person claiming the exemption is an underwriter. Along this line, it is important to remember that for purposes of the underwriter definition, the term "issuer" includes persons in "control" of the issuer. The term "control" has been broadly construed to mean "direct or indirect" power to determine the management and policies of a person or business, whether through ownership of voting securities or otherwise. Clearly, ownership of more than 51% of the voting stock of a corporation constitutes control. However, far less than 51%—even as little as 10% or less—may establish control where the remainder of the corporate stock is widely held (i. e., distributed among numerous owners). Other facts tending to show control are control of the proxy machinery of a corporation (again, especially where the corporate securities are widely held) and membership in a control group (a group that together exercises control).

Thus, a person is an underwriter if he or she purchases securities from a "control" person with a view toward, or offers or sells for a "control" person in connection with, the distribution of any security. Secondary distributions of securities held by control persons are subject to the registration and prospectus requirements of the 1933 Act because they are considered to have as much potential for fraud and abuse as initial public offerings by issuers. And because "control" persons either directly or indirectly control the issuer's actions, they are generally civilly liable anytime the issuer is liable under the anti-fraud provisions of both the 1933 and 1934 Securities Acts (these are discussed later in the chapter).

However, the Securities Act does not go so far as to state that "control" persons can never make casual sales of their securities without going through the registration process. The SEC permits "control" persons to sell strictly limited quantities of their securities without registration (in no event to exceed 1% of the total class of shares outstanding) if they sell them exclusively through brokers' transactions; do not solicit or arrange for solicitation of orders; and make no payments other than to a broker who executes the order to sell. Also, there must be available to purchasers adequate information about the securities and the issuer of the securities. And the control person must file notice of intent to make the sale with the SEC at the same time as he or she places the order to sell with the broker.

(k) *Small offerings under Regulation A (not over $1,500,000).* If the total amount of offerings made by an issuer during any 12 month period does not exceed $1,500,000,[5] the offering is exempt from the usual registration requirements. However, under SEC Regulation A, the issuer must still file a simplified "registration statement" for the small offering with the SEC. (Thus, there is not a complete exemption for small offerings, but merely a simplified form of registration.)

To take advantage of the Regulation A procedure, an issuer must file a "notification" of intent to do so with the SEC regional office nearest the issuer's principal place of business. The notification must be submitted in quadruplicate on SEC Standard Form 1–A (which calls for much of the information required on a registration statement but in much less detail). The issuer must also file an "offering circular" similar to a prospectus.

The issuer must file the notification and offering circular at least ten working days (excluding Saturdays, Sundays, and holidays) prior to the initial date of the offering (contrast this with the 20 day period that elapses before a registration statement becomes effective). However, the SEC responds to a notification and offering circular in much the same way as it responds to a registration statement; and an issuer will generally await SEC comments and approval before commencing offers and sales of the securities. The issuer must provide a copy of the offering circular to every person to whom a written offer is made or a sale confirmed at least 48 hours before confirmation of the sale.

(1) *Very small offerings under Rule 240 (not over $100,000).* In 1975, the SEC adopted SA Rule 240 which provides that an issuer can sell up to $100,000 of securities to up to 100 beneficial (actual) owners in any 12 month period without going through even the Regulation A requirements. Rule 240 provides a complete exemption for very

5. Acting on authority given by Congress, the SEC increased the small offering ceiling from $500,000 to $1,500,000 in September of 1978. It should also be pointed out that the SEC is just beginning to use a new registration form—the S–18—which will allow companies to offer up to $5 million without going through the full S–1 requirements (while "S–18" is less complicated than an S–1 filing, it is more onerous that a Regulation A filing, with S–18 calling for a more substantial prospectus than the Regulation A offering circular).

small offerings—there are no purchaser residency requirements or rules requiring public access to information about the issuer of the securities. However, no advertising or sales commissions are permitted. And the issuer must file a report of all sales made under Rule 240 during any year in which such sales are made with the nearest SEC regional office.

(m) *Private placement of securities.* The Securities Act of 1933 specifically exempts "transactions by an issuer not involving any public offering." The problem here has been to determine what is a "public" and what is a "private" offering. In 1974, the SEC adopted SA Rule 146 to provide objective standards for making this determination. Under Rule 146, an offering is private (and therefore not subject to federal registration requirements) only if the following conditions are met:

First, no more than 35 people must purchase the securities. However, a person who purchases more than $150,000 of securities in the offering will not be counted for purposes of the 35. From a practical standpoint, this means that an issuer can privately place securities with any number of large institutions such as insurance companies or pension funds (that purchase more than $150,000 of securities) without going through the federal registration process. The law permits this because such purchasers are in a position to insist that the issuer provide them with even more extensive information than is required in a registration statement—the Securities Act disclosure requirements are not for the benefit of financially sophisticated investors, but for the benefit of uninformed investors.

Second, there must be no general advertising of the issue and no general solicitation of purchasers. Where general advertising or solicitation occurs, the placement is public, not private.

Third, the issuer must offer and sell the securities only to people who, in the issuer's honest opinion, are sufficiently experienced to evaluate the risks of the investment and financially able to bear the potential losses.

Fourth, each person who is offered the securities must be furnished with or have access to the kind of information that would be supplied in a registration statement.

Fifth, all the purchasers must buy the securities for investment purposes and not with the view of re-selling them. Generally, the issuer requires the purchasers to sign "investment letters" stating that they are buying for investment only (for this reason, shares issued pursuant to the private placement exemption are commonly referred to as "lettered stock"). And the securities themselves generally bear a legend calling attention to the fact that the purchasers represented that they were purchasing for investment pursuant to the private placement exemption (the legend has the effect of making the securities largely unmarketable).

However, such statements by the purchasers are not conclusive as to their actual intent; and where the issuer knows or should know that the purchasers are acquiring the securities with an eye to re-selling them, the fact that the issuer obtained "investment letters" and imprinted "legends" on the security certificates will not establish a private placement. The SEC has stated that such measures are precautions only and will not, by themselves, serve as the basis for exemption from registration requirements.

If a purchaser in fact acquires the securities with a view to re-selling them, notwithstanding his or her assertions to the contrary, the issuer may be held liable for violating the Securities Act. In determining whether the issuer *should have known* of the purchaser's noninvestment intent, the SEC will look at the relationship between the issuer and the purchaser, and the nature of the purchaser's business (e. g., the past investment and trading practices of the purchaser may be inconsistent with the purchase of a large block of securities for investment).

This is not to say that privately placed securities can never be resold. Under SEC Rule 144, such "restricted securities" may be resold without being deemed part of a public distribution (offering) if certain conditions are met. First, the securities must be owned and fully paid for for a period of at least two years prior to resale. Second, the amount of securities sold during any six month period following the two year "holding period" must not exceed one percent of the class outstanding (if the securities are sold on a stock exchange where the securities are actively traded, the amount must not exceed the lesser of one percent of the class outstanding or the average weekly volume on all such exchanges during the four weeks preceding the sale). Third, the sale may be made only through brokers' transactions. Fourth, there must be available to the public current information about the issuer of the securities. And finally, notice of the sale must be filed with the SEC on a prescribed form concurrently with the sale.

(n) *Dealer and broker transactions.* Under the 1933 Act, dealers or brokers who acquire issued securities during the distribution period may not solicit purchasers for the securities without furnishing the purchasers with a prospectus. The Securities Act does not differentiate between dealers and brokers (as you will learn later, the Securities Exchange Act of 1934 does so). Generally, a dealer or broker is any person who engages in the business of offering, buying, selling, or otherwise dealing or trading in securities issued by another.

To distinguish broker-dealer distribution trading from post-distribution trading, the SEC has established an arbitrary

"40 day" rule: brokers or dealers who solicit sales of securities within 40 days after the effective date of a registration statement covering the securities must comply with the same prospectus requirements as issuers and underwriters of the securities.

However, the Securities Act does not intend to prohibit *unsolicited* dealer or broker transactions at any time, and the Act expressly exempts all brokers' transactions that are executed upon an unsolicited customer's order to buy or sell securities. A "broker's transaction" is defined as any transaction by a broker in which the broker does no more than execute a customer's order to buy or sell securities; the broker receives no more than the usual or customary broker's commission; the broker neither solicits nor arranges for the solicitation of the customer's order; and the broker, after reasonable inquiry, is not aware of circumstances indicating that the customer is an underwriter with respect to the securities or that the transaction is part of a distribution of securities of an issuer.

The broker-dealer exemption is designed to insure that individuals may dispose of their securities freely without registration and to assure an open market for securities at all times. However, the exemption applies only to the dealer's or broker's part in the transaction—the customer must find his or her own exemption from registration or he or she will be liable under the Act (usually, the customer can rely on the "casual sales" exemption).

Any person who claims an exception under (a) through (n) above has the burden of establishing all the facts necessary to support the exemption. If there is the slightest variation from the exemption requirements, the basis for the exemption will be gone, and every offer or sale will violate Section 5 of the Securities Act. A person who violates Section 5 is liable to the purchaser and must refund the full purchase price. (This will obviously work out to the advantage of the purchaser if the investment has declined in value subsequent to the sale.)

And even if all exemption requirements have been fully complied with, the exemption will not be available if the offering is shown to be part of a plan or scheme to evade the registration provisions of the Act.

(4) *The civil liability of people who fail to make full disclosure.* Section 5 of the Securities Act of 1933 makes it unlawful for any person to sell nonexempt securities in interstate commerce unless a registration statement covering the securities has been filed with the SEC and is in effect. Section 11 of the Act puts teeth into the law by providing civil liabilities "on account of any false registration statement" as follows.

The Act provides:

CIVIL LIABILITIES ON ACCOUNT OF FALSE REGISTRATION STATEMENT

Section 11

(a) In case any part of the registration statement, when such part became effective, contained an untrue statement of a material fact or omitted to state a material fact required to be stated therein or necessary to make the statements therein not misleading, any person acquiring such security (unless it is proved that at the time of such acquisition he knew of such untruth or omission) may, either at law or in equity, in any court of competent jurisdiction, sue—

(1) every person who signed the registration statement;

(2) every person who was a director of (or person performing similar functions) or partner in, the issuer at the time of the filing of the part of the registration statement with respect to which his liability is asserted;

(3) every person who, with his consent, is named in the registration statement as being or about to become a director or person performing similar functions, or partner;

(4) every accountant, engineer, or appraiser, or any person whose profession gives authority to a statement made by him, who has with his consent been named as having prepared or certified any part of the registration statement, or as having prepared or certified any report or valuation which is used in connection with the registration statement, with respect to the statement in such registration statement, report, or valuation, which purports to have been prepared or certified by him;

(5) every underwriter with respect to such security.

If such person acquired the security after the issuer has made generally available to its security holders an earning statement covering at least twelve months beginning after the effective date of the registration statement, then the right of recovery under this subsection shall be conditioned on proof that such person acquired the security relying upon such untrue statement in the registration statement or relying upon the registration statement and not knowing of such omission, but such reliance may be established without proof of the reading of the registration statement by such person.

(b) Notwithstanding the provisions of subsection (a) no person other than the issuer, shall be liable as provided therein who shall sustain the burden of proof—

(1) that before the effective date of the part of the registration statement with respect to which his liability is asserted (A) he had resigned from or had taken such

steps as are permitted by law to resign from, or ceased or refused to act in, every office, capacity, or relationship in which he was described in the registration statement as acting or agreeing to act, and

(B) he had advised the Commission and the issuer in writing that he had taken such action and that he would not be responsible for such part of the registration statement; or

(2) that if such part of the registration statement became effective without his knowledge, upon becoming aware of such fact he forthwith acted and advised the Commission, in accordance with (1) and, in addition, gave reasonable public notice that such part of the registration statement had become effective without his knowledge; or

(3) that (A) as regards any part of the registration statement not purporting to be made on the authority of an expert, and not purporting to be a copy of or extract from a report or valuation of an expert, and not purporting to be made on the authority of a public official document or statement, he had, after reasonable investigation, reasonable ground to believe and did believe, at the time such part of the registration statement became effective, that the statements therein were true and that there was no omission to state a material fact required to be stated therein or necessary to make the statements therein not misleading; and

(B) as regards any part of the registration statement purporting to be made upon his authority as an expert or purporting to

be a copy of or extract from a report or valuation of himself as an expert,

(i) he had, after reasonable investigation, reasonable ground to believe and did believe, at the time such part of the registration statement became effective, that the statements therein were true and that there was no omission to state a material fact required to be stated therein or necessary to make the statements therein not misleading, or

(ii) such part of the registration statement did not fairly represent his statement as an expert or was not a fair copy of or extract from his report or valuation as an expert; and

(C) as regards any part of the registration statement purporting to be made on the authority of an expert (other than himself) or purporting to be a copy of or extract from a report or valuation of an expert (other than himself), he had no reasonable ground to believe, and did not believe, at the time such part of the registration statement became effective, that the statements therein were untrue or that there was an omission to state a material fact required to be stated therein or necessary to make the statements therein not misleading, or that such part of the registration statement did not fairly represent the statement of the expert or was not a fair copy of or extract from the report or valuation of the expert; and

(D) as regards any part of the registration statement purporting to be a statement made by an official person or purporting to be a copy of or extract from a public official document, he had no reasonable ground to believe and did not believe, at the time such part of the registration statement became effective, an omission to state a material fact required to be stated therein or necessary to make the statements therein not misleading, or that such part of the registration statement did not fairly represent the statement made by the official person or was not a fair copy of or extract from the public official document.

* * *

(g) In no case shall the amount recoverable under this section exceed the price at which the security was offered to the public.

————

Under Section 11, *any person* who acquires a security issued pursuant to a registration statement (including a prospectus) containing a misrepresentation or omission of a material fact may sue *any or all persons* connected with the preparation or publication of the statement. The term "material" has been interpreted by the courts to mean "a fact which if it had been correctly stated or disclosed would have deterred or tended to deter the average prudent investor from purchasing the securities in question." Escott v. Barchris Constr. Corp., 283 F. Supp. 643 (S.D.N.Y.1968).

The right to sue under Section 11 is thus not limited to the original issuee (purchaser) of the security—any person who subsequently acquires the security from the original issuee or his or her transferee may also sue under the Section.

To recover, the security holder must prove only that some material fact was omitted or misrepresented in the registration statement, resulting in money loss to the security holder. The security holder does not have to prove that he or she relied on the omission or misrepresentation in making the purchase (with the exception of where the security holder purchased the security after the issuer had made generally available to security holders an earnings statement covering at least 12 months beginning after the effective date of the registration statement).

As to who is liable under Section 11, the *issuer* of the securities is strictly liable for any loss resulting from the omission or misrepresentation (i. e., the issuer is liable regardless of how much care he or she exercised in preparing and publishing the statement). Also liable, but not strictly so, are (1) any *underwriter* of the securities, (2) any person who *signed* the registration statement, (3) *officers, directors, or partners* of the issuer at the time the registration statement was filed (including those who agreed to be named and were named on the registration statement as prospective directors or partners), and (4) any *professional* such as an accountant, engineer, appraiser, or the like who is named in the registration statement as having certified the portion of the statement containing the omission or misrepresentation.

The people listed in (1) through (4) above are not strictly liable under Section 11, but are liable only if they failed to exercise "due diligence" with respect to the information contained in the registration statement. Section 11(c) of the Securities Act states:

In determining * * * what constitutes reasonable investigation and reasonable ground for belief [that all statements in the registration statement were complete and accurate—in other words, "due diligence"], the standard or reasonableness shall be that required of a prudent man in the management of his own property.

———

As to the portions of the registration statement made on the authority of an expert, "due diligence" is established as long as the defendant had no reasonable ground to disbelieve the expert's statements. As to all other portions, the burden is on the defendant to show that he or she personally investigated the accuracy of the statement—he or she cannot escape liability on the basis that he or she accepted the management's representations at face value.

The type and extent of investigation required of a particular defendant depends on his or her degree of expertise as well as his or her relationship to the issuer. Obviously, a director who is actively engaged in management of the business will have more responsibility than a director who has little to do with management. As for an accountant, he or she is expected to use the generally accepted principles of the accounting profession in making his or her expert judgment.

Note that a defendant has a good defense to liability under Section 11 if he or she can show that the purchaser had knowledge of the misstatement or omission at the time of making the purchase. The defendant also has a good defense to the extent that he or she can show that the security declined in value for reasons apart from the misstatement or omission (e. g., where the entire industry is depressed, and all stocks have declined in value).

As for a "control" person who is sued under Section 11, he or she has a good defense to liability if he or she can show that he or she had no knowledge of or reason to believe in the existence of the facts resulting in the controlled person's liability.

Section 12 of the Securities Act of 1933 provides additional protection for the original issuee (purchaser) of the securities. The Section reads in part:

Any person who—

(1) offers or sells a security in violation of Section 5, or

(2) offers or sells a security (whether or not exempted * * *) * * * by means of a prospectus or oral communication, which includes an untrue statement of a material fact or omits to state a material fact * * * and who shall not sustain the burden of proof that he did not know, and in the exercise of reasonable care could not have known, of such untruth or omission,

shall be liable to the person purchasing such security from him, who may sue * * * to recover the consideration paid for such security with interest thereon, less the amount of any income received thereon * * *

———

Thus, under Section 12, the original purchaser can sue his or her immediate seller (the issuer, underwriter, or dealer) for any loss resulting from any misrepresentation or omission of a material fact in any communication, oral or written, made in connection with the offer or sale of the securities. (Compare with Section 11 where *any holder* of the securities may sue *any person* connected with the preparation or publication of a registration statement containing a material misrepresentation or omission.) Unlike Section 11, Section 12 applies even to securities that are exempt from the registration requirements of the 1933 Act (with the exception of securities issued by certain governmental bodies).

Again, to recover under Section 12, the purchaser must prove only that his or her immediate seller made an oral or written misrepresentation or omission of a material fact in connection with the offer or sale, the misrepresentation or omission resulting in money loss to the purchaser. The purchaser does not have to prove that he or she relied on the misstatement or omission in making the purchase. However, the seller has a complete defense to an action under Section 12 if he or she can show that he or she exercised "due diligence" with regard to the information contained in the communication. The seller will be liable only if he or she knew or should have known (using reasonable care) that the statement was false or that material information was omitted. And, of course, the purchaser cannot recover if he or she had knowledge of the misstatement or omission at the time of the purchase.

Are there any rules governing dealings in securities after their initial issue?

As we have seen, the Securities Act of 1933 controls *initial* issues of securities: the Act requires full disclosure through use of a registration statement, including a prospectus. The Securities Exchange Act of 1934, on the other hand, governs dealing in securities *subsequent* to their initial issue. The 1934 Act has the following purposes:

(1) To regulate the securities exchanges and the securities market;

(2) To make information about issuers of securities available to buyers and sellers of securities;

(3) to prevent fraud in securities trading and halt manipulation of markets; and

(4) To protect the national credit by controlling the amount of credit allowable in the securities market.

The continuing regulation of publicly held securities under the Securities Exchange Act of 1934 may be summarized as follows:

Continuing disclosure requirements. The Securities Act of 1934 requires all companies having at least 500 or more shareholders of "equity" securities and total assets [6] of at least $1,000,000 to register their securities with the Securities and Exchange Commission and file quarterly reports with the Commission providing a complete up-to-date statement of all business operations and matters affecting the value of the securities (the quarterly reports must be filed on Form 10–Q for each of the first three quarters of the fiscal year, and on Form 10–K for the final quarter making up the annual report). The information required in the reports closely parallels that required in the 1933 Act registration statement, including detailed information as to the nature of the registrant's business; any significant changes in the business during the preceding fiscal year; a description of the physical properties of the registrant; current financial reports; identification of the registrant's executive directors and officers and their holdings in the corporation; and identification of other principal holders of the corporate securities.

A corporation must register its securities within 120 days after the first fiscal year in which the "total assets" and stock criteria are met. The registration becomes effective 60 days after filing. Thereafter, the issuer may trade its securities, but must continue to make quarterly reports.

Also, any person who owns more than five percent of any class of securities of

---

6. "Total assets" means gross assets as shown on the issuer's balance sheet or on

the balance sheet of the issuer and its subsidiaries consolidated, whichever is larger.

the corporation must file an individual report with the SEC disclosing his or her holdings. In this way, the investing public has access to information that will help it spot attempts by an investor to take over corporate management by gaining control of at least 51% of the voting stock.

A company that is subject to SEC registration and continuing disclosure requirements must furnish its shareholders with an annual report containing substantially the same information as is required in the quarterly reports filed with the SEC (including current financial reports).

It should be pointed out that the annual report is in addition to any proxy information that must be provided to the shareholders under SEC proxy rules. As you will recall from Ch. 23, many large corporations solicit proxies from shareholders who cannot personally attend shareholder meetings. The use of proxies is essential to conducting corporate business at the annual shareholders meeting. The Securities Exchange Act of 1934 provides that, prior to every meeting of its shareholders, a registered company must furnish each shareholder with a "proxy statement" containing full information regarding all matters to be voted on at the meeting. The form of proxy must be such that each shareholder can indicate his or her approval or disapproval of each proposal to be presented at the meeting. Preliminary copies of the proxy statement and form of proxy must be filed with the SEC at least ten days before they are sent to the shareholders. If the SEC finds the proxy information to be inadequate, it will require changes before the statement and proxy form can be mailed to the shareholders. A final copy of the statement and form must be filed with the SEC at the time of mailing.

More than 10,000 companies are subject to SEC registration and continuing disclosure. About one-third of these have securities listed on the securities exchanges.

Requirements for registration on stock exchanges. The Securities Exchange Act of 1934 defines the term "exchange" as "any organization, association, or group of persons, whether incorporated or unincorporated, which constitutes, maintains, or provides a marketplace or facilities for bringing together purchasers and sellers of securities * * *" The 1934 Act makes it unlawful for anyone, including a broker or dealer, to use the mails or any other instrumentality of interstate commerce to effect a security transaction using the facilities of an "exchange" unless the exchange is registered as a "national securities exchange" with the Securities and Exchange Commission.

The Securities Exchange Act provides that any exchange may register with the SEC as a "national securities exchange" by filing a registration statement with the Commission containing such agreements and information as the Commission may prescribe. Ordinarily, the registration statement must include extensive data as to the exchange's organization, its rules of operation and membership, and any other information the SEC requires in the public interest and for the protection of investors. To become registered, an exchange must meet the standards established by the SEC, and, once registered, it is subject to continuing regulation and control. For example, SEC rules and regulations control what is required by way of financial responsibility of exchanges and exchange members; the hours of trading; the manner, method, and place of soliciting business; the time and method of making settlements for customers; the amount of minimum deposits on margin accounts,[7] and so on. A registered exchange that violates SEC rules and regulations may be suspended or terminated.

There are more than a dozen national exchanges registered with the SEC, the largest being the New York and American Exchanges, the smallest being the Pacific, Midwest, Boston, and Honolulu exchanges. Each exchange provides a market for various corporate securities that have been listed with the exchange as a place where the securities can be purchased or sold (there are over 6,000 listed securities). The main function of an exchange is to provide a trading room where brokers can bring their orders regarding a given list of securities. Brokers as a group generally have a large number of customer "buy" and "sell" orders which can easily be matched at an exchange. Brokers earn a commission for providing this easy trading facility.

Each national exchange establishes its own requirements for listing stock on the exchange—and the requirements are generally quite strict. For a corporation to list its securities on the New York Stock Exchange, for example, the corporation must have a minumum of 2,000 shareholders each owning at least 100 shares of securities; it must have a minimum of 1,000,000 publicly traded shares, having a market value of at least $16,000,000; it must have net tangible assets of at least $16,000,000, and it must have earned at least $2,500,000 during the latest fiscal year and at least $2,000,000 during each of the two preceding years.

Corporations often find it desirable to list their stock with an exchange because listed stock generally has a better stand-ing with investors. Investors know that the stock meets the strict exchange standards and that it has more collateral value than unlisted stock (i. e., it is easier to use as security for obtaining a loan). In addition, there is available a constant quotation about the value of listed stock; and the stock can be converted into cash at any time. The advantages of listing also rub off on the issuer-corporation as listed stock generally sells at a higher price than unlisted. Too, the corporation will attain a wider distribution of owners which will result in a wider interest in prosperity of the company. And just from the trading of its securities in the exchange market, the company will receive a large amount of advertising which should result in better sales of its products. Future financing of the corporation should also be easier once the company's securities are well known.

But remember, only about one-third of the companies that must register with the SEC list their securities with an exchange. Two-thirds choose not to list their securities or cannot list them because they cannot meet the exchange requirements.

The sale of unlisted securities is accomplished in what is termed the "over-the-counter" market. Securities dealers maintain this market by buying and selling unlisted stocks (or unlisted bonds or other securities) and carrying them in their inventory. Dealers in the over-the-counter market generally specialize in a particular type of security such as municipal bonds, bank stocks, or utility stocks, or else they deal in all the securities of a particular local community. Typically, a dealer carrying unlisted stock announces that he or she will buy additional shares

7. In a margin account, the customer pays only a portion of the full cash price of the security and borrows the balance from the stock brokerage house; the company charges the customer interest on the amount borrowed. Margin requirements (i. e., the percentage of the purchase price that the customer must pay in cash) are set by the Federal Reserve Board (see Ch. 15) and change from time to time (e. g., the margin requirements might be 50 to 65% on listed stocks, 90% on government bonds, and 100% on new issues).

of the stock at what is termed its "bid" price whenever the stock is offered to the dealer by the public or other securities houses; and the dealer announces that he or she will sell the stock at its "ask" price. The difference between the "bid" and "ask" prices is the dealer's "spread" or gross profit margin. The ask price typically runs from 1 to 5% more than the bid price, so that the investor must see his or her investment go up at least that much before he or she will break even. For example, say that the common stock of Ray Chamberlain Sports, Inc. is being traded in the over-the-counter market. A dealer with an inventory of the stock "asks" $20.00, but provides a "bid" price of $18.50. If Lois Investor buys 100 shares at $20.00 a share, she will have to see the bid price rise to $20.00 before she will break even on the investment (without regard to any commission that might be payable on the purchase). If, rather than wait, Lois immediately re-sells the stock at its quoted bid price, she will receive only $18.50 a share (though she herself paid the ask price of $20.00).

It should be pointed out that there exists a nationwide, computer-based automatic quotation service that provides up-to-the-second bid and ask prices throughout the trading day on over 3,500 over-the-counter securities.

The listed and over-the-counter securities markets in the United States function through over 5,000 security houses or firms along with the many hundreds of employees who work for the firms. The firms handle hundreds of billions of dollars of transactions annually. The Securities Exchange Act of 1934 was passed in part to regulate this industry and to protect the investing public from fraud and other abuse in the resale of securities.

The anti-fraud provisions of the Securities Exchange Act of 1934. Section 10(b) of the Securities Exchange Act of 1934 makes it unlawful for any person who is using the mails or any other facility of interstate commerce in purchasing or selling securities "to use or employ, in connection with the purchase or sale of any security * * * any manipulative or deceptive device or contrivance in contravention of such rules and regulations as the Commission may prescribe as necessary or appropriate in the public interest or for the protection of investors."

In order to effectuate Section 10(b), the Securities and Exchange Commission has promulgated Rule 10(b)–5 which has become the basic anti-fraud provision of the Securities Exchange Act (the Rule was referred to briefly in Chapter 23 insofar as it relates to the recovery of insider profits).

The Rule provides:

It shall be unlawful for any person, directly or indirectly, by the use of any means or instrumentality of interstate commerce, or of the mails, or of any facility of any national securities exchange,

(1) to employ any device, scheme, or artifice to defraud,

(2) to make any [oral or written] untrue statement of a material fact or to omit to state a material fact necessary in order to make the statements made, in the light of circumstances under which they were made, not misleading, or

(3) to engage in any act, practice, or course of business which operates or would operate as a fraud or deceit upon any person

in connection with the purchase or sale of any security.

————————

Unlike Sections 11 and 12 of the 1933 Securities Act, Section 10(b) and Rule 10(b)–5 do not expressly provide a civil action remedy for violations of the Rule.

However, the law implies such a remedy (and also finds therein a basis for criminal sanctions).

The language of Rule 10(b)–5 is all encompassing. So long as the interstate commerce requirement is met ("the use of any means or instrumentality of interstate commerce, or of the mails, or of any facility of any national securities exchange"), the Rule applies to *any* purchase or sale by *any* person of *any* security. There are no exemptions. All securities—whether publicly traded or closely held, registered or unregistered, listed or traded over the counter—fall within the scope of the Rule.

The Rule covers not only the original issuance of securities, but also every subsequent resale—even a redemption or repurchase by the issuer corporation. It applies to every transfer or exchange of securities, including the "exchange of stock" that occurs in a merger or consolidation.

As to who may sue under the Rule, any *buyer* or *seller* of securities who suffers a money loss as the result of another's fraudulent activity in connection with the purchase or sale may sue (under Sections 11 and 12 of the 1933 Act, only the *buyer* may sue).

As to who may be sued, any person who violates the Rule may be whether or not he or she actively participated in the purchase or sale. All that is required is that the party's activity be "connected with" the purchase or sale (meaning any activity that would cause a reasonable investor to rely thereon in making a purchase or sale). No privity between the plaintiff and the defendant (i. e., no contract or other direct dealings) is required. Depending on the circumstances, any of the following may be sued: buyer, seller, issuer, underwriter, broker, dealer, accountant, lawyer, even a complete outsider (e. g., a stock brokerage house that publishes false information concerning a security prompting a purchaser to buy the security from another party). A "control" person who is sued under Rule 10(b)–5 has a good defense to liability if he or she can show that he or she acted in good faith and did not directly or indirectly induce the activity resulting in the "controlled" person's liability.

To recover under Rule 10(b)–5, the plaintiff purchaser or seller must prove that:

(1) The defendant misrepresented or failed to disclose a material fact or otherwise acted so as to cheat or defraud the plaintiff in connection with the purchase or sale. An alleged omission or misrepresentation may be oral or written; the latter may be found in a registration statement, prospectus, annual report, proxy statement, press release, or any other document.

(2) The omission or misrepresentation was material (such that a reasonable investor would have attached importance to it in deciding whether to purchase or sell).

(3) The defendant's activity was intentional (which, in some cases, may include a situation where the defendant acted in reckless disregard of the truth).

(4) The plaintiff relied on the defendant's manipulative or deceptive device or conduct in making the purchase or sale (contrast this with the anti-fraud provisions of the 1933 Act where reliance need not be shown).

Rule 10(b)–5 has been given a very expansive interpretation by the courts and is the leading anti-fraud provision of the federal securities acts. It has been applied to hold accountable underwriters, dealers, accountants, and lawyers who have published misleading information about securities. Issuer corporations have sued their promoters under Rule 10(b)–5 to recover for "watered stock" violations (i. e., where the promoters have transferred overvalued personal property to the corporation in exchange for shares). Shareholders have brought class actions to recover for 10(b)–5 violations. They have maintained derivative suits (on behalf of the corporation) under the Rule against corporate directors who have engaged in fraudulent activity in connection with the purchase or sale of securities to the shareholders. For example, in Bailes v. Colonial Press, Inc., 444 F.2d 1241 (5th Cir. 1971), shareholders brought a derivative suit against the directors and former shareholders of a corporation for fraud in connection with the public offering of stock to the shareholders. The corporation (originally closely held) had issued stock to the former shareholders who had paid nothing for the shares as a first step in a fraudulent plan to offer the stock subsequently to the public.

Because there are no exemptions under Rule 10(b)–5, even a closely held corporation that is not subject to the registration requirements of the SEC is still subject to Rule 10(b)–5. For example, suppose that Ray Chamberlain Sports, Inc. has only two shareholders—Ray Chamberlain and Lola Forthright—and assets of only $250,000. Though the corporation does not have to register with the SEC (remember, only a corporation having at least 500 shareholders and total assets of at least $1,000,000 must register), it is nevertheless subject to Rule 10(b)–5. If Lola Forthright mails a "doctored" (fraudulent) profit and loss statement to her sister, inducing her sister to purchase a portion of her stock, Lola violates Rule 10(b)–5 and can be held civilly and criminally liable.

The list of actions brought under Rule 10(b)–5 goes on and on. The Rule provides an invaluable tool for the protection of buyers and sellers of securities.

Regulation of the securities industry. A substantial portion of the Securities Exchange Act of 1934 is devoted to regulation of the people who are involved in the securities industry. And about 25% of the SEC staff works full-time in this area. The following important rules apply:

(1) No person may engage in business as a broker or dealer unless he or she is registered with the Securities and Exchange Commission (an exception is made for a broker-dealer who deals only in exempt securities or whose business is totally intrastate). The 1934 Act defines a "broker" as a "person engaged in the business of effecting transactions in securities for the *account of others*", and a "dealer" as a "person engaged in the business of buying and selling securities for *his or her own account.*" (Emphasis added.) The Securities and Exchange Commission may revoke or suspend the registration of any broker-dealer who is found to have violated the federal securities laws.

(2) A firm that acts as both a broker and a dealer is a fiduciary of its customers at all times, even when acting as a dealer in the over-the-counter market. It follows that a broker-dealer cannot take the position that he or she is dealing with his or her customers "at arm's length" but must provide full disclosure regarding *all transactions at all times.* A failure to provide such disclosure is a violation of the anti-fraud provisions of Rule 10(b)–5. The disclosure requirement is based on the "shingle theory" that a broker-dealer hangs out his or her "shingle" declaring himself or herself to be an expert in the securities business who will provide customers with expert advice, full disclosure, and no conflict of interest on the broker-dealer's part.

(3) A broker-dealer must furnish his or her customers with a written confirmation of each transaction disclosing all material terms and commissions and stating whether the broker-dealer was acting as a broker for the customer or as a dealer for his or her own account.

(4) A broker-dealer may be held liable under the anti-fraud provisions of Rule 10(b)–5 for inducing a customer to engage in an excessive number of transactions. This is referred to as "churning" a customer's account and is done by a broker-dealer to generate more commissions for himself or herself. Securities Exchange Act (SEA) Rule 15C1–7 makes it illegal to churn: it defines "churning" as effecting transactions "which are excessive in size or frequency in view of the financial resources and character of the account."

(5) It is unlawful for a broker-dealer to purchase securities, then, without disclosing the purchase, recommend the securities to customers, holding on and selling the securities for a profit after the price rises because of the recommendation. This illegal practice is referred to as "scalping".

(6) It is also unlawful for a broker-dealer to recommend the purchase of a security unless the broker-dealer has a firm and sound basis (of reliable information about the security and its issuer) for making the recommendation. This rule prevents the use of "boiler-room operations" (high pressure sales techniques, such as telephoning "lists" of customers and recommending a particular security without having any basis for believing the security to be a good investment). And it forms the basis for holding a broker-dealer liable under anti-fraud Rule 10(b)–5 when a customer relies upon an unfounded recommendation to his or her detriment.

(7) A broker-dealer who holds customers' funds and/or securities must maintain net capital (i. e., an excess of assets over liabilities) of at least $25,000. A broker-dealer who holds neither customers' funds nor securities need maintain net capital of only $5,000. In no case may a broker-dealer let his or her aggregate indebtedness exceed 1500% of his or her net capital.

(8) A broker who has agreed to hold securities for a customer must act promptly to take possession of the securities; and, of course, the broker must take proper care of the securities and provide adequate facilities for their safekeeping.

(9) A broker must maintain a "Special Reserve Bank Account for the Exclusive Benefit of Customers" in which he or she holds cash or U.S. Government securities in an amount equal to the total credit balance of cash in his or her customers' accounts (the total "credit balance" being the net amount owing to customers after all amounts owed by customers to the broker-dealer have been deducted.)

(10) Under the Securities Investor Protection Act passed by Congress in 1970, every broker-dealer must become a member of the Securities Investor Protection Corporation (SIPC). Each broker-dealer must pay the SIPC an annual assessment equal to one-half of 1% of the member's gross revenues until a member fund of 150 million dollars is accumulated. Thereafter, each broker-dealer must pay whatever additional assessments are necessary to maintain the fund at that level. If a broker-dealer becomes insolvent, the SIPC will stand behind his or her customers' accounts and claims to the extent of $50,000 per customer for losses involving both securities and cash, and to the extent of $20,000 per customer for losses involving cash only.

(11) With regard to margin accounts, a broker-dealer is permitted to charge interest on the amount of credit extended to a customer. However, the broker-dealer must disclose to the customer the rate and method of computing interest on the account balance, any additional collateral requirements, and the broker-dealer's rights to make margin calls. A "margin call" is a demand made upon a margin customer to reduce the amount of his or her loan from the broker-dealer so as to maintain the prop-

er margin requirement where the securities have declined in value. For example, say that a customer buys $10,000 of stock on margin. The margin requirement being 50% (i. e., 50% of the value of the securities), the customer pays $5,000 down and owes the balance to the broker-dealer. Subsequently, the stock declines in value from $10,000 to $8,000. The customer receives a margin call requiring him or her to reduce his or her indebtedness by $1,000 so as to maintain the 50% margin.

(12) It should also be pointed out that there is much self-regulation within the securities industry. Stock exchanges have extensive rules and regulations governing their internal operations and dealings with customers as well as that of their member firms. Also, the National Association of Securities Dealers (NASD) has adopted "Rules of Fair Practice" covering the operation of the over-the-counter market. Broker-dealers who are exchange or NASD members may be held liable for violating rules of these associations, and the associations themselves may be held liable for failing to enforce the rules they have promulgated among their members.

(13) Investment companies are regulated by the Investment Company Act of 1940. The Act defines an "investment company" as a company which is "engaged primarily * * * in the business of investing, reinvesting, or trading in securities, or is engaged in that business and more than 40% of its assets consist of investment securities." [8] Under the terms of the Act, every investment company must register with the SEC, and there are substantial registration requirements. Following registration, the companies are closely supervised by the SEC and are subject to civil and other sanctions for violations of the securities acts.

Enforcement of the federal securities laws by the Securities and Exchange Commission. The Securities and Exchange Commission has broad power to investigate violations of the federal securities laws. This includes power to hold formal hearings, subpoena witnesses and place them under oath, and require the production of books and records.

Before holding a formal hearing, the Commission generally conducts an informal inquiry to determine whether a violation has occurred. If the inquiry reveals a violation, the SEC will call a formal hearing to which it will subpoena witnesses who may appear with counsel, but who may not be present during the examination of other witnesses. Of course, the witnesses are entitled to all of the federal constitutional protections, including the Fourth Amendment's guarantee against unreasonable searches and seizures and the Fifth Amendment's privilege against self-incrimination (see Appendix A).

Generally, SEC formal proceedings are conducted in private to protect the people under investigation. If the SEC finds that a public investigation is necessary, it must afford the witnesses every opportunity for cross-examination of witnesses and presentation of rebuttal evidence.

Based on its hearing findings, the SEC may revoke a security registration. And it may bar from association with broker-dealers any person who has violated the federal securities laws (this being a sanction against employees of broker-dealer firms). The SEC may also disqualify professionals who have violated the securities laws (e. g., lawyers and accountants) from practicing or appearing before the Securities and Exchange Commission.

---

8. Investment companies are in the business of investing; they generally set up "mutual funds" in which investors pool their money; the company invests the money to produce a profit for the investors.

Of course, any final order of the SEC may be appealed to the U.S. Circuit Courts for judicial review (see Appendix A on "judicial review").

The SEC may also bring action in the federal district courts to enjoin violations of the securities laws. The courts will issue an injunction if there appears to be a reasonable likelihood of further violation. Any person or firm that violates a court ordered injunction may be held in contempt of court and fined or imprisoned (or both).

In addition to requesting an injunction, the SEC may ask the court to appoint independent directors or a special agent for a corporation to make certain that the corporation complies with the law.

Enforcement by the Justice Department. The Securities and Exchange Commission has no power to prosecute criminal cases involving violations of the federal securities laws. Rather, the Commission turns evidence of criminal violations over to the Justice Department (the U.S. Attorney General's office) for prosecution.

As you know from previous sections, "willful" violations of the federal securities laws are criminal offenses punishable by fine, imprisonment, or both. This includes "willful" violations of any provision of either Act, or of any rule or regulation promulgated pursuant to the Acts; and it includes "willful" misrepresentations or omissions of material fact in any application, registration statement, report, or document that must be filed under the Acts (including misrepresentations or omissions made by engineers, C.P.A.'s, or other professionals). The "willful" requirement means only that the defendant must have intended to do the act in question (negligence is not enough). However, it is not necessary to show that the defendant knew that he or she was violating a specific provision of the securities acts.

Thus, Section 24 of the Securities Act of 1933 provides:

Any person who willfully violates any of the provisions of this Title, or the rules and regulations promulgated by the Commission under authority thereof, or any person who willfully, in a registration statement filed under this Title, makes any untrue statement of a material fact or omits to state any material fact required to be stated therein or necessary to make the statements therein not misleading, shall upon conviction be fined not more than $5,000 or imprisoned not more than five years, or both.

And Section 32(a) of the Securities Exchange Act of 1934 states:

Any person who willfully violates any provisions of this title, or any rule or regulation thereunder the violation of which is made unlawful or the observance of which is required under the terms of this title, or any person who willfully and knowingly makes, or causes to be made, any statement in any application, report, or document required to be filed under this title or any rule or regulation thereunder or any undertaking contained in a registration statement as provided in subsection (d) of Section 15 of this title or by any self-regulatory organization in connection with an application for membership or participation therein or to become associated with a member thereof, which statement was false or misleading with respect to any material fact shall upon conviction be fined not more than $10,000, or imprisoned not more than five years, or both, except that when such person is an exchange, a fine not exceeding $500,000 may be imposed; but no person shall be subject to imprisonment under this section for the violation of any rule or regulation if he proves that he had no knowledge of such rule or regulation.

Private Actions. You also know that a private individual who is injured by a violation of the federal securities laws may generally bring a civil action [9] to recover money damages from the violator. There are probably more private actions brought under the Statutes than there are SEC suits (for injunctions) or government criminal prosecutions.

You will recall that under Section 11 of the Securities Act of 1933, a buyer may sue any person who is connected with the preparation and publication of a registration statement (including a prospectus) containing a misrepresentation or omission of a material fact. If the buyer is the original issuee of the securities, he or she may rescind the transaction or sue for money damages; subsequent purchasers can only sue for money damages. The buyer's measure of damages under Section 11 is the difference between the amount the buyer paid for the security (not exceeding the price at which the security was offered to the public) and the security's fair market value at the time the suit is brought or, if the security is resold prior to initiation of the suit, its resale price. If the security is resold after initiation of the suit, but before judgment, the first formula is applied, except that where the buyer's damages would be lowered by using the resale price, the resale price is used. In no case will the buyer's measure of damages exceed the public offering price of the securities.

Under Section 12 of the 1933 Act, the original issuee (purchaser) may sue his or her immediate seller for violating the registration requirements of the Act, or for misrepresenting or omitting a material fact in any communication, oral or written, made in connection with the sale of the security. Upon tender of the security, the buyer may recover any consideration paid for the security, with inter-

est, less any income received (in effect, a rescission). If the buyer has already resold the security, he or she may sue for money damages.[10]

Section 18 of the Securities Exchange Act of 1934 provides that any person who misrepresents or omits a material fact in any application, report, registration statement, or other document filed pursuant to the Act (or any rule or regulation promulgated thereunder) may be liable in damages to any person who purchases or sells a security *in reliance on* the omission or misrepresentation. To recover damages, the plaintiff buyer or seller must prove that he or she in fact relied on the omission or misrepresentation to his or her detriment, and that the defendant knew or should have known of the statement's false or misleading nature. Liability is limited, however, in the important respect that the defendant is accorded the defense that he or she acted in "good faith" and had no knowledge that such statement was false or misleading. Section 18 makes no reference to the measure of damages recoverable—the result is that the plaintiff may recover whatever actual damages he or she sustains.

Finally, under Rule 10(b)–5 (adopted pursuant to Section 10 of the 1934 Act), any buyer or seller who is injured by another's manipulative or deceptive activity in connection with the purchase or sale of any security may sue to rescind the transaction (if privity exists between the plaintiff and defendant) or to recover money damages. For example, a seller who sues for damages under 10(b)–5 is entitled to the difference between the price he or she received for the securities and the price he or she would have received had there been no fraud. The latter is often determined on the basis of the fair market value of the securities at

---

9. See Appendix A for a description of the civil action procedure.

10. Any action under the Securities Act of 1933 must be brought within one year after discovery of the untrue statement or omis-

sion or after such discovery should have been made by the exercise of reasonable diligence. In no event can an action be brought more than three years after the security was brought in good faith.

the time suit is initiated. Where the fraud involves the concealment or omission of a material fact, the courts will generally look to the value the securities attained after the facts became known and the market had a reasonable time to absorb the new information.

As for punitive damages, most courts hold that they are not recoverable in civil actions based on violations of the securities laws (see Appendix A for a discussion of "punitive damages").

Because securities law violations frequently injure a large number of individuals, "class actions" by plaintiffs are favored. In cases involving corporate mismanagement, shareholders may bring a derivative suit against the corporate directors and officers to recover on behalf of the corporation.

What is the Foreign Corrupt Practices Act?

The Foreign Corrupt Practices Act was passed by Congress in 1977 as an amendment to the Securities Exchange Act of 1934. The Act is designed to prevent the use of corporate funds for corrupt purposes. Among other things, the Act requires companies that are subject to the registration and continuing disclosure requirements of the Securities Exchange Act of 1934 to maintain strict accounting standards and management control over their assets; and it makes it a crime for U. S. companies to bribe foreign government officials for specified corrupt purposes. Companies violating the criminal prohibitions face a maximum fine of $1,-000,000. Individuals acting on behalf of such companies face a maximum fine of $10,000 and five years in jail.

Prior to passage of the legislation, investigations by the SEC had revealed corrupt foreign payments by over 300 U. S. companies involving hundreds of millions of dollars. This corporate bribery had tarnished the reputation and image of all U. S. businesspersons and had affected the very stability of overseas business. A strong anti-bribery law was urgently needed to bring these corrupt practices to a halt and to restore public confidence in the integrity of the American business system.

Section 102 of the Foreign Corrupt Practices Act amended Section 13(b) of the Securities Exchange Act of 1934 by adding the following Subparagraph (2).

(2) Every issuer which has a class of securities registered pursuant to section 12 of this title and every issuer which is required to file reports pursuant to section 15(d) of this title shall—

(A) make and keep books, records, and accounts, which, in reasonable detail, accurately and fairly reflect the transactions and dispositions of the assets of the issuer; and

(B) devise and maintain a system of internal accounting controls sufficient to provide reasonable assurances that—

(i) transactions are executed in accordance with management's general or specific authorization;

(ii) transactions are recorded as necessary (I) to permit preparation of financial statements in conformity with generally accepted accounting principles or any other criteria applicable to such statements, and (II) to maintain accountability for assets;

(iii) access to assets is permitted only in accordance with management's general or specific authorization; and

(iv) the recorded accountability for assets is compared with the existing assets at reasonable intervals and appropriate action is taken with respect to any differences.[11]

Subparagraph (2) imposes affirmative duties on issuers (subject to registration and continuing disclosure under the 1934 Securities Act) to maintain books, records, and accounts which, in reasonable detail, accurately and fairly reflect the transactions of the corporation; and it requires the issuers to design an adequate system of internal accounting controls to assure, among other things, that the assets of the issuer are used for proper corporate purposes. The system of internal controls must be sufficient to provide reasonable assurances that:

(1) **Transactions are executed in accordance with management directions;**

(2) Transactions are recorded in a manner that permits the company to prepare its financial statements in accordance with generally accepted accounting principles or other applicable criteria and to maintain accountability for assets;

(3) Access to company assets is permitted only in accordance with management authorization; and

(4) The recorded accountability for assets is compared with existing assets at reasonable intervals, and appropriate action is taken with respect to differences.

The Act makes it clear that the establishment and maintenance of a system of internal controls and the maintenance of

accurate books and records are important management obligations. Along this line, standards of reasonableness apply. The term "accurately" does not mean exact precision as measured by some abstract principle. Rather, it means that an issuer's records should reflect transactions in conformity with generally accepted accounting principles or other criteria. The size of the business, diversity of operations, degree of centralization of financial and operating management, amount of contact by top management with day-to-day operations, and numerous other circumstances are factors which management must consider in establishing and maintaining an internal accounting controls system. And the accounting profession is expected to use its professional judgment in evaluating the systems maintained by issuers.

The purpose of the Subparagraph (2) requirements is to strengthen the accuracy of the corporate books and records and the reliability of the audit process which form the foundations of our system of corporate disclosure. Too often in the past, corporate bribery has been concealed by the falsification of corporate books and records. Under the Foreign Corrupt Practices Act, an issuer's records must reflect transactions in conformity with accepted methods of recording economic events; this should effectively prevent "off-the-books" slush funds and payments of bribes.

Section 103 of the Foreign Corrupt Practices Act amended the Securities Exchange Act of 1934 by inserting after Section 30 the following new section.

Foreign Corrupt Practices by Issuers
Sec. 30A. (a) It shall be unlawful for any issuer which has a class of

---

11. A limited exemption from these requirements may be obtained for an issuer involved in an endeavor related to national security upon the specific written directive of an agency or department responsible for national security matters (pursuant to Presidential authority to issue such directives).

securities registered pursuant to section 12 of this title or which is required to file reports under section 15(d) of this title, or for any officer, director, employee, or agent of such issuer or any stockholder thereof acting on behalf of such issuer, to make use of the mails or any means or instrumentality of interstate commerce *corruptly in furtherance of an offer, payment, promise to pay, or authorization of the payment of any money, or offer, gift, promise to give, or authorization of the giving of anything of value to—*

(1) *any foreign official* for purposes of—

(A) influencing any act or decision of such foreign official in his official capacity, including a decision to fail to perform his official functions; or

(B) inducing such foreign official to use his influence with a foreign government or instrumentality thereof to affect or influence any act or decision of such government or instrumentality,

in order to assist such issuer in obtaining or retaining business for or with, or directing business to, any person;

(2) *any foreign political party or official thereof or any candidate for foreign political* office for purposes of—

(A) influencing any act or decision of such party, official, or candidate in its or his official capacity, including a decision to fail to perform its or his official functions; or

(B) inducing such party, official, or candidate to use its or his influence with a foreign government or instrumental-

ity thereof to affect or influence any act or decision of such government or instrumentality,

in order to assist such issuer in obtaining or retaining business for or with, or directing business to, any person; or

(3) *any person,* while knowing or having reason to know that all or a portion of such money or thing of value will be offered, given, or promised, directly, or indirectly, to any foreign official, to any foreign political party or official thereof, or to any candidate for foreign political office, for purposes of—

(A) influencing any act or decision of such foreign official, political party, party official, or candidate in his or its official capacity, including a decision to fail to perform his or its official functions; or

(B) inducing such foreign official, political party, party official, or candidate to use his or its influence with a foreign government or instrumentality thereof to affect or influence any act or decision of such government or instrumentality,

in order to assist such issuer in obtaining or retaining business for or with, or directing business to, any person.

———

The new Section 30A prohibits a "covered" corporation (i. e., one that is subject to registration and continuing disclosure with the SEC) from making corrupt use of the mails or other means of interstate commerce in furtherance of an offer, payment, promise to pay, or authorization of payment of anything of value to any foreign official, foreign political party, candidate for foreign political office, or any other person (e. g., an agent) which the issuer knows or has reason to know will make such an offer, promise, or payment. Note that the use of interstate commerce need only be *in furtherance of* making the corrupt payment. The purpose of the payment must be to influence an act or decision of a foreign official, party, candidate, etc. (including a decision not to act) or to induce such official, party, candidate, etc. to use his or her influence to affect a government act or decision so as to assist the issuer in obtaining, retaining, or directing business to any person. The word "corruptly" is used to make it clear that the offer, payment, promise, or gift must be intended to induce the recipient to *misuse* his or her official position in order to *wrongfully* direct business to the payor or his or her client, or to obtain preferential legislation or a favorable regulation. The word "corruptly" connotes an evil motive or purpose—an intent to wrongfully influence the recipient. However, it does not require that the act be fully consummated. And it covers payments or gifts regardless of who first suggested them. Thus, it is no defense that the payment was demanded as a price for gaining entry into a market or to obtain a contract since, at some point, the U. S. company would have to make a conscious decision whether or not to bribe.

As used in the Act, the term "foreign official" means "any officer or employee of a foreign government or any department, agency, or instrumentality thereof, or any person acting in an official capacity for or on behalf of such government or department, agency, or instrumentality." However, it does not include an employee whose duties are primarily ministerial or clerical.

With regard to penalties for violations of Section 30A, the Foreign Corrupt Practices Act amended Section 32(a) of the Securities Exchange Act of 1934 to provide:

(c)(1) Any issuer which violates section 30A(a) of this title shall, upon conviction, be fined not more than $1,000,000.

(2) Any officer or director of an issuer, or any stockholder acting on behalf of such issuer, who willfully violates section 30A(a) of this title shall, upon conviction, be fined not more than $10,000, or imprisoned not more than five years, or both.

(3) Whenever an issuer is found to have violated section 30A(a) of this title, any employee or agent of such issuer who is a United States citizen, national, or resident or is otherwise subject to the jurisdiction of the United States (other than an officer, director, or stockholder of such issuer), and who willfully carried out the act or practice constituting such violation shall, upon conviction, be fined not more than $10,000 or imprisoned not more than five years, or both.

(4) Whenever a fine is imposed under paragraph (2) or (3) of this subsection upon any officer, director, stockholder, employee, or agent of an issuer, *such fine shall not be paid, directly or indirectly, by such issuer.*

Section 104 of the Foreign Corrupt Practices Act made the same provisions and penalties (as are found under Sections 30A and 32(a)) applicable to "domestic concerns" other than those subject to SEC jurisdiction. As used here, a "domestic concern" means "any individual who is a citizen, national, or resident of the United States * * * or any corporation, partnership, association, joint-stock company, business trust, unincorporated organization, or sole proprietorship which has its principal place of business in the United States, or which is organized under the laws of a State of the United States or a territory, possession, or commonwealth of the United States." The result is that the same strong anti-bribery laws apply to all domestic concerns, whether or not they are subject to registration and continuing disclosure under the 1934 Securities Act.

It should be pointed out that the Foreign Corrupt Practices Act will not reach all corrupt overseas payments. Certainly, it is clear that any issuer or domestic concern that engages in bribery of foreign officials indirectly through any other person or entity (e. g., through a foreign subsidiary) will itself be liable under the Act. However, the Act will not cover payments by foreign nationals acting solely on behalf of a foreign subsidiary where there is no connection with U. S. interstate commerce or use of U. S. mails, and where the issuer, reporting company, or domestic concern had no knowledge of the payment. But a U. S. company that "looks the other way" in order to be able to raise the defense that it was ignorant of bribes made by its foreign subsidiary may well be in violation of the Subparagraph (2) requirement of devising and maintaining adequate accounting controls (assuming it is a "covered" corporation). Under Subparagraph (2), no "off-the-books" accounting fund could be lawfully maintained either by a U. S. parent or its foreign subsidiary, and no improper payment could be lawfully disguised.

Whether or not a particular situation involves bribery by a corporation or by an individual acting on his or her own will depend on all the facts and circumstances, including the position of the employee, the care with which the board supervises management, the care with which management supervises employees in sensitive positions, and the corporation's adherence to the strict accounting standards established in Subparagraph (2).

The Subparagraph (2) requirements, taken together with the strong anti-bribery provisions of Sections 30A and 32 (a), should effectively put an end to foreign corrupt practices. With regard to "covered" corporations, it is the SEC's responsibility to conduct investigations, bring civil actions for injunction and refer criminal cases to the Justice Department for prosecution. The Justice Department retains sole investigative and prosecutorial jurisdiction over domestic concerns that are not otherwise within the jurisdiction of the SEC.

What are "Blue Sky" laws?

In addition to the federal securities laws, each state has its own legislation regulating securities activities. The 1917 case of Hall v. Geiger-Jones Co., 242 U. S. 539, 37 S.Ct. 217, 61 L.Ed. 480, stated the purpose of such legislation as being to prevent "speculative schemes which have no more basis than so many feet of *blue sky*." (Emphasis added.) Following the *Geiger-Jones* case, state securities laws have become widely known as "Blue Sky" laws.

Blue Sky laws evidence the strong public interest in protecting people from promoters of worthless securities and from deceit and fraud in securities transactions. In a great many cases, an issuer will have to comply with both state and federal securities laws. For example, an underwriting group that intends to make a national distribution of a new issue of securities may have to comply, first, with the federal registration requirements under the 1933 Securities Act, and, second, with the Blue Sky legislation in each state where the issue is to be offered.

While Blue Sky laws vary somewhat from state to state, most all do the following three things:

(1) Prohibit fraud in the offering and sale of securities;

(2) Require brokers and dealers to register with the state before they engage in the securities business; and

(3) Require registration of securities with the state before the securities can be sold in the state.

Unlike the SEC, the state has power to deny registration though full disclosure is made. Some states go so far as to forbid the offer or sale of securities within the state unless the issuer obtains a permit from the state.

A few states dispense with registration and simply impose civil and criminal liability for any fraud in connection with the sale or issuance of securities.

A state Uniform Securities Act was drafted in 1958 and about two-thirds of the states have since adopted it. The Uniform Statute adopts the anti-fraud language of SEC Rule 10(b)–5: its anti-fraud sanctions thus apply to "any offer, sale, or purchase of any security". The effect is that, in states having adopted the Uniform Securities Act, the same anti-fraud provisions apply whether a transaction is interstate or wholly intrastate. Part I, Section 101 of the Uniform Securities Act provides:

UNIFORM SECURITIES ACT

An Act

[PURPOSE] Relating to securities; prohibiting fraudulent practices in relation thereto; requiring the registration of broker-dealers, agents, investment advisers, and securities; and making uniform the law with reference thereto.

Part I

Fraudulent and Other Prohibited Practices

Section 101.   (Sales and Purchases)

It is unlawful for any person, in connection with the offer, sale or purchase of any security, directly or indirectly

(1) to employ any device, scheme, or artifice to defraud.

(2) to make any untrue statement of a material fact or to omit to state a material fact necessary in order to make the statements made, in the light of the circumstances under which they are made, not misleading, or

(3) to engage in any act, practice, or course of business which operates or would operate as a fraud or deceit upon any person.

––––––

Part II of the Uniform Securities Act, entitled "Registration of Broker-Dealers, Agents, and Investment Advisers", makes it unlawful for any person to transact business in the state as a broker-dealer or agent unless he or she is registered with the state. Part II also requires broker-dealers and agents to keep appropriate records and to file annual financial reports and other information with the state administrative agency.

Part III of the Act, entitled "Registration of Securities", makes it unlawful for any person to offer or sell any non-exempt security in the state unless it is registered under the Act with the state administrative agency.

Part IV, "General Provisions", specifies what securities and securities transactions are exempt from the registration statement requirements. The exemptions are similar to those under the federal law: they include government issued securities; securities issued by certain financial institutions, nonprofit organizations, and insurance companies; short-term commercial paper; casual or isolated sales; private placements (Section 402(b)(10) exempts any "transaction pursuant to an offer directed by the offeror to not more than ten persons * * * in this state during any period of twelve consecutive months"); etc.

Part IV of the Act also creates an administrative agency to administer the law. It provides the agency with investigative and injunctive power to root out violations of the Act and put a stop to them. Part IV additionally provides criminal penalties for willful violations of the Act (a fine of up to $5,000 and/or imprisonment for up to three years). And Section 410 provides for civil liability as follows.

Alabama
Alaska
Arkansas
Colorado
Delaware
District of Columbia
Hawaii
Idaho
Indiana
Iowa
Kansas
Kentucky
Maryland
Massachusetts
Michigan
Minnesota
Missouri

Montana
Nebraska
Nevada
New Jersey
New Mexico
North Carolina
Oklahoma
Oregon
Pennsylvania
South Carolina
Utah
Virginia
Washington
West Virginia
Wisconsin
Wyoming

The Act provides:

Section 410. (Civil Liabilities)

(a) Any person who

(1) offers or sells a security in violation [of the Act] * * *

(2) offers or sells a security by means of any untrue statement of a material fact or any omission to state a material fact * * * is liable to the person buying the security from him, who may sue either at law or in equity to recover the consideration paid for the security, together with interest * * * costs, and reasonable attorney's fees * * * or for damages if he no longer owns the security.

The following states (including the District of Columbia) have adopted the Uniform Securities Act:

You will note that some of the great commercial states such as New York, California, Illinois, and Texas have not adopted the Uniform Securities Act. However, all of these states have "Blue Sky" laws that are similar to the Uniform Act at least insofar as they prohibit fraud and require registration of (non-exempt) securities and broker-dealers.

The Uniform Securities Act provides for three methods of registration of securities (states not adopting the Act generally have similar methods):

(1) *Registration by notification.* A company that can meet certain stability and earnings tests can take advantage of a simplified registration procedure called *registration by notification.* This involves filing an abbreviated registration statement with the state agency, acknowledging compliance with the statutory tests and describing the securities to be offered and the terms of the offering. To register with the state by notification, an issuer-company must "pass" the following tests:

(a) The issuer-company must have been in continuous operation for at least five years.

(b) The issuer must not have defaulted during the current fiscal year or within the three preceding fiscal years in the payment of principal, interest, or dividends on any security having a fixed maturity, fixed interest, or fixed dividend provision.

(c) During the three preceding years, the issuer must have had average earnings of at least five percent on its common stock.

The notification statement must acknowledge that the above tests have been met; and it must list the issuer's name, address, and form and date of organization; the general character and location of the business; a description of the securities being offered; the offering price, and the method of determining the offering price. The issuer must attach to the statement a copy of any prospectus, pamphlet, circular, advertisement, form letter, or the like that is to be used in connection with the offering.

Depending on the particular state, a registration by notification becomes effective immediately upon filing, or from two to three business days thereafter (assuming, of course, that the state administrator does not object to the statement).

(2) *Registration by co-ordination.* A security is eligible for *registration by co-ordination* under the Uniform Securities Act if a registration statement has been filed under the federal Securities Act of 1933 in connection with the same offering. (In other words, registration by co-ordination is available if the security offering is subject to the federal Securities Act of 1933, requiring the filing of a registration statement, including a prospectus, with the Securities and Exchange Commission.)

To register securities by co-ordination, an issuer must file with the state agency copies of the latest form or prospectus filed under the federal Securities Act of 1933 along with a promise to forward all future amendments to the prospectus no later than the first business day after they are filed with the Securities and Exchange Commission. Generally, that is all that is required, although the Uniform Securities Act empowers the state agency to require the filing of other information.

A registration by co-ordination becomes effective automatically when the federal registration statement becomes effective provided that the prospectus and other required information has been on file with the state agency for at least ten days, and the state has not issued a stop order (rendering the registration statement ineffective) or initiated proceedings with respect to a possible denial of registration. The issuer must promptly notify the state agency by telephone or telegram of the date and time when the federal registration becomes effective. And the issuer must furnish the state agency with precise information as to the maximum and minimum proposed offering prices and the commissions to be paid at least two full business days before the offering is made.

(3) *Registration by qualification.* A nonexempt security that does not qualify for registration by notification or co-ordi-

nation must be registered by *qualification*. Registration by qualification is similar to registration under the federal Securities Act of 1933: much of the same extensive information that is required in a federal registration statement must be filed with the state agency, the objective again being full disclosure of all relevant facts. The state registration statement must include complete and accurate information as to the general character and location of the business; a description of its physical properties and equipment; general competitive conditions in the industry; capitalization of the business; longterm debt; all material contracts, including management contracts; pending litigation; financial information including a balance sheet as of a date within four months prior to the filing of the statement, a profit and loss statement, and an analysis of surplus for each of the three fiscal years preceding the date of the balance sheet; information relating to promoters and amounts paid to them for services or properties; information about any person who owns 10% or more of the outstanding stock of the corporation; and any additional information the state administration deems necessary for protection of the public. If an expert (e. g., an accountant, appraiser, or engineer) is named as having certified any report or valuation in the statement, his or her written consent must also be filed with the state.

Registration by qualification becomes effective when the state administrator orders it effective.

Prospectus. Unlike the federal Securities Act of 1933, the State Uniform Securities Act does not *require* the use of a prospectus in each and every case. Rather, the Act leaves it up to the state agency to determine when and where a prospectus is needed. Thus, the agency may or may not require that a prospectus (containing certain of the information contained in the registration statement) be given to each and every offeree of the securities. However, many of the states that have not adopted the Uniform Securities Act do require a prospectus.

Denial or revocation of registration effectiveness. If the state agency finds that the registration statement contains false or misleading information or omits material facts, the agency can issue a stop order denying, suspending, or revoking the effectiveness of the statement. The same is true where the agency determines that the issuance, if conducted, would work or tend to work a fraud on purchasers or would be made with "unreasonable" amounts of commissions, promoters' profits, or the like. Notice that under Blue Sky laws, the state may deny an application for registration of a security even though full disclosure is made (e. g., on the basis of "unreasonable" commissions). Under the federal securities laws, the SEC has no power to deny registration so long as full disclosure is made.

The state agency may enter a final stop order only if the registrant has been given notice and an opportunity for a hearing. Like all other administrative rulings (see Appendix A), the agency's orders are subject to review by the courts.

What is the federal Interstate Land Sales Full Disclosure Act?

It was in 1917 that the court in *Hall v. Geiger-Jones* spoke of the "speculative schemes" in the securities industry that had no more basis than "so many feet of blue sky". Sixteen years later, in 1933, the federal Congress passed the Securities Act requiring full disclosure in public offerings of securities made in interstate commerce. It was not until the 1960's that widespread sales of undeveloped land began to be made interstate to purchasers who discovered that they had been the victims of false advertising. The federal Congress responded in 1968 with the Interstate Land Sales Full Disclosure Act which became effective in 1969. The Statute is very similar in its requirements to the Securities Act of 1933 and was doubtless patterned after that law.

Section 1703 of the Interstate Land Sales Full Disclosure Act makes it unlawful for any land developer to use any instrument of interstate commerce or the mails to sell or lease any lot in any subdivision unless the land is registered with the Department of Housing and Urban Development (HUD) and a printed "property report" (similar to a prospectus) is furnished to the purchaser or lessee in advance of the signing of the sales or lease agreement. Section 1703 also prohibits fraud or deceit on the part of the developer.

The Section states:

Section 1703. Prohibitions Relating to Sale or Lease of Lots in Subdivisions; Voidability of Contracts or Agreements

(a) It shall be unlawful for any developer or agent, directly or indirectly, to make use of any means or instruments of transportation or communication in interstate commerce, or of the mails—

    (1) to sell or lease any lot in any subdivision unless a *statement of record* with respect to such lot is in effect * * * and a printed property report * * * is furnished to the purchaser in advance of the signing of any contract or agreement for sale or lease by the purchaser; and

    (2) in selling or leasing, or offering to sell or lease, any lot in a subdivision

        (A) to employ any device, scheme, or artifice to defraud, or

        (B) to obtain money or property by means of a material misrepresentation with respect to any information included in the statement of record or the property report or with respect to any other information pertinent to the lot or the subdivision and upon which the purchaser relies, or

        (C) to engage in any transaction, practice, or course of business which operates or would operate as a fraud or deceit upon a purchaser.

(b) Any contract or agreement for the purchase or leasing of a lot in a subdivision covered * * * where the property report has not been given to the purchaser in advance or at the time of his signing, shall be voidable at the option of the purchaser. A purchaser may revoke such contract or agreement within forty-eight hours, where he has received the property report less than forty-eight hours before he signed the contract or agreement, and the contract or agreement shall so provide, except that the contract or agreement may stipulate that the foregoing revocation authority shall not apply in the case of a purchaser who (1) has received the property report and inspected the lot to be purchased or leased in advance of signing the contract or agreement, and (2) acknowledges by his signature that he has made such inspection and has read and understood such report. (Emphasis added.)

The "statement of record" (which is similar to the registration statement under the 1933 Securities Act) must make full disclosure of the following: the legal description of the land and maps of the land showing the proposed division, lot dimensions, and streets and roads; complete information regarding any debts owing on the land; terms and conditions for sale or lease of the lots; any unusual noise or safety conditions; the availability of sewage facilities and other public utilities; copies of deeds, easements, or other land restrictions; financial statements; and any other information HUD deems necessary for the protection of the public.

The statement of record becomes effective 30 days after filing unless HUD finds it to be incomplete or inaccurate and requires additional information. HUD, in this case, will advise the developer, and the effective date will be postponed until 30 days after the additional or corrected information is filed. A developer who is advised that his or her statement of record is unsatisfactory has a right to request a hearing and must be granted one within 20 days after the date of the request. The developer may appeal the final HUD order to the U.S. Circuit Court of Appeals.

If HUD at any time determines that a statement of record contains a misstatement or omission of material fact, it will "suspend" the statement, meaning that the statement will become ineffective and no land sales or leases may proceed. A suspension order is also reviewable to the U.S. Circuit Court of Appeals.

The information contained in a statement of record is a matter of public record and will be furnished to anyone who wants to see it. The property report (a copy of which must be given to each potential purchaser or lessee) must reproduce most of the information required in the statement. Section 1707 of the Interstate Land Sales Full Disclosure Act provides:

Section 1707. Information Required in Property Report; Use For Promotional Purposes

(a) A property report relating to the lots in a subdivision shall contain such information contained in the statement of record * * * as the Secretary (of HUD) may deem necessary * * *. A property report shall also contain such other information as the Secretary may by rules or regulations require as being necessary or appropriate in the public interest or for the protection of purchasers.

(b) The property report shall not be used for any promotional purposes before the statement of record becomes effective and then only if it is used in its entirety. No person may advertise or represent that the Secretary (of HUD) approves or recommends the subdivision or the sale or lease of lots therein. No portion of the property report shall be underscored, italicized, or printed in larger or bolder type than the balance of the statement unless the Secretary requires or permits it.

Like the federal Securities Act of 1933, the Interstate Land Sales Full Disclosure Act provides for certain exemptions. They are listed at Section 1702 as follows:

Section 1702. Exemptions

(a) Unless the method of disposition is adopted for the purpose of evasion * * *, the provisions * * * shall not apply to—

(1) the sale or lease of real estate not pursuant to a common promotional plan to offer or sell *fifty* or more lots in a subdivision;

(2) the sale or lease of lots in a subdivision, all of which are *five acres or more* in size;

(3) the sale or lease of any *improved land* on which there is a residential, commercial, or industrial building, or to the *sale or lease of land under a contract obligating the seller to erect such a building thereon within a period of two years*;

(4) the sale or lease of real estate under or pursuant to *court order*;

(5) the sale of evidences of indebtedness secured by a *mortgage or deed of trust* on real estate; [See Ch. 27 for a discussion of the use of real estate as security for debts.]

       *   *   *

(7) the sale or lease of real estate by any *government* or government agency;

(8) the sale or lease of *cemetery lots*;

(9) the sale or lease of lots to any person who acquires such lots for the *purpose of engaging in the business of constructing residential, commercial, or industrial buildings.* *   *   *;

(10) the sale or lease of real estate which is free and clear of all liens, encumbrances, and adverse claims if each and every purchaser or his or her spouse has made a personal on-the-lot inspection of the real estate which he purchased and if the developer executes a written affirmation to that effect to be made a matter of record in accordance with rules and regulations of the Secretary *   *   *

(b) The Secretary may from time to time *   *   * exempt [other sales or leases of land] *   *   * if he finds that the enforcement *   *   * with respect to such subdivision or lots is not necessary in the public interest and for the protection of purchasers by reason of the small amount involved or the limited character of the public offering.

————

Also exempt are purely intrastate sales and leases of subdivision lots.

A person who purchases or leases a subdivision lot covered by a statement of record or property report containing a misstatement or omission of material fact may bring a civil action for damages against the developer. Section 1709 of the Act states:

Section 1709. Civil Liabilities—Suit For Untrue Statement or Omission to State Material Fact in Statement of Record

(a) Where any part of the statement of record, when such part became effective, contained an untrue statement of a material fact or omitted to state a material fact required to be stated therein, any person acquiring a lot in the subdivision covered by such statement of record from the developer or his agent during such period the statement remained uncorrected, unless it is proved that at the time of such acquisition he knew of such untruth (or omission) may, either at law or in equity, in any court of competent jurisdiction, sue the developer.

(b) Any developer or agent, who sells or leases a lot in a subdivision—

    (1) in violation of Section 1703 of this title, or

    (2) by means of a property report which contained an untrue statement of a material fact or omitted to state a material fact required to be stated therein, may be sued by the purchaser of such lot.

(c) The suit authorized under subsection (a) or (b) of this section may be to recover such damages as shall represent the difference between the amount paid for the lot and the reasonable cost of any improvements thereto, and the lesser of (1) the value thereof as of the time such suit was brought, or (2) the price at which such lot shall have been disposed of in a bona fide market transaction before suit, or (3) the price at which such lot shall have been disposed of after suit in a bona fide market transaction but before judgment.

*   *   *

(e) In no case shall the amount recoverable under this section exceed the sum of the purchase price of the lot, the reasonable cost of improvements, and reasonable court costs.

An injured party must bring an action under Section 1709 within one year after the misstatement or omission should have been discovered by the exercise of reasonable diligence. In no event may an injured party bring an action more than three years after the sale or lease is entered into.

HUD is authorized to conduct investigations to determine if violations of the Interstate Land Sales Full Disclosure Act have occurred and to seek injunctions to stop violations. Any person who willfully violates the Act may be found guilty of a felony and may be fined (up to $5,000) or imprisoned (up to five years) or both.

CASES

CASE 1—*An offering of securities to all red-headed men is no less "public" than an unrestricted offering to the world at large.*

SECURITIES & EXCHANGE COMM. v. RALSTON PURINA CO.

Certiorari to the United States Court of Appeals for the Eighth Circuit, 1953.
346 U.S. 119, 73 S.Ct. 981, 97 L.Ed. 1494.

Mr. Justice CLARK delivered the opinion of the Court.

Section 4(1) of the Securities Act of 1933 exempts "transactions by an issuer not involving any public offering" from the registration requirements of § 5.[2] We must decide whether Ralston Purina's offerings of treasury stock to its "key employees" are within this exemption. On a com-

---

2. "Sec. 5. (a) Unless a registration statement is in effect as to a security, it shall be unlawful for any person, directly or indirectly—

  "(1) to make use of any means or instruments of transportation or communication in interstate commerce or of the mails to sell or offer to buy such securi-

ty through the use or medium of any prospectus or otherwise; or

  "(2) to carry or cause to be carried through the mails or in interstate commerce, by any means or instruments of transportation, any such security for the purpose of sale or for delivery after sale. * * *" 48 Stat. 77, 15 U.S.C.A. § 77e.

plaint brought by the Commission under § 20(b) of the Act seeking to enjoin respondent's unregistered offerings, the District Court held the exemption applicable and dismissed the suit. The Court of Appeals affirmed. The question has arisen many times since the Act was passed; an apparent need to define the scope of the private offering exemption prompted certiorari.

Ralston Purina manufactures and distributes various feed and cereal products. Its processing and distribution facilities are scattered throughout the United States and Canada, staffed by some 7,000 employees. At least since 1911 the company has had a policy of encouraging stock ownership among its employees; more particularly, since 1942 it has made authorized but unissued common shares available to some of them. Between 1947 and 1951, the period covered by the record in this case, Ralston Purina sold nearly $2,000,000 of stock to employees without registration and in so doing made use of the mails.

In each of these years, a corporate resolution authorized the sale of common stock "to employees * * * who shall, without any solicitation by the Company or its officers or employees, inquire of any of them as to how to purchase common stock of Ralston Purina Company." A memorandum sent to branch and store managers after the resolution was adopted advised that "The only employees to whom this stock will be available will be those who take the initiative and are interested in buying stock at present market prices." Among those responding to these offers were employees with the duties of artist, bakeshop foreman, chow loading foreman, clerical assistant, copywriter, electrician, stock clerk, mill office clerk, order credit trainee, production trainee, stenographer, and veterinarian. The buyers lived in over fifty widely separated communities scattered from Garland, Texas, to Nashua, New Hampshire, and Visalia, California. The lowest salary bracket of those purchasing was $2,700 in 1949, $2,435 in 1950 and $3,107 in 1951. The record shows that in 1947, 243 employees bought stock, 20 in 1948, 414 in 1949, 411 in 1950, and the 1951 offer, interrupted by this litigation, produced 165 applications to purchase. No records were kept of those to whom the offers were made; the estimated number in 1951 was 500.

The company bottoms its exemption claim on the classification of all offerees as "key employees" in its organization. Its position on trial was that "A key employee * * * is not confined to an organization chart. It would include an individual who is eligible for promotion, an individual who especially influences others or who advises others, a person whom the employees look to in some special way, an individual, of course, who carries some special responsibility, who is sympathetic to management and who is ambitious and who the management feels is likely to be promoted to a greater responsibility." That an offering to all of its employees would be public is conceded.

The Securities Act nowhere defines the scope of § 4(1)'s private offering exemption. Nor is the legislative history of much help in staking out its boundaries. The problem was first dealt with in § 4(1) of the House Bill, which exempted "transactions by an issuer not with or through an underwriter * * *." The bill, as reported by the House Committee, added "and not involving any public offering." This was thought to be one of those transactions "where there is no practical need for [the bill's] application or where the public benefits are too remote." The exemption as thus delimited became law.

*   *   *

Decisions under comparable exemptions in the English Companies Acts and state "blue sky" laws, the statutory antecedents of federal securities legislation, have made one thing clear—to be public an offer need not be open to the whole world. In Securities and Exchange Comm'n v. Sunbeam Gold Mines Co., 95 F.2d 699 (C.A. 9th Cir. 1938), this point was made in dealing with an offering to the stockholders of two corporations about to be merged. Judge Denman observed that:

> "In its broadest meaning the term 'public' distinguishes the populace at large from groups of individual members of the public segregated because of some common interest or characteristic. Yet such a distinction is inadequate for practical purposes; manifestly, an offering of securities to all red-headed men, to all residents of Chicago or San Francisco, to all existing stockholders of the General Motors Corporation or the American Telephone & Telegraph Company, is no less 'public', in every realistic sense of the word, than an unrestricted offering to the world at large. Such an offering, though not open to everyone who may choose to apply, is nonetheless 'public' in character, for the means used to select the particular individuals to whom the offering is to be made bear no sensible relation to the purposes for which the selection is made. * * * To determine the distinction between 'public' and 'private' in any particular context, it is essential to examine the circumstances under which the distinction is sought to be established and to consider the purposes sought to be achieved by such distinction."

The courts below purported to apply this test. The District Court held, in the language of the *Sunbeam* decision, that "The purpose of the selection bears a 'sensible relation' to the class chosen," finding that "The sole purpose of the 'selection' is to keep part stock ownership of the business within the operating personnel of the business and to spread ownership throughout all departments and activities of the business." The Court of Appeals treated the case as involving "an offering, without solicitation, of common stock to a selected group of key employees of the issuer, most of whom are already stockholders when the offering is made, with the sole purpose of enabling them to secure a proprietary interest in the company or to increase the interest already held by them."

Exemption from the registration requirements of the Securities Act is the question. The design of the statute is to protect investors by promoting full disclosure of information thought necessary to informed investment decisions.[10] The natural way to interpret the private offering exemption is in light of the statutory purpose. Since exempt transactions are those as to which "there is no practical need for [the bill's] application," the applicability of § 4(1) should turn on whether the particular class of persons affected needs the protection of the Act. An offering to those who are shown to be able to fend for themselves is a transaction "not involving any public offering."

---

10. The words of the preamble are helpful: "An Act to provide full and fair disclosure of the character of securities sold in interstate and foreign commerce and through the mails, and to prevent frauds in the sale thereof, and for other purposes." 48 Stat. 74.

The Commission would have us go one step further and hold that "an offering to a substantial number of the public" is not exempt under § 4(1). We are advised that "whatever the special circumstances, the Commission has consistently interpreted the exemption as being inapplicable when a large number of offerees in involved." But the statute would seem to apply to a "public offering" whether to few or many.[11] It may well be that offerings to a substantial number of persons would rarely be exempt. Indeed nothing prevents the commission, in enforcing the statute, from using some kind of numerical test in deciding when to investigate particular exemption claims. But there is no warrant for superimposing a quantity limit on private offerings as a matter of statutory interpretation.

The exemption, as we construe it, does not deprive corporate employees, as a class, of the safeguards of the Act. We agree that some employee offerings may come within § 4(1), e. g., one made to executive personnel who because of their position have access to the same kind of information that the Act would make available in the form of a registration statement.[12] Absent such a showing of special circumstances, employees are just as much members of the investing "public" as any of their neighbors in the community. * * * "[T]he participants in employees' stock-investment plans may be in as great need of the protection afforded by availability of information concerning the issuer for which they work as are most other members of the public."

Keeping in mind the broadly remedial purposes of federal securities legislation, imposition of the burden of proof on an issuer who would plead the exemption seems to us fair and reasonable. Agreeing, the court below thought the burden met primarily because of the respondent's purpose in singling out its key employees for stock offerings. But once it is seen that the exemption question turns on the knowledge of the offerees, the issuer's motives, laudable though they may be, fade into irrelevance. The focus of inquiry should be on the need of the offerees for the protections afforded by registration. The employees here were not shown to have access to the kind of information which registration would disclose. The obvious opportunities for pressure and imposition make it advisable that they be entitled to compliance with § 5.

Reversed.

11. See Viscount Sumner's frequently quoted dictum in Nash v. Lynde: " 'The public' * * * is of course a general word. No particular numbers are prescribed. Anything from two to infinity may serve: perhaps even one, if he is intended to be the first of a series of subscribers, but makes further proceedings needless by himself subscribing the whole." [1929] A. C. 158, 169.

12. This was one of the factors stressed in an advisory opinion rendered by the Commission's General Counsel in 1935. "I also regard as significant the relationship between the issuer and the offerees. Thus, an offering to the members of a class who should have special knowledge of the issuer is less likely to be a public offering than is an offering to the members of a class of the same size who do not have this advantage. This factor would be particularly important in offerings to employees, where a class of high executive officers would have a special relationship to the issuer which subordinate employees would not enjoy." 11 Fed.Reg. 10952.

CASE 2—*Is the independent auditor liable even though he or she does not benefit from the inflated price of the security?*

DRAKE v. THOR POWER TOOL CO.

United States District Court, N.D. Illinois, E.D., 1967.
282 F.Supp. 94.

PARSONS, District Judge.

Plaintiff Drake complains that he purchased Thor stock through the facilities of the New York Stock Exchange at a time when the assets and profits of Defendant Thor were being fictitiously reported in its financial statements and thereupon promulgated to the public as well as to Thor's stockholders, and that when the true financial condition became known the price of Thor shares as then traded on the New York and Midwest Stock Exchanges dropped precipitously. Thor is charged with falsification of its inventory and sales figures and issuing financial statements reflecting such false figures. Peat, Marwick, Mitchell & Co., Thor's independent accounting firm, is charged with applying inappropriate accounting procedures with respect to the Thor audits and uttering untrue certifications of Thor's false financial statements. The cause is a class action on behalf of certain persons similar to plaintiff who had bought and subsequently sold their shares. * * *

A Rule 10b–5 claim is alleged as well [a claim] under § 18 * * * of the Securities Exchange Act of 1934 * * *

The Defendant, Peat, Marwick, has filed a motion to dismiss the action * * *.

Section 10(b) of the 1934 Act, provides:

It shall be unlawful for any person, directly or indirectly, by the use of any means or instrumentality of interstate commerce or of the mails, or of any facility of any national securities exchange—

(b) To use or employ in connection with the purchase or sale of any security registered on a national securities exchange or any security not so registered, any manipulative or deceptive device or contrivance in contravention of such rules and regulations as the Commission may prescribe as necessary or appropriate in the public interest or for the protection of investors.

Rule 10b–5 as promulgated by the Securities and Exchange Commission, provides:

It shall be unlawful for any person, directly or indirectly, by the use of any means or instrumentality of interstate commerce, or of the mails, or of any facility of any national securities exchange—

(a) To employ any device, scheme or artifice to defraud.

(b) To make any untrue statement of a material fact or to omit to state a material fact necessary in order to make the statement made, in the light of the circumstances under which they were made, not misleading, or

(c) To engage in any act, practice, or course of business which operates or would operate as a fraud or deceit upon any person, in connection with the purchase or sale of any security.

* * * The Federal securities legislation was designed to protect the investor, maintain integrity and honesty in the securities market, and curb "unnecessary, unwise, and destructive speculation." Where Congress expressly created civil liabilities to implement these policies, two aims predominated: to compensate the innocent investor who had lost money on falsely valued securities and to deter the proscribed practices by effective civil sanctions which complemented injunctive and criminal remedies. * * *

Neither congressional intent nor the statutory scheme will be distorted by granting the plaintiffs a remedy under Rule 10b–5. The Rule functions as a reservoir in an interstate economy with transactions occurring all over the country in situations where there simply would not be a remedy without it. Rule 10b–5 is particularly applicable to this case.

The defendant has argued that because the complaint states a cause of action which is assertable under Section 18 of the 1934 Act, plaintiff is precluded from asserting Section 10(b) and Rule 10b–5. This contention is disposed of by Judge Lord's decision in Miller v. Bargain City, U.S.A., 229 F.Supp. 33.

> * * * [I]t is true that the specific conduct alleged in the complaint would appear to amount to the type of fraud which is covered by Section 18. However, it is also true that the complaint alleges that defendants employed "a device, scheme, or artifice to defraud" and that they engaged in an "act, practice or course of business" which operated as a fraud or deceit. These allegations are certainly broad enough to permit evidence of conduct violative of Rule 10b–5. Discovery may reveal that plaintiffs have evidence of conduct that transcends the specific conduct embraced in Section 18.

Likewise, in the present case, though the complaint alleges conduct which would be covered by Section 18, the complaint also alleges that defendants' officers "devised a plan, scheme and artifice to artificially increase the assets, net worth and the net profit of Thor for the years 1961, 1962, 1963 and 1964." The complaint also alleges that Defendant Peat, Marwick "failed to exercise the proper or appropriate auditing procedures," which implies an allegation of negligence which may also transcend * * * Section 18.

> * * *

Section 10(b) and Rule 10b–5 are aimed at prohibiting fraudulent schemes in trading in securities and were designed in protecting both investors and the public interest. * * *

* * * The purpose of the financial statements is to inform the man on the street, and the underlying policy of the Securities and Exchange Acts and of Rule 10b–5 is to assure that he can have truthful information in buying securities. * * * [T]he defendants have set themselves up to be independent certified public auditors. As such, they have assumed a peculiar relationship with the investing public. * * *

Defendant Peat, Marwick, in independently auditing Thor's financial statement, remains liable regardless of whether it had benefited from the supposedly inflated market price. * * *

In Fischer et al. v. Kletz et al., 266 F.Supp. 180 (S.D.N.Y.1967), which also involved the Defendant Peat, Marwick in an allegation that it failed to disclose that financial statements which it certified contained false and misleading figures and that interim statements were false and misleading[,] Judge Tyler refused to dismiss a common law fraud allegation and also found the defendant liable under Rule 10b–5. The Court clearly placed no weight on the absence of any allegation of gain.

* * *

The Court denies Defendant's Motion to Dismiss.

PROBLEMS

1. Answer the following "True" or "False" and give reasons for your answers:

   (a) It is not necessary to use an underwriter in making a public offering of securities.

   (b) An issuer who receives a "bed-bug" letter in response to a registration statement filed with the SEC must either re-write the registration statement or forego the public offering.

   (c) Privately placed securities can never be resold.

   (d) The SEC is authorized to prosecute criminal cases involving violations of the federal securities laws.

   (e) The SEC may prohibit a public offering of securities even though full disclosure is made by the issuer of the securities.

   (f) The state may prohibit a public offering of securities even though full disclosure is made by the issuer of the securities.

   (g) In states having adopted the State Uniform Securities Act, the same anti-fraud provisions apply whether a transaction is interstate or wholly intrastate.

   (h) Like the federal Securities Act of 1933, the State Uniform Securities Act requires the use of a prospectus in every public offering of securities.

   (i) The federal Interstate Land Sales Full Disclosure Act is very similar in its requirements to the federal Securities Act of 1933.

   (j) A person who purchases or leases a subdivision lot covered by a statement of record or property report containing a misstatement of material fact may bring a civil action for damages against the developer.

   (k) All corporations, whatever their size, are subject to SEC registration and continuing disclosure requirements under the federal Securities Exchange Act of 1934.

   (l) Any broker's transaction that is executed upon an unsolicited customer's order to buy or sell securities is exempt from the registration requirements of the Securities Act of 1933.

2. Briefly define the following: The *Howey* test; "red herring" prospectus; "tombstone ads"; "lettered stock"; exchange; margin call; listed securities; over-the-counter market; "shingle theory"; "churning"; "scalping"; Special Reserve Bank Account for the Exclusive Benefit of Customers; registration by notification; registration by co-ordination; registration by qualification; statement of record; property report.

3. (a) Marx, Inc., a closely held corporation engaged in the manufacture of hospital supplies, is contemplating making a public offering of securities. What is a closely held corporation? And why might such a corporation decide to "go public"?

(b) Midas Marx owns 75% of the shares in the closely held Marx, Inc.; his brother Martin owns the remaining 25%. Martin Marx, his sister Molly, and his other brother Milton serve as directors of the corporation. Martin is also President of the corporation, Molly is Vice-President, and Milton is Secretary-Treasurer. The corporation decides to make a public offering of $10,000,000 of common stock in the corporation to residents in a three state area. Martin, acting on behalf of the corporation, prepares a registration statement (including a prospectus) covering the proposed securities offering and files it with the SEC. Although Martin knows that another company's new invention will soon render one of Marx's major products obsolete, he makes no mention of this fact in the registration statement. The statement nevertheless passes SEC scrutiny, and it becomes effective 20 days after filing. Molly Marx, who is being paid a $1,000 bonus over and above her regular salary for helping sell the securities, telephones Norma Carswell and persuades her to purchase $10,000 worth of stock. Norma, who will invest in anything, does not read the prospectus covering the securities, and does not take Marx' productline into consideration in making the purchase. When it becomes apparent that Marx omitted information concerning its productline from the registration statement, and the securities decline in value, Norma's attorney advises her to sue under the federal securities laws. Marx, however, contends that the SEC approved the statement, relieving Marx of any responsibility for omissions of fact. What are Norma's rights, if any, against Marx, Inc., Midas, Martin, Molly, and Milton Marx under Sections 11 and 12 of the federal Securities Act of 1933? Under Section 10(b) of the Securities Exchange Act of 1934? Explain fully, discussing the liability of each party separately.

(c) Assume the same facts as in (b) except that the offering is made only to residents of the state in which Marx, Inc. is incorporated and doing business, and the registration statement is filed with the state securities agency pursuant to the State Uniform Securities Act. Again, what are Norma's rights, if any against Marx, Inc., Midas, Martin, Molly, and Milton Marx under Sections 11 and 12 of the federal Securities Act of 1933? Under Section 10(b) of the Securities Exchange Act of 1934? Under the State Uniform Securities Act?

4. The partnership of Maxim & Rose, CPAs, has been engaged by their largest client, a limited partnership, to examine the financial statements in connection with the offering of 2,000 limited-partnership interests to the public at $5,000 per subscription. Under these circumstances, which of the following is true?

a. Maxim & Rose may disclaim any liability under the federal securities acts by an unambiguous, bold-faced disclaimer of liability on its audit report.

b. Under the Securities Act of 1933, Maxim & Rose has responsibility only for the financial statements as of the close of the fiscal year in question.

c. The dollar amount in question is sufficiently small so as to provide an exemption from the Securities Act of 1933.

d. The Securities Act of 1933 requires a registration despite the fact that the client is *not* selling stock or another traditional "security."

[# 6, November 1977 CPA Exam]

5. Under the Securities Act of 1933, subject to some exceptions and limitations, it is unlawful to use the mails or instruments of interstate commerce to sell or offer to sell a security to the public *unless*

a. A surety bond sufficient to cover potential liability to investors is obtained and filed with the Securities and Exchange Commission.

b. The offer is made through underwriters qualified to offer the securities on a nationwide basis.

c. A registration statement has been properly filed with the Securities and Exchange Commission, has been found to be acceptable, and is in effect.

d. The Securities and Exchange Commission approves of the financial merit of the offering.

[# 3, May 1977 CPA Exam]

6. Under which of the following circumstances is a public offering of securities exempt from the registration requirements of the Securities Act of 1933?

a. There was a prior registration within one year.

b. The corporation is a public utility subject to regulation by the Federal Power Commission.

c. The corporation was closely held prior to the offering.

d. The issuing corporation and all prospective security owners are located within one state, and the entire offering, sale, and distribution is made within that state.

[# 4, May 1977 CPA Exam]

7. An exemption from the full registration requirements under federal securities law is generally accorded those offerings by an issuer whose aggregate offering price during any twelve-month period

a. Does *not* exceed $90,000.

b. Does *not* exceed $300,000.

c. Does *not* exceed $1,500,000.

d. Does *not* exceed 10 percent of the value of the issuer's securities then outstanding.

[# 14, May 1975 CPA Exam as modified to reflect changes in the law.]

8. Issuer, Inc., a New York corporation engaged in retail sales within New York City, was interested in raising $2,500,000 in capital. In this connection it approached through personal letters eighty-eight people in New York, New Jersey, and Connecticut, and then followed up with face-to-face negotiations where it seemed promising to do so. After extensive efforts in which Issuer disclosed all the information that these people requested, nineteen people from these areas purchased Issuer's securities. Issuer did *not* limit its offers to insiders, their relatives, or wealthy or sophisticated investors. In regard to this securities issuance,

a. The offering is probably exempt from registration under federal securities law as a private placement.

b. The offering is probably exempt from registration under federal securities law as a small offering.

c. The offering is probably exempt from registration under federal securities law as an intrastate offering.

d. The offering probably is *not* exempt from registration under federal securities law.

[# 15, May 1975 CPA Exam as modified to reflect changes in the law.]

9. Mr. Jackson owns approximately 40% of the shares of common stock of Triad Corporation. The rest of the shares are widely distributed among over 2,000 shareholders. Jackson has had a number of personal problems related to other business ventures and would like to raise about $2,000,000 through the sale of some of his shares. He accordingly approached Underwood & Sons, an investment banking house in which he knew one of the principals, to purchase his Triad shares and distribute the shares to the public at a reasonable price through its offices in the United States. Any profit on the sales could be retained by Underwood pursuant to an agreement reached between Jackson and Underwood. In this situation

a. The securities to be sold probably do not need to be registered with the Securities and Exchange Commission.

b. Underwood & Sons probably is *not* an underwriter as defined in the federal securities law.

c. Jackson probably is considered the issuer under federal securities law.

d. Under federal securities law, *no* prospectus is required to be filed in connection with this contemplated transaction.

[# 16, May 1975 CPA Exam]

10. **Part a.** Your client, Lux Corporation, is a small food manufacturing company with a single plant located in its state of incorporation and has outstanding 200,000 shares of $10 par value common stock which is selling at about that price in infrequent sales. Lux desires to raise $500,000 of additional working capital and is considering the following alternatives:

1. Sale of $500,000 of a new issue of convertible debentures to Kelly, a sophisticated investor who formerly had been an executive of the Company. Kelly retired and now lives in a neighboring state.

2. Sale of $500,000 of additional common stock to local businessmen and other local investors.

3. Borrowing of $500,000 from a local bank on a nonnegotiable demand note.

Required: In separately numbered paragraphs discuss the impact of the registration requirements of the Securities Act of 1933 as it applies to each of the above alternatives.

Part b. Mekto Corporation's sole issue of stock is traded on a national exchange. In conducting the year-end examination of its financial statements, the auditor learned that Mekto's research department had perfected a manufacturing process which would have a very positive and material effect on future earnings. Mekto reported the new process as an asset at its nominal development cost and made no announcement of the development.

When a rumor about the new process started in late January, Mekto's president promptly telephoned financial papers in several states and announced that there was no substance to the rumor. A number of papers reported the president's denial of the rumor. Thereafter Mekto's stock traded in its normal narrow range. In February, relying on the information reported in the financial press, Howard sold a large block of his Mekto stock at the current market price.

Mekto's president made a public announcement about the perfection of the new process the following June. The announcement precipitated a dramatic increase in both the price and volume of trading of Mekto's stock. Neither Mekto nor any person with knowledge of the process engaged in trading Mekto's stock prior to the public announcement of the discovery.

Required: Discuss Howard's rights against Mekto and its president under federal securities law.

[# 5.b. & c., May 1974 CPA Exam]

Chapter 25

ANTITRUST AND LABOR LAW

Introduction

In the late 1800's, the social theory of "laissez-faire" prevailed in the United States. The basic rule of "laissez-faire" was that people are best served by letting them go about their business with as little government interference as possible. In a free market, laissez-faire theorists insisted, individuals can pursue their own self-interests, and unfettered competition will maintain prices and wages at the proper levels. In the case of prices, firms will compete for the consumer's dollar; and, as to wages, workers will compete for jobs, and bargain individually with employers to obtain the best working conditions possible. Laissez-faire, however, did not and could not work. Neither competition nor individual bargaining can produce the desired results where the parties are not even close to being evenly matched. If a very large firm competes with a very small one, for example, the small firm will end up going under, and competition will be effectively eliminated. And if the large firm bargains individually with its workers, it is in a position to dictate terms of employment, and will frequently do so to the detriment of the employees. By the late 1800's, it had become increasingly clear that government regulation was necessary both for purposes of maintaining competition and for protecting the rights of unorganized employees. Beginning with the Sherman Act in 1890, many laws have been enacted to accomplish these objectives.

This chapter will deal, first, with the antitrust laws that are designed to outlaw or control business practices tending to restrain trade and impair free competition. And, second, it will deal with labor law—the laws designed to protect the rights of employees to self-organize and bargain collectively with their employers.

Antitrust and labor law are of interest to all people whether they are business people, consumers, employers, or employees. Antitrust law is designed to insure competition in business. Competition means better consumer products at lower prices. Antitrust law achieves its goal by prohibiting anti-competitive business practices and unfair methods of competition.

Labor law, on the other hand, is designed to keep the peace between workers and management—i. e., between employers and their employees. Business people and employees alike need to know about the rights of employees to organize and bargain collectively.

Antitrust and labor law are treated together here, because, historically, they were closely tied together. Let us begin our study by looking back to post Civil War America.

What was business like in post Civil War America?

After the Civil War ended in 1865, and until 1914, the American economy underwent a period of rapid industrialization. Hundreds of new corporations emerged during this time—corporations larger than ever before; and "industrial empires" flourished under the control of a few powerful people. As these industrial giants gained monopolistic control of the marketplace, they began to charge the public more while, at the same time, giving the public less. Public dissatisfaction soon turned to outrage as the "giants" used unfair methods to force their smaller competitors out of business. Frequently, for example, they cut prices to such an extent that the small competitors simply could not afford to stay in business. But once the competition was gone, prices would skyrocket. Farmers, too, found much to complain about in the way the "giants" ran business. The role of agriculture had greatly diminished throughout the country. With lower prices for their crops, and higher costs for the manufactured goods and railroad services they so desperately needed, the farmers began to organize and make demands upon the industrial "giants".

The individual worker, however, found that he or she had little or no ability to bargain with the "giant": the personal relationship that had once existed between employer and employee had come to an end with industrialization. At the same time, the Western Frontier disappeared and thousands of workers began to migrate to the cities where they became more and more dependent on wages for survival. Unskilled European immigrants also came into the country in droves and began to flood the labor market.

The net result was that "big" business —really big business—had everything going for it at the expense of the two groups making up the bulk of the population—the consumers and the workers. These groups suffered low wages and high prices all because of monopoly—the elimination of effective competition.

The common law (unwritten law) was completely ineffective in dealing with the competitive abuses crying out for reform. While the common law outlawed certain combinations between companies or corporations and thus rendered them unenforceable (the companies could not force each other to combine by going to court after entering into such an agreement— theirs would be an illegal bargain, and they would be left in pari delicto—i. e., "in equal fault" and without remedy), it did not provide an absolute prohibition against unfair competition that could be enforced by both government and private parties. Statutory laws—acts of Congress —were urgently needed.

Was the Sherman Antitrust Act, passed in 1890, initially effective in curbing the abuses of big business?

Under strong public pressure to curtail business abuses, Congress passed the Sherman Antitrust Act in 1890. This Act is still in effect today, and, along with a few other statutes, it forms our basic antitrust law. Although the Sherman Act was designed to outlaw certain types of big business conduct (notably monopolies and monopolizing), big business wielded great power; and, as unbelievable as it may seem, the Act was first used not against big business, but against organized labor. How did this come about?

Well, in 1880, both workers and farmers joined in the first effort to organize against the abuses of the new industrial society. Their organization was called the Knights of Labor, and it included workers from almost every kind of occupation—skilled and unskilled laborers, farmers, and even small business people. Membership in the Knights had grown to 700,000 by 1886 only to break down and almost disappear by 1890: the alliance between groups as diverse as workers and farmers simply could not hold together. In 1886, skilled workers formed the American Federation of Labor and elected the renowned Samuel Gompers as the organization's first president. Gompers led the AFL for the next 40 years and greatly influenced the development of labor unions in this country. The AFL was composed of national craft unions, and by 1914 had more than 2,000,000 members concentrated in skilled trades and a few industries.

During the 1880's, business went to court to get injunctions against labor union activity—and business usually won. In the case of Vegelahn v. Guntner, 167 Mass. 92, 44 N.E. 1077 (1896), for example, the court agreed with management that employee picketing had to be stopped, for "no one can lawfully prevent employers or persons wishing to be employed from the exercise of their rights." And courts throughout the country repeatedly insisted that employers had the right to "be free of molestation".

After passage of the Sherman Act in 1890, it was not difficult to convince an already biased court system that unions posed a greater threat than did big business. In 1893, for example, the American Railway Union was organized under the leadership of Eugene Debs. The purpose of the Union was to organize railroad industry employees. When the Pullman Palace Car Company refused to negotiate with the Union, many employees walked off the job, and much violence and damage resulted. Finally, a Sherman Act injunction was obtained against the Union, and Debs and others were jailed for failing to obey it. The court held that the Sherman Act language prohibiting "combinations or conspiracies in restraint of trade", applied to labor union as well as business activities. This was in 1894.

During the next 20 years, up until 1914, the Sherman Act was used as a strike-breaking weapon against the labor union. And in the "Danbury Hatters" case (Loewe v. Lawlor, 208 U.S. 274, 28 S.Ct. 301, 52 L.Ed. 488 (1908)), the United States Supreme Court seemed to say that trade unions themselves were illegal under the Sherman Act.

What happened in 1914?

When Congress passed the Sherman Act in 1890, it did not intend to use the Act against labor unions. What it did intend was to curb the abuses of big business. But the courts interpreted the Sherman Act so that not only was it not used to curb big business abuses, but it was used to prevent effective labor union organization. By 1914, Congress was clearly unhappy with these results. And the public was furious! Two acts were passed to make it clear that big business unfair competition had to stop, and that antitrust laws were not to be used against labor organizations. These acts were the Clayton Act and the Federal Trade Commission Act (presented in detail later in this chapter).

The Clayton Act is often called "labor's Magna Carta" because of two sections of the Act which apply specifically to labor organizations:

Section 6 provides that antitrust laws are not to be interpreted so as to prohibit the existence of labor organizations from "lawfully carrying out the legitimate objects thereof." This Section effectively exempts labor unions and agricultural organizations from the Sherman and Clayton Acts.

Section 20 specifically prohibits the use of injunctions by the federal courts in any case between an employer and employees, or between employers or employees involving a dispute over terms and conditions of employment.

Union membership rose sharply after passage of the Clayton Act. Today, union members number in the millions. As you can see, the antitrust laws and labor's first efforts to organize were closely tied together from post Civil War times up until the passage of the Clayton Act in 1914. Since that time, however, antitrust laws have generally been used to curb anti-competitive behavior on the part of business. And labor law has gone its own way with other federal statutes. Because of this, we will now consider antitrust and labor law independently of each other in the text sections that follow.

A. ANTITRUST LAW

What is the purpose of antitrust law?

Antitrust law is founded on three basic statutes: the Sherman Act, the Clayton Act, and the Federal Trade Commission Act.

The Sherman Act makes unlawful "every contract, combination or conspiracy *in restraint of trade* in interstate or foreign commerce". It also prohibits monopolizing and attempts to monopolize. Violators of the Act are subject to fine or imprisonment, or both. And any property in transit in interstate commerce which is subject to any contract or conspiracy violative of the Act is subject to forfeiture to the United States. The Sherman Act empowers the federal district courts to issue injunctions restraining violations. And it provides that anyone who is injured by a violation of the Act may sue in a civil action and recover treble damages (i. e., three times the amount of the actual loss sustained).

More specific is the Clayton Act which prohibits certain practices *if the effect of the practices might be to substantially lessen competition.* Price discrimination, mergers and consolidations, "tie-in" sales, and exclusive dealing arrangements are all prohibited where they are found to be anti-competitive in nature (see the following section).

The Federal Trade Commission Act (passed in 1914 at the same time as the Clayton Act) created the Federal Trade Commission. This administrative agency is broadly authorized to enforce the antitrust laws, including both the Sherman and Clayton Acts.[1] In addition, the FTC may, on its own, identify and restrain any anti-competitive business or corporate conduct. The Commission initiates enforcement proceedings by serving a complaint on the alleged violator. If the FTC finds a violation of the antitrust laws, it issues a "cease and desist order" which becomes final unless the defendant seeks judicial review.

What specific practices fall within the meaning of unfair competition?

"Unfair competition" includes, but is not limited to, the following:

(1) *Monopolizing.* Probably all of you have played the game of "Monopoly" where your goal was to gain control of the most property and drive your competitors out of business. However, the kinds of "ruthless tactics" that enabled you to win the game would not be permitted in real life—the government would not let you get away with them. Monopoly power is defined as the power to control prices or exclude competitors in a particular market. But unless the monopolist deliberately and purposefully exercises his or her monopoly power to acquire or maintain the market, there is no "unfair competition" in the sense of an antitrust violation. Innocent or natural monopolies are not illegal (e. g., a small town newspaper where the town market can support only one paper; a professional basketball team in a city where there are insufficient sports fans to support more than one team; or a manufacturer who alone possesses the particular facilities required to supply a market).

(2) *Attempts to monopolize.* The U.S. Supreme Court has defined "attempt to monopolize" as "the employment of methods, means, and practices which would, if successful, accomplish monopolization." An attempt is illegal, however, only where it involves "unfair conduct" and not merely good business know-how. Sometimes, for example, a really good competitor can eliminate his

---

1. The Justice Department also enforces antitrust law independently of the Federal Trade Commission.

or her competition without doing anything unfair, and there is certainly nothing wrong with this. But a business person who tries to induce others to boycott his or her competitors, or who uses discriminatory pricing in an effort to drive the competitors out of business, is guilty of unfair conduct—of an attempt to monopolize. He or she may be enjoined by a court of equity, criminally prosecuted, or sued in a civil action for treble damages.

(3) *Collaboration among competitors —horizontal restraints of trade.* Competitors in the same industry who get together and agree to eliminate or lessen the competition between or among themselves are said to create a horizontal restraint of trade. For example, if Ford, General Motors, and Chrysler collaborate (get together and agree) to fix auto prices, or to divide up the U.S. market for cars, they are creating a horizontal restraint of trade since all compete directly in the auto market. Horizontal restraints of trade may take any of the following forms:

(a) *Price fixing among competitors.* The U.S. Supreme Court has stated that any combination or agreement between competitors, formed for the purpose of raising, depressing, fixing, pegging, or stabilizing the price of a commodity in interstate or foreign commerce is illegal per se (i. e., illegal without regard to its effect on competition). Thus it is no defense that the price fixed was a "reasonable" price: "price fixing" among competitors is simply illegal under antitrust law.

(b) *Division of markets.* Any agreement among businesses performing similar services or dealing in similar products to divide up and share the available market is also illegal per se. And, just as with price fixing, no justifications or defenses are allowed.

(c) *Group boycotts.* People are generally free to refuse to deal with others —except where their actions constitute "unfair competition". Any agreement among a group of competitors not to deal with a person or firm outside the group is an unlawful group boycott. And a group boycott, like price-fixing and division of markets, is illegal per se.

(d) *Exchange of information among competitors on prices, costs, production, inventories, etc.* An agreement to fix prices, divide markets, or boycott certain goods may be inferred from an exchange of information among competitors. In the case of American Column and Lumber Co. v. United States, 257 U.S. 377, 42 S.Ct. 114, 66 L.Ed. 284 (1921), for example, the Court held unlawful an exchange of product, inventory, and current price list information among 365 hardwood manufacturers who controlled one-third of the market. The Court's decision was influenced by the fact that, after the exchange, prices among the group members increased substantially.

(4) *Vertical restraints.* Unlike a horizontal restraint of trade which involves anti-competitive agreements within the same level of industry, a vertical restraint refers to anti-competitive dealings on different levels. For example, before a car is sold to a consumer:

(1) The iron ore is mined;

(2) The ore is refined into steel ingots;

(3) The ingots are processed into sheets of steel;

(4) The steel, along with fabrics, paints, etc., is manufactured into an automobile;

(5) The auto is distributed to a dealer; and

(6) The dealer holds the auto for sale.

None of these processes directly compete on a horizontal level. Rather, the relationships are "vertical"—on different levels of industry—and some vertical restraints of trade are illegal.

(a) *Resale price maintenance by sellers.* It is a per se violation of antitrust law for a seller (e. g., a manufacturer) to set by contract the price at which the buyer (e. g., the retailer) can resell his or her product. "State Fair Trade Laws" used to exempt from illegality resale price maintenance agreements as to commodities which: (1) bore the trademark, brand, or name of the producer or distributor; and (2) were in free and open competition with other commodities of the same general class. These laws went so far as to say that any seller who knew about such an agreement was bound by it—whether or not he or she signed it! However, in 1975, the federal Congress disallowed State Fair Trade Laws, and such contracts are now illegal. Congress has made it clear that buyers must remain free to resell at prices *they* set based on the competitive conditions of the retail market.

(b) *Customer and territorial restrictions.* Formerly, the U.S. Supreme Court held that it was a per se antitrust violation for a manufacturer to impose territorial and customer restrictions upon dealers (e. g., a manufacturer could not require dealers to resell his or her products only to customers residing within a certain geographical area). However, the U.S. Supreme Court has overruled its earlier decisions, and now holds that such territorial and customer restrictions violate antitrust law only if their effect might be to unreasonably restrain trade.

(c) *Tying agreements.* In a tying agreement, a seller refuses to sell one of his or her products (the "tying" product) to a customer unless the customer agrees to buy a second product (the "tied" product) as well. Tying agreements are illegal per se under the Clayton Act. Thus it is a violation of antitrust law for a computer manufacturer to "tie" the use of its computer cards to the purchase of its computers.

(5) *Mergers and Consolidations.* Any merger or consolidation (horizontal or vertical) the effect of which might be to substantially lessen competition is illegal. For example, a merger which results in a firm controlling an undue percentage share of the market is likely to substantially lessen competition and is thus subject to an unjunction.

The above list of anti-competitive behavior is not exclusive. Remember, the Federal Trade Commission may find that certain conduct is an unfair method of competition even though it violates neither the letter nor the spirit of existing antitrust laws. And once the Commission identifies the new anti-competitive behavior, it may issue a cease and desist order against it. Of course, Federal Trade Commission decisions are always subject to judicial review by the U.S. Circuit Courts of Appeal.

What is the Robinson-Patman Act?

The Robinson-Patman Act was passed by Congress in 1936 as an amendment to the Clayton Act; it is properly thought of as part of the Clayton Act. Robinson-Patman specifically outlaws certain activities by buyers and sellers. With regard to sellers, the Act makes it unlawful for any seller engaged in commerce to *directly* or *indirectly* discriminate in prices charged to purchasers on the sale of commodities of like grade and quality where the effect *may be* to injure, destroy, or prevent competition. Prior to passage of Robinson-Patman, the Clayton Act had already outlawed price discrimination intended to drive *direct* competitors out of the market—i. e., price discrimination designed to do what is called "primary line" injury. Thus, it was unlawful under the original Clayton Act for large nationwide firms to engage in local price cutting in an effort to injure smaller local competitors or force them out of the market. But it was unclear whether the original Clayton Act covered what is called "secondary line" injury—i. e., competition at the buyer's level. Secondary line injury occurs where one buyer is given a more favorable price than his or her competitors. For example, for a manufacturer to give a better price to chain stores than to the chain stores' small store competitors is price discrimination at the secondary level. The Robinson-Patman Act outlaws this kind of discrimination.

Unlawful secondary line discrimination results because a customer who receives a better price is able to resell at a lower price than his or her competitors. For example, in FTC v. Morton Salt Co., 334 U.S. 37, 68 S.Ct. 822, 92 L.Ed. 1196 (1948), it was held that even though salt represents a very small portion of a retail grocer's business, the effect of selling salt at a reduced price to a favored buyer was to allow that grocer to divert business and cause competitive injury.

And even if a favored buyer does not sell at a lower price than his or her competitors, it may still be unlawful because the favored party may have lower manufacturing costs than his or her competitors and thus achieve a higher profit—again with the result that competition is injured.

The Robinson-Patman Act also provides that a seller who provides or pays for advertising (e. g., handbills, window and floor displays, demonstrations, and the like) must do so through a plan under which all buyers are notified and can receive a payment or service proportional to their purchases. In other words, a seller who offers advertising services for his or her products must offer them to all buyers on proportionally equal terms (i. e., on terms based on the buyers' relative volume of purchases and the relative amount of sales of the seller's products). To do otherwise is a per se violation of the Robinson-Patman Act—no showing of adverse competitive effect is required.

With regard to buyers, the Robinson-Patman Act makes it per se unlawful for a buyer to exact price concessions in the form of brokerage commissions either personally or through an agent. This is unlawful regardless of its effect on competition.

There are two important defenses to Robinson-Patman violations:

(1) *Justification based on cost.* There is no violation of Robinson-Patman if prices are different because costs are different. The Act states that "differentials which make only due allowance for differences in the cost of manufacture, sale, or delivery resulting from the differing methods or quantities" in which commodities are sold or delivered do not result in illegal price discrimination. Rather, the differences are *functional discounts.* Some purchasers may have special needs requiring special manufacture and justifying additional costs. And others may merit a higher charge because of higher freight and delivery costs (e. g., a buyer who receives large quantities in carload lots).

However, the defense based on difference in costs applies only to the price discrimination portion of Robinson-Patman. It is no defense to the granting of a brokerage payment or to discriminatory payments for advertising or to discriminatory promotional services.

(2) *Justification based on meeting competition.* It is a complete defense to a charge of price discrimination or of furnishing unequal advertising or promotional payments or services that the action was taken to meet a competitor's equally low price or to match a competitor's advertising or promotional services or facilities (however, it is no defense to a charge of providing brokerage payments).

The defense is available even though the price charge is somewhat lower than the competitor's so long as it is shown that the price was set based on a reasonable belief that it was required to meet the competitor's price. This is because competitors may not be able to determine all the information needed to come up with identical prices. And if they exchange information to do so, the exchange itself may be a violation of the Sherman Act.

One final note about Robinson-Patman. The Statute specifically applies to both buyers and sellers. Section 2(f) of the Clayton Act, as amended by Robinson-Patman, makes it unlawful for a buyer "knowingly to induce or receive a discrimination in price which is prohibited * * *." Section 2(c) specifically provides that it is unlawful "to receive or accept" as well as "to pay or grant" brokerage commissions as price concessions. A violation of Robinson-Patman, like any other Clayton Act violation, may result in fine, imprisonment, or both for the offender, and treble damages for the injured party or parties.

B. LABOR LAW

What is labor law?

Labor law is designed to control and govern the continuous process by which workers and management decide the terms and conditions of employment. It is based almost entirely on federal statutes passed by Congress during the last 45 years. The idea behind labor law is to keep peace between workers and management through the process known as *collective bargaining*—i. e., the settlement of industrial disputes through peaceful negotiation between employers and employee representatives. Successful collective bargaining requires two things: (1) self-organization of employees; and (2) equal bargaining power between workers and management. Labor law encourages and promotes these goals by placing statutory limitations on employer interference with the right of employees to self-organize and bargain collectively. And, because unions, too, may abuse their power, labor law also acts to curb and control certain union activities.

What federal statutes make up our "labor law"?

Labor law is presently based on four statutes:

(1) The Norris-LaGuardia Act of 1932;

(2) The National-Labor Relations (or Wagner) Act of 1935;

(3) The Labor Management Relations (or Taft-Hartley) Act of 1947; and

(4) The Labor-Management Reporting and Disclosure (or Landrum-Griffin) Act of 1959.

The Norris-LaGuardia Act declares that the worker "though he should be free to decline to associate with his fellows must have full freedom of association, self-organization, and designation of representatives of his own choosing, to negotiate the terms and conditions of his employment; and must be free from the interference, restraint, or coercion of employers of labor in these activities." The Norris-LaGuardia Act thus promotes union organization and collective bargaining: it permits unions to exert effective economic pressure against employers.

The National Labor Relations Act of 1935 guarantees employees the right (1) to form, join, or assist labor organizations; (2) to bargain collectively with the employer; and (3) to engage in concerted activity for the purpose of collective bargaining or mutual aid and protection. The National Labor Relations Act is the heart of labor law. Just twelve years after its passage in 1935, union membership had increased from 3 million to 15 million employees.

After World War II came to an end, unions began to strike on a nationwide basis in some of our most important industries, including coal mining, oil refining, lumber, rail, auto, etc. The strikes were designed to force employers into making great concessions at a time when almost every kind of product was in very short supply. This was a poor time for employees to take their employers to task. The War was over. Americans had been waiting patiently to start living again—to be able to buy the many things they had done so long without. When organized labor used strikes to force higher wages and other concessions at this peak of consumer demand, the general public turned with fury on the unions. They blamed the unions and they blamed the strikes for delays in the production of consumer goods. Growing sentiment arose to prohibit, or, at least, restrict certain union activities. Congress responded with the third major part of our labor legislation —the Taft-Hartley Act of 1947.

The Taft-Hartley Act enables the government to combat union "unfair labor practices" and to intervene in strikes that threaten the national welfare. The Federal Mediation and Conciliation Service, created by the Act to assist in labor disputes, must be notified by labor and/or management anytime either party desires to make a change in the terms or conditions of employment as previously fixed by a collective bargaining agreement.

Taft-Hartley also authorizes the president to intervene in labor disputes by appointing a Board of Inquiry to investigate and report on the issues involved. If the president concludes from the report that the national health, welfare, or security of the country is threatened, he may ask a federal district court to issue an 80 day injunction against the strike or work stoppage. Where granted, the injunction will dissolve after the 80 days, and the strike may thereafter continue.

Taft-Hartley additionally outlaws the *closed shop*. In a closed shop, union membership is a condition of employment—that is, membership is required before hiring. Membership in a *union shop* is also compulsory, but only *after* employment. And union shop arrangements are legal so long as there is a 30 day "grace" period after hiring before membership is required. Thus a collective bargaining agreement between labor and management may require new employees, as a condition of their employment, to join the union "on or after" the 30th day of employment. But it cannot require them to join the union before they are hired.

During the 1950's, the Senate investigated a number of unions on charges of corruption, unethical behavior, and a lack of democratic procedures. The result of the investigation was the Landrum-Griffin Act passed in 1959 to protect the rights and interests of individual workers as well as of the public from infringement by powerful union leaders. Landrum-Griffin makes specific election procedures mandatory for unions; and it requires substantial disclosures by labor unions and their officers. The Act also provides penalties for fraud or corruption or misuse of union funds.

What are the goals of labor law?

The goals of labor law are four:

(1) Industrial peace—continued production uninterrupted by strikes and lockouts.

(2) Collective bargaining—the settlement of industrial disputes through peaceful negotiations between employers and employee representatives. Where collective bargaining proves ineffective to settle a dispute, other methods of settlement, including conciliation and mediation through the Federal Mediation and Conciliation Service, and waiting or "cooling off" periods should be attempted.

(3) Self-organization of employees—self-organization accomplished free from employer interference and union coercion.

(4) Quick settlement of disputes that imperil the national health or safety.

With these four goals in mind, let us consider some of the specific problems that arise in labor-management relations.

How do federal labor law statutes protect employees?

Protection of the right of employees to band together to form unions and to bargain collectively is the underlying purpose of the National Labor Relations Act. The job of implementing this protection is given to the National Labor Relations Board along with its general counsel (made up of a great many lawyers) and its numerous field agents. The Board itself is composed of five members, each appointed by the president of the United States (with Senate approval) to serve for a term of five years. The two major functions of the Board are (1) to determine employee representation for industries, and (2) to decide whether certain challenged actions are unfair labor practices.

Representation cases refer to the actual decision as to which union is representing the workers. The law states that the employer must bargain collectively when asked to do so by his or her workers' designated representative. The workers must select this representative by secret ballot in an election administered by the National Labor Relations Board. Before an election can be held, the Board must first determine the appropriate bargaining unit—that is, which group of employees makes up the union. Similarity of skills is generally the most important factor here, since it usually reflects a similarity of problems and interests among the employees. The law specifically prohibits the Board, however, from placing professional employees with nonprofes-

sionals, and from placing plant guards (who enforce security rules) with other employees. After the Board determines who belongs in the bargaining unit, it will direct an election in which the employees pick the union they want to represent them. Administration of the election is delegated by the Board to its field agents and regional directors. Once the regional director certifies the results, his or her decision is final unless a party seeks review by the full National Labor Relations Board.

In "unfair labor practice" cases, the Board's authority is more formally exercised. A trial or hearing examiner conducts a hearing on the issues involved and enters a report with recommended findings and suggested remedies. If neither party objects to the report, it becomes the decision of the Board. Where objections are filed, the Board assumes complete control over the case, reviews the record, and makes its own determination. A party who objects to the Board's decision may appeal his or her case to the U.S. Court of Appeals.

If the National Labor Relations Board believes that an injunction is necessary to put an end to the unfair labor practice, it will go to the federal district court and allege: (1) the filing of an unfair labor practice charge; (2) the issuance of a complaint on the charge; (3) the facts supporting the charge; and (4) the likelihood that the unfair practice will continue unless an injunction is issued to restrain it. If the court agrees with the Board, the injunction will issue.

What are some unfair labor practices?

(1) *Employer questioning of employees and related problems.* It is not an unfair labor practice for an employer to merely question an employee about his or her union activities. But if the employer uses spies or informers to obtain such information, he or she does run foul of the law. And while an employer can

make and enforce rules that prevent an employee from distributing union literature or soliciting union membership during the employee's working hours, or in areas where work is being performed, the employer cannot ban such activities altogether. The employee's right to pursue union activities during his or her nonwork hours and in nonwork areas must be recognized.

Suppose an employer releases anti-union literature containing false statements. The release, in itself, is not an unfair labor practice; but the Board will set aside an election in which the release or other propaganda has made it impossible for the employees to reach a free and fair decision on the issues or candidates.

(2) *Union coercion of employees.* Unions, too, must respect the rights of employees. Section 8(b) of the National Labor Relations Act prohibits a union from restraining or otherwise coercing employees in the exercise of their right to self-organize. In one case, for example, a union representative trying to organize workers stated that "those who do not join the union will lose their jobs," and that "we have ways of dealing with people like you guys." The representative's statements were found to be unfair labor practices.

Section 8(b)(1)(A) of the NLRA also prohibits unions or their agents from threatening employees with physical harm, or committing actual violence upon them for refusal to cooperate with union directives. The Section applies to any threat of bodily harm, and even to destruction of company property by a union agent (on the theory that the destruction constitutes an implied threat of physical violence to the employees). And although peaceful picketing does not amount to coercion for purposes of the Act, mass picketing calculated to deter nonstrikers from working does violate the Section as does the blocking of plant entrances and exists.

(3) *Employer or union discrimination.* It is illegal for either employers or unions to use discrimination as a means of denying employees their rights to self-organize. Thus, an employer may not legally hire or fire an employee on the basis of his or her membership, or lack of membership, in a labor union. Nor may an employer discharge, lay off, transfer, or otherwise change terms of employment in order to encourage or discourage union membership. It is also unlawful for a union to cause or attempt to cause an employer to discriminate against an employee.

In summary, the National Labor Relations Act provides that it is an unfair labor practice to do the following:

Employers:

To—

(1) Interfere with, restrain, or coerce employees in the exercise of their rights to form, join, or assist unions, or to bargain collectively, or to act in any concerted fashion for their mutual aid or protection; or to interfere, restrain, or coerce employees who choose to refrain from any such union activities.

(2) Dominate or interfere with the formation or administration of any labor organization, or to contribute financial or other support to it.

(3) Discriminate in hiring, in granting tenure, or regarding any other condition of employment in order to encourage or discourage union membership (but remember, the "union shop" is an exception to this rule).

(4) Discriminate against any employee because he or she has filed charges or given testimony under the Act (such as by firing the employee or discriminating against him or her with respect to pay or promotion).

(5) Refuse to bargain with a labor organization that represents a majority of the employees in the bargaining unit.

Unions:

To—

(1) Restrain or coerce employees in their right to join or to refuse to join a union.

(2) Restrain or otherwise coerce an employer in his or her selection of a collective bargaining representative who will arbitrate or adjust grievances on behalf of the company.

(3) Cause or attempt to cause an employer to discriminate against an employee in violation of the rule that an employer shall not discriminate in order to encourage or discourage union membership.

(4) Refuse to bargain collectively in good faith with an employer.

(5) Strike or terminate a contract without giving notice to the employer and to the Federal Mediation and Conciliation Service.

What is the law on collective bargaining?

A union that is duly elected by a majority of employees has exclusive authority to represent all employees on matters properly the subject of collective bargaining. The employer must bargain directly with the certified union—he or she may not negotiate individual contracts with his or her employees. The employees, too, are bound by the union election and must thereafter deal with their employer through their elected union representatives. Because unions are not infallible and may abuse their power, the law provides that the union has a duty to bargain fairly on behalf of all employees (including nonunion members). Failure to do so constitutes an unfair labor practice.

It is also an unfair labor practice for employers or unions to refuse to bargain at all, or to refuse to bargain "in good faith". Each side must make a sincere effort to reach an agreement, and must actively participate in negotiations to that

end. An employer who has a "take it or leave it" attitude or offers terms that no responsible employee representative could accept is not bargaining in good faith.

What are the three subjects of collective bargaining?

The National Labor Relations Act divides collective bargaining into three subject matter areas:

(1) *Compulsory subjects.* These are areas where bargaining is required by statute. NLRA Section 8(d) requires employers and unions to bargain collectively on "wages, hours, and other terms and conditions of employment, or the negotiation of an agreement or any question arising thereunder." Retirement plan benefits fall within the meaning of "wages, rates of pay, hours of employment or other conditions of employment" and are thus the proper subject of compulsory collective bargaining.

(2) *Permissive subjects.* These are subjects that fall within the discretion of the employer and the union who may choose whether or not to bargain about them. Subjects such as corporate structure, general business practice, and plant location, for example, may be the subject of collective bargaining, but they don't have to be.

(3) *Illegal subjects.* These are areas forbidden to the employer and union who cannot bargain here because it would be illegal to do so (e. g., an attempt to bargain about a "closed shop" as outlawed by the Taft-Hartley Act).

How can a collective bargaining agreement be changed or terminated?

Suppose the employer or the union wants to change or terminate a collective bargaining agreement. The party desiring the change must do the following:

(1) Notify the other party in writing of his or her desire to make the change at least 60 days prior to the expiration date of the contract;

(2) Offer to meet and confer with the other party for the purpose of negotiating a new or altered contract;

(3) Notify the appropriate federal and state mediation agencies within 30 days of the first notice, unless an agreement has been reached by that time;

(4) Continue in full force and effect, without resorting to strike or lockout, all the terms and conditions of the existing contract for the period of 60 days after the first notice is given, or until the expiration date of the contract, whichever occurs later.

How are collective bargaining agreements enforced?

Under the Taft-Hartley Act, a union may sue or be sued on behalf of the employees it represents. Thus either party (employer or union) may sue the other for breach of the collective bargaining agreement. The suit may be brought in any federal district court having jurisdiction over the parties, regardless of diversity of citizenship or federal jurisdictional amount.

What is the law on strikes and picketing?

The National Labor Relations Act guarantees employees the right to strike and picket. The Act further provides that strikers retain their status as "employees" even while on strike. Of course, the employees can always agree with their employer not to strike as part of a collective bargaining agreement.

Still, a strike or boycott is illegal if its objective is to enforce what would amount to an unfair labor practice (e. g., a strike to force the employer to discriminate against employees on the basis of race).

And under the NLRA, the following strikes are also illegal:

(1) *Violent strikes.* Strikes that are violent in nature receive no protection under the law. Sitdown strikes, where workers occupy the employer's premises and refuse to work, are also illegal. And strikers found guilty of violence in connection with a strike may be discharged.

(2) *Strikes occurring prior to expiration of the 60 day cooling off period.* The NLRA makes it unlawful for a union to strike to terminate or change a collective bargaining agreement without first giving the employer 60 days notice thereof and offering to negotiate a new contract. The reason for the notice requirement is to create a "cooling off" period during which time tempers may "cool" and a drastic strike may be averted. Where the contract is for a fixed term, the union cannot strike prior to the contract termination date; and it may strike then only if the 60 days notice requirement has been met.

(3) *Partial strikes.* Employees may either continue to work and negotiate or they can strike; but they cannot remain on the job and occasionally disrupt or shut down the employer's operations.

(4) *Strikes undertaken to force employers to make other nonunion employees join the union.*

(5) *Strikes undertaken to force an employer to pay for unnecessary services.* Called "featherbedding", this is the practice of forcing employers to hire or retain more workers than the employer needs to operate his or her business.

Can an employer hire replacements during a strike and refuse to take the strikers back after the strike is over?

It is an unfair labor practice under the NLRA for an employer to interfere with his or her employees' right to strike. Obviously, workers would be reluctant to strike if they thought they might lose their jobs as a result. Yet, on the other side of the coin, the employer has a legitimate right and interest in keeping his or her business operating when his or her workers walk off the job. Certainly, it is not unreasonable for the employer to hire other employees to work in place of the strikers. But what happens when the strike is over, and the strikers desire to return to their jobs? Does the employer have to take the strikers back? The answer here depends on why the workers went on strike in the first place. If the workers went on strike because of an *unfair labor practice,* they are entitled to come back to work even if it is necessary to fire their replacements. But if the workers struck only for increased benefits (such as higher wages), the employer does not have to reinstate them if replacements have taken over their jobs.

Employers may also discharge employees for "slowdowns", partial strikes or "wildcat strikes". A slowdown occurs when workers remain on the job but refuse to perform their duties or to work at the regular pace. A partial strike takes place when employees come to work, work a short time, then feign illness or other disability in order to cause a work stoppage. And a "wildcat strike" arises when a minority of union members strike without union authorization.

As far as picketing is concerned, any picketing carried out by violent means is unlawful. The National Labor Relations Act additionally prohibits mass picketing designed to deter employees from entering or leaving a plant as well as any picketing accompanied by threats or violence. Obstructing plant entrances to keep nonstrikers from entering or leaving is also unlawful.

What requirements must a union election meet?

The Landrum-Griffin Act of 1959 was passed in part to guarantee fair union elections. The Act sets forth the following minimal requirements for conducting the nomination and election of union officials in a free and democratic manner:

(1) All union members in good standing must be allowed to vote ("one man, one vote").

(2) Local officers must be elected at least every three years, and national officers every five.

(3) Union officers must be elected by secret ballot.

(4) Reasonable opportunity to nominate candidates must be provided.

(5) Every union member in good standing must be eligible to be a candidate, subject to reasonable qualifications uniformly imposed.

(6) Members must be notified at least 15 days prior to the election.

(7) If the union distributes campaign literature, it must do so at the expense of the candidates and without discrimination between or among them.

(8) Adequate safeguards must be provided for the election itself, including the right of any candidate to have observers at the polls and at the ballot counting.

(9) Candidates must not use union funds to finance their campaigns. Landrum-Griffin authorizes the Secretary of Labor in conjunction with the courts to protect the rights of union members in connection with union elections. Although the Secretary may initiate his or her own investigation into election violations, he or she usually acts upon complaints filed by disgruntled members of the union. If, upon investigation, the Secretary finds "probable cause" to believe that the law was violated, he or she will bring suit in federal court (within 60 days of the complaint's filing date) to set aside the election. The federal court will then decide whether the law was violated; and if it decides that it was, a new election will be ordered. The Secretary of Labor will supervise the new election and certify the names of the winners to the court.

What about corruption in unions?

The Landrum-Griffin Act also requires union disclosure of certain basic information, including the names of officers and union finance materials. This information must be made available to union members. Willful violation of the Act's reporting provisions is punishable by a fine of up to $10,000, and/or imprisonment for up to one year. The Secretary of Labor has the right to inspect union records, and to question such persons as he or she believes necessary to determine if violations have occurred.

Title V of the Landrum-Griffin Act, entitled "Safeguards for Labor Organiza-

tions", imposes fiduciary duties upon union officers, agents, shop stewards, and other union representatives. Union officials are also prohibited from using union funds for personal expenditures, and from acquiring financial or other interests that conflict with the interests of the labor union. To help enforce these provisions, the law permits individual union members to sue union officials for damages, for an accounting, or for any other appropriate relief where the union itself fails to do so. Union officials found guilty of embezzling, stealing, or otherwise willfully misappropriating union funds may be fined up to $10,000 and imprisoned up to five years.

CASES

CASE 1—*"Smokey and the Bandit"—the Coors Beer case.*

ADOLPH COORS CO. v. FEDERAL TRADE COMM.

United States Court of Appeals, Tenth Circuit, 1974.
497 F.2d 1178.

BARRETT, Circuit Judge.

Adolph Coors Company appeals an Order to Cease and Desist issued by the Federal Trade Commission. The FTC filed a complaint alleging that Coors was engaged in anticompetitive practices in violation of Section 5 of the Federal Trade Commission Act.[1] An Initial Decision was issued by the Administrative Law Judge after hearings were conducted in Denver extending over a period of thirty days. The Law Judge found that Coors had not violated the Act. He recommended that the complaint be dismissed. The FTC appealed the Initial Decision to the five-member Federal Trade Commission. The Commission substituted its findings for those of the Law Judge and found, as a matter of Law, that Coors had violated Section 5 of the Act.

Adolph Coors Company, a Colorado corporation, is engaged in brewing, distribution and sale of beer, using the trade name of "Coors". Coors has one brewery in Golden, Colorado, and distributes its beer in an eleven-state area. The beer is sold to the distributors who in turn sell to retailers. While Coors is the fourth largest beer brewer in the United States, it alone among the nation's some 70 brewers is a "shipping" brewery, i. e., Coors ships all of the beer brewed at its single "regional" brewing plant at Gold-

---

1. Section 5 of the Federal Trade Commission Act, 15 U.S.C.A. § 45, provides in part:

   (a)(1) Unfair methods of competition in commerce, and unfair or deceptive acts or practices in commerce, are declared unlawful.

* * *

   (6) The Commission is empowered and directed to prevent persons, partnerships, or corporations, * * * from using unfair methods of competition in commerce and unfair or deceptive acts or practices in commerce.

en, Colorado, F.O.B. to the various distributors in Arizona, California, Colorado, Idaho, Kansas, Nevada, New Mexico, Oklahoma, Texas (some counties only), Utah and Wyoming. In 1971 the average barrel of Coors beer traveled 961 miles to its market place.

The beer is made by the aseptic brewing process which requires refrigerated marketing. It is uncontroverted that Coors beer is substantially more expensive than any other beer consumed in the United States, and yet because of its popularity, Coors has climbed from the 49th largest brewery in 1948 to its number 4 position today. Coors maintains market leadership in total sales against all competitors except in its territory served in Texas. Because of the delicacy of the product, it is essential that the refrigeration controls and expeditious marketing techniques be strictly monitored. Once the beer is delivered to the distributors, this obligation is assumed by them under an agreement with Coors. It is the distributor who is required to protect the "integrity" of the Coors beer quality by guarding against a retailer's failure to rotate the beer, and failure to insure proper refrigerated storage. Coors beer retained over 90 days must be destroyed.

Coors has 35 area representatives to help market the product. Each representative is assigned certain distributors to work with and to see that Coors' Policy Manual is followed. The price Coors charges to its distributors is set by Coors. Coors suggests to its distributors and retailers the price at which to sell its beer.

Each distributor is assigned a territory in which to market Coors' products. Coors may reduce the territory or add distributors to a particular territory. There are 166 independent distributors and one wholly owned subsidiary company.

In 1964 Coors eliminated sales to central warehouse accounts. Central warehouse accounts are either retailers such as large chain supermarkets who buy for redelivery to their own outlets, or independents who purchase for redelivery to nonaffiliated retail outlets or retailer warehouses.

Coors favors draught accounts. It has a draught policy in which tavern owners are given 30 days to discontinue handling other brands of light draught beer. If the owner-retailer continues to sell another brand of light draught beer, Coors discontinues its supply of light draught beer to the tavern.

The contract between Coors and the distributors enables Coors to cancel its contract for any breach by the distributor, with a five-day notice. Either Coors or the distributor may cancel the contract without cause with a 30-day notice.

Coors contends that: (1) it did not engage in wholesale or retail price fixing; (2) its vertically imposed territories are reasonable and legal; (3) it has no policy of requiring exclusive draught accounts; (4) it has the right to protect its quality product and not distribute its beer through central warehousing; (5) its contract termination rights are reasonable and legal; * * *.

Coors contends that it did not engage in price fixing agreements with its distributors. Its practices are set out in the Coors Policy Manual which states as follows:

> In order to maintain a successful wholesale or retail business, pricing integrity is essential. Pricing integrity will result in an

adequate and equitable profit to both Distributor and retailer and is fair to the ultimate consumer.

It is the policy of the Adolph Coors Company to suggest, if it so chooses, to either the wholesaler or retailer level, suggested minimum pricing. We reserve the right to further that policy by simply refusing to deal with anyone who doesn't adhere to said policy.

The Adolph Coors Company and its agents must only state the policy. They cannot make agreements, threaten, coerce, or intimidate wholesalers or retailers in any manner. They can enforce the policy only by reserving the right to refuse to deal with those who don't adhere to the suggested prices.

Coors' sales manager, Harvey Gorman, testified that the product is controlled by agreeing individually with each distributor. This policy is enforced by a provision in the contract between Coors and the distributor enabling Coors to terminate a distributorship in 30 days without cause. Since there are about 7,000 applicants for distributorships, any distributor who does not conform to Coors' pricing policies could readily be replaced. Coors' area representatives constantly obtain wholesale price information and send the information to the home office in Golden. The area representatives also resolve any conflicts between the prices proposed by a distributor and those suggested by Coors.

John Hemphill, a former Coors distributor, testified that he would only go so far in making a request to use his own prices, knowing that Coors could terminate him in 30 days. He also testified that a Coors' area representative told him that the best thing for him to do is not to be a distributor if he could not agree to Coors' policies on pricing and territories.
* * *

Jay Wagnon, a Coors' distributor, testified that Coors insisted on controlling distributor price increases and that when he refused to adopt wholesale prices suggested by the Coors' area representative he was summoned to Golden and requested to change his prices. He stated that Coors' personnel told him to bring his prices in line with Coors' recommendations or they could put another distributor in his area. He testified that he was afraid; that he had been threatened; and that he therefore conformed to the suggested prices. * * *

Jay Thurman, a former distributor, testified that he was given pricing sheets by the area representative which were to be followed. He was told that if the prices were changed, it would go through Mr. Straight, a Coors official, who, in turn, would determine if the changes were justified.

Peter Tinetti, a former distributor, testified that Coors sent him the prices at which to sell Coors beer.

The area representatives submitted reports to the Golden headquarters about agreements or understandings they had made with distributors on wholesale prices.

Price fixing is illegal *per se* under the Sherman Antitrust Act. Price fixing is also illegal *per se* under Section 5 of the Federal Trade Commission Act. Prices are fixed when they are agreed upon. The agreement to fix prices renders the conspiracy illegal. The agreement may be inferred or implied from the acts and conduct of the parties, as well as from surrounding circumstances.

* * * the test * * * is whether the agreement, or conduct, interferes with the freedom of sellers or traders in such a manner as to prohibit or restrain their ability to sell in accordance with their own judgment, and not what particular effect the agreement or conduct, has on the actual prices.

* * *

There is substantial evidence from the record as a whole to support the Commission's findings of price fixing agreements between Coors and its distributors.

Coors also challenges the Commission's finding that Coors has a resale price maintenance program and that it has in some cases secured adherence to its suggested retail prices by unlawful means. There is substantial evidence to support the Commission's finding.

Coors' policy is to establish pricing integrity which means that a certain profit is allowed on each level of resale. Pricing integrity is not possible with price discounting. Coors implements pricing integrity by refusing to deal with anyone not adhering to its price suggestions. A Coors' area representative threatened to refuse further sales to an offending retailer unless he would adhere to the prices suggested by Coors. Coors used its distributors to secure retailers' adherence to suggested minimum prices. One area representative reported that a retailer was cut off by a distributor because the retailer was advertising Coors beer at cut prices. Another area representative reported that a distributor planned to take appropriate action against a retailer who refused to sell at suggested prices. A distributor reported that Coors beer was not delivered to a retailer who cut prices. An area representative reported that action would be taken against a retailer who refused to raise his prices to a profit level.

Mr. Letcher, a retailer, testified that he was selling Coors at special weekend prices and that he was warned by the Coors distributor to discontinue the practice. Letcher refused to cooperate and the distributor terminated deliveries to his store. The distributor told Letcher that deliveries would be received if he would agree not to discount the beer, and that Letcher might lose the retail account if he continued to discount the beer. Letcher was also told by the distributor that Coors does not tolerate price cutting. Letcher sold his business. The distributor resumed deliveries to the new owners who agreed not to discount the beer. The distributor did not act independently in cutting off Letcher as Coors suggests, but cut him off in accordance with Coors' pricing policies.

United States Supreme Court decisions hold that if a manufacturer advances beyond a simple refusal to deal and takes affirmative action to secure compliance with its prices, a combination in violation of Section 1 of the Sherman Antitrust Act and Section 5 of the Federal Trade Commission Act occurs. Any trespass on the independence of a reseller or wholesaler to set his own prices is a violation of the Sherman Act. A seller may refuse to deal with one failing to adhere to its specified prices, but where a concerted effort is used to interfere with the distributors' pricing independence and to compel them to adhere to suggested prices, there is a violation of the Sherman Antitrust Act. A manufacturer may choose those to whom it will sell to as long as its conduct has no monopolistic purposes.

The Commission found that:

* * * [Coors] has pursued a policy of fixing, controlling and maintaining prices at which Coors beer is sold at both the wholesale and retail level, that in furtherance of this policy it has engaged in various acts and practices such as: suggested resale prices to both distributors and retailers, checking prices at which distributors and retailers sell Coors beer, advising distributors and retailers that it is contrary to Coors pricing policy for them to deviate from prices approved by respondent, threatening to terminate distributorships and threatening to force distributors to sell their businesses for refusing to adhere to suggested retail prices, entering into agreements and understandings with distributors as to the wholesale prices which the distributors will charge for Coors beer, joining with distributors in attempting to coerce retailers to refrain from selling Coors beer at prices below those approved by respondent, encouraging distributors to prevent retail price cutting by refusing to deliver Coors beer to price cutters, or to reduce the amount of beer delivered, and entering into agreements and understandings with retailers as to the retail prices or range of prices at which such retailers will sell Coors beer.

There is substantial evidence in the record to support the Commission's findings.

II.

Coors alleges that its vertically imposed territories are reasonable and legal. The Commission held that Coors vigorously enforces its territorial restrictions and that it has engaged in unlawful price fixing which is:

* * * [s]trong grounds for presuming that the most injurious effects of vertical territorial divisions may be operative, and, therefore, for holding the entire arrangement of territories with price fixing illegal per se.

The Coors' distributor contract provides, in part, as follows:

While this agreement is in effect the Distributor will conduct the business of wholesale distribution of Coors Beer in the above territory only * * *.

In United States v. Arnold, Schwinn & Co., 388 U.S. 365, 87 S.Ct. 1856, 18 L.Ed.2d 1249 (1967), the United States brought an antitrust action against Arnold, Schwinn & Co., an association of Schwinn distributors and a Schwinn distributor, seeking a declaratory judgment to invalidate the distribution franchising system of its products. Schwinn bicycles are shipped directly to franchised retailers who agree to sell only to ultimate consumers. Schwinn also distributed its bicycles to franchised distributors who agreed not to resell to anyone outside their assigned territories. The Court held that:

Under the Sherman Act, it is unreasonable without more for a manufacturer to seek to restrict and confine areas or persons with whom an article may be traded after the manufacturer has parted with dominion over it. Such restraints are so obviously destructive of competition that their mere existence is enough. If the

manufacturer parts with dominion over his product or transfers
risk of loss to another, he may not reserve control over its destiny
or the conditions of its resale.

The rule of law in *Schwinn* is clear and unequivocal.

> Once the manufacturer has parted with title and risk, he has
> parted with dominion over the product, and his effort thereafter to
> restrict territory or persons to whom the product may be trans-
> ferred—whether by explicit agreement or by silent combination or
> understanding with his vendee—is a *per se* violation of § 1 of the
> Sherman Act.

Coors, a manufacturer, enters into an agreement with its distributors
to distribute Coors beer in the assigned territory only. Coors maintains
that the territorial restrictions are necessary to retain the quality and proper refrigerated handling of its beer, and that the territorial restrictions are
legal. However, since Coors parts with title and risk to the product when it
sells and delivers the beer to distributors, and thus has parted with dominion over the product, its further effort to restrict the territories or persons
to whom the product can be transferred is a *per se* violation of Section 1 of
the Sherman Act and Section 5 of the Federal Trade Commission Act.
Coors may still condition its sales to distributors and others upon maintenance of procedures necessary to control the quality of the product.

Although we are compelled to follow the *Schwinn per se* rule rendering
Coors' territorial restrictions on resale illegal *per se*, we believe that the *per
se* rule should yield to situations where a unique product requires territorial
restrictions to remain in business. For example, speed of delivery, quality
control of the product, refrigerated delivery, and condition of the Coors
product at the time of delivery may justify restraints on trade that would
be unreasonable when applied to marketing standardized products. Perhaps
the Supreme Court may see the wisdom of grafting an exception to the *per
se* rule when a product is unique and where the manufacturer can justify
its territorial restraints under the rule of reason.

The dissenters in *Schwinn* contended that the new *per se* rule cannot be
justified, automatically invalidating vertical restraints in a distribution system based on sales to wholesalers and retailers.

> * * * the Court has, *sua sponte* created a bluntly indiscrimi-
> nate and destructive weapon which can be used to dismantle a vast
> variety of distributional systems—competitive and anticompetitive,
> reasonable and unreasonable.

Thus we are foreclosed from considering the reasonableness of the restriction or its business justification. We are cognizant of the unpredictability
which is created in relationship to the Coors operation. [The Supreme Court
did change the Schwinn *per se* rule in the case of Continental T. V. Inc. v.
GTE Sylvania, Inc., 433 U.S. 36, 97 S.Ct. 2549, 53 L.Ed.2d 568 (1977).]

Coors contends that it has no policy of requiring exclusive draught accounts. The Commission found that Coors combined with its distributors
in the practice of encouraging and coercing retailers to sell Coors draught
beer to the exclusion of light draught beer competitors in violation of Section 5 of the Federal Trade Commission Act.

Mr. Coors testified that exclusive draught accounts were desirable.
Several distributors testified that the purpose of obtaining exclusive

draught accounts is to encourage draught customers to buy beer to take home. To implement the policy, Coors threatened to terminate a retailer's supply of Coors draught beer unless he eliminated competitive draught beers within 30 days. Coors' distributors did, in fact, take out their Coors draught beer if the retailer did not comply with the policy.

The policy of pursuing an exclusive draught policy violates Section 5 of the Federal Trade Commission Act. There is substantial evidence in the record to support the Commission's finding.

Coors asserts that it has the right to protect its quality product and not distribute its beer through central warehousing. The Commission held that Coors' prohibition of central warehouse sales, or a requirement that wholesale prices to those accounts equal those to other retailers is a substantial restraint on the capacity of the distributor to resell to whomever he chooses and threatens the same anticompetitive results as other illegal restraints on alienation. Therefore, the Commission found that the practices are unfair methods of competition in violation of Section 5 of the Federal Trade Commission Act.

The central warehouse method of distribution involves purchase by the warehouser of beer from the brewer or the distributor. The beer is delivered by the retailer to its outlets. This method of distribution could cut the price of the beer to the retailer and consumer. Coors eliminated sales to central warehouse accounts in 1964. The distributors viewed central warehousing as a threat to the integrity of their territorial restrictions. Coors alleges that sales to central warehousers affects the quality of its beer because of poor procedures used by the warehousers.

The Order imposed by the FTC does not prevent Coors' distributors from conditioning its sales to central warehouse accounts on the maintenance of procedures necessary to the quality control of its products. The Order only enjoins Coors from requiring its distributors from refusing to sell to central warehouse accounts. The restriction by Coors, limiting those with whom the distributors may deal, amounts to a restriction on resale and violates the mandates of *Schwinn* and the Federal Trade Commission Act. There is substantial evidence in the record to support the FTC's finding.

Coors alleges that its contract termination rights are reasonable and legal and that its conduct in the rare instances of its use has been proper and legal in every respect. The Commission held that:

> Whether or not any actual terminations of Coors distributors, or sales forced by threat of termination can be ascribed entirely, solely and unambiguously to the failure of the terminated or coerced distributor to participate in an antitrust violation, it is abundantly clear from the record in this case that Coors representatives have used the explicit or implicit threat of speedy termination in often successful efforts to force the acquiescence of its distributors in anti-competitive behavior.

The Coors distributor contract provides in part as follows:

> This agreement and any supplements now or hereafter effective (whether fixing prices and terms to the Distributor, or otherwise) may be cancelled in entirety at any time by the Company for any breach by the Distributor on five (5) days' written notice to the Distributor. This agreement and such supplements may be can-

celled in entirety by either party without cause upon the giving of notice to that effect to the other party, in which event termination shall become effective thirty (30) days after delivery or the mailing of the written notice of cancellation, whichever first occurs.
* * *

The Commission held that Coors used the threat of speedy termination to force its distributors into anticompetitive behavior. There is substantial evidence in the record to support the Commission's holding.

Coors has the right to terminate distributors according to the contract provisions which the distributors have agreed to. However, it may not use the contract termination provisions to force its distributors into anticompetitive behavior.

[Affirmed.]

CASE 2—*"Ma Bell is a cheap mother."*

SOUTHWESTERN BELL TELEPHONE CO.

200 NLRB No. 101, Case No. 14–CA–6595, Samuel M. Singer,
Administrative Law Judge, 1972.

1973 CCH # 24859.

Before MILLER, KENNEDY and PENELLO.

Judge's Findings and Conclusions

A telephone company was charged with violating Section 8(a)(1) and (3) of the Act by directing employees to leave its premises unless they ceased displaying sweatshirts containing a slogan that the employer deemed objectionable.

It is stipulated that, during discussions toward a new bargaining agreement, employees appeared at work wearing sweatshirts with the slogan, "Ma Bell is a Cheap Mother." It is further stipulated that the slogan is capable of more than a single interpretation, with one of those meanings being considered obscene, derisive and insulting. Even some employees complained that the shirts were vulgar and in poor taste.

The employees wearing the shirts were directed to leave unless they removed the shirts or somehow covered up the slogans. All of the shirt-wearers chose to leave. The company did not pay them for the time they lost. The company told workers and the union that the men were not suspended, but could return to work whenever they satisfied the directive.

The union did not encourage, but neither did it discourage the wearing of the shirts. The union sponsored and distributed other insignia such as "big potato" buttons and automobile stickers. It did approve "Cheap Mother" bumper stickers. The company never prohibited the wearing of union insignia or slogans of any kind other than the "Cheap Mother" slogan. It did not object to the "big potato" buttons. No employee was ever previously disciplined for union activity. The employer has encouraged employees to wear sweatshirts with company slogans.

Section 7 of the Act guarantees to employees the right to engage in concerted activities for the purpose of collective bargaining or other mutual aid or protection. The fact that the employees wore the shirts on the first day of contract negotiations clearly shows that their objective was to support the union's bargaining position. It is not material that the union did not sponsor the activity or that the sweatshirts did not name the union, since employees can act concertedly for their mutual aid or protection independently of a union.

However, some concerted activities may be so "indefensible" as to warrant the disciplining of participants. Although the display of union insignia at work is a valid form of concerted or union activity, considerations of plant production or discipline may justify restrictions on such activity.

It is acknowledged that the slogan had a double interpretation and that the word "mother" can be used in a derisive and insulting manner. Management officials thought the slogan vulgar and profane, and designed to taunt supervisors. In view of the controversial nature of the language and its susceptibility to a derisive and profane construction, management could legitimately ban the use of the "provocative" slogan as a reasonable precaution against discord and bitterness between employees and management, and to assure plant discipline. The subjective intent of the employees is not controlling.

The offensive language was worn on shirts to be exposed to employees and management for the entire working day. The fact that supervisors may occasionally use an obscene epithet to give vent to strong feelings does not legitimize such a continuous display. The company's directive was a reasonable and protected management prerogative. It did not matter that the order came before the actual disruption of discipline.

There is no merit to the contention that the slogan was privileged free speech. The protection of the Act is not co-extensive with the protection accorded citizens under the Constitution or other laws. The Act deals only with the employer-employee relationship. "Freedom of Speech" does not preclude an employer from prohibiting the distribution of defamatory and insulting statements that tend to disrupt discipline.

It is noted that the company has never been known as an antiunion employer, and that the employees were not discharged or disciplined for wearing the sweatshirts, except to the extent they lost wages for the hours they chose to be absent from the plant.

It is concluded that the employer did not violate either Section 8(a)(1) or (3) of the Act. The employer's request that the slogans be removed or covered up was unrelated to opposition to protected concerted activity.

Board's Decision

The Board has decided to affirm the rulings, findings, and conclusions of the Administrative Law Judge and to adopt his recommended order.

PROBLEMS

1. Answer the following "True" or "False" and give reasons for your answers:

   (a) The Sherman Act was originally used as a strike-breaking weapon against the unions.

   (b) All monopolies are illegal.

   (c) It is illegal per se for a manufacturer to impose customer and territorial restrictions upon dealers.

   (d) The FTC may find that certain conduct is an unfair method of competition (and issue a cease and desist order against it) even though the conduct violates neither the letter nor the spirit of existing antitrust law.

(e) The president may intervene in labor disputes that threaten the national health, welfare, or security.

(f) Strikers retain their status as "employees" even while on strike.

(g) The Taft-Hartley Act outlaws the *union shop*.

(h) It is an unfair labor practice for an employer to question an employee about his or her union activities.

(i) A union that is duly elected by a majority of employees has *exclusive* authority to represent all employees on matters properly the subject of collective bargaining.

(j) It is an unfair labor practice for employers or unions to bargain in "bad faith".

2.   Don McCready, the President and General Manager of Thompson, Inc. posts the following sign in the employee lounge:

      "No union solicitation or distribution of union materials at any time on employer's premises—by order of management."

McCready also discharges employee Doug Sorenson for encouraging union members to strike for higher wages and a better pension plan. Union representative Tina Summers seeks your advice. Is the employer's ban on union solicitation and distribution of union materials enforceable? What action, if any, would you advise the employees to take? What are Doug Sorenson's rights, if any, against Thompson, Inc.? What action, if any, would you advise Doug to take?

3.   (a) The employees of "Buy Smart" Grocery Stores decide to strike for higher wages. Their current contract is set to expire on June 1st, so on May 15th, the employees' union notifies Buy Smart in writing of their intention to strike for higher wages. The union offers to meet and confer with representatives of Buy Smart for the purpose of negotiating a new contract. On June 1st, the employees' union has not yet reached an agreement with Buy Smart, so the employees go on strike. What are Buy Smart's legal rights, if any, against the employees? Assuming Buy Smart hires replacement workers during the strike, does it have to fire the replacements and allow the strikers to return when the strike is over? Explain.

   (b) Suppose instead that the Buy Smart employees strike because of several threats made by management to discourage new employees from joining the union. A total of 500 workers walk off the job. They take turns picketing the Buy Smart Stores in a peaceable and orderly fashion. Assuming Buy Smart hires replacement workers during the strike, does it have to fire the replacements and allow the strikers to return when the strike is over? Explain. Would your answer differ if 50 of the striking employees had blocked the store entrances and exits during the strike and verbally and physically abused both Buy Smart customers and management? Explain.

   (c) After the strike, it comes to light that Union President Dolores Fisher threatened several employees with physical harm unless they would agree to help picket the stores. It is also discovered that Dolores used union funds to finance her re-election campaign and that she has been using union monies for personal travel expenditures. What are the union members' rights, if any, against Dolores Fisher? What action, if any, would you advise them to take?

4. *Define the following:* collective bargaining; compulsory, permissive, and illegal subjects of collective bargaining; "featherbedding"; closed shop; "labor's Magna Carta"; vertical restraint of trade; horizontal restraint of trade; "wildcat" strike; partial strike; "slowdown".

5. White Corporation acquired 100% of the stock of King Corporation, a competitor of White. Both companies are of substantial size with respect to their involvement in interstate commerce. This acquisition would

    a.   Be legal under the Clayton Act unless the acquisition were certain to create a monopoly in any line of commerce in any section of the country.

    b.   Constitute a *per se* violation under the Clayton Act.

    c.   Be illegal under the Clayton Act if its effect might be to substantially lessen competition.

    d.   Be illegal under the Clayton Act only if its effect were certain to lessen competition substantially.

    [# 47, November 1974 CPA Exam]

6. You were the auditor examining the financial statements of Mason Corporation and noted an extraordinary increase in the sales of certain items. Further inquiry revealed that Mason sold various interrelated products which it manufactured. One of the items was manufactured almost exclusively by them. This unique product was in great demand and was sold throughout the United States. Mason realized the importance of the product to its purchasers and decided to capitalize on the situation by requiring all purchasers to take at least two of its other products if they wished to obtain the item over which it had almost complete market control. At the spring sales meeting the president of Mason informed the entire sales force that they were to henceforth sell only to those customers who agreed to take the additional products. He indicated that this was a great opportunity to substantially increase sales of other items. Under the circumstances, which of the following *best* describes the situation?

    a.   The plan is both ingenious and legal and should have been resorted to long ago.

    b.   The arrangement is an illegal tying agreement; hence per se illegal.

    c.   Since Mason did *not* have complete market control over the unique product in question, the arrangement is legal.

    d.   As long as the other products which must be taken are sold at a fair price to the buyers, the arrangement is legal.

    [# 46, November 1977 CPA Exam]

7. The Diablo Oven Company entered into agreements with retail merchants whereby they agreed not to sell beneath Diablo's minimum "suggested" retail price of $85 in exchange for Diablo's agreeing not to sell its ovens at retail in their respective territories. The agreement does not preclude the retail merchants from selling competing ovens. What is the legal status of the agreement?

    a.   It is legal if the product is a trade name or trademarked item.

b. It is legal if the power to fix maximum prices is *not* relinquished.

c. It is illegal unless it can be shown that the parties to the agreement were preventing cutthroat competition.

d. It is illegal even though the price fixed is reasonable.

[# 12, May 1978 CPA Exam]

8. Blackstone Corporation entered into a price fixing arrangement with several of its competitors. Blackstone is engaged in interstate commerce as are its competitors. The Justice Department has obtained proof of the agreement. Under the circumstances, which of the following is Blacksone or its officers *not* liable for or subject to?

a. Fines and/or imprisonment.

b. Treble damages.

c. Seizure of its goods shipped in interstate commerce pursuant to the arrangement.

d. Forfeiture of its right to do business in interstate commerce.

[# 48, November 1977 CPA Exam]

9. Devold Enterprises, Inc., sells frozen baked goods to chain stores, wholesalers, restaurant suppliers, and retailers in interstate commerce. It naturally seeks to avoid violation of the Robinson-Patman Act which proscribes price discrimination. Which of the following will permit Devold to *avoid* potential violations of the Act?

a. Its volume of sales is less than $300,000 per year.

b. It pays for local advertising of selected large volume retailers.

c. It provides free marketing advice and provides displays to its customers strictly based on their relative volume of purchases and the relative amount of sales of its products.

d. It pays brokerage commissions to favored customers.

[# 41, November 1977 CPA Exam]

10. **Part a.** During the audit of the accounts receivable of the Flint Charcoal Company, it was learned that one of the customers, Cranston, refused to pay for the charcoal purchased over the past six months. An analysis of the correspondence revealed the following facts.

Flint is a large manufacturer and distributor of charcoal briquettes. It sells the briquettes in interstate commerce to wholesalers, jobbers, and directly to retail outlets. Several of the wholesalers have recently opened up their own retail outlets in the area in which Cranston's store is located. Six months ago, Better Buy Charcoal, one of Flint's major competitors, uniformly reduced the price of charcoal briquettes to its wholesalers. Better Buy sells exclusively to wholesalers. When Flint's wholesale customers learned of the cheaper prices offered by Better Buy they told Flint "it had better lower its prices or they would switch to Better Buy." Flint promptly matched Better Buy's price reduction in order to retain its wholesale customers. Flint could not totally justify on a cost basis the difference in price at which it sold to wholesalers as compared with retailers. Cranston, upon discovering the unfavorable price differential, refused to pay on the orders he received and notified Flint that he would not pay more than the price charged to the wholesalers. Cranston warned Flint that if legal action were taken by Flint, he would counterclaim for damages based upon Flint's "illegal pricing policies."

Required: Answer the following, setting forth reasons for any conclusions stated.

What are the legal problems and implications of the above facts?

Part b. The CPA firm of Christopher and Diana was engaged to audit the books of Starr Antenna Company. An examination of Starr's files revealed the threat of a lawsuit by Charles Grimm, the owner of Grimm's TV Sales and Service Company. An analysis of the pertinent facts revealed the following.

Grimm's complaint arose because Grimm could not obtain the quantity of television antennas ordered from Starr. The three other antenna manufacturers, who supplied the tri-state area in which Starr did business, would not sell antennas to Grimm. Grimm knows that several other retailers are encountering similar problems with Starr and the three major competitors. Diana, the partner in charge of the audit, found this to be a strange situation and talked with Baxter, Starr's Vice President of Marketing. Baxter explained that about a year ago there had been a period of "cutthroat" competition among the four major antenna manufacturers involved. In order to avoid a repetition of this disastrous situation, they had entered into an unwritten gentlemen's agreement to "limit output per manufacturer to the amount produced in the year immediately preceeding that in which the cutthroat competition had occurred." They also agreed that each manufacturer would not sell to the acknowledged customers of the others. Baxter said there was still plenty of competition for new customers in the tri-state area and that they were contemplating raising the production limitation by 25%. He said that "this arrangement had made life a lot easier and profitable for all concerned." He also indicated that the prices charged were "reasonable" to the purchasers.

Required: Answer the following, setting forth reasons for any conclusions stated.

What are the legal problems and implications of the above facts?

Part c. The General Pen Company is one of the largest manufacturers of fountain pens and does business in every state in the United States. General developed a new line of prestige pens called the "Diamond Line" which it sold at a very high price. In order to uphold its prestige and quality appeal, General decided to maintain a high resale price. Consequently, it obtained agreements from department stores, jewelers, and other outlets not to sell the pen below the $15 suggested retail price. The Double Discount Department Store refused to sign the agreement and used the pen as a sales gimmick to attract customers. Double advertised and sold Diamond Line pens for $12, to which General objected. Double threatened General with a treble damage action for price-fixing if it did not withdraw its objections.

Required: Answer the following, setting forth reasons for any conclusions stated.

What are the legal problems and implications of the above facts?

[# 6 a.b. & c., May 1977 CPA Exam]

Chapter 26

CREDITORS AND BANKRUPTCY UNDER THE 1979 BANKRUPTCY ACT

Neither a borrower, nor a lender be;
For loan oft loses both itself and
friend,
And borrowing dulls the edge of
husbandry.

Shakespeare
Hamlet, Act I, Scene 3

Despite these words of the immortal Shakespeare, people have been borrowing and lending for thousands of years. Even the earliest civilizations recognized the legal relationship of debtor and creditor. Recognition, however, did not mean leniency for the debtor who would not or could not pay his or her debts. Up until the last few hundred years, the law dealt harshly with the delinquent debtor. For example, the early Roman Law (as founded on the Twelve Tables about 450 B.C.) provided that a creditor who was unable to collect on his or her claim from a debtor could cut up the debtor's body and divide the pieces—or, better yet, leave the debtor alive and sell him or her into slavery. Even after the law prohibited dismemberment for failure to pay debts, it still allowed the debtor to pledge his or her person, spouse, or children as security for debts; and if payment was not made as promised, the pledged persons were turned over to the creditor to work in bondage. This practice went on for hundreds of years.

Under the English common law system that we have inherited, it was never possible for a debtor to pledge his or her person or family as security for debts. But under the Statute of Merchants (1285), a debtor who did not pay his or her debts could be immediately imprisoned; and it was not necessary for the creditor to look first to the debtor's property for payment. It was not until the 18th Century that the practice of jailing debtors and holding them "hostage" until their debts were paid was finally abolished.

The debtor's position further improved in 1705 when the first bankruptcy laws came into existence. These laws gave the honest debtor an opportunity to secure a discharge of his or her debts and to retain a portion of his or her estate exempt from the claims of creditors.

Modern bankruptcy law, which we will study in this chapter, accomplishes the same results. It permits a debtor who is "snowed under" by his or her debts to go bankrupt and start over unencumbered by past financial obligations. Bankruptcy, however, does not wipe the slate clean of all debts. Though most debts are discharged (i. e., eliminated) in bankruptcy, the bankrupt remains liable for any unpaid alimony and child support; for taxes that fall due within three years preceding the bankruptcy; for liabilities arising out of obtaining money or property by false pretenses, or from securing a loan or credit on the basis of a materially fraudulent statement of financial condition; for debts resulting from the bankrupt's willful or malicious injuries to the person or property of another; and for educational loans due within five years preceding the bankruptcy.

And the debtor who goes bankrupt must give up most of his or her property. Any property he or she owns under a secured transaction or installment sale backed by a lien on the goods (subjects covered in detail in the following sections) may be repossessed by the specific creditor involved (e. g., the mortgagor of the bankrupt's home may foreclose on the house). Assets not subject to a lien are turned over to the court and sold; and the proceeds are used to pay off the bankrupt's debts. Still, the debtor is not stripped totally naked: some of his or her property is exempt from sale for his or her debts. For example, the bankrupt can generally keep his or her home if it is not worth too much; some household furnishings and personal clothing; and some tools and other property used in a trade or profession. But most of the bankrupt's debts and most of his or her property are gone. What is more, having been given a new start in life, the debtor cannot repeat the bankruptcy process for a period of six years following discharge.

In 1978, over 200,000 hard-pressed individuals and companies in the United States went into court and declared themselves bankrupt. A single law firm in Los Angeles handled nearly 4,000 bankruptcies last year. And bankruptcy is no longer considered to be a stigma—no more so than is divorce. People at all income levels and in all kinds of occupations are going bankrupt in ever growing numbers. It generally costs from $300 to $500 for an individual to go through bankruptcy with the assistance of an attorney. While an individual can go it alone with a "do it yourself" bankruptcy form, it is risky to do so.

Of course, not everyone who is having financial difficulties wants or needs to have his or her debts completely discharged (i. e., go through straight bankruptcy). An individual who has a few good assets and can work to pay off his or her debts should do so in order to retain a portion of his or her property, and because the bankruptcy court cannot discharge a bankrupt's debts again for six years (if more serious financial problems arise during the six year period, the bank-

rupt will not be able to escape his or her creditors). Chapter 13 of the federal Bankruptcy Act allows a debtor who feels that he or she can work out his or her problems to do so according to an agreed-upon repayment schedule. Only when a debtor is flat broke is straight bankruptcy the answer.

There are many laws affecting debtors and creditors apart from federal bankruptcy law. In this chapter, we will first explore the pre-bankruptcy remedies of creditors as well as the state law regarding debtors. Next, we will consider federal bankruptcy law in some detail. The federal Bankruptcy Act of 1898 remained relatively unchanged until November of 1978 when President Jimmy Carter signed into law an entirely new bankruptcy law. The new Act became effective October 1, 1979. It is the new bankruptcy law that we will be concerned with in our study.

What kinds of creditors are there?

Creditors fall into three basic categories: general, governmental, and lien creditors. All three kinds of creditors share in common a desire to be paid as soon as possible; but each, under the law, is provided with different rights and remedies.

A *government creditor* is any government entity to which a debt is owed, whether the debt arises out of a contract with the government or is based on a tax owing. A government creditor can be either a lien creditor or a general creditor depending on whether or not the government has a lien against the debtor's property. A lien is simply a charge on the debtor's property that secures the lien creditor's claim. The lien gives the creditor the right to have his or her claim satisfied from the specific property which is subject to the lien before the property can be used to satisfy the claims of general creditors (creditors having no lien or security on the debtor's assets). However, a creditor is a lien creditor only to the extent of the value of his or her lien on specific property. If the value of the property subject to the lien is insufficient to satisfy the creditor's claim, the creditor will become a general creditor as to the balance owing.

How do liens arise (i. e., how does one become a secured creditor?)

Liens are created in several different ways, the first of which is by agreement. Frequently, for example, liens are created between parties to a sales contract for the purchase of goods. Here, a party may want to purchase goods but does not have the cash price or sufficient credit standing to buy the goods on open credit. So, instead, the party makes a down payment on the purchase price and promises to pay the balance to the seller in installments over a specified period of time. The seller, during this time, may retain a lien or security interest in the goods; and the buyer enjoys possession and use of the goods while he or she pays off the credit balance. As will be seen in Ch. 27, one way the creditor can protect his or her security interest (which lasts until the full balance is paid) is by filing a "financing statement" (usually in the Secretary of State's Office, although the place of filing varies from state to state). The financing statement generally includes the names and addresses of the parties to the agreement, a description of the collateral (the property to which the lien attaches), and the signatures of the parties. By filing this statement, the secured creditor puts the world on notice that the described collateral, though it is in the debtor's possession, is subject to the creditor's lien. However, the financing statement must be filed before the debtor is petitioned into bankruptcy. A filing made after that time is invalid (see Ch. 27), and the creditor who makes the filing remains a general, unsecured creditor.

The *security interest* as described above is the lien created by agreement when personal property is used as collateral When the secured property is real estate (land and buildings), the lien created by the agreement is called a *mortgage.*

Liens are created not only by agreement, but by judicial process as well. These so-called "judicial liens" result from a creditor's efforts to collect his or her debt. As you will see in the following sections, many of these efforts involve activity prior to obtaining a courtroom judgment. Prejudgment efforts resulting in liens include "attachment" and "garnishment". And if the creditor obtains a judgment against the debtor, the judgment, too, will create a lien. Suppose the debtor fails to pay the judgment, and the creditor must resort to post-judgment procedure such as "execution". Again, a lien may result. Where any of these—prejudgment, judgment, and post-judgment efforts—result in liens, the liens are called judicial liens.

Finally, liens may be created by statute. The most common statutory liens include: (1) the employee's lien on the employer's personalty to secure payment of back wages; (2) the landlord's lien on the tenant's property to secure payment of back rent (although, as you will recall from Ch. 2, most states have abolished this lien); (3) the materialman's and mechanic's liens on land and improvements on land to secure the compensation of those who contributed labor or materials to improving the land; and (4) tax liens on the property of people who have not paid their lawful taxes. For example, Section 6321 of the federal Internal Revenue Code provides that all federal taxes are liens on all of the taxpayer's property. Generally, a demand for payment of the tax must be made, but the lien itself dates from the time the tax is assessed. After demand, the lien becomes one of the many possible claims competing to be satisfied out of the taxpayer's property. Priorities regarding statutory liens are considered in a later section. For now, it is enough to say that until notice of the tax lien is properly filed, the lien is not enforceable against many competing claimants. Tax lien notices affecting real property must be filed in the office designated by the state wherein the property is located. Notices affecting personal property must be filed in the office designated by the state wherein the individual property owner lives, or where the corporation or partnership has its principal executive office at the time the lien is filed. If a state fails to specify an office for filing, the tax lien is filed with the clerk of the U.S. district court for the judicial district wherein the property is located or where the taxpayer resides. Notice of the tax lien must be refiled every six years to keep the lien in force.

A similar procedure is required to perfect other statutory liens such as the employee's lien, landlord's lien, and mechanic's lien.

Any lienholder, whether he or she holds a consensual lien (security interest or mortgage), a judicial lien (because of the creditor's efforts to collect the debt), or a statutory lien (an employee's lien, landlord's lien, mechanic's lien, tax lien, etc.) stands in a much better position regarding the debtor's assets than does a general creditor, at least to the extent that the lien holder's security covers his or her claim.

What is a creditor likely to do first if his or her claim against a debtor is not paid on time?

It is a fact of modern life that credit is easy to obtain, and that too many people over-extend themselves and get into financial difficulty. While unpaid creditors can resort to legally prescribed methods of collection, they usually do so only as a last resort. First, they generally attempt to collect payment by writing letters, making phone calls, threatening lawsuits, personally visiting the debtor at home, and, sometimes, by communicating with the debtor's employer.

The so-called "dunning" letter is used first. To "dun" is to demand payment of a debt again and again; and the dunning letter is designed to pester or plague someone into paying his or her debts. Dunning letters can be quite hostile, as can the other efforts of creditors to collect. For many years, the law provided little protection for the debtor against annoying collection practices unless the practices were so unreasonable as to constitute a tort (i. e., socially unreasonable conduct for which a civil action for money damages lies). Using tort as the theory for recovery, debtors could sometimes recover for defamation of character, invasion of privacy, or intentional infliction of mental distress. However, it is generally difficult to prove such torts against creditors. Defamation, for example, is a tort designed to prevent one person from publishing false facts about another. But if the debtor really owes the debt, the statements made by the creditor are true, and truth is a good defense. Sometimes, however, a creditor will make other damaging statements, unrelated to his or her financial claim, that will serve as the basis for a defamation action. Or invasion of privacy may be found where a creditor makes an unreasonable number of contacts with the debtor's neighbors, employers, family members, or with the debtor personally. But the contacts must be unreasonable or a tort action will not lie. If the contacts are outrageously hostile, causing the debtor severe emotional distress, the debtor may be able to recover for intentional infliction of mental distress. But again, these torts are often difficult to prove. And many times, the debtor lacks the money and legal education needed to pursue the remedies.

To help the debtor in these situations, Congress passed the Fair Debt Collection Practices Act, which became effective March of 1978. The Act prohibits collection agencies from engaging in many of the unscrupulous practices that have plagued debtors, and that have made the collection agency business notorious. Some of the prohibited practices include:

(1) Harassing or abusive telephone calls to the debtor, particularly at his or her place of employment;

(2) Falsely implying that the debtor's wages are about to be seized;

(3) Falsely implying that the collector is a lawyer;

(4) Making unauthorized calls to the debtor's employer, neighbors, and friends.

On its face, the Act applies only to collection agencies (companies in the business of collecting creditor's claims)—not to creditors or collection lawyers. However, Congress has declared that the practices are contrary to the public interest, and that is all that is required to establish that each abusive and unfair debt collection practice (whether by a collection agency, a creditor, or a collection lawyer) comes within the meaning of Section 5(a) of the Federal Trade Commission Act. The Act authorizes the FTC to investigate unfair and deceptive practices that are found to be against the public interest, and to outlaw and punish the commission of such practices. Any debtor who feels that he or she has been unfairly or abusively treated by his or her creditors should contact the Federal Trade Commission in Washington D.C., or the nearest FTC regional office.

Where a creditor is unable to collect his or her debt by using reasonable "pressuring" techniques, the creditor must resort to legally prescribed collection procedures. There are three areas of creditors'

remedies that must be explored here, including:

(1) Remedies prior to judgment;

(2) The judgment itself; and

(3) Post-judgment remedies.

What are the prejudgment remedies?

There are three prejudgment remedies that a creditor can sometimes pursue before his or her claim is reduced to judgment. These are attachment, garnishment, and prejudgment receivership. Each is a procedure that enables the creditor to preserve property belonging to the debtor until the creditor can prove the validity of his or her claim. The idea here is to prevent the debtor from disposing of his or her property, or from concealing or destroying it so it cannot be used to pay off the debt. The creditor may have a legitimate claim that he or she can reduce to judgment by bringing an action against the debtor in a court of law. And the debtor may have sufficient property with which to satisfy the claim once the judgment is granted by the court. What the creditor worries about is what the debtor might do with the property during the time the court is considering the case and before the judgment is rendered against the debtor. Suppose the debtor disposes of the property, conceals it, or destroys it. Prejudgment remedies are designed to prevent this from happening.

These remedies are available only upon the commencement of the case against the debtor.

Attachment. A writ of attachment seizes the debtor's property so as to secure the creditor's claim in case judgment is later rendered in the creditor's favor. Attachments are strictly controlled by statute in all our states. They are generally granted only if (1) the plaintiff is unable to obtain personal service on the defendant (see Appendix A regarding jurisdiction over the person of the defendant by service of process) because the defendant is out of the state hiding or is a nonresident; or (2) where there are special or extraordinary circumstances indicating that the defendant is about to dispose of or secret his or her property to defraud creditors. Where either situation is present, the plaintiff-creditor can get the clerk of the court in which the action is being processed to issue a writ of attachment by filing a bond and an affidavit stating that the statutory grounds for attachment exist. The order of attachment is then directed to the sheriff of the county in which the defendant's property is located. The order instructs the sheriff to satisfy the plaintiff's claim once the judgment has been granted by the court.

The act of the sheriff in taking the property into custody is called a *levy*. Where real property is involved, the sheriff is generally required to post notice of the attachment on the property and to leave a copy of the attachment order with the person in possession of the land. With personal property that can by physically possessed, the sheriff takes the property into actual custody.

A levy on property creates a lien on the property. But although the lien dates from the time of the levy, it becomes effective only if the attaching creditor in fact secures a judgment against the debtor. Once a judgment is granted, the lien gives the attaching creditor a secured creditor's position as to that specific property and thus a preferred position as against other competing creditors who are unsecured.

The debtor can obtain a termination of the attachment by posting a bond called a "discharging" bond in which the debtor promises to pay the claim if judgment is entered against him or her; the issuer of the bond promises to pay if the debtor does not.

The creditor, however, must exercise care in using attachment as a prejudg-

ment remedy. If the debtor can prove that the plaintiff-creditor maliciously obtained the order of attachment without probable cause for believing that the statutory grounds existed, the debtor can sue the creditor for the tort of malicious and wrongful attachment.

Prejudgment garnishment. An order of attachment directs the sheriff to seize the defendant's property. In a prejudgment garnishment, the order is directed at a third party, called the garnishee, who either owes the debtor money or other property, or who is in possession of property belonging to the debtor. The garnishment informs the garnishee that the plaintiff-creditor has a right to satisfy a claim out of what the garnishee holds for the debtor or owes to him or her. The order directs the garnishee to hold the property or to refuse to pay the principal debtor until the creditor's case has been decided and the resulting judgment in favor of the creditor (if, in fact, it is in his or her favor) has been satisfied by the principal debtor.

Most often, the garnishment order is directed to the debtor's employer, or to the bank at which the debtor has a savings or checking account. Like an attachment, the garnishment generally creates a lien when the creditor obtains a judgment against the debtor. And once again, tort actions may lie for improper garnishment.

Prejudgment receivership. A receivership is generally created to preserve or manage property removed from the possession of a debtor. Thus, in an attachment, the sheriff seizes the debtor's property in order to make it available to satisfy the creditor's claim if and when the creditor obtains a judgment. In a prejudgment garnishment, a third party holding property belonging to the debtor is ordered to keep the property for use in satisfying the creditor's claim, again, if and when the creditor obtains a judgment. In the case of an order appointing a receiver and creating a receivership, a third party is given possession of the debtor's property along with authority to preserve and manage it. The receiver may be authorized, for example, to continue the operation of a business, to collect rents, or even to sell the property.

A receivership differs from an attachment and garnishment in that the creditor does not obtain a lien on the property subject to the receivership.

Are there any limitations on the use of attachment, garnishment, and prejudgment receivership?

The U.S. Supreme Court has ruled that the use of prejudgment remedies must conform to the requirements of "due process" of law. This means that before the debtor's property can become subject to attachment, garnishment, or receivership, the debtor must be notified of the claim against him or her, and must be given an opportunity to be heard on the matter. The notice and hearing requirement is designed to establish the validity of the creditor's claim before the debtor can be deprived of his or her property in any manner.

But there are exceptions. The U.S. Supreme Court has stated that notice and hearing may be constitutionally dispensed with in "extraordinary situations" demanding special protection for state or creditor interests. Thus, a government agency may seize property in order to protect the public welfare—and it may do so without notice and hearing. So, too, may property be attached or garnished or become subject to prejudgment receivership where such action is necessary to obtain jurisdiction over a nonresident who cannot be reached by the usual service of summons. Finally, if it can be shown that there is immediate danger that a debtor will destroy or conceal disputed goods, the prejudgment remedies may be resorted to without preliminary notice or hearing.

The use of garnishment is additionally limited by the federal Consumer Credit Protection Act (this "Truth in Lending" Act is further described in Appendix A) passed in 1968, and containing a section on garnishment that became effective July 1, 1970. The Act exempts a certain amount of an individual's disposable earnings for any work week from being subject to garnishment. The exemption is the greater of either:

(1) Seventy-five percent of the individual's disposable earnings for that week; or

(2) Thirty times the federal minimum hourly wage prescribed under the Wage and Hour Act at the time such earnings are payable. The minimum wage was $2.65 an hour in 1978 and became $2.90 an hour on January 1, 1979. Thus, in 1979, the minimum protected income (i. e., income not subject to garnishment) is $87.00 a week.

The Act also prohibits an employer from discharging an employee because his or her earnings have been garnished for a single indebtedness. And it provides that where state law is more restrictive than the federal law, the provisions of the state law will govern. In New York, for example, the amount of earnings subject to garnishment remained at the 10 percent figure in effect prior to passage of the federal law and did not rise to 25 percent. In New York, too, a creditor must obtain a courtroom judgment before he or she can garnish wages: the New York City Consumer Protection Law prohibits lawyers who are attempting to collect debts for creditors from even getting in touch with the debtor's employer before a final courtroom judgment has been obtained against the debtor.

How does the creditor obtain a judgment?

If the debtor fails to pay despite pressures from the creditor (and despite the use of any prejudgment remedies available), the creditor will have to seek a courtroom judgment against the debtor (see Appendix A for a description of the four stage litigation process and an explanation of how a judgment results at the end of the trial stage of litigation).

Obviously, upon serving the debtor with a copy of the summons and complaint, the creditor would prefer that the debtor fail to respond at all. For if the debtor fails to respond, a default judgment will be entered against him or her (see Appendix A on "default judgments"). A default judgment provides a fast and relatively inexpensive remedy for the creditor; and such judgments are fairly common. Many debtors do in fact fail to respond after service of process upon them, and many judgments are entered by default against debtors.

Unscrupulous creditors have often resorted to an illegal practice known as "sewer service" in order to assure a default judgment. In this situation, the process server (the person hired to find the defendant and hand him or her the summons and complaint) makes no effort to find the defendant debtor, but instead files a false affidavit that the process has been served. The process server then simply throws the summons and complaint away. The procedure is called "sewer service" because the discarded papers are likely to come to rest in the sewer. Of course, "sewer service" is illegal: it not only constitutes criminal perjury, but it is a federal crime involving violation of civil rights as well. In the case of United States v. Brand Jewelers, Inc., 318 F.Supp. 1293 (S.D.N.Y.1970), it was held that the United States government, through the federal attorney's office, has the power to correct abuses resulting from "sewer service" so as to prevent a denial of due process. Still, this practice continues to plague debtors, particularly poor debtors. Anyone who is a witness to "sewer service" should bring it to the attention of his or her local federal and district attorneys' offices.

Another practice that consumers should be aware of is the use of what is called a "confession of judgment" (or "cognovit judgment"). In this situation, the parties to a contract creating an indebtedness consent to a confession of judgment within the written contract itself. The contract specifically states that if the debt is not paid when due, the creditor can appear in court and obtain a judgment against the debtor based on the "confession of judgment" without having to serve the debtor with a summons, complaint, or any other notice. A confession of judgment in a written contract violates due process only where one party takes advantage of the other in obtaining the provision—for example, where the creditor, because of a stronger bargaining position, more or less forces the debtor to accept its inclusion. But where the debtor and creditor have equal bargaining power, and the "confession of judgment" is included as a result of arms length and good faith bargaining, there is no due process violation. Still, the "confession of judgment" is looked upon with disfavor in the usual consumer transaction, and may well prove to be a denial of due process in most of these situations.

Does a valid judgment create a lien?

Yes. A "valid" judgment creates a lien on the debtor's real property (only in the three southern states of Alabama, Georgia and Mississippi is a judgment lien good against both the real and personal property of the debtor). The judgment lien gives the creditor a position of priority as to the specific real property to which the lien attaches over other creditors whose claims arise after the judgment. But the key to the answer here is "valid". A judgment that results from "sewer service" or from other denial of due process (e. g., lack of jurisdiction) is no judgment at all: it creates no real property lien, and has no other binding legal effect. It is up to the debtor, in each case, to establish the due process violation.

How is a judgment collected?

Once a creditor obtains a valid judgment, he or she can actually collect the money through either "execution" or "after-judgment garnishment".

Execution. A writ of execution is issued, upon a judgment creditor's request, by the clerk of the court in which the judgment was granted. The granting of the writ requires no hearing: it is a completely ministerial act, and the court clerk exercises no discretion in granting the writ. Based on the writ of execution, the sheriff levies on the property described, and, after appraisal and notice of sale, sells the property at public auction. In most states, the writ of execution extends to both the real and personal property of the debtor; and it applies for a period of from 60 to 90 days, during which time the property must be sold. After the expenses of the sale are subtracted from the sale proceeds, the judgment creditor is paid, assuming there are no lien creditors who take priority over him or her with respect to the specific property sold (if there are such creditors, they will be paid first). Any excess that remains goes to the judgment debtor.

Statutes in most states prohibit the execution sale of property at an unfair price. After appraisal, the property must be sold for a dollar amount not less than a certain percentage of the appraised value. And in several states (see Ch. 27), the debtor is specifically granted a statutory right of redemption allowing him or her to repurchase any real property sold at

execution within a certain period of time following the sale (generally one year). In only a very few states does this right of redemption extend to personal property.

After-judgment garnishment. An execution results in sale of the debtor's property. But sometimes the debtor has no property to sell. Where this is the case, the creditor will still be able to collect the judgment if he or she can pinpoint property, funds, or earnings belonging to the debtor in the hands of some third party. Once the judgment creditor locates the property, he or she can obtain a writ of garnishment from the court by filing an affidavit declaring that he or she has a judgment unpaid by the judgment debtor, and that the garnishee holds some of the debtor's property or earnings. The writ of garnishment is then served on the garnishee who must answer within a certain time and set out what property or earnings of the debtor he or she holds. If the garnishee fails to answer the writ of garnishment, the court will either enter a judgment against the garnishee for the amount alleged to be in his or her possession, or it will compel the garnishee to answer by use of contempt proceedings. If the garnishee answers and denies that he or she has such property or earnings, the issue as to whether the garnishee does or does not will be tried in court like any other case. If the garnishee admits to possession, the court will issue a judgment against the garnishee for the property or earnings, and the property will be ordered turned over to the court for sale to satisfy the claim of the judgment creditor. But remember, the Consumer Credit Protection Act (Truth in Lending) exempts a minimum of 75% of the debtor's weekly earnings from garnishment. And it prohibits an employer from discharging an employee because of garnishment of earnings for a single debt.

Do other laws exempt part of the debtor's property from being subject to his or her debts?

We have seen that part of a debtor's wages are exempt from garnishment under the Consumer Credit Protection Act. Exemptions, however, do not stop there. Statutes in all states exempt certain other properties of the debtor from being subject to sale for his or her debts. The purpose of such laws is to prevent the debtor and his or her family from becoming public charges. To begin with, all states exempt certain personal property from the claims of creditors (in some cases, the property is exempt up to a certain value only). An exemption is generally created for life insurance as well, and for wages up to a certain amount (the amount can be greater than the federal law requires, but it cannot be less).

A typical state statute might provide for the following exemptions:

(1) For a head of a family, or a person 65 years of age or older, equity (ownership interest) in a home of up to $20,000. For any other person, equity up to $10,000. Or, in the alternative, equity up to $5,000 in a house trailer in which the debtor or his or her family lives. (The exemption covering the family home is called the "homestead" exemption. In most states, the debtor can claim this exemption only if he or she has a family, uses the property as a residence, and possesses an ownership interest in the home. However, if there is a mortgage on the property, the mortgage is not affected by the exemption statute; and the financial institution financing the purchase of the home can foreclose on the property and sell it notwithstanding that the home falls within the "homestead" exemption as to other creditors.)

(2) All household furnishings, appliances, and personal wearing apparel are exempt if they are reasonably necessary to and personally used by the debtor or his or her family (including a piano, radio, TV set, shotgun, rifle, and enough provisions and fuel to cover the debtor's needs for up to three months time).

(3) Equity up to $300 in an automobile so long as the vehicle is not worth more than $1,000.

(4) Savings of up to $1,000 in a financial institution (savings account).

(5) Life insurance that can be purchased with premiums of up to $500 a year.

(6) Up to $2,500 of actual cash value, over and above all liens and other creditors' interests, of tools and any other property used by a debtor in his or her trade, business, or profession (including, for example, a boat, truck, or car that the debtor uses for business purposes).

A debtor who wants to take advantage of these exemptions when a writ of execution has been issued to sell his or her property must claim the exemption within a certain period of time after the levy.

Also, the exemptions do not apply equally to all creditors. A federal tax lien is good as against all property owned by the deficient taxpayer. And if a debtor puts up exempt property as collateral for a loan, the debtor is generally deemed to have waived his or her right of exemption with respect to that loan.

In addition to the state exemptions described above, Social Security and veterans benefits are exempt under federal statute.

Have any states passed additional laws protecting the consumer with regard to credit transactions?

A few states including Colorado, Idaho, Indiana, Oklahoma, Utah, and Wyoming have passed the Uniform Consumer Credit Code (Oregon has passed a modified version of the Statute) which serves to protect the consumer in buying and selling goods on credit. The Code includes the following provisions:

(1) A buyer has a right to cancel a home solicitation sale until 12 midnight of the third business day following the day on which the buyer signs the agreement to purchase. This provision protects the consumer against high pressured door-to-door salespeople by giving the consumer the right to avoid any contract obtained in such a manner (however, the consumer who avoids does have to pay a cancellation fee of five percent of the purchase price). The seller must present the buyer with the following statement in a conspicuous type, 8-point or larger:

BUYER'S RIGHT TO CANCEL

If this agreement was solicited at your residence and you do not want the goods or services, you may cancel this agreement by mailing a notice to the seller. The notice must say that you do not want the goods or services and must be mailed before midnight of the third business day after you sign this agreement. The notice must be mailed to: _____

(insert name and mailing address of seller)

IF YOU CANCEL, THE SELLER MAY RETAIN AS A CANCELLATION FEE 5 PERCENT OF THE CASH PRICE, BUT NOT EXCEEDING YOUR CASH DOWN PAYMENT, OR $25 WHICHEVER IS THE LESSER.

However: you may not cancel if you have requested the seller to provide goods or services without delay because of an emergency, and

(1) The seller in good faith makes a substantial beginning of performance of the contract before you give notice of cancellation, and

(2) In the case of goods, the goods cannot be returned to the seller in substantially as good condition as when received by the buyer.

Generally, the buyer's "right to cancel" does not extend to goods and services purchased for less than $50.

(2) Referral selling schemes in which the buyer is told that his or her purchase price will be reduced if he or she can get a certain number of friends to sign up for the product or service are outlawed.

(3) Confession of judgment clauses are also outlawed.

(4) Where the buyer defaults in a credit sale under $1,000, the seller has an option to either sue the buyer for the balance due or repossess the goods, but he or she cannot do both (i. e., the seller cannot repossess the goods, resell them, and then obtain a judgment against the defaulting buyer for the unpaid balance). Where the sale is over $1,000, on the other hand, the seller can repossess the goods and still obtain a deficiency judgment against the buyer. In Oregon, if the unpaid time balance at the time of default is over $500, the seller is entitled to repossess and obtain a deficiency judgment for any amount remaining after deducting the fair market value of the goods from the unpaid time balance.

Can a debtor in financial difficulty defeat his or her creditors' rights to attach or execute against his or her property by conveying the property away to friends or relatives?

The answer is no. The law has long stated (since the Statute of 13 Elizabeth enacted in 1570) that a debtor is not free to conceal or transfer his or her property so as to prevent creditors from satisfying their legal claims. Such a transfer is called a *fraudulent conveyance*—that is, a conveyance intended to delay, hinder, or defraud creditors. A fraudulent conveyance is void and of no effect against the persons hindered, delayed, or defrauded. Fraudulent conveyances include not only selling the property to others, but also giving it away at a creditor's expense. A debtor must be just before he or she is generous. The leading case involving fraudulent conveyances dates back to 1601 in England and is known as *Twyne's* case. The court in this case considered a debtor's efforts to transfer his property in order to defraud a creditor. The court found six specific "signs and marks" of fraud, which have become known in modern law as "badges of fraud". The following six circumstances, the court stated, indicated the debtor's intent to defraud:

(1) The conveyance was general (the debtor did not even except such items as wearing apparel and other necessities thus arousing a suspicion that no real intention to transfer property was present);

(2) The debtor remained in possession of the property after the transfer and continued to deal with the property as his own (if a real transfer was intended, the debtor would not have kept possession);

(3) The conveyance was made while a creditor's action was pending against the debtor (a transfer made after litigation has begun or immediately prior to anticipated litigation is also highly suspicious);

(4) The transaction was secret;

(5) The transferee took only a legal interest in the property and held the property for the equitable benefit of the transferor, in effect creating a trust (see Ch. 29) for the debtor (the passage of bare legal title hinders and delays the judgment creditor by depriving him or her of legal remedies while, at the same time, allowing the debtor to keep the complete beneficial interest);

(6) The deed itself contained statements that it was made honestly and truly, and that it was bona fide (such unusual recitals are suspicious).

Today, all jurisdictions recognize these "badges of fraud" in determining whether a particular conveyance has been made to defeat creditors. Courts also carefully scrutinize intra-family transfers, voluntary transfers, transfers without consideration, and transfers made immediately prior to the start of litigation against the debtor.

If a fraudulent conveyance has been made, the defrauded creditor can either bring a legal action to set the conveyance aside, or he or she can completely ignore the transfer and levy on and sell the property despite the conveyance. Generally, where the creditor has a lien on the property, he or she can also recover damages in tort against anyone who hinders him or her in execution of the lien.

Apart from bankruptcy, what legal alternatives are available to an individual who cannot pay his or her debts?

Before resorting to federal bankruptcy law, a debtor who is unable to pay his or her debts as they fall due should first try to work out an acceptable repayment plan with his or her creditors. The debtor should contact the creditors, explain his or her financial situation, and try to obtain a voluntary extension of time. To eliminate a few of the debts, the debtor might also encourage certain secured creditors to repossess purchased items that the debtor can get along without. Sometimes, the debtor will place the operation of a business and his or her financial affairs under control of a creditor's committee which may be able to provide sound management, allowing both the creditors and the debtor to benefit.

State law also provides the debtor with a number of alternatives to bankruptcy, including assignments for the benefit of creditors, a composition for the benefit of creditors, and, in some states, a state wage earner receivership.

Assignments for the benefit of creditors. A debtor may voluntarily assign (transfer) all his or her assets (with the exclusion of exempt property) to another party who is given the job of liquidating the assets and distributing the proceeds to the creditors. Any surplus remaining in the hands of the assignee (the party to whom the property is transferred) after the creditors are paid goes back to the debtor.

A purported assignment for the benefit of creditors is a fraudulent conveyance where it is not really made for the creditors' benefit. To be valid, the assignment must be complete; and the debtor must not retain any interest or advantage in or control over the property. If the debtor attempts to retain the power to revoke the assignment, or to tell the assignee to delay liquidation of the assets, the assignment will be a fraudulent conveyance. Partial assignments in which the debtor transfers only a part of his or her property are generally considered fraudulent in that the creditors are hindered and delayed if they must go, first, to the assignee to satisfy their claims, and then back to the debtor when liquidation of the transferred assets proves insufficient to cover their debts.

In more than 40 states, assignments for the benefit of creditors are strictly regulated by statute. The statutes generally provide for recording of the assignment, filing of the debtor's assets and debts, and bonding by the assignee. In addition, the debtor must properly notify the creditors of the assignment; and the transfer must take place under the watchful eyes of the court.

The assignee's primary duty is to sell the debtor's property and convert it into cash for distribution among the creditors as expeditiously as possible. The transfer and sale of assets, however, is subject to any existing liens, claims, or encumbrances valid as against the debtor. Thus, if there are any lien creditors, they will be paid first; and the general creditors will share the balance.

Of course, it is possible that the creditors may not wish to have the debts and assets administered through a general assignment. If this is so, the creditors can force the debtor into bankruptcy (involuntary bankruptcy is discussed in a following section). If the creditors force the debtor into bankruptcy after the assignment has been made, the assignee is required to turn over the debtor's estate to the bankruptcy receiver or trustee. The bankruptcy court then examines the estate and determines the propriety and reasonableness of disbursements made out of the assets by the assignee.

In conclusion, there are certain advantages and disadvantages to a general assignment for the benefit of creditors. Since assignment is informal, it may be less expensive and less time consuming than formal bankruptcy proceedings. And because assignment is flexible, it may result in higher sales proceeds (sufficient to pay off the creditors in full and still leave the debtor with some excess). But while bankruptcy costs more and results in less, it does result in a discharge of the debtor's debts which an assignment for the benefit of creditors does not do. Thus, in the assignment situation, if the creditors are not paid in full out of the sales proceeds of the transferred assets, the debtor remains liable for the deficiencies. This inability to obtain a discharge is the biggest disadvantage of making a general assignment. It is for this reason that assignments for the benefit of creditors are seldom used.

What is a composition of creditors?

A composition of creditors is simply a contract between the debtor and his or her creditors, and between and among the creditors themselves, that each creditor will accept a lesser sum immediately in full payment of the total amount owing. Thus, unlike an assignment for the benefit of creditors, a composition of creditors effects a discharge of the debtor from the remaining debts he or she owes to creditors who agree to the plan. The discharge occurs at the time the debtor pays the creditors in accord with the plan. And as a composition is not statutory in nature, there is nothing to prevent a debtor whose debts have been discharged by composition from later going through bankruptcy (a debtor whose debts have been discharged in bankruptcy, on the other hand, cannot go through bankruptcy again for another six years).

What is an extension?

An extension is much like a composition in that it, too, is based on an agreement or contract between or among the debtor and his or her creditors. It is unlike a composition in that the debtor pays his or her creditors not in part, but in full. An extension simply gives the debtor more time—that is, it results in payment in full, but over a period of time extended beyond the original due date. Sometimes, the debtor bargains for a combination composition and extension contract with his or her creditors which permits the debtor to pay less in full satisfaction of the debts over an extended period of time. This is not a true composition contract because the creditors are not immediately paid; nor is it a true extension since it does not result in full payment to the creditors.

What is a state wage earner receivership?

Statutes in a few states provide for a voluntary state wage earner receivership. In Ohio, for example, the court will appoint someone, upon the debtor's request, to act as a receiver in collecting all non-exempt wages of the debtor and distributing them pro rata among the debtor's creditors until all debts are paid in full. During the time the wage earner receivership is in effect, all repossessions and wage garnishments against the debtor are prohibited (as will be seen in a following section, a similar type of federal receivership may be available under Chapter 13 of the federal Bankruptcy Act).

What is bankruptcy?

So far in this chapter, we have dealt with debtor-creditor law on the state level. We have seen that state law generally rewards the creditor who acts most quickly with respect to the debtor and the debtor's property. Thus, the creditor who acts first to obtain a lien or attach the debtor's property will most likely obtain payment before the other creditors. Bankruptcy law, on the other hand, is federal law, and it does not emphasize the "first in time" concept. Rather, it attempts to treat all creditors within the same class as equals: thus, whatever property the debtor owns will be shared equally by all creditors within the same class. In addition, the federal law emphasizes a "discharge" of the debtor's debts. The idea behind the law is to give the debtor a chance to start over. The basic Bankruptcy Act was originally passed by Congress in 1898. In November of 1978 (80 years later), President Carter signed into law a completely new Bankruptcy Act which became effective on October 1, 1979. While the new law continues the basic philosophy of the old and accomplishes the same basic results, many of the specifics have changed. We will study these specifics throughout the remainder of the chapter as we study bankruptcy law.

Bankruptcy law may be divided into two main areas. The first is the so-called "straight bankruptcy" which, as described earlier, is designed to liquidate the debtor's property, pay off his or her creditors, and discharge the debtor from any remaining debts. Straight bankruptcy can be either "voluntary" or "involuntary". The new Bankruptcy Act deals with straight bankruptcy in Chapters 3, 5, and 7.

The second main area of bankruptcy law is "debtor rehabilitation". Debtor rehabilitation does not work to liquidate the debtor's property and discharge the debtor's debts. Rather, it serves to reorganize his or her holdings and instruct his or her creditors to look to the debtor's future earnings for payment. The new Bankruptcy Act deals with debtor reorganization and rehabilitation in Chapters 11 and 13 (the old law dealt with these subjects in several chapters). Chapter 11 is concerned specifically with debtor reorganizations, including railroad reorganizations under Subchapter IV. Chapter 13, entitled "Adjustment of Debts of an Individual with Regular Income", deals with debtor rehabilitation and resembles the state law composition, extension, and wage earner receivership plans discussed previously in the chapter.

In the sections that follow, we will deal with straight bankruptcy, both voluntary and involuntary, as well as with debtor reorganization and rehabilitation.

What is straight bankruptcy?

Straight bankruptcy does two things:

(1) *It liquidates the debtor's non-exempt property.* To accomplish this, the bankruptcy court usually appoints a "trustee" whose job is to collect the bankrupt's property, sell it, and distribute the proceeds among the bankrupt's creditors. Where the debtor has very little property, or the situation is otherwise uncomplicated, a trustee may not be needed and will not be appointed.

(2) *It discharges the bankrupt from any remaining debts that are not specifically excluded from discharge from the Bankruptcy Act.* The old law provided that contingent claims which were not capable of liquidation or of reasonable estimate were not "provable" and could not be discharged—the 1979 law makes no such exception.

Section 101(4) of the new law states: Claim means—

(A) the right to payment, whether or not such right is reduced to judgment, liquidated, unliquidated, fixed, contingent, matured, unmatured, disputed, undisputed, legal, equitable, secured, or unsecured. * * *

Nearly all straight bankruptcies are voluntarily initiated by the debtor. Involuntary bankruptcies, initiated by the debtor's creditors, are unusual by comparison. The debtor begins a voluntary straight bankruptcy by filing a petition with the federal district court in the area where the debtor's domicile, residence, or principal place of business has existed for the longest period of time during the preceding 180 days as provided by Section 1472 of the 1979 Act. The debtor's solvency is immaterial, as is the amount of his or her liabilities, so long as the debtor has debts. The debtor must include in the petition a list of all his or her creditors so that they may be sent a notice of the first creditors' meeting. The new bankruptcy law lists the debtor's duties as follows:

Section 521. Debtor's Duties
The debtor shall—

(1) file a list of creditors, and unless the court orders otherwise, a schedule of assets and liabilities, and a statement of the debtor's financial affairs;

(2) if a trustee is serving in the case, cooperate with the trustee as necessary to enable the trustee to perform the trustee's duties. * * *

(3) if a trustee is serving in the case, surrender to the trustee all property of the estate and any recorded information, including books, documents, records, and papers, relating to the property of the estate; and

(4) appear at the hearing required.

* * *

———

Once the debtor has filed the petition, he or she is automatically declared a bankrupt (called an "order for relief" under the new law), and the first creditors' meeting is called.

Section 301 reads:

Section 301. Voluntary Cases

A voluntary case * * * is commenced by the filing with the bankruptcy court of a petition * * * by an entity that may be a debtor. * * * The commencement of a voluntary case * * * constitutes an order for relief. * * *

———

Where the straight bankruptcy is involuntary, the debtor can be declared a bankrupt, and the first creditors' meeting can be called, only if the following conditions are met:

(1) The debtor must not be a railroad, insurance company, bank, savings and loan association, credit union, farmer, or a corporation that is not a "moneyed business or commercial" enterprise (Sections 109 and 303 of the 1979 Act).

(2) The bankruptcy petition must be filed by the proper number of creditors holding certain minimum claims that are not contingent as to liability. If the debtor has twelve or more creditors, at least three of them must join in filing the petition; if the debtor has less than twelve creditors, a single creditor may legally file. In determining whether the debtor has twelve or more creditors, several kinds of creditors are not counted, including the debtor's own employees or relatives; fully secured creditors; officers, directors, or stockholders of the debtor; and any creditor who has received a lien, transfer, or preference that can be avoided under the law. The creditors who file (whether three or more or a single creditor) must hold claims that are not contingent as to liability and that amount to at least $5,000 beyond the value of any property securing such claims.

(3) Finally, the debtor must be properly served with the petition. If the debtor is properly served but does not respond to the petition, he or she may be declared a bankrupt by default. If the debtor responds and controverts the petition, he or she may be declared a bankrupt in a judicial trial only if it is shown that (1) the debtor is generally not paying his or her debts as they fall due, *or* (2) a custodian took possession of the debtor's property within 120 days of the filing of the petition under a general assignment for the benefit of creditors, a receivership, or the like.

Under the old bankruptcy law, a debtor could not be forced into involuntary bankruptcy unless he or she had committed one of more of six so-called "acts of bankruptcy". This is no longer a part of the law. The 1979 Bankruptcy Act allows creditors to petition a debtor into bankruptcy if the above requirements are met without regard to the old acts of bankruptcy. However, if the debtor successfully controverts the creditors' petition (by showing that he or she is generally paying his or her debts as they fall due and that his or her property has not been taken over by or transferred to any custodian as described above), then the debtor may have judgment against the creditors who filed the petition for costs, attorneys' fees, and other damages, including punitive damages if the creditors filed in bad faith. Section 303 of the new bankruptcy law provides for the law on involuntary cases as follows:

Section 303. Involuntary Cases

* * *

(b) An involuntary case is commenced by the filing with the bankruptcy court of a petition * * *

(1) by three or more entities, each of which is either a holder of a claim against such person that is not contingent as to liability * * * if such claims aggregate at least $5,000 more than the value of any lien on property of the debtor securing such claims * * *;

(2) if there are fewer than 12 such holders, excluding any employee or insider of such person and any transferee of a transfer which is voidable * * * by one or more of such holders that hold in the aggregate at least $5,000 of such claims;

* * *

(d) The debtor * * * may file an answer to a petition under this section.

(e) After notice and a hearing, and for cause, the court may require the petitioners under this section to file a bond to indemnify the debtor for such amounts as the court may later allow under subsection (i) of this section.

(f) * * * [E]xcept to the extent that the court orders otherwise, and until an order for relief in the case, any business of the debtor may continue to operate, and the debtor may continue to use, acquire, or dispose of property as if an involuntary case concerning the debtor had not been commenced.

(g) At any time after the commencement of an involuntary case * * * but before an order for relief in the case, the court, on request of a party in interest, after notice to the debtor and a hearing, and if necessary to preserve the property of the estate or to prevent loss to the estate, may appoint an interim trustee * * * to take possession of the property of the estate and to operate any business of the debtor. Before an order for relief, the debtor may regain possession of property if the debtor files such bond as the court requires, conditioned on the debtor's accounting for and delivering to the trustee, if there is an order for relief in the case, such property, or the value, as of the date the debtor regains possession of the property.

(h) If the petition is not timely controverted, the court shall order relief against the debtor in an involuntary case. * * * Otherwise, after trial, the court shall order relief against the debtor in an involuntary case * * * only if —

(1) the debtor is generally not paying such debtor's debts as such debts become due; or

(2) within 120 days before the due date of the filing of the petition, a custodian, other than a trustee * * * was appointed or took possession.

(i) If the court dismisses a petition under this section other than on consent of all petitioners and the debtor, and if the debtor does not waive the right to judgment under this subsection, the court may grant judgment—

(1) against the petitioner and in favor of the debtor for—

(A) costs;

(B) a reasonable attorney's fee; or

(C) any damages proximately caused by the taking of possession of the debtor's property by a trustee * * *

(2) against any petitioner that filed the petition in bad faith for—

(A) any damages proximately caused by such filings; or

(B) punitive damages.

(j) Only after notice to all creditors and a hearing may the court dismiss a petition under this section—

   (1) on the motion of a petitioner;

   (2) on consent of all petitioners and the debtor; or

   (3) for want of prosecution.

How does straight bankruptcy proceed once the debtor has been adjudged a bankrupt?

Once the debtor has been adjudged a bankrupt, the straight bankruptcy procedure is the same whether the debtor originally filed for bankruptcy voluntarily or was forced into bankruptcy upon the petition of his or her creditors. The debtor's creditors file their claims, and the claims are allowed or disallowed according to the specific procedure set forth in Sections 501 and 502 of the 1979 Bankruptcy Act.

The Act provides:

Section 501. Filing of Proofs of Claims or Interests

(a) A creditor * * * may file a proof of a claim. An equity security holder may file a proof of interest.

* * *

(c) If a creditor does not timely file a proof of such creditor's claim, the debtor or the trustee may file a proof of such claim.

Section 502. Allowance of claims or interest

(a) A claim or interest, proof of which is filed * * * is deemed allowed, unless a party in interest * * * objects.

(b) * * * [I]f such objection to a claim is made, the court after notice and a hearing shall determine the amount of such claim as of the date of the filing of the petition, and shall allow such claim in such amount, except to the extent that—

(1) such claim is unenforceable against the debtor * * * ;

(2) such claim is for unmatured interest;

(3) such claim may be offset * * * against a debt owing to the debtor;

(4) if such claim is for tax assessed against property of the estate, such claim exceeds the value of the interest of the estate in such property;

(5) if such claim is for services of an insider or attorney of the debtor, such claim exceeds the reasonable value of such services;

* * *

(7) if such claim is the claim of a lessor for damages resulting from the termination of a lease of real property, such claim exceeds—

   (A) the rent * * * for the greater of one year, or 15 percent not to exceed three years, of the remaining term of such lease * * * plus * * *

   (B) any unpaid rent due under such lease * * *

(8) if such claim is for damages resulting from the termination of an employment contract, such claim exceeds—

   (A) the compensation provided by such contract * * * for one year * * * plus

   (B) the unpaid compensation due under such contract * * *

(9) such claim results from a reduction, due to late payment, in the amount of an otherwise applicable credit available to the debtor in connection with

an employment tax on wages, salaries, or commissions earned from the debtor.

(c) There shall be estimated for purpose of allowance under this section—

(1) any contingent or unliquidated claim; fixing or liquidation of which, as the case may be, would unduly delay the closing of the case. * * *

Notice that claims for unmatured interest will not be allowed, and that claims for rent on leases of real estate will generally be allowed only for one year's rent beyond what was owing at the time of the filing of the petition (e. g., if the debtor had a lease to pay rent on a building for four more years at the time of the filing, the lessor's claim would only be allowed for unpaid rent due under the lease at the time of the filing plus one year's rent). The same is true for long term employment contracts.

Once the creditor's claims have been determined, the first creditors' meeting is scheduled; all creditors are notified as to when the meeting will take place.

Sections 341, 342, and 343 provide:

Section 341. Meetings of Creditors and Equity Security Holders

(a) Within a reasonable time after the order for relief * * * there shall be a meeting of creditors.

Section 342. Notice

There shall be given such notice as is appropriate * * *

Section 343. Examination of the Debtor

The debtor shall appear and submit to examination under oath at the meeting of creditors * * * Creditors * * * may examine the debtor.

At the first meeting, the creditors question the bankrupt regarding the location and value of his or her assets. The creditors hope to discover, through their questions, whether the debtor has made any fraudulent conveyances or preferential transfers (discussed below).

In addition to questioning the debtor, the creditors also elect a trustee to act as their representative. Creditors holding at least 20% of the total claims must vote in the election, and the trustee must receive a majority of the votes. If no one person receives a majority, the court will appoint the trustee.

Section 702 states in part:

Section 702. Election of Trustee
* * *

(b) At the meeting of creditors * * * creditors may elect one person to serve as trustee in the case if election of a trustee is requested by creditors that may vote * * * and that hold at least 20 percent in amount of the claims * * *

(c) A candidate for trustee is elected trustee if—

(1) creditors holding at least 20 percent in amount of the claims * * * vote; and

(2) such candidate receives the votes of creditors holding a majority in amount of claims specified * * *

(d) If a trustee is not elected under subsection (c) of this section, then the interim trustee shall serve as trustee in the case.

The trustee's job, in any case, is to collect the bankrupt's assets. After conducting whatever investigation is necessary to uncover the assets, the trustee is empowered to avoid, in court, any transfers that prove to be fraudulent or preferential. You will recall the state law definition of a "fraudulent conveyance" from earlier in the chapter. The federal Bankruptcy

Act defines a "fraudulent transfer" and "fraudulent obligation" as follows:

Section 548. Fraudulent Transfers and Obligations

(a) The trustee may avoid any transfer of an interest of the debtor in property, or any obligation incurred by the debtor, that *was made or incurred on or within one year before the date of the filing of the petition*, if the debtor—

(1) made such transfer or incurred such obligation with actual intent to hinder, delay or defraud any entity to which the debtor was or became, on or after the date that such transfer occurred or such obligation was incurred, indebted; or

(2) (A) received less than a reasonably equivalent value in exchange for such transfer or obligation; and

(B)(i) was insolvent on the date that such transfer was made or such obligation was incurred, or became insolvent as a result of such transfer or obligation;

(ii) was engaged in business, or was about to engage in business or a transaction, for which any property remaining with the debtor was an unreasonably small capital; or

(iii) intended to incur, or believed that the debtor would incur, debts that would be beyond the debtor's ability to pay as such debts matured. [Emphasis added.]

Thus, the trustee may set aside a transfer made or obligation incurred by the debtor within one year of the filing of the bankruptcy petition if the debtor made the transfer or incurred the obligation with actual intent to defraud *or* if the debtor received less than reasonably equivalent consideration for the transfer or obligation and was insolvent at the time (or became insolvent as the result of the transfer or obligation).

The trustee may also set aside any *preferential transfer* made by the debtor. A preferential transfer is a transfer of the bankrupt's nonexempt property for the benefit of a creditor on account of an antecedent (previous) debt. The transfer is preferential only if the debtor was insolvent at the time he or she made the transfer. Section 101(26) of the 1979 Bankruptcy Act defines "insolvent" as a "financial condition such that the sum of [one's] debts is greater than all of [one's] property, at a fair valuation, exclusive of (i) property transferred, concealed or removed with intent to hinder, delay, or defraud [one's] creditors; and (ii) property that may be exempted from property of the estate". To be preferential, the transfer must also operate to permit the transferee creditor to obtain a greater percentage of his or her claim than some other creditor in the same class. Since, by definition, a "preference" requires a transfer on account of an antecedent debt, the creation of a new debt through execution of a mortgage or by buying more goods on account would not be a preference. Nor would a gift transfer constitute a preference since a gift would not involve a creditor (however, a gift might well constitute a fraudulent conveyance). Also, to be preferential, the transfer must generally be made within 90 days before the bankruptcy filing, but may go up to one year prior to filing if an insider is involved. Section 547 of the new law is the "preferences" section.

It reads in part:

Section 547. Preferences
* * *

(b) * * * [T]he trustee may avoid any transfer of property of the debtor—

(1) to or for the benefit of a creditor;

(2) for or on account of an antecedent debt owed by the debtor before such transfer was made;

(3) made while the debtor was insolvent;

(4) made—

(A) on or within 90 days before the date of the filing of the petition; or

(B) between 90 days and one year before the date of the filing of the petition, if such creditor, at the time of such transfer—

(i) was an *insider*; and

(ii) had reasonable cause to believe the debtor was insolvent at the time of such transfer; and

(5) that enables such creditor to receive more than such creditor would receive if
* * *

(B) the transfer had not been made; and

(C) such creditor received payment of such debt to the extent provided by the provisions of this title [i. e., if the creditor received no more than he or she would have received through the straight bankruptcy pro-

ceedings, the transfer may not be avoided by the trustee].

———

And Section 101(25) of the Act defines "insider" as follows:

(25) "Insider" includes

(A) if the debtor is an individual—

(i) relative of the debtor or of a general partner of

(ii) partnership in which the debtor is a general partner;

(iii) general partner of the debtor; or

(iv) corporation of which the debtor is a director, officer, or person in control;

(B) if the debtor is a corporation—

(i) director of the debtor;

(ii) officer of the debtor;

(iii) person in control of the debtor;

(iv) partnership in which the debtor is a general partner;

(v) general partner of the debtor; or

(vi) relative of a general partner, director, officer, or person in control of the debtor;

(C) if the debtor is a partnership—

(i) general partner in the debtor;

(ii) relative of a general partner in, general partner of, or person in control of the debtor;

    (iii) partnership in which the debtor is a general partner;

    (iv) general partner of the debtor; or

    (v) person in control of the debtor.

———

Notice that with regard to a transfer made on or within 90 days before the date of filing of the bankruptcy petition, the transferee need not know or have reason to believe that the debtor is insolvent at the time of the transfer. With regard to a transfer made to an insider between 90 days and one year before the date of filing, the insider must have reasonable cause to believe that the debtor is insolvent at the time of the transfer or the transfer will not be preferential.

It is the duty of the trustee in bankruptcy to sell the property of the bankrupt's estate so as to be able to distribute the money to the bankrupt's creditors. The creditors, if they choose, may elect a committee to work with the trustee. Sections 704 and 705 of the 1979 Act set forth the duties of the trustee and the creditors' committee as follows:

Section 704. Duties of Trustee
The trustee shall

(1) collect and reduce to money the property of the estate for which such trustee serves, and close up such estate as expeditiously as is compatible with the best interests of parties in interest;

(2) be accountable for all property received;

(3) investigate the financial affairs of the debtor;

(4) if a purpose would be served, examine proofs of claims and object to the allowance of any claim that is improper;

(5) if advisable, oppose the discharge of the debtor;

(6) unless the court orders otherwise, furnish such information concerning the estate and the estate's administration as is requested by a party in interest;

(7) if the business of the debtor is authorized to be operated, file with the court and with any governmental unit charged with responsibility for collection or determination of any tax arising out of such operation, periodic reports and summaries of the operation of such business, including a statement of receipts and disbursements, and such other information as the court requires; and

(8) make final report and file a final account of the administration of the estate with the court.

Section 705. Creditors' Committee
(a) At the meeting under section 341 * * * creditors that may vote for a trustee under section 702 * * * may elect a committee of not fewer than three, and not more than eleven, creditors, each of whom holds an allowable unsecured claim * * *

(b) A committee elected under subsection (a) of this section may consult with the trustee in connection with the administration of the estate, make recommendations to the trustee respecting the performance of the trustee's duties, and submit to the court any question affecting the administration of the estate.

———

After all the bankrupt's nonexempt property is liquidated, the bankrupt's "estate" is formally closed. The trustee makes a final report which, when approved by the court, permits cash disbursement of the sales proceeds to the creditors. Any remaining debts of the bankrupt are discharged, with the exception of those specifically excluded by the Bankruptcy Act.

Is any of the bankrupt's property exempt from the bankruptcy sale?

It was pointed out earlier in the chapter that all states exempt certain property from the claims of creditors. These exemptions apply to bankruptcy proceedings as well. Thus, all or part of the bankrupt's equity in his or her home, auto, household furnishings, savings, life insurance, tools, etc. are exempt from the bankruptcy sale even where the bankrupt's other assets are nowhere near sufficient to cover the bankrupt's debts. The 1979 Bankruptcy Act specifically provides for certain exemptions that the debtor may choose as an alternative to the exemptions provided by his or her own state law.

Section 522 of the Act provides:

Section 522. Exemptions

* * *

(b) * * * [A]n individual debtor may exempt from property of the estate either—

(1) property that is specified under subsection (d) of this section * * * or, in the alternative,

(2) * * * any property that is exempt under * * * State or local law that is applicable * * * at the place in which the debtor's domicile has been located for the 180 days immediately preceding the date of the filing of the petition, or for a longer portion of such 180 day period than in any other place;

* * *

(d) The following property may be exempted under subsection (b)(1) of this section:

(1) The debtor's aggregate interest, not to exceed $7,500 in value, in real property or personal property that the debtor or a dependent of the debtor uses as a residence * * *

(2) The debtor's interest, not to exceed $1,200 in value, in one motor vehicle.

(3) The debtor's interest, not to exceed $200 in value in any particular item, in household furnishings, household goods, wearing apparel, appliances, books, animals, crops, or musical instruments, that are held primarily for the personal, family, or household use of the debtor or a dependent of the debtor.

(4) The debtor's aggregate interest, not to exceed $500 in value, in jewelry held primarily for the personal, family, or household use of the debtor or a dependent of the debtor.

(5) The debtor's aggregate interest, not to exceed in value $400 plus any unused amount of the exemption provided under paragraph (1) of this subsection, in any property.

(6) The debtor's aggregate interest, not to exceed $750 in value, in any implements, professional books, or tools, of the trade of the debtor or the trade of a dependent of the debtor.

(7) Any unmatured life insurance contract owned by the debtor, other than a credit life insurance contract.

(8) The debtor's aggregate interest, not to exceed in value $4,000 * * * in any accrued dividend or interest under or loan value of, any unmatured life insurance contract owned by the

debtor under which the insured is the debtor or an individual of whom the debtor is a dependent.

(9) Professionally prescribed health aids for the debtor or a dependent of the debtor.

(10) The debtor's right to receive

  (A)   a social security benefit, unemployment compensation, or a local public assistance benefit;

  (B)   a veteran's benefit;

  (C)   a disability, illness, or unemployment benefit;

  (D)   alimony, support, or separate maintenance, to the extent reasonably necessary for the support of the debtor and any dependent of the debtor;

  (E)   a payment under a stock bonus, pension, profit sharing, annuity, or similar plan or contract on account of illness, disability, death, age, or length of service, to the extent reasonably necessary for the support of the debtor and any dependent of the debtor;

(11) The debtor's right to receive, or property that is traceable to—

  (A)   an award under a crime victim's reparation law;

  (B)   a payment on account of the wrongful death of an individual of whom the debtor was a dependent, to the extent reasonably necessary for the support of the debtor and any dependent of the debtor;

  (C)   a payment under a life insurance contract that insured the life of an individual of whom the debtor was a dependent on the date of such individual's death, to the extent reasonably necessary for

the support of the debtor and any dependent of the debtor;

  (D)   a payment, not to exceed $7,500, on account of personal bodily injury, not including pain and suffering or compensation for actual pecuniary loss, of the debtor or an individual of whom the debtor is a dependent; or

  (E)   a payment in compensation of loss of future earnings of the debtor or an individual of whom the debtor is or was a dependent, to the extent reasonably necessary for the support of the debtor and any dependent of the debtor.

(e) A waiver of exemptions executed in favor of a creditor that holds an unsecured claim against the debtor is unenforceable * * * with respect to such claim against property that the debtor may exempt under subsection (b) of this section.

———

Thus, Section 522 provides a minimum amount of exemptions that the debtor may claim. If the debtor's own state law provides larger or more beneficial exemptions, the debtor may claim the state exemptions as an alternative to Section 522. In either event, the exempt properties are not subject to sale for the debtor's debts with two exceptions: all the debtor's property—even exempt property—can be reached to satisfy tax debts and support obligations of the debtor (alimony and child support).

What is a "discharge" in bankruptcy?

One of the main purposes of the Bankruptcy Act is to discharge debtors from their remaining debts so that the debtors can start over fresh in life. To "discharge" a debt is to completely eliminate it. This means that once a bankrupt's debts are discharged in bankruptcy, he or she has no further obligation with respect to payment. Debts listed by the debtor may be discharged even though the creditor files no proof of claim under Section 501. Still, not all debts are dischargeable in bankruptcy; and, sometimes, an objection to discharge may be raised with the result that there is no discharge at all. Our study of discharge will be divided into four parts: (1) objections to discharge; (2) exceptions to discharge; (3) effect of discharge; and (4) revocation of discharge.

OBJECTIONS TO DISCHARGE

The 1979 Bankruptcy Act spells out several grounds for denying a debtor a discharge in bankruptcy. Section 727(c) of the Act states that either the trustee or a creditor may object to discharge on any of the following grounds:

(1) The debtor's effort to conceal or destroy property within one year before the filing of the petition or after the petition is filed;

(2) The debtor's effort to destroy or falsify financial records or his or her failure to keep or preserve such records or information;

(3) The debtor's fraudulent act in making false oaths, false claims, attempting to obtain money or property by false pretenses, or in withholding information relating to his or her property or financial affairs;

(4) The debtor's failure to explain satisfactorily any loss or deficiency of assets to meet his or her liabilities.

(5) The debtor's refusal to obey an order of the court requiring him or her to answer questions material to the bankruptcy proceeding. Of course, the bankrupt has a constitutional, Fifth Amendment right to refuse to answer where the answer might tend to incriminate him or her. But if the court grants the debtor immunity so that there can be no incrimination, his or her continued failure to answer will serve as grounds for denial of discharge.

(6) The debtor's previous discharge in bankruptcy within the last 6 years (measured from filing date to filing date).

Under the old law, the fact that the debtor had failed to pay his or her filing fees was also grounds for denying discharge. This is no longer the law under the 1979 Act, and was probably unconstitutional in any case in that it denied equal protection of the laws to those persons who could not afford the filing fees.

If the bankruptcy court finds that any one of the six grounds listed in Section 727 exists, the court will deny the debtor a discharge, and the debtor will leave the bankruptcy proceeding still owing the same debts that he or she owed prior to the proceeding (of course, the debts will be less in amount since the creditors will have received a distribution from sale of the debtor's nonexempt property). The specific language of Section 727 is as follows:

Section 727. Discharge

(a) The court shall grant the debtor a discharge, unless

* * *

(2) the debtor, with intent to hinder, delay, or defraud a creditor or an officer of the estate charged with custody of property * * * has transferred, removed, destroyed, mutilated, or concealed, or has permitted to be transferred, removed, destroyed, mutilated, or concealed—

(A) property of the debtor, within one year before the date of the filing of the petition; or

(B) property of the estate, after the date of the filing of the petition.

(3) the debtor has concealed, destroyed, mutilated, falsified, or failed to keep or preserve any recorded information, including books, documents, records, and papers, from which the debtor's financial condition or business transactions might be ascertained, unless such act or failure to act was justified under all the circumstances of the case;

(4) the debtor knowingly and fraudulently, in or in connection with the case—

(A) made a false oath or account;

(B) presented or used a false claim;

(C) gave, offered, received, or attempted to obtain money, property, or advantage, or a promise of money, property, or advantage, for acting or forbearing to act; or

(D) withheld from an officer of the estate entitled to possession * * * any recorded information, including books, documents, records, and papers, relating to the debtor's property or financial affairs;

(5) the debtor has failed to explain satisfactorily, before determination of denial of discharge under this paragraph, any loss of assets or deficiency of assets to meet the debtor's liabilities;

(6) the debtor has refused, in the case —

(A) to obey any lawful order of the court, other than an order to respond to a material question or to testify;

(B) on the ground of privilege against self incrimination to respond to a material question approved by the court or to testify, after the debtor has been granted immunity with respect to the matter concerning which such privilege was invoked; or

(C) on a ground other than the properly invoked privilege against self-incrimination, to respond to a material question approved by the court or to testify;

(7) the debtor has committed any act specified in paragraph (2), (3), (4), (5), or (6) of this subsection, on or within one year before the date of the filing of the petition, or during the case commenced within six years before the date of the filing of the petition, or during the case, in connection with another case concerning an insider;

(8) the debtor has been granted a discharge * * * in a case commenced within six years before the date of the filing of the petition;

* * *

(b) Except as provided in Section 523 * * * a discharge * * * discharges the debtor from all debts that arose before the date of the order for relief * * * whether or not a proof of claim based on such debt or liability is filed * * * and whether or not a claim based on any such debt or liability is allowed * * *

EXCEPTIONS TO DISCHARGE

As stated previously, not all debts are dischargeable in bankruptcy. Section 523 of the Bankruptcy Act specifically excepts nine types of debts from discharge; and any creditor who can show that his or her claim falls within one of these nine categories can collect any unpaid portion of the claim from the debtor personally. The nine statutory exceptions include:

(1) Back taxes the debtor-bankrupt owes (unless the taxes became due and owing more than three years before the bankruptcy) or taxes for which no tax returns were filed.

(2) Debts that arise from obtaining money by false pretenses or false representation (including "innocent" misrepresentation) and debts that result from obtaining credit on the basis of materially false financial statements.

(3) Debts that are not properly scheduled, unless the creditor has notice of the bankruptcy proceeding before the time to file claims has expired. This means that if the bankrupt fails to schedule all of his or her creditors, and gives an incomplete list of creditors to the bankruptcy court, the debts owing to the unscheduled creditors will not be discharged unless the creditors have other actual notice of the proceeding.

(4) Debts resulting from the bankrupt's misconduct as a public or corporate officer or as a result of breach of fiduciary duty. This would include, for example, debts arising from fraud, embezzlement, or larceny.

(5) Unpaid support obligations such as alimony, maintenance, or child support.

(6) Claims resulting from the debtor-bankrupt's willful and malicious injury to the person or property of another.

(7) Fines or other penalties owed to the government and not classified as taxes.

(8) Educational loans due within the last five years unless this would result in undue hardship to the debtor or his or her dependents.

(9) Debts that could have been listed in a previous bankruptcy proceeding of the debtor or for which discharge was waived in a previous bankruptcy proceeding.

The old bankruptcy law provided that wages the bankrupt owed to his or her employees could not be discharged. The new Act does not recognize this exception. Section 523, which deals with exceptions to discharge, provides as follows:

Section 523. Exceptions to discharge

(a) A discharge * * * does not discharge an individual debtor from any debt—

(1) for a tax or a customs duty—

(A) of the kind and for the periods specified in section 507 [three years] * * *

(B) with respect to which a return, is required—

(i) was not filed; * * *

(C) with respect to which the debtor made a fraudulent return or willfully attempted in any manner to evade or defeat such tax;

(2) for obtaining money, property, services, or an extension, renewal, or refinance of credit, by—

(A) false pretenses, a false representation, or actual fraud, other than a statement respecting the debtor's or an insider's financial condition; or

(B) use of a statement in writing—

(i) that is materially false;

(ii) respecting the debtor's or an insider's financial condition;

(iii) on which the creditor to whom the debtor is liable for obtaining such money, property, services, or credit reasonably relied; and

(iv) that the debtor caused to be made or published with intent to deceive;

(3) neither listed nor scheduled * * * unless such creditor had notice or actual knowledge of the case in time for * * * timely filing;

(4) for fraud or defalcation while acting in a fiduciary capacity, embezzlement, or larceny;

(5) to a spouse, former spouse, or child of the debtor, for alimony to, maintenance for, or support of such spouse or child, in connection with a separation agreement, divorce decree, or property settlement agreement * * *;

(6) for willful and malicious injury by the debtor to another entity or to the property of another entity;

(7) to the extent such debt is for a fine, penalty, or forfeiture payable to and for the benefit of a governmental unit * * * other than a tax penalty * * *;

(8) to a governmental unit, or a nonprofit institution of higher education, for an educational loan, unless

(A) such loan first became due before five years before the date of the filing of the petition; or

(B) excepting such debt from discharge under this paragraph will impose an undue hardship on the debtor and the debtor's dependents; or

(9) that was or could have been listed or scheduled by the debtor in a prior case * * * under the Bankruptcy Act in which the debtor waived discharge or was denied discharge * * *

EFFECT OF DISCHARGE

Section 524 of the 1979 Bankruptcy Act is entitled "Effect of Discharge". The Section states clearly that discharged debts are no longer collectible. In a new provision of the law, the Statute also makes it clear that promises made by a debtor *after* discharge to pay discharged debts are not enforceable. Under prior law, such promises were enforceable even in the absence of consideration (see Ch. 9). The debtor may enter into an agreement *prior to discharge* to pay such debts, but even then, he or she may rescind the agreement for a period of 30 days. Also, before entering into the agreement, a hearing must be held in which the court explains that the debtor need not promise to repay the debt. And if the debt is a "consumer debt", the court must approve the agreement as not involving undue hardship for the debtor and as being in the debtor's best interests. Section 101 (7) defines a "consumer debt" as a "debt incurred by an individual primarily for a personal, family, or household purpose".

Section 524 reads in part:

Section 524. Effect of Discharge

(a) A discharge in a case under this title—

(1) voids any judgment at any time obtained, to the extent that such judgment is a determination of the personal liability of the debtor with respect to any debt discharged under section 727 * * *;

(2) operates as an injunction against the commencement or continuation of an action, the employment of process, or any act, to collect,

recover, or offset any such debt as a personal liability of the debtor, or from property of the debtor * * * ;

* * *

(c) An agreement between a holder of a claim and the debtor, the consideration for which in whole or in part, is based on a debt that is dischargeable in a case under this title is enforceable only to any extent enforceable under applicable nonbankruptcy law, whether or not discharge of such debt is waived, only if—

(1) such agreement was made before the granting of the discharge * * * ;

(2) the debtor has not rescinded such agreement within 30 days after such agreement becomes enforceable;

(3) the provisions of subsection (d) of this section have been complied with; and

(4) in a case concerning an individual, to the extent that such debt is a consumer debt that is not secured by real property of the debtor, the court approves such agreement as—

(A)(i) not imposing an undue hardship on the debtor or a dependent of the debtor; and

(ii) in the best interest of the debtor; * * *

REVOCATION OF DISCHARGE

Once a discharge has been granted, there are only three grounds for its revocation. A creditor, trustee, or other interested party can obtain a revocation of discharge if he or she can prove that the discharge was obtained through fraud; or that the bankrupt fraudulently failed to tell the trustee that he or she had other properties; or that the bankrupt failed to answer material questions during the bankruptcy proceedings or within one year after discharge. Generally, the court has power to revoke a discharge upon proof of any one of these three grounds for a period of one year following entry of discharge.

Section 727 of the 1979 Act provides:

* * *

(d) On request of the trustee or a creditor, and after notice and a hearing, the court shall revoke a discharge * * * if—

(1) such discharge was obtained through the fraud of the debtor, and the requesting party did not know of such fraud until after the granting of such discharge;

(2) the debtor acquired property that is property of the estate or became entitled to acquire property that would be property of the estate, and knowingly and fraudulently failed to report the acquisition of, or entitlement to, such property, or to deliver or surrender such property to the trustee; or

(3) the debtor committed an act specified in subsection (a)(6) of this section * * * failed to answer material questions * * *

(e) The trustee or a creditor may request a revocation of a discharge—

(1) under subsection (d)(1) of this section, within one year after such discharge was granted; or

(2) under subsection (d)(2) or (d)(3) of this section before the later of

(A) one year after the granting of such discharge; and

(B) the date the case is closed.

In what order are creditors paid?

Early in the chapter, we classified creditors into secured (lien), government, and general creditors. Now we must further classify general creditors into five classes according to the priority in which they will be paid under federal bankruptcy law.

You will recall that the bankrupt's creditors are paid after the trustee has reduced all the bankrupt's nonexempt property into cash. The secured creditors always have the first right to payment, at least insofar as the security covers their claims. To the extent that a secured creditor's security does not cover his or her claim, the secured creditor becomes a general creditor. When there is more than one secured creditor as to the same specific property (i. e., more than one creditor has a lien against the same property), state law governs the order of payment. Generally, the "first in time, first in right" rule controls as to liens on the same property (Ch. 27 deals with the "secured creditor" in detail). And, again, when the proceeds from the particular property run out, the lien (secured) creditor becomes a general creditor for the balance.

In the case of a federal tax lien which attaches to all the debtor's property, Section 6323(a) of the federal Internal Revenue Code recognizes and protects "purchasers, holders of security interests, mechanics lienors, and judgment lien creditors" whose secured interests arose before notice of the tax lien was filed. In other words, specific liens on particular parts of the property, which liens arose prior to perfection of the tax lien (by proper filing as described previously in the chapter), will take priority over the tax lien as to the particular property involved.

So you see that lien creditors are also general creditors to the extent that their liens do not cover their claims. And government, for example, is a general

creditor for any unpaid taxes that remain unassessed at the time the bankruptcy procedure begins. This is so because a tax lien is conditioned on three things: first, assessment by the government of the taxes owing; second, demand upon the taxpayer for payment of the taxes; and third, a failure by the taxpayer to pay. The tax lien itself dates from the time the assessment is made. But suppose that a taxpayer inaccurately reports his or her income and understates his or her taxes by a considerable amount. Months or even years may go by before an audit of the taxpayer's return uncovers the deficiency. Even after the taxpayer has been notified by the government that he or she owes more taxes, another 90 days must pass before the tax deficiency can be legally assessed. By this time, the taxpayer may have gone into bankruptcy. The government, in this case, will not have a lien (as no assessment has been made), but will have only the rights of a general creditor as to the taxes owing. Even so, the government will be in a better position than some general creditors because the Federal Bankruptcy Act categorizes general creditors' claims according to priority. Once the secured creditors have been paid, what cash is left will go to the general creditors, but in the following order:

(1) *First priority*—administrative expenses of handling the bankruptcy. Included are filing fees, costs and expenses incurred in the trustee's administration of the bankruptcy, and any money spent to recover property rightfully belonging to the bankrupt's estate. But remember, even these expenses will not be paid until the claims of all lien creditors have been fully satisfied. However, to the extent that a secured creditor was benefited by an administrative expenditure (e. g., where the trustee incurred an expense to preserve secured property), the trustee may recover the expense from the secured creditor.

(2) *Second priority*—in an involuntary bankruptcy proceeding only, debts incurred in the ordinary course of the debtor's business or financial affairs after filing of the bankruptcy but before the appointment of the trustee.

(3) *Third priority*—certain wage claims arising within 90 days preceding the filing of the bankruptcy petition or the termination of the debtor's business, whichever occurs first. Wages are covered only to the extent of $2,000 per any one claimant. However, wages of all types of employees are covered under the 1979 Bankruptcy Act (prior law covered only nonmanagement employees). Also, "wages" include claims for vacations, severance, and sick pay as well as the usual wages, salaries, or commissions.

(4) *Fourth priority*—unsecured claims for contributions to employee benefit plans up to $2,000 for each employee but less any amount paid such employee for wages under the third priority.

(5) *Fifth priority*—unsecured claims up to a maximum of $900 arising from deposits of money made by people with the debtor in order to purchase or rent property or to purchase services for personal, family, or household use which property or services were not delivered or provided.

(6) *Sixth priority*—taxes legally due and owing within three years of the bankruptcy to the United States or to any state or other political subdivision.

These are taxes for which the government has no lien or secured status.

Only after these six priority claims have been fully covered do the rest of the general creditors share in the balance of the proceeds.

For example, consider the following situation. Joe Bankrupt owns an apartment house worth $350,000 that is mortgaged for $275,000. Joe's total other assets including his $25,000 home will sell for $40,000. Assume that Joe's state provides for a homestead exemption of $5,000, but remember that the 1979 Bankruptcy Act provides for a $7,500 exemption. Assume that Joe has total other exempt property of $2,500. Joe owes the janitor of his apartment house $400 in wages for last month. He owes bills in the amount of $3,200 to department stores, utility companies, and BankAmericard. Joe speculated in the stock market over the past year (buying on margin) and has just lost a total of $105,000 which he now owes to a local stock broker. Joe suffered an uninsured fire loss and owes $22,000 to creditors for business inventory that was destroyed in the fire. He also had an auto accident and is being sued for negligence. Joe failed to properly report his income for last year and has underpaid his taxes. Joe voluntarily files for bankruptcy. Within a month, a $50,000 judgment is entered against Joe for negligence in the auto accident; and the government files a tax claim against him for $12,300 additional income taxes for last year.

Joe's Assets		Joe's Debts	
Apartment house	$350,000	Mortgage	$275,000
Others	40,000	Janitor wages	400
	$390,000	Bills—general	3,200
		Owed to others	
		Fire loss	22,000
		Broker	105,000
		Balance owing at time of filing bankruptcy	$405,600
		Plus	
		Negligence judgment	50,000
		Tax claim	12,300
total assets	$390,000	total debts	$467,900

Administration expenses of the bankruptcy totaled $1,850. Joe's assets brought $390,000. How will the $390,000 be distributed?

First, Joe keeps $10,000 as exempt assets.

Balance of $380,000 goes:

		$380,000
First—to secured creditor on mortgage		−275,000
	Balance	$105,000
Second—priorities among general creditors		
(1) Administration expenses		−1,850
	Balance	$103,150
(2) Janitor's wage claim		−400
	Balance	$102,750
(3) Taxes owing to government		−12,300
	Balance	$ 90,450

The $90,450 will go to Joe's remaining general creditors who are as follows:

General bills owing	$ 3,200
Fire loss creditors	22,000
Broker	105,000
Judgment creditor	50,000
(judgment came too late to give lien)	
Total	$180,200

Thus, there is $90,450 in cash to divide among the remaining general creditors who have claims totaling $180,200. Dividing $90,450 by $180,200, we see that each creditor will receive a little over 50 cents on the dollar (.5016) or about one-half of the amount owing. Joe Bankrupt will be discharged from all his remaining debts and will be left with only $10,000 of assets representing his exempt property.

What is the difference between straight bankruptcy and debtor relief under debtor rehabilitation provisions?

In addition to straight bankruptcy, the Bankruptcy Act offers the debtor alternative methods by which he or she may work to pay off his or her debts without losing all of his or her property. The methods are similar to the composition, extension, and wage earner receivership agreements found in most states. As you will recall, a composition is a contract between the debtor and his or her creditors, and among the creditors themselves, by which the creditors agree to accept a lesser sum immediately in full payment of the amount owing. An extension is an agreement between and among the debtor and his or her creditors whereby the debtor agrees to pay his or her debts in full, but over an extended period of time.

Chapters 11 and 13 of the new Bankruptcy Act deal with "debtor rehabilitation". These chapters incorporate the ideas of composition, extension, and receivership for purposes of providing debtor relief. Chapter 11, entitled "Reorganization", allows a debtor to set up a payment plan involving such devices as composition, extension, and receivership; Chapter 11 is available to debtor individuals, corporations, and partnerships alike. Chapter 13, entitled "Adjustment of Debts of an Individual with Regular Income", provides relief for individual debtors who desire to effect a composition or extension out of future earnings or wages. A debtor may use either Chapter—11 or 13—even after straight bankruptcy proceedings have begun if deemed appropriate by the court (the straight bankruptcy is simply "converted" into a Chapter 11 or 13 case). We will consider both Chapters in the sections that follow.

How does a Chapter 11 reorganization work?

A Chapter 11 "reorganization" permits a debtor to work out a court supervised plan with his or her creditors usually in the nature of a composition (reduction in debt), an extension (more time to pay off the debt), or a receivership (involving the continuing management of

the debtor's business or property). Chapter 11 is purely voluntary on the part of the debtor, and can be utilized by an individual, a partnership, or a corporation. The debtor elects to go under Chapter 11 by filing a petition in the U. S. district court where the debtor would file for straight bankruptcy. Frequently, the court permits the debtor to continue operating his or her own business during the time the Chapter 11 reorganization is in effect.

The debtor must then, within 120 days, file a plan stating the terms of the proposed reorganization. The debtor may propose almost anything, including changes or modifications in the rights of the creditors (both secured and unsecured)—even their division into different classes (e. g., creditors with claims of less than $1,000, or creditors with wage claims, rent claims, or the like). The debtor will generally state how he or she plans to make a living or carry on his or her business, and what payment schedule he or she intends to follow during the period of extension. A debtor corporation may provide, as part of the plan, for the issuance of new securities or for the amendment of the corporate charter.

Sections 1121 and 1123 of the 1979 Act provide:

Section 1121.   Who May File a Plan

(a) The debtor may file a plan with a petition commencing a voluntary case, or at any time in a voluntary case or an involuntary case.

(b) Except as otherwise provided in this section, only the debtor may file a plan until after 120 days after the date of the order for relief under this chapter.

(c) Any party in interest, including the debtor, the trustee, a creditors' committee, * * * may file a plan if and only if—

(1) a trustee has been appointed under this chapter;

(2) the debtor has not filed a plan before 120 days after the date of the order for relief under this chapter; or

(3) the debtor has not filed a plan that has been accepted, before 180 days after the date of the order for relief under this chapter, by each class the claims or interest of which are impaired under the plan.

(d) On request of a party in interest and after notice and a hearing, the court may for cause reduce or increase the 120 day period or the 180 day period referred to in this section.

Section 1123. Contents of plan

(a) A plan shall—

(1) designate * * * classes of claims * * * and classes of interests;

(2) specify any class of claims or interest that is not impaired under the plan [Section 1124 states that "a class of claims is impaired under a plan, unless the plan leaves unaltered the legal, equitable, and contractual rights to which such claim or interest entitles the holder of such claim or interest"];

(3) shall specify the treatment of any class of claims or interests that is impaired under the plan;

(4) provide the same treatment for each claim or interest of a particular class, unless the holder of a particular claim or interest agrees to a less favorable treatment of such particular claim or interest;

(5) provide adequate means for the plan's execution, such as—

(A) retention by the debtor of all or any part of the property of the estate;

(B) transfer of all or any part of the property of the estate to one or more entities, whether organized before or after the confirmation of such plan;

(C) merger or consolidation of the debtor with one or more persons;

(D) sale of all or any part of the property of the estate either subject to or free of any lien, or the distribution of all or any part of the property of the estate among those having an interest in such property of the estate;

(E) satisfaction or modification of any lien;

(F) cancellation or modification of any indenture or similar instrument;

(G) curing or waiving any default;

(H) extension of a maturity date or a change in an interest rate or other term of outstanding securities;

(I) amendment of the debtor's charter; or

(J) issuance of securities of the debtor * * * for cash, for property, for existing securities, or in exchange for claims or interests, or for any other appropriate purpose;

(b) subject to subsection (a) of this section, a plan may

(1) impair or leave unimpaired any class of claims, secured or unsecured, or of interests;

* * *

(3) provide for

(A) the settlement or adjustment of any claim or interest belonging to the debtor or to the estate;

* * *

(4) provide for the sale of all or substantially all of the property of

the estate, and the distribution of the proceeds of such sale among holders of claims or interests;

* * *.

The debtor's creditors may either accept or reject the plan. Section 1126 of the 1979 Act provides that a class of creditors accepts the plan where there is majority creditor approval in number and two-thirds in amount of claims. Thus, if there are 50 creditors in a particular class, at least 26 must approve. And if the aggregate amount of claims within the class is $30,000, the approval must come from creditors holding claims of at least $20,000.

Section 1126 states:

Section 1126.   Acceptance of Plan

(a) The holder of a claim or interest allowed * * * may accept or reject a plan. If the United States is a creditor * * * the Secretary of the Treasury may accept or reject the plan on behalf of the United States.

* * *

(c) A class of claims has accepted a plan if such plan has been accepted by creditors * * * that hold at least two-thirds in amount and more than one-half in number of the allowed claims of such class held by creditors * * *

* * *

(f) Notwithstanding any other provision of this section, a class that is not impaired under a plan is deemed to have accepted the plan, and solicitation of acceptance with respect to such class from the holders of claims or interests of such class is not required.

Notice that Subsection (f) states that if a class of creditors is not "impaired", then no acceptance of the plan by this class is required. Again, "a class of claims is impaired under a plan unless the plan leaves unaltered the legal, equitable, and contractual rights to which such claim or interest entitles the holder of such claim or interest".

Section 1125 of the Act provides that the creditors must be sent copies or summaries of the plan prior to their voting on it.

The Act provides:

Section 1125.   Postpetition Disclosure and Solicitation

(a) In this section—

(1) "adequate information" means information of a kind, and in sufficient detail, as far as is reasonably practicable in light of the nature and history of the debtor and the condition of the debtor's books and records, that would enable a hypothetical reasonable investor typical of holders of claims or interests of the relevant class to make an informed judgment about the plan; and

(2) "investor typical of holders of claims or interests of the relevant class" means investor having—

(A) a claim or interest of the relevant class;

(B) such a relationship with the debtor as the holders of other claims or interests of such class generally have; and

(C) such ability to obtain such information from sources other than the disclosure required by this section as holders' claims or interest in such class generally have.

(b) An acceptance or rejection of a plan may not be solicited after the commencement of the case under this title from a holder of a claim or interest with respect to such claim or interest, unless at the time of or before such solicitation, there is transmitted to such holder the plan or a summary of the plan, and a written disclosure statement approved, after notice and a hearing, by the court as containing adequate information. The court may approve a disclosure statement without a valuation of the debtor or an appraisal of the debtor's assets.

(c) The same disclosure statement shall be transmitted to each holder of a claim or interest of a particular class, but there may be transmitted different disclosure statements, differing in amount, detail or kind of information, as between classes.

(d) Whether a disclosure statement contains adequate information is not governed by any otherwise applicable nonbankruptcy law, rule, or regulation but an agency or official whose duty is to administer or enforce such a law, rule, or regulation may be heard on the issue whether a disclosure statement contains adequate information. Such an agency or official may not appeal from an order approving a disclosure statement.

Under Chapter 11, a trustee need not be appointed. The 1979 Act provides that a trustee will be appointed under the Chapter only for cause such as fraud, incompetence, or (if a company) gross mismanagement, or if the court otherwise decides that it is in the best interests of the creditors or shareholders (in the case of a corporate debtor). Where a trustee is not appointed, the debtor continues to possess his or her assets and continues to operate any business involved in the reorganization.

Under the old Bankruptcy Act, the reorganization sections were divided into two chapters—10 and 11. Chapter 10 dealt strictly with rehabilitation of corporations and *required* the appointment of a trustee to manage the corporation during reorganization if the corporation owed debts of more than $250,000. The

SEC had to be advised of Chapter 10 plans and give its opinion to the court as to whether the plans should be approved. Because of the SEC's interest in protecting the investing public, the Commission could sue (under the old law) to convert a Chapter 11 case (where appointment of a trustee was discretionary with the court) to a Chapter 10 case (where appointment of a trustee was automatic) so long as the corporation owed debts of more than $250,000. Now that there is no longer a Chapter 10, there will be fewer trustees appointed, and corporate management will more often continue to operate the business during the carrying out of the reorganization plan. The SEC can still request that a trustee be appointed, but the court will not comply with the request unless it is convinced that the corporate management is either fraudulent or incompetent. However, at any time after commencement of the case, the court may, upon petition of any interested party, appoint an "examiner" with similar powers to the trustee if the court determines this to be in the best interest of the creditors, or if the debtor's unsecured debts exceed $5,000,000.

Section 1104 reads in part:

Section 1104. Appointment of Trustee or Examiner

(a) At any time after the commencement of the case but before confirmation of a plan, on request of a party in interest, and after notice and a hearing, the court shall order the appointment of a trustee—

(1) for cause, including fraud, dishonesty, incompetence, or gross mismanagement, of the affairs of the debtor by current management, either before or after the commencement of the case, or similar cause, but not including the number of holders of securities of the debtor or the amount of assets or liabilities of the debtor; or

(2) if such appointment is in the interests of creditors, any equity security holders, and other interests of the estate, without regard to the number of holders of securities of the debtor or the amount of assets or liabilities of the debtor.

(b) If the court does not order the appointment of a trustee under this section, then at any time before the confirmation of a plan, on request of a party in interest, and after notice and a hearing, the court shall order the appointment of an examiner to conduct such an investigation of the debtor as is appropriate, including an investigation of any allegations of fraud, dishonesty, incompetence, misconduct, mismanagement, or irregularity in the management of the affairs of the debtor of or by current or former management of the debtor, if

(1) such appointment is in the interest of creditors, any equity security holders, and other interests of the estate; or

(2) the debtor's fixed, liquidated, unsecured debts, other than debts for goods, services, or taxes, or owing to an insider, exceed $5,000,000.

———

Whether or not a trustee is appointed, the law does require the appointment of at least one creditors' committee made up of unsecured creditors (including those holding the seven largest claims of the type represented by the committee). The committee's job is to work with the trustee or debtor in possession in carrying out the reorganization plan.

Sections 1102 and 1103 of Chapter 11 provide:

Section 1102.　Creditors'　*　*　*　Committees

(a)(1) As soon as practicable after the order for relief under this chapter, the court shall appoint a committee of creditors holding unsecured claims.

(2) On request of a party in interest, the court may order the appointment of additional committees of creditors　*　*　* to assure adequate representation of creditors　*　*　*

(b)(1) A committee of creditors appointed under subsection (a) of this section shall ordinarily consist of the persons, willing to serve, that hold the seven largest claims against the debtor of the kinds represented on such committee, *　*　*

Section 1103.　Powers and Duties of Committees

(a) At a scheduled meeting of a committee appointed under section 1102 of this title, *　*　* such committee may select and authorize the employment by such committee of one or more attorneys, accountants, or other agents, to represent or perform services for such committee.

*　*　*

(c) A committee appointed under section 1102 of this title may—

(1) consult with the trustee or debtor in possession concerning the administration of the case;

(2) investigate the acts, conduct, assets, liabilities, and financial condition of the debtor, the operation of the debtor's business and the desirability of the continuance of such business, and any other matter relevant to the case or the formulation of a plan;

(3) participate in the formulation of a plan, advise those represented by such committee of such committee's recommendations as to any plan formulated,

and collect and file with the court acceptances of a plan;

(4) request the appointment of a trustee or examiner under section 1104 of this title, if a trustee or examiner, as the case may be, has not previously been appointed under this chapter in the case; and

(5) perform such other services as are in the interest of those represented.

The bankruptcy court "confirms" the debtor's plan only if it is satisfied that the proposal is in the best interests of the creditors; that the debtor will faithfully carry out the plan; that the debtor has not committed any act that would bar him or her from discharge in a straight bankruptcy proceeding (if necessary, review "objections to discharge"); that the plan provides for payment to creditors in the order of priority as described earlier in the chapter; and that the creditors have *either accepted the plan* (as explained previously or, if they have not accepted, *that they will receive or retain as much as they would have received or retained under a straight bankruptcy proceeding*. Section 1129 of Chapter 11 provides:

Section 1129. Confirmation of Plan

(a) The court shall confirm a plan only if all of the following requirements are met:

* * *

(7) With respect to each class

(A) each holder of a claim or interest of such class—

(i) has accepted the plan; or

(ii) will receive or retain under the plan on account of such claim or interest property of a value, as of the effective date of the plan, that is not less than the amount that such holder would

so receive or retain if the debtor were liquidated under Chapter 7 [straight bankruptcy] of this title on such date;

* * *

(8) With respect to each class—

(A) such class has accepted the plan; or

(B) such class is not impaired under the plan.

* * *

(b)(1) * * * [I]f all of the applicable requirements of subsection (a) of this section other than paragraph (8) are met with respect to a plan, the court, on request of the proponent of the plan, shall confirm the plan notwithstanding the requirements of such paragraph if the plan does not discriminate unfairly, and is fair and equitable, with respect to each class of claims or interests that is impaired under, and has not accepted, the plan.

(2) For the purpose of this subsection, the condition that a plan be fair and equitable with respect to a class includes the following requirements:

(A) With respect to a class of secured claims, the plan provides—

(i)(I) that the holders of such claims retain the lien securing such claims, whether the property subject to such lien is retained by the debtor or transferred to another entity, to the extent of the allowed amount of such claims: and

(II) that each holder of a claim of such class receive on account of such claim deferred cash payments totaling at least the allowed amount of such claim, of a value, as of the effective date of the plan, of at least the value of such holder's interest in the estate's interest in such property;

(ii) for the sale * * * of any property that is subject to the lien securing such claims, free and clear of such lien, with such lien to attach to the proceeds of such sale, and the treatment of such lien on proceeds under clause (i) or (iii) of this subparagraph; or

(iii) for the realization by such holders of the indubitable equivalent of such claims.

(B) With respect to a class of unsecured claims—

(i) the plan provides that each holder of a claim of such class receive or retain on account of such claim property of a value, as of the effective date of the plan, equal to the allowed amount of such claim; or

(ii) the holder of any claim or interest that is junior to the claims of such class will not receive or retain on account of such junior claim or interest any property.

Even after the plan has been confirmed by the court, the case may be converted to straight bankruptcy if the plan proves to be unworkable. Chapter 11, Section 1112.

The effect of confirmation, apart from exceptions provided in the plan itself, is to discharge the debtor in the same manner as does a straight bankruptcy proceeding.

Section 1141 provides:

Section 1141. Effect of Confirmation
* * *

(c) After confirmation of a plan, the property dealt with by the plan is free and clear of all claims and interests of creditors, * * * except as otherwise provided in the plan or in the order confirming the plan.

(d)(1) except as otherwise provided in this subsection, in the plan, or in the order confirming the plan, the confirmation of a plan—

(A) discharges the debtor from any debt that arose before the date of such confirmation * * * whether or not—

(i) a proof of claim based on such debt is filed
* * *

(iii) the holder of such claim has accepted the plan;

* * *

(2) The confirmation of a plan does not discharge an individual from any debt excepted from discharge under Section 523 of this title.

What is Chapter 13 of the 1979 Bankruptcy Act?

Chapter 13 of the 1979 Bankruptcy Act provides debtor rehabilitation for an "individual with regular income". Section 101(24) defines an "individual with regular income" as an "individual whose income is sufficiently stable and regular to enable such individual to make payments under a plan under Chapter 13 of this title * * *." Chapter 13 of the old bankruptcy law applied only to "wage earners" (employees); the new law has greatly expanded coverage to include self-employed persons and anyone else with "regular" income. An individual debtor elects to go under Chapter 13 by filing (with the U.S. district court) a "plan" providing for the use of all or part of the debtor's future earnings for payment of his or her debts. Generally, the proposed payment period may not exceed three years. Under Chapter 13, the court appoints a trustee to administer the plan.

The plan must recognize and provide for payment in full of all Section 507 priority claims. Other debts may be classified in the same manner as under Chapter 11.

Sections 1321 and 1322 provide:

Section 1321. Filing of Plan

The debtor shall file a plan.

Section 1322. Contents of Plan

(a) the plan shall—

(1) provide for the submission of all or such portion of future income of the debtor to the supervision and control of the trustee as is necessary for the execution of the plan;

(2) provide for the full payment, in deferred cash payments of all claims entitled to priority under Section 507 of this title, unless the holder of a particular claim agrees to a different treatment of such claim; and

(3) if the plan classifies claims, provide the same treatment for each claim within a particular class.

(b) Subject to subsections (a) and (c) of this section, the plan may—

(1) designate a class or classes of unsecured claims, as provided in Section 1122 of this title, but may not discriminate unfairly against any class so designated;

(2) modify the rights of holders of secured claims, other than a claim secured only by a security interest in real property that is the debtor's principal residence, or of holders of unsecured claims;

(3) provide for curing or waiving of any default;

(4) provide for payment on any unsecured claim to be made con-

currently with payments on any secured claim or any unsecured claim;

* * *

(10) include any other appropriate provision not inconsistent with this title.

(c) The plan may not provide for payment over a period that is longer than three years, unless the court, for cause, approves a longer period, but the court may not approve a period that is longer than five years.

———

Notice that the rights of both secured and unsecured creditors can be modified with the single exception of a secured interest in the debtor's residence.

After notice to the creditors, a confirmation hearing must be held (under Section 1324), and any creditor or party in interest may object to confirmation. However, creditor approval is not required—it is up to the court to decide whether or not to confirm the plan.

Generally, the plan will ask for a combination composition and extension affording the debtor a longer time to pay a lesser amount of his or her debts. However, the amount of cash or property to be distributed to unsecured creditors under the plan must not be less than the amount the creditors would receive under a straight bankruptcy proceeding. Each secured creditor must either accept the plan, or the plan must allow the creditor to retain his or her lien and ultimately receive the secured amount, or the plan must provide for the creditor to receive the actual property securing the claim.

Section 1325 reads in part:

Section 1325. Confirmation of Plan

(a) The court shall confirm a plan if

(1) the plan complies with the provisions of this chapter and with other applicable provisions of this title;

* * *

(3) the plan has been proposed in good faith and not by any means forbidden by law;

(4) the value, as of the effective date of the plan, of property to be distributed under the plan on account of each allowed unsecured claim is not less than the amount that would be paid on such claim if the estate of the debtor were liquidated under chapter 7 [straight bankruptcy] of this title on such date;

(5) with respect to each allowed secured claim provided for by the plan—

(A) the holder of such claim has accepted the plan;

(B)(i) the plan provides that the holder of such claim retain the lien securing such claim; and

(ii) the value, as of the effective date of the plan, of property to be distributed under the plan on account of such claim is not less than the allowed amount of such claim; or

(C) the debtor surrenders the property securing such claim to such holder; and

(6) the debtor will be able to make all payments under the plan and comply with the plan.

Again, all Section 507 claims must be paid first.

Section 1326 states:

Section 1326. Payments

(a) Before or at the time of each payment to creditors under the plan, there shall be paid—

(1) any unpaid claim of the kind specified in section 507(a)(1) of this title; * * *.

(b) Except as otherwise provided in the plan or in the order confirming the plan, the trustee shall make payments to creditors under the plan.

Once confirmed, the plan binds the debtor and each creditor.

The Act provides:

Section 1327. Effect of Confirmation

(a) The provisions of a confirmed plan bind the debtor and each creditor, whether or not the claim of such creditor is provided for by the plan, and whether or not such creditor has objected to, has accepted, or has rejected the plan.

While the plan is in effect, it may be modified to increase or reduce payments or claims of a particular class or to extend or reduce the time for such payments.

Section 1329. Modification of Plan After Confirmation

(a) At any time after confirmation but before completion of payments under a plan, the plan may be modified * * *;

* * *

(c) A plan modified under this section may not provide for payments over a period that expires after three years after the time that the first payment under the original plan was due, unless the court, for cause, approves a longer period, but the court may not approve a period that expires after five years after such time.

Once the debtor has made all payments called for under the plan, the court will order a discharge of his or her remaining debts (except those that are not dischargeable in a straight bankruptcy proceeding). If the debtor fails to make all the required payments, discharge will be denied unless (1) the debtor is blameless, *and* (2) the creditors are in as good a position as they would have been under a straight bankruptcy proceeding.

Section 1328 provides:

Section 1328. Discharge

(a) As soon as practicable after completion by the debtor of all payments under the plan, unless the court approves a written waiver of discharge executed by the debtor after the order for relief under this chapter, the court shall grant the debtor a discharge of all debts provided for by the plan * * *.

(b) At any time after the confirmation of the plan and after notice and hearing, the court may grant a discharge to a debtor that has not completed payments under the plan only if—

(1) the debtor's failure to complete such payments is due to circumstances for which the debtor should not justify be held accountable;

(2) the value, as of the effective date of the plan, of property actually distributed under the plan on account of each allowed unsecured claim is not less than the amount that would have been paid on such claim if the estate of the debtor had been liquidated under chapter 7 [straight bankruptcy] of this title on such date;
* * *

(c) A discharge granted under subsection (b) of this section discharges the debtor from all unsecured debts provided for by the plan * * * except any debt—

* * * (2) of a kind specified in section 523 (a) of this title.

———

In many cases, a Chapter 13 "plan" is preferable to straight bankruptcy. While straight bankruptcy results in discharge of the bankrupt's debts, the bankrupt will usually lose all of his or her property.

In a Chapter 13 proceeding, on the other hand, the debtor receives a discharge but is usually able to retain at least a portion of his or her assets.

Are there any other new and unique aspects to the 1979 Bankruptcy Act?

The Bankruptcy Act of 1979 accomplishes two other new things:

First, Section 104 of the Act provides that the dollar amounts stated in the Act will be adjusted periodically to reflect changes in the value of the dollar.

Section 104. Adjustment of Dollar Amounts

The judicial Conference of the United States shall transmit to the Congress and to the President before May 1, 1985, and before May 1 of every sixth year after May 1, 1985, a recommendation for the uniform percentage adjustment of each dollar amount in this title * * *.

———

Second, the Act provides for the creation of "Bankruptcy Courts" as special courts to handle bankruptcy matters. The Act states that a Bankruptcy Court shall be created in every judicial district where there is located a federal district court (district courts are located in every state and in the District of Columbia— see Appendix A). The Bankruptcy Courts are scheduled to come into existence on April 1, 1984. Bankruptcy Judges will be appointed by the president of the United States, subject to Senate confirmation, and will serve for terms of 14 years.

Finally, Section 1930 of the Bankruptcy Act prescribes filing fees in the amount of $60.00 for a case under Chapter 7 (straight bankruptcy) or Chapter 13 (adjustment of debts of an individual with regular income), and $200.00 for a reorganization case under Chapter 11 (unless the case involves a railroad in which event the fee is $500.00).

CASES

CASE 1—*Notice and opportunity to be heard must be given before garnishment.*

SNIADACH v. FAMILY FINANCE CORP. OF BAY VIEW

Supreme Court of the United States, 1969.
395 U.S. 337, 89 S.Ct. 1820, 23 L.Ed.2d 349.

Mr. Justice DOUGLAS delivered the opinion of the Court.

Respondents instituted a garnishment action against petitioner as defendant and Miller Harris Instrument Co., her employer, as garnishee. The complaint alleged a claim of $420 on a promissory note. The garnishee filed its answer stating it had wages of $63.18 under its control earned by petitioner and unpaid, and that it would pay one-half to petitioner as a subsistence allowance [1] and hold the other half subject to the order of the court.

Petitioner moved that the garnishment proceedings be dismissed for failure to satisfy the due process requirements of the Fourteenth Amendment. The Wisconsin Supreme Court sustained the lower state court in approving the procedure. The case is here on a petition for a writ of certiorari.

The Wisconsin statute gives a plaintiff 10 days in which to serve the summons and complaint on the defendant after service on the garnishee. In this case petitioner was served the same day as the garnishee. She nonetheless claims that the Wisconsin garnishment procedure violates that due process required by the Fourteenth Amendment, in that notice and an opportunity to be heard are not given before * * * seizure of the wages. What happens in Wisconsin is that the clerk of the court issues the summons at the request of the creditor's lawyer; and it is the latter who by serving the garnishee sets in motion the machinery whereby the wages are frozen. They may, it is true, be unfrozen if the trial of the main suit is ever had and the wage earner wins on the merits. But in the interim the wage earner is deprived of his enjoyment of earned wages without any opportunity to be heard and to tender any defense he may have, whether it be fraud or otherwise.

Such summary procedure may well meet the requirements of due process in extraordinary situations. But in the present case no situation requiring special protection to a state or creditor interest is presented by the facts; nor is the Wisconsin statute narrowly drawn to meet any such unusual condition. * * *

The question is not whether the Wisconsin law is a wise law or unwise law. Our concern is not what philosophy Wisconsin should or should not embrace. We do not sit as a super-legislative body. In this case the sole ques-

---

1. Wis.Stat. § 267.18(2)(a) provides:
   "When wages or salary are the subject of garnishment action, the garnishee shall pay over to the principal defendant on the date when such wages or salary would normally be payable a subsistence allowance, out of the wages or salary then owing in the sum of $25 in the case of an individual without dependents or $40 in the case of an individual with dependents; but in no event in excess of 50 per cent of the wages or salary owing. Said subsistence allowance shall be applied to the first wages or salary earned in the period subject to said garnishment action."

tion is whether there has been a taking of property without that procedural due process that is required by the Fourteenth Amendment. We have dealt over and over again with the question of what constitutes "the right to be heard" within the meaning of procedural due process. * * * [W]e said that the right to be heard "has little reality or worth unless one is informed that the matter is pending and can choose for himself whether to appear or default, acquiesce or contest." In the context of this case the question is whether the interim freezing of the wages without a chance to be heard violates procedural due process.

A procedural rule that may satisfy due process for attachments in general does not necessarily satisfy procedural due process in every case. The fact that a procedure would pass muster under a feudal regime does not mean it gives necessary protection to all property in its modern forms. We deal here with wages—a specialized type of property presenting distinct problems in our economic system. We turn then to the nature of that property and problems of procedural due process.

A prejudgment garnishment of the Wisconsin type is a taking which may impose tremendous hardship on wage earners with families to support. Until a recent Act of Congress [Truth in Lending Law], § 304 of which forbids discharge of employees on the ground that their wages have been garnished, garnishment often meant the loss of a job. Over and beyond that was the great drain on family income. As stated by Congressman Reuss:

> "The idea of wage garnishment in advance of judgment, of trustee process, of wage attachment, or whatever it is called is a most inhuman doctrine. It compels the wage earner, trying to keep his family together, to be driven below the poverty level."

Recent investigations of the problem have disclosed the grave injustices made possible by prejudgment garnishment whereby the sole opportunity to be heard comes after the taking. Congressman Sullivan, Chairman of the House Subcommittee on Consumer Affairs who held extensive hearings on this and related problems stated:

> "What we know from our study of this problem is that in a vast number of cases the debt is a fraudulent one, saddled on a poor ignorant person who is trapped in an easy credit nightmare, in which he is charged double for something he could not pay for even if the proper price was called for, and then hounded into giving up his pound of flesh, and being fired besides."

The leverage of the creditor on the wage earner is enormous. The creditor tenders not only the original debt but the "collection fees" incurred by his attorneys in the garnishment proceedings:

> "The debtor whose wages are tied up by a writ of garnishment, and who is usually in need of money, is in no position to resist demands for collection fees. If the debt is small, the debtor will be under considerable pressure to pay the debt and collection charges in order to get his wages back. If the debt is large, he will often sign a new contract of 'payment schedule' which incorporates these additional charges."

Apart from those collateral consequences, it appears that in Wisconsin the statutory exemption granted the wage earner is "generally insufficient to support the debtor for any one week."

The result is that a prejudgment garnishment of the Wisconsin type may as a practical matter drive a wage-earning family to the wall. Where the taking of one's property is so obvious, it needs no extended argument to conclude that absent notice and a prior hearing this prejudgment garnishment procedure violates the fundamental principles of due process.

Reversed.

CASE 2—*Does Arizona's Motor Vehicle Act conflict with the federal bankruptcy law?*

PEREZ v. CAMPBELL

Certiorari to the United States Court of Appeals for the Ninth Circuit, 1971.
402 U.S. 637, 91 S.Ct. 1704, 29 L.Ed.2d 233.

Mr. Justice WHITE delivered the opinion of the Court.

This case raises an important issue concerning the construction of the Supremacy Clause of the Constitution—whether Ariz.Rev.Stat.Ann. § 28–1163(B) (1956), which is part of Arizona's Motor Vehicle Safety Responsibility Act, is invalid under that clause as being in conflict with the mandate of * * * the Bankruptcy Act, providing that receipt of a discharge in bankruptcy fully discharges all but certain specified judgments. * * *

On July 8, 1965, petitioner Adolfo Perez, driving a car registered in his name, was involved in an automobile accident in Tucson, Arizona. The Perez automobile was not covered by liability insurance at the time of the collision. The driver of the second car was the minor daughter of Leonard Pinkerton, and in September 1966 the Pinkertons sued Mr. and Mrs. Perez in state court for personal injuries and property damage sustained in the accident. On October 31, 1967, the petitioners confessed judgment in this suit, and a judgment order was entered against them on November 8, 1967, for $2,425.98 plus court costs.

Mr. and Mrs. Perez each filed a voluntary petition in bankruptcy in Federal District Court on November 6, 1967. Each of them duly scheduled the judgment debt to the Pinkertons. The District Court entered orders on July 8, 1968, discharging both Mr. and Mrs. Perez from all debts and claims provable against their estates, including the Pinkerton judgment.

During the pendency of the bankruptcy proceedings, the provisions of the Arizona Motor Vehicle Safety Responsibility Act came into play. * * * § 28–1142 provides that within 60 days of the receipt of an accident report the Superintendent of the Motor Vehicle Division of the Highway Department shall suspend the driver's license of the operator and the registration of the owner of a car involved in an accident "unless such operator or owner or both shall deposit security in a sum which is sufficient in the judgment of the superindendent to satisfy any judgment or judgments for damages resulting from the accident as may be recovered against the operator or owner." * * *

Article 4 of the Arizona Act, which includes the only provision at issue here, deals with suspension of licenses and registrations for nonpayment of judgments. Interestingly, it is only when the judgment debtor in an automobile accident lawsuit—usually an owner-operator like Mr. Perez—fails to respond to a judgment entered against him that he must overcome two hurdles in order to regain his driving privileges. Section 28–1161, the first section of Art. 4, requires the state court clerk or judge, when a judgment has remained unsatisfied for 60 days after entry, to forward a certified copy of the judgment to the superintendent. This was done in the present case, and on March 13, 1968, Mr. and Mrs. Perez were served with notice that their drivers' licenses and registration were suspended pursuant to § 28–1162(A). Under other provisions of Art. 4, such suspension is to continue until the judgment is paid, and § 28–1163(B) specifically provides that "[a] discharge in bankruptcy following the rendering of any such judgment shall not relieve the judgment debtor from any of the requirements of this article." In addition to requiring satisfaction of the judgment debt, § 28–1163(A) provides that the license and registration "shall remain suspended and shall not be renewed, nor shall any license or registration be thereafter issued in the name of the person * * * until the person gives proof of financial responsibility" for a future period. Again, the validity of this limited requirement that some drivers post evidence of financial responsibility for the future in order to regain driving privileges is not questioned here. Nor is the broader issue of whether a State may require proof of financial responsibility as a precondition for granting driving privileges to anyone before us for decision. What is at issue here is the power of a State to include as part of this comprehensive enactment designed to secure compensation for automobile accident victims a section providing that a discharge in bankruptcy of the automobile accident tort judgment shall have no effect on the judgment debtor's obligation to repay the judgment creditor, at least insofar as such repayment may be enforced by the withholding of driving privileges by the State. It was that question, among others, which petitioners raised after suspension of their licenses and registration by filing a complaint in Federal District Court seeking declaratory and injunctive relief and requesting a three-judge court. They asserted several constitutional violations, and also alleged that § 28–1163(B) was in direct conflict with the Bankruptcy Act and was thus violative of the Supremacy Clause of the Constitution. In support of their complaint, Mr. and Mrs. Perez filed affidavits stating that the suspension of their licenses and registration worked both physical and financial hardship upon them and their children. * * *

* * * [T]he construction of the Bankruptcy Act is * * * clear. This Court on numerous occasions has stated that "[o]ne of the primary purposes of the bankruptcy act" is to give debtors "a new opportunity in life and a clear field for future effort, unhampered by the pressure and discouragement of preëxisting debt." There can be no doubt that Congress intended this "new opportunity" to include freedom from most kinds of preexisting tort judgments.

* * * [W]e proceed immediately to the constitutional question whether a state statute that protects judgment creditors from "financially irresponsible persons" is in conflict with a federal statute that gives discharged debtors a new start "unhampered by the pressure and discouragement of preëxisting debt." As early as Gibbons v. Ogden, 9 Wheat. 1 (1824), Chief Justice Marshall stated the governing principle—that "acts of the State Legislatures * * * [which] *interfere with,* or are contrary to the laws of Congress, made in pursuance of the constitution," are invalid under the Supremacy Clause. * * *

From the foregoing, we think it clear that § 28–1163(B) of the Arizona Safety Responsibility Act is constitutionally invalid. The judgment of the Court of Appeals is reversed and the case is remanded for further proceedings consistent with this opinion.

It is so ordered.

PROBLEMS

1. Carl Henry is driving along Wiltshire Road in his sportscar when Jenny Metcalfe negligently collides with his car; Jenny is driving an old pickup truck at the time. Carl suffers minor injuries in the accident, and the damage to his car is estimated at $1,195. Carl consults a lawyer and decides to sue Jenny for $3,500. However, before bringing suit, Carl learns that Jenny is planning to leave town to escape paying him: her plans include picking up her two week paycheck in the amount of $280 from Connor Medical Supply; withdrawing her $2,000 in savings from First State Bank; loading up her pickup with her few personal belongings and leaving the state. What action, if any, can Carl take immediately to protect his interests?

   Assume that Jenny has no plans to leave town. Carl sues her for negligence and obtains a judgment in the amount of $3,500. When Jenny refuses to pay the judgment, Carl seeks your advice. How can Carl enforce the judgment?

2. Harvey Fine has been forced into straight bankruptcy by his creditors. The court appoints Mona Carswell to serve as trustee.

   (a) Can Mona set aside any of the following pre-bankruptcy transfers made by Harvey? Explain fully.

      (1) Eight months before the involuntary bankruptcy petition was filed, Harvey repaid a $20,000 personal loan to his brother, Morton. The loan, which was unsecured, was originally made to enable Harvey to go into business on his own. At the time of repayment, Morton knew that Harvey's liabilities exceeded his assets; it was for this reason that Morton insisted upon repayment in full.

      (2) Two months before the involuntary petition was filed, Harvey paid off $3,000 owing on open account to Francine McCrea, a business supplier and personal friend of Harvey's. At the time of repayment, Harvey's liabilities exceeded his assets, but Francine did not know this.

      (3) Seven months prior to filing of the petition, Harvey gave his mountain cabin to his daughter, Sheila. The deed stated that the transfer was "bona fide and honestly and truly made". After the transfer, Harvey continued to use the cabin on weekends. At the time of the transfer to Sheila, Harvey's liabilities exceeded his assets, but Sheila did not know this.

   (b) In the bankruptcy proceeding, several of Harvey's creditors object to two claims which have been filed with the court. Will the following claims be allowed? Explain fully.

      (1) Nancy Green claims $13,000 in rent owing under a lease of property (office space) to Harvey. $1,000 is for past due rent at the time of filing of the petition, and $12,000 represents the $500/month rent due for the two years remaining on the lease.

      (2) Mitch Conaway claims $15,000 for personal injuries suffered in an automobile accident caused by Harvey's negligence. The claim has never been reduced to judgment.

(c) Harvey hopes to retain at least a portion of his property even though he is going through straight bankruptcy. However, he is discouraged when he finds that his state law provides for the following exemptions only:

(1) Equity in a residence up to $5,000.

(2) Equity in one motor vehicle up to $500.

(3) Equity in household goods and furnishings up to $100.

Harvey's equity in his home is $15,000; his equity in his car, $1,100; his equity in household goods and furnishings, $8,000; and in family jewelry, $1,000. How much of this "equity" will Harvey be able to keep even as he goes through bankruptcy? Be specific in your answer.

(d) Which of the following of Harvey's debts will be discharged in bankruptcy? Explain.

(1) Back taxes owing for the five year period prior to filing of the petition.

(2) $6,000 in unpaid alimony and child support.

(3) $2,500 that Harvey embezzled three years ago when he worked as Treasurer of Sebert Corporation.

(4) A $3,000 judgment against Harvey for negligent driving.

(5) A $5,000 unsecured contract debt for the purchase of office machinery.

(6) A $1,500 claim for damages resulting from Harvey's intentional assault and battery upon the claimant.

(e) Suppose that six months after Harvey's discharge in bankruptcy, Mona discovers that Harvey failed to disclose the existence and whereabouts of certain substantial properties belonging to him. What is Mona likely to do?

(f) Suppose that during the straight bankruptcy proceeding, it becomes clear that Harvey's sole proprietorship operation could be successful if provided with sound management and supervision, and that Harvey could pay off his debts with future earnings from the operation. Discuss any viable alternative Harvey has under federal bankruptcy law to going through with the straight bankruptcy.

3. Answer the following "True" or "False" and give reasons for your answers:

(a) Home solicitation sales are illegal in states having adopted the Uniform Consumer Credit Code.

(b) A "confession of judgment clause" in a written contract is illegal in states having adopted the Uniform Consumer Credit Code.

(c) Only "provable" debts can be discharged in bankruptcy.

(d) A bankrupt's promise to pay a debt discharged in bankruptcy is not enforceable where the promise is made subsequent to discharge.

(e) Even if a debtor's creditors do not approve a Chapter 11 reorganization plan, the court may confirm the plan if the creditors will receive or retain as much as they would receive or retain under a straight bankruptcy proceeding.

(f) A trustee must be appointed to help carry out a Chapter 11 reorganization plan.

(g) The rights of both secured and unsecured creditors can be modified under a Chapter 13 plan with the exception of a secured interest in the debtor's residence.

(h) At least one creditors' committee composed of unsecured creditors must be appointed to help carry out a Chapter 11 reorganization plan.

(i) Liens are frequently created by judicial process.

(j) A lien creditor stands in a much better position regarding a debtor's assets than does a general creditor.

(k) A debtor who is harassed by a creditor has no legal remedies.

(*l*) An employer may discharge an employee whose wages are garnished for a single indebtedness.

(m) A valid judgment creates a lien on the debtor's real and personal property.

(n) Generally, a Chapter 11 plan must provide the same treatment for each creditor within a particular class.

(*o*) Confirmation of a Chapter 11 reorganization plan works to discharge the debtor in much the same way as does a straight bankruptcy proceeding.

(p) Once the debtor has made all payments called for under a Chapter 13 plan, the court will order a discharge of the debtor's remaining debts.

4. A client has joined other creditors of the Ajax Demolition Company in a composition agreement seeking to avoid the necessity of a bankruptcy proceeding against Ajax. Which statement describes the composition agreement?

   a. It provides for the appointment of a receiver to take over and operate the debtor's business.

   b. It must be approved by all creditors.

   c. It does *not* discharge any of the debts included until performance by the debtor has taken place.

   d. It provides a temporary delay, *not* to exceed six months, insofar as the debtor's obligation to repay the debts included in the composition.

   [# 24, May 1978 CPA Exam]

5. A voluntary petition in bankruptcy may

   a. *Not* be filed by a person who has income in excess of $10,000 per year.

   b. *Not* be filed by a self-employed professional.

   c. Be filed only if insolvency, in the bankruptcy sense, is at least $1,500.

   d. Be filed by an individual who is solvent in the bankruptcy sense.

   [# 19, May 1974 CPA Exam]

6. A bankrupt can be denied a discharge in bankruptcy if

   a. He had failed to keep or preserve books of account or records.

     b.   He was discharged in bankruptcy eight years earlier.

     c.   He permitted a creditor to obtain a lien on his property three months prior to bankruptcy and did *not* act to discharge it.

     d.   General creditors with provable claims will be unable to receive more than 10% of the amount of their claims.

     [# 28, May 1974 CPA Exam]

7.   Under Chapter [11] of the Bankruptcy Act, a plan to be accepted and confirmed by the Court

     a.   Must be accepted by all creditors.

     b.   May be approved by a majority of creditors by number.

     c.   May be approved by one-third of the creditors by number if their claims equal two-thirds of provable claims.

     d.   May be approved by a majority as to number of creditors and two-thirds as to amount of claims with regard to a particular class of claims.

     [Modified from # 31, May 1974 CPA Exam to reflect 1979 Bankruptcy Act.]

8.   You are setting up the accounts for Barkum Enterprises, which operates a retail novelties business. Barkum wants all true liabilities shown. He recently received a discharge in bankruptcy, but the following [allowed] claims were unpaid because of lack of funds. Which would you consider to be a claim against him and his new venture?

     a.   The unpaid amount owed to a secured creditor who received less than the full amount after resorting to his security interest.

     b.   The unpaid amounts owed to his trade suppliers for goods sold by him in the ordinary course of his prior business.

     c.   A personal loan by his father made in an attempt to stave off bankruptcy.

     d.   The unpaid amount on the claim of a creditor who extended credit on the strength of a fraudulent financial statement.

     [Modified from #32, May 1978 CPA Exam to reflect 1979 Bankruptcy Act.]

9.   In the course of examining the financial statements of Superior Systems, Inc., the financial vice president discloses that the corporation has a serious collection problem with one of its customers, Vizar Components, Inc. Vizar is approximately $10,000 in arrears; its checks have been returned for insufficient funds. Other creditors have similar claims against Vizar.

     You have also learned that the principal creditors, including Superior, have held a meeting to consider possible alternative courses of action. During the meeting, an examination of the financial statements of Vizar revealed that it was in a difficult current position, but that it had sufficient assets to meet liabilities in the event of a bankruptcy proceeding. The meeting also revealed that Vizar's problems had built up over the past two years due to poor management. The company appears to have significant potential to return to profitability if properly managed.

Required:

1. Can the creditors of Vizar Components, Inc. (including Superior Systems) force Vizar Components into straight bankruptcy? Explain. Assuming Vizar's creditors file an involuntary petition, and Vizar successfully controverts the petition, what are Vizar's rights, if any, against the creditors?

2. What are the viable alternatives to a straight bankruptcy proceeding? Explain.

[Modified from # 7.d., November 1973 CPA Exam to reflect 1979 Bankruptcy Act.]

10. The MIB Corporation has been petitioned into bankruptcy. The petition was filed February 1, 1977. Among its creditors are the following:

A. *Viscount Machine, Inc.*
Viscount put an $8,600 deposit down on certain heavy machinery to be purchased from MIB. MIB was petitioned into bankruptcy, and the machinery (which was never identified to the contract) was not delivered.

B. *Second National County Bank*
Second National holds a first mortgage on the real estate where MIB has its principal plant, office, and warehouse. The mortgage is for $280,750 representing the unpaid balance due on the original $350,000 mortgage. The property was sold for $290,000, its fair market value as established by bids received by the trustee. The mortgage was taken out two years ago and duly filed and recorded at that time.

C. *Marvel Supply Company*
Marvel, a major supplier of parts, delivered $10,000 worth of parts to MIB on January 17, 1977. Upon delivery Marvel received 50% cash and insisted on the balance by the end of the month. When the balance was not paid, Marvel obtained from MIB a duly executed financing statement which Marvel filed on February 2, 1977.

D. *Sixty-one wage earners*
Sixty machine operators employed in MIB's plant and warehouse were not paid for the final month. Each has a claim for $400 which equals $24,000 in total. Also, the Executive Assistant to the President of the Corporation was not paid for the final month and has a claim for $2,400 against MIB.

E. *Federal, state, and local taxing authorities*
MIB owes $6,800 in back taxes.

F. *Administration costs*
These total $12,000.

G. *Various general creditors*
Excluding items A through F above, general creditors have allowable claims of $1,614,900. The bankrupt's total estate consists of $850,000 of assets in addition to the real estate described in B.

Required: Answer the following, setting forth reasons for any conclusions stated.

1. Discuss the legal implications and the resulting rights of each of the persons or entities described above in A

through G as a result of the facts given and the application of bankruptcy law to them.

2. What is the bankruptcy dividend (percentage on the dollar) that each general creditor will receive? Show calculations in good form.

[Modified from #7.a., May 1977 CPA Exam to reflect 1979 Bankruptcy Act.]

Chapter 27

LEGAL DEVICES USED TO PROTECT CREDITORS: SECURITY INTERESTS IN PERSONAL PROPERTY UNDER ARTICLE 9 OF THE UNIFORM COMMERCIAL CODE; MORTGAGES ON REAL ESTATE; SURETYSHIP ARRANGEMENTS; AND THE BULK SALES RULES

How easy is it to borrow money or buy on credit?

"He who goes a borrowing, goes a sorrowing."

Benjamin Franklin from
Poor Richard's Almanac

In 1941, consumer credit in the United States totaled 9 billion dollars (i. e., the entire consumer population owed a total of 9 billion dollars on homes, cars, and loans). Today, the consumer credit figure is well over 500 billion dollars and going up. Credit is easy to obtain in our society because merchants know that charge account customers and customers who buy on time under installment contracts tend to return to the same stores where they have existing accounts and can get possession of what they want now and pay later. Perhaps 80% of all goods sold by furniture stores, appliance stores, and jewelry stores are financed with consumer credit. About 60% of all clothing sales, and from 60 to 70% of all department store sales are also credit financed. Approximately three-fourths of all cars purchased in the United States are purchased under some credit arrangement. And nearly all people who buy homes make a down payment of from 5 to 25% of the purchase price and owe the balance; they pay off their "mortgage" on the property in equal monthly installments over a period of 25 to 30 years.

People know that buying on time costs more because of interest and other finance charges. A person who takes out a $40,000 mortgage to finance a home will end up paying more than $100,000 for the home over a 30 year period. So why do people borrow? Quite simply, they want to have the use of homes, cars, refrigerators, clothes, and other property NOW—the "now use" of these items is considered to be worth the extra costs of borrowing.

And for the most part, credit works well and materially adds to the enjoyment of life. Benjamin Franklin's quote from *Poor Richard's Almanac* is not necessarily valid anymore. More than 50% of the Nation's families are in debt, but are not "sorrowing" because of it. Rather, borrowing enables them to enjoy homes, cars, TV sets, and college educations for their children. This is not to say that people never get into financial difficulty because of too much borrowing. As you know from the last chapter, many people do over-extend themselves financially and end up having to go through bankruptcy. Still, this is the exception rather than the rule—most people borrow, repay, borrow again and enjoy life all the more because of it.

But not only consumers borrow money. Businesses, too, often need to borrow cash in order to expand or diversify, or they need to purchase inventory on credit simply to stay in business. Thus, a business that has many credit customer accounts may itself have many creditors. Business financing is a natural, ongoing part of business involving many millions of dollars of debtor-creditor transactions daily.

Despite the fact that credit is needed, and that it increases sales, there would be no credit if creditors could find no protection in the law for their interests. Understandably, creditors would be unwilling to loan money to finance the purchase of "big ticket" items (expensive items such as refrigerators, TV sets, automobiles, homes, entire inventories, and other large items posing a considerable risk of loss) if they had no *legal* assurance of repayment. Knowing this, the law provides creditors with legal procedures and devices to protect them from losing the values they have extended. In the last chapter, we considered several creditor procedures that protect creditors, whether secured or unsecured, including attachments, garnishments, judgments, creditors' committees, assignments for the benefit of creditors, and so on. In this chapter, we will look closely at a number of legal devices that enable creditors to feel more "secure" about their lending. The most important such methods or devices include those allowing a creditor to reach specific property owned by the debtor before any other creditor can reach it; those permitting a creditor to collect the debt from a third party if the primary debtor refuses to pay or cannot pay; and those protecting the creditors of a business in the event that the entire business or a major part of it is sold to another party. These special creditor protections are considered in four main chapter parts as follows:

Part I. The use of personal property as security: secured transactions under Article 9 of the Uniform Commercial Code;

Part II. The use of real property as security: mortgages;

Part III. Having a third party agree to pay in the event that the debtor does not: suretyship; and

Part IV. Protecting creditors of a business when the business is sold: bulk transfers under Article 6 of the Uniform Commercial Code.

PART I

THE USE OF PERSONAL PROPERTY AS SECURITY: SECURED TRANSACTIONS UNDER ARTICLE 9 OF THE UNIFORM COMMERCIAL CODE

What transactions are covered by Article 9 of the Uniform Commercial Code?

Money lenders have been around for thousands of years. Moneylending is a good business: the lender loans money to a debtor and charges the debtor interest on the loan. When the debtor repays the loan along with interest, the lender makes a profit. It is as simple as that.

However, the risk is that the debtor may not repay the loan. While the creditor may go to court to obtain a judgment against the debtor for breach of contract, the judgment will be worth little if the debtor is insolvent (the debtor, in this case, may go through bankruptcy and have the judgment discharged).

To protect against the risk of nonpayment, creditors in the past worked to establish legal means of obtaining "security" so that, even if a loan was not repaid, the creditor would not lose the value of the loan. The obvious method was for the creditor to take a "security interest" for the amount of the loan in property already belonging to the debtor. But what "security devices" could be used?

Prior to the 19th Century, only two security devices existed in the law. The first was a real property *mortgage* in which a real property owner would put up his or her land as security for a loan. If the loan was not repaid, the creditor could have the land sold and take his or her payment from the proceeds (mortgages are discussed in Part II of the chapter).

The second security device available prior to the 19th Century was a *pledge*. In a pledge, a personal property owner would transfer possession of his or her tangible personal property ("chattels") to a creditor as security for the repayment of a loan (or other promised performance). "Tangible personal property" was defined in Ch. 3 as follows:

A tangible personal property right refers to something with material substance—something you can touch. This book, for example, is a tangible or chose in possession. And so is a table, a lamp, a telephone, a TV set, an automobile, an airplane, and an ocean liner. An intangible, on the other hand, has no material substance. It is called a chose in "action" * * * Intangible personal property rights include patents, copyrights, common stock rights, bonds, accounts receivable, business goodwill, and any other transferable contract right.

———————

Modernly, an intangible may also be pledged if it is represented by an indispensable instrument such that enjoyment, transfer, or enforcement of the intangible is dependent on possession of the instrument (e. g., a promissory note or stock certificate).

Neither the real estate mortgage nor the pledge provided sufficient protection for creditors because, in many cases, the debtor had no land to mortgage and/or needed to retain possession of his or her personal property (e. g., the debtor might need the goods for use as inventory or equipment). Thus, a third security de-

vice, a *chattel mortgage,* was developed in the 19th Century. Like a pledge, a chattel mortgage was a mortgage or security interest in the debtor's personal property; its advantage over the pledge was that it did not require a transfer of possession of the property to the creditor. Thus, a debtor could borrow money, giving a chattel mortgage in his or her personal property as security for the loan. At the same time, the debtor could retain possession of the property for use as inventory, equipment, etc. Many states passed chattel mortgage acts providing that if the creditor properly recorded the chattel mortgage in the public records, the creditor would have priority over other creditors of the debtor with regard to the specific collateral. In other words, if the debtor did not repay the loan, the secured creditor who recorded would have first claim to proceeds from sale of the chattel.

The 19th Century also saw the development of yet a fourth security device— the *conditional sale.* In a conditional sale, a seller would sell tangible personal property on credit to a buyer, with the seller retaining title to the merchandise until the purchase price was paid in full (as opposed to selling on open account with no security device). Generally, the seller would have a right to repossess the goods upon any default in payment by the buyer. The conditional sale differed from the chattel mortgage in that only a seller of goods could make use of it. Of course, a seller could take a chattel mortgage in the property sold rather than use a conditional sale. However, at least at early law, sellers preferred the conditional sale because it did not have to be filed in the public records to give the creditor priority as to the chattel. (In later law, many states required the filing of conditional sales as well as chattel mortgages.)

Modernly, Article 9 of the Uniform Commercial Code, entitled "Secured

Transactions", has replaced the statutes dealing with chattel mortgages and conditional sales. The Article is extremely broad in scope: it covers all transactions involving the creation of a security interest in personal property. The Article applies regardless of the form of the transaction and irrespective of the terms the debtor and creditor use to describe it (e. g., "pledge", "chattel mortgage", "conditional sale", etc.).

Section 9–102 of the Uniform Commercial Code states:

Section 9–102. Policy and Subject Matter of Article

(1) Except as otherwise provided in Section 9–104 on excluded transactions, this Article applies

   (a) to any transaction (regardless of its form) which is intended to create a security interest in personal property or fixtures including goods, documents, instruments, general intangibles, chattel paper or accounts; and also

   (b) to any sale of accounts or chattel paper.

(2) This Article applies to security interests created by contract including pledge, assignment, chattel mortgage, chattel trust, trust deed, factor's lien, equipment trust, conditional sale, trust receipt, other lien or title retention contract and lease or consignment intended as security. This Article does not apply to statutory liens except as provided in Section 9–310.

———

It is clear from Section 9–102 that Article 9 is not limited to transactions involving the creation of security interests in *chattels*—the Section allows (and governs) the creation of security interests in *any personal property*. Personal property includes, first of all, "goods", which encompass not only chattels, but also growing crops, standing timber to be cut and removed, and the unborn young of animals (see Ch. 2). "Goods" include "consumer goods", "equipment", "farm products", and "inventory", defined at Section 9–109 of the Code as follows:

Section 9–109. Classification of Goods; "Consumer Goods"; "Equipment"; "Farm Products"; "Inventory"

Goods are

(1) "consumer goods" if they are used or bought for use primarily for personal, family or household purposes;

(2) "equipment" if they are used or bought for use primarily in business (including farming or a profession) or by a debtor who is a non-profit organization or a governmental subdivision or agency or if the goods are not included in the definitions of inventory, farm products or consumer goods;

(3) "farm products" if they are crops or livestock or supplies used in farming operations or if they are products of crops or livestock in their unmanufactured states (such as ginned cotton, wool-clip, maple syrup, milk and eggs), and if they are in the possession of a debtor engaged in raising, fattening, grazing or other farming operations. If goods are farm products they are neither equipment nor inventory;

(4) "inventory" if they are held by a person who holds them for sale or lease or to be furnished under contracts of service or if he has so furnished them, or if they are raw materials, work in process, or

materials used or consumed in a business. Inventory of a person is not to be classified as his equipment.

Note that, under Section 9–102, a security interest can be created in *fixtures* (as you will recall from Ch. 2, a "fixture" is an article that started out as personal property but was connected to real property in such a manner, or with such intent, that it became a part of the real property—a real property "fixture"). Section 9–313 of the UCC provides that a person who holds a security interest in goods that later become fixtures may be protected even after the goods have become real property (security interests in "fixtures" are discussed later in the chapter). The same Section states that no security interest can be created in ordinary building materials that are incorporated into an improvement on land (i. e., made an integral and inseparable part of the improvement, as to put bricks into a wall).

Article 9 of the UCC applies not only to the use of *goods* as collateral, but also to other kinds of personal property, including "documents, instruments, general intangibles, chattel paper or accounts." Thus, a security interest can be created in "documents", meaning documents of title such as bills of lading and warehouse receipts (as studied in Ch. 16).

A security interest can also be created in "instruments", meaning negotiable promissory notes and drafts (see Chapters 13 and 14) and security certificates representing investments in stocks, bonds, and other securities (see Ch. 24). For example, a shareholder will often put up his or her common stock as collateral when taking out a bank loan.

"General intangibles" such as goodwill, trademarks, copyrights, patents, or even blueprints or literary rights can also serve as collateral for the creation of a security interest.

So can "chattel paper". "Chattel paper" is any writing that sets forth the terms of a security agreement and contains the debtor's promise to pay the secured party. The most common source of chattel paper is a purchase money security interest in personal property. Section 9–107 of the Code defines a "purchase money security interest" as follows:

Section 9–107. Definitions: "Purchase Money Security Interest"

A security interest is a "purchase money security interest" to the extent that it is

(a) taken or retained by the seller of the collateral to secure all or part of its price; or

(b) taken by a person who by making advances or incurring an obligation gives value to enable the debtor to acquire rights in or the use of collateral if such value is in fact so used.

Subsection (a) describes the typical "conditional sale" in which a purchaser buys goods on credit and signs a statement in which he or she promises to pay the purchase price (usually in installments) and agrees to give the seller a security interest in the goods until they are paid for. The statement the buyer signs is "chattel paper". Frequently, the secured party seller uses the chattel paper as collateral in order to obtain a loan or buy on credit. The chattel paper, in this case, not only embodies the original security interest in the goods (i. e., the security interest that resulted when the goods were sold on credit to the buyer whose promise to repay is contained in the paper), but it also serves as collateral in the second financing transaction between the holder of the chattel paper and the buyer of the paper.

With regard to the use of "accounts" as collateral, most businesses sell on credit to customers without using any security device. A business simply bills its customers periodically for the amounts owing on their accounts (e. g., most people have one or more charge accounts and a number of utility company accounts for electric, water, gas, and telephone service). The Uniform Commercial Code defines an "account" at Section 9–106 as "any right to payment for goods sold or leased or for services rendered which is not evidenced by an instrument or chattel paper, whether or not it has been earned by performance." Sometimes, a business uses its "accounts receivable" (i. e., the amounts owing to the business from its customers) as collateral for taking out a loan or buying on credit. The secured party lender, in this case, will have priority as to the accounts only if he or she complies with all Article 9 requirements for protecting the interest.

It should be pointed out that both accounts and chattel paper may also be sold outright (as opposed to being used as collateral for obtaining a loan or buying on credit).[1] Where the sale is made in order to finance the seller's ongoing business operations (e. g., to purchase inventory), the sale is treated as a secured transaction under UCC Article 9–102 (1)(b). In other words, the buyer's interest in the accounts and chattel paper is considered to be a security interest only, and the buyer must comply with all Article 9 requirements in order to have priority over other creditors of the seller who claim ownership of or a security interest in the accounts or chattel paper.

Sometimes, what appears to be a personal property lease agreement (i. e., rental of personal property for a term) is really an Article 9 security transaction. Leases are often structured so that the lessee is entitled to purchase the "leased" goods at the end of the term. If the "purchase price" to be paid is nominal (so little as to be negligible in relation to the value of the property), the substance of the transaction is a sale and not a lease. In other words, the so-called lessor sells the property to the so-called lessee, but calls the transaction a lease so as to protect himself or herself until full payment is made (by retaining title, the so-called lessor prevents other creditors of the lessee from reaching the leased property).

Under Article 9, such a lease arrangement is a security agreement, and the so-called lessor will take priority over other creditors of the "lessee" only if he or she complies with the requirements of Article 9. The same result follows where the so-called lessee has an option to renew at the end of the lease term for a nominal rental. By way of example, suppose that Bill Businessperson "leases" a new Chevrolet from Linda Lease-A-Car Company. The monthly rental is set at $150 and Bill is given an option to purchase the car for $150 at the end of the four year term (or an option to renew the lease for another four years by making one additional rental payment of $150). Here, the substance of the "rental" transaction looks to be a sale (the purchase or renewal price is nominal), and the lease is a security agreement. Linda must thus comply with the requirements of Article 9 if she is to take priority over other creditors of Bill Businessperson with regard to the leased auto (e. g., upon default in "rental" by an insolvent Bill Businessperson).

In conclusion, Article 9 covers any security transaction involving the use of any kind of personal property as collateral. The Article does not apply to the use

---

1. Accounts and chattel paper are usually sold at a discount in the same way negotiable instruments that are not yet due are sold.

of real property as collateral (this is the subject of "mortgages" as discussed in Part II of the chapter). And it expressly exempts from its coverage certain security transactions, including security interests governed by federal statutes (e. g., the Federal Aviation Act provides a method for recording title to airplanes); claims that arise out of judicial proceedings, such as judgments claims; the use of insurance policies as loan collateral; and the sale of accounts or chattel paper where the sale is made as part of the sale of the entire business (such "bulk sales" are considered in Part IV of the chapter).

Being broad in coverage, Article 9 provides a simple and unified structure within which the many secured financing transactions involving personal property can be handled with minimum cost and maximum certainty. The two most common types of secured transactions under Article 9 are (1) loans made to personal property owners, with the personal property securing the loan, and (2) purchases of personal property on credit, with the buyer giving a security interest in the purchased property to the seller (i. e., purchase money security interests). While language of "chattel mortgage" and "conditional sale" still crops up from time to time in describing such transactions, the Uniform Commercial Code does not use these terms. Rather, the Code uses the following terminology to describe secured transactions in personal property:

(1) *Security interest.* The Code defines "security interest" as every interest "in personal property or fixtures which secures payment or performance of an obligation." UCC 1–201(37). Pledges, chattel mortgages, conditional sales—all are included within the definition and will create superior rights in the secured party if the rules of Article 9 are complied with.

(2) *Security agreement.* The "security agreement" is the agreement which creates the security interest. The security agreement is required in every case no matter what the form of transaction (pledge, chattel mortgage, conditional sale, etc.). It is usually in writing, but may be oral if the secured party has possession of the collateral as in a pledge (the specifics of the security agreement are considered in the following section).

(3) *Secured party.* The "secured party" is the lender, seller, purchaser, or other person in whose favor the security interest is created; he or she possesses the security interest in the collateral according to the terms of the security agreement.

(4) *Debtor.* The "debtor" is the party who must pay or otherwise perform the obligation embodied in the security agreement.

(5) *Financing statement.* Sometimes, but not always, the secured party must file a document called a *financing statement* describing the collateral in order to maintain a position of priority over other creditors of the debtor. The financing statement should not be confused with the security agreement. The financing statement is much less detailed; it is not required in every case (the security agreement is), and it does not create the security interest but merely gives public notice of the interest when filed in the proper local or statewide office.

No matter what terminology the parties themselves use to describe their personal property security transaction, the provisions of Article 9 are controlling.

What is meant by the statement that an Article 9 security interest "attaches" to the collateral?

Section 9–203 of the Uniform Commercial Code states in part:

Section 9–203. Attachment and Enforceability of Security Interests;

(1) * * * [A] security interest is not enforceable against the debtor

or third parties with respect to the collateral and does not attach unless

(a) the collateral is in the possession of the secured party pursuant to agreement, or the debtor has signed a security agreement which contains a description of the collateral and in addition, when the security interest covers crops growing or to be grown or timber to be cut, a description of the land concerned; and

(b) value has been given; and

(c) the debtor has rights in the collateral.

(2) A security interest attaches when it becomes enforceable against the debtor with respect to the collateral. Attachment occurs as soon as all of the events specified in subsection (1) have taken place

*   *   *

———————

Thus, under the UCC, "attachment" of a security interest is synonymous with *creation* of the interest. Unless and until a security interest attaches, the interest simply does not exist. Attachment (creation) of a security interest requires three things:

(1) The debtor and the secured party must enter into a security agreement (sometimes oral, but usually in writing);

(2) The secured party must give value for the security interest; and

(3) The debtor must have rights in the collateral.

A security agreement. In all cases, the debtor and the secured party must enter into a security agreement. Where the collateral is in the secured party's *possession,* the security agreement does not have to be in writing—a completely oral agreement will suffice. This is the typi-

cal pledge transaction where the debtor transfers possession of the collateral to the secured party. For example, someone who pawns his or her guitar for $100.00 is likely to receive only a pawn ticket and not a written security agreement. Still, the pawn shop will have a security interest in the guitar by virtue of having possession of it and by reason of having entered into an oral security agreement.

But sometimes it is impractical or undesirable for the secured party to have possession of the collateral. Where, pursuant to agreement, the collateral is not in the secured party's possession, the security interest will attach only if the parties have a written security agreement that describes the collateral and is signed by the debtor (under UCC Section 1–201(39), "signed" includes any symbol executed or adopted by a party with present intention to authenticate a writing). The requirement of a writing in the absence of possession by the secured party is like the Statute of Frauds requirement (see Ch. 10) with regard to certain contracts: a contract that falls within the Statute is enforceable only if it is supported by a written memo signed by the party to be charged. Thus, where the secured party does not have possession of the collateral, the security interest is enforceable only if it is evidenced by a written security agreement signed by the debtor. It is not necessary for the secured party to sign, although, as a practical matter, most secured parties do so.

The written security agreement must contain a reasonably definite description of the collateral, UCC Section 9–110 stating that "any description of personal property * * * is sufficient whether or not it is specific if it reasonably identifies what is described." For example, in one case, a written security agreement that described the collateral in general terms as "the contents" of the debtor's luncheonette and all "property used in" operation of the luncheonette was held sufficiently definite to cover a cash register used in operation of the business. National Cash Register Co. v. Firestone & Co., Inc., 346 Mass. 255, 191 N.E.2d 471 (1963).

Where the security interest covers crops or timber, the written security agreement must also include a description of the land involved. Again, a detailed legal description is not required so long as the security agreement reasonably identified the land. A description by street number or location is usually sufficient.

It is not necessary for the written agreement to expressly mention "proceeds". It is presumed that the parties intend the security interest to extend to any proceeds (cash or other property) that result when the specific collateral is sold or exchanged.

UCC Section 9–306 provides in part:

Section 9–306. "Proceeds"; Secured Party's Rights on Disposition of Collateral

(1) "Proceeds" includes whatever is received upon the sale, exchange, collection or other disposition of collateral or proceeds * * *

(2) * * * [A] security interest continues in collateral notwithstanding sale, exchange or other disposition thereof * * * and also continues in any identifiable proceeds * * * received by the debtor.

The written security agreement must also contain language that clearly shows that the debtor *intended* to create a security interest in the collateral. If it does not, no interest will be created. For example, in the case of American Card Co., Inc. v. H.M.H. Co., 97 R.I. 59, 196 A. 2d 150 (1963), the debtor borrowed $10,000 from the creditor, signing a promissory note and a standard-form fi-

nancing statement which listed the collateral; the secured party filed the financing statement. The statement, however, did not show any agreement between the parties or any intent on the part of the debtor to confer on the creditor a security interest in the collateral. As a result, the court held that the creditor had no such interest. The caveat is that while a written security agreement may be used as a financing statement, the reverse is not true. Generally, a financing statement does not purport to grant a security interest to a creditor but serves only as notice that a security interest has been claimed. (It should be pointed out that most secured parties do not file their written security agreement as a financing statement because they do not want all the details of their transaction to become a matter of public record.)

Two provisions—an "after-acquired property" clause and a "future advances" clause—are often used in written security agreements to facilitate the financing of inventory and accounts receivable. The first allows the security interest to extend to the debtor's after-acquired property; the second permits the interest to cover additional loans to be made in the future by the secured party ("future advances").

With regard to after-acquired property, Section 9-204(1) of the Code states that "a security agreement may provide that any or all obligations covered by the security agreement are to be secured by after-acquired collateral." For example, a security agreement might include a clause stating that the security interest applies to "all inventory now or hereafter acquired by the debtor" or to "all accounts due or to become due to the debtor." Of course, the security interest will not attach to the after-acquired property until the debtor acquires the property (remember, the debtor must have rights in the collateral for the security interest to attach).

With regard to future advances, Section 9–204(3) states that "obligations covered by a security agreement may include future advances or other value whether or not the advances or value are given pursuant to commitment." For example, a security agreement might provide: "The security interest herein created shall also secure all other indebtedness, obligations and liabilities of the debtor to the secured party, now existing and hereafter arising, including future advances, howsoever evidenced or created, actual, direct, contingent or otherwise."

"After-acquired" property clauses and "future advance" clauses work together with the provisions of Section 9–205 to enable the debtor whose inventory is subject to a security interest to transfer and dispose of individual items of the inventory while acquiring other inventory with which to replace it. The security interest, in this case, is on the whole of the inventory (whatever items the inventory consists of at any particular time); periodically, the secured creditor loans additional money on the inventory. The arrangement is called a *floating lien:* the lien is said to "float" over the collateral, attaching to each item of inventory as it comes into the debtor's possession and ending when the item is sold (or if the item is an account, when the account is collected). Thus, in a "floating lien", there is a constant turnover of collateral, with the security interest resting on a shifting stock of goods or accounts. The secured party makes present and future advances to the debtor with the advances secured by both present and after-acquired inventory and/or accounts.

The UCC Section 9–205 provides:

Section 9–205. Use or Disposition of Collateral Without Accounting Permissible

A security interest is not invalid or fraudulent against creditors by reason of liberty in the debtor to use, commingle or dispose of all or part of the collateral * * * or to collect or compromise accounts or chattel paper, or to accept the return of goods or make repossessions, or to use, commingle or dispose of proceeds, or by reason of the failure of the secured party to require the debtor to account for proceeds or replace collateral. This section does not relax the requirements of possession where perfection of a security interest depends upon possession of the collateral by the secured party or by a bailee.

———

The *Official Comment* states in part:

The UCC provides:

This Article expressly validates the floating charge or lien on shifting stock. This section provides that a security interest is not invalid or fraudulent by reason of liberty in the debtor to dispose of the collateral without being required to account for proceeds or substitute new collateral.

———

It should be pointed out that the Uniform Commercial Code limits the operation of after-acquired property clauses against consumers. Section 9–204(2) provides that no security interest will attach under an after-acquired property clause to consumer goods other than accessions unless the consumer-debtor acquires rights in the goods within 10 days after the secured party gives value. The Section reads:

(2) No security interest attaches under an after-acquired property clause to consumer goods other than accessions * * * when given as additional security unless the debtor acquires rights in them within ten days after the secured party gives value.

Section 9–204(2) is designed to protect consumers from encumbering all of their present and future assets when they buy consumer goods on credit. But note that accessions are not exempt from operation of the after-acquired property clause (as you will recall from Ch. 3, accessions are items of personal property that are added to property already in existence—e. g., crops, the offspring of animals, materials added to a chattel in repairing it, and materials manufactured into a finished product).

The secured party must give value. The Uniform Commercial Code defines "value" at Section 1–201(44) as follows:

(44) "Value" * * * [A] person gives "value" for rights if he acquires them

(a) in return for a binding commitment to extend credit or for the extension of immediately available credit whether or not drawn upon and whether or not a chargeback is provided for in the event of difficulties in collection; or

(b) as security for or in total or partial satisfaction of a pre-existing claim; or

(c) by accepting delivery pursuant to a pre-existing contract for purchase; or

(d) generally, in return for any consideration sufficient to support a simple contract.

As you can see, the term "value" has a much broader meaning with regard to the creation of a security interest than it has with regard to the consideration required for a valid contract. You will recall from Ch. 9 that past consideration is no consideration for a contract. However, under Section 1–201(44)(b), "a person gives 'value' for rights if he or she acquires them as security for a pre-existing claim." Thus, a person who takes a security interest for an antecedent debt (i. e., past consideration furnished by the secured party) gives "value" within the

meaning of the Section. For example, say that Bill Businessperson purchases a car from Cora Cardealer on an open credit with no agreement regarding any security. One month later, Bill is unable to pay for the car, and he enters into a security agreement with Cora, giving Cora a security interest in the car. Though Cora extended the credit a month ago, she is considered to give "value" now for purposes of creating the security interest, and the interest attaches to the automobile. (Cora, of course, is not promising to do anything new or different, and there is no consideration in the contract law sense.)

The debtor must have rights in the collateral. To say that the debtor must have rights in the collateral is not to say that he or she must own the property (i. e., have legal title to it). It is true that, in most cases, the debtor owns the property that he or she puts up as collateral, and has rights in the property on the basis of title. But title is not required. The debtor may have far less than complete ownership of the property and still have "rights" in the collateral for purposes of creating a security interest. For example, a person who contracts to buy goods acquires a "special property" interest in the goods at the time they are identified to the contract of sale (see Ch. 17). This "special property" is not complete ownership, but it will serve as "rights in the collateral" for purposes of creating a security interest in the goods.

Similarly, a person in rightful possession of personal property has rights in the property though legal title is vested in another—even in the secured party himself or herself. For example, a person who purchases a car on credit generally gives a purchase money security interest in the car to the person who finances the purchase. The secured party will retain title to the automobile, though the debtor has possession of the car, until such time as the loan is fully paid. Along this line, Section 9–202 of the

Uniform Commercial Code specifically states: "Each provision of this Article with regard to rights, obligations and remedies applies whether title to collateral is in the secured party or in the debtor."

Having considered each of the three requirements for attachment in detail, let's look now at an example. Say that Bill Businessperson enters into a written agreement with Lisa Lender wherein Lisa agrees to loan Bill $25,000 on July 1st, the loan to be secured by Bill's factory equipment (which Bill owns and is using in the business); at the same time, Lisa agrees to loan Bill another $15,000 on his inventory together with an automobile Bill plans to buy in the next few weeks. On July 1st, Lisa loans Bill $25,000; on August 15th, she loans Bill another $15,000; and, on September 1st, Bill purchases the car. Lisa has a security interest in the factory equipment, in the inventory, and in the car—however, each interest attached (i. e., came into existence) at a different time. Lisa's security interest in the equipment attached on July 1st because all three requirements for attachment were met on that date: the parties had a written security agreement; Lisa gave value in the amount of $25,000; and Bill had rights in his factory equipment. Lisa's security interest in the inventory attached on August 15th: though the security agreement was entered into on July 1st, Lisa did not give value (loan the $15,000) until August 15th. And, finally, Lisa's security interest in the car attached on September 1st: though the security agreement was reached on July 1st, and though Lisa gave value on August 15th, the debtor Bill did not have rights in the collateral (the car) until September 1st.

What is meant by the statement that an Article 9 security interest is "perfected"?

A creditor who extends credit in relation to personal property looking to obtain a security interest in the property will end up in one of three positions.

First, the security interest may not attach (because one or more of the three requirements for attachment have not been met), in which case the creditor will receive no security interest. The creditor will be in the same position as any other unsecured creditor (see Ch. 26). If the debtor does not pay, the creditor may sue the debtor to obtain a money judgment. However, if the debtor is unable to pay the judgment, the creditor's only right will be to share in the debtor's non-exempt assets with other general, unsecured creditors of the debtor.

Second, the security interest may attach, but it may not be perfected. Here, the creditor will be secured and have something more than an unsecured creditor—but not much more. A secured creditor with an unperfected security interest will have rights to proceed against the specific collateral if the debtor does not pay (i. e., if the debtor defaults). However, the creditor will enjoy little protection as against *other* claimants to the same collateral. While the creditor will have priority over other unperfected security interest holders if his or her interest attached first, his or her claim will generally be subordinate to that of perfected security interest holders and bona fide purchasers for value (i. e., purchasers who take the collateral for value without knowledge of the security interest).

Third, the security interest may attach, and it may be perfected, in which case the creditor will be in the best position possible with respect to the collateral. The holder of a security interest who does whatever is necessary to "perfect" the interest maximizes his or her rights against third party claimants to the same collateral. In most cases, the holder of a perfected security interest will have priority over the claims of subsequent lien creditors of the debtor or a creditors' representative such as a receiver, trustee in bankruptcy, or assignee for the benefit of creditors (see Ch. 26). The secured party will also prevail over holders of unperfected security interests and interests perfected at a later date and time. In many cases, the holder of a perfected security interest will even prevail over a bona fide purchaser of the collateral.

Sometimes, however, not even perfection will serve to protect the creditor. Section 9–307(1) of the Uniform Commercial Code provides that a person who buys goods in the ordinary course of business from a seller who deals in goods of that kind will take the goods free of any existing security interest (perfected or unperfected) even where the buyer knows of the interest at the time of the purchase.[2]

Section 9–307(1) states:

> (1) A buyer in ordinary course of business * * * other than a person buying farm products from a person engaged in farming operations takes free of a security interest created by his seller even though the security interest is perfected and even though the buyer knows of its existence.

To come under the Section, the sale must be in the regular course of the seller's business and the buyer must give value for the goods (and, here, value does not include total or partial satisfaction of a pre-existing debt or claim). Usually, the buyer is purchasing some product or item from the dealer's inventory. Thus, a person who buys a car from an automobile dealer in the ordinary course of business will take the car free of any existing security interest in the car, whether perfected or unperfected.

As to how a security interest is perfected, the Uniform Commercial Code provides for three methods of perfection:

(1) Taking possession of the collateral;

(2) Filing a "financing statement" giving public notice of the security interest with the appropriate state or local agency; and, in some cases,

(3) By simple attachment of the security interest.

Taking possession of the collateral. In the typical pledge situation, the secured party's *possession* of the collateral, without more, serves to perfect the security interest. You will recall that a pledge is a bailment or delivery of personal property by way of security for a debt or other promised performance. Not only goods may be pledged, but also money, documents of title (e. g., warehouse receipts and bills of lading), negotiable instruments (e. g., promissory notes and drafts, and investment securities), and chattel paper (when transferred to third parties to secure a second credit transaction).

Remember that the secured party's possession of the collateral (pursuant to agreement with the debtor) eliminates the need for a *written* security agreement —the secured party's possession of the collateral also serves to perfect the security interest (i. e., maximize the secured party's rights with respect to collateral). *Everything that can be done to secure a creditor is thus achieved by possession alone.* This is a very important fact to remember (and one students often forget!).

A security interest is perfected by possession from the moment possession is taken; it remains perfected only as long as the possession continues. Of course, the secured party, as a bailee, must use reasonable care in storing and preserving the collateral. He or she may charge the debtor for any reasonable expenses incurred in caring for the property, includ-

---

2. While the buyer takes free of the security interest if he or she merely knows that a security interest covers the goods, he or she takes subject to the interest if he or she also knows that the sale is in violation of some term of the security agreement.

ing insurance costs (the collateral secures payment of these expenses as well as payment of the original debt).

Most items that can be pledged can also be perfected by filing a "financing statement". However, security interests in money or negotiable instruments (including negotiable money instruments and negotiable investment securities) can only be perfected by taking possession of the collateral. Section 9–304(1) of the Uniform Commercial Code states: "A security interest in chattel paper or negotiable documents may be perfected by filing. A security interest in money or instruments (other than instruments which form a part of chattel paper) can be perfected only by the secured party's taking possession * * *" However, possession of the instruments may be relinquished to the debtor for purposes of sale, exchange, collection, or renewal without losing the perfection for a period of 21 days. UCC 9–304(5)(b).

On the other hand, some intangible items such as accounts receivable cannot be pledged because they are not represented by any tangible document or instrument. Perfection as to such collateral is by filing only.

Quite often, when inventory is used as collateral, possession (and hence perfection) is accomplished by the use of "field warehousing" as discussed in Ch. 16: the secured party in the "floating lien" situation takes over part of the debtor's facilities and controls what is sold from the inventory and what is added to it.

Filing a financing statement. It is frequently impractical for the secured party to take possession of the collateral. The secured party, in this case, can perfect his or her security interest by filing a *financing statement.* A financing statement is a document designed to put the debtor's creditors "on notice" that a security agreement is in effect as to certain of the debtor's property. The statement briefly notes the secured party's interest

in the property and describes in general terms the type of collateral included under the security agreement. The secured party files the financing statement in the local or statewide government office as prescribed by the Uniform Commercial Code. While the secured party may use the written security agreement as the financing statement, most secured parties prefer not to. The security agreement is generally much more detailed than the financing statement (which gives little specific information about the underlying transaction), and most parties prefer not to have the "detail" of their transaction on file publicly.

Section 9–402 of the Uniform Commercial Code lists the requirements of the financing statement as follows:

Section 9–402. Formal Requisites of Financing Statement

(1) A financing statement is sufficient if it gives the names of the debtor and the secured party, is signed by the debtor, gives an address of the secured party from which information concerning the security interest may be obtained, gives a mailing address of the debtor and contains a statement indicating the types, or describthe items, of collateral * * * A copy of the security agreement is sufficient as a financing statement if it contains the above information and is signed by the debtor.

* * *

(3) A form substantially as follows is sufficient to comply with subsection (1):
Name of Debtor (or assignor) _____
Address _____
Name of secured party (or assignee) _____
Address _____

1. This financing statement covers the following types (or items) of property:
    (Describe) _____

2. (If collateral is crops) The above described crops are growing or are to be grown on:
    (Describe Real Estate) _____

3. (If applicable) The above goods are to become fixtures on *
    (Describe Real Estate) _____
    and this financing statement is to be filed (for record) in the real estate records. (If the debtor does not have an interest of record.) The name of a record owner is _____

4. (If products of collateral are claimed) Products of the collateral are also covered.

_____
        Signature of Debtor
        (or Assignor)

_____

The *Official Comment* to Section 9–402 states in part.

What is required to be filed is not * * * the security agreement itself, but only a simple notice which may be filed before the security interest attaches or thereafter. The notice itself indicates merely that the secured party who has filed may have a security interest in the collateral described. Further inquiry from the parties concerned will be necessary to disclose the complete state of affairs.

Note that the financing state must include:

(1) The names of both the debtor and the secured party;

(2) An address for the secured party from which information concerning the security interest may be obtained;

(3) A statement indicating the types of or describing the items of collateral; and

(4) The signature of the debtor alone.

_____

Where the collateral is crops (either growing or to be grown) or goods that are to become fixtures, the financing statement must also include a description of the real estate involved.

A financing statement that substantially complies with the requirements of Section 9–402 will be effective even though it contains minor errors (i. e., errors not so misleading as to seriously jeopardize the rights of third parties).

The financing statement need not make mention of the fact that the security agreement covers after-acquired property as long as the types of collateral subject to the after-acquired property clause are adequately described. Thus, a financing statement that refers to "inventory" is sufficient to cover both present and after-acquired inventory. And, with but limited exception, filing as to collateral automatically covers proceeds. (UCC Section 9–306(3).)

The place of filing varies from state to state and even within a particular state depending on the type of collateral involved. The Uniform Commercial Code at Section 9–401 sets forth three alternative filing systems for states to choose from. Most states have adopted Alternative 2 which provides for a combination of local and statewide filing. Alternative 2 requires local filing in the office of a designated county official in the county of the debtor's residence for se-

_____

* Where appropriate substitute either "The above timber is standing on _____" or "The above minerals or the like (including oil and gas) or accounts will be financed at the wellhead or minehead of the well or mine located on _____".

curity interests in consumer goods, farm equipment, and farm products; local filing in a designated county office in the county where the land is located for security interests in fixtures, minerals, timber, or growing crops; and statewide filing with the secretary of state for all other collateral. Needless to say, this combination of local and statewide filing is confusing. When in doubt, it is wise to file both locally and statewide since filing in the wrong place will be ineffective.

UCC Section 9–401(3) states that if the creditor files correctly in light of the existing circumstances, the filing remains effective though the debtor's residence or place of business, or the use or (intrastate) location of the collateral is thereafter changed. However, if the debtor moves the collateral to another state, the secured party must re-perfect his or her interest in the new state (by filing or taking possession of the collateral) within four months after the removal. So long as the secured party re-perfects within the four month period, his or her interest will be deemed perfected in the new state from the date of the original perfection. If he or she fails to re-perfect within the four month period, his or her interest will become unperfected as against anyone who purchases the collateral or takes a security in it after its removal from the state. UCC Section 9–303(2).

Under Section 9–403(2) of the Code, a properly filed financing statement is effective for a period of five years from the date of filing. Unless a new financing statement or a *continuation statement* is filed before the expiration of the five year period, the security interest will become unperfected. Where this occurs, all third parties having liens against the collateral will gain priority over the interest. In most cases, the secured party elects to file a continuation statement because, unlike the original financing statement, it does not have to be signed by the

debtor (only the secured party must sign it). The continuation statement must identify the original financing statement by file number. The statement adds another five year period of perfection to the security interest; succeeding continuation statements may be filed to add additional five year periods.

Before moving on to perfection by attachment alone, it should be pointed out that Section 9–302(3) of the UCC expressly exempts from the Article 9 *filing* requirements security interests in property subject to a state certificate of title law. In many states, automobiles, boats, mobile homes, and the like are subject to laws requiring that a security interest in the property be noted on a certificate of title covering the property (or be otherwise filed centrally under the statute). Compliance with the certificate of title law is the exclusive method of perfection in this case and filing in the normal way under the UCC is ineffective.

Perfection by attachment of the security interest. To this point, we have considered two ways of perfecting a security interest: (1) by taking possession of the collateral; and (2) by filing a financial statement covering the security interest.

In a few situations, there is yet a third method of perfection and that is by mere attachment (creation) of the interest. In other words, mere attachment of the security interest will serve to perfect the interest. The most important such transaction is the purchase money security interest in consumer goods. You will recall that, in a purchase money security interest, the secured party advances money or credit to the debtor to enable him or her to purchase the collateral. Where the transaction involves the purchase of consumer goods (i. e., goods used or bought primarily for personal, family, or household purposes), it is not necessary for the secured party to file a financing statement to perfect his or her security interest. The security interest is perfected automatically upon its attachment to the collateral. UCC Section 9–302(1)(d).

This is not to say that a written security agreement is not required—a written agreement is always required unless the secured party has possession of the collateral. And, of course, in the purchase money security interest situation, the very purpose of the transaction is to give the *debtor* possession of the consumer goods. By way of example, suppose that Harvey Consumer buys a TV set on credit so that his family can watch television. Harvey agrees to pay off the purchase price in installments; he signs a written security agreement giving the seller a security interest in the set until the purchase price is paid. The creditor-seller has a perfected security interest in the TV set upon attachment. Because the interest is a purchase money security interest in consumer goods, no filing is required.

The general rule is that a secured party with a perfected interest has priority over all subsequent claimants to the same collateral. However, where perfection occurs by attachment alone in the case of consumer goods, there is one "subsequent claimant" against whom the secured party will not be protected. And that is a buyer who subsequently purchases the goods from any seller without knowledge of the security interest and for his or her own personal, family, or household use. A subsequent consumer buyer who purchases the goods without knowledge of the security interest will take them free of the interest unless the secured party has also perfected by filing a financing statement.

For example, suppose that Harvey Consumer sells the TV set to his neighbor, Sheila, who plans to use the set for family viewing purposes. Sheila has no knowledge of the creditor-seller's purchase money security interest in the set (perfected by attachment only) and takes the set free of the interest. However, if the creditor-seller had filed a financing statement covering the set (and not relied on attachment alone for perfection), Sheila's interest in the set would be subject to the creditor-seller's interest.

This should be contrasted with the situation where a buyer purchases goods in the ordinary course of business from a dealer in goods of that kind. As stated previously, the buyer takes the goods free of any existing security interest (perfected or unperfected) in them even where the buyer has knowledge of the interest at the time of the purchase. Filing, in this case, won't protect the secured creditor.

What are the priorities of Article 9 secured creditors?

Sometimes, more than one person claims a security interest in the same collateral. As to who has priority with respect to the collateral, the general rule is that the first secured party to "file or perfect" has priority. Section 9–312 of the Code states the "first to file or perfect" rule as follows:

Section 9–312. Priorities Among Conflicting Security Interests in the Same Collateral

* * *

(5) In all cases not governed by other rules stated in this section * * * priority between conflicting security interests in the same collateral shall be determined according to the following rules:

(a) Conflicting security interests rank according to priority in time of filing or perfection. Priority dates from the time a filing is first made covering the collateral or the time the security interest is first perfected, whichever is earlier.

Thus, the first party to file *or* perfect his or her security interest will have priority. As you know, a secured party may file a financing statement before his or her security interest attaches (remember, attachment requires three things: a security agreement, the giving of value by the secured party, and the debtor acquiring rights in the collateral). So long as the security interest ultimately comes into being, the early "filing" date will govern priorities under the "first to file or perfect" rule. For example, suppose that, on July 1st, Debra Debtor arranges to borrow $20,000 from Frank Financer, the loan to be made on August 1st, and to be secured by Debra's collection of valuable paintings; Debra is to retain possession of the paintings. Frank files a financing statement on July 1st describing the paintings as collateral. On July 10th, Debra transfers possession of the paintings to Artis Artcollecter as security for a $20,000 loan made by Artis to Debra on that day. On August 1st, Frank Financer loans Debra $20,000. Nine months later, Debra is insolvent and cannot repay either loan. As between Frank and Artis, who has priority with regard to the paintings? You know that Artis took possession of the paintings on July 10th, the day she loaned the $20,000 to Debra: thus, her security interest in the collateral both attached and was perfected on that day. Frank, on the other hand, filed a financing statement on July 1st, but did not loan the $20,000 (i. e., give value) until August 1st: thus, his security interest in the collateral did not attach until August 1st (and therefore could not be perfected until that time). However, Section 9–312 of the Uniform Commercial Code states that the "first to file *or* perfect" takes priority, and Frank, though his security interest attached and was perfected after Artis', was first to file or perfect. He therefore takes priority as to the collateral. Assuming the paintings bring $18,000 when sold, Frank will receive all of the money and Artis none of

it. (And it makes no difference whether Frank knew of Artis' interest at the time he advanced the $20,000 to Debra.)

On the other hand, if Artis had taken possession of the paintings (i. e., perfected her interest) before Frank filed, then Artis would have priority as to the collateral because she was first to *perfect* or file.

The UCC creates certain exceptions to the "first to file or perfect" rule as follows:

(1) *A purchase money security interest in collateral other than inventory.* You will recall that in the purchase money security interest situation, the secured party finances the debtor's purchase of property, the property then serving as collateral for the loan. For example, Bill Businessperson might borrow money from First State Bank with which to purchase machinery for use in his business. The bank retains a purchase money security interest in the machinery. Since the purchase money security interest is in collateral other than consumer goods, attachment alone will not serve to perfect the interest. And perfection by possession is impractical since the very purpose of the purchase money security interest is to give immediate possession of the machinery to the debtor Bill for use in his business. Thus, the bank must file a financing statement in order to perfect the security interest.

But suppose that five days after he purchases the machinery, and before the bank files, the debtor Bill takes out a second loan from another financial institution, the same machinery serving as collateral for the loan. The second financial institution immediately files a financing statement covering the security interest. First State Bank subsequently files. As between First State Bank (the bank that financed the purchase of the machinery) and the second financial institution, who prevails as to the collateral in the event that Bill is unable to repay either loan? Under the first to file or perfect rule, the second financial institution would prevail since it was the first to file. However, Section 9–312(4) of the Uniform Commercial Code provides an exception to the "first to file or perfect" rule in the case of a purchase money security interest in goods other than collateral.

The Section states:

———

A purchase money security interest in collateral other than inventory has priority over a conflicting security interest in the same collateral or its proceeds if the purchase money security interest is perfected at the time the debtor receives possession of the collateral or within ten days thereafter.

———

Thus, under Section 9–312(4), First State Bank has a "10 day" grace period within which to perfect: so long as the bank perfects its interest by the time the debtor receives possession of the collateral or within 10 days thereafter, the bank takes priority.

Where the purchase money secured party fails to file or perfect before the debtor receives possession of the collateral or within 10 days thereafter, the priorities are governed by the "first to file or perfect" rule.

(2) *A purchase money security interest in inventory.* There is no 10 day grace period with regard to a purchase money security interest in inventory. The purchase money secured party will have priority over a prior perfected interest in the debtor's inventory (e. g., a "floating lien") only if the purchase money secured party's interest is perfected at the time the debtor receives possession of the inventory *and* the purchase money secured party gives written notice of his or her claim to the existing security

interest holder before the debtor receives possession. The notice must describe the inventory collateral by item or type.

For example, say that Molly Merchant has a substantial inventory of drugs and sundries; Martha Supplier has a "floating lien" on the inventory. Molly purchases additional inventory on credit from George Newproducts, with George retaining a purchase money security interest in the inventory. To protect his interest from Martha's "floating lien", George must perfect it before Molly receives possession of the new products, and he must notify Martha Supplier in writing that he has a security interest in the products. If George does this, he will have priority over Martha's "floating lien" as to the new inventory items in the event that they (George and Martha) are not paid and must look to the collateral (the inventory) for payment. This is the rule of UCC Section 9–312(3) which is explained in the *Official Comment* as follows:

———

Under subsection (3) the same rule of priority, but without the ten day grace period for filing, applies to a purchase money security interest in inventory, with the additional requirement that the purchase money secured party give notification, as stated in subsection (3), to any other secured party who filed earlier for the same item or type of inventory. The reason for the additional requirement of notification is that typically the arrangement between an inventory secured party and his debtor will require the secured party to make periodic advances against incoming inventory or periodic releases of old inventory as new inventory is received. * * * The notification requirement protects the inventory financer in such a situation: if he has received notification, he will presumably not make an advance; if he has not received notification (or if the other interest does not qualify as a purchase money interest) any advance he may make will have priority. Since an arrangement for periodic advances against incoming property is unusual outside the inventory field no notification requirement is included in subsection (4).

----

(3) *Where one person holds a security interest in inventory and another holds a security interest in present and future accounts (i. e., accounts receivable).* Another priority problem may arise where one party has a security interest in the debtor's inventory and another has a security interest in the debtor's accounts. In selling his or her inventory, the debtor may receive not only cash proceeds, but also accounts receivable (from selling on credit to customers). You know that the inventory secured party's security interest extends to the cash proceeds from sale of the inventory. But does it extend to the accounts receivable proceeds? As between the inventory secured party and the accounts secured party, who has priority with regard to these "accounts" proceeds in the event that the debtor cannot pay his or her debts? UCC Section 9–312(3) provides the answer. It first acknowledges that the inventory secured party has priority with respect to cash (or check) proceeds that are deposited in an earmarked bank account as proceeds of an inventory sale (or are otherwise identifiable as such proceeds). But as to the accounts receivable resulting from an inventory sale, the accounts secured party has priority so long as he or she was first to file a financing statement covering his or her interest. The accounts secured party, in this case, will also have priority as to the cash received when the accounts are finally paid.

(4) *Priority of a security interest in chattel paper.* An inventory secured party's security interest also extends to pro-

ceeds in the form of chattel paper and instruments. If the debtor sells the chattel paper or instruments to a purchaser, who has priority with respect to the paper and instruments as between the inventory secured party and the purchaser?

UCC Section 9–308 states:

Section 9–308. Purchase of Chattel Paper and Instruments

A purchaser of chattel paper or an instrument who gives new value and takes possession of it in the ordinary course of his business has priority over a security interest in the chattel paper or instrument

(a) which is perfected under Section 9–304 (* * * temporary perfection) or under Section 9–306 (perfection as to proceeds) if he acts without knowledge that the specific paper or instrument is subject to a security interest; or

(b) which is claimed merely as proceeds of inventory subject to a security interest (Section 9–306) even though he knows that the specific paper or instrument is subject to the security interest.

The *Official Comment* to the Section states:

* * * Clause (b) of the section deals with the case where the security interest in the chattel paper is claimed merely as proceeds—i. e., on behalf of an inventory financer who has not by some new transaction with the debtor acquired a specific interest in the chattel paper. In that case a purchaser, even though he knows of the inventory financer's proceeds interest, takes priority provided he gives new value and

takes possession of the paper in the ordinary course of his business.

The same basic rule applies in favor of a purchaser of other instruments who claims priority against a proceeds interest therein of which he has knowledge. Thus a purchaser of a negotiable instrument might prevail under clause (b) even though his knowledge of the conflicting proceeds claim precluded his having holder in due course status. * * *

* * * Clause (a) deals with the case where the non-possessory security interest in the chattel paper is more than a mere claim to proceeds—i. e., exists in favor of a secured party who has given value against the paper, whether or not he financed the inventory sale whose sale gave rise to it. In this case the purchaser, to take priority, must not only give new value and take possession in the ordinary course of his business; he must also take without knowledge of the existing security interest.

———

(5) *Priority between a secured party and a lien creditor.* In Ch. 26, we discussed methods used by creditors to obtain payment, including attachment and garnishment. Such creditors' remedies frequently result in liens on the debtor's property. Say that a lien arises on property in which a secured party already holds a security interest. As between the lien creditor and the secured party, who has priority? Section 9–301(1)(b) of the Uniform Commercial Code states that "an unperfected security interest is subordinate to the rights of a person who becomes a lien creditor before the security interest is perfected." In other words, if the secured party perfects his or her interest before the creditor obtains the lien, the secured party has priority. If, on the other hand, the lien arises before the se-

cured party perfects, the lien creditor has priority.

(6) *Priority in the case of a federal tax lien.* The Federal Tax Lien Act creates a lien in favor of the United States on all property belonging to a person who fails to pay his or her federal taxes. However, until notice of the lien is filed, the lien is inferior to the interest of any purchaser, security interest holder (whether the interest is perfected or unperfected), mechanic's lienor, or judgment lien creditor. A perfected security interest is always superior to a subsequently filed federal tax lien. If the secured party makes future advances after the federal tax lien is filed, the secured party's priority will extend to the advances so long as the secured party makes them without knowledge of the federal filing and not more than 45 days after the filing.

(7) *The priority of the repairer.* The Uniform Commercial Code, Section 9–310, states:

> When a person in the ordinary course of his business furnishes services or materials with respect to goods subject to a security interest, a lien upon goods in the possession of such person given by statute or rule of law for such materials or services takes priority over a perfected security interest unless the lien is statutory and the statute expressly provides otherwise.

———

In nearly all states, a person who repairs goods has a statutory right to retain possession of the goods until the repairs are paid for. The repairer has a lien on the repaired goods which is superior even to a perfected security interest. The idea is that the repairer's work has either preserved or increased the value of the collateral; thus, the security interest holder should not complain if the collateral serves first as security for payment of the repairs.

(8) *Priority of a security interest in fixtures.* Sometimes, one person has a security interest in personal property that becomes a fixture, while another has a mortgage on the real property itself (remember, a "fixture" is an item that started out as personal property but became real property by reason of its attachment to land). Special "fixture filing" rules under the Uniform Commercial Code govern priorities in this case. Under all three UCC alternative filing systems, a security interest in goods "which are or are to become fixtures   *   *   *   must be filed in the office where a mortgage on the real estate would be filed or recorded." (See Part II.) The fixture filing must be made in the real estate records in such a way that a person who is making a title search of the real property will locate the filing.

The most common security interest in fixtures is a purchase money interest in which the secured party finances the debtor's purchase of fixtures, taking a purchase money security interest in the fixtures (the debtor being the owner or lessee of the real property). Under Section 9–313 of the Code, the purchase money security interest has priority over any conflicting interest (perfected or unperfected) of the real property owner or mortgagee as long as the purchase money security interest is perfected by a fixture filing before the goods become fixtures or within 10 days thereafter. In other words, the holder of the purchase money security interest has a 10 day grace period after installation of the fixtures within which to make an effective fixture filing.

Of course, even where the fixture filing is made after the 10 day grace period, the purchase money security interest will still have priority over *subsequently* recorded interests in the real property (see Ch. 6 regarding recordation of deeds and other interests in real property).

Without regard to the fixture filing requirements, a security interest in fixtures has priority over conflicting interests if the fixtures are "readily removable factory or office machines or readily removable replacements of domestic appliances which are consumer goods, and before the goods become fixtures, the security interest is perfected by any method permitted." UCC Section 9–313(4)(c). Thus, the secured party need not make a fixture filing in the real estate records where the fixtures are readily removable factory or office machines—a chattel filing as for any other "equipment" will serve to perfect the interest. And where the goods are consumer goods, attachment alone (without filing) will perfect the interest. In any case, perfection must occur *before* the goods become fixtures for the interest to take priority over existing claims of record.

Sometimes, a mortgage holder or purchaser of property clearly has priority over a security interest in fixtures on the property, but consents in writing to let the fixtures take priority. Such agreements are routinely enforced by the courts. Also, a security interest in fixtures has priority if the debtor has a right to remove the fixtures as against the mortgage holder or owner of the real property (e. g., where the debtor is the lessee of the property and has a right to remove the fixtures—e. g., in the case of mobile homes).

However, a security interest in fixtures (even a purchase money security interest) is subordinate to a construction mortgage recorded before the goods become fixtures if the goods become fixtures before completion of the construction. (In a construction mortgage, the secured party mortgagee loans money to the debtor to finance construction on real property, the land and resulting buildings serving as security for repayment of the loan.) The holder of the mortgage is given priority to prevent the debtor from using the same collateral for two loans—first, obtaining funds from the construction mortgagee ostensibly to purchase the fixtures (e. g., the construction mortgagee advancing $2,000 to purchase built-in electricals such as stoves, refrigerators, and dishwashers); then, second, purchasing the items on credit from the supplier, giving the supplier a security interest in them.

(9) *Priority of a security interest in accessions.* You will recall that an accession is personal property that is added to or affixed to already existing personal property (e. g., a new motor placed in an airplane). Sometimes, one person has a security interest in the accession (the motor), while another has a security interest in the item as a whole (the airplane). Section 9–314 of the Uniform Commercial Code governs priorities in this situation. Essentially, the Section provides that where a security interest in an accession *attaches and is perfected before installation or affixation* of the property to the item as a whole, the accession security interest has priority with respect to the accession over any conflicting interest, perfected or unperfected, existing or created subsequently, in the whole of the goods.

Where a security interest in an accession *attaches, but is not perfected prior to installation or affixation,* the interest has priority as to competing interests (perfected or unperfected) existing at the time of installation; but the interest is subordinate to competing claims subsequently acquired without knowledge of the accession security interest (and before perfection of the interest).

And, finally, where a security interest in an accession *attaches after installation or affixation,* the interest has no priority over existing claims (perfected or unperfected) to the whole, nor any priority over subsequently acquired claims unless the accession interest is perfected first in time.

(10) *Priority of a security interest in goods which become part of a product or mass.* Sometimes, a secured party will help finance a manufacturing process by loaning on certain of the raw materials that are to go into the finished product. With regard to a security interest taken by the party in the raw materials, Section 9–315(1) of the Uniform Commercial Code states:

(1) If a security interest in goods was perfected and subsequently the goods or a part thereof have become part of a product or mass, the security interest continues in the product or mass if

(a) the goods are so manufactured, processed, assembled or commingled that their identity is lost in the product or mass; or

(b) a financing statement covering the original goods also covers the product into which the goods have been manufactured, processed or assembled.

*   *   *

(2) When under subsection (1) more than one security interest attaches to the product or mass, they rank equally according to the ratio that the cost of the goods to which each interest originally attached bears to the cost of the total product or mass.

———

(11) *Priority of a security interest in goods that are returned or repossessed.* As you know, security interests may be created both in the inventory of a business (e. g., a "floating lien") and in the business accounts that result when the inventory is sold on credit to customers. As between the inventory secured party and the account secured party, who prevails as to goods that are returned by cus-

tomers or that are repossessed upon default by the debtor (repossession is discussed in a later section)? The rule is that the inventory secured party automatically acquires a security interest in the returned goods if the original debt is unpaid. However, the inventory secured party will have to refile or take possession to perfect the interest unless he or she still has an effective financing statement on file with the appropriate local or statewide office.

Are there any special problems for the Article 9 secured creditor if his or her debtor goes bankrupt?

As discussed in Ch. 26, bankruptcy procedure is designed to distribute all of a bankrupt's nonexempt assets to his or her creditors and to discharge the bankrupt's remaining debts. A trustee in bankruptcy is elected to represent the creditors; the trustee is responsible for collecting and liquidating the bankrupt's assets and for distributing the cash to the bankrupt's unsecured creditors. Because of this, the interests of the trustee may often be adverse to that of a party claiming a security interest in a particular asset owned by the bankrupt. Obviously, if the asset is used first to pay off the secured party's interest, there will be less money available for distribution to the unsecured creditors.

When the interests of the trustee and a secured party conflict, the trustee may attempt to set aside the secured party's lien on the debtor's property. You will recall that Section 9–301 (b) of the Code states:

* * * [A]n unperfected security interest is subordinate to the rights of

(b) A person who becomes a lien creditor before the security interest is perfected; * * *

And Section 544 of the 1979 federal Bankruptcy Act states in part:

(a) The trustee shall have, as of the commencement of the case, * * * the rights and powers of * * *

(1) a creditor that extends credit to the debtor at the time of the commencement of the case, and that obtains, at such time and with respect to such credit, a judicial lien on all property on which a creditor on a simple contract could have obtained a judicial lien, whether or not such a creditor exists; * * *.

Section 70(c) of the old bankruptcy law, the predecessor of Section 544, was known as the "strong-arm" clause because it placed the trustee in bankruptcy in the position of a lien creditor even though the creditors the trustee represents are general unsecured creditors (i. e., creditors without liens). Section 544 of the new bankruptcy law accomplishes the same result. Putting Section 9–301 (b) of the UCC together with the "strong-arm" clause of the federal Bankruptcy Act (Section 544), you can see that the trustee in bankruptcy takes priority over a secured creditor with an *unperfected* interest.

For example, suppose that Martha Supplier sells machinery on credit to Bill Businessperson for use in his business. Martha takes a purchase money security interest in the machinery pursuant to agreement on January 15th, the date of the sale. However, Martha neglects to file a financing statement (and filing is the only way this interest can be perfected since Martha does not have possession and the collateral is other than consumer goods). On March 15th, an insolvent Bill Businessperson files a petition in bankruptcy. On April 1st, Martha files a financing statement covering the purchase money security agreement. Under the "strong-arm" clause, the trustee in bankruptcy is in the position of a lien creditor as of March 15th—the date the petition in bankruptcy was filed. Since Martha Supplier did not perfect by filing until April 1st, the trustee in bankruptcy will take the machinery under the "strong-arm" clause, and Martha will be relegated to the status of an unsecured creditor (i. e., she will be entitled to share ratably with other unsecured creditors in Bill Businessperson's nonexempt assets). If, on the other hand, Martha had perfected the security interest prior to March 15th, she would prevail over the trustee.

While the trustee in bankruptcy cannot attack a perfected security interest under the "strong-arm" clause, he or she can attack a perfected interest on the grounds that it is a "preferential transfer" under Section 547 of the 1979 Bankruptcy Act. In Ch. 26, we described a "preferential transfer" as follows:

A preferential transfer * * * is a transfer of the bankrupt's nonexempt property for the benefit of a creditor on account of a previous or antecedent debt. The transfer is preferential only if the debtor was insolvent at the time he or she made the transfer. * * * To be preferential, the transfer must also operate to permit the transferee creditor to obtain a greater percentage of his or her claim than some other creditor in the same class. Since, by definition, a preference requires a transfer on account of an antecedent (previous) debt, the creation of a new debt through execution of a mortgage or by buying more goods on account would not be a pref-

erence. Nor would a gift transfer constitute a preference since a gift would not involve a creditor.

The trustee in bankruptcy may avoid (set aside) any preferential transfer made by the bankrupt within 90 days of the bankruptcy filing (and up to one year if the transferee is an "insider" who had reasonable cause to believe that the debtor was insolvent at the time of the transfer —see Section 547 in Ch. 26). The 1979 Bankruptcy Act defines "transfer" at Section 101(40):

(40) "Transfer" means every mode, direct or indirect, absolute or conditional, voluntary or involuntary, of disposing of or parting with property or with an interest in property, including retention of title as a security interest.

Thus, an insolvent debtor who gives a security interest in collateral to an unsecured creditor on account of an antecedent debt within 90 days of bankruptcy makes a preferential transfer which may be set aside by the trustee in bankruptcy. By way of example, suppose that Martha Supplier sells $5,000 worth of goods on open account to Bill Businessperson (Martha is thus a general unsecured creditor). The sale takes place on December 20th. By Feburary 1st, Bill has become insolvent and cannot pay any of the $5,000 owing on the account. Martha agrees to take a security interest in goods belonging to Bill valued at $5,000 on account of the antecedent debt (remember, an antecedent debt constitutes "value" for purposes of attachment of a security interest). Martha files a financing statement covering the security interest the same day. On April 15th, Bill Businessperson files a petition in bankruptcy. The trustee in bankruptcy may set aside Martha Supplier's security interest on the grounds that it is a preferential transfer. The result is that Martha will be back in the position of a general unsecured creditor.

In the past, trustees in bankruptcy attempted to use Section 60 of the old Bankruptcy Act (the predecessor to Section 547 which now governs preferential transfers) to attack security interests in "after-acquired" property under a "floating lien" arrangement where the property was acquired by the debtor within 90 days of bankruptcy. The trustees' argument was that, though the original security agreement was entered into prior to 90 days of filing the bankruptcy petition, the security interest in the after-acquired property came into existence only when it is was actually acquired by the debtor; and if this was within 90 days of bankruptcy, the security interest should be attackable as a preferential transfer. The courts, however, rejected this argument, holding that the security interest in the "floating lien" situation is on the entire mass of inventory, not on individual items, and that the lien involves the mere substitution of collateral as collateral is sold and then replaced with new collateral (the courts assuming that there is no major fluctuation in the value of the collateral during the 90 day period before bankruptcy). This has now been codified by Section 547(c)(5) of the 1979 Bankruptcy Act, but with built-in protection for unsecured creditors who might actually be hurt by such transfers.

Section 547(c)(5) reads in part:

(c) The trustee may not avoid under this section a transfer—

(5) of a perfected security interest in inventory or a receivable or the proceeds of either, except to the extent that the aggregate of all such transfers to the

transferee caused a reduction, as of the date of the filing of the petition and to the prejudice of other creditors holding unsecured claims, of any amount by which the debt secured by such security interest exceeded the value of all security interest for such debt.

* * *

———————

Finally, the trustee in bankruptcy may try to proceed under Section 548 of the 1979 Bankruptcy Act which allows the trustee to set aside any fraudulent transfer made by the bankrupt within one year of the filing of the bankruptcy petition. However, to prevail, the trustee must show that the security interest was given fraudulently (i. e., without fair consideration or with the intent to hinder, delay, or defraud creditors).

What can the Article 9 secured creditor do by way of enforcement if his or her debtor "defaults"?

Apart from priority or bankruptcy problems, what are the secured party's rights when the debtor fails to make payment when due or otherwise breaches the terms of the security agreement (as by making an unauthorized sale of the collateral)? Many times, the security agreement expressly provides that if the debtor misses an installment payment, the secured party has a right to *accelerate* payment (i. e., require immediate payment of the entire balance owing). Or the secured party may simply treat the debtor as being in default.

Where a default occurs, the secured party obviously has all the rights of any general unsecured creditor. Thus, the secured party can go to court and reduce his or her claim against the debtor to judgment (see Ch. 26). The secured party may then execute the judgment on all the debtor's nonexempt assets, including the specific collateral securing the debt. If the debtor is solvent, proceeding against him or her as an unsecured creditor will result in full payment and it will make little difference that the creditor is secured.

However, over and above the rights of an unsecured creditor, the secured party has certain special rights against the collateral itself under Article 9 of the Uniform Commercial Code. Sections 9–501 through 9–507 provide that upon default, the secured creditor may take what is called "default action" against the specific collateral. And in the great majority of cases, the secured party will want to proceed against the specific collateral rather than obtain a general judgment against all the debtor's nonexempt property. If the secured creditor places himself or herself in the position of an unsecured creditor, and it turns out that the debtor is insolvent, the creditor will end up sharing the debtor's nonexempt assets with all the debtor's other general creditors. The secured creditor may end up receiving only a small part of the amount owing. Proceeding against the collateral itself, on the other hand, will generally result in full (or at least substantial) payment for the creditor. And many times, it can be accomplished without going to court.

A good example is found where accounts receivable are used as security. Section 9–318 of the Uniform Commercial Code provides that, *upon default* by the debtor, a secured party who holds a security interest in the debtor's accounts receivable may notify the parties who owe money on the accounts (the accounts receivable debtors) to make payment directly to the secured party rather than to the debtor (their creditor). Until such notice is given, the secured party has no right to direct payment; this is so even where the accounts receivable debtors know that a security interest has been created by assignment of their accounts to

the secured party. Upon receiving notice, the accounts receivable debtors have a right to demand proof of the assignment (creation of the security interest) from the secured party.

Section 9–318(3) provides:

(3) The account debtor is authorized to pay the assignor until the account debtor receives notification that the amount due or to become due has been assigned and that payment is to be made to the assignee. A notification which does not reasonably identify the right assigned is ineffective. If requested by the account debtor, the assignee must seasonably furnish reasonable proof that the assignment has been made and unless he does so the account debtor may pay the assignor.

Also, with regard to "default action", Section 9–503 of the Code states:

Section 9–503. Secured Party's Right to Take Possession After Default

Unless otherwise agreed a secured party has on default the right to take possession of the collateral. In taking possession a secured party may proceed without judicial process if this can be done without breach of the peace * * *

Upon default by the debtor, Section 9–503 allows the secured party to personally take possession of the collateral without going to court if this can be done without a breach of the peace. For example, where the security interest is in the debtor's automobile, the secured party may, on default by the debtor, remove the automobile from its street or parking lot location without notifying the debtor or obtaining his or her permission. However, the secured party may not remove the collateral over the debtor's express objection even though physical violence is not required to effect removal. Nor may the secured party enter the debtor's place of business, or his or her home or garage, without the debtor's consent, in order to remove the collateral. Any breaking and entering is improper, as are threats and active deception (e. g., posing as a law enforcement officer in order to remove the collateral).

You will recall from Ch. 26 that prejudgment remedies must conform to the requirements of due process of law: that is to say, before a debtor's property can become subject to attachment, garnishment, or receivership, the debtor must be notified of the claim and given an opportunity to be heard on the matter. Along this line, debtors have challenged the use of "self-help" repossession by secured parties under Section 9–503 of the Code as being a taking of property without due process of law. However, the courts have upheld the "self-help" remedy, declaring that there is no due process violation because there is no "state" (governmental) action involved where the secured party personally repossesses the collateral.

Where repossession is not physically possible (e. g., where the collateral is very heavy equipment), the Code authorizes the secured party to render the equipment inoperative on the debtor's premises and/or dispose of it there without a breach of the peace. If a breach of peace is inevitable, the secured party must resort to the courts.

If the collateral is a fixture, and the secured party has priority over all competing claims to the real property, the secured party may, on default, remove the fixture from the realty. However, the secured party must reimburse any owner or mortgage holder (other than the debtor) for physical damage caused the real property by reason of the removal. An owner or mortgage holder who would be entitled to reimbursement in the event of damage may refuse the secured party permission to remove the fixture until he or she has given adequate security for payment of the repairs (as by posting a "repair" bond). For example, suppose that Martha Supplier sells 25 "built-in" style ranges on credit to Arnie Apartment-Owner, Martha retaining a security interest in the ranges, and making a "fixture filing" covering the interest before the ranges are installed in Arnie's apartment house. Clark Mortgagee holds a mortgage on the apartment house, but Martha's security interest as to the ranges takes priority over the mortgage. Upon default by Arnie in paying for the ranges, Martha may remove the ranges from the apartment house subject only to a duty to reimburse Clark Mortgagee for any physical damage to the real property caused by the removal. However, Clark has a right to insist, prior to removal of the ranges, that Martha give adequate security for payment of repairs.

Of course, a secured party must always exercise great care in repossessing collateral. If the debtor has not, in fact, defaulted, the secured party will be liable to the debtor for money damage. In the case of Whisenhunt v. Allen Parker Co., 119 Ga.App. 813, 168 S.E.2d 827 (1969), the creditor had a security interest in the debtor's inventory, with the security agreement calling for monthly installment payments. The debtor made several monthly payments, then suddenly died. No payments were in arrears at the time of the debtor's death, and nothing in the security agreement provided that death was an event of default. Still, the creditor treated the death as a default and took immediate action to repossess the collateral. The court held this to be improper and ordered the creditor liable to the debtor's estate for losses sustained by reason of the repossession (and wrongful repossession of business inventory can easily result in substantial losses).

Once the collateral has been (rightfully) repossessed, the secured party generally has two alternatives:

(1) *The secured party may retain the collateral in satisfaction of the debt (this is referred to as "strict foreclosure").* In most cases, the secured party may simply retain the collateral in satisfaction of the debt—this is called *strict foreclosure.* The secured party must notify the debtor in writing of his or her intent to foreclose; and where the collateral is other than consumer goods, the secured party must also send written notice to any other secured creditor who has notified the secured party in writing of a claim to the collateral. If, after sending notice, the secured party does not receive a written objection to his or her retention of the collateral within 21 days from any of the parties who have been notified, the secured party may retain the collateral in satisfaction of the debt. Where the secured party retains the collateral, the obligation is completely discharged, and the secured party abandons any claim to a deficiency. If, on the other hand, the secured party receives a written objection within the 21 day period, he or she must proceed to the second alternative and sell the collateral in satisfaction of the debt.

Also, the secured party cannot retain the collateral but must sell it if the collateral is consumer goods and the debtor has paid 60% of the cash price (in the case of a purchase money security interest) or 60% of the loan (in the case of a security interest other than a purchase money security interest). The reasoning is that, if the debtor has paid more than 60% of the cash price or loan, he or she can probably have the collateral sold for more

than what is owing (the 40%) and receive the surplus. If the secured party fails to sell the collateral within 90 days of the repossession, the debtor may bring a tort action for conversion (see Ch. 1) against the secured party.

(2) *Or the secured party may elect to sell the collateral and apply the sales proceeds to the unpaid debt.* As an alternative to retaining the collateral, the secured party may always choose to sell the collateral and apply the sales proceeds to the unpaid debt. And, in some cases, the secured party must do this as where written objection is made to his or her retention of the collateral or the debtor has paid 60% of the purchase price.

Where the secured party chooses to sell the collateral, every aspect of the sale "including the method, manner, time, place and terms must be commercially reasonable." The secured party must give notice of the sale to the debtor and to any other secured party who has given notice to the secured party of having a claim to the collateral (except in the case of consumer goods where notice need be given only to the debtor). The sale of the collateral to a purchaser for value transfers all of the debtor's rights in the collateral to the purchaser and discharges the security interest (along with any junior security interests in the collateral).

As to the sales proceeds, they must be applied in the following order:

First, to pay the secured party's reasonable expenses (including attorneys fees) in repossessing and disposing of the collateral;

Second, to pay the debt owed to the secured party;

Third, to pay the debt owed to any junior security interest holder (i. e., a person with a security interest that is subordinate to the secured party's) who has made a written demand and furnished reasonable proof of the security interest; and

Fourth, and, finally, any remaining surplus must be turned over to the debtor.

In many states, if the sale does not result in sufficient proceeds to cover the secured party's reasonable expenses along with the amount of the debt owing, the debtor will be liable to the secured party for the deficiency. However, statutes in a number of states (including California, Illinois, and Washington) provide that a creditor who repossesses and sells consumer goods may not collect any deficiency in proceeds from the debtor. The secured party, in these states, must elect between obtaining a judgment against the debtor and attempting to collect the full debt or repossessing and reselling the collateral with the risk of a deficiency in proceeds.

A secured party who fails to comply with the default provisions of Article 9 (as by using force to repossess the collateral, failing to give proper notice of sale to the debtor, selling the collateral in some "commercially unreasonable" way, etc.) is liable to the debtor for any losses that he or she suffers. UCC 9–507(1). If the collateral is consumer goods, UCC Section 9–506(1) allows the debtor to recover a minimum of the credit service charge plus 10 percent of the principal amount of the debt *or* the time price diffential plus 10 percent of the cash price. For example, suppose that a debtor borrows $5,000 to buy a camper-truck for use on a cross-country vacation; the creditor takes a purchase money security interest in the camper. The debtor, who is to pay $9.00 per $100 over a period of three years, defaults in payment. The secured party repossesses the camper, using physical force to do so. Under UCC Section 9–507(1), the debtor may sue the secured party for a minimum of $500 (10% of the $5,000 principal) plus $1,380 (the $9.00 credit charge x 50 hundreds x 3 years) for a total of $1,850. And if the debtor has suffered actual loss greater than this, he or she may recover the full amount of the loss.

A debtor whose property has been repossessed has a "right of redemption" under Section 9–506 of the Uniform Commercial Code. The right of redemption is the right to free the collateral from any lien or encumbrance and regain absolute ownership by payment of the amount due. The debtor exercises the right by tendering an amount sufficient to cover the debt as well as any expenses incurred by the secured party in repossessing the collateral (e. g., attorneys fees or other legal expenses). However, the right must be exercised before the secured party has sold the collateral or entered into a contract to do so. And it must be exercised before the secured party has taken steps to retain the collateral in satisfaction of the debt (as by giving the required notice to the debtor and other claimants to the property).

PART II

THE USE OF REAL PROPERTY AS SECURITY: MORTGAGES

What is the law of mortgages?

In Part I of this chapter, we considered the use of *personal property* as collateral for securing a debt or other promised performance. We saw that Article 9 of the Uniform Commercial Code controls the creation and perfection of security interests in personal property, determines security interest priorities, and provides for remedies upon default by the debtor. In Part II, we will consider the use of *real property* as collateral for securing a debt or other promised performance.

The Uniform Commercial Code does not govern mortgages (i. e., the use of real property as security). Rather, state common law and statutory law (other than the UCC) controls. Generally speaking, real property secures much larger debts than personal property; and the debts are usually paid off over a longer period of time (20 to 30 years as opposed to the comparatively shorter time periods involved when personal property serves as collateral).

In broad terms, a *mortgage* is a conveyance of land given as security for payment of a debt. The debtor (the "mortgagor") borrows money from the creditor (the "mortgagee"), and conveys his or her real property to the mortgagee as security for the loan. Right at the outset, it is important to understand that the "conveyance" aspect of the transaction must be minimized. For all intents and purposes, the debtor (mortgagor) retains complete ownership of the land—he or she retains possession and use of the land though having created a lien or encumbrance on the property. This lien or security aspect is the dominant feature of a mortgage. When the mortgage debt is repaid, the mortgagee's interest in the land immediately and automatically terminates, and the mortgagor once again holds the property free of the lien. The immediate and automatic extinguishment of the mortgagee's security interest upon payment of the debt is called the *condition of defeasance* and is a part of every mortgage.

Mortgages are used to borrow against all kinds of real property, with the loan proceeds used for countless purposes. By far and away the most common use of a mortgage is to aid in purchase of a home. Nearly everyone who owns a home has a mortgage on the home. Most home mortgages are made by savings and loan associations (i. e., companies in the business of obtaining savings from the public and putting the money to work earning interest by lending it out on mortgages, mostly on homes). Usually, a home mortgage calls for level monthly payments over a period of 25 to 30 years; the early payments are mostly interest with only small amounts applied to repayment of the mortgage principal. Of course, as the principal is gradually re-

duced, a greater portion of the monthly payment goes toward principal until, finally, after 25 or 30 years, the entire loan is repaid and the condition of defeasance extinguishes the mortgage.

Our study of mortgage law will be divided into the following four parts:

(1) The creation of the mortgage;

(2) The rights and duties of the mortgagor and mortgagee during the term of the mortgage;

(3) The legal effect of paying the debt on time in accord with the mortgage; and

(4) The rights and duties of the mortgagor and mortgagee upon default by the mortgagor.

The creation of the mortgage. No prescribed words are necessary to create a mortgage. However, in most cases, the basic structure of the mortgage is very similar to that of a deed. You will recall from Ch. 6 that a deed must be in writing; it must describe the grantee as well as the land conveyed; it must contain words of grant; it must be signed by the grantor and his or her spouse (if any); it must be acknowledged by the grantor; and it must be delivered to the grantee.

Much the same items are required in a valid mortgage. Like a grantor, a mortgagor is usually joined by his or her spouse in executing the mortgage. The mortgage must be evidenced by a writing sufficient to satisfy the Statute of Frauds. You will recall from Ch. 10 that a contract creating an interest in land must be evidenced by a written memo containing the essential terms of the agreement and signed by the party to be charged in order to be enforceable under the Statute of Frauds. A mortgage contract certainly creates an interest in the mortgagor's land (a security interest) and must therefore be supported by a written memo signed by the mortgagor if it is to be enforceable. The writing must reasonably identify the mortgagee and describe the debt and land involved. The writing need not contain all the specifics of the agreement: usually, the parties do not want all the details put into the writing because the writing is generally recorded in the public records. For example, the exact amount of the debt need not be stated so long as the debt is described with sufficient particularity so that it is identifiable. Nor must the interest rate be stated (except in North Dakota where this is required by statute).

The lack of detail in the writing is unimportant because most mortgages are also represented by a negotiable promissory note. In other words, there is usually (but not always) both a mortgage and a note, and the note specifies the "sum certain" and the interest rate (see Ch. 13). Obviously, there is more security with a promissory note, and it is always prudent to have the mortgagor sign one. At the same time, a note is not required (however, in this case, the written mortgage will have to be more specific to satisfy the Statute of Frauds).

Some states demand that the mortgagor's signature be witnessed by at least two competent parties. All states provide that a mortgage (like a deed) must be acknowledged or it cannot be recorded. You will recall the following discussion of "acknowledgment" from Ch. 6:

> "Acknowledgment" refers to a formal declaration made by the grantor in front of a public officer, usually a notary public, that he or she has signed the deed, and is transferring the property voluntarily. Upon acknowledgment, the notary public will attach a certificate of acknowledgment to the deed, reciting that the grantor has freely appeared and executed the instrument as his or her voluntary act and deed.

Because an unacknowledged mortgage cannot be recorded, a mortgagee should always insist that the mortgagor acknowledge the mortgage.

Also like a deed, a mortgage must be delivered. An effective delivery is made when the mortgagor surrenders the mortgage in complete form to the mortgagee with the intention that it operate as a security interest in the real property.

Words of grant are also found in mortgages the same as in deeds. While a deed usually contains such language as "give, grant, bargain, or sell", a mortgage generally states that the mortgagor "mortgages and warrants" the property. Generally, a mortgage also specifically states that the transfer is "conditional and defeasible" (in other words, that the transfer is subject to the condition subsequent of repayment of the debt whereupon the security interest will immediately and automatically terminate).

A mortgage, again like a deed, must describe the real property with sufficient certainty that it can be located on the basis of the description. The description may be by "metes and bounds" (actual measurements and boundaries); by reference to government surveys; by recorded plats (maps or other representations of property subdivided into lots); by streets and numbers; by name of the property; by reference to adjacent property; or by any other nucleus of description.

In Ch. 6, it was pointed out that consideration is not required for a valid deed (e. g., a gift transfer of real property by deed requires no consideration). However, a deed will often be supported by consideration because most transfers by deed are contracts of sale, and consideration is necessary for a valid contract. The same is true with regard to mortgages. Consideration is not required for a valid mortgage, but it is usually present because most mortgages involve a contract loan of money. Of course, mortgages are occasionally given as security for pre-existing debts. For example, suppose that Tom Lender loans Barbara

Borrower $5,000 in a completely unsecured transaction; Barbara promises to repay the money in ten months time. Six months later, Barbara fears that she will be unable to repay the money (or Tom decides he needs some security), and Barbara gives Tom a mortgage on some real property she owns to secure the debt. Since Tom gives no new value for the mortgage, there is no consideration for the mortgage. Nevertheless, the mortgage (like a security interest in personal property given for an antecedent debt) is valid.

However, this would be an unusual case, as mortgages are generally contracts subject to all the rules covered in Chapters 7 through 10. Thus, the defenses of fraud, duress, mistake, and unconscionability are generally available to mortgagors (and lenders are sometimes in a position to take unconscionable advantage of a debtor who desperately needs money).

As stated previously, a mortgagor frequently executes a mortgage on land contemporaneously with acquiring ownership of the property in order to secure the purchase price. This is the typical home purchase transaction. A mortgage that is executed to secure the purchase price of land is referred to as a *purchase money mortgage*. A special rule applies to such mortgages. The general rule is that a purchase money mortgage takes priority over all prior claims existing against the mortgagor at the time of the purchase. By way of example, suppose that Barbara Borrower buys land, putting $8,000 down, and mortgaging the purchased land for $20,000 to provide the balance of the purchase price. The mortgage Barbara gives the mortgagee will take preference over any existing judgments, liens, or other debts outstanding against Barbara at the time of the purchase. However, the special priority of the purchase money mortgage is subject to the recording acts: if, after taking the mort-

gage, the mortgagee fails to record it, the mortgagee's interest will be subordinate to *subsequent*, recorded interests.

In contrast to a purchase money mortgage is a construction mortgage which is executed for the purpose of financing construction on land: the mortgagee is empowered and obligated to disburse funds to the builder or contractor as the construction progresses. The mortgage secures all future advances, and the building that results along with the land itself serves as security for the mortgage. Frequently, the ultimate purchaser of the property "assumes" the construction mortgage ("assumption" of mortgages is discussed later).

Mortgages, like deeds, should always be recorded. As you will recall from Ch. 6, recording statutes in all states provide for the recordation of deeds and other documents, such as mortgages, affecting title to real property. To "record" is to officially file a copy of a deed or other instrument with the County Land Recorder's Office. While recording is not essential to making a deed or other instrument valid as between the grantor and grantee, it does serve as "constructive notice" (i. e., inferred or implied notice) to the world at large that there is an outstanding interest in the land. Like a grantee who records, a mortgagee who records is protected against the claims of all subsequent mortgagees and other security interest holders. A mortgagee who fails to record may be in a position subordinate to later mortgagees.

To this point, we have been describing the form of the usual or customary mortgage. However, it is important to understand that a mortgage can result even though its form is not cast in the usual or regular way. Sometimes, an instrument that looks to be a deed absolute is really a mortgage. The fact that the instrument looks to be a deed will not prevent a determination that it is a mortgage if there is clear and convincing evidence that the parties *intended* to create a security interest only and not to actually sell the land. If such proof is available, the courts will find a mortgage, and the borrower-mortgagor will have a right to pay the debt and regain clear title to the property (because the instrument looks to be a deed absolute, the mortgagor should demand a "reconveyance" from the mortgagee to protect himself or herself from sale of the property to a bona fide purchaser). And if the borrower fails to repay the debt, the mortgagee must go through the foreclosure process (hereafter described) just as if a regular mortgage had been used.

Usually, where a mortgage is intended, the mortgagor retains possession of the property. This, in itself, will prevent the mortgagee from selling the land to a bona fide purchaser: possession by one other than the purported owner is held to be constructive notice of a claim to the land, requiring an inquiry from anyone contemplating a purchase of the property (it would therefore be impossible to take without notice). Of course, if the land is vacant, and the mortgagee looks to have an absolute deed, he or she can convey good and complete ownership to an innocent purchaser for value. The mortgagor's only remedy, in this case, is against the mortgagee.

A *deed of trust* is a security device that is commonly used (particularly in 9 states) instead of a regular mortgage. Instead of giving a mortgage to a creditor, the borrower deeds the land to a third party (the trustee) who holds title to the land solely for the purpose of returning it to the borrower once the loan is paid off. If the borrower fails to repay the loan, the trustee is empowered to sell the property at a public auction without going through the courts and apply the proceeds of the sale to the debt. Generally, the mortgagee notifies the trustee of any default by the mortgagor whereupon the trustee is required to publish notice

of the sale for the benefit of the debtor and prospective purchasers.

In many ways, using a trust deed makes it easier for the mortgagee (the creditor) to collect his or her money upon default by the debtor. With a regular mortgage, as you will learn shortly, a judicial proceeding is often required to effect a sale of the property upon default.

Also, a trust deed provides special protections for both mortgagor and mortgagee. Whereas a regular mortgage involves two parties, a trust deed is a three party transaction: mortgagor, mortgagee, and trustee. The trustee is very similar to an escrow agent in that he or she is an independent party who will act only upon objective proof of default. If there are surplus proceeds resulting from sale of the property, the trustee will turn them over to the mortgagor.

A trust deed is also advantageous in that it facilitates the borrowing of large sums of money. For example, a corporation might borrow money from several individuals through the use of bonds secured by real estate owned by the corporation. While it would be impractical to give each bondholder a separate mortgage, it is a simple matter to deed the land to a trustee with a deed of trust securing the bonds purchased by the investors.

The rights and duties of the mortgagor and mortgagee during the term of the mortgage. Whether a mortgage is cast in regular form or as a deed of trust, it is regarded as a mere lien upon the property—that is to say, a mere security interest in the land, with the mortgagee having no right to possession of the property. This right of possession remains in the mortgagor unless and until there has been a rightful foreclosure and sale of the property. Of course, the parties may always agree as part of the mortgage contract that the mortgagee is to have possession of the land, but this seldom occurs.

Though the mortgagee is not entitled to possession of the land, he or she does have a right to prevent impairment of his or her interest by the mortgagor. Thus, the mortgagor may not damage the property or commit acts of waste that impair the mortgagee's security. For example, while the mortgagor may cut timber from the land for firewood or repairs, or in the course of good husbandry, he or she may not cut additional timber if the result would be to impair the mortgagee's security interest in the land. An injured mortgagee may sue the mortgagor for money damages or petition the court for an injunction against further injury to the premises.

Generally, under the terms of the mortgage agreement, the mortgagor has a duty to pay the taxes that come due upon the real property, to keep the property in repair, and to keep it properly insured (it is well settled in the law that both the mortgagor and mortgagee have insurable interests in the mortgaged land—see Ch. 11). If the mortgagor fails to pay the taxes, make repairs, or provide adequate insurance, the mortgagee may generally accelerate payment and declare the entire debt due. This permits the mortgagee to foreclose and have the property sold to satisfy the mortgage debt. Or, rather than accelerate, the mortgagee may simply pay such expenses and add them to the amount of the debt secured by the mortgage.

Sometimes, a real property owner places more than one mortgage on the same property. Under the recording acts, a person who takes a mortgage for value without knowledge of a prior, unrecorded mortgage *and* records his or her mortgage will have priority over the prior interest. In other words, if the debtor-mortgagor cannot pay either debt, the holder of the subsequent, recorded mortgage will take priority over the prior, unrecorded mortgage. But remember, to be protected under the recording acts, a person must take *for value* and *without notice*, and must subsequently *record* his or her interest. Many times, these requirements are not met, and the prior mortgage will take priority even though it is unrecorded (the general rule being, without regard to the recording acts, that the first mortgage takes priority over subsequent mortgages, liens, or encumbrances).

The legal effect of paying the debt on time in accord with the mortgage. The typical mortgage provides a definite time when the debt must be paid. The mortgage is said to reach "maturity" at that time. Very often when the mortgage debt is a large one, the mortgage agreement calls for payment in installments (with each installment being part interest and part principal). A mortgage payable in installments generally contains an *acceleration* clause stating that, upon failure of the mortgagor to pay any installment when due, the entire debt shall become due and payable immediately.

Many times, the mortgagor has an option to pay off the debt at its maturity date or to prepay it at an earlier time. However, in the absence of a specific provision allowing prepayment, the mortgagor has no right to insist that the mortgagee accept payment prior to the maturity date. Many mortgages allow prepayment subject to the condition that the mortgagor pay a penalty upon prepayment. Such prepayment penalties are generally upheld on the basis that the mortgagee entered into the mortgage contract expecting to receive interest over a number of years, and where prepayment is made, the mortgagee loses this interest.

At some point in time, the mortgage debt will mature and the mortgagor will either pay the debt or be in default. If the mortgagor pays the debt, the mortgagee's security interest in the real estate will automatically terminate (remember, the mortgagee's interest is subject from the outset to termination by payment of the debt). No conveyance by the mortgagee is required to perfect the mortgagor's estate: the mortgagee's interest in the land immediately reverts to the mortgagor by operation of law.

Nevertheless, statutes in many states require a mortgagee who has received payment to file a "satisfaction" of the mortgage (i. e., a statement that the mortgage has been paid) in the public mortgage records. If the mortgagee fails to file a satisfaction within a specified period of time following a request by the mortgagor that he or she do so, the mortgagee will be liable in damages to the mortgagor (for a definite sum set by statute and for any additional damages the mortgagor sustains by reason of the failure to file).

The rights and duties of the mortgagor and mortgagee upon default by the mortgagor. In most cases, the mortgage is paid, a "satisfaction" is entered, and the transaction is complete. Sometimes, however the mortgagor fails to make payment when the obligation matures and is considered to be in default. The rights and duties of the mortgagor and mortgagee in this case are summarized below:

(1) Upon default by the mortgagor, the mortgagee does not automatically acquire ownership of the land. However, this was not always the case. In England, in the 14th Century, and for a couple hundred years thereafter, if a mortgage debt was not paid when due, the default served to extinguish the mortgagor's interest in the land, and the mortgagee automatically succeeded to ownership of the property by operation of law. After a time, the law recognized that this was too harsh a result and permitted the mortgagor who had defaulted to reacquire ownership of the land by paying the debt in full (along with interest). This was called the mortgagor's *equity of redemption* and was a right that could be sold by the mortgagor or even passed on to his or her heirs at death.

Of course, the result of the mortgagor's equity of redemption was to place the mortgagee in a position of uncertainty: the mortgagor, or his or her heir, could come in and repurchase the property at any time. To remedy this situation, the law developed a new practice called a "foreclosure suit" which allowed the mortgagee to go to court to obtain a judge's order stating that the mortgagor's equity of redemption would be cut off if it was not exercised within a specified period of time (typically, six months to 1 year). If the mortgagor failed to redeem the property within this time, the equity of redemption was forever barred and the mortgagee became the owner absolute of the real property. Today, this method of foreclosure is known as *strict foreclosure.*

A majority of states prohibit strict foreclosure by statute. However, in Connecticut and Vermont, it is still used as customary remedy. Illinois permits strict foreclosure if three conditions are met: the value of the real estate must not exceed the amount of the debt plus interest and costs; the mortgagee must be willing to take the property in full satisfaction of the debt; and the mortgagor must be insolvent. Strict foreclosure is little used elsewhere although it would appear to be allowed in at least 16 other states under some circumstances. In the four New England states of Massachusetts, Maine, New Hampshire, and Rhode Island, what is called *foreclosure by entry and continued possession* is permitted. In these states, if the debt is not paid when due, the mortgagee may enter upon the property and take possession of the land, assuming this can be done without a breach of the peace. If the mortgagee continues in possession, and the mortgagor does not pay the mortgage debt within a specified time (3 years in Massachusetts and 1 year in Maine and New Hampshire), the mortgagor's equity of redemption will be forever barred. But, again, the mortgagee's entry must be peaceable (if this is not possible, the mortgagee must resort to the courts); and, after the entry, the mortgagee must record the fact of entry in the public land records.

Most courts disfavor the strict foreclosure remedy because of the harsh result of turning the land over to the mortgagee even though it may be worth considerably more than the debt owing, with the result that the mortgagor loses his or her surplus equity. The preferred remedy is foreclosure by judicial sale of the property with any surplus proceeds (proceeds over and above the amount of the debt) turned over to the mortgagor.

It should be pointed out that the mortgagor cannot lawfully waive his or her equity of redemption. The courts will simply not permit a mortgagor to contract away this right and allow the land to go immediately and absolutely to the mortgagee if the debt is not paid when due. The doctrine is expressed, "Once a mortgage, always a mortgage," and one of the characteristics of a mortgage is the mortgagor's right to redeem.

Of course, the equity of redemption will be cut off by foreclosure: strict foreclosure in the few states that permit it; foreclosure by entry and possession in the four New England states; and foreclosure by judicial sale of the property in all other states. The equity of redemption will also be cut off if the mortgagee has possession of the land and meets all the requirements of adverse possession as described in Ch. 6. The same is true where the mortgagor fails to exercise the right for a very long period of time. For example, in one case, the court held that the mortgagor lost the equitable right to redeem where he or she failed to exercise the right for a period of some twenty years, during which time he or she did not even acknowledge that a mortgage existed.

But apart from foreclosure, adverse possession, and special circumstances, the mortgagor's equity of redemption will continue on and, even if the mortgagor does not exercise the right, he or she may assign it or pass it on to his or her heirs at death.

(2) By far and away the most common way for the mortgagee to obtain his or her money upon default by the mortgagor is through judicial sale of the property. Sale under court action (i. e., judicial sale), which is regulated by statute in all states, is the preferred method of foreclosure in a substantial majority of states, and the exclusive method in several states. It may be used whether the mortgage is cast in regular form or as a trust deed. Its only drawback is that it is costly and time-consuming because it requires going to court.

The specifics of the statutes regulating "judicial sale" vary from state to state but generally call for public sale of the property after compliance with certain notice requirements as to time, place, manner, and terms of the sale. The sale itself is usually done at the direction of the county sheriff in the county where the land is located. Generally, the court must confirm the sale and will not do so if it determines that the price received for the property was so low as to be unconscionable. However, the court will not refuse to confirm simply because a depression exists or because a higher price might be received at a later time—it will refuse to confirm only where the price is so low as to raise a presumption of unfairness or a lack of protection for the mortgagor.

Sometimes, a power of sale is written into a mortgage or trust deed, authorizing the mortgagee to sell the property upon default by the buyer without going through a judicial sale. Several states specifically prohibit the use of such a power. And the power is commonly used in only about a third of the states. Even where allowed, the power of sale is regarded with suspicion by the courts and its exercise is closely scrutinized. In any case, the sale must be conducted fairly to produce as good a price as possible, and it is must be preceded by proper notice to the debtor as to time, place, and other terms of the sale.

If the sales proceeds are not sufficient to cover the mortgage debt (and related costs and interest), the mortgagee may in some states obtain a judgment against the mortgagor for the deficiency. However, most states have either abolished or sharply restricted deficiency judgments. Too often, the mortgaged property does not bring its true value at a forced sale. And, sometimes, the mortgagee himself or herself is the purchaser. To allow a mortgagee to buy the property at less than its actual value and then to obtain a deficiency judgment is to allow a recovery beyond the amount of the mortgage debt. The states are particularly strict in prohibiting deficiency judgments in the case of purchase money mortgages. Remember, in a purchase money mortgage, the seller-mortgagor sells the land on credit to the purchaser, taking a mortgage in the land as security for the purchase price. If a foreclosure ultimately results, and there is a deficiency, it can be inferred that the seller-mortgagee originally sold the land at a price beyond its true value and thus overreached (i. e., took advantage of) the buyer-mortgagor.

Occasionally, the sale of the land will result in surplus proceeds beyond the amount of the mortgage debt and related costs and interests. Such surplus belongs to the mortgagor.

(3) A foreclosure sale cuts off the mortgagor's equitable right of redemption. However, in 26 states, the mortgagor has a statutory right of redemption following a foreclosure sale enabling him or her to redeem the property (by paying the sales price plus reasonable costs and expenses) for a certain period of time (usually one year). Statutory redemption nullifies the foreclosure sale and restores title of the land to the mortgagor. *The mortgagor's statutory right of redemption should not be confused with his or her equitable right of redemption prior to the foreclosure sale.* Statutes recognizing the statutory right of redemption include: Alabama, Arizona, Arkansas, California, Colorado, Idaho, Illinois, Indiana, Iowa, Kansas, Kentucky, Maine, Michigan, Minnesota, Missouri, Montana, Nevada, New Mexico, North Dakota, Oregon, South Dakota, Tennessee, Utah, Vermont, Washington, and Wyoming.

In all other states, the foreclosure sale is final and cannot be set aside.

Who is responsible for paying the mortgage debt when the mortgagor sells the mortgaged property to a third party purchaser (i. e., what is the difference between selling the land "subject to the mortgage" and selling it with the mortgage "assumed")?

Since the mortgagor owns the mortgaged property subject only to a security interest in the mortgagee, the mortgagor may freely sell or otherwise transfer the property. However, the mortgagor can never delegate his or her duty of performance under the mortgage. Thus, the mortgagor will always be liable on the mortgage even if he or she sells the property.

Whether or not the purchaser of the property will also be liable on the mortgage will depend on whether the purchaser took the land "subject to the mortgage" or took it with an "assumption" of the mortgage.

A purchaser takes the land "subject to the mortgage" when he or she pays the mortgagor the value of the property less the amount of the mortgage debt owing, but does not assume any personal liability for the mortgage debt. The purchaser, in this case, is not bound on the mortgage either to the mortgagor or mortgagee. Of course, the land still serves as security for the mortgage debt. But if there is a deficiency following a foreclosure sale, the mortgagee cannot look to the purchaser for the deficiency but can go only against the mortgagor.

In contrast, a purchaser takes the land and "assumes" the mortgage when he or she pays the mortgagor the value of the land less the amount of the mortgage debt owing, and also promises the mortgagor that he or she will pay the mortgage debt. The purchaser's promise is said to be an "assumption" of the mortgage. Of course, the mortgagor is not relieved of his or her own duty to pay the debt; but where the purchaser "assumes" the mortgage, the mortgagor does have a right to insist that the purchaser make payment. The mortgagee can look to either party for payment—the mortgagor on the basis of the original mortgage agreement, and the purchaser on the basis of being a third party beneficiary of the assumption agreement (see Ch. 10) or by reason of suretyship (see Part III of this chapter). If the mortgagee collects from the mortgagor, the mortgagor has a right to reimbursement from the purchaser.

It is apparent that the purchaser of mortgaged real property is in a better position (i. e., a less risky one) if he or she takes the land "subject to the mortgage" rather than with an "assumption" of the mortgage.

PART III

HAVING A THIRD PARTY AGREE TO PAY IN THE EVENT THAT THE DEBTOR DOES NOT: SURETYSHIP

What is suretyship?

In Parts I and II of this chapter, we discussed the use of property as security for the payment of a debt or other promised performance. Part I dealt with the use of personal property as collateral in creating security interests under Article 9 of the Uniform Commercial Code; Part II dealt with the use of real estate as collateral in creating security interests using mortgages or trust deeds.

Now we find that there is yet a third way for a creditor to provide security for a debt or other promised performance—a method not involving the use of property as security. Rather, a third person, called a *surety*, agrees to repay the debt (or perform the promise) owed to the creditor assuming the debtor (the *principal*) does not. This security device is known as the suretyship contract and it always involves three parties: the debtor-principal, the creditor, and the surety.

By way of example, suppose that Sylvia Student wants to borrow $3,000 from a bank to help her with her college expenses. Sylvia applies for a loan but finds that she does not have sufficient credit standing to obtain an unsecured loan nor adequate real or personal property to use as collateral in obtaining a loan. Sylvia goes to her employer, Bill Businessperson, who agrees to "back" the loan with his own personal credit: this time, not only Sylvia promises to repay the loan to the bank, but Bill also promises to repay the loan. And this time, the bank, knowing of Bill's sound financial position, agrees to make the loan.

Thus, in the suretyship relationship, the surety becomes legally bound to the creditor on the principal's debt, with the result that both parties are liable. The creditor is entitled to payment from the principal or the surety; however, the ultimate burden of the debt remains on the principal who must reimburse the surety if the surety is required to pay it. In our example, Sylvia is the principal and thus has the ultimate duty to pay the loan to the creditor bank. However, the bank may also look to the surety, Bill, for payment.

The surety's obligation to the creditor may be absolute and unconditional so that the creditor has an option to go against either the surety or the principal in the first instance. Or the surety's promise may be conditioned upon the creditor first trying to collect from the principal (as we shall see, this is required in some states). Suretyship may also be tied into the use of property as security as where a third person provides collateral to secure the debt of another.

Thus, in the broad sense, the term "suretyship" includes any relationship wherein one person agrees to answer for the debt of another—for example, assuming a mortgage, indorsing a check, or signing a note as an accommodation maker.

Suretyship is first of all a contract and therefore subject to all the contract law rules presented in Chapters 7 through 10. It follows that a person without legal capacity cannot serve as a surety. If a person agrees to act as a surety because of fraud, duress, undue influence, mistake, or unconscionable act, the person has a good defense to performance. The same is true where there is a material variance of the surety's undertaking as a result of a modification in the principal's obligation (in other words, the surety's obligation cannot be materially changed).[4] And contract law rules regarding consideration, legality, capacity, impossibility, and so on may all be relevant to determining the rights and duties of the three parties in the suretyship relationship.

Though suretyship is a contract, it is to some extent unique as a legal concept—it has been a part of law even to the time of the Bible. Originally, a surety was used personally as a human hostage to secure payment of a debt: if the debt was not paid, the surety would be imprisoned, tortured, or even put to death. After a time, the person of the surety ceased to be used as the security, and, instead, the surety's promise became the security. Still, it was not considered particularly

intelligent to become a surety and promise to pay for another's debt. The Bible, Proverbs 11:15, states: "He that is surety for a stranger shall smart for it; and he that hateth suretyship is sure." The fact is, sureties were often inexperienced and did the foolish thing and ended up having to pay for their friends' debts. It is partly for this reason that there are special protections in the law for the surety. Before we review these special rules and principles, it is a good idea to look at how suretyship differs from some other legal relationships.

How does suretyship differ from "guaranty", "warranty", "indorsement", and "indemnity"?

The following legal relationships are often confused with suretyship:

Guaranty. To understand the difference between guaranty and suretyship, it is necessary to distinguish between a primary obligation and a secondary one. A *primary obligation* is one in which the promisor makes a direct and unconditional promise to perform personally; the promisor's performance is not conditioned upon another party's failure to perform. A *secondary obligation* is one in which the promisor promises to perform only in the event that another person fails to perform his or her duty; the promise, in this case, is clearly conditional. Thus, if Bill Businessperson says, "I promise to pay Sylvia Student's debt", this is a primary promise or primary obligation. Strictly speaking, all contracts of suretyship are primary obligations. If Bill Businessperson says, "I promise to pay Sylvia Student's debt only in the event that she does not pay it", this is a secondary promise or secondary obligation. All contracts of guaranty are secondary obligations.

In nearly all states, the consequences of suretyship and guaranty are the same. In many states, both terms are used in the

---

4. Also, a valid tender of performance by the principal debtor releases the surety from his or her obligation. And though it does

not release the principal (assuming the tender is not accepted), it does stop the running of interest from the date of tender.

law as part of the suretyship concept. Section 82 of the *Restatement of Security* defines the meaning of the word "surety" to include all undertakings for the obligation of another, including suretyship and guaranty. Along this line, several states have passed statutes abolishing the distinction between guaranty and suretyship.

The California statute provides:

> The distinction between sureties and guarantors is hereby abolished. The terms and their derivatives, wherever used in this Code or any other statute or law of this State now in force or hereafter enacted, shall have the same meaning, as hereafter in this section defined. A surety or guarantor is one who promises to answer for the debt, default, or miscarriage of another, or hypothecates property as security therefor. Guaranties of collection and continuing guaranties are forms of suretyship obligations, and * * * shall be subject to all provisions of law relating to suretyship in general.

———

Thus, in the broad sense, a "surety" may be defined as one who is liable for the debt of another, whether primarily or secondarily so, whether conditionally or unconditionally so. As defined, the term "surety" would include a guarantor.

Warranty. You will recall from Ch. 18 that a warranty is a promise or affirmation of fact regarding products or instruments (e. g., with regard to goods, there are warranties of title, quality, quantity, fitness for a particular purpose, etc.). A warranty has nothing to do with suretyship and should not be confused with that relationship.

Indorsement. You will recall from our study of negotiable instruments law that a person who indorses a negotiable instrument makes a promise by virtue of the indorsement that he or she will pay the debt (the sum certain of the note,

check, or draft) if the person primarily liable does not. An indorser's promise is very similar to a surety's promise and perhaps could be properly classified as such except for the fact that indorsements (along with negotiable instruments generally) are strictly controlled by Article 3 of the Uniform Commercial Code. Thus, there are special rules that apply to indorsements that do not apply to suretyship contracts generally. For example, an indorsement must be on the negotiable instrument itself or on a paper attached to the instrument; a suretyship promise, on the other hand, need not be embodied in the same instrument or document containing the principal's promise. Also, in a suretyship relationship, there are no conditions precedent to the surety's liability; with regard to the indorser's liability, there are conditions precedent of presentment and notice of dishonor. And finally, suretyship contracts, generally relate to nonnegotiable promises rather than negotiable instruments.

Indemnity. As you will recall from Ch. 11, a contract of indemnity is designed to provide compensation in the event of loss.

It was stated in that chapter:

> The fundamental and underlying principle of insurance is the concept of indemnity * * * "payment for damage, loss or expense incurred" * * *. And *Black's Law Dictionary* defines "indemnity" as "a collateral contract assurance by which one person engages to secure another against an anticipated loss or to prevent him from being damnified by the legal consequences of an act."

———

Thus, if you have car insurance, and you hit a telephone pole while driving your car, your insurance company will indemnify you for your losses. Unlike a suretyship contract which involves three parties (the principal, the creditor, and the surety), a contract of indemnity involves only two parties (the insurer and the insured). And while a contract of indemnity generally does not fall within the Statute of Frauds, a suretyship contract (as will be seen in the next section) is within the Statute.

What are the special rules of suretyship?

The following special rules and principles apply to the suretyship contract:

Statute of Frauds. You will recall from Ch. 10 that certain promises are enforceable under the Statute of Frauds only if they are supported by a written memo signed by the party to be charged. The suretyship obligation is one such promise and must be evidenced by a written memo signed by the surety in order to be enforceable.

Ch. 10 stated:

* * * [The] Statute of Frauds applies to suretyship promises. You will recall that two of the situations falling within the Statute are promises to answer for the debt of another, and promises by a personal representative of a decedent's estate to answer for the decedent's debts out of the personal representative's own funds. These are suretyship promises and require a written and signed memorandum in order to be enforceable.

———

Creditor's collection precedure. The general rule is that the creditor does not have to proceed first against the principal upon default but may proceed directly and immediately against the surety to collect the debt. In other words, the surety cannot force the creditor to try to collect first from the principal.[3] States following the general rule include Connecticut,

Delaware, Louisiana, Maine, Massachusetts, Michigan, Minnesota, New Hampshire, New Jersey, New Mexico, Oregon, Rhode Island, South Carolina, Vermont, Wisconsin, and others.

In about half the states, the general rule has been changed by judicial decision or statute. In the following states, if the surety notifies the creditor to proceed first against the principal, and the creditor does not do so, but attempts to collect instead from the surety, the surety will be discharged: Alabama, Arizona, Arkansas, California, Colorado, Georgia, Illinois, Indiana, Iowa, Kentucky, Mississippi, Missouri, Montana, New York, North Carolina, North Dakota, Ohio, Oklahoma, Pennsylvania, South Dakota, Tennessee, Texas, Virginia, Washington, West Virginia, and Wyoming.

Exoneration. To exonerate means to free from responsibility. The principal owes a duty to the surety to perform as soon as performance is due so that the surety will be exonerated and will not be sued by the creditor. Thus, it is a principle of surety law that a surety may compel his or her principal to perform the obligation when it is due. If the principal fails to perform, the surety may bring a suit against the principal and obtain a decree from the court requiring the principal to pay the creditor. This is so even though (as we shall see) the principal has a duty to indemnify (reimburse) the surety if the surety is required to pay the debt. Reimbursement is not an adequate remedy because the surety may suffer considerable loss by reason of having to raise the money to pay the debt.

Reimbursement. A surety who pays the principal's debt has a right of reimbursement from the principal. And the right is not conditioned upon the surety being forced to pay the debt. The surety

---

3. However, in most states, if a party promises merely to "guarantee collection", he or she, as a typical conditional guarantor, is liable only after the creditor has

proceeded against the principal and obtained a judgment that is returned unsatisfied.

may voluntarily make payment, then go to court to seek reimbursement from the principal.

However, a surety is not allowed to make a profit at the principal's expense. If the surety discharges the principal's debt with property worth less than the amount owing, or compromises the debt for a smaller sum than what is owed, the surety can recover only the value of the property or the amount paid to the creditor.

If the surety discharges the debt by giving the creditor his or her personal promissory note, the majority rule is that the surety may sue the principal for the face value of the note even though the surety has not yet paid the note.

Subrogation. Subrogation is the substitution of one person in the legal position of another with respect to a lawful claim, demand, or right. Subrogation was discussed in Ch. 11 (dealing with insurance) as follows:

> [A]n insurance company that pays for an insured's loss is *subrogated* to the legal rights of the insured against the party who caused the loss.

Black's Law Dictionary defines "subrogation" as follows:

> It is the substitution of one person in the place of another with reference to a lawful claim, demand or right, or that he who is substituted succeeds to the rights of the other in relation to the debt or claim, and its rights, remedies, or securities.

> Thus, if an insured suffers a loss, he or she may look to his or her insurance company for payment; the insurance company, in turn, will receive whatever legal rights the insured may have * * * to recover money damages in or out of court from the party who caused the loss.

Upon paying the principal's debt, the surety has a right to be subrogated to the creditor's lawful claims against the principal. Subrogation entitles the surety to use any legal remedy against the principal that the creditor could have used, and to enjoy any benefit or advantage that the creditor would have had in proceeding against the principal. Thus, if the creditor was holding the debtor-principal's collateral as security, the surety will have the creditor's right to proceed against the collateral by reason of the subrogation.[5] The surety will succeed to any position of priority that the creditor has against the debtor. If the suretyship relates to a mortgage, and the surety pays the mortgage debt, the surety has all the rights of the mortgagee (see Part II of this chapter relating to foreclosure).

Contribution. Where there are co-sureties, and one surety pays the principal's entire debt, or more than his or her share of the debt, that surety is entitled to contribution from his or her co-sureties to the extent of their ratable shares.[6]

This right of contribution exists between all who are liable as sureties as to the *same obligation* of a principal; it does not exist where the sureties are liable on *different obligations* of a principal.

PART IV
PROTECTING CREDITORS OF A BUSINESS WHEN THE BUSINESS IS SOLD: BULK TRANSFERS UNDER ARTICLE 6 OF THE UNIFORM COMMERCIAL CODE

What is the purpose of bulk sales law?

As we have seen, creditors may protect themselves by using property as security or by having a third party serve as surety for a debtor. Still, many creditors sell on open account without using any security device. This is particularly true of suppliers who provide inventory mer-

---

5. Note that the creditor need not proceed against the collateral first before looking to the surety for payment.

6. Co-sureties are liable jointly and severally and may be sued by the creditor as a group or individually.

chandise. Most inventory suppliers sell to merchants on credit, expecting to be paid in the ordinary course of business as the inventory is sold to customers. As long as the merchant-debtor's business operates smoothly, and the merchant pays the supplier as the inventory is sold, the supplier has nothing to worry about. However, if the merchant decides to sell his or her business or a "major part" of his or her materials, supplies, merchandise, or other inventory, the supplier may justifiably worry about whether or not he or she will be repaid. As long as the inventory is present, the supplier, upon default by the buyer, can use all of the remedies discussed in Ch. 26 to collect his or her debt from the merchant. As you will recall, these include the prejudgment remedies of attachment, garnishment, and prejudgment receivership—remedies designed "to prevent the debtor from disposing of his or her property, or from concealing or destroying it, so it cannot be used to pay his or her debt."

The difficulty arises where the merchant, without warning, sells the entire business (or a major part of it) and there is no longer any inventory to attach or place in receivership. What is more, the merchant-debtor may have squandered the proceeds resulting from sale of the business and/or left the state. In the ordinary case, the merchant's creditors cannot reach the transferred assets in the buyer's hands unless the creditors can show that the transfer was a fraudulent conveyance or preferential transfer (see Ch. 26). A good faith purchaser of the assets would take them free of the creditors' claims.

Yet, if the creditors have adequate warning of a planned bulk sale, they can take action prior to the sale to protect their interests. The purpose of bulk sales law under Article 6 of the Uniform Commercial Code is to provide such notice. Bulk sales law does not prescribe specific remedies for creditors; rather, it

is designed to give notice to suppliers and other creditors of a going business that the business or a major part of it is going to be sold. Once notified, the creditors can take whatever action they deem necessary (if any) to protect their interests. Of course, in many cases, the creditors will take no special action because they know that the seller is solvent and responsible and will pay them anyway. But if the creditors fear that they will not be paid, they may pressure the seller and buyer to pay them off as part of the bulk sale transaction, or they may resort to any other available legal remedies (including the prejudgment remedies).

To what transactions does the bulk sales law apply?

Section 6–102 of the Uniform Commercial Code defines a "bulk transfer" as follows:

Section 6–102. "Bulk Transfers"; Transfers of Equipment; Enterprises Subject to This Article; Bulk Transfers Subject to This Article

(1) A "bulk transfer" is any transfer in bulk and not in the ordinary course of the transferor's business or a major part of the materials, supplies, merchandise or other inventory * * * of an enterprise subject to this Article.

(2) A transfer of a substantial part of the equipment * * * of such an enterprise is a bulk transfer if it is made in connection with a bulk transfer of inventory, but not otherwise.

(3) The enterprises subject to this Article are all those whose principal business is the sale of merchandise from stock, including those who manufacture what they sell.

Note that the law applies only to businesses whose principal business is the sale of merchandise from stock, including businesses that manufacture what they sell. The *Official Comment* to Section 6–102 states:

> 2. The businesses covered are defined in subsection (3). Notice that they do not include farming nor contracting nor professional services, nor such things as cleaning shops, barber shops, pool halls, hotels, restaurants, and the like whose principal business is the sale not of merchandise but of services. While some bulk sales risk exists in the excluded businesses, they have in common the fact that unsecured credit is not commonly extended on the faith of a stock of merchandise.
>
> 3. The transfers included are of "materials, supplies, merchandise or other inventory" that is, of goods. Transfers of investment securities are not covered by the Article, nor are transfers of money, accounts receivable, chattel paper, contract rights, negotiable instruments, nor things in action generally.

Also note that the law applies to the transfer of a *major part* of a business' materials, supplies, merchandise, or other inventory. The Code nowhere defines "major part"—rather, the courts must, in each case, look at the impact the transfer will have on creditors. Some courts apply an arbitrary rule, stating that anything over 50% of a business' materials, supplies, merchandise, or other inventory is a "major part" of the business (meaning over 50% of the value of the materials, supplies, merchandise, etc.). However, it would appear that less than this could also be a major part; thus, a seller of a business would be well advised to

follow the bulk sales requirements whenever he or she is transferring a substantial bulk of materials, supplies, merchandise, or other inventory.

Finally, note that equipment is included under the bulk sales rules only if it is transferred in connection with a bulk transfer of inventory.

What must be done to comply with Article 6 when a bulk sale is made?

The "bulk sales" requirements of Article 6 come into play when a person whose principal business is selling merchandise from stock decides to sell his or her business (or transfer a major part of his or her materials, supplies, merchandise, or other inventory). Article 6 sets forth the following four requirements, imposing duties on both the seller and buyer in the bulk sales situation:

(1) The buyer-transferee of the business must require the seller-transferor to furnish him or her with a list of the existing creditors of the business. The list must include all creditors, whether trade creditors (those who furnish inventory on credit); creditors who claim on the basis of other contracts, torts, or tax claims; even creditors who claim amounts that are disputed by the seller. Each creditor's name and business address must be listed together with the amount of his or her claim. And the list must be signed and sworn to by the seller.

(2) The buyer and seller must together prepare a schedule of the property to be transferred.

(3) The buyer must preserve the creditors' list and property schedule for six months following the transfer. During this time, the buyer must either permit creditors to inspect and copy from the list and schedule at all reasonable hours or the creditor must file the list and schedule in a public office (such as the county clerk's office) in the area where the business is located.

(4) The buyer must give notice of the sale to the listed creditors and any other parties known to have claims against the business. The notice must either be delivered personally or "sent" by registered or certified mail at least ten days before the buyer takes possession of the property transferred in bulk.

Sections 6–104, 6–105, and 6–107 are the relevant Uniform Commercial Code provisions.

The UCC provides:

Section 6–104. Schedule of Property, List of Creditors

(1) * * * [A] bulk transfer * * * is ineffective against any creditor of the transferor unless:

(a) The transferee requires the transferor to furnish a list of his existing creditors prepared as stated in this section; and

(b) The parties prepare a schedule of the property transferred sufficient to identify it; and

(c) the transferee preserves the list and schedule for six months next following the transfer and permits inspection of either or both and copying therefrom at all reasonable hours by any creditor of the transferor, or files the list and schedule * * *

(2) The list of creditors must be signed and sworn to or affirmed by the transferor or his agent. It must contain the names and business addresses of all creditors of the transferor, with the amounts when known, and also the names of all persons who are known to the transferor to assert claims against him even though such claims are disputed * * *

(3) Responsibility for the completeness and accuracy of the list of creditors rests on the transferor, and the transfer is not rendered ineffective by errors or omissions therein unless the transferee is shown to have had knowledge.

Section 6–105. Notice to Creditors

In addition to the requirements of the preceding section, any bulk transfer subject to this Article * * * is ineffective against any creditor of the transferor unless at least ten days before he takes possession of the goods or pays for them, whichever happens first, the transferee gives notice of the transfer in the manner and to the persons hereafter provided (Section 6–107).

Section 6–107. The Notice

(1) The notice of creditors (Section 6–105) shall state:

(a) that a bulk transfer is about to be made; and

(b) the names and business addresses of the transferor and transferee, and all other business names and addresses used by the transferor within three years last past so far as known to the transferee; and

(c) whether or not all the debts of the transferor are to be paid in full as they fall due as a result of the transaction, and if so, the address to which creditors should send their bills.

(2) If the debts of the transferor are not to be paid in full as they fall due or if the transferee is in doubt on that point then the notice shall state further:

(a) the location and general description of the property to be transferred and the estimated total of the transferor's debts;

(b) the address where the schedule of property and list of creditors (Section 6–104) may be inspected;

(c) whether the transfer is to pay existing debts and if so the amount of such debts and to whom owing;

(d) whether the transfer is for new consideration and if so the amount of such consideration and place of payment;

(3) The notice in any case shall be delivered personally or sent by registered or certified mail to all the persons shown on the list of creditors furnished by the transferor (Section 6–104) and to all other persons who are known to the transferee to hold or assert claims against the transferor.

In addition to the above four requirements, some 18 states have passed as part of Article 6 optional Section 6–106 requiring that part of the bulk sales proceeds be distributed to the transferor's creditors. States having passed this Section include Alaska, Florida, Idaho, Kansas, Kentucky, Maryland, Mississippi, Montana, New Jersey, North Dakota, Oklahoma, Pennsylvania, South Dakota, Tennessee, Texas, Utah, Washington, and West Virginia.

The Section provides:

Section 6–106. Application of the Proceeds

(1) Upon every bulk transfer * * * it is the duty of the transferee to assure that such consideration is applied so far as necessary to pay those debts of the transferor which are either shown on the list furnished by the transferor (Section 6–104) or filed in writing in the place stated in the notice (Section 6–107) within

thirty days after the mailing of such notice * * *

(2) If any of said debts are in dispute the necessary sum may be withheld from distribution until the dispute is settled or adjudicated.

(3) If the consideration payable is not enough to pay all of the said debts in full distributions shall be made pro rata.

What is the result of failure to comply with the bulk sales rules?

Assuming the buyer and seller fully comply with the bulk sales rules of Article 6, the creditors of the business, having been notified of the bulk sale, can do whatever they deem necessary (if anything) to protect their interests. It may be that the seller-transferor is solvent and responsible and that the creditors will be paid off completely with no difficulty. The creditors, in this case, are likely to do nothing.

However, if it appears that the inventory is being sold for far less than it is actually worth, or that the seller is going to flee the state with all the proceeds of the sale, the creditors will want to act immediately to protect themselves. If the creditors do nothing, and the bulk sale is made in full conformity with Article 6, the creditors will have no claim to the goods transferred in bulk to the transferee-buyer.

A creditor who is worried about an impending bulk sale may try to get the parties to agree to pay him or her off as part of the bulk sale transaction. If this does not work, the creditor may threaten legal action. However, unless there has been a breach of contract, the creditor will have no basis for going to court to obtain a judgment (in other words, the debt must be overdue or the creditor will have no cause to complain). And to use a prejudgment remedy (e. g., attachment), the creditor must show that he or she is in imminent danger of losing his or her claim by reason of the transferor hiding the proceeds, spending them, or leaving the state. Of course, the creditor may threaten to force the transferor into bankruptcy, but to do this, the creditor must show that the transferor has debts of at least $5,000, and that he or she is not paying his or her debts as they fall due or has had his or her property taken over by a legal custodian (see Ch. 26). If the creditor cannot show this, he or she can do nothing more to fight the bulk sale (the creditor, in this case, probably has little to worry about anyway by reason of the sale).

But suppose that the parties (buyer and seller) fail to comply fully with the requirements of Article 6. The Uniform Commercial Code states that noncomplying transfers are ineffective. The result is that the seller's creditors can still reach the inventory or other goods transferred just as if they never left the seller's hands. Thus, though the goods are in the possession of the buyer-transferee, the creditors can levy [4] upon the goods and have them sold to satisfy judgments against the seller-transferor. The creditors can also obtain an injunction against the transferee to prevent him or her from reselling the goods, or if the goods have

already been resold, to prevent the transferee from disposing of the proceeds.

Of course, a bona fide purchaser of the goods (i. e., one who takes the goods for value without knowledge of the failure to comply with the bulk sales rules) will acquire ownership (title) of the property free of the creditors' claims. Any other person taking the property will be an assignee only in the same position as the transferee.

Any action or levy by a creditor under the bulk sales law must be brought or maintained within six months after the date on which the transferee takes possession of the goods unless the transfer has been concealed. In the latter case, creditors' actions or levies may be maintained up to six months after discovery of the bulk transfer.

In conclusion, remember that the bulk sales rules are designed to give the creditors of a business prior notice that a bulk sale is to occur so that the creditors can take whatever action they deem necessary to protect their interests. It is important to remember that the bulk sales rules do not affect any remedies a creditor might have as a secured creditor (under Article 9 of the UCC or as a mortgage holder) nor any remedies a creditor might have by reason of federal Bankruptcy law or state creditor remedy law.

---

4. Levies include attachment, garnishment, receivership, and any other state process or proceeding used to apply a debtor's property to payment of his or her debts (see Ch. 26).

CASES

CASE 1—*Wolf's purchase money security interest has priority under Article 9.*

IN RE ULTRA PRECISION INDUSTRIES, INC.

United States Court of Appeals, Ninth Circuit, 1974.
503 F.2d 414.

EAST, Senior District Judge:

THE APPEAL

National Acceptance Company of California (National) appeals from the two several orders of the District Court denying its Petition for Review and affirming the referee's two several rulings or orders that the security interest held by Community Bank (Bank) and Wolf Machinery Company (Wolf) in three large Rigid Hydro Copy Profiling Machines, numbered 5890 and 5910 (Bank) and machine numbered 5934 (Wolf), respectively,[1] had priority over a conflicting security interest held by National. § 9312 (4) of the Uniform Commercial Code of California (Code). We affirm.

FACTS

The pertinent facts are:

National loaned Ultra Precision Industries, Inc. (Ultra) $692,000, and to secure the repayment of that sum, Ultra on or about March 7, 1967, executed in favor of National a Chattel Mortgage Security Agreement covering specifically described equipment of Ultra. National perfected its security interest by timely filing a Financing Statement. The Chattel Mortgage Security Agreement and the Financing Statement contained the usual after-acquired equipment security clauses; however, without reference to any specific property.

Subsequent to the acquisition of National's security interest and during 1967 and 1968, Ultra placed orders with Wolf for two of the machines, later identified as machines numbered 5890 and 5910. It was agreed between Ultra and Wolf that after those machines had been shipped to Ultra and installed, Ultra would be given an opportunity to test them in their operations during a reasonable testing period,[2] and, further, that arrangements satisfactory to Ultra for outside financing was a condition precedent to the ultimate purchase of those machines. The machines were delivered to Ultra on April 30, 1968 and June 20, 1968, respectively, satisfactory testing was accomplished, outside financing obtained, and on July 31, 1968, Ultra and Wolf executed a Purchase Money Security Interest Conditional Sales Agreement (Security Interest Agreement) covering the sale of those two machines by Wolf to Ultra, and as a part of the outside financing arrangement, Wolf in consideration of the payment of $128,122.20 assigned the Security

1. These machines are large complicated precision pieces of equipment, weighing 16,000 to 20,000 pounds each.

2. The machines were shipped directly from Europe by Cosa (a distributor) to the plant of Ultra as a matter of convenience, rather than to Wolf and then to Ultra. This practice is customary in the industry with respect to machines of the size and weight involved.

Interest Agreement to Bank. Bank's security interest was perfected by the filing of a Financing Statement on August 5, 1968.[3]

In June, 1968, Ultra placed another order with Wolf for a similar machine, later identified as machine numbered 5934, under identical terms of testing and purchase as those for the purchase of the above numbered machines 5890 and 5910. The machine was delivered to Ultra on August 7, 1968, satisfactory testing was accomplished, outside financing obtained, and on October 23, 1968, Ultra and Wolf executed a similar Security Interest Agreement covering the sale of the machine numbered 5934 by Wolf to Ultra, and as a part of the outside financing arrangement, Wolf, for value received, assigned the Security Interest Agreement to C.I.T. Corporation. C.I.T. Corporation's security interest was perfected by the filing of a Financing Statement on October 30, 1968. On October 7, 1969, C.I.T. Corporation reassigned the Security Interest Agreement to Wolf when Ultra became bankrupt.

ISSUE

The priorities among the three security interests involved are determined by the application of § 9312(4), which reads:

"A purchase money security interest in collateral other than inventory has priority over a conflicting security interest in the same collateral *if the purchase money security interest is perfected at the time the debtor receives possession of the collateral or within 10 days thereafter.* (emphasis added):"

The sole issue presented by the facts and the contention of the parties on appeal is: On what dates did Ultra become "the debtor [receiving] possession of the collateral [the three respective machines]" within the meaning of § 9312(4)?

DISCUSSION

Briefly stated, National contends that Ultra was its "debtor" in "possession of the collateral" at the moment it received physical delivery of the respective three machines, without regard to any agreement to the contrary between Wolf and Ultra as to the terms and conditions of the ultimate sale and purchase of the machines respectively; hence, the machines were within the grasp of the after-acquired property clause. Since the Security Interest Agreements held by Bank and Wolf were not perfected within ten days "thereafter" as commanded by § 9312(4), they are unenforceable as against National's perfected security interest.

Bank and Wolf each contend that Ultra did not become their "debtor" in "possession of the collateral" (the three respective machines) until the terms and conditions of the proposed sales and purchases thereof had been met and the Security Interest Agreement had been executed and delivered. We subscribe to that contention.

---

3. The general purpose of the Uniform Commercial Code is to create a precise guide for commercial transactions under which businessmen may predict with confidence the results of their dealings and avoid the confusion arising from a debtor's ostensible dominion of property then burdened with an outstanding secret security interest. The requirement of strict compliance with the filing provisions is the prime virtue of the Code. Today filing is required to perfect the security interest so that creditors may learn of pre-existing security interests.

Section 9105(1) of the Code provides:

"(1) In this division unless the context otherwise requires:

"(d) 'Debtor' means the person who owes payment or other performance of the obligation secured   *   *   *."

National urges that the term "debtor" as used in § 9312(4) means the debtor under its "conflicting security interest." Such an interpretation does violence to the clear language of the section * * *. To us, the word "debtor" in § 9312(4) means the debtor of the seller or holder of the "purchase money security interest in collateral" (the thing sold).

It is manifest that Ultra was not a "debtor" of Wolf and did not owe payment or other performance of the obligation secured unto Wolf until the moment of the execution and delivery of the Security Interest Agreements on July 31, 1968 and October 23, 1968, respectively. Suffice to say that prior to those dates, (a) Wolf held no definitive security interest in the machines which could be perfected by the filing of a Financing Statement, and (b) Ultra held no assignable legal interest in the machines which could fall into the grasp of National's after-acquired property security clause.

We hold that Ultra became the purchase money security interest "debtor [receiving] possession of the collateral [the three respective machines]" at the instant of the execution and delivery of the Security Interest Agreements, respectively, and not before; and, further, that since each of the Security Interest Agreements were timely perfected, the security interests of Wolf and Bank, respectively, are each prior and superior to the conflicting security interest held by National.

* * *

The record as a whole reveals good faith, above board, uninvolved commercial credit transactions, without any withholding on the part of or secret equities among the parties. National was in no way misled by any acts of Wolf or Bank giving rise to an estoppel, and National advanced no money or credit on the strength of Ultra's pre-Security Interest Agreement possession of the machines. Wolf was entitled to abide with the terms and conditions of the proposed sales and purchases of its machines and to perfect its ultimate Security Interest Agreements in accordance with § 9312(4).

Affirmed.

CASE 2—*The purchaser at the "bulk sale" received an affidavit of "no creditors."*

ADRIAN TABIN CORP. v. CLIMAX BOUTIQUE, INC.

Supreme Court, Appellate Division, Second Department, 1972.
40 A.D.2d 146, 338 N.Y.S.2d 59.

SHAPIRO, Justice.

The novel issue posed by this appeal is whether a purchaser at a bulk sale, who receives an affidavit of "no creditors" is nevertheless under a duty to make careful inquiry as to the possible existence of creditors, of whom he has no actual knowledge. The plaintiff, a creditor of the seller, was not notified of the sale and hence seeks an adjudication that, as to it, the sale is void.

Defendant L.D.J. Dresses, Inc. (hereinafter referred to as "the seller") operated a dress shop in Jamaica, Queens. The seller was indebted to the plaintiff, a garment supplier, at the time it sold its business in bulk to defendant Paul Warman, who in turn sold the business to defendant Climax Boutique, Inc., in which he was a principal. (Warman and Climax will hereafter be referred to as "the purchasers".)

Prior to the consummation of the bulk sale the purchasers received an affidavit from Joseph Marino, the president of the seller, which stated that the seller was not indebted to anyone and had no creditors. The purchasers caused a lien search to be conducted and determined that there were no outstanding liens.

At the trial, the purchasers' attorney testified as follows:

"I knew * * * the attorney for the seller for at least fifteen years, knew him well, had seen him in court maybe once a month for fifteen years so knew his voice well. In fact I had matters with him too from the past. At the closing * * * [the seller's attorney] and I spoke on the telephone and I said, 'What about the general creditors? you have told me already there are none but I think I should have some necessary affidavit to cover.' Then he said, 'Well, to begin with,' he said, 'I am going to give you a bill of sale sworn to by the seller and notarized by me as an attorney that there are absolutely no creditors. He has shown me checks that he had sent to all his creditors because I checked it with him in order to close out the business for the end of the year and I am satisfied that there are none and as an attorney I would never let my client sign such a affidavit if I thought there were, and there are no creditors.' "

The parties stipulated that the purchasers had no knowledge of the plaintiff prior to the sale.

In setting aside the sale the Special Term noted that the purchasers had not requested an examination of the seller's books and had not questioned the source of the garments involved in the sale. It held that the purchasers had not made careful inquiry of the seller as to existing creditors and that, failing such careful inquiry, the purchasers had acted at their peril. The appeal is from the ensuing judgment * * *.

A bulk sale is ineffective against creditors of the seller unless the purchaser requires the seller to furnish a list (signed and sworn to or affirmed) of his existing creditors (Uniform Commercial Code, § 6–104) and notifies such creditors of the impending sale (Uniform Commercial Code, §§ 6–105, 6–107). * * *

* * * Subdivision (3) of section 6–104 of the Uniform Commercial Code provides that "responsibility for the completeness and accuracy of the list of creditors rests on the transferor, and the transfer is not rendered ineffective by errors or omissions therein *unless the transferee is shown to have had knowledge*" (emphasis supplied). Section 1–201 of the Uniform Commercial Code, the general definitions section of that code, provides, in subdivision (25), that "a person 'knows' or has 'knowledge' of a fact when he has actual knowledge of it." It is therefore apparent that a bulk sale may not be set aside as to creditors not listed by the seller in the affidavit requested by the purchaser, of whom the purchaser had no actual knowledge. As the purchasers concededly had no actual knowledge of the plain-

tiff, the possibility of whose existence as a creditor was denied by the seller in an affidavit (the purchasers having no reason to disbelieve the truthfulness of the affidavit), the bulk sale may not be set aside as to the plaintiff.

We note, in passing, that even were the purchasers under a duty to make careful inquiry, they complied with that responsibility in this case by making a lien search and by making inquiry of the seller's attorney, who represented that all creditors had been paid and that he had seen the checks sent out to them in payment of the seller's obligations.

The judgment should be reversed * * *.

PROBLEMS

1. Answer the following "True" or "False" and give reasons for your answers:

   (a) Bulk sales law prescribes specific remedies for creditors to take when the debtor sells his or her business or a major part of his or her materials, supplies, merchandise, or other inventory.

   (b) Bulk sales law does not apply to businesses whose principal business is the sale of services.

   (c) A suretyship obligation must be evidenced by a written memo in order to be enforceable.

   (d) When a mortgage debt is repaid, the mortgagee's interest in the land immediately and automatically terminates and the mortgagor again holds the property free of the lien.

   (e) To be valid, a mortgage must be represented by a negotiable promissory note.

   (f) An unacknowledged mortgage cannot be recorded.

   (g) Consideration is required for a valid mortgage.

   (h) A deed of trust is commonly used in place of a regular mortgage.

   (i) Article 9 of the Uniform Commercial Code covers any security transaction involving the use of personal property as collateral.

   (j) Most secured parties simply file the security agreement as the financing statement.

   (k) The security agreement must always be in writing.

   (l) Everything that can be done to secure a creditor is accomplished by possession alone.

   (m) Security interests in money and negotiable instruments can only be perfected by filing a financing statement.

   (n) An inventory secured party takes priority over an accounts secured party with regard to accounts received as "proceeds" from inventory sales.

   (o) Upon default by the debtor, the secured party may use self-help to repossess the collateral if it can be done without a breach of the peace.

   (p) A debtor whose personal property has been repossessed may generally regain ownership by paying the amount owing.

2. (a) On March 1st, Marla Mitchell obtains a $10,000 civil judgment (arising out of a negligence action) against Sid Smith. On April 1st, Ben Barker loans Sid $55,000 to enable him to purchase a two-bedroom

rental property. Sid executes a mortgage on the property in favor of Ben, with the mortgage evidenced by a negotiable installment note. Ben does not record the mortgage. Sid subsequently executes a second mortgage against the property in favor of Jim Zell in return for a $10,000 loan. Jim, who has no knowledge of the first mortgage, immediately records his mortgage. As between Marla and Ben, who has priority with respect to the property in the event that Sid fails to pay them? As between Ben and Jim? As between Marla and Jim? Explain your answers fully. Assuming Sid defaults on the mortgage agreements, what foreclosure remedies are available to Ben and Jim? What rights, if any, does Sid have following foreclosure?

Suppose that Sid purchases a "built-in" style air conditioning system on credit from Walker, Inc. Walker takes a purchase money security interest in the system; it installs the system and "builds it into" the rental property. Six days after installation, Walker makes a proper fixture filing in the county real estate records. As between Walker and the mortgagees, who has priority with regard to the air conditioning system? Explain.

(b) By the terms of its security agreement with Fisher Furniture Company, First State Bank has a security interest in "all inventory now or hereafter acquired by Fisher Furniture Company." The security agreement further states that "the security interest herein created shall also secure all other indebtedness, obligations, and liabilities of Fisher Furniture to First State Bank, now existing and hereafter arising, including future advances." On August 5th, First State Bank files a financing statement covering the interest. The statement purports to cover Fisher's "inventory": it makes no mention of "inventory hereafter acquired"; nor does it refer to "future advances". On August 20th, Pete Seely purchases a five piece set of livingroom furniture from the Fisher Company for $2,500. What type of security interest does First State Bank have in Fisher's inventory? Explain fully. Does the fact that the financing statement makes no mention of "inventory hereafter acquired" or "future advances" impair the Bank's security agreement in any way? Explain. Does Pete Seely take the furniture subject to the Bank's security interest? Explain.

Suppose that Fisher Furniture makes a credit purchase of 15 waterbeds to add to its inventory from Atlantis Manufacturing, Inc. Atlantis takes a purchase money security interest in the beds. It files a financing statement covering the beds five days after Fisher takes possession of the furniture. As between First State Bank and Atlantis Manufacturing, who takes priority with regard to the beds? Explain. Would your answer differ if the Bank's interest was in Fisher's "equipment", and Atlantis had taken a purchase money security interest in equipment it had sold to Fisher? Explain.

(c) Dana Smith purchases a refrigerator-freezer on credit from Apple Appliance, Inc. The Apple Company takes a security interest in the refrigerator-freezer, but does not file any financing statement regarding the interest. Dana uses the appliance for a few weeks in her home and then sells it to her neighbor Fred Stoner for $450 cash. Fred, who plans to use the appliance in his own home, is unaware of Apple's security interest. Does Fred take the set subject to Apple's security interest? Explain.

(d) On September 10th, Jane Dolan agrees to loan David Jackson $5,000 on September 20th, the loan to be secured by David's collection of valuable coins; by the terms of the written security agreement, David is to keep possession of the coins. Jane files a financing statement covering the security interest on September 11th. On September 15th, David borrows $6,000 from Bill Bosley; the same day, David transfers possession of the coins to Bill as security for the loan. On September 20th Jane loans David $5,000. As between Jane and Bill, who has priority with respect to the coins? Explain fully.

Assume that Jane Dolan has a perfected security interest in David's coins, and that David is in possession of the coins. If David leaves the state, taking his coins with him, does Jane lose her perfected status? Explain fully.

3. Weatherall seeks to create a valid perfected security interest in goods under the provisions of the Uniform Commercial Code. Which of the following acts or actions will establish this?

   a. Weatherall obtains a written agreement under which Weatherall takes possession of the security.

   b. Weatherall obtains an unsigned written security agreement.

   c. Weatherall obtains a security agreement signed only by the debtor.

   d. Weatherall files a financing statement which is *not* in itself a security agreement.

   [# 28, November 1977 CPA Exam]

4. Vega Manufacturing, Inc., manufactures and sells hi-fi systems and components to the trade and at retail. Repossession is frequently made from customers who are in default. Which of the following statements is correct concerning the rights of the defaulting debtors who have had property repossessed by Vega?

   a. Vega has the right to retain all the goods repossessed as long as it gives notice and cancels the debt.

   b. It is unimportant whether the goods repossessed are defined as consumer goods, inventory, or something else in respect to the debtor's rights upon repossession.

   c. If the defaulting debtor voluntarily signs a statement renouncing his rights in the collateral, the creditor must nevertheless resell them for the debtor's benefit.

   d. If a debtor has paid sixty percent or more of the purchase price of consumer goods in satisfaction of a purchase money security interest, the debtor has the right to have the creditor dispose of the goods.

   [# 50, May 1978 CPA Exam]

5. Miltown borrowed $60,000 from Strauss upon the security of a first mortgage on a business building owned by Miltown. The mortgage has been amortized down to $50,000. Sanchez is buying the building from Miltown for $80,000. Sanchez is paying only the $30,000 excess over and above the mortgage. Sanchez may buy it either "subject to" the mortgage, or he may "assume" the mortgage. Which is a correct statement under these circumstances?

a. The financing agreement ultimately decided upon must be recorded in order to be binding upon the parties.

b. The financing arrangement is covered by the Uniform Commercial Code if Sanchez takes "subject to" the existing first mortgage.

c. Sanchez will acquire *no* interest in the property if he takes "subject to" instead of "assuming" the mortgage.

d. Sanchez would be better advised to take "subject to" the mortgage rather than to "assume" the mortgage.

[# 21, November 1977 CPA Exam]

6. The facts are the same as those stated above in number 5, but the property purchased by Sanchez has declined in value and the mortgage is in default. It has now been amortized to $43,000. The property is sold under foreclosure proceedings and $39,000, net of costs, is received. Which is a correct legal conclusion if Sanchez acquired the property "subject to" the mortgage?

a. Sanchez has *no* further liability after foreclosure.

b. Miltown can *not* be held personally liable by Strauss for the $4,000 deficiency.

c. Sanchez is *not* liable to Strauss, but is personally liable to Miltown if Miltown pays the deficiency.

d. Miltown and Sanchez will have to satisfy the deficiency equally, that is, each owes $2,000.

[# 22, November 1977 CPA Exam]

7. Which of the following defenses asserted by a surety should be effective in a suit by a creditor?

a. Insolvency of the creditor and the principal debtor.

b. Death of the principal debtor.

c. Failure of the creditor to foreclose a mortgage on property which he holds to secure the principal debtor's performance.

d. A material variance of the surety's undertaking as a result of a modification in the principal debtor's obligation.

[# 15, May 1976 CPA Exam]

8. Casper, Inc., has just purchased the entire stock in trade of Marvel Toy Company. The purchase price was very low due to Marvel's poor financial condition. Casper failed to notify known creditors of Marvel. The president and sole stockholder of Marvel has disappeared without paying any of Marvel's suppliers. Casper has received letters from several of Marvel's creditors demanding that it pay the Marvel debts. These facts arose during your annual examination of the financial statements of Casper.

Required: What responsibility, if any, does Casper have for Marvel's debts?

[# 6.c., November 1973 CPA Exam]

9. **Part a.** Monolith Industries, Inc., manufactures appliances and has been the major supplier of appliances to Wilber Force Corporation, a chain of retail appliance stores. The financing arrangement between Monolith and Wilber Force calls for the sale of Monolith to Wilber Force of appliances to be

resold to the public through Wilber Force's chain of appliance stores. Title to the merchandise has been retained by Monolith until receipt of payment. Monthly accountings and payments have been rendered by Wilber Force to Monolith.

Monolith filed a financing statement with the appropriate jurisdictions involved pursuant to the Uniform Commercial Code. The financing statement clearly revealed the debtor-creditor relationship between the parties, described the goods in general terms, and set forth Monolith's security interest in the various appliances sold to Wilber Force. It also contained a provision asserting Monolith's rights against any and all proceeds arising from the sale of said appliances by Wilber Force.

Wilber Force is in financial difficulty. Monolith is asserting rights to certain chattel paper (i. e., installment-sales contracts and non negotiable notes) received by Wilber Force arising from the sale of Monolith appliances to its retail customers. Double Discount Corporation purchased the chattel paper in question from Wilber Force in the ordinary course of its business and took possession of all the paper at the time it was purchased. Double Discount was aware of Monolith's security interest in the inventory. Both Monolith and Double Discount claim ownership of the paper.

Required: 1. Does Monolith have a perfected security interest? Explain.

2. Assuming Monolith has a perfected security interest, does it include proceeds? Explain.

3. Does Monolith have any rights against Double Discount regarding the chattel paper? Explain.

Part b. While examining accounts receivable during the current audit of Dodson Corporation you encountered the following situation involving Excelsior Sales Distributors, Inc., one of Dodson's customers.

In the past, Dodson had sold Excelsior various hi-fi components for sale to its retail customers in the ordinary course of business. The credit arrangement between the parties provided for payment by Excelsior on a 2/10, net/30 basis. Excelsior fell behind on payments for merchandise it had purchased, and Dodson demanded a security interest in the merchandise for which payment had not been received. Negotiations between the parties resulted in the following plan which has been executed.

• Excelsior returned to Dodson all of the unsold merchandise in its possession which had been delivered by Dodson. (This was insufficient to cover the outstanding obligation to Dodson because merchandise which previously had been delivered had been sold by Excelsior and was not available for repossession.) Dodson placed the merchandise in a bonded warehouse retaining a negotiable warehouse receipt for the items repossessed from Excelsior. The merchandise was segregated in the warehouse for identification.

• Excelsior agreed to pay all storage and delivery costs on the repossessed merchandise.

• Dodson agreed to release the repossessed merchandise to Excelsior upon payment in cash for each delivery.

- Dodson agreed not to file a financing statement on the repossessed merchandise.

- All future sales were to be made on a cash basis, but only after Excelsior satisfied all outstanding debts to Dodson.

Subsequently, under a separate agreement, Excelsior's owners, who were also its directors and officers, guaranteed all outstanding obligations of Excelsior to Dodson including any deficiency which may arise on disposition of the repossessed merchandise.

Six months later, Excelsior filed a voluntary petition in bankruptcy. Dodson is asserting rights to the merchandise it sold and repossessed. Dodson also seeks to collect from Excelsior's owners on their guarantee for the deficiency resulting from merchandise previously delivered less the proceeds from the sale of merchandise repossessed.

Required: 1. Does Dodson have a perfected security interest in the repossessed merchandise? Explain.

2. Assuming Dodson is a secured creditor of Excelsior, can the duly appointed trustee in bankruptcy set aside Dodson's security interest in the repossessed merchandise? Explain.

3. Can Dodson recover against Excelsior's owners upon their guarantee for any remaining deficiency after a valid auction sale of the repossessed merchandise? Explain.

[# 7.a. & b., May 1974 CPA Exam]

10. During its annual examination of the financial statements of Ramrod Corporation, Farr & Williamson, CPAs, discovered the following problem involving an account receivable from DeMars Corporation. As of December 31, 1974, DeMars was three months in arrears on purchases of $21,690 made in late September 1974. In addition, a letter dated November 30, 1974, indicated that DeMars would not be able to pay its outstanding obligations because an involuntary petition in bankruptcy had been filed on November 21, 1974. The trustee in bankruptcy has indicated that, based upon a conservative estimate, DeMars will pay 10 cents on the dollar.

Further investigation revealed that DeMars was one of Ramrod's oldest and most-cherished customers. Not only that, but Fairmont, Ramrod's president, was a close personal friend and golfing partner of Goodson, DeMars' president. As a result of this relationship, Goodson had telephoned Fairmont on November 12, 1974, and informed him that DeMars' other creditors were in the process of preparing and filing an involuntary bankruptcy petition against it and that its financial condition had badly deteriorated. It was agreed by the two parties that Ramrod should take a secured position on the $21,690 arrearage via the assignment of $21,690 of DeMars' accounts receivable. This was done and a financing statement was duly signed by the parties and filed on November 15, 1974.

Later in its examination of Ramrod's financial statements, Farr & Williamson learned of another problem related to DeMars. Because of the close relationship between the companies and their presidents, Fairmont had urged Ramrod's board of directors in early January 1974 to authorize him to sign the corporate name as surety for $200,000 loan which DeMars was negotiating with Local Lending Corporation. The loan was to be secured by a first mortgage on DeMars' real property. The fair market value of the real property at that time was $200,000; however, because it was Local Lending's policy not to loan in excess of 75% of the security's fair market value, it was insisting upon a satisfactory surety on the loan. Additionally, Local Lending was worried about DeMars' financial condition. On January 10, 1974, Fairmont was authorized to sign the corporate name as an accommodation indorser on the $200,000 loan which was consummated that day. The current fair market value of the real property is approximately $180,-000. DeMars is in default and Local Lending has demanded that Ramrod satisfy the debt.

Required: 1. Will Ramrod be able to successfully assert the standing of a secured creditor in the bankruptcy proceeding in respect to the $21,690 account receivable? Explain.

2. Assuming Ramrod is liable on its accommodation indorsement, can Ramrod force Local Lending to first resort to its mortgage before proceeding against Ramrod? Explain.

3. Assuming Ramrod is liable on its accommodation indorsement and has paid Local Lending the balance due ($190,260) on the loan by Local Lending to DeMars, what rights and standing does Ramrod have in bankruptcy as a result? Explain.

[# 6.a, d, & e, May 1975 CPA Exam]

Chapter 28

BUSINESS AND PROFESSIONAL RESPONSIBILITY: BUSINESS TORTS, THE DUTIES AND LIABILITIES OF CPA'S, AND LEGAL ETHICS

What is the meaning of "responsibility" as used in this chapter?

The word "responsibility", like many other words, has more than one meaning. Funk & Wagnalls New Practical Standard Dictionary gives this definition of the term:

RESPONSIBILITY * * * 1. The state of being responsible or accountable. 2. That for which one is answerable; a duty or trust. 3. Ability to meet obligations or to act without superior authority or guidance. See synonyms under duty.[1]

And the term "responsible" is defined as follows.

RESPONSIBLE * * * 1. Answerable *legally* or morally for the discharge of a *duty,* trust, or debt. 2. Having capacity to perceive the distinctions of right and wrong; having ethical discrimination. 3. Able to meet legitimate claims; having sufficient property or means for the payment of debts. 4. *Involving accountability or obligation.* (Emphasis added.) [2]

Our text is a law book. For this reason, our use of the term "responsibility" will emphasize that which is *required* by

law—numbers (1) and (4) in the above definition of "responsible", i. e., to be "answerable legally * * * for the discharge of a duty" and "involving accountability or obligation". Looking to a thesaurus for words that express this meaning of "responsibility", we find: "obligatory, binding, imperative, mandatory, must." [3] Thus, in our study, we will not be concerned with moral obligation or perhaps what *ought* to be done beyond that which is *legally required* of businesspeople, accountants, and lawyers by way of responsibility. While the "ought" may properly be the subject of business and professional morality and ethics, it is not the subject of law. And, without regard to morality and ethics, the law *requires* a tremendous amount of responsibility and provides for substantial civil and criminal penalties if business and professional responsibility is not discharged. In other words, the law makes certain responsibilities obligatory and binding and a person who fails to carry out his or her responsibility will be held legally accountable for such failure.

Our study of business and professional responsibility will be divided into the following parts:

Part I. The legal responsibility of businesspeople;

Part II. The legal responsibility of accountants; and

Part III. The legal responsibility of lawyers.

---

1. Funk & Wagnalls *New Practical Standard Dictionary,* American Press, 1946, p. 1116.

2. Ibid.

3. Roget's *International Thesaurus,* Volume 1, Thomas Y. Crowell Co., 1970, p. 225.

PART I
THE LEGAL RESPONSIBILITY OF BUSINESSPEOPLE

To whom do businesspeople owe legal responsibility?

Earlier in the text in discussing methods of doing business, we stated that only those who actually *own* the business (and therefore participate in its profits and losses) are "doing business" within our meaning. Here, again, in talking about the responsibility of businesspeople, we are talking about the people who own the business enterprise (including those who represent the owners in the operation of the business). Of course, when the owners choose the corporate form of business organization and separate ownership from management, both the shareholder-owners and the director-managers have distinct legal duties or responsibilities (see Ch. 23).

A businessperson owes specific legal responsibilities to:

(1) Owners of the business;

(2) Suppliers;

(3) Competitors;

(4) Consumers;

(5) Employees;

(6) Members of society; and

(7) Government.

Much of the law governing the businessperson's responsibility in these seven areas has already been covered in the text of this book. In this chapter, we can only briefly summarize some of the more important principles of law requiring a businessperson to act in a legally responsible manner.

(1) *Owners.*

There are three ways of doing business —as a sole proprietorship, partnership, or corporation. At first blush, one might wonder whether a sole proprietor, being an individual business owner, has any legal responsibility to himself or herself. The answer is yes. A person who has been successful in accumulating some wealth has a legal responsibility to maintain sufficient property so that he or she, or his or her family, does not become a charge of the state. Thus, if a sole proprietor becomes incompetent or is a spendthrift (a "spendthrift" being a person whose excessive drinking, idleness, gambling, or debauchery so spends, wastes, or lessens the person's estate that he or she or his or her family is exposed to want or suffering) the court may appoint a guardian to handle his or her affairs (e. g., upon petition of an adult child to prevent the parent from squandering his or her assets). This is most obvious where the sole proprietor is married. A married person with children owes certain support obligations to his or her family. Statutes in most states provide that family expenses, including children's education expenses, are the responsibility of both spouses. A person may not only have a legal responsibility to support a spouse during marriage but also afterwards, with a continuing duty of support in the form of alimony. A variety of remedies are used to enforce support responsibilities. A child, through his or her attorney, may sue the parent directly in a civil suit if support is not provided. And in most states, criminal nonsupport statutes make it a misdemeanor for a parent to refuse to support his or her children if he or she is financially able to do so. And, again, if the parent is incompetent or a spendthrift, a child, through his or her attorney, may petition the court to appoint a guardian to manage the parent's properties and business affairs.

With regard to the partnership method of doing business, partners have responsibilities not only to themselves as individuals, but also to each other regarding the partnership business and partnership property. In Ch. 22, it was stated:

Each partner is a fiduciary of every other partner. * * * A fiduciary is a person in a position of trust and confidence with another. A partner is in a position of trust and confidence with his or her co-partners * * * and must act with utmost loyalty and care * * *. It follows that a partner may not compete with the partnership (as by engaging in a competitive business) or "self-deal" in partnership transactions without the consent of *all* the partners. If the partner does so, he or she will have to account to the partnership for any profits derived.

* * * [I]f all the partners have died and the personal representative of the last surviving partner is liquidating the partnership, the personal representative is a fiduciary as to the survivors of the deceased partners and their interests.

The many common law and statutory rules creating responsibility between and among partners are set out in detail in Ch. 22. These laws make partners jointly liable on all contract obligations of the partnership and jointly and severally liable for all partnership torts committed by co-partners within the ordinary scope of partnership business. Again, the law imposes obligation (i. e., responsibility) upon the partners to prevent them from taking advantage of each other.

The owners and representatives of a corporation also have substantial legal responsibilities to each other. To begin with, the law requires responsibility in use of the corporate form. By using the corporate method of doing business, the corporate entity is created separate and distinct from its shareholder owners. The corporate entity or "veil" serves as a shield to protect the shareholders from liability beyond the amount of their in-

vestments. However, the "veil" will operate only if the corporate business is conducted in good faith. If the corporation is being used to defraud creditors, the courts will pierce the "corporate veil" and hold the shareholders personally liable.

Also, corporate promoters are fiduciaries of each other and owe one another full disclosure regarding all formation activities. Promoters are also fiduciaries of the corporation itself, and must make full disclosure to an independent board of directors when selling property to the corporation or taking shares in return for services. A failure to disclose constitutes a fraud upon the corporation, and the law will permit rescission of the contract. Furthermore, if "watered stock" results (see Ch. 23), the promoters may be subject to criminal liability under state "Blue Sky" laws and federal securities laws. Shareholders of the corporation who suffer loss by reason of the promoters' activity may also recover damages.

Like promoters, directors and officers of a corporation are fiduciaries and are held to high standards of good faith and care in all matters relating to the corporate management.[4] The "corporate opportunity doctrine" prevents directors (and other insiders) from personally taking advantage of business opportunities that would be beneficial to the corporation. The Securities Exchange Act of 1934 also prohibits insiders from using any manipulative or deceptive device in connection with the purchase or sale of any security (Rule 10(b)–5) and from making "short swing" profits (Rule 16—where made, such profits will belong to the corporation so that all owners may share in the corporate successes).

The corporate directors may also breach their fiduciary duties to the owners of the corporation by refusing to declare dividends though a large surplus

---

4. Regarding foreign markets, the 1977 Foreign Corrupt Practices Act provides for up to a $1,000,000 fine on companies attempting to bribe foreign officials. (See chapter 24.)

has accumulated; the courts, in such case, may require payment of a dividend.

And the directors may be held criminally liable under state statutes making it a crime to knowingly be a party to false statements or entries in corporate records that present the corporation in a false financial light. Such laws protect shareholders as well as creditors.

The law further protects shareholders by providing them with pre-emptive rights so that they can preserve their respective positions of ownership when new stock is issued. Cumulative voting rights assure minority interests of representation on the board of directors. And shareholders may bring derivative suits if management refuses to act to protect the corporation.

Also, no major change in corporate structure by way of merger or consolidation can take place unless the shareholder-owners approve by a two-thirds majority vote; any shareholder who does not approve may demand that the corporation purchase his or her shares.

The law prohibits any absolute restriction on transfer of shares; and it provides that the majority shareholders have fiduciary responsibilities to the minority. Thus, the majority may not use its power to control the corporation so as to produce a profit for itself at the expense of the minority. Nor may the majority sell property to the corporation at inflated values or "freeze out" the minority by dissolving and reincorporating. The majority must exercise "inherent fairness" and provide equal opportunity to the minority when selling out its majority interest or exchanging its stock for shares in other corporations.

Finally, with regard to the issuance and sale of securities, the federal Securities Act of 1933 and the Securities Exchange Act of 1934, and state "Blue Sky" laws, impose substantial responsibilities on issuers of securities. These statutes require full and fair disclosure regarding the character of the securities sold and provide stiff penalties for failures to disclose and for offering and selling securities in fraud of the investing public. The specific requirements regarding "registration statements" and "prospectus" materials are set forth in detail in Ch. 24.

(2) *Suppliers.*

The relationship between a business and its suppliers is governed by three legal concepts: contracts, sales, and creditors' rights. The relationship is based, first of all, on a *contract* between the business and the supplier of inventory, supplies, equipment, or other items necessary to the business (Chapters 7 through 10). Usually, the contract involves a *sale of goods* under Article 2 of the Uniform Commercial Code (Chapters 17 through 19). And the goods are usually sold on *credit,* bringing into play creditors' rights, including prejudgment remedies, secured transactions, and the bulk sales rules (Chapters 26 and 27). Again, in this chapter, we can only mention some of the more important rules by way of indicating the many standards and principles that are built into common and statutory law requiring responsibility on the part of business in its dealings with suppliers.

You will recall from Ch. 7 that contracts are legally recognized promises or bargains made by two or more persons, including all rights and duties resulting from the promises or bargains. The purpose of contract law is to ensure that people will receive their reasonable expectations from the promises and bargains they enter into. It is important that people be able to plan and project, secure in the knowledge that their business dealings and agreements with others will be legally binding and enforceable. A valid contract requires four things—mutual assent, consideration, capacity, and legality. This in and of itself makes business responsible to its suppliers and suppliers responsible to their business customers. For the parties know when they are bound. Of course, sometimes, all four elements appear to be present, yet there is still no binding contract because of the presence of fraud, duress, undue influence, or mutual mistake. And even in the absence of such factors, a transaction may be so unfair and unconscionable that the courts will refuse to enforce it. The "unconscionability" doctrine is built into the Uniform Commercial Code at Section 2–302. Most of the cases under the Section involve an "adhesion contract" in which one of the parties was forced to adhere to the other's terms because of being in an inferior bargaining position; the party lacked any meaningful choice and agreed to terms that were unreasonably favorable to the other party. The *Official Comment* to Section 2–302 of the Uniform Commercial Code states:

> * * * The basic test is whether, in the light of the general commercial background and the commercial needs of the particular trade or case, the clauses involved are so one-sided as to be unconscionable under the circumstances existing at the time of the making of the contract. * * * The principle is one of the prevention of oppression and unfair surprise. The rules regarding fraud, duress, undue influence, unconscionability, etc., place increased responsibility on contracting parties so as to prevent people from being forced or tricked into binding obligations.

———

On the other hand, some contracts are enforced though bargain theory consideration (the usual form of consideration) is not present. Thus, a party who induces another to rely on a promise to his or her substantial economic detriment will be estopped from denying that consideration exists. This is the "promissory estoppel" substitute for bargain theory consideration. And under the principles of quasi-contract, responsibility or obligation may be imposed, despite a lack of bargain theory consideration, where one person has substantially and unjustly benefited at another's expense (e. g., as where a person mistakenly pays money or erroneously delivers goods to another who knows or has reason to know that a mistake has been made).

So you see, contract law and sales law impose great responsibility on the businessperson insofar as his or her dealings with suppliers are concerned. There are rules on illegal transactions; dealings with minors; performance and discharge of contract obligations; insurable interests and principles of indemnity in insurance contracts; risk of loss rules in sales of goods; buyers' and sellers' remedies when sales contracts are breached; and special responsibilities of carriers, warehousemen, and other bailees, etc. All these rules serve to make the businessperson responsible in dealing with suppliers. And running through all these transactions is the ever-present obligation of "good faith". Section 1–203 of the Uniform Commercial Code states that "every contract or duty * * * imposes an obligation of good faith in its performance or enforcement". And Section 2–103 provides that "good faith" in the case of a merchant means honesty in fact and the observance of reasonable commercial standards of fair dealing in the trade.

And if in the process of selling goods to a business, the supplier becomes a creditor, you know that there are extensive laws protecting the creditor and requiring responsibility from the businessperson-debtor. For example, the debtor cannot conceal or transfer his or her property so as to prevent creditors from satisfying legal claims. A transfer designed to delay, hinder, or defraud creditors is a "fraudulent conveyance" and is void and of no effect. Also, you will recall that bankruptcy law creates responsibility in the debtor with regard to his or her nonexempt assets. Chapters 11 and 13 of the federal Bankruptcy Act are concerned with "Debtor Rehabilitation": these chapters permit a debtor to work out a court-supervised plan with his or her creditors so as to reduce and pay off his or her debts.

Overall, it may be said that a large part of commercial law is devoted to controlling transactions between a business and its suppliers. The law obligates the parties on both sides of the transaction to responsibility and good faith dealing.

(3) Competitors.

You know from Ch. 25 that the social theory of laissez-faire (i. e., allowing business to compete without government interference or regulation) did not work. History showed that large businesses, left unregulated, took advantage of their positions to the detriment of smaller firms and consumers. As a result of anti-competitive behavior, some firms gained positions of monopoly with the result that consumers paid higher prices for poorer products. The federal government stepped in with antitrust laws to require responsibility in business competition. The Sherman Act of 1890 provides that monopolizing or attempting to monopolize is illegal if the result is to unreasonably restrain competition. Under the Sherman Act, the Clayton Act and other antitrust laws, the following practices are illegal: price-fixing, division of markets, group boycotts, resale price maintenance, tying agreements, and even exchanges of information among competitors with the purpose of fixing prices or dividing markets. Antitrust laws provide a powerful incentive for product innovation and development as well as incentive for reduced costs. The net effect of the laws is that no one seller or group of sellers acting together may exclude competitors

from the market or set profit levels by giving less and charging more. Fledgling businesses may thus compete with lower prices and better services or products or better selling activities and gain a foothold in the market. In placing responsibility on business for maintaining competitive markets, the antitrust laws benefit not only business but also society as a whole.

(4) Consumers.

Business also owes substantial responsibilities to consumers. In the area of contract law, business may not use fraud, duress, or unconscionable techniques to induce consumers to enter into contracts. A contract so induced is voidable to the consumer; and it may render the business liable in damages for tort (e. g., for misrepresentation). The fact that the consumer had little education, or that the seller used fine print contract forms or charged an excessive price (e. g., a price two or three times greater than the average retail price elsewhere) is strong evidence of unconscionability.

Contract law also prevents businesspeople from taking advantage of minors, mentally ill people, and other incompetent parties. In most states, the common law contract rules have been supplanted by unfair trade practice statutes.

Too, the Uniform Commercial Code protects a consumer who buys merchandise in good faith from a merchant who does not have title to the goods. Under the entruster rule, the merchant has power to transfer title to a good faith purchaser for value though the goods were originally entrusted to the merchant for a purpose other than sale. Along the same line, a person with voidable title to goods may transfer full title to a good faith purchaser for value.

Business also has considerable responsibility to consumers with regard to defective products. Under rules of negligence, warranty, and strict liability, the seller of a defective product is responsible in damages for any harm resulting from the defect. "Consumer protection" or responsibility is a relatively new legal concept. It was only in 1962 that President John F. Kennedy first enunciated the four basic consumer rights in his consumer message to Congress. These rights are:

(1) The right to safety—the right to be protected against the marketing of goods that are hazardous to health or life;

(2) The right to be informed—the right to be given sufficient facts to make an informed choice, and to be protected against fraudulent, deceitful, and grossly misleading advertising and labeling practices;

(3) The right to choose—the right to be provided access, wherever possible, to a variety of good quality products and services at fair, competitive prices; and

(4) The right to be heard—the right to be assured that consumer interests will receive full and sympathetic consideration in the formulation of government policy, and fair and speedy treatment in its administrative tribunals.

Since 1962, countless consumer protection statutes have been passed, one of the most important being the federal Consumer Credit Protection Act of 1968, also called "Truth-in-Lending". Truth-in-Lending requires full disclosure of annual interest rates and other finance charges on all consumer loans and credit buying, including the revolving charge accounts so often used by business. The full disclosure requirements apply to all business, whether banks, savings and loan associations, department stores, credit card issuers, automobile dealers, doctors, dentists, other professional people, etc.

Truth-in-Lending also limits a credit cardholder's liability to $50.00 on lost or stolen credit cards even where the consumer does not promptly notify the issuer of loss or unauthorized use of the card. And, in all cases, the cardholder's liability terminates upon notification of the loss to the issuer. Federal law also provides that unsolicited merchandise received in the mail may be used or disposed of with no legal obligation to the sender. (See Appendix A, *The American Legal Environment in a Nutshell,* for further discussion of consumer protection.)

Finally, business is responsible to consumers in the sense that it is responsible to third parties for torts committed by business employees while acting in the scope of their employment. The employer's responsibility flows from the doctrine of respondeat superior (see Ch. 20).

The penalties for business not meeting its obligations to consumers are so substantial that most businesspeople make every effort to carry out their responsibilities.

(5) *Employees.*

Business also owes considerable responsibility to employees. Workmen's Compensation Statutes in every state require business to pay into a fund to compensate employees who are injured on the job. More than a billion dollars of medical expenses are paid each year under Workmen's Compensation Statutes; and disability benefits are paid to workers who suffer disability and cannot return to work. Employer contributions to the fund are based on numbers and kinds of injuries so that business has a profit motive incentive in keeping work-related injury to a minimum. The result is that business takes protective measures to prevent injury to employees.

Also in every state, business must contribute to government operated funds set up for the protection of workers who become unemployed. Unemployment Compensation laws provide benefits for such workers; the laws require employer contributions as an obligation or responsibility of doing business.

What is more, the Fair Labor Standards Act (see Ch. 20) guarantees workers certain minimum employment standards including a minimum wage and a maximum length work week. The law also outlaws oppressive child labor. Along the same line, the Civil Rights Act of 1964 and the federal Age Discrimination in Employment Act of 1967 make it illegal to discriminate in employment on the basis of race, color, religion, sex, national origin, or age.

With regard to labor law, there are four federal labor law statutes (see Ch. 25) which prevent a business from interfering with its employees' efforts to self-organize (form unions) and bargain collectively. An employer may not use unfair labor practices to prevent employees from forming unions; nor may an employer discriminate in hiring in order to encourage or discourage union membership. And the statutes require a business to bargain with a labor organization that represents a majority of the employees in the bargaining unit.

(6) Members of society.

Business additionally owes responsibilities to members of the public who live in the area where the business operates. These responsibilities are set out in the thousands of statutory enactments dealing with the protection of our environment. Under these statutes, business must comply with rigid standards designed to prevent pollution of the air and water. Businesses that violate the standards may be fined or even closed down. In addition, private parties may bring actions based on nuisance, trespass, and negligence to stop business from polluting and to recover money damages. Where several parties are injured, they may bring a single "class action" suit (see Appendix A for further discussion of environmental law).

(7) Government.

Federal and state governments provide services for the people of this country in areas of defense, human resource programs (including health, income security, education, veterans benefits, and welfare) and physical resource programs (including agriculture and rural development, natural resources and environment, commerce and transportation, and community development and housing). The federal government alone spends over 500 billion dollars a year in these areas. About one-fifth of these dollars is obtained by the government through corporation taxes. And if the sole proprietorship and partnership methods of doing business are taken into account, business provides about 50% of all government tax dollars. Business must pay income taxes, property taxes on its real property (and on its business inventory in many communities), and frequently consumption taxes (customs, excise, sales, and use taxes—for a description of these taxes and how they are levied and collected, see Appendix A, *The American Legal Environment in a Nutshell*).

Thus, business not only provides livings for most of our people, it also furnishes the taxes that operate our government. Business must take care to maintain complete and accurate records so as to be able to meet its tax responsibilities. Penalties for failure to do so include fine and imprisonment.

What additional concept of law creates business responsibility?

In the previous section, we identified seven groups to whom business is legally responsible. To complete our picture of business responsibility, we must look now at a special concept of law that imposes further obligation on business—the concept of *commercial torts*. You will recall the definition of a "tort" from Ch. 1.

It says:

Any unreasonable interference with another's personal or property interests is called a legal "tort". Simply put, a "tort" is socially unreasonable conduct —conduct society will not tolerate— that adversely affects another's interest, causing personal loss or property loss. The legal concept of tort law is designed to measure the amount of loss sustained, and to equitably "adjust" the loss by providing compensation for the tort victim.

———

A "commercial tort" or "business tort" is socially unreasonable business conduct that adversely affects a consumer, competitor, or other party. As with any other tort, the injured party may sue the tortfeasor (the businessperson who commits the tort) for money damages.

The law recognizes seven specific "commercial torts" or business wrongs:

(1) *The commercial tort of infringing on another's trademark or tradename.*

You will recall the following discussion of trademarks and tradenames from Ch. 3.

It says:

According to the federal Lanham Act of 1946, a "trademark" is "any work, name, symbol, or device or any combination thereof adopted and used by a manufacturer or merchant to identify his goods and distinguish them from those manufactured or sold by others." Tradenames, on the other hand, do not identify the goods themselves, but rather, relate to the business or business goodwill.

An exclusive, 20 year right to use a trademark or tradename may be obtained by registering the mark or name

with the Patent Office in Washington, D.C. If the right is infringed, the owner may obtain a court ordered injunction in addition to money damages.

———

One reason the law protects trademarks and tradenames is to protect consumers. Symbols and names relating to products provide valuable product identification for consumers and prevent unscrupulous businesses from "palming off" their goods as products of another. The idea is to protect consumers from buying goods they do not intend to buy. Knowing the trademark or tradename of a product makes it easy for a retailer to provide continuity of product quality. And by reference to trademarks and tradenames, consumers can avoid buying products they have found to be unsatisfactory in the past.

The law also protects trademarks and tradenames to protect manufacturers. A manufacturer who produces a superior product can use a trademark or tradename to identify the product; the mark or name will obviously have great value to the manufacturer. When another business copies the mark or name, it not only confuses the public, but it causes loss to the business that owns the mark or name. Such copying constitutes socially unreasonable conduct and is a tort—a commercial tort—for which the owner of the mark or name may obtain money damages. Section 37 of the Lanham Act specifically provides for tort damages as follows.

The Act provides:

Section 35. When a violation of any right of the registrant of a mark registered in the patent office shall have been established in any civil action arising under this Act, the plaintiff shall be entitled * * * to recover

(1) defendant's profits,

(2) any damages sustained by the plaintiff, and

(3) the costs of the action.

* * *   In assessing damages the court may enter judgment, according to the circumstances of the case, for any sum above the amount found as actual damages, not exceeding three times such amount.

———

There are numerous examples in the law of the tort of infringing another's trademark or tradename. In Maier Brewing Co. v. Fleischmann Distilling Corp., 390 F.2d 117 (9th Cir. 1968), the plaintiff Fleischmann successfully sued the defendant Brewing Company for selling beer under the same name and label as the plaintiff sold scotch whiskey ("Black and White"). In Armco Steel Corp. v. International Armament Corp., 249 F. Supp. 954 (D.C.1966), Armco Steel brought suit when the defendant used the name "Interarmco" to describe its products. And in Safeway Stores, Inc. v. Safeway Quality Foods, Inc., 433 F.2d 99 (7th Cir. 1970), the plaintiff sued the defendant for using the same tradename "safeway".

In cases brought under Section 35 of the Lanham Act, the plaintiff seeks an order enjoining the defendant from further use of the trademark or tradename; an order requiring the defendant to destroy or deliver up any products or containers bearing such mark or name; a judgment for the defendant's profits obtained from such use; and judgment for treble damages (i. e., three times the damages sustained by the plaintiff) together with the costs of the action including attorney's fees.

(2) *The commercial tort of imitating product design or product packaging.*

You know from Ch. 3 that Congress has created a patent system under which an inventor can obtain a patent to his or her invention for a limited period of time (17 years). Anyone who infringes upon the patentee's right during this period is subject to court ordered injunction and damages under the U.S. patent laws.

But many times, it is not possible to patent an idea either because the idea is not something "new and never before used" or because it will not result in a "new and useful art, machine, manufacture, or composition of matter, or any new and useful improvement thereof." And, sometimes, an idea may simply be too costly to patent. Yet unpatented ideas are often very valuable and result in highly saleable products. However, because the products have not been patented, they may be copied.

It is well established in the law that copying unpatented products and selling the copies does not in and of itself constitute a tort. The social policy favoring business competition and the availability of competing products for consumers is held sufficient justification for allowing the copying and sale. However, while business may copy unpatented products, it may not intentionally "palm off" the copies as being the "original" manufactured items. A false representation that the goods are the originals rather than copies, which representation is likely to confuse or deceive the public, constitutes the tort of unfair competition for which injunctive relief and damages may be sought. However, it must be emphasized that the mere inability of the public to tell two identical items apart will not support an injunction against copying or an award of damages—there must be some false representation or intentional "palming off" of the items as the originals.

(3) *The commercial tort of misappropriating another's trade secret.*

To obtain patent protection, a patent applicant must make full disclosure of his or her invention to the U.S. Patent Office. Assuming the patent is granted, it will be available publicly for anyone to inspect. In contrast, a "trade secret" is protected and kept exclusive by means of keeping it secret from the public. The *Restatement of Torts,* Section 757, Comment (b), (1939), defines a "trade secret" as follows.

The Restatement provides:

A trade secret may consist of any formula, pattern, device or compilation of information which is used in one's business, and which gives him an opportunity to obtain an advantage over competitors who do not know or use it. It may be a formula for a chemical compound, a process of manufacturing, treating or preserving materials, a pattern for a machine or other device, or a list of customers.

Thus, almost any knowledge or information can be a trade secret. Frequently, an inventor must make a choice between patenting a process or protecting it as a trade secret. If he or she chooses the latter course, protection will exist only as long as the process remains a secret.

The law provides limited protection for trade secrets. A business has responsibility not to *wrongfully* appropriate another's trade secrets, as by stealing them, or inducing an employee or former employee of the other to wrongfully divulge the secrets. A wrongful appropriation will render the taker liable in tort damages. However, there is no liability where a business *rightfully* discovers another's trade secrets as by independently developing the same ideas, or studying the other party's marketed products. Once a product is placed on the market, anyone is free to look at it, reverse engineer it, take it apart, figure it out, and copy it. Remember, a trade secret is protected only so long as it remains secret.

However, substantial—not absolute—secrecy is all that is required. A business possessing a trade secret may entrust it to any number of individuals as long as the disclosure is made pursuant to an obligation of trust and confidence. For example, an employee has fiduciary duties to his or her employer by reason of the employment contract and may not divulge the employer's trade secrets. And, frequently, the employment contract expressly prohibits the employee from disclosing trade secrets upon leaving the employment. As you know from Ch. 9, such an agreement will be enforced by the courts unless it constitutes an unreasonable restraint on trade. In each case, the courts must balance the employer's interest in maintaining the secrecy of customer lists and other information with the employee's interest in using his or her job-learned skills in making a living.

Beyond prohibiting the "palming off" of copies as originals, and imposing liability for wrongfully appropriating another's trade secrets, the law favors full disclosure of ideas and inventions in order that competition may be fostered. True, the patent law grants a 17 year monopoly but *only* in return for free availability and use of the invention at the end of the 17 year period.

(4) *The commercial tort of misrepresentation and false advertising.*

You will recall from Ch. 8 that the presence of fraud will vitiate or prevent mutual assent, making a contract voidable.

It was stated in that chapter:

Fraud * * * requires four things:

(1) A material misrepresentation;

(2) Intent on the part of the party making the misrepresentation that the other party rely on it;

(3) Justifiable reliance by the other party (it would not be justifiable, for example, to rely upon a state-

ment one knows to be false); and

(4) Inducement of the agreement by the misrepresentation (i. e., the misrepresentation must prompt the party to enter into the transaction).

* * *

Modernly, all courts permit avoidance on the basis of fraud * * * where the misrepresentation is made with * * * *actual* knowledge or *imputed* knowledge. A party has actual knowledge who makes a misrepresentation intentionally or knowingly; a party has imputed or chargeable knowledge who makes a misrepresentation negligently because of a careless failure to discover the statement's truth or falsity. A growing number of courts even go so far as to provide a legal remedy on a strict liability basis for a completely *innocent* misrepresentation that is made unintentionally and without carelessness of any kind.

* * *

A person induced to enter into a contract because of the fraudulent misrepresentation of another has what is termed a "voidable" agreement. This means that the party has an election of remedies: he or she may either rescind the contract and seek restitution, or he or she may affirm the contract and request money damages.

* * *

In order to recover money damages, a party who elects to affirm a contract induced by fraud must bring a legal action in court for the tort involved * * *. A "tort" is any socially unreasonable conduct, and this certainly includes misrepresentation. Where the misrepresentation is intentionally made with knowledge of its falsity, either by written or spoken word or by active concealment of the truth, the tort involved is the tort of "deceit." Where the misrepresentation is based on a careless failure to discover the falsity of the representation, the tort at issue is "negligence" (see Ch. 1 for the four elements required in order to prove any negligent action). Generally speaking, only a party who is in the business of supplying information for the guidance of others (e. g., an accountant, stock broker, lawyer, or the like) will be held responsible in money damages for his or her negligent misrepresentations.

As for a completely innocent misrepresentation (one that is unintentional and nonnegligent), a growing number of courts hold the speaker liable in damages on a "strict liability" basis, particularly where the misstatement is made in connection with the sale of a chattel.

———

In the area of commercial torts, false advertising that results in the purchase of goods will serve as the basis for a tort action based on misrepresentation. Of course, the misrepresentation must be of a material fact—something more than mere "puffing" of wares or a statement of opinion. And the buyer must rely on the false advertising in making the purchase. If the buyer was unaware of the advertising or did not rely on it (e. g., because he or she didn't believe it), there can be no recovery. The misrepresentation may be found in national advertising or on labels on the goods themselves.

Besides purchasers, competitors may also have a tort action against a business that falsely advertises; to recover, a competitor must show that the false advertising diverted customers away from his or her business.

(5) *The commercial tort of product defamation, producer defamation, or invasion of privacy.*

A businessperson may lawfully promote his or her product by critically comparing it to another's. However, the comparison must be honest and accurate. False assertions about another's product, made with intent to injure the other's business, constitute the tort of *disparagement*. Disparagement is similar to false advertising in that it involves giving false information to potential customers. It differs from false advertising in that the false statements are made about another's product and not one's own. A businessperson who disparages the quality, purity, or value of another's product is liable in tort for any pecuniary damage directly caused by the disparagement. If the false statements also defame the other party in the operation of his or her trade or business (by imputing dishonesty, fraud, deception, or other misconduct to the party so as to reflect poorly on his or her business character or reputation), the businessperson may additionally be liable for libel or slander (see Appendix A, *The American Legal Environment in a Nutshell,* for a discussion of libel and slander).

With regard to the right of privacy, using another's name, portrait, or picture without his or her consent for purposes of trade or advertising constitutes a tortious invasion of the party's right of privacy and is compensable in damages as a commercial tort. A person's right to the exclusive use of his or her own name, portrait, or picture for these purposes is often referred to as a "right of publicity". The case of Haelan Laboratories, Inc. v. Topps Chewing Gum, Inc., 202 F.2d 866, 868 (2nd Cir. 1953) stated it this way.

The Court stated:

This right might be called a "right of publicity". For it is common knowledge that many prominent persons (especially actors and ballplayers), far from having their feelings bruised through public exposure of their likenesses, would feel sorely deprived if they no longer received mon-

ey for authorizing advertisements, popularizing their countenances, displayed in newspapers, magazines, buses, trains, and subways. This right of publicity would usually yield them no money unless it could be made the subject of an exclusive grant which barred any other advertiser from using their pictures.

---

(6) *The commercial "prima facie" tort, including interference with contractual relations and interference with prospective advantage.*

Competition is inherently desirable within our economic system because it makes for better products at reduced costs. A person may be such a successful competitor that others simply cannot compete, and, generally, there is nothing tortious in this. But where the sole purpose of the competition is to use economic advantage to destroy the livelihood of another, it is a social wrong within the meaning of tort law—it is "unfair competition". And business has a responsibility to compete fairly. For example, in the famous case of Tuttle v. Buck, 107 Minn. 145, 119 N.W. 946 (1909), a banker set up a barber shop with the sole purpose of putting the local barber out of business. The court held that the banker had committed an actionable tort.

The court stated:

[The] defendant is possessed of large means, and is engaged in the business of a banker in said village of Howard Lake * * * and is nowise interested in the occupation of a barber; yet in the pursuance of the wicked, malicious, and unlawful purpose * * *, and for the sole and only purpose of injuring the trade of the plaintiff, and of accomplishing his purpose and threats of ruining the plaintiff's said business and driving him out of said village, the defendant fitted up and furnished a barber shop in said village for conducting the trade of barbering * * * said defendant * * * hired two barbers in succession for a stated salary, paid by him, to occupy said shop * * * with the sole design of injuring the plaintiff, and of destroying his said business, and not for the purpose of serving any legitimate interest of his own * * * and * * * to the plaintiff's damage in the sum of $10,-000.

* * * [W]hen a man starts an opposition place of business, not for the sake of profit to himself, but regardless of loss to himself, and for the sole purpose of driving his competitor out of business, and with the intention of himself retiring upon the accomplishment of his malevolent purpose, he is guilty of wanton wrong and an actionable tort.

———

Though the defendant's conduct in the *Tuttle* case did not fall within any established classification of tort, the court held that his conduct was "prima facie" (on its face) tortious. Remember, a tort is any socially unreasonable conduct; and any intentional act that is solely designed to damage another's property or trade is socially unreasonable and tortious whether or not it fits within any established tort classification. In the case of Ledwith v. International Paper Co., 64 N.Y. S.2d 810 (1946), the defendant acted from malicious motives to prevent the plaintiff from receiving an increase in pay, then to have the plaintiff demoted and later discharged. The court imposed liability on the defendant, stating that his conduct was a "prima facie" tort.

Two specific kinds of unfair or "prima facie" tortious competition are *interference with contractual relations* and *interference with prospective advantage*. A person interferes with a party's contrac-

tual relations when he or she intentionally causes a third party to breach an existing contract with the party. Thus, a person who induces a skilled worker to breach his or her employment contract has interfered with the employer's contractual relations and is liable in damages. The same is true of a retailer who persuades a supplier to breach a contract with another retailer so as to provide him or her with a commodity in short supply: the first retailer has interfered with the other's contractual relations and is liable to the party in damages.

A person interferes with another's prospective advantage when he or she intentionally deprives that other of an economic advantage that the person would otherwise have. This would include inducing another not to enter into a contract with the party. But the examples go far beyond this. In one case, the defendant destroyed the only bridge over to an island; this had the effect of severely injuring the plaintiff's business (i. e., depriving him of an economic advantage). In another case, the defendant fraudulently precipitated the plaintiff's election defeat. In still another case, a defendant telegraph company failed to deliver a message inviting the plaintiff to enter into an advantageous contract. Any method of unfair competition that results in a loss of profits may constitute interference with prospective advantage: a breach of trust, a boycott, an illegal conspiracy, threats or intimidation—all may be tortious within the meaning of "prima facie" tort.

(7) *Commercial tort action based on violation of antitrust law.*

In Ch. 25, we studied antitrust law, with emphasis on the Sherman Act, Clayton Act, and Federal Trade Commission Act. Two of these statutes, the Sherman Act and Clayton Act, provide a civil remedy in tort for private persons who are injured by violations of the Acts. The

Sherman Act makes illegal " * * * every contract, combination in the form of trust or otherwise or conspiracy, in restraint of trade or commerce among the several states or with foreign nations." The Statute also outlaws any attempt to restrain trade, stating that violators include " * * * every individual who shall monopolize, or attempt to monopolize or combine or conspire with any other person or persons, to monopolize any part of the trade or commerce among the several states or with foreign nations." The Sherman Act contains the following enforcement provisions:

(1) Any person who violates the law is subject to criminal prosecution for a misdemeanor and upon conviction to a fine not exceeding $5,000 or imprisonment not exceeding one year or both;

(2) The government has power to enjoin violations of the Act;

(3) Property in transit in interstate commerce is subject to forfeiture to the United States if it is subject to any contract or conspiracy violative of the Sherman Act; and

(4) A private party who is injured by a violation of the Act may bring suit against the violator and recover treble damages (i. e., three times the amount of damages sustained).

The Clayton Act specifically outlaws price discrimination, tying agreements, corporate acquisitions, and membership on more than one board of directors where the effect is to substantially lessen competition. As with the Sherman Act, anyone injured by a violation of the Clayton Act may sue the guilty party for treble damages.

Most of the specific commercial torts described in this section would also violate the Sherman Act permitting the injured party (the tort victim) to sue under the federal statute for treble damages.

For example, in Perryton Wholesale, Inc. v. Pioneer Distributing Co. of Kansas, Inc., 353 F.2d 618 (10th Cir. 1965), the court held that enticing away a competitor's employees not only amounts to unfair competition, but is also a violation of the Sherman Act. Even conduct inspired for political or social reasons may violate the antitrust laws if it affects commercial activity. For example, in McBeath v. Inter-American Citizens for Decency Committee, 374 F.2d 359 (5th Cir. 1967), the defendant diverted customers from the plaintiff's business to make a political point; the court held that the defendant had violated the antitrust laws and awarded the plaintiff treble damages. And in Bratcher v. Akron Area Bd. of Realtors, 381 F.2d 723 (6th Cir. 1967), the court held that the defendant's efforts to prevent blacks from owning or renting property in white neighborhoods also violated the antitrust laws, again entitling the plaintiff to treble damages.

What is the Uniform Deceptive Trade Practices Act?

Several states have adopted the Uniform Deceptive Trade Practices Act which allows individuals to obtain an injunction against a number of deceptive trade practices.

Section 3(a) of the Act provides:

A person likely to be damaged by a deceptive trade practice of another may be granted an injunction against it * * * . Proof of monetary damage, loss of profits, or intent to deceive is not required. Relief granted for the copying of an article is limited to the prevention of confusion or misunderstanding as to source.

———

Section 3(b) of the Statute defines "deceptive trade practices" as follows:

A person engages in a deceptive trade practice when, in the course of his business, vocation, or occupation, he:

(1) passes off goods or services as those of another;

(2) causes likelihood of confusion or of misunderstanding as to the source, sponsorship, approval, or certification of goods or services;

(3) causes likelihood of confusion or of misunderstanding as to affiliation, connection, or association with, or certification by, another;

(4) uses deceptive representations or designations of geographic origin in connection with goods or services;

(5) represents that goods or services have sponsorship, approval, characteristics, ingredients, uses, benefits or quantities that they do not have or that a person has a sponsorship, approval, status, affiliation, or connection that he does not have;

(6) represents that goods are original or new if they are deteriorated, altered, reconditioned, reclaimed, used or second-hand;

(7) represents that goods or services are of a particular standard, quality, or grade, or that goods are of a particular style or model, if they are of another;

(8) disparages the goods, services, or business of another by false or misleading representation of fact;

(9) advertises goods or services with intent not to sell them as advertised;

(10) advertises goods or services with intent not to supply reasonably expectable public demand, unless the advertisement discloses a limitation of quantity;

(11) makes false or misleading statements of fact concerning the existence of, or amounts of price reductions; or

(12) engages in any other conduct which similarly creates a likelihood of confusion or of misunderstanding.

In addition to injunctive relief, some of the state statutes provide criminal penalties for engaging in deceptive trade practices (and, of course, any of these acts may also constitute a commercial tort providing the injured party with a civil action for money damages).

Overall, and in conclusion, we see that the law—common, statutory, and administrative—imposes tremendous responsibility on business. The legal consequences of being irresponsible are severe for a business—the payment of money damages, the loss of profits, bankruptcy, the payment of a fine, or even going to jail. The result is that business remains responsible most of the time.

PART II

THE LEGAL RESPONSIBILITY OF ACCOUNTANTS: THE DUTIES AND LIABILITIES OF CPA'S

What is the basic responsibility of a public accountant?

Perhaps the key word in describing the role of a public accountant is the word "independent". The work of the public accountant in *independently* examining, verifying, and certifying business accounts and financial data and statements makes it possible for the private enterprise system to function. The private enterprise system is based on the continuing confidence of investors and creditors in the reliability of such statements.

A public accountant is responsible not only to the client who pays his or her fee, but also to investors, creditors, and other members of the public who rely on his or her reports. As you know, the federal securities laws impose both civil and criminal liability on auditors for certain failures of responsibility. To help guide accountants, the American Institute of Certified Public Accountants (AICPA) promulgates "generally accepted accounting principles" (GAAP) and "generally accepted auditing standards" (GAAS). However, the Securities and Exchange Commission (SEC), which administers the securities laws, takes the position that the auditor's obligation goes beyond the GAAP and GAAS. The SEC states that it is the auditor's duty to (1) detect any gross overstatement of assets and profits, and (2) to communicate the results of his or her audit so that even lay investors (people without accounting training) can make meaningful investment decisions.

The courts agree with the SEC, stating that the test is not simply whether GAAP and GAAS have been followed, but whether the financial statements, data, and disclosures tell the investor what he or she needs to know in order to make a meaningful decision regarding whether or not to invest. If they do not, the accountant may be liable despite the fact that he or she has complied with GAAP or GAAS. Judge MacMahon stated it this way in the case of Hertzfeld v. Laventhol, Krekstein, Horwath & Horwath, CCH Fed.Sec.L.Rep. #94,574 (S.D.N.Y. 1974):

Much has been said by the parties about generally accepted accounting principles and the proper way for an accountant to report real estate transactions. We think this misses the point. Our inquiry is properly focused not on whether Laventhol's report satisfies esoteric accounting norms, comprehensible only to the initiate, but whether the report fairly presents the true financial position of Firestone, as of November 30, 1969, to the untutored eye of an ordinary investor.

It may be concluded that the courts will not hesitate to require a higher standard than GAAP or GAAS, particularly where the investing public is reading and relying on the accountant's financial data and reports.

Three types of improper accounting that can result in both civil and criminal liability are "artful accounting", "creative accounting", and "salami accounting". "Artful accounting" refers to the incomplete disclosure of information or the hiding of information so that an investor or creditor looking at the financial report is not likely to see it. An important disclosure may be buried in a footnote, or it may be phrased in such sophisticated financial terminology that a lay person (one not educated in accounting) cannot understand it. For example, saying that certain customers' accounts are "subject to realization" may be an artful way of saying that they are uncollectible.

"Creative accounting" means structuring transactions so as to create a false picture of financial health (e. g., creating "paper profits" through transactions with your own subsidiaries).

Finally, "salami accounting" is taking up a past accounting error gradually over future periods so as to prevent immediate full disclosure of the error (the error is said to be "sliced very thin" and taken up gradually into the financial picture so as not to distort "the mainfare").

Because public accounting is important to the economic system and affects the public welfare, it is regulated by statute in all states. For example, all states regulate use of the title "certified public accountant" (CPA). To become a CPA an accountant must pass a 24-hour exam prepared and graded by the American Institute of Certified Public Accountants The exam contains two parts on accounting practice, and one part each on accounting theory, auditing, and business law. Many states additionally require an accountant to have from 1 to 6 years of accounting experience and/or a college degree in specified courses to become a CPA. And an increasing number of states require continuing education as a condition to continued licensing of CPA's.

The American Institute of Certified Public Accountants regulates its membership with the Code of Professional Ethics. The courts look upon these rules as minimum standards required of all public accountants. Because they are minimum standards, the courts and the Securities and Exchange Commission are free to impose additional standards with regard to financial data and statements submitted in connection with the federal securities laws.

Whether civil or criminal liability is at issue, the courts are involved in regulating the accounting profession. In determining an accountant's liability, it is necessary to look at:

(1) The CPA's responsibility to his or her client;

(2) The CPA's responsibility to third parties; and

(3) the CPA's potential criminal liability.

What is the CPA's responsibility to his or her client?

The CPA's responsibility to his or her client is based on the *contract* between the parties. The CPA is an independent contractor who promises to perform certain services for a fee. The CPA's duty under the contract is to perform the services properly and with due care. For example, a contract to perform an audit implies duties to verify the cash, confirm accounts receivable, check the physical inventories, and follow generally accepted

accounting principles (GAAP) and standards (GAAS).[5] If the CPA fails to carry out these duties properly and with due care, the CPA not only breaches the contract but also commits the tort of negligence (malpractice).

And it may make a difference whether a client brings an action based on contract versus tort. For example, contract damages are designed to put the parties in the positions they would have been in had the contract been carried out (subject to the rule of remoteness). Tort damages for negligence, on the other hand, include any damages proximately caused by the breach of duty, and, if gross negligence is involved, may even include punitive damages. Also, the statute of limitations time period for bringing suit generally differs for contract and tort actions. It should be pointed out that the problem has been obviated under modern pleading statutes which allow a plaintiff to sue for both breach of contract and the tort of negligence in one legal action.

An accountant's responsibility to his or her client may be summarized as follows:

(1) The standard of care required of an accountant is that of an average accountant performing his or her work with reasonable care. An accountant is not an insurer or guarantor and is not liable for an honest error in judgment, assuming reasonable care has been exercised. However, reasonable care means more than simply verifying the arithmetical accuracy of a client's financial data and statements. The accountant must inquire into the *substantial accuracy* of the data, using reasonable care and skill in making inquiries and investigations. Also, the accountant's own accounting procedures and mathematical computations must be *substantially accurate*; if they are not, this shows a lack of due care. In addition, the accountant must not certify material that he or she knows to be inaccur-

---

5. The CPA should avoid relying on oral understandings with clients. Understand- ings should be stated in writing in what is ordinarily termed an "engagement letter."

ate. And the accountant must use reasonable care and skill in forming his or her opinion about the material's accuracy. This is not to say that an auditor must approach his or her work with suspicion —an auditor is a "watchdog", not a "bloodhound"—but merely that he or she must use more care if his or her suspicions are aroused.

Along the same line, an accountant is not strictly liable for discovering fraud, but a negligent failure to uncover fraud will result in liability (e. g., where the fraud is undetected because of the accountant's failure to follow GAAP or GAAS).

(2) An auditor has a duty to *communicate* the information obtained from his or her audit to the client (and to any third parties the auditor knows will rely on the information). While a CPA is an independent contractor, he or she has contract duties of loyalty and honesty to the client. Thus, if the CPA discovers that fraud exists, he or she has a duty to disclose this fact to the client.

(3) An accountant who is being sued by a client for negligence may assert the client's contributory negligence as a defense to liability (e. g., a client who fails to follow his or her accountant's advice or refuses to allow the accountant to perform necessary procedures may be guilty of contributory negligence).

(4) An accountant who materially breaches a contract with a client is not entitled to any fee and may be sued by the client for breach of contract and/or the tort of negligence. If the breach is willful or grossly negligent, the client may recover punitive damages in the tort action (such damages are not recoverable in a breach of contract action).

If the breach is minor (e. g., a minor error or inaccuracy in the report), the account will still be entitled to a fee, but the client may "set-off" reasonable damages from the amount owing.

(5) Apart from negligence, an accountant will be liable for the intentional tort of deceit if he or she actively deceives the client or shows a reckless disregard for the truth (i. e., gross negligence bordering on intentional deceit). An example of "reckless disregard" would be failing to carry out a vital procedure such as bank reconciliation. The accountant, in this case, may be sued not only for actual damages but also for punitive damages.

(6) Where the accountant dies or becomes disabled and is unable to perform the contract, the contract obligations of both parties are discharged. The contract calls for services of a personal nature and it would be objectively impossible for anyone else to perform.

(7) To avoid liability to third parties when doing "unaudited" financial statements or mere "write-up" work (bookkeeping functions or creating basic financial records), an accountant must make it clear: (1) that the work is not based on an audit; (2) that it is for the internal use of the client only; and (3) that the accountant expresses no opinion about the substantial accuracy of the work. Under AICPA standards, an accountant is associated with any unaudited financial statements or write-up work he or she prepares whether the work is on plain paper or letterhead. To disclaim liability to third parties, the accountant must mark each page of the work "unaudited" and must make a disclaimer of opinion either on the work itself or on a separate sheet. Where a financial statement is prepared on an accountant's letterhead without any qualifications, anyone using the material can assume it is the result of an audit and impose liability on this basis.

Even with unaudited financial statements or write-up work, the accountant is still under a duty of loyalty and honesty to the client and must disclose any information (e. g., evidence of fraud) resulting from the work.

(8) With regard to tax work, a CPA must sign any tax return that he or she prepares whether or not he or she receives a fee for the work. However, the CPA must not sign until he or she is completely satisfied that all relevant information has been provided and all relevant questions have been answered. The following preparer's declaration is found on a tax return, and the CPA must not modify the declaration.

It provides:

> Under penalties of perjury, I declare that I have examined this return, including accompanying schedules and statements, and to the best of my knowledge and belief, it is true, correct, and complete. Declaration of preparer (other than taxpayer) is based on all information of which preparer has any knowledge.

In signing a tax return, a CPA need not provide a disclaimer of opinion for unaudited data or the like: a tax return is not a financial statement, and the preparer's signature does not constitute an opinion as to the taxpayer's financial condition or the accuracy of his or her financial statements.

However, if the CPA is negligent in preparing the return, or fails to file it on time, he or she will be liable for malpractice and will have to pay any penalties and interest assessed by the government.

Incorrect tax advice will also result in liability for negligence (malpractice). For example, in the case of Rassieur v. Charles, 354 Mo. 117, 188 S.W.2d 817 (1945), an accountant incorrectly advised his client that she had realized a taxable profit on the sale of certain securities and should sell certain other securities so as to create a tax loss before the end of the year. The client had, in fact, incurred a tax loss on sale of the securities and suffered increased loss as a result of selling the additional securities. The court ruled that the accountant was liable for the difference in the sales price of the stock and its repurchase price when the correct facts came to light.

An accountant who discovers that he or she has given incorrect tax advice has a duty to advise the client of the error immediately. An accountant who is performing continuous services for a client also has a duty to inform the client of any changes in the law affecting previous tax advice (an accountant who is not performing continuous services is not expected to follow up with changes in the law when the contract relationship with the client no longer exists).

(9) At common law, there exists no accountant-client privilege (like that of a doctor-patient, attorney-client, priest-penitent, etc.) that may be invoked by a client to prevent disclosure of his or her communications to the account. Thus, if an accountant is subpoenaed to testify in state or federal court about a client's communications, the accountant may not refuse to testify the way that a doctor, lawyer, or priest may refuse with regard to the communications of a patient, client, or penitent. The reasoning here is that it is not in the public interest to impede the courts in the administration of justice by preventing them from calling accountants as witnesses.

However, 15 states and Puerto Rico [6] have passed statutes creating a limited accountant-client privilege, including Arizona, Colorado, Florida, Georgia, Illinois, Iowa, Kentucky, Louisiana, Maryland, Michigan, Missouri, Nevada, New Mexico, Pennsylvania, and Tennessee. The statutes vary in many respects. Some cover all public accountants, while others cover only CPA's; some apply to all accounting sources, while others are restricted in coverage. Some do not apply to criminal cases or bankruptcy proceedings. All are alike in that they pro-

---

6. Notice that there is no accountant-client privilege in any federal court other than in Puerto Rico.

tect only communications that are *intended* to be confidential.[7]

The Rules of Ethics of the American Institute of Certified Public Accountants prohibits the disclosure of confidential client data unless: (1) the client consents; (2) the disclosure is necessary to avoid violation of generally accepted accounting principles (GAAP) or standards (GAAS); (3) the disclosure is in response to an enforceable subpoena from a state or federal court (and there is no statute creating an accountant-client privilege); or (4) the disclosure is in response to an inquiry made by the Ethics Division or Trial Board of the AICPA or any state CPA or other regulatory agency.

It is interesting to note that a taxpayer may refuse to surrender his or her tax records and documents to a court of law or other investigatory authority on the basis of the 5th and 14th Amendment privilege against self-incrimination. However, the privilege does not apply if the taxpayer entrusts the records or documents to a third party such as an accountant, and the third party may not withhold possession on the basis of the taxpayer's privilege.

Finally, it should be pointed out that an accountant *may not* retain client records in order to enforce payment of a fee.

(10) An accountant's "working papers" belong to the accountant, and not to the client. The American Institute of Certified Public Accountants defines "working papers" in the following language:

Working papers are the records kept by the independent auditor of the procedures he followed, the tests he performed, the information he obtained, and the conclusions he reached pertinent to his examination. Working papers, accordingly, may include work programs, analyses, memoranda, letters of confirmation and representation, abstracts of company documents, and schedules of commentaries prepared or obtained by the auditor [from Statement of Auditing Standards No. 1, p. 68 AICPA guidelines].

However, an accountant's ownership of "working papers" is basically custodial, and the accountant may not transfer the papers to a third party without the client's consent. Nor may the accountant turn over the papers to a government agency (e. g., the Internal Revenue Service) without the client's consent unless in response to an enforceable subpoena. The accountant has a duty to keep the information contained in the papers confidential. Thus, before selling his or her accounting practice, an accountant must obtain his or her clients' permission to transfer their working papers.

Where a partner in an accounting firm dies, the working papers of the firm belong to the surviving partners. The working papers of a deceased sole proprietor accountant, on the other hand, must be destroyed once the deceased's estate has no further need for them.

(11) Internal accounting and auditing manuals developed by an accounting firm are considered "trade secrets" under the law and a court will require their production only upon a showing by the plaintiff of some actual need or necessity for the manuals in the case before the court. In the case of Rosen v. Dick, CCH Fed.L. Rep. #94,989 (1975) the court held that the plaintiff had made such a showing.

The court stated:

The internal accounting and auditing manuals of Andersen are properly termed "trade secrets". Clearly, they are carefully protected internally and are the product of much effort on the part of Andersen.

---

7. Furthermore, only the client can invoke the privilege (it is for his or her protection); the accountant cannot.

However, in this case, I think a showing of necessity has been made. In order to show fraud or negligence, even measured against generally accepted accounting practices, plaintiff must establish by a preponderance of the evidence that Andersen's actions did not meet that standard. It will be necessary for plaintiff to be aware of these procedures to conduct a meaningful deposition of the accountants who worked on the audits in question. Evidence that is acquired from those depositions will have a direct bearing on the outcome of the case. I find sufficient need, therefore, to overcome the trade secret barrier, protected, of course, by the proper restrictive order.

————

(12) An accountant who performs auditing services is generally covered by a fidelity bond purchased through a surety company. Usually, an accountant also carries malpractice insurance to cover losses resulting from negligence (e. g., losses resulting from the auditor's negligent failure to discover fraud). In many cases, if the surety company has to pay on the fidelity bond it will be entitled to reimbursement from the accountant's malpractice insurance. Typically, the surety company has a right to reimbursement for loss resulting from the accountant's dishonest, criminal, or grossly negligent acts but not for loss resulting from his or her ordinary negligence.

Frequently, a client carries insurance against embezzlement within his or her company. If the insurer has to pay for a loss, the insurer will be subrogated (see Ch. 11) to the rights of the insured against the embezzler and any other party who contributed to the loss. Thus, if the insured's accountant negligently failed to discover the embezzlement, the insurer will have a right (the insured's right) to sue the accountant and recover for the negligence.

What is the CPA's responsibility to third parties?

In addition to an accountant's client, many third parties also rely on the accountant's reports, including creditors, suppliers, investors, and regulatory agencies. The accountant's liability to such third parties for negligence or fraud in preparing for reports is summarized below.

(1) *Negligence.* Whether a third party can hold an accountant liable for ordinary negligence depends on the relationship existing between the accountant and the third party. The early rule was that a third party could recover from an accountant for ordinary negligence only if the third party was identified as the *primary beneficiary* of the audit contract. In other words, the accountant had to know prior to submitting the work that it was being done *primarily* for the benefit of a particular, *identified* third party. Justice Cardozo, speaking for the court in Ultramares Corp. v. Touche, 255 N.Y. 170, 174 N.E. 441 (1931), stated that an accountant should not be held liable "in an indeterminate amount for an indeterminate time to an indeterminate class" for losses that are the result of ordinary negligence.

The modern rule, stated in the case of Ryan v. Kanne, 170 N.W.2d 395 (Iowa, 1969), is that a third party can recover from an accountant for ordinary negligence, whether or not the third party was identified as the *primary* beneficiary of the contract, so long as the accountant knew that the reports were intended for the use or guidance of a third party and the third party was identified before the accountant submitted the reports. In the *Ryan* case, the CPA's had orally guaranteed the accuracy of "accounts payable" within $5,000; the accounts were off by more than $20,000. Though no third party had been identified as the *primary* beneficiary of the contract, the accountants knew that particular third parties would be using and relying on the report in deciding whether or not to invest in the client's business. Judgment was awarded against the accountants for some $30,000 despite their contention that the third parties were not parties to the contract.

The court stated:

When the accountant is aware that the balance sheet to be prepared is to be used by a certain party or parties who will rely thereon in extending credit or in assuming liability for obligations of the party audited, the lack of privity should be no valid defense to claim for damages due to the accountant's negligence. We know of no good reason why accountants should not accept the legal responsibility to known third parties who reasonably rely upon financial statements prepared and submitted by them.

———

The trend in the law is to carry the accountant's potential liability for ordinary negligence still further and hold him or her responsible even to *unidentified* third parties so long as:

(1) The accountant knew the reports would be used by third parties;

(2) The accountant had knowledge of the *class* of users (e. g., banks) and the *type of transaction* (e. g., loans) contemplated; and

(3) The third party who suffers the loss is a member of the *class* and he or she relied on the reports in entering into the contemplated *transaction.*

(2) *Fraud.* The general rule stated in the *Ultramares* case (see above) is that an accountant is liable for fraudulent or deceitful reports to any and all third parties who rely upon the reports to their loss. The third parties do not have to be intended users, and they do not have to

be identified (compare this with the accountant's liability to third parties for ordinary negligence).

As used here, fraud encompasses not only intentional deceit but also reckless misstatement or omission of facts (gross negligence). Fraud based on gross negligence is referred to as "constructive" fraud. An example would be certifying financial statements without any basis for a belief in their accuracy. In State Street Trust Co. v. Ernst, 278 N.Y. 104, 15 N. E.2d 416 (1938), the court stated:

Accountants, however, may be liable to third parties, even where there is lacking deliberate or active fraud. A representation certified as true to the knowledge of the accountants when knowledge there is none, a reckless misstatement, or an opinion based on grounds so flimsy as to lead to the conclusion that there was no genuine belief in its truth, are all sufficient upon which to base liability. A refusal to see the obvious, a failure to investigate the doubtful, if sufficiently gross, may furnish evidence leading to an inference of fraud so as to impose liability for losses suffered by those who rely on the balance sheet. In other words, heedlessness and reckless disregard of consequence may take the place of deliberate intention.

In *Ultramares* * * * we said with no uncertainty that negligence, if gross, or blindness, even though not equivalent to fraud, was sufficient to sustain an inference of fraud. Our exact words were: "In this connection we are to bear in mind the principle already stated in the course of this opinion that negligence or blindness, even when not equivalent to fraud, is none the less evidence to sustain an inference of fraud. At least this is so if the negligence is gross.

———

Remember that when fraud or constructive fraud is proved, the accountant is liable to anyone who suffered loss as a result of the fraud.

(3) In most states, an accountant who incurs liability to third parties has a right of contribution against any parties who wrongfully helped cause the loss (e. g., the client or other party).

(4) Where two or more accountants audit portions of the same report, the report must clearly indicate who bears responsibility for which part of the work. And an accountant may not rely on the unaudited data of another accountant where the data could materially affect his or her opinion as to the total financial statement or report. If the accountant does rely on the data, he or she must *disclaim* an opinion or face liability to third parties for making statements without knowledge or in reckless disregard of the truth.

(5) The trend in the law is to hold an accountant responsible for notifying parties known to be relying on his or her completed reports of any information that subsequently comes to light, making the reports inaccurate or misleading.

(6) *The Securities Act of 1933.* As you know from Ch. 24, the Securities Act of 1933 (the "truth in securities" law) regulates initial sales of securities to the public in interstate commerce. The primary purpose of the Act is to protect the investing public. The Act requires registration of initial issuances of securities with the Securities and Exchange Commission, and demands the filing of a registration statement, including a prospectus, containing financial statements certified by an independent public accountant.

Under Section 11 of the Act, an accountant who misrepresents or omits a material fact in a registration statement or prospectus filed under the Act is civilly liable to third parties who purchase the covered securities. The purchaser need not prove fraud, negligence, or reliance in order to recover (except that the purchaser must prove reliance where he or she bought the securities after the issuance of an earnings statement covering a period of at least 12 months following the effective date of the registration statement). However, an accountant can avoid liability under Section 11 by showing "due diligence"—i. e., by showing that, after reasonable investigation, the accountant had reason to believe that the statements contained in the statement were true and complete *at the time the registration statement became effective.* Note that the accuracy of the statement is measured as of the statement's effective date. This puts a duty of due diligence on the accountant up to the time the registration statement becomes effective. In other words, the accountant has a continuing duty to investigate until the effective date of the registration statement. And if the accountant discovers or learns of new information which materially affects the accuracy of the financial statements filed with the SEC, he or she must file amended statements with the SEC.

A purchaser must bring a civil action under Section 11 within one year after discovering the misrepresentation or omission (or within one year after it should have been discovered), but in no event more than three years after the security was offered to the public. The purchaser's measure of damages (and the accountant's liability) is the difference between the amount paid for the security and its market value at the time of suit. If the purchaser has resold the security, his or her measure of damages will be the difference between the amount paid and the resale price. However, in no case can the measure of damages exceed the price at which the security was offered to the public.

Section 11 does not apply to periodic reports filed with the SEC or annual reports distributed to shareholders.

(7) *The Securities Exchange Act of 1934.* Under the Securities Exchange Act of 1934, any company having at least 500 shareholders (of equity securities) and total assets of at least 1 million dollars must register its securities with the SEC and furnish the Commission with an annual report, including financial statements certified by an independent public accountant. Several thousand companies provide continuous disclosure under the Act regarding their investment securities.

An accountant may incur liability under Section 18 of the Act which provides civil liability for making any false or misleading statement in any document required to be *filed* under the Act. Liability extends to any person who *relies* on the false statement in purchasing or selling a covered security.

Liability under Section 10(b) and Rule 10(b)–5 of the Act is much broader. Section 10(b) and Rule 10(b)–5 provide civil liability for making any false statement or using any other deceptive device in connection with the purchase or sale of any security. These rules apply to all securities, whether listed on a national exchange or traded over-the-counter, and regardless of whether they are subject to the filing requirements of the securities laws. However, an accountant is liable under the rules only upon a showing of *willful* or *intentional* conduct designed to deceive or defraud investors (i. e., the accountant must have knowledge of the fraud, which, in some cases, may include a situation where the accountant acted in reckless disregard of the truth).

(8) A class action is the favored remedy where several third parties are injured by an accountant's fraud, negligence, or securities law violation, and there is a common question of law or fact.

What is the CPA's potential criminal liability?

Accountants have potential criminal liability under both state and federal statutes. Many states have statutes providing criminal penalties for willfully falsifying reports or making false statements in a prospectus. And four federal statutes provide for criminal penalties as follows:

(1) *The Securities Act of 1933 (Registration statements).*

Section 24

Any person who willfully violates any of the provisions of this title, or the rules and regulations promulgated by the Commission under authority thereof, or any person who willfully, in a registration statement filed under this title, makes any untrue statement of a material fact or omits to state any material fact required to be stated therein or necessary to make the statements therein not misleading, shall upon conviction be fined not more than $10,000 or imprisoned not more than five years, or both.

---

(2) *The Securities Exchange Act of 1934 (Section 10(b) violations).*

Section 32(a)

Any person who willfully violates any provisions of this title, or any rule or regulation thereunder the violation of which is made unlawful or the observance of which is required under the terms of this title, or any person who willfully and knowingly makes, or causes to be made, any statement in any application, report, or document required to be filed under this title or any rule or regulation thereunder or any undertaking contained in a registration statement as provided in subsection (d) of Section 15 of this title or by any self-regulatory organization in connection with an application for membership or participation therein or to become associated with a member thereof, which statement was false or misleading with respect to any material fact shall upon conviction be fined not more than $10,000, or imprisoned not more than five years, or both, except that when such person is an exchange, a fine not exceeding $500,000 may be imposed; but no person shall be subject to imprisonment under this section for the violation of any rule or regulation if he proves that he had no knowledge of such rule or regulation.

(3) *The Federal False Statements Statute (false statements within the jurisdiction of any federal department or agency).*

Section 1001

Whoever, in any matter within the jurisdiction of any department or agency of the United States knowingly and willfully falsifies, conceals or covers up by any trick, scheme, or device a material fact, or makes any false, fictitious or fraudulent statements or representations, or makes or uses any false writing or document knowing the same to contain any false, fictitious or fraudulent statement or entry, shall be fined not more than $10,000 or imprisoned not more than five years, or both.

(4) *The Federal Mail Fraud Statute (mailing false financial statements).*

Section 1341

Whoever, having devised or intending to devise any scheme or artifice to defraud, for obtaining money or property by false or fraudulent pretenses, representations, or promises, or to sell, dispose of, loan, exchange, alter, give away, distribute, supply or furnish or procure for unlawful use any counterfeit or spurious coin, obligation, security, or other article, or anything represented to be or intimated or held out to be such counterfeit or spurious article, for the purpose of executing such scheme or artifice or attempting so to do, places in any post office or authorized depository for mail matter, any matter or thing whatever to be sent or delivered by the Postal Service, or takes or receives therefrom, any such matter or thing, or knowingly causes to be delivered by mail according to the direction thereon, or at the place at which it is directed to be delivered by the person to whom it is addressed, any such matter or thing, shall be fined not more than $1,000 or imprisoned not more than five years, or both.

A CPA who aids or assists others in violating the federal laws may be subject to criminal liability for conspiracy to commit an offense against the United States. And an accountant who willfully prepares false tax returns, or assists others in evading their taxes is subject to fine and imprisonment under the federal tax laws.

The courts will "infer" that an accountant has acted "willfully" where his or her actions show a reckless disregard for the truth. And compliance with generally accepted accounting principles (GAAP) is not a defense to a criminal charge where the auditor had knowledge of but failed to disclose improper activities of the client that would affect the audited financial statements. An auditor who makes an honest mistake is under a duty to disclose the error when he or she discovers it: failure to disclose may result in both civil and criminal liability (as failure to disclose evidences an intent to mislead).

PART III

THE LEGAL RESPONSIBILITY OF LAWYERS

The practice of law, like the practice of accounting, affects the public interest and is therefore subject to regulation by the states. However, unlike accounting and other professions which are regulated by the state legislatures, the practice of law is regulated by the judicial branch of government. It is the judiciary which has ultimate responsibility for regulating the legal profession: the highest court of each jurisdiction generally sets standards for the practice of law. This is not to say that the legislative branch never passes statutes affecting legal practice, but only that such statutes are in aid of the judiciary which has power to set higher standards than the legislature (a statute attempting to reduce standards set by the judiciary is invalid). Statutes in most states create a state bar association to which anyone practicing law in the state must belong. The bar association is given power to set standards for admission to practice and to formulate disciplinary rules for regulating members of the bar. The bar association is responsible for most of the actual regulation of the legal profession.

In most states, an applicant for admission to the practice of law must have a degree from a law school that has been accredited by the American Bar Association (the ABA is a voluntary group with about 150,000 lawyer members representing approximately half the attorneys who are members of state bar associations

throughout the United States). Law school consists of three years of postgraduate study following an undergraduate college degree. After finishing law school, an applicant must take and pass a state bar exam which is prepared and administered by the state bar association. Most states administer as part of the exam the "Multistate Bar Exam" which is an objective test prepared by the National Conference of Bar Examiners. The bar exam is generally a three day affair comparable in length to the CPA exam.

Before being admitted to practice, bar applicants who pass the bar exam are thoroughly investigated to determine whether they possess the high moral standards and mental and emotional stability needed to represent clients properly. The state bar committee generally interviews applicants and requires them to fill out detailed questionnaires as well as provide references who will be contacted by the committee. The applicant must cooperate fully and make all required disclosures. If, after reviewing the questionnaires and contacting the references, the bar committee determines that a particular applicant is of bad moral character, it will refuse to admit the applicant. Conviction of certain crimes in and of itself constitutes basis for finding "moral turpitude" and preventing admission to the bar. Included is any kind of crime involving intentional dishonesty such as forgery, embezzlement, and robbery, and any crime of violence such as murder, rape, or aggravated assault. Conviction of possession of substantial amounts of marijuana for purposes of sale has been held sufficient to bar admission to the practice of law; conviction of mere possession of marijuana for one's own use has been held insufficient. While juvenile delinquency and other improper adolescent behavior will not necessarily preclude admission to practice, such behavior will be closely scrutinized. Of course, if an applicant can demonstrate that he or she has been rehabilitated and is presently a person of good moral character, he or she may be admitted to practice despite past crimes or improper behavior. And an applicant always has a right to judicial review (generally by the highest state court) of any decision against his or her admission to practice. Still, it must be stressed how very carefully the bar committee investigates an applicant's background—every effort is made to admit only those persons who are known to possess high moral standards.

Even after an applicant has become a lawyer (i. e., has been admitted to practice law in a state), he or she is subject to continuing regulation as each state has adopted a code of professional responsibility for lawyers. Most states have adopted the *Code of Professional Ethics* formulated by the American Bar Association. The *Code* consists of Nine Canons of Ethics, each Canon supplemented by a large number of "Ethical Considerations" and "Disciplinary Rules". The Nine Canons set forth an attorney's *general* responsibilities. The Ethical Considerations are *aspirational* principles: an attorney has a duty to try to meet them. In contrast, the Disciplinary Rules are *mandatory* minimum standards of conduct; an attorney who fails to comply with the Rules is subject to disciplinary action (including temporary suspension from practice and permanent disbarment) from the bar association and the courts.

The Nine Canons of Ethics are as follows:

CANONS OF ETHICS

Canon 1.   A lawyer should assist in maintaining the integrity and competence of the legal profession.

Canon 2.   A lawyer should assist the legal profession in fulfilling its duty to make legal counsel available.

Canon 3.   A lawyer should assist in preventing the unauthorized practice of law.

Canon 4.   A lawyer should preserve the confidence and secrets of a client.

Canon 5.   A lawyer should exercise independent professional judgment on behalf of a client.

Canon 6.   A lawyer should represent a client competently.

Canon 7.   A lawyer should represent a client zealously within the bounds of the law.

Canon 8.   A lawyer should assist in improving the legal system.

Canon 9.   A lawyer should avoid even the appearance of professional impropriety.

Each Canon or general rule is supplemented by a number of Ethical Considerations and Disciplinary Rules. For example, Canon 4 ("A lawyer should preserve the confidence and secrets of a client") is supplemented by the following Ethical Consideration:

EC 4–1

Both the fiduciary relationship existing between lawyer and client and the proper functioning of the legal system require the preservation by the lawyer of confidences and secrets of one who has employed or sought to employ him. A client must feel free to discuss whatever he wishes with his lawyer and a lawyer must be equally free to obtain information beyond that volunteered by his client. A lawyer should be fully informed of all the facts of the matter he is handling in order for his client to obtain the full advantage of our legal system. It is for the lawyer in the exercise of his independent professional judgment to separate the relevant and important from the irrelevant and unimportant. The observance of the ethical obligation of a lawyer to hold inviolate the confidences and secrets of his client not only facilitates the full development of facts essential to proper representation of the client but also encourages laymen to seek early legal assistance.

Canon 4 and Ethical Consideration 4–1 set down general guidelines for an attorney in preserving the confidence and secrets of a client. Disciplinary Rule 4–101, which also supplements Canon 4, is much more specific and it is mandatory.

"DR" 4–101 provides in part:

DR 4–101

* * * A lawyer shall not knowingly:

(1) Reveal a confidence or secret of his client.

(2) Use a confidence or secret of his client to the disadvantage of the client.

(3) Use a confidence or secret of his client for the advantage of himself or of a third person, unless the client consents after full disclosure.

* * * A lawyer shall exercise reasonable care to prevent his employees, associates, and others whose services are utilized by him from disclosing or using confidences or secrets of a client * * *

Looking now at Canon 7 ("A lawyer should represent a client zealously within

the bounds of the law"), we find that it is supplemented by Ethical Consideration 7–10.

EC 7–10

The duty of a lawyer to represent his client with zeal does not militate against his concurrent obligation to treat with consideration all persons involved in the legal process and to avoid the infliction of needless harm.

Again, Canon 7 and "EC" 7–10 present the general responsibility of a lawyer in representing clients. Disciplinary Rule 7–102, which also supplements Canon 7, is more specific.

It reads in part:

DR 7–102

* * * In his representation of a client, a lawyer shall not:

(1) File a suit, assert a position, conduct a defense, delay a trial, or take other action on behalf of his client when he knows or when it is obvious that such action would serve merely to harass or maliciously injure another.

(2) Knowingly advance a claim or defense that is unwarranted under existing law * * *

* * *

(5) Knowingly make a false statement of law or fact * * *

(7) Counsel or assist his client in conduct that the lawyer knows to be illegal or fraudulent.

Each Canon is supplemented by a large number of Ethical Considerations and Disciplinary Rules. In the pages that follow, we can only briefly summarize a few of these rules and principles. Keep in mind as you read that, while Ethical

Considerations are aspirational, Disciplinary Rules are mandatory minimum standards: an attorney who violates the Disciplinary Rules is subject to disciplinary action by the state bar association and the courts. Such action is designed primarily to protect the public and safeguard the reputation of the legal profession; it is designed secondarily to punish the attorney for his or her objectionable conduct. Generally speaking, an attorney may be disciplined for any one of the following reasons:

(1) Violation of a disciplinary rule (and mistake or ignorance of the rule is no defense);

(2) Conviction of a crime involving moral turpitude whether or not the crime is connected with the attorney's practice;

(3) Commission of any other act involving moral turpitude whether or not it constitutes a crime (in other words, doing something that brings the legal profession into disrepute).

Usually, disciplinary proceedings are initiated by a complaint to the state bar association. It may be an unsatisfied client who is complaining or a fellow lawyer or judge who has knowledge of a lawyer's misconduct. Along this line, a lawyer has a duty to disclose any conduct of another lawyer that looks to be in violation of the rules of professional responsibility. An attorney is obligated not only to reveal such information but also to testify about it in court and before appropriate disciplinary bodies.

An attorney who is brought up on disciplinary charges has a right to due process, including adequate notice of the charges, right to be heard, right to counsel, etc. An attorney has no right to a jury trial in disciplinary proceedings. However, all disciplinary actions are reviewable by the highest state court, and only that court can impose disciplinary sanctions against the attorney. Possible sanctions include temporary suspension from practice (in some states, an attorney may be suspended for up to three years) and permanent disbarment (meaning that the attorney's license to practice is permanently revoked).

And, of course, if the attorney's conduct also constitutes a crime, the attorney may be charged with the crime and, upon conviction, may be fined or imprisoned. Statutes in most states make certain kinds of attorney actions criminal, including efforts to hinder prosecution (e. g., trying to bribe jurors—see Ch. 9) and practicing law while suspended or disbarred.

(a) *Accepting employment.*

An attorney has a duty to accept employment unless he or she has a valid reason for not accepting. This means that a lawyer has a duty to take on unpopular cases, to represent clients who have committed the worst type of crimes, and to represent indigents. Representation must be provided in these cases, and it is the duty of every attorney to provide such services if called upon.

On the other hand, an attorney has a duty to refuse employment if he or she knows that he or she cannot provide adequate or competent representation; and an attorney must never accept or continue employment involving illegal activity.

(b) *Advertising.*

Bar associations traditionally prohibited lawyers from advertising for fear that they would exaggerate their abilities and prompt a loss of respect for the legal profession. However, in recent years, consumer groups have maintained that the public's "right and need to know" takes precedence—that the public has a right to adequate information about lawyers and legal services so as to know when a lawyer is needed, where to find one, and what charges will be made for basic services. The U. S. Supreme Court, in reviewing the issue, has ruled that certain lawyer advertising is permissible so long as it is not misleading. As a result of the decision, lawyers may now advertise that they are limiting their practice to one or more fields of law and may publish hourly rates and fees for given services. However, a lawyer may not use endorsements by previous clients or show statistical data on past performance in an effort to predict future successes. Legal advertising must not create any unjustified expectations nor give any impression that the lawyer is in a position to influence improperly any court, tribunal, or other public body or official.

(c) *Solicitation.*

A lawyer may not solicit clients (i. e., approach potential clients and offer to represent them) either directly (personally) or indirectly (through an investigator or other party—sometimes called a "runner"). Thus, neither an attorney nor his or her employee may seek out an accident victim and suggest that he or she needs a lawyer (referred to as "ambulance chasing"). Mutual referral services also run afoul of the anti-solicitation rule. For example, a doctor may not send patients to a particular attorney in return for having the attorney do the legal work in collecting the doctor's unpaid accounts.

However, a single exception to the rule is recognized. It is generally agreed that an attorney may offer services free of charge to an unpopular defendant who may not otherwise receive adequate legal representation.

(d) *Minimum fee schedules.*

In Goldfarb v. Virginia State Bar, 421 U.S. 773, 95 S.Ct. 2004, 44 L.Ed.2d 572 (1975), the U. S. Supreme Court held that the legal profession is not exempt from the antitrust laws. The case involved a minimum fee schedule established by the Virginia State Bar; attorneys were required to observe the minimum fees and not "undercut" them (charge less). The Court ruled that the

minimum fee schedule was an unreasonable restraint on trade and violative of the Sherman Act. As a result of the *Goldfarb* decision, lawyers are free to compete by charging whatever fees they deem to be appropriate under the circumstances.

(e) *Reasonable fees.*

Although lawyers are free to set their own fees, they must still observe certain basic fee rules established by the courts to protect the public. Ethical Consideration 2–19 states that the basis of the legal fee should be agreed upon between the attorney and client at the outset of the relationship. Generally, a fee is *fixed* or *contingent*. A fixed fee is a flat rate for a specific legal service or a specified hourly rate. Some fixed fees are set by statute for particular legal services such as probating estates and handling workmen's compensation claims and the like. A contingent fee is one that is dependent upon the case turning out successfully: typically, if the lawyer's client wins the case, the lawyer will take a specified percentage of the client's recovery; if the client loses the case, the lawyer will receive nothing by way of a fee. Contingent fees are not permitted in criminal cases or divorce cases; and lawyers are urged not to accept contingent fees in other cases where the client is able to pay a reasonable fixed fee. However, contingent fees are widely used in many civil actions, and for a client who has limited funds, a contingent fee may be the best means of ensuring that he or she will have a day in court.

Whether fixed or contingent, the courts will not enforce a fee agreement that is obviously excessive or unconscionable. And if the attorney waits to set the fee until after he or she has begun or completed the work, the burden will be on the attorney to prove that the fee is fair (the courts holding that the attorney had undue influence over the client at the time of setting the fee). Thus, if the client is old or ill or otherwise susceptible to undue influence, the courts will closely scrutinize a large fixed fee to determine if it is reasonable. With regard to contingent fees, the courts will look closely at situations where the plaintiff is helpless or inexperienced and the fee seems disproportionate to the amount of recovery and the amount of work performed by the attorney. However, the courts recognize that a lawyer who works on a contingent fee basis receives nothing if his or her client loses the case, and that the lawyer's income from a successful case also reflects work done on many unsuccessful cases. So the standards of "reasonableness" are not quite as strict in the area of contingent fees.

A lawyer who charges clearly excessive or unreasonable fees is subject to professional discipline.

(f) *Sharing fees with nonlawyers.*

A lawyer may not share legal fees with nonlawyers. This prevents solicitation and ensures that lawyers will be able to carry out their responsibilities free from the influence of nonlawyers.

Fee sharing between lawyers is permitted so long as the fee division reflects the work performed by each.

(g) *Confidential communications.*

A lawyer is a fiduciary of his or her client and must keep in confidence all client communications. This obligation continues even after termination of the attorney-client relationship. Thus, an attorney may not accept employment where secrets of a former client could be put to the client's disadvantage. Nor may an attorney sell his or her practice (in other words, his or her client's files) without the consent of the clients.

As you know, there exists no common law accountant-client privilege. However, the law does recognize an attorney-client privilege. Thus, an attorney may lawfully refuse to disclose client confidences and secrets in court. On the basis

of the privilege, an attorney may refuse to disclose the physical location of his or her client; the privilege even protects client communications regarding the commission of prior crimes. However, the privilege does not extend to communications in which the client seeks advice in order to plan the commission of a crime or other illegality. The attorney-client privilege stems from the public policy favoring adequate representation. The successful operation of our legal system requires that every person be able to confide freely to an attorney without fear of subsequent disclosure.

(h) *The duty of loyalty.*

As a fiduciary, an attorney has a duty of loyalty to his or her client, meaning that the attorney must not allow his or her personal interests or the interests of a third party to detract from his or her responsibility to the client.

Disciplinary Rule 5–101 states in part:

DR 5–101. Refusing Employment When the Interests of the Lawyer May Impair His Independent Professional Judgment

A. Except with the consent of his client after full disclosure, a lawyer shall not accept employment if the exercise of his professional judgment on behalf of his client will be or reasonably may be affected by his own financial, business, property, or personal interests.

A lawyer who has accepted employment must refrain from acquiring any interest in the claim or property which is the subject matter of the litigation he or she is conducting. And, of course, the lawyer may not accept any "kickbacks" or any other fee or compensation from any third party with whom the attorney is dealing on behalf of the client.

A lawyer who knows that he or she is likely to be called as a witness in a court action must decline or discontinue employment for any client or potential client involved in the action. Social policy states that it is more important for the lawyer to serve as a witness than to act as an advocate. Suppose that an attorney does not anticipate being called as a witness but it later turns out that the attorney's testimony is needed to prevent injustice. The general rule is that the attorney must testify despite the fact that he or she represents a party involved in the action.

Finally, an attorney must disregard any third party interests that interfere with his or her loyalty to the client. For example, a lawyer who is representing a minor in juvenile proceedings must remember at all times that he or she is representing the minor and not the minor's parents or family. The lawyer must make all decisions in what he or she believes to be the best interests of the minor.

(i) *Maintaining the client's funds or other properties.*

An attorney is under an absolute duty to keep his or her client's funds and other property safe and entirely separate from his or her own assets. Disciplinary Rule 9–102 states that all funds belonging to the client must be deposited in one or more separately identified bank accounts.

The Rule further states:

A lawyer shall:

(1) Promptly notify a client of the receipt of his funds, securities or other properties.

(2) Identify and label securities and properties of a client promptly upon receipt and place them in a safe deposit box or other place of safekeeping as soon as practicable.

(3) Maintain complete records of all funds, securities, and other properties of a client coming into the possession of the lawyer and render appropriate accounts to his client regarding them.

(4) Promptly pay or deliver to the client as requested by a client the funds, securities, or other properties in the possession of the lawyer which the client is entitled to receive.

———

An attorney who commingles a client's funds with his or her personal funds is subject to disciplinary action even though the attorney acted in good faith and made full restitution to the client. Usually, a single conversion of a client's funds, however small, will result in complete and total disbarment.

(j) *Providing competent representation.*

A lawyer has a duty to perform legal services properly and with care. If a lawyer lacks competence in a particular area of law, he or she must either associate with an attorney who is competent (with the client's consent, of course) or decline the employment.

A lawyer's duty to perform with care means something more than lack of negligence.

Ethical Consideration 6–5 states:

EC 6–5

A lawyer should have pride in his professional endeavors. His obligation to act competently calls for higher motivation than that arising from fear of civil liability or disciplinary penalty.

———

However, to recover damages from an attorney for breach of care or competence, a client must prove either the tort of negligence or breach of contract (i. e., breach of implied promise to use reasonable care and skill). The standard of care or competence required of an attorney is that of a lawyer of ordinary skill and capacity performing similar services in the same or a similar community. A lawyer is expected to possess the knowledge of a reasonably well-informed attorney as well as ordinary legal research skills (i. e., the ability of an ordinary lawyer to "research" or uncover the rules of law that apply to the particular legal problem). Of course, if an attorney holds himself or herself out as a specialist in tax, labor law, patent law, or the like, the attorney will be held to the standard of care required of a specialist and not merely that of an ordinary lawyer.

To win a malpractice case, a client must prove not only that the lawyer breached the duty of competence, but also that the breach resulted in the client losing the case.

Generally speaking, an attorney is not subject to disciplinary action for simple negligence (although the attorney will be liable to the client in a malpractice action). However, if an attorney attempts to conceal his or her negligence by making misrepresentations to the client, the misrepresentations will constitute sufficient grounds for suspension or disbarment.

Incompetent counsel may be a basis for setting aside the judgment of a court, particularly in a criminal conviction. Juan Corona, the alleged mass murderer of more than 20 migrant workers in California, had his conviction overturned in 1978 because of the determined incompetency of his lawyer. For incompetency to justify setting aside a criminal conviction, the defense counsel's errors must be so substantial that the accused was effectively deprived of his or her constitutional rights. The Disciplinary Rules regarding competency provide as follows:

DR 6-101. Failing to Act Competently

A.   A lawyer shall not:

(1) Handle a legal matter which he knows or should know that he is not competent to handle, without associating with him a lawyer who is competent to handle it.

(2) Handle a legal matter without preparation adequate in the circumstance.

(3) Neglect a legal matter entrusted to him.

DR 6-102.   Limiting Liability to Client

A.   A lawyer shall not attempt to exonerate himself from or limit his liability to his client for his personal malpractice.

---

(1) *Ending the attorney-client relationship.*

The rules for terminating the attorney-client relationship differ depending on whether the party desiring to end the relationship is the attorney or the client. Once an attorney starts to represent a client, the attorney may not end the relationship at will; this is so even where the attorney has no specific or formal contract with the client. The attorney must continue in the employment until the job is done unless the client refuses to cooperate or unless the attorney's health makes it impossible for him or her to provide proper representation.

And of course, in some cases, an attorney *must* withdraw from employment: (1) where the work to be done is clearly illegal; (2) where it would violate a Disciplinary Rule; (3) where its sole purpose is to harass or maliciously injure a person; (4) where the attorney's mental or physical condition makes it unreasonably difficult for him or her to perform the work; and (5) where the client discharges the attorney.

Even when properly withdrawing from representation, an attorney must notify the client so that he or she can hire another lawyer. The withdrawing attorney must also refund any paid but unearned fees and promptly return any documents or other property belonging to the client. If an attorney withdraws without a proper basis for doing so, the attorney may be liable to the client for breach of contract.

With regard to an attorney's withdrawal from employment, Disciplinary Rule 2-110 provides:

DR 2-110. Withdrawal from Employment

A. In general

    (1) If permission for withdrawal from employment is required by the rules of a tribunal, a lawyer shall not withdraw from employment in a proceeding before that tribunal without its permission.

    (2) In any event, a lawyer shall not withdraw from employment until he has taken reasonable steps to avoid foreseeable prejudice to the rights of his client, including giving due notice to his client, allowing time for employment of other counsel, delivering to the client all papers and property to which the clients is entitled, and complying with applicable laws and rules.

    (3) A lawyer who withdraws from employment shall refund promptly any part of a fee paid in advance that has not been earned.

B. Mandatory withdrawal

    A lawyer representing a client before a tribunal, with its permission if required by its rules, shall withdraw from employment, and a lawyer representing a client in other matters shall withdraw from employment, if:

    (1) He knows or it is obvious that his client is bringing the legal action, conducting the defense, or asserting a position in the litigation, or is otherwise having steps taken for him, merely for the purpose of harassing or maliciously injuring any person.

    (2) He knows or it is obvious that his continued employment will result in a violation of a Disciplinary Rule.

    (3) His mental or physical condition renders it unreasonably difficult for him to carry out the employment effectively.

    (4) He is discharged by his client.

C. Permissive withdrawal

    If DR 2-110 (B) is not applicable, a lawyer may not request permission to withdraw in matters pending before a tribunal, and may not withdraw in other matters, unless such request or such withdrawal is because:

    (1) His client:

        (a) Insists upon presenting a claim or defense that is not warranted under existing law and cannot be supported by good faith argument for an extension, modification, or reversal of existing law.

        (b) Personally seeks to pursue an illegal course of conduct.

        (c) Insists that the lawyer pursue a course of conduct that is illegal or that is prohibited under the Disciplinary Rules.

        (d) By other conduct renders it unreasonably difficult for the lawyer to carry out his employment effectively.

        (e) Insists, in a matter not pending before a tribunal, that the lawyer engage in conduct that is contrary to the judgment and advice of the lawyer but not prohibited under the Disciplinary Rules.

   (f) Deliberately disregards an agreement or obligation to the lawyer as to expenses or fees.

(2) His continued employment is likely to result in a violation of a Disciplinary Rule.

(3) His inability to work with co-counsel indicates that the best interests of the client likely will be served by withdrawal.

(4) His mental or physical condition renders it difficult for him to carry out the employment effectively.

(5) His client knowingly and freely assents to termination of his employment.

(6) He believes in good faith, in a proceeding pending before a tribunal, that the tribunal will find the existence of other good cause for withdrawal.

In contrast to the strict rules regarding an attorney's withdrawal from a case a client has a right to end the attorney-client relationship at any time with or without a reason. However, a client who discharges his or her attorney without cause may be liable in damages for breach of employment contract.

Conclusion. Perhaps contrary to the belief of many, the legal profession is highly responsible; it is more strictly regulated than any other profession. Whether practicing law or conducting private business or personal affairs, an attorney is bound to the same strict professional standards and must always conduct himself or herself so as to reflect credit upon the legal profession. As Ethical Consideration 9–6 states it, an attorney must make every effort to avoid even the appearance of impropriety.

The Rule provides:

EC 9–6

    Every lawyer owes a solemn duty to uphold the integrity and honor of his profession; to encourage respect for the law and for the courts and the judges thereof; to observe the Code of Professional Responsibility; to act as a member of a learned profession, one dedicated to public service; to cooperate with his brother lawyers in supporting the organized bar through the devoting of his time, efforts, and financial support as his professional standing and ability reasonably permit; to conduct himself so as to reflect credit on the legal profession and to inspire the confidence, respect, and trust of his clients and of the public; and to strive to avoid not only professional impropriety but also the appearance of impropriety.

CASES

CASE 1—*Even lawful acts done maliciously can be the basis for going to court.*

J. J. THEATRES, INC. v. V. R. O. K. CO.

Supreme Court, Special Term, New York County, Part III, 1950.
96 N.Y.S.2d 271.

STEUER, Justice.

The complaint alleges that plaintiffs are tenants and subtenants of a theatre and that they have duly performed according to the terms of their respective leases. It further alleges that the corporate defendant is the owner of the fee and one of the individuals is its moving spirit. The complaint alleges that defendants agreed among themselves to harass plaintiffs to the end that they would abandon their leases. The means of harassment were the bringing of baseless lawsuits in connection with the leases, and it is alleged that four dispossess proceedings and two actions for additional rent were brought, all of which resulted in judgments for the plaintiffs herein, defendants in those actions. The remaining defendant Weinstock is alleged to have concurred in the bringing of the suits and to have advanced money for that purpose in the expectation that when plaintiffs were forced to vacate the premises that he would become the tenant.

* * * Motions to dismiss are made by Weinstock and the other defendants separately.

* * * In effect the complaint alleges an actional wrong, namely, interference with the plaintiff's business. Opera on Tour, Inc. v. Weber, 285 N.Y. 348, 34 N.E.2d 349, 136 A.L.R. 267. The means of interference are not actionable, as plaintiff concedes that the bringing of suits does not amount to malicious prosecution. The question, therefore, is, can an action for unlawful interference be predicated upon acts which themselves can form no basis for recovery no matter how wrongful may be the motive which induces them.

The answer is in the affirmative. Even lawful acts if done maliciously and with intent to injure can be the subject of a cause of action. Al Raschid v. News Syndicate Co., 265 N.Y. 1, 191 N.E. 713, and authorities therein collected. But, it may be argued, a baseless suit is always an annoyance and the source of some damage * * *. [W]here the suit results in no appreciable effect on plaintiff's business there is no damage beyond the costs collectible in the suit and hence no cause of action. Where it is otherwise, recovery may be had.

* * * [I]t is alleged that their business has decreased and the value of their leasehold lessened as a result of the public knowledge of the suits. * * * [T]his makes out a cause of action.

The motions are * * * denied * * *.

CASE 2—*Can another copy what is not patented?*

SEARS, ROEBUCK & CO. v. STIFFEL CO.
Supreme Court of the United States, 1964.
376 U.S. 225, 84 S.Ct. 784, 11 L.Ed.2d 661.

Mr. Justice BLACK delivered the opinion of the Court.

The question in this case is whether a State's unfair competition law can, consistently with the federal patent laws, impose liability for or prohibit the copying of an article which is protected by neither a federal patent nor a copyright. The respondent, Stiffel Company, secured design and mechanical patents on a "pole lamp"—a vertical tube having lamp fixtures along the outside, the tube being made so that it will stand upright between the floor and ceiling of a room. Pole lamps proved a decided commercial success, and soon after Stiffel brought them on the market Sears, Roebuck & Company put on the market a substantially identical lamp, which it sold more cheaply, Sears' retail price being about the same as Stiffel's wholesale price. Stiffel then brought this action against Sears in the United States District Court for the Northern District of Illinois, claiming in its first count that by copying its design Sears had infringed Stiffel's patents and in its second count that by selling copies of Stiffel's lamp Sears had caused confusion in the trade as to the source of the lamps and had thereby engaged in unfair competition under Illinois law. There was evidence that identifying tags were not attached to the Sears lamps although labels appeared on the cartons in which they were delivered to customers, that customers had asked Stiffel whether its lamps differed from Sears', and that in two cases customers who had bought Stiffel lamps had complained to Stiffel on learning that Sears was selling substantially identical lamps at a much lower price.

The District Court, after holding the patents invalid for want of invention, went on to find as a fact that Sears' lamp was "a substantially exact copy" of Stiffel's and that the two lamps were so much alike, both in appearance and in functional details, "that confusion between them is likely, and some confusion has already occurred." On these findings the court held Sears guilty of unfair competition, enjoined Sears "from unfairly competing with [Stiffel] by selling or attempting to sell pole lamps identical to or confusingly similar to" Stiffel's lamp, and ordered an accounting to fix profits and damages resulting from Sears' "unfair competition."

The Court of Appeals affirmed.[1] 313 F.2d 115. That court held that, to make out a case of unfair competition under Illinois law, there was no need to show that Sears had been "palming off" its lamps as Stiffel lamps; Stiffel had only to prove that there was a "likelihood of confusion as to the source of the products"—that the two articles were sufficiently identical that customers could not tell who had made a particular one. Impressed by the "remarkable sameness of appearance" of the lamps, the Court of Appeals upheld the trial court's findings of likelihood of confusion and some actual confusion, findings which the appellate court construed to mean confusion "as to the source of the lamps." The Court of Appeals thought this enough under Illinois law to sustain the trial court's holding of unfair competition, and thus held Sears liable under Illinois law for doing no more

---

1. No review is sought here of the ruling affirming the District Court's holding that the patent is invalid.

than copying and marketing an unpatented article. We granted certiorari to consider whether this use of a State's law of unfair competition is compatible with the federal patent law.

Before the Constitution was adopted, some States had granted patents either by special act or by general statute, but when the Constitution was adopted provision for a federal patent law was made one of the enumerated powers of Congress because, as Madison put it in The Federalist No. 43, the States "cannot separately make effectual provision" for either patents or copyrights. That constitutional provision is Art. I, § 8, cl. 8, which empowers Congress "To promote the Progress of Science and useful Arts, by securing for limited Times to Authors and Inventors the exclusive Right to their respective Writings and Discoveries." Pursuant to this constitutional authority, Congress in 1790 enacted the first federal patent and copyright law, 1 Stat. 109, and ever since that time has fixed the conditions upon which patents and copyrights shall be granted. These laws, like other laws of the United States enacted pursuant to constitutional authority, are the supreme law of the land. When state law touches upon the area of these federal statutes, it is "familiar doctrine" that the federal policy "may not be set at naught, or its benefits denied" by the state law. This is true, of course, even if the state law is enacted in the exercise of otherwise undoubted state power.

The grant of a patent is the grant of a statutory monopoly; indeed, the grant of patents in England was an explicit exception to the statute of James I prohibiting monopolies. Patents are not given as favors, as was the case of monopolies given by the Tudor monarchs but are meant to encourage invention by rewarding the inventor with the right, limited to a term of years fixed by the patent, to exclude others from the use of his invention. During that period of time no one may make use, or sell the patented product without the patentee's authority. But in rewarding useful invention, the "rights and welfare of the community must be fairly dealt with and effectually guarded." To that end the prerequisites to obtaining a patent are strictly observed, and when the patent has issued the limitations on its exercise are equally strictly enforced. To begin with, a genuine "invention" or "discovery" must be demonstrated "lest in the constant demand for new appliances the heavy hand of tribute be laid on each slight technological advance in an art." Once the patent issues, it is strictly construed. [I]t cannot be used to secure any monopoly beyond that contained in the patent, the patentee's control over the product when it leaves his hands is sharply limited, and the patent monopoly may not be used in disregard of the antitrust laws. Finally, and especially relevant here, when the patent expires the monopoly created by it expires, too, and the right to make the article—including the right to make it in precisely the shape it carried when patented—passes to the public.

Thus the patent system is one in which uniform federal standards are carefully used to promote invention while at the same time preserving free competition. Obviously a State could not, consistently with the Supremacy Clause of the Constitution, extend the life of a patent beyond its expiration date or give a patent on an article which lacked the level of invention required for federal patents. To do either would run counter to the policy of Congress of granting patents only to true inventions, and then only for a limited time. Just as a State cannot encroach upon the federal patent laws directly, it cannot, under some other law, such as that forbidding unfair competition, give protection of a kind that clashes with the objectives of the federal patent laws.

In the present case the "pole lamp" sold by Stiffel has been held not to be entitled to the protection of either a mechanical or a design patent. An unpatentable article, like an article on which the patent has expired, is in the public domain and may be made and sold by whoever chooses to do so. What Sears did was to copy Stiffel's design and to sell lamps almost identical to those sold by Stiffel. This it had every right to do under the federal patent laws. That Stiffel originated the pole lamp and made it popular is immaterial. "Sharing in the goodwill of an article unprotected by patent or trade-mark is the exercise of a right possessed by all—and in the free exercise of which the consuming public is deeply interested." To allow a State by use of its law of unfair competition to prevent the copying of an article which represents too slight an advance to be patented would be to permit the State to block off from the public something which federal law has said belongs to the public. The result would be that while federal law grants only * * * 17 years' protection to genuine inventions, States could allow perpetual protection to articles too lacking in novelty to merit any patent at all under federal constitutional standards. This would be too great an encroachment on the federal patent system to be tolerated.

Sears has been held liable here for unfair competition because of a finding of likelihood of confusion based only on the fact that Sears' lamp was copied from Stiffel's unpatented lamp and that consequently the two looked exactly alike. Of course there could be "confusion" as to who had manufactured these nearly identical articles. But mere inability of the public to tell two identical articles apart is not enough to support an injunction against copying or an award of damages for copying that which the federal patent laws permit to be copied. Doubtless a State may, in appropriate circumstances, require that goods, whether patented or unpatented, be labeled or that other precautionary steps be taken to prevent customers from being misled as to the source, just as it may protect businesses in the use of their trademarks, labels, or distinctive dress in the packaging of goods so as to prevent others, by imitating such markings, from misleading purchasers as to the source of the goods. But because of the federal patent laws a State may not, when the article is unpatented and uncopyrighted, prohibit the copying of the article itself or award damages for such copying. The judgment below did both and in so doing gave Stiffel the equivalent of a patent monopoly on its unpatented lamp. That was error, and Sears is entitled to a judgment in its favor.

Reversed.

CASE 3—*A person who does not meet the requirements of the "Public Accountancy Act" may not hold himself or herself out to the public as an accountant.*

TEXAS STATE BD. OF PUBLIC ACCOUNTANCY v. FULCHER

Court of Civil Appeals of Texas, Corpus Christi, 1974.
515 S.W.2d 950.

BISSETT, Justice.

This suit was instituted by the Texas State Board of Public Accountancy against W. L. Fulcher to enjoin him from holding himself out to the public as an "accountant" on the ground that he was violating certain provisions of the Public Accountancy Act of 1945. The Texas Society of Certified Public Accountants intervened as a party plaintiff. The trial court, after a trial before the court without a jury, denied the application for injunction on grounds that the Act was unconstitutional, and dismissed the action. Plaintiff and intervenor, hereinafter sometimes called "appellants", have appealed.

The Board alleged that appellee is not registered with the Texas State Board of Public Accountancy either as a public accountant or certified public accountant, that he does not now hold and has never held a live permit for the practice of public accounting issued under any section of the Act, and that he has violated certain provisions of the Act by unlawfully holding himself out as an "accountant". The prayer was that appellee "be enjoined from holding himself out as a public accountant and engaging in the business of public accountancy" until he has complied with the provisions of the Act.

Appellee denied generally the allegations contained in the petition. He further pled that the Act violates rights guaranteed him and others by both the Federal and State Constitutions because it is "ambiguous, contradictory, and prohibitory, rather than regulatory".

The issue here presented is whether the Act, as it is applied to appellee, violates any right or rights guaranteed to appellee by the Constitution of Texas and of the United States. * * *

Appellee is not a certified public accountant nor is he a licensed or registered public accountant under any of the provisions of the Act. He does not hold a permit for the practice of public accounting under the Act. Appellee admits that he performs accounting services for the general public and uses the designation "accountants" in his business. He further admits that he has held himself out to the public as an "accountant". In addition to preparing income tax returns and furnishing bookkeeping services to his clients, appellee renders general accounting services to the public, which include preparation of financial statements and reports, and designing and implementing accounting and bookkeeping systems. He does not make and prepare certified audits nor does he affix his signature to financial reports or statements in such a manner as to indicate that they are based upon a certified audit. He does, however, sign his name to financial reports and statements. The words "Fulcher & Fulcher, Accountants" appear on both the building directory in the office building where appellee maintains his place of business and on the entrance door to his office. The words "Fulcher & Company, Accountants" appear as the return address on his business envelopes. Appellee agreed that if a member of the public was seeking an accountant, his business envelope and the sign would be sufficient notice that he was holding himself out to the public as an accountant.
    * * *
It is well settled that accounting is a highly skilled and technical profession that affects the public welfare, and which the state, in the exercise of its police power, may regulate. Statutes which prohibit anyone from holding himself out as a "public accountant" or a "certified accountant" without having actually received a certificate or permit to practice public accountancy have generally been upheld. * * * As the affairs of the people change and progress, the police power progresses to meet the needs. Today, the need to protect the public against fraud, deception as the conse-

quences of ignorance or incompetence in the practice of most professions makes regulation necessary. The state may exact the requisite degree of skill and learning in professions which affect the public, or at least a substantial portion of the public, such as the practice of law, medicine, engineering, dentistry, and many others. The Act before us recognizes public accountancy as one of such professions. Public accountancy now embraces many intricate and technical matters dealing with many kinds of tax laws, unfair trade practices, rate regulations, stock exchange regulations, reports required by many governmental agencies, financial statements and the like. So, in this view of the practice of public accounting, the public welfare of this State demands that it be regulated, as is done by Article 41a, V.A.C.S.

* * *

We hold that the Public Accountancy Act of 1945, as amended, is constitutional. It, as applied to appellee, does not amount to an unwarranted regulation of private business and the right of a citizen to pursue an ordinary occupation. It does not abridge rights of private property and does not infringe upon rights of contract in matters of purely private concern bearing no perceptible relation to the public welfare. It is not unreasonable, arbitrary, vague or ambiguous. It does not deny appellee equal protection of the law, nor does it violate any guarantees to appellee under the Bill of Rights, nor does it benefit only a single class, licensed accountants, at the expense of unlicensed accountants and the public as a whole. Every licensing act creates a hardship on those who do not meet its requirements and works to the benefit of those who do, and every licensing act involves a legislative determination that there is or is not a public need for unlicensed practitioners in the profession that is being regulated. The decision by the legislature should not be disturbed unless it is patently violative of constitutional prohibitions and guarantees, or is so ambiguous or vague to the extent that a potential actor cannot determine the point at which his lawful conduct becomes proscribed conduct. That is not the case here.

The Act's prohibitions bear a reasonable relationship to the expressed purpose to be accomplished by the Act, to-wit: "the regulation and licensing of persons to practice public accounting in this state", as stated in the caption of the 1961 amendment. Clearly, it was the intention of the legislature to protect the public by regulating the practice of public accounting in this State through the issuance of permits and licenses to only those who, in the judgment of the legislature, are qualified to engage in such practice. The Act, as now amended, sets forth certain educational and training standards for the obtaining of a permit to practice public accountancy, which operate equally on all within the same class. That such standards are reasonable and legitimate bases for classifying persons who would engage in the practice of public accountancy is not open to question.

* * *

Appellee, by offering and furnishing accounting services for pay to the general public was engaged as an accountant in the practice of public accounting. The use of the word "accountants" by appellee on his office signs and business envelopes constituted a holding out to the public that he was an "accountant", which under the undisputed facts before us, was in violation of Section 8(e) of the Act. The State Board of Public Accountancy is entitled to the injunctive relief sought by it.

* * *

Reversed.

PROBLEMS

1. To attract clients, attorney Frank Broadmore places the following advertisement in the local newspaper:

    Simple wills --$120
    Uncontested divorces --$150
        & Other reasonably priced legal services ------CALL 221–1451
    When the ad proves ineffective, Frank approaches Lyn Gardner, the survivor of a major airplane crash, and tells Lyn that she needs an attorney. Frank offers to represent her for 40% of any recovery she receives from the airline; Lyn accepts the offer. Frank also approaches B.J. Riley, an indigent accused of a horrendous mass murder, and offers to defend B.J. against the charges; B.J. also accepts. Frank is successful in negotiating a $60,000 settlement on Lyn's behalf with the airline. Frank needs more than his 40% share of the settlement to purchase some real property in the area so he uses $5,000 of Lyn's share to help in making the purchase. Within a week's time, Frank's cash flow problem is gone and he pays Lyn (who is none the wiser) her full 60% share. Meanwhile, Ron Morley contacts Frank and asks him to represent him in a negligence action. The case looks to be a good one with a potentially large recovery so Frank agrees to represent Ron. In order to have more time to devote to Ron's case, Frank contacts B.J. Riley and informs her that he will no longer be representing her. B.J. is angry and complains to the state bar association. Lyn Gardner also complains to the bar, having discovered that Frank borrowed $5,000 of her money without her permission. An investigation into Frank's practice begins. Is Frank subject to disciplinary action for any of the following? Explain fully.

    (a) For having advertised his services in the local newspaper;

    (b) For approaching Lyn and offering to represent her;

    (c) For approaching B.J. and offering to represent her;

    (d) For setting up a fee arrangement with Lyn whereby he would receive 40% of any recovery from the airline;

    (e) For "borrowing" $5,000 of Lyn's money for a week's time;

    (f) For withdrawing from B.J.'s case.

2. Oliver's Shoes, Inc. markets a pair of wooden sandals with a specially designed arch that serves to exercise the foot and keep it in good health. Though the sandals are not patented, they sell well across the country under the trademark of "Lo-Mar" Sandals. Percy Enterprises, in an effort to increase its profits, manufactures and sells a wooden sandal that is identical in appearance to the "Lo-Mar" shoes. The Percy Company sells the shoes under the name "Low-Marr" Sandals; it does a good business as many consumers who intend to buy the Oliver Company product pick up the Percy shoes by mistake. When Oliver Shoes discovers what Percy Enterprises is up to, it seeks your legal advice. What rights, if any, does the Company have against Percy Enterprises? Explain fully. Would your answer differ if the Oliver Company's product was patented? Explain.

3. Percy Enterprises also manufactures and sells a canvas sports shoe which directly competes with a shoe sold by Paulson Bros. Shoes. To increase its sales at Paulson's expense, the Percy Company tells several

retail shoe stores that the Paulson manufacturing process is "shoddy", and that the Paulson Company is on its last financial legs. The Percy Company, in fact, has no knowledge about the Paulson operation or finances; nevertheless, its sales increase and Paulsons' sales decrease. The Percy Company also advertises its shoes as being "the first choice of sports favorite Jim Doherty." Jim Doherty, in fact, knows nothing about the shoes, and has not consented to having his name used for advertising purposes. What rights, if any, does Paulson Bros. Shoes have against the Percy Company? Explain fully. What rights, if any, does Jim Doherty have against the Percy Company? Explain fully.

4. (a) To what seven groups is business legally responsible? Explain fully.

  (b) Define: *artful accounting; creative accounting; salami accounting.*

5. Answer the following "True" or "False" and give reasons for your answer:

  (a) Ethical Considerations are mandatory minimum standards of conduct for attorneys.

  (b) The law requires tremendous business and professional responsibility and imposes substantial civil and criminal penalties if such responsibility is not discharged.

  (c) An accountant may be held liable under Rule 10(b)–5 (promulgated under Section 10(b) of the Securities Exchange Act of 1934) on the basis of intent or negligence.

  (d) A trade secret is protected only so long as it remains secret.

  (e) A private individual who is injured by a violation of the Sherman Act may bring suit under the Act and recover treble damages.

  (f) With regard to an accountant's liability, the courts will never impose a higher standard of care than GAAP and GAAS.

  (g) An accountant cannot avoid liability to third parties when doing "unaudited" financial statements or mere "write-up" work.

  (h) An accountant is liable for fraudulent or deceitful reports to any and all third parties who rely upon the reports to their detriment.

  (i) A bar applicant who was convicted of embezzlement in the past may be denied admission to the bar on the basis of the conviction.

  (j) A lawyer is subject to disciplinary action for knowingly revealing a confidence or secret of his or her client.

  (k) The courts will not enforce a lawyer's fee agreement where the fee is obviously excessive or unconscionable.

6. Winslow Manufacturing, Inc. sought a $200,000 loan from National Lending Corporation. National Lending insisted that audited financial statements be submitted before it would extend credit. Winslow agreed to this and also agreed to pay the audit fee. An audit was performed by an independent CPA who submitted his report to Winslow to be used solely for the purpose of negotiating a loan from National. National, upon reviewing the audited financial statements, decided in good faith *not* to extend the credit desired. Certain ratios, which as a matter of policy were used by National in reaching its decision, were deemed too low. Winslow used copies of the audited financial statements to obtain credit elsewhere. It was subsequently learned that the CPA, despite the

exercise of reasonable care, had failed to discover a sophisticated embezzlement scheme by Winslow's chief accountant. Under these circumstances, what liability does the CPA have?

a. The CPA is liable to third parties who extended credit to Winslow based upon the audited financial statements.

b. The CPA is liable to Winslow to repay the audit fee because credit was *not* extended by National.

c. The CPA is liable to Winslow for any losses Winslow suffered as a result of failure to discover the embezzlement.

d. The CPA is *not* liable to any of the parties.

[# 3, November 1976 CPA Exam]

7. Martinson is a duly licensed CPA. One of his clients is suing him for negligence alleging that he failed to meet generally accepted auditing standards in the current year's audit thereby failing to discover large thefts of inventory. Under the circumstances

a. Martinson is *not* bound by generally accepted auditing standards unless he is a member of the AICPA.

b. Martinson's failure to meet generally accepted auditing standards would result in liability.

c. Generally accepted auditing standards do *not* currently cover the procedures which must be used in verifying inventory for balance-sheet purposes.

d. If Martinson failed to meet generally accepted auditing standards, he would undoubtedly be found to have committed the tort of fraud.

[# 21, November 1975 CPA Exam]

8. A third party-purchaser of securities has brought suit based upon the Securities Act of 1933 against a CPA firm. The CPA firm will prevail in the suit brought by the third party even though the CPA firm issued an unqualified opinion on materially incorrect financial statements if

a. The CPA firm was unaware of the defects.

b. The third-party plaintiff had *no* direct dealings with the CPA firm.

c. The CPA firm can show that the third-party plaintiff did *not* rely upon the audited financial statements.

d. The CPA firm can establish that it was *not* guilty of actual fraud.

[# 19, November 1975 CPA Exam]

9. Whitlow and Wyatt, CPA's, has been the independent auditors of Interstate Land Development Corporation for several years. During these years, Interstate prepared and filed its own annual income tax returns.

During 1974, Interstate requested Whitlow and Wyatt to examine all the necessary financial statements of the corporation to be submitted to the Securities and Exchange Commission (SEC) in connection with a multi-state public offering of one-million shares of Interstate common stock. This public offering came under the provisions of the Securities Act of 1933. The examination was performed carefully and the financial statements were fairly presented for the respective periods. These financial statements were included in the registration statement filed with the SEC.

While the registration statement was being processed by the SEC but prior to the effective date, the Internal Revenue Service (IRS) subpoenaed Whitlow and Wyatt to turn over all its working papers relating to Interstate for the years 1971–1973. Whitlow and Wyatt initially refused to comply for two reasons. First, Whitlow and Wyatt did not prepare Interstate's tax returns. Second, Whitlow and Wyatt claimed that the working papers were confidential matters subject to the privileged-communications rule. Subsequently, however, Whitlow and Wyatt did relinquish the subpoenaed working papers.

Upon receiving the subpoena, Wyatt called Dunkirk, the chairman of Interstate's board of directors and asked him about the IRS investigation. Dunkirk responded, "I'm sure the IRS people are on a fishing expedition and that they will not find any material deficiencies."

A few days later Dunkirk received written confirmation from the IRS that it was contending that Interstate had underpaid its taxes during the period under review. The confirmation revealed that Interstate was being assessed $800,000 including penalties and interest for the three years.

* * *

Required:

1. Discuss the additional liability assumed by Whitlow and Wyatt in connection with this SEC registration engagement.

2. Discuss the implications to Whitlow and Wyatt and its responsibilities with respect to the IRS assessment.

3. Could Whitlow and Wyatt have validly refused to surrender the subpoenaed materials? Explain.

[# 5.b., 1975 CPA Exam]

10. Duval was the agent for Sunshine Pools, Inc. He sold pools, related equipment, and accessories for Sunshine. Holmes, president of Tilden Sporting Equipment, Inc., approached Duval and offered him an excellent deal on a commission basis if he would secretly sell their brand of diving boards and platforms instead of the Sunshine products. Duval agreed. The arrangement which was worked out between them was to have Duval continue to act as a general sales agent for Sunshine and concurrently act as the agent for an "undisclosed" principal in respect to Tilden diving boards. He could then sell both lines to new pool customers and then go back to prior customers to solicit sales of the Tilden boards. Duval was not to mention his relationship with Tilden to the prospective customers, and of course, no mention of these facts would be made to Sunshine. Duval was told to use his discretion insofar as effectively misleading the prospective customers about whose diving board they were purchasing.

Things went smoothly for the first several months until Tilden began to manufacture and ship defective diving boards. Subsequently, Tilden became insolvent, and Holmes absconded with advance payments made by purchasers including those who had purchased from Duval.

Required: Answer the following, setting forth reasons for any conclusions stated.

a. What are the rights of the various customers against Duval?

b. What are the rights of the various customers against Tilden and/or Holmes?

c. What rights does Sunshine have against Duval?

d. What rights does Sunshine have against Tilden and/or Holmes?

[# 5.a. b. c. & d., November 1977 CPA Exam]

Chapter 29

MANAGING THE PROPERTY OF OTHERS: TRUSTS

What is the scope of this chapter?

You will recall that the first six chapters of our text dealt with property, a most fascinating legal concept. We learned in those chapters that every individual needs at least a minimal amount of property to survive in this world. Many people, however, want more than a bare subsistence, and so spend many of their waking hours working hard in order to acquire money and possessions (both of which are forms of property).

We learned, too, that property is a complex bundle of rights protected by the 14th Amendment to the U.S. Constitution which states that "life, liberty, and property cannot be taken without due process of law". While, traditionally, property referred only to transferable rights, it has come to include, under the meaning and protection of the 14th Amendment, nontransferable government entitlements, such as licenses, franchises, welfare benefits, and subsidies. Commercial law and criminal law statutes have further expanded the meaning of the term "property".

As to the protection of property interests, we saw that the legal concepts of tort and crime are designed to protect people against unreasonable interference with their use and enjoyment of property. The crimes of burglary, arson, theft, and robbery, as well as the torts of trespass, nuisance, conversion, and negligence provide property owners with legal remedies in the case of interference with their ownership interests.

We next studied the distinction between personal and real property, covering in depth the subject of "meshing" the two kinds of property (i. e., the occa-

sions where personal property becomes real property and vice versa). We fully explored the acquisition of ownership of both personal and real property rights. With regard to acquisition of personal property, we studied finder's rights, accession, confusion, gifts, patents, and copyrights. With regard to acquisition of real property, we looked at the many real property interests, including chattels real (leaseholds) and possessory rights in land, such as the fee simple, the life estate, and future interests.

Before leaving the area of property and moving on to contracts, we learned that a person may own property in severalty or concurrently with others; that a person may own water rights or enjoy rights to support from a neighbor's land; and that a person may have a right to profits, covenants, or easements.

Also, we took a look at the transfer of land by deed and adverse possession. And we considered land use planning as it is achieved through zoning and subdivision control.

Having begun our study of commercial law with an in depth overview of property law, it is only fitting that we end our study with a comprehensive treatment of the two remaining aspects of the law of property—(1) the management and use of property for the benefit of another (i. e., trusts); and (2) the deathtime transfer of property by will or intestacy (including the process of probate). Trusts are dealt with in this chapter, while wills, intestacy and probate are considered in the following and final chapter of the text.

Both remaining areas of property law are very practical areas of study. In a trust, for example, one person holds property for the benefit of another. A trust arrangement is often desirable for a spouse or child who is incapable of managing property, or who is simply unwilling to assume such responsibility. With the property placed in trust, the trustee (the person who holds the property) is solely responsible for managing and caring for the property, while the spouse or child (the "beneficiary" of the trust) is entitled to all the benefits and income derived from the property. And trust provisions can be very flexible to suit the needs of the particular situation. The trustee, for example, may be given broad discretion to make investments, or very little discretion. The beneficiaries may have a right to all the income, or only a portion; and they may or may not have a right to reach the trust property itself.

As to deathtime transfers of property, a person may control the disposition of his or her property to a great extent by owning property jointly with the right of survivorship, or, as is more common, by leaving a valid will. A person who leaves a will frequently writes a trust into the will for the benefit of his or her surviving spouse or minor children. The testator (person leaving the will) may prefer that a trustee manage the property for the benefit of his or her lawfully designated beneficiaries rather than have responsibility for management directly on the beneficiaries. In the case of minor children, it is not unusual for the testator to provide that the trust is to continue until the children reach the age of 21, 25, or 30.

Where a person dies intestate (i. e., without a will), the decedent's properties will pass to his or her heirs as determined by reference to state "intestacy" laws. These laws specifically define who shall inherit, how much they shall inherit, and when the state itself is entitled to take the property.

What kinds of trusts are there?

Black's Law Dictionary defines "trust" as follows:

A right of property, real or personal, held by one party for the benefit of another * * *. Any arrangement whereby property is transferred with intention that it be administered by trustee for another's benefit.[1]

Trusts may be either express, implied, or constructive. An "express" trust is a trust that comes into existence when a party externally manifests an intent to create a trust. The party creating the trust is called a "trustor", and his or her expression of intent may be by words or conduct.

An "implied" trust, on the other hand, is a trust that arises by operation of law when a party who transfers property truly intends to create a trust, but fails to externally manifest or express such intent. The trust is called a "resulting" trust and is dealt with in detail in a later section of this chapter.

Finally, a "constructive" trust is a trust that is neither express nor implied but is created by law to prevent a wrong or remedy an injustice. For example, where a person fraudulently obtains title to property, the wrongdoer will be forced by the courts to hold the property in a "constructive" trust for the benefit of the former owner. Like resulting trusts, constructive trusts are dealt with in a later section.

------

1. Henry Campbell Black, *Black's Law Dictionary*, Revised Fourth Edition, West Publishing Co., 1968, p. 1680.

What are the five specific elements of an express trust?

There are five elements necessary to create an express trust, including: (1) intent to create a trust; (2) a valid trust purpose; (3) designation of a trust property (called the trust "res" or "corpus"); (4) designation of a trustee (a person who holds a trust res for the benefit of another called a "beneficiary"); and (5) determination of one or more trust beneficiaries.

Intent. As previously stated, the trustor must externally manifest an intent to presently create a trust with respect to a particular property. This means that the trustor must make clear either by words or conduct that he or she intends to presently transfer legal title to property to a trustee who must hold the property for the benefit of another. No special technical language is required—the words "trust" or "trustee" need not be used. Nor is it necessary that the trustor notify the beneficiary of the trust's creation. A trust is not a contract, and consideration is not required between trustor-trustee or trustor-beneficiary.

However, the trustor's intent must be to *presently* create a trust, or a trust will not arise. This means that the trustor most intend that the trust take effect immediately rather than at some future date. For example, there is no trust created where Ed Brown states to his corporate business manager, "As soon as I return from Europe, I want you to have the business for the benefit of my children". Of course, once Ed returns from Europe and delivers the corporate common stock to his business manager, the trust will go into effect.

Additionally, the trustee must intend to create a legal obligation in the trustee to hold the property for the benefit of another. The trustor's "hope", "wish", "request", or "suggestion" that the transferee hold for the benefit of another is generally insufficient. Such language is termed "precatory" language (words "requesting" or "suggesting" rather than clearly and positively commanding) and will not give rise to an express trust. Thus, where Ed Brown transfers his ranch to "my wife, Leona, with the hope that she will use the ranch to care for our children", there is no express trust created, and Leona is free to disregard Ed's wishes.

However, there are exceptions where even precatory language will result in creation of an express trust. For example, the courts have held that the more specific and definite the trust instructions, the more likely it is that the trustor intended to create a legal obligation in the transferee to hold for the benefit of another notwithstanding his or her use of precatory language. Also, where the result of ruling out a trust is to place complete ownership and beneficial use of the property in a stranger as opposed to a spouse or child, a trust is likely to be upheld even where the language is merely "wishful" or "hopeful". This is particularly so where the precatory instructions are given to a personal representative (an executor or administrator of a decedent's estate as will be explained in Ch. 30) who is not also a natural beneficiary of the transferor. And, finally, where the tranferor has for some time taken care of the purported beneficiary, the court is likely to find an express trust even in the presence of equivocal and precatory language.

Purpose. Generally speaking, a trust may be created for any lawful purpose. Most often, the purpose is to provide for the welfare of some private individual, such as the trustor's spouse or child. Where the purpose is to promote the public welfare or to benefit a charity, the trust is a "charitable" trust to which special rules apply (charitable trusts are considered in a following section).

Where a transferor of property attempts to create a trust for what the law determines to be an improper purpose, the trust will be held invalid because it is contrary to public policy. Thus, trusts designed to induce criminal or tortious acts, or to encourage immorality or divorce are invalid. Similarly, trusts created for the purpose of hindering or defrauding creditors are impermissible and invalid. As you know, creditors have a right to set aside any such transfer as a fraudulent conveyance.

Trusts in violation of the Rule Against Perpetuities are also invalid. In other words, a trustor may not use a "perpetual trust" to tie up property for an indefinite period of time. The trust interest must vest within the maximum period of lives in being plus 21 years. (At this time, you may wish to review the Rule Against Perpetuities in Ch. 4 of the text). Thus, if a *childless* Ed Brown makes an inter vivos transfer of his ranch to "the Bank of Illinois in trust for my grandchildren", the attempted trust is invalid as a violation of the Rule Against Perpetuities. Ed's grandchildren can be ascertained only when Ed's children die, and since Ed's children must necessarily be born after creation of the trust, the trust will vest, if at all, in a grandchild born after the period of all measuring lives and 21 years has elapsed. For example, suppose that Ed creates the trust this year, fathers a child the following year, then dies the next year. If Ed's child has a child 30 years later, and Ed's child dies 35 years thereafter, Ed's grandchild will receive the beneficial interest more than 21 years after the death of Ed, the measuring life. Because of this, the trust violates the Rule Against Perpetuities and is invalid.

Trust Property. The property placed into trust is called trust *res* or *corpus*. Generally, any transferable property may form a part of the trust res or corpus whether the property is real or personal, tangible or intangible, presently possessory or a future interest. All that is required is that the property satisfy the following three requirements:

First, the trustor must own the property at the time he or she creates the trust. Ed Brown's son, Tom, for example, cannot create a trust by transferring "all the property I will inherit from my father Ed Brown's estate, upon my father's death, in trust for the benefit of my wife, Mary". Tom has no present interest in the property to transfer, and Tom cannot create a trust with respect to property that he does not own.

Second, the trustor's property interest must be transferable (i. e., alienable). Of course, most property interests are transferable. But once in a while, a legal provision or contract term will render a valuable property interest nonalienable. Federal Treasury Regulations, for example, provide that certain U.S. Savings Bonds cannot be transferred—as a result, they cannot be placed into trust. Similarly, some life insurance policies prohibit any transfer of the ownership interest, thus ruling out a transfer in trust to a trustee.

Third, the assets comprising the trust res or corpus must be identifiable—that is, they must be sufficiently described so that the property can be identified. Thus, where Ed Brown transfers "in trust, $100,000 of assets from my stocks, bonds, and farm equipment", the trust will fail for lack of definiteness.

Designation of a trustee. To become a trustee, a person must have capacity not only to take ownership of the property but to properly manage it as well. While the trustor may specifically name or designate a trustee, the trust will not fail for lack of definiteness if the trustor should fail to do so. The court, under such circumstances, will simply appoint an appropriate trustee. And the court will appoint a new trustee any time the death or resignation of a trustee gives rise to a vacancy in the trusteeship during the active period of the trust. The only exception to this rule is where the trustor makes it clear that he or she intends the trust to fail if a particular named trustee declines to serve, cannot serve, or later becomes unable to continue serving.

As to the trustee's ownership interest in the trust res, it is "bare legal title" only. Bare legal title permits the trustee to manage and use the property to the extent necessary to carry out the trust purpose. Generally, the trust instrument will spell out in detail the trustee's powers with regard to the property (e. g., the instrument may provide that the trustee has the power of sale). Because the trustee's interest is one of bare legal title, with all beneficial ownership belonging to the beneficiaries of the trust, creditors of the trustee cannot reach the trust res or corpus in any way.

Where a specifically designated trustee refuses to accept the trusteeship, as he or she has every right to do, the trustee is said to "disclaim" the position. Disclaimer is impossible, however, once the trustee has accepted the duties; and, having accepted, the trustee cannot resign without a court order relieving him or her of further responsibility.

As to removal, the court may remove a trustee who breaches his or her responsibilities of proper management and accounting, or who has a conflict of interest in remaining in the position. And the trust instrument itself may provide that the beneficiaries of the trust have power to remove the trustee and to require appointment of a new one.

In the event that the trustee ever becomes the sole beneficiary of the trust, the trustee's bare legal title will merge with the beneficiary's beneficial interest, and the trustee-beneficiary will become the fee simple absolute owner of the property, free and clear of any trust arrangement.

Designation of beneficiary. A private express trust will fail in the absence of a named or identifiable beneficiary, called a *cestui que trust,* who is capable of enforcing the trust terms. Again, the beneficiary need not be specifically named or even be in existence at the time the trust is created so long as enough information is given so that the beneficiary may be identified either now or later with reasonable certainty. Thus, a transfer of property by Ed Brown to "the First National Bank of New York in trust for the benefit of my son, Tom Brown, for his life, and remainder in trust to Tom's children" is valid even though Tom Brown has no children at the time of creation of the trust—it will be easy enough to identify the children at a later date. If children are never born to Tom Brown, the trust res or corpus will simply go back to Ed Brown or his heirs by means of a resulting trust (to be explained later in this chapter).

Where one or more persons are designated beneficiaries by means of reference to a "class" of persons, the class must be sufficiently described that the court can determine who is entitled to enforce the trust. The terms "children", "brothers and sisters", and "family" (i. e., a spouse and children) are sufficiently definite; "relatives" may be too indefinite. "Friends" is unquestionably vague, and the trust will fail for lack of definiteness.

Any person, including a minor and an incompetent, may be a beneficiary. In addition to having enforcement rights against the trustee, a beneficiary has an actual property interest (the beneficial use of the property) in the trust res or corpus. The interest may be for years, for life, or forever. It may be contingent, vested, determinable, or subject to a condition. Where there is more than one beneficiary, the co-beneficiaries are presumed to hold their interests as tenants in common unless the trustor has expressly indicated that they are to hold in another form of concurrent ownership.

In the absence of a provision to the contrary, a beneficiary is free to transfer his or her interest in the trust to another. The beneficiary may borrow money on the interest, or even transfer the interest in trust for the benefit of some other person. Where the beneficiary has more than a life estate interest, the beneficiary may transfer the interest at death by will or intestacy. And creditors of the beneficiary can reach the interest to satisfy their lawful claims (an exception arises under a "spendthrift" trust as will be explained in a later section).

Finally, a person who benefits only incidentally from the existence of a trust is not a beneficiary, and has no rights under the terms of the trust (e. g., the spouse or creditor of a beneficiary).

How are trusts created?

A property owner may create a trust simply by declaring that he or she holds property for the benefit of another, in which case the trustor is also the trustee. Where this occurs, there is no need for delivery of the trust res to the trustee since the trustor-trustee is already in possession of the property interest. All that is required is that the trustor-trustee separate the trust res from his or her other property. If real estate is involved, the trustor must generally execute and record a deed of the land to himself or herself as trustee.

Where the trustee is someone other than the trustor, delivery of the trust res to the trustee is required. This is so whether the transfer in trust is made inter vivos or at death (a deathtime transfer by will is called a *testamentary* transfer). With regard to personal property, delivery generally means actual physical transfer of the property. Where actual physical delivery is impossible, a symbolic

or constructive delivery as described in Ch. 3 will suffice. With regard to real property, a written deed or other effective writing is needed to transfer the real property to the trustee who will hold it in trust for the benefit of the cestui que trust.

A trust will come into existence regardless of notice to or express acceptance by either the trustee or beneficiary. Like the trustee, the beneficiary is free to disclaim the interest, and, if he or she chooses to do so, a resulting trust in favor of the trustor or his or her estate will be declared. If the beneficiary says nothing, but acquiesces in receiving benefits from the trust, the beneficiary's acceptance will be presumed.

As stated previously, a trust is not a contract, and no consideration between or among parties is required (the great majority of trusts are created gratuitously as gifts). If a beneficiary does in fact give something in return for creation of the trust, and all other elements of a contract are present, the beneficiary will have legal rights to enforce the trust the same as with any other enforceable contract.

A trust may be created orally or in writing. The only difficulty with an oral trust is in the area of real property. Say that a trustor transfers real property to a trustee with oral instructions that the trustee is to hold the property in trust for the benefit of another. While the oral trust is valid, it will be unenforceable under the Statute of Frauds in the event that the trustee does not voluntarily comply with the trustor's orders. An exception arises where the oral trust is evidenced by a writing, signed by the trustor, containing the essential terms of the trust agreement in a reasonably complete and definite form, including a description of the land and designation of the beneficiaries (usually, a deed signed by the trustor will accomplish this purpose). Another exception arises where the beneficiary, relying on the oral trust, takes possession of the land and makes repairs, improvements, or pays real property taxes. In the case of either exception, the trustee can be made to perform the terms of a completely oral trust.

In any event, so long as the trustee is willing to perform the trust, no one can object that the trust is oral—not the trustor, not the beneficiaries, nor any other party whether related or unrelated to the transaction.

What is a spendthrift trust?

Earlier in the chapter, we pointed out that a beneficiary's ownership interest in the trust res is generally transferable and can usually be "reached" by the beneficiary's creditors. We also suggested that the trustor may use what is termed a "spendthrift" trust to limit the beneficiary's interest, making it nontransferable and not subject to the claims of creditors.

A "spendthrift" trust may be defined as a trust that prohibits the beneficiary from voluntarily or involuntarily transferring his or her interest in the trust res. Thus, the beneficiary of such a trust may not sell or give away his or her right to trust income or principal; nor can the beneficiary's creditors reach the trust in any way.

As a practical matter, spendthrift trusts are used to protect financially incompetent beneficiaries from their own financial mismanagement. Such trusts are recognized in almost all states. However, a few states, such as California, permit creditors of the spendthrift to reach at least a part of the trust income, although not any of the trust res or corpus. Of course, once trust income or principal is paid to a spendthrift beneficiary, it becomes an asset just like any other and may be transferred or reached by creditors.

On the grounds of public policy, some courts permit certain creditors of the ben-

eficiary to reach the trust even where there is a valid spendthrift provision. For example, the wife or child of a "husband/father beneficiary" may reach the trust income or principal insofar as is necessary for their support. Additionally, anyone who furnishes "necessaries" for the beneficiary may reach the trust. And tax claims of state and federal governments are routinely permitted against the trust income and principal.

In conclusion, it should be pointed out that a trustor cannot create a spendthrift trust for himself or herself. It would be contrary to public policy to permit a person, by means of a trust device, to place his or her property beyond the reach of creditors.

What is a discretionary trust?

A "discretionary" trust is one in which the trustee has absolute discretion to either pay or refuse to pay trust income or principal (i. e., trust res or corpus) to a beneficiary. Generally, where the trustee decides not to pay, he or she is bound by the terms of the trust to distribute to another beneficiary instead.

A particular beneficiary under a discretionary trust may thus receive no interest whatsoever. And unless and until the trustee decides to pay the beneficiary, the beneficiary has no interest to transfer, and creditors of the beneficiary have no interest to reach. But suppose that the beneficiary nevertheless attempts to transfer his or her "interest" in the trust, or a creditor of the beneficiary attaches the beneficiary's "interest". Once notified of the transfer or attachment, the trustee must either pay the transferee or the attaching creditor, or pay no one. If the trustee pays the beneficiary subsequent to receiving notice of the third party's claim, he or she will be personally liable to the transferee or creditor. Of course, the trustee may simply decide within his or her discretion not to pay that particular beneficiary (or his or her transferee or creditor), but to pay another beneficiary instead. In this case, the transferee or creditor will be out of luck.

Unlike a spendthrift trust, then, a discretionary trust does not prohibit a beneficiary from transferring his or her interest; nor does it make it impossible for creditors of the beneficiary to reach the beneficiary's interest. What it does do is render such actions meaningless unless and until the trustee decides to exercise discretion in favor of the beneficiary.

The discretionary trust is used often in states that do not recognize spendthrift trusts. To accomplish a result similar to the spendthrift provision, the trustor will name an alternative beneficiary who can be counted on to come to the spendthrift beneficiary's assistance should the latter get into financial trouble (in which case distribution to the spendthrift would be of benefit only to his or her creditors). For example, Ed Brown might transfer property in trust to Linda Thompson who is given discretion to pay trust income and portions of the principal to either Ed's son, Tom Brown, or Ed's friend and Tom's godfather, Jim Johnson. If Tom Brown gets into financial difficulties, and his creditors attach his interest in the trust, Linda Thompson can exercise discretion in favor of Jim Johnson. Jim, who is Tom's godfather and has Tom's interests at heart, can be counted on by Ed to take care of Tom through a sense of moral obligation.

What is a protective trust?

A "protective" trust is an ordinary trust that automatically becomes discretionary (giving the trustee discretion to distribute the trust income to any or all of a group of beneficiaries, including the original beneficiary) at such time as the original beneficiary becomes insolvent or attempts to transfer his or her interest in the trust, or a creditor of the beneficiary attempts to reach the trust interest. A good example of a protective trust is found in the following transfer by Ed Brown:

> To the United States National Bank in trust for my son Tom Brown, but if Tom ever cannot pay his debts as they fall due, or if Tom's creditors ever try to reach his interest in this trust, or if Tom ever tries to voluntarily transfer his interest in this trust to another, then in trust for Tom Brown, his wife Mary, or Tom's older sister Suzie, or his younger sister Betty, as the trustee believes best under the circumstances.

As in all protective trusts, the only way that Tom, the original beneficiary, can be certain of receiving benefits is by remaining solvent and making no effort to transfer his trust interest.

Because the protective trust indirectly accomplishes the objectives of a spendthrift trust, it is used often in jurisdictions that do not recognize spendthrift provisions.

What is a support trust?

A "support" trust is one in which the trustee has the power to pay the beneficiary only so much of the trust income as is necessary for the beneficiary's support, education, and maintenance. The trust income may be spent for these purposes and no others. Like the spendthrift beneficiary, the support beneficiary cannot transfer his or her interest in the trust; nor may creditors of the beneficiary reach the interest. Payment by the trustee to the beneficiary's transferee or creditor would not accomplish the support of the beneficiary, and, under the terms of the support trust, every payment must do this and only this.

What is a blended trust?

A "blended" trust is a trust designed by its terms to benefit a group of people rather than individual beneficiaries (e.

g., "in trust for the Jones family"). The trust is nonseparable or "blended", meaning that no one member of the group has an individual interest distinct and separable from the interest of the group. Accordingly, no one member can transfer an interest in the property; and no creditor of an individual member may reach the trust income or corpus.

What is a charitable trust?

A "charitable" trust, or trust created for a charitable purpose, is created in much the same manner as a private express trust. The trustor of a charitable trust must intend to transfer a trust res to a trustee to be held for the benefit of another. However, unlike a private express trust, a charitable trust will not fail for lack of a definite, designated beneficiary. All that is required is that the trust be created for the benefit of some group (which may be indefinite in number) large enough to produce a public benefit. The fact that a single individual or a small group is the direct recipient of the trust fund monies will not be fatal to the charitable trust so long as the recipient is selected from a group "substantial" enough in size to produce the required public benefit. For example, a charitable trust will be upheld in a transfer of funds in trust to the Milton Meyer School of Business for the establishment of an annual scholarship program for well qualified business students who show an interest in the insurance profession. The fact that one or two students will be singled out each year as scholarship recipients does not destroy the charitable nature of the trust.

As to the requirement of a charitable purpose, it is generally agreed that a valid charitable trust may be created for any of the following purposes:

(1) Relief of poverty;

(2) Advancement of education;

(3) Advancement of religion;

(4) Promotion of health;

(5) Government or municipal purposes; and

(6) Purposes resulting in benefit to the community (e. g., animal care, maintenance of public ceme- fountains).

Thus, any purposes promoting religion, education, health, arts, sciences, etc. are valid charitable purposes.

Whatever the charitable purpose, it must be clearly expressed in the trust instrument: a trust created simply "for charity", "for benevolent purposes", or "for the benefit of all mankind" will fail for indefiniteness.

The trustee of a charitable trust need not be a charitable organization—in most cases, the trustee is a financial institution or other financial expert. In any case, the trustee must be empowered to use the trust funds only for the charitable, nonprofit making purpose.

In some states, a trustor may be prohibited by statute from creating charitable trusts by will. Such statutes, called "Mortmain" or "fear of hell" statutes, are designed to protect a decedent's close relatives (e. g., a spouse and children) from the decedent's "eve of death" decision to leave his or her property to charity in an effort to increase his or her chances for "eternal salvation". The statutes vary from state to state: some prohibit the decedent trustor from leaving more than one-third to one-half of his or her estate to charity, while others prohibit any charitable gifts in a will executed by the decedent within a short period of time (typically 30 days) before death. In all states, such statutes do not apply unless the decedent is survived by close relatives who would otherwise stand to inherit the property. And many states have altogether eliminated Mortmain statutes, thus abolishing any statutory restriction on testamentary gifts to charities.

The Rule Against Perpetuities does not apply to charitable trusts. As a result, a charitable trust may be created to last forever. However, this does not mean that a trustor may postpone a gift in trust to a charity until some future period beyond lives in being and 21 years. Thus, while it is permissible for Ed Brown to transfer property in trust "for the University of Texas forever", it is impermissible for him to transfer the property in trust "for my son Tom Brown for life, then for Tom's children for life, then for Tom's grandchildren for life, then for the University of Texas forever". To postpone the charitable gift in trust in this manner is to violate the Rule Against Perpetuities.

Because a charitable trust may last forever, it sometimes happens that a charitable trust "outlives" its charitable purpose (for example, where a trust is established to found and maintain a "girls" school, and the girls school is ultimately made coeducational). Where this occurs, the courts may turn to the special charitable trust doctrine of *cy pres* which enables the courts to apply the charitable trust funds to another, similar charitable purpose in the event the original trust purpose cannot be carried out. *Cy pres* applies only to charitable trusts, and it will not be invoked where the trustor clearly intended to strictly limit use of the trust funds to the original charitable purpose. Where the doctrine is found to apply, the courts will make every effort to locate a charitable purpose as close to the trustor's original purpose and intent as possible. In the example above, the courts might well find that the trustor's intent would be to continue to benefit the school even though it had become coeducational.

Finally, a charitable trust containing a provision discriminating on the basis of race or sex will fail for violating the U.S. Constitution.

What is an honorary trust?

An "honorary" trust falls somewhere in between a charitable trust and a private express trust. It is not a charitable trust because it is created for a noncharitable purpose; nor is it a private express trust because it has no specific, designated beneficiary capable of compelling enforcement of the trust. The typical example of an honorary trust is a transfer of property in trust for the benefit or care of an animal. For example, suppose that Ed Brown transfers property in trust to Jim Johnson for the benefit and care of Ed's pet dog, Samson. The transfer is an honorary trust and not a charitable trust because there is no charitable purpose (a transfer in trust for the benefit of "stray animals" or "to prevent cruelty to animals" would be a valid charitable purpose and a valid charitable trust).

Because honorary trusts lack a beneficiary, and because they frequently violate the Rule Against Perpetuities ("lives in being plus 21 years" cannot be measured by animal lives), most jurisdictions do not recognize their validity. Generally, however, where the transferee "trustee" voluntarily carries out the transferor "trustor's" intent, the courts will allow the transfer to stand, although they will not acknowledge the transfer as a valid trust. Where the transferee fails to carry out the transferor's instructions, the property will return to the transferor or his heirs by means of a resulting trust.

What is a resulting trust?

A "resulting" trust is a trust that arises by operation of law when a person transfers property, intending that someone other than the transferee should have the beneficial interest but failing to clearly express such intent. Although the transferor expresses no intent that a trust should come into existence, and while no valid express trust arises, the courts will imply a "resulting" trust in favor of the intended beneficiary, and the transferee will serve as a trustee for that person. The resulting trust may be based entirely on oral evidence—it need not be evidenced by a writing—even where real property is involved.

Basically, there are three situations where a resulting trust will arise:

(1) *Failure of an express trust.* Where a trustor intends to create an express trust, but the trust, for some reason, fails (e. g., because it fails to designate a beneficiary, or because land is involved and there is no evidentiary writing), the court will imply a resulting trust in favor of the trustor on the basis that the trustor intended either to create a valid express trust or to keep the property for himself or herself. The transferee of the property, in such case, will hold the property in a resulting trust for the transferor ("trustor") or his or her estate.

(2) *Fulfillment of the trust purpose.* Similarly, where a trustor transfers more property in trust than is needed to accomplish the trust purpose, any excess trust res will be held in a resulting trust for the trustor or his or her estate. Again, the theory is that the trustor intends any surplus to revert to his or her own use, rather than to the benefit of the trustee. For example, suppose that Ed Brown transfers property to Jim Johnson in trust for Ed's son, Tom Brown, for life. If, at Tom's death, there is property remaining in the trust, a resulting trust will be declared in favor of Ed Brown or his successors in interest. Jim Johnson will have no claim to the property.

Another example arises where there are charitable trust funds remaining after the specific charitable purpose of the trust has been carried out. Assuming that the doctrine of cy pres cannot be applied to extend the trust, the trustee will hold the leftover property in a resulting trust for the benefit of the original trustor or his or her estate.

(3) *Purchase money resulting trust.* A resulting trust will sometimes be declared in favor of a person who pays all or a substantial part of the purchase price for property while another person succeeds to legal ownership and title of the property (e. g., where Ed Brown hands Jim Johnson $25,000 and tells him to pay the money to Bill Girod who will then transfer owership of his three bedroom home to Jim; or where Ed simply pays $25,000 to Bill with instructions that he should transfer title to the property to Jim Johnson). Where this occurs, the person acquiring legal title to the property will hold the property in trust for the benefit of the person who supplied the purchase price.

Purchase money resulting trusts are not favored by the courts, and, where possible, the courts will find that the purchaser did not intend such a trust to arise. Thus, a purchase money resulting trust will generally be ruled out where there is a close family relationship between the person who furnishes the purchase price and the person who acquires legal title. The person acquiring title, in this case, is said to be a natural object of the purchaser's bounty (particularly so in the case of a spouse or child), and it is natural to assume that a gift of the property was intended and not a trust relationship. This strong presumption in favor of gifts, coupled with the fact that many "purchasers" intend to merely loan money rather than obtain the benefit of the property, serves to defeat the purchase money resulting trust in a good majority of cases.

Along the same line, where the effect of finding a resulting trust in favor of the purchaser would be to help the purchaser accomplish an unlawful purpose, such as defrauding creditors or evading taxes, a purchase money resulting trust will not be declared. For example, suppose that Ed Brown purchases a 100 acre farm and directs that the property be legally transferred to Ed's friend,

Jim Johnson, because Ed is in trouble with his creditors and wants to prevent them from "reaching" the farm property. Ed cannot later ask the court to declare a purchase money resulting trust in his favor. Rather, the entire conveyance will be set aside as a fraudulent conveyance.

Suppose that Ed Brown pays $75,000 and Jim Johnson pays $25,000 towards the purchase price of a 150 acre ranch which is transferred over into the legal ownership of Johnson. In the event a purchase money resulting trust is declared, Jim Johnson will hold a ¾th's undivided interest in the property in trust for Ed Brown. Remember, the "purchaser" does not have to pay the entire price —only a substantial part.

What is a constructive trust?

A "constructive" trust, like a resulting trust, is one that arises by operation of law. However, a constructive trust is imposed by the courts not to comply with the trustor's probable intent (as is a resulting trust) but to prevent a wrong or remedy an injustice that our legal system will not tolerate.

Thus, where a murderer inherits property from his or her victim's estate, the courts will impose a constructive trust in favor of those next entitled to the property, with the murderer in the position of trustee.

A constructive trust will also be declared where a person uses improper methods such as fraud, force, or trickery to acquire another's property: the transferee will hold the property in constructive trust for the person who was fooled, tricked, or otherwise improperly influenced into parting with his or her property.

Similarly, a constructive trust will be imposed where a *fiduciary,* a person who stands in a position of responsibility, trust, and confidence with another, takes advantage of his or her "special position" to gain or acquire control of property that rightfully belongs to the other party. As you will recall from Ch. 21, *Black's Law Dictionary* defines "fiduciary" as follows:

A person having duty, created by his undertaking, to act primarily for another's benefit in matters connected with such undertaking   *   *   *. As an adjective it means   *   *   * relating to or founded upon a trust or confidence.   *   *   *

[A] relationship implying and necessitating great confidence and trust on the one part and a high degree of good faith on the other part   *   *   *

A relation subsisting between two persons in regard to a business contract, or piece of property, or in regard to the general business or estate of one of them, of such a character that each must repose trust and confidence in the other and must exercise a corresponding degree of fairness and good faith.

Out of such a relation, the law raises the rule that neither party may exert influence or pressure upon the other, take selfish advantage of his trust, or deal with the subject matter of the trust in such a way as to benefit himself or prejudice the other except in the exercise of the utmost good faith and with the full knowledge and consent of that other,   *   *   * to take advantage of the forgetfulness or negligence of another being totally prohibited as between persons standing in such a relation to each other. Examples of fiduciary relations are those existing between attorney and client, guardian and ward, principal and agent, executor and heir, trustee and *cestui que trust*, landlord and tenant, etc.[2]

Thus, if an agent who is employed to purchase property for a principal takes title to the property in his or her own name, the courts will impose a constructive trust on the property in favor of the principal. The agent has breached his or her fiduciary relationship and should not be permitted to benefit from the wrongdoing. Similarly, a corporate officer who uses his or her special position to acquire property that the corporation has expressed an interest in will be required to hold the property in a constructive trust for the corporate shareholders. And an employee who acquires title to property on the basis of confidential information disclosed to him or her during the course of employment will be required to hold such property in a constructive trust for the employer.

How long does a resulting trust or constructive trust last?

Generally, where a resulting or constructive trust has been declared, the courts will order the "trustee" to transfer the "trust res" to the "beneficiary" as soon as is practicable. Once the transfer is accomplished, the trust will terminate by operation of law as one and the same person will hold both bare legal title and beneficial use (with such a merger of the legal and beneficial interests, there is no need for the trust to continue).

What are the powers of a trustee?

A trustee has whatever powers are specifically spelled out in the trust instrument (if any), as well as whatever powers are "necessary or appropriate" to accomplishing the purpose of the trust. Thus, even in an oral trust or in a written trust containing no specific powers, the trustee will be deemed to have the following implied powers unless they are expressly withheld at the time of creation of the trust:

(1) *Power of sale.* The trustee has an implied power to sell both the real and personal property making up part of the trust res.

(2) *Power to lease.* The trustee also has an implied power to lease trust property for reasonable periods of time under reasonable lease provisions. Where the trust is to terminate at a specific future date, it is not reasonable to lease the property for a period that will extend beyond the duration of the trust. Where the trust has no fixed term, the trustee is still under a duty of care to see that the property is not leased for a period that will extend beyond the "probable" period of the trust. For example, suppose that Ed Brown transfers property in trust for the benefit of his five year old son, Tom. If the trust is to last for the life of Tom, the trustee could reasonably lease the trust property for a period of 20 years: although it is possible, it is not likely that Tom will die before the period of the lease has elapsed. However, where Ed transfers the same property in trust for the life of his 87 year old grandmother, a lease for 20 years would clearly be unreasonable (Ed's grandmother is likely to die before 20 years has elapsed) and would be beyond the trustee's powers.

(3) *Power to pay expenses.* The trustee has an implied power to incur and pay for the reasonable expenses of managing the trust corpus. Under this power, the trustee may take whatever action is necessary to utilize and preserve the trust property, including making improvements to the property.

The power to borrow against the trust res, on the other hand, is never implied,

---

2. Henry Campbell Black, *Black's Law Dictionary*, Revised Fourth Edition, West Publishing Co., 1968, pp. 753–754.

and must be expressly conferred at the time of creation of the trust. Also, the power to accumulate income is not an implied power, and, in the absence of express power to accumulate, the trustee must at reasonable intervals pay all of the net income from the trust to the income beneficiary pursuant to the terms of the trust.

Is the trustee required to exercise the trust powers? Occasionally, a trust will include what are called "imperative" powers that the trustee must exercise. For example, the trustee may be directed to purchase the beneficiary a new automobile every three years. The trustee has no choice in the matter, and must either exercise the power (i. e., make the purchases) or the court will order him or her to do so. More typically, however, the powers granted to the trustee are "discretionary", and the trustee is free to either exercise a particular power or ignore it completely. The court, in this case, may require the trustee to make a decision (exercise discretion) as to whether or not to exercise the power, but the court will never interfere with the decision the trustee makes.

Trust powers, whether discretionary or imperative, are not considered personal to a particular trustee but are a part of the trustee's office. Thus, if the named trustee dies, any new trustee who is appointed will assume all the old trustee's powers.

A trustee is free to delegate the actual exercise of a power to an employee or agent so long as the trustee exercises a high degree of care in making the delegation. Generally, a trustee is said to exercise proper care in delegating authority where a reasonably prudent businessperson would employ others to help in the same or similar circumstances. The delegation must be of a "ministerial" as opposed to a "discretionary" function: while the trustee can hire others to do "routine" or "ministerial" tasks, he or she must personally exercise discretion. And the trustee must prudently and very carefully select the employee or agent who is to do the work. In any event, the trustee will be personally liable for any losses that occur as a result of an improper delegation—improper because a ministerial function has been carelessly delegated, or because a discretionary function has been wrongfully delegated.

What are the duties of a trustee?

As stated previously, a trustee stands in a fiduciary relationship to the cestui que trust (i. e., the trust beneficiary). The trustee's fiduciary duties with regard to management of the trust estate include:

(1) *Duty of loyalty.* The duty of loyalty refers to the trustee's duty to manage the trust solely in the interest of the beneficiary. The duty is one of absolute loyalty, and the trustee must scrupulously avoid obtaining any personal advantage because of his or her position as trustee. Thus, the trustee may not use or deal with the trust property for his or her own profit or for any other purpose unconnected with the trust. For example, the trustee may not loan personal funds to the trust or borrow money from the trust even if he or she agrees to repay the loan with interest. Nor may the trustee accept a commission from any third party in a trust-related transaction. Similarly, the trustee must not employ a spouse or relative to render services for the trust. And if the trustee is a corporate trustee, such as a bank or trust company, the trustee must not deposit trust funds in its own bank or company; nor may the corporate trustee invest trust funds in the purchase of its own shares (some states do permit investment in corporate shares by statute).

Where a breach of loyalty question arises, the burden of proof will be upon the trustee to come forward with evidence showing that the duty of loyalty has not been violated.

(2) *Duty to properly manage the trust*. The trustee is generally required to exercise that degree of care and skill in managing the trust that a reasonably prudent businessperson would exercise in dealing with his or her own property. Of course, where the trustee represents that he or she has greater skill than a man or woman of ordinary prudence, the trustee will be held to the higher standard of care (for example, a higher standard of care may be required of a lawyer or investment broker). And where the trustee is a corporate trustee (e. g., a bank with a trust department), some courts demand a higher degree of care and skill on the theory that corporate trustees hold themselves out as being specially qualified to manage trust funds.

(3) *Duty to safeguard the trust res*. The trustee is also obligated to properly secure and safeguard the trust res. Again, the standard of care required is that of a reasonably prudent person in caring for his or her own property and safeguarding it from loss or deterioration. Thus, the trustee is required to pay all bills and property taxes on time, and to provide for needed repairs. And if claims are made against the trust assets, jeopardizing the trust corpus, the trustee must hasten to the defense of the trust property.

(4) *Duty to earmark*. The trustee must take special care to keep the trust assets separate from his or her individual assets and the assets of any other trust that he or she is managing. This is called the trustee's "duty to earmark", and the trustee will be liable for any losses that result from a failure to earmark trust funds or assets. However, most states do allow corporate trustees to place property from several trusts in a single common fund to allow for greater flexibility in purchasing common investments.

(5) *Duty to invest*. A trustee is generally obliged to manage the trust and invest the trust properties so as to produce income from the assets of the trust res. The trustee must use reasonable care and skill in making the investments; he or she will be liable for any losses sustained because of a failure to exercise reasonable care. If the trustee simply fails to invest, he or she will be liable for the amount of income that would have been produced had suitable investments been made. Typically, real property must be rented or farmed, and where the property cannot be made productive, it must be sold (of course, the trustor is always free to provide in the trust instrument that the land is to be held onto whether or not it is productive). Unproductive chattels must also be sold; and money must be invested. In making investments, the trustee may be guided by one of the following three standards:

(a) *Express direction*. The trust instrument may specifically authorize the trustee to make investments of a particular nature, or it may limit the trustee to a particular class or type of investment.

(b) *Statutory or legal list*. In some states, there are statutory lists, or "legal lists" as they are sometimes called, that specify the kinds of investments that a trustee can make (the lists are usually confined to the more conservative investments such as government bonds or guaranteed savings). Some of the statutes take a "mandatory" approach and require the trustee to invest only in the areas prescribed. Other statutes are "permissive" and allow the trustee to invest in areas not on the list so long as the investment is proper and prudent for the particular trust purpose. In "straying" from the "permissive" list, the trustee must still use the statute as his or her guide, and must exercise great care in choosing an alternative investment.

(c) *Prudent investor rule*. A majority of states restrict trustee investment, not by statutory list, but by the *prudent investor rule*. Under the prudent investor rule, a trustee is required to use good faith and sound discretion in making investments—he or she must generally do what a prudent businessperson would do in making a permanent disposition of his or her own funds considering both the probable income from and the probable safety of the investment. Thus, in making investments, the "prudent" trustee must consider a variety of factors, including liquidation of the investment (i. e., reduction to cash), diversification, security, and taxation. The trustee must also continuously review whatever investments are made to ensure that they do not become unproductive.

It should be pointed out that government bonds are safe investments whether a statutory list or prudent investor rule is followed. The same is true with respect to a well secured first mortgage on land, although a second mortgage on real property would not necessarily be acceptable. Unsecured loans are generally improper under either rule, and so is investment in real property except where the land is necessary to some other trust purpose such as running a particular business. As to corporate common stocks, they are generally excluded from statutory investment lists, but are permissible investments under the prudent investor rule.

(6) *Duty to properly account.* The trustee has a duty to keep accurate accounts and to present accurate accountings to the beneficiary. Suppose that A delivers property to B to be held in trust for the life of C, all income from the trust res to be distributed quarterly to C, and, upon C's death, the trust res or "principal" to be distributed to remainderman D. Here, the trust instrument provides that one beneficiary, C, is to receive only income from the trust res, while another beneficiary, D, is to receive "principal". If the trust instrument also specifies that it is up to the trustee to determine what is "income" and what is "principal", and what expenses are to be charged to "income" and what expenses to "principal" for purposes of accounting, the trustee's determinations will be deemed conclusive so long as the trustee makes the decisions in good faith.

However, where the trust instrument does not provide that the trustee is to make these determinations on his or her own, the trustee is governed by the following rules which are designed to protect the interests of both life beneficiary and remainderman:

(a) The life beneficiary is entitled to all trust "income", and the remainderman is entitled to all trust "capital" or "principal".

(b) All "ordinary" receipts such as rent, interest, and cash dividends are trust income.

(c) All "extraordinary" receipts such as monies resulting from the sale of trust assets are trust capital or principal.

(d) In a testamentary trust that takes effect upon the trustor's death, all trust earnings resulting from the moment of death are payable as income to the life beneficiary even though the trustee may not receive the trust res until several months after the trustor's death because of the time involved in probate. Thus, trust earnings during the period of probate, will not increase the size of the trust res, but will be distributed as income to the life beneficiary.

(e) A variety of rules have been applied in the situation where a life beneficiary dies, and, at the moment of his or her death, there exists earned (i. e., accrued) income on the trust property that has not yet been received by the trustee. The common law rule was that unless the trustee had actually received the income at the time of the life beneficiary's death, the income would become a part of the trust res for the benefit of the remainderman and the life beneficiary's estate would not be entitled to any of it. The only exception to this rule was for interest deemed earned on a day-to-day basis —whoever was entitled to the interest each day would receive it. Thus, interest that had accrued on a $10,000 savings account for three months prior to the life beneficiary's death would belong to the life beneficiary's estate whether or not the trustee had received the interest at the time of the beneficiary's death.

In contrast to the common law rule, the Revised Uniform Principal and Income Act, a statute in effect in many states today, provides that all income is apportionable except dividends. This means that the life beneficiary's estate is entitled to all income accrued up to the moment of death regardless of receipt by the trustee.

As for dividends, all "ordinary" cash dividends are treated as income and not as principal. "Extraordinary" dividends, on the other hand, may be either income or principal (at least to a certain extent) depending upon the rule that is followed in the particular jurisdiction. The majority or "Massachusetts Rule" states that all cash dividends, whether ordinary or extraordinary, are income belonging to the life beneficiary, while all stock dividends, which are always extraordinary, are a part of trust capital or principal. A cash dividend is considered extraordinary where it is unusual in size or in timing. A stock dividend, which is always extraordinary, refers to the payment of a dividend in stock rather than in money. For example, suppose that trustee B holds 100 shares of General Motors stock in trust for the life of C, all trust income to be paid quarterly to C, and upon C's death, the trust principal to be distributed to D. General Motors may issue additional common stock as a dividend, and give the trustee one share for every 50 shares owned—that is, two shares. Under the majority rule, the two shares form a part of the trust principal and cannot be distributed as income to the life beneficiary C.

The "Pennsylvania Rule" (a minority view) is that extraordinary dividends, stock or cash, are "principal" payments to the extent that they reduce the book value of the shares from what it was when the stock was acquired by the trust. The minority differs considerably from the majority: to the extent that an extraordinary cash dividend reduces the acquisition date book value of the shares of stock held in trust, the dividend forms a part of the trust capital or principal and will ultimately be distributed to the trust remainderman. Any balance remaining will be currently distributed as income to the life beneficiary. Acquisition date book value is found by totaling the assets of the dividend distributing corporation as of the date the trust acquired stock in the corporation, deducting all corporate liabilities as of the same date, and dividing the difference by the number of shares of stock outstanding at that time. For example, suppose that ABC Corporation has total ownership assets of $1,000,000, total debts owing of $700,000 and 300 shares of stock outstanding at the time 50 shares of ABC stock are placed into trust for the life of D, all income from the trust to be distributed quarterly to D, and, upon the death of D, the trust corpus to be distributed to E, the trust remainderman. Acquisition date book value of each of the 50 shares of stock held in trust is determined by subtracting $700,000 from $1,000,000 and dividing the difference (i. e., the net book value) of $300,000 by the 300 shares of stock outstanding—the result, a per share book value of $1,000. Now assume that in Year Y, ABC Corporation has a net income of $50,000 and distributes cash dividends of $50,000 to its shareholders. If ABC Corporation started Year Y with $1,000,000 of assets and $700,000 of debts, and finished the year with the same amount of debts but $1,050,000 of assets because of its income, the $50,000 cash distribution will not result in a reduction of the acquisition date book value of the 50 shares of stock held in trust. The $50,000 dividend will have been paid solely out of the earnings and profits of Year Y. However, if, using the same figures, ABC Corporation distributes, not $50,000, but $100,000 in Year Y, there will be a reduction in acquisition date book value of the stock. This follows because the Corporation will finish the year, after payment of the dividend, with only $950,000 of assets and $700,000 of debts. Subtracting $700,000 from $950,000 and dividing by 300 (the shares of stock outstanding), it can be seen that the per share book value of the stock is now $833.33—a reduction in value of $166.67 per share. Thus, out of the $333.33 dividend ($100,000 divided by 300) paid on each of the 50 shares of stock held in trust, the "extraordinary" portion of $166.67 must be allotted to trust capital or principal in order to maintain a $1,000 per share value for the benefit of the trust remainderman. The remaining cash distribution of $166.66 per share becomes trust income payable to the life beneficiary D.

Because of the many difficulties inherent in determining whether a particular cash dividend has been paid out of corporate earnings or profits so as not to reduce the acquisition date book value of trust held shares, most states follow the Massachusetts Rule and hold that such dividends are in their entirety trust income fully payable to the life beneficiary regardless of reduction in book value. The majority rule may not be the most equitable rule, but it is certainly the easiest to apply.

(f) Proceeds from the sale of trust assets generally become a part of trust capital or principal. The only time any portion of the proceeds will be allocable to trust income is where the trustee unreasonably delays in selling unproductive trust property. You will recall that the trustee has a duty to sell unproductive property so as to convert that part of the trust corpus to productive use. Under the Revised Uniform Principal and Income Act, "unproductive" property is defined as property producing an annual income of less than 1% of its original appraised value or market cost. If the trustee delays in selling such property, he or she must apportion the proceeds of the sale between trust income and principal so as to reflect the income that would have resulted had the trustee sold the property immediately and properly invested the proceeds. In any event, the trustee may be personally liable to the beneficiaries for breaching his or her duty to properly invest.

(g) The general rule is that current expenses are chargeable against trust income while extraordinary expenses (expenses that benefit only the remainderman) are chargeable against trust principal. Thus, extraordinary expenses incurred at the time of creation of a trust in putting the trust property into an income-producing condition are chargeable to the trust capital account. Thereafter, current repairs, maintenance expense, and current insurance premiums are chargeable to trust income. As for taxes, ordinary taxes are payable out of trust income, while assessments for permanent improvements that will last until the trust remainderman comes into possession are payable out of principal. Mortgage interest, another current expense, is chargeable to income, while payment against the mortgage debt itself is chargeable to principal.[3]

Administration expenses of the trust, including compensation for the trustee's services, are generally apportioned between income and principal accounts. Some statutes provide that the administration expenses should be evenly divided between the two accounts, while other statutes maintain that the costs should be

3. Costs incurred in selling trust assets and in defending title to such assets is also chargeable to the principal account (this being "for the benefit" of the capital account).

split on the basis of the services rendered and the respective benefits received by the life beneficiary and trust remainderman. Allocation of expenses under the latter statutes is thus left to the discretion of the trustee and the courts.

As a means of keeping the corpus intact for the remainderman, most courts also require the trustee to deduct from the income account for depreciation of the trust assets, and to add the amount deducted to the principal account. Depreciation, of course, refers to the decline in value of an asset as the result of normal wear and tear or the like. By deducting depreciation loss from the income account and adding back into the principal reserve, the trust remainderman will ultimately receive a well-preserved res rather than a trust corpus depleted in value by the mere passage of time.

Is it possible to change or terminate an existing trust?

An existing trust may be changed or terminated as follows:

(1) *By the trustor.* The general rule is that a trustor has no power to change or revoke an existing trust unless the trustor expressly reserved such rights at the time of creating the trust (a few states hold to the contrary and say that a trust is revocable unless it is expressly stated to be irrevocable). Merely reserving a right to change or modify the trust does not in itself create a right to terminate the trust. However, expressly reserving a right to terminate or revoke the trust does bestow upon the trustor the right to change or modify the terms of the trust. By statute in several states, the creditors of a trustor who reserves a power to revoke can reach the trust corpus even though the trustor has failed to exercise his or her power.

(2) *By the trustee.* A trustee cannot change or terminate a trust unless the trust instrument specifically authorizes him or her to do so.

(3) *By the beneficiaries.* Generally, the beneficiaries of a trust can change or terminate the trust if the following three conditions are met:

First, all the beneficiaries, however remote or contingent their interests, must consent to the change or termination. If, for any reason, one or more beneficiaries cannot or will not consent, any suit to bring about change or termination will fail.

Second, all the beneficiaries must be legally competent to consent to the change or termination. A mentally incompetent beneficiary or one under legal age cannot consent, and a change or termination of the trust cannot take place (occasionally, the court will appoint a guardian ad litem to represent the interests of an underaged beneficiary, in which case, upon the guardian's consent, the change or termination may be granted).

Third, the contemplated change or termination must not defeat a "material purpose" of the trust as orginally contemplated by the trustor. Thus, a spendthrift trust, by its very nature, cannot be terminated because the trustor's original and material intent was that the beneficiary be protected from himself or herself. And where the trustor provides that a trust set up for the benefit of a child is not to terminate until the child reaches a specified age (for example, 45 years), to permit termination prior to that date would obviously defeat a material purpose of the trustor.

(4) *By the courts.* The courts will never disturb trust provisions as to beneficiaries and their respective shares. However, the courts will sometimes modify the management or administration of a trust where an unforeseen change in circumstances renders the prescribed administration harmful to a material purpose of the trust. For example, suppose that Ed Brown places his farm in

trust for the benefit of his ten year old son, Tom, with a provision that Tom should not receive any income or principal from the trust until he reaches 21 years of age. Now suppose that Ed Brown dies immediately thereafter in an accident that leaves young Tom badly injured. If the cost of Tom's medical care is substantial and longterm, the courts are likely to permit distribution of trust income and principal to the boy even though he is only ten years old. Had Ed Brown been able to "foresee" events, he would have wanted to provide for his son's care; and withholding distribution until Tom reaches 21 would defeat the material purpose of Ed Brown's trust—namely, to provide funds at a time when Tom needs them.

Similarly, if Ed Brown's trust provides that the farm is to be operated as a farm for the duration of the trust, and it later becomes apparent that unforeseen changes in the surrounding area make it impossible to continue operating profitably as a farm, the courts may modify the terms of the trust and permit an alternative use of the land.

(5) *By operation of law.* A trust automatically terminates by operation of law once the specified term of trust is over (e. g., a trust created "for ten years", "for the life of A", or "until C is 30 years old"). A trust will also terminate automatically if the trust purpose is fulfilled. Thus, where Ed Brown places property in trust "for my son Tom Brown until he finishes law school and becomes an attorney", the trust will terminate by operation of law once Tom finishes law school and is admitted to the practice of law.

Termination by operation of law additionally occurs where the legal title of the trustee merges with the equitable, beneficial interest of the beneficiary (i. e., where the trustee becomes the only beneficiary, the trust terminates, and the trustee owns the entire "bundle of sticks" in what was formerly the trust res).

And, finally, where the trust res is completely used up or destroyed, the trust can no longer exist and so ceases to be by operation of law.

CASES

CASE 1—*After Alice gave the ring back Angelo claimed a "resulting trust."*

PRASSA v. CORCORAN

Supreme Court of Illinois, 1962.
24 Ill.2d 288, 181 N.E.2d 138.

DAILY, Justice.

The plaintiff, Angelo Prassa, instituted this action in the superior court of Cook County against his ex-fiancee, Alice Patricia Corcoran, and her father, H. James Corcoran, seeking to impress a trust on an improved parcel of real estate, title to which is jointly in plaintiff and Alice, for an accounting, and for a decree compelling conveyance of the property to him. Alice Corcoran appeals from a decree finding that a resulting trust arose in favor of the plaintiff and directing that she execute a deed in favor of the plaintiff. * * *

The uncontroverted evidence indicates plaintiff and defendant became engaged to be married in July, 1959. As a token of the engagement plaintiff gave her a ring. In contemplation of the marriage it was decided that a two-flat building in which they could live after marriage be purchased. It was at the suggestion of defendant's father that plaintiff decided to purchase the apartment building in which Alice resided with her parents. It was planned that after the marriage plaintiff and Alice would live in the second floor apartment and her parents would continue to live downstairs. Negotiations were handled by defendant's father and the sellers, but it was contemplated by the parties that plaintiff alone would pay the consideration for the building. Having reached an agreement on the price, a contract was prepared by the attorney for the sellers. On September 1, 1959, plaintiff and his fiancee signed the contract and plaintiff paid the sellers' attorney $2,000 as earnest money. The balance of $18,750 was to be paid by plaintiff on the passing of the deed. Defendant signed the contract "Alice Patricia Prassa" even though at the time she was a single woman. Pursuant to the contract, the sellers, on October 1, delivered a warranty deed conveying the property in question to "Angelo Prassa and Alice Patricia Prassa, his wife, not in tenancy in common but in joint tenancy." The plaintiff then paid to the sellers the balance of the purchase price in cash. Plaintiff testified he told the sellers or their representatives how he wanted the contract and deed to be made out, the manner chosen being due to the fact that "we were going to get married the following month and we figured why go through all the expense of having it changed after we were married." Plaintiff had no conversation with the defendant as to how she was to be designated in the documents, but had only discussed it with her father and the lawyer. Defendant testified she signed the documents in the manner directed by the plaintiff. She had never signed her name that way before and was not aware of any legal rights possessed by her under the contract until the present litigation ensued.

On November 4 plaintiff and his fiancee, in the course of decorating and furnishing the apartment which they were going to occupy, had a dispute. She gave the engagement ring back to the plaintiff. Plaintiff that same evening attempted to return the ring to defendant, but she refused it. Defendant's parents were informed of the occurrence that evening. The following day plaintiff sent flowers to Alice and visited her that evening for the purpose of attempting a reconciliation. Plaintiff told her if she wouldn't take the ring he wouldn't come back. She again refused to accept the ring. Three days later Alice called plaintiff telling him that she would now accept the ring. At this time plaintiff agreed to drive her to work and discuss the matter. Thereafter unavailing discussions between themselves and with a clergyman were held concerning possible reconciliation. They were fruitless and upon defendant's refusal to convey to plaintiff her interest in the building, plaintiff instituted this suit.

The character of the trust relied upon by plaintiff is that of a resulting trust created by operation of law. The applicable rules of law have been frequently stated. A resulting trust arises by operation of law where one person pays or furnishes the consideration for a deed conveying real estate to another. Whether or not such a trust arises depends in every case upon the intention, at the time of the conveyance, of the person who furnishes the purchase price. Such a trust arises, if it arises at all, the instant the legal title is taken, and is founded upon the natural equity that he who pays for the property should enjoy it, unless he intended by the vesting of title to confer a beneficial interest upon the grantee. The payment of the consideration raises a *prima facie* presumption in favor of a resulting trust. This presumption, however, may be rebutted by parol proof of an intention on the part of the payor that the grantee shall take the beneficial interest and not merely the legal title. No general rule can be stated that will determine when a conveyance made to one other than the person furnishing the consideration will carry with it a beneficial interest and when it will be construed to create a trust, but the intention must be gathered from the facts and circumstances as shown by the record in each case. Where a deed absolute in terms and without condition or reservation conveys real estate to two persons as joint tenants, the language of the deed is sufficient to show an express intent to convey both the legal title and the beneficial interests to the two grantees as joint tenants, but if the purchase price was paid by only one of such grantees, this indicates an intention that that grantee is the only one beneficially interested in the property, and under such facts, the expressed intent as shown by the deed must give way to the rule of equity which protects the party paying the purchase price by raising a resulting trust in his favor.

* * *

Where * * * the uncontroverted evidence is that the plaintiff paid the original payment and sole consideration for the property, and that title to the property in question was conveyed to the plaintiff and defendant, as joint tenants, such facts bring this case within the resulting trust doctrine.

* * *

Upon the foregoing facts and considerations the law raises a *prima facie* presumption in favor of a resulting trust, and imposes upon the grantee the burden of going forward with the evidence and showing an intention on the part of the grantor that she was to have some beneficial interest in the property.

* * * [T]here is clear proof in support that plaintiff did not intend to vest in defendant a beneficial interest in the property at the time of the conveyance.

The contract and deed indicate that the intended interest of the defendant in the property was to be as plaintiff's wife and not as Alice Patricia Corcoran. Such conclusion is also evident from Alice's concern over whether she should sign the contract in that manner and then doing so pursuant to plaintiff's verbal request. Defendant herself testified that plaintiff had told her prior to the conveyance that he "had saved money for a home when he was to marry"; moreover, the property was to serve as a home for plaintiff and defendant as well as her parents. Plaintiff's testimony that he chose the particular form of the contract for convenience is additional corroboration of a nondonative intention at the time of the conveyance.

Although a resulting trust cannot be predicated upon a condition subsequent to the conveyance, subsequent conduct and attitude toward the act in question and the property acquired may be used to shed light upon the true intention of the plaintiff. Defendant's father, who was integrally involved in the negotiations and consummation of the purchase transaction, testified that after the marriage appeared definitely off he stated that he wished to buy the property from plaintiff "for what he (plaintiff) paid for it." Alice testified that pursuant to her father's offer she made efforts to secure funds with which to purchase the building. From such evidence the only reasonable inference to be drawn is in support of an intention held by plaintiff not to make a gift prior to consummation of marriage. This certainly is not to suggest that a gift cannot be given by one engaged individual to the other in contemplation of marriage. Rather, under the circumstances here presented, the chancellor was warranted in finding that plaintiff did not intend a gift. In determining that no gift was contemplated and therefore not consummated during the period of engagement, it is immaterial which of the parties was responsible for the breaking of the engagement.

*   *   *

Decree affirmed.

CASE 2—*Were the "Happy Birthday" checks from dad properly charged to the trust?*

JIMENEZ v. LEE

Supreme Court of Oregon, In Banc, 1976.
274 Or. 457, 547 P.2d 126.

O'CONNELL, Chief Justice.

This is a suit brought by plaintiff against her father to compel him to account for assets which she alleges were held by defendant as trustee for her. Plaintiff appeals from a decree dismissing her complaint.

Plaintiff's claim against her father is based upon the theory that a trust arose in her favor when two separate gifts were made for her benefit. The first of these gifts was made in 1945, shortly after plaintiff's birth, when her paternal grandmother purchased a $1,000 face value U.S. Savings Bond which was registered in the names of defendant "and/or" plaintiff "and/or" Dorothy Lee, plaintiff's mother. It is uncontradicted that the bond was purchased to provide funds to be used for plaintiff's educational needs. A second gift in the amount of $500 was made in 1956 by Mrs. Adolph Diercks, one of defendant's clients. At the same time Mrs. Diercks made identical gifts for the benefit of defendant's two other children. The $1,500 was deposited by the donor in a savings account in the names of defendant and his three children.

In 1960 defendant cashed the savings bond and invested the proceeds in common stock of the Commercial Bank of Salem, Oregon. Ownership of the shares was registered as "Jason Lee, Custodian under the Laws of Oregon for Betsy Lee [plaintiff]." At the same time, the joint savings account containing the client's gifts to defendant's children was closed and $1,000 of the proceeds invested in Commercial Bank stock.[1] Defendant also took title to this stock as "custodian" for his children.

The trial court found that defendant did not hold either the savings bond or the savings account in trust for the benefit of plaintiff and that defendant held the shares of the Commercial Bank stock as custodian for plaintiff under the Uniform Gift to Minors Act (ORS 126.805–126.880). Plaintiff contends that the gifts for her educational needs created trusts in each instance and that the trusts survived defendant's investment of the trust assets in the Commercial Bank stock.

It is undisputed that the gifts were made for the educational needs of plaintiff. The respective donors did not expressly direct defendant to hold

---

1. The specific disposition of the balance of this account is not revealed in the record. Defendant testified that the portion of the gift not invested in the stock "was used for other unusual needs of the children." Defendant could not recall exactly how the money was used but thought some of it was spent for family vacations to Victoria, British Columbia and to satisfiy his children's expensive taste in clothing.

1152   MANAGING THE PROPERTY OF OTHERS   Ch. 29

the subject matter of the gift "in trust" but this is not essential to create a trust relationship. It is enough if the transfer of the property is made with the intent to vest the beneficial ownership in a third person. That was clearly shown in the present case. Even defendant's own testimony establishes such intent. When he was asked whether there was a stated purpose for the gift, he replied:

> " * * * Mother said that she felt that the children should all be treated equally and that she was going to supply a bond to help with Elizabeth's educational needs and that she was naming me and Dorothy, the ex-wife and mother of Elizabeth, to use the funds as may be most conducive to the educational needs of Elizabeth."

Defendant also admitted that the gift from Mrs. Diercks was "for the educational needs of the children." There was nothing about either of the gifts which would suggest that the beneficial ownership of the subject matter of the gift was to vest in defendant to use as he pleased with an obligation only to pay out of his own funds a similar amount for plaintiff's educational needs.

Defendant himself demonstrated that he knew that the savings bond was held by him in trust. In a letter to his mother, the donor, he wrote: "Dave and Bitsie [plaintiff] & Dorothy are aware of the fact that I hold $1,000 each for Dave & Bitsie in trust for them on account of your E-Bond gifts." It is fair to indulge in the presumption that defendant, as a lawyer, used the word "trust" in the ordinary legal sense of that term.

Defendant further contends that even if the respective donors intended to create trusts, the doctrine of merger defeated that intent because plaintiff acquired both legal and equitable title when the savings bond was registered in her name along with her parents names and when Mrs. Diercks' gift was deposited in the savings account in the name of plaintiff and her father, brother and sister. The answer to this contention is found in II Scott on Trusts § 99.4, p. 811 (3d ed 1967):

> "A trust may be created in which the trustees are A and B and the sole beneficiary is A. In such a case it might be argued that there is automatically a partial extinguishment of the trust, and that A holds an undivided half interest as joint tenant free of trust, although B holds a similar interest in trust for A. The better view is, however, that there is no such partial merger, and that A and B will hold the property as joint tenants in trust for A. * * *"

Having decided that a trust was created for the benefit of plaintiff, it follows that defendant's purchase of the Commercial Bank stock as "custodian" for plaintiff under the Uniform Gift to Minors Act was ineffectual to expand defendant's powers over the trust property from that of trustee to that of custodian.[4]

4. If defendant were "custodian" of the gifts, he would have the power under the Uniform Gift to Minors Act (ORS 126.820) to use the property "as he may deem advisable for the support, maintenance, education and general use and benefit of the minor, in such manner, at such time or times, and to such extent as the custodian in his absolute discretion may deem advisable and proper, without court order or without regard to the duty of any person to support the minor, and without regard to any other funds which may be applicable or available for the purpose." As custodian defendant would not be required to account for his stewardship of the funds unless a petition for accounting were filed in circuit court no later than two years after the end

Defendant's attempt to broaden his powers over the trust estate by investing the trust funds as custodian violated his duty to the beneficiary "to administer the trust solely in the interest of the beneficiary."

The money from the savings bond and savings account are clearly traceable into the bank stock. Therefore, plaintiff was entitled to impose a constructive trust or an equitable lien upon the stock so acquired. Plaintiff is also entitled to be credited for any dividends or increment in the value of that part of the stock representing plaintiff's proportional interest. Whether or not the assets of plaintiff's trust are traceable into a product, defendant is personally liable for that amount which would have accrued to plaintiff had there been no breach of trust. Defendant is, of course, entitled to deduct the amount which he expended out of the trust estate for plaintiff's educational needs. However, before he is entitled to be credited for such expenditures, he has the duty as trustee to identify them specifically and prove that they were made for trust purposes. A trustee's duty to maintain and render accurate accounts is a strict one. This strict standard is described in Bogert on Trusts and Trustees § 962, pp. 10–13 (2d ed 1962):

> "It is the duty of the trustees to keep full, accurate and orderly records of the status of the trust administration and of all acts thereunder. * * * 'The general rule of law applicable to a trustee burdens him with the duty of showing that the account which he renders and the expenditures which he claims to have been made were correct, just and necessary. * * * He is bound to keep clear and accurate accounts, and if he does not the presumptions are all against him, obscurities and doubts being resolved adversely to him.' He has the burden of showing on the accounting how much principal and income he has received and from whom, how much disbursed and to whom, and what is on hand at the time."

Defendant did not keep separate records of trust income and trust expenditures. He introduced into evidence a summary of various expenditures which he claimed were made for the benefit of plaintiff. It appears that the summary was prepared for the most part from cancelled checks gathered together for the purpose of defending the present suit. This obviously did not meet the requirement that a trustee "maintain records of his transactions so complete and accurate that he can show by them his faithfulness to his trust."

In an even more general way defendant purported to account for the trust assets in a letter dated February 9, 1966, written to plaintiff shortly after her 21st birthday when she was in Europe where she had been receiving instruction and training in ballet. In that letter defendant revealed to plaintiff, apparently for the first time, that her grandmother had made a gift to her of a savings bond and that the proceeds of the bond had been invested in stock. Without revealing the name of the stock, defendant represented that it had doubled in value of the bond from $750 to $1,500. The letter went on to suggest that plaintiff allocate $1,000 to defray the cost of additional ballet classes and that the remaining $500 be held in reserve to defray expenses in returning to the United States and in getting settled in a college or in a ballet company.

of plaintiff's minority. ORS 126.875. As the trustee of an educational trust, however, defendant has the power to use the trust funds for educational purposes only and has the duty to render clear and accurate accounts showing the funds have been used for trust purposes. See ORS 128.010; Restatement (Second) of Trusts § 172 (1959).

Defendant's letter was in no sense a trust accounting. In the first place, it was incomplete; it made no mention of Mrs. Diercks' gift. Moreover, it was inaccurate since it failed to reveal the true value attributable to the Commercial Bank stock. There was evidence which would put the value of plaintiff's interest in the stock at considerably more than $1,500.[9]

Defendant contends that even if a trust is found to exist and that the value of the trust assets is the amount claimed by plaintiff there is sufficient evidence to prove that the trust estate was exhausted by expenditures for legitimate trust purposes. Considering the character of the evidence presented by defendant, it is difficult to understand how such a result could be reached. As we noted above, the trust was for the educational needs of plaintiff. Some of the expenditures made by defendant would seem to fall clearly within the purposes of the trust. These would include the cost of ballet lessons, the cost of subscribing to a ballet magazine, and other items of expenditure related to plaintiff's education. But many of the items defendant lists as trust expenditures are either questionable or clearly outside the purpose of an educational trust. For instance, defendant seeks credit against the trust for tickets to ballet performances on three different occasions while plaintiff was in high school. The cost of plaintiff's ticket to a ballet performance might be regarded as a part of plaintiff's educational program in learning the art of ballet, but defendant claims credit for expenditures made to purchase ballet tickets for himself and other members of the family, disbursements clearly beyond the purposes of the trust.

Other expenditures claimed by defendant in his "accounting" are clearly not in furtherance of the purposes of the trust. Included in the cancelled checks introduced into evidence in support of defendant's claimed offset against the trust assets were: (1) checks made by defendant in payment of numerous medical bills dating from the time plaintiff was 15 years old (these were obligations which a parent owes to his minor children); (2) checks containing the notation "Happy Birthday" which plaintiff received from her parents on her 17th, 18th and 22nd birthdays; (3) a 1963 check with a notation "Honor Roll, Congratulations, Mom and Dad"; (4) defendant's check to a clothier which contains the notation "Betsy's Slacks and Sweater, Pat's Sweater, Dot's Sweater" (defendant attempted to charge the entire amount against the trust); (5) defendant's check to a Canadian Rotary Club for a meeting attended when he joined plaintiff in Banff after a summer ballet program; (6) $60 sent to plaintiff to enable her to travel from France, where she was studying ballet, to Austria to help care for her sister's newborn babies. There were also other items improperly claimed as expenditures for plaintiff's educational benefit, either because the purpose of the outlay could not be identified or because defendant claimed a double credit.[11]

It is apparent from the foregoing description of defendant's evidence that the trial court erred in finding that "Plaintiff in these proceedings has

9. It appears that with the accumulation of cash and stock dividends the total value of plaintiff's interest at the time she received defendant's letter would amount to as much as $2,135. This figure is an approximation derived from the incomplete stock price information before us. It is important only to demonstrate that defendant did not render an adequate accounting. Our calculation does not include the value of plaintiff's interest in stock purchased with the proceeds of Mrs. Diercks' gift.

11. The double counting occurs where defendant claims credit for cashier's checks sent to plaintiff while she was staying in Europe and at the same time also claims credit for his personal checks used to purchase the cashier's checks.

received the accounting which she sought and * * * is entitled to no further accounting." The trial court also erred in finding that "Defendant did not hold in trust for the benefit of Plaintiff" the product traceable to the two gifts.

The case must, therefore, be remanded for an accounting to be predicated upon a trustee's duty to account, and the trustee's burden to prove that the expenditures were made for trust purposes. There is a moral obligation and in proper cases a legal obligation for a parent to furnish his child with higher education. Where a parent is a trustee of an educational trust, as in the present case, and he makes expenditures out of his own funds, his intent on one hand may be to discharge his moral or legal obligation to educate his child or on the other hand to follow the directions of the trust.[13] It is a question of fact in each case as to which of these two purposes the parent-trustee had in mind at the time of making the expenditures.[14] In determining whether defendant has met this strict burden of proof, the trial court must adhere to the rule that all doubts are resolved against a trustee who maintains an inadequate accounting system.

The decree of the trial court is reversed and the cause is remanded for further proceedings consistent with this opinion.

PROBLEMS

1. Answer the following "True" or "False" and give reasons for your answers:

   (a) In a trust, the trustee holds equitable title to the trust res while the beneficiary holds bare legal title.

   (b) A trust is not a contract, and no consideration between or among parties is required.

   (c) The Rule Against Perpetuities does not apply to charitable trusts.

   (d) The trustee of a charitable trust must be a charitable organization.

   (e) Generally, creditors of a trust beneficiary are able to "reach" the beneficiary's interest in the trust.

13. The rule stated by Bogert indicates why different's intent is important:

"The trustee is entitled to be credited on the accounting with all sums paid or property transferred by him from trust funds, and with sums advanced by him from his own funds, when such payments or transfers were in the exercise of powers expressly or impliedly granted to him by the trust instrument, or powers given him by statute or court order, or reasonably incidental to the exercise of such powers." Bogert on Trusts and Trustees § 972(1) (2d ed 1962), pp. 218–220.

If defendant made expenditures out of his own funds intending to discharge his obligation to educate his child, the payments were not "sums advanced by him from his own funds * * * in the exercise of [trust] powers." Such expenditures would be in his capacity as plaintiff's father and not as trustee.

14. There is evidence that defendant considered expenditures made prior to February 9, 1966 (the date of defendant's letter to plaintiff which we previously described) as not being for trust purposes because at that date he regarded the proceeds from the savings bond still intact. The letter read:

"I believe that it would be fair and realistic that I should henceforth offset against this $1500 such further funds as you may need to continue with your ballet instruction, or to travel to New York or elsewhere to commence your ballet career on an independent, self-supporting basis.

"The situation is comparable to that of the mother bird that finally nudges the baby out of the nest so that it, too, may learn to fly."

(f) Discretionary trusts are used often in states that do not recognize spendthrift trusts.

(g) A trustee may not delegate his or her ministerial duties to third parties.

(h) No matter how much care a trustee exercises in making investments, if the investments result in loss, the trustee will be liable to the trust beneficiaries.

(i) A trustor has no power to change or revoke an existing trust unless he or she reserved such rights at the time of creating the trust.

(j) A beneficiary has no power to change or terminate an existing trust.

2. What five elements are required for an express trust? Explain.

3. What trusts, if any, arise in the following situations? Explain.

(a) Minnie Waverly hands her adult son, Robert, a check for $5,000 and orally tells him, "Here, Robert, I hope you will use this to help put Cindy (Robert's daughter) through college."

(b) Lori Saunders dies leaving a will which provides for the transfer of $50,000 in real and personal property "to First State Bank for the care and benefit of the Hank Simmons family."

(c) Marsha Hunter conveys a parcel of real property to Mike Lolly. Marsha orally tells Mike, "You are to hold this land in trust for Grace Goodfellow."

(d) Nick Jones dies leaving a will which provides for the transfer of $100,000 "to First State Bank for the care and benefit of my friends."

(e) Nick's will also provides for the transfer of $20,000 "to Sara Johnson in trust for the benefit and care of my cat, Mittens."

4. *Define the following*: protective trust; support trust; purchase money resulting trust; constructive trust; Mortmain Statutes; cestui que trust.

5. Hacker is considering the creation of either a lifetime (intervivos) or testamentary (by his will) trust. In deciding what to do, which of the following statements is correct?

a. An intervivos trust must meet the same legal requirements as one created by a will.

b. Property transferred to a testamentary trust upon the grantor's (creator's) death is *not* included in the decedent's gross estate for federal tax purposes.

c. Hacker can retain the power to revoke an intervivos trust.

d. If the trust is an intervivos trust, the trustee must file papers in the appropriate state office roughly similar to those required to be filed by a corporation.

[# 35, May 1978 CPA Exam]

6. Allgood is a trustee of a trust in which Lance is the life beneficiary and Ronald is the remainderman who is entitled to the corpus (principal) upon the death of Lance. Five thousand shares of stock in Parkard Company make up a portion of the trust. In September 1977, Parkard

declared a 10% stock dividend out of the earnings accumulated after the trust was created. Parkard also issued rights to subscribe to new stock, and the trustee sold these stock rights for $5,000. Regarding Allgood's duties as the trustee, which of the following is correct, assuming there is no express provision covering the point in the trust indenture?

a. The proceeds from the subsequent sale of the 10% stock dividend must be divided proportionately between the beneficiaries.

b. The proceeds from the sale of the stock rights must be added to the corpus (principal) of the trust.

c. Allgood has discretion insofar as determining the proper share the beneficiaries are to receive in connection with the $5,000.

d. Allgood was obligated to obtain the consent of the beneficiaries prior to selling the stock rights.

[# 44, November 1977 CPA Exam]

7. When Wayne died in 1976 his will created a testamentary trust out of the residue of his estate for the benefit of his wife during her lifetime and the remainder to his son, Eric, upon Mrs. Wayne's death. The residue of the estate included rental property subject to a $45,000 first mortgage. Probate of the estate has been completed, and the property deeded to the trustee to hold pursuant to the terms of the will. Carlton, Wayne's attorney and advisor, was named as executor and the Jefferson Trust Company was named as the sole trustee. Which of the following parties does *not* have an interest in the trust property sufficient to obtain fire insurance on said property?

a. The son, Eric.

b. Wayne's wife.

c. The first mortgagee.

d. Eric's wife.

[# 47, November 1977 CPA Exam (See also Chapter 11 on insurable interests and Chapter 27 on mortgages.)]

8. Harris is the trustee named in Filmore's trust. The trust named Filmore as the life beneficiary, remainder to his children at age 21. The trust consists of stocks, bonds, and three pieces of rental income property. Which of the following statements best describes the trustee's legal relationships or duties?

a. The trustee has legal and equitable title to the rental property.

b. The trustee must automatically reinvest the proceeds from the sale of one of the rental properties in like property.

c. The trustee is a fiduciary with respect to the trust and the beneficiaries.

d. The trustee must divide among all the beneficiaries any insurance proceeds received in the event the real property is destroyed.

[# 30, May 1978 CPA Exam]

9. *TRUE-FALSE QUESTION.* If during his life X establishes a trust, he may not authorize his trustee

a. To keep all trust assets invested in a particular stock.

b. To allocate stock dividends received to principal rather than to income.

c. To lend money to the trust.

d. To withhold income from one beneficiary and pay it to another.

e. To accumulate income for a minor.

[# H., 156, 157, 158, 159, 160, May 1966 CPA Exam]

10. You have been assigned by a CPA firm to work with the trustees of a large trust in the preparation of the first annual accounting to the court. The income beneficiaries and the remaindermen are in dispute as to the proper allocation of the following items on which the trust indenture is silent:

(1) Costs incurred in expanding the garage facilities of an apartment house owned by the trust and held for rental income.

(2) Real estate taxes on the apartment house.

(3) Cost of casualty insurance premiums on the apartment house.

(4) A two-for-one stock split of common stock held by the trust for investment.

(5) Insurance proceeds received as the result of a partial destruction of an office building which the trust owned and held for rental income.

(6) Costs incurred by the trust in the sale of a tract of land.

(7) Costs incurred to defend title to real property held by the trust.

Required: 1. Explain briefly the nature of a trust, the underlying concepts in the allocation between principal and income, and the importance of such allocations.

2. Indicate the allocations between principal and income to be made for each of the above items.

[# 7.b., May 1976 CPA Exam]

Chapter 30

TRANSFERRING PROPERTY AT DEATH: WILLS

Does a person have a right to control the disposition of his or her property at death?

Based upon all available and relevant evidence, the old saying that "you can't take it with you" is true. Because we cannot take our property with us at death, it is only natural that we should want to provide for its disposition to others. Thus, under our American legal system, one of the most important rights and characteristics of private property ownership is the right of every person to determine and control the disposition of his or her property at death.

We have already learned that many individuals use the joint tenancy with the right of survivorship as a means of avoiding probate and automatically transferring property interests at death to surviving joint tenants. We also know that inter vivos trusts may be used to transfer property interests (e. g., Marcus Peabody may transfer property to Harry Hemlock in trust for Marcus Peabody for life, and upon Marcus Peabody's death, the trust res to be distributed to Marcus' wife, Marlene).

However, the subject matter of this chapter is the testamentary (deathtime) transfer of property by will or intestacy —wills, will substitutes, intestate death, and probate procedure [1] are all consid-

ered in detail in this final chapter of our text.

What is a will?

A "will", as defined by Black's Law Dictionary, is:

The legal expression or declaration of a person's mind or wishes as to the disposition of his property, to be performed or take effect after his death * * * [It is] a revocable instrument by which a person makes disposition of his property to take effect after his death * * * [It is] a written instrument executed with the formalities of law, whereby a person makes a disposition of his property to take effect after his death. * * * [T]he form of an instrument is of little consequence in determining whether it is a will, but if it is executed with formalities required by statute, and if it is to operate only after death of maker, it is a "will." [2]

A will, therefore, may be defined as a written instrument executed in accordance with the formalities prescribed by state statute whereby a property owner (called a "testator") directs the disposition of his or her real and personal property to take effect upon death. Because a will does not effectively transfer property

1. In 1969, in an attempt to encourage uniformity of probate laws throughout the United States, the National Conference of Commissioners on Uniform State Laws and the American Bar Association gave their approval to the Uniform Probate Code (UPC). Although the UPC was designed to uniformly reduce the time and expense of probate, and to increase its efficiency and flexibility, the Code has not yet achieved widespread acceptance (some eleven states had adopted all or part of the UPC as of January 1, 1977) and so cannot be considered a "uniform" law in the same sense as is the UCC. Thus, the testamentary transfer of property and the administration of decedents' estates are still very much subject to varying regulation on a state by state basis.

2. Henry Campbell Black, *Black's Law Dictionary*, Revised Fourth Edition, West Publishing Co., 1968, p. 1772.

until the testator's death, the testator is free to revoke or modify the will at any time during life. As a result of this right to revoke, the beneficiaries named in the will have no interest in the property until the testator dies, and, until that time, are said to have but a "mere expectancy".

Although wills are revocable and legally ineffective until death, the law provides that the meaning of words and phrases used in a will are to be construed or interpreted according to the language usuage and law in effect at the time of execution of the will rather than at the time of the testator's death.[3]

What are the requirements of a valid will?

Generally, there are four requirements for a valid will:

(1) Testamentary intent;

(2) Testamentary capacity at the time of execution of the will;

(3) Execution without fraud, duress, undue influence, or mistake; and

(4) Execution in full compliance with the statutory formalities.

If any one of these four requirements is lacking, the decedent's property will pass as if there is no will.

(1) *Testamentary intent.* The testator must intend that the instrument presently operate as his or her last will and testament. This means that the testator must specifically intend (a) to provide for the disposition of his or her property (b) to take effect only upon death (c) according to the terms of the written "will". Testamentary intent is a subjective test, and if it can be shown that a particular decedent did not have the required intent to presently create a will, the will will fail despite the fact that, on its face, the instrument appears proper in every respect.

Where a will is executed in full compliance with statutory formalities, a presumption arises that the instrument was also executed with the required testamentary intent. In most states, the presumption is rebuttable, and evidence tending to show lack of intent is always admissible. Thus, evidence that a decedent-testator orally stated that he or she did not intend to execute a valid will but only to play a joke on his or her relatives (or accomplish some other similar objective) will rebut the presumption of testamentary intent and rule out a valid will.

Testamentary intent is also lacking where the words used in the writing indicate an intent to execute a will at some time in the future rather than to presently provide for the disposition of property at death. For example, suppose that Sidney Smith signs and witnesses a document that states, "It is my intention to make a will, leaving all my property to my friend, Mary Lewis". The document is not a valid will because Sidney Smith indicates no intent that the signed and witnessed writing serve as his last will and testament—Sidney's expressed intention is to execute a will in the future. Even if Sidney sends a letter to his attorney, instructing the attorney to prepare a will leaving all his property to Mary Lewis, the letter itself will not be effective to transfer Sidney's property in the event that Sidney dies before the will is drawn up and executed. Sidney does not intend the letter to serve as a valid will: he intends merely to execute a will in the future.

However, the requirement of a *present* intent does not prohibit a testator from including will provisions that are conditioned upon the happening of some specified event or contingency. For example, one spouse will often provide by will that the other spouse is to receive real and personal properties only if he or she survives the testator-spouse. Similarly, it is perfectly proper for Sidney Smith to execute a will containing a provision that his properties are to be transferred to Mary

---

3. However, the law to be applied is generally the law in effect at the time of the testator's death.

Lewis only if Mary marries him. If the condition occurs (i. e., if Mary marries Sidney), Mary will be entitled to Sidney's property upon his death; if the condition does not occur, the will provision will be inoperative, and Mary will receive nothing.

The only time a condition will not be acceptable in a will is where the condition is contrary to public policy. Thus, a provision in a will providing for a transfer of property to Mary Lewis "only if Mary divorces her husband, Lance", is contrary to public policy and will be legally disregarded. In most jurisdictions, the named beneficiary (in this case Mary) will still be entitled to the property after deletion of the condition so long as all four requirements for a valid will are otherwise present.

(2) *Testamentary capacity.* To make a valid will, a person must be of sound mind. "Sound mind" does not demand a superior intelligence, or even an average mentality. All that is required is that the testator have, if not actual knowledge, at least the capacity to generally understand and remember:

(a) The nature and extent of his or her property;

(b) The people who are the natural objects of his or her bounty or generosity (e. g., relatives and close friends); and

(c) The disposition that he or she is making of the property.

It is essential that the testator have the capacity to understand and interrelate these factors so as to come up with an orderly plan for the disposition of his or her property.

Because of the requirement of testamentary capacity, many wills begin with a statement by the testator that he or she is of "sound mind". Such language suggests that the testator has the required testamentary capacity to make a will, but evidence tending to show the contrary is al-ways admissible. In some states, a showing of capacity must be made before a will will be admitted to probate. In most states, however, there is a rebuttable presumption of competency that effectively forces those who would contest capacity to disprove its existence. Rumor has it that one old fellow decided to bypass all question of his capacity by beginning his will as follows: "I, _____, being of sound mind, used all of my property and spent all of my money, before I died." Needless to say, the old fellow's proclamation took his relatives by surprise and obviated all need for a will contest.

While a person may lack capacity to make a will for many reasons, the most common reasons are lack of legal age, presence of mental deficiency, and presence of mental derangement or delusion.

Underage. All states provide by statute that a person under a certain age (usually 18 or 21) cannot make a valid will.

Mental deficiency. As previously stated, the test of mental competency is whether a person has the mental capacity to understand and interrelate the nature and extent of his or her property, the natural objects of his or her bounty, and the disposition of property that he or she is making. It takes no great mental giant to satisfy this test, and a person possessing but minor mental deficiencies will not be prevented from making a will on the grounds of testamentary incapacity. Thus, a person who is incompetent to manage a business, or even his or her own affairs, is not necessarily incompetent to make a valid will.

Mental derangement or delusion. A delusion or irrational belief held by a testator will invalidate only that portion of the will affected. However, a belief is irrational only where it is so contrary to reason and good sense that it indicates mental derangement. Thus, if the testator had any rational basis, however tenuous, for the belief, it will not be considered irrational. If the testator had any facts to reason from (incorrect though the reasoning might be), the belief will not be considered a mental delusion. But a testator who disinherits his only daughter because he concluded without benefit of any facts that his wife of 35 years was once unfaithful and gave birth to the girl as a result, the testator is probably suffering from an insane delusion regarding the child, and the disinheritance provision will likely be disregarded.

(3) *Absence of fraud, duress, undue influence, and mistake.* A person who believes that a testator executed a will as a result of fraud, duress, undue influence, or mistake may petition the probate court upon the testator's death to disregard the will in whole or in part. If the person who alleges the existence of one of these four factors proves facts sufficient to substantiate the charge, the probate court will set aside the affected portions of the will, which may very well be the will in its entirety.

You will recall our extensive study of fraud, duress, undue influence, and mistake in Ch. 8, "Factors Preventing Mutual Assent in Contracts". By way of review, the important elements of these four factors are summarized below.

Fraud. Fraud, as it relates to the execution of a will, refers to an intentional misrepresentation of a material fact made with intention that a testator rely upon the misrepresentation in executing a will, and in fact resulting in the testator's execution of a will in justifiable reliance thereon. Again, there are two kinds of fraud: fraud in the execution and fraud in the inducement.

Fraud in the execution, also called "fraud in the factum", usually involves the surreptitious substitution of one document for another. For example, a testator may be tricked into signing a document without realizing that the instru-ment is a will. Or the testator may be fooled into signing one will, believing it to be another. In both cases, the testator is deceived as to the nature of the instrument or its contents and has no testamentary intent as that term is defined in the law.

A testator who intentionally and knowingly signs and executes a will in justifiable reliance upon another's fraudulent misrepresentation is a victim of *fraud in the inducement.* For example, suppose that Sidney Smith's son, Robert, is killed in an automobile accident while touring Europe. If one Gina Smith suddenly shows up and persuades Sidney to execute a will in her favor by falsely representing that she is Robert's widow, Sidney's will will be a product of fraud in the inducement. In this case, the testator has not been deceived as to the nature of the instrument; nor does he lack the required testamentary intent. Rather, his testamentary intent and execution have been fraudulently induced, and the resulting will or affected portions are invalid.

Upon a showing of fraud in the execution or fraud in the inducement, the probate court will set aside the will in whole or in part. The court may also use the remedy of constructive trust (as defined in Ch. 29) to carry out the testator's probable intent. Thus, where the testator has been fraudulently persuaded to change beneficiaries, the court may impose a constructive trust for the benefit of the party who would have received the property but for the fraud. For example, where Sidney Smith is persuaded to execute a will in favor of his niece, Freda, rather than his son, Robert, on the basis of Freda's fraudulent assertion that Robert has been killed in Europe, the court may impose a constructive trust in favor of Robert. A constructive trust may be imposed whether the fraud affects the entire will or merely a portion of the will.

Duress. Black's Law Dictionary defines duress in this manner:

> Unlawful constraint exercised upon a man whereby he is forced to do some act that he otherwise would not have done. It may be either "duress of imprisonment," where the person is deprived of his liberty in order to force him to compliance, or by violence, beating, or other actual injury, or duress "per minas", consisting in threats of imprisonment or great physical injury or death. Duress may also include the same injuries, threats, or restraint exercised upon the man's wife, child, or parent. * * * Duress consists of any illegal imprisonment, or legal imprisonment used for an illegal purpose, or threats of bodily or other harm, or other means amounting to or tending to coerce the will of another, and actually inducing him to do an act contrary to his free will. * * * And it is never duress to threaten to do that which a party has a legal right to do * * * such as, instituting or threatening to institute civil actions.[4]

Thus, "duress" is physical or mental coercion that deprives a testator of his or her own free will and forces the testator to execute a will or portions of a will that he or she would not otherwise execute. The key word here is "coerce". Where duress or coercion can be established, the will or its affected portions will be declared invalid by the court.

Undue influence. Like duress, undue influence demands an overpowering of the testator's own free will. However, it does not require the element of coercion or actual force that is needed for a showing of duress. Undue influence may be defined as persuasion, pressure, or influence, short of actual force, but stronger than mere advice, that so overpowers the testator's own free will that he or she cannot act intelligently, understandingly, and voluntarily, but acts, instead, subject to the will or purposes of another in executing a will. Generally, the courts require a combination of the following four factors as proof of undue influence:

(1) The testator was in a weakened physical or mental state and thus susceptible to the undue persuasion of others;

(2) The person accused of exercising undue influence was in a position to personally benefit or gain from its exercise;

(3) The person had an opportunity to exercise the undue influence; and

(4) The will, as written, provided for an unnatural disposition of the testator's property, rather than a disposition to the natural objects of the testator's bounty, such as a spouse and children.

Undue influence does not require the existence of a confidential or fiduciary relationship (e. g., attorney and client, or trustee and beneficiary) between testator and influencer, but the presence of such a relationship certainly makes undue influence easier to establish. This is because a person who stands in a relationship of trust and confidence with the testator is likely to have more opportunity to unduly influence the provisions of the testator's will than is a complete stranger or casual friend. Thus, where a person in a confidential or fiduciary relationship benefits from provisions in a testator's will at the expense of the testator's natural bounty, the court is likely to declare the provisions invalid as a result of undue influence. The courts will impose a constructive trust for the benefit of the testator's close friends or relatives.

4. Henry Campbell Black, *Black's Law Dictionary*, Revised Fourth Edition, West Publishing Co., 1968, p. 594.

Mistake. A testator who mistakenly signs an instrument not realizing that it is a will has no testamentary intent, and the will is void. However, the will of a testator who merely makes a mistake as to who his or her living relatives are, or what their health and financial status might be, will not be invalid in whole or in part unless the mistake appears on the face of the will. For example, if, upon hearing that his cousin, Ruth, has died in Europe, Sidney Smith provides by will, "I leave all my property to the American Red Cross", the will will not be set aside if it later turns out that Ruth is alive and well. However, if Sidney provides, "I leave all my property to the American Red Cross because my cousin, Ruth, has died in Europe", and Ruth later turns up alive, the will will be declared invalid and a constructive trust imposed for her benefit.

(4) *Proper statutory formalities.* The statutory formalities for execution of a will are essentially the same from state to state. Typically, there are four: (a) signature of testator; (b) publication by the testator; (c) competent witnesses; and (d) signature of witnesses.

Signature. The testator may sign the will in any manner so long as he or she intends what is written to serve as his or her complete signature. A full name, a nickname, or initials may be used; even a mark or rubber stamp will be sufficient if the testator intends it to serve as his or her signature. If the testator is too ill to sign the will, or is illiterate and cannot sign, he or she can direct another person to sign for him or her: so long as the other person signs in the presence of and at the direction of the testator, the signature will be valid. Again, a full name, a nickname, initials, a rubber stamp or mark will be acceptable.

Some states do not require the testator to sign at the end of the will (a signature at the end of an instrument is called a "subscription"). Thus, a full name, a

nickname, or a rubber stamp anywhere on the instrument will serve as a valid signature so long as that is the testator's clear intent. Other states do require a subscription, and hold that if anything appears after the testator's signature other than an attestation clause (a statement by the witnesses affirming the testator's signature), the entire will is void (a minority of these states hold that only the provisions appearing after the signature are void). Of course, even where subscription is not required, the testator cannot simply add on to the will or make changes in the will after the will has been executed. Change or modification must be accomplished by a valid *codicil* (i. e., a properly executed amendment as will be explained in a later section).

Finally, the testator must either sign in the presence of the required witnesses, or acknowledge (i. e., declare as genuine) in their presence a signature previously placed on the instrument by himself or herself or by another at his or her direction.

Publication. Required in but a minority of states, "publication" refers to a declaration by the testator to the assembled witnesses that the instrument is the testator's will. The publication may be by words or conduct so long as the nature of the instrument is communicated to the witnesses. Usually, the attestation clause will acknowledge that the testator has declared the writing to be his or her last will and testament.

In no case is it necessary for the witnesses to be familiar with the contents of the will.

Witnesses. A will must generally be witnessed by two (in a few states, three) competent witnesses. The testator must sign or acknowledge the will, and publish the will, where necessary, in their assembled presence.

A "competent" witness is a witness old enough and of sufficient mental capacity to understand the nature of what he or she is witnessing. No minimum age is required.

So long as a person is mature enough to understand the proceedings so as to be able to testify in court regarding them should the need ever arise, the person's youth will be no bar to competency. Also, the fact that a witness who was competent at the time of execution of the will later becomes incompetent will not affect the validity of the will.

A witness must have no beneficial interest in the will—that is, he or she must receive no direct interest by the terms of the instrument. However, the effect of an "interested" party witnessing the will is not to invalidate the entire will, but only the gift to that particular witness. Thus, a person who by the terms of the will is to receive $5,000 in cash cannot witness the will or he or she will forfeit the interest. However, a person who stands but to indirectly benefit from the will (e. g., a spouse or creditor of a beneficiary) is not an "interested" party and may freely serve as a witness. Similarly, an attorney who prepares a will is not considered an interested party merely because he or she will ultimately receive a probate fee from the testator's estate. Nor is an intestate heir (one who would receive property if the testator had no will) an interested party unless, of course, he or she is also named as a beneficiary under the will.

The only time a gift to an interested witness will be upheld is where more than the required number of witnesses attest to the will, and the interested witness can be legally disregarded. A disregarded witness is called a "supernumerary" witness (i. e., an extra witness over and above the statutory requirement). Where more than one witness is interested, all must be supernumerary or none will be: unless there are sufficient witnesses apart from the interested parties to satisfy the statutory requirement, all gifts to the interested witnesses will be voided.

Signature of witnesses. The witnesses must also sign the will, attesting to the testator's signature and to the publication, where required. Where publication is called for, the witnesses must attest to (affirm) their knowledge of the nature of the instrument. Where it is not required, the witnesses need only attest to the testator's execution of a document— not to their knowledge of the kind of document.

Most states require the witnesses to sign the will in the presence of the testator, although not necessarily within each other's presence. As to what constitutes "presence", the courts use two tests: the "scope of vision" test, and the conscious presence" test. A witness is present for purposes of the "scope of vision" test only if he or she signs the will in the testator's physical presence and within the scope of his or her vision. Whether or not the testator *actually* sees, he or she must be *able* to see the will, the witnesses, and the signing.

The "conscious presence" test, on the other hand, is satisfied where the testator can either see or hear what is being done, the testator is conscious of what is occurring, and the signing is a continuous transaction that takes but a brief moment of time.

It generally makes no difference whether the witnesses sign before or after the testator signs, or whether their signatures appear on the will before or after his or her signature appears (although their signatures almost always appear after). Although it is usually not required by statute, most wills contain a formal "attestation clause" immediately after the testator's signature and immediately preceding the signatures of the attesting witnesses. The attestation clause expressly affirms the testator's signature or acknowledgment in the presence of the witnesses, as well as his or her publication of the document (where required) as his or her last will and testament. A typical attestation clause might read as follows:

> The foregoing instrument, consisting of three pages, was on the date above mentioned, signed, published and declared by the said SIDNEY AARON SMITH as and for his Last Will and Testament, in the presence of us, who at his request, and in his presence, and in the presence of each other, do hereunto subscribe our names as witnesses thereto.

In most jurisdictions, the use of an attestation clause serves to raise a rebuttable presumption of proper execution of a will: a person who would contest the will for lack of proper execution must show facts to rebut the presumption and substantiate the charge.

The four requirements of a valid will —testator's signature, publication, competent witnesses, and attestation—are designed to accomplish several things. First, they are designed to prevent fraud and forgery in the execution of a will and to provide the best evidence possible for establishing testamentary intent. Second, they are ritualistically fashioned to impress upon the testator the importance of his or her act in providing for an orderly, deathtime disposition of property. And, finally, they are structured to reduce the likelihood of undue influence or duress being exercised upon the testator (particularly the requirement of competent witnesses who are disinterested in the testamentary plan).

Does every page of a will have to be separately signed and attested to?

Where a will contains more than one page (and many wills contain many pages), all the pages may be validated by one proper execution—that is, by one sig-

nature of the testator somewhere on the instrument, one publication where required, and a single attestation by two or three competent witnesses.

The validation of several pages as the testator's will is referred to as *integration* of the will. Pages may be integrated (i. e., unified into a single whole) only where they are physically present at the time of execution of the will, and only where they are intended by the testator to form a part of the will.

Usually, the attestation clause states the total number of pages of the will, and, where there is so, a rebuttable presumption of integration arises. Such a presumption also arises where the pages of a will are physically attached (e. g., stapled pages) or where the pages are numbered in sequence.

Does the testator's reference in a will to another document make the other document a part of the will?

Where a testator makes reference in a will to another document such as a deed, a letter, or a prior invalid will, the document will become part of the will though it is not executed with the testamentary formalities so long as the document was in existence at the time of execution of the will, the will specifically describes the document so that it may be readily identified, and the testator expresses an intent in the will that the document become part of it. Where these conditions are met, the document is said to be *incorporated by reference* into the will. For example, where Sidney Smith's will provides, "To my son, Robert, I leave the personal property described in a letter to Robert, dated March 3rd, 1978, the letter to be found in my safety deposit box", the letter referred to in the will is incorporated by reference and becomes a part of the will. However, where Sidney's will provides, "I want my son, Robert, to have some specific items of personal property that I will list in a letter sometime within the next year, said letter to be placed into my safety deposit box", the letter will not be incorporated by reference because it was not in existence at the time the will was executed.

May a testator determine his or her beneficiaries or the interests they will receive by reference in the will to extrinsic (i. e., outside) acts or events?

The "extrinsic facts" doctrine provides that a testator may determine beneficiaries or their interests by reference in a will to extrinsic acts or events so long as the acts or events have an "independent legal significance" apart from the will itself. An act or event has independent legal significance where it is fundamentally nontestamentary in nature. For example, Sidney Smith may provide by will, "I leave $1,000 to each employee working on my ranch at the time of my death". Determination of beneficiaries by reference to employment at a particular time is perfectly proper because employees are ordinarily selected because of their business skills—not because they are desired as beneficiaries. The act of employment thus has an independent significance apart from its impact on Sidney's testamentary disposition. The same is true where Sidney's will provides, "I leave all my property to whichever of my children I am living with at the time of my death". Again, it is unlikely that Sidney will live with a particular child merely to designate him or her as a beneficiary.

However, where Sidney provides by will, "I am going to write a letter sometime in the future and designate which of my children are to receive my property", the determination of beneficiaries by letter has no independent legal significance apart from furthering Sidney's testamentary scheme, and the determination cannot be upheld on the basis of the "extrinsic facts" doctrine. Nor can the provision be upheld as a valid incorporation by reference: the letter was not in exis-

tence at the time the will was written. (However, the letter, once written, may constitute a valid holographic will as will be explained in a later section.)

Are trusts ever written into wills?

As stated in Ch. 29, trusts are frequently written into wills as a means of providing property management for beneficiaries such as a spouse or children who are either too young or incompetent to manage their own property or simply unwilling to do so. A trust created by will is called a *testamentary trust* and takes effect only upon the testator's death. A testamentary trust must satisfy the requirements of a valid trust as well as the requirements of a valid will.

What is a "pour-over" trust provision in a will?

A provision in a will providing that all or a portion of the testator's property should be added to the trust res or corpus of a trust established during the lifetime of the decedent is called a "pour-over" trust provision. For example, Sidney Smith might provide by will that $50,000 and 750 shares of General Motors stock should be added to the trust res of an inter vivos trust Sidney created ten years ago for the benefit of his invalid younger sister, Angela. Upon Sidney's death, the "pour-over" trust provision would operate to transfer the designated property into the trust res or corpus to be administered and distributed as part of the inter vivos trust.

Pour-over trust provisions may be upheld on the basis of incorporation by reference (i. e., the inter vivos trust is made a part of the will by the testator's express reference to it), or as an act of independent significance under the "extrinsic facts" doctrine (i. e., the inter vivos trust is fundamentally nontestamentary in nature and has independent significance apart from the testator's dispository scheme).

What is a power of appointment?

An owner of property may give another person the power to designate who should own the property. Such a power is called a *power of appointment*. A power of appointment may be created by deed or by will. And the power itself may be an authorization to make the appointment by will only (called a "testamentary power of appointment"), or by inter vivos appointment only, or by either method. Some states, including California, provide that, unless the creating instrument expressly provides to the contrary, a power stated to be exercisable by an inter vivos instrument is also exercisable by a written will.

The property owner who creates the power of appointment is called the *donor* of the power; the person to whom the power is given is the *donee*. And the individuals who are designated as takers of the property by the donee are the *appointees*.

A power of appointment may thus be defined as a power created by a donor and conferred on a donee enabling the donee either to appoint persons to take the property or to appoint the proportionate shares which designated persons shall take in the property.

The power of appointment may give the donee the power to exercise the appointment in favor of the donee himself or herself or in favor of the donee's estate. Such a power is called a *general power*. A general power is very close to ownership itself since the donee may appoint the property to himself or herself during life or control its disposition upon death. Because of this, a general power is said to be "tantamount to ownership", and the value of the property subject to the general power is included in the donee's estate for purposes of death taxes.

A general power of appointment is most frequently created by will. This is particularly true of a donor-testator who wants to leave the income from property to one person for life, and also to give that person the power to reach the principal of the property if necessary for his or her protection and to control what happens to the property when he or she dies. Typically, this is what one spouse might do for a surviving spouse in his or her last will and testament. For example, Mary Wife's last will and testament might read as follows:

LAST WILL AND TESTAMENT OF MARY WIFE

I, MARY WIFE, do hereby make, publish, and declare this to be my Last Will and Testament, and do revoke all wills and codicils heretofore made by me.

I.

I nominate and appoint my husband, STANLEY HUSBAND, as executor of my estate.

II.

I direct my Executor to pay from my estate all my just debts, the expenses of my last illness and funeral and final interment and the expenses of administration of my estate.

III.

I direct my Executor to pay from my estate all inheritance, estate, transfer and succession taxes which become payable by reason of my death and authorize him to contest or compromise any claims for such taxes.

* * *

IV.

I give, devise, and bequeath all of my property, both real and personal, to the trustee hereinafter named, in trust on the terms and conditions and for the uses and purposes following:

* * * The trust fund shall be held by my trustee on the following terms:

(1) The net income shall be paid to or applied for the benefit of my husband in quarterly or more frequent installments during his lifetime. In addition, my trustee shall have the authority, in his discretion, to pay to or apply on behalf of my husband such principal sums as he may determine to be necessary and proper for his maintenance and welfare in order that he may maintain the standard of living to which he was accustomed at the time of my death.

(2) Upon the death of my husband all the assets of the trust fund then remaining shall be distributed as my said husband *shall appoint by his Last Will and Testament, which power he may exercise in favor of his estate or of any other person or persons.* In default of such appointment, or subject to any partial appointment by my husband, the trust fund remaining shall be distributed outright in equal shares to my children then living at my husband's death.

Note that in Article VI(2), Mary has created a general power of appointment in her husband Stanley, the donee of the power. Mary also adds the following provision to enable Stanley to have complete power to reach the trust principal during his lifetime:

During the lifetime of my said husband, he shall have the absolute power to withdraw all of the principal of the trust estate or portions thereof from time to time. Such withdrawals shall be made by an instrument in writing, signed by my husband and filed with the trustee. Any principal so withdrawn shall be distributed to my said husband free of the trust herein provided.

Clearly, a general power of appointment gives the donee what is "tantamount to ownership" of the property. Still, use of the trust and the power of appointment allows for management by other than the trust beneficiary (the husband, in this case); and it permits division of the decedent's estate to provide maximum deductions for computing death taxes. The first $250,000 of property left to a surviving spouse is not taxed for death tax purposes by the federal government. However, if more than $250,000 is left to a surviving spouse, up to 50% of the adjusted gross estate is not taxed if at least that much or more is left to the spouse.[5] The allowable deduction for property going to a surviving spouse is called the *marital deduction*. Often, a trust is written into a will so as to provide two funds, with one fund going to the surviving spouse and providing the maximum marital deduction, and the other fund going to other beneficiaries.

In contrast to a general power of appointment (which may be exercised in favor of the donee or his or her estate) is a *special power of appointment*. A special power is one that cannot be exercised in favor of the donee or his or her estate, but may be exercised only in favor of identifiable person(s) other than the donee. For example, suppose that Mary Wife used this language in Article VI(2):

(2) Upon the death of my husband all the assets of the trust fund then remaining shall be distrib-

---

5. "Adjusted gross estate" is the entire gross estate less the deductions allowed for funeral, administration, and other expenses.

uted as my said husband shall appoint by his Last Will and Testament, which power he may only exercise in favor of our children Tom, Dick, Harry, Mary, and Ann.

Here, Mary has created a special power of appointment. The husband, as donee of the power, may exercise it only in favor of the named children. A special power is *exclusive* if the donee is authorized to exclude one or more of the designated appointees from receiving any of the property. If some benefit must be conferred upon all of the appointees, then the power is *nonexclusive*. Most courts hold that, unless the creating instrument expressly provides that the donee must include all appointees, the special power is exclusive, and the donee may completely exclude one or more of the appointees or give the property entirely to one appointee. (A minority of courts hold that a power is presumed to be nonexclusive.) Thus, in the example above, most courts would hold this to be an exclusive power, and Stanley could exercise the power in his will so as to exclude one or more of the children.

Where a power is found to be nonexclusive, there is still a question as to what share an appointee must receive. Again, there is a split of authority with some courts saying that a mere "token share" is sufficient while others require each appointee to receive a "substantial share" though not an equal share.

Whether the special power is exclusive or nonexclusive, if the donee fails to exercise the power, the designated appointees will take equally.

Creditors of a donee of a special power of appointment cannot reach the property that is subject to the special power. Creditors of a donee of a general power of appointment, on the other hand, can reach the property that is subject to the

general power, but only if the power has been exercised in favor of the donee, or in favor of a volunteer (one who pays no consideration) or a creditor of the donee at a time when the donee was insolvent. It should be pointed out that a creditor is classified as a volunteer within the meaning of this rule. So if an appointment is made in favor of one creditor when the donee is insolvent, all of the creditors will be entitled to share equally.

Sometimes, a power of appointment is neither general nor special. It is not general because it does not allow the donee to appoint to himself or herself or his or her estate. It is not special because it does not identify the appointee or appointees (remember, the appointees must be identifiable). Rather, it is a *hybrid* or *limited* power and is generally treated as a special power insofar as creditors are concerned.

What is a codicil?

A "codicil" is a legally effective amendment to a will. Whether a codicil is a separate instrument (the usual case) or simply an addition to the original will itself, the codicil must be executed with full testamentary formalities—that is, signature of the testator, publication where required, and attestation by two or three competent witnesses.

Generally, a valid codicil has the effect of republishing or re-executing the original will. This means that the will, as amended by the codicil, will be interpreted as of the date of the codicil rather than as of the date of execution of the will. This change in effective date of interpretation may have a substantial impact on specific provisions of the will. For example, suppose that Sidney Smith provides by will that Sandy Granstrom is to receive $1,000 in cash from his estate. Unfortunately, Sandy witnesses the will, and because she cannot qualify as a supernumerary, she stands to forfeit her $1,000 interest. However, if Sidney later executes a codicil to the will that Sandy does not witness, the gift to Sandy will be valid because the effect of the codicil is to republish the will as of the later date: the courts will look only to the attesting witnesses of the codicil, and the prior attestation will be disregarded.

Or suppose that Sidney Smith provides by will, "I am going to write a letter sometime in the future and designate which of my children is to receive my property". You will recall that the letter, once written, cannot be incorporated by reference into the will because the letter was not in existence at the time of execution of the will. However, if, after the letter is written, Sidney executes a codicil to the will, the letter will be incorporated by reference because the effect of the codicil is to republish the will as of the codicil's effective date, and the letter is in existence at the time.

The only time republication will not apply is where its application is clearly contrary to the testator's expressed intent.

How are testamentary gifts legally designated?

A gift of personal property under a will is called a "bequest" or "legacy"; a gift of real property is called a "devise". Bequests and devises may be classified as follows:

(1) *Specific bequest or devise.* A specific bequest or devise under a will is a gift of identifiable property. For example, a gift of "my 12 gauge Browning over and under shotgun" or "my apartment house located at 12th and Market in Mandan, North Dakota" is, in the first instance, a specific bequest of the shotgun, and in the second, a specific devise of the land.

Unless a will provides otherwise, the beneficiary of a specific bequest or devise is entitled to the specified gift free and clear of the testator's debts (the testator's debts will be satisfied out of the general

assets of the estate). This is called the beneficiary's "right to exoneration". An exception to the right arises where the specified property is subject to a security interest in another party, in which case the beneficiary takes the property subject to the interest. Thus, if in the example above, the apartment house is mortgaged, the beneficiary will take the real property subject to the mortgage.

(2) *General bequest or devise.* A general bequest or devise is not a gift of specific, identifiable property, but a gift of fixed or calculable value that may be satisfied out of any of the general assets of a decedent's estate (e. g., a bequest of $2,500 or of "all the personal property I own at the time of my death", or a devise of "all my land").

(3) *Demonstrative bequest.* A demonstrative bequest is both specific and general. It is a gift of personal property, usually money, that is to be paid first out of a particular fund, and, second, out of the general assets of the estate to the extent that the particular fund is insufficient. An example of a demonstrative bequest is a gift of "$2,500 to my son, John, from my savings account at the First National Bank, but, if that fund is insufficient, out of my other properties".

(4) *Residuary bequest and devise.* A residuary bequest and devise is a gift of whatever personal and real property is left after all specific, general, or demonstrative gifts have been satisfied. The residuary gift must be worded so as to pass all the testator's remaining property (however, it is possible for a testator to satisfy this requirement by bequeathing all his or her remaining personal property to one person, and all his or her remaining real property to another). While no special words or language are required to create a residuary gift, the words "the rest, residue, and remainder of my property" are usually employed.

What is ademption by extinction?

To "adeem" is to destroy. Ademption by extinction is the destruction of a specific bequest or devise that occurs when the specified personal property or realty is not to be found in the testator's estate upon his or her death. The gift, in this case, fails completely, and the beneficiary who was to receive the property receives nothing. Where only a portion of the property is missing, the gift is adeemed *pro tanto* (to the extent of that portion), and the beneficiary is entitled to whatever portion remains.

Ademption by extinction applies only to specific bequests and devises. A minority of courts make its operation dependent upon the intent of the testator: unless it can be shown that the testator transferred or otherwise disposed of the property with the intent that the specific bequest or devise be destroyed, ademption by extinction will not operate to deprive the beneficiary of his or her interest. For example, if a testator *in a minority jurisdiction* makes a specific bequest of an automobile, then sells the car for $5,000 and places the proceeds into a savings account, the beneficiary of the specific bequest will probably receive the $5,000.

Wherever possible, the courts will classify gifts as general bequests and devises rather than specific gifts of property in order to avoid the hardship of ademption by extinction.

What is ademption by satisfaction?

General and demonstrative bequests are considered "adeemed by satisfaction" where the testator, subsequent to execution of the will, makes an inter vivos gift to the designated beneficiary, intending the gift to satisfy in whole or in part the testamentary bequest. Ademption by satisfaction does not apply to specific bequests because an inter vivos transfer of the property to the beneficiary would re-move the property from the estate and result in ademption by extinction. (Although the doctrine of ademption by satisfaction would appear to logically apply to general devises of real property, the courts have so far chosen not to apply it in this area.)

Unlike ademption by extinction which, in a majority of jurisdictions, takes place regardless of the testator's intent, ademption by satisfaction will occur only where the testator intends the inter vivos gift to reduce or take the place of the testamentary bequest. If the testator does not intend this result, the general or demonstrative bequest will still be valid.

Where ademption by satisfaction is found to apply, the value of the inter vivos gift will be deducted from the bequest, and the beneficiary will receive whatever balance, if any, remains. Some special rules apply where a class gift is involved. For example, suppose that Robert Smith provides by will, "I leave $50,000 to my children". After Robert executes the will, two of his children get into financial difficulty and persuade Robert to give them some of the money before he dies. Prior to death, Robert transfers a total of $5,000 to his son, James, and $8,000 to his daughter, Carla, intending that the transfers be deducted from the testamentary bequest. Robert transfers nothing to his other two children, Mark and Karen. Upon Robert's death, the doctrine of ademption by satisfaction applies because Robert intended the inter vivos transfers to reduce the testamentary bequests to his son and daughter. Because a class gift is involved, the court will throw everything into *hotchpot*. This means that the court will add together the total value of the inter vivos gifts ($13,000) and the original amount of the testamentary bequest ($50,000). The court will then divide the total by the number of people in the class ($63,000 ÷ 4) to come up with the amount of money or property ($15,750) that each member of the class should receive. Class members who have received a portion of their share inter vivos (James and Carla) will have that amount ($5,000 and $8,000 respectively) subtracted from their share of the hotchpot. Thus, upon Robert's death, James will receive a total of $10,750; Carla will receive $7,750; and Mark and Karen will each receive $15,750. As you can see, the result of applying ademption by satisfaction is to treat all members of the class equally, taking into account that some of the members received a portion of their interest inter vivos.

In what order are testamentary gifts distributed? What happens when there are insufficient assets to fully satisfy all gifts?

Testamentary gifts are distributed in the following order: first, specific bequests and devises (a demonstrative gift is specific to the extent of the specified fund); second, general bequests or devises (including a demonstrative gift in excess of the specified fund); and, third and last, residuary gifts.

Where there are insufficient assets to fully satisfy all gifts, the courts generally resort to *abatement* (i. e., proportionate reduction) of gifts within a particular class. The order of abatement is normally just the reverse of the order of distribution—that is, residuary gifts are first reduced, then general gifts, then, finally, specific bequests and devises. In some states, all personal property gifts are abated before real property gifts; in other states, specific and general gifts are abated ratably rather than general gifts first.

Where abatement of a class gift is required, each class member generally loses a proportionate share of the property. Suppose that Robert Smith provides by will that his children are to receive $50,000 upon his death, but Robert dies, leaving only $40,000 available for distri-

bution to his two sons and two daughters. Assuming no inter vivos gifts have been made, each child's $12,500 share will be ratably reduced by $2,500 for a total of $10,000 for each child.

In some states, where the class consists only partially of blood relatives of the testator, the shares of the blood relatives will be paid in full and the shares of the other class members will be abated. Thus, if in our example above, two of the class members are Robert's children, and two are friends of the family, Robert's children will each receive a full $12,500 while Robert's friends will receive but $7,500 each ($12,500–$5,000).

What is a lapsed gift?

A "lapsed" gift is a gift that fails because the named beneficiary is either unwilling to accept the gift, or unable to take the property because he or she is dead at the time the will takes effect. If the will does not specify an alternative beneficiary, a lapsed specific, general, or demonstrative gift will become a part of the residuary; a lapsed residuary gift will be treated as intestate property and will pass according to the state intestacy laws (intestacy is discussed in a later section).

A class gift will not lapse so long as any members of the class are alive and willing to take the property. Thus, if Robert Smith leaves "$50,000 to my children", the gift will be valid even if three of Robert's four children die before Robert dies so long as the fourth and last child is willing to accept the $50,000 at the time of Robert's death. However, where Robert leaves "$50,000 to my children, James, Carla, Mark, and Karen", the court may construe the gift, not as a class gift, but as a specific bequest of $12,500 to each child: the gift of any child who dies before Robert dies will thus lapse in the absence of an alternative beneficiary.

Most states have now passed "anti-lapse" statutes which generally provide that a testamentary gift to a blood relative of the testator will not lapse in the event that the relative predeceases the testator. Rather, the gift will pass to the deceased beneficiary's heirs or beneficiaries.

Are there any restrictions on a testator's disposition of his or her property?

With the following limited exceptions, a testator is free to dispose of his or her property in any manner he or she chooses so long as the proper will formalities are observed.

(1) *Spouses.* In most states, a surviving spouse has a statutory right to claim a designated portion or share (usually $\frac{1}{4}$th to $\frac{1}{2}$) of a decedent's spouse's property regardless of the provisions of the decedent spouse's will. Thus, if the surviving spouse receives nothing by the terms of the will, he or she can make an "election" against the will and receive from $\frac{1}{4}$th to $\frac{1}{2}$ of the estate. The same is true where the surviving spouse receives some property by the terms of will, but less than his or her statutory share: he or she can elect against the will, renouncing all the testamentary gifts provided, and receive, again, from $\frac{1}{4}$th to $\frac{1}{2}$ the decedent spouse's estate. A surviving spouse who makes a "renunciation" of the gifts provided by will may lose the specific bequests and devises made in his or her favor, but the spouse will gain an increased overall share of the estate property.

Where a surviving spouse chooses to elect against the will, the probate court must generally abate the testamentary gifts made to others (residuary gifts first, then general gifts, then specific gifts) in order to provide the spouse with his or her proper statutory share.

It might also be pointed out that election against the will and renunciation are usually not provided for by statute in community property states: as each spouse already has an undivided ownership interest in all property, other than separate property, acquired during the marriage, a statutory forced share is not considered necessary.

(2) *Children.* "Pretermitted heir" statutes in nearly all states provide that where the testator's child is not mentioned in a will, the will will be disregarded to the extent that the child will be permitted to receive his or her intestate share of the decedent's property (i. e., that share he or she would be entitled to receive had the testator left no will). For example, suppose that Robert Smith executes a will, leaving property to his sons, James and Mark, and his daughter, Carla. Robert leaves nothing to his daughter, Karen—in fact, he fails to mention her anywhere in the will. Upon Robert's death, the probate court will declare Karen to be a "pretermitted" (i. e., omitted) heir and permit her to take her intestate share of Robert's property. If necessary, the gifts to James, Mark, and Carla will be abated to provide Karen with her lawful share.

The "pretermitted heir" statute applies whether the pretermitted child was born before or after execution of the will. The theory behind the statute is that the testator has merely forgotten to provide for the child, and that, in disregarding the child's omission from the will, the law is simply carrying out the testator's intent.

It follows that the pretermitted heir statute does not apply where it is apparent from the will that the testator clearly intended to disinherit the child. For example, a specific statement in a will that "I hereby disinherit my son, Robert" is sufficient to accomplish the task—the "pretermitted heir" statute will not be used to defeat the testator's expressed intent.

(3) *Debtors.* The "doctrine of retainer" is the rule of law that a monetary bequest to a debtor of the testator (and

thus a debtor of the testator's estate) should be reduced by the amount of the debt outstanding. For example, suppose that Sidney Smith loans $5,000 to his friend, Peter Carson; Peter still owes Sidney the money at the time of Sidney's death. If Sidney's will provides that Peter is to receive $10,000 from Sidney's estate, the doctrine of retainer will operate to reduce the $10,000 bequest by the $5,000 debt outstanding for a total bequest to Peter of $5,000.

(4) *Creditors.* A testamentary bequest to a creditor of the testator in an amount equal to or greater than the debt owing is rebuttably presumed to be in satisfaction of the debt. Unless the creditor can show that the testator intended the bequest to be separate from and in addition to satisfaction of the debt, the creditor cannot collect twice from the testator's estate.

(5) *Charities.* As pointed out in Ch. 29, Mortmain Statutes in some states restrict or prohibit a testator's testamentary gifts to charity. You will recall that some of the statutes provide that a testator may give no more than one-third or one-half of his or her estate to charity. Other statutes declare that any testamentary gift made within a short period of time before the testator's death (such as 30 days) is invalid.

Of course, many states have modernly repealed such laws and permit the free and unrestricted testamentary transfer of property to charity so long as the proper will formalities, including testamentary intent and capacity, are present.

How are wills revoked?

Because a will takes effect only at death, it is revocable up until the moment of death. A will may be revoked in three ways:

(1) *By a later will or codicil.* Most wills begin with a statement that the testator "hereby revokes all wills and codicils

heretofore made by me". In the absence of such an express revocation clause, a later will will totally revoke an earlier will only if the later will is entirely inconsistent with the earlier instrument. If the later will is only partially inconsistent, the later instrument will supersede the prior will as to the inconsistencies. But the earlier instrument will continue to operate to the extent that it does not conflict with terms of the subsequent will.

A codicil, too, changes, or revokes a prior will or codicil to the extent that the codicil is inconsistent with the prior instruments.

(2) *By destruction of a will.* A physical act of destruction performed upon a will by a testator, such as burning, tearing, or otherwise obliterating the instrument, will serve to revoke the will where the physical act is simultaneously accompanied by the testator's intent to revoke. The intent to revoke must be present— the physical act alone will not revoke the will. (A lost will, or a will accidentally destroyed without an intent to revoke can always be proved by a copy of the will, or by the testimony of witnesses familiar with its contents.)

Generally, some material part of the will must be damaged by the physical act. However, in the case of destruction by burning, the burning of any portion of the will, material or immaterial, is sufficient to revoke the will so long as the intent to revoke is present.

(3) *By operation of law.* A will may be revoked by operation of law where there has been a substantial change in circumstances since the will was executed, and the testator dies without writing a new will taking the change into account. For example, suppose that a testator marries after executing a will, and then dies, leaving a surviving spouse. The surviving spouse, though not mentioned in the will, is modernly entitled to a share of

the decedent spouse's property equivalent to his or her intestate share (i. e., the share the surviving spouse would have received had there been no will). Insofar as the decedent's will fails to provide for the surviving spouse, the will is revoked by operation of law.

Suppose that Sidney Smith executes a will leaving a sizeable portion of his estate to his wife, Marjorie. Sidney and Marjorie later obtain a divorce, then Sidney dies, without having executed a new will revoking the gifts to Marjorie. Are the gifts to Marjorie valid? In some states, a divorce or dissolution of marriage results in automatic revocation of testamentary gifts to a former spouse; in those states, the gifts to Marjorie would be invalid. The majority rule, however, is that divorce or dissolution of marriage does not by itself constitute such a change in circumstances as to warrant the automatic revocation of testamentary gifts executed in favor of a former spouse prior to the divorce. Where, however, the divorce or dissolution is accompanied by a property settlement, many courts agree that the change in circumstances is sufficient, and the testamentary gifts are revoked by operation of law. In the example above, the Smith's divorce was not accompanied by a property settlement, thus the testamentary gifts to Marjorie are valid.

Some changes in circumstances are never sufficient to effect an automatic revocation of all or part of a will. These include insanity of the testator, the testator's increased wealth, or the testator's change in feeling toward a spouse or other beneficiary.

Does revocation of a second will serve to republish or "revive" a prior will?

There exists a split of authority as to whether revocation of a second will automatically revives a prior will. Most states hold that revocation of Will #2

does not impliedly revive Will #1, and, that if Will #1 is to be effective, it must itself be re-executed or republished by codicil.

It might also be pointed out that where a person mistakenly revokes a will, the law may imply that the revocation was conditional, being dependent upon the mistake of law or fact, and thus disregard the revocation when the revoking testator's expectations are not met. This is called the "doctrine of dependent relative revocation". For example, if Sidney Smith tears up his will, intending to revoke it because he erroneously believes that his son and primary beneficiary has been killed in Europe, the doctrine of dependent relative revocation will operate upon Sidney's death to disregard the revocation by destruction and give the will effect.

What is a nuncupative will?

Statutes in many jurisdictions permit the use of *nuncupative* (i. e., oral) wills for a number of limited purposes. Generally, a nuncupative will may be made only by a soldier in the battlefield, a sailor in action at sea, or a civilian in fear of imminent death from injuries received on the day of execution of the oral will. Such a will may be used to transfer personal property only—never real property. (Some jurisdictions even set a limit upon the amount of personal property that may be transferred, e. g., in California, $1,000.)

A nuncupative will must usually be witnessed by two disinterested parties who are instructed by the testator that he or she is intending and attempting to make a valid will. The witnesses must reduce the will to writing within a short period of time (such as 30 days) and offer it to the court for probate (administration) within six months. Thus, if the testator does not die within six months of execution of the oral will, the will will be automatically revoked by operation of law.

What is a holographic will?

A *holographic* will is a written will that lacks the statutory requirements for formal execution. Holographic wills are recognized as valid in a minority of states so long as the following three requirements are met in addition to testamentary intent:

(1) The will must be written entirely in the testator's own handwriting. However, most courts will uphold the validity of a holographic will containing material in other than the testator's own handwriting so long as the material is not essential to the will (e. g., a typed heading such as "My Will" is not essential and will not affect the validity of the will). Most courts will also permit a testator to incorporate by reference into the will nonholographic material (e. g., a typewritten list of property).

(2) The will must be dated in the handwriting of the testator. The date must include the day, month, and year— so long as the date is complete, it need not be correct.

(3) Finally, the will must be signed in the testator's own handwriting. The testator may sign anywhere on the instrument, and he or she may use any nickname, initials, mark, etc., so long as he or she intends what is written to serve as a full and complete signature.

Are there any effective "will substitutes"—that is, means of transferring property at death other than by will?

While a will is certainly the most publicized means of controlling the disposition of property at death, there are a number of "will substitutes" that may be preferable to a will in one or more situations. These include:

(a) Inter vivos gifts;

(b) Gifts causa mortis;

(c) Concurrent tenancies with the right of survivorship;

(d) Deeds;

(e) Inter vivos trusts;

(f) Life insurance;

(g) Totten trusts.

With the exception of the so-called "Totten trust", all the will substitutes listed above have been dealt with to some extent in previous chapters of the text. You will recall from Ch. 3 that an inter vivos gift is a voluntary lifetime transfer of property without consideration. An inter vivos gift requires donative intent on the part of the donor, delivery of the property to the donee, and acceptance by the donee. Such a gift is an effective will substitute in the sense that a person who gives away all or part of his or her property during life has little or nothing left to transfer at death. And for people who can afford to give away a good deal of their property during life and still maintain an adequate standard of living, there is the added lifetime benefit of being able to see their children and close friends enjoy their property as opposed to merely passing it on to them at death.

You will also recall from Ch. 3 that a gift causa mortis is a conditional gift of personal property that is solely motivated by the donor's anticipation of imminent death. Because the donor intends the gift to take effect only if he or she dies, the gift causa mortis is automatically revoked by operation of law if the donor fails to die from the feared peril. A gift causa mortis is an effective will substitute only insofar as personal property is concerned (real property cannot be the subject of a gift causa mortis). Assuming the donor dies as anticipated, the gift causa mortis will prevail even over a specific bequest of the same property in the donor's will: the property which is subject to the specific bequest will be considered adeemed by extinction.

In Ch. 5, we discussed the joint tenancy with the right of survivorship and the tenancy by the entirety, also with the survivorship characteristic. We learned that property held with the survivorship characteristic passes, not to the deceased cotenant's heirs or beneficiaries, but to the surviving cotenant or cotenants automatically by operation of law. Because the interest passes automatically at the moment of death, the deceased joint tenant or tenant by the entirety has nothing left to transfer by will or intestacy, and a will provision purporting to transfer property held concurrently with the right of survivorship is void and of no effect. One elderly woman, for example, hired an attorney to draft her a will leaving her $80,000 cash estate to her nine grandchildren. At the same time, however, and without realizing the legal effect of her actions, the woman placed the $80,000 into a savings account which she held jointly with her son and daughter, all with the right of survivorship. When the woman died a few months later, the $80,000 automatically passed to her son and daughter, the surviving joint tenants —despite the terms of the will, the woman's grandchildren received nothing. As you can see, a person who owns all his or her property concurrently with the right of survivorship has no need for a will. Such ownership is a very effective will substitute, and a popular one as well.

From Chapters 4 and 6, we know that a grantor may presently convey by inter vivos deed a future interest in fee simple to a specified grantee, reserving in himself or herself a life estate in the property. So long as the grantor delivers a valid deed of conveyance to the grantee, intending the deed to *presently* create a future interest (a vested remainder in fee simple), the transfer will be an effective will substitute, and, upon the grantor's death, the property will belong to the grantee in fee simple absolute. The grantor may even deposit the deed into escrow with delivery conditioned upon the grantor's death without rendering the transfer testamentary (i. e., without making the transfer a deathtime transfer requiring the statutory will formalities).

As explained in Ch. 29, and as mentioned previously in this chapter, an inter vivos (or "living") trust may be used to transfer real and/or personal property interest to a trustee for the benefit of another. A property owner who places all his or her property into an inter vivos trust may effectively avoid the need for a will. For example, it is not unusual for a trustor to transfer property in trust for the lifetime benefit of himself or herself, and, upon his or her death, for the benefit of a surviving spouse or children. As long as the Rule Against Perpetuities is not violated, the trust can continue on uninterrupted at the death of the trustor for the benefit of the named beneficiaries for several lifetimes. Even completely revocable trusts are effective will substitutes so long as the trustor does not retain unlimited control over the trust property.

It follows from our discussion of life insurance in Ch. 11 that a person who purchases life insurance, naming as beneficiary someone other than his or her own estate, has an effective will substitute at least insofar as the life insurance proceeds payable upon the death of the insured are concerned. Thus, a person may control the disposition of all his or her property by converting the property into cash and using the cash to purchase life insurance, whether ordinary life, term insurance, limited-payment life, endowment contracts, or annuity contracts. Upon the insured's death, the insurance company will pay all policy proceeds to the beneficiary named in the policy, and the insured's will, if he or she has one, will have no effect upon the disposition of the property.

Frequently, an insured will transfer ownership of a life insurance policy to a trustee for the benefit of another. Upon the death of the insured, the life insurance proceeds become a part of the trust res (the proceeds are payable directly to the trust, the named beneficiary of the insurance policy), and will be managed by the trustee according to the conditions and purposes stated in the trust. Life insurance trusts are not considered testamentary even though there is an absence of any significant trust res prior to the trustor-insured's death. They are nontestamentary and valid will substitutes even where the insured retains the power to revoke or modify the trust, or to change its beneficiaries.

Finally, we come to the so-called "Totten" trust, also called the "savings bank deposit trust" or "tentative trust". Suppose, for a moment, that Sidney Smith deposits $10,000 in an account at the First National Bank for "Sidney Smith in trust for my son, Robert". Has Sidney created a valid trust in favor of Robert, with himself appointed as trustee? If so, does Robert have an immediate right to the money or any portion of it, or do Robert's rights arise only when Sidney dies? If Robert's rights do not arise until Sidney's death, and if Sidney has unlimited power over the $10,000 until that time, the transfer would appear testamentary in nature, and, in the absence of the proper will formalities, would be invalid.

Nevertheless, a majority of states follow the "tentative trust doctrine" established in the New York case of Matter of Totten, 179 N.Y. 112, 71 N.E. 748 (1904) (the case from which the term "Totten" trust derives). The tentative trust doctrine provides that a deposit of funds by a person in his or her own name as trustee for another creates a revocable inter vivos trust. The depositor can revoke the trust in whole or in part at anytime simply by making withdrawals from the account. And so long as the depositor is alive, his or her creditors can reach the deposit even though the depositor is technically deemed a trustee for another. Whatever is left in the account (if anything) at the time of the depositor's death will go to the named beneficiary if he or she is still alive.

Because the deposit is held to create a valid, though revocable inter vivos trust, and because the balance of the account will pass to the named beneficiary rather than remain in the decedent-depositor's estate, the Totten trust is an effective will substitute and one readily available to property owners of even the most limited means.

It should be pointed out that if the named beneficiary of the trust predeceases the depositor, the trust will terminate and the beneficiary's heirs or beneficiaries will have no rights to the account balance upon the depositor-trustor's death.

Also, if the depositor-trustor specifically provides by will that the account balance is to go to someone other than the trust beneficiary, the will will control, and the trust beneficiary will receive nothing. However, a statement that "all my property" is to go to some other named individual is not sufficiently specific to affect the rights of the Totten trust beneficiary—the statement must specifically refer to the Totten trust account.

Finally, the revocable Totten trust will become irrevocable if the depositor-trustor turns control of the account over to the beneficiary by giving the beneficiary the savings account passbook.

Why is a transfer of property that appears so testamentary in character given the legal status of a valid, revocable inter vivos trust and will substitute in a majority of jurisdictions? Despite the fact that the depositor retains almost unlimited control over the deposited funds, and despite the fact that the beneficiary has no interest, if any, until the depositor-trustor dies, the Totten trust is a socially desirable device that enables people of limited means to obtain the advantages of a will without the expense and delay of a testamentary disposition of property.

In the minority of jurisdictions where Totten trusts are not recognized because of their testamentary nature, the account balance is deemed an asset of the decedent-depositor's estate, and the account beneficiary has no rights to the property.

What are the significant consequences of using a will substitute?

The use of will substitutes—inter vivos gifts, gifts causa mortis, concurrent tenancies with the right of survivorship, deeds, inter vivos trusts, life insurance, or Totten trusts—may have significant consequences in the areas of taxation and probate.

Tax consequences. As you know from previous chapters, both state and federal governments tax the transfer of property, whether a person gives the property away inter vivos or passes it on only at death. For the most part, any irrevocable transfer of property without adequate consideration in money or money's worth is a gift. Any revocable transfer or transfer effective only at death forms part of a decedent's estate for death tax purposes (e. g., a transfer at the time of death by Totten trust or other revocable inter vivos trust, a transfer of property by the right of survivorship, a transfer of life insurance proceeds to a beneficiary, a transfer of property in fee simple upon the expiration of the deceased grantor's reserved life estate interest, etc.).

The federal gift and estate taxes were combined in the Tax Reform Act of 1976, and the same rate of tax now applies whether a person gives property away or transfers it effective at death. The rate varies from 18% on a very small transfer to 70% on a large transfer of property worth $5,000,000 or more. However, there is a unified gift and estate tax credit of $47,000 that is applied directly against any gift and estate tax

owing, with the result that an individual may give away inter vivos or pass on at death a combined total of $175,625 worth of property without incurring any federal gift or estate tax liability.

Additionally, there is a federal gift and estate tax "marital deduction" which permits a spouse to make inter vivos gifts to the other spouse of up to $100,000 worth of property without incurring gift tax liability, or to transfer to a surviving spouse at death up to $250,000 worth of property without incurring death tax liability.

The result of the combined and complicated federal gift and estate tax is that, unless an individual owns upwards of $175,000 worth of property ($250,000 where property is left to a surviving spouse), the tax implications of transferring property by inter vivos gift, or by deathtime transfer, are not very important. (Of course, upon the death of a surviving spouse, there may be taxes to worry about.)

However, for property owners whose estates are substantially larger than $175,000–$250,000, the use of will substitutes and/or the execution of a will may have significant and possibly adverse tax consequences—estate planning is essential if the property owner's assets are to be transferred at the lowest possible cost in order to provide the maximum possible security for the property owner's surviving family.

Probate consequences. Probate, as explained in Ch. 5, is simply the process of legally transferring a deceased person's property to the deceased's lawfully designated heirs or beneficiaries. The probate process ensures that the right people end up with the property, and it serves to protect creditors of the deceased, including governmental taxing authorities.

However, probate is a time-consuming process (usually 8 to 10 months), and it is also expensive (perhaps 3–5% of the value of the estate). Because of this, many people use will substitutes to avoid probate. Property that is given away during life is not in the decedent's estate at death and so is not subject to probate. Nor is property that is placed in trust or held jointly with the right of survivorship probated as part of the decedent's estate. Similarly, life insurance proceeds paid directly to the decedent's beneficiary by an insurance company also escape probate.

For a property owner who owns a small to average estate, and thus has little or no tax liability to worry about, the savings in probate costs that may be achieved through the use of will substitutes is often a very desirable result. However, a property owner with a very large estate who uses will substitutes in order to avoid probate may find that the probate costs saved amount to very little in comparison to the death taxes that result. It may be more important for the property owner to hold the property in severalty or in tenancy in common so as to achieve special tax effects, than to transfer the property so as to avoid probate: the net result, though probate costs will be paid,

may be to save thousands of dollars in death taxes (particularly where both spouses have substantial holdings and the tax potential is considerable).

What are the rules on intestacy?

It is amazing how many people erroneously believe that the property of a person who dies without a will goes, in every case, to the state. Certainly, property *escheats* (i. e., passes) to the state if a person dies without a will, and without surviving relatives to inherit the property. But, as a practical matter, this seldom occurs. Generally, the property of a person who dies without a will passes to the decedent's nearest surviving relatives as prescribed by state intestacy laws—first, to the decedent's spouse and children; if none, to the decedent's parents; and, if neither—to the decedent's brothers and sisters. It is only when the intestate decedent has no living relatives to inherit his or her property (and state statutes often cut off the more remote relatives such as second cousins or great uncles and aunts from inheriting) that the property will escheat to the state.

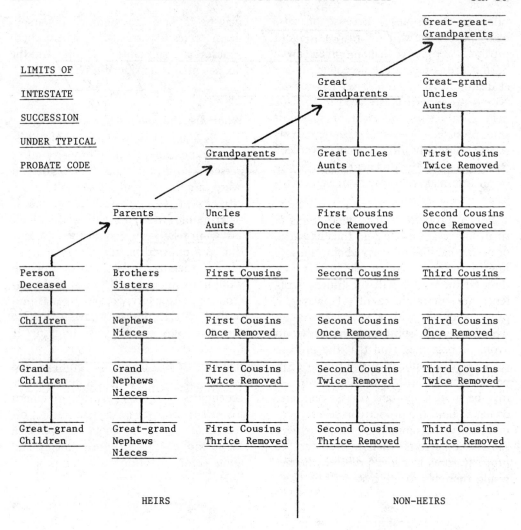

LIMITS OF

INTESTATE

SUCCESSION

UNDER TYPICAL

PROBATE CODE

				Great-great- Grandparents
			Great Grandparents	Great-grand Uncles Aunts
		Grandparents	Great Uncles Aunts	First Cousins Twice Removed
	Parents	Uncles Aunts	First Cousins Once Removed	Second Cousins Once Removed
Person Deceased	Brothers Sisters	First Cousins	Second Cousins	Third Cousins
Children	Nephews Nieces	First Cousins Once Removed	Second Cousins Once Removed	Third Cousins Once Removed
Grand Children	Grand Nephews Nieces	First Cousins Twice Removed	Second Cousins Twice Removed	Third Cousins Twice Removed
Great-grand Children	Great-grand Nephews Nieces	First Cousins Thrice Removed	Second Cousins Thrice Removed	Third Cousins Thrice Removed

HEIRS   NON-HEIRS

Note that the deceased's property will go first to children, then to grandchildren, then to great grandchildren. It is only when there are none of these that the property will go to those listed in the second column, brothers and sisters, etc. And it is only when there are no living relatives in any of the first three columns that the property will escheat to the state. Individuals in the fourth and fifth columns are not closely enough related to be classified as heirs.

Note further that a wife or husband is not an "heir" because a spouse is not a blood relative However, a wife or husband does receive the decedent's property

—generally all of it if there are no children, and half of it if there are children —if the decedent dies intestate.

By way of example, suppose that Robert Smith dies intestate (i. e., without a will), leaving a surviving wife, Peg, an unmarried daughter, Karen, and two grandchildren, Peter and Brian, the children of Robert's son, Mark, who predeceased Robert. Because Robert has no will, state statute determines who gets the property. While state intestacy laws differ from state to state, a typical statute might provide for the following distribution of property.

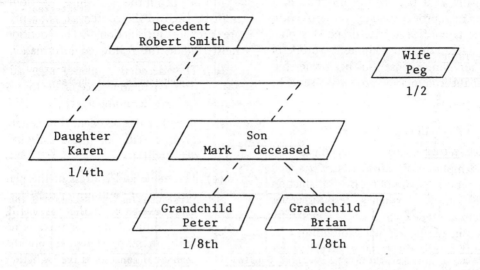

THIS IS PER STIRPES

Note that the grandchildren Peter and Brian take the share of their deceased father Mark. They are said to take their father's share "per stirpes" which means by right of representation.

In most states, if the heirs are all in the same class (i. e., all children or all granchildren, etc.), they do not take "per stirpes", but rather "per capita" which means in their own right in equal shares. Thus, in our example, if daughter Karen was also deceased, leaving a surviving child Susan, the three grandchildren, being in the same class, would take "per capita" and each receive ⅙th of the estate as follows:

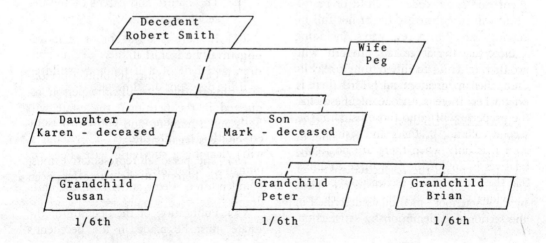

THIS IS PER CAPITA

Finally, if a person dies intestate in a community property state, the surviving spouse is entitled to the decedent's one-half interest in the community property (the surviving spouse thus has ownership of all the community property—see Ch. 5).

What is an "advancement"?

An "advancement" is very much like an ademption by satisfaction. As you will recall, ademption by satisfaction comes into play when a testator gives property inter vivos to a beneficiary named in his or her will, intending that the gift satisfy the testamentary bequest in whole or in part (the testamentary bequest is reduced by the amount of the inter vivos gift). Similarly, an "advancement" is an inter vivos gift made by a property owner (who later dies intestate) to a child or grandchild with the intention that the gift constitute prepayment toward the donee's intestate portion of the decedent's estate. The advancement operates to reduce the intestate share by the value of the inter vivos gift.

However, unless the decedent *intends* that the gift reduce the intestate share, the gift will not qualify as an advancement, and the decedent's child or grandchild will be entitled to his or her full intestate share. In a few states, including California, a gift to any person who would qualify as an intestate heir may be treated as an advancement only if there is written evidence of the decedent's intent.

If a class of children or grandchildren qualify as intestate heirs, and one or more members of the class have received an advancement, the respective shares of the individual members will be calculated by the "hotchpot" method as described in the section on ademption by satisfaction.

What is basic probate procedure?

The following is a brief summary of basic probate procedure.

(1) To begin the procedure, a petition must be filed in the court with appropriate probate jurisdiction. The petition must contain the following information:

(a) The decedent's name, age, address, date and place of death, social security number, etc.;

(b) Whether the decedent died testate (with a will) or intestate (without a will);

(c) The name and address of the person who will administer the estate (the "executor" if there is a will, the "administrator" if there is no will; in many states, simply the "personal representative" whether the decedent dies testate or intestate). The personal representative is a fiduciary and is generally required to post a surety bond with the court unless the will of the decedent exempts him or her from this responsibility. The personal representative has an affirmative duty to discover, collect, and distribute all the decedent's assets;

(d) The names, relationships, and addresses of the heirs; and

(e) The nature and extent of the decedent's assets.

(2) If there is a will, proof of its validity must be furnished.

(3) Once the court appoints a personal representative (usually the person requested in the petition), the estate will be issued a number, and will be formally opened as a legal entity.

(4) The personal representative must notify the heirs that the estate has been opened.

(5) Publication of the opening of the estate must be made in the decedent's county newspaper (e. g., once in each of four consecutive weeks) to give creditors an opportunity (usually 4 to 6 months) to file claims.

(6) The personal representative must next file an inventory of the decedent's assets (frequently an appraisal of the assets is required).

(7) The court may provide temporary support for the decedent's spouse or children.

(8) Claims, expenses, debts, and taxes of the estate are paid. If necessary, a portion of the estate properties will be sold to effect payment.

(9) The remaining estate properties are then distributed to the proper persons.

(10) Accountings showing the following information are generally required:

    (a) The time covered;

    (b) The value of the inventoried property;

    (c) All money or property received during the period covered;

    (d) All disbursements made during this period; and

    (e) A statement that taxes have been paid.

(11) The estate is closed.

Who is entitled to income earned by an estate during the period of probate?

Obviously, a decedent's property will continue to produce income during the period of administration or probate of the estate, which may take many months, or even years. Such income is taxable to the estate which is a taxable entity that must report its income and pay income taxes like any other taxpayer. The estate reports its income on what is called a "fiduciary income tax return". (Inter vivos and testamentary trusts must also report their income on a "fiduciary income tax return" and pay income taxes just like any other taxable entity. A trust which, by its terms must distribute income to beneficiaries receives a deduction for the income distributed to the beneficiaries who must report the income they receive on their own personal returns.) Of course, income earned and taxed to the estate will not be taxed again when it is distributed to the beneficiaries of the estate at the end of the probate period.

As to who is entitled to the earnings and profits of the estate during this period, it is necessary to return to our previous classification of testamentary gifts.

Specific gifts. Specific gifts, such as bank accounts, stocks, bonds, real estate, etc. carry with them the right to all earnings and profits produced by the specific property *after* the death of the testator (any accrued, but unpaid interest on the property at the time of the testator's death also goes to the specific beneficiary).

For example, rent due and owing prior to the testator's death is not payable to the specific devisee of the rental property, but rent falling due after the testator's death is. Similarly, dividends declared on stock prior to the testator's death do not belong to the stock beneficiary, but dividends declared after the testator's death do. Suppose that there is a split of stock resulting in an increased number of shares—does the stock beneficiary have a right to the added shares? The beneficiary will have a right to the shares whether the stock split is declared before or after the testator's death so long as the gift of stock is truly a *specific* bequest of particular shares rather than a *general* bequest that may be satisfied out of any number of shares. For example, if Sidney Smith bequeaths "*my* 100 shares of General Motors stock to my son, Robert", and, prior to Sidney's death, the stock splits two for one, Robert will be entitled to the full 200 shares upon Sidney's death because the specific 100 shares Sidney intended Robert to receive are now represented by 200 shares. However, a bequest of "100 shares of General Motors stock to my son, Robert" is probably a general gift of stock that may be satisfied out of any General Motors stock in Sidney's estate, and Robert would not be entitled to any additional stock resulting from a stock split prior to Sidney's death. The courts, in any case, will try to give effect to the testator's probable intent. And a gift of stock in a closely held or family corporation will more than likely be held a specific rather than a general bequest.

General gifts. In most states, general bequests begin to bear interest at the legal rate in favor of the general gift beneficiary starting one year after the testator's death.

Residuary gifts. Residuary gifts do not bear interest. However, all earnings and profits that do not belong to the specific gift beneficiaries, and that are not payable as interest to the general gift beneficiaries belong to the residuary beneficiary.

In what order are claims against the decedent's estate or other interests in the estate satisfied?

While probate statutes vary somewhat from state to state, the following order of payment is typical:

(1) Expenses of administration, including court costs (probate fees), attorneys fees, and personal representative fees;

(2) The decedent's funeral expenses;

(3) Medical bills and other expenses of the decedent's last illness;

(4) Family support allowances provided during the administration of the estate for the support of the decedent's surviving spouse and children;

(5) Taxes owing to the government;

(6) Any wages owing to employees of the decedent for work during the three months immediately preceding their employer's death;

(7) All mortgages or secured liens or claims against the estate in the order of their priority;

(8) All inter vivos judgments against the decedent in the order of their priority (first in time, first in priority);

(9) All other valid claims against the estate;

(10) And finally, the beneficiaries or heirs are paid.

With regard to payment of beneficiaries or heirs, if the decedent died testate, the specific gifts are distributed first, then the general, and, finally, the residuary. If the decedent died intestate, the intestate heirs are paid their respective shares or portions of the estate.

In most states, taxes must be equitably apportioned against the shares of all beneficiaries of the estate unless the decedent's will provides otherwise. As a result, it is very common to find a provision in a will that all taxes are to be paid out of the residuary portion of the estate so as not to affect the specific, demonstrative, and general bequests and devises.

May a beneficiary or heir refuse to take his or her share of a decedent's estate?

Both a beneficiary under a will and an intestate heir of a decedent may refuse to accept their lawful share of the decedent's estate, with the following results:

Beneficiary's disclaimer. In most states, a beneficiary under a will is not automatically vested with ownership of a testamentary gift upon the testator's death. The beneficiary must first accept the gift, although acceptance will be presumed if the beneficiary fails to reject the gift within a reasonable period of time after learning of his or her rights under the will. The beneficiary's rejection of a gift is called a "renunciation" or "disclaimer", and it relates back to the time of the testator's death with the result that the beneficiary is never considered to have held an ownership right in the property disclaimed.

Intestate heir's disclaimer. In contrast to the ownership rights of a beneficiary, the ownership rights of an intestate heir are considered to vest automatically by operation of law at the time of the decedent's death. As a result, an heir who thereafter renounces or disclaims the interest is in effect giving the property back to the decedent's estate. Thus, the heir may be liable for inheritance taxes for having received the property in the first place, and he or she may be liable for gift taxes for having given the property back. Additionally, if the heir is insolvent, his or her creditors may be able to set the transfer aside as a fraudulent conveyance as as to reach the property in satisfaction of their claims. (A minority of jurisdictions treats an intestate heir's disclaimer the same as a beneficiary's disclaimer, and a minority of jurisdictions vice versa).

To prevent some of the inequities that may arise when an intestate heir disclaims his or her intestate share, or a beneficiary in a minority jurisdiction renounces his or her testamentary gift, the Tax Reform Act of 1976 provides as follows: an heir or beneficiary who disclaims will not be treated as having made a gift to the person to whom the interest passes upon disclaimer so long as the following four conditions are satisfied:

(1) The refusal to accept is in writing;

(2) The written disclaimer is received by the person transferring the interest or his or her legal representative no later than nine months after the interest is created;

(3) The heir or beneficiary accepts no part of the interest or any of its benefits prior to disclaiming; and

(4) The interest passes to someone other than the heir or beneficiary or his or her appointee (i. e., the disclaiming party cannot direct the transfer to another person).

May a person transfer a testamentary gift or intestate share that he or she expects to receive in the future prior to the death of the testator or intestate decedent?

Closely related to the question of whether an heir or beneficiary may disclaim his or her lawful interest in a decedent's estate is the question of whether an expectant heir or beneficiary may transfer his or her "expectancy" prior to the death of the testator or intestate decedent. The majority rule is that such interests are freely assignable and can be transferred at any time prior to the death of the testator or intestate decedent and up until the time of distribution of the estate assets. (To prevent a beneficiary from assigning his or her expectancy, a testator will often resort to a trust device as explained in the previous chapter.)

What is a will contest?

Once a will has been offered for probate, parties with a direct interest in the decedent's estate may contest the will (i. e., challenge its validity) for a period of time set by statute (often six months). A party with a direct interest in the estate is one who will benefit economically if the will is set aside. This does not include creditors of the decedent whose claims will be paid in any event; nor does it include a party who stands to receive more under the will than he or she would receive by the laws of intestacy (the result of an effective will contest is to determine distribution on the basis of the intestacy laws unless there is an earlier, valid will that controls).

To effectively challenge the validity of a will, the contesting party must introduce evidence that the testator lacked capacity to make a will; that he or she was unduly influenced; that he or she executed the will as a result of duress, fraud, or mistake; or that the testator failed to observe the proper statutory formalities.

Sometimes, a testator will attempt to forestall will contests by providing in the will itself that any person who contests the will shall forfeit all rights that he or she may have under the will. Some courts hold such clauses invalid as being contrary to the public policy of probating only valid wills. Other courts permit such clauses but construe them narrowly so that a beneficiary may raise a question of interpretation under the will without losing his or her rights thereunder. In any event, a beneficiary who successfully challenges a will does not lose the rights that he or she may have under the laws of intestacy or under the terms of another valid will.

What happens if a decedent and his or her beneficiaries are killed in a simultaneous death?

For a person to receive property under a will or by virtue of the laws of intestacy, it is necessary for the person to survive the decedent, if only for a moment of time. Sometimes, however, where a common disaster occurs, it is difficult to determine who died first. Thus, the Uniform Simultaneous Death Act, the law in effect in a great many states, provides that where it is impossible to determine who died first in a common accident, the property of *each* decedent will be distributed as if he or she had survived. The effect of the Act is to prevent a double probate. For example, suppose that Sidney Smith executes a will leaving one-half of his property to his wife, Mary, and one-half to his son, Robert. Sidney's wife, Mary, executes a will leaving one-half of her estate to Sidney, and one-half to Robert. Subsequently, Sidney, Mary, and Robert all die in an

automobile accident with no evidence of who died first. Under the USDA, Sidney will be deemed to have survived both his wife and son insofar as his estate is concerned; and Mary will be deemed to have survived both her husband and son with regard to her property. As a result, all gifts under both wills will lapse, and both Sidney and Mary will be deemed to have died intestate.

Life and accidental insurance are handled the same way: where both insured and beneficiary die in the same accident, it is presumed that the beneficiary died first so as to permit distribution of the insurance proceeds to the alternate beneficiary.

Sometimes, for tax reasons, it is desirable that a spouse be deemed the survivor in a common accident situation so as to achieve the marital deduction for estate tax purposes. As the USDA presumption will not operate if the will provides to the contrary, a testator may provide that "if my spouse and I are killed in an accident where it is impossible to determine who dies first, this will is to be construed as though I predeceased my spouse." The will will be given effect according to its terms and the property will pass, upon the simultaneous death of both spouses, to the "surviving" spouse as provided in the will (thus permitting operation of the marital deduction).

A provision of the 1976 Tax Reform Act, called the "orphans exclusion", permits a special deduction in computing the federal death tax where a decedent leaves at least one surviving minor child (under 21) with no known living parent to care for him or her. The deduction is $5,000 times the difference between 21 and the child's age in years at the time of the decedent's death (i. e., $5,000 x 21 — the child's age in years at the time of the decedent's death). For example, suppose that Robert Smith and his wife, Peg, are killed in a common accident, leaving as orphans their four surviving children: James, age 17; Carla, age 15; Mark, age 12; and Karen, age 10. James will not be 21 for 4 years, Carla for 6 years, Mark for 9, and Karen for 11—for a total of 30 years. $5,000 times 30 provides a special "orphans" deduction of $150,000.

Can a decedent's murderer take property as a beneficiary under the decedent's will or as an intestate heir in the case of an intestate decedent?

No. Just as a joint tenant who murders his or her cotenant will not be permitted to acquire ownership of the cotenant's property by the right of survivorship, a person who murders another cannot share in his or her victim's estate either as a beneficiary under the decedent's will or as the decedent's lawful intestate heir. The murderer will not be permitted to profit from his or her wrongful act. Generally, he or she will be treated as though he or she predeceased the decedent, in which the case the murderer's gifts under the will will lapse, and his or her intestate gifts will be distributed to the victim's other intestate heirs.

Are there any tax implications in transferring property to one person for life, with remainder interests to later generations?

Prior to the Tax Reform Act of 1976, a transfer of property to one person for life with a remainder interest to future generations was a popular method of postponing the payment of death taxes upon the death of the life tenant. The usual procedure was to place property in trust (often a testamentary trust in a will) for the life of one person with a remainder to that person's children. Upon the life tenant's death, the life tenant had nothing left to transfer and so was not subject to estate tax. And the remainderman, who was merely coming into possession of a future interest he or she already

owned, was not subject to inheritance tax. In this manner, death tax could be postponed for a whole generation. And where the trustor created a remainder for life in the life tenant's children, and a further remainder in the children's children, death tax could be postponed for two generations. For example, if Sidney Smith executed a will containing a provision creating a testamentary trust for the benefit of Sidney's nephew for life, remainder to Sidney's grandnephew for life, and, finally, a remainder in fee simple to Sidney's great grandnephew, there would be no death tax payable upon the death of Sidney's nephew or grandnephew—the tax would not be payable until the death of Sidney's great grandnephew.

The Tax Reform Act of 1976, however, created what is called a "generation skipping transfer tax" which is substantially equivalent to the estate or gift tax that would be imposed upon property transferred outright. The value of the property subject to the generation skipping tax is simply added to the other taxable transfers (either gift or death-time transfers) made by the life tenant. A tentative tax is computed on the total of the transfers, then the tax on all transfers other than the generation skipping transfer in question is subtracted to arrive at the generation skipping transfer tax (this process is repeated for each life remainderman). The life tenants, or "deemed transferors" are not personally liable for the tax: the tax must be paid out of the proceeds of the trust property. Thus, in the example above, a "transfer" tax will be imposed when the nephew dies and also when the grandnephew dies. Obviously, much of the incentive for transferring property in this manner has been taken away.

It might be pointed out that the generation skipping tax does provide a sizeable exclusion for generation skipping transfers to grandchildren (e. g., Robert Smith executes a will containing a testamentary trust provision for the lifetime benefit of his daughter, Carla, remainder in fee simple to Carla's children). Generation skipping transfers to grandchildren are not subject to the tax to the extent that the total transfers do not exceed $250,000 through each of the trustor's children (regardless of how many children each of the trustor's children might have). If Robert Smith has four children, for example, he can transfer $250,000 tax free through each of the children for the benefit of his grandchildren—a total tax free transfer of $1,000,000.

Can property be placed in trust for a limited period of time so as to make the income taxable to someone other than the grantor for that limited period?

Yes—if certain conditions are met. A taxpayer in a high tax bracket may want to reduce his or her income tax liability by placing income producing property into what is termed a "grantor trust" for the benefit of a family member (or perhaps a close friend) who is in a much lower tax bracket. A taxpayer can effectively "split his or her income" in this

manner only if he or she places the property into trust for a minimum of ten years: so long as the grantor-trustor has no reversionary interest in the trust during this period of time, all income from the trust will be taxed to the trust beneficiary—not to the grantor.

Of course, the grantor-trustor may provide for a reversionary interest in himself or herself after the ten year period, and a provision in the trust that the property will revert to the grantor prior to this time if the income beneficiary dies within the ten year period is also permissible. However, other than this, the grantor must have no power to direct the beneficial enjoyment of the trust income during the ten year period, either to himself or herself, or to others.

In conclusion, use of a "grantor trust" is particularly desirable for individuals in high income tax brackets with minor children in low income tax brackets (although the grantor will be taxed on any portion of the trust income that is used for the support and maintenance of the children as the grantor is already legally obligated to provide for their support).

CASES

CASE 1—*She feared that if we went to the attorney who prepared her former will her daughter would find out about it and "raise Hell."*

IN RE ESTATE OF WEIR

Court of Appeals of Oregon, 1975.
21 Or.App. 476, 535 P.2d 119.

TONGUE, Judge Pro Tem.

This is a proceeding to contest the will of Sophia Weir, a resident of Coos County. The mental capacity of the Testator is conceded, but it is contended that the will was the result of the undue influence of the sole beneficiary, Wayne Clawson, alias Bill Wolf. As in most will contest cases, the facts are of extreme importance.

The facts.

A previous will was executed by Mrs. Weir on December 28, 1971, naming one of her two daughters, Louise Carlton, as her sole beneficiary. At that time Mrs. Weir and a hired man lived on her farm. In May 1972,

Wayne Clawson became manager of the farm. He had come to Oregon from California where he had a criminal record of several convictions, with the result that he had assumed the name of Bill Wolf. From June 1972, until her death on November 23, 1973, Mrs. Weir and Wolf occupied the old two-story house on the farm.

Mrs. Weir was then 77 years of age and in poor health suffering from diabetes, high blood pressure, chronic urinary infection, diarrhea and progressive cataracts; but she was mentally "sharp" and strong willed, according to the testimony. Shortly after Wolf came to the farm Mrs. Weir fell and broke her hip. She was a heavy woman and thus had to be helped. As a result of these disabilities, Mr. Wolf helped her take her baths and helped her to bed, among other things. He took good care of her, according to the testimony.

Shortly after he became manager of the farm Mr. Wolf had an attorney prepare a "management agreement," which he took to the farm, where it was signed by him and Mrs. Weir. By the terms of that agreement Mr. Wolf was to be the manager of the farm for five years, with "full authority" to manage it "within [his] sole discretion." The agreement also provided that as compensation he was to be furnished living quarters, rent free, for the five-year period, as well as title to all timber on the premises, to be removed within five years. There was no testimony as to the amount or value of that timber.

Mrs. Carlton, Mrs. Weir's daughter, became concerned about developing problems between herself and Mr. Wolf when she visited her mother on the farm. Although there is no evidence that she knew of the management agreement, she took her mother to the office of the attorney who had prepared her previous will. That attorney testified that he talked to Mrs. Weir alone and that she told him that she wanted to stay on the ranch and have Mr. Wolf take care of her, but that she did not want him to be in a "position to lay claim to the ranch as a result of services provided for her." She said nothing, however, about the written management agreement.

He then wrote a letter to Mr. Wolf as attorney for Mrs. Weir stating his understanding that "in return for taking care of Mrs. Weir and her ranch operation," Mr. Wolf was to receive "full tenancy at the premises," subject to termination at any time, and stating that if this was not a correct statement of the agreement between him and Mrs. Weir, to "contact me at your early convenience to discuss what you feel to be the true and correct nature of the agreement." Mr. Wolf did not respond to that letter because, as he testified, he thought it "not important enough."

Considerable testimony was offered from several witnesses to the effect that as of that time Mrs. Weir did not want to sell the farm, which had been "in the family" for over 100 years, but wanted to keep it in "the family" for "the kids," in accordance with the provisions of her previous will leaving it to her daughter and that she made such statements as late as within three months prior to her death. Mr. Wolf, however, testified that she never told him that she wanted to keep the farm in the family, but said that "they would never take care of it," but would sell it and were "just waiting for her to die."

There was testimony that in "conversations" with Mrs. Weir, Mr. Wolf was critical of Mrs. Carlton for failing to devote sufficient attention to her mother; that this was the subject of "frequent conversations," and that Mrs. Weir was also critical of her daughter. Mrs. Carlton apparently visited her mother once each week "for the eggs" and also drove her to see the doctor. There were also difficulties between Mr. Wolf and one of Mrs. Carlton's sons, who was accused by Wolf of stealing from Mrs. Weir.

It also appears that a friend of Mr. Wolf, a Mr. Ogden, also originally from California, where he had once been convicted of a crime, was a frequent visitor at the farm. He stayed there on his days off from work "almost every week," and played cribbage and pinochle with Mrs. Weir. Another frequent visitor to the farm was Eldred Clawson, father of Mr. Wolf, who was retired and "came up" from California to visit his son. He also had a criminal record in California. According to Mr. Ogden, he, Mr. Wolf and Wolf's father, Mr. Clawson, were all "living" at the farm in November 1973 when the contested will was executed and when Mrs. Weir died.

Except for the testimony of one other witness, the only evidence of any statements by Mrs. Weir prior to the preparation and execution of the contested will indicating a change of her previous desire to leave the farm "in the family" was the testimony of Mr. Wolf himself. He testified that over a period of "a couple of months" he and Mrs. Weir "talked over the possibility of [his] becoming the owner of the place" and that she "asked me if I would keep the place going if I owned it and I told her I would try my very best." Mr. Wolf also told his friend, Mr. Ogden, that he would "like to own something like this" and also told his father that Mrs. Weir said that there was a possibility that she would "will the place to him." He denied, however, that he had any conversations with her about preparing a will to accomplish that purpose.

There was also testimony that on occasion Mr. Wolf would give Mrs. Weir an affectionate pat or hug and refer to her as "Mom." He also testified that Mrs. Weir trusted him, had "much confidence" in him, and that she confided most of her problems to him.

Just when and under what circumstances she finally decided to change her previous will is not entirely clear, even under the testimony of the proponents of the contested will. Mr. Ogden testified that he typed the will on a typewriter that he had taken to the farm and that he got the information for the will from Mrs. Weir, who said she was "very unhappy" with her daughter; that this was the reason for changing her will, and that she definitely wanted to make a new will and leave it to Mr. Wolf." He testified that he suggested that she go to a lawyer but that she asked him to "do it." He also said that he typed two or three drafts of the one-page will and that Mrs. Weir finally said that "it would do all right." Ogden also said that he got the description of the farm for the purposes of the will from tax statements that were "on the table" and that he did not know if they were provided by Mr. Wolf.

Mr. Wolf's father, Mr. Clawson, who also had lived at the farm for some time before the contested will was executed, said that he heard no discussions between Mrs. Weir, Ogden and Wolf about the will and knew nothing about it other than that Ogden typed it "upstairs" and then brought it down to show her to read and make any necessary changes.

Mr. Wolf testified that he gave the tax statement to Ogden for the purposes of using in the will its description of the farm, but that he did so at the request of Mrs. Weir, and that he did not tell Ogden what to "say" in the will, but that Mrs. Weir did. He also testified that about one month before he had tried, "at her request," to get the attorney who prepared his management contract to come to the farm and prepare a will, but that the attorney refused to do so and suggested that Mrs. Weir come to his office. Wolf said that he also previously talked to another attorney, who declined to prepare the will and suggested that he go to another attorney. Mr. Wolf testified that Mrs. Weir did not want anyone to know about the new will and feared that if she went to the attorney who prepared her former will her daughter would find out about it and would "raise Hell." These were the reasons, according to Mr. Wolf, that she asked Ogden to "do it."

Apparently the will was typed by Ogden on Sunday, November 18, 1973. On the following day Mr. Wolf requested a notary public whom he had previously known to come to the farm to notarize the will. Upon arrival of the notary, and in the presence of Mr. Ogden and Mr. Clawson, Wolf's father, the will was signed by Mrs. Weir and was witnessed by them. According to the testimony, Mr. Wolf, the sole beneficiary of the will, was "in and out" of the room both when the will was prepared and when it was signed and witnessed. According to the notary, Wolf spoke to Mrs. Weir at that time as "Mom" and asked if he could get her another cup of coffee.

The notary and the other witnesses, Ogden and Clawson, identified their signatures and that of Mrs. Weir, but were not asked the usual questions whether she appeared to have the necessary testamentary capacity and whether she appeared to be acting of her own free will. They testified, however, that the notary read the will to Mrs. Weir before she signed it. There was other testimony that because of cataracts she had considerable difficulty in reading.

On November 23, 1973, four days after the execution of the will on November 19, Mrs. Weir died in the farmhouse of an apparent heart attack. Mr. Wolf was alone with her at that time. At that time the natural heirs of Mrs. Weir, in addition to the daughter who had been named as the sole beneficiary in her previous will, included another daughter and several grandchildren.

In its decree denying the "petition to revoke probate" of the will of November 19, 1973, and in admitting that will to probate "in solemn form" the trial court made no findings of fact other than general findings that Mrs. Weir was competent and that "said will was not the result of undue influence."

It was established by the evidence that the will was the product of undue influence.

The Supreme Court of Oregon held in In re Reddaway's Estate, that:

> "Definitions of undue influence couched in terms of the testator's freedom of will are subject to criticism in that they invite us to think in terms of coercion and duress, when the emphasis should be on the unfairness of the advantage which is reaped as the result of wrongful conduct. 'Undue influence does not negative consent by the donor. Equity acts because there is want of conscience on the part of the donee, not want of consent on the part of the donor.' Said in another way, undue influence has a closer kinship to fraud than to duress. It has been characterized as 'a species of fraud.'

> " * * * This court has held that where a confidential relation exists between a testator and the beneficiary, slight evidence

is sufficient to establish undue influence. The rule is more specifically stated in In re Southman's Estate, as follows:

> " 'The existence of a confidential relationship * * * when taken in connection with other suspicious circumstances may justify a suspicion of undue influence so as to require the beneficiary to go forward with the proof and present evidence sufficient to overcome the adverse inference. * * *'

"It will be noted that the burden does not exist unless there are circumstances in addition to the confidential relation. * * *"

As in *Reddaway*, we find that there was a confidential relationship between Mrs. Weir and Mr. Wolf and that the "relationship [was] such as to indicate a position of dominance by the one in whom confidence [was] reposed over the other." As in *Reddaway*, we also find that in this case "suspicious circumstances are abundant."

In *Reddaway* the Oregon Supreme Court listed and discussed the various "factors of importance" to be considered in determining whether undue influence was exercised. Upon considering those various factors we find that enough of them were sufficiently established so as to require the conclusion that the will of Sophia Weir was the product of undue influence by Bill Wolf, for reasons which we shall next discuss.

(1) *Procurement, i. e., "participation [by] the beneficiary in the preparation of the will."* Wolf provided for Ogden the description of the farm for the purposes of the will, despite his contention that he did so at the request of Mrs. Weir. Aside from the fact that Wolf's friend Ogden typed the will and Wolf's own father and his friend Ogden witnessed the will, he also procured a notary public to witness the will and was "in and out" of the room during its execution, at which time he called Mrs. Weir "Mom" and offered to get her a cup of coffee.

(2) *Independent advice.* No independent advice was provided to Mrs. Weir relative to the preparation of the will.

(3) *Secrecy and haste.* One reason that no lawyer was engaged to prepare the will was the desire to keep it a secret. The circumstances are such as also to indicate considerable haste in its preparation. The only reason for waiting until the next day for the execution of the will was the mistaken belief of Wolf that it had to be witnessed by a notary public.

(4) *Change in decedent's attitude toward others.* As in *Reddaway*, there was a change in the attitude of the testator toward her own child. Although Wolf testified that the reason for the change was her displeasure with her daughter, it is "just as probable" in this case that Wolf "played a part in effecting this change in attitude," as it was that similar conduct played a similar part in *Reddaway*.

(5) *Change in the testator's plan of disposing of her property.* As in *Reddaway*, there was such a change in the plan of the testator and there was evidence of a previously "settled intent in the disposition of [her] estate" and of a "variance" between the testator's previous will and the will in question.

(6) *Unnatural or unjust gift.* Although, as recognized in *Reddaway*, one may make a legal disposition of his estate which reasonable men would regard as "unfair," it is a "circumstance" to be weighed in determining whether undue influence existed. This is not a case in which the benefici-

ary who cared for an ill and aged testator was rewarded by the will for faithful service and would otherwise have received little or no compensation. Wolf already had procured a five year "management agreement," including title to all timber on the property.

(7) *Susceptibility to influence.* Finally, as in *Reddaway*, this testator, although a person of "strong will," was physically sick and infirm and was susceptible to influence by reason of her dependence upon Wolf as the result of her physical infirmities.

As in *Reddaway*, there was also other evidence in the record which was relevant to the issue of undue influence, including other "suspicious circumstances," but the combination of the foregoing circumstances is sufficient, in our judgment, to require that this court sustain the contention of the contestants that undue influence was exercised upon this testator.

* * * [T]he will of Sophia Weir was the product of undue influence by Bill Wolf.

Accordingly, the decree of the trial court is reversed and this case is remanded for further proceedings not inconsistent with this opinion.

CASE 2—A *"Totten"* trust.

IN RE PETRALIA'S ESTATE

Supreme Court of Illinois, 1965.
32 Ill.2d 134, 204 N.E.2d 1.

HERSHEY, Justice.

In 1948 Antonio Petralia opened a savings account in the First National Bank of Chicago, naming himself as "trustee" for the benefit of his daughter, Dominica Di Maggio, to whom the balance in the account at his death was to be paid. After Petralia's death, Dominica Di Maggio, plaintiff herein, instituted a citation proceeding against the defendant administrator of the estate of Antonio Petralia in the probate court of Cook County in which she claimed title to the account. The probate court held that a valid trust had been created and that under the terms thereof the plaintiff was entitled to the balance of $17,189.15 in the account. The Appellate Court affirmed, and we granted leave to appeal.

This is the first occasion on which we have been called upon to consider the validity of savings bank or "Totten" trusts. The defendant urges the court to reverse the judgments below on two grounds: (1) that the execution of the signature card was insufficient to establish an intent on the part of Antonio Petralia to create a trust; and (2) "that the form of trust attempted to be executed by the savings accounts trusts is an attempt at a testamentary disposition and not operative, due to the failure to conform with the Statute of wills."

The record indicates that for a number of years prior to 1948 Antonio Petralia was the sole owner of a regular savings account which he had opened in his name at the First National Bank of Chicago. On November 8, 1948, he closed the account and transferred all the funds therein to the savings account trust which is the subject of this litigation. The new account was entitled "Tony Petralia, Trustee," and on the first side of the signature card appeared the signature "Tony Petralia" with the word "trustee" written beneath. On the reverse side of the card was the following language:

> "All deposits in this account are made for the benefit of Domenica Di Maggio to whom or to whose legal representative said deposits or any part thereof, together with the interest thereon, may be paid in the event of the death of the undersigned Trustee."

The signature "Tony Petralia" again appeared below the language on a line designated "trustee". Beneath the signature was written "Mrs. Domenica Di Maggio", "July 29, 1909" and "Daughter."

Introduced in evidence were facsimile ledger sheets of the First National Bank which showed that from the date the account was opened to the date of his death, Antonio Petralia alone made numerous deposits to and infrequent withdrawals from the account. The balance in the account steadily increased.

In support of his contention that the execution of the signature card was insufficient to show an intent to create a trust, the administrator emphasizes the fact that the printed agreement on the card provided that the bank "may", rather than "shall", pay the balance to the plaintiff at his death. The use of the word "may" is said to show a lack of intent that the plaintiff was definitely to receive the benefit of the account.

The reason for the inclusion of the word "may" in the agreement is not clear. * * * Whatever the reason for the use of the word "may", however, we think that the general tenor of the agreement indicates an intent to create a trust and that the settlor intended that the funds be paid to his daughter at his death. This conclusion is confirmed by the fact that the settlor changed his regular savings account to a savings account in trust form, an act which would have been unnecessary if he intended to maintain the account solely for his own benefit. We think it significant also that Antonio Petralia did not in fact withdraw the funds in the account and use them for his own benefit during his lifetime but instead followed a regular pattern of making deposits, thereby steadily increasing the size of the account, apparently for the benefit of his daughter. Although there was testimony by Antonio Petralia's nephew that Petralia had told him the account was opened so that his daughter could make deposits for him, the fact that Petralia alone made all deposits greatly discredits the persuasiveness of such evidence. We think there was ample evidence to support the trial court's finding that Antonio Petralia intended to create a trust.

This brings us to a consideration of the defendant's contention that the trust was invalid as an attempted testamentary disposition without compliance with the Statute of Wills. Since the trust agreement was not executed in accordance with the formalities required by the Statute of Wills, the determinative issue becomes whether a valid *inter vivos* trust was created. One of the requirements for the establishment of a valid *inter vivos* trust is that the beneficiary acquire a present interest during the lifetime of the settlor. The defendant argues that since the settlor alone retained the power to withdraw interest and principal from the account during his lifetime, the trust was illusory and testamentary in that the beneficiary never obtained any present interest during the settlor's lifetime.

It is true that Antonio Petralia, as settlor and trustee, retained extensive control over the savings account trust which he established. However, in this respect it is not significantly different in substance from other revocable *inter vivos* trusts which have been held valid in this and other jurisdictions. The nature of the beneficiary's present interest under such trusts is well stated in 1 Scott, The Law of Trusts, 353–354: "The declaration of trust immediately creates an equitable interest in the beneficiaries although the enjoyment of the interest is postponed until the death of the settlor, and although the interest may be divested by the exercise of the power of revocation." The fact that the beneficiary's actual enjoyment of the trust is contingent on Antonio Petralia's death without first having revoked the trust by withdrawing the balance in the account does not negate the existence of a present interest in the plaintiff during her father's lifetime, even though that interest may have been highly destructible.

We conclude that the instrument executed by Antonio Petralia on November 8, 1948, was sufficient to create a valid and enforceable *inter vivos* savings account trust. In so holding we accept the position adopted by the American Law Institute in § 58 of the Restatement (Second) of Trusts: "Where a person makes a deposit in a savings account in a bank or other savings organization in his own name as trustee for another person intending to reserve a power to withdraw the whole or any part of the deposit at any time during his lifetime and to use as his own whatever he may withdraw, or otherwise to revoke the trust, the intended trust is enforceable by the beneficiary upon the death of the depositor as to any part remaining on deposit on his death if he has not revoked the trust."

The judgment of the Appellate Court affirming the order of the probate court of Cook County is affirmed.

Judgment affirmed.

CASE 3—*There may be many reasons for a parent to think that one child should receive more—this was not an advancement.*

CLEMENT v. BLYTHE

Supreme Court of Arkansas, 1952.
220 Ark. 551, 248 S.W.2d 883.

George Rose SMITH, Justice.

This is a controversy between W. R. Blythe's three daughters and his one son with reference to the division of the 310 acres that Blythe owned at his death intestate in 1932. Blythe's widow died in 1948, and after her death this partition suit was brought. The only disputed issue is whether an additional 75 acres, which Blythe conveyed to his son, the appellee, in 1930, should be treated as an advancement and considered as part of the estate in the partition. The chancellor, holding that the 1930 conveyance was not an advancement, awarded the appellee a one-fourth interest in the 310 acres without regard to the fact that he had received the 75-acre tract during his father's lifetime.

In 1929 Blythe and his wife were living alone in Faulkner County, the four children having married and moved away. In December of that year Blythe proposed to his son that if the latter and his wife would come back and live in the vicinity of his parents they would convey to the son the 75-acre tract. The appellee accepted this offer, gave up his job in Pulaski County, and went back to Faulkner County. Mr. and Mrs. Blythe then conveyed the tract to their son, the deed reciting that the son should live with and take care of his parents for the rest of their lives, else the deed would be void. The appellee lived in the family home until 1934, when he built a house on the 75-acre tract. This land is only a few hundred yards from the homestead and was occupied by the appellee until his mother's death in 1948. Neither parent is shown to have complained that their son failed to carry out his bargain in any respect, and the appellants do not ask that the 1930 deed be canceled on the theory that the appellee should have done more for his parents than he did.

To this point the testimony does not show an advancement. An advancement is a gift—usually a substantial gift—which the parent intends to be charged against the donee's share of the parental estate if the donor should die intestate. But if the conveyance does not amount to a gift, for the reason that full value is given by the child, then it is not an advancement. In this case the appellee gave up his work in Pulaski County and lived with or near his parents for eighteen years, in return for property that was worth about $900 in 1930. There is lacking that absence of consideration that is an essential element of a gift.

Nevertheless the appellants insist that Blythe, Sr., was attempting to divide his holdings among his children when he conveyed the 75-acre tract to the appellee in 1930. There is proof that on the same day Blythe executed three deeds: First, the deed to his son, which we have described; second, an undelivered deed to one of his daughters which would have conveyed eighty acres; and third, an undelivered deed to his wife and a second daughter which would have conveyed the same land that was given to the appellee. It is forcefully argued that the simultaneous execution of these three deeds shows that Blythe's purpose was to divide his estate among his children.

There is a presumption that a parent's substantial gift to one of his children is intended as an advancement. This presumption is based on the belief that a parent means to treat all his children alike, but by its nature the presumption is not an especially strong one. There may evidently be many reasons for a parent to think that one of his children should receive more than an exact share of the estate. Hence it has been said that "all such presumptions may be readily overcome by proof of actual intent."

* * *

We agree with Schouler's view that the presumption may be readily overcome. In the case at bar a preponderance of the testimony shows that the conveyance to the appellee was not meant as an advancement. Indeed, the contemporaneous execution of the other two deeds supports this conclusion. Those deeds were not introduced at the trial; the witnesses testified only as to their recollection of a transaction that occurred twenty years earlier. Since the deed to the appellee required him to live with his parents for the rest of their lives, it is fair to suppose that Blythe, Sr., inserted a similar clause in the deeds to his daughters. When we note that neither daughter returned to Faulkner County in 1930 and that neither of the other deeds was delivered, we think the natural inference is that the conveyances were offered as an inducement for the return of the children and that the appellee alone accepted the offer.

Affirmed.

CASE 4—*Does a husband who murders his wife have a right to share in her estate when she dies intestate?*

ESTATE OF KALFUS v. KALFUS

Superior Court of New Jersey, Chancery Division, 1963.
81 N.J.Super. 435, 195 A.2d 903.

PASHMAN, J. S. C.

This is a summary proceeding to determine the　*　*　*　the rights of defendant Richard H. Kalfus under the New Jersey statute of descent and distribution. A brief factual résumé is necessary to an understanding of the present controversy.

On November 20, 1962 Domenica Kalfus was murdered by her defendant husband. Domenica died intestate. Following a plea defendant was sentenced to the New Jersey State Prison, where he is presently confined, for a term of 15 to 20 years.

Domenica died seized of an estate comprising personal property and the equity in the family home in Cliffside Park which she owned in fee simple. The equity in the house was approximately $25,500 and the personal estate about $6,800. She was survived by her husband and two infant children, Michele, age seven, and Jane, age three. Bernard Natalino, a brother of the deceased intestate, was appointed guardian of the infants and administrator of the estate. This court ordered the real property sold as being in the best interests of the infants, and the proceeds of the sale were deposited into court pending a determination of the following　*　*　*　question　*　*　*.

Does a husband who murders his wife have a right to share in her personal estate where the wife dies intestate?

*　*　*

Under our statute of descent and distribution, an intestate's husband is entitled to one-third of the intestate's personal property if a child or children also survive the deceased parent.

*　*　*

In the insurance cases the courts have impressed a constructive trust on the proceeds of the policy by invoking the age-old maxim of the common law that "no man can profit by his own wrongdoing."

*　*　*

[T]heory allows the legal title to pass but equity treats the wrongdoer as a constructive trustee because of his unconscionable conduct, and will compel the wrongdoer to convey the property to the heirs or next of kin of the deceased.

This　*　*　*　view was adopted in Sherman v. Weber, where the nature of the property was a tenancy by the entirety, and in Whitney v. Lott, a situation involving a devise from deceased wife, to husband-murderer. More recently the doctrine of constructive trust was used in Neiman v. Hurff, where a husband murdered his wife. The husband and wife held real property as tenants by the entirety and shares of stock as joint tenants.

In the Whitney case the effect of the statute of wills was circumvented by the use of the constructive trust whereby title would pass, subject however to the imposition of the trust *ex maleficio*.

* * * Even in the absence of a specific statute, it has been held that a murderer cannot inherit from his victim under the statute of descent and distribution.

* * *

Based upon the reasoning of our courts in analogous situations and upon the cases in those jurisdictions which deny recovery to a murderer who takes the life of a spouse or the person from whom he or she is to inherit under the statutes of descent and distribution, this court holds that * * * defendant is a constructive trustee of the afore-mentioned property because of his unconscionable method of acquiring the property. He is therefore ordered to transfer and convey the legal title to the property to the minor plaintiffs.

* * *

Counsel may submit a judgment in accordance with this opinion.

PROBLEMS

1. What are the four requirements for a valid will? Explain fully.

2. Answer the following "True" or "False" and give reasons for your answers:

   (a) A valid codicil has the effect of republishing or re-executing the original will.

   (b) Holographic wills are valid in a majority of jurisdictions.

   (c) Only a party with a direct interest in the decedent's estate can contest the decedent's will.

   (d) A person who is incompetent to manage his or her own affairs is necessarily incompetent to make a valid will.

   (e) Generally, use of an attestation clause raises a rebuttable presumption of proper execution of a will.

   (f) Ademption by extinction applies only to general bequests and devises.

   (g) The order of abatement of testamentary gifts is normally just the reverse of the order of distribution.

   (h) A nuncupative will can only be used to transfer real property.

   (i) An advancement is very much like an ademption by satisfaction.

   (j) One spouse cannot by will cut his or her surviving spouse out of his or her estate.

3. Discuss the legal implications of each of the following:

   (a) Pat Cross provides by will, "I leave all my property to my sister, Jean, because my daughter, Kathy, was killed in a climbing accident." Kathy, in fact, survived the accident and appears on the scene to contest the will.

   (b) Pat Cross provides by will, "I leave all my property to my daughter, Kathy." When Pat is informed that Kathy was killed in a climbing accident, he tears up the will. Pat dies, and it is discovered that Kathy is still alive.

   (c) Pat Cross dies without a will and without any surviving heirs.

   (d) Pat Cross provides by will, "I leave $5,000 to each of my children who are living in the City of Missoula at the time of my death."

(e) In his will, Pat Cross directs that $55,000 be added to an inter vivos trust established by Pat five years ago for the benefit of his grandson, Richard.

(f) Pat Cross provides by will, "I leave $75,000 to my children." After Pat executes the will, his daughter Kate gets into financial trouble and asks Pat for $8,000. Pat gives her the money. Pat then dies, leaving four children—Kathy, Kate, Jon, and Sandy.

4. *Define the following:* incorporation by reference; anti-lapse statute; supernumerary witness; doctrine of retainer; Totten Trust; Uniform Simultaneous Death Act; generation skipping tax; pretermitted heir.

5. Madison died 15 years after executing a valid will. He named his son, Walker, as the executor of his will. He left two-thirds of his estate to his wife and the balance equally to his children. Which of the following is a right or duty of Walker as executor?

   a. Walker must post a surety bond even if a provision in the will attempts to exempt him from this responsibility.

   b. Walker has an affirmative duty to discover, collect, and distribute all the decedent's assets.

   c. If the will is silent on the point, Walker has complete discretion insofar as investing the estate's assets during the term of his administration.

   d. Walker can sell real property without a court order, even though he has *not* been expressly authorized to do so.

   [# 41, May 1977 CPA Exam]

6. The normal types of questions relating to estates and trusts which might be referred from a law firm to a CPA firm would include problems which involve

   a. The order of distribution under the intestate succession laws.

   b. Whether an ancillary proceeding is required.

   c. The amount of property or money to be received by the income beneficiaries as contrasted with the amount to be accumulated for the remainderman.

   d. Whether a will has been effectively revoked.

   [# 46, November 1976 CPA Exam]

7. Fifteen years ago, Madison executed a valid will. He named his son, Walker, as the executor of his will and left two-thirds of his estate to his wife and the balance equally to his children. Madison is now dead and the approximate size of his estate is one million dollars. Which of the following statements is correct?

   a. The will is invalid because it was executed at a time which is beyond the general statute of limitations.

   b. The estate is *not* recognized as a taxable entity for tax purposes.

   c. All the property bequeathed to his wife will be excluded from the decedent's estate for federal estate tax purposes.

   d. Walker must, in addition to being named in the will, be appointed or approved by the appropriate state court to serve as the executor.

   [# 34, May 1978 CPA Exam]

8. You have been the CPA for Arnold Smith, who has died. Mr. Smith, a widower, left surviving, his mother, age 86, and a son, Donald, age 26. Arnold Smith's daughter, Rita, died one year before his death leaving surviving her husband, Bob, and two children, Alice and Marie. At the time of Mr. Smith's death, Bob remains a widower and Alice and Marie are minors.

Mr. Smith's will, which was duly probated, provides, in part:
"All the property which I shall own at the time of my death or which shall be subject to disposition under my will is hereinafter referred to as my Residuary Estate.

"If any descendant of mine shall survive me, my Residuary Estate shall be divided and set apart for my descendants who shall survive me, in equal shares *per stirpes*. The shares so set apart shall be dealt with as hereinafter provided in this Article, and I bequeath and devise them accordingly.

"(1) In the case of each share set apart for a descendant of mine who shall be under age of twenty-five (25) years and who shall have been in being at the time of my death, my trustee shall hold such share as the principal of a separate trust for the primary benefit of such descendant, shall invest and reinvest such principal and shall pay the net income therefrom to such descendant. Such trust shall continue until such descendant shall attain the age of twenty-five (25) years or shall sooner die. Thereupon my trustee shall distribute the entire principal of such trust to such descendant, or if he shall not be living, shall distribute or otherwise deal with such principal as such descendant, by his last will duly admitted to probate and not otherwise shall direct (except that the power so granted to such descendant shall not be exercisable, to any extent, in favor of such descendant, his estate, his creditors or the creditors of his estate), and, to the extent, if any, that such principal shall not be disposed of effectively through the exercise by such descendant of the power granted to him, my trustee shall distribute such principal to the XYZ charity, a home for foster children.

"(2) In the case of each share set apart for any other descendant of mine, such share shall be distributed to such descendant.

"If no descendant of mine shall survive me, I bequeath and devise my Residuary Estate to the XYZ charity."

Mr. Smith's Residuary Estate equals $100,000. The executor and the attorney for the estate have asked you to assist in preparing financial reports for the estate.

Required: a. Under the above terms of the will, who are the beneficiaries and what is the amount and nature of each of their legacies? Explain.

b. Assume that a beneficiary's share has been placed in trust under the terms of the will:

1. If the trustee believes that the beneficiary is not in need of income currently, under the above terms of the will may he accumulate income for the ben-

eficiary so that it can be paid to the beneficiary at a later time when he is in need? Explain.

2. Describe the power which a beneficiary of this trust is given over the disposition of the principal of his trust.

c. Assume that a beneficiary of a trust dies before attaining the age of twenty-five years and did not effectively exercise his power under the trust so that XYZ charity becomes entitled to receive the principal of the trust. If at that time XYZ charity is no longer in existence, explain what would happen to the trust fund if the *cy pres* doctrine is applied.

d. Do the trust provisions of the will possibly violate the rules against perpetuities? Explain.

[# 8.a, b, c, & d, November 1966 CPA Exam (See also Chapter 4 on the Rule Against Perpetuities and Chapter 29 on Trusts.)]

9. Kilgore created an irrevocable fifteen-year trust for the benefit of his minor children. At the end of the fifteen years, the principal (corpus) reverts to Kilgore. Kilgore named the Reliable Trust Company as trustee and provided that Reliable would serve without the necessity of posting a bond. In understanding the trust and rules applicable to it, which of the following is correct?

a. The trust is *not* a separate legal entity for federal tax purposes.

b. The facts indicate that the trust is a separate legal entity for both tax and non-tax purposes.

c. Kilgore may revoke the trust after eleven years, since he created it, and the principal reverts to him at the expiration of the fifteen years.

d. If Kilgore dies ten years after creation of the trust, it is automatically revoked and the property is distributed to the beneficiaries of his trust upon their attaining age 21.

[# 33, May 1978 CPA Exam (see also Chapter 29 on trusts).]

10. **Part a.** Frugal, for whom you perform accounting services, told you that he plans to create his own *inter vivos* trust (living trust) and that he plans to name you the trustee.

Frugal showed you the following provision in a draft of the disposition he plans for the trust principal at his death.

"On my death the then principal of the trust shall be distributed to my then living descendants, in equal shares *per stirpes*."

Required: 1. Would such a trust instrument have to be probated as a will at Frugal's death since the trust instrument provides for disposition of the property at death? Explain.

2. If you do not wish to serve as trustee is there any way of your avoiding the responsibility even if Frugal insists that he will name you as trustee over your objection? Explain.

3. State the percentage of trust principal which each party would receive at Frugal's death if during his life Frugal had only two children, Rita and Selma, and was survived by

(i) John, his brother,

(ii) Susan, his sister,

(iii) Rita, his daughter,

(iv) Thomas and Mary, his grandchildren whose mother is Rita, and

(v) Albert, his grandchild (whose mother, Selma, predeceased Frugal).

Part b. Wellington purchased several thousand dollars worth of corporate securities in the joint names of "Wellington and Potter or the survivor."

Later, Wellington decided that Potter should not receive the corporate securities at Wellington's death because Potter had become wealthy. Wellington, therefore, went to his attorney and executed a codicil to his Last Will and Testament naming his brother as the party to receive the securities upon his death.

Wellington is now dead.

Required: Who is entitled to the securities in question? Explain.

[# 4.a & b, May 1968 CPA Exam]

Appendix A

THE AMERICAN LEGAL ENVIRONMENT
IN A NUTSHELL

(This is a digest of the text entitled The American Legal Environment—Individuals, Their Business and Their Government, written by William T. Schantz and published by West Publishing Company in 1976.)

WHAT IS THE MEANING AND FUNCTION OF LAW?

The word law describes almost any principle that should be obeyed, whether it be the law of hospitality or the law of grammar. The term is always used to express rules or principles that govern conduct, action or arrangement. Law is some type of plan, method, scheme, or system of controlling the conduct of people. Within this plan or system of control, there exist many rules and procedures. Law may be odious, repulsive or offensive, but it is still law as long as it is an effective way to control the conduct of people. Law must direct, guide, manage and restrain, in both personal behavior and deportment, those persons subject to it.

To achieve a system of law, there must be built into that system some means of authority, control or power to insure that people will act, for the most part, in the manner desired. The power or authority required to effectively control human conduct is not simply physical force. The threat of force is usually sufficient. People feel mentally coerced to obey the law. They voluntarily obey it, in order to avoid the unpleasant consequences. Power is necessary for effective control. This power may be lodged in the hands of one individual, in the hands of a few, or in the hands of all the people.

In considering different systems of power and control it is necessary to look at three specific questions: Who has the power? Where does the power originate? How is the power used?

The power can be held by one person, by a few persons or by many persons. Power may exist simply because it has been taken by force or by some other method not involving the consent of the people. A system is legitimate only if the people have freely consented to the power structure within the structure. If the people in authority benefit by reason of having the power at the expense of the people subject to that authority, the system is corrupt.

Many terms apply to the various power structures that have been used or are now being used throughout the world to create and enforce law. If one person takes complete power and control without the consent of the people subject to that control, the government is called an autocracy. If this person occupies an inherited throne, he is a monarch and the government is a monarchy. Historically, control was often lodged in the hands of a few individuals, as opposed to just one. Those few, supposedly rulers of superior intelligence, ability and character, often simply had more wealth and the system was known as an aristocracy.

A system in which the supreme power is in the hands of the people is a democracy. In a pure democracy, the people make the laws themselves. In a republican government, on the other hand, the people exert their power indirectly through elected representatives who make the law. Democracy generally results in the preservation of more individual freedom through the limitation of power.

If people are to live together amicably, law must be an essential part of their lives. Every action one takes affects others either directly or indirectly and may cause them involvement or even injury. Controversies and conflicts can and will result that must be settled in a peaceable manner. If they cannot be settled peaceably using rules of law, people will resort to other means, and expose themselves to harm, enslavement or death. We must have rules if we are to live together. However, rules take away from freedom. Every time a rule is made, freedom to act in a certain way is somewhat restricted. People in authority must determine how far the rules can go before the cost in both freedom and money becomes too great.

Every rule of law must be considered in light of how much freedom will be lost.

There are four legitimate and proper functions of law. They are: the settlement of disputes; the establishment and maintenance of order; the protection of the individual and his or her property; and the promotion of the general welfare. The settlement of disputes is critical to a system of control. Just as essential is the establishment and maintenance of order. Once a dispute makes its way to the courtroom, it must be settled, even there, under orderly rules of procedure. The achievement of order—the establishment of a universal standard of conduct—permits all of us to operate daily with less confusion and anxiety and with a foreseeable expectation regarding the conduct of others. The protection of person and property is perhaps even more important than the first two functions of law. Freedom to live without fear is essential. The function of law—to protect persons and their property—is not carried out with perfection. But without law, there would be much more crime and many more people would be hurt, either physically or through loss of property. Even limited security and protection is much better than no security or protection at all. The promotion of the general welfare involves activities that protect and help people as a group rather than as individuals. For example, the criminal law, in addition to providing individual protection, affects the entire public interest in the prevention and punishment of crime. Education laws, pollution laws, conservation laws, health laws, and numerous others—fit within this function of the law and promote the general welfare.

An ideal system of law must include at the least the following ten characteristics: (1) The law must be based on the free consent of the people subject to that system of control. (2) The law must strive to achieve a system of limited control in order to preserve a maximum amount of freedom. (3) The law must stay within and effectively carry out the four legitimate functions we have previously defined. (4) The law must provide clearly defined sources of power based upon the consent of the people, wherein the general power and authority are spelled out. No authority will be recognized unless it can be traced to a source, and exercise of power will depend upon the popular consent found within these sources. (5) The law must apply to all men equally and without exception. (6) The law must be knowable, understandable, and reasonable. People will accept the law only if they know and understand it to some considerable extent. In addition, the law must be reasonable to insure the voluntary compliance of those subject to it. (7) The law must be flexible, adaptable, and changeable through orderly procedure. The ability to effect change by those subject to the law is essential. (8) The law must provide for and encourage active and meaningful participation by the governed. All persons must be eligible to hold positions of authority. They must be able to vote to determine who will hold these positions of power. (9) The law must provide for rule by the majority of the people, while at the same time, safeguarding individual rights even as against the will of the majority or of the government itself. (10) The law must provide for efficient and effective control without wasting the resources of its people. Without efficient operation, there is no effective control. The ideal system has limited control with minimum cost and maximum efficiency.

The system of law in the United States is properly called a constitutional system with a republican form of government. On paper, the system is close to ideal based as it is on the consent of the governed, with direct and active involvement by the people and constitutional safeguards of individual rights. Its operation and administration, however, is less than ideal, for it depends on people for its accomplishments. Accepting the limitations and imperfections of people, it results that the system operates imperfectly.

It is clear, however, that a person can wield authority under United States law only if he derives his power from well defined sources of law. The sources of law in the United States are three: written law; common law; and administrative law.

The written law is narrowly defined to include federal and state constitutions, treaties made by the President with foreign nations, and statutes written and passed by the federal Congress, state legislatures, or local governmental units. To be written, therefore, a law must be found in one of three formal documents—a constitution, treaty or statute. A constitution, or supreme law of the land governed, sets out in formal written terms the fundamental system of power, i.e., the rules of and principles for that area. A treaty is a formal written agreement between the United States and one or more foreign nations or sovereigns. Treaties are made by the President with the advice and consent of the Senate. A statute is a formal written enactment of a legislative body, whether it be federal, state, city or county.

Written law is a source of great power in the United States. Still, there are many situations that are not regulated by constitution, treaty or statute. This is where common law comes into the picture. Common law comes into play when a judge has to make a decision—settle a dispute—without written law to guide him. The judge will decide the case by looking to the rules of the common law—rules that were applied to similar cases in the past. This is how the common law developed and continues to develop. If other judges follow this decision, the decision is considered a precedent; and if a large number of judges follow the precedent and decide the same question in the same way, it becomes part of the common law. Common law rules are subject to change as the common beliefs in the community change. They can also be superceded and modified by statute (by the written law).

The third source of law in the United States is that which results from the work of an administrative agency. An administrative agency may be defined as any governmental authority which is not a court or a legislature but which acts like one because it directly affects the rights and duties of persons by making rules or deciding cases. Administrative agencies can only be created by statute. They are created for two very important reasons. First, the regulation of certain fields requires a nonlegal expertise. The agency makes rules and decides cases in the same manner as do legislatures and courts but also provides the technical know-how to make its binding rules and decisions meaningful. Secondly, agencies empowered with the authority to resolve disputes between parties or to determine the rights of an individual provide a means to settle the many thousands of mechanical questions that would otherwise overwhelm the courts by their volume. This makes good sense, because it allows the courts to devote their attention to more controversial matters. All power to act within the United States system of law must be derived from written, common, or administrative law.

The law relates to every aspect of a person's life. This, of course, applies to both the conduct of business and to a customer's dealings with business. The administration of business involves decision making. To make informed decisions, a business manager must understand the legal ramifications involved. The customer, also, must know when he is binding himself to a contract to buy a product, and what to do if the product proves defective. A complete basic understanding of the legal environment in the United States should enable one to achieve a better way of life.

HOW IS LAW MADE IN THE UNITED STATES?

Law is a system of control over the conduct of people. Developing the specifics of that system is called lawmaking and involves four distinct categories of activity: rulemaking (making general rules); interpreting (determining what the general rule means); adjudicating (deciding cases or settling disputes); and executing (carrying out and enforcing the rules).

Rulemaking is the creation of principles governing conduct—principles that tell people what they can and cannot do. Rules are made either through legislation or through the common law. Legislative rules are prospective and general in application. Common law rules are retrospective and specific in application. Rules are made on all governmental levels— from city and county to the national level. The administrative agency, too, makes rules in carrying out the job outlined in its enabling statute. The people themselves share in rulemaking independently of the legislature through use of the initiative and referendum.

While it is important to use general terms in defining rules, certain difficulties may arise in deciding whether the rule does in fact apply to a particular situation. Interpretation of the general words used is necessary. The job of interpretation is chiefly the responsibility of the courts. Adjudication, the act of settling disputes and controversies, means the ability to decide the case completely and to dispose of it. A great part of lawmaking is the settling of controversies between people in an orderly, peaceful and final manner. This, also, is primarily the responsibility of the courts.

Execution of the law, which involves enforcing and carrying the law into effect, is primarily the task of the executive branch of government.

No person may engage in lawmaking in the United States unless he possesses the power or authority to do so. The power to make law originates in the words of the United States Constitution, which is the fundamental and supreme law of the land. Any law not in harmony with it is invalid. So to determine where the power to make law originates, the first place to look to is the United States Constitution.

The Constitution defines the power of each branch of government and specifies how change is to be made in the Constitution, etc. The Constitution, therefore, provides Congress with the power to make general rules within certain subject areas; the President with power to execute these rules; and the federal courts with power to interpret them, and to decide cases and controversies on defined subject matters. All power not specifically given to the federal Congress, the President, or the federal courts is reserved to the states and the people. The entire authority to make law must be traced to federal and state constitutions.

The Constitution sets up three branches of government—legislative, executive and judicial—each with lawmaking functions and each checking and balancing the others.

Congress, granted legislative powers, has only those specific powers that are enumerated in the Constitution. These powers belong only to the Congress and may not be transferred to either of the other branches. Congress may, however, delegate rulemaking power to an administrative agency as long as it is giving the agency only the power to "fill up the details" of the statute passed by Congress. What is not specifically granted to the federal Congress is retained by the individual states and is subject to rulemaking by the state legislatures.

Included in the powers of the Congress, which are enumerated in Sections 8 and 9 of the Constitution, are the power to: collect taxes; pay U. S. debts; provide for the U. S. defense; provide for the general welfare; borrow money; regulate commerce; establish immigration and naturalization laws; coin and regulate money; grant patents and copyrights; establish courts; declare war; govern federal lands; and make laws necessary to carry out the above powers.

Congress also has broad powers to investigate to determine what legislation should be passed. State legislatures also have power to make rules on all kinds of subject matters. Crime, divorce, adoption, transfer of property, mortgaging property, operation of business, pollution, and many others—all are subject to state and local rulemaking power.

Constitutions also limit the power of government, protect the individual from misuse of governmental authority, and guarantee fundamental individual rights. They guarantee that no person will be denied the writ of habeas corpus. This prevents unjust imprisonment or detention by authorities. They forbid the passage of bills of attainder. This prevents punishment of persons without trial. Constitutions prohibit ex post facto laws from being passed. Ex post facto laws are those which apply retrospectively. Constitutions state that laws impairing the obligation of contracts may not be passed, and that no law may restrict the free exercise of religion, abridge the freedom of speech or of the press, or prevent peaceable assembly. Constitutions guarantee freedom from unreasonable search and seizure. No persons may be deprived of life, liberty, or property without due process of law. Slavery is outlawed, and equal protection of the law to all persons is guaranteed by the Constitution.

Primary responsibility for writing the general rules rests with the legislature; complete responsibility for determining general rules of the common law is with the courts, as is primary responsibility for interpreting written and common law and deciding cases and controversies. The chief responsibility for carrying the law into effect and enforcing it belongs to the executive branch.

Congress uses a specific procedure for enactment of statutes, and similar steps are followed by state legislatures. An idea for a law is written into a bill. The bill must be introduced into Congress, either to the Senate or the House (an exception is made for revenue bills which may be introduced only in the House). The bill is then considered by a committee which may either recommend it or table it. If tabled, it is forgotten unless the majority of the Senate or House insist that it be considered. If not tabled, the bill is read and voted on. If passed, it is sent to the other chamber for identical consideration. If the second chamber disagrees with the first, a committee comprised of members of both chambers will reconcile the differences and the bill will be sent back to both chambers. If the second chamber approves of the original bill, it is sent to the President.

The President either signs, vetoes, or ignores the bill. If signed, the bill becomes law. If vetoed, the bill is sent back to Congress where it can be passed over the President's head by a two-thirds majority vote. If ignored, the bill becomes law within 10 days as long as Congress is in session; if Congress adjourns within 10 days, the bill is automatically vetoed by a "pocket veto". The pocket veto applies only when Congress is adjourning, not when recessing.

Statutes must be written in broad, general terms that will apply to a great number of fact situations, but necessarily, this results in a need for interpretation. In determining what legislation means, a judge first looks to the legislative history. When there is doubt about the meaning of words in statutes, courts use "rules of construction" which are, for the most part, rules of common law. Included among the many rules of construction are: words are presumed to be used in their common sense; the government is not generally included in the scope of a statute; statutes in general terms apply only to future situations; where the statute is plain, it must be given effect according to its plain meaning; the meaning of a doubtful word may be decided by looking at words with which it is associated; criminal laws are strictly construed; remedial laws are liberally construed; where a general word follows specific words it takes its meaning from them.

Besides using rules of construction to decide the meaning of words found in statutes, judges also ask themselves two questions. Since words have many possible meanings, what can the word mean? And what is the context in which the word appears? The idea is that judges should interpret the word in such a manner as to give effect to its underlying purpose as reflected in its textual (in what kind of statute was the word found) and circumstantial contexts (what were the circumstances that caused the statute to be passed). In this way, the legislative intent will be carried out.

In deciding if general rules of legislation are valid and constitutional, courts apply the doctrine of judicial review. Judicial review is the power to declare a law unconstitutional. The power, drawn from the Constitution, has always been controversial since it was first exercised by the courts in Marbury vs. Madison. Judicial review, now an integral part of our system, allows the courts to make law by striking down other law. Courts will review a statute and exercise judicial review only where there is a real case or controversy (an honest and actual antagonistic fight for one's rights), and the constitutionality of a statute becomes important to determination of basic rights.

Common law is law resulting from court cases when there is no written law applicable—hence it is often called "unwritten law." A court decision becomes part of the common law only when it serves as precedent for other legal decisions. The use of precedent in deciding court cases is the doctrine of stare decisis. This comes from a Latin phrase which means "to adhere to precedents and not unsettle things that are settled." Courts use precedent not only in deciding cases, but also in interpreting statutes. Courts, however, are not required to follow precedent—although they usually do. From time to time, they find that conditions have changed and that new precedent should be established. Judicial reasoning by example, using precedents, involves three steps: a past case is recognized as being similar to a present case; the rule of the precedent case is stated; the rule is applied to the current case.

The power to settle disputes between private persons in the United States has been delegated primarily to courts, but agencies also adjudicate to some extent. Adjudication—the determination of issues—affects people more directly than legislative rulemaking. Whenever a court decides a case, the result is called a judgment or a decree.

The general rules made by Congress and the specific decisions reached by courts would mean very little if they were unenforceable. The executive branch has primary responsibility for enforcing the laws. The executive branch has two major components—the Executive Office and the Executive Departments. The executive office includes fourteen specific bureaus and the executive branch includes twelve departments to assist in administering the law. Numerous agencies apart from the President (independent in the sense that they are not controlled by the President) help carry out the laws. And, in addition to the federal law, there exist countless other state and local governmental operations that enforce the law and carry it into effect.

The federal and state system of law administration undertakes to carry out and enforce the law as it is defined by the legislative and judicial branches of our government. As in any vast system, the possibility for abuse is considerable. The system must provide its own safeguards. The statutes themselves provide built-in checks and safeguards in the system to minimize corruption. Judicial review also applies to the enforcement of the law. The President must remain within his constitutional powers or the powers given him by the Congress. Administrative agencies, too, may not exceed the power conferred by their statutes. If governmental employees violate constitutional rights, the employee and perhaps the government may be liable. The Justice Department, headed by the Attorney General, actively investigates government administration. Although all officials who break the law obviously don't get caught, the law does apply equally to all persons and no one is above the law. It is a basic principle in the United States system that "we have a government of law, not of men."

The Constitution gives power to make agreements with other countries to the President. The President may make executive agreements without Congressional consent, but treaties require concurrence by $\frac{2}{3}$ of the Senators. While statutes passed by Congress must be made in pursuance of the Constitution and therefore subject to all of its limitations, treaties are not so restricted and need only be made "under the authority of the United States." Treaties deal with every sort of subject matter, from war and peace to international trade, patents, and copyrights. Treaties, unlike statutes, cannot be enforced. Countries keep them as a matter of good faith.

The general law of business in the United States can be traced to England, where several hundred years ago, mercantile courts (the merchants themselves) settled disputes between merchants. Their decisions were based on a system of rules and customs generally accepted by businessmen (called "the law merchant"). This system was eventually incorporated into the common law. Common law dealing with business has generally now been codified into statutory form. All state legislatures have adopted the Uniform Commercial Code (although Louisiana has adopted only parts), an extremely detailed code with more than 400 sections covering many areas of commercial law with greatest emphasis on the law of sales and the use of checks and promissory notes. Both the Uniform Commercial Code and the common law are important in the study of business law.

The legal system in the United States is one of checks and balances designed to diffuse control and responsibility among the several branches of government. The President may veto acts of Congress, but Congress may override his veto. The President appoints judges who must be approved by Congress; the judges may exercise judicial review over the Congress and the President, but Congress controls the courts' budgets. Congress can additionally impeach the President and judges or investigate his activities or those of the court. Congress can also create administrative agencies with power to make rules and decisions. The President appoints the people who serve on such an agency; and the court can determine if that agency has exceeded its power. Locally, people can not only vote for representatives but can also vote to recall them, and can "initiate" legislation themselves.

The checks and balances are designed to prevent any government body from obtaining excessive power and to insure that the supreme power remains with the people, with the law continuing to apply to all men whatever their positions of power.

WHAT IS THE PRIMARY CONCEPT OF OUR LAW?

No lawyer can ever know all the law. But he or she does understand the primary concept in our legal system and is able to recognize which specific legal concept applies to a particular fact situation. A concept is a general thought or idea. It is a mental formulation on a broad scale and in some detail. The primary concept in law is the notion of rights and duties. A right is a legal capacity to act or to demand action or forbearance on the part of another. An act is a voluntary physical movement of a human being. A forbearance is a consciously willed absence of physical movement. A legal duty is a legal obligation to act or to refrain from acting. Rights and duties always go together. Whenever there is a right in one person or group, there is always a correlative duty in some other person or group. All legal concepts are concerned with rights and duties and must be thought of in those terms.

The whole of our law may be classified in two parts—the substantive law that defines rights and duties and the adjective or procedural law by which rights and duties may be enforced.

A specific legal concept is an authoritatively defined category or division of the law. Division of the law into categories (legal concepts) enables the lawyer to place a fact situation into a specific area of law so that certain rules, unique to that area or category, will apply. The lawyer's special talent is the ability to categorize problems and therefore to know what rules will apply to resolve the dispute. Every fact situation must be placed within a specific legal concept defined in one or more of the legal sources: common law, written law and administrative law. There are a great many legal concepts in our legal system. These concepts or categories are traditionally divided into areas of public and private law. Public law involves the rights of society as a whole and includes criminal, administrative, and constitutional law. Private law deals with the legal relationships between people and involves the concepts of torts and contracts. Torts deal with wrongs committed by one person against another, and contracts deal with rights and duties of individuals created through their own agreement. There are many other specific legal concepts in addition to tort, crime, and contract such as property law, labor law, tax law, environmental law, domestic relations law, etc.

The law library is the source of many answers to lawyers' quest for applicable law. Law libraries contain all state and federal statutes, appellate court opinions, legal encyclopedias, and other legal books and documents. Lawyers must know how to find the appropriate law or court case among all this information. The law library is designed to allow the lawyer to quickly find the relevant cases and laws. The West key number system of indexing provides the lawyer with easy access to appellate court opinions. Also available to the lawyer is the complete statutory law of the U.S. published in the U.S. Code Annotated, and Shepherd's Citations which give the judicial history of every reported decision and statute. The lawyer then, is able to find up-to-date law regarding any particular legal concept or subject matter he or she chooses.

The primary concept of our law is that of rights and duties. The protection of and guarantee of individual rights is the most important single objective of our legal system. The two types of individual rights are personal and property rights. Personal rights are those which are not transferable. They are divided into two classes: first, those rights one has solely by virtue of being a person and citizen (rights to free speech, religion, due process, and rights to vote, get married or make a will); and second, those rights acquired through contract with another (such as the right to have someone work for you), but which rights cannot be sold or given away.

Property rights, or those which can be transferred, include personal property rights and real property rights. Real property rights refer to real estate (land and things permanently attached to land). Personal property rights, not to be confused with personal rights, can be divided into two categories: tangibles, or choses in possession, which are material possessions; and intangibles, which are choses in action or rights with no material substance (e. g., patents, copyrights, stocks, bonds, etc.).

Once you have a legally recognized right, you are entitled to voluntary performance of the corresponding duty. But if that performance is not forthcoming, the law provides you with the courts and all available legal procedure to make certain that person performs. Rights are worthless unless they are protected. Courts resolve disputes, interpret written law and establish principles of common law, but they are used as well to make persons perform their duties. It is in the trial court that the matter in dispute is first considered and resolved. Trial courts determine the facts and attempt to settle the dispute once and for all. If both parties are satisfied after the trial, the case goes no further.

Appellate courts only review decisions after the original trial is over. The loser at trial level tries to persuade the appellate court that the case was decided incorrectly. At appellate level there are no juries or witnesses. Judges make their decisions from transcripts, briefs and oral argument of the lawyers. All appellate court opinions are preserved in law libraries and are available to lawyers who seek precedents for future cases.

WHAT IS "JURISDICTION"?

Before a court can decide a case, it must have the power to do so. This power is called jurisdiction. Two requirements must be met before a court has jurisdiction to settle a dispute. First, the court must have jurisdiction over the person, which is obtained through service of process on the party being sued. Second, the case must fall within the designated powers of the court—designated in constitutions and statutes—called jurisdiction over the subject matter.

A court must have power to consider a particular question before it can legitimately dispose of it. There are two systems of courts in the United States, state and federal, as provided by statute and constitution. State and federal court systems result from dual sovereignty, that is, government at both the state and federal level. Some matters are the province of state courts; others, the province of federal courts as designated in federal and state constitutions and statutes. If a court does not have the designated power it cannot decide the case.

State court systems vary somewhat from state to state, but the basic framework in every state is the same. The lowest level trial courts handle minor crimes, or cases involving small amounts of money. These lower courts often have small-claims divisions where the smallest kind of money claim can be disposed of in one final decision (there is usually no right to appeal from a small claims court). In the small claims division, parties represent themselves without lawyers.

The next level is the main state trial courts. These courts handle serious criminal, tax, probate, divorce, tort and contract cases, etc. Trial court decisions are reviewed for error in state appellate courts. A person who loses at the state trial level has the right to at least one trial and one appeal based on the concept of "due process"—as explained in the 14th Amendment. Many states have more than one appellate court. The highest reviewing state court is usually known as the Supreme Court, Court of Appeals, or something similar.

The federal court system deals only with federal questions or diversity of citizenship cases. Diversity of citizenship cases must involve amounts over $10,000 before federal courts have jurisdiction. Federal questions are those involving the U.S. Constitution, federal statutes or federal treaties. The federal system has three basic levels of courts. The district court is the main federal trial court. It decides all federal questions and can hear all diversity of citizenship (cases involving citizens of different states) cases involving more than $10,000. Appeals from district courts (found in every state) go to the U.S. Court of Appeals. There are 11 of these circuit courts and each court has three judges.

The United States Supreme Court is the highest court in the land. Cases may get to this court by writ of certiorari—a petition asking the Court to hear the case because a federal question is involved—only if the court decides to hear them. While the writ of certiorari is discretionary with the Supreme Court, the Court must hear an appeal from the highest state court if the state court has ruled a federal statute or treaty invalid.

There are also administrative agencies and special courts on the federal level which hear cases. Administrative agencies can decide cases within their jurisdiction. Examples are the Federal Trade Commission and National Labor Relations Board. These cases may also be reviewed by federal appellate courts. The United States Customs Court has jurisdiction only over matters involving customs. The Court of Claims deals only with money claims against the United States. There is also a Court of Customs and Patent Appeals. Appeals from these special federal courts may be taken to the Supreme Court. Removal (for trial as opposed to appeal) from a state court to a federal court may be done only prior to the beginning of trial in the state court and only if the case could have been brought originally in the federal court. Furthermore, only the defendant has a right to remove the case to Federal court—the plaintiff does not.

The United States system of law is based largely on the English system. The English system established both law courts (for money damages) and equity courts (for other remedy such as injunction). Generally, in the United States, separate courts of law and equity were not established. Each court, however, has the power of both the law and equity courts of England. An action at law is brought to obtain money damages. A suit at equity is brought to obtain relief other than money damages. There is no jury in equity cases and the rules aren't nearly as strict as those in law actions. Decrees are granted in equity cases ordering actions to be done or not to be done (injunctions). Both actions at law and suits in equity involve private law—that is, cases brought between individuals as opposed to criminal cases where the state attempts to prove someone guilty of a crime, and where the procedure involved is quite different.

Before a court can decide a case, it must have jurisdiction or power to do so. In addition to requiring that the case fall within an area of law over which the court has power (jurisdiction over the subject matter), the court must also have jurisdiction over the person of the defendant. If the defendant can be found, he is served with a summons to "appear and defend". But if his whereabouts are unknown, service sometimes can be accomplished by publication of notice and mailing a summons to his last known address. Service by such publication can be done only to a very limited extent for such things as achieving a divorce based on desertion. If property is at issue, jurisdiction over the defendant requires personal service in nearly all cases. This is because the purpose of the summons is to provide the defendant with notice that he is being sued, and to provide him with an opportunity to defend himself. This is part of the due process of law. In some states, the summons must be personally delivered to the defendant, while in other states, it may be mailed, published, or left at his home or business. After summons has been served, the defendant must respond before a certain time or lose the case by default. In certain cases, summons are allowed to be served out of state by "long arm" statutes which require the defendant to come back to the state where he or she committed conduct which is the basis for the case and defend there.

A class action is one brought by or against one or more members of a class or group of persons sharing a common interest. Class actions originated in courts of equity to promote justice when the persons affected by a decree were too numerous to bring them all before the court. The Federal Rules of Civil Procedure for federal courts state that a class action may be brought only if: the class is so numerous that joinder of all members is impracticable; there are questions of law or fact common to the class; the claims or defenses of the representative parties are typical of the claims or defenses of the class; and the representative parties will fairly and adequately protect the interests of the class.

Several states have adopted the federal class action rule as part of their own law and use of the class action has become widespread in areas of social control—antitrust, civil rights, consumer protection, and matters involving the environment.

WHAT IS THE CIVIL ACTION PROCEDURE FOR MONEY DAMAGES?

Adjective law is the procedural law by which rights and duties are enforced by courts and governmental authorities. The civil action for money damages is the usual dispute between individuals. Civil actions may be based on breach of contract or tort. Or they may arise from a property dispute or any other legal concept involving private law. Much of what applies to civil actions applies to other legal procedures also, such as suits in equity, so it is important to understand the civil action.

If jurisdiction can be established in several places (several courts would properly have jurisdiction over the subject matter), determining the proper or best place for the trial to be held is called venue. While the court must have proper jurisdiction or its decision is invalid, venue is mostly a matter of convenience. Improper venue can be waived, so if a court has proper jurisdiction, and the parties do not object to venue, the court can render a valid judgment. Determination of proper venue may be prescribed by statute, or it may be based simply on convenience or avoiding prejudice. The federal statute states that proper venue is the district in which either plaintiff or defendant resides, or the district where the injury occurred. Venue can always be objected to on grounds of prejudice of either judge or prospective jury. This occurs frequently in criminal cases where substantial pre-trial publicity makes it difficult for a defendant to receive a fair trial in a particular area of the country. Another ground for change of venue is the doctrine of "forum non conveniens," which means the place selected for trial is not convenient for the witnesses or parties.

Federal trial courts (District Courts) are found in every state to hear cases involving federal questions or diversity of citizenship. In determining what substantive law a federal trial court must follow, several things must be considered. If the case involves a federal question, then federal law applies to that issue. If the federal court has jurisdiction because of diversity of citizenship (the plaintiff is from one state and the defendant from another), and there is no federal question, the court must apply the substantive law of the state in which the court resides. Even though state law applies in this case, federal procedural rules still govern courtroom mechanics.

Litigation is the carrying on of a lawsuit. It is the courtroom contest for the purpose of enforcing a right. Litigation involves four stages or steps: the pleading stage, which determines the facts at issue; the discovery stage, which investigates the facts, prepares evidence for trial, and attempts to settle the controversy before trial; the trial stage, which resolves the issues of fact; and the appellate stage, which reviews the trial court proceedings for error.

Pleading is the process that brings the case initially before the court. The parties are "pleading" or arguing for or against a position by presenting their version of the facts in writing. Pleadings notify, in writing, the court and the parties of the nature of the case, define the controversy, and narrow and formulate the issues in dispute. Most importantly, they set the boundary lines of the litigation, as nothing can be introduced at trial that is irrelevant to the disputed facts as contained in the pleadings. There are three basic pleadings: complaint, answer, and reply. The plaintiff files the complaint to inform the defendant why he is being sued. The complaint alleges facts which form the basis for recovery. The answer is the response to the complaint either denying or admitting the alleged facts. One type of answer is the general denial of the entire complaint. This forces the plaintiff to prove everything. Usually the defendant will admit some facts, such as that the court has jurisdiction, and deny others. What is denied must be proved. Also, the defendant can assert new facts in his answer, if he wishes, by way of "affirmative" defense as to allege that the plaintiff, not the defendant, was the party at fault. Only in this case does the plaintiff "reply." This final pleading, or reply, is the plaintiff's admittance or denial of new facts alleged in the answer. Once the pleadings are filed, the case is said to be "at issue." If the defendant believes the plaintiff's claim has no legal basis, that is, if the complaint does not allege facts recognized to be within any specific legal concept providing an enforceable right, he or she may file a demurrer or motion for dismissal instead of an answer. The demurrer says "so what" to the plaintiff, i. e., even if the facts are true, the plaintiff still cannot win.

Discovery is the stage that takes surprise out of the trial and insures full disclosure of the facts prior to the trial. Discovery, which is now mandatory in most states, also encourages pre-trial settlement of cases by making both parties fully aware of all facts. The philosophy of pre-trial discovery was written into the law with the 1938 adoption of the Federal Rules of Civil Procedure. The four basic tools for discovery include: depositions, which are sworn witness testimony taken out of court; interrogatories, which are written questions which must be answered under oath; production of documents—either party may upon request receive and copy documents in the hands of the other party; and physical and mental examinations, which may be ordered of a party by the court.

If settlement out of court is impossible, the trial stage of litigation begins. To understand a trial, one must first understand the United States adversary system. In an adversary system, each side is responsible for presenting his side of the case and each must have an opportunity to be heard. The court's decision is based on what the parties themselves, through their attorneys, have brought forth through evidence. The judge does not get involved with the presentation of evidence, but acts only as an impartial referee. The jury simply listens, observes, and makes a decision based on what it hears.

The actual court procedure involves eleven parts. First the jury is selected. Trial by jury is constitutionally guaranteed for certain types of trials. Juries usually contain twelve members but can constitutionally contain fewer. Juries must be randomly selected from a fair cross-section of the community. Every person who is called for jury service has a duty to serve except for certain persons who are exempt, including lawyers and doctors. Prospective jurors are routinely questioned in a "voir dire" examination so the judge and attorneys may attempt to determine whether the juror is impartial and qualified. If the judge believes a prospective juror is prejudiced, he will dismiss him for cause. Both sides are allowed to dismiss a certain number of prospective jurors for any reason they wish by means of "peremptory challenges." A jury is eventually impaneled from unchallenged qualified jurors.

After jury selection, the attorneys make their opening statements. The plaintiff's attorney first gives the jury an overall picture of his version of the case. The defendant's attorney may make his statement immediately after the plaintiff's statement or may wait until the plaintiff finishes his complete presentation.

Presentation of the plaintiff's case is next. Evidence is presented by examining witnesses and producing documents. The plaintiff first directly examines the witness; the defendant may then cross-examine; the plaintiff may then recross-examine, etc. until a party desires to ask no more questions. The examination in each case is limited to what was previously discussed. Only expert witnesses may give opinions. After the plaintiff has presented all his evidence, he or she rests his or her case.

A motion for a directed verdict will frequently be made by the defendant at this stage. Such a motion is in effect saying that the plaintiff has not proved sufficient facts to possibly win so there is no need to go on. This motion is similar to the demurrer in the pleading stage. If the motion is granted, the plaintiff automatically loses.

The defendant now presents his case in the same manner as did the plaintiff. Then the plaintiff may bring in rebuttal evidence if he wishes. The defendant may bring in evidence to counter the rebuttal. This pattern may continue until one party has completely exhausted his evidence.

Each party gives a closing argument to the jury. The plaintiff speaks first and last. This argument frequently attacks the opponent's evidence for unreliability. The arguments must stay within the record or be based on facts supported by evidence.

The judge instructs the jury to base its verdict upon the evidence presented and the laws involved as recited by the judge. The jury reaches and delivers its verdict. The jury is locked up until it reaches the verdict. If the jury cannot agree, a mistrial will be declared.

After the verdict, the losing party may make a motion for a retrial. The judge will grant a new trial only if he or she thinks the jury's verdict goes against the weight of the evidence. As an alternative, the judge may grant a "remittitur" which gives the plaintiff the option of either taking less in damages or going through a new trial.

During the course of the trial, rules of evidence establishing which facts may or may not be presented to the jury must be used. Their purpose is to allow the jury to hear only evidence which is competent and relevant to the dispute. One rule says that only experts can give their opinions in court. Jury verdicts should not be based on nonexpert opinions. Another rule is that the attorney may not prompt his witness by asking a leading question, i. e., a question which suggests the answer the attorney wants to hear. Hearsay evidence or evidence based on the personal knowledge of the witness is not admissable. Irrelevant evidence may not be introduced in court. Confidential communications between persons in certain relationships, such as husband-wife, doctor-patient, clergy-penitent and attorney-client, do not have to be disclosed in court. If an attorney refers to a written document, contract, or other writing, he must produce that writing itself (this is "the best evidence" rule). Repetitious evidence may not be admitted. These are just a few of the rules of evidence; there are others which also may apply. It is up to each attorney to object if the opposing party does not adhere to the rules. The plaintiff must prove his case by a preponderance of the evidence while staying within the rules of evidence.

If one party believes that an error of law (such as the admitting of improper evidence over objection or the giving of incorrect jury instructions) was made during the trial, but is unable to convince the judge on post trial motion that a new trial should be granted, he has a right to appeal to a higher court of law. The appeal must be filed within a time limit, and the appellant must notify the respondent (the winner at the trial). The appellant is the party who lost the case in the trial court and is now appealing.

A transcript and briefs are prepared and submitted to the appellate court. These briefs contain the parties' arguments as to why the case should be reversed or affirmed. In addition to reading the briefs, the appellate court listens to brief oral arguments from the attorneys, after which the judges take a vote of first impression. Based on this vote, the case is assigned by the chief judge to himself or herself or to one of the other judges for preparation of an opinion. One judge presents the opinion which is circulated. Other judges may write dissenting opinions, but if no dissent is made, the opinion becomes the official opinion of the court. The final opinion is announced and the appellate court decision is sent to the trial court for enforcement (either to affirm, reverse, or reverse and remand for a new trial). If a new trial is granted, its result may again be appealed.

Once a case is decided, appealed, and no further appeal is available, it would not make sense to allow the parties to start all over again. For this reason, a judgment is said to be final once all possibility of further appeal is gone. This is the meaning of res judicata—literally, that the thing has been decided. Further suits involving the same question of law between the same parties may not take place again. However, res judicata applies only to civil actions for money damages and not to other procedures.

In order to enforce a judgment for money damages, the first step is to obtain a writ of execution from the court. This writ is a routine court order that directs the appropriate officer to take and sell as much of the defendant's property as is necessary to pay the judgment. If you cannot collect all of your judgment at the present time, you may wait and collect it later. A judgment generally lasts for a long period of time—such as ten years by statute. And it can be renewed for additional periods of time.

WHAT ARE THE PROCEDURES INVOLVED IN EQUITY, DIVORCE, PROBATE, CRIME, JUVENILE COURT, ADMINISTRATIVE AGENCY, AND IMPEACHMENT CASES?

Often, monetary damages in a settlement are not enough. The plaintiff may want something in addition to money, or perhaps something altogether different. Procedure in other than civil cases for money includes: the equity case in which an injunction is sought; the domestic relations case, which deals with divorce, custody, support and alimony; the probate case, which deals with administration of estates; the criminal case which prosecutes those charged with crime; the juvenile court case, which deals with juveniles in trouble; the administrative agency case, which is one in which an agency acts like a court; and the impeachment case, which deals with the removal of a public officer.

Equity. When the plaintiff asks for something other than money, the court must apply the principles of equity. Several changes exist in the four stages of litigation. Pleading is basically the same in equity as in civil cases for money. However, the plaintiff in an equity case must allege in his complaint why money damages are an insufficient remedy. Discovery in equity is the same as in money damage cases. Trials in equity are similar, but there are differences. There is no jury at equity. The judge decides the case. The rules of evidence are relaxed in equity cases. The judge applies equitable maxims (principles designed to do what is best and right for all parties including the community) in equity cases. The judge in an equity case issues a decree rather than a judgment. The court will often issue a temporary injunction for immediate relief to the plaintiff as soon as the case is filed, with the injunction becoming final if the plaintiff wins. The principle of res judicata doesn't apply to equitable decrees.

Divorce. Like many other areas of law, United States divorce law is derived from English law. In England, church law controlled the marriage relationship. In the U.S., traditional grounds for and defenses to divorce come from church law. Many decisions, however, place divorce law in the equity courts. Still other courts state that divorce is primarily statutory. As a result, divorce law and procedure is a blend of equity, ecclesiastical law, and statutory law.

There are important differences between divorce proceedings and civil litigation procedure. Some of them include: Minors may bring and defend divorce actions. The defendant in a divorce case may be served by a public notice though property matters won't be determined without personal service—only the divorce will be granted. Federal courts have no jurisdiction to grant divorces but they may enforce alimony or property decrees of state courts. Parties often must wait for a specified time after filing the complaint before the court will hear the divorce. Immediately after filing for divorce, the court may, if necessary, issue a temporary injunction to protect the parties from harm or harassment. A divorce may not be obtained by default. The privileged communication between husband and wife rule does not apply in divorce actions. Divorce decrees usually do not become final for a period of time. Most states have residence requirements for divorce. The courts may modify child support and alimony decrees because of changed conditions.

There is a growing trend toward no-fault divorces. These laws eliminate the traditional grounds for divorce. Parties need only show that irreconcilable differences exist between them.

Probate. The administration of a dead person's estate is the main problem of probate. If a dead person leaves a valid will, the courts will enforce it. But if no will is left, the property will pass according to the laws of intestacy (if a spouse and children survive, the spouse will typically get ½ the decedent's estate and the children ½). If a person dies without a will, and there are no relatives, the property escheats to the state. The only exception to the rule that the courts will enforce a valid will occurs when a married person attempts to cut his spouse out of the will. Statutes will allow the spouse to receive up to one-half by contesting the will. The main purpose of probate is to get the decedent's property to the rightful owners. To do this, probate procedure is followed.

Specific probate procedure is as follows. A petition is filed with the proper court. If there is a will, proof of its validity is furnished. A personal representative is appointed and he notifies the heirs that the estate has been opened. Publication is made in a local newspaper. An inventory of decedent's assets is filed. Temporary support for family is provided. Claims are paid (including taxes) and the remaining properties are distributed to the proper persons. The estate is closed.

Guardianships and conservatorships are another problem within the concept of probate. The guardianship or conservatorship is created to protect and manage the property of someone who can't do it himself (the guardian is appointed on the petition of someone other than the ward, while the conservator is appointed on the petition of the ward himself or herself). The guardian or conservator must protect, preserve, and manage the estate. His or her duties continue as long as the ward remains incapacitated. Both guardians and conservators are closely supervised by the court to make certain the property is adequately protected.

Crime. A criminal conviction results in extremely grave consequences for the convicted individual who may be locked in jail for months, years or for life. The law of criminal procedure is designed to protect the *innocent* from harsh criminal measures, even if some guilty people go free as a result. The burden of proof in our system is on the government. The defendant is assumed innocent until proved guilty. The guilt must be proved beyond a reasonable doubt—a far greater burden of proof than in civil litigation.

Law enforcement officials must adhere to strict, constitutionally founded rules while obtaining evidence so as not to infringe upon anyone's basic rights. Evidence obtained by an unlawful search cannot be used in criminal prosecution. To be lawful, a search must usually be authorized by a warrant. Involuntary or coerced confessions may not be used as evidence in a criminal trial. Before any questioning, a person must be warned that he has a right to remain silent and that he has a right to an attorney. Otherwise, any statement he makes may not be used as evidence. The police may not induce criminal conduct just to obtain a conviction. Such police action is called entrapment and is a legitimate defense to a crime. Improper identification procedures can violate due process of law.

Actual criminal procedural treatment of the defendant from time of arrest involves the following steps.

Pretrial procedure includes arrest, arraignment, and other special procedures. The arrest is the starting point of criminal procedure. The arrest may be made with or without a warrant. An arrest may be made without a warrant if the officer reasonably believes the person has actually committed a felony, or under other specified circumstances. A warrant for arrest may be obtained by grand jury indictment or by filing a complaint before a judge showing probable cause for arrest. A person arrested for a criminal misdemeanor may obtain his release by posting bail. Only some of those arrested for felonies may be released on bail. Generally, an individual may be released on his own recognizance (without monetary bail) if the judge believes there is no danger of his or her not appearing for arraignment. Once the accused has been charged and arrested, he or she must be called into court and informed of the charges. This is called the arraignment. At this time, the accused is informed of his constitutional rights. The defendant is given an opportunity to plead guilty or not guilty. If the defendant's attorney requests from the prosecution evidence that is favorable to the defendant, the prosecution must comply with the request. Some courts require complete disclosure of all evidence even without request.

The rights of the accused must be protected during the course of the trial against him or her. The defendant has a constitutionally guaranteed right to an attorney and if he or she cannot afford one, the court must appoint one. The constitution guarantees the accused a speedy trial. The defendant has a right to a fair and impartial trial which may be violated by pre-trial publicity. The defendant in this situation should ask for a change of venue before trial. Our legal system provides for public trials in all criminal cases. The accused in a criminal prosecution cannot be compelled to testify against himself or herself, but may waive this right by taking the stand in his or her own defense. The Constitution provides for confrontation of witnesses by the accused. This means that the defendant has a right to be physically present in the courtroom and his or her attorney has a right to cross-examine any witnesses. Another important rule is that the accused can neither be tried, sentenced, nor punished unless he or she is sane at the time of trial.

After trial, judgment and sentencing of a convicted criminal takes place. Sentence in a criminal trial is always imposed by the court. The Constitution prohibits cruel and inhuman punishment. The Constitution also forbids imposing greater punishment on a poor person than on a rich one.

Upon conviction, the defendant may ask for a new trial, or he or she may appeal his conviction. The principles of res judicata do not apply to criminal cases as a convicted criminal can always seek further review of his or her case by petitioning for habeas corpus. The right to appeal from a criminal conviction is guaranteed for the indigent as well as for the wealthy. If a person is too poor to pay the court costs of appeal, they will be paid for him or her. The defendant is also entitled to a hearing and a chance to speak out on his or her own behalf before probation or parole can be revoked.

There are several specific rules and procedures dealing with criminal cases. The court in a criminal case must have territorial jurisdiction which means that the case must be tried in the state where the crime took place. Venue can be changed to assure fair trial. The Constitution prohibits anyone from being tried twice for the same offense (double jeopardy). The statute of limitations sets certain time limits within which criminal prosecutions must be initiated. These vary from state to state.

Juvenile Court. Procedure differs when a juvenile is involved with crime. Juvenile court rules provide special protection for the young criminal offender. Juvenile courts deal with delinquency, truancy, incorrigibility, and neglect. They generally have jurisdiction over children up to a certain age limit. Juvenile courts are usually simply branches of other courts. The purpose of the juvenile court is not to punish but to help the child. At the same time, the rights of juveniles must be safeguarded. To insure this, the following rules for dealing with accused juveniles have been set down.

Detention of juveniles is permitted only where it is necessary to protect human life or property, to prevent the child from running away or to supervise and return him to court. Juveniles may be taken to jail only if they are kept separate from adults and if the juvenile court has specifically ordered jail. The police are required to notify the parents of their child's arrest. The Miranda rights must be observed. Officials must inform the juvenile of his or her right to remain silent; that anything he or she does say can be used against him or her; that he or she has a right to an attorney, etc. Where the juvenile is charged with a crime, the prosecution must prove guilt beyond a reasonable doubt. The juvenile, however, does not have a right to a trial by jury, or to a public trial.

Probation is always a favored alternative to a reform school in dealing with juveniles.

Administrative Agency. An administrative agency is any government authority that is not a court or legislature but that acts like one by making rules or deciding cases. Administrative agencies affect all of us much more than do courts or legislatures. Agencies dispose of many times the number of court-handled cases. Administrative rules are part of the law. Their validity may be challenged, however, by taking the case to the courts of review. Equity procedure applies to administrative review once the case is taken from the agency to the courts. Administrative agency procedure prior to judicial involvement includes the following aspects.

An agency can make rules as long as it stays within its enabling statute. The administrative agency has investigative powers and may have access to any factual materials it needs to carry out programs. The examiner who acts as a judge may preside over hearings. The examiner usually sits alone and the hearing proceeds according to special rules. Once administrative remedies are exhausted, a higher court can review the action of an agency.

Impeachment. The terms impeachment and conviction are often used interchangeably by the ignorant. But the distinction between the two is crucial. Impeachment is merely an accusation. A person in public office is impeached when an authorized legislative body charges him with conduct that is improper or unworthy of his or her office. The official is not removed unless and until tried and found guilty or convicted. The Constitution vested sole power to impeach in the House of Representatives, where a majority vote is sufficient to bring the accusation. The President, Vice President, and government officials may be removed for treason, bribery and other high crimes and misdemeanors. An impeached official may later be tried and convicted of crime for the same conduct. There is no jury in impeachment cases. Less misconduct is required to impeach a judge than to impeach a President. This is because a judge may serve on the court for terms of "good behavior", which indicates that a judge may be removed from office for "bad behavior", which can be considerably less serious than "high crimes."

WHAT IS DUE PROCESS?

The Fourteenth Amendment of the Constitution states that life, liberty and property cannot be taken away without due process of law. Five factors enter into the meaning of due process.

The first factor of due process involves the principle that power must be based on one of the three sources of law. The power to take life, liberty or property must come from written, common, or administrative law. The second factor involves the principle that everyone is entitled to his day in court. A person must be given notice and a hearing. Courts must be available to resolve disputes. Thirdly, a court must have jurisdiction before it can render a valid judgment. Established rules of evidence must be followed within the courtroom. Finally, constitutional rights must be carefully safeguarded. The rights to counsel, to protection against improper search and seizure, to public trial by jury, to confront and cross-examine witnesses, the privilege against self-incrimination—all are essential to due process of law.

WHAT IS THE SUBSTANTIVE LAW ON TORTS AND DAMAGES?

Tort and crime, two of the legal concepts defined earlier, are both broad categories covering a wide range of human activity: but, while they are distinct legal concepts, they are interrelated as well since the same act is frequently both a tort and crime. A tort is any conduct that is socially unreasonable. The purpose of tort law is to determine and adjust losses caused by torts. Crime, unlike tort, is an offense against the public, and results in government prosecution of the accused. Unlike tort law, criminal law in no way compensates the injured victim. Burden of proof in a tort action is much less than the state's burden of proof in the criminal action. A person may be held liable for a tort when the plaintiff proves he or she committed the socially unreasonable conduct by "a preponderance of the evidence." The state must prove crime "beyond a reasonable doubt." A tort may be intentional or negligent and often includes criminal conduct.

A person may be held liable for tortious conduct on any of the following three grounds. (1) Intentional interference with the plaintiff's interests. The intent required is not a hostile one, but merely an intent to bring about a certain result. The defendant in a tort action is said to intend those results that a reasonable man in his position would believe substantially certain to follow from his actions. (2) A person may also be held liable for harm that results from his carelessness. Negligence does not include an unavoidable accident and is always based on a departure from reasonable conduct—the conduct of a reasonable, prudent man under the same or similar circumstances. But, there is no negligence involved in an unavoidable accident. (3) A person may also be held liable based on the theory of strict liability—liability without fault. Under strict liability theory, a defendant may be held responsible where his actions are neither intentional nor negligent, simply because he caused the harmful result. Strict liability applies in situations where the defendant's conduct involves a very substantial risk of harm to others.

Certain types of intentional behavior have been recognized as torts, but not all torts have names: any socially unreasonable conduct is a tort and new torts are recognized from time to time. Some with names include: battery, an unpermitted, offensive, or unprivileged touching of another's person; assault, any act that places a person in actual apprehension or fear of an imminent battery (requires ability to carry out threat by defendant, mere words being generally insufficient); false imprisonment, which takes place when one person confines another person within a certain area and refuses to let him leave (includes arrest without legal authority if restraint of liberty takes place); infliction of mental distress, which includes the ability to seek legal redress for outrageous acts that induce feelings of grief, anxiety, or shame when unaccompanied by physical injury, but which requires an especially flagrant act of outrageous misconduct in order to establish liability; defamation, which occurs when one person invades the interest in reputation and good name of another. It may take two forms, libel—written defamation, or slander—oral defamation. A defamatory statement must be communicated to someone other than the plaintiff, and slander or libel must generally be supported by proof of special damages. Also tortious is invasion of the right of privacy, which may include using a person's name, portrait, or picture without his consent for purposes of trade or advertising; invading another's privacy by intruding on his solitude or seclusion; public disclosure of private facts about a person; or publicly and falsely attributing an opinion, poem, or work of art to the person.

Another type of tort is intentional interference with property. Examples include: trespass to land, which is any physical entry upon the surface of land (includes entry to buildings); nuisance, which occurs when a person uses his property in a manner that unreasonably interferes with the plaintiff's use and enjoyment of his land; and conversion, which involves serious interference with another's personal property. The interference must be intentional. When conversion occurs, the person who has committed the act may be forced by a court of law to purchase the property at its fair market value. But if the interference is less than serious, it is called trespass to chattels rather than conversion, and a forced sale does not result. Trespass to chattels, which is intentional damage to a chattel that is insufficient to be termed a conversion, results only in payment for the damages.

Intentional interference with economic relations is also tortious and in-includes: injurious falsehood, which involves the disparagement by one person of another person's business for which actual pecuniary loss is proven; interference with contractual relations, which occurs when a person induces another to breach a contract with the plaintiff or causes him not to enter into a contract with the plaintiff at all; and interference with the prospective advantage, which occurs when one person deprives another of an economic advantage he might otherwise have received.

A defendant who engages in normally tortious conduct is not liable if he is privileged to commit the act. Consent is sometimes implied from the plaintiff's conduct. The defense is good only so long as the defendant remains within the boundaries of the consent given. A defendant may escape liability for an otherwise tortious act if it was done in self-defense. According to the theory of self-defense, a person is privileged to use whatever force is reasonably necessary to prevent harmful contact or confinement. The privilege to use force in self-defense extends not only to real danger but to apparent danger as well—so long as there is reasonable ground to believe that the danger is real. It is necessary, however, to stay within the boundaries of the defense. Force cannot be used once the danger has passed.

A person may also escape liability from an act done to defend others or to protect others from real or apparent danger. A person is not liable for an act committed in defense of property if he has used only reasonable force that is not likely to cause death or great bodily injury. Recapture of chattels is another defense to tort. A person whose property has been wrongfully taken may use reasonable force to retake it if he does so immediately. The defense of necessity applies when a person commits an otherwise tortious act to protect the entire community. The interest protected, however, must be a public, not personal one.

The defense of legal process applies when an officer or policeman acts tortiously while attempting to arrest an individual or while acting otherwise within his duties. If the officer employs unreasonable force, or acts improperly in any way, he may still be liable for damages. A private citizen making an arrest may claim this defense, but he or she must be very careful to have an adequate basis for making the arrest.

A parent or person who stands in the place of a parent may claim the defense of discipline for any *reasonable* force used in disciplining and controlling a child. The force must be reasonable, however; child beating is a battery.

There are four defenses for slander and libel, two of which are complete defenses. Absolute privilege or immunity exists in a few limited situations where there is a good reason to permit complete freedom of expression. Some of those who are absolutely privileged in what they say are judges, grand jurors, witnesses, attorneys and legislators in the course of judicial or legislative proceedings. The purpose of this rule is to insure complete freedom of access to the courts and to legislatures. Truth is a complete defense to slander and libel. In most jurisdictions, the defendant cannot be held liable for a statement that is proven to be true (truth is not a defense to tort actions brought because of invasion of privacy). Evidence of retraction of the defamatory statement generally reduces the plaintiff's damage award. The retraction must be an honest effort to repair the wrong. Constitutional privilege presents an important defense in defamation and privacy cases involving public officials or matters of public concern. It extends to fair comment upon the conduct and qualifications of public officers and employees. This defense is based on the First Amendment guarantee of freedom of speech and press and is not limited to opinion, but extends even to misstatements of fact if made for the public benefit and with an honest belief in their truth.

A person whose carelessness results in injury is liable for the tort of negligence. Negligence is unintentional conduct that falls below the standard established by law for the protection of others against unreasonably great risk of harm. To constitute negligence, the risk must be foreseeable at the time the conduct occurs, and in light of that risk, the defendant's actions must be unreasonable. There must be a failure to do what a reasonable man would do in the same circumstances. Next, the plaintiff must prove that this breach of duty caused the injury to him. When this proof is difficult, the court sometimes applies the doctrine of "res ipsa loquitur," which means the thing speaks for itself. To apply this, the following conditions must be met. The event must be one that normally does not occur in the absence of negligence; the injury must be caused by something within the exclusive control of the defendant; it must be impossible for the plaintiff to have negligently caused his own injury; and evidence of the event's true explanation must be more accessible to the defendant than to the plaintiff. Finally, the plaintiff must prove that he suffered actual loss or damage. Once these conditions are shown to exist, the burden of proof shifts to the defendant who must either disprove negligence or be held liable.

The two most common defenses to negligence are contributory negligence and assumption of risk. Contributory negligence is conduct by the plaintiff that contributes to the harm he suffers; conduct that falls below the standard imposed upon him by law for his own protection. If both the plaintiff and defendant are at fault, the plaintiff is usually barred from recovery (some states have "comparative negligence" statutes where if both parties are negligent, the one less so can still recover). Many courts also hold that even where the plaintiff himself is negligent, he may still recover damages if the defendant had the "last clear chance" to avoid the harm. Of course, the plaintiff must do whatever he can to avoid furthering the damages after the initial injury if he wishes to recover full damages. This is called the rule of avoidable consequences.

Another defense to negligence is assumption of risk. The plaintiff who assumes the risk of the defendant's negligence may be barred from recovery. Where the plaintiff agrees to accept the risk, he may be unable to recover damages if injury later results. Assumption of risk is generally not an express assumption, but one implied from the plaintiff's conduct. At times, the plaintiff knows that the defendant has been negligent but, aware of the risk, he still voluntarily encounters it. In this case, he is generally barred from recovery.

The third theory of tort liability is strict liability, which holds the defendant responsible for unintentional conduct he has taken every precaution to prevent. The action usually involves a substantial risk of harm and is neither intentionally harmful nor negligent. Liability exists simply because the actions cause a harmful result. The three traditional areas of strict liability include animals, abnormally dangerous things, and food and drink.

A person who owns animals that are likely to roam and cause damage may be held strictly liable for the harm that results from their wanderings. A person who keeps a naturally wild animal is strictly liable for any damage the animal causes. A person who does an abnormally dangerous act is strictly liable for damages. The act must be ultra-hazardous, and must be one unnatural to its surroundings for strict liability to apply. The seller of food and drink is strictly liable for damages caused by defective goods.

In the past few years, strict liability has been applied to any kind of defective product (not just food and drink products) that is recognizably dangerous to those who may come in contact with it. Strict liability applies to the seller of defective goods when the following conditions are met. The seller must be engaged in the business of selling such a product. The product is expected to and does reach the user or consumer without substantial change in the condition in which it is sold. Strict liability may apply to sellers even though the seller has exercised all possible care in the preparation and sale of his product and the user or consumer has not bought the product from or entered into any contractual relation with the seller. It will make the seller liable for all damage that results because the product is defective when sold.

The purpose of the tort action is to compensate the plaintiff for his loss. Determination of this loss is based on the law of damages—that is, the rules and standards used by courts to measure compensation for injury. The measure of damages in a personal injury action includes the reasonable cost of care for doctors, nurses, and other medical expenses. The expenses must be traceable to the injury. When the injury forces the plaintiff to lose time from work, his lost earnings are also part of these damages. The plaintiff who suffers bodily injury may also recover damages for past and future pain and serious mental suffering.

Punitive damages, which are awarded only when the defendant's actions are absolutely outrageous, are designed to punish the defendant and to deter others from following his example—sometimes called "smart money." Punitive damages are taxable; compensatory damages are not.

Survival statutes now allow compensation to personal representatives or surviving families of decedents for pre-death injuries, loss of earnings, etc. of the now-deceased person. The purpose of damages is to compensate the plaintiff for his loss.

There are various rules of compensation for particular situations. In oral defamation cases, material damages must be proved. When personal property is wrongfully destroyed, the usual measure of damages is the value of the property. Where the plaintiff has suffered no compensatory loss, he may still be awarded nominal damages. Statutes of limitation in all our states set maximum time limits for bringing tort actions.

With respect to suits for torts involving family members, several rules apply. Spouses can sue each other for torts involving property interests, but many states prohibit personal tort suits between spouses. The growing trend in the law is toward complete freedom of action between spouses. A child may sue his parents for torts affecting his property, but most laws still forbid unemancipated children from bringing personal tort actions against their parents. Only emancipated (no longer living at home) children may usually bring such torts. Parents, likewise, generally cannot sue their children for personal torts. Other family members generally can sue each other.

Several other classes of defendants are also immune from tort liability. The federal government cannot be sued without its consent. It has given consent to liability only for negligent or wrongful acts of employees acting within the scope of their employment at the operational level of government. Among the areas of federal immunity from suit is the area of government policy actions. Policy makers are exempt from suits for all discretionary acts. Strict liability in any of its traditional areas is not imposed upon the federal government. States and municipalities also share in this governmental immunity, but the trend in law is toward abrogation of governmental immunity.

The higher ranked administrative and public officials in government are generally immune from liability for torts committed in the performance of official functions. Charitable organizations involved in public service are often at least partially immune from tort liability. Minors are liable for their own torts, but lenient standards of intent or negligence may be applied to them. Parents are not liable for their children's torts except in some places to a limited extent for vandalism by statute ($100–$500).

A person may pay an insurance company to indemnify him for the losses he sustains through legal liability to others. This insurance is especially important to businessmen, property owners, professional practitioners, and automobile drivers. Without insurance, these persons could be financially ruined by a tort suit. Some states have now adopted "no fault" auto insurance laws which are designed to compensate victims for personal injury and property damage without regard to fault.

WHAT IS THE SUBSTANTIVE LAW ON CRIME AND PUNISHMENT?

A crime is any act or omission prohibited by public law in order to protect the public. A crime is punishable by fine, imprisonment or death. Substantive law declares and defines what conduct is criminal, and prescribes punishment for conviction of crime.

Criminal law is found in all three sources of law: common, administrative and written. The roots of criminal law are found in English common law. Many states now, however, have comprehensive criminal codes that abolish common law crime. A violation of rules of an agency is called an administrative crime. While state and federal criminal statutes vary, the general principles and applications remain the same.

The three classes of crime are treasons, felonies and misdemeanors. Treason against the United States consists of levying war against the U.S. or adhering to U.S. enemies, giving them aid and comfort. Treason, therefore, is an intentional act of betrayal that strikes at the very heart of government. A felony is a very serious crime. Generally a felony is defined as any offense punishable by death or confinement in the state penitentiary. Crimes other than treasons or felonies are misdemeanors.

Crimes are usually classified according to punishment, length of sentence, and place of confinement. Statutes seldom label a specific crime as either a misdemeanor or felony. Even so, the classification of a crime can make a big difference in some situations. Convicted felons often lose many rights, including that of holding office, to vote, to serve on a jury, and to practice as an attorney. The Oregon criminal code enacted in 1971 is a good example of a modern criminal code and will be referred to here to illustrate recent trends in criminal law.

Some specific crimes and their punishments are as follows. Murder is unlawfully killing another human being with malice aforethought. Intent to kill a human being, a form of malice aforethought, may be gathered from all the circumstances of the killing. Intentional use of a deadly weapon is generally sufficient evidence of intent to kill, but even where no weapon is used, an intent to kill may still be established. Another state of mind which may constitute malice aforethought is intent to cause grievous bodily harm. A person who intends to inflict great bodily harm upon another and accidentally kills him is guilty of murder. A third form of malice aforethought is intent to act with gross recklessness or in wanton and willful disregard of a known and substantial risk to human life—called "depraved heart" murder; bombing a building is an example. Intent to oppose by force an officer making a lawful arrest also provides malice aforethought. And, intent to commit a dangerous or violent felony constitutes malice aforethought. However, a homicide occurring during the commission of a crime is murder only when the homicide and felony are closely connected in point of time, place, and causal relation. In order for murder to occur, the defendant's conduct must cause the death of a living human being. This leads to the issue of when life begins and ends. Thus, killing an unborn fetus is not usually murder; nor is mutilating a corpse. The legal trend is toward adoption of brain death as the proper criterion for establishing time of death. Under most state laws, death is murder only if it occurred within a year and a day from the time the injury was inflicted (3 years in California). Many states distinguish between murder in the first and second degrees. First degree murder is generally defined as any willful, deliberate, and premeditated killing.

Voluntary manslaughter is intentional homicide provoked in a sudden passion or heat of blood. The provocation must be sufficient to excite the ordinary man's passion and to cause him to act rashly and without reflection.

If the homicide is justifiable or excusable as in cases of accident and self-defense, no criminal responsibility will be incurred. Involuntary manslaughter includes all criminal killing other than murder or voluntary manslaughter. It usually involves very reckless or negligent conduct.

The Oregon Code provides an example of a modern statutory treatment of murder and manslaughter. The Oregon Code classifies criminal homicide into murder, manslaughter and criminally negligent homicide. Criminal homicide is murder under Oregon law when it is intentionally committed, or recklessly committed under circumstances manifesting extreme indifference to the value of human life, or when it takes place during commission or attempted commission of a felony. Criminal homicide is manslaughter under the Oregon Code where the homicide is committed under the influence of an extreme emotional disturbance that is susceptible of reasonable explanation, or where a person intentionally causes or aids another person to commit suicide. Under the Oregon law, criminally negligent homicide occurs when, with criminal negligence, a person causes the death of another.

Assault, under the common law, is an attempt to harm another with force and violence, with or without a weapon. Under Oregon law, a person is guilty of menacing (the term for the old common law assault) if by word or conduct he intentionally attempts to place another person in fear of imminent serious physical injury. At common law, battery is any unlawful injury, however slight, to another's person. The injury need not be serious. Since every battery includes an assault, a person indicted for both can be convicted of assault alone where the battery cannot be proved. Mayhem occurred at common law when one person violently deprived another of the use of some part of his body so as to render him less able to fight. American statutes have expanded the crime to include disfigurement as well as dismemberment. The Oregon Statute has reclassified assault, battery and mayhem into "assault and related offenses." The Statute defines three degrees of assault, two of which are felonies.

Rape at common law was defined as unlawful sexual intercourse with a woman without her consent. A woman who consents to sex has not been raped. There can be no consent where a woman is insane, idiotic, insensible, or asleep at the time of the act. Statutory rape is defined as unlawful sexual intercourse with a female under the age of consent. Sexual misdemeanors under common law include adultery, fornication, illicit cohabitation, and seduction. The trend in the law is to make legal any sex act between consenting adults.

Kidnapping under the common law was defined as forcibly abducting a person from his or her country. Under the Oregon law, it is defined as taking a person from one place to another or secretly confining him or her in a place where he or she is not likely to be found with intent to interfere substantially with his or her liberty, and without that person's consent or legal authority.

Besides offenses against the person, there are also offenses against property, some of which are discussed below. Under the Oregon law, larceny is classified under theft. Theft is defined as intentionally depriving another person of his or her property or appropriating it by any means. Oregon law classifies theft into degrees, according to seriousness. Theft by receiving is also an Oregon statutory crime. Theft of services occurs when one person uses deception to obtain services or to avoid paying for them. Common law burglary was breaking and entering into the dwelling of another at nighttime with intent to commit a felony. Burglary has been expanded by statute to include breaking into buildings other than houses, in the daytime as well as night; to entering without intent to commit crime; and even to mere possession of burglary tools. Arson at common law was the willful and malicious burning of another's dwelling. Statute has expanded this crime to include buildings other than dwellings. Robbery was a common law felony defined as the taking and carrying away of another's personal property from his person, or in his presence, by means of violence or threats of violence.

Other criminal offenses involve fraud or deception. Forgery is falsely making or altering a written instrument. Criminal simulation is making or altering an object to give it a false appearance of antiquity, rarity, source or authorship. Other fraudulent offenses include: negotiating a bad check, fraudulent use of a credit card; falsifying business records; sports bribery; issuing a false financial statement; opening a telegram addressed to another; opening, reading or publishing a letter; and misrepresentation of age by a minor.

Examples of offenses against the public order include the following. Riot is engaging in tumultuous and violent conduct with five or more persons and thus intentionally or recklessly creating a grave risk of causing public alarm. Disorderly conduct includes such things as fighting, using abusive language, obstructing traffic, etc. Public intoxication takes place when, because of drinking, a person creates any public disturbance. Loitering occurs when a person unreasonably lingers or prowls in a public place under circumstances warranting justifiable alarm, and refuses upon inquiry to identify himself or herself to account for his or her presence. Other offenses against the public order include harassment, abuse of venerated objects, pointing a firearm at another, carrying a concealed weapon, and discharging a firearm on or across a highway. Offenses against the public decency and health include prostitution, furnishing obscene material for minors, promoting gambling, criminal activity in drugs, cruelty to animals and violating liquor laws pertaining to minors.

Commission of a crime generally requires two elements—mens rea (criminal intent) and actus reus (criminal act). While most crimes are affirmatively committed, some crimes are defined in terms of omission to act. But liability for nonaction may be imposed only where a legal duty to act can first be established. There are legal duties based upon the family relationship. Parents have duties to their children and husbands have duties to their wives. Statutes also impose legal duties upon certain classes of people.

Attempts, solicitations and conspiracies are crimes in themselves. An attempt is a substantial step taken in a course of conduct planned to culminate in the commission of a crime. Criminal solicitation takes place when a person intentionally entices, advises, incites, orders or otherwise encourages another person to commit a crime. It is also criminal for two or more persons to conspire or combine to commit a crime.

To incur criminal liability for his or her conduct, a person must generally act with intent to commit a crime. Motive, however, is not an essential element of any crime. A person may have a good motive and still intentionally commit a crime. Many statutory crimes in the areas of negligence and strict liability do not require specific intent.

There are two areas of criminal law that help determine when a person is guilty of crime. These are: responsibility and parties to crime. A person can only be guilty of crime when he or she is responsible for his or her actions. Thus the defense of insanity is used when a defendant denies responsibility for his or her conduct. According to the McNaughten case, a person is insane if, at the time of committing the act, he was laboring under such a defect of reason as to not know the nature or quality of the act, or as not to know that what he or she was doing was wrong. Some states say a person is insane if mental disease has kept him or her from controlling his or her conduct (Durham rule). Under Oregon law, a person is insane if, at the time of the crime, he lacks substantial capacity to appreciate the criminality of his or her conduct or to conform his or her conduct to the requirements of law (Model Penal Code test). A defendant may also claim as a defense to crime that he or she was not responsible due to intoxication or lack of consciousness. Children up to a certain age are generally considered incapable of committing crime. Another important rule of law states that if several persons combine or conspire to commit a crime, or if they command or counsel a crime, or aid or abet in any attempt to commit a crime, each is responsible for all the acts committed by all parties in execution of the common purpose so long as the acts are a natural or probable consequence of the unlawful undertaking.

Many criminal offenses relate to the administration of criminal law and to the obstruction of justice. The Oregon Criminal Code lists the following offenses against the state and public justice. Bribe giving involves the offering to confer pecuniary benefit upon a public servant with intent to influence that servant's official exercise of discretion. Bribe receiving is also in this class of crime. Perjury, another crime in this class, occurs when a person makes a false sworn statement in regard to a material issue that he or she knows to be false. Escape is committed when a person, aided by another person present, uses, or threatens to use, physical force in escaping from custody, or uses or threatens to use a dangerous or deadly weapon in his or her escape. Other crimes against the state and public justice are bail jumping, bribing a witness, hindering prosecution, compounding a felony, and obstructing governmental administration.

The ultimate end of criminal law is the prevention of harm to individual and social interests. Four particular goals stand out. Deterrence involves discouraging others from crime by making an example of the offender, or by authorizing severe punishment for crime. Incapacitation involves removing the offender from society and thus denying him or her any further opportunity to commit crime. Rehabilitation involves preparing the person for his or her return to society and to a useful life. Retribution inflicts justly deserved punishment.

Criminal law, in its broadest sense, seeks to prevent injury to the public health, safety, morals, and welfare. It uses punishment and the threat of punishment to achieve its purposes.

WHAT IS THE LAW REGARDING THE PAYMENT OF TAXES FOR GOVERNMENT SERVICES AND PROTECTION?

Taxation is a very complicated legal concept. The source of the power to tax is found in the constitutional provision giving Congress the power to require payment of taxes. As government has grown and has taken on increasing responsibility for the protection and welfare of the people, the revenue-generating need has also grown, causing a heavier tax burden. A tax may be defined as a compulsory contribution levied by the state upon persons, property, income and privileges for the purpose of defraying the expenses of government. Only an authorized legislative body may levy a tax, and it must do so according to established legal principles. A basic understanding of taxation and public regulation is essential to successful living in our society.

For a tax to be valid, it must be levied not only by a duly constituted public authority but also for the public good.

The tax rate is the percentage of the tax base that must be paid by the taxpayer to the government. A tax base is an object upon which a tax is levied and to which a tax rate is applied. The amount of tax due is determined simply by multiplying the base by the tax rate.

Taxation involves three basic rate structures. A tax rate structure is a pattern that shows how a rate behaves as the tax base increases or decreases. In a progressive tax rate structure, the rate increases as the base increases. In a proportional rate structure, the rate remains constant whether the base is large or small, and regardless of whether it increases or decreases. In a regressive rate structure, the rate decreases as the base increases. Actually, there are no regressive rate structures used in this country. Our system is basically one of progressive taxation. The advantage to this is that taxpayers in the middle and upper income tax brackets help the government provide services and benefits for low income producers. The disadvantage is that it diminishes desire to work and incentive to invest. Tax rate structures have always been a subject of controversy.

Property taxes. Property tax is the substance of *local* tax structures. School districts rely heavily on property taxes. There are no federal property taxes, and only a few state property taxes. Property tax is generally levied on real property, but it is sometimes levied on some personal property. Property is often assessed in terms of fair market value or actual cash value. The primary assessment district is the governmental unit that carries out the original assessment activity. It determines the value of the property, and levies and collects the taxes.

General administrative procedure in execution of a property tax is as follows. The assessor makes the original assessment or values all property within a district on a particular day. Assessments are reviewed by the district boards who have power to alter the assessments on grounds of unjust valuation. The specific tax rate to be applied against property is determined and collection of the property taxes takes place at the local level. The funds are distributed to the particular governmental units. Taxpayers who feel they have been unjustly treated may always seek judicial review of assessment and other taxing procedures. Certain properties are exempted altogether from property tax.

A tax sale resulting from nonpayment of delinquent tax is not a final loss of the property usually. A taxpayer may, for a certain length of time after his property has been sold for taxes, pay the costs and get his property back.

Income taxes. The Constitution grants Congress the power to collect income taxes. The first step in arriving at taxable income is to determine gross income. There are regulations concerning exactly what is considered income for tax purposes but nearly all receipts are income with the exception of such items as gifts, inheritances, insurance settlements, etc. The second step is to deduct from gross income all allowable deductions (such things as medical expense, interest, taxes, and charitable deductions) and exemptions to arrive at net or taxable income. The third step is to apply the tax structure rate to this taxable income to determine tax liability. The last step is to apply the credits allowed, including taxes already paid to determine the specific amount owed to the government.

Applying the rate against the base is not difficult but one must be careful to use the correct schedule, depending on whether one is single, married, or a "head of household." Avoiding difficulty in income tax reporting may be accomplished by following these rules. Fill in all necessary schedules, forms and explanations in detail. Wherever an unusual item is likely to raise a question, attach an explanation. Preserve all records, receipts, etc. that are relevant to proving your position. Retain a copy of your return for your own reference. Be consistent each year on any continuous item such as depreciation. The income tax is the backbone of the United States tax system with individuals, corporations, and trusts paying income taxes.

Estate and gift taxes. Estate and gift taxes tax the transfer of property by gifts or death. The mechanics of the federal estate tax are similar to those of the income tax. The gross value of the estate must be first established. Next, certain allowable deductions are subtracted. There is a marital deduction for the first $250,000 left to a surviving spouse—also there are deductions for expenses, debts, taxes owing, etc., which can be subtracted from the gross estate. The progressive tax schedule is next applied to the net estate. Certain credits are allowed against the tax itself. Since a person could otherwise avoid death taxes altogether by giving all his property away before his death, the government has also enacted gift tax laws. The federal gift tax law is unified with the estate tax law and the same rate from 18% to 70% applies, depending on the size of the gift or estate. Approximately $175,000 can be transferred by gift or at death without tax.

Consumption taxes. Consumption taxes are levied against expenditures for consumption in four general areas: customs, excise, sales and use. Customs or tariffs are levied on goods that cross national boundaries. They include specific duties, those levied on certain goods, and ad valorem duties, those levied on the value of goods imported. Excise taxes are those on the making or selling of goods. This tax is paid by the producer or distributor, and passed on to the consumer. The sales tax is a more general tax levied on all goods, or on all goods with some minor exceptions, such as food. Use taxes are imposed on the use, storage, or consumption of all goods bought in a neighboring state without sales tax that would be subject to the sales tax if purchased within the state that does have sales tax. Motor vehicle tax and highway taxes (the gas tax) supply money for the construction and maintenance of U.S. highways.

Social security taxes. Social security taxes are paid by almost all Americans as a result of the Social Security Act of 1935. Employers and employees share equally in the payment of this tax. There are three basic types of social security benefits: retirement, survivors, and disability payments. Social security benefits, by reason of disability benefits, are important to the young person as well as to the elderly.

As a taxpayer, you have a legal duty to pay your taxes in full, but not a penny more. If the government makes a mistake in computing your taxes, you have not only a right but a duty to protest. But, if called in for an audit, it is best to cooperate in resolving the dispute. If it is impossible to reach a settlement and your position is sound, you may take your case to court to have your tax dispute settled.

The federal government spends a great deal of money on government services, programs, and general government. The three biggest budget items are the human resources programs, national defense, and our physical resource programs. The energy program is one of the main federal government expenditure programs. The federal budget provides funds for a comprehensive national energy program policy to deal with current shortages. One of the goals of the program has been to reestablish the nation's self-sufficiency in energy by 1980.

Another major expenditure program is the national defense (although not as big as human resource programs). Our national security programs contribute toward the goal of world peace by deterring other nations from initiating conflict with our interests. Even though a great deal is still spent on national defense, in recent years defense programs have taken a much smaller percentage of the gross national product than they did 25 years ago. There is much government money spent on international affairs and finance. International security assistance programs help friendly developing countries establish and maintain their capacity for self-defense. Money is also spent on international development assistance programs that support the economic advancement of underdeveloped countries. The Peace Corps sends volunteers to developing countries to help meet their need for trained manpower and to promote better international understanding. The United States also donates and sells agricultural commodities on favorable terms to friendly nations.

The federal budget provides for a well-balanced program of space research and technology. Advancements are rapidly being made in many technological areas. There are also expenditures for agricultural and rural development. Agricultural programs provide income protection for the farmer, food assistance for the needy, and wholesome food supplies for the consumer. Natural resources and environmental programs encourage wise use of the nation's water, timber, and other resources while protecting and improving the environment. Federal money is also spent on commerce and transportation programs, which include mass transit programs and highway funding programs. Federal disaster aid requires heavy expenditures. Community development and housing programs have several goals. They aim to help alleviate current high interest rates on housing loans; try to improve and expand support for community development and management; experiment with cash assistance to low income families in their areas of housing need; and try to continue the phase-out of ineffective federal programs.

Spending for education, general science, and manpower increases the nation's capacity to achieve social and economic progress. State and local governments still have the primary responsibility for public education. Federal aid to students of higher education, however, has been rapidly expanding. The federal government also assists states and localities in hiring the unemployed or under-employed. Other programs assist recipients of welfare and help reduce job-related accidents and disease.

A great deal is spent on federal health programs and such things as cancer research and other disease research, hospital construction and medical assistance. Income security programs benefit retired and disabled workers and the survivors of deceased workers. There are programs for unemployment compensation, supplemental security income, food assistance (food stamps) and other social service programs. The federal government also provides for veteran benefits and services.

In addition, much money is spent on general government programs including revenue collection, law enforcement, protection of civil rights, drug enforcement, tax collection, etc.

Under general revenue sharing programs, within each state, one-third of all funds go to the state government and two-thirds to local governments. Federal payments are made to states and localities with minimal restrictions and controls. The government closest to the people can thus deal with its own problems. In many cases, the funds have enabled state and local governments to reduce local taxes and still provide much needed services.

WHAT IS THE BASIC LAW ON CONSUMER PROTECTION AND THE ENVIRONMENT?

Consumer protection and environmental law are two of the newest concepts in our legal system. Consumerism is defined as the organized effort to seek redress, restitution, and remedy for dissatisfaction related to the acquisition of goods or services. Society has rejected the once pre-eminent doctrine of caveat emptor which states "let the buyer beware." In place of the doctrine, a consumer bill of rights has emerged. The four basic consumer rights include the right to safety, the right to be informed, the right to choose, and the right to be heard.

The government has also become increasingly involved with preserving the environment in the last several years. Government agencies concerned with protecting the environment have sprung up with increasing rapidity. Thousands of environmental laws have been passed.

Consumer protection. The consumer movement was originally concerned with the consumer's safety and needs, but now the movement is also demanding better products. The mounting political support for the movement has increased the movement's effectiveness. The consumer movement is primarily concerned with legal power since the consumer needs laws to protect his rights. The consumer movement directs a large proportion of its activities toward influencing government action as the best way to get results. One of the tactics used by consumers to effect their right to be heard is use of the exposé. The exposé is a means of revealing inside information through the press. Another tactic consumers use is the lawsuit. The consumer uses the legal process to make companies compensate consumers who are injured while using their products; to help publicize consumer controversies in some cases; and to seek court injunctions or orders to help further the consumer movement. Consumers often lobby in an attempt to influence government policies. Besides this, the consumer sometimes attempts to influence the manner in which government conducts its own business and use boycotts and advertising to force change.

The consumer's final tactic is the proxy fight in which consumer issues are passed on directly to the owners of a corporation who, hopefully, will resolve a conflict between increased dividends and an improved product in favor of the product. In a proxy fight, each shareholder may vote his own stock, or he may give his vote or proxy to another. A proxy is simply a person who substitutes for another by acting or voting for him. Even if consumers lose in a proxy fight, they still may get the consumer message across and assert their right to be heard.

The consumer's right to safety is the right to be protected against the marketing of goods that are hazardous to health or life. The risk of harm through the use of a defective product is growing, so the right to safety also increases in importance. Federal concern with the consumer's right to safety is increasing and many statutes have been passed in the areas of food and drugs, toys, fabrics, traffic, meats, and boats. The Consumer Product Safety Act of 1972 is the legislation that will have the greatest impact on protecting the consumer's right to safety. The act created a Consumer Product Commission with broad powers to conduct research, develop and enforce standards of product safety, etc. The act prohibits the maufacture, sale, distribution, or import of any consumer product that does not conform to product safety standards or that has been banned as a hazardous product. Thus the commission has power to prescribe mandatory safety standards for virtually all consumer products. One section of the act dealing with product certification requires the manufacturer to conduct a reasonable testing program to make certain that the product conforms to established safety standards. Another section of the act requires the manufacturer to take corrective steps if he learns that the product is defective. The manufacturer must notify the commission and then repair or replace the product, or refund the consumer's money. The commission is authorized to inspect facilities where consumer goods are manufactured, stored, or transported. Among its accomplishments, the commission has published the "Consumer Product Hazard Index", established a toll-free product-safety information line, and has taken long range steps to develop safety standards for a long and varied list of products used in and around the home.

The consumer can also find protection in the tort law of negligence and strict liability, and in contract law dealing with warranty. Advertisement claims, sales literature, labels, instructions and oral sales presentations will be held legally binding on the manufacturer as an express warranty if the purchaser relied on the claims in making his purchase. In the area of strict liability in tort, the doctrine of privity in product liability has been abolished, meaning that either the purchaser or any user of the defective product may now recover damages when injured by reason of a defective product.

The consumer's right to be informed is the right to be given sufficient information to make an informed choice—to be protected against fraudulent, deceitful or grossly misleading information, advertising, labeling and other practices. The federal government has enacted various legislation to aid the consumer in realizing this right, but the act that has had the greatest impact on the consumer's right to be informed is the Consumer Credit Protection Act of 1968, also known as "Truth in Lending." The Act includes credit disclosure regulations; it prohibits extortionate credit transactions; and it places certain limitations on the garnishment of wages. The purpose of truth in lending is to inform borrowers and customers of the cost of credit so they can compare these costs with those of other credit sources. Specific responsibilities for enforcing the Act are divided among nine federal agencies. Any credit extended for personal, family, household, or agricultural use not exceeding $25,000 is included within the Act, as are any real estate credit transactions for these purposes regardless of the amount. Not affected by the Act are business and commercial credit, credit to federal, state and local governments, transactions in securities and commodities accounts with a broker, transactions under certain public utility tariffs and credit over $25,000.

Where credit is covered by the law, the customer must be informed of the finance charge and the annual percentage rate. The finance charge is the total cost the customer must pay either directly or indirectly for obtaining the credit. A person who fails to make the disclosures required under this law may be sued by the customer for twice the amount of the finance charge plus court costs and attorney fees. Real estate credit in any amount is covered under truth in lending when it is extended to an individual for other than business purposes. In many instances, a customer may cancel a credit arrangement within three business days if his residence is used as collateral for credit.

The federal credit card law, an amendment to truth in lending, limits the cardholder's liability to $50 on lost or stolen credit cards even where the consumer does not promptly notify the card's issuer of its loss. Liability ends in all cases upon notification of loss. The Federal Trade Commission is pursuing a vigorous course of action in enforcing the provisions of the Truth in Lending Act.

Since federal regulation is limited to interstate commerce, an increasing number of states, counties, and municipalities have established some form of consumer affairs office. The structure and responsibilities of state consumer protection offices vary considerably. Some merely advise, while others actively enforce consumer protection laws. Usually, however, they are located in the attorney general's office and share in the responsibility for implementing unfair and deceptive trade practices statutes. Some states limit use of the deficiency judgment. This means that the creditor is limited in his ability to repossess and sell an article and then also sue the buyer where the buyer has failed to meet his sales contract payments.

Environmental law. Environmental protection was traditionally the job of state and local governments as it was considered a proper exercise of their "police power." But in recent years, the federal government has taken on increasing responsibility for pollution control and enforcement. Federal authority to impose environmental regulations and controls stems from three constitutional powers: the power to tax and spend; the commerce power; and the treaty power. While the spending power may be used only for the general welfare, the environment is actually the epitome of what is general. The power to tax is equally broad. So these powers may be used to control pollution. Under the commerce power, Congress can regulate virtually every activity that tends to contaminate the environment. Finally, the treaty power may be exercised where other grants of power are insufficient. Congress can implement a treaty through legislation that, previously, it had no power to enact.

Federal agencies concerned with environmental regulation have sprung up with increasing speed in recent years. The key federal agency effort to protect the environment is presently centered in the Environmental Protection Agency which brought together for the first time in a single agency the major environmental problems of air and water pollution, solid wastes management, pesticides, radiation and noise. EPA is primarily a regulatory agency, since it must establish and enforce environmental standards. Included among these standards are definitions of the pollutant levels that must be prevented from entering our air and water, as well as limitations required on radiation emissions and pesticide control. But research, too, is an important part of EPA, and the latest EPA advancements in control technology are made available to the public in workshops and seminars attended by state and local officials and other interested people. Among the EPA's many activities are: providing financial assistance and manpower development to combat environmental problems, working with local officials to inspect and maintain emission controls, helping the cities boost their mass transit programs, establishing traffic-free zones and imposing parking bans.

The Council on Environmental Quality was established to formulate and recommend national policies for the promotion of and improvement of the quality of the environment. The Council's activities include the development and recommendation to the President of policies that promote environmental equality. To assist the Council in its review of federal activities, and to insure consideration of environmental factors in federal decision making, each federal agency is required to submit to the Council an *environmental impact statement* on any proposed legislation or other major action that might significantly affect the environment. Recent Council guidelines stipulate that all federal agencies should evaluate the impact of federally supported projects on population and growth. The Council has identified a modeling technique for assessing energy policy alternatives. To devise an energy program that will have a minimum impact on the environment, the Council insists that it is necessary to analyze the entire energy system, not just one element of the system.

The Department of Agriculture consists of a variety of administrations and services, each responsible for particular areas of environmental control. The Farmers Home Administration provides loans to farmers, and grants for the construction of rural community water and waste disposal systems. The Forest Service manages national forests and grasslands. The Soil Conservation Service works to protect the environment in many ways such as taking soil surveys and conducting conservation operations. The Agricultural Research Service conducts various research programs.

The National Oceanic and Atmospheric Administration, located within the Dept. of Commerce, is the key agency involved in protecting our oceans. The agency's mission is stated as the mapping and charting of the global oceans, as well as the management, use and conservation of ocean animals and mineral resources. The agency also alerts us to impending environmental hazards, including hurricanes, tornadoes, floods and other destructive natural events.

Other federal agencies with environmental functions include the Dept. of the Army, the Dept. of Health, Education and Welfare, the Dept. of Housing and Urban Development, the Dept. of Justice, the Dept. of the Interior, the Atomic Energy Commission, the Federal Power Commission, and other independent agencies.

The National Environmental Policy Act requires all federal agencies to prepare an environmental impact statement if any of their proposed activities might significantly affect the environment. The purpose of the act is to establish a national environmental policy, to authorize research concerning natural resources, and to establish a council of environmental advisors. The act outlines the government's responsibilities as far as environmental preservation is concerned. The act requires agencies to consider the environmental repercussions of their proposed actions and to discuss their proposals with federal and state agencies well versed in environmental matters. The agencies must then prepare an environmental impact statement on the conclusions they arrive at. Exceptions are made only for agencies that deal with security and military institutions or when temporary or emergency actions are involved. The act also establishes the Council on Environmental Quality which is designed to provide the President with objective advice and to closely supervise federal activities affecting the environment. The act requires the President to submit an annual Environmental Quality report to Congress.

Federal law presently provides for several air pollution abatement procedures. They are listed below. Where the air pollution problem is intrastate, the EPA Administrator may take action only if requested to do so by the governor of the affected state. Where interstate air pollution is involved, and where there is evidence of imminent and substantial danger to human health, the Administrator may seek immediate court action to stop the emission of pollutants if state or local authorities fail to act. Where interstate air pollution exists in an air quality control region that has fallen below prescribed air quality standards, federal enforcement of these standards is authorized if the state itself fails to take reasonable action. In case of interstate air pollution where the source of the pollution is in one state and the adverse effect is in another, the Administrator is required to call an interstate air pollution conference if requested to do so by the state governor or by a state air pollution agency. A formal hearing board may then be appointed to decide the case.

The Federal Air Pollution Program has only been developed in the past 20 years through the passage of various air pollution laws. The legislation requires reduction of automobile pollution and the EPA has power to enforce these auto regulations. The EPA also has power to establish standards for civil aircraft.

Most pollution control regulations are enforced at state and local levels of government. In the majority of states, the state health department is primarily responsible for environmental controls. Much of the traditional machinery for public health enforcement is outdated and inappropriate for use in pollution control however. In the past, cities often have been the chief governmental units dealing with air pollution control. State programs have only recently developed. Today, every state has developed air pollution control plans. Local government attempts to regulate air pollution range from the very primitive to the complex multi-million dollar operation.

There are still many problems in air pollution regulation. One difficulty has been in determining the proper role of the court in environmental law—in determining whether a judge can impose requirements or prohibitions more stringent than those detailed in federal legislation. Another problem is that the nation lacks sufficient air quality information. Finally, shortages in energy have sharply affected air pollution control programs.

The Federal government has two statutory programs for water pollution control. The first is based on the Rivers and Harbors Act dealing with navigable waterways. The Act was designed to protect navigability, but it has been interpreted to permit pollution control. The major effect of the Act is to forbid the dumping of refuse into any navigable water or its tributary. The first major legislation directed toward a serious federal water pollution control program was the Water Quality Act creating the Federal Water Pollution Control Administration. This Act directed the states to prepare stream quality standards and to draw up corresponding plans to meet the standards. A subsequent act imposed statewide water quality standards, expanded federal grant funds, authorized studies on water pollution control, etc. Finally, Congress passed the Federal Water Pollution Control Act Amendments of 1972, a comprehensive program for water pollution control. The act's goal is to eliminate all pollution in navigable waters by 1985. According to the Amendments, industry must apply the best practicable control technology currently available. There are many water pollution programs at the state and local level. The municipality is generally responsible for the purity of local water within the state. Presently, every state has a water pollution control agency. State penalties for failure to comply with water quality standards vary greatly.

The Solid Waste Disposal Act of 1968 vested major responsibility for solid waste programs of the Environmental Protection Agency. The Act was designed to "develop efficient means of disposing of the tons of solid wastes that clog the nation's cities and countryside." Its most significant provisions are those requiring EPA to report to Congress on National Disposal Sites; requiring the director of EPA to promulgate guidelines and model statutes for solid waste recovery, collection, separation and disposal; and establishing a National Materials Policy for the conservation and wise use of our limited natural resources. State law generally places responsibility for solid waste disposal enforcement on the municipality.

Although a variety of noise sources are now controlled at the federal level, the Noise Pollution and Abatement Act of 1970 was the first federal effort at overall environmental noise abatement. Under the provisions of the Act, the Office of Noise Abatement and Control was established to conduct research and investigation into environmental noise. Federal efforts to abate transportation noise are directed primarily at aircraft noise. The Dept. of Transportation Act directs the Secretary of Transportation to promote and undertake research and development relating to transportation including noise abatement, with particular emphasis on aircraft noise. Federal action in the area of highway noise abatement is also significant.

There are three federal acts which govern occupational noise control and abatement. Construction noise regulation is concerned with construction site noise, and with noise related to the accoustical characteristics of building. Enforcement of noise control was traditionally a matter of local concern. The states have long exercised jurisdiction over industrial noise through industrial codes administered by the state labor department. Large numbers of state laws regarding noise pollution have been enacted. There are, nonetheless, still many gaps in state regulation. Cities, too, have responded to increased noise levels by enacting more laws.

Several remedies may be used in controlling the environment. A class action may be brought where a wrong has been committed against a group of persons so numerous that it is impractical to bring all the parties before the court. The class action is a potentially useful tool in the fight for a decent environment. The shareholder action is a special type of class action that shareholders of a corporation, as opposed to the general public, have a right to maintain against corporate management.

The common law doctrine of nuisance may be of some limited value in environmental litigation. A person whose property rights have been invaded can bring a private nuisance action. The law has long recognized the right of a private citizen to bring a tort action for a public nuisance. But to do so, he must show that the nuisance is public, that he has suffered special damages over and above ordinary damage caused to the public, and that his injury is different in kind from that of the general public. The individual confronted with a nuisance may seek money damages or equitable relief by injunction, or he can abate the nuisance by self-help.

The common law doctrine of trespass has also been used in environmental litigation as has a legal theory based on the tort of negligence.

One of the new remedies in environmental litigation is called "inverse condemnation." Where the government acts to seriously damage or materially diminish the value of property, the owner of the property may sue the government defendant for its full value, even where there has been no physical occupancy or formal taking through the power of eminent domain. Still, another new environmental remedy is based on the public trust doctrine. This doctrine states that the government has a duty as a trustee of the people to protect our nation's natural resources. If the government breaches its trust, court action may be instituted. The doctrine has been applied not only to public lands and waters, but to cases involving wildlife protection and public roads.

WHAT IS THE LAW ON MARRIAGE, WOMEN'S RIGHTS, CHILDREN, AND DIVORCE?

Marriage. Where common law marriage is still recognized in the United States, it is generally agreed that in order for the marriage to be valid, the parties must agree that they are man and wife; they must publicly live as man and wife in a mutual and open manner. Common law marriage, however, is on the decline in this country and at least 35 states do not recognize it. Even in the states where this type of marriage does exist, proving the existence of marriage can be difficult. In attempting to determine in a certain situation whether a common law marriage exists or not, the court is more likely to find that it exists where children have been born from the relationship, or where the parties have maintained their relationship for a long time prior to the death of one of the parties. The whole idea behind common law marriage is to treat as married those persons who have agreed to act as man and wife and who appear to be married.

Marriage has always been regulated in the United States by the government as a constitutional exercise of state power to "promote the general welfare." All states require the parties to procure a marriage license before the ceremony can take place. There is generally a waiting period ranging from one to five days between the application for the license and its issuance. Before the license will be issued, the parties must also submit to a physical examination and produce a physician's statement that they are free from V.D. Certain individuals, including civil officers and religious leaders, are authorized by statute to solemnize marriages. Since few states require any special form for the marriage ceremony, more and more couples are writing and using their own marriage vows. No particular place is required for the marriage ceremony in most states, but most states do require at least two witnesses. All states require recordation of the license or marriage certificate. A ceremonial marriage is valid notwithstanding the failure of the parties to consummate the marriage. Once there is proof of a contractual or common law marriage then the law presumes that the legal formalities of marriage were complied with; the parties had capacity to marry; the person who celebrated the marriage was authorized to do so; and the latest in a number of successive marriages is the valid one. However, these are rebuttable presumptions only, placing the burden of proof upon the person who attacks the validity of the marriage. In no event can a person be legally married to two persons at the same time. Thus, there is also a legal presumption that a marriage, once contracted, continues in force until it is proven to have ended. Where this presumption conflicts with the presumption concerning successive marriages, the latter prevails, but only so long as no convincing proof is offered rebutting it.

A proxy marriage is one that takes place in the absence of one or both of the parties. Proxy marriages are presently invalid, but have been limitedly approved in some states during times of war.

There exist special marriage laws regarding incest, nonage, venereal disease and impotence. Concerning incest, all states prohibit marriages between parent and child, brother and sister, and grandparent and grandchild. Most states forbid marriages between first cousins, uncles and nieces, and aunts and nephews. Such marriages are invalid.

Statutes typically provide that a man under 21 or a woman under 18 may marry only with the written consent of a parent or guardian. There is also a minimum age under which no marriage is valid. This is the area of nonage. A person below the minimum age who manages to get married may have the marriage annulled. Where the marriage is not annulled, and the couple live together until the underaged party reaches the minimum age of consent, the marriage becomes valid. If one party to a marriage is of age and one is not, the party of age may not have the marriage annulled. Only the underaged party may do so.

Under a few state laws, a person with a venereal disease has no capacity to get married. Where this is so, V.D. is a grounds for an annulment. Impotence (the permanent inability to copulate) is a grounds for annulment in many states. Under the common law, husbands were obligated to support their wives and the traditional roles of husband and wife were recognized. In about half the states, "Family Expense Acts" now impose the burden of family support on both parties. These statutes provide that family expenses are chargeable against the property of both spouses. The position of most of these states, however, is that the husband is still primarily liable for family expenses. The wife is liable only if the husband refuses or fails to pay.

At common law, the father was under no obligation to support his children. This rule, however, has been changed by statute in the United States, and now the father owes his offspring the duty of support. The mother, again, is liable only where the father fails. If a father fails in his support responsibilities, a child may sue him in a civil suit, or he may be criminally prosecuted. The husband is also liable, under support laws, for his wife's necessaries. The law is unsettled as to whether a husband must support a wife who has an independent income. The recent trend in the law is toward an equality of the sexes. Nearly all states require the close relatives of indigent persons to help out with their support if the relatives are able.

Consortium is a term used to describe all the incidents of a family relationship, including such things as the husband's rights to the wife's services, companionship, and sexual relations, as well as the wife's right to her husband's society, affection, and financial support. Consortium also embraces the parent-child relationship of mutual affection, companionship and love. Rights of consortium may be indirectly enforced by bringing a legal action for money damages against an interfering third party. The general rule is that one cannot enforce the rights of consortium by suing for specific enforcement or performance of those rights. A third party may be sued for "alienation of affection" where it is possible to prove that the third party acted to cause the spouse to transfer his or her affection and feeling away from the other spouse. Several states have abolished the alienation of affection suit considering that it produces bad social results. A negligent interference with the husband and wife relationship is also actionable in most states. Thus, a husband whose wife is injured might be able to maintain his own action for loss of consortium. A parent's interest in his or her child's society is also legally protected. If someone wrongfully takes a child from his or her parents, the parent may recover custody by means of habeas corpus. This is an order requiring a person to appear in court and show why he or she is holding someone, and, if there is no legal basis for doing so, to give up the custody.

Women's rights. In the past 150 years, the rights of women have changed drastically. Under the common law, an unmarried woman had few rights. She could make contracts and own property, and she could sue or be sued. However, she could not vote, hold public office, or sit on a jury. A married woman, at common law, had even fewer rights. Her personal property became her husband's and he was entitled to all profits of her lands. She could not make contracts, sue, or make a will. Today, these legal disabilities have been removed by statute. A woman can acquire, own, and transfer all kinds of property; she can make contracts, sue or be sued, make a will, testify in court, and she is responsible for all her own torts and crimes. All women have rights to vote, to hold office, to sit on juries, to engage in business and to keep their own earnings. But enforcement of many laws continues to be difficult. Women still face de facto discrimination in employment.

In 1972, Congress submitted an Equal Rights Amendment to the states for ratification. The proposed constitutional amendment guarantees that "equality of rights under the law shall not be abridged on account of sex." The purpose of the amendment is to eliminate all discrimination on the basis of sex. The Equal Rights Amendment has not yet been ratified by the states, but, if passed, will have the following effects. A uniform minimum marriage age for both sexes will probably be adopted by all legislatures. Wives will no longer have to adopt their husband's surnames if they don't want to (in most places this is already true). The wife will be assured the right to choose her own legal domicile instead of being forced to have the same legal domicile as her husband. A few laws will probably be changed so that one parent is not given preference in child custody disputes. Women will probably become subject to the draft. It is not certain whether or not women will be sent into combat if the E.R.A. is passed. Married women in the service will be eligible for the same fringe benefits as married men. A quicker movement toward equal pay and promotions can be expected for women in the job market. Women will probably lose any special benefits which have formerly been provided them. The social security regulations will change. But, it is not certain how the passage of the E.R.A. will change or affect the separation of sexes in restrooms, dorms, etc. Each spouse will continue to own and control his or her own property in most states. In community property states, the E.R.A. will demand equal control of property for the wife. States which grant widows a share in the husband's estate will have to grant equal rights to widowers. No schools will be able to be segregated according to sex. Tax supported schools won't be able to set any kind of admission standards which are different for men and women. Technical or trade schools will have to admit women. Sports competitions will be opened up to anyone qualified, regardless of sex.

As of 1980, a few of the needed 38 states had still not ratified the E. R.A. The battle between E.R.A. proponents and opponents is a close and heated one. The amendment is extremely controversial. Opponents think the E.R.A. threatens motherhood, the family, and woman's traditional position in society. Proponents believe the E.R.A. will wipe out laws which still sanction sex discrimination. The E.R.A. is an important campaign issue, and may or may not be passed.

Title IX of the Educational Amendments of 1972 states that equal educational opportunities should be available to students of either sex at any educational institution receiving federal assistance. Many complex legal brambles have grown out of this provision and the Department of Health, Education and Welfare has finally translated the provisions into specific regulations. A summary of the regulations follows.

All professional, graduate, and vocational schools must admit students without regard to sex. So must all public undergraduate schools. If a district keeps separate-sex high schools, it must provide equal facilities and courses to males and females. After admission, a school must treat students of both sexes equally if it wants to receive federal aid. There are exceptions for military and religious schools. Non-academic activities must not be segregated if they receive financial help from the school. Schools are free to maintain certain separate facilities for males and females, such as showers, housing, etc., but they must be of comparable quality. Scholarship money must be apportioned without regard to sex. Females must be subject to the same graduation requirements, the same rules, and the same discipline as males. Counseling must be equitable. Pregnancy must be treated as any other temporary disability. The regulations concerning athletics are the most controversial. They say that, if a school provides a sporting team for students of one sex and there is enough interest to form a team of the opposite sex, the school must do so. If too few women are interested to form a full team, and it is a noncontact sport, women must be permitted to try out for the men's team. Equal opportunity does not necessarily mean equal expenditures, however. HEW has pointedly ignored sex-biased textbooks in its regulations, arguing that it does not want to play "federal censor" in possible violation of the First Amendment.

Population control. The United States birthrate is at an all-time low. This is partly because families realize they cannot afford many children and partly because women are choosing to postpone or forget about having children. In spite of this, there still exists a population problem, and though not critical in the United States, of serious concern in the world. Population control is a difficult task to accomplish. A controversial subject, it stirs strong emotional response reflecting not only concern for ecology and the environment, but religious and political viewpoints as well. The country has taken many important steps toward controlling population in the past 15 years. In 1964, the Supreme Court overturned a state law prohibiting use and prescription of contraceptives. In 1972, the Court reversed the conviction of a defendant found guilty of supplying contraceptives to an unmarried woman. In 1969, the President called for the creation of a Commission on Population Growth to research population growth and family planning. In 1970, Congress passed an act establishing the commission and setting up a study on population problems.

The 1973 Supreme Court decisions on abortion drastically altered existing abortion law in the United States. Under the common law, abortion was not generally a crime. In the mid-1800's, the first criminal abortion laws were passed. Only therapeutic abortions were legal then. The laws became stricter and the penalties more severe as time went on. Illegal abortions increased in number and many deaths and injuries resulted from the work of illegal abortionists. Finally, a few states softened their abortion laws. This is where abortion stood in 1973 when the Supreme Court held unconstitutional an abortion law prohibiting almost all abortions. The Court decision was based on the constitutional right of privacy. The Court ruled that only at the end of the first trimester of pregnancy can the state regulate the abortion procedure, and only at the end of the second trimester can the state proscribe abortion. In 1973, in the Doe v. Wade case, the Court struck down an abortion law because it imposed regulations that were not reasonably related to the mother's health. The court decisions made clear that states cannot prohibit abortions nor can they set up procedural barriers that make abortions difficult to obtain. Abortion is a very sensitive topic and many people oppose the recent court decisions.

Anti-abortion groups believe that a fetus has a right to life. The anti-abortion groups have tried to have the Constitution amended making abortions illegal, but so far have failed. The Supreme Court has ruled that it is unconstitutional for a state to require the husband's consent to his wife's abortion, or to require parental consent in the case of a minor.

However, a woman on welfare is not entitled to have the government pay for her abortion.

In most states, there are abortion referral services to help out in counseling the pregnant woman who wants an abortion.

Illegitimate children. An illegitimate child is one born out of wedlock. Unfortunately, the illegitimate child has long been punished by the law in order to encourage marriage and legitimacy. Under the common law, for example, a father had no duty to support his illegitimate child unless he could be forced to acknowledge paternity by means of a paternity suit. The paternity suit proceeding is still retained in most of our states today, and it may be brought against a married man as well as a single man. Proof of paternity is very difficult in most cases, and when the paternity suit fails, the father has no duty of support. Even if the court decides that the man is the father of the child, the court will order him to pay monetary support expenses, but never anything more. Of course, the parents can always legitimize their illegitimate children by consent. The procedure for doing this varies from state to state. The illegitimate child suffered most because he had no common law right to inherit from his father. In most states, the child could inherit from his mother but not from his father. However, a recent Supreme Court decision struck down state laws prohibiting an illegitimate child from inheriting from his father, and now all children—legitimate and illegitimate—have equal rights of inheritance. In some states, all children are considered legitimate when born even though there is no proof as to who is the father.

Adoption. A legal adoption extinguishes all the relationship, rights, and duties existing between a child and his natural parents—and it creates rights and duties between the child and his adoptive ones. Adoption statutes are designed to protect the rights of the child, and the interests of both the real and adoptive parents. Adoption is an involved process, and the law on adoption may be divided into several categories. One category of adoption law is adoption with consent. Statutes typically provide that a legitimate child may be adopted only with the consent of both parents. Only the mother must consent to her illegitimate child's adoption. Another area of adoption law is adoption without consent. Statutes generally provide that children who have been abandoned or neglected by their parents can be put up for adoption without the parents' consent. The placement process in adoption is usually handled by a public or private child-placing agency. It involves obtaining consent from the natural parents, and finding a good home for the child. Adoptions may also be privately arranged. Private placements are risky, however, because of potential interferences between the natural parents and the adoptive ones. In order to adopt a child, the prospective parents must be financially secure adults in reasonably good health. Sometimes other factors are taken into account, such as marital status, age, race, and religion.

Adoption procedure involves several steps. The proceedings begin when the adoptive parents file a petition with the court. Next, a hearing in the judge's chambers is usually held. The judge must determine whether the adoptive parents are suitable to take the child. Most states require an investigation of adoptive parents, the results of which must be made available to the court. The judge must then decide whether he or she is in favor of adoption, and if so, will enter an interlocutory (temporary) decree which gives the adoptive parents custody of the child. Since the decree is interlocutory, it is still subject to change. In most states, the adoption decree becomes final after a period of time if the situation has worked out well for the child and the adoptive parents. But even where this time has passed, the child can be removed from the adoptive parents if his or her welfare so demands.

The results of adoption are these: the parents obtain legal custody; the child obtains a new name; the state issues a new birth certificate; the child acquires a right to inherit from his or her new parents; and the adopted child may recover for the wrongful death of the adoptive parents.

Equitable adoption occurs when a child lives with people who agree to care for the child but who never formally go through with an adoption. Sometimes, the child can still claim an inheritance based on the theory that the law should honor his or her "parents'" intent and treat the child as though he or she were formally adopted. Adults are sometimes adopted in order to establish a right of inheritance.

Divorce. There are several traditional grounds for divorce based on the fault of one of the parties. One of the traditional grounds for divorce is adultery. This grounds for divorce is seldom used anymore. Another traditional ground is desertion or abandonment by one of the parties. Cruelty was the most widely used traditional grounds for divorce for a long time before no-fault divorce. Living apart and separate can be grounds for divorce in many states. Other grounds for divorce include nonsupport, criminal conviction, insanity, etc.

The most significant change in divorce law has been the widespread addition of the no-fault and irreconcilable differences provisions in laws defining grounds for divorce. About two-thirds of the states now have no-fault divorce laws. The principle of fault of the parties is then abolished in deciding whether the marriage should be ended and in dividing the property.

A marriage wholly dissolved may still give rise to a continuing duty of support in the form of alimony. Alimony was originally designed to give the wife the support she was entitled to during marriage. Now, women are usually less dependent on their husbands financially, and so are awarded alimony less often. Courts take several factors into account in determining how much alimony to award. The husband's ability to pay is considered, as are the needs of the wife. The wife is generally considered to be entitled to an amount that will support her in the manner to which she has become accustomed during marriage. The fault of the parties is investigated in some (fault) states. The age, health, and length of marriage of the spouses are considered. Sometimes alimony is awarded to the husband if he has been dependent upon the wife for support. Divorce decrees often contain property settlements in addition to alimony orders. There are tax considerations whether the situation involves alimony, child support, or property settlement. Alimony is taxable money. The husband, however, may generally deduct any alimony payments made to his ex-wife. In order to qualify as taxable income to the wife, the alimony must be payable in periodic payments. Child support payments are not taxable to the wife or deductible to the husband. Generally, the parent who has custody of the child most of the time is entitled to the tax exemption for dependent children.

The father is primarily responsible for support of the children unless he becomes unable, then the duty falls upon the mother. The duty of support ends when the child becomes of age.   In determining the award, the court looks at the family's standard of living before the divorce.

Alimony decrees are modifiable only upon proof of changed circumstances.   Decrees have been modified in face of the wife's remarriage, the husband's remarriage, a change in either the needs of the wife or the income of the husband, or the death of the husband.   Where the husband refuses to meet his alimony or child support obligations, the court will enforce its order with a contempt proceeding.

When a family breaks up, and custody of the children must be decided, the most important consideration is the child's welfare.   If both parents have died, the courts will usually appoint a guardian.   If the parents have named a guardian by will, their choice will usually be honored.   In a custody battle between divorced parents, each will be given an opportunity to be heard before a custody order is made.   In deciding which parent should have custody, courts consider several factors.   In nearly all states, both spouses have an equal right to custody.   Courts frequently conclude that a child should be placed with the parent of the same sex.   When one of the parents is morally unfit, the court is likely to award custody to the other.   If a spouse has remarried, the courts ask how willing the new spouse would be to accept the children.   The court considers the health, age, home conditions and ability to care for children of both parties.   Wherever possible, courts like to keep brothers and sisters together.   Some courts award custody to the parent who plans to remain within the state.   The wishes of the child are sometimes considered, especially where the child is older.

The main objective of the court is to do what is best for the child. The custody order may be modified if the court thinks it is best for the child's welfare.

Appendix B

GLOSSARY

Abandoned Property. Property intentionally and permanently given up by its owner.

Abatement. Proportionate reduction of testamentary gifts within a particular class.

Abstract of Title. A summary of the record title of real property, including all outstanding liens, mortgages, judgments, and similar claims.

Acceptance. Response to an offer in the manner requested by the offeror; valid and effective only if it is unequivocal and unqualified.

Accession. A means of acquiring ownership or title to personal property that is "added to" property already in existence.

Accommodation Party. An additional party who indorses an instrument thereby becoming secondarily liable for repayment if the maker fails to pay.

Accord and Satisfaction. An agreement wherein a party with an existing duty of performance under a contract promises to do something other than perform the duty as a means of discharging the contractual obligation.

Account. Any right to payment for goods sold or leased or for services rendered which is not evidenced by an instrument or chattel paper, whether or not it has been earned by performance.

Account Stated. Where a debtor and creditor who have entered into a series of transactions agree upon an account balance, the debtor agreeing to pay the stated amount, and the creditor agreeing to accept the amount as payment in full.

Accretion. Acquiring property through the deposit of new soil or through the gradual receding of the water so as to expose soil already existing there.

Acknowledge. To declare a will as genuine.

Acknowledgment. A formal declaration made by the grantor in front of a public officer that he or she has signed a deed and is transferring the property voluntarily.

Ademption by Extinction. The destruction of a specific bequest or devise that occurs when the specified personal property or realty is not to be found in the testator's estate upon his or her death.

Ademption by Satisfaction. Where the testator, subsequent to execution of the will, makes an inter vivos gift to the designated beneficiary, intending the gift to satisfy in whole or in part the testamentary bequest (only in cases of general and demonstrative bequest).

Ademption Pro Tanto. The partial destruction of a specific bequest or devise that occurs when a portion of the specified personal property or realty is missing, resulting with the beneficiary being entitled to whatever portion is left.

Adhesion Contract. A one-sided contract in which the offeror and offeree occupy substantially unequal bargaining positions. The offeree is forced to adhere to the terms dictated by the offeror in order to acquire some essential property or service.

Administrative Law. Law resulting from the work of an administrative agency.

Administrator. The person who will administer an estate if there is no will.

Advance. A capital contribution by a partner beyond the amount the partner agreed to contribute in the partnership agreement.

Advancement. An inter vivos gift made by a property owner (who later dies intestate) to a child or grandchild with the intention that the gift constitute prepayment toward the donee's intestate portion of the decedent's estate.

Adverse Possession. A method of acquiring ownership of real property by merely possessing the property in a manner prescribed by statute for a specific period of time.

Affidavit. A sworn statement.

"Affirmative Action". A program initiated by the federal government to eliminate discrimination in employment against women and minorities. By threatening to terminate supply and research contracts, the federal government has pressured employers to take specific steps to hire and promote minorities and women in percentages roughly equal to their representation in the local community.

Affirmative Warranty. Warranty stating a condition that need exist only at the time the contract is entered into.

Affirmative Waste. A voluntary act on the part of the tenant that damages the premises.

After-Acquired Property Clause. A clause in a security agreement allowing the security interest to extend to the debtor's after-acquired property.

Agent. A person who is authorized to make contracts on behalf of another called a principal.

"All-Line" Companies. Companies that sell life insurance as well as casualty and fire and marine insurance.

Alluvion. The landowner's gaining of land as new soil is gradually deposited from the water and onto his or her property.

Ameliorating Waste. A material change in the use of the land which improves the land. However, it is unauthorized and so wrongful.

Antitrust Laws. Laws used to curb anti-competitive behavior on the part of big business.

Apparent Authority. Authority that results from an appearance of authority created by the principal.

Arbitration Clause. A contract provision providing for arbitration of disputes without going to court.

Artful Accounting. The incomplete disclosure of information or the hiding of information so that an investor or creditor looking at the financial report is not likely to see it.

Articles of Partnership. A formal, written partnership agreement.

Assigned Risk Plan. A means of providing auto insurance for bad risk drivers.

Assignee. Party who receives the rights of an existing contract that is transferred.

Assignment. A transfer of rights under an existing contract from one of the original parties to a third party.

Assignment for the Benefit of Creditors. A debtor's voluntarily transfer of all his assets (with the exclusion of exempt property) to another party who is given the job of liquidating the assets and distributing the proceeds to the creditors.

Assignor. The party who transfers the rights of an existing contract.

Assumption of a Mortgage. A purchaser takes land and assumes the mortgage when he or she pays the mortgagor the value of the land less the amount of the mortgage debt owing, and also promises the mortgagor that he or she will pay the mortgage debt.

Attempt to Monopolize. The employment of methods, means, and practices which would, if successful, accomplish monopolization.

Authority by Necessity. In an emergency situation where someone is injured, a servant may have real authority by necessity to summon medical aid on behalf of his or her employer, binding the employer to pay for the aid.

Automobile Medical Payments Insurance. Insurance that reimburses the insured and others riding in his or her automobile for personal injury resulting from an automobile accident.

Avulsion. A sudden change in the land that does not result in a change of ownership or boundary.

Baggage. Those items that a passenger takes on a common carrier for his or her personal use and convenience either during the journey or afterwards.

Bailee. The party in possession of bailed property.

Bailment. The rightful possession of another's personal property.

Bailment Container Rule. The rule that where a bailed chattel is a closed container or other item containing property not visible to the bailee, the bailee is responsible for the chattel's contents only where he or she should know as a reasonable person that the contents are present.

Bailment for the Sole Benefit of the Bailee. A bailment that benefits only the bailee. The bailee is required to exercise extraordinary care and is liable for slight negligence.

Bailment for the Sole Benefit of the Bailor. A bailment that benefits only the bailor. The bailee must exercise slight care and is liable for gross negligence.

Bailor. The owner of bailed property.

Bargain and Sale Deed. A deed purporting to convey the grantor's interest in land, but making no promise he or she has good title to the property.

Bargain Theory of Consideration. The most common basis for enforcing promises. Bargain theory is what is usually meant when the term consideration is used. It requires two things: (1) the consideration must be the motive for the promise, and the promise the motive for the consideration; and (2) the consideration must be legally sufficient (i. e., either a benefit to the promisor or a detriment to the promisee).

Bearer. An unnamed payee.

Bearer Paper. An instrument that is made payable "to bearer" and can be freely negotiated without indorsement.

Bed-Bug Letter. A written notice from the SEC that a registration statement is not acceptable.

Benefit. When the promisor legally bargains for and receives a return promise or act that he or she was not previously entitled to receive.

Benefit-of-the-Bargain Rule. The rule of damages which awards the injured party the difference between the value actually received and the value that would have been received had the subject matter of the agreement been as represented.

Bequest. A gift of personal property under a will.

Bilateral Contract. A promise for a promise. The offerer promises to do something in exchange for the offeree's return promise to do something or not to do something.

Bill of Lading. A document evidencing the receipt of goods for shipment issued by a person engaged in the business of transporting or forwarding goods.

Binder. An oral agreement between applicant and insurer, with regard to insurance other than life, that the applicant will be insured temporarily during the period between application for and issuance of the policy.

Blank Indorsement. An indorsement by a named payee wherein the named payee signs his or her name on the back of the instrument, converting it from order to bearer paper.

Blended Trust. A trust designed by its terms to benefit a group of people rather than individual beneficiaries.

Blue Sky Laws. Securities laws designed to protect people from promoters of worthless securities and from deceit and fraud in securities transactions.

Bodily Injury Liability Insurance. Insurance that protects the insured and those who drive the insured's car with his or her permission against liability to third parties who suffer bodily injury as a result of the negligent operation of the insured's motor vehicle.

Bona Fide Purchaser. One who takes property for value and in good faith, without knowledge or notice that there is anything wrong with the title or that there are any defenses to its validity.

Bond. A borrower's written promise given in return for money to pay a fixed sum of money at a specified future time, with stated interest payable at fixed intervals.

Breach of Contract. A failure by a party, under contractual obligation, to perform at the time and place called for in the agreement.

Broker. A person engaged in the business of effecting transactions in securities for the account of others.

Broker's Transaction. Any transaction by a broker in which the broker does not more than execute a customer's order to buy or sell securities.

Bulk Transfer. Any transfer in bulk and not in the ordinary course of the transferor's business of a major part of the materials, supplies, merchandise, or other inventory.

By-Laws. Written rules decided upon by corporate directors that govern corporate activities and operations.

Cancellation. Marking an instrument (note, draft, check, etc.) "paid" on its face so as to void any further liability on the instrument.

Capital Surplus. Any amount paid for par value stock over and beyond its par value.

Capture. Obtaining the identified goods from the seller without going to court.

Cashier's Check. A check issued by the bank itself.

C. & F. A maritime shipment contract where the buyer promises to pay a price for the goods that includes their cost and freight charges.

C.I.F. A maritime shipping contract where the buyer promises to pay a price for the goods that includes their cost, the freight charges, and insurance for the goods until they are delivered.

C.O.D. Means collect on delivery with the buyer being required to pay for the goods and their transportation before delivery is made.

Certificate of Deposit. A writing that is an acknowledgment by a bank of receipt of money with an engagement to repay it along with interest to the order of a payee or to bearer.

Certified Check. A check that is formally accepted by the bank which makes the bank primarily liable on the instrument.

Cestui que Trust. A named or identifiable beneficiary who is capable of enforcing the trust terms.

Champerty. An illegal bargain in which one person pays another's costs and expenses in bringing a case to court with the understanding that if the party bringing the case is successful, the party putting up the money will share in the proceeds.

Charitable Trust. A trust created for a charitable purpose; the trustor must intend to transfer a trust res to a trustee to be held for the benefit of another.

Chattel. An article of personal property.

Chattel Mortgage. A security interest in the debtor's personal property that does not require a transfer of possession of the property to the creditor.

Chattel Paper. Any writing that sets forth the terms of a security agreement and contains the debtor's promise to pay the secured party.

Check. A draft drawn on a bank and payable on demand.

Chose in Action. An intangible personal property right; something that has no material substance.

Chose in Possession. A tangible personal property right; something with material substance.

Churning. The illegal act of a broker-dealer inducing a customer to engage in an excessive number of transactions so as to generate more and more commissions for the broker-dealer.

Clayton Act. Federal act passed in 1914 prohibiting certain practices if they might substantially lessen competition. (Price discrimination, mergers and consolidations, tie in sales, exclusive dealing arrangements are all prohibited where they are found to be anti-competitive in nature.)

Closed Shop. Union membership is a condition of employment; membership is required before hiring.

Closely Held Corporation. A corporation whose shares have not been offered or sold to the public, but are held by a relatively small group of private shareholders.

Codicil. A properly executed amendment; a legally effective amendment to a will.

Co-insurance Clause. Clause in a fire policy requiring the insured to maintain a certain amount of insurance on the property.

Collateral Note. A note secured by a pledge of personal property.

Collateral Promise. A promise to discharge or answer for the debt of another.

Collecting Bank. Any bank handling the item for collection, except the payor bank.

"Collection Guaranteed". Words that an indorser may add to his or her indorsement promising that if the instrument is not paid when due, he or she will pay the instrument provided that the holder reduces his or her claim against the maker or acceptor to judgment and the judgment is returned unsatisfied, or the maker or acceptor has become insolvent, or it is otherwise apparent that it is useless to proceed against the maker or acceptor.

Collective Bargaining. The settlement of industrial disputes through peaceful negotiation between employers and employee representatives.

Collision Insurance. Insurance that compensates the insured for collision damage done to his or her own automobile.

Co-maker. An additional party who signs on the front of an instrument, thereby becoming primarily responsible along with the maker for repaying the note.

Commercial Paper. Checks, drafts, and notes (negotiable instruments) serving as basic means of payment in most commercial transactions.

Commercial Reasonableness. An objective standard measured by the sound business judgment of reasonable persons familiar with the customary practices in the type of transaction involved.

Commercial Tort. Socially unreasonable business conduct that adversely affects a consumer, competitor, or other party.

Common Carrier. One engaged in transporting goods for the general public without discrimination and for compensation.

Common Law. "Unwritten", judgemade rules that guide a judge in making a decision or settling a dispute.

Common Stock. The ordinary stock of a corporation.

Compensatory Damages. Damages designed to compensate or recompense the injured party for his or her loss.

Competent Witness. A witness old enough (*no* minimum age) and of sufficient mental capacity to understand the nature of what he or she is witnessing.

Composition of Creditors. A contract between the debtor and his creditors, and between the creditors themselves, that each creditor will accept a lesser sum immediately in full payment of the total amount owing.

Comprehensive Physical Damage Insurance. Insurance that reimburses for loss or damage to an automobile resulting from damage other than collision—theft, fire, vandalism, windstorm, etc.

Compulsory Subjects of Collective Bargaining. Areas where bargaining is required by statute.

Concealment. An active effort to hide facts; an affirmative act intended to prevent another from learning a fact significant or relevant to a contemplated transaction. With regard to insurance, an insured's intentional failure to disclose a material fact.

Concurrent Ownership. Owning real or personal property with one or more other individuals.

Condition. A fact or event, the happening or non-happening of which creates or terminates a promisor's duty of performance under a contract.

Condition Concurrent. Conditions, either express or implied by law, that must be performed at the same time.

Condition of Defeasance. The immediate and automatic extinguishment of the mortgagee's security interest upon payment of the mortgage debt.

Condition Implied in Fact. An unstated condition that the parties would have expressly agreed to had they thought about it at the time of entering into the contract.

Condition Precedent. A condition that must occur before a party will have an absolute duty to perform under a contract.

Condition Subsequent. An event the happening of which terminates any further duty of performance under a contract.

Conditional Binding Receipt. A written memorandum of the essential terms of the life insurance contract that provides that the insurance coverage is effective as of the date of application so long as certain conditions are met.

Conditional Indorsement. An indorsement requiring the indorsee to perform a duty owed to the indorser.

Conditional Sale. A sale of goods in which the seller of goods sells tangible personal property on credit to a buyer, with the seller retaining title to the merchandise until the purchase price is paid in full.

Conforming Goods. Goods in accord with the terms of the contract.

Confusion. Title to personal property may be acquired by confusion when goods owned by different parties are intermingled so that the property of each is no longer distinguishable.

Conscious Presence Test. "Test" of a witness's presence. Satisfied by the testator seeing or hearing what is being done, the testator being conscious of what is occuring and the signing being a continuous transaction that takes but a brief moment of time.

Consensual Lien. A lien that arises by *agreement* between the parties.

Consequential Damages. Damages directly caused by the wrongful act.

Conservator. A special guardian appointed by petition of the ward when the ward feels unable, whether for physical, mental, or emotional reasons, to properly care for his or her own business or property.

Consideration. The requirement that a party either do something that he or she was not already bound to do, or that the party promise to do something or not to do something that he or she was not already bound to do or to refrain from doing. The second element required for a valid contract.

Consignee. The person to whom goods are shipped by a common carrier.

Consignment. A bailment arrangement in which the owner of goods delivers them to a bailee with authority to sell the goods on behalf of the owner.

Consolidation. A consolidation occurs when a new corporation is formed from one or more existing corporations: the new or consolidated corporation absorbs both existing corporations which cease to exist as separate entities.

Conspicuous. A term or clause is conspicuous when it is so written that a reasonable person against whom it is to operate ought to have noticed it.

Constructive Bailment. A bailment where the bailor loses the property and the finder takes possession of it.

Constructive Eviction. When a landlord so seriously interferes with the tenant's use and enjoyment of the land that the tenant is forced to leave the property.

Constructive Notice. Inferred or implied notice.

Constructive Trust. A trust that is neither express nor implied but is created by law to prevent a wrong or remedy an injustice.

Contest a Will. To challenge the validity of a will.

Contingent Fees. Payment arrangement wherein an attorney takes a percentage of any recovery in a legal action.

Contingent Remainder. A remainder granted to one or more unascertained individuals or created subject to a condition precedent.

Contract. Legally recognized promises or bargains made by two or more persons and including all rights and duties resulting from the promises or bargains.

Contract Under Seal. A formal contract binding because of its form, needing no consideration at common law to be binding. It required a sufficient writing, a seal, and a delivery.

Contractual Capacity. The power that a person has to enter into a contract.

Conversion. A serious interference with another's personal property. This is an intentional tort.

Conversion Rights. Rights of preferred stockholders to convert their stock to common stock at certain times or under certain circumstances.

Corporate Charter. A written instrument in certificate form creating the corporation and permitting it to operate.

Corporate Opportunity Doctrine. A director or officer cannot take personal advantage of a business opportunity that would be advantageous to the corporation without first offering the corporation a right of first refusal.

Corporate Promoter. A person who participates in forming the corporation, selling its stock, and organizing its initial business activities.

Corporation. An artificial being, invisible, intangible and existing only in contemplation of law. Being the mere creature of law, it possesses only those properties which the charter of its creation confers upon it.

Counteroffer. Response to an offer in which the offeree proposes his or her own definite conditional undertaking containing terms different from or at variance with those of the original offer.

Covenant. An absolute and unconditional promise to perform; a promise to do something or not to do something.

Cover. The purchase of substitute goods in the event the seller breaches the contract.

Creative Accounting. Structuring transactions so as to create a false picture of financial health.

Creditor Beneficiary Contract. Contract in which the promisee's primary intent in entering into the agreement is to discharge an obligation owed or believed to be owed to the third party.

Cumulative Preferred Stock. Stock in which the shareholder's right to the stated dividend will carry over to the next year (and subsequent years) until it is paid.

Cumulative Voting. Under cumulative voting, each share of common stock has as many votes as there are directors to be elected. And a shareholder can distribute his or her votes among the candidates in any way that he or she chooses.

Current Profits. The profits of the current year.

Custody. Actual physical control of thep roperty, but no intent to control.

Dealer of Securities. Any person who is engaged in the business of offering, selling, dealing, or otherwise trading in securities issued by another.

Death Taxes. Transfer taxes imposed by the government upon the estate of the deceased, taxing the transfer of the decedent's property either to his or her beneficiaries, heirs and/or surviving cotenants.

Debenture. A bond that is not secured by specific assets.

Debtor. The party who must pay or otherwise perform the obligation embodied in the security agreement.

Dedication. The voluntary transfer of privately owned land to the government for a public purpose.

Deed. An instrument required by law to evidence the transfer of real property by gift, contract of sale, or contract of exchange.

Deed of Trust. A security device in which the borrower deeds the land to a third party (the trustee) who holds title to the land solely for the purpose of returning it to the borrower once the mortgage is paid off.

De Facto Corporation. A corporation that is not organized in compliance with all statutory requirements, but one in which the incorporators made a good faith attempt to comply with the statute, and made some actual use of the corporation.

Defendant. The party being sued.

De Jure Corporation. One that is organized in compliance with the statutory requirements for incorporation.

Demonstrative Bequest. A gift of personal property, usually money, that is to be paid first out of a particular fund, and, second, out of the general assets of the estate to the extent that the particular fund is insufficient.

Depositary Bank. The bank where the check is deposited.

Deposited Acceptance Rule. Rule which states that, unless the offeror expressly provides to the contrary in his or her offer, the offeree's acceptance of the offer is effective when properly dispatched.

Depreciation. The decline in value of an asset as the result of wear and tear or the like.

Dereliction. The gaining of land as water gradually recedes from the land, thus exposing soil already there.

Derivative Suit. An action brought by one or more shareholders on behalf of the corporation to recover damages for the corporation.

Destination Contract. The seller must deliver the goods to a particular destination and he or she bears the risk and expense until such delivery.

Determinable Fee. A qualified fee that conditions the grantee's use of the land by words such as "so long as" or "until".

Detriment. When the promisee does something or promises to do something that he or she was not previously legally bound to do or if he or she refrains from doing something or promises to refrain from doing something that he or she has a legal right to do.

Devise. A gift of real property under a will.

Direct Beneficiary. One who benefits directly from the contract and who acquires rights of enforcement as well.

Disabling Restraint. A provision in a transfer of land that prohibits further alienation of the land. This is illegal.

Discharge of Contract Duties. When a person who enters into a valid contract performs the contract obligations. Other methods of discharge include objective impossibility, novation, or the occurrence of a condition subsequent.

Discharged. Freed of any further obligation to perform his or her contract obligations.

Discharging Bond. Bond used to terminate an attachment in which the debtor promises to pay the claim if judgment is entered against him (the issuer of the bond promises to pay if the debtor does not).

Disclaimer of Warranty. When the seller absolves or tries to absolve him or herself from liability on the basis of warranty.

Disclosed Agency. An agency relationship in which the third party who deals with the agent has knowledge of the existence of the agency and of the identity of the principal.

Discount Note. Note where the maker promises to pay the lender in installments a lump sum representing both loan principal and interest; the maker receives a cash amount less than the face value of the note because the interest to be paid is deducted from the face value and only the balance remaining is given to the maker.

Dishonored. A holder takes an instrument with knowledge that it has been dishonored when the holder knows or has reason to know that demand for acceptance or payment of the instrument has been properly made upon the party expected to pay, and acceptance or payment has been refused.

Disparagement. A commercial tort in which false assertions are made about another's product with intent to injure the other's business.

Dissolution of a Partnership. The change in the relation of the partners caused by any partner ceasing to be associated in the carrying on as distinguished from the winding up of the business.

Distraint. A landlord's right to lock a tenant out of the rented real property.

Distress. A landlord's right to seize his tenant's personal property.

Divestment. A reducing or taking away of an interest in land.

Division of Markets. Any agreement among businesses performing similar services or dealing in similar products to divide up and share the available market.

Doctrine of Cy Pres. A special charitable trust rule which states that the courts may apply the charitable trust funds to another similar charitable purpose in the event the original trust purpose cannot be carried out.

Doctrine of Finality. Payment or acceptance of any instrument is final in favor of a holder in due course, or a person who has in good faith changed his position in reliance on the payment. (Except for liability for breach of warranty on presentment.)

Doctrine of Impracticability. A small minority of courts allow discharge of contract duties even in the event of subjective impossibility if performance of the contract would be many times more difficult or expensive than the parties originally contemplated.

Doctrine of Prior Appropriation. A rule of law stating the first riparian owner to appropriate the water is entitled to use it all.

Doctrine of Respondeat Superior. The rule of law that a master or employer must respond in damages for all torts committed by his or her employees while acting within the scope of his or her employment.

Doctrine of Retainer. The rule of law that a monetary bequest to a debtor of the testator should be reduced by the amount of the debt outstanding.

Doctrine of Riparian Rights. A rule of law stating that a riparian owner is entitled to the flow of the river or stream water in its natural condition to, by, through, and over his or her land, free from unreasonable diminution in quantity and free from unreasonable pollution in quality.

Document of Title. Includes bill of lading, dock warrant, dock receipt, warehouse receipt or order for the delivery of goods, and also any other document which in the regular course of business is treated as adequately evidencing that the person in possession of it is entitled to receive, hold, and dispose of the document and the goods it covers.

Domiciled Paper. An instrument that has a definite due date and is payable at a special place.

Domitae Naturae. Domestic animals.

Donee. One receiving the gift.

Donee Beneficiary Contract. Contract in which the promisee's primary intent in entering into the agreement is to confer a gift on the third party.

Donor. One making the gift.

Double Indemnity Clause. Clause in a life insurance policy providing that the amount of insurance will double if the insured dies as the result of an accident within 90 days of the accident.

Draft. A writing that is a negotiable order to pay.

Due Diligence. The standard of reasonableness required of a prudent man in the management of his own property.

Duress. Any physical or mental coercion that deprives a person of his or her own free will and forces him or her to act contrary to his or her free will.

Duty. A legal obligation to act or refrain from acting.

Earned Surplus. Undistributed profits from previous years.

Easement. This is a genuine, though nonpossessory, interest in real property. It is a right to use another's land that cannot be revoked by the landowner.

Easement Appurtenant. This involves two adjoining parcels of land in which the dominant estate is in some way benefited by the servient estate.

Easement by Necessity. This arises when an easement is strictly necessary to the use or enjoyment of land.

Easement by Prescription. This is acquiring an easement by adverse use of the property.

Easement in Gross. This involves one parcel of land belonging to someone other than the easement holder, and benefits the holder personally.

Eminent Domain. The right of the government to take private property for public use by means of a condemnation proceeding.

Encroachment. The trespass on land of a physical structure or fixture.

Endowment Insurance. A contract wherein an insurer promises to pay an insured a lump sum of money when the insured reaches a specific age, and if the insured fails to reach that age, to pay the lump sum to the insured's beneficiary.

Entrepreneur Theory. Theory that since the employer has created the risk of harm by hiring the employee to work for him, he should assume full financial responsibility if the employee's tortious conduct, that is within the scope of his or her employment, causes injury to a third party.

Entrust. To aquiesce in any retention of possession of the goods by the merchant.

Entruster Rule. Any entrusting of possession of goods to a merchant who deals in goods of that kind gives him the power to transfer all rights of the entruster to a buyer in the ordinary course of business.

Equity of Redemption. The right of a mortgagor who has defaulted to reacquire ownership of the land subject to the mortgage by paying the debt in full.

Escheat. When you die without a will and without heirs, your property passes (escheats) to the state.

Estop. To deny someone the ability to assert a particular fact.

Estoppel by Deed. The rule of law that a person who purports to convey an interest in real property that he or she does not own will be later "estopped" from denying transfer of that interest to the grantee if the grantor subsequently acquires ownership of the land.

Estovers. The use of natural resources for repair maintenance.

Exchange. The difference between the values of two currencies from different countries.

Exclusive Dealing Contract. Contract wherein a buyer and seller agree to sell the goods of the seller in a particular area or under franchise.

Exculpatory Clause. A contract provision whereby one party to a contract agrees as part of the contract not to hold the other party liable for his or her negligent misconduct.

Executor. The person who will administer an estate if there is a will.

Executory Interest. Any presently owned future interest that does not qualify as a reversion, remainder, a possibility of reverter, or a right of re-entry for condition broken.

Express Condition. A condition that is explicitly stated by the parties.

Express Contract. An oral or written contract.

Express Trust. A trust that comes into existence when a party externally manifests an intent to create a trust.

Express Warranty. Any affirmation of fact, and any promise or description pertaining to the goods in question, that is made orally or in writing.

Ex-ship. A destination contract where the risk of loss passes to the buyer when the goods are unloaded at the specified destination.

Extended Coverage. Insurance coverage, beyond the normal coverage under a fire policy, at an added cost for such perils as hail, explosion, riot, aircraft damage, smoke damage, vandalism, etc.

Extension. An extension allows the debtor to pay his creditors in full, but over a period of time extended beyond the original due date.

Extrinsic Facts Doctrine. Doctrine providing that a testator may determine beneficiaries or their interests by reference in a will to extrinsic acts or events so long as the acts or events have an independent legal significance apart from the will itself.

F.A.S. Means free alongside and a seller who agrees to ship F.A.S. must deliver the goods free of expense to the buyer alongside the vessel on which they are to be loaded.

F.O.B. Free on board.

Factor. A consignee in the business of selling goods on consignment (also called a commission merchant).

Featherbedding. The practice of forcing employers to hire or retain more workers than the employer needs to operate his business.

Federal Reserve System. Created by the Federal Reserve Act of 1913, this system establishes monetary and credit policy throughout the United States.

Federal Trade Commission. Administrative agency broadly authorized to enforce the antitrust laws, including both the Sherman and the Clayton Acts. The FTC may identify and restrain any anticompetitive business or corporate conduct.

Fee Simple Absolute. A possessory estate that has the potential of lasting forever; the maximum interest one can have in land (the whole bundle of sticks).

Fee Simple Subject to a Condition Subsequent. A qualified fee that conditions the grantee's use of the land by words such as "on condition that", "but if", or "provided that".

Ferae Naturae. Wild animals.

Fertile Octogenarian Rule. For purposes of the rule against perpetuities, every single person is presumed capable of producing children.

Feudalism. A system of real property ownership and control instituted by William the Conqueror.

Fiduciary. A person who has a legal duty to act primarily for the benefit of another with whom he or she stands in a position of responsibility, trust and confidence.

Financial Responsibility Laws. State laws requiring drivers involved in accidents to furnish proof of their financial responsibility (usually by purchasing insurance or by posting a bond) as a condition to continued driving in the state.

Financing Statement. A brief statement describing the collateral subject to a security agreement. It is designed to put the debtor's creditors on notice that a security interest is in effect as to certain of the debtor's property.

Firm Offer. Written offer to buy or sell goods made and signed by a merchant and containing an express promise that the offer will be kept open for a period of time.

Fixture. An article, once personal property, that has become so closely connected to real property that it becomes a part of the land.

Floating Lien. A security agreement in which there is a constant turnover of collateral, with the security interest resting on a shifting stock of goods or accounts.

Forced Sale. A sale of property required by law to satisfy a debt or other obligation of the seller.

Forced Share. The statutory right of a spouse to a specific fraction of his or her decedent spouse's real and personal property.

Foreclosure Suit. A court action brought by the mortgagee to obtain a judge's order stating that the mortgagor's equity of redemption will be cut off if it is not exercised within a specified period of time.

Forgery. Unauthorized signature.

Fraternal Society. A nonprofit organization established for the benefit of its members.

Fraudulent Conveyance. A conveyance that is intended to delay, hinder, or defraud creditors; it is void and of no effect against the persons defrauded, hindered, or delayed.

Freehold Estate. An interest in land of potentially infinite or lifetime duration.

Friendly Fire. An intentional fire that remains under control; usually this is not covered in a policy unless by special endorsement.

Fructus Industriales. Annual crops produced by labor as opposed to growing naturally.

Fructus Naturales. Trees, bushes, etc. that do not require annual cultivation.

Frustration of Purpose. The rule that an event may so change or destroy the purpose and value of a performance that, even though performance is still possible, the duty of performance will be discharged.

Fully Executory Contract. A contract wherein both parties have yet to perform.

Fungible Goods. Goods of the same quality and value, any one unit of which is the same as any other unit, which are customarily sold by weight and measure.

Future-Advances Clause. A clause in a security agreement allowing the security interest to cover additional loans to be made in the future by the secured party.

Future Interest. An interest in land that is presently owned, but possession of which is postponed to some future date.

Futures. A transaction in futures occurs where a person contracts to deliver, in the future, goods that he or she does not own at the time of contracting.

General Agent. An agent authorized to contract for more than a single transaction and/or a continuing period of time.

General Bequest. A gift of personal property of fixed or calculable value that may be satisfied out of any of the general assets of a decedent's estate.

General Devise. A gift of real property of fixed or calculable value that may be satisfied out of any of the general assets of a decedent's estate.

General Lien. A lien that secures payment of any and all debts owed by the debtor to the secured party creditor.

General Plan Restrictions. Restrictions placed upon all lots within a single subdivision as part of a general plan to benefit all lot owners.

General Warranty Deed. A deed transferring the land to a grantee and warranting that the grantor has good title to the property.

Gift. A voluntary transfer of ownership of property without consideration.

Gift Causa Mortis. A conditional gift of personal property made by a person anticipating imminent death.

Good Faith. Honesty in fact in the conduct or transaction concerned.

Good Record Title. Marketable title based on public land records.

Goods. All things which are movable at the time of identification to the contract for sale, including animals, their unborn young, growing crops, timber, and other things to be severed from land or realty.

Government Creditor. Any government entity to which a debt is owed, whether the debt arises out of a contract with the government, or is based on a tax owing.

Grantor Trust. Trust created when a taxpayer in a high tax bracket reduces his or her income tax liability by placing income producing property into trust for the benefit of a family member or close friend who is in a much lower tax bracket. (Trust must be for at least ten years.)

Gratuitous Bailment. A bailment not supported by consideration.

Group Boycott. Any agreement among a group of competitors not to deal with a person or firm outside the group.

Guardian. In a guardianship, the party appointed to look out for the ward's interests.

Guardianship. A legal relationship created by the courts to protect and manage the person and/or property of a living person who is too young, too old, too ill, or too incompetent to handle his or her affairs.

Half-truths. Disclosure of part of the facts; an incomplete statement of facts.

Holder. A person who is in possession of an instument drawn, issued or indorsed to him or to his order or to bearer or in blank.

Holder in Due Course. A holder who takes a negotiable instrument for value, in good faith and without notice that it is overdue or has been dishonored or that there is any defense against or claim to it on the part of any person.

Holographic Will. A will written entirely in the testator's own handwriting.

Homeowners' Policy. Combines fire insurance with extended coverage including coverage for loss from theft, glass breakage, collapse of building, accidental overflow of water or heating from plumbing or heating systems, and freezing perils. This also provides property owners with liability insurance for protection against claims of bodily injury and property damage asserted by parties coming onto the land.

Honorary Trust. A trust created for a noncharitable purpose with no specific designated beneficiary capable of compelling enforcement of the trust.

Horizontal Restraint of Trade. An agreement between competitors in the same level of industry to eliminate or lessen the competition between or among themselves.

Hostile Fire. An accidental fire or an intentional one that has escaped, broken out, or become uncontrollable.

Hotel Guest. One who takes up quarters at a hotel or motel intending to live there but temporarily.

Hotelkeeper. Anyone in the business of providing living accommodations for transient persons.

Identification of Goods. Selection of the specific goods to be sold under a contract of sale.

Illegal Subjects-Collective Bargaining. Areas forbidden to the employer and union who cannot bargain here because it would be illegal to do so.

Illusory Promise. A "promise" where, in actuality, the promisor promises nothing, undertaking no obligation and setting no limit on his or her future course of conduct.

Implied in Fact Contract. A contract in which the mutual assent is manifested by conduct alone.

Implied Trust. A trust that arises by operation of law when a party who transfers property truly intends to create a trust, but fails to externally manifest or express such intent.

Implied Warranty Against Patent or Trademark Infringement. A seller who is a merchant regularly dealing in goods of the kind warrants that the goods shall be free of the rightful claim of any third person by way of infringement or the like; but a buyer who furnishes specifications to the seller must hold the seller harmless against any such claim which arises out of compliance with the specifications.

Implied Warranty of Authority. One who purports to be an agent impliedly warrants to third parties that he or she has authority to represent that principal with regard to the particular transaction.

Implied Warranty of Fitness for a Particular Purpose. If the seller at the time of contracting has reason to know any particular purpose for which the goods are required and that the buyer is relying on the seller's skill or judgment to select or furnish suitable goods, there is an implied warranty that the goods shall be fit for such purpose.

Implied Warranty of Merchantability. A seller of goods who deals in goods of that kind warrants the goods to be fit for the general purpose they are to be used for.

Impossibility of Performance. Where the promised performance becomes objectively impossible to perform after the contract has been entered into, the duty of performance is discharged.

Incidental Authority. Additional authority that enables the agent to carry out his or her express agency duties.

Incidental Beneficiary. One who benefits only indirectly from the contract and who acquires no rights of enforcement whatsoever.

Incidental Damages. Expenses the injured party incurs in reasonably seeking to mitigate the damages.

Incompetent. Any person who is personally unable to care for his or her property for any reason, including mental illness, advanced age, or disease.

Incontestable Clause. Clause providing that after two years' time, the insurer cannot contest or challenge the validity of the life insurance policy.

Indemnity Insurance. A collateral contract assurance by which one person engages to secure another against an anticipated loss or to prevent him from being damnified by the legal consequences of an act; also compensation for a loss already sustained.

Independent Contractor. One who works physically for the employer but is under no control of the employer other than as to the results to be accomplished.

Independent Legal Significance. Act or event is said to have "independent legal significance" where it is fundamentally nontestamentary in nature.

Indorse. To sign one's signature on an instrument thereby assuming contractual liability.

Information Return. A tax return filed by a partnership, specifying how much income the partnership had for the year, and what each partner's share of the income was.

Innocent Misrepresentation. A misrepresentation that is made unintentionally and without carelessness of any kind.

Insider Profits. A director, officer, or other "insider" of a corporation uses his or her inside information to make a personal profit.

Insolvent. A person is insolvent when he or she cannot pay his or her debts as they fall due, or has ceased to pay his or her debts in the ordinary course of business, or if the person comes within the meaning of insolvency given in the Federal Bankruptcy Act (liabilities exceed assets).

Installment Note. A promissory note that calls for monthly payments (the fact that the note is payable monthly does not make the note nonnegotiable).

Insurable Interest in Life. A person has an insurable interest in his or her own life and also in the life of another to the extent that death of that other will result in measurable economic loss to the person.

Insurable Interest in Property. Whenever damage or destruction of property will result in measurable economic loss to a person, the person has an insurable interest in the property.

Insurance. An arrangement for transferring and distributing risk.

Insurance Agent. A person authorized by an insurance company to negotiate and enter into insurance contracts on behalf of the company.

Insurance Broker. An independent contractor whose business it is to determine what insurance needs are present, then place those insurance needs with the appropriate companies.

Insurance Policy. A written contract of the insurer's promise to pay in the event of loss, and the insured's promise to pay premiums and give proper notice of the loss.

Insurer. A company that contracts to pay for the loss of a person.

Integrated Agreement. A writing that the parties intend to be the final and complete expression of their contract.

Integration. The validation of several pages of a testator's will.

Inter-insurance Exchange. Where several individuals protect themselves against a particular risk by joining together as a group or syndicate and setting up an indemnity fund to compensate group members for their losses.

Interested Party. A person who has a beneficial interest in a will.

Interference with Contractual Relations. A commercial tort in which a person causes a third party to breach an existing contract with the plaintiff.

Interference with Prospective Advantage. A commercial tort in which a person intentionally deprives another person of an economic advantage that he or she would otherwise have.

Interlocking Directorate. The situation in which a director serves on the boards of two corporations that deal with each other.

Intermediary Bank. Any bank to which an item is transferred in course of collection except the depositary or payor bank.

Inter vivos Gift. A gift made when the donor is alive.

Interwoven Tort. When the result of holding a minor liable for a tort is to achieve the same effect as enforcing the contract, the tort action is not allowed. The tort is said to be "interwoven" with the contract.

Intestate. Dying without a will.

Intrastate Offering of Securities. An issue that is offered and sold only to residents within one state by an issuer who resides and does business within the state, or in the case of a corporation, is incorporated in and doing business in the state.

Investment Company. A company which is engaged primarily in the business of investing, reinvesting, or trading in securities, or is engaged in that business and more than 40% of its assets consist of investment securities.

Involuntary Bailment. A bailment where the bailor unintentionally turns over possession of the property to the bailee.

Issuer of Credit. Bank or other person issuing a credit.

Issuer of Securities. Any person who issues or proposes to issue a security.

Joint and Survivorship Annuity. Annuity that continues for the joint lives of a husband and wife (i. e., the annuity continues until the second spouse dies).

Joint Liability. Liability together as a group; all parties must be named in any court action to enforce the obligation.

Justifiable Reliance. A party who relies upon another's misrepresentation must have reasonable basis for doing so or fraud in the inducement will not be found.

Key Employee. An employee crucial to the operation of the business.

Knights of Labor. First organization made up of both workers and farmers in an effort to organize against the abuses of the new industrial society (formed in 1880).

Labor Law. Laws made to keep peace between workers and management —based on four statutes.

Laissez-Faire. Social theory, prevalent in the U.S. in the late 1800's, that the people are best served by letting them go about their business with as little government interference as possible.

Landrum-Griffin Act. Federal act passed in 1959 to protect the rights and interest of individual workers as well as of the public from infringement by powerful union leaders; outlaws corrupt union practices.

Lapsed Gift. A gift that fails because the named beneficiary is either unwilling to accept the gift, or unable to take the property because he or she is dead at the time the will takes effect.

Latent Ambiguity. A mistake as to the existing facts that prevents the formation of mutual assent; the uncertainty arises from extrinsic facts showing that the parties involved were thinking of different things at the time of contracting.

Lateral Support. An absolute right of every landowner to support from adjoining land.

Lease. A binding agreement by a landlord to rent real property to a tenant, coupled with a conveyance to the tenant of the right to exclusive possession of the property.

Legacy. A gift of personal property under a will.

Legal Concept. A specifically defined division or part of the whole law.

Legal Life Estate. Life estate created by operation of law.

Legal List. A list specifying the kinds of investments that a trustee can make.

Legal Possession. Actual physical control over the property plus intent to assume or exercise control.

Legal Responsibility. The obligations legally required of businesspeople, accountants, and lawyers.

Legally Sufficient Consideration. Consideration that is either a benefit to the promisor or a detriment to the promisee.

Lessee. One who leases property from another.

Lessor. One who leases property to another.

Letter of Credit. A special device used often in sales transactions both as a method of payment and as a means of financing the sale. It is an engagement by a bank or other person made at the request of a customer that the issuer/bank will honor drafts or other demands for payment upon compliance with the conditions specified in the credit.

Levy. The act of the sheriff in taking the judgment debtor's property into his custody.

License. A privilege of one person, called a licensee, to go onto another's land for a specific purpose.

Lien. A claim or charge against real or personal property that secures payment of a debt or performance of some other act.

Lien Creditor. A creditor holding a lien against the debtor's property. A lien creditor has the right to have his claim satisfied from the specific property against which he holds the lien before the property can be used to satisfy the claims of general creditors.

Life Estate. A possessory estate that is limited in duration to the life-time or combined lifetimes of one or more designated individuals.

Life Estate Pur Autre Vie. A life estate measured by the life of someone other than the grantee.

Limited Partnership. A partnership consisting of one or more general partners and one or more limited partners. The limited partner is liable only to the extent of his or her investment in the partnership.

Limited-Payment Life. Insurance protection against death for the entire life of the insured with the insured's payment of premiums limited to a fixed number of years—10, 20, 30, etc.

Liquidated Damages. Where a contract includes a provision stipulating a specific amount of damages.

Liquidated Debt. A debt where it is certain what is due and how much is due.

Lloyd's of London. An organization that will write insurance on almost any known risk. Lloyd's operates through syndicates of individuals who agree to insure particular risks, each individual being personally liable for a fraction of the risk assumed.

Locus in Quo. Place in which a chattel is found.

Lost Property. Property unintentionally or accidentally lost or left behind by its owner.

Main Purpose/Leading Object Rule. Where a promisor's main purpose or leading object in making a collateral promise is to secure an advantage for himself or herself or otherwise directly benefit, the promise is not truly a promise to answer for the debt of another, and so is enforceable without written evidence.

Maintenance. An agreement merely to pay the costs and expenses of legal action without sharing in the proceeds.

Maker. The party issuing a promissory note.

Malum in se. Against good morals.

Malum Prohibitum. In violation of a statute or rule but not against good morals.

Market Value of Stock. The price that a willing buyer would pay a willing seller for the stock.

Marketable Title. Title reasonably free from doubt; title that a prudent buyer would accept.

Marshaling of Assets. The arranging or ranking of assets in a certain order toward payment of debts.

Master. Employer who retains control or the right to control the employee in how he renders the services.

Master-Servant. The relationship of employer to employee.

Material Alteration. Any alteration of an instrument is material which changes the contract of any party thereto, including any change in the number or relations of the parties; or an incomplete instrument, by completing it otherwise than authorized; or the writing as signed, by adding to it or by removing any part of it.

Massachusetts Rule. The rule that all cash dividends, whether ordinary or extraordinary, are income belonging to the life beneficiary, while all stock dividends, which are always extraordinary, are a part of trust "capital" or "principal".

Memorandum. Written evidence of the essential terms of the agreement including the identity of the contracting parties, a description of the subject matter of the contract, the terms and conditions of the agreement, a recital of the consideration, and the signature of the party to be charged.

Merchant. A person who deals in goods of the kind or otherwise by his occupation holds himself out as having knowledge or skill peculiar to the practices or goods involved in the transaction or to whom such knowledge or skill may be attributed by his employment of an agent or broker or other intermediary who by his occupation holds himself out as having such knowledge or skill. UCC 2–104.

Mere Inquiry. A question, suggestion, or request anticipating a change from the original terms of the offer.

Merger. A merger takes place when an existing corporation absorbs one or more existing corporations: the absorbing corporation survives the merger; the absorbed corporations cease to exist.

Metes and Bounds Description. Description of land by actual measurements and boundaries.

Minor. A person under the age of 18, 19, 20, or 21 depending on state law.

Mislaid Property. Property that the owner has intentionally put down in a particular location only to subsequently forget where he or she has placed the property.

Mistake. An erroneous belief relating to the facts as they exist at the time that an agreement is made or entered into.

Mitigation of Damages Rule. The injured party is legally obligated to make a reasonable effort to minimize the damages flowing from the breach of contract.

Mixed Defense. A defense that is sometimes personal and sometimes real, depending on the circumstances involved.

Modified or Substituted Contract. Where parties agree, prior to performance, to modify the original agreement or to substitute an entirely new contract in its place.

Money. A medium of exchange authorized or adopted by a domestic or foreign government as part of its currency.

Monopolizing. Deliberate and purposeful execution of power to control prices or exclude competitors in a particular market.

Mortgage. A conveyance of land given as security for the payment of a debt. The debtor borrows money from the creditor and conveys his or her real property to the creditor as security for the loan.

Mortgagee. The creditor in a mortgage agreement.

Mortgagor. The debtor in a mortgage agreement.

Multiple-Line Companies. Companies that sell all kinds of insurance other than life insurance.

Mutual Assent. The agreement of the parties, usually manifested by an offer and an acceptance.

Mutual Benefit Bailment. A bailment in which both parties benefit from the bailment relationship. The bailee is required to exercise ordinary care and is liable for ordinary negligence.

Mutual Corporation. Several individuals joining together, to protect against risk, as a syndicate or group and setting up an indemnity fund to compensate group members for their losses. This differs from an inter-insurance exchange in that the mutual corporation is much larger and permanent and the policyholders elect directors who manage the company.

Mutual Mistake. When both parties involved in a contract agreement are mistaken as to a material fact; the mistake prevents formation of mutual assent.

Mutual Rescission. An agreement to forget an existing contract.

National Labor Relations Act. A federal statute passed in 1935 that guarantees employees the right (1) to form, join, or assist labor organizations, (2) to bargain collectively with the employer, and (3) to engage in concerted activity for the purpose of collective bargaining or mutual aid and protection.

Necessaries. Certain support obligations a husband owes to his wife and children, including such articles as food, shelter, and clothing.

Negligence. Unintentional conduct that falls below the standard established by law for the protection of others against unreasonably great risk of harm to either person or property.

Negotiable Draft. A written instrument in which one party (drawer) unconditionally orders a second party (drawee) to pay "to the order of" a named payee or "to bearer" a sum certain in money on demand or at a definite time in the future.

Negotiable Instrument. A contract designed to serve as a substitute for money and to help facilitate credit transactions.

Negotiable Promissory Note. A written instrument in which one party unconditionally promises to pay "to the order of" another party or "to bearer" a sum certain in money upon demand or at a definite time in the future.

Negotiation. The subsequent transfer of a negotiable instrument to a third party so as to make the party a holder; order paper is negotiated by indorsement and delivery, bearer paper by delivery alone.

No Arrival, No Sale Contract. The seller must ship the goods, but if they do not arrive, the seller will not be liable; the seller makes no promise that the goods will arrive.

No Fault Automobile Insurance. Where an insurance company pays, not for the loss of a third party bearing a lawful claim against the insured, but for the loss of its own policy holder without regard to the fault of the parties.

Nonconforming Goods. Goods not in the condition contracted for when delivered to the carrier.

Noncumulative Preferred Stock. Stock in which the shareholder's right to the stated dividend does not carry over to subsequent years.

No-par Value Stock. Stock that is issued without any stated value on the certificate.

Norris-LaGuardia Act. A federal act passed in 1932 providing that the worker "though he should be free to decline to associate with his fellows must have full freedom of association, self-organization, and designation of representatives of his own choosing, to negotiate the terms and conditions of his employment, and must be free from the interference, restraint, or coercion of employers of labor in these activities".

Novation. Where, with the agreement of all parties, a new party fully substitutes for one of the original parties to a contract, and the original party is fully discharged from any further duty of performance under the old contract.

Nuisance. The use of one's own land in such a manner as to unreasonably interfere with another's use and enjoyment of his or her land. This is an intentional tort.

Nuncupative Will. An oral will.

Objective Impossibility. Impossibility of anyone to perform the particular promise made.

Obstruction of Justice. Agreement to obstruct the administration of justice; an illegal bargain.

Occupation. Acquiring title to personal property by taking possession of either wild things or abandoned property.

Offer. A definite conditional undertaking, i. e., a *definite* proposal made by one party (the offeror) to another party (the offeree) indicating the offering party's present intent to enter into a contract, conditioned upon the offeree's completion of the contract by acceptance, his or her power to accept being created by the offer itself.

Oppressive Child Labor. A condition of employment under which any employee under the age of 16 years is employed by an employer, other than a parent, in any occupation, or any employee between the ages of 16 and 18 years is employed by any employer in any occupation which the Secretary of Labor shall find and by order declare to be particularly hazardous for the employment of children between such ages or detrimental to their health or well being.

Option Contract. A contract in which the subject matter is to keep an offer open.

Order Paper. A note made payable "to the order of" a named payee; the payee must indorse it in order to negotiate it.

Order to Pay. A direction to pay and must be more than an authorization or request. It must identify the person to pay with reasonable certainty.

Ordinary Life Insurance. Insurance protection against death for the entire life of the insured; insured pays premiums throughout life.

Original Tenor. Original terms of the instrument.

Out-of-Pocket Rule. The rule of damages which awards the injured party the difference between the value paid and the value actually received.

Overissue. The issue of securities in excess of the amount which the issuer has corporate power to issue.

Ownership. Generally referred to as title which confers upon the owner the exclusive right to use, possess, and dispose of the property owned.

Par Value Stock. Stock that is assigned a specific value.

Pari Delicto. Equal fault; parties to an illegal bargain are generally said to be in "pari delicto".

Parol Evidence. Oral testimony; however in parol evidence rule, it encompasses both oral and written evidence contradictory to the fully and finally written contract.

Parol Evidence Rule. States that a fully written integrated contract may not be changed, altered, varied, or modified by any oral or written evidence (apart from the writing) occurring prior to or at the time of the signing of the agreement.

Partial Strike. Employees come to work but, after working a short time, feign illness or other disability in order to cause a work stoppage.

Partially Disclosed Principal. An agency relationship in which the agent reveals the existence of the relationship, but does not identify the principal.

Participating Preferred Stock. Preferred stock in which the shareholder is entitled to participate in any dividends paid to the common stockholders beyond the preferred shareholder's own annual rate.

Partition. To actually divide property into severalty interests, or, where this cannot be physically accomplished, to sell the property and divide up the proceeds.

Partnership. An association of two or more persons to carry on as co-owners a business for profit.

Partnership at Will. A partnership with no fixed or determinable period of duration.

Partnership for Term. A partnership with a fixed term of duration.

Partnership Property. All property originally brought into the partnership stock or subsequently acquired by purchase or otherwise on account of the partnership.

Passenger. A person who comes upon the carrier's premises with the intention of traveling using the carrier's facilities under contract with the carrier.

Payee. A named party to whom a negotiable instrument is made payable.

"Payment Guaranteed". Words that an indorser may add to his or her indorsement, promising that if the instrument is not paid when due, he or she will immediately pay it without any conditions precedent.

Payor Bank. A bank by which an item is payable as drawn or accepted.

Permanent Lodger. One who takes up residence at a hotel or boarding house, intending to stay there permanently.

Permissive Subjects of Collective Bargaining. Subjects that fall within the discretion of the employer and the union who may choose whether or not to bargain about them.

Permissive Waste. A negligent failure to act by the tenant which results in damage or decay to the property.

Personal Defense. A defense good as against all holders but a holder in due course; "personal" in the sense that it arises out of a breach of agreement between former parties to the instrument.

Plaintiff. The party who brings a legal action.

Pledge. The placement of personal property in the possession of another as security for some act by the bailor.

Police Power. The inherent authority of the government to do whatever is deemed necessary to protect public health, welfare, and morals.

Possession. To legally possess personal property, a person must intend to exercise control over the chattel and he or she must physically control the chattel to an appreciable extent.

Possibility of Reverter. If the condition stated in a determinable fee is broken, this is the grantor's right of automatic return of his or her property.

Pour-Over Trust Provision. A provision in a will providing that all or a portion of the testator's property should be added to the trust res or corpus of a trust established during the lifetime of the decedent.

Pre-emptive Right. The right of a shareholder to purchase a percentage of the new issue of stock equal to his or her present holdings.

Preferential Transfer. A transfer of the bankrupt's nonexempt property for the benefit of a creditor on account of a previous or antecedent debt.

Preferred Stock. Stock with a preference as to earnings and/or net assets.

Prejudgment Remedy. A procedure that enables the creditor to preserve the property belonging to the debtor until the creditor can prove the validity of his claim.

Preliminary Negotiation. The initial bantering back and forth of ideas before entering into a contract.

Premiums. Specified monetary amounts paid by the insured into a general fund.

Presenting Bank. Any bank presenting an item except a payor bank.

Pretermitted Heir Statute. Statute providing that where a child of a testator is not mentioned in the will, the will will be disregarded to the extent that the child will be permitted to receive his or her intestate share of the decedent's property (the share he or she would have been entitled to had the testator left no will).

Price-Fixing. An agreement between competitors to raise, depress, fix, peg, or stabilize the price of a commodity.

Prima Facie. A fact presumed to be true unless disproved by some evidence to the contrary.

Prima Facie Case. A case that is sufficient to prove itself, unless and until it is refuted.

Primary Promise. A promise to answer for one's own debt.

Private Contract Carrier. One who carries goods for a limited number of customers under contract but does not hold himself or herself out to transport goods for the general public.

Privity of Contract. Parties who have contracted with each other are said to be in "privity" of contract.

Probate. The legal process of transferring a decedent's property to those people lawfully entitled to the property upon the decedent's death.

Profit. An irrevocable right to take something away from the land, such as minerals, trees, etc.

Promise to Pay. An undertaking to pay and must be more than an acknowledgment of an obligation.

Promissory Estoppel. Where the bargain theory of consideration does not apply, the promisor will still be held to his or her promise if the promisee has substantially changed his or her position in reliance upon the promise.

Promissory Warranty. Warranty stating a condition that must be maintained throughout the period of the insurance policy.

Property Damage Liability Insurance. Insurance that protects the insured and those who drive the insured's car with his/her permission against liability to third parties who incur property damage as a result of the negligent operation of the insured's motor vehicle. (Does not cover insured's vehicle—only third party's motor vehicle.)

Protective Trust. An ordinary trust that automatically becomes discretionary (giving the trustee discretion to distribute the trust income to any or all of a group of beneficiaries, including the original beneficiary) at such time as the original beneficiary becomes insolvent or attempts to transfer his or her interest in the trust, or a creditor of the beneficiary attempts to reach the trust interest.

Protest. A formal notice of dishonor required only when dealing with drafts (not including checks) drawn or payable in a foreign country.

Provisional Settlement. The initial crediting of a check on the day of deposit to the customer's account; provisional in that the bank may charge back the item against the customer's account if it cannot collect on the check.

Proxy. A power of attorney given by a shareholder to another party authorizing the party to exercise the voting rights of the shares.

Prudent Investor Rule. The rule that a trustee must use good faith and sound discretion in making investments.

Publication. A declaration by the testator to the assembled witnesses that the instrument is the testator's will.

Publicly Held Corporation. A corporation whose shares have been offered and sold to the public.

Punitive Damages. Penalty damages designed to punish the wrongdoer and deter others from acting in a similar manner; they vary in amount according to the outrageousness of the wrongdoer's conduct.

Purchase Money Mortgage. A mortgage that is executed to secure the purchase price of land.

Purchase Money Security Interest. A security interest that is (1) taken or retained by the seller of the collateral to secure all or part of its purchase price; or (2) taken by a person who by making advances or incurring an obligation gives value to enable the debtor to acquire rights in or other use of collateral if such value is in fact so used.

Put Up. To describe goods to the people present at an auction and to open up bidding on the goods.

Qualified Fee. An estate that confers upon its owner all the ordinary rights of a fee simple absolute, but that is subject to completely ending or terminating upon the happening of a specified contingency.

Qualified Indorsement. An indorsement "without recourse" which eliminates all secondary liability for that particular indorser.

Quasi Contract. An agreement implied in law to prevent unjust enrichment.

Quitclaim Deed. A deed purporting to convey only what interest, if any, the grantor has in a specified piece of real property.

Quo Warranto Action. An action by the state forcing a corporation into involuntary dissolution. This action requires forfeiture of the corporate charter.

Quorum. A simple majority of the board of directors.

Real Authority. Authority manifested by the principal to the agent either expressly or by implication.

Real Defense. A defense good against even a holder in due course.

Reclamation. The seller's right to reclaim goods given to the buyer upon discovery of the buyer's insolvency.

Recognizance. A formal acknowledgement in court by a recognizor that he or she is bound to make a certain payment unless a specified condition is performed.

Redemption of Shares. A corporation redeems shares when it purchases shares of its stock from shareholders and cancels the shares.

Rejection. A definite statement by the offeree that he or she does not intend to accept the offer.

Release. An agreement to give up or relinquish existing rights.

Remainder. A future interest expressly created by the terms of a conveyance that remains away from the grantor and becomes possessory in another party upon the termination of a preceding possessory estate created by the same conveyance.

Renter's Insurance. Insurance purchased by a renter to protect against loss to his or her personal property from burglary, fire, or vandalism.

Renunciation. The holder of an instrument may discharge any party by renouncing his rights by a writing signed and delivered or by surrender of the instrument to the party to be discharged.

Rescission. The avoidance or annulment of a contract. The effect is to restore the parties to the positions they were in prior to the agreement—to make it just as though no contract had been entered into.

Residuary Bequest and Devise. A gift of whatever personal (bequest) and real (devise) property is left after all specific, general, and demonstrative gifts have been satisfied.

Restitution. The restoration of anything to its rightful owner. With regard to breach of contract, the restoration of the parties, insofar as is practicable, to the positions they were in prior to entering into the contract.

Restoration in Specie. Restoration of whatever actual property is left in whatever condition it is in.

Restrictive Indorsement. An indorsement is restrictive which either is conditional; or purports to prohibit further transfer of the instrument; or includes the words "for collection", "for deposit", "pay any bank", or like terms signifying a purpose of deposit or collection; or otherwise states that it is for the benefit or use of the indorser or of another person.

Restricted Surplus. A portion of the earned surplus set aside by the board of directors for special purposes.

Resulting Trust. A trust that arises by operation of law where a person transfers property, intending that someone other than the transferee should have the beneficial interest, but failing to clearly express such intent.

Retirement Income Insurance (also called annuity contracts). Where the insurer must pay the annuitant (insured) a fixed sum of money at periodic intervals commencing upon a certain date and continuing until the annuitant dies, at which time a final lump sum must be paid by the company.

Reverse Unilateral Contract. An act for a promise: the offeror offers to perform an act in return for a requested promise from the offeree to do something or not to do something.

Reversion. A future interest retained by a grantor who conveys away less than he or she owns.

Rider. A separate sheet of paper containing a change of terms of a written insurance contract; attached to the policy.

Right of First Refusal. A director or officer must offer the corporation a "right of first refusal" on any business opportunity that he or she learns of that would be of benefit to the corporation.

Right of Redemption. The right of the debtor to free the collateral from any lien or encumbrance and regain absolute ownership by payment of the amount due.

Right of Re-entry for Condition Broken. If the condition stated in a fee simple subject to a condition subsequent is broken, this is the right of the grantor to re-enter and repossess the property.

Right of Survivorship. Upon the death of any joint tenant, the deceased tenant's interest passes, not to the tenant's lawfully designated beneficiaries or heirs, but to the surviving joint tenants.

Riparian Owner. A person who owns land next to water.

Rule Against Perpetuities. A contingent or conditional interest in land will be valid only if the interest must vest, if at all, within lives in being plus 21 years.

Rule in Shelley's Case. A specific grant of a life estate to a grantee followed by a remainder to the grantee's heirs will be effective to convey the full fee simple interest to the grantee, and nothing to the heirs.

Rule of Remoteness. An injured party should be compensated only for losses that are reasonably foreseeable to the parties at the time they enter into the contract.

Salami Accounting. Taking up a past accounting error gradually over future periods so as to prevent immediate full disclosure of the error.

Sale. A contract by which the ownership of goods is transferred from a seller to a buyer.

Sale on Approval. The goods are delivered to a buyer for a stated period of time, during which the buyer may use the goods for the purpose of determining whether or not to purchase them.

Sale or Return. Goods are delivered to a buyer with an option to return them to the seller. The goods must be delivered primarily for resale.

Satisfaction of a Mortgage. A statement that the mortgage has been paid.

Scalping. An illegal act in which a broker-dealer purchases securities, then without disclosing the purchase, recommends the securities to customers, holding on and selling the securities for a profit after the price rises because of the recommendation.

Scheduled Injuries. Certain types of injuries involving partial disability that are specifically covered in state workmen's compensation statutes, each which has a predetermined amount of compensation that will be paid for an employee experiencing that injury.

Scope of Vision Test. Test of a witness's presence whereby the witness is considered present only if he or she signs the will in the testator's physical presence and within the scope of his or her vision.

Section. A piece of real property one square mile in area (640 acres).

Secured Party. The lender, seller, purchaser, or other person in whose favor the security interest is created.

Securities and Exchange Commission. A commission created by the Securities Exchange Act of 1934 to enforce and administer all federal securities laws.

Security. Any note, stock, treasury stock, bond, debenture, evidence of indebtedness, certificate of interest or participation in any profit-sharing agreement, collateral-trust certificate, preorganization certificate or subscription, transferable share, investment contract, voting-trust certificate, certificate of deposit for a security, fractional undivided interest in oil, gas, or other mineral rights, or in general, any interest or instrument commonly known as a "security", or any certificate of interest or participation in temporary or interim certificate for, receipt for, guarantee of, or warrant or right to subscribe to or purchase, any of the foregoing.

Security Interest. Every interest in personal property or fixtures which secures payment or performance of an obligation.

Self-dealing. An agent "self-deals" when he or she acts for himself or herself in a transaction.

Seller's Right to Cure. The seller can cure (i. e., remedy the nonconformity) if the contract time for performance has not yet expired or if the contract time has expired but the seller had reasonable grounds to believe the goods would be acceptable.

Separate Property. In a community property state, property belonging entirely to one spouse who is free to sell the property, mortgage it, or otherwise exercise control over the property irrespective of the wishes of the other spouse.

Servant. Person employed to render services of any type to a master (employer) subject to the master's right of control.

Set-off. To deduct from the purchase price for damages incurred.

Several Liability. Where each of the parties specifically promises to be individually bound, using language such as "each of us makes this promise severally, not jointly".

Severalty. Owning real or personal property without anyone else sharing in the ownership.

Sewer Service. An illegal practice where the process servers make no effort to find the defendant debtor, but instead file false affidavits that the process has been served and then simply throw the summons and complaint away.

Shelter Provision. Provides that where the assignor of a negotiable instrument is a holder in due course, the assignee will acquire the rights of such a holder as will subsequent transferees of the instrument.

Sherman Act. Federal act passed in 1890 which makes unlawful every contract, combination or conspiracy in restraint of trade in interstate or foreign commerce. It also prohibits monopolizing and attempts to monopolize.

Shipment Contract. The seller is required to deliver the goods merely to a carrier at the place of shipment rather than to a particular destination.

Sight Draft. A draft payable on demand (upon presentation to the drawee).

Sitdown Strike. A strike where workers occupy the employer's premises and refuse to work.

Slowdown. Workers remain on the job but refuse to perform their duties or to work at the regular pace.

Sole Proprietorship. A business that is owned and operated by one person.

Special Agent. An agent authorized to conduct but a single transaction not involving any continuity of service.

Special Goods. Goods unsuitable for sale to others in the ordinary course of the seller's business.

Special Indorsement. An indorsement directing the maker or drawee to pay a specific named individual.

Special Lien. A lien that secures payment only for the work or service performed on the particular chattel.

Special Place. A place specific in nature such as a specific branch of a specific bank located in a specific city.

Special Property Right. The right acquired by the buyer upon identification of the goods to the contract of sale. Includes three rights as set out in the UCC: (1) the right to inspect the goods; (2) the right to replevin the goods; and (3) the right to recover damages from any third party who converts the goods or otherwise interferes with the property.

Specific Bequest. A gift of identifiable personal property under a will.

Specific Devise. A gift of identifiable real property under a will.

Specific Performance. Performance in the exact manner specified by the contract.

Spendthrift. A person whose excessive drinking, idleness, gambling, or debauchery so spends, wastes, or lessens his or her estate that the person's family is exposed to want or suffering.

Spendthrift Trust. A trust that prohibits the beneficiary from voluntarily or involuntarily transferring his or her interest in the trust.

Spoliation. Alteration of an instrument by a meddling stranger.

"Stand in the Shoes" of an Assignor. The assignee of contract rights stands in the same position as the assignor and stands subject to the same defenses as existed prior to the assignment.

Stale Check. A check that has been outstanding more than six months.

State Wage Earner Receivership. The court appoints someone, upon the debtor's request, to act as a receiver in collecting all nonexempt wages of the debtor and distributing them pro rata among the debtor's creditors until all debts are paid in full.

Stated Capital. The total par value of all issued par value shares plus the total value received for all no-par value shares.

Statute of Frauds. A statute specifically providing that certain contracts are not enforceable in the absence of special written evidence.

Statute of Limitations. A statute specifying a time period in which legal action on a particular claim must be initiated.

Statutory Right of Redemption. The right of a mortgagor following a foreclosure sale to redeem the property by paying the sales price plus reasonable costs and expenses for a certain period of time (usually one year).

Stock Certificate in Registered Form. A stock certificate issued in the name of a specific person whose name appears on the face of the certificate itself.

Stock Corporation. A life insurance company that is owned and controlled by stockholders; operates to make a profit for its owners.

Stock Dividend. The distribution of additional stock to each shareholder.

Stock Exchange. Any organization, association, or group of persons, whether incorporated or unincorporated, which constitutes, maintains, or provides a marketplace or facilities for bringing together purchasers and sellers of securities.

Stock Split. Each share of outstanding stock is split into a larger number of shares, thus increasing the total number of outstanding shares.

Stock Subscription. An agreement by a party called a subscriber to purchase a certain amount of capital stock of a corporation.

Stoppage in Transit. The seller's right to stop the goods while they are in transit and retake possession of them.

Stop Payment. An order to the bank not to pay a check.

Straight Bankruptcy. A proceeding designed to liquidate the debtor's property, pay off his or her creditors, and discharge the debtor from his or her other debts. It can be either voluntary (started by the debtor himself or herself) or involuntary (started by the debtor's creditors).

Straight Bill of Lading. A nonnegotiable bill of lading that specifies a consignee to whom the goods are to be delivered—the carrier is contractually obligated to deliver the goods to that person only.

Straight Voting. Each common stockholder generally has the right to cast one vote for each share of stock that he or she owns.

Strict Foreclosure. The situation in which a debtor defaults and the secured party simply retains the collateral in satisfaction of the debt.

Strict Liability. Liability for conduct that is unintentional and without fault.

Subagent. A party to whom an agent delegates his or her authority.

Subjacent Support. A landowner's right to support of his or her property by the land lying under it.

Subjective Impossibility. Personal inability of the promisor to perform the promise made.

Subrogation. The substitution of one person in the place of another with reference to a lawful claim, demand, or right, so that he who is substituted succeeds to the rights of the other in relation to the debt or claim, and its rights, remedies, or securities.

Subscription. A signature at the end of an instrument.

Sunday Laws. Statutes making it illegal to enter into contracts or perform contracts on Sunday.

Supernumerary Witness. An extra witness over and above the statutory requirement.

Support Trust. A trust in which the trustee has the power to pay the beneficiary only so much of the trust income as is necessary for the beneficiary's support, education and maintenance.

Surety. A third person who agrees to repay the debt owed to the creditor, assuming the debtor does not.

Suretyship. A contract wherein a third person agrees to repay the debt owed to the creditor, assuming the debtor does not.

Suretyship Promises. Promises to answer for the debt of another; legally enforceable only if the promise is supported by a written memo signed by the promisor.

Syndicate. An association of brokerage firms with each member firm offering the securities to its customers.

Taft-Hartley Act. Federal act passed in 1947 that enables government to combat union "unfair labor practices" and to intervene in strikes that threaten the national welfare.

Tenancy at Sufferance. An "estate" that results when a tenant in lawful possession of property under one of the other three leasehold estates remains in possession of the leased property after expiration of the term of the lease without the consent of the landlord.

Tenancy at Will. An estate that is terminable at the will of either landlord or tenant.

Tenancy for Years. A tenancy that has a fixed or definite beginning and end at the time of the creation of the tenancy.

Tenancy from Period to Period. An estate that continues from year to year or successive fractions of a year until terminated by proper notice from either party.

Tenant. A renter of land, buildings, or apartments.

Tender. A conditional offer to perform.

Term Insurance. Life insurance protection against death for a specified period of time, such as five to ten years.

Testamentary Capacity. Requirement for a valid will that a person be of sound mind. He or she must be able to generally understand and remember the nature and extent of his or her property, the people who are natural objects (relatives and friends) of his or her bounty or generosity, and the disposition that he or she is making of the property.

Testamentary Intent. Requirement for a valid will that the testator must intend that the instrument presently operate as his or her last will and testament.

Testamentary Transfer. Transfer of a person's property at the time of his or her death.

Testamentary Trust. A trust created by a will which takes effect only upon the testator's death. The trust must satisfy requirements of both a valid trust and a valid will.

Testate. Dying with a will.

Third Party Beneficiary Contract. Contract entered into for the purpose of directly benefiting a third person who is not a party to the contract.

Time Draft. A draft payable at a definite time in the future.

Title. Ownership of real or personal property.

Title Insurance. Insurance protection against loss arising from a defect in title or from a lack of good title.

Title Search. A search of public land records for all recorded ownership rights and outstanding interests in a particular piece of real property.

Tombstone Ad. An advertisement by an issuer of stock that a public offering of stock is about to be made.

Tort. Socially unreasonable conduct.

Tort of Deceit. Tort where a misrepresentation is intentionally made with knowledge of its falsity, either by written or spoken word or by active concealment of the truth.

Total Assets. Gross assets as shown on the issuer's balance sheet or on the balance sheet of the issuer and its subsidiaries consolidated, whichever is larger.

Township. A piece of real property six square miles in area. The township is divided into 36 sections.

Trade Acceptance. A special kind of draft used to finance the movement of goods in commerce; the drawer of this type of draft names himself as payee.

Treasure Trove. Coin, bullion, or paper money that is found buried in the ground.

Treasury Stock. A corporation repurchases shares when it buys shares of its stock from shareholders, but does not cancel the shares. The stock is held by the corporation itself, and is known as treasury stock.

Trespass to Chattels. Intentional interference with personal property not serious enough to justify a forced sale of the property.

Trespass to Land. Any physical entry upon the surface of land. This is an intentional tort.

Trust. A right of property, real or personal, held by one party for the benefit of another.

Trust Beneficiary. The person entitled to all the benefits and income derived from trust property.

Trustee. The person who holds trust property and is solely responsible for managing and caring for the property.

Trustor. The party creating a trust.

Trust "res" or "corpus". The property placed into trust.

"Truth in Lending". Act requiring all lenders to spell out their finance charges—to inform borrowers and customers of the cost of credit.

Tying Agreement. Where a seller refuses to sell one of his products (the tying product) to a customer unless the customer agrees to buy a second product (the tied product) as well.

Ultra Vires Act. An act by a corporation that goes beyond the powers of the corporation.

Unconscionable Contract. A contract containing provisions extremely unfair to one party to the contract who had little bargaining power in entering into the agreement.

Underwriter. A financing specialist who is paid to offer advice regarding the need for public financing, the best types of securities to offer, the best time to offer them, and the best offering price.

Undisclosed Agency. An agency relationship in which the third party has no knowledge of the existence of the agency.

Undue Influence. Persuasion, pressure, or influence short of actual force, but stronger than mere advice, that so overpowers the dominated party's free will or judgment that he or she cannot act intelligently and voluntarily, but acts, instead, subject to the will or purposes of the dominating party.

Unfair Competition. The use of economic advantage to destroy the livelihood of another.

Unfair Conduct. When a businessperson tries to induce others to boycott his competitors or uses discriminatory pricing in an effort to drive his or her competitors out of business.

Unilateral Contract. A promise for an act; the offeror promises to do something or not to do something in exchange for the offeree's performance of a requested act.

Uninsured Motorist Coverage. Insurance that compensates for *bodily* injury resulting from the negligent driving of an uninsured motorist.

Union Shop. Union membership is compulsory, but only *after* employment.

Unlawful Detainer Proceeding. A statutory procedure by which a landlord can legally evict a tenant in default on his or her rent.

Unliquidated Debt. A debt not ascertained in amount; not determined; remaining unsettled.

Usury. The illegal lending of money at a rate higher than that allowed by statute.

Variable Annuity. Annuity where the insurer promises to pay, not a fixed sum at periodic intervals, but a variable amount dependent upon the company's success at investing its annuitant's premium dollars in stocks, bonds, real estate, etc.

Vertical Restraint of Trade. Anticompetitive agreements on different levels of industry.

Vest. A future interest in land is said to "vest" when an ascertained grantee has the unconditional right to possession of the interest upon the expiration of all prior estates in the land.

Vested Remainder. An unconditional remainder granted to an ascertained person.

Voidable Contract. A contract which may be either ratified or rescinded.

Voidable Transaction. A transaction that one of the parties may avoid or ratify at his option.

Void Transaction. One that has absolutely no force and effect and is incapable of legal enforcement.

Voluntary Bailment. A bailment where the bailor intentionally delivers personal property to the bailee.

Waiver of Defenses. The nontransferring party agrees not to assert existing defenses against the assignee of contract rights.

Ward. The party, in a guardianship, that has the incapacity.

Warehouse Receipt. A receipt for goods issued by a person engaged in the business of storing goods for hire.

Warehouseman. A person in the business of storing the goods of others for compensation.

Warranty. A promise that a proposition of fact is true.

Warranty of Title. A seller of goods impliedly warrants that he or she has good title to the goods and that the transfer is rightful.

Waste. Damage done to land to the detriment of the future interest holder.

Watered Stock. Stock issued by corporation for less than full and adequate consideration.

Wildcat Strike. A minority of union members strike without union authorization.

Wild Deed. A deed not in the chain of title.

Will. A written instrument executed in accordance with the formalities prescribed by state statute whereby a property owner (testator) directs the disposition of his or her real and personal property to take effect upon death.

Without Recourse. Words that may be used by a drawer in signing a draft or check so as to completely eliminate the drawer's secondary liability.

Words of Limitation. Words that limit or define the interest in land that a grantee receives such as "and his heirs".

Words of Purchase. Words that effectively create an immediate future interest in relatives or other people.

Working Papers. The records kept by an independent auditor of the procedures followed, tests performed, information obtained, and conclusions reached pertinent to his or her examination.

Workmen's Compensation Statutes. Provide for the injured worker to receive an amount of money (worked out in advance by a state agency) to use for medical expense and support after each and every accident that arises out of and in the course of employment.

Writ of Attachment. An order to seize a debtor's property in order to secure the claim of a creditor.

Written Law. Includes federal and state constitutions; treaties made by the president with foreign nations; and statutes passed by the federal Congress, the state legislatures, and by local governmental units.

*

INDEX

1296   INDEX
References are to Pages

SALES—Cont'd

Performance,

Delivery,

Conforming goods, 576, 583–584, 596.

Non-conforming goods, 576, 583–584, 596–597.

Substantial non-conformity, 583, 600–601.

Inability to perform to contract,

Commercial impracticability, 572.

Doctrine of impracticability, 572.

Objective impossibility, 571.

Subjective impossibility, 571.

Remedies of buyer and seller when contract is breached (chart), 646.

Retraction of an anticipatory breach, 630.

Risk of loss,

Acceptance of non-conforming goods by buyer, 583–584.

Agreement of the parties, 580–581.

C. & F. shipments, 578–580.

C.O.D. shipments, 577.

Contract, effect of breach on, 583–584.

Delivery to carrier, 575–576, 580–581.

Destination contracts, 577.

Ex-ship contracts, 580.

F.A.S. shipments, 578.

F.O.B. shipments, 577–578.

Goods in possession of bailee, 580, 584–585.

Goods that are lost, damaged or stolen,

Fault of one party, 571.

No fault of the parties, 571–574.

No agreement of the parties, 575.

"No arrival, no sale" contracts, 573–574.

Sale on approval, 581–583.

Sale on consignment, 582–583.

Sale or return, 581–583.

Shipment contracts, 575–576.

Shipments by common carriers, 575–580.

Summary, 584–585.

Upon tender to buyer, 575–576, 581.

Wrongful repudiation or breach of contract by buyer, 584.

Security interest in goods, 576.

Sellers,

Damages for nonacceptance or repudiation by buyer, 638–640.

Delivers non-conforming goods, 595–596.

Duties,

Hold goods for buyer, 642.

Resell goods, 642.

Supply goods to buyer, 258.

Fails to deliver goods, 595.

Insolvency causing non-performance, 595.

Insurable interest in goods, 569–570.

Lacks title to document, 670.

Measure of damages for buyer's breach, 641–642.

SALES—Cont'd

Sellers—Cont'd

Obligation to transfer and deliver goods, 593.

Remedies for buyer's breach,

Cancel contract, 642–643.

Collect the price of the goods accepted, 641–642.

Complete the manufacturing of the goods, 641.

Demand cash before delivery, 632–633.

Identify goods to the contract for resale, 637–638.

Incidental damages, 634, 644.

Interpleader action in court, 636.

Reclaim the goods, 633–634.

Refuse credit to buyer, 631.

Resell or salvage goods in incomplete form, 640–641.

Restitution for overpayment for goods, 645.

Retaining deposit from purchase price, 644.

Right to resell goods, 637–640.

Scrap or resell goods for value, 640–641.

Stop manufacturing of goods, 641.

Stoppage of goods in transit, 635–637.

Suit for replevin, 634.

Summary, 631–632, 643.

Withholding delivery of goods, 631–632.

Remedies or damages established by agreement,

Consequential damages, 643.

Exclusive remedies, 643.

Liquidated damages, 644.

Measure of damages, 644–645.

Repudiation of contract by, 595.

Revesting title of goods in seller, 667.

Rights,

Buyer refuses to accept goods, 593.

Buyer refuses to pay for goods, 593.

To cure defects in goods, 603.

To cure non-conforming goods, 599–601.

Security interest in goods, 570.

Voidable title to document, 670.

Wrongful selling of goods, 669.

Title,

See also Title.

Importance of, 52.

Legal concept of, 52.

Passage of title,

Property interests of buyer, 52.

Security interests of seller, 52.

Statutory procedures for acquiring title, 58.

Title certificate, 52.

TITLE—Cont'd
Title insurance, 149–150.
  Lawyer-title policies, 149.
  Title-plant policies, 149.
Title recordation, 146–147.
Title search, 148–149.
Unmarketable title, 138.

TORTS
Deceit, 231.
Defamation of character, 10.
Defenses,
  Defense of property, 12.
  Recapture of chattels, 12–13.
  Self defense, 12.
Defined, 10.
Intentional torts,
  Assault, 10.
  Battery, 10.
  Conversion, 12, 54, 59–61, 68, 474–475.
  Defined, 658.
  False imprisonment, 10.
  Mental distress, 10.
  Trespass to chattels, 12, 54, 59, 68.
  Trespass to land, 11.
Invasion of privacy, 10.
Liability for intentional actions, 341–342.
Minors liability for torts, 341–342.
Negligence,
  Defined, 10–11, 658.
  Elements of, 11, 659.
  Test of, 6, 658.
Nuisance, 11–12.
Purpose of tort law, 659.
Statute of limitations, 266–267.
Strict liability, 663–666.

TRADEMARKS, 68–69

TRUSTS
Blended trust, 1136–1137.
Changing a trust, by, 1147–1148.
  Beneficiary, 1147.
  Courts, 1147–1148.
  Operation of law, 1148.
  Trustee, 1147.
  Trustor, 1147.
Charitable trust, 1137–1138.
Constructive trust, 1130, 1140–1141.
Creation of, 1134–1135.
Defined, 1130.
Discretionary trust, 1135–1136.
Express trust,
  Defined, 1130.
  Elements of, 1131–1133.
    Designation of a trust property, 1132.
    Designation of a trustee, 1132–1133.
    Determination of trust beneficiaries, 1133.
    Intent to create a trust, 1131.
    Valid trust purpose, 1131–1132.
Grantor trust, 1190.
Implied trust, 1130.
Life beneficiary interests, 1144–1146.
Protective trust, 1136.

TRUSTS—Cont'd
Remainderman interests, 1144–1147.
Resulting trust, 1138–1141.
Rule against perpetuities, 1132, 1138.
Spendthrift trust, 1135.
Support trust, 1135.
Termination of a trust by, 1147–1148.
  Beneficiary, 1147.
  Court, 1147–1148.
  Operation of law, 1148.
  Trustee, 1147.
  Trustor, 1147.
Testamentary trust, 1167.
Trustee,
  Defined, 1131.
  Designation of a, 1132–1133.
  Duties,
    Loyalty, 1142.
    Properly account, 1144–1147.
    Properly manage trust, 1143.
    Safeguard the trust res, 1143.
    To earmark, 1143.
    To invest, 1143–1144.
  Power to,
    Lease, 1141.
    Pay expenses, 1141–1142.
    Sale, 1141.

TRUTH IN LENDING ACT, 977, 1088

UNEMPLOYMENT COMPENSATION, 697–700

UNFAIR COMPETITION, 947–949

UNFAIR LABOR PRACTICES, 953–955

UNIFORM COMMERCIAL CODE
See also Bailment; Contracts; Sales.
Adoption of, 3–4.
Articles of, 176–177.
Purpose of, 4.
Sale of goods, 177.
Supplementing common law, 177.
Uniformity of, 177.

UNIFORM CONSUMER CREDIT CODE, 279–281

UNIFORM DECEPTIVE TRADE PRACTICES ACT, 1096–1097

UNIFORM GIFT TO MINORS ACT, 65

UNIFORM LIMITED PARTNERS ACT, 819–822

UNIFORM PROBATE CODE, 1159

UNIFORM SECURITIES ACT
See also Securities.
Administrative agency to enforce act, 927.
Fraudulent practices, 926.
General provisions, 926–929.
Methods of registering securities with state, 928–929.
Prohibited practices, 426.
Purpose of, 926.

†